The Faber Book of English History in Verse

The Faber Book of

ENGLISH HISTORY IN VERSE

Edited by Kenneth Baker

faber and faber

LONDON · BOSTON

First published in 1988
by Faber and Faber Limited
3 Queen Square London WC1N 3AU
Reprinted in 1988
This paperback edition (with corrections)
first published in 1989

Photoset by Parker Typesetting Service Leicester
Printed in Great Britain by Richard Clay Ltd Bungay Suffolk

British Library Cataloguing in Publication Data

The Faber book of English history in verse.
1. English poetry 2. England — History — Poetry
I. Baker, Kenneth, *1934–*
821'.008'0358 PR1195.E52
ISBN 0-571-15062-4

For all those people, including my family, who have contributed to my education.

Contents

King Charles I (1625–49)

The Commonwealth (1649–60)

King Charles II (1660–85)

King James II (1685–8)

William and Mary (1688–1702)

THE HOUSE OF WINDSOR

King Edward VII (1901–10)

King George V (1910–36)

Introduction

Anthologies grow slowly. I started to compile this history of England in verse some years ago, as I was struck by the great wealth and range of poetry which has been given over to telling the story of our country. The poems I had in mind spoke of great events and great figures, and I could see how they could be brought together in such a way as to offer a true sense of the narrative flow of our history. It is important for people living today to understand how they came to be what they are, to appreciate the forces and events that have shaped the institutions which guide and govern us, and generally to recognize how our rich and complex past has shaped what we think of as our national identity.

Each age has added something to the total picture. Roman roads, Anglo-Saxon kingship, Norman architecture, the Tudor Church of England, the rise of Parliament under the Stuarts, the thrust for empire in Hanoverian times, the satanic mills, Victorian prosperity and the wars of the twentieth century – all these have some direct bearing on how we live today. At one level the story is of kings and queens, of wars and battles, of famous victories like Trafalgar and near disasters like Dunkirk. Events of this sort are fixed in people's memories, together with a number of significant dates: 1066, 1215, 1603, 1815, 1940. A constant theme is man's mortality, and the transience of fame and fortune:

> For God's sake let us sit upon the ground,
> And tell sad stories of the death of kings –
> How some have been deposed, some slain in war,
> Some haunted by the ghosts they have deposed,
> Some poisoned by their wives, some sleeping killed;
> All murdered – for within the Hollow Crown
> That rounds the mortal temples of a king,
> Keeps Death his court . . .

Shakespeare, of course, had an incomparable understanding of history and most of his judgements stand up well to the test of modern scholarship, although he was far too harsh on Richard III. He is such a good guide that the Duke of Marlborough observed: 'Shakespeare, the only history of England I ever read.'

Running alongside the decisive events of history, and approachable, too, through the writings of poets, are the lives of the ordinary people of England. These must form part of any serious account, and so I have included an extract from *Piers Plowman* in 1370 in which William Langland pleads for the numerous poor of his time; a ballad from the Peasants' Revolt; the thoughts of a Berkshire farmer on Napoleon's invasion plans; the poem of George Loveless, the leader of the Tolpuddle Martyrs; the humour of Lancashire textile workers from Bury; the pride of an East End schoolboy wearing a red tie during the General Strike; and the sadness of a father who has lost his son in the blitz. This sea of men and women flows through our history, shaping and defining our national character. Edward Thomas's poem 'Lob' conveys something of the dogged cheerfulness of our people, and the sense of continuity their presence lends to historical events:

> The man you saw, – Lob-lie-by-the-fire, Jack Cade,
> Jack Smith, Jack Moon, poor Jack of every trade,
> Young Jack, or old Jack, or Jack What-d'ye-call,
> Jack-in-the-hedge, or Robin-run-by-the-wall,
> Robin Hood, Ragged Robin, lazy Bob,
> One of the lords of No Man's Land, good Lob, –
> Although he was seen dying at Waterloo,
> Hastings, Agincourt, and Sedgemoor too, –
> Lives yet. He never will admit he is dead
> Till millers cease to grind men's bones for bread,
> Nor till our weathercock crows once again
> And I remove my house out of the lane
> On to the road.

An appreciation of history in all its aspects, and particularly of the history of one's own country, is an essential part of life. It helps general understanding, it promotes tolerance and it gives delight. A Tudor historian, Polydor Vergil, in dedicating his book on the Welsh monk Gildas to Henry VIII, described history as 'the only unique, certain and faithful witness of times and things'. He added that it is 'not only useful and enriching, but positively essential', and that it 'displays eternally to the living those events which should be an example and those which should be a warning'. T. S. Eliot said it so well in 'Little Gidding':

> The moment of the rose and the moment of the yew-tree
> Are of equal duration. A people without history
> Is not redeemed from time, for history is a pattern
> Of timeless moments. So, while the light fails
> On a winter's afternoon, in a secluded chapel
> History is now and England.

I should make it clear that what lies in these pages is the story of England. I have not attempted to include the histories of Scotland or Wales or Northern Ireland, each of which has a great store of fine poetry and deserves an anthology of its own. I have brought them in only at those points where the history of England becomes intertwined with theirs – Edward I's invasion of Wales, for instance, and the Battle of the Boyne, and Bonnie Prince Charlie's uprising. This is essentially the history of the 'True-Born Englishman', that mongrel character whose antecedents Daniel Defoe identified so sharply:

> Thus from a mixture of all kinds began
> That heterogeneous thing, an Englishman:
> In eager rapes and furious lusts begot
> Betwixt a painted Briton and a Scot:
> Whose gend'ring offspring quickly learn'd to bow
> And yoke their heifers to the Roman plow;
> From whence a mongrel, half-bred race there came,
> With neither name nor nation, speech or fame,
> In whose hot veins new mixtures quickly ran,
> Infus'd betwixt a Saxon and a Dane;
> While their rank daughters, to their parents just,
> Receiv'd all nations with promiscuous lust.
> This nauseous brood directly did contain
> The well-extracted blood of Englishmen.

The language which the English people shaped by means of assimilation and change developed into the marvellous instrument of communication which is now used throughout the world. It is also one of the potent forces which unites us as a nation. Caxton helped to regulate the spelling of words by employing what was common practice in London in the 1480s; Shakespeare developed the usages of the Court and of the common people to extraordinary effect; the translators of the King James Bible attuned the language to the needs of worship; and Kipling found poetry in the slang of the ordinary soldier. Yet Kipling also reminds us of another trait of the English – their leaning towards taciturnity, reserve and caution:

For undemocratic reasons and for motives not of State,
They arrive at their conclusions – largely inarticulate.
Being void of self-expression they confide their views to none;
But sometimes in a smoking-room, one learns why things were done.

Yes, sometimes in a smoking-room, through clouds of 'Ers' and 'Ums,'
Obliquely and by inference, illumination comes,
On some step that they have taken, or some action they approve –
Embellished with the *argot* of the Upper Fourth Remove.

In telegraphic sentences, half nodded to their friends,
They hint a matter's inwardness – and there the matter ends.
And while the Celt is talking from Valencia to Kirkwall,
The English – ah, the English! – don't say anything at all.

Just a word on how I have put this book together: throughout the text I have provided notes of explanation which are also designed to carry the narrative forward chronologically. I cannot be blamed for the views of the poets, but those expressed in the notes are mine. I have included, along with contemporary poems, many that were written long after the events concerned, for example: Chesterton on King Alfred, Philip Larkin on the figures depicted on a medieval tombstone, Kipling on James I, Robert Graves on Nelson's funeral, Noël Coward on the death of Queen Victoria, Gavin Ewart on the 1920s, and so on. Anglo-Saxon and Latin pieces have been translated, but I have left most of the medieval verse in its original form, as with a little effort it can be understood and translation usually saps its vigour.

I decided to end this anthology at the accession of our Queen Elizabeth II. There has been a remarkable shortage of good, straight – as opposed to satirical – verse about public events in England over the past thirty years. One could name exceptions: Larkin on Britain's withdrawal from East of Suez in 1968, Adrian Mitchell on Nye Bevan's change of heart, or C. H. Sisson on the loss of the old county names through the local government reforms of 1974. It could be, too, that the immediacy of the news as it is reported on television has blunted the poetic imagination, but perhaps more public poetry will come to be written in retrospect.

I should like to take this opportunity to thank the many people who have helped and given advice to me over the years. These are principally my family, who insisted that I should let Middle English texts stand as they were; Jonathan Barker at the Poetry Library of the Arts Council; David Cook, who checked many of the historical facts; and Christopher Reid at Faber and Faber.

PRE-NORMAN

AD 61

Boadicea

When the British warrior queen,
  Bleeding from the Roman rods,
Sought, with an indignant mien,
  Counsel of her country's gods,

Sage beneath a spreading oak
  Sat the Druid, hoary chief;
Every burning word he spoke
  Full of rage, and full of grief.

'Princess! if our agèd eyes
  Weep upon thy matchless wrongs,
'Tis because resentment ties
  All the terrors of our tongues.

Rome shall perish – write that word
  In the blood that she has spilt;
Perish, hopeless and abhorred,
  Deep in ruin as in guilt.

Rome, for empire far renowned,
  Tramples on a thousand states;
Soon her pride shall kiss the ground –
  Hark! the Gaul is at her gates!

Other Romans shall arise,
  Heedless of a soldier's name;
Sounds, not arms, shall win the prize –
  Harmony the path to fame.

Then the progeny that springs
  From the forests of our land,
Armed with thunder, clad with wings,
  Shall a wider world command.

Regions Caesar never knew
  Thy posterity shall sway,
Where his eagles never flew,
  None invincible as they.'

Such the bard's prophetic words,
  Pregnant with celestial fire,
Bending, as he swept the chords
  Of his sweet but awful lyre.

She, with all a monarch's pride,
  Felt them in her bosom glow;
Rushed to battle, fought, and died;
  Dying, hurled them at the foe.

'Ruffians, pitiless as proud,
  Heaven awards the vengeance due;
Empire is on us bestowed,
  Shame and ruin wait for you.'

William Cowper

Julius Caesar invaded England in 55 BC and again in 54 BC. The Romans then returned to Gaul. The real invasion started under the Emperor Claudius in AD 43 and the Romans controlled Britain for the next 360 years. Several rebellions were crushed, including the one led by Boadicea, Queen of the Iceni, who ruled part of East Anglia. To avoid capture and the humiliation of a triumph in Rome, she took poison.

c. 300

THE ROMAN OCCUPATION

from **The Roman Centurion's Song**

Legate, I had the news last night – my Cohort ordered home
By ship to Portus Itius and thence by road to Rome.
I've marched the Companies aboard, the arms are stowed
 below:
Now let another take my sword. Command me not to go!

I've served in Britain forty years, from Vectis to the Wall.
I have none other home than this, nor any life at all.
Last night I did not understand, but, now the hour draws near
That calls me to my native land, I feel that land is here.

Here where men say my name was made, here where my work
 was done,
Here where my dearest dead are laid – my wife – my wife and
 son;
Here where time, custom, grief and toil, age, memory, service,
 love,
Have rooted me in British soil. Ah, how can I remove?

*

Let me work here for Britain's sake – at any task you will –
A marsh to drain, a road to make or native troops to drill.
Some Western camp (I know the Pict) or granite Border keep,
Mid seas of heather derelict, where our old messmates sleep.

Legate, I come to you in tears – My Cohort ordered home!
I've served in Britain forty years. What should I do in Rome?
Here is my heart, my soul, my mind – the only life I know.
I cannot leave it all behind. Command me not to go!

Rudyard Kipling

At the peak of its power, Rome kept a garrison of 50,000 soldiers in Britain, but as the Barbarians advanced from other quarters they had gradually to be withdrawn. Kipling's poem shows one soldier who wanted to stay. The Romans left behind them a network of straight roads, the ineradicable traces of their language, a capital called Londinium and many buildings. The first three of these survived, but the buildings were pillaged and razed by invaders from the North and the East and only their foundations survived the Dark Ages.

Roman wall blues

Over the heather the wet wind blows,
I've lice in my tunic and a cold in my nose.

The rain comes pattering out of the sky,
I'm a Wall soldier, I don't know why.

The mist creeps over the hard grey stone,
My girl's in Tungria; I sleep alone.

Aulus goes hanging around her place,
I don't like his manners, I don't like his face.

Piso's a Christian, he worships a fish;
There'd be no kissing if he had his wish.

She gave me a ring but I diced it away;
I want my girl and I want my pay.

When I'm a veteran with only one eye
I shall do nothing but look at the sky.

W. H. Auden

after 500

KING ARTHUR

from Idylls of the King

And slowly answered Arthur from the barge:
'The old order changeth, yielding place to new,
And God fulfils Himself in many ways,
Lest one good custom should corrupt the world.
Comfort thyself: what comfort is in me?
I have lived my life, and that which I have done
May He within Himself make pure! but thou,
If thou shouldst never see my face again,
Pray for my soul. More things are wrought by prayer
Than this world dreams of. Wherefore, let thy voice
Rise like a fountain for me night and day.
For what are men better than sheep or goats
That nourish a blind life within the brain,
If, knowing God, they lift not hands of prayer
Both for themselves and those who call them friend?
For so the whole round earth is every way
Bound by gold chains about the feet of God.
But now farewell. I am going a long way
With these thou seëst – if indeed I go
(For all my mind is clouded with a doubt) –
To the island-valley of Avilion;
Where falls not hail, or rain, or any snow,
Nor ever wind blows loudly; but it lies
Deep-meadowed, happy, fair with orchard-lawns
And bowery hollows crowned with summer sea,
Where I will heal me of my grievous wound.'

So said he, and the barge with oar and sail
Moved from the brink, like some full-breasted swan
That, fluting a wild carol ere her death,
Ruffles her pure cold plume, and takes the flood
With swarthy webs. Long stood Sir Bedivere
Revolving many memories, till the hull
Looked one black dot against the verge of dawn,
And on the mere the wailing died away.

Alfred, Lord Tennyson

In the fourth and fifth centuries small bands of Anglo-Saxons set sail from Denmark and North Germany to settle in Britain. The local inhabitants put up some resistance, and we have the name of at least one of their leaders, Ambrosius Aurelianus, who seems to have been a Roman 'staying on'. The one whom everybody knows, King Arthur, has achieved the status of a legend. The legend itself was written down after the Norman Conquest, and much later written up by Tennyson. One certain fact is that Arthur defeated the Anglo-Saxons at Badon, possibly on a hilltop near Bath, at some time in the early sixth century.

Tennyson drew upon the accounts of Geoffrey of Monmouth and Thomas Malory to recreate his ideal of Romantic chivalry. He wrote:

> How much of history we have in the story of Arthur is doubtful. Let not my readers press too hard on details, whether for history or for allegory . . . He is meant to be a man who spent himself in the cause of honour, duty and self-sacrifice.

c. 670

Cædmon's Hymn

Nū scylun hergan hefænrīcaes Uard,
Metudæs mæcti end His mōdgidanc,
uerc Uuldurfadur, suē Hē uundra gihuæs,
ēci Dryctin, ōr āstelidæ.
Hē ǣrist scōp ælda barnum
heben til hrōfe, hāleg Scepen.
Thā middungeard moncynnæs Uard,
ēci Dryctin, æfter tīadæ
fīrum foldu, Frēa allmectig.

Now we must praise the Guardian of Heaven,
the might of the Lord and His purpose of mind,
the work of the Glorious Father; for He,
God Eternal, established each wonder,
He, Holy Creator, first fashioned
heaven as a roof for the sons of men.
Then the Guardian of Mankind adorned
this middle-earth below, the world for men,
Everlasting Lord, Almighty King.

translated by Kevin Crossley-Holland

I include this as it is said to be the first poem in Old English, or more particularly in the Northumbrian dialect. It was written between 657 and 680. Bede relates that Cædmon, a tuneless old cowherd, was told in a vision to 'sing Creation', which he duly did. Hilda, the Abbess of Whitby, was so impressed that she got her monks to read Cædmon passages from the Scriptures, which he then sang into verse. Whatever the truth of the matter, the significance of it is that this is the first recorded use of heroic, pagan, Germanic-style poetry for Christian purposes. It started a tradition and introduced phrases that were to be used again and again as Christianity spread over England.

c. 880

THE VIKING INVASIONS

from The Ballad of the White Horse

The Northmen came about our land
  A Christless chivalry:
Who knew not of the arch or pen,
Great, beautiful half-witted men
  From the sunrise and the sea.

Misshapen ships stood on the deep
  Full of strange gold and fire,
And hairy men, as huge as sin
With hornèd heads, came wading in
  Through the long, low sea-mire.

Our towns were shaken of tall kings
  With scarlet beards like blood:
The world turned empty where they trod,
They took the kindly cross of God
  And cut it up for wood.

And there was death on the Emperor
  And night upon the Pope:
And Alfred, hiding in deep grass,
  Hardened his heart with hope.

A sea-folk blinder than the sea
  Broke all about his land,
But Alfred up against them bare
And gripped the ground and grasped the air,
  Staggered, and strove to stand.

He bent them back with spear and spade,
  With desperate dyke and wall,
With foemen leaning on his shield
And roaring on him when he reeled;
  And no help came at all.

He broke them with a broken sword
  A little towards the sea,
And for one hour of panting peace,
Ringed with a roar that would not cease,
With golden crown and girded fleece
  Made laws under a tree.

G. K. Chesterton

Alfred came to the throne in 871, at the age of twenty-three. The Vikings had conquered the rest of the country and he was driven back to a small area in Somerset, the Athelney Marshes. He decided to retaliate. He built up his army, organized a network of fortified boroughs, and had ships made which were longer and faster than those of the Norsemen. He succeeded in confining the Vikings to the so-called Danelaw, comprising Northern and Eastern England, and forced their leader Guthrum to sue for peace after his great victory at Edington in 878. He restored Christianity and even began its dissemination among the pagan Vikings, cherished the scholarship which produced the *Anglo-Saxon Chronicle*, and laid down laws enforcing loyalty to the new state. He may be said to have created the English nation and certainly deserves his title of 'Alfred the Great'.

KING ALFRED AND THE CAKES

Where lying on the hearth to bake
By chance the cake did burn:
'What! canst thou not, thou lout,' quoth she,
'Take pains the same to turn?
But serve me such another trick,
I'll thwack thee on the snout.'
Which made the patient king, good man,
Of her to stand in doubt?

Anonymous

At the time of Alfred's refuge in the Athelney Marshes, a rumour grew up which was later recorded as fact. It was said that he had to disguise himself as a peasant and live with a swineherd and his wife. One day, either preoccupied with his plans or cleaning his weapons, he let some cakes burn. The wife was angry and belaboured him, saying, 'Turn the loaves over so that they don't burn, for I see every day that you have a huge appetite.'

937

The Battle of Brunanburh

This year King Athelstan, ring-giver, lord
of earls, and Prince Eadmund his brother, earned
lasting battle-fame with blade-edge
at Brunanburh; son of Eadweard, they sundered
the shield-wall, shattered the linden shields
with smithied brands: as often in battle,
true to their lineage, they guarded treasure, land
and villages from all invaders. Enemies
fell, both Scot and seafarer sank
doomed; that field, blood-sluiced, grew slippery
from sun-rise – the famous radiance,
God's dazzling candle, soaring
over morning earth – to the setting of that fair
creation.

There, many warriors, many a Scot
and war-worn North-man alike, lay
spear-pierced above his shield,
dead-beat. All day, West Saxon bands
ran down the foe, hacking the spines of fugitives
with swords rasped fine. No Mercian refused
the hard sword-play with hostile heroes,
Anlaf's shipment over the heaving waves,
fated to the fray. Five young kings
lay on that field, dead by the sword,
in the slump of death, with seven earls
of Anlaf, and a countless glut of Scots
and seamen. There, the North-men's leader
was put to flight, with few survivors,
driven to his prow, a quick escape
by galley across the gloomed sea. Also
Constantine, old hand at sword-play, fled
to his native North: the old
war-king drained of swagger, his kinsmen
and friends slain in the field, his own son
left dead of wounds. That grey-aged

veteran could no more vaunt of sword-clash
than could Anlaf. Neither had cause for laughter
among their army-remnants, as victors
after battle-clamour, strenuous combat
on that reddled turf with Eadweard's
sons. Then in nailed boats the North-men,
bleeding survivors of javelins, set sail
with sapped prides through slapping seas
to Dublin, Ireland. Likewise, both brothers,
king and prince battle-proud and boisterous,
returned to their own terrain,
the meadows of Mercia. They left the dark
raven behind, charcoal-coated, horny-beaked,
to jab that carrion, and the grey-coat eagle,
the white-tailed ravening war-hawk, to have
his will of the dead, and that grizzled wolf
of the wood.
            Never was wilder carnage
seen on this island, of soldiery sword-felled,
such as the tomes of clerics tell,
since Angles and Saxons came here seeking
the Britons across broad sea, when proud
warriors whelmed the Welsh-men, and brave
earls laid hold on this land.

translated from the Anglo-Saxon by Harold Massingham

King Athelstan of Wessex and his brother, Eadmund, who were grandsons of Alfred, fought off an invasion from the North led by Olaf Guthfrithson, the Norse King of Dublin, Constantine, King of the Scots and Picts, and Owen, King of the Strathclyde Welsh. The defenders won at Brunanburh, and this great triumph was dutifully and beautifully recorded in the regimental magazine of the House of Alfred, the *Anglo-Saxon Chronicle*. In this 'slump of death' the raven, the eagle and the wolf had their fill, but Olaf escaped to trouble England again after Athelstan's death in 939.

954

ERIC BLOODAXE

from **Briggflatts**

Loaded with mail of linked lies,
what weapon can the king lift to fight
when chance-met enemies employ sly
sword and shoulder-piercing pike,
pressed into the mire,
trampled and hewn till a knife
– in whose hand? – severs tight
neck cords? Axe rusts. Spine
picked bare by ravens, agile
maggots devour the slack side
and inert brain, never wise.
What witnesses he had life,
ravelled and worn past splice,
yarns falling to staple? Rime
on the bent, the beck ice,
there will be nothing on Stainmore to hide
void, no sable to disguise
what he wore under the lies,
king of Orkney, king of Dublin, twice
king of York, where the tide
stopped till long flight
from who knows what smile,
scowl, disgust or delight
ended in bale on the fellside.

Basil Bunting

After a short and violent reign as King of Norway, Eric Bloodaxe fled to Northumbria where the Norsemen welcomed him as their king. The last adventurer of a savage society, he tried to bring together an alliance of Dublin and York against the English. Eadred, the King of the

English, forced Eric out in 948, and again in 954 when he was betrayed by Earl Oswulf, who was given Southern Northumbria as his prize.

c. 980–1016

Danegeld

It is always a temptation to an armed and agile nation,
  To call upon a neighbour and to say:
'We invaded you last night – we are quite prepared to fight,
  Unless you pay us cash to go away.'

And that is called asking for Dane-geld,
  And the people who ask it explain
That you've only to pay 'em the Dane-geld
  And then you'll get rid of the Dane!

It is always a temptation to a rich and lazy nation,
  To puff and look important and to say: –
'Though we know we should defeat you, we have not the time
    to meet you.
  We will therefore pay you cash to go away.'

And that is called paying the Dane-geld;
  But we've proved it again and again,
That if once you have paid him the Dane-geld
  You never get rid of the Dane.

It is wrong to put temptation in the path of any nation,
  For fear they should succumb and go astray,
So when you are requested to pay up or be molested,
  You will find it better policy to say: –

'We never pay *any* one Dane-geld,
No matter how trifling the cost,
For the end of that game is oppression and shame,
And the nation that plays it is lost!'

Rudyard Kipling

In 978, Ethelred the Unready succeeded to the English throne upon the murder of his brother, Edward, at Corfe Castle. Ethelred was weak and tried to buy off the invading Danes by giving them money – the famous Danegeld. Each time, the Danes asked for more, and eventually their king, Canute, became King of England in 1016. The Saxon period had come to an end and it seemed as if the country would submit to a long period of Scandinavian rule. Family rivalries, however, and the chaotic politics of the next fifty years provided an opportunity for the thrustful, well-organized and confident Normans to conquer Britain and to tie her to the French political system for nearly 400 years.

991

from **The Battle of Maldon**

Then the brave warrior raised his spear,
gripped his shield and stepped towards a seafarer;
thus the brave earl advanced on the churl;
each had evil designs on the other.
The Viking was the quicker – he hurled his foreign spear
wounding the lord of the warriors.
Byrhtnoth broke the shaft on the edge of his shield;
the imbedded spear-head sprang out of his wound.
Then he flung his spear in fury at the proud Viking
who dared inflict such pain. His aim was skilful.
The spear split open the warrior's neck.
Thus Byrhtnoth put paid to his enemy's life.
Then he swiftly hurled a second spear
which burst the Viking's breastplate, wounding him cruelly
in the chest; the deadly point pierced his heart.
The brave earl, Byrhtnoth, was delighted at this;
he laughed out loud and gave thanks to the Lord
that such good fortune had been granted to him.
But one of the seafarers sent a sharp javelin
speeding from his hand; it pierced the body
of earl Byrhtnoth, Ethelred's brave thane.

translated from the Anglo-Saxon by Kevin Crossley-Holland

The Old English poem from which this episode is taken records a fight between Vikings and an army of English warriors under the leadership of Byrhtnoth, the Ealdorman of Essex. The Vikings had demanded a sum of money as their price for moving on and, when the English refused to pay, a bloody battle took place at Maldon in Essex, where Byrhtnoth was killed and the Vikings prevailed.

c. 1020

from King Canute

King Canute was weary-hearted; he had reigned for years a score,
Battling, struggling, pushing, fighting, killing much and robbing more;
And he thought upon his actions, walking by the wild sea-shore.

'Twixt the chancellor and bishop walked the king with steps sedate,
Chamberlains and grooms came after, silversticks and goldsticks great,
Chaplains, aides-de-camp, and pages – all the officers of state,

Sliding after like his shadow, pausing when he chose to pause:
If a frown his face contracted, straight the courtiers dropped their jaws;
If to laugh the king was minded, out they burst in loud hee-haws.

But that day a something vexed him, that was clear to old and young:
Thrice his grace had yawned at table, when his favourite gleemen sung,
Once the queen would have consoled him, but he bade her hold her tongue.

'Something ails my gracious master,' cried the keeper of the seal.
'Sure, my lord, it is the lampreys served at dinner, or the veal?'
'Pshaw!' exclaimed the angry monarch. 'Keeper, 'tis not that I feel.

''Tis the *heart*, and not the dinner, fool, that doth my rest impair:
Can a king be great as I am, prithee, and yet know no care?
Oh, I'm sick, and tired, and weary.' – Someone cried, 'The king's arm-chair!'

Then towards the lackeys turning, quick my lord the keeper
nodded,
Straight the king's great chair was brought him, by two footmen
able-bodied;
Languidly he sank into it: it was comfortably wadded.

'Leading on my fierce companions,' cried he, 'over storm and
brine,
I have fought and I have conquered! Where was glory like to
mine?'
Loudly all the courtiers echoed: 'Where is glory like to thine?'

*

'Might I stay the sun above us, good Sir Bishop?' Canute cried;
'Could I bid the silver moon to pause upon her heavenly ride?
If the moon obeys my orders, sure I can command the tide.

'Will the advancing waves obey me, bishop, if I make the sign?'
Said the bishop, bowing lowly, 'Land and sea, my lord, are
thine.'
Canute turned towards the ocean – 'Back!' he said, 'thou
foaming brine.

'From the sacred shore I stand on, I command thee to retreat;
Venture not, thou stormy rebel, to approach thy master's seat:
Ocean, be thou still! I bid thee come not nearer to my feet!'

But the sullen ocean answered with a louder, deeper roar,
And the rapid waves drew nearer, falling sounding on the
shore;
Back the keeper and the bishop, back the king and courtiers
bore.

And he sternly bade them never more to kneel to human clay,
But alone to praise and worship That which earth and seas obey:
And his golden crown of empire never wore he from that day.
. . . King Canute is dead and gone: parasites exist alway.

William Makepeace Thackeray

Canute, whose name was also spelt Cnut, was King of Denmark and Norway, as well as of England from 1016 to 1035. Much of his reign was spent in holding this large empire together. Canute's rule in England was beneficial: he encoded the law, supported the Church and maintained peace. He was a courageous and powerful figure whose reign appears as a golden interlude shining through the Dark Ages. Powerful, though not omnipotent!

1057

Godiva

I waited for the train at Coventry;
I hung with grooms and porters on the bridge,
To watch the three tall spires; and there I shaped
The city's ancient legend into this: –

Not only we, the latest seed of Time,
New men, that in the flying of a wheel
Cry down the past, not only we, that prate
Of rights and wrongs, have loved the people well,
And loathed to see them overtax'd; but she
Did more, and underwent, and overcame,
The woman of a thousand summers back,
Godiva, wife to that grim Earl, who ruled
In Coventry: for when he laid a tax
Upon his town, and all the mothers brought
Their children, clamouring, 'If we pay, we starve.'
She sought her lord, and found him, where he strode
About the hall, among his dogs, alone,
His beard a foot before him, and his hair
A yard behind. She told him of their tears,
And pray'd him, 'If they pay this tax, they starve.'
Whereat he stared, replying, half-amazed,
'You would not let your little finger ache
For such as *these?*' – 'But I would die,' said she.
He laugh'd, and swore by Peter and by Paul:
Then fillip'd at the diamond in her ear;
'O ay, ay, ay, you talk!' – 'Alas!' she said,
'But prove me what it is I would not do.'
And from a heart as rough as Esau's hand,
He answer'd, 'Ride you naked thro' the town,
And I repeal it'; and nodding, as in scorn,
He parted, with great strides among his dogs.
So left alone, the passions of her mind,
As winds from all the compass shift and blow,
Made war upon each other for an hour,

Till pity won. She sent a herald forth,
And bade him cry, with sound of trumpet, all
The hard condition; but that she would loose
The people: therefore, as they loved her well,
From then till noon no foot should pace the street,
No eye look down, she passing; but that all
Should keep within, door shut, and window barr'd.
  Then fled she to her inmost bower, and there
Unclasp'd the wedded eagles of her belt,
The grim Earl's gift; but ever at a breath
She linger'd, looking like a summer moon
Half-dipt in cloud: anon she shook her head,
And shower'd the rippled ringlets to her knee;
Unclad herself in haste; adown the stair
Stole on; and, like a creeping sunbeam, slid
From pillar unto pillar, until she reach'd
The gateway; there she found her palfrey trapt
In purple blazon'd with armorial gold.
  Then she rode forth, clothed on with chastity:
The deep air listen'd round her as she rode,
And all the low wind hardly breathed for fear.
The little wide-mouth'd heads upon the spout
Had cunning eyes to see; the barking cur
Made her cheek flame; her palfrey's footfall shot
Light horrors thro' her pulses; the blind walls
Were full of chinks and holes; and overhead
Fantastic gables, crowding, stared: but she
Not less thro' all bore up, till, last, she saw
The white-flower'd elder-thicket from the field
Gleam thro' the Gothic archway in the wall.
  Then she rode back, clothed on with chastity:
And one low churl, compact of thankless earth,
The fatal byword of all years to come,
Boring a little auger-hole in fear,
Peep'd – but his eyes, before they had their will,
Were shrivell'd into darkness in his head,
And dropt before him. So the Powers, who wait
On noble deeds, cancell'd a sense misused;
And she, that knew not, pass'd; and all at once,

With twelve great shocks of sound, the shameless noon
Was clash'd and hammered from a hundred towers,
One after one: but even then she gain'd
Her bower; whence reissuing, robed and crown'd,
To meet her lord, she took the tax away,
And built herself an everlasting name.

Alfred, Lord Tennyson

There are so many sources for this legend that we may assume something like it actually happened.

NORMANS AND PLANTAGENETS

The Kings and Queens of England after the Conquest

Willie, Willie, Harry, Ste,
Harry, Dick, John, Harry 3;
1, 2, 3 Neds, Richard 2,
Harries 4, 5, 6 – then who?
Edwards 4, 5, Dick the Bad,
Harries twain, and then the lad;
Mary, Bessie, James the Vain,
Charlie, Charlie, James again;
William and Mary, Anne, and *gloria!* –
4 Georges, William and Victoria,
Ned and George; repeat again;
And then Elizabeth comes to reign.

Anonymous

William the Conqueror, 1066–87

1066

THE BATTLE OF HASTINGS AND THE NORMAN CONQUEST

The Anvil

England's on the anvil – hear the hammers ring –
    Clanging from the Severn to the Tyne!
Never was a blacksmith like our Norman King –
    England's being hammered, hammered, hammered into line!

England's on the anvil! Heavy are the blows!
    (But the work will be a marvel when it's done)
Little bits of Kingdoms cannot stand against their foes.
    England's being hammered, hammered, hammered into one!

There shall be one people – it shall serve one Lord –
    (Neither Priest nor Baron shall escape!)
It shall have one speech and law, soul and strength and sword.
    England's being hammered, hammered, hammered into shape!

Rudyard Kipling

The one date that every schoolchild knows is 1066. In that year Edward the Confessor died without issue. Harold, Earl of Wessex, had only a distant claim to the throne, but because he was in the country at the time he quickly got himself crowned. After beating off a rival contender, Harold of Norway, at the Battle of Stamford Bridge, he marched south to fight off another, William, Duke of Normandy, who had a rather better claim, and to whom, moreover, Harold had once sworn allegiance. William had landed at Pevensey Bay, and the two armies met at Hastings, where Harold was killed probably by an arrow in the eye. His body was not given to his mother, as would have been customary, but at William's command it was buried at the top of a cliff with a stone bearing the inscription:

> By the Duke's command, O Harold, you rest here a king,
> That you may still be guardian of the shore and sea.

Three Norman kings ruled England until 1135. The Norman Conquest was very thorough. The Domesday survey, started by William in 1085, showed that the rental value of England was £37,000 per year and that about 250 individuals with incomes of over £100 a year in effect controlled the country. Virtually all of these were Normans. During their supremacy, only 10,000 Normans lived in England, but their grip was complete. They built castles as fortified residences for the barons. The barons exacted loyalty from their knights, and the knights from their peasants. The barons swore loyalty to the King, who in return granted them the use of his land. This feudal system of interlocking obligations was the foundation of English society for over 300 years.

At the Statue of William the Conqueror, Falaise

See him ride the roaring air
In an iron moustache and emerald hair,
Furious with flowers on a foundry cob
The bastard son of the late Lord Bob.

He writes his name with a five-flagged spear
On skies of infantry in the rear
And fixed at his feet, in chainmail stations,
Six unshaven Norman relations:

Rollo, Guillaume Longue-Épée,
Le Bon, Sans Peur, Richard Three,
Robert the Devil; and over them all
The horse's tail, like a waterfall.

Many a shell struck Talbot's Tower
From Henry the Fifth to Eisenhower,
But never a splinter scratched the heel
Of the bully in bronze at the Hôtel de Ville.

On the chocolate wall of the tall château
Tansy, pimpernel, strawberry grow;
And down by the tanyard the washing hangs wet
As it did in the dirty days of Arlette.

Hubert and Arthur and Holy Joan
Knew this staring stack of stone
Where William scowls in a Saracen cap
And sat out the fight for the famous Gap.

Gallop on, General with cider eyes,
Until the snow-coasts of Sussex rise!
Silence the tearful and smiling with thunder
As you spring from the sea, bringing history under.

Charles Causley

THE NORMANS IN ENGLAND

from **The True-Born Englishman**

He rais'd no Money, for he paid in Land.
He gave his Legions their Eternal Station,
And made them all Freeholders of the Nation.
He canton'd out the Country to his Men,
And ev'ry Soldier was a Denizen.
The Rascals thus enrich'd, he call'd them *Lords*,
To please their Upstart Pride with new-made Words:
And *Doomsday-Book* his Tyranny records.
And here begins the Ancient Pedigree
That so exalts our Poor Nobility:
'Tis that from some *French* Trooper they derive,
Who with the *Norman* Bastard did arrive:
The Trophies of the Families appear;
Some show the Sword, the Bow, and some the Spear,
Which their Great Ancestor, *forsooth*, did wear.
These in the Heralds Register remain,
Their Noble Mean Extraction to explain.
Yet who the Hero was, no man can tell,
Whether a Drummer or a Colonel:
The silent Record blushes to reveal
Their Undescended Dark Original.
But grant the best, How came the Change to pass;
A *True-Born Englishman* of *Norman* Race?
A *Turkish* Horse can show more History,
To prove his Well-descended Family.
Conquest, as by the Moderns 'tis exprest,
May give a Title to the Lands possest:
But that the Longest Sword shou'd be so Civil,
To make a *Frenchman English*, that's the Devil.

Daniel Defoe

1087

DEATH OF WILLIAM THE CONQUEROR

He ordered the poor to build castles.
This was very hard work.
The king was a tough man
And he took many gold coins from his people
And many more hundreds of pounds in silver . . .
This was most unfair, and he did not really need the money . . .
He marked out a huge area for deer, and made laws about it.
Anyone who killed a hart or a hind
Was to be blinded . . .
He loved the stags as dearly
As though he had been their father . . .
The rich complained and the poor wept.
But he was too merciless to care if everyone hated him.
And they just had to obey him.
Otherwise, they lost their lives and their lands
And their goods and their king's friendship.
Alas! that any man should behave in this proud way
And declare that he is so far above all other men!
May Almighty God show mercy on his soul
And pardon him his sins.

The Peterborough Chronicler

This chronicler, who in fact wrote in prose, but of a kind that suggests the rhythms of verse, as it has been set out here, noted both the good and the bad things of William's reign. The King had a powerful physical presence, and indeed this was an essential element of medieval kingship. William of Malmesbury recorded that he had 'a fierce face', and that 'he was majestic . . . although his pot-belly rather spoiled his appearance'.

King William II, 1087–1100

1100

The Death of Rufus

To hunt rode fierce King Rufus,
  Upon a holy morn –
The Church had summon'd him to pray,
  But he held the Church in scorn.
Sir Walter Tyrrel rode with him,
  And drew his good bow-string;
He drew the string to smite a deer,
  But his arrow smote the king!

Hurl'd from his trembling charger,
  The death-struck monarch lay;
While fast, as flees the startled deer,
  Rash Tyrrel fled away:
On the spot where his strong hand had made
  So many desolate,
He died with none to pity him –
  Such was the tyrant's fate!

None mourn'd for cruel Rufus:
  With pomp they buried him;
But no heart grieved beside his bier –
  No kindly eye grew dim;
But poor men lifted up their heads,
  And clasp'd their hands, and said:
'Thank God, the ruthless Conqueror
  And his stern son are dead!'

Menella Smedley

The most memorable thing about William Rufus's reign was his mysterious death in the New Forest. While alive, he had debased the coinage, fallen out with the Church and disinherited many baronial families. His chroniclers, mainly churchmen, deplored the morals of the royal court and lamented the oppressive nature of the King's rule. Nevertheless, he was a shrewd and successful politician and, further to his credit, he started building one of the finest and most important civic edifices of medieval times, Westminster Hall. This poem, by a little-known Victorian writer, is the only one on the subject that I have been able to find.

King Stephen, 1135–54

from King Stephen

ACT I

Scene I. – Field of Battle.

Alarum. Enter King STEPHEN, *Knights, and Soldiers.*

STEPHEN: If shame can on a soldier's vein-swoll'n front
Spread deeper crimson than the battle's toil,
Blush in your casing helmets! for see, see!
Yonder my chivalry, my pride of war,
Wrench'd with an iron hand from firm array,
Are routed loose about the plashy meads,
Of honour forfeit. O that my known voice
Could reach your dastard ears, and fright you more!
Fly, cowards, fly! Gloucester is at your backs!
Throw your slack bridles o'er the flurried manes,
Ply well the rowel with faint trembling heels,
Scampering to death at last!
1ST KNIGHT: The enemy
Bears his flaunt standard close upon their ear.
2ND KNIGHT: Sure of a bloody prey, seeing the fens
Will swamp them girth-deep.
STEPHEN: Over head and ears,
No matter! 'Tis a gallant enemy;
How like a comet he goes streaming on.
But we must plague him in the flank, – hey, friends?
We are well-breath'd – follow!

*

Scene III. – The Field of Battle. Enter STEPHEN *unarmed.*
STEPHEN: Another sword! And what if I could seize
One from Bellona's gleaming armoury,
Or choose the fairest of her sheaved spears!
Where are my enemies? Here, close at hand,
Here come the testy brood. O, for a sword!
I'm faint – a biting sword! A noble sword!
A hedge-stake – or a ponderous stone to hurl
With brawny vengeance, like the labourer Cain.
Come on! Farewell my kingdom, and all hail
Thou superb, plumed, and helmeted renown!
All hail! I would not truck this brilliant day
To rule in Pylos with a Nestor's beard –
Come on!

John Keats

In 1819, Keats started to write a play for Edmund Kean, the great actor. Kean, alas, left for a tour of America, and so the poet abandoned it after only three scenes. But these are enough to show the heroic character of his protagonist, Stephen. Henry I's son had died in the wreck of the White Ship in 1120, leaving as heir to the throne his sister, Matilda, to whom Henry made his nobles swear allegiance. On his death, however, they lent their support to Stephen, and a civil war started, in the course of which Stephen was himself captured at the battle of Lincoln in 1141. A brave and courageous warrior, he was able to regain the kingdom, but he never fully controlled his nobles, and when his own son died he accepted Matilda's son, Henry, as his heir.

King Henry II, 1154–88

1172

THE MURDER OF THOMAS À BECKET

from **Murder in the Cathedral**

KNIGHTS: Where is Becket, the traitor to the King?
  Where is Becket, the meddling priest?
Come down Daniel to the lion's den,
  Come down Daniel for the mark of the
    beast.

Are you washed in the blood of the Lamb?
  Are you marked with the mark of the
    beast?
Come down Daniel to the lions' den,
  Come down Daniel and join in the feast.

Where is Becket the Cheapside brat?
  Where is Becket the faithless priest?
Come down Daniel to the lions' den,
  Come down Daniel and join in the feast.

THOMAS: It is the just man who
Like a bold lion, should be without fear.
I am here.
No traitor to the King. I am a priest,
A Christian, saved by the blood of Christ,
Ready to suffer with my blood.
This is the sign of the Church always,
The sign of blood. Blood for blood.
His blood given to buy my life,
My blood given to pay for His death,
My death for His death.

FIRST KNIGHT: Absolve all those you have excommunicated.

SECOND KNIGHT: Resign the powers you have arrogated.
THIRD KNIGHT: Restore to the King the money you
appropriated.
FOURTH KNIGHT: Renew the obedience you have violated.
THOMAS: For my Lord I am now ready to die,
That his Church may have peace and liberty.
Do with me as you will, to your hurt and
shame;
But none of my people, in God's name,
Whether layman or clerk, shall you touch.
This I forbid.
KNIGHTS: Traitor! traitor! traitor!
THOMAS: You, Reginald, three times traitor you:
Traitor to me as my temporal vassal,
Traitor to me as your spiritual lord,
Traitor to God in desecrating His Church.
FIRST KNIGHT: No faith do I owe to a renegade,
And what I owe shall now be paid.

T. S. Eliot

Henry II and Thomas à Becket had been close friends, but the latter, who was made Chancellor of England as well as Archbishop of Canterbury, underwent a marked change, becoming increasingly devout and aloof. He defended the power of the Catholic Church against the growing secular authority of Henry's state. Becket fled to France, but was then coaxed back and, after a short reconciliation with the King, was murdered in Canterbury Cathedral. Within three years he was canonized, in time becoming England's most popular saint.

King Richard I, 1189–99

1191

THE THIRD CRUSADE

With numberless rich pennons streaming
And flags and banners of fair seeming
Then thirty thousand Turkish troops
And more, ranged in well ordered groups,
Garbed and accoutred splendidly,
Dashed on the host impetuously.
Like lightning speed their horses fleet,
And dust rose thick before their feet.
Moving ahead of the emirs
There came a band of trumpeters
And other men with drums and tabors
There were, who had no other labours
Except upon their drums to hammer
And hoot, and shriek and make great clamour.
So loud their tabors did discord
They had drowned the thunder of the Lord.

Ambroise the Chronicler

Richard the Lionheart looked upon England as a treasure house from which to fund his campaigns abroad. He spent only two years of his reign in the country, which has earned him a splendid statue outside the Houses of Parliament. In 1190 he set out at the head of the Third Crusade with the purpose of seizing Jerusalem, recapturing a piece of wood from the Holy Cross, and, more to the point, acquiring as much gold and silver as possible. He forced the Turks' leader, Saladin, to abandon the city of Acre in Palestine. This poem describes the battle of Arsuf, a triumph for Richard, though he was unable to capture Jerusalem itself. On the way back to England, he was imprisoned in

Germany and had to be ransomed. After a short spell in England in 1194, he spent the rest of his reign fighting in France. He was wounded by a bolt from a crossbow shot by a man whose shield was a frying-pan. The wound turned septic and Richard died, forgiving his assailant.

King John, 1199–1216

1215

MAGNA CHARTA

The Reeds of Runnymede

At Runnymede, at Runnymede,
   What say the reeds at Runnymede?
The lissom reeds that give and take,
That bend so far, but never break.
They keep the sleepy Thames awake
   With tales of John at Runnymede.

At Runnymede, at Runnymede,
   Oh hear the reeds at Runnymede: –
'You mustn't sell, delay, deny,
A freeman's right or liberty,
It wakes the stubborn Englishry,
   We saw 'em roused at Runnymede!

'When through our ranks the Barons came,
With little thought of praise or blame,
But resolute to play the game,
   They lumbered up to Runnymede;
And there they launched in solid line,
The first attack on Right Divine –
The curt, uncompromising "Sign!"
   That settled John at Runnymede.

'At Runnymede, at Runnymede,
Your rights were won at Runnymede!
No freeman shall be fined or bound,
Or dispossessed of freehold ground,
Except by lawful judgment found
And passed upon him by his peers!
Forget not, after all these years,
The Charter signed at Runnymede.'

And still when Mob or Monarch lays
Too rude a hand on English ways,
The whisper wakes, the shudder plays,
Across the reeds at Runnymede.
And Thames, that knows the moods of kings,
And crowds and priests and suchlike things,
Rolls deep and dreadful as he brings
Their warning down from Runnymede!

Rudyard Kipling

Unlike his brother Richard, King John lost too many battles. He was nicknamed 'Softsword' after surrendering Normandy in 1204. He tried to intimidate the over-mighty barons by keeping their sons as hostages, and he exacted high taxes from them. In 1215, on an island in the Thames at Runnymede, they replied by making him sign a list of promises which came to be known as Magna Charta. Some clauses were trivial – concerning, for instance, fish traps in the Medway – but the thirty-ninth declared: 'No free man shall be arrested, or imprisoned, or have his property taken away, or be outlawed, or exiled, or in any way ruined, except by lawful judgment . . . or by the law of the land.' Future kings of England had to swear to accept the terms of Magna Charta. Although 'King John was not a good man', one good thing he did was to proclaim that the Jews should not be persecuted.

1216

THE DEATH OF KING JOHN

from **King John**

ACT V *Scene VII*
The Orchard of Swinstead Abbey.
Enter the BASTARD

BAST: O, I am scalded with my violent motion,
And spleen of speed to see your majesty!
K. JOHN: O cousin, thou art come to set mine eye:
The tackle of my heart is crack'd and burn'd,
And all the shrouds wherewith my life should sail
Are turned to one thread, one little hair;
My heart hath one poor string to stay it by,
Which holds but till thy news be uttered;
And then all this thou seest is but a clod
And module of confounded royalty.
BAST: The Dauphin is preparing hitherward,
Where heaven He knows how we shall answer him;
For in a night the best part of my power,
As I upon advantage did remove,
Were in the Washes all unwarily
Devoured by the unexpected flood.

[*The* KING *dies.*]

*

PRINCE HENRY: At Worcester must his body be interr'd;
For so he will'd it.
BAST: Thither shall it then:
And happily may your sweet self put on
The lineal state and glory of the land!
To whom, with all submission, on my knee,
I do bequeath my faithful services
And true subjection everlastingly.
SALISBURY: And the like tender of our love we make,
To rest without a spot for evermore.
P. HEN: I have a kind soul that would give you thanks,
And knows not how to do it but with tears.
BAST: O, let us pay the time but needful woe
Since it hath been beforehand with our griefs.
This England never did, nor never shall,
Lie at the proud foot of a conqueror,
But when it first did help to wound itself.
Now these her princes are come home again,
Come the three corners of the world in arms,
And we shall shock them. Nought shall make us rue,
If England to itself do rest but true. [*Exeunt*]

William Shakespeare

King Henry III, 1216–72

1264

SIMON DE MONTFORT'S REBELLION

from **The Song of Lewes**

So whether it is that the King, misled
By flattering talk to giving his consent,
And truly ignorant of their designs
Unknowingly approves such wrongs as these
Whose only end can be destruction, and
The ruin of his land; or whether he,
With malice in his heart, and ill-intent,
Commits these shameful crimes by raising up
His royal state and power far beyond
The reach of all his country's laws, so that
His whim is satisfied by the abuse
Of royal privilege and strength; if thus
Or otherwise this land of ours is brought
To total rack and ruin, and at last
The kingdom is left destitute, it is
The duty of the great and noble men
To rescue it, to purge the land of all
Corruption and all false authority.

*

For in this year of grace, twelve sixty-four,
The feast of Good Saint Pancras four days past,
The English army rode the heavy storm
Of mighty war, at Lewes' Castle walls.
Then reason to blind fury did give way,
And life to the bright sword. They battle joined
The fourteenth day of May, and dreadful was
The strife in Sussex County, and the See
Of Chichester's Lord Bishop. Hundreds fell,
For mighty was the sword; virtue prevailed,
And evil men took to their heels and fled.
Against these wicked men, our great good Lord
Stood firm, and with the radiant shield of truth
Endued with righteous strength the pure of heart.
Routed their foes, by strength of arms without,
And craven fear within, on them did shine,
More to increase their valour, Heaven's smile.

Roger de Berksted

Henry III had accepted Magna Charta, but his reckless and extravagant behaviour as king led to bankruptcy and he resorted to arbitrary levies and taxes. The nobles, with the former royal favourite Simon de Montfort at their head, sought to control Henry through regular meetings of their Council, sometimes called Parliament, but he resisted and civil war broke out. In 1264 de Montfort won a victory over the royal army at Lewes, capturing both Henry and his heir, Edward. But his success was short-lived. Several of his principal supporters found him insufferably arrogant and deserted him. Within a year he was defeated and killed at Evesham by Edward, a man of sterner stuff than his father. This poem, thought to be by a Franciscan friar, and written in Latin, gives voice to the rebels' grievances and would seem to indicate the strength of feeling against the king.

King Edward I, 1272–1307

1276

THE SUBJUGATION OF WALES

from **The Bard**

'Ruin seize thee, ruthless King!
   Confusion on thy banners wait;
Tho' fann'd by Conquest's crimson wing,
   They mock the air with idle state.
Helm, nor hauberk's twisted mail,
Nor e'en thy virtues, Tyrant shall avail
   To save thy secret soul from nightly fears,
   From Cambria's curse, from Cambria's tears!'
Such were the sounds that o'er the crested pride
   Of the first Edward scatter'd wild dismay,
As down the steep of Snowdon's shaggy side,
   He wound with toilsome march his long array.
Stout Glo'ster stood aghast in speechless trance:
'To arms!' cried Mortimer, and couch'd his quiv'ring lance.

   On a rock whose haughty brow
Frowns o'er cold Conway's foaming flood,
   Robed in the sable garb of woe,
With haggard eyes the poet stood;
(Loose his beard, and hoary hair
Stream'd, like a meteor, to the troubled air;)
And with a master's hand, and prophet's fire,
Struck the deep sorrows of his lyre.

'Hark, how each giant-oak, and desert cave,
Sighs to the torrent's awful voice beneath!
O'er thee, oh King! their hundred arms they wave,
Revenge on thee in hoarser murmurs breathe;
Vocal no more, since Cambria's fatal day,
To high-born Hoel's harp, or soft Llewellyn's lay.

'Cold is Cadwallo's tongue,
That hush'd the stormy main:
Brave Urien sleeps upon his craggy bed:
Mountains, ye mourn in vain
Modred, whose magic song
Made huge Plinlimmon bow his cloud-topt head.
On dreary Arvon's shore they lie,
Smear'd with gore, and ghastly pale:
Far, far aloof th' affrighted ravens sail;
The famish'd eagle screams, and passes by.
Dear lost companions of my tuneful art,
Dear as the light that visits these sad eyes,
Dear as the ruddy drops that warm my heart,
Ye died amidst your dying country's cries –

No more I weep. They do not sleep.
On yonder cliffs, a grisly band,
I see them sit, they linger yet,
Avengers of their native land:
With me in dreadful harmony they join,
And weave with bloody hands the tissue of thy line . . .'

Thomas Gray

Gray was the author of a famous poem, but this is not it. Here he depicts a bard cursing the advance of Edward I's armies into Snowdonia, which had been the bastion of Welsh resistance to English rule. The cause of Llewellyn, the Welsh prince, was lost, and a string of fine castles was built to make permanent the conquest of Wales. At the most magnificent of these, Caernarvon, Edward's son was proclaimed Prince of Wales.

ROBIN HOOD

The Ballad of Robin Hood and the Bishop of Hereford

Come, gentlemen all, and listen a while;
A story I'll to you unfold –
How Robin Hood servèd the Bishop,
When he robb'd him of his gold.

As it befel in merry Barnsdale,
And under the green-wood tree,
The Bishop of Hereford was to come by,
With all his companye.

'Come, kill a ven'son,' said bold Robin Hood,
'Come, kill me a good fat deer;
The Bishop's to dine with me to day,
And he shall pay well for his cheer.

'We'll kill a fat ven'son,' said bold Robin Hood,
'And dress't by the highway-side,
And narrowly watch for the Bishop,
Lest some other way he should ride.'

He dress'd himself up in shepherd's attire,
With six of his men also;
And the Bishop of Hereford came thereby,
As about the fire they did go.

'What matter is this?' said the Bishop;
'Or for whom do you make this a-do?
Or why do you kill the King's ven'son,
When your company is so few?'

'We are shepherds,' said bold Robin Hood,
'And we keep sheep all the year;
And we are disposed to be merry this day,
And to kill of the King's fat deer.'

'You are brave fellowes,' said the Bishop,
 'And the King of your doings shall know;
Therefore make haste, come along with me,
 For before the King you shall go.'

'O pardon, O pardon,' says bold Robin Hood,
 'O pardon, I thee pray!
For it never becomes your lordship's coat
 To take so many lives away.'

'No pardon, no pardon!' the Bishop says;
 'No pardon I thee owe;
Therefore make haste, come along with me,
 For before the King you shall go.'

Robin set his back against a tree,
 And his foot against a thorn,
And from underneath his shepherd's coat
 He pull'd out a bugle horn.

He put the little end to his mouth,
 And a loud blast did he blow,
Till threescore and ten of bold Robin's men
 Came running all on a row;

All making obeisance to bold Robin Hood;
 – 'Twas a comely sight for to see:
'What matter, my master,' said Little John,
 'That you blow so hastilye?' –

'O here is the Bishop of Hereford,
 And no pardon we shall have.' –
'Cut off his head, master,' said Little John,
 'And throw him into his grave.' –

'O pardon, O pardon,' said the Bishop,
 'O pardon, I thee pray!
For if I had known it had been you,
 I'd have gone some other way.' –

'No pardon, no pardon!' said Robin Hood;
  'No pardon I thee owe;
Therefore make haste, come along with me,
  For to merry Barnsdale you shall go.'

Then Robin has taken the Bishop's hand
  And led him to merry Barnsdale;
He made him to stay and sup with him that night,
  And to drink wine, beer and ale.

'Call in the reckoning,' said the Bishòp,
  'For methinks it grows wondrous high.' –
'Lend me your purse, Bishop,' said Little John,
  'And I'll tell you by-and-by.'

Then Little John took the Bishop's cloak,
  And spread it upon the ground,
And out of the Bishop's portmantua
  He told three hundred pound.

'So now let him go,' said Robin Hood;
  Said Little John, 'That may not be;
For I vow and protest he shall sing us a mass
  Before that he go from me.'

Robin Hood took the Bishop by the hand,
  And bound him fast to a tree,
And made him to sing a mass, God wot,
  To him and his yeomandrye.

Then Robin Hood brought him through the wood
  And causèd the music to play,
And he made the Bishop to dance in his boots,
  And they set him on 's dapple-grey,
And they gave the tail within his hand –
  And glad he could so get away!

Anonymous

The legend of Robin Hood was spread by word of mouth in the Middle Ages. The first written reference dates from the 1370s, and scholars have argued over whether he lived in the reign of King John, Edward I, or Edward III. The only certainty is that he operated as an outlaw in Sherwood Forest, north of Nottingham. Over the centuries, his status as a highway robber was transformed into that of a social hero and freedom fighter. His enemies were the enemies of the common people: grasping landlords, corrupt sheriffs and corpulent clergy. Highway robbery was rife in the Middle Ages and in 1390 the poet Chaucer was pounced upon and relieved of £20. No wonder the pilgrims travelled to Canterbury in convoy. Posterity is unlikely to treat the muggers of the twentieth century so fondly.

King Edward II, 1307–27

1314

THE BATTLE OF BANNOCKBURN

Robert Bruce's March to Bannockburn

Scots, wha hae wi' Wallace bled,
    Scots, wham Bruce has aften led;
Welcome to your gory bed,
    Or to victorie.

Now's the day, and now's the hour;
See the front o' battle lower,
See approach proud Edward's power –
    Chains and slaverie!

Wha will be a traitor knave?
Wha can fill a coward's grave?
Wha sae base as be a slave?
    Let him turn and flee!

Wha for Scotland's King and law,
Freedom's sword will strongly draw,
Free-man stand, or free-man fa'?
    Let him follow me!

By oppression's woes and pains!
By your sons in servile chains!
We will drain our dearest veins,
    But they shall be free!

Lay the proud usurpers low!
Tyrants fall in every foe!
Liberty's in every blow!
Let us do, or die!

Robert Burns

In 1306, a year after Wallace's beheading in London, a great Scottish landowner, Robert Bruce, was crowned King of Scotland at Scone. At last a leader had emerged who could avenge his country's shameful submission to English conquest. Edward I died fighting on his way to crush Bruce's rebellion, and his son, Edward II, was decisively beaten at Bannockburn in 1314. Bruce's armies ravaged the North of England, reaching as far as York. In 1328 the English recognized Scotland's independence, but in the following year Bruce died from leprosy, leaving the kingdom to his six-year-old son, David, and his heart to an old friend, James Douglas, who took it with him on a crusade.

PIERS GAVESTON

from **Vita Edwardi Secundi**

Though handsome, rich and clever you may be,
Through insolence we may your ruin see.

translated from the Latin by N. Denholm-Young

On his accession in 1307 Edward II recalled his favourite, Piers Gaveston, who had been in exile, and loaded him with titles, honours and jewels. Contemporary chroniclers were quite clear that the two were lovers. In 1312 the nobles ganged up against Gaveston and took him prisoner at Scarborough and the Earl of Warwick later had him executed as a traitor at Blacklow Hill near the town of Warwick. His body lay where it had fallen until four cobblers raised it on a ladder, sewed the head back on, and took it to the only people who would receive it, the Dominicans at Oxford. It could not, however, be buried, as Gaveston had been excommunicated.

EDWARD AGAINST THE NOBLES

from **Edward the Second**

K. EDW: Now, lusty lords now, not by chance of war,
But justice of the quarrel and the cause,
Vailed is your pride; methinks you hang the heads,
But we'll advance them, traitors; now 'tis time
To be avenged on you for all your braves,
And for the murder of my dearest friend,
To whom right well you knew our soul was knit,
Good Pierce of Gaveston, my sweet favourite.
Ah, rebels! recreants! you made him away.
Accursèd wretches, was't in regard of us,
When we had sent our messenger to request
He might be spared to come to speak with us,
And Pembroke undertook for his return,
That thou, proud Warwick, watched the prisoner,
Poor Pierce, and headed him 'gainst law of arms?
For which thy head shall overlook the rest,
As much as though in rage outwent'st the rest.

Christopher Marlowe

THE FALL OF EDWARD

In winter woe befell me;
By cruel Fortune thwarted,
My life now lies a ruin.
Full oft have I experienced,
There's none so fair, so wise,
So courteous nor so highly famed,
But, if Fortune cease to favour,
Will be a fool proclaimed.

Edward II,
translated from the Norman by A. R. Myers

Edward's Queen, Isabella, deserted his side and, with the help of her lover, Mortimer, contrived to depose him in favour of the King's son. Edward wrote this poem in captivity, before being brutally murdered at Berkeley Castle by having a red-hot poker thrust into his bowels.

King Edward III, 1327–77

1348–9

THE BLACK DEATH

The Shilling in the Armpit

We see death coming into our midst like black smoke,
a plague which cuts off the young, and has no mercy for the fair of face.
Woe is me of the shilling in the armpit:
it is seething, terrible, wherever it may come,
a white lump that gives pain and causes a loud cry,
a burden carried under the arms, a painful angry knob.
It is of the form of an apple, like the head of an onion,
a small boil that spares no one.
Great is its seething, like a burning cinder . . .

Ieuan Gethyn

The Black Death started in Asia in the 1330s, reaching Turkey in 1347. From there it spread quickly through Italy and France, arriving in England in 1348, and Scotland in 1349. It lasted for only two years, although it reappeared on several occasions in England before the Great Plague of London in 1665. The bubonic plague was carried by fleas that lived on rats, and as soon as humans were bitten it became contagious. As described by this Welsh poet, boils, oozing pus and patchy blackening of the skin were symptoms of the disease. Death followed in a few days. According to some estimates, one third of the population of Europe died in consequence.

c. 1370

THE KNIGHTHOOD

from **The General Prologue to the Canterbury Tales**

A Knyght ther was and that a worthy man,
That fro the tyme that he first bigan
To riden out, he loved chivalrie,
Trouthe and honour, fredom and curteisie.
Ful worthy was he in his lordes werre,
And therto had he riden, no man ferre,
As wel in cristendom as in the hethenesse,
And ever honoured for his worthynesse.
At Alisaundre he was whan it was wonne;
Ful ofte tyme he hadde the bord bigonne
Aboven alle nacions in Pruce.
In Lettow had he reysed and in Ruce,
No cristen man so ofte in his degree.
In Gernade at the seege eek hadde he be
Of Algezir, and riden in Belmarye.
At Lyeys was he, and at Satalye,
Whan they were wonne; and in the Grete See
At many a noble armee hadde he be.
At mortal batailles hadde he been fiftene,
And foughten for our feith at Tramyssene
In lystes thries, and ay slayn his foo.
This ilke worthy knyght hadde been also
Somtyme with the lord of Palatye
Agayn another hethen in Turkye;
And evermoore he hadde a sovereyn prys.
And though that he were worthy, he was wys,
And of his port as meeke as is a mayde,
He never yet no vileynye ne sayde,
In al hys lyf, unto no maner wight.
He was a verray parfit, gentil knyght.

Geoffrey Chaucer

Chaucer, the Father of English Poetry, started to write in the 1360s. He had been a minor courtier, occasionally a diplomat, and for a while he was Comptroller of Customs. He lost his post in 1386 when his patron, John of Gaunt, was temporarily out of favour, and it is possible that this was when, with time on his hands, he felt he could start to put together *The Canterbury Tales*. During Edward III's reign he had been allowed a pitcher of wine every day, but this was later changed to a tun once a year, which is what our present Poet Laureate now receives. When Chaucer died in 1400, he was buried in Westminster Abbey, the first writer to be so honoured.

The General Prologue to *The Canterbury Tales* offers a most vivid picture of some of the people who made up the England of the Middle Ages. Each portrait is precise and memorable. Among those represented is the Knight, who was indeed a valiant Crusader, with fifteen 'mortal battles' to his credit. Algeciras (1344), Attalia (1352), Alexandria (1365) and Armenia (1367) are among those cited by Chaucer.

THE NOBILITY

An Arundel Tomb

Side by side, their faces blurred,
The earl and countess lie in stone,
Their proper habits vaguely shown
As jointed armour, stiffened pleat,
And that faint hint of the absurd –
The little dogs under their feet.

Such plainness of the pre-baroque
Hardly involves the eye, until
It meets his left-hand gauntlet, still
Clasped empty in the other; and
One sees, with a sharp tender shock,
His hand withdrawn, holding her hand.

They would not think to lie so long.
Such faithfulness in effigy
Was just a detail friends would see:
A sculptor's sweet commissioned grace
Thrown off in helping to prolong
The Latin names around the base.

They would not guess how early in
Their supine stationary voyage
The air would change to soundless damage,
Turn the old tenantry away;
How soon succeeding eyes begin
To look, not read. Rigidly they

Persisted, linked, through lengths and breadths
Of time. Snow fell, undated. Light
Each summer thronged the glass. A bright
Litter of birdcalls strewed the same
Bone-riddled ground. And up the paths
The endless altered people came,

Washing at their identity.
Now, helpless in the hollow of
An unarmorial age, a trough
Of smoke in slow suspended skeins
Above their scrap of history,
Only an attitude remains:

Time has transfigured them into
Untruth. The stone fidelity
They hardly meant has come to be
Their final blazon, and to prove
Our almost-instinct almost true:
What will survive of us is love.

Philip Larkin

the 1370s

THE POOR

from **Piers Plowman**

The most needy aren oure neighbores, and we nime good
  heede,
As prisones in pittes, and poure folke in cotes,
Charged with children and chef lordes rente:
That they with spinninge may spare, spenen hit in hous-hire;
Bothe in milk and in mele to make with papelotes,
To aglotie with here gurles that greden after foode.
Also hemselve suffren muche hunger,
And wo in winter-time with wakinge a nightes
To rise to the ruel to rocke the cradel,
Both to carde and to cembe, to clouten and to washe,
To ribbe and to reli, rushes to pilie,
That reuthe is to rede othere in rime shewe
The wo of these women that wonieth in cotes;
And of meny other men that muche wo suffren,
Bothe afingrede and afurst to turne the faire outwarde,
And beth abashed for to begge, and wolle nat be aknowe
What hem needeth at here neighbores at noon and at even.
This ich wot witerly, as the worlde techeth,
What other bihoveth that hath meny children,
And hath no catel bote his crafte to clothy hem and to fede,
And fele to fonge therto, and fewe pans taketh.
Ther is pain and peny-ale as for a pitaunce ytake,
Colde flesh and cold fish for veneson ybake;
Fridayes and fasting-dayes a ferthing-worth of muscles
Were a feste for suche folke, other so fele cockes.

William Langland

The great medieval poem from which these lines come was written by a monk from the Midlands in about the 1370s. It is full of revealing details of the social life of the time.

1376

THE DEATH OF THE BLACK PRINCE

Such as thou art, some time was I
Such as I am, such shalt thou be.
I little thought on the hour of death
So long as I enjoyed breath.

Great riches here I did possess
Whereof I made great nobleness.
I had gold, silver, wardrobes and
Great treasure, horses, houses, land

But now a caitiff poor am I,
Deep in the ground, lo here I lie.
My beauty great is all quite gone,
My flesh is wasted to the bone.

*

And if ye should see me this day
I do not think but ye would say
That I had never been a man;
So much altered now I am.

For God's sake pray to the heavenly King
That he my soul to heaven would bring.
All they that pray and make accord
For me unto my God and Lord,
God place them in his Paradise,
Wherein no wretched caitiff lies.

Richard Barber

Edward III's son, the Black Prince, led his father's armies to victory in France and earned the reputation of being 'the flower of chivalry of all the world'. He developed dropsy and died at the age of forty-six, leaving as heir to the old, sick and tired King his young son, Richard of

Bordeaux. The Black Prince had laid down instructions for his funeral, including these words to be inscribed on his tomb.

1377

THE DEATH OF EDWARD III

Sum tyme an Englis schip we had,
  Nobel hit was, and heih of tour;
Thorw al Christendom hit was drad,
  And stif wold stonde in uch a stour,
  And best dorst byde a scharp schour,
And other stormes smale and grete;
  Nou is that schip, that bar the flour,
Selden seiȝe and sone forȝete.

*

The rother was nouther ok ne elm,
  Hit was Edward the thridde the noble kniht;
The prince his sone bar up his helm,
  That never scoumfited was in fiht.
  The king him rod and rouwed ariht,
The prince dredde nouther stok nor streete.
  Nou of hem we lete ful liht;
That selden is seiȝe is sone forȝete.

Anonymous

Edward III had been a great king and a commanding personality. He possessed a fierce temper and it was rumoured that he had once killed a servant with his own hands in a fit of rage. His armies won great victories at Crécy in 1346 and Poitiers in 1356, and in 1347 the key French port of Calais was captured for the English. But the last years of his reign went badly, so that by 1375 England held only Calais, a few ports in Brittany, and a part of Gascony – less than he had inherited on his accession to the throne. For all that, his reign was looked upon by the Tudors as a golden age.

King Richard II, 1377–99

1381

THE PEASANTS' REVOLT

from **A Prologue to the play 'Watt Tyler'**

Too seldom, if the righteous fight is won,
Rebellion boasts a Tell or Washington;
But if the champion of the People fail,
Foes only live to tell Misfortune's tale,
And meanness blots, while none to praise is nigh.
The hero's virtues, with a coward's lie.
Tonight we bring, from his insulted grave,
A man too honest to become a slave:
How few admire him! few, perhaps, bewail'd!
He was a vulgar hero – for he fail'd:
Such glorious honours soothe the patriot's shade!
Of such materials History is made!
But had his followers triumph'd, where he fell
Fame would have hymn'd her village Hampden well,
And Watt the Tyler been a William Tell.

Ebenezer Elliott

This uprising started in Kent and was led by a priest, John Ball, together with Jack Straw and Wat Tyler. The people were oppressed by taxes and alarmed by a series of military setbacks in France. They marched from Kent, pillaging manors, and as they advanced on London they killed the Treasurer and the Archbishop of Canterbury. The King issued letters of pardon and briefly rode out to meet the rebel forces at Smithfield. When Jack Straw and Wat Tyler approached the King, the Lord Mayor of London, Sir William Walworth, struck off Tyler's head. The mob was leaderless and the King rode among them saying, 'Sirs, will you shoot your own king? I will be your captain.'

This was a genuine revolt of ordinary people. Ball preached an early form of Communism, and he caught the nobles and yeomen farmers on the hop. He was hanged, drawn and quartered, and his remains were put on show around the country. His egalitarian philosophy is summed up in the little rhyme of which he was the author:

When Adam delved and Eve span,
Who was then the gentleman?

from The Peasants' Revolt

Tax has tenet us alle,
probat hoc mors tot validorum,
The kyng therof hade smalle,
fuit in manibus cupidorum;
Hit hade harde honsalle,
dans causam fine dolorum;
Revrawnce nede most falle,
propter peccata malorum.

In Kent this kare began,
mox infestando potentes,
In rowte the rybawdus ran,
sua pompis arma ferentes;
Folus dred no mon,
regni regem neque gentes,
Churles were hor chevetan,
vulgo pure dominantes.

*

Laddus loude thay loȝe,
clamantes voce sonora,
The bisschop wen thay sloȝe,
et corpora plura decora;
Maners down thay drowȝe,
in regno non meliora;
Harme thay dud inoȝe,
habuerunt libera lora.

*

Owre kyng hadde no rest,
alii latuere caverna,
To ride he was ful prest,
recolendo gesta paterna;
Jak Straw down he kest
Smythfield virtute superna.
Lord, as thou may best,
regem defende guberna.

Anonymous

This is the only poem about the Peasants' Revolt that we know to be by a contemporary. With a little poetic licence, and omitting the Latin, I have made a modern English version of it that preserves something of the effect of the abrupt rhyming lines of the original:

Tax has hit us all;
The King's revenue is small;
It bears hard on us all;
Reverence now must fall.

In Kent this trouble began:
In riot the rebels ran,
For fools fear no man.
Churls were their chieftain.

Loud the lads did bray,
When the bishop they did slay.
Manors they burnt in a day –
Harm that won't go away.

Our King had no rest;
To ride forth he was pressed.
Jack Straw was a pest.
May his Majesty be blessed!

1399

THE STATE OF ENGLAND

from **King Richard the Second**

ACT II *Scene I.*
London. A Room in Ely House.
GAUNT *on a couch; the* DUKE OF YORK, *and others, standing by him.*

GAUNT: Methinks, I am a prophet new inspired;
And thus, expiring, do foretell of him:
His rash fierce blaze of riot cannot last;
For violent fires soon burn out themselves:
Small showers last long, but sudden storms are short;
He tires betimes, that spurs too fast betimes;
With eager feeding, food doth choke the feeder;
Light vanity, insatiate cormorant,
Consuming means, soon preys upon itself.
This royal throne of kings, this scepter'd isle,
This earth of majesty, this seat of Mars,
This other Eden, demi-paradise;
This fortress, built by nature for herself
Against infection, and the hand of war;
This happy breed of men, this little world;
This precious stone set in the silver sea,
Which serves it in the office of a wall,
Or as a moat defensive to a house,
Against the envy of less happier lands;
This blessed plot, this earth, this realm, this England,
This nurse, this teeming womb of royal kings,
Fear'd by their breed, and famous by their birth,
Renowned for their deeds as far from home,
(For Christian service, and true chivalry,)
As is the sepulchre in stubborn Jewry,
Of the world's ransom, blessed Mary's son:
This land of such dear souls, this dear dear land,
Dear for her reputation through the world,
Is now leased out, (I die pronouncing it,)
Like to a tenement, or pelting farm:

England, bound in with the triumphant sea,
Whose rocky shore beats back to the envious siege
Of watery Neptune, is now bound in with shame,
With inky blots, and rotten parchment bonds;
That England, that was wont to conquer others,
Hath made a shameful conquest of itself:
O, would the scandal vanish with my life,
How happy then were my ensuing death!

William Shakespeare

THE DEPOSITION OF RICHARD II

from **King Richard the Second**

ACT IV. *Scene I.*
Westminster Hall.
BOLINGBROKE *in Council with the Lords and Commons.*
Re-enter YORK, *with* KING RICHARD, *and* OFFICERS
bearing the crown, etc.

K. RICH: Alack, why am I sent for to a king,
Before I have shook off the regal thoughts
Wherewith I reign'd? I hardly yet have learn'd
To insinuate, flatter, bow, and bend my knee; –
Give sorrow leave a while to tutor me
To this submission. Yet I will remember
The favours of these men: Were they not mine?
Did they not sometimes cry, All hail! to me?
So Judas did to Christ: but he, in twelve,
Found truth in all but one; I, in twelve thousand none.
God save the king! – Will no man say Amen?
Am I both priest and clerk? well then, Amen.
God save the king! although I be not he;
And yet, Amen, if Heaven do think him me. –
To do what service am I sent for hither?
YORK: To do that office, of thine own good will,
Which tired majesty did make thee offer, –
The resignation of thy state and crown
To Henry Bolingbroke.
K. RICH: Give me the crown: – Here, cousin, seize the crown;
Here, on this side, my hand; on that side, thine.
Now is this golden crown like a deep well,
That owes two buckets filling one another;
The emptier ever dancing in the air,
The other down, unseen, and full of water:
The bucket down, and full of tears, am I,
Drinking my griefs, whilst you mount up on high.
BOLING: I thought you had been willing to resign.

K. RICH: My crown I am; but still my griefs are mine:
You may my glories and my state depose,
But not my griefs; still am I king of those.
BOLING: Part of your cares you give me with your crown.
K. RICH: Your cares set up, do not pluck my cares down.
My care is – loss of care, by old care done;
Your care is – gain of care, by new care won;
The cares I give, I have, though given away;
They tend the crown, yet still with me they stay.
BOLING: Are you contented to resign the crown?
K. RICH: Ay, no; – no, ay: for I must nothing be;
Therefore no no, for I resign to thee.
Now mark me how I will undo myself: –
I give this heavy weight from off my head,
And this unwieldy sceptre from my hand,
The pride of kingly sway from out my heart;
With mine own tears I wash away my balm,
With mine own hand I give away my crown,
With mine own tongue deny my sacred state,
With mine own breath release all duteous oaths:
All pomp and majesty I do forswear;
My manors, rents, and revenues, I forego;
My acts, decrees, and statutes, I deny;
God pardon all oaths, that are broke to me!
God keep all vows unbroke, are made to thee!
Make me, that nothing have, with nothing grieved;
And thou with all pleased, that hast all achieved
Long may'st thou live in Richard's seat to sit,
And soon lie Richard in an earthly pit!
God save King Henry, unking'd Richard says,
And send him many years of sunshine days! –
What more remains?

William Shakespeare

A weak king was the curse of medieval England. When Richard II succeeded his grandfather, Edward III – one of the strongest of our monarchs – he was a boy of eleven. He was by nature an aesthete who created a cultured court hospitable to writers and painters, and the beautiful hammer-beam roof in Westminster Hall dates from his reign. He failed, however, to control the great baronial families, and so resorted to a series of arbitrary and quixotic ploys in order to maintain his rule. In 1399, on the death of his uncle, John of Gaunt, he seized the lands of Gaunt's son, Henry of Lancaster, who had fled to Paris. No one, it appeared, was safe. But Henry returned to England, where the King, deserted by the rest of the nobles and loathed by the merchants for his forced loans, found himself isolated among his own subjects. Henry thereupon claimed the throne by right of descent, vindicated by conquest. The thirty-three-year-old Richard, last of the Plantagenets, was taken to Pontefract Castle where he was either starved to death or suffocated. Henry said a solemn requiem mass for him at St Paul's.

The House of Lancaster had started its reign and Shakespeare was to be its retrospective Poet Laureate.

Requiem for the Plantagenet Kings

For whom the possessed sea littered, on both shores,
Ruinous arms; being fired, and for good,
To sound the constitution of just wars,
Men, in their eloquent fashion, understood.

Relieved of soul, the dropping-back of dust,
Their usage, pride, admitted within doors;
At home, under caved chantries, set in trust,
With well-dressed alabaster and proved spurs
They lie; they lie; secure in the decay
Of blood, blood-marks, crowns hacked and coveted,
Before the scouring fires of trial-day
Alight on men; before sleeked groin, gored head,
Budge through the clay and gravel, and the sea
Across daubed rock evacuates its dead.

Geoffrey Hill

LANCASTER AND YORK

King Henry IV, 1399–1413

from An Address to the King

O worthi noble kyng, Henry the ferthe,
In whom the glade fortune is befalle
The poeple to governe uppon this erthe,
God hath the chose in comfort of ous alle:
The worschipe of this lond, which was doun falle,
Now stant upriht thurgh grace of thi goodnesse,
Which every man is holde forto blesse.

The highe god of his justice allone
The right which longeth to thi regalie
Declared hath to stonde in thi persone,
And more than god may no man justefie.
Thi title is knowe uppon thin ancestrie,
The londes folk hath ek thy riht affermed;
So stant thi regne of god and man confermed.

John Gower

This is the beginning of a long poem, most of which urges Henry to follow a policy of peace and to avoid war. Apart from dealing with several rebellions at home, however, Henry did embark on costly foreign warfare at the end of his reign. Gower takes care to emphasize Henry's claim to the throne through descent from John of Gaunt, Edward III's third son, adding for good measure that God had chosen him and that he had the support of the people of the land. Even so, the new king was looked upon as a usurper. In Shakespeare's words, 'Uneasy lies the head that wears a crown.'

PRINCE HAL

from **King Henry the Fourth, Part Two**

ACT IV *Scene V*

KING HENRY *lying on a bed.*

PRINCE: I never thought to hear you speak again.
K. HEN.: Thy wish was father, Harry, to that thought:
I stay too long by thee, I weary thee.
Dost thou so hunger for my empty chair
That thou wilt needs invest thee with mine honours.
Before thy hour be ripe? O foolish youth!
Thou seek'st the greatness that will overwhelm thee.
Stay but a little; for my cloud of dignity
Is held from falling with so weak a wind
That it will quickly drop: my day is dim.
Thou has stol'n that which after some few hours
Were thine without offence; and at my death
Thou hast seal'd up my expectation:
Thy life did manifest thou lov'dst me not,
And thou wilt have me die assur'd of it.
Thou hid'st a thousand daggers in thy thoughts,
Which thou hast whetted on thy stony heart,
To stab at half an hour of my life.
What! canst thou not forbear me half an hour?
Then get thee gone and dig my grave thyself,
And bid the merry bells ring to thine ear
That thou art crowned, not that I am dead.
Let all the tears that should bedew my hearse
Be drops of balm to sanctify thy head:
Only compound me with forgotten dust;
Give that which gave thee life unto the worms.
Pluck down my officers, break my decrees;
For now a time is come to mock at form.
Harry the Fifth is crown'd! Up, vanity!
Down, royal state! all you sage counsellors, hence!
And to the English court assemble now,
From every region, apes of idleness!

Now, neighbour confines, purge you of your scum:
Have you a ruffian that will swear, drink, dance,
Revel the night, rob, murder, and commit
The oldest sins the newest kind of ways?
Be happy, he will trouble you no more:
England shall double gild his treble guilt,
England shall give him office, honour, might;
For the fifth Harry from curb'd licence plucks
The muzzle of restraint, and the wild dog
Shall flesh his tooth in every innocent.
O my poor kingdom! sick with civil blows.
When that my care could not withhold thy riots,
What wilt thou do when riot is thy care?
O! thou wilt be a wilderness again,
Peopled with wolves, thy old inhabitants.

William Shakespeare

In the famous scene from which this passage is taken, Prince Hal, son and heir to Henry IV, believing his father to be dead, tries on the crown, but the old king wakes and delivers this majestic rebuke. After leading a riotous life with such companions as Sir John Falstaff, and the mercenary soldiers Pistol and Bardolph, the prince acceded to the throne as Henry V, cast off his old friends and became a national hero – or so the genius of Shakespeare would have it.

King Henry V, 1413–22

1415

from The Battle of Agincourt

Fair stood the wind for France
When we our sails advance,
Nor now to prove our chance
    Longer will tarry;
But putting to the main,
At Caux, the mouth of Seine,
With all his martial train
    Landed King Harry.

And taking many a fort,
Furnished in warlike sort,
Marcheth towards Agincourt
    In happy hour;
Skirmishing day by day
With those that stopped his way,
Where the French general lay
    With all his power;

*

And turning to his men,
Quoth our brave Henry then,
'Though they to one be ten,
    Be not amazëd;
Yet have we well begun,
Battles so bravely won
Have ever to the sun
    By fame been raisëd.

*

'Poitiers and Cressy tell,
When most their pride did swell,
Under our swords they fell;
    No less our skill is
Than when our grandsire great,
Claiming the regal seat,
By many a warlike feat
    Lopped the French lilies.'

*

They now to fight are gone,
Armour on armour shone,
Drum now to drum did groan,
    To hear was wonder:
That with the cries they make
The very earth did shake;
Trumpet to trumpet spake,
    Thunder to thunder.

Well it thine age became,
O noble Erpingham,
Which didst the signal aim
    To our hid forces!
When, from a meadow by,
Like a storm suddenly
The English archery
    Struck the French horses:

With Spanish yew so strong,
Arrows a cloth-yard long,
That like to serpents stung,
    Piercing the weather;
None from his fellow starts,
But, playing manly parts,
And like true English hearts,
    Stuck close together.

When down their bows they threw,
And forth their bilbos drew,
And on the French they flew,
Not one was tardy;
Arms were from shoulders sent,
Scalps to the teeth were rent,
Down the French peasants went:
Our men were hardy.

This while our noble King,
His broad sword brandishing,
Down the French host did ding
As to o'erwhelm it;
And many a deep wound lent,
His arms with blood besprent,
And many a cruel dent
Bruisëd his helmet.

*

Upon Saint Crispin's day
Fought was this noble fray,
Which fame did not delay
To England to carry;
Oh, when shall English men
With such acts fill a pen?
Or England breed again
Such a King Harry?

Michael Drayton

from **King Henry the Fifth**

ACT IV *Scene III*
The English camp.

KING HENRY: . . . This day is call'd the feast of Crispian:
He that outlives this day, and comes safe home,
Will stand a tip-toe when this day is nam'd,
And rouse him at the name of Crispian.
He that shall live this day, and see old age,
Will yearly on the vigil feast his neighbours,
And say, 'To-morrow is Saint Crispian':
Then will he strip his sleeve and show his scars,
And say, 'These wounds I had on Crispin's day.'
Old men forget: yet all shall be forgot,
But he'll remember with advantages
What feats he did that day. Then shall our names,
Familiar in his mouth as household words,
Harry the king, Bedford and Exeter,
Warwick and Talbot, Salisbury and Gloucester,
Be in their flowing cups freshly remember'd.
This story shall the good man teach his son;
And Crispin Crispian shall ne'er go by,
From this day to the ending of the world,
But we in it shall be remembered;
We few, we happy few, we band of brothers;
For he to-day that sheds his blood with me
Shall be my brother; be he ne'er so vile
This day shall gentle his condition:
And gentlemen in England, now a-bed
Shall think themselves accurs'd they were not here,
And hold their manhoods cheap whiles any speaks
That fought with us upon Saint Crispin's day.

William Shakespeare

Henry V showed himself determined to reclaim for England the old Angevin Empire in France, and in 1415 he set sail for that purpose with

1,500 ships and 10,000 fighting men. Within a few months, however, after capturing the fortified town of Harfleur, the number of his men had been reduced to 6,000 by death in battle and dysentery. Withdrawing to the coast, this small army met a much larger French one and, through Henry's personal inspiration and skilful use of the long bow, defeated it. Thereafter England was committed to a ruinously expensive war on the Continent: in 1418 alone the army ordered one million goose feathers for its arrows. In 1420 the Treaty of Troyes established Henry as heir to the French throne through his marriage to Catherine of Valois. From England's point of view, that represented the high point of the Hundred Years War, and from then on it was downhill all the way until at last Mary Tudor lost Calais. Henry died in 1422, from dysentery caught on the campaign, and he made the unforgivable mistake, for a medieval king, of leaving an heir just one year old.

1420

DICK WHITTINGTON'S THIRD TERM AS LORD MAYOR OF LONDON

Here must I tell the praise
  Of worthy Whittington,
Known to be in his age
  Thrice Mayor of London.
But of poor parentage
  Born was he, as we hear,
And in his tender age
  Bred up in Lancashire.

Poorly to London than
  Came up this simple lad,
Where with a merchant-man,
  Soon he a dwelling had;
And in a kitchen placed,
  A scullion for to be,
Whereas long time he past
  In labour drudgingly.

His daily service was
  Turning spits at the fire;
And to scour pots of brass,
  For a poor scullion's hire.
Meat and drink all his pay,
  Of coin he had no store;
Therefore to run away,
  In secret thought he bore.

So from this merchant-man
  Whittington secretly
Towards his country ran,
  To purchase liberty.
But as he went along,
  In a fair summer's morn
London bells sweetly rung,
  'Whittington, back return!'

Evermore sounding so,
  'Turn again Whittington:
For thou in time shall grow
  Lord-Mayor of London.'
Whereupon back again
  Whittington came with speed.
A 'prentice to remain,
  As the Lord had decreed.

*

But see his happy chance!
  This scullion had a cat,
Which did his state advance,
  And by it wealth he gat.
His master ventured forth,
  To a land far unknown,
With merchandise of worth,
  As is in stories shown.

Whittington had no more
But this poor cat as than,
Which to the ship he bore,
Like a brave merchant-man,
'Venturing the same,' quoth he,
'I may get store of gold,
And Mayor of London be;
As the bells have me told.'

Whittington's merchandise
Carried was to a land
Troubled with rats and mice,
As they did understand.
The king of that country there,
As he at dinner sat,
Daily remained in fear
Of many a mouse and rat.

Meat that on trenchers lay,
No way they could keep safe;
But by rats borne away,
Fearing no wand or staff.
Whereupon soon they brought
Whittington's nimble cat;
Which by the king was bought;
Heaps of gold given for that.

Home again came these men
With their ships loaden so,
Whittington's wealth began
By this cat thus to grow.
Scullion's life he forsook
To be a merchant good,
And soon began to look
How well his credit stood.

After that he was chose
  Sheriff of the city here,
And then full quickly rose
  Higher, as did appear.
For to this cities praise,
  Sir Richard Whittington
Came to be in his day,
  Thrice Mayor of London.

Anonymous

The eponymous pantomime hero had his origins in verifiable history, catching the popular imagination as an archetype of the rags-to-riches story.

King Henry VI, 1422–61

1430

from To the King on his Coronation

Most noble prince of cristen princes alle,
  Flowryng in yowthe and vertuous innocence,
Whom God above list of his grace calle
  This day to estate of knyghtly excellence,
  And to be crowned with diewe reverence,
To grete gladness of al this regioun,
  Lawde and honour to thy magnificence,
And goode fortune unto thy high renoun.

Royal braunched, descended from two lynes,
  Of seynt Edward and of seynt Lowys;
Holy seyntes, translated in theyr shrynes,
  In theyr tyme manly, prudent, and wys;
  Arthur was knyghtly, and Charles of grete prys,
And of all these thy grene tender age,
  By the grace of God and by his advys,
Of manly prowesse shal taken tarage.

*

Prince excelent, be feythful, triewe, and stable;
  Drede God, do lawe, chastice extorcioun;
Be liberal of courage, unmutable;
  Cherisshe the chirche with hole affeccioun;
  Love thy lieges of eyther regioun;
Preferre the pees, eschewe werre and debate;
  And God shal sende from the heven downe
Grace and goode hure to thy royal estate.

attributed to John Lydgate

Lydgate, the monk of Bury St Edmunds, may have written this ode of welcome to the young King Henry who was crowned at seven years of age. Not only does the poet ascribe to him qualities which, sadly, Henry VI was not to possess, but he takes the opportunity to make a political point by stressing the dual inheritance and its legitimacy.

1436

from Plea for a Navy

The trewe processe of Englysh polycye,
  Of utterwarde to kepe thys regne in rest
Of oure England, that no man may denye,
  Nere saye of soth but one of the best
  Is thys, that who seith southe, northe, est, and west,
Cheryshe marchandyse, kepe thamyralté,
That we bee masteres of the narowe see.

*

Where bene oure shippes? where bene oure swerdes become?
  Owre enmyes bid for the shippe sette a shepe.
Allas! oure reule halteth, hit is benome;
  Who dare weel say that lordeshyppe shulde take kepe?
  I wolle asaye, thoughe myne herte gynne to wepe,
To do thys werke, yf we wole ever the,
Ffor verry shame, to kepe aboute the see.

Anonymous

For the next fifteen years England was under the control of a minority government led by Henry's brothers and Cardinal Beaufort. The English armies in France were pushed back, particularly after 1429. Paris fell in 1436, but few in England wished to give up revenue to the merchants who argued strongly for a subsidized navy.

King Edward IV, 1461–83

1461

THE RISE OF THE HOUSE OF YORK

Also scripture saithe, woo be to that regyon
  Where ys a kyng unwyse or innocent;
Moreovyr it ys right a gret abusion,
  A womman of a land to be a regent,
  Qwene Margrete I mene, that ever hathe ment
To governe alle Engeland with myght and poure,
  And to destroye the ryght lyne was here entent,
Wherfore sche hathe a fal, to here gret langoure.

*

Wherfore I lykken England to a gardayne,
  Whiche that hathe ben overgrowen many yere
Withe wedys, whiche must be mowen doune playne,
  And than schul the pleasant swete herbes appere.
  Wherfore alle trewe Englyshe peuple, pray yn fere
For kyng Edward of Rouen, oure comfortoure,
  That he kepe justice and make wedis clere,
Avoydyng the blak cloudys of langoure.

A gret signe it ys that God lovythe that knyght,
  For alle thoo that woold have destroyed hym utterly,
Alle they ar myschyeved and put to flyght.
  Than remembre hys fortune with chevalry
  Whiche at Northamptoun gate the victory,
And at Mortimers Crosse he had the honnour;
  On Palme Sonday he wan the palme of glorye,
And put hys enemyes to endelez langour.

Anonymous

Embedded in this piece of Yorkist propaganda is a very pleasant verse of poetry. The Wars of the Roses lasted from 1455 to 1485. The Yorkists triumphed at Northampton in 1460 when they captured Henry VI, but the Duke of York was himself killed at Wakefield in the same year. His son, Edward of March, regained the initiative and beat the Lancastrians at Mortimers Cross and Towton in 1461. These victories cleared the way for his coronation as Edward IV, the first Yorkist king of England.

1478

THE MURDER OF THE DUKE OF CLARENCE

from **King Richard the Third**

ACT I *Scene IV*
London. The Tower.

FIRST MURDERER: Who made thee then a bloody minister,
When gallant-springing, brave Plantagenet,
That princely novice, was struck dead by thee?
CLARENCE: My brother's love, the devil, and my rage.
FIRST MURD: Thy brother's love, our duty, and thy fault,
Provoke us hither now to slaughter thee.
CLAR: If you do love my brother, hate not me;
I am his brother, and I love him well.
If you be hir'd for meed, go back again,
And I will send you to my brother Gloucester,
Who shall reward you better for my life
Than Edward will for tidings of my death.
SECOND MURD: You are deceiv'd, your brother Gloucester hates you.
CLAR: O, no! he loves me, and he holds me dear: Go you to him from me.
BOTH MURD: Ay, so we will.
CLAR: Tell him, when that our princely father York
Bless'd his three sons with his victorious arm,
And charg'd us from his soul to love each other,
He little thought of this divided friendship:
Bid Gloucester think on this, and he will weep.
FIRST MURD: Ay, millstones; as he lesson'd us to weep.
CLAR: O! do not slander him, for he is kind.
FIRST MURD: Right,
As snow in harvest. Thou deceiv'st thyself:
'Tis he that sends us to destroy you here.
CLAR: It cannot be; for he bewept my fortune,
And hugg'd me in his arms, and swore, with sobs,
That he would labour my delivery.

FIRST MURD: Why, so he doth, now he delivers you
From this earth's thraldom to the joys of heaven.
SECOND MURD: Make peace with God, for you must die, my lord.
CLAR: Have you that holy feeling in thy soul,
To counsel me to make my peace with God,
And art thou yet to thy own soul so blind,
That thou wilt war with God by murdering me?
O! sirs, consider, they that set you on
To do this deed will hate you for the deed.
SECOND MURD: What shall we do?
CLAR: Relent and save your souls.
FIRST MURD: Relent! 'tis cowardly and womanish.
CLAR: Not to relent, is beastly, savage, devilish.
Which of you, if you were a prince's son,
Being pent from liberty, as I am now,
If two such murderers as yourselves came to you,
Would not entreat for life?
My friend, I spy some pity in thy looks;
O! if thine eye be not a flatterer,
Come thou on my side, and entreat for me,
As you would beg, were you in my distress:
A begging prince what beggar pities not?
SECOND MURD: Look behind you, my lord.
FIRST MURD: Take that, and that: (*Stabs him.*)
If all this will not do,
I'll drown you in the malmsey-butt within.
(*Exit, with the body.*)

William Shakespeare

If the Duke of Clarence had not met his end in a butt of malmsey wine, his death would no doubt have been forgotten amid the baronial mayhem of the fifteenth century. He was a younger brother of Edward IV and was of an ambitious and unstable disposition. He supported Warwick the Kingmaker during his rebellion of 1469–71, but upon Edward's return from exile in 1471 defected back to his brother and fought alongside him at Barnet and Tewkesbury. Although restored to favour, he was never satisfied with his power, and in 1478 Edward had him arrested for high treason. Tradition relates that he was executed by drowning in his favourite wine. Shakespeare depicted Richard of Gloucester as his murderer, but there is no external evidence for this and the full responsibility must lie with Edward.

King Edward V, 1483, and King Richard III, 1483–5

THE MURDER OF THE PRINCES IN THE TOWER

from **King Richard the Third**

ACT IV *Scene III*
London. A Room of State in the Palace.
(*Enter* TYRREL)

TYR: The tyrannous and bloody act is done;
The most arch deed of piteous massacre,
That ever yet this land was guilty of,
Dighton, and Forest, whom I did suborn
To do this piece of ruthless butchery,
Albeit they were flesh'd villains, bloody dogs,
Melting with tenderness and mild compassion,
Wept like two children, in their death's sad story.
O thus, quoth Dighton, *lay the gentle babes,–*
Thus, thus, quoth Forrest, *girdling one another*
Within their alabaster innocent arms:
Their lips were four red roses on a stalk,
Which, in their summer beauty, kiss'd each other.
A book of prayers on their pillow lay;
Which once, quoth Forrest, *almost changed my mind:*
But, O, the devil – there the villain stopp'd;
When Dighton thus told on, – *we smothered*
The most replenished sweet work of nature.
That, from the prime creation e'er she framed. –
Hence both are gone with conscience and remorse,
They could not speak; and so I left them both,
To bear this tidings to the bloody king:
And here he comes.
(*Enter* KING RICHARD)
All health, my sovereign lord!
K. RICH: Kind Tyrrel! am I happy in thy news?

William Shakespeare

In April 1483 Edward IV died and was succeeded by his twelve-year-old son, Edward V, whose coronation was planned for 22 June. Richard of Gloucester, Edward IV's brother and the young King's uncle, was made Protector. He realized that the Woodville family, relations of Edward, would wait until the King came of age and then turn upon Richard himself. So he moved quickly to place Edward and his younger brother under guard in the Tower of London, an act which had the full support of the Archbishop of Canterbury. With that accomplished, he claimed the throne and was crowned in July. Tudor propaganda accused him of suffocating the princes in the Tower; of killing Henry VI; and of having his brother, the Duke of Clarence, murdered. So bad was his reputation that he was obliged personally to deny that he had done away with his wife, Anne, in order to marry his niece.

The Cat, the Rat and Lovel our dog
Rule all England under the Hog.

William Collingbourne

This scathing couplet was found pinned to the door of St Paul's Cathedral in London. It alludes to Catesby, Ratcliffe and Lovel, ministers of the King, who is represented here by his heraldic emblem, a white boar. But this was no age for satire. Collingbourne, who had also tried to persuade Henry Tudor to lead a revolt against Richard, was caught and, on a new gallows specially constructed on Tower Hill, he was hanged. According to report, he was cut down while still alive to have 'his bowels ripped out of his belly and cast into the fire there by him', and even so he 'lived till the butcher put his hand into the bulk of his body; insomuch that he said in the same instant, "O Lord Jesus, yet more trouble," and so died to the great compassion of much people'. As another couplet has it:

The axe was sharp, the block was hard,
In the fourth year of King Richard.

1485

THE BATTLE OF BOSWORTH

from **King Richard the Third**

SCENE IV

Another part of the field.

Alarum; excursions. Enter NORFOLK *and forces fighting; to him* CATESBY.

CATESBY: Rescue, my Lord of Norfolk, rescue, rescue!
The king enacts more wonders than a man,
Daring an opposite to every danger:
His horse is slain, and all on foot he fights,
Seeking for Richmond in the throat of death.
Rescue, fair lord, or else the day is lost!

(*Alarums. Enter* KING RICHARD)

KING RICHARD: A horse! a horse! my kingdom for a horse!
CATESBY: Withdraw, my lord; I'll help you to a horse.
KING RICHARD: Slave, I have set my life upon a cast,
And I will stand the hazard of the die.
I think there be six Richmonds in the field;
Five have I slain to-day instead of him.
A horse! a horse! my kingdom for a horse! [*Exeunt.*]

Another part of the field.

Alarum. Enter KING RICHARD *and* RICHMOND; *they fight.* RICHARD *is slain. Retreat and flourish. Re-enter* RICHMOND, DERBY *bearing the crown, with divers other Lords.*

RICHMOND: God and your arms be praised, victorious friends!
The day is ours; the bloody dog is dead.
DERBY: Courageous Richmond, well hast thou acquit thee.
Lo, here, this long usurped royalty
From the dead temples of this bloody wretch
Have I pluck'd off, to grace thy brows withal;
Wear it, enjoy it, and make much of it.

*

RICHMOND: O now, let Richmond and Elizabeth,
The true succeeders of each royal house,
By God's fair ordinance conjoin together;
And let their heirs, (God, if thy will be so,)
Enrich the time to come with smooth-faced peace,
With smiling plenty, and fair prosperous days;
Now civil wounds are stopp'd, peace lives again:
That she may long live here, God say – Amen.
[*Exeunt.*]

William Shakespeare

Richard was feared and detested by many of the noble families. In August 1485 Henry Tudor, Earl of Richmond, landed at Milford Haven, and within three weeks was King. The decisive factors in Richard's defeat at Bosworth were the inertia of the Earl of Northumberland, who failed to appear, and the treachery of the Stanley family who, in spite of having been handsomely rewarded by Richard, switched their allegiance to Henry. So ended Richard III's reign. Some historians have tried to restore his good name, but it's no easy match to take on Shakespeare.

THE TUDORS

King Henry VII, 1485–1509

THE TUDOR ROSE

'I loue the rose both red & white.'
'Is that your pure perfite appetite?'
'To here talke of them is my delite!'
'Ioyed may we be,
oure prince to se,
& rosys thre!'

Anonymous

Henry Tudor, of the red rose of Lancaster, married Elizabeth, daughter of Edward IV, of the white rose of York, and thereby brought the dynastic Wars of the Roses to an end. The resulting hybrid, the Tudor rose, the third alluded to here, was personified in the figure of Arthur, Henry's heir, who, however, died young, leaving the succession to his brother, Henry VIII.

1491

THE DEATH OF CAXTON

Fiat Lux

Thy prayer was 'Light – more Light – while Time shall last!'
Thou sawest a glory growing on the night,
But not the shadows which that light would cast,
Till shadows vanish in the Light of Light.

Alfred, Lord Tennyson

William Caxton had been a merchant and a diplomat, but in 1476, after his retirement, he set up a printing press in the precincts of Westminster Abbey, the first in the country. There he printed works by Chaucer, Lydgate, Gower and Malory, and anything else he thought he could sell. By adopting the spelling that was common in London, he helped to regularize that of the whole English language. The invention of printing had a revolutionary effect on communications. Hitherto the business of scholarship had been a monopoly of the clergy, by whom it was jealously guarded as being the main source of their influence and power. Now it was to be available to anyone. Tennyson wrote this epitaph for Caxton's tomb in St Margaret's, Westminster.

King Henry VIII, 1509–47

HENRY'S WIVES

Divorced, beheaded, died,
Divorced, beheaded, survived.

Anonymous

This simple mnemonic describes the fate of each of the six wives of Henry VIII: Catherine of Aragon, Anne Boleyn, Jane Seymour, Anne of Cleves, Catherine Howard and Catherine Parr.

c. 1510

A TUDOR TEXTILE FACTORY

from **The Pleasant History of Jack of Newbury**

Within one roome, being large and long
There stood two hundred Loomes full strong.
Two hundred men, the truth is so,
Wrought in the Loomes all in a row.
By every one a pretty boy
Sate making quilts with mickle joy,
And in another place hard by
A hundred women merrily
Were carding hard with joyful cheere
Who singing sate with voyces cleere,
And in a chamber close beside
Two hundred maidens did abide,
In petticoats of Stammell red,
And milk white kerchiefs on their head.
Their smocke-sleeves like to winter snow
That on the Westerne mountaines flow,
And each sleeve with a silken band
Was featly tied at the hand.
These pretty maids did never lin
But in that place all day did spin,
And spinning so with voyces meet
Like nightingales they sang full sweet.
Then to another roome, came they
Where children were in poore aray;
And every one sate picking wool
The finest from the course to cull:
The number was sevenscore and ten
The children of poore silly men:
And these their labours to requite
Had every one a penny at night,
Beside their meat and drinke all day,
Which was to them a wondrous stay.
Within another place likewise

Full fifty proper men he spies
And these were sheremen everyone,
Whose skill and cunning there was showne:
And hard by them there did remaine
Full four-score rowers taking paine.
A Dye-house likewise had he then,
Wherein he kept full forty men:
And likewise in his Fulling Mill
Full twenty persons kept he still.

Thomas Deloney

Deloney's poem was written in 1597 and achieved great popularity. It celebrates a legendary figure of the Tudor cloth industry, John Winchcombe, who lived in the reign of Henry VIII and, among other things, led one hundred of his apprentices into battle at Flodden Field in 1513. The manufacture of cloth was the major economic activity of Tudor England. In the Middle Ages the various processes involved in the making of cloth were organized by separate guilds. In the sixteenth century, however, rich merchants began the practice of gathering the various trades under a single roof, while weavers regularly petitioned Parliament against this early manifestation of capitalism.

1515–29

CARDINAL WOLSEY'S ASCENDANCY

from **Why Come Ye not to Courte?**

To tell the truth plainly
He is so ambitious,
So shameless and so vicious,
And so superstitious
And so much oblivious
From whence that he came
That he falleth into a *caeciam*
Which, truly to express,
Is a forgetfulness,
Or wilful blindness.

*

Howbeit the primordial
Of his wretched original
And his base progeny
And his greasy genealogy
He came of the sang royall
That was cast out of a butcher's stall.

*

Such is a kinges power
To make within an hour
And work such a miracle
That shall be a spectacle
Of renown and wordly fame.
In likewise now the same
Cardinal is promoted,
Yet with lewd conditions coated
As hereafter ben noted,
Presumption and vainglory,
Envy, wrath, and lechery,
Couvetise and gluttony,
Slothful to do good,
Now frantic, now starke wood.

Set up a wretch on high
In a throne triumphantly,
Make him a great estate
And he will play checkmate
With royal majesty.

John Skelton

The son of an Ipswich butcher, Thomas Wolsey more or less ran the country in the early years of Henry's reign. As a Cardinal, Archbishop of York, and Lord Chancellor of England, he lived in sumptuous style, the envy of the nobility and, eventually, of the King himself. He dined off gold plate, had his red hat carried before him, and built Hampton Court; but he failed, when required, to obtain for his master a divorce from Catherine of Aragon. He fell from grace and was arrested, but died while being taken to be tried in London.

1518

THE FRENCH FASHION OF THE ENGLISH GALLANT

He struts about
In cloaks of fashion French. His girdle, purse,
And sword are French. His hat is French.
His nether limbs are cased in French costume.
His shoes are French. In short, from top to toe
He stands the Frenchman.

*

With accent French he speaks the Latin tongue,
With accent French the tongue of Lombardy,
To Spanish words he gives an accent French,
German he speaks with his same accent French,
In truth he seems to speak with accent French,
All but the French itself. The French he speaks
With accent British.

translated from the Latin of Thomas More

Henry VIII admired French clothes and French manners, and he made French the language of his courtiers. Thomas More, in a Latin poem, pointed out the spuriousness of this attempted conversion, all the more untimely when the national consciousness of England was being formed through the break from Rome, and William Tyndale was about to start his translation of the Bible into English.

c. 1520

TUDOR FOOTBALL

Eche time and season hath his delite and joyes,
Loke in the stretes, behold the little boyes,
Howe in fruite season for joy they sing and hop,
In Lent is each one full busy with his top
And nowe in winter for all the greevous colde
All rent and ragged a man may them beholde,
They have great pleasour supposing well to dine,
When men be busied in killing of fat swine,
They get the bladder and blowe it great and thin,
With many beanes or peason put within,
It ratleth, soundeth, and shineth clere and fayre,
While it is throwen and caste up in the ayre,
Eche one contendeth and hath a great delite
With foote and with hande the bladder for to smite,
If it fall to grounde, they lifte it up agayne,
This wise to labour they count it for no payne,
Renning and leaping they drive away the colde,
The sturdie plowmen lustie, strong and bolde
Ouercommeth the winter with driving the foote-ball,
Forgetting labour and many a grevous fall.

Alexander Barclay

THE KING'S PLEASURES

The Hunt is Up

The hunt is up, the hunt is up,
And it is well nigh day;
And Harry our King is gone hunting
To bring his deer to bay.

The east is bright with morning light,
And darkness it is fled,
The merry horn wakes up the morn
To leave his idle bed.

The horses snort to be at the sport,
The dogs are running free,
The woods rejoice at the merry noise
Of hay-taranta-tee-ree.

The sun is glad to see us clad
All in our lusty green,
And smiles in the sky as he rideth high
To see and to be seen.

Awake all men, I say again
Be merry as you may:
For Harry our king is gone hunting
To bring his deer to bay.

Anonymous

The most extrovert of English kings, Henry VIII, threw himself into vigorous physical activity of all kinds. The chronicler Edward Hall notes that, during a royal progress in 1511, the King indulged 'in shooting, singing, dancing, wrestling, casting the bar, playing at the recorders, flute and virginals, and in setting of songs and making of ballads, and did set two godly masses'. He spent many days of his life in the saddle. In 1524 he was almost killed in a joust with the Duke of Suffolk because he had refused to put his visor down. In the next year, while out hawking – his favourite pastime – he tried to leap over a ditch with a pole, but fell into the mud head first and was only just saved from drowning. In 1536, at the age of forty-four, he was unseated in a joust and lay unconscious for two hours after his horse had rolled over him. But the big, heavy, old body withstood all this, and even managed to survive that most dreadful thing, Tudor medicine, until Henry's fifty-fifth year.

1529

THE FALL OF WOLSEY

from **King Henry the Eighth**

ACT III *Scene II*

Antechamber to the KING'*s Apartment*.

CARDINAL WOLSEY: . . . I have ventur'd,
Like little wanton boys that swim on bladders,
This many summers in a sea of glory;
But far beyond my depth: my high-blown pride
At length broke under me; and now has left me,
Weary and old with service, to the mercy
Of a rude stream, that must for ever hide me.
Vain pomp and glory of this world, I hate ye!
I feel my heart new open'd. O, how wretched
Is that poor man that hangs on princes' favours!
There is, betwixt that smile we would aspire to,
That sweet aspéct of princes, and their ruin,
More pangs and fears than wars or women have;
And when he falls, he falls like Lucifer,
Never to hope again.

*

WOLSEY: (*To* CROMWELL) . . . Serve the king;
And, – pr'ythee, lead me in:
There take an inventory of all I have;
To the last penny, 't is the king's: my robe,
And my integrity to heaven, is all
I dare now call mine own. O Cromwell, Cromwell!
Had I but serv'd my God with half the zeal
I serv'd my king, he would not in mine age
Have left me naked to mine enemies.

William Shakespeare

1533

THE RISE OF CRANMER

Cranmer

Cranmer was parson of this parish
And said Our Father beside barns
Where my grandfather worked without praying.

From the valley came the ring of metal
And the horses clopped down the track by the stream
As my mother saw them.

The Wiltshire voices floated up to him
How should they not overcome his proud Latin
With We depart answering his *Nunc Dimittis*?

One evening he came over the hillock
To the edge of the churchyard already filled with bones
And saw in the smithy his own fire burning.

C. H. Sisson

Thomas Cranmer's studies for the priesthood at Cambridge were interrupted by his marriage to an innkeeper's daughter, who later died. During the 1520s he was associated with scholars who were questioning the supremacy and infallibility of the Pope. He was used by Henry VIII in the matter of his first divorce and in 1533 he was appointed Archbishop of Canterbury. It was he, in effect, who founded the Church of England, establishing the Bible in English, translating the Prayer Book himself, and promulgating the Thirty-nine Articles. On the death of Edward VI he foolishly supported Lady Jane Grey and was condemned for treason. Mary wanted to punish him for heresy and he was duly convicted, but under duress he recanted and this was seen as a great triumph for Catholicism. Though it did not save him from the stake, he finally regained his courage, renounced his recantation and, approaching the flames that were to consume him, thrust in first the hand which had signed it.

1535

THE EXECUTION OF SIR THOMAS MORE

Sir Thomas More

Holbein's More, my patron saint as a convert,
the gold chain of *S's*, the golden rose,
the plush cap, the brow's damp feathertips of hair,
the good eyes' stern, facetious twinkle, ready
to turn from executioner to martyr –
or saunter with the great King's bluff arm on your neck,
feeling that friend-slaying, terror-dazzled heart
balooning off into its awful dream –
a noble saying, 'How the King must love you!'
And you, 'If it were a question of my head,
or losing his meanest village in France . . .'
then by the scaffold and the headsman's axe –
'Friend, give me your hand for the first step,
as for coming down, I'll shift for myself.'

Robert Lowell

Thomas More was a true Renaissance man – a scholar, a poet, a philosopher, a Member of Parliament and a diplomat. He succeeded Wolsey as Lord Chancellor in 1529, but resigned the post in 1532. In 1534 he refused to take the oath asserting Henry VIII's supremacy over the Pope and legitimizing his divorce from Catherine of Aragon. More knew that this refusal to compromise his principles would cost him his life, and it did.

1536

THE DEATH OF ANNE BOLEYN

As for them all I do not thus lament,
But as of right my reason doth me bind;
But as the most doth all their deaths repent,
Even so do I by force of mourning mind.
Some say, 'Rochford, haddest thou been not so proud,
For thy great wit each man would thee bemoan,
Since as it is so, many cry aloud
It is great loss that thou art dead and gone.'

Ah! Norris, Norris, my tears begin to run
To think what hap did thee so lead or guide
Whereby thou hast both thee and thine undone
That is bewailed in court of every side;
In place also where thou hast never been
Both man and child doth piteously thee moan.
They say, 'Alas, thou art far overseen
By thine offences to be thus dead and gone.'

Ah! Weston, Weston, that pleasant was and young,
In active things who might with thee compare?
All words accept that thou diddest speak with tongue,
So well esteemed with each where thou diddest fare.

And we that now in court doth lead our life
Most part in mind doth thee lament and moan;
But that thy faults we daily hear so rife,
All we should weep that thou are dead and gone.

*

Ah! Mark, what moan should I for thee make more,
Since that thy death thou hast deserved best,
Save only that mine eye is forced sore
With piteous plaint to moan thee with the rest?
A time thou haddest above thy poor degree,
The fall whereof thy friends may well bemoan:
A rotten twig upon so high a tree
Hath slipped thy hold, and thou art dead and gone.

And thus farewell each one in hearty wise!
The axe is home, your heads be in the street;
The trickling tears doth fall so from my eyes
I scarce may write, my paper is so wet.
But what can hope when death hath played his part,
Though nature's course will thus lament and moan?
Leave sobs therefore, and every Christian heart
Pray for the souls of those be dead and gone.

attributed to Thomas Wyatt

A FINAL WORD FROM HER OWN BOOK OF HOURS

Remember me when you do pray,
That hope doth lead from day to day.

Anne Boleyn

In 1525 Henry became infatuated with one of the Ladies of the Court, Anne Boleyn. She was beautiful, ambitious and resolute. In 1529 she played an important role in the downfall of Wolsey. Henry showered her with gifts and she went out riding and hunting with him. Around 1531 they started to sleep together and in 1532 she found herself pregnant. Henry, in the mean time, had proclaimed himself the head of the Church in England, and arranged for his divorce from Catherine. He married Anne secretly in January, 1533; her coronation took place in June; and in September she gave birth to a daughter, Elizabeth, who was to prove the most notable Queen in English history.

Henry, however, wanted a son to secure the stability of his succession. Anne suffered a miscarriage in 1534, and again in 1536. But already the King's eye had alighted on another Lady of the Court, Jane Seymour. Anne's position grew increasingly isolated. Henry's chief minister, Thomas Cromwell, divined his master's wish that she must go, either by divorce or by some other means. At Easter in 1536 Henry and Anne quarrelled in public and Cromwell decided to act. Within four weeks Anne was arrested, tried, executed and buried in the Tower. The charges brought against her included incest with her brother Rochford, and adultery with the various courtiers named in the poem which is attributed to Thomas Wyatt. Wyatt himself was arrested on the grounds that he had been Anne's lover before her marriage, but he was later released.

Cromwell manufactured whatever evidence he needed, and rigged the juries. Anne may have been flirtatious, but it is unlikely that she was so rash as to have actively deceived Henry. The coup against her worked because she had so many enemies – the friends of Mary Tudor, of the late Thomas More, and of the up-and-coming Seymours. But her greatest enemy was no doubt the King himself, who had grown bored with her and was able to exploit the services of Cromwell, one of the most efficient civil servants of the Tudor period. Anne did not have a chance.

She was executed on 19 May. On the next day Henry was betrothed to Jane Seymour, and on 30 May they were married.

1537

THE DEATH OF QUEEN JANE

Queen Jane was in travail
For six weeks or more,
Till the women grew tired,
And fain would give o'er.
'O women! O women!
Good wives if ye be,
Go, send for King Henrie,
And bring him to me.'

King Henrie was sent for,
He came with all speed,
In a gownd of green velvet
From heel to the head.
'King Henrie! King Henrie!
If kind Henrie you be,
Send for a surgeon,
And bring him to me.'

The surgeon was sent for,
He came with all speed,
In a gownd of black velvet
From heel to the head.
He gave her rich caudle,
But the death-sleep slept she.
Then her right side was opened,
And the babe was set free.

The babe it was christened,
And put out and nursed,
While the royal Queen Jane
She lay cold in the dust.

*

So black was the mourning,
And white were the wands,
Yellow, yellow the torches,
They bore in their hands.
The bells they were muffled,
And mournful did play,
While the royal Queen Jane
She lay cold in the clay.

Six knights and six lords
Bore her corpse through the grounds;
Six dukes followed after,
In black mourning gownds.
The flower of Old England
Was laid in cold clay,
Whilst the royal King Henrie
Came weeping away.

Anonymous

Historically speaking, this poem is quite inaccurate. In October of the year in question, Henry and Jane were separated by the outbreak of plague and Jane was without the King's company when her son Edward was born by Caesarean section. Nor did she die in childbirth. She lived for a further twelve days, and Cromwell blamed her death on the Queen's attendants who, he said, 'had suffered her to take great cold and to eat things her fantasy called for'. At last Henry had a legitimate son. Jane had done her duty and could be laid to rest. He paid her the compliment of remaining single for two years, but he soon tired of the role of widower.

1539

THE DISSOLUTION OF THE MONASTERIES

Little Jack Horner
Sat in the corner,
Eating a Christmas pie;
He put in his thumb,
And pulled out a plum,
And said, What a good boy am I!

Anonymous

According to one interpretation of this otherwise puzzling nursery rhyme, Jack Horner was steward to the last Abbot of Glastonbury. Hoping to appease Henry VIII's insatiable greed for Church property, at a time when the King was presiding over the wholesale dissolution of old monastic institutions, the Abbot sent Jack to London with a pie in which the title deeds of twelve manors were concealed. On the way, Jack opened the pie and extracted the title deed to the manor of Mells. The Horner family did in fact acquire the manor of Mells at the time of the Dissolution, but always claimed that the title was fairly bought.

THE ACHIEVEMENTS OF HENRY VIII

As I walked alone
and mused on things,
That have in my time
been done by great kings,
I bethought me of abbeys
that sometime I saw,
Which are now suppressed
all by a law.
O Lord, (thought I then)
what occasion was here
To provide for learning
and make poverty clear.
The lands and the jewels
that hereby were had
Would have found godly preachers
which might well have led
The people aright
that now go astray
And have fed the poor
that famish every day.

Robert Crowley

Opinions on Henry VIII are sharply divided. His defenders argue that he created the Church of England, built up the power of Parliament as the agent of his Protestant Reformation, made England a force to be reckoned with in European politics, established a strong monarchy, and encouraged the arts. His detractors point out that he pillaged the monasteries to pay off the nobility and his own supporters, and that he was vain, greedy, cruel, lecherous, self-pitying, and treacherous to his friends and ministers. The more one reads about him, indeed, the less attractive does he appear. Dickens was unequivocal: 'The plain truth is, that he was a most intolerable ruffian, a disgrace to human nature, and a blot of blood and grease upon the History of England.'

King Edward VI, 1547–53

EDWARD VI'S SHILLING

About my circle, I a Posie have
The title God unto the King first gave.
The circle that encompasseth my face
Declares my Soveraigne's title, by God's grace.

*

You see my face is beardless, smoothe and plaine.
Because my soveraigne was a child 'tis knowne
When as he did put on the English Crowne.
But had my stamp been bearded, as with haire,
Long before this it had beene worne and bare.
For why? With me the unthrifts every day,
With my face downwards do at shove-board play . . .

John Taylor

The shillings of Henry VIII had become clipped and debased. Edward VI issued new ones, which proved very popular until they too became debased. Pistol in *The Merry Wives of Windsor* confirms what we are told by the seventeenth-century poet John Taylor, that they were widely used in the game of shove halfpenny.

1549

Kett's Rebellion

On Mousehold Heath they gathered
Kett's ragtail army, 30,000 peasants.
Below them the city of Norwich
trembled, a mirage in the summer heat.
Mayor Codd and his burgesses
flapping like chickens overcircled by a hawk
sent deputies bowing up the hillside
to bargain for time with bread and meat,
meanwhile sunk their valuables in wells
and out of a secret gate
sped messengers to London squawking for help
against Kett 'that Captain of Mischief'
and his 'parcel of vagabonds . . . brute beasts.'

For six weeks up on Mousehold Heath they sat
high on heather, sky and hope.
''Twas a merry world when we were yonder
eating of mutton' one would look back.
The sun poured down like honey

and there was work for work-shaped hands, –
stakes to be sharpened, trenches to be dug,
a New Jerusalem of turf thrown up.
Hacking down the hated fences
and rounding up gentry was for sport.
Meanwhile the Dreamer under the Oak
wrote these words with the tip of his tongue:
'We desire that Bondmen may be free
as Christ made all free, His precious blood shedding.'
The sentries lay back on cupped palms.
Crickets in the dry grass wound their watch.
City-men crawled like ants.
Clouds coasted round the edge . . .

'The country gnoffs, Hob, Dick, and Hick
With clubs and clouted shoon
Shall fill the Vale of Dussindale
With slaughtered bodies soon.'

August 27th, 1549.
A long black cloud against the blood-red sunrise
Warwick and his mounted Landsknechts showed up.
One puff of their cannon
took the skull of Mousehold Heath clean off.
Then down the hill they tumbled
with their pitchforks, their birdslings, their billhooks.
They had no chance, – less
than rabbits making a run for it
when the combine rips into the last patch
and the Guns stand by, about to make laconic remarks.
So they laid themselves down, ripe for sacrifice,
till the brook got tired of undertaking
and Dussindale was bloodily fulfilled.
Kett, found shivering in a barn,
was dragged through the city in ankle-chains
then hung upside down from the castle wall, –
they made fun of Death in those days.

Then Mayor Codd called for a Thanksgiving Mass
followed by feasting in the streets.
While many a poor cottage-woman
waiting for her menfolk to come back
heard tapping on the shutters that night
but it was handfuls of rain.

Keith Chandler

During Edward VI's troubled reign there were risings in the West Country against the Reformation, and in Norfolk against the enclosing of land by capitalist farmers. Kett was a well-off East Anglian tanner; but he put himself at the head of what was in effect a peasants' revolt that posed a major threat to local shire governors. His ragged army captured Norwich. This was the only act of rebellion in the whole of the Tudor period to have social aims – the lowering of rents and the abolition of bond men, game laws and enclosures. The regency government saw it as a serious challenge to the stability of the realm and it was suppressed mercilessly, German mercenaries being used to kill 3,000 of those involved. A further 300 were hanged, for Tudor justice was not tempered by leniency.

Mary Tudor, 1553–8

from Lady Jane Grey

An apartment in the Castle of Framlingham.
(*enter* QUEEN MARY, *with a prayer-book in her hand, like a nun.*)

MARY: Thus like a nun, not like a princess born,
Descended from the royal Henry's loins,
Live I environ'd in a house of stone.
My brother Edward lives in pomp and state;
I in a mansion here all ruinate.
Their rich attire, delicious banqueting,
Their several pleasures, all their pride and honour,
I have forsaken for a rich prayer-book.
The golden mines of wealthy India
Are all as dross comparèd to thy sweetness:
Thou art the joy and comfort of the poor;
The everlasting bliss in thee we find.
This little volume enclosèd in this hand,
Is richer than the empire of this land.

John Webster

When Edward VI died, the Duke of Northumberland tried to place his daughter-in-law, Lady Jane Grey, upon the throne, but the country rallied to Mary Tudor, Henry VIII's elder daughter and, according to his will, the rightful heir. Mary married Philip II of Spain, eleven years her junior, and their child was expected to inherit England, Burgundy and the Netherlands.

MARY AND PHILIP

Still amorous, and fond, and billing,
Like Philip and Mary on a shilling.

Samuel Butler

from The Alchemist

FACE: Have you provided for her grace's servants?
DAPPER: Yes, here are six score Edward shillings.
FACE: Good!
DAPPER: And an old Harry's sovereign.
FACE: Very good!
DAPPER: And three James shillings, and an Elizabeth groat. Just twenty nobles.
FACE: O, you are too just. I would you had had the other noble in Maries.
DAPPER: I have some Philip and Maries.
FACE: Ay, those same are best of all: where are they?

Ben Jonson

After Mary's marriage to Philip, coins were struck showing husband and wife facing each other. The inscription around the rim declared that Philip was not only King of England, but also King of Naples and Prince of Spain. On the reverse, the arms of England were matched by those of the House of Habsburg. But this so alarmed people that new coins were quickly struck, simply recording that Philip was the King of England – a country he visited only twice.

1554

ELIZABETH'S IMPRISONMENT

Oh, Fortune! how thy restlesse wavering state
Hath fraught with cares my troubled witt!
Witnes this present prisonn, wither fate
  Could beare me, and the joys I quit.
Thus causedst the guiltie to be losed
From bandes, wherein are innocents inclosed:
  Causing the guiltles to be straite reserved.
  And freeing those that death hath well deserved.
But by her envie can be nothing wroughte,
So God send to my foes all they have thoughte.

Elizabeth I

In 1554 Mary's sister, Elizabeth, was imprisoned after the discovery of a plot to overthrow the Queen, who would also have liked to debar her from succession to the throne. Living throughout Mary's reign under the shadow of the scaffold, Elizabeth devoted herself to her studies and was to become one of the most learned of England's monarchs, able to address universities in Latin and ambassadors in their own tongues.

THE PROTESTANT MARTYRS

The Martyrdom of Bishop Farrar

Burned by Bloody Mary's men at Caermarthen. 'If I flinch from the pain of the burning, believe not the doctrine that I have preached.' (His words on being chained to the stake.)

Bloody Mary's venomous flames can curl;
They can shrivel sinew and char bone
Of foot, ankle, knee, and thigh, and boil
Bowels, and drop his heart a cinder down;
And her soldiers can cry, as they hurl
Logs in the red rush: 'This is her sermon.'

The sullen-jowled watching Welsh townspeople
Hear him crack in the fire's mouth; they see what
Black oozing twist of stuff bubbles the smell
That tars and retches their lungs: no pulpit
Of his ever held their eyes so still,
Never, as now his agony, his wit.

An ignorant means to establish ownership
Of his flock! Thus their shepherd she seized
And knotted him into this blazing shape
In their eyes, as if such could have cauterized
The trust they turned towards him, and branded on
Its stump her claim, to outlaw question.

So it might have been: seeing their exemplar
And teacher burned for his lessons to black bits,
Their silence might have disowned him to her,
And hung up what he had taught with their Welsh hats:
Who sees his blasphemous father struck by fire
From heaven, might well be heard to speak no oaths.

But the fire that struck here, come from Hell even,
Kindled little heavens in his words
As he fed his body to the flame alive.
Words which, before they will be dumbly spared,
Will burn their body and be tongued with fire
Make paltry folly of flesh and this world's air.

When they saw what annuities of hours
And comfortable blood he burned to get
His words a bare honouring in their ears,
The shrewd townsfolk pocketed them hot:
Stamp was not current but they rang and shone
As good gold as any queen's crown.

Gave all he had, and yet the bargain struck
To a merest farthing his whole agony,
His body's cold-kept miserdom of shrieks
He gave uncounted, while out of his eyes,
Out of his mouth, fire like a glory broke,
And smoke burned his sermons into the skies.

Ted Hughes

from The Register of the Martyrs

1555
February
When raging reign of tyrants stout,
Causeless, did cruelly conspire
To rend and root the simple out,
With furious force of sword and fire;
When man and wife were put to death:
We wished for our Queen ELIZABETH.

February
4 When ROGERS ruefully was brent;
8 When SAUNDERS did the like sustain;
When faithful FARRAR forth was sent
His life to lose, with grievous pain;
22 When constant HOOPER died the death:
We wished for our ELIZABETH.

*

October
When learned RIDLEY, and LATIMER,
16 Without regard, were swiftly slain;
When furious foes could not confer
But with revenge and mortal pain.
When these two Fathers were put to death:
We wished for our ELIZABETH.

*

1556
February
When two women in Ipswich town,
19 Joyfully did the fire embrace;
When they sang out with cheerful sound,
Their fixed foes for to deface;
When NORWICH NO-BODY put them to death,
We wished for our ELIZABETH.

March
12 When constant CRANMER lost his life
And held his hand into the fire;
When streams of tears for him were rife
And yet did miss their just desire:
When Popish power put him to death,
We wished for our ELIZABETH.

*

1557
July
2 When GEORGE EGLES, at Chelmsford town,
Was hanged, drawn, and quarterèd;
His quarters carried up and down,
And on a pole they set his head.
When wrestèd law put him to death,
We wished for our ELIZABETH.

*

1558
November
5 When JOHN DAVY, and eke his brother,
5 With PHILIP HUMFREY kissed the cross;
When they did comfort one another
Against all fear, and worldly loss;
When these, at Bury, were put to death,
We wished for our ELIZABETH.

November
When, last of all (to take their leave!),
At Canterbury, they did some consume,
Who constantly to CHRIST did cleave;
Therefore were fried with fiery fume:
But, six days after these were put to death,
GOD sent us our ELIZABETH!

Our wished wealth hath brought us peace.
Our joy is full; our hope obtained;
The blazing brands of fire do cease,
The slaying sword also restrained.
The simple sheep, preserved from death
By our good Queen, ELIZABETH.

Thomas Bright

Mary was determined to restore England to the Catholic faith, and she got Parliament to revive the medieval heresy laws which would enable Protestants to be rooted out and saved from eternal perdition by being burned in this world rather than the next. In 1555 seventy condemned heretics were burned at the stake, and by the end of Mary's reign the total had exceeded 300. The victims included the bishops Ridley and Latimer, who died in the town ditch at Oxford, and Thomas Cranmer. Such a programme of persecution was politically disastrous, and from it sprang one of the great works of Protestant literature, Foxe's *Book of Martyrs*. When, in 1558, France waged war on Spain, the last British possession on the Continent, Calais, was lost. Mary died with the name 'Calais' supposedly engraved on her heart, and her subjects celebrated her passing with bonfires in the streets of London.

1558

THE DEATH OF MARY TUDOR

Cruel Behold my Heavy Ending

Goodnight is Queen Mary's death:
a lute that bore her heavy end
through city-prisoning towers
and martyrs' candles.

Without her father's desperate gaiety
she clung to confessors
and watched the ghost of a dog
flung through her window at night
ear-clipped
howling the hanging of priests.

Then the lute resolved
the tragic cadence unfulfilled
and the Queen merciful
in all matters but religion
heard the flame of Latimer's cry
and died.

Peter Jones

Queen Elizabeth I, 1558–1603

LORD BURGHLEY

To Mistress Anne Cecil, upon Making Her a New Year's Gift

As years do grow, so cares increase;
And time will move to look to thrift!
Though years in me work nothing less;
Yet, for your years, and New Year's gift,
This housewife's toy is now my shift!
To set you on work, some thrift to feel;
I send you now a Spinning Wheel!

But one thing first, I wish and pray,
Lest thirst of thrift might soon you tire,
Only to spin one pound a day;
And play the rest, as time require!
Sweat not! (O, fie!) fling rock in fire!
God send, who sendeth all thrift and wealth,
You, long years; and your father health!

William Cecil, Lord Burghley

William Cecil was Elizabeth's intimately trusted chief minister and he provided the solid core of government for most of her long reign. His successor in this role was his son, Robert, who served both Elizabeth and James I. As this poem indicates, he could also, in common with many other public figures of the time, turn his hand to versification.

1569

THE NORTHERN REBELLION

The Daughter of Debate

The doubt of future foes exiles my present joy,
And Wit me warns to shun such snares as threaten my annoy,
For falsehood now doth flow, and subjects' faith doth ebb
Which would not be if Reason ruled, or Wisdom move the web,
But clouds of toys untried to cloak aspiring minds,
Which turn to rain of late repent by course of changed winds.
The top of hope supposed, the root of ruth will be,
And fruitless all their grafted guiles, as ye shall shortly see.
Those dazzled eyes with pride, which great ambition blinds,
Shall be unsealed by worthy wights, whose foresight falsehood blinds.
The daughter of debate, that eke discord doth sow,
Shall reap no gain where former rule hath taught still peace to grow.
No foreign banish'd wight shall anchor in this port;
Our realm it brooks no stranger's force, let them elsewhere resort;
Our rusty sword, with rest, shall first his edge employ,
To poll their tops that seek such change, and gape for joy.

Elizabeth I

In 1569 the Northern Earls, Westmorland and Northumberland, tried to raise the North in the Catholic cause. Their figurehead was Mary Stuart, Queen of Scots, whom they planned to marry to Elizabeth's cousin, the Duke of Norfolk. They took the city of Durham and said Mass there, but in the cold winter months that followed, the spirit of revolt petered out and the rebels fled to Scotland. The vast estates which they left behind were divided among those who had remained loyal to Elizabeth. She had survived the most dangerous threat to her sovereignty and she celebrated by writing this poem.

1583

Sir Humphrey Gilbert

Southward with fleet of ice
Sailed the corsair Death;
Wild and fast blew the blast,
And the east-wind was his breath.

His lordly ships of ice
Glisten in the sun;
On each side, like pennons wide,
Flashing crystal streamlets run.

His sails of white sea-mist
Dripped with silver rain;
But where he passed there were cast
Leaden shadows o'er the main.

Eastward from Campobello
Sir Humphrey Gilbert sailed;
Three days or more seaward he bore,
Then, alas! the land-wind failed.

Alas! the land-wind failed,
And ice-cold grew the night;
And never more, on sea or shore,
Should Sir Humphrey see the light.

He sat upon the deck,
The Book was in his hand:
'Do not fear! Heaven is as near,'
He said, 'by water as by land!'

In the first watch of the night,
  Without a signal's sound,
Out of the sea, mysteriously,
  The fleet of Death rose all around.

The moon and the evening star
  Were hanging in the shrouds;
Every mast, as it passed,
  Seemed to rake the passing clouds.

They grappled with their prize,
  At midnight black and cold!
As of a rock was the shock;
  Heavily the ground-swell rolled.

Southward through day and dark
  They drift in close embrace,
With mist and rain o'er the open main;
  Yet there seems no change of place.

Southward, for ever southward,
  They drift through dark and day;
And like a dream, in the Gulf-Stream
  Sinking, vanish all away.

Henry Wadsworth Longfellow

Humphrey Gilbert was Sir Walter Ralegh's half-brother, and they journeyed together on voyages of discovery. In 1583 Gilbert established the first British colony in North America at Newfoundland. He published a treatise urging the discovery of the so-called North West Passage to the Indies and he perished looking for it.

1587

THE EXECUTION OF MARY, QUEEN OF SCOTS

Elizabeth Reflects on Hearing of Mary's Execution

She was my heir. Her severed head they say
    Was old and grey, and wigged: That Queen of France
And Scotland, who long dreamed to reign today
    On England's throne. Courage she had. Her dance

Led men to die: her death may lead still more.
    What was arranged is done. Our sorrow shows
Itself. Queens should not lightly die. The store
    And show of our distress may keep the throws

Of anguish fresh before all governments.
    What moves upon this news will Europe make?
Too many troops may strike their cantonments.
    And for ourselves? At least we must ask Drake

To fleece (with our support obscure) and bleed
Those ships by Spanish shore. Oh this land we lead!

John Loveridge

Alas! Poor Queen

She was skilled in music and the dance
And the old arts of love
At the court of the poisoned rose
And the perfumed glove,
And gave her beautiful hand
To the pale Dauphin
A triple crown to win –
And she loved little dogs
And parrots
And red-legged partridges
And the golden fishes of the Duc de Guise
And a pigeon with a blue ruff
She had from Monsieur d'Elbœuf.

Master John Knox was no friend to her;
She spoke him soft and kind,
Her honeyed words were Satan's lure
The unwary soul to bind.
'Good sir, doth a lissome shape
And a comely face
Offend your God His Grace
Whose Wisdom maketh these
Golden fishes of the Duc de Guise?'

She rode through Liddesdale with a song;
'Ye streams sae wondrous strang,
Oh, mak' me a wrack as I come back
But spare me as I gang.'
While a hill-bird cried and cried
Like a spirit lost
By the grey storm-wind tost.

Consider the way she had to go,
Think of the hungry snare,
The net she herself had woven,
Aware or unaware,
Of the dancing feet grown still,
The blinded eyes –
Queens should be cold and wise,
And she loved little things,
        Parrots
      And red-legged partridges
And the golden fishes of the Duc de Guise
And the pigeon with the blue ruff
She had from Monsieur d'Elbœuf.

Marion Angus

Mary Stuart was in fact Elizabeth's heir, but she was excluded from succession to the throne by the Act of Supremacy, passed in 1534. Elizabeth saw her as a constant threat none the less. Although kept in virtual imprisonment in England for almost the last twenty years of her life, she continued to inspire plots against the English Queen, and at last, on 1 February 1587, Elizabeth signed her death warrant. Mary was executed on 8 February and her son, James VI of Scotland, who had been brought up by Calvinists, in turn became Elizabeth's heir.

Mary, Mary, quite contrary,
How does your garden grow?
With silver bells and cockle shells,
And pretty maids all in a row.

Anonymous

The old nursery rhyme is supposed to be about Mary Stuart, the 'silver bells' alluding to those used in the Mass, the 'cockle shells' to the badge of St James of Compostela, worn by pilgrims, and the 'pretty maids' to the famous four Marys who attended the Queen of Scots.

THE PUBLIC EXECUTIONER

Portraits of Tudor Statesmen

Surviving is keeping your eyes open,
Controlling the twitchy apparatus
Of iris, white, cornea, lash and lid.

So the literal painter set it down –
The sharp raptorial look; strained eyeball;
And mail, ruff, bands, beard, anything, to hide
The violently vulnerable neck.

U. A. Fanthorpe

The Public Executioner was one of the busiest public servants in Tudor England. Three Queens were beheaded – Anne Boleyn, Catherine Howard and Mary, Queen of Scots – and one who aspired to be queen, Lady Jane Grey. Other victims were prominent statesmen such as Thomas More and Thomas Cromwell; bishops such as Cranmer, Latimer and Ridley; courtiers such as Surrey and Essex; and many thousands besides.

THE ELIZABETHAN ARMY

An Old Soldier of the Queen's

Of an old Soldier of the Queen's,
With an old motley coat, and a Malmsey nose,
And an old jerkin that's out at the elbows,
And an old pair of boots, drawn on without hose
Stuft with rags instead of toes;
  And an old Soldier of the Queen's,
  And the Queen's old Soldier.

With an old rusty sword that's hackt with blows,
And an old dagger to scare away the crows,
And an old horse that reels as he goes,
And an old saddle that no man knows,
  And an old Soldier of the Queen's,
  And the Queen's old Soldier.

With his old wounds in Eighty Eight,
Which he recover'd, at Tilbury fight;
With an old Passport that never was read,
That in his old travels stood him in great stead;
  And an old Soldier of the Queen's,
  And the Queen's old Soldier.

With his old gun, and his bandeliers,
And an old head-piece to keep warm his ears,
With an old shirt is grown to wrack,
With a huge louse, with a great list on his back,
Is able to carry a pedlar and his pack;
  And an old Soldier of the Queen's,
  And the Queen's old Soldier.

Anonymous

While Philip II of Spain did his best to stir up trouble in Scotland and among the English Catholics, Elizabeth had her eye on the Netherlands, which formed a crucial part of the Habsburg Empire. Her ingenious diplomacy was directed towards maintaining peace for England, at the same time as keeping France and Spain at loggerheads. She was able to play a significant part in European politics because her credit was good: she borrowed at between 8 and 9 per cent, while Philip was obliged to pay interest at 12 or even 18 per cent. In 1586, however, meaning to lend active support to the Protestants, she sent a military expedition to the Netherlands which ended in miserable failure. Her soldiers appear to have been as feeble as her sailors were brilliant.

SIR FRANCIS DRAKE

Drake's Drum

Drake he's in his hammock an' a thousand mile away,
(Capten, art tha sleepin' there below?),
Slung atween the round shot in Nombre Dios Bay,
An' dreamin' arl the time o' Plymouth Hoe.
Yarnder lumes the Island, yarnder lie the ships,
Wi' sailor lads a dancin' heel-an'-toe,
An' the shore-lights flashin', an' the night-tide dashin',
He sees et arl so plainly as he saw et long ago.

Drake he was a Devon man, an' rüled the Devon seas,
(Capten, art tha sleepin' there below?),
Rovin' tho' his death fell, he went wi' heart at ease,
An' dreamin' arl the time o' Plymouth Hoe.
'Take my drum to England, hang et by the shore,
Strike et when your powder's runnin' low;
If the Dons sight Devon, I'll quit the port o' Heaven,
An' drum them up the Channel as we drummed them long ago.'

Drake he's in his hammock till the great Armadas come,
(Capten, art tha sleepin' there below?),
Slung atween the round shot, listenin' for the drum,
An' dreamin' arl the time o' Plymouth Hoe.

Call him on the deep sea, call him up the Sound,
Call him when ye sail to meet the foe;
Where the old trade's plyin' an' the old flag flyin'
They shall find him ware an' wakin', as they found him long ago!

Henry Newbolt

Elizabethan seamen carried the English flag across the world. Ralegh settled Virginia as a colony of the Crown, Gilbert claimed Newfoundland, John Hawkins shipped slaves from Portuguese West Africa to the Caribbean, and English merchants searching for the North-East Passage to the Indies reached Moscow. In 1572 Francis Drake delivered a severe blow to England's major rival in foreign trade and colonial expansion, Spain, when at Nombre de Dios on the Panama isthmus he intercepted the Spanish mule convoy bearing silver from Peru. From 1577 to 1580 he sailed his ship, *The Golden Hind*, around the world and was knighted by the Queen on his return, Elizabeth being not only proud of her merchant adventurers, but also a shareholder in several of their expeditions. In 1587 Drake made a daring pre-emptive strike against the Spanish fleet where it lay in the harbour of Cadiz, and in 1588 he helped destroy the Armada as it sailed to invade England.

1588

THE SPANISH ARMADA

Our gracious Queen
  doth greet you everyone
And saith 'She will among you be
  in every bitter storm.
Desiring you
  true English hearts to bear
To God, to her, and to the land
  Wherein you nursèd were.'

Thomas Deloney

The Spanish Armada of 197 ships sailed up the English Channel with the intention of uniting with the Spanish army in the Netherlands and forming the great force that would invade England. The English army was drawn up at Tilbury to protect London. Elizabeth, putting on a metal breastplate, joined her troops there and delivered one of the most heroic speeches in English history, including the famous sentence: 'I know I have the body of a weak and feeble woman, but I have the heart and stomach of a King, and a King of England too.' The English admiral, Lord Howard, ordered fireships to be launched against the Spanish fleet, creating chaos, and by the end of the affair only thirty-four Spanish ships remained in commission.

The Armada

Attend, all ye who list to hear our noble England's praise;
I tell of the thrice famous deeds she wrought in ancient days,
When that great fleet invincible against her bore in vain
The richest spoils of Mexico, the stoutest hearts of Spain.

It was about the lovely close of a warm summer day,
There came a gallant merchant-ship full sail to Plymouth Bay;
Her crew hath seen Castile's black fleet, beyond Aurigny's isle,
At earliest twilight, on the waves lie heaving many a mile.
At sunrise she escaped their van, by God's especial grace;
And the tall Pinta, till the noon, had held her close in chase.
Forthwith a guard at every gun was placed along the wall;
The beacon blazed upon the roof of Edgecumbe's lofty hall;
Many a light fishing-bark put out to pry along the coast,
And with loose rein and bloody spur rode inland many a post.
With his white hair unbonneted, the stout old sheriff comes;
Behind him march the halberdiers; before him sound the drums;
His yeomen round the market cross make clear an ample space;
For there behoves him to set up the standard of Her Grace.
And haughtily the trumpets peal, and gaily dance the bells,
As slow upon the labouring wind the royal blazon swells.
Look how the Lion of the sea lifts up his ancient crown,
And underneath his deadly paw treads the gay lilies down.
So stalked he when he turned to flight, on that famed Picard field,
Bohemia's plume, and Genoa's bow, and Cæsar's eagle shield.
So glared he when at Agincourt in wrath he turned to bay,
And crushed and torn beneath his claws the princely hunters lay.
Ho! strike the flagstaff deep, sir Knight: ho! scatter flowers, fair maids:
Ho! gunners, fire a loud salute: ho! gallants, draw your blades:
Thou sun, shine on her joyously; ye breezes, waft her wide;

Our glorious SEMPER EADEM, the banner of our pride.
The freshening breeze of eve unfurled that banner's massy fold;
The parting gleam of sunshine kissed that haughty scroll of gold;
Night sank upon the dusky beach, and on the purple sea,
Such night in England ne'er had been, nor e'er again shall be.
From Eddystone to Berwick bounds, from Lynn to Milford Bay,
That time of slumber was as bright and busy as the day;
For swift to east and swift to west the ghastly war-flame spread,
High on St Michael's Mount it shone: it shone on Beachy Head.
Far on the deep the Spaniard saw, along each southern shire,
Cape beyond cape, in endless range, those twinkling points of fire.
The fisher left his skiff to rock on Tamar's glittering waves:
The rugged miners poured to war from Mendip's sunless caves:
O'er Longleat's towers, o'er Cranbourne's oaks, the fiery herald flew:
He roused the shepherds of Stonehenge, the rangers of Beaulieu.
Right sharp and quick the bells all night rang out from Bristol town,
And ere the day three hundred horse had met on Clifton down;
The sentinel on Whitehall gate looked forth into the night,
And saw o'erhanging Richmond Hill the streak of blood-red light.
Then bugle's note and cannon's roar the deathlike silence broke,
And with one start, and with one cry, the royal city woke.
At once on all her stately gates arose the answering fires;
At once the wild alarum clashed from all her reeling spires;
From all the batteries of the Tower pealed loud the voice of fear;
And all the thousand masts of Thames sent back a louder cheer:
And from the furthest wards was heard the rush of hurrying feet,
And the broad streams of pikes and flags rushed down each roaring street;
And broader still became the blaze, and louder still the din,
As fast from every village round the horse came spurring in:
And eastward straight from wild Blackheath the warlike errand went,
And roused in many an ancient hall the gallant squires of Kent.
Southward from Surrey's pleasant hills flew those bright couriers forth;
High on bleak Hampstead's swarthy moor they started for the north;
And on, and on, without a pause, untired they bounded still:

All night from tower to tower they sprang; they sprang from hill to hill:
Till the proud peak unfurled the flag o'er Darwin's rocky dales,
Till like volcanoes flared to heaven the stormy hills of Wales,
Till twelve fair counties saw the blaze on Malvern's lonely height,
Till streamed in crimson on the wind the Wrekin's crest of light.
Till broad and fierce the star came forth on Ely's stately fane,
And tower and hamlet rose in arms o'er all the boundless plain;
Till Belvoir's lordly terraces the sign to Lincoln sent,
And Lincoln sped the message on o'er the wide vale of Trent;
Till Skiddaw saw the fire that burned on Gaunt's embattled pile,
And the red glare on Skiddaw roused the burghers of Carlisle.

Thomas Babington, Lord Macaulay

THE EARL OF LEICESTER

Here lieth the worthy warrior
Who never bloodied sword;
Here lieth the noble counsellor,
Who never held his word.

Here lieth his Excellency,
Who ruled all the state;
Here lieth the Earl of Leicester,
Whom all the world did hate.

Anonymous

Robert Dudley, Earl of Leicester, was a handsome, proud and ambitious man. He had witnessed his father's execution after the attempt to place Lady Jane Grey on the throne and had only just been reprieved from the same fate. Rumour accused him of having killed his first wife, Amy Robsart, who in 1560 was found dead, with her neck broken, at the bottom of a staircase in an empty house at Cumnor. Another rumour suggested that he had killed the husband of his mistress and it was pointed out that the husband of his second wife had died in mysterious circumstances. According to yet another rumour, he used crushed pearls and amber as an aphrodisiac. What is certainly true is that he enraptured the Queen and, as her favourite, was forgiven almost all his mistakes. Not, however, his disastrous leadership of the Netherlands campaign in 1586. After his death in 1588, the Queen locked herself in her room for seven days until eventually the door had to be forced. When she died, a little ring-box covered with pearls was found beside her bed, and in it a letter from Leicester on which the Queen had written, 'His last letter'.

The Looking-Glass

(A Country Dance)

Queen Bess was Harry's daughter. Stand forward partners all!
In ruff and stomacher and gown
She danced King Philip down-a-down,
And left her shoe to show 'twas true –
(The very tune I'm playing you)
In Norgem at Brickwall!

The Queen was in her chamber, and she was middling old.
Her petticoat was satin, and her stomacher was gold.
Backwards and forwards and sideways did she pass,
Making up her mind to face the cruel looking-glass.
The cruel looking-glass that will never show a lass
As comely or as kindly or as young as what she was!

Queen Bess was Harry's daughter. Now hand your partners all!

The Queen was in her chamber, a-combing of her hair.
There came Queen Mary's spirit and It stood behind her chair,
Singing 'Backwards and forwards and sideways may you pass,
But I will stand behind you till you face the looking-glass.
The cruel looking-glass that will never show a lass
As lovely or unlucky or as lonely as I was!'

Queen Bess was Harry's daughter. Now turn your partners all!

The Queen was in her chamber, a-weeping very sore,
There came Lord Leicester's spirit and It scratched upon the
door,
Singing 'Backwards and forwards and sideways may you pass,
But I will walk beside you till you face the looking-glass.
The cruel looking-glass that will never show a lass,
As hard and unforgiving or as wicked as you was!'

Queen Bess was Harry's daughter. Now kiss your partners all!

The Queen was in her chamber, her sins were on her head.
She looked the spirits up and down and statelily she said: –
'Backwards and forwards and sideways though I've been,
Yet I am Harry's daughter and I am England's Queen!'
And she faced the looking-glass (and whatever else there was)
And she saw her day was over and she saw her beauty pass
In the cruel looking-glass, that can always hurt a lass
More hard than any ghost there is or any man there was!

Rudyard Kipling

1591

THE DEATH OF SIR RICHARD GRENVILLE

The Revenge

A Ballad of the Fleet

At Flores in the Azores Sir Richard Grenville lay,
And a pinnace, like a fluttered bird, came flying from far away:
'Spanish ships of war at sea! we have sighted fifty-three!'
Then sware Lord Thomas Howard: "Fore God I am no coward;
But I cannot meet them here, for my ships are out of gear,
And the half my men are sick. I must fly, but follow quick.
We are six ships of the line; can we fight with fifty-three?'

Then spake Sir Richard Grenville: 'I know you are no coward;
You fly them for a moment to fight with them again.
But I've ninety men and more that are lying sick ashore.
I should count myself the coward if I left them, my Lord
Howard,
To these Inquisition dogs and the devildoms of Spain.'

So Lord Howard passed away with five ships of war that day,
Till he melted like a cloud in the silent summer heaven;
But Sir Richard bore in hand all his sick men from the land
Very carefully and slow,
Men of Bideford in Devon,
And we laid them on the ballast down below;
For we brought them all aboard,
And they blest him in their pain, that they were not left to
Spain,
To the thumbscrew and the stake for the glory of the Lord.

He had only a hundred seamen to work the ship and to fight,
And he sailed away from Flores till the Spaniard came in sight,
With his huge sea-castles heaving upon the weather bow.
'Shall we fight or shall we fly?
Good Sir Richard, tell us now,
For to fight is but to die!
There'll be little of us left by the time this sun be set.'
And Sir Richard said again: 'We be all good English men.
Let us bang those dogs of Seville, the children of the devil,
For I never turned my back upon Don or devil yet.'

Sir Richard spoke and he laughed, and we roared a hurrah, and
so
The little Revenge ran on sheer into the heart of the foe,
With her hundred fighters on deck, and her ninety sick below;
For half their fleet to the right and half to the left were seen,
And the little Revenge ran on through the long sea-lane
between.

Thousands of their soldiers looked down from their decks and
laughed,
Thousands of their seamen made mock at the mad little craft
Running on and on, till delayed
By their mountain-like San Philip that, of fifteen hundred tons,
And up-shadowing high above us with her yawning tiers of
guns,
Took the breath from our sails, and we stayed.

And while now the great San Philip hung above us like a cloud
Whence the thunderbolt will fall
Long and loud,
Four galleons drew away
From the Spanish fleet that day,
And two upon the larboard and two upon the starboard lay,
And the battle thunder broke from them all.

But anon the great San Philip, she bethought herself and went,
Having that within her womb that had left her ill content;
And the rest they came aboard us, and they fought us hand to
hand,
For a dozen times they came with their pikes and musqueteers,
And a dozen times we shook 'em off as a dog that shakes his
ears
When he leaps from the water to the land.

And the sun went down, and the stars came out far over the
summer sea,
But never a moment ceased the fight of the one and the fifty-
three.
Ship after ship, the whole night long, their high-built galleons
came,
Ship after ship, the whole night long, with her battle-thunder
and flame;
Ship after ship, the whole night long, drew back with her dead
and her shame.
For some were sunk and many were shattered, and so could
fight us no more –
God of battles, was ever a battle like this in the world before?

For he said, 'Fight on! fight on!'
Though his vessel was all but a wreck;
And it chanced that, when half of the short summer night was gone,
With a grisly wound to be drest he had left the deck,
But a bullet struck him that was dressing it suddenly dead,
And himself he was wounded again in the side and the head,
And he said, 'Fight on! fight on!'

And the night went down and the sun smiled out far over the summer sea,
And the Spanish fleet with broken sides lay round us all in a ring;
But they dared not touch us again, for they feared that we still could sting.
So they watched what the end would be.
And we had not fought them in vain,
But in perilous plight were we,
Seeing forty of our poor hundred were slain,
And half of the rest of us maimed for life
In the crash of the cannonades and the desperate strife;
And the sick men down in the hold were most of them stark and cold,
And the pikes were all broken or bent, and the powder was all of it spent;
And the masts and the rigging were lying over the side;
But Sir Richard cried in his English pride:
'We have fought such a fight for a day and a night
As may never be fought again!
We have one great glory, my men!
And a day less or more
At sea or ashore,
We die – does it matter when?
Sink me the ship, Master Gunner – sink her, split her in twain!
Fall into the hands of God, not into the hands of Spain!'

And the gunner said, 'Ay, ay,' but the seamen made reply:
'We have children, we have wives,
And the Lord hath spared our lives.
We will make the Spaniard promise, if we yield, to let us go;
We shall live to fight again and to strike another blow.'
And the lion there lay dying, and they yielded to the foe.

And the stately Spanish men to their flagship bore him then,
Where they laid him by the mast, old Sir Richard caught at last,
And they praised him to his face with their courtly foreign grace;
But he rose upon their decks, and he cried:
'I have fought for Queen and Faith like a valiant man and true;
I have only done my duty as a man is bound to do:
With a joyful spirit I Sir Richard Grenville die!'
And he fell upon their decks and he died.

And they stared at the dead that had been so valiant and true,
And had holden the power and glory of Spain so cheap
That he dared her with one little ship and his English few;
Was he devil or man? He was devil for aught they knew,
But they sank his body with honour down into the deep,
And they manned the Revenge with a swarthier alien crew,
And away she sailed with her loss and longed for her own;
When a wind from the lands they had ruined awoke from sleep,
And the water began to heave and the weather to moan,
And or ever that evening ended a great gale blew,
And a wave like the wave that is raised by an earthquake grew,
Till it smote on their hulls and their sails and their masts and
their flags,
And the whole sea plunged and fell on the shot-shattered navy
of Spain,
And the little Revenge herself went down by the island crags
to be lost evermore in the main.

Alfred, Lord Tennyson

All the great sailors of Elizabethan England were engaged in the lucrative business of pillaging the Spanish treasure-fleets. Such exploits earned the approval and financial backing of the Queen and the city of London. To meet the threat, the Spanish arranged to sail in convoys protected by large galleons. It was a fleet of this kind that fell upon the much smaller English one, of which all ships, except the *Revenge*, escaped. Its master, Grenville, died heroically.

ELIZABETHAN LETTERS

from **Master Francis Beaumont to Ben Jonson**

What things have we seen
Done at the Mermaid! heard words that have been
So nimble, and so full of subtle flame,
As if that every one from whence they came
Had meant to put his whole wit in a jest,
And had resolved to live a fool the rest
Of his dull life.

Francis Beaumont

from **Lines on the Mermaid Tavern**

Souls of Poets dead and gone,
What Elysium have ye known,
Happy field or mossy cavern,
Choicer than the Mermaid Tavern?

John Keats

The Mermaid Tavern in Bread Street was a favourite meeting-place for the poets and playwrights of Elizabethan London. Ralegh, Shakespeare, Donne and Jonson were among its habitués. This was a time of extraordinary literary achievement. The English theatre, in particular, was one of the great glories of Elizabeth's reign. Such dramatists as Kyd, Marlowe and Greene came to it from the academic world, but

Shakespeare was an actor-manager who turned to writing plays. Noblemen financed their own groups of players and the public flocked into the 'wooden O' to be shocked, thrilled, amused and stirred to pride by what was often fairly undisguised political propaganda. Francis Beaumont, of the Beaumont and Fletcher team of playwrights, witnessed this creative abundance at first hand, while Keats looks back on it wistfully.

1601

THE FALL OF ESSEX

from Polyhymnia

Then proudly shocks amid the martial throng
Of lusty lanciers, all in sable sad,
Drawn on with coal-black steeds of dusky hue,
In stately chariot full of deep device,
Where gloomy Time sat whipping on the team,
Just back to back with this great champion. –
Young Essex, that thrice-honourable Earl:
Y-clad in mighty arms of mourner's dye,
And plume as black as is a raven's wing,
That from his armour borrow'd such a light
As boughs of yew receive from shady stream:
His staves were such, or of such hue at least,
As are those banner-staves that mourners beat;
And all his company in funeral black;
As if he mourn'd to think of him he miss'd,
Sweet Sidney, fairest shepherd of our green,
Well-letter'd warrior, whose successor he
In love and arms, had ever vow'd to be:
In love and arms, O, may he so succeed
As his deserts, as his desires would speed!

Robert Peele

Robert Devereux, second Earl of Essex, was a protégé of the courtier and poet Sir Philip Sidney. Sidney died from a gangrenous wound after the battle of Zutphen in 1586, the occasion on which he is reported to have yielded a drink to a more grievously wounded soldier with the immortal words: 'Thy need is yet greater than mine.' The court went into mourning for him, and soon afterwards the Earl of Essex was able to attend a tournament in an outfit of the most fetching deep black with which he caught the eye of the Queen, later going on to become her last favourite. In 1599 he was appointed to quell the uprising of the Earl of Tyrone in Ireland, but he failed disastrously. On his return to England, he was rebuffed after bursting into the Queen's own apartments while she was in the middle of dressing. He planned to take over the government from Cecil, but his attempted coup was a botched affair and the loyal people of London refused to support him. He was tried and found guilty, and on Shrove Tuesday, after attending the performance of a play, Elizabeth signed the death warrant of one of the two men for whom she had deeply cared. The following verse from a street ballad shows that Essex had at least a measure of popular support:

Count him not like Campion,
   (those traitrous men), or Babington;
Not like the Earl of Westmorland
   By whom a number were undone.
He never yet hurt mother's son –
   His quarrell still maintained the right;
For which the tears my cheeks down run
   When I think on his last Goodnight.

1603

THE DEATH OF ELIZABETH I

Gloriana Dying

None shall gainsay me. I will lie on the floor.
Hitherto from horseback, throne, balcony,
I have looked down upon your looking up.
Those sands are run. Now I reverse the glass
And bid henceforth your homage downward, falling
Obedient and unheeded as leaves in autumn
To quilt the wakeful study I must make
Examining my kingdom from below.
How tall my people are! Like a race of trees
They sway, sigh, nod heads, rustle above me,
And their attentive eyes are distant as starshine.
I have still cherished the handsome and well-made:
No queen has better masts within her forests
Growing, nor prouder and more restive minds
Scabbarded in the loyalty of subjects;
No virgin has had better worship than I.
No, no! Leave me alone, woman! I will not
Be put into a bed. Do you suppose
That I who've ridden through all weathers, danced
Under a treasury's weight of jewels, sat
Myself to stone through sermons and addresses,
Shall come to harm by sleeping on a floor?
Not that I sleep. A bed were good enough
If that were in my mind. But I am here
For a deep study and contemplation,
And as Persephone, and the red vixen,
Go underground to sharpen their wits,
I have left my dais to learn a new policy
Through watching of your feet, and as the Indian
Lays all his listening body along the earth
I lie in wait for the reverberation
Of things to come and dangers threatening.
Is that the Bishop praying? Let him pray on.

If his knees tire his faith can cushion them.
How the poor man grieves Heaven with news of me!
Deposuit superbos. But no hand
Other than my own has put me down –
Not feebleness enforced on brain or limb,
Not fear, misgiving, fantasy, age, palsy,
Has felled me. I lie here by my own will,
And by the curiosity of a queen.
I dare say there is not in all England
One who lies closer to the ground than I.
Not the traitor in the condemned hold
Whose few straws edge away from under his weight
Of ironed fatality; not the shepherd
Huddled for cold under the hawthorn bush,
Nor the long dreaming country lad who lies
Scorching his book before the dying brand.

Sylvia Townsend Warner

You poets all, brave Shakespeare, Jonson, Green,
Bestow your time to write for England's Queen. . . .
Return your songs and sonnets and your says,
To set forth sweet Elizabetha's praise.

Anonymous

Nor doth the silver-tonguèd Melicert
Drop from his honeyed muse one sable tear,
To mourn her death that gracèd his desert
And to his lays opened her royal ear.
  Shepherd, remember our Elizabeth,
  And sing her Rape, done by that Tarquin, Death.

Henry Chettle

Elizabeth died at Richmond Palace on 24 March 1603. She had attained the great age of seventy. A horseman waiting below her room was thrown one of the rings she had been wearing, and with this proof of her death galloped off to Scotland where James VI was expecting it. In the library at Chequers there is a ring in the shape of a skull which is said to be that ring. The anonymous popular ballad quoted above urges the great poets of the time to sing her praises, but, as Henry Chettle noted, the greatest of them all remained silent. This is not entirely surprising, as only two years earlier Shakespeare's patron, the Earl of Southampton, had been sentenced to death for his part in the Essex affair, and reprieved only at the last minute.

THE STUARTS

King James I, 1603–25

James I

The child of Mary Queen of Scots,
  A shifty mother's shiftless son,
Bred up among intrigues and plots,
  Learnèd in all things, wise in none.
Ungainly, babbling, wasteful, weak,
  Shrewd, clever, cowardly, pedantic,
The sight of steel would blanch his cheek,
  The smell of baccy drive him frantic,
He was the author of his line –
  He wrote that witches should be burnt;
He wrote that monarchs were divine,
  And left a son who – proved they weren't!

Rudyard Kipling

James VI of Scotland was crowned James I of England. The two most enduring achievements of his reign were literary: the publication in 1611 of the King James Version of the English Bible, on which a committee had been working since 1604, and in 1623 of the First Folio of Shakespeare's plays. Both served to enlarge, enrich and enshrine the great glory of the English language. Early settlers in Jamestown, Virginia, and in New England had as their resource what was to become the mother tongue of a mighty continent.

James himself was strong in opinions, but weak in action; and he was much taken up with two favourites, Robert Carr, Earl of Somerset, and George Villiers, Duke of Buckingham. Kipling's contempt for James had been preceded by that of Dickens, who wrote: 'A creature like his Sowship on the throne is like the Plague, and everybody receives infection from him.' And to other writers his name had been a by-word for pedantry.

from The Dunciad

Oh (cry'd the Goddess) for some pedant Reign!
Some gentle JAMES, to bless the land again;
To stick the Doctor's Chair into the Throne,
Give law to Words, or war with Words alone,
Senates and Courts with Greek and Latin rule,
And turn the council to a Grammar School!
For sure, if Dulness sees a grateful Day,
'Tis in the shade of Arbitrary Sway.
O! if my sons may learn one earthly thing,
Teach but that one, sufficient for a King;
That which my Priests, and mine alone, maintain,
Which as it dies, or lives, we fall, or reign:
May you, may Cam, and Isis preach it long!
'The RIGHT DIVINE of Kings to govern wrong.'

Alexander Pope

1605

Gunpowder Plot Day

Please to remember
The Fifth of November,
Gunpowder, treason and plot;
I see no reason
Why gunpowder treason
Should ever be forgot.

Anonymous

The Gunpowder Plotters were driven to action by disappointment that James, whose wife had secretly turned Catholic, had not relaxed the laws against Catholics in general. They prepared plans to do away with King and Parliament together, but these were betrayed by Francis Tresham, who could not bear the thought of his own kinsmen being blown to eternity by the barrels of gunpowder which Guido Fawkes was to ignite. After the plot had been discovered, Catholics were debarred from all public office and forbidden to venture more than five miles from their homes.

1605

ENGLISH SETTLEMENTS IN AMERICA

from **To the Virginian Voyage**

You brave heroic minds,
Worthy your country's name,
That honour still pursue,
Go and subdue;
Whilst loitering hinds
Lurk here at home with shame.

Britons, you stay too long;
Quickly aboard bestow you,
And with a merry gale
Swell your stretched sail,
With vows as strong,
As the winds that blow you.

Your course securely steer;
West and by South forth keep:
Rocks, lee shores, nor shoals,
When Eolus scolds,
You need not fear,
So absolute the deep.

And cheerfully at sea
Success you still entice
    To get the pearl and gold;
    And ours to hold
Virginia,
Earth's only paradise.

Where nature has in store
Fowl, venison and fish;
    And the fruitfullest soil,
    Without your toil,
Three harvests more,
All greater than your wish.

*

And in regions far
Such heroes bring you forth,
    As those from whom we came;
    And plant our name
Under the star
Not known unto our North.

Michael Drayton

In 1603 England had no colonies, but by 1660 she had the beginnings of an empire. The Elizabethan settlements had all failed. In James's reign the flag was raised in India, the East Indies, Virginia and Massachusetts. Colonies were founded by private-enterprise companies set up to develop the wealth of the new lands. In 1601 a company was formed to finance an expedition to Virginia. The pioneers landed at Chesapeake Bay, sailed up what was to be called the James River and landed at the site of Jamestown. Their early years proved a struggle and their numbers were soon reduced from 143 to 38; but in 1617 they sent back to England what was to be the source of their subsequent wealth – a cargo of Virginian tobacco.

The first colonists were people who sought adventure, land, wealth and religious freedom. In 1620 a band of Puritans, the 'Pilgrim Fathers', sailed from Plymouth in the *Mayflower* to found a new plantation which, after twenty years, amounted to some 600 souls. James I did little to help this colonial expansion, his only gesture being to order the exportation of criminals to Virginia. Charles I did scarcely better. It was left to Oliver Cromwell to be the first real imperialist, when he recognized the necessity for an efficient organization of sea power that would enable England to defend its colonies and attack the colonies of others.

1607

THE SCOTTISH INVASION OF ENGLAND UNDER JAMES I

from **The True-Born Englishman**

The Offspring of this Miscellaneous Crowd,
Had not their new Plantations long enjoy'd,
But they grew *Englishmen*, and rais'd their Votes
At Foreign Shoals of *Interloping Scots*.
The Royal Branch from *Pict-land* did succeed,
With Troops of *Scots* and Scabs from *North-by-Tweed*.
The Seven first Years of his Pacifick Reign,
Made him and half his Nation *Englishmen*.
Scots from the *Northern* Frozen Banks of *Tay*,
With Packs and Plods came *Whigging* all away:
Thick as the Locusts which in *Egypt* swarm'd,
With Pride and hungry Hopes compleatly arm'd:
With Native Truth, Diseases, and No Money,
Plunder'd our *Canaan* of the Milk and Honey.
Here they grew quickly Lords and Gentlemen,
And all their Race are *True-Born Englishmen*.

Daniel Defoe

In 1607 James tried to unite England and Scotland as one country. Debates in the House of Commons brought out the worst of English bigotry. It was variously alleged that the Scots were sly and beggarly, but it was the London merchants who prevailed when they shrewdly argued that, once the Scots were let in, they would take over the best English companies. Plans for the Union were shelved for a further hundred years.

1609

THE DIVINE ORDER

from **Troilus and Cressida**

ACT I *Scene III*
The Grecian camp.

ULYSSES: . . . The heavens themselves, the planets, and this centre
Observe degree, priority and place,
Insisture, course, proportion, season, form,
Office and custom, in all line of order;
And therefore is the glorious planet Sol
In noble eminence enthron'd and spher'd
Amidst the other, whose med'cinable eye
Corrects the ill aspects of planets evil,
And posts, like the commandment of a king,
Sans check, to good and bad: but when the planets
In evil mixture to disorder wander,
What plagues and what portents, what mutiny,
What raging of the sea, shaking of earth,
Commotion in the winds! Frights, changes, horrors,
Divert and crack, rend and deracinate,
The unity and married calm of states
Quite from their fixture! O, when degree is shak'd,
Which is the ladder to all high designs,
The enterprise is sick! How could communities,
Degrees in schools, and brotherhoods in cities,
Peaceful commerce from dividable shores,
The primogenitive and due of birth,
Prerogative of age, crowns, sceptres, laurels,
But by degree, stand in authentic place?
Take but degree away, untune that string,
And, hark! what discord follows; each thing meets

In mere oppugnancy: the bounded waters
Should lift their bosoms higher than the shores,
And make a sop of all this solid globe;
Strength should be lord of imbecility,
And the rude son should strike his father dead;
Force should be right; or, rather, right and wrong –
Between whose endless jar justice resides –
Should lose their names, and so should justice too.

William Shakespeare

In the famous speech which he gives to the character of Ulysses in *Troilus and Cressida* (1609), Shakespeare emphasizes to his Jacobean audience the importance of an authority which is divinely ordained and which is maintained by the hierarchical nature of society. It is not quite a text for the Divine Right of Kings, but it does offer a clear warning of what would happen should the state of things be undermined.

1611

THE AUTHORIZED VERSION OF THE ENGLISH BIBLE

Ecclesiasticus XLIV, 1–14

Let us now praise famous men, and our fathers that begate us.

The Lorde hath wrought great glory by them through his great power from the beginning.

Such as did beare rule in the kingdomes, men renowned for their power, giving counsell by their understanding, and declaring prophecies:

Leaders of the people by their counsels, and by their knowledge of learning meet for the people, wise and eloquent in their instructions.

Such as found out musical tunes and recited verses in writing.

Rich men furnished with ability, living peaceably in their habitations.

All these were honoured in their generations, and were the glory of their times.

There be of them, that have left a name behind them, that their praises might be reported.

And some there be, which have no memorial, who are perished as though they had never bene, and are become as though they had never bene borne, and their children after them.

But these were mercifull men, whose righteousness hath not beene forgotten.

With their seede shall continually remaine a good inheritance, and their children are within the covenant.

Their seed stands fast, and their children for their sakes.

Their seed shall remaine for ever, and their glory shall not be blotted out.

Their bodies are buried in peace, but their name liveth for evermore.

From 1604 scholars had been working at Oxford, Cambridge and Westminster to make an authoritative translation of the Bible into English, in an attempt to bridge the gap between Protestant and Puritan factions of the Church. The leading scholar was John Bois of Cambridge, whose particular job it was to translate the Apocrypha, where the book of Ecclesiasticus is to be found. The first English translation of the Bible had been made by John Wyclif in the 1380s and it had been condemned as heretical. Tyndale published his in 1525, and in the next forty years another five versions appeared. The King James committee, however, produced a work of outstanding beauty. The scholars used a relatively small vocabulary of some 8,000 words, which may account for the directness of its appeal. Shakespeare used a much wider vocabulary of some 30,000 words, a number of which he invented himself. The plays of Shakespeare and the King James Bible established the English language as the greatest glory of Western civilization.

1615

THE FALL OF SOMERSET

Upon the Sudden Restraint of the Earl of Somerset

Dazzled thus with height of place,
Whilst our hopes our wits beguile,
No man marks the narrow space
'Twixt a prison and a smile.

Then, since Fortune's favours fade,
You that in her arms do sleep;
Learn to swim, and not to wade,
For the hearts of Kings are deep.

But, if Greatness be so blind
As to trust in towers of air,
Let it be with Goodness lined,
That at least the fall be fair.

Then, though darkened, you shall say,
When friends fail, and Princes frown,
Virtue is the roughest way,
But proves at night a bed of down.

Henry Wotton

Robert Carr, a blond and handsome page, became James's favourite, was made the Earl of Somerset, and in 1613 was one of the King's principal advisers. Another courtier, Sir Thomas Overbury, expressed his resentment at Somerset's infatuation with Frances Howard, the Countess of Essex, who was reputed to be a witch and whom Somerset wanted to marry. Overbury was thrown in the Tower, where he was poisoned by the Countess. She then secured a divorce and married Somerset, but the scandal leaked abroad and not even James could save the couple from public disgrace. This led the way for the Duke of Buckingham to become the new favourite.

1616

THE DEATH OF SHAKESPEARE

To the Memory of my Beloved Mr William Shakespeare

I, therefore, will begin. Soul of the Age!
  The applause, delight, the wonder of our Stage!
My Shakespeare, rise; I will not lodge thee by
  Chaucer, or Spenser, or bid Beaumont lie
A little further, to make thee a room:
  Thou art a monument, without a tomb,
And art alive still, while thy book doth live,
  And we have wits to read and praise to give.
That I not mix thee so, my brain excuses;
  I mean with great, but disproportioned Muses:
For, if I thought my judgement were of years,
  I should commit thee surely with thy peers,
And tell how far thou didst our Lyly out-shine,
  Or sporting Kyd, or Marlowe's mighty line.
And though thou hadst small Latin and less Greek,
  From thence to honour thee, I would not seek
For names; but call forth thundering Æschylus,
  Euripides, and Sophocles to us,
Paccuvius, Accius, him of Cordova dead,
  To life again, to hear thy buskin tread,
And shake a stage; or, when thy socks were on,
  Leave thee alone, for the comparison
Of all that insolent Greece or haughty Rome
  Sent forth, or since did from their ashes come.
Triumph, my Britain, thou hast one to show
  To whom all scenes of Europe homage owe.
He was not of an age but for all time!
  And all the Muses still were in their prime
When, like Apollo, he came forth to warm
  Our ears, or, like a Mercury, to charm!

Ben Jonson

1618

THE EXECUTION OF SIR WALTER RALEGH

His Epitaph

Which He Writ the Night Before His Execution

Even such is time, that takes in trust
  Our youth, our joys, our all we have,
And pays us but with age and dust;
  Who in the dark and silent grave,
When we have wandered all our ways,
Shuts up the story of our days!
But from this earth, this grave, this dust,
The Lord shall raise me up, I trust!

Walter Ralegh

Ralegh had been condemned to death in 1603 on trumped-up charges. Reprieved, he lived in the Tower of London until 1616, when he was released and put in charge of a disastrous expedition to find Eldorado. Spiteful and petty as ever, James I took it upon himself to strike down the last of the Elizabethans, who by then was nearly seventy years old. When, at the second stroke of the axe, Ralegh's head fell from his body, a voice from the crowd in the New Palace Yard cried out, 'We have not such another head to be cut off.'

King Charles I, 1625–49

Ten years the world upon him falsely smiled,
Sheathing in fawning looks the deadly knife . . .

Richard Fanshawe

James I had expounded the theory of the Divine Right of Kings, and his son Charles tried to implement it in the 1630s. The question was whether the King could rule without Parliament. The Members of Parliament themselves, moneyed and landed men, asserted their representative rights against royal absolutism. The principles for which they stood were a far cry from democracy and general suffrage, but those ideals have their beginnings in this conflict and the Civil War to which it eventually led probably prevented revolution at a later date. Colonel Thomas Rainborough, MP for Droitwich, pointed the way forward when he said: 'I think the meanest He that is in England hath a life as well as the greatest He; and therefore, truly sir, I think that every man that is to live under a government ought, first, by his own consent to put himself under that government.'

THE THREAT TO THE KING

from **The Secret People**

The face of the King's servants grew greater than the King.
He tricked them and they trapped him and drew round him in a ring;
The new grave lords closed round him that had eaten the abbey's fruits,
And the men of the new religion with their Bibles in their boots,
We saw their shoulders moving to menace and discuss.
And some were pure and some were vile, but none took heed of us;
We saw the King when they killed him, and his face was proud and pale,
And a few men talked of freedom while England talked of ale.

G. K. Chesterton

the 1630s

THE PURITANS

Here lies the corpse of William Prynne,
A bencher late of Lincoln's Inn,
Who restless ran through thick and thin.

This grand scripturient paper-spiller,
This endless, needless margin-filler,
Was strangely tost from post to pillar.

His brain's career was never stopping,
But pen with rheum of gall still dropping,
Till hand o'er head brought ears to cropping.

Nor would he yet surcease such themes,
But prostitute new virgin reams
To types of his fanatic dreams.

But whilst he this hot humour hugs,
And for more length of tedder tugs,
Death fang'd the remnant of his lugs.

Samuel Butler

William Prynne was a fully paid-up member of God's awkward squad. He was a thorough-going Puritan who, in 1632, wrote a 1,000-page attack on the theatre. The Puritans had a special dislike of theatres. In 1642 they ordained that all such places of entertainment should be closed, and in 1647 that actors should be pursued as rogues. When these measures failed, they proposed that playgoers should be liable to a fine of five shillings.

In 1634 Prynne was sentenced to life imprisonment and his ears to be cut off in the pillory. This did not, however, stop the flow of pamphlets, and in 1637 he was sentenced to have the stumps of his ears shorn and to be branded. Released by the Long Parliament, he led the prosecution of Archbishop Laud and urged the execution of Charles, but he managed to fall out with Cromwell, who put him back in prison. Prynne died in 1669.

1641

THE EXECUTION OF STRAFFORD

Epitaph on the Earl of Strafford

Here lies wise and valiant dust,
Huddled up 'twixt fit and just,
Strafford, who was hurried hence
'Twixt treason and convenience.
He spent his time here in a mist,
A Papist, yet a Calvinist;
His Prince's nearest joy and grief,
He had, yet wanted, all relief;
The prop and ruin of the State,
The people's violent love and hate;
One in extremes loved and abhorred.
Riddles lie here, or in a word,
Here lies blood, and let it lie
Speechless still, and never cry.

John Cleveland

As a Member of Parliament, the Earl of Strafford had prepared the Petition of Right against Charles in 1628, but in the next year he went over to the Royalist side and served as the King's most able and devoted minister. In the 1630s he governed Ireland, returning in 1639 to help his master in the struggle to retain his personal authority. But it was too late. The royal army was defeated in an encounter with Scottish rebels and the King had to recall Parliament, which had been in abeyance throughout the decade. Parliament used Strafford as the King's scapegoat and took revenge on his earlier defection by passing an Act of Attainder which Charles was forced to sign, thereby in effect signing Strafford's death warrant. In a letter to Charles before the signing, Strafford did not plead for mercy, but instead offered himself as a sacrifice to appease Parliament's wrath. This is one of the most heroic documents of British history. Strafford wrote:

> I do most humbly beseech your Majesty . . . to pass this Bill, and by this means remove, I cannot say this accursed, but I confess this

> unfortunate, thing forth of the way towards that blessed agreement which God, I trust, shall ever establish between you and your subjects.

Archbishop Laud, who was also to be executed, wrote of Strafford: 'He served a mild and gracious Prince, who knew not how to be or to be made great.'

1642

RAISING MONEY FOR THE CIVIL WAR

from **Hudibras**

Did Saints, for this, bring in their Plate,
And crowd as if they came too late.
For when they thought the Cause had need on't,
Happy was he that could be rid on't,
Did they coin Piss-Pots, Bowls, and Flaggons,
Int' officers of horse and dragoons;
And into pikes and musquetteers,
Stamp beakers, cups, and porringers?
A thimble, bodkin, and a spoon,
Did start up living men, as soon
As in the furnace they were thrown,
Just like the dragon's teeth being sown.
Then was the Cause of Gold and Plate,
The brethren's offerings, consecrate,
Like th' Hebrew Calf, and down before it
The Saints fell prostrate, to adore it,
So say the wicked.

Samuel Butler

Both the King and Parliament needed metal to mint the coins that would fund their armies during the inevitable conflict. Londoners were urged by Parliament to bring their gold and silver to the Guildhall, and so great was the success of the appeal that the Royalists called the Roundheads 'the Thimble and Bodkin Army'. Charles established his mint at Oxford and required the Colleges to lend him their plate, promising to repay them 'as soon as God shall enable Us'.

1642

THE BATTLE OF EDGEHILL

After Edgehill, 1642

1 Villagers Report 'The Late Apparitions'

A December Saturday, star-clear
at Kineton. Three months since the battle,
the village collects itself – Christmas
perhaps a demarcation, a control
in the blood-letting. Yet on the ridge
of Edge Hill, the night resounds,
armies grinding one against the other
re-enacting the action, re-dying the deaths.

Shepherds hear trumpets, drums –
expect a visitation of holy kings with retinues.
Instead, the spectral soldiers strike,
icy night skies crack with cries,
steel clashing and the sput of muskets.
A knot of Kineton men watch, witness;
Samuel Marshall, the Minister, says
the Devil's apparitions seize the dead.

2 *A Ghost Speaks*

I am unplanted, my world this waste –
the heath where bone was split, undressed of flesh,
where arteries unleashed their flood, the colour
of death. What is the colour of honour? The blue
in which we dissolve into air? the white of ashes?
Can I be woven into the braids of her hair, my lady,
or exist in the quick of my son's fingernails?
I, who carried the Standard, once drove the plough,
turning up earth, the harvest of worms. Now I envy
the seeds in the furrow, their dark cradle.

My blood is this Midlands field, this hacked hedgerow
where I lie, hearing the drumbeat of the dead,
corpses strewn rotting, graveless.
I glide up and down these rows of human manure,
the faces of soldiers like fallen cameos.
Here is Sir Edmund Verney, Thomas Transome –
they look skywards, lolling near my own wistful face.
Sir Edmund is grimacing slightly as he did in life,
Thomas Transome's skull a broken eggshell.

The brittle linnet flies from me. Dry leaves relinquish
their hold on twigs. A hare sits motionless, watching,
listening to last groans forever in the wind.

I see a troop of Horse on the skyline – Parliament's.
They charge our pikemen; now they vanish
like moving cloud-shadows across the field.
I cannot follow the clouds; I am chained to my carcass
hovering, as others are, above their unburied selves.

3 *A Dragoon Observes Colonel Cromwell*

Like a falcon from the gauntlet, he throws off these deaths.
He tells us 'Smile out to God in Praise', for his is the sword
of the Lord. I see his horse, piebald with blood.

Gladys Mary Coles

In August 1642 Charles raised his standard at Nottingham and the first battle of the Civil War took place at Edgehill on 23 October. Charles's German nephew, Prince Rupert, led one of his famous cavalry charges, which swept everything before it, but ran out of control. The foot-soldiers of the Parliamentary army held on doggedly. The Royalist Sir Edmund Verney was killed clutching the standard so firmly that his right hand had to be cut off. William Harvey, the scientist, who also fought, pulled a dead body over himself as he lay wounded, to protect himself against the freezing cold. Oliver Cromwell did not take part in this battle, for it seems that he arrived too late, but he took notice of what had happened and resolved to reorganize his army accordingly. Strange rumours soon began to circulate about Edgehill: shepherds claimed to have heard unaccountable sounds of battle – shots, trumpets and drums – while ghostly soldiers were seen riding and fighting. Charles sent agents to investigate these reports and pamphlets were written by both sides alleging that divine messages could be read in them.

1643

To Lucasta, Going to the Wars

Tell me not, Sweet, I am unkind,
That from the nunnery
Of thy chaste breast and quiet mind
To war and arms I fly.

True, a new mistress now I chase,
The first foe in the field;
And with a stronger faith embrace
A sword, a horse, a shield.

Yet this inconstancy is such
As thou too shalt adore;
I could not love thee, Dear, so much,
Loved I not Honour more.

Richard Lovelace

WOMEN TO THE DEFENCE OF LONDON

from **Hudibras**

What have they done or what left undone,
That might advance the Cause at London?
March'd rank and file with Drum and Ensign,
T'entrench the City for defence in;
Rais'd Rampiers with their own soft hands,
To put the enemy to stands;
From Ladies down to Oyster-wenches
Labour'd like Pioneers in Trenches,
Fell to their Pick-axes and Tools,
And help'd the men to dig like Moles?

Samuel Butler

The Cavalier poet Lovelace expresses the romance of service to the Royalist cause, while Butler describes the equal determination of the women of London to resist the King's advance.

1645

The Battle of Naseby

Oh! wherefore come ye forth, in triumph from the North,
With your hands, and your feet, and your raiment all red?
And wherefore doth your rout sent forth a joyous shout?
And whence be the grapes of the wine-press which ye tread?

Oh evil was the root, and bitter was the fruit,
And crimson was the juice of the vintage that we trod;
For we trampled on the throng of the haughty and the strong,
Who sate in the high places, and slew the saints of God.

It was about the noon of a glorious day in June,
  That we saw their banners dance, and their cuirasses shine,
And the Man of Blood was there, with his long essenced hair,
  And Astley, and Sir Marmaduke, and Rupert of the Rhine.

Like a servant of the Lord, with his Bible and his sword,
  The General rode along us to form us to the fight,
When a murmuring sound broke out, and swell'd into a shout,
  Among the godless horsemen upon the tyrant's right.

And hark! like the roar of the billows on the shore,
  The cry of battle rises along their charging line!
For God! for the Cause! for the Church, for the Laws!
  For Charles King of England, and Rupert of the Rhine!

The furious German comes, with his clarions and his drums,
  His bravoes of Alsatia, and pages of Whitehall;
They are bursting on our flanks. Grasp your pikes, close your ranks;
  For Rupert never comes but to conquer or to fall.

They are here! They rush on! We are broken! We are gone!
  Our left is borne before them like stubble on the blast.
O Lord, put forth thy might! O Lord, defend the right!
  Stand back to back, in God's name, and fight it to the last.

Stout Skippon hath a wound; the centre hath given ground:
  Hark! hark! – What means the trampling of horsemen on our rear?
Whose banner do I see, boys? 'Tis he, thank God! 'tis he, boys,
  Bear up another minute: brave Oliver is here.

Their heads all stooping low, their points all in a row,
  Like a whirlwind on the trees, like a deluge on the dikes,
Our cuirassiers have burst on the ranks of the accurst,
  And at a shock have scattered the forest of his pikes.

Fast, fast, the gallants ride, in some safe nook to hide
  Their coward heads, predestined to rot on Temple Bar:
And he – he turns, he flies: – shame on those cruel eyes
  That bore to look on torture, and dare not look on war.

Ho! comrades, scour the plain; and, ere ye strip the slain,
  First give another stab to make your search secure,
Then shake from sleeves and pockets their broadpieces and
    lockets,
  The tokens of the wanton, the plunder of the poor.

Fools, your doublets shone with gold, and your hearts were gay
    and bold,
  When you kissed your lily hands to your lemans today;
And tomorrow shall the fox, from her chambers in the rocks,
  Lead forth her tawny cubs to howl above the prey.

Where be your tongues that late mocked at heaven and hell and
    fate,
  And the fingers that once were so busy with your blades,
Your perfumed satin clothes, your catches and your oaths,
  Your stage-plays and your sonnets, your diamonds and your
    spades?

Down, down, for ever down with the mitre and the crown,
  With the Belial of the Court, and the Mammon of the Pope;
There is woe in Oxford Halls; there is wail in Durham's Stalls:
  The Jesuit smites his bosom; the Bishop rends his cope.

And She of the seven hills shall mourn her children's ills,
  And tremble when she thinks of the edge of England's sword;
And the Kings of earth in fear shall shudder when they hear.
  What the hand of God hath wrought for the Houses and the
    Word.

Thomas Babington, Lord Macaulay

This splendid poem describes the decisive battle of the Civil War. The Royalist troops were heavily outnumbered by Roundheads, largely because the forces led by Lord Goring, who was jealous of Prince Rupert, failed to turn up. A brilliant charge by Rupert nearly won the day, but Cromwell's cavalry stood firm. Macaulay, in his enthusiasm for the Protestant and Parliamentary cause, overlooked the fact that Cromwell's men brutally murdered as many of the Royalist women camp-followers as they could lay their hands on. As usual, Cromwell had no doubts about the reason for his victory: 'Sir, there is none other than the hand of God.'

1646

THE LONG PARLIAMENT

On the New Forcers of Conscience under the Long Parliament

Because you have thrown off your Prelate Lord,
And with stiff vows renounced his Liturgy,
To seize the widow'd whore Plurality
From them whose sin ye envied, not abhorr'd;
Dare ye for this adjure the civil sword
To force our consciences that Christ set free,
And ride us with a classic hierarchy
Taught ye by mere A. S. and Rutherford?
Men whose life, learning, faith and pure intent
Would have been held in high esteem with Paul
Must now be named and printed heretics
By shallow Edwards and Scotch What-d'ye-call.
But we do hope to find out all your tricks,
Your plots and packings, worse than those of Trent,
That so the Parliament
May with their wholesome and preventive shears
Clip your phylacteries, though baulk your ears,
And succour our just fears,
When they shall read this clearly in your charge:
New Presbyter is but old Priest writ large.

John Milton

In the 1640s, the Long Parliament allowed the Presbyterians to dismantle the Church of England. They proved to be quite as intolerant as the Catholics and attacked all who would not conform, including Milton, who had become an Independent. The Presbyterians mentioned in this poem had denounced Milton's tracts on divorce. In 1649 Rutherford advocated the death penalty for heresy, proving the truth of Milton's famous last line.

1648

FAIRFAX

On the Lord General Fairfax, at the Siege of Colchester

Fairfax, whose name in arms through Europe rings
Filling each mouth with envy or with praise,
And all her jealous monarchs with amaze
And rumours loud, that daunt remotest kings;
Thy firm unshaken virtue ever brings
Victory home, though new rebellions raise
Their Hydra heads, and the false North displays
Her broken league, to imp their serpent wings.
O yet a nobler task awaits thy hand;
For what can war but endless war still breed,
Till truth and right from violence be freed,
And public faith clear'd from the shameful brand
Of public fraud? In vain doth Valour bleed,
While Avarice and Rapine share the land.

John Milton

Fairfax was the great general who with Cromwell had created the New Model Army, victorious at the battles of Marston Moor and Naseby. In the second part of the Civil War he fought the Royalists in the South-east and starved Colchester to surrender. After Charles's execution, he withdrew from public life and lived peacefully for twenty years.

1649

THE EXECUTION OF CHARLES I

from **An Horatian Ode upon Cromwell's Return from Ireland**

What field of all the civil wars
Where his were not the deepest scars?
    And Hampton shows what part
    He had of wiser art;

Where, twining subtle fears with hope,
He wove a net of such a scope
    That Charles himself might chase
    To Car'sbrook's narrow case;

That thence the Royal Actor borne
The tragic scaffold might adorn:
    While round the armèd bands
    Did clap their bloody hands.

He nothing common did or mean
Upon that memorable scene,
    But with his keener eye
    The axe's edge did try;

Nor called the Gods, with vulgar spite,
To vindicate his helpless right;
    But bowed his comely head
    Down, as upon a bed.

This was that memorable hour
Which first assured the forcèd power:
    So when they did design
    The Capitol's first line,

A bleeding head, where they begun,
Did fright the architects to run;
    And yet in that the State
    Foresaw its happy fate!

Andrew Marvell

This is an extract from a poem written to celebrate Cromwell's triumphant return from Ireland in 1650. Marvell recognizes Charles's courage and serenity, but has no doubts about the justice of the Parliamentarian cause.

Oh let that day from time be blotted quite,
And let belief of't in next age be waived.
In deepest silence th'act concealed might,
So that the Kingdom's credit might be saved.

*

But if the Power Divine permitted this,
His Will's the law and ours must acquiesce.

Lord General Fairfax

Fairfax was at the Banqueting Hall in Whitehall on the morning of Charles's execution and spoke with the King a few hours before the event. On the night preceding it, he had been approached by several people, including two Dutch ambassadors, who had urged him to save the King. But the entire area had been filled with troops by Cromwell and, although Fairfax had no wish to be responsible for the King's death, he did nothing to prevent it. In a great fit of hand-wringing and guilt-assuaging he composed these verses, and even managed to pass the buck to God.

Samuel Pepys, who was present at the King's death, was also in 1660 a witness at the execution of one of the leading Parliamentarians. In his diary he wrote:

> I went out to Charing cross to see Maj.-Gen. Harrison hanged, drawn, and quartered – which was done there – he looking as cheerfully as any man could do in that condition. He was presently cut down and his head and his heart shown to the people, at which there was great shouts of joy . . . Thus it was my chance to see the King beheaded at Whitehall and to see the first blood shed in revenge for the blood of the King at Charing cross. From thence to my Lord's and took Capt. Cuttance and Mr. Sheply to the Sun taverne and did give them some oysters.

By the Statue of King Charles I at Charing Cross

Sombre and rich, the skies;
Great glooms, and starry plains.
Gently the night wind sighs;
Else a vast silence reigns.

The splendid silence clings
Around me; and around
The saddest of all kings
Crowned, and again discrowned.

Comely and calm, he rides
Hard by his own Whitehall:
Only the night wind glides:
No crowds, nor rebels, brawl . . .

Which are more full of fate:
The stars; or those sad eyes?
Which are more still and great:
Those brows; or the dark skies?

Although his whole heart yearns
In passionate tragedy:
Never was face so stern
With sweet austerity.

Vanquished in life, his death
By beauty made amends:
The passing of his breath
Won his defeated ends.

Brief life, and hapless? Nay:
Through death, life grew sublime.
Speak after sentence? Yea:
And to the end of time . . .

Lionel Johnson

This famous equestrian statue was commissioned from the sculptor Le Sueur in 1630 and erected in 1648. After Charles's execution, Parliament sold it to a brass merchant, John Rivet of Holborn, with orders that it should be destroyed. Rivet buried it and then sold spoons and knife-handles allegedly made from its metal. After the Restoration, Rivet presented it intact to Charles II who had it erected at the top of Whitehall, where his father had been executed. On 30 January each year devout Royalists and Catholics place flowers at the base of the monument. Lionel Johnson wrote his poem towards the end of the nineteenth century.

The Commonwealth, 1649–60

OLIVER CROMWELL

Rupert of the Rhine
Thought Cromwell was a swine.
He felt quite sure
After Marston Moor

E. C. Bentley

To the Lord General Cromwell

Cromwell, our chief of men, who through a cloud
Not of war only, but detractions rude,
Guided by faith and matchless fortitude,
To peace and truth thy glorious way hast ploughed,
And on the neck of crownèd Fortune proud
Hast reared God's trophies, and his work pursued;
While Darwen stream, with blood of Scots imbrued,
And Dunbar field resounds thy praises loud,
And Worcester's laureate wreath: yet much remains
To conquer still; Peace hath her victories
No less renowned than War: new foes arise,
Threatening to bind our souls with secular chains.
Help us to save free conscience from the paw
Of hireling wolves, whose Gospel is their maw.

John Milton

Cromwell, a wealthy East Anglian farmer, became an MP in the Long Parliament, but emerged after the Roundhead victories in 1644 and 1645 as the leader of the Protestant revolution. He routed the Royalists in the second civil war of 1648, and then came to accept that Charles must be executed. He ruthlessly crushed the uprisings that took place after Charles's death: in Ireland in 1650; among the Scots in the same year; and in England in 1651 – this last ending with his victory at Worcester. In 1653 he became Lord Protector and, even more quickly than Charles, fell out with Parliament, crying: 'Take away that fool's bauble, the mace!' Thereafter he ruled England, not with MPs, but with Major-Generals. His devotion to the cause of parliamentary democracy is recognized by the statue of him erected outside the public entrance to the House of Commons.

1649

from The Diggers' Song

'You noble Diggers all, stand up now, stand up now,
You noble Diggers all, stand up now,
The waste land to maintain, seeing Cavaliers by name
Your digging do disdain and persons all defame.
Stand up now, stand up now.

Your houses they pull down, stand up now, stand up now,
Your houses they pull down, stand up now;
Your houses they pull down to fright poor men in town,
But the Gentry must come down, and the poor shall wear the crown.
Stand up now, Diggers all!

*

The Lawyers they conjoin, stand up now, stand up now,
The Lawyers they conjoin, stand up now!
To arrest you they advise, such fury they devise,
The devil in them lies, and hath blinded both their eyes.
Stand up now, stand up now.

The Clergy they come in, stand up now, stand up now,
The Clergy they come in, stand up now;
The Clergy they come in, and say it is a sin
That we should now begin our freedom for to win.
Stand up now, Diggers all!

*

The Cavaliers are foes, stand up now, stand up now,
The Cavaliers are foes, stand up now;
The Cavaliers are foes, themselves they do disclose
By verses, not in prose, to please the singing boys.
Stand up now, Diggers all!

To conquer them by love, come in now, come in now,
To conquer them by love, come in now;
To conquer them by love, as it does you behove,
For He is King above, no Power is like to Love.
Glory here, Diggers all!'

Gerrard Winstanley

A ferment of revolutionary ideas was released during the 1640s. The Levellers, led by John Lilburne, advocated egalitarianism, but a weaver from Wigan, Gerrard Winstanley, went further. He demanded the communal ownership of all property. In 1649, with a band of twenty followers, he occupied some common land on St George's Hill in Surrey, his stated purpose being 'to sow corn for the succour of men'. Cromwell would not have any of this, and the Diggers were moved on and dispersed a year later. In the same year he crushed the Levellers at Burford, and after that the Ranters, who had carried their libertarian views to the extent of sharing their wives.

The Leveller's Rant

To the hall, to the hall,
For justice we call,
On the king and his pow'rful adherents and friends,
Who still have endeavour'd, but we work their ends.
'Tis we will pull down whate'er is above us,
And make them to fear us, that never did love us,
We'll level the proud, and make very degree,
To our royalty bow the knee,
'Tis no less than treason,
'Gainst freedom and reason
for our brethren to be higher than we.

First the thing, call'd a king,
To judgment we bring,
And the spawn of the court, that were prouder than he,
And next the two Houses united shall be:
It does to the Roman religion inveigle,
For the state to be two-headed like the spread-eagle;
We'll purge the superfluous members away,
They are too many kings to sway,
And as we all teach,
'Tis our liberty's breach,
For the free-born saints to obey.

Not a claw, in the law,
Shall keep us in awe;
We'll have no cushion-cuffers to tell us of Hell,
For we are all gifted to do it as well:
'Tis freedom that we do hold forth to the nation
To enjoy our fellow-creatures as at the creation;
The carnal men's wives are for men of the spirit,
Their wealth is our own by merit,
For we that have right,
By the law called might,
Are the saints that must judge and inherit.

Alexander Brome

This is a spirited response by a Cavalier poet to the Levellers and Ranters.

1653

A Prophecy

The land shall be free of all taxation
And men in their minds shall be freed of all vexation . . .
Sorrow and care shall torment us no more,
Some men shall grow rich and some shall grow poor . . .
Men shall next year be kind to their wives
That women shall live most excellent lives . . .
If a traveller chance to be weary, he may
Call at the first ale-house he find in his way
And there for his money he welcome may be,
All this next year you are certain to see.

Will Lilly

Lilly, a pedlar of almanacs, wrote this while in prison.

from On the Victory obtained by *Blake* over the *Spaniards*, in the Bay of *Sanctacruze*, in the Island of *Teneriff*. 1657

Now does *Spains* Fleet her spatious wings unfold,
Leaves the new World and hastens for the old:
But though the wind was fair, they slowly swoome
Frayted with acted Guilt, and Guilt to come:
For this rich load, of which so proud they are,
Was rais'd by Tyranny, and rais'd for War;
Every capatious Gallions womb was fill'd,
With what the Womb of wealthy Kingdomes yield,
The new Worlds wounded Intrails they had tore,
For wealth wherewith to wound the old once more.

*

They dreaded to behold, Least the Sun's light,
With *English* Streamers, should salute their sight:
In thickest darkness they would choose to steer,
So that such darkness might suppress their fear;
At length theirs vanishes, and fortune smiles;
For they behold the sweet Canary Isles.

*

For *Sanctacruze* the glad Fleet takes her way,
And safely there casts Anchor in the Bay.
Never so many with one joyful cry,
That place saluted, where they all must dye.
Deluded men! Fate with you did but sport,
You scap't the Sea, to perish in your Port.

*

With hast they therefore all their Gallions moar,
And flank with Cannon from the Neighbouring shore.
Forts, Lines, and Sconces all the Bay along,
They build and act all that can make them strong.

*

Those forts, which there, so high and strong appear,
Do not so much suppress, as shew their fear.
Of Speedy Victory let no man doubt,
Our worst works past, now we have found them out.
Behold their Navy does at Anchor lye,
And they are ours, for now they cannot fly.

*

The Thund'ring Cannon now begins the Fight,
And though it be at Noon, creates a Night.
The Air was soon after the fight begun,
Far more enflam'd by it, then by the Sun.
Never so burning was that Climate known,
War turn'd the temperate, to the Torrid Zone.
Fate these two Fleets, between both Worlds had brought.
Who fight, as if for both those Worlds they fought.
Thousands of wayes, Thousands of men there dye,
Some Ships are sunk, some blown up in the skie.
Nature ne'r made Cedars so high aspire,
As Oakes did then, Urg'd by the active fire.
Which by quick powders force, so high was sent,
That it return'd to its own Element.
Torn Limbs some leagues into the Island fly,
Whilst others lower, in the Sea do lye.
Scarce souls from bodies sever'd are so far,
By death, as bodies there were by the War.
Th' all-seeing Sun, neer gaz'd on such a sight,
Two dreadful Navies there at Anchor Fight.

*

Our Cannon now tears every Ship and Sconce,
And o're two Elements Triumphs at once.
Their Gallions sunk, their wealth the Sea does fill,
The only place where it can cause no Ill.
Ah would those Treasures which both Indies have,
Were buryed in as large, and deep a grave,
Wars chief support with them would buried be,
And the Land owe her peace unto the Sea.
Ages to come, your conquering Arms will bless,
There they destroy, what had destroy'd their Peace.
And in one War the present age may boast,
The certain seeds of many Wars are lost.
All the Foes Ships destroy'd, by Sea or fire,
Victorious *Blake*, does from the Bay retire,
His Seige of *Spain* he then again pursues,
And there first brings of his success the news;
The saddest news that ere to *Spain* was brought,
Their rich Fleet sunk, and ours with Lawrel fraught.
Whilst fame in every place, her Trumpet blowes,
And tell the World, how much to you it owes.

Andrew Marvell

Cromwell studiously built up the navy, and Robert Blake was the great admiral who reasserted England's supremacy at sea by defeating the Dutch fleet under its veteran commander, van Tromp, in 1653. In the next year Jamaica was captured from Spain. As Elizabeth I had done, Cromwell set about harassing the great Spanish treasure-fleets. One was captured off Cadiz and another was sunk by Blake in harbour at the Canaries, as Marvell relates. Spain's power was crippled, but as the English fleet headed back to Plymouth Blake died on board.

1658

THE DEATH OF CROMWELL

from A Poem upon the Death of His late Highnesse the Lord Protector

I saw him dead, a leaden slumber lyes
And mortall sleep over those wakefull eys:
Those gentle Rayes under the lidds were fled
Which through his lookes that piercing sweetnesse shed:
That port which so Majestique was and strong,
Loose and depriv'd of vigour stretch'd along:
All wither'd, all discolour'd, pale and wan,
How much another thing, no more that man?
Oh human glory vaine, Oh death, Oh wings,
Oh worthless world, Oh transitory things!

*

Thee many ages hence in martiall verse
Shall th'English souldier ere he charge rehearse:
Singing of thee inflame themselvs to fight
And with the name of Cromwell armyes fright.
As long as rivers to the seas shall runne,
As long as Cynthia shall relieve the sunne,
While staggs shall fly unto the forests thick,
While sheep delight the grassy downs to pick,
As long as future time succeeds the past,
Always thy honour, praise and name shall last.

Andrew Marvell

Cromwell suffered from malaria, called marsh-fever in his day. During the 1630s the wife of a Spanish envoy in Lima, who had been cured of malaria by the use of quinine, popularized it in Europe. Quinine is a powder made from the bark of a tree, the Cinchona, named after her. It also came to be known as 'Jesuit's Bark'. Cromwell could have taken it and been cured, but he died, as he had lived, a Protestant bigot, calling quinine 'the powder of the Devil'.

King Charles II, 1660–85

In 1660 the Puritan Revolution had exhausted all public enthusiasm for it and in effect it petered out. So another experiment was tried – the restoration of the monarchy. Charles I's son returned from exile and became Charles II. Cromwell's body was exhumed and those who had signed the death warrant of the previous King were mercilessly pursued. The Book of Common Prayer was reintroduced, and the Test Acts were passed to keep Dissenters and Catholics alike out of office.

Parliament struggled to reassert its power and denied the supply of money to the King. Charles circumvented this by taking large bribes from Louis XIV of France. England fought Holland and allied herself with France, though many people would have preferred the opposite. The political situation was dominated by Charles's inability to produce an heir, although this was not for want of trying. It appeared more and more likely that his brother, a declared Catholic sympathizer, would succeed him.

Whig historians have praised the Puritan Revolution, while condemning the profligacy, deceitfulness and self-indulgence of the court of Charles II. Yet this was also an age which produced England's greatest scientist, Newton, its greatest architect, Wren, and its greatest political poet, Dryden.

1660

THE RESTORATION

from **Iter Boreale**

Now sing the triumphs of the men of war,
The glorious rays of the bright Northern Star,
Created for the nonce by Heav'n to bring
The wise men of three nations to their King.
Monck! the great Monck! that syllable outshines
Plantagenet's bright name or Constantine's.
'Twas at his rising that our day begun;
Be he the morning star to Charles our sun.
He took rebellion rampant by the throat,
And made the canting Quaker change his note.
His hand it was that wrote (we saw no more)
Exit tyrannus over Lambert's door.
Like to some subtle lightning, so his words
Dissolved in their scabbards rebels' swords.
He with success the sov'reign skill hath found
To dress the weapon and so heal the wound.
George and his boys, as spirits do, they say,
Only by walking scare our foes away.

Robert Wild

Wild's poem celebrates Charles II's return to London in May 1660. George Monck, one of Cromwell's generals, played the key role in Charles's restoration. After Cromwell's death, his son, Richard, briefly took over, but those who wanted the Republic to continue decided to recall the Rump Parliament, which Cromwell had dissolved. The army under General Lambert suppressed some Royalist uprisings in 1659. Returning with his army from Scotland to London, Monck played his cards so close to his chest throughout the subsequent negotiations that few knew whether he favoured Parliament or Charles. In 1660, however, he resolved the issue and went to Breda in Holland to bring the King back to England.

THE CHARACTER OF THE KING

Epitaph on Charles II

In the Isle of Great *Britain* long since famous known,
For breeding the best C[ully] in *Christendom;*
There reigns, and long may he reign and thrive,
The easiest prince and best bred man alive:
Him no ambition moves to seek renown,
Like the *French* fool to wander up and down,
Starving his subjects, hazarding his crown.
Nor are his high desires above his strength,
His scepter and his p... are of a length,
And she that plays with one may sway the other,
And make him little wiser than his brother.
I hate all monarchs and the thrones they sit on,
From the Hector of *France* to the Cully of *Britain.*
Poor Prince, thy p... like the buffoons at court,
It governs thee, because it makes thee sport;
Tho' safety, law, religion, life lay on't,
'Twill break through all to its way to c...
Restless he rolls about from whore to whore,
A merry Monarch, scandalous and poor.
To *Carewell* the most dear of all thy dears.
The sure relief of thy declining years;
Oft he bewails his fortune and her fate,
To love so well, and to be lov'd so late;
For when in her he settles well his t...
Yet his dull graceless buttocks hang an Arse.
This you'd believe, had I but time to tell you,
The pain it costs to poor laborious *Nelly,*
While she employs hands, fingers, lips and thighs,
E'er she can raise the member she enjoys.

John Wilmot, Earl of Rochester

1665

THE GREAT PLAGUE

Ring-a-ring o' roses,
A pocket full of posies,
  A-tishoo! A-tishoo!
We all fall down

Anonymous

Pindarique Ode Made in the Time of the Great Sickness

I thought on every pensive thing,
That might my passion strongly move,
That might the sweetness sadness bring;
Oft did I think on death, and oft on Love,
The triumphs of the *little God*, and that same *ghastly King*.
The ghastly King, what has he done?
How his pale Territories spread!
Strait scantlings now of consecrated ground
His swelling Empire cannot bound,
But every day new *Colonies* of dead
Enhance his Conquests, and advance his Throne.
The mighty *City* sav'd from storms of war,
Exempted from the Crimson floud,
When all the Land o'reflow'd with blood,
Stoops yet once more to a new Conqueror:
The *City* which so many Rivals bred,
Sackcloth is on her loyns, and ashes on her head.

When will the frowning heav'n begin to smile;
Those pitchy clouds be overblown,
That hide the mighty Town,
That I may see the mighty pyle?
When will the angry Angel cease to slay;
And turn his brandisht sword away
From that illustrous *Golgotha* . . .?

Thomas Flatman

The nursery rhyme is said to date from the time of the Great Plague itself. The give-away symptom was a rash of red spots, and people tried to fend off the infection by carrying nosegays of herbs. As the sickness developed, breathing became more difficult before the inevitability of death.

1666

THE GREAT FIRE OF LONDON

from **Annus Mirabilis**

The fire, mean time, walks in a broader gross,
To either hand his wings he opens wide:
He wades the streets, and straight he reaches cross,
And plays his longing flames on th' other side.

At first they warm, then scorch, and then they take:
Now with long necks from side to side they feed:
At length, grown strong, their Mother fire forsake,
And a new Collony of flames succeed.

To every nobler portion of the Town,
The curling billows roul their restless Tyde:
In parties now they straggle up and down,
As Armies, unoppos'd, for prey divide.

One mighty Squadron, with a side wind sped,
  Through narrow lanes his cumber'd fire does haste:
By pow'rful charms of gold and silver led,
  The *Lombard* Banquers and the *Change* to waste.

Another backward to the *Tow'r* would go,
  And slowly eats his way against the wind:
But the main body of the marching foe
  Against th' Imperial Palace is design'd.

Now day appears, and with the day the King,
  Whose early care had robb'd him of his rest:
Far off the cracks of falling houses ring,
  And shrieks of subjects pierce his tender breast.

Near as he draws, thick harbingers of smoke,
  With gloomy pillars, cover all the place:
Whose little intervals of night are broke
  By sparks that drive against his Sacred Face.

*

Nor with an idle care did he behold:
  (Subjects may grieve, but Monarchs must redress.)
He chears the fearful, and commends the bold,
  And makes despairers hope for good success.

Himself directs what first is to be done,
  And orders all the succours which they bring.
The helpful and the good about him run,
  And form an Army worthy such a King.

He sees the dire contagion spread so fast,
  That where it seizes, all relief is vain:
And therefore must unwillingly lay waste
  That Country which would, else, the foe maintain.

The powder blows up all before the fire:
  Th' amazed flames stand gather'd on a heap;
And from the precipices brinck retire,
  Afraid to venture on so large a leap.

Thus fighting fires a while themselves consume,
  But straight, like *Turks*, forc'd on to win or die,
They first lay tender bridges of their fume,
  And o'r the breach in unctuous vapours flie.

Part stays for passage till a gust of wind
  Ships o'r their forces in a shining sheet:
Part, creeping under ground, their journey blind,
  And, climbing from below, their fellows meet.

Thus, to some desart plain, or old wood side,
  Dire night-hags come from far to dance their round:
And o'r brode Rivers on their fiends they ride,
  Or sweep in clowds above the blasted ground.

No help avails: for, *Hydra*-like, the fire,
  Lifts up his hundred heads to aim his way.
And scarce the wealthy can one half retire,
  Before he rushes in to share the prey.

John Dryden

LONDON AFTER THE GREAT FIRE

from **Annus Mirabilis**

Me-thinks already, from this Chymick flame,
  I see a City of more precious mold:
Rich as the Town which gives the *Indies* name,
  With Silver pav'd, and all divine with Gold.

Already, Labouring with a mighty fate,
  She shakes the rubbish from her mounting brow,
And seems to have renew'd her Charters date,
  Which Heav'n will to the death of time allow.

More great then humane, now, and more *August*,
New deifi'd she from her fires does rise:
Her widening streets on new foundations trust,
And, opening, into larger parts she flies.

Before, she like some Shepherdess did show,
Who sate to bathe her by a River's side:
Not answering to her fame, but rude and low,
Nor taught the beauteous Arts of Modern pride.

Now, like a Maiden Queen, she will behold,
From her high Turrets, hourly Sutors come:
The East with Incense, and the West with Gold,
Will stand, like Suppliants, to receive her doom.

John Dryden

The Great Plague had carried off as many as 68,000 Londoners and in the following year the Great Fire destroyed the heart of the city. Yet this provided the opportunity for the architects of the time, most notably Sir Christopher Wren, to redesign London in a more planned way and to erect some of the most beautiful buildings since the medieval cathedrals. Wren's epitaph, composed by his son, is inscribed over the north door inside St Paul's Cathedral and reads: 'Si monumentum requiris, circumspice' ('If you seek his monument, look around').

1667

THE DUTCH IN THE MEDWAY

from **The Last Instructions to a Painter**

Ruyter the while, that had our ocean curb'd,
Sail'd now among our rivers undisturb'd,
Survey'd their crystal streams and banks so green
And beauties ere this never naked seen.
Through the vain sedge the bashful nymphs he ey'd:
Bosoms and all which from themselves they hide.
The sun much brighter, and the skies more clear,
He finds the air and all things sweeter here.
The sudden change and such a tempting sight
Swells his old veins with fresh blood, fresh delight.
Like am'rous victors he begins to shave,
And his new face looks in the English wave.
His sporting navy all about him swim
And witness their complacence in their trim.
Their streaming silks play through the weather fair
And with inveigling colors court the air,
While the red flags breathe on their top-masts high
Terror and war but want an enemy.
Among the shrouds the seamen sit and sing,
And wanton boys on every rope do cling.

Andrew Marvell

England and Holland went to war over the control of trade routes. At first England showed the upper hand. She defeated the Dutch at the battle of Lowestoft in 1665, but the Lord High Admiral, Charles II's brother James, Duke of York, failed to follow up the advantage and let the Dutch fleet escape. This did not stop Parliament voting him a payment of £120,000. In 1666 there was further, inconclusive fighting, but in 1667 England suffered its most humiliating naval defeat when the ageing Dutch Admiral De Ruyter broke through the chain defences at Chatham and sailed up the Medway. There was enormous incompetence on the English side, but the admiral concerned, Monck, now the Duke of Albemarle, may have been incapacitated by a singularly painful wound received the year before. As Marvell delicately put it:

Most with story of his hand or thumb
Conceal (as Honor would) his Grace's bum,
When the rude bullet a large collop tore
Out of that buttock never turn'd before.
Fortune, it seem'd, would give him by that lash
Gentle correction for his fight so rash,
But should the Rump perceiv't, they'd say that Mars
Had now reveng'd them upon Aumarle's arse.

1671

THE ATTEMPT ON THE CROWN JEWELS

On Blood's Stealing the Crown

When daring Blood, his rents to have regain'd
Upon the English diadem distrain'd,
He chose the cassock, surcingle, and gown
(No mask so fit for one that robs a crown),
But his lay-pity underneath prevail'd,
And while he spar'd the Keeper's life, he fail'd.
With the priest's vestments had he but put on
A bishop's cruelty, the crown was gone.

Andrew Marvell

Colonel Blood, an adventurer, seeking redress over a land dispute, made an ingenious plan to steal the Crown Jewels. Under the disguise of a priest, he ingratiated himself with the Keeper of the Jewel House, Talbot Edwards, and was granted a special viewing, whereupon he and his companions turned upon Edwards and bound and gagged him. One stuffed the Orb down his breeches, another tried to saw the Sceptre in half, and Blood popped the Crown under his priest's cloak. Unfortunately for them, at that very moment Edwards's son returned on leave from Flanders and they were captured. Charles II pardoned Blood, possibly because he had proven himself too valuable as a spy.

1672

RELATIONS WITH FRANCE

Lines Written in a Lincoln's Inn Boghouse

From peace with the French and war with the Dutch,
From a new mouth which will cost us as much,
And from councils of wits which advise us to such,
Libera nos, Domine.

From Pope and from priests which lead men astray,
From fools that by cheats will be so led away,
From saints that 'Go to the Devil' will pray,
Libera nos, Domine.

From Parliament-sellers elected for ale,
Who sell the weal public to get themselves bail,
And if e'er it be dissolv'd will die in a jail,
Libera nos, Domine.

Anonymous

From 1670 Charles II followed a policy of being friendly to France, of encouraging Catholicism, and of having as little as possible to do with Parliament. None of this was popular, and his relations with the French king, Louis XIV, whose territorial ambitions many Englishmen thought should be checked, caused particular suspicion.

THE KING'S WHORES

Barbara Palmer, Duchess of Cleveland

Let Ancients boast no more
Their lewd Imperial Whore
Whose everlasting Lust
Surviv'd her Body's latest thrust,
And when that Transitory dust
Had no more vigour left in Store
Was still as fresh and active as before.

*

When shee had jaded quite
Her allmost boundless Appetite,
Cloy'd with the choicest Banquetts of delight,
She'l still drudge on in Tastless vice
As if shee sinn'd for Exercise
Disabling stoutest Stallions ev'ry hour,
And when they can perform no more
She'l rail at 'em and kick 'em out of door.

Monmouth and *Candish* droop
As first did *Henningham* and *Scroop*
Nay Scabby *Ned* looks thinn and pale
And sturdy *Frank* himself begins to fail
But Woe betide him if he does
She'l sett her *Jocky* on his Toes
And he shall end the Quarell without Blows . . .

attributed to John Wilmot, Earl of Rochester

Nell Gwynne

Hard by Pall Mall lives a wench call'd Nell.
  King Charles the Second he kept her.
She hath got a trick to handle his p—,
  But never lays hands on his sceptre.
All matters of state from her soul she does hate,
  And leave to the politic bitches.
The whore's in the right, for 'tis her delight
  To be scratching just where it itches.

Anonymous

Nell Gwynne, the orange-seller from Covent Garden, became the King's mistress in 1669. Her rags-to-riches story made her popular with the crowds. As distinct from the King's other whores, she was not a Catholic. She once escaped from a mob in Oxford, after being mistaken for the Duchess of Portsmouth, by saying: 'Pray, good people, be civil – I am the Protestant whore.'

1673–80

THE POPISH PLOT

from **Absalom and Achitophel**

From hence began that Plot, the nation's curse,
Bad in itself, but represented worse.
Rais'd in extremes, and in extremes decri'd;
With oaths affirm'd, with dying vows deni'd.
Not weigh'd or winnow'd by the multitude;
But swallow'd in the mass, unchew'd and crude.
Some truth there was, but dash'd and brew'd with lies,
To please the fools, and puzzle all the wise.
Succeeding times did equal folly call
Believing nothing, or believing all.

John Dryden

TITUS OATES

from **Absalom and Achitophel**

Sunk were his eyes, his voice was harsh and loud,
Sure signs he neither choleric was nor proud.
His long chin prov'd his wit; his saintlike grace
A church vermilion, and a Moses' face.
His memory, miraculously great,
Could plots exceeding man's belief repeat;
Which therefore cannot be accounted lies,
For human wit could never such devise.
Some future truths are mingl'd in his book;
But, where the witness fail'd, the prophet spoke.
Some things like visionary flights appear;
The spirit caught him up, the Lord knows where,
And gave him his Rabbinical degree
Unknown to foreign university.
His judgement yet his mem'ry did excel;
Which piec'd his wondrous evidence so well,
And suited to the temper of the times,
Then groaning under Jebusitic crimes.

John Dryden

In October 1678 Titus Oates, a charlatan, made accusations before a magistrate, Sir Edmund Berry Godfrey, that a plot had been hatched by Papists to kill the King and put his brother James on the throne. Three weeks later the body of Godfrey was found on Primrose Hill, impaled on his own sword. A cursory medical examination indicated that he could have been strangled as well. The murder hunt was on. A Catholic suspect under torture confessed, declaring that Godfrey had been strangled in front of three Catholic priests. Those found guilty were executed. Some years later Oates admitted that all his evidence had been fabricated and he was sentenced to be whipped from Newgate to Tyburn. The affair created a wave of mass hysteria which was exploited by the politicians of the time, most notably the Earl of Shaftesbury.

1681

THE EARL OF SHAFTESBURY

from **Absalom and Achitophel**

Of these the false Achitophel was first,
A name to all succeeding ages curst.
For close designs and crooked counsels fit;
Sagacious, bold, and turbulent of wit.
Restless, unfix'd in principles and place;
In pow'r unpleas'd, impatient of disgrace.
A fiery soul which, working out its way,
Fretted the pigmy body to decay,
And o'er-inform'd the tenement of clay.
A daring pilot in extremity;
Pleas'd with the danger, when the waves went high
He sought the storms; but, for a calm unfit,
Would steer too nigh the sands to boast his wit.
Great wits are sure to madness near alli'd,
And thin partitions do their bounds divide;
Else why should he, with wealth and honor blest,
Refuse his age the needful hours of rest?
Punish a body which he could not please;
Bankrupt of life, yet prodigal of ease?
And all to leave what with his toil he won
To that unfeather'd, two-legg'd thing, a son,
Got while his soul did huddl'd notions try,
And born a shapeless lump, like anarchy.
In friendship false, implacable in hate;
Resolv'd to ruin or to rule the state;
To compass this the triple bond he broke,
The pillars of the public safety shook,
And fitted Israel for a foreign yoke.
Then, seiz'd with fear, yet still affecting fame,
Usurp'd a Patriot's all-atoning name.
So easy still it proves in factious times
With public zeal to cancel private crimes.
How safe is treason, and how sacred ill,

Where none can sin against the people's will;
Where crowds can wink, and no offense be known,
Since in another's guilt they find their own!

John Dryden

'Absalom and Achitophel' is perhaps the finest political poem in the English language. Asked to write it by the King, Dryden applied his majestic Augustan couplets to satirizing the Whigs, and particularly, in the figure of Achitophel, Anthony Ashley Cooper, the Earl of Shaftesbury, who had been arrested for high treason in July 1681. Shaftesbury had led the Whig opposition to the King, openly supporting the Duke of Monmouth as Protestant heir to the throne; masterminding the campaign to exclude the King's brother, James; exploiting the public feeling stirred up by the Popish Plot; and striving to ensure that Parliament was not suspended. He had, in effect, created the post of Leader of the Opposition. It was he who first made use of the slogan that 'Popery and slavery, like two sisters, go hand in hand.'

WHIGS AND TORIES

My Opinion

After thinking this fortnight of Whig and of Tory,
This to me is the long and the short of the story:
They are all fools or knaves, and they keep up this pother
On both sides, designing to cheat one another.

Poor Rowley (whose maxims of state are a riddle)
Has plac'd himself much like the pin in the middle;
Let which corner soever be tumbl'd down first,
'Tis ten thousand to one but he comes by the worst.

'Twixt brother and bastard (those Dukes of renown)
He'll make a wise shift to get rid of his crown;
Had he half common sense (were it ne'er so uncivil)
He'd have had 'em long since tipp'd down to the Devil.

The first is a Prince well-fashion'd, well-featur'd,
No bigot to speak of, not false, nor ill-natur'd;
The other for government can't be unfit,
He's so little a fop, and so plaguy a wit.

Had I this soft son, and this dangerous brother,
I'd hang up the one, then I'd piss upon t'other;
I'd make this the long and the short of the story:
The fools might be Whigs, none but knaves should be Tories.

Charles Sackville, Earl of Dorset

The last ten years of Charles's reign were a period of bitter political conflict and they saw the birth of two dominant parties – Whigs and Tories. When in 1679 Parliament failed to renew the Licensing Act, bitterness was increased as virulent lampoons and satires flooded from the presses. The country party, or Whigs, supported Monmouth as Protestant heir, while the Court party, or Tories, backed James. Charles, in the middle, cunningly exploited the royal prerogative and ruled without Parliament for the last four years of his reign.

CHARLES II

We have a pritty witty king
  And whose word no man relys on:
He never said a foolish thing,
  And never did a wise one.

John Wilmot, Earl of Rochester

King James II, 1685–8

from The Statue in Stocks-Market

But with all his faults restore us our King,
If ever you hope in December for Spring;
For though all the world cannot show such another,
Yet we'd rather have him than his bigoted brother.

Andrew Marvell

1685

The Humble Address of the Loyal Professors of Divinity and Law that Want Preferment and Practice

Great sir, our poor hearts were ready to burst
For the loss of your brother when we heard it at first.
But when we were told that you were to reign
We all fell a roaring out huzzas again.
With hearts full of joy, as our glasses of wine,
In this loyal address both professions do join.

May Jeffreys swagger on the bench
And James upon the throne,
Till we become slaves to the French
And Rome's dominion own;

May no man sit in Parliament
But by a false return,
Till Lords and Commons by consent
Their Magna Charta burn.
Though Smithfield now neglected lie,
Oh, may it once more shine
With Whigs in flaming heaps that fry
Of books they call divine;
From whence may such a blaze proceed,
So glorious and so bright,
That the next parish priest may read
His mass by Bible light.
Then holy water pots shall cheer
Our hearts like aqua vitae
Whilst singing monks in triumph bear
Their little God Almighty.
More blessings we could yet foretell
In this most happy reign,
But hark, the King's own chapel bell
Calls us to prayers again.
May trade and industry decay,
But may the plague increase,
Till it hath swept those Whigs away
That sign not this address.

Anonymous

James II set out to restore Catholicism to England at breakneck speed. Within ten days of his accession, he attended a Mass in public, which occasioned the ironical 'Humble Address'. The Test Acts, excluding all Dissenters from state office, were his main stumbling-block, and so he revived the power to dispense with inconvenient laws, just as his father, Charles I, had tried to do. He suspended Parliament and strengthened the standing army. When seven Protestant bishops refused to read one of his declarations from the pulpit, he had them arrested and put on trial. Although they were acquitted, this gesture did more than anything to turn opinion against the King. But the last straw was the birth of a son as Prince of Wales in June 1688, which in effect barred James's two Protestant daughters – Mary, married to William of Orange, and Anne, married to Prince George of Denmark – from the throne. William, however, had been making his own preparations, egged on by Protestant exiles, and in 1688 the people of England appealed to him to release them from 'Popery and slavery'.

1685

MONMOUTH'S REBELLION

Monmouth Degraded

(Or, James Scott, the Little King in Lyme)

Come beat alarm, sound a charge
As well without as in the verge,
Let every sword and soul be large
  To make our monarch shine, boys.
Let's leave off whores and drunken souls
And windy words o'er brimming bowls,
Let English hearts exceed the Poles'
  'Gainst Perkin, King in Lyme, boys.

Such a fop-king was ne'er before
Is landed on our western shore,
Which our black saints do all adore,
  Inspir'd by Tub-Divine, boys.
Let us assume the souls of Mars
And march in order, foot and horse,
Pull down the standard at the cross
  Of Perkin, King in Lyme, boys.

Pretended son unto a King,
Subject of delights in sin,
The most ungrateful wretch of men;
   Dishonour to the shrine, boys.
Of Charles, and James the undoubted right
Of England's crown and honours bright:
While he can find us work, let's fight
   'Gainst Perkin, King in Lyme, boys.

The Sainted Sisters now look blue,
Their cant's all false if God be true;
Their teaching stallions dare not do
   No more but squeeze and whine, boys;
Exhorting all the clowns to fight
Against their God, King, Church, and Right,
Takes care, for all their wives at night,
   For Perkin, King in Lyme, boys.

'Poor Perkin' now he is no more,
But James Scott as he was before;
No honour left but soul to soar
   Till quite expir'd with time, boys.
But first he'll call his parliament
By Ferguson and Grey's consent,
Trenchard and all the boors in's tent,
   Fit for the King in Lyme, boys.

'Gainst these mock kings, each draw his sword;
In blood we'll print them on record,
'Traitors against their sovereign lord';
   Let's always fight and join, boys.
Now they're block'd up by sea and land,
By treason they must fall or stand,
We only wait the King's command
   To burn the rogues in Lyme, boys.

But now we hear they're salli'd forth,
Front and flank 'em, south and north,
Nobles of brave England's worth,
  Let your bright honours shine, boys.
Let guns and cannons roar and ring
The music of a warlike King,
And all the gods just conquest bring
  Against the rogues in Lyme, boys.

Anonymous

The handsome bastard son of Charles II, the Duke of Monmouth left his mistress in Holland after she had sold her jewels to support his cause, and set sail with just three ships and a few hundred men to seize the throne of England. On 11 June 1685, he landed at Lyme in Dorset, raised his blue banner, and was proclaimed King at Taunton. On 6 July James II's regular army met Monmouth's straggling forces at Sedgemoor and crushed them. On 15 July, after a grovelling plea to his uncle, Monmouth died bravely on Tower Hill, telling the executioner that his blade was not sharp enough – which proved to be right, as it took seven strokes to kill him.

JUDGE JEFFREYS

A True Englishman

Let a lewd judge come reeking from a wench
To vent a wilder lust upon the bench;
Bawl out the venom of his rotten heart,
Swell'd up with envy, over-act his part;
Condemn the innocent by laws ne'er fram'd
And study to be more than doubly damn'd.

Anonymous

Jeffreys was made Lord Chief Justice in 1683 after presiding over the trial of Titus Oates. James II made him Lord Chancellor, and in the aftermath of Sedgemoor he conducted what came to be known as the Bloody Assizes in the West Country.

THE MORALS OF THE TIMES

from **A Faithful Catalogue of Our Most Eminent Ninnies**

Curs'd be those dull, unpointed, dogg'rel rhymes,
Whose harmless rage has lash'd our impious times.
Rise thou, my muse, and with the sharpest thorn,
Instead of peaceful bays, my brows adorn;
Inspir'd with just disdain and mortal hate,
Who long have been my plague, shall feel thy weight.
I scorn a giddy and unsafe applause,
But this, ye gods, is fighting in your cause;
Let Sodom speak, and let Gomorrah tell,
If their curs'd walls deserv'd their flames so well.
Go on, my muse, and with bold voice proclaim
The vicious lives and long detested fame
Of scoundrel lords, and their lewd wives' amours,
Pimp-statesmen, bugg'ring priests, court bawds, and whores.

*

Oh, sacred James! may thy dread noddle be
As free from danger as from wit 'tis free!
But if that good and gracious Monarch's charms
Could ne'er confine one woman to his arms,
What strange, mysterious spell, what strong defense,
Can guard that front which has not half his sense?
Poor Sedley's fall e'en her own sex deplore,
Who with so small temptation turn'd thy whore.
But Grafton bravely does revenge her fate
And says, thou court'st her thirty years too late;
She scorns such dwindles, her capacious arse
Is fitter for thy scepter, than thy tarse.

Charles Sackville, Earl of Dorset

Dorset was a noted libertine, but this did not prevent him from writing a scurrilous attack on his contemporaries, including James II. On his accession, James promised his demure wife that he would put aside his mistress, Catherine Sedley, whom he had ennobled as the Countess of Dorchester. It was James's luck to have a succession of singularly unattractive mistresses, which led his brother Charles to quip: 'James had his mistresses given him by his priests for penance.'

1688

THE TRIAL OF THE SEVEN BISHOPS

A New Catch in Praise of the Reverend Bishops

True Englishmen, drink a good health to the miter;
Let our church ever flourish, though her enemies spite her.
May their cunning and forces no longer prevail;
And their malice, as well as their arguments, fail.
Then remember the Seven, which supported our cause,
As stout as our martyrs and as just as our laws!

Anonymous

The Song of the Western Men

A good sword and a trusty hand!
  A merry heart and true!
King James's men shall understand
  What Cornish lads can do.

And have they fixed the where and when?
  And shall Trelawny die?
Here's twenty thousand Cornish men
  Will know the reason why!

Out spake their captain brave and bold,
  A merry wight was he:
'If London Tower were Michael's hold,
  We'll set Trelawny free!

We'll cross the Tamar, land to land,
  The Severn is no stay,
With "one and all", and hand in hand,
  And who shall bid us nay?

And when we come to London Wall,
  A pleasant sight to view,
Come forth! come forth, ye cowards all,
  Here's men as good as you!

Trelawny he's in keep and hold,
  Trelawny he may die;
But twenty thousand Cornish bold
  Will know the reason why.'

R. S. Hawker

Trelawny was the Bishop of Bristol, and one of the seven bishops to defy James and be imprisoned in the Tower. On the evening of their acquittal, seven English magnates signed an invitation to William of Orange to become their King and establish 'free Parliaments and the Protestant religion' in the land. Hawker was a nineteenth-century vicar of Morwenstow. Each of the chimneys on the house he built there was of a different medieval design.

William and Mary, 1688–1702

On 5 November 1688, William, Prince of Orange, landed at Torbay in Devon, not far from where Monmouth had landed three years earlier. James II's army outnumbered his by two to one, but at Salisbury the King was incapacitated by severe nose-bleeding and decided not to march against William at Exeter. This delay was a great mistake. His military commander, John Churchill, defected, and James fled back to London where he threw the Great Seal of England into the Thames. He never put up a fight.

Lilli Burlero

Ho, brother Teague, dost hear de decree,
  Lilli burlero, bullen a-la;
Dat we shall have a new debittie,
  Lilli burlero bullen a-la,
  Lero lero, lero lero, lilli burlero, bullen a-la;
  Lero lero, lero lero, lilli burlero, bullen a-la.

Ho, by my shoul, it is a Talbot,
And he will cut de Englishman's troat.

Though, by my shoul, de English do prat,
De law's on dare side, and Chreist knows what.

But if dispense do come from de Pope,
Weel hang Magno Cart and demselves on a rope.

And the good Talbot is made a lord,
And he with brave lads is coming aboard.

Who'll all in France have taken a swear,
Dat day will have no Protestant heir.

Oh, but why does he stay behind,
Ho, by my shoul, 'tis a Protestant wind.

Now Tyrconnel is come a-shore,
And we shall have commissions gillore.

And he dat will not go to mass,
Shall turn out and look like an ass.

Now, now, de heretics all go down,
By Chreist and St Patrick, the nation's our own!

attributed to Thomas Wharton

The words of 'Lilli Burlero', possibly by Thomas Wharton, were written in 1687 as an attack on the new Governor of Ireland, Tyrconnel, and an arrangement of the tune was published by Henry Purcell. But the song instantly transcended its topical purpose and became extraordinarily popular everywhere, especially among soldiers. It has been said that it 'sang a deluded Prince out of three Kingdoms'.

1689

A CATHOLIC VIEW OF THE CORONATION

A Dainty Fine King Indeed

The eleventh of April has come about,
To Westminster went a rabble rout,
In order to crown a bundle of clouts;
A dainty fine king indeed.

He's half a knave and half a fool,
The Protestant joyner's crooked tool,
Oh! its splutters, and nails shall such an one rule;
A dainty fine king indeed.

He has gotten part of the shape of a man,
But more of a monkey, deny it who can;
He has the head of a goose, but the legs of a cran;
A dainty fine king indeed.

In Hide Park he rides like a hog in armour,
In Whitehall he creeps like a country farmer,
Old England may boast of a godly reformer;
A dainty fine king indeed.

Anonymous

THE PROTESTANT VIEW OF WILLIAM III

A New Song of an Orange

Good People come buy
The Fruit that I cry,
That now is in Season, tho' Winter is nigh;
'Twill do you all good
And sweeten your Blood,
I'm sure it will please when you've once understood
'tis an *Orange*.

It's Cordial Juice,
Does much Vigour produce,
I may well recommend it to every Mans use,
Tho' some it quite chills,
And with fear almost kills,
Yet certain each Healthy Man benefit feels
by an *Orange*.

To make Claret go down,
Sometimes there is found
A jolly good Health, to pass pleasantly round;
But yet, I'll protest,
Without any Jest,
No Flavour is better then that of the taste
of an *Orange*.

Anonymous

WILLIAM III'S VIEW OF HIMSELF

As I walk'd by my self
And talk'd to my self,
My self said unto me,
Look to thy self,
Take care of thy self,
For nobody cares for Thee.

I answer'd my self,
And said to my self,
In the self-same Repartee,
Look to thy self
Or not look to thy self,
The self-same thing will be.

William III

1689

Bonnie Dundee

To the Lords of Convention 'twas Claver'se who spoke,
'Ere the King's crown shall fall there are crowns to be broke;
Then each cavalier who loves honour and me,
Let him follow the bonnet of Bonnie Dundee.
  'Come fill up my cup, come fill up my can,
  Come saddle your horses, and call up your men;
  Come open the West Port, and let me gang free,
And it's room for the bonnets of Bonnie Dundee!'

Dundee he is mounted, he rides up the street,
The bells are rung backward, the drums they are beat;
But the Provost, douce man, said, 'Just e'en let him be,
The Gude Town is weel quit o' that De'il of Dundee.'
  'Come fill up my cup,' etc.

'There are hills beyond Pentland, and lands beyond Forth.
If there's lords in the Lowlands, there's chiefs in the north;
There are wild Duniewassals, three thousand times three,
Will cry "hoigh!" for the bonnet of Bonnie Dundee.
  'Come fill up my cup,' etc.

'Away to the hills, to the caves, to the rocks –
Ere I own an usurper. I'll couch with the fox;
And tremble, false Whigs, in the midst of your glee.
You have not seen the last of my bonnet and me.
  'Come fill up my cup,' etc.

Walter Scott

The Convention was the Parliamentary assembly which formalized the abdication of James II. There the Presbyterians of the Scottish Lowlands, who had been persecuted under James, were glad to proclaim William as the new King. The leader of the Catholics, Claverhouse,

Viscount Dundee, rode out of the West Port of Edinburgh to raise the Highlands in the Stuart cause. The King's troops marched north to capture Blair Atholl Castle, but were met in the narrow pass of Killiecrankie by the Highlanders, who charged down upon the Redcoats only half an hour before sunset. Their heavy claymores cut through the Royalist army, which withdrew to Stirling. At the moment of victory, however, Bonny Dundee was shot and killed, as some said, by a silver bullet.

1690

THE BATTLE OF THE BOYNE

from **The Boyne Water**

July the First, of a morning clear, one thousand six hundred and ninety,
King William did his men prepare, of thousands he had thirty;
To fight King James and all his foes, encamped near the Boyne Water,
He little fear'd though two to one, their multitudes to scatter.

King William call'd his officers, saying: 'Gentlemen, mind your station,
And let your valour here be shown before this Irish nation;
My brazen walls let no man break, and your subtle foes you'll scatter,
Be sure you show them good English play as you go over the water.'

*

Within four yards of our fore-front, before a shot was fired,
A sudden snuff they got that day, which little they desired;
For horse and man fell to the ground, and some hung in their saddle;
Others turn'd up their forked ends, which we call 'coup de ladle'.

Prince Eugene's regiment was the next, on our right hand advanced,
Into a field of standing wheat, where Irish horses pranced –
But the brandy ran so in their heads, their senses all did scatter,
They little thought to leave their bones that day at the Boyne Water.

Both men and horse lay on the ground, and many there lay bleeding;
I saw no sickles there that day – but, sure, there was sharp shearing.

*

So praise God, all true Protestants, and I will say no further,
But had the Papists gain'd the day there would have been open murder.
Although King James and many more were ne'er that way inclined,
It was not in their power to stop what the rabble they designed.

Anonymous

Three months after William had landed in England, James left France to lead an uprising of his supporters in Ireland. He laid siege to Londonderry, which bravely held out for fifteen weeks, and then had to withdraw to Dublin where he was reinforced by 6,000 French troops. William landed in the north and marched on Dublin, but found his path blocked by James's army where it was drawn up by the River Boyne, in a strong defensive position. However, William's 36,000 soldiers crossed the river and defeated James's 25,000. It proved a decisive victory, for it established the ascendancy of the Protestant minority all over Ireland, until the forces unleashed by the French Revolution led to an independent Catholic Ireland.

1698

New Year's Day Song

Chorus

What then should happy Britain do?
Blest with the gift and giver too.

On warlike enterprizes bent
To foreign fields the hero went;
  The dreadful part he there perform'd
  Of battles fought, and cities storm'd:
But now the drum and trumpet cease,
  And wish'd success his sword has sheath'd,
  To us returns, with olive wreath'd,
To practice here the milder arts of peace.

Grand chorus

  Happy, happy, past expressing,
Britain, if thou know'st thy blessing;
Home-bred discord ne'er alarm thee,
Other mischief cannot harm thee.
Happy, if thou know'st thy blessing
Happy, happy, past expressing.

Nahum Tate

William was almost constantly engaged in protecting his Seven Provinces against the predatory ambitions of Louis XIV. He undertook campaigns in 1691, 1692, 1693 and 1694, and negotiated an advantageous peace in 1697. This lasted until 1702, when the fight against Louis was resumed in the War of the Spanish Succession, and after Louis had proclaimed his support for James II's son, the 'Old Pretender', as heir to the English throne. William was essentially a military commander, but it says much for his political acumen, too, that he managed to maintain a large standing army in spite of Parliament's suspicions and fears. It was this army which John Churchill, the Duke of Marlborough, was to lead so brilliantly.

1701

THE EXECUTION OF CAPTAIN KIDD

Great Black-backed Gulls

Said Cap'n Morgan to Cap'n Kidd:
'Remember the grand times, Cap'n, when
The Jolly Roger flapped on the tropic breeze,
And we were the terrors of the Spanish Main?'
And Cap'n Kidd replied: 'Aye when our restless souls
Were steeped in human flesh and bone;
But now we range the seven seas, and fight
For galley scraps that men throw overboard.'

Two black-backed gulls, that perched
On a half-sunken spar –
Their eyes were gleaming-cold and through
The morning fog that crept upon the grey-green waves
Their wicked laughter sounded.

John Heath-Stubbs

Sir Henry Morgan and William Kidd were the two most notorious pirates of the Spanish Main. They plundered the merchant ships engaged in the circular trade of slaves from Africa and sugar to Europe. Morgan died as Lieutenant-Governor of Jamaica, but Kidd was hanged at Execution Dock on the Thames in 1701.

1702

THE DEATH OF WILLIAM III

But *William* had not Govern'd Fourteen Year,
To be an unconcern'd Spectator here:
His Works like Providence were all Compleat,
And made a Harmony we Wonder'd at.
The Legislative Power he set Free,
And led them step by step to Liberty,
'Twas not his Fault if they cou'd not Agree.
Impartial Justice He protected so,
The Laws did in their Native Channels flow,
From whence our sure Establishment begun,
And *William* laid the first Foundation Stone:
On which the stately Fabrick soon appear'd,
How cou'd they sink when such a Pilot steer'd?
He taught them due defences to prepare,
And make their future Peace their present care:
By him directed, Wisely they Decreed,
What Lines shou'd be expell'd, and what succeed;
That now he's Dead, there's nothing to be done,
But to take up the Scepter he laid down.

Daniel Defoe

William served England well, but by the winter of 1701 he was worn out and did not expect to see another summer. In February 1702 his horse, Sorrel, stumbled, it is said, on a molehill, and threw the King off, breaking his collar-bone. Within three weeks he was dead. He had never been a popular figure: people did not like his asthmatic cough, his hooked nose, his solitariness, or the fact that he was foreign. An elegy on his horse appeared promptly, but Defoe tried to set the record straight.

Queen Anne, 1702–14

from An Ode Humbly Inscrib'd to the Queen

But, Greatest *Anna*! while Thy Arms pursue
Paths of Renown, and climb Ascents of Fame
Which nor *Augustus* nor *Eliza* knew;
What *Poet* shall be found to sing Thy Name?
What Numbers shall Record? What Tongue shall say
Thy Wars on Land, Thy Triumphs on the Main?
Oh Fairest Model of Imperial Sway!
What Equal Pen shall write Thy wond'rous Reign?
Who shall Attempts and Victories rehearse
By Story yet untold, unparallell'd by Verse?

Matthew Prior

Anne ruled for twelve years and, for eleven of those, British armies were busy fighting Louis XIV and winning great victories. The politics of Anne's reign were Byzantine, but they saw the consolidation of identifiable groupings of Whigs and Tories. It was a glittering period in terms of military and literary achievement, but the Queen herself remains a shadowy figure. As much as most people are able to say about her is that 'Queen Anne is dead'. In 1712 her statue was erected outside St Paul's and there it stands to this day. As an anonymous squib-writer put it:

Brandy Nan, Brandy Nan,
You're left in the lurch
With your face to the gin shop
And your back to the Church.

1704

THE BATTLE OF BLENHEIM

from **The Campaign**

But O, my muse, what numbers wilt thou find
To sing the furious troops in battle joined?
Methinks I hear the drum's tumultuous sound
The victor's shouts and dying groans confound,
The dreadful burst of cannon rend the skies,
And all the thunder of the battle rise.
'Twas then great Marlborough's mighty soul was proved,
That, in the shock of changing hosts unmoved,
Amidst confusion, horror and despair,
Examined all the dreadful scenes of war;
In peaceful thought the field of death surveyed,
To fainting squadrons sent the timely aid,
Inspired repulsed battalions to engage,
And taught the doubtful battle where to rage.
So when an angel by divine command
With rising tempests shakes a guilty land,
Such as of late o'er pale Britannia past,
Calm and serene he drives the furious blast;
And, pleased th' Almighty's orders to perform,
Rides in the whirlwind, and directs the storm.

Joseph Addison

The Duke of Marlborough led a huge army of English and European troops on the long march from Cologne to Austria, where one of Louis XIV's armies was threatening to capture the Habsburg capital, Vienna. A battle was fought over a three-mile front and through the village of Blenheim, between armies of much the same size – about 60,000 men each. It was indeed a bloody contest, for about half of the French force was killed. After seventeen hours in the saddle, Marlborough was able to scribble a note on the back of a tavern bill: 'Let the Queen know, her Army has had a Glorious Victory.' The power of Louis XIV, the Sun

King, had suffered a serious set-back for the first time in forty years. In 1705 the Queen, with the consent of Parliament, granted her Captain-General the royal manor of Woodstock – 16,000 acres on which Marlborough asked Sir John Vanbrugh, the playwright and architect, to build him a palace.

On Sir John Vanbrugh

Under this stone, reader, survey
Dead Sir John Vanbrugh's house of clay.
Lie heavy on him, earth! for he
Laid many heavy loads on thee.

Abel Evans

from After Blenheim

'Twas a summer evening,
  Old Kaspar's work was done,
And he before his cottage door
  Was sitting in the sun,
And by him sported on the green
His little grandchild, Wilhelmine.

She saw her brother Peterkin
  Roll something large and round,
Which he beside the rivulet
  In playing there had found;
He came to ask what he had found
That was so large, and smooth, and round.

Old Kaspar took it from the boy
  Who stood expectant by;
And then the old man shook his hand.
  And with a natural sigh –
''Tis some poor fellow's skull,' said he,
'Who fell in that great victory.'

'I find them in the garden,
For there's many here about;
And often when I go to plough
  The ploughshare turns them out.
For many thousand men,' said he,
'Were slain in that great victory.'

'Now tell us what 'twas all about,'
  Young Peterkin, he cries;
And little Wilhelmine looks up
  With wonder-waiting eyes;
'Now tell us all about the war,
And what they fought each other for.'

'It was the English,' Kaspar cried,
  'Who put the French to rout;
But what they fought each other for
  I could not well make out;
But everybody said,' quoth he,
'That 'twas a famous victory.

*

'And everybody praised the Duke
  Who this great fight did win.'
'But what good came of it at last?'
  Quoth little Peterkin.
'Why, that I cannot tell,' said he,
'But 'twas a famous victory.'

Robert Southey

1707

THE UNION

Just such a happy Change, our Nation finds:
If we Unite, our once Contented Minds,
With our rich Neighbour: then, doth dawn the day,
Which drives all Feuds and enmities away.
Let base Revenge and Damn'd Envy be gone,
And all our Int'rests be conjoyn'd in one.
No *Mastiff Devil* can our good withstand,
If as true Friends, we do join hand to hand,
That so no more of jealousies be known;
And in our Isle, no more Dissention sown,
And each now, more than Self, his Country mind,
So henceforth, we that Blessedness shall find,
Which, n'ere before, we luckily cou'd reach,
No *Wonder.* Since so damnable a breach,
Did two brave *Neighbours* fatally divide;
What cou'd but war and Poverty betide?
Yet there's no State, in the vast *Universe,*
Might more enjoy of bless or happiness,
Than we, the *Natives* of this admir'd Isle:
If we would banish prejudice and guile,
And let no more, our foolish ears be stunn'd,
With lies, mistakes, and fears, that have no ground.
'Tis true, oft *England* hath us roughly us'd,
And has our ruine and destruction chus'd;
Stop, *Envy*, stop, *Scotland* is guilty too;
How oft did she her Warlike hands imbrue
In *English* Blood? We can't Excuse pretend.
But let's no more 'bout former Strifes contend:
For if we Search, our Histories can tell,
Both have resisted one another *Well.*

Daniel Defoe

Various rulers had tried to unite England and Scotland: Edward I by conquest, James I by parliamentary agreement, Cromwell by force, William III by hope. It was left to Anne to see it achieved. She offered the Scots a guarantee of the Protestant Succession, and the Whig Lords secured guarantees against the Jacobites. Defoe himself was sent to Scotland as a spy by the Tory leader, Robert Harley, his mission being to penetrate Jacobite groups and send reports on their activities back to London. This he did with no thanks or subsequent recognition from Harley.

On the Union

The Queen has lately lost a Part
Of her entirely-*English* Heart,
For want of which by way of Botch,
She piec'd it up again with *Scotch*.
Blest Revolution, which creates
Divided Hearts, united States.
See how the double Nation lies;
Like a rich Coat with Skirts of Frize:
As if a Man in making Posies
Should bundle Thistles up with Roses.
Whoever yet a Union saw
Of Kingdoms, without Faith or Law.
Henceforward let no Statesman dare,
A Kingdom to a Ship compare;
Lest he should call our Commonweal,
A Vessel with a double Keel:
Which just like ours, new rigg'd and man'd,
And got about a League from Land,
By Change of Wind to Leeward Side
The Pilot knew not how to guide.
So tossing Faction will o'erwhelm
One crazy double-bottom'd Realm.

Jonathan Swift

Swift could not abide the Union, as is clear from this poem, which, however, was not published until after his death in 1745. The double keel to which he refers was invented by Sir William Petty, the founder of the Royal Society. Petty had settled in Ireland, where he designed and built boats with this peculiarity. The last of these was launched in Dublin in 1684. It was hopelessly unseaworthy and never got beyond the bar of Dublin harbour.

THE WHIG JUNTO

An Acrostick on Wharton

Whig's the first Letter of his odious Name;
Hypocrisy's the second of the same;
Anarchy's his Darling; and his Aim
Rebellion, Discord, Mutiny, and Faction;
T*om*, Captain of the Mob in Soul and Action;
O'ergrown in Sin, cornuted, old, in Debt,
N*oll*'s Soul and *Ireton*'s live within him yet.

Anonymous

Thomas Wharton was a leading Whig politician and one of the five members of the party's so-called Junto, or inner circle. He is thought to have written the words of 'Lilli Burlero' and had been a drinking companion of William III. A shrewd and successful organizer of elections, he liked to be called 'Honest Tom', but the Tories dubbed him 'King Tom'. He gambled, fornicated, hunted and raced on an extravagant scale, and his morals were such that Macaulay later commented that 'to the end of his long life the wives and daughters of his nearest friends were not safe from his lecherous plots'. On the day after he became Lord Lieutenant of Ireland, the bailiffs moved into his London house to seize his furniture in payment of debts. He thought like a Roundhead, but lived like a Cavalier.

HAMPTON COURT

from **The Rape of the Lock**

Close by those meads, for ever crowned with flowers,
Where Thames with pride surveys his rising towers,
There stands a structure of majestic frame,
Which from the neighb'ring Hampton takes its name.
Here Britain's statesmen oft the fall foredoom
Of foreign tyrants and of nymphs at home;
Here thou, great Anna! whom three realms obey,
Dost sometimes counsel take – and sometimes tea.
Hither the heroes and the nymphs resort,
To taste awhile the pleasures of a court;
In various talk the instructive hours they passed,
Who gave the ball, or paid the visit last;
One speaks the glory of the British Queen,
And one describes a charming Indian screen;
A third interprets motions, looks, and eyes;
At every word a reputation dies.
Snuff, or the fan, supply each pause of chat,
With singing, laughing, ogling, and all that.
Meanwhile, declining from the noon of day,
The sun obliquely shoots his burning ray;
The hungry judges soon the sentence sign,
And wretches hang that jury-men may dine;
The merchant from the Exchange returns in peace,
And the long labours of the toilet cease.

Alexander Pope

Christopher Wren had designed a great and elegant extension to the Tudor palace of Hampton Court. It was this which nearly burnt down on Easter Monday 1986, when a fire was accidentally started by a candle. William III and Queen Anne both spent a lot of time there, and their courtiers indulged in the comparatively new fashion of taking tea. Tea, coffee and cocoa were introduced to England in the middle of the seventeenth century. The East India Company had been given the monopoly of trade to the Far East and by Queen Anne's reign it had pushed the Dutch into second place in that field. Thousands of tons of tea were imported each year, with porcelain as a makeweight, and at its height tea accounted for 5 per cent of British imports. Britain was well on its way to becoming a nation of tea-drinkers. The tea which Queen Anne drank came from China, for Indian tea reached these shores only as late as 1840, and she would have drunk it from a Chinese bowl without handles – these were not added until 1750.

THE HANOVERIAN HEIR

The crown's far too weighty
For shoulders of eighty;
She could not sustain such a trophy;
Her hand, too, already
Has grown so unsteady
She can't hold a sceptre;
So Providence kept her
Away. – Poor old Dowager Sophy.

Thomas D'Urfey

Queen Anne's seven children had all died. The last, a boy, the Duke of Gloucester, was born in 1689. When he died in 1700 Parliament passed the Act of Settlement which named the ageing Sophia Dorothea, Electress and Dowager Duchess of Hanover, as Anne's successor since she was a Protestant. Anne did not care for this distant relative, and D'Urfey got fifty guineas as a reward for singing her the song from which this snatch is taken. As it happened, Sophia died before Anne, and so her son, George, succeeded.

1714

QUEEN ANNE DIES

A Farewell to the Year

Farewell old year, for Thou canst ne're return,
No more than the great Queen for whom we mourn;
Farewell old year, with thee the Stuart race
Its Exit made, which long our Isle did grace;
Farewell old year, the Church hath lost in Thee
The best Defender it will ever see;
Farewell old year, for Thou to us did bring
Strange changes in our State, a stranger King;
Farewell old year, for thou with Broomstick hard
Hast drove poor Tory from St James's Yard;
Farewell old year, old Monarch, and old Tory,
Farewell old England, Thou hast lost thy glory.

Anonymous

THE HOUSE OF HANOVER

King George I, 1714–27

George I – Star of Brunswick

He preferr'd Hanover to England,
He preferr'd two hideous mistresses
To a beautiful and innocent wife.
He hated arts and despised literature;
But he liked train-oil in his salads,
And gave an enlighten'd patronage to bad oysters.
And he had Walpole as a minister;
Consistent in his preference for every kind of corruption.

H. J. Daniel

At the age of fifty-four, George, the Elector of Hanover, came to the throne of a country he had never visited, whose language he never spoke and whose people he never loved. He had divorced his wife, the mother of George II twenty years earlier and he brought with him his long established mistress, Melusine von der Schulenburg, who had borne him three daughters and was later made the Duchess of Kendal. It was also alleged that he had another mistress, his half-sister, Sophie Charlotte, who became the Countess of Darlington. As Kendal was tall and thin, and Darlington was short and fat, they were known as 'The Maypole and the Elephant'.

England came under the sway of three great statesmen: Stanhope and Walpole until 1742, and then the elder Pitt. Walpole presided over a period of peace, prosperity and stability; Pitt had a vision of a great and powerful empire spreading over the world and he set about achieving it. During this time the power of the House of Commons was established firmly, and the royal veto was never used after 1714. It became the task of the Duke of Newcastle to provide through his enormous wealth and patronage a majority for the government of the day, a service he undertook for over forty years. On a journey back to Hanover in 1727, George I suffered a stroke in his coach and died. It was said that his death was induced by a letter which he had just read from his divorced wife, who had died a year earlier, in which she forecast that he would die within a year of her. He did.

The Wee, Wee German Lairdie

Wha the deil hae we gotten for a king,
  But a wee, wee German lairdie?
And, when we gaed to bring him hame,
  He was delving in his yardie;
Sheughing kail and laying leeks,
  But the hose and but the breeks;
And up his beggar duds he cleeks –
  This wee, wee German lairdie.

And he's clapt doun in our guidman's chair,
  The wee, wee German lairdie;
And he's brought fouth o' foreign trash
  And dibbled them in his yardie.
He's pu'd the rose o' English loons,
  And broken the harp o' Irish clowns;
But our thistle taps will jag his thumbs –
  This wee, wee German lairdie.

Come up amang our Highland hills,
  Thou wee, wee German lairdie,
And see how the Stuarts' lang-kail thrive
  They dibbled in our yardie;
And if a stock ye dare to pu',
  Or haud the yoking o' a plough,
We'll break your sceptre ower your mou',
  Thou wee bit German lairdie.

Our hills are steep, our glens are deep,
  Nae fitting for a yardie;
And our Norland thistles winna pu',
  Thou wee bit German lairdie;
And we've the trenching blades o' weir,
  Was prune ye o' your German gear –
We'll pass ye 'neath the claymore's shear,
  Thou feckless German lairdie!

Auld Scotland, thou'rt ower cauld a hole
  For nursin' siccan vermin;
But the very dogs o' England's court
  They bark and howl in German.
Then keep thy dibble in thy ain hand,
  Thy spade but and thy hardie;
For wha the deil now claims your land,
  But a wee, wee German lairdie?

Allan Cunningham

1715

THE FIRST JACOBITE UPRISING

A Jacobite's Epitaph

To my true king I offered free from stain
Courage and faith; vain faith, and courage vain.
For him I threw lands, honours, wealth, away,
And one dear hope, that was more prized then they.
For him I languished in a foreign clime,
Grey-haired with sorrow in my manhood's prime;
Heard on Lavernia Scargill's whispering trees,
And pined by Arno for my lovelier Tees;
Beheld each night my home in fevered sleep,
Each morning started from the dream to weep;
Till God, who saw me tried too sorely, gave
The resting-place I asked, an early grave.
O thou, whom chance leads to this nameless stone,
From that proud country which was once mine own,
By those white cliffs I never more must see,
By that dear language which I spake like thee,
Forget all feuds, and shed one English tear.
O'er English dust. A broken heart lies here.

Thomas Babington, Lord Maucaulay

The Stuart cause was kept alive by the son of James II. Known as the Old Pretender and kept in Paris by the favour of Louis XIV, he became the hope of all malcontents in England. And he failed them all. Nine months after the accession of George I, he encouraged the Earl of Mar to raise a rebellion in the Highlands. It was a botched and bungled affair and, although some rebels reached Preston, they were trounced and fled northwards again. James himself eventually arrived in Perth, just in time to retreat to Dundee, and within four weeks he was back in France, before finally settling in Italy.

1720

THE SOUTH SEA BUBBLE

from The Bubble

Ye wise philosophers, explain
   What magic makes our money rise,
When dropt into the Southern main;
   Or do these jugglers cheat our eyes?

Put in your money fairly told;
   Presto! be gone – 'Tis here again:
Ladies and gentlemen, behold,
   Here's every piece as big as ten.

Thus in a basin drop a shilling,
   Then fill the vessel to the brim,
You shall observe, as you are filling,
   The pond'rous metal seems to swim.

It rises both in bulk and height,
   Behold it mounting to the top;
The liquid medium cheats your sight:
   Behold it swelling like a sop.

In stock three hundred thousand pounds,
 I have in view a Lord's estate;
My manors all contiguous round,
 A coach and six, and served in plate!

Thus the deluded bankrupt raves,
 Puts all upon a desperate bet,
Then plunges in the Southern waves,
 Dipt over head and ears – in debt.

*

The sea is richer than the land,
 I heard it from my Grannam's mouth,
Which now I clearly understand,
 For by the sea she meant the South.

Thus by Directors we are told,
 Pray, Gentlemen, believe your eyes:
Our ocean's covered o'er with gold;
 Look round about how thick it lies.

We, Gentlemen, are your assisters,
 We'll come and hold you by the chin;
Alas! all is not gold that glisters:
 Ten thousand sunk by leaping in.

*

May he, whom Nature's laws obey,
 Who lifts the poor, and sinks the proud,
Quiet the raging of the sea,
 And still the madness of the crowd!

But never shall our isle have rest,
 Till those devouring swine run down,
(The devils leaving the possest)
 And headlong in the waters drown.

The nation then too late will find,
   Computing all their cost and trouble,
Directors' promises but wind,
   South Sea at best a mighty bubble.

Jonathan Swift

In 1719 the South Sea Company, which in 1711 had been assigned the monopoly of England's trade with Spanish America, proposed a scheme to convert part of the National Debt into its shares. The Commons approved it and in 1720 stocks were issued to, among others, the King's mistresses, the Chancellor of the Exchequer, and various ministers. The directors of the Company had to keep the price of the stock high and a wild boom started, with the price rising from £130 to £1,050 between February and June. Bubble companies sprang up and, when Parliament banned them, the market slumped, so that by November the price was down to £135. The Chancellor of the Exchequer was sent to the Tower, but the crash made Sir Robert Walpole First Lord of the Treasury, and our first Prime Minister.

1722

THE DEATH OF MARLBOROUGH

A Satirical Elegy on the Death of a Late Famous General

His Grace! impossible! what dead!
Of old age too, and in his bed!
And could that Mighty Warrior fall?
And so inglorious after all!

Well, since he's gone, no matter how,
The last loud trump must wake him now:
And, trust me, as the noise grows stronger,
He'd wish to sleep a little longer.
And could he be indeed so old
As by the news-papers we're told:
Threescore, I think, is pretty high;
'Twas time in conscience he should die.
This world he cumber'd long enough;
He burnt his candle to the snuff;
And that's the reason, some folks think,
He left behind *so great a s—k*.
Behold his funeral appears,
Nor widow's sighs, nor orphan's tears,
Wont at such times each heart to pierce,
Attend the progress of his herse.
But what of that, his friends may say,
He had those honours in his day.
True to his profit and his pride,
He made them weep before he dy'd.

Come hither, all ye empty things,
Ye bubbles rais'd by breath of Kings;
Who float upon the tide of state,
Come hither, and behold your fate.
Let pride be taught by this rebuke,
How very mean a thing's a Duke;
From all his ill-got honours flung,
Turn'd to that dirt from whence he sprung.

Jonathan Swift

After Blenheim, Marlborough went on to win three more celebrated victories – at Ramallies (1706), Oudenarde (1708) and Malplaquet (1709). Swift loathed Marlborough, who had started penniless and died the richest man in England. In the winter of 1711 Swift joined with the Tories Harley and Bolingbroke in a move to overthrow the great Duke, and they succeeded. This was the only time in his life that Swift was really at the centre of political affairs. He expected a good reward, especially for the brilliant pamphlet he had written under the title 'The Conduct of the Allies', but no bishopric came his way, only the deanery of St Patrick's in Dublin. How lucky for the world, as it was there, in virtual exile, that he wrote *Gulliver's Travels*. When Marlborough died in 1721, Swift could not resist another burst of spleen against his old enemy.

1727

THE DEATH OF SIR ISAAC NEWTON

from **To the Memory of Sir Isaac Newton**

Even *Light itself*, which every thing displays,
Shone undiscover'd, till his brighter mind
Untwisted all the shining robe of day;
And, from the whitening undistinguish'd blaze,
Collecting every ray into his kind,
To the charm'd eye educ'd the gorgeous train
Of *Parent-Colours*. First the flaming *Red*
Sprung vivid forth; the tawny *Orange* next;
And next delicious *Yellow*; by whose side
Fell the kind beams of all-refreshing *Green*.
Then the pure *Blue*, that swells autumnal skies,
Ethereal play'd; and then, of sadder hue,
Emerg'd the deepen'd *Indico*, as when
The heavy-skirted evening droops with frost.
While the last gleamings of refracted light
Dy'd in the fainting *Violet* away.
These, when the clouds distil the rosy shower,
Shine out distinct adown the watry bow;
While o'er our heads the dewy vision bends
Delightful, melting on the fields beneath.
Myriads of mingling dies from these result,
And myriads still remain – Infinite source
Of beauty, ever-flushing, ever-new!
   Did ever poet image ought so fair,
Dreaming in whispering groves, by the hoarse brook!
Or prophet, to whose rapture heaven descends!
Even now the setting sun and shifting clouds,
Seen, *Greenwich*, from thy lovely heights, declare
How just, how beauteous the *refractive Law*.

James Thomson

Newton was a genius in mathematics, physics, astronomy and philosophy. His great works were *Philosophiae naturalis principia mathematica* (1687) and *Opticks* (1704). He formulated the Law of Gravity and the three Laws of Motion, established that white light consists of a mixture of all colours, and developed calculus. Voltaire, who was at Newton's funeral, commended the English for honouring a scientist of heretical religious views with burial in Westminster Abbey. Einstein's view of Newton was that he 'determined the course of Western thought, research and practice to an extent that nobody before or since can touch'.

Epitaph Intended for Sir Isaac Newton, in Westminster Abbey

Nature, and Nature's laws lay hid in night:
God said, *Let Newton be!* and all was light.

Alexander Pope

It did not last: the Devil howling 'Ho!
Let Einstein be!' restored the status quo.

J. C. Squire

King George II, 1727–60

In most things I did as my father had done,
I was false to my wife and I hated my son:
My spending was small, and my avarice much,
My kingdom was English, my heart was High-Dutch:
At Dettingen fight I was not known to blench,
I butcher'd the Scotch, and I bearded the French:
I neither had morals, nor manners, nor wit;
I wasn't much miss'd when I died in a fit.
Here set up my statue, and make it complete,
With Pitt on his knees at my dirty old feet.

H. J. Daniels

George II had been bullied by his father, and in turn he tried to bully his son. He was lucky to have a loving and clever wife, Caroline. Walpole used the Queen to persuade the King to support his policies, or, as he put it in his earthy Norfolk way, he 'took the right sow by the ear'. George II was the last monarch to lead a British army to victory, which he did at Dettingen in Bavaria. He liked all things military and was able to recall in detail the uniforms of European regiments. His great love, however, was for music, and he made it possible for Handel to live in England. In his will he asked that his coffin be laid alongside that of his wife, with the two near sides open so that their dusts might mingle.

SIR ROBERT WALPOLE

Two Character Studies

1

With favour and fortune fastidiously blest,
He's loud in his laugh and he's coarse in his jest;
Of favour and fortune unmerited vain,
A sharper in trifles, a dupe in the main.
Achieving of nothing, still promising wonders,
By dint of experience improving in blunders;
Oppressing true merit, exalting the base,
And selling his country to purchase his peace.
A jobber of stocks by retailing false news,
A prater at court in the style of the stews,
Of virtue and worth by profession a giber,
Of juries and senates the bully and briber:
Though I name not the wretch you know who I mean –
'Tis the cur dog of Britain and spaniel of Spain.

2

And first: to make my observation right,
I place a statesman full before my sight,
A bloated minister in all his geer,
With shameless visage, and perfidious leer;
Two rows of teeth arm each devouring jaw;
And, ostrich-like, his all-digesting maw,
My fancy drags this monster to my view
To shew the world his chief reverse in you.
Of loud unmeaning sounds a rapid flood
Rolls from his mouth in plenteous streams of mud;
With these the court and senate-house he plies,
Made up of noise, and impudence, and lies.

Jonathan Swift

Walpole was Prime Minister from 1721 to 1742, which is a record yet to be surpassed. His policy was, proverbially, to let sleeping dogs lie – to avoid war, encourage trade and reduce taxation. He exercised enormous patronage, finding so many jobs for his sons, brothers, cousins and friends that his administration came to be known as the 'Robinocracy'. He was also the last PM to make a huge personal fortune while in office: government surpluses passed though his own account and enabled him to speculate on a grand scale. He amassed some superb paintings, which one of his descendants sold to Catherine the Great of Russia and which now form the heart of the Hermitage Museum in Leningrad. For all this, he gave England peace for eighteen years; he reinforced the power of the House of Commons; he consolidated the achievements of the Whig revolution; and he eliminated from politics the savagery and vindictiveness which in previous generations could lead those who had fallen on misfortune to the gallows or into exile. Swift saw Walpole as the barrier to his preferment in England, and loathed him for it.

1739

THE LAST DAYS OF DICK TURPIN

My Poor Black Bess

When fortune, blind goddess, she fled my abode,
Old friends proved ungrateful, I took to the road;
To plunder the wealthy to aid my distress,
I bought thee to aid me, my poor Black Bess.

When dark sable night its mantle had thrown
O'er the bright face of nature, how oft we have gone
To famed Hounslow Heath, though an unwelcome guest
To the minions of fortune, my poor Black Bess.

How silent thou stood when a carriage I've stopped,
And their gold and their jewels its inmates I've dropped;
No poor man I plundered or e'er did oppress
The widow or orphan, my poor Black Bess.

When Argus-eyed justice did me hotly pursue,
From London to York like lightning we flew;
No toll-bar could stop thee, thou the river didst breast,
And in twelve hours reached it, my poor Black Bess.

Anonymous

Tradition has transformed Dick Turpin into romantic figure, but in real life he was no more than a poacher, thief, highwayman and murderer. He did not even make the famous twelve-hour ride to York which has been attributed to him: that was the feat of another highwayman in 1676. For a while, Turpin lived in York under the name of Palmer, but he was discovered after a quarrel with an innkeeper over a gamecock. He was executed in 1739, having paid five people to mourn for him.

1740

THE GROWTH OF THE BRITISH EMPIRE

from The Masque of Alfred

When Britain first at Heaven's command
  Arose from out the azure main,
This was the charter of the land,
  And guardian angels sang this strain,.
    'Rule, Britannia, rule the waves,
    Britons never will be slaves.

'The nations not so blest as thee
  Must in their turn to tyrants fall,
While thou shalt flourish great and free,
  The dread and envy of them all.

'Still more majestic shalt thou rise,
  More dreadful from each foreign stroke;
As the loud blast that tears the skies
  Serves but to root thy native oak.

'Thee haughty tyrants ne'er shall tame;
  All their attempts to bend thee down
Will but arouse thy generous flame,
  But work their woe and thy renown.

'To thee belongs the rural reign,
  Thy cities shall with commerce shine;
All thine shall be the subject main,
  And every shore it circles thine.

'The muses, still with freedom found,
  Shall to thy happy coast repair;
Blest Isle! with matchless beauty crowned,
  And manly hearts to guard the fair!
    'Rule, Britannia, rule the waves,
    Britons never will be slaves.'

James Thomson

George II's reign saw the steady expansion and consolidation of the British Empire, although only one new colony was founded, namely Georgia, which was initially settled by debtors from the Fleet Prison. In the 1750s British armies won sweeping victories in Europe, as well as in India under Clive and in Canada under Wolfe.

1745

THE SECOND JACOBITE UPRISING

Charlie is my Darling

Charlie is my darling, my darling, my darling,
Charlie is my darling, the young Chevalier.

'Twas on a Monday morning,
Right early in the year,
When Charlie came to our toun,
The young Chevalier.

As he came marching up the street,
The pipes played loud and clear,
And a' the folk came running out
To meet the Chevalier.

We' Hieland bonnets on their heads,
And claymores bright and clear,
They came to fight for Scotland's right,
And the young Chevalier.

They've left their bonnie Hieland hills,
Their wives and bairnies dear,
To draw the sword for Scotland's lord,
The young Chevalier.

Oh, there were mony beating hearts,
And mony a hope and fear:
And mony were the pray'rs put up
For the young Chevalier.

Lady Nairne

In July 1745 Prince Charles Edward Stuart, the Young Pretender, landed in Scotland with the intention of recapturing the three kingdoms lost by his grandfather, James II. He had no troops with him, no money, and only seven friends. The Highland clans, led by the Macdonalds, rallied to him, and by September he had entered Edinburgh and won the skirmish of Prestonpans. Then he made the mistake of marching into England, passing through Preston and Manchester, and finally reaching Derby where his men refused to go further. England failed to rally to him and he retreated north, pursued by the Duke of Cumberland.

In 1746 the opposing armies met at Culloden, where Cumberland's 9,000 men ran down and slaughtered Charles's 5,000. For five months the Prince wandered through the Highlands, sheltered by poor crofters and rescued at one point by the now famous Flora Macdonald, but at last he returned to the Continent. The whole rash escapade had been poorly planned, poorly financed and poorly conducted. It was sustained by a romantic myth, but it led to the deaths of many thousands of Scots at the hands of 'Butcher' Cumberland. A flower in England is called Sweet William but the Scots named a weed Stinking Billy in memory of his savage reprisals.

1746

THE BATTLE OF CULLODEN

Lament for Culloden

The lovely lass o' Inverness,
Nae joy nor pleasure can she see;
For e'en and morn she cries, Alas!
And aye the saut tear blins her ee:
Drumossie moor – Drumossie day –
A waefu' day it was to me!
For there I lost my father dear,
My father dear, and brethren three.

Their winding-sheet the bluidy clay,
Their graves are growing green to see:
And by them lies the dearest lad
That ever blest a woman's ee!
Now wae to thee, thou cruel lord,
A bluidy man I trow thou be,
For mony a heart thou hast made sair
That ne'er did wrang to thine or thee.

Robert Burns

Bonnie Charlie's Now Awa

Bonnie Charlie's now awa,
Safely owre the friendly main;
Mony a heart will break in twa,
Should he ne'er come back again.
  Will ye no come back again?
  Will ye no come back again?
  Better lo'ed ye canna be,
  Will ye no come back again?

Lady Nairne

1759

THE BRITISH CONQUEST OF CANADA

Bold General Wolfe to his men did say,
Come, come, my lads and follow me,
To yonder mountains that are so high
All for the honour, all for the honour,
Of your king and country.

The French they are on the mountains high,
While we poor lads in the vallies laid,
I see them falling like moths in the sun,
Thro' smoke and fire, thro' smoke and fire
All from our British guns.

The very first volley they gave to us,
Wounded our General in his left breast,
Yonder he sits for he cannot stand,
Fight on so boldly, fight on so boldly,
For whilst I've life I'll have command.

Here is my treasure lies all in gold,
Take it and part it, for my blood runs cold,
Take it and part it, General Wolfe did say,
You lads of honour, you lads of honour,
Who made such gallant play.

Anonymous

Wolfe landed in Canada in 1759 to overthrow the French. He surprised them by scaling the Heights of Abraham and defeated their general, Montcalme. Quebec surrendered and Canada, with its rich trade in fish and fur, became British. Wolfe died in the battle, and his murmured last words were, 'Now God be praised, I will die in peace.' Pitt, Prime Minister of the time, trusted daring and unconventional soldiers like Wolfe. George II was once told that Wolfe was a mad dog, to which he replied that he should bite some of his other generals.

from **Stanzas on the Taking of Quebec**

Alive, the foe thy dreadful vigour fled,
  And saw thee fall with joy-pronouncing eyes;
Yet they shall know thou conquerest, though dead!
  Since from thy tomb a thousand heroes rise.

Oliver Goldsmith

1759

QUIBERON BAY

Hawke

In seventeen hundred and fifty nine,
When Hawke came swooping from the West,
The French King's Admiral with twenty of the line,
Was sailing forth, to sack us, out of Brest.
The ports of France were crowded, the quays of France a-hum
With thirty thousand soldiers marching to the drum,
For bragging time was over and fighting time was come
When Hawke came swooping from the West.

'Twas long past noon of a wild November day
When Hawke came swooping from the West;
He heard the breakers thundering in Quiberon Bay
But he flew the flag for battle, line abreast.
Down upon the quicksands roaring out of sight
Fiercely beat the storm-wind, darkly fell the night,
But they took the foe for pilot and the cannon's glare for light
When Hawke came swooping from the West.

The Frenchmen turned like a covey down the wind
When Hawke came swooping from the West;
One he sank with all hands, one he caught and pinned,
And the shallows and the storm took the rest.
The guns that should have conquered us they rusted on the shore,
The men that would have mastered us they drummed and marched no more,
For England was England, and a mighty brood she bore
When Hawke came swooping from the West.

Henry Newbolt

In 1759 France planned what was to be her last attempt of the Seven Years War to invade Britain. Admiral Sir Edward Hawke blockaded one of the French fleets at Brest for over six months, but then because of bad weather he relaxed his hold and the French admiral Conflans steered his ships out of port on 14 November. Hawke gave chase, forcing the French to head south, and six days later he caught up with them at Belle-Ile, where he pushed Conflans into Quiberon Bay. By the dawn of 21 November the French fleet had scattered, its flagship having run aground, three other vessels being sunk and one captured. Hawke wrote: 'Had we but two hours' more daylight, the whole had been totally destroyed or taken.' He had broken common navy practice by keeping a blockade up well into winter; he had turned French tactics on their head by joining battle in a storm along the most dangerous coast in France; and he had crushed all hopes France had of invading Britain.

SEA POWER

Heart of Oak

Come cheer up my lads, 'tis to glory we steer,
To add something new to this wonderful year;
To honour we call you, not press you like slaves,
For who are so free as the sons of the waves?

Heart of Oak are our ships, Heart of Oak are our men,
We always are ready,
Steady, boys, steady,
We'll fight and we'll conquer again and again.

We ne'er meet our foes but we wish them to stay,
They ne'er meet us but they wish us away;
If they run, then we follow, and drive them ashore,
For if they won't fight us, we cannot do more.
Heart of Oak, &c.

*

They talk to invade us, these terrible foes,
They frighten our women, our children, and beaux;
But, if their flat bottoms in darkness come o'er,
Sure Britons they'll find to receive them on shore.
Heart of Oak, &c.

We'll make them to run, and we'll make them to sweat,
In spite of the Devil and Russel's Gazette;
Then cheer up my lads, with one heart let us sing,
Our soldiers, our sailors, our statesmen, our king.
Heart of Oak, &c.

David Garrick

The great actor-manager David Garrick wrote this song for his pantomime, *Harlequin's Invasion*, to celebrate British victories over the French at Lagos, Quiberon Bay and Quebec.

WRECKING

Song of the Cornish Wreckers

Not that they shall, but if they must –
Be just, Lord, wreck them off St Just.

Scythes beneath the water, Brisons,
Reap us a good crop in all seasons.

We would be meek, but meat we lack.
Pile wrecks on Castle Kenidjack.

Our children's mouths gape like a zawn.
Fog, hide the sharp fangs of Pendeen.

You put Your own Son first, Jehovah,
And so do we. Send bread to Morvah.

Crowbar of oceans, stove the wood
Treasure-troves on Gurnard's Head.

Mermaids, Mary-Anne, Morwenna,
Sing them to the crags of Zennor.

Food, Lord, food! Our starving flock
Looks for manna but finds a rock.

Hard land you give us. Mist and stones.
Not enough trees to bury our bones.

To save the drowning we'll risk our lives.
But hurl their ships upon St Ives.

Guide us, when through death we sail,
Past the burning cliffs of Hell.

Soul nor sailor mean we harm.
But our blue sky is their black storm.

D. M. Thomas

SMUGGLING

A Smuggler's Song

If you wake at midnight, and hear a horse's feet,
Don't go drawing back the blind, or looking in the street
Them that ask no questions isn't told a lie.
Watch the wall, my darling, while the Gentlemen go by!
Five and twenty ponies,
Trotting through the dark –
Brandy for the Parson,
'Baccy for the Clerk;
Laces for a lady, letters for a spy,
And watch the wall, my darling, while the Gentlemen go by!

Running round the woodlump if you chance to find
Little barrels, roped and tarred, all full of brandy-wine,
Don't you shout to come and look, nor use 'em for your play.
Put the brushwood back again – and they'll be gone next day!

If you see the stable-door setting open wide;
If you see a tired horse lying down inside;
If your mother mends a coat cut about and tore;
If the lining's wet and warm – don't you ask no more!

If you meet King George's men, dressed in blue and red,
You be careful what you say, and mindful what is said.
If they call you 'pretty maid,' and chuck you 'neath the chin,
Don't you tell where no one is, nor yet where no one's been!

Knocks and footsteps round the house – whistles after dark –
You've no call for running out till the house-dogs bark.
Trusty's here, and *Pincher's* here, and see how dumb they lie –
They don't fret to follow when the Gentlemen go by!

If you do as you've been told, 'likely there's a chance,
You'll be given a dainty doll, all the way from France,
With a cap of Valenciennes, and a velvet hood –
A present from the Gentlemen, along o' being good!
Five and twenty ponies,
Trotting through the dark –
Brandy for the Parson,
'Baccy for the Clerk.
Them that asks no questions isn't told a lie –
Watch the wall, my darling, while the Gentlemen go by!

Rudyard Kipling

In the eighteenth century British sailors ruled the seas, dominating trade, extending empire and beating off all comers in the competition for naval supremacy. These two poems show the darker side of things – the business of wrecking and smuggling. The places mentioned in Thomas's poem are on the north-west coast of Cornwall, near to Land's End. There was a medieval law which stated that the goods salvaged from a wreck belonged to those who got possession of them. Some ships were lured on to the rocks by false beacons, and when in trouble were followed along the cliff-tops by entire village communities, ready to pounce on what floated ashore. Sailors escaping a wreck knew that they would also have to flee the locals, who would be quite prepared to push them under as they grabbed what was going.

King George III, 1760–1820

George III's long reign was one of the most momentous in English history. Britannia really did rule the waves, though not well enough to hold the American colonies. Britain was the only major European country which was not overrun by Napoleon. The Napoleonic Wars called forth Britain's most famous sailor, Nelson, who died at the moment of victory at Trafalgar in 1805, bequeathing his mistress, Lady Hamilton, to the nation; and its most famous soldier, Wellington, who survived his victory at Waterloo in 1815 to become Prime Minister and godfather to the future King Edward VII.

George III himself was a conscientious but inadequate monarch. He had fifteen children, more than any other British king, but was sadly let down by them, for they proved a gaggle of spendthrifts, drunkards and adulterers. He suffered from bouts of madness and was permanently insane for the last eleven years of his reign. He had what has now been diagnosed as Porphyria, which can be treated, but he was forced to endure seclusion and strait-jackets, although his doctors did also advise him to bathe in the sea for therapeutic purposes, which incidentally started the fashion of the seaside holiday.

George the Third
Ought never to have occurred.
One can only wonder
At so grotesque a blunder.

E. C. Bentley

A PORTRAIT OF THE KING

from **Mr Whitbread's Brewhouse**

Now Majesty into a pump so deep
Did with an opera-glass so curious peep,
Examining with care each won'drous matter
That brought up water!

Thus have I seen a magpie in the street,
A chatt'ring bird we often meet,
A bird for curiosity well known,
            With head awry,
            And cunning eye,
Peep knowingly into a marrow-bone.

And now his curious Majesty did stoop
To count the nails on ev'ry hoop;
And lo! no single one came in his way,
That, full of deep research, he did not say,
'What's this? hae, hae? what's that? what's this? what's that?'
So quick the words too, when he deign'd to speak,
As if each syllable would break its neck.

*

To Whitbread now deign's Majesty to say,
'Whitbread, are all your horses fond of hay?'
'Yes, please your Majesty,' in humble notes,
The Brewer answer'd – 'also, Sir, of oats:
Another thing my horses too maintains,
And that, an't please your Majesty, are grains.'

'Grains, grains,' said Majesty, 'to fill their crops?
Grains, grains? – that comes from hops – yes, hops, hops,
  hops?'

Here was the King, like hounds sometimes, at fault –
'Sire,' cry'd the humble Brewer, 'give me leave
Your sacred Majesty to undeceive:
Grains, Sire, are never made from hops, but malt.'

'True,' said the cautious Monarch, with a smile;
From malt, malt, malt – I meant malt all the while.'
'Yes,' with the sweetest now, rejoin'd the Brewer,
'An't please your Majesty, you did, I'm sure.'
'Yes,' answer'd Majesty, with quick reply,
'I did, I did, I did, I, I, I, I.'

Peter Pindar

Writing under the pseudonym of Peter Pindar, John Wolcot, a Devonshire clergyman, launched frequent satirical attacks on the slow-wittedness of the King, here depicted on a tour of Whitbread's Brewery in Islington.

1770

AGRICULTURAL DECLINE

from **The Deserted Village**

Sweet smiling village, loveliest of the lawn,
Thy sports are fled, and all thy charms withdrawn;
Amidst thy bowers the tyrant's hand is seen,
And desolation saddens all thy green:
One only master grasps the whole domain,
And half a tillage stints thy smiling plain:
No more thy glassy brook reflects the day,
But chok'd with sedges, works its weedy way.
Along thy glades, a solitary guest,
The hollow-sounding bittern guards its nest;
Amidst thy desert walks the lapwing flies,
And tires their echoes with unvaried cries.
Sunk are thy bowers, in shapeless ruin all,
And the long grass o'ertops the mouldering wall;
And, trembling, shrinking from the spoiler's hand,
Far, far away, thy children leave the land.

Ill fares the land, to hastening ills a prey,
Where wealth accumulates, and men decay:
Princes and lords may flourish, or may fade;
A breath can make them, as a breath has made;
But a bold peasantry, their country's pride,
When once destroy'd, can never be supplied.

A time there was, ere England's griefs began,
When every rood of ground maintain'd its man;
For him light labour spread her wholesome store,
Just gave what life requir'd, but gave no more:
His best companions, innocence and health;
And his best riches, ignorance of wealth.

But times are alter'd; trade's unfeeling train
Usurp the land and dispossess the swain;
Along the lawn, where scatter'd hamlets rose,
Unwieldy wealth, and cumbrous pomp repose;
And every want to opulence allied,
And every pang that folly pays to pride.

Oliver Goldsmith

The Lincolnshire Poacher

When I was bound apprentice in famous Lincolnshire,
Full well I served my Master for more than seven year,
Till I took up with poaching, as you shall quickly hear:
Oh! 'tis my delight on a shiny night in the season of the year!

As me and my comrades were setting of a snare,
'Twas then we seed the gamekeeper – for him we did not care,
For we can wrestle and fight, my boys, and jump o'er
anywhere,
Oh! 'tis my delight, *etc.*

As me and my comrades were setting four or five,
And taking on him up again, we caught the hare alive;
We caught the hare alive, my boys, and through the woods did
steer:
Oh! 'tis my delight, *etc.*

I threw him on my shoulder, and then we trudged home,
We took him to a neighbour's house and sold him for a crown;
We sold him for a crown, my boys, but I did not tell you
where,
Oh! 'tis my delight, *etc.*

Bad luck to every magistrate that lives in Lincolnshire,
Success to every poacher that wants to sell a hare;
Bad luck to every gamekeeper that will not sell his deer:
Oh! 'tis my delight, *etc.*

Anonymous

During George III's reign, poaching was such a menace that more than fifty statutes were passed in the effort to suppress it. Yet as more and more common land was enclosed, the rural poor had increasing need to practise it. Heavy sentences were passed, and even the death penalty was applied, but with the discovery of Australia a new possibility arose, and English magistrates started to populate the colony with poachers. This folk song became a favourite of George IV, probably because he enjoyed neither shooting nor hunting.

1775

THE AMERICAN WAR OF INDEPENDENCE

Concord Hymn

By the rude bridge that arched the flood,
Their flag to April's breeze unfurled,
Here once the embattled farmers stood,
And fired the shot heard round the world.

The foe long since in silence slept;
Alike the conqueror silent sleeps;
And Time the ruined bridge has swept
Down the dark stream which seaward creeps.

On this green bank, by this soft stream,
  We set to-day a votive stone;
That memory may their deed redeem,
  When, like our sires, our sons are gone.

Spirit, that made those heroes dare
  To die, or leave their children free,
Bid Time and Nature gently spare
  The shaft we raise to them and thee.

Ralph Waldo Emerson

In the 1770s Lord North's government, in an attempt to reassert the sovereignty of the English crown over the American colonies, which had shown an increasingly independent spirit, took various unpopular measures, including the levying of duty on tea. In London, Lord Chatham pleaded for moderation and the withdrawal of troops, and Burke in a famous speech declared: 'Magnanimity in politics is not seldom the truest wisdom, and a great Empire and little minds go ill together.' But by 1775 open conflict was inevitable. Massachusetts had armed its militia against the troops of the English general, Gage, who set out to seize its armoury at Concord. On the way there a skirmish took place at Lexington, and the first shots of the war were fired. Sixty Americans and 273 British soldiers were killed. In July George Washington was recognized as Commander-in-Chief of the rebels and a year later the Declaration of Independence was signed. In 1777 a British army under 'Gentleman Johnny' Burgoyne surrendered at Saratoga Springs, and in 1781 another, under Lord Cornwallis, surrendered at Yorktown.

The British government's policy of imposing taxes without consent had been foolish, and its agents, from North to Gage, Burgoyne and Cornwallis, were inadequate to the task of seeing it through. Cornwallis went on to become Governor-General of India, where his heavy hand all but provoked rebellion in Bengal.

1781

A Prophecy, *from* America

The Guardian Prince of Albion burns in his nightly tent,
Sullen fires across the Atlantic glow to America's shore,
Piercing the souls of warlike men who rise in silent night.
Washington, Franklin, Paine & Warren, Gates, Hancock & Green
Meet on the coast glowing with blood from Albion's fiery Prince.

Washington spoke: 'Friends of America, look over the Atlantic sea!
A bended bow is lifted in heaven, & a heavy iron chain
Descends link by link from Albion's cliffs across the sea to bind
Brothers & sons of America, till our faces pale and yellow,
Heads deprest, voices weak, eyes downcast, hands work-bruis'd,
Feet bleeding on the sultry sands, and the furrows of the whip
Descend to generations that in future times forget.'

The strong voice ceas'd, for a terrible blast swept over the heaving sea:
The eastern cloud rent: on his cliffs stood Albion's wrathful Prince,
A dragon form, clashing his scales; at midnight he arose,
And flam'd red meteors round the land of Albion beneath:
His voice, his locks, his awful shoulders and his glowing eyes
Appear to the Americans upon the cloudy night.

Solemn heave the Atlantic waves between the gloomy nations,
Swelling, belching from its deeps red clouds & raging fires.
Albion is sick! America faints! enrag'd the Zenith grew.
As human blood shooting its veins all round the orbèd heaven,
Red rose the clouds from the Atlantic in vast wheels of blood,
And in the red clouds rose a Wonder o'er the Atlantic sea,
Intense, naked, a Human fire, fierce glowing as the wedge
Of iron heated in the furnace; his terrible limbs were fire,
With myriads of cloudy terrors, banners dark & towers
Surrounded; heat but not light went thro' the murky
  atmosphere.

The King of England, looking westward, trembles at the vision.

William Blake

In this prophetic statement, written some years after the War of Independence, Blake interprets the spirit of rebellion as a far more radical force than Washington himself is likely to have considered it.

1782

EIGHTEENTH-CENTURY CONSCRIPTION

The Press-gang

Oh, where will you hurry my dearest?
  Say, say, to what clime or what shore?
You tear him from me, the sincerest
  That ever lov'd mortal before.

Ah! cruel, hard-hearted to press him
  And force the dear youth from my arms!
Restore him, that I may caress him,
  And shield him from future alarms.

In vain you insult and deride me
  And make but a scoff of my woes;
You ne'er from my dear shall divide me –
  I'll follow wherever he goes.

Think not of the merciless ocean –
  My soul any terror can brave,
For soon as the ship makes its motion,
  So soon shall the sea be my grave.

Charles Dibdin

Service in the British navy was so unpopular that men had to be pressed into it. Recruiting parties toured the ports, seizing the gullible and the unemployed, drunk or sober. Through the invocation of an Elizabethan Vagrancy Act, the prisons were emptied to man the fleet. Merchant ships were stopped on the high seas and crew forcibly transferred. Such treatment was one of the major sources of discontent among the American colonies. It was remarkable that there were so few mutinies, although one that took place at the Nore in 1797 almost brought the war effort to an end. Impressment ceased in practice in 1815, and in law in 1853, with the introduction of the service system.

1783

The Condemned Cell at Newgate

All you that in the condemned hole do lie,
Prepare you for tomorrow you shall die.
Watch all and pray; the hour is drawing near
That you before the Almighty must appear.
Examine well yourselves, in time repent,
That you may not to eternal flames be sent,
And when St Sepulchre's bell in the morning tolls
The Lord have mercy on your souls.

Anonymous

The night before an execution, a gaoler at Newgate Prison would pronounce these cheering words outside the cell of the condemned. At least until 1783, those to be hanged were taken by cart on the long journey to the Tyburn gallows at Marble Arch. The cart would be stopped outside St Sepulchre's, where the great bell was rung – one of the bells of Old Bailey. Only Jack Shepherd ever escaped from Newgate. Other distinguished residents had been Ben Jonson, Christopher Marlowe and Daniel Defoe.

1784

PITT THE YOUNGER

But mark what he did
  For to get to his station:
He told a damned lie
  In the ear of the king.
Then a shite on his name,
  For I'm all for the nation,
So don't bother me
  With the name of the thing.
His taxes now prove
  His great love for the people,
So wisely they're managed
  To starve the poor souls.
Sure the praise of the man
  Should be rung in each steeple
That would rob them of daylight,
  Of candles and coals. . .

Charles Morris

The National Saviour

When Faction threaten'd Britain's land,
Thy new-made friends – a desperate band,
    Like Ahab – stood reprov'd:
Pitt's powerful tongue their rage could check;
His counsel sav'd, 'midst general wreck,
    The Israel that he loved.

Anonymous

After a period of squabbling among the Whigs, a general election took place in 1784 and William Pitt the Younger became Prime Minister at the age of twenty-five. He held this office until 1801, seeing the country through the period of the French Revolution and the beginning of the Napoleonic Wars. He died during an additional term of office in 1806, his last words being, 'My country! Oh, my country!' His great political rival was Charles James Fox, who got one of his cronies, Charles Morris, to write the piece above, so as to remind the electorate that Pitt had promised not to raise taxes on windows or candles, but had done just that within months of his victory at the polls. Fox himself barely held office, but by opposing Pitt on almost every single issue with eloquent attacks in the House of Commons, he may be said to have defined for later ages the role of leader of His Majesty's Opposition.

1790

THE KING'S MADNESS

from **For the King's Birthday, 1790**

And lo, amid the watery roar
In Thetis' car she skims the shore,
Where Portland's brows, embattled high
With rocks, in rugged majesty
Frown o'er the billows, and the storm restrain,
She beckons Britain's scepter'd pair
Her treasures of the deep to share!
Hail then, on this glad morn, the mighty main!
Which leads the boon divine of lengthen'd days
To those who wear the noblest regal bays:
That mighty main, which on its conscious tide
Their boundless commerce pours on every clime,
Their dauntless banner bears sublime;
And wafts their pomp of war, and spreads their thunder wide!

Thomas Warton

This Poet Laureate faced something of a problem, for in 1788 the King had gone mad. In 1789 he and Queen Charlotte visited Weymouth in the hope that sea bathing would cure him, as his doctors had recommended. The diarist Fanny Burney, who had seen one of the newfangled bathing machines, recorded that it 'follows the Royal one into the sea, filled with fiddlers, who play God Save the King as his Majesty takes the plunge'.

1791

THE RIGHTS OF MAN

from **God Save Great Thomas Paine**

God save great Thomas Paine,
His 'Rights of Man' explain
To every soul.
He makes the blind to see
What dupes and slaves they be,
And points out liberty,
From pole to pole.

Thousands cry 'Church and King'
That well deserve to swing,
All must allow:
Birmingham blush for shame,
Manchester do the same,
Infamous is your name,
Patriots vow.

Pull proud oppressors down,
Knock off each tyrant's crown,
And break his sword;
Down aristocracy,
Set up democracy,
And from hypocrisy
Save us good Lord.

*

Despots may howl and yell,
Though they're in league with hell
They'll not reign long;
Satan may lead the van,
And do the worst he can,
Paine and his 'Rights of Man'
Shall be my song.

Joseph Mather

In 1791 the radical Thomas Paine published the first part of *The Rights of Man* in reply to Edmund Burke's *Reflections on the Revolution in France.* To avoid persecution for it, Paine fled to France, but soon fell out with the revolutionaries there and narrowly escaped the guillotine. He died in New York, but not before he had fallen out with the colonial rebels whose cause he had earlier espoused.

1792

THE DEATH OF SIR JOSHUA REYNOLDS

from **Retaliation**

Here Reynolds is laid and, to tell you my mind,
He has not left a better or wiser behind:
His pencil was striking, resistless and grand;
His manners were gentle, complying and bland;
Still born to improve us in every part,
His pencil our faces, his manners our heart;
To coxcombs averse, yet most civilly steering,
When they judged without skill he was still hard of hearing;
When they talked of their Raphaels, Correggios and stuff,
He shifted his trumpet and only took snuff.

Oliver Goldsmith

When Goldsmith died in 1774, it was found that he had written a series of sketches of his closest friends in the form of epitaphs. This is what he wrote about the great painter Reynolds. Reynolds had settled in London in 1753 and had come to dominate British painting. In 1768 he enhanced the status of his profession by establishing the Royal Academy, of which he was the first President. He was very deaf and much preferred the company of literary men like Johnson, Goldsmith and Burke to that of painters. When Goldsmith's death was announced, Burke burst into tears and Reynolds threw down his palette and stopped painting for the day.

1793

THE SLAVE TRADE

The Negro's Complaint

Forc'd from home, and all its pleasures,
  Afric's coast I left forlorn;
To increase a stranger's treasures,
  O'er the raging billows borne,
Men from England bought and sold me.
  Paid my price in paltry gold;
But though theirs they have enroll'd me,
  Minds are never to be sold.

Still in thought as free as ever,
  What are England's rights, I ask,
Me from my delights to sever,
  Me to torture, me to task?
Fleecy locks, and black complexion
  Cannot forfeit nature's claim;
Skins may differ, but affection
  Dwells in white and black the same.

Why did all-creating Nature
  Make the plant for which we toil?
Sighs must fan it, tears must water,
  Sweat of ours must dress the soil.
Think, ye masters, iron-hearted,
  Lolling at your jovial boards;
Think how many backs have smarted
  For the sweets your cane affords.

Is there, as ye sometimes tell us,
   Is there one who reigns on high?
Has he bid you buy and sell us,
   Speaking from his throne the sky?
Ask him, if your knotted scourges,
   Matches, blood-extorting screws,
Are the means which duty urges
   Agents of his will to use!

Hark! he answers – Wild tornadoes,
   Strewing yonder sea with wrecks;
Wasting towns, plantations, meadows,
   Are the voice with which he speaks.
He, forseeing what vexations
   Afric's sons should undergo,
Fix'd their tyrants' habitations
   Where his whirlwinds answer – No.

By our blood in Afric wasted,
   Ere our necks receiv'd the chain;
By the mis'ries we have tasted,
   Crossing in your barks the main;
By our suff'rings since ye brought us
   To the man-degrading mart;
All sustain'd by patience, taught us
   Only by a broken heart:

Deem our nation brutes no longer
   Till some reason ye shall find
Worthier of regard and stronger
   Than the colour of our kind.
Slaves of gold, whose sordid dealings
   Tarnish all your boasted pow'rs,
Prove that you have human feelings,
   Ere you proudly question ours!

William Cowper

In the triangular trade-system of the eighteenth century, ships from Europe took cloth, salt and guns to West Africa, then slaves from Africa to the Caribbean, and lastly sugar from the Caribbean back to Europe. This trade was based upon Europe's addiction to sugar and it was that addiction which required and sustained the appalling institution of slavery. More than twenty million slaves crossed the Atlantic and an even greater number died on the journey. One slave produced about a ton of sugar in the course of his lifetime. The Quakers were among the first to condemn slavery, and Dr Johnson proposed a toast at Oxford to 'success to the next revolt of the Negroes in the West Indies'.

In 1772, the great Chief Justice Lord Mansfield had given his judgment against slavery: 'The Black must go free.' Adam Smith condemned the traffic and William Wilberforce, Pitt's close friend, moved bill after bill to ban it. In 1807 the Ministry of All Talents passed an act banning the trade and British ships were deputed to see that this was observed. Yet the traffic continued, and it was not until 1833 that an act was passed to outlaw slavery in all British possessions. Even then a young MP, W. E. Gladstone, whose family had Caribbean interests, predicted evil consequences for the West Indies and for the slaves themselves.

1797

THE DEATH OF EDMUND BURKE

from **Retaliation**

Here lies our good Edmund, whose genius was such,
We scarcely can praise it or blame it too much;
Who, born for the universe, narrowed his mind,
And to party gave up what was meant for mankind;
Though fraught with all learning, yet straining his throat
To persuade Tommy Townshend to lend him a vote;
Who, too deep for his hearers, still went on refining,
And thought of convincing, while they thought of dining;
Though equal to all things, for all things unfit;
Too nice for a statesman, too proud for a wit;
For a patriot, too cool; for a drudge, disobedient;
And too fond of the *right* to pursue the *expedient*;
In short, 'twas his fate, unemployed or in place, sir,
To eat mutton cold and cut blocks with a razor.

Oliver Goldsmith

Edmund Burke was more important as a political philosopher than as a politician. He held office for only a short time, during the extraordinary coalition between Fox and North in 1783. Burke's writings, however, have had a profund influence. He set out the classic definition of an MP, as being a representative rather than a delegate. As he said in his address to the electors of Bristol in 1774: 'You choose a member indeed, but when you have chosen him, he is not a member of Bristol, but he is a member of Parliament.' He opposed the power of the Crown and asserted the need for political parties: 'Parties must ever exist in a free country.' In his famous *Reflections on the Revolution in France* (1790), he warned that revolutions would inevitably lead to despotism and he reaffirmed the value of tradition, moderation and slow harmonious change. When Disraeli was ennobled, he chose for his title the name of Burke's village, Beaconsfield.

1799

THE INCOME TAX

Oh what wonders, what novels in this age there be,
And the man that lives longest the most he will see;
For fifty years back pray what man would have thought,
That a tax upon income would be brought.
Sing, tantara rara new tax.

We're engag'd in a war who can say but 'tis just,
That some thousands of Britons as laid in the dust,
And the nation of millions it's made shift to drain,
Yet to go on with vigour each nerve we will strain.
Sing, tantara rara will strain.

From the peer so down to the mechanical man,
They must all come beneath our minister's plan,
And curtail their expences to pay their share,
To preserve their great rights & their liberties dear.
Sing tantara rara how dear.

If you've not 60 l. you'll have nothing to pay,
That's an income too small to take any away,
But from that to a hundred does gradually rise,
All above, nothing less than the tenth will suffice,
Sing tantara rara one tenth.

This tax had produc'd what most wish to conceal,
The true state of their income few love to reveal,
What long faces it's caus'd, and of oaths not a few
Whilst papers they sign'd for to pay in their due.
Sing tantara rara long face.

Anonymous

Pitt introduced Income Tax in 1799. It was intended as a temporary measure to help pay for the French wars, but although it was waived for a short while between 1802 and 1803, and later from 1816 to 1842, it was brought back then and is still with us today.

1803

THE NAPOLEONIC WARS

The Berkshire Farmer's Thoughts on Invasion

So! Bonaparte's coming, as folks seem to say,
(But I hope to have time to get in my hay).
And while he's caballing, and making a parley,
Perhaps I shall house all my wheat and my barley.
Fal la de ral, &c.

Then I shall have time to attend to my duty,
And keep the starved dogs from making a booty
Of what I've been toiling for, both late and early,
To support my old woman, whom I love so dearly.
Fal la de ral, &c.

Then, there are my children, and some of them feeble,
I wish, from my soul, that they were more able
To assist their old father, in drubbing the knaves,
For we ne'er will submit to become their tame slaves.
Fal la de ral, &c.

But then, there's son Dick, who is both strong and lusty,
And towards the French he is damnable crusty;
If you give him a pitchfork or any such thing,
He will fight till he's dead, in defence of his King.
Fal la de ral, &c.

And I'll answer for Ned, too, he'll never give out;
He should eat no more bacon, if I had a doubt.
And wish every one, who's not staunch in the cause,
May ne'er get a bit more to put in their jaws.
Fal la de ral, &c.

So you see, Bonaparte, how you are mistaken,
In your *big little* notions of stealing our bacon.
And your *straight way to London*, I this will you tell,
Your straight way to London is your short way to Hell.
Fal la de ral, &c.

Anonymous

From 1793 to 1815 Britain was almost continually at war with France. Napoleon rapidly came to dominate the whole of Europe. It was the British navy under Horatio Nelson which checked the French advance on different fronts at the Battle of the Nile in 1798, and again at Copenhagen in 1801. In 1803 Napoleon was ready to invade England and, with a huge army of 160,000 men gathered in Northern Europe, he practised embarking and landing. Pitt, out of office since 1801, was recalled and the country prepared to meet the invasion. Nelson saved the day. In 1805 he commanded the force which destroyed the French and Spanish fleets off Cape Trafalgar. With his twenty-seven ships he out-manoeuvred, out-gunned and out-fought the considerably greater numbers against him, but died from a sniper's wound at the hour of victory.

1805

At Viscount Nelson's lavish funeral,
While the mob milled and yelled about the Abbey,
A General chatted with an Admiral:

'One of your Colleagues, Sir, remarked today
That Nelson's *exit*, though to be lamented,
Falls not inopportunely, in its way.'

'He was a thorn in our flesh,' came the reply –
  'The most bird-witted, unaccountable,
Odd little runt that ever I did spy.

'One arm, one peeper, vain as Pretty Poll,
  A meddler, too, in foreign politics
And gave his heart in pawn to a plain moll.

'He would dare lecture us Sea Lords, and then
  Would treat his ratings as though men of honour
And play at leap-frog with his midshipmen!

'We tried to box him down, but up he popped,
  And when he'd banged Napoleon at the Nile
Became too much the hero to be dropped.

'You've heard that Copenhagen "blind eye" story?
  We'd tied him to Nurse Parker's apron-strings –
By G–d, he snipped them through and snatched the glory!'

'Yet,' cried the General, 'six-and-twenty sail
  Captured or sunk by him off Trafalgar –
That writes a handsome *finis* to the tale.'

'Handsome enough. The seas are England's now.
  That fellow's foibles need no longer plague us.
He died most creditably, I'll allow.'

'And, Sir, the secret of his victories?'
  'By his unServicelike, familiar ways, Sir,
He made the whole Fleet love him, damn his eyes!'

Robert Graves

1809

THE BATTLE OF CORUNNA

The Burial of Sir John Moore after Corunna

Not a drum was heard, not a funeral note,
As his corpse to the rampart we hurried;
Not a soldier discharged his farewell shot
O'er the grave where our hero we buried.

We buried him darkly at dead of night,
The sods with our bayonets turning,
By the struggling moonbeam's misty light
And the lanthorn dimly burning.

No useless coffin enclosed his breast,
Not in sheet or in shroud we wound him;
But he lay like a warrior taking his rest
With his martial cloak around him.

Few and short were the prayers we said,
And we spoke not a word of sorrow;
But we steadfastly gazed on the face that was dead,
And we bitterly thought of the morrow.

We thought, as we hollowed his narrow bed
And smoothed down his lonely pillow,
That the foe and the stranger would tread o'er his head,
And we far away on the billow!

Lightly they'll talk of the spirit that's gone,
And o'er his cold ashes upbraid him –
But little he'll reck, if they let him sleep on
In the grave where a Briton has laid him.

But half of our heavy task was done
  When the clock struck the hour for retiring;
And we heard the distant and random gun
  That the foe was sullenly firing.

Slowly and sadly we laid him down,
  From the field of his fame fresh and gory;
We carved not a line, and we raised not a stone,
  But we left him alone with his glory.

Charles Wolfe

In 1803 Napoleon annexed Spain and installed one of his brothers as King. In reply, the Duke of Wellington led a British army from Portugal to victory at Vimiera, but Napoleon then burst into Spain with 200,000 veterans, captured Madrid and forced the British, now under the command of Sir John Moore, to retreat. They marched 250 miles in nineteen days. Moore fought a rearguard action at Corunna while what was left of his army embarked. It was the Dunkirk of the Peninsular Wars, which Wellington eventually won in 1813.

1812

THE ASSASSINATION OF THE PRIME MINISTER

Lines on the Death of Mr P–R–C–V–L

In the dirge we sung o'er him no censure was heard,
  Unembittered and free did the tear-drop descend;
We forgot in that hour how the statesman had erred,
  And wept, for the husband, the father and friend.

Oh! proud was the meed his integrity won,
  And generous indeed were the tears that we shed,
When in grief we forgot all the ill he had done,
  And though wronged by him living, bewailed him when
    dead.

Even now, if one harsher emotion intrude,
'Tis to wish he had chosen some lowlier state –
Had known what he was, and, content to be good,
Had ne'er for our ruin aspired to be great.

So, left through their own little orbit to move,
His years might have rolled inoffensive away;
His children might still have been blessed with his love,
And England would ne'er have been cursed with his sway.

Thomas Moore

If Spencer Percival had not been assassinated as he entered the House of Commons on 11 May 1812, he would probably have joined the ranks of the now forgotten Prime Ministers. He had been PM for two years and was a politician of strong reactionary views. He was shot by a madman, John Bellingham, who was tried and publicly executed within a week. The House of Commons voted Percival's widow a capital sum of £50,000, but the country as a whole took the matter rather differently. In Bolton the mob ran wild with joy; in Nottingham a crowd paraded with drums beating and colours flying; while in the Potteries a man ran down the streets, shouting: 'Percival is shot. Hurrah!'

THE LUDDITES

from **General Ludd's Triumph**

Chant no more your old rhymes about bold Robin Hood,
His feats I but little admire,
I will sing the Achievements of General Ludd,
Now the Hero of Nottinghamshire.

*

Now by force unsubdued, and by threats undismay'd
Death itself can't his ardour repress
The presence of Armies can't make him afraid
Nor impede his career of success
Whilst the news of his conquests is spread far and near
How his Enemies take the alarm
His courage, his fortitude, strikes them with fear
For they dread his Omnipotent Arm . . .
And when in the work of destruction employed
He himself to no method confines,
By fire and by water he gets them destroyed
For the Elements aid his designs.
Whether guarded by Soldiers along the Highway
Or closely secured in the room,
He shivers them up both by night and by day,
And nothing can soften their doom.

Anonymous

Enoch Made Them – Enoch Shall Break Them

And night by night when all is still,
And the moon is hid behind the hill,
We forward march to do our will
  With hatchet, pike and gun!
Oh, the cropper lads for me,
The gallant lads for me,
Who with lusty stroke
The shear frames broke,
The cropper lads for me!

Great Enoch still shall lead the van
Stop him who dare! stop him who can!
Press forward every gallant man
  With hatchet, pike, and gun!
Oh, the cropper lads for me . . .

Anonymous

In 1811 the textile and hosiery trades were depressed for three reasons: the trade embargo imposed as a punishment upon America for supporting Napoleon had slashed exports; men's fashions were changing and the old fabrics were no longer in such heavy demand; and new machinery threatened the jobs of skilled craftsmen. Well-organized gangs went from village to village in Lancashire, Yorkshire and Nottinghamshire, breaking up machines. Many of the hammers they used for this task had been made by Enoch Taylor of Marsden, a blacksmith, who also manufactured the new frames, which gave rise to the slogan quoted above. The Government, rattled by the recent assassination of the Prime Minister, declared frame-breaking a capital offence and sent 12,000 troops to police the North – more than Wellington had commanded in Spain four years earlier. George Mellor, who led a famous, if futile, attack on Rawfold's Mill in the Spen Valley, was captured and, with sixteen other men, was hanged at York in January 1813.

Song for the Luddites

As the Liberty lads o'er the sea
Bought their freedom, and cheaply, with blood,
So we, boys, we
Will die fighting, or live free,
And down with all kings but King Ludd!

When the web that we weave is complete,
And the shuttle exchanged for the sword,
We will fling the winding sheet
O'er the despot at our feet,
And dye it deep in the gore he has pour'd.

Though black as his heart its hue,
Since his veins are corrupted to mud,
Yet this is the dew
Which the tree shall renew
Of Liberty, planted by Ludd!

George Gordon, Lord Byron

Luddism remained fitfully alive for a few years, ending in an outburst in 1816. But it achieved little. As the war ended, trade picked up, wages rose and more machines were needed to meet higher demand. In 1817, in Yorkshire, there were at least sixty more gig mills, and 1,300 more mechanical shears, than there had been before the troubles. There was, of course, no such figure as General Ludd in reality. The Nottinghamshire men had adopted the name of a legendary apprentice, said to have broken his stocking frame after he had been unfairly punished by his father.

1813

A DIVERSION OF THE TIMES

Song in Praise of Gowfing

O rural diversions, too long has the chace,
All the honours usurp'd, and assum'd the chief place;
But truth bids the Muse from henceforward proclaim,
That Gowf, first of sports, shall stand foremost in fame.

At Gowf we contend, without rancour or spleen,
And bloodless the laurels we reap on the green;
From vig'rous exertion our pleasures arise,
And to crown our delights no poor fugitive dies.

O'er the heath see our heroes in uniform clad,
In parties well match'd, how they gracefully spread;
While with long strokes and short strokes they tend to the goal,
And with put well-directed plump into the hole.

From exercise strong, from strength active and bold,
We'll traverse the green, and forget to grow old.
Blue devils, diseases, dull sorrow and care,
Knock'd down by our balls as they whizz thro' the air.

Health, happiness, harmony, friendship, and fame,
Are the fruits and rewards of our favourite game;
A sport so distinguish'd, the fair must approve,
Then to Gowf give the day, and the evening to love.

Andrew Duncan

Duncan wrote this for the Blackheath Club, near London. James I had played golf on Blackheath Common in 1608 and the club now established there claims to be the oldest in the world, although the one founded at St Andrews in 1754 is more famous. It is curious to note that the game was flourishing during the Napoleonic Wars.

1815

THE BATTLE OF WATERLOO

from **Childe Harold's Pilgrimage**

There was a sound of revelry by night,
  And Belgium's Capital had gathered then
  Her Beauty and her Chivalry, and bright
  The lamps shone o'er fair women and brave men;
  A thousand hearts beat happily; and when
  Music arose with its voluptuous swell,
  Soft eyes looked love to eyes which spake again,
And all went merry as a marriage bell;
But hush! hark! a deep sound strikes like a rising knell!

Did ye not hear it? – No; 'twas but the wind,
Or the car rattling o'er the stony street;
On with the dance! let joy be unconfined;
No sleep till morn, when Youth and Pleasure meet
To chase the glowing Hours with flying feet –
But hark – that heavy sound breaks in once more,
As if the clouds its echo would repeat;
And nearer, clearer, deadlier than before!
Arm! Arm! it is – it is – the cannon's opening roar!

*

And there was mounting in hot haste: the steed,
The mustering squadron, and the clattering car,
Went pouring forward with impetuous speed,
And swiftly forming in the ranks of war;
And the deep thunder peal on peal afar;
And near, the beat of the alarming drum
Roused up the soldier ere the morning star;
While thronged the citizens with terror dumb,
Or whispering, with white lips – The foe! They come! they come!'

*

Last noon beheld them full of lusty life,
Last eve in Beauty's circle proudly gay,
The midnight brought the signal-sound of strife,
The morn the marshalling in arms, – the day
Battle's magnificently-stern array!
The thunder-clouds close o'er it, which when rent
The earth is covered thick with other clay
Which her own clay shall cover, heaped and pent,
Rider and horse, – friend, foe, – in one red burial blent!

George Gordon, Lord Byron

After the failure of his Russian campaign in 1812, Napoleon had abdicated and gone into exile on the island of Elba. But in 1815 he contrived a brilliant return and his old soldiers flocked to rejoin him.

The nations of Europe rallied in opposition and the two armies met at Waterloo in Belgium. It was a hard-fought battle, which the allied army under Wellington came close to losing on two occasions, but as the sun set at 8.15 the Duke gave the order for a general advance and won the day. Interestingly, although Waterloo tends to be acclaimed as a British victory, in an allied army of 67,000 men only 21,000 were in fact British.

THE 'CHORUS OF THE YEARS' SURVEYS THE FIELD OF WATERLOO BEFORE THE BATTLE

from **The Dynasts**

Yea, the coneys are scared by the thud of hoofs,
And their white scuts flash at their vanishing heels,
And swallows abandon the hamlet-roofs.

The mole's tunnelled chambers are crushed by wheels,
The lark's eggs scattered, their owners fled;
And the hedgehog's household the sapper unseals.

The snail draws in at the terrible tread,
But in vain; he is crushed by the felloe-rim;
The worm asks what can be overhead,

And wriggles deep from a scene so grim,
And guesses him safe; for he does not know
What a foul red flood will be soaking him!

Beaten about by the heel and toe
Are butterflies, sick of the day's long rheum,
To die of a worse than the weather-foe.

Trodden and bruised to a miry tomb
Are ears that have greened but will never be gold,
And flowers in the bud that will never bloom.

Thomas Hardy

NAPOLEON'S CAREER

Boney was a warrior,
Way-aye-yah!
A warrior, a terrier,
Johnny Franswor!

Boney beat the Prussians,
The Osstrians and the Rooshians.

He beat the Prussians squarely,
He whacked the English nearly.

We licked him in Trafalgar's bay,
Carried his main topm'st away,

'Twas on the plains of Waterloo,
He met the boy who put him through.

He met the Duke of Wellington,
That day his downfall had begun.

Boney went a-cruisin',
Aboard the Billy Ruffian.

Boney went to Saint Helen',
An' he never came back agen.

They sent him into exile,
He died on Saint Helena's isle.

Boney broke his heart an' died,
In Corsica he wisht he styed.

He wuz a rorty general,
A rorty, snorty general.

Anonymous

Lines Written during the Time of the Spy System

I saw great Satan like a Sexton stand,
With his intolerable spade in hand,
Digging three graves. Of coffin shape they were
For those who coffinless must enter there,
With unblest rites. The shrouds were of that cloth
Which Clotho weaveth in her blackest wrath.
The pillows to these baleful beds were toads,
Large, living, livid, melancholy loads,
Whose softness shocked. Worms of all monstrous size
Crawled round; and one, upcoiled, that never coils.
A dismal bell, inculcating despair,
Was always ringing in the heavy air:
And all about the detestable pit
Strange headless ghosts, and quarter'd forms did flit;
Rivers of blood from dripping traitors spilt,
By treachery stung from poverty to guilt.
I asked the Fiend, for whom those rites were meant?
'These graves,' quoth he, 'when life's short oil is spent, –
When the dark night comes, and they're sinking bedwards –
I mean for Castles, Oliver and Edwards.'

Charles Lamb

From 1792 to 1820 the Government used spies extensively to get information about revolutionary groups. Of the spies named here by Lamb, Castles was busy in London and betrayed the leaders of the Spa Fields Riots in 1816, as Edwards did for the Cato Street Conspirators, while Oliver, the most infamous, reported directly to the Home Secretary on details of the Pentridge rising in Nottingham in 1817. Juries in London refused to convict men on the evidence of such informers, but this was not so at Nottingham, where those found guilty were hanged. The years immediately following Waterloo saw economic distress and political turmoil, as tens of thousands of soldiers and sailors joined the ranks of the workless. In 1817 habeas corpus was suspended; the embryonic trade unions were banned; and England only just escaped revolution.

1819

THE PETERLOO MASSACRE

With Henry Hunt We'll Go

With Henry Hunt we'll go, my boys,
With Henry Hunt we'll go;
We'll mount the cap of liberty
In spite of Nadin Joe.

'Twas on the sixteenth day of August,
Eighteen hundred and nineteen,
A meeting held in Peter Street
Was glorious to be seen;
Joe Nadin and his big bull-dogs,
Which you might plainly see,
And on the other side
Stood the bloody cavalry.

Anonymous

Orator Hunt was a radical reformer who advocated annual Parliaments and universal suffrage. He was billed to speak to a mass meeting at St Peter's Fields, Manchester, on 16 August 1819. Alarmed at the possibility of a general uprising, the authorities ordered the Manchester Yeomanry, which consisted largely of merchants, farmers and small tradesmen, to charge the mob that had gathered. In this famous engagement, known as the Peterloo Massacre, eleven people were killed. Hunt was arrested and imprisoned for two and a half years. This is the only surviving fragment of a popular song commemorating the event. Joe Nadin was the Deputy Constable of Manchester.

ANARCHY

from **The Mask of Anarchy**

As I lay asleep in Italy
There came a voice from over the Sea,
And with great power it forth led me
To walk in the visions of Poesy.

I met Murder on the way –
He had a mask like Castlereagh –
Very smooth he looked, yet grim;
Seven blood-hounds followed him:

All were fat; and well they might
Be in admirable plight,
For one by one, and two by two,
He tossed them human hearts to chew
Which from his wide cloak he drew.

Next came Fraud, and he had on,
Like Eldon, an ermined gown;
His big tears, for he wept well,
Turned to mill-stones as they fell.

And the little children, who
Round his feet played to and fro,
Thinking every tear a gem,
Had their brains knocked out by them.

Clothed with the Bible, as with light,
And the shadows of the night,
Like Sidmouth, next Hypocrisy
On a crocodile rode by.

And many more Destructions played
In this ghastly masquerade,
All disguised, even to the eyes,
Like Bishops, lawyers, peers, or spies.

Last came Anarchy: he rode
On a white horse, splashed with blood;
He was pale even to the lips,
Like Death in the Apocalypse.

And he wore a kingly crown;
And in his grasp a sceptre shone;
On his brow this mark I saw –
'I AM GOD, AND KING, AND LAW!'

With a pace stately and fast,
Over English land he passed,
Trampling to a mire of blood
The adoring multitude.

And a mighty troop around,
With their trampling shook the ground,
Waving each a bloody sword,
For the service of their Lord.

And with glorious triumph, they
Rode through England proud and gay,
Drunk as with intoxication
Of the wine of desolation.

O'er fields and towns, from sea to sea,
Passed the Pageant swift and free,
Tearing up, and trampling down;
Till they came to London town.

And each dweller, panic-stricken,
Felt his heart with terror sicken
Hearing the tempestuous cry
Of the triumph of Anarchy.

Percy Bysshe Shelley

Written 'on the occasion of the massacre at Manchester', the poem from which these first stanzas are taken serves as a passionate incitement to revolution and expresses the dismay shared by many of the more advanced thinkers of the time.

England in 1819

An old, mad, blind, despised, and dying king, –
Princes, the dregs of their dull race, who flow
Through public scorn, – mud from a muddy spring, –
Rulers who neither see, nor feel, nor know,
But leech-like to their fainting country cling,
Till they drop, blind in blood, without a blow, –
A people starved and stabbed in the untilled field, –
An army, which liberticide and prey
Makes as a two-edged sword to all who wield, –
Golden and sanguine laws which tempt and slay;
Religion Christless, Godless – a book sealed;
A Senate, – Time's worst statute unrepealed, –
Are graves, from which a glorious Phantom may
Burst, to illumine our tempestuous day.

Percy Bysshe Shelley

King George IV, 1820–30

1820

THE PRINCE REGENT

from **The Political House that Jack Built**

This is THE MAN – all shaven and shorn,
All cover'd with Orders – and all forlorn;
THE DANDY OF SIXTY, who bows with a grace,
And has *taste* in wigs, collars, cuirasses and lace;
Who, to tricksters, and fools, leaves the State and its treasure,
And, when Britain's in tears, sails about at his pleasure;
Who spurn'd from his presence the Friends of his youth,
And now has not one who will tell him the truth;
Who took to his counsels, in evil hour,
The Friends to the Reasons of lawless Power;
That back the Public Informer, who
Would put down the *Thing*, that, in spite of new Acts,
And attempts to restrain it, by Soldiers of Tax,
Will *poison* the Vermin,
That plunder the Wealth,
That lay in the House,
That Jack built.

William Hone

William Hone started out as a bookseller, but went on to become a radical publisher. He published William Hazlitt's *Political Essays* and was made to stand trial on three occasions. In 1820 he issued what was to be the most popular satirical pamphlet of the nineteenth century, 'The Political House that Jack Built', illustrated by George Cruikshank, who later achieved fame with his illustrations for *Oliver Twist*. Hone's pamphlet satirized many famous people, and within a year it had run into fifty-two editions.

QUEEN CAROLINE

The Bath

'. . . The wide sea
Hath drops too few to wash her clean'

William Shakespeare

The weather's hot – the cabin's free!
And she's as free and hot as either!
And Berghy is as hot as she!
In short, they all are hot together!
Bring then a large capacious tub,
And pour great pails of water in,
In which the frowzy nymph may rub
The itchings of her royal skin.

Let none but Berghy's hand untie
The garter, or unlace the boddice;
Let none but Berghy's faithful eye
Survey the beauties of the goddess.

While *she* receives the copious shower
He gets a step in honour's path,
And grows from this auspicious hour
A K-night Companion of the Bath.

William Hone

George had married Caroline in 1795 and, after the birth of a daughter, Charlotte, they separated. When he became Regent in 1811, Caroline went to live on the Continent, accompanied by her major-domo, Bartolomeo Bergami, who served, it was said, all her needs. In 1820, on George's accession, she returned, and the luckless Prime Minister, Lord Liverpool, had to move a Bill dissolving the marriage and depriving her of the title of Queen. Her case was taken up by the Whigs and she became as popular as her husband was unpopular. The Bill was dropped, but she was refused entry to Westminster Abbey at the

Coronation and died a year later. Max Beerbohm said of Caroline that she had been cast for a tragic role, but played it in tights.

On the Queen

Most Gracious Queen, we thee implore
To go away and sin no more,
But if that effort be too great,
To go away at any rate.

Anonymous

ENCLOSURES

from The Fallen Elm

Thus came enclosure – ruin was its guide
But freedoms clapping hands enjoyed the sight
Though comforts cottage soon was thrust aside
& workhouse prisons raised upon the scite
Een natures dwellings far away from men
The common heath became the spoilers prey
The rabbit had not where to make his den
& labours only cow was drove away
No matter – wrong was right & right was wrong
& freedoms bawl was sanction to the song
– Such was thy ruin music making elm
The rights of freedom was to injure thine
As thou wert served so would they overwhelm
In freedoms name the little that is mine
& there are knaves that brawl for better laws
& cant of tyranny in stronger powers
Who glue their vile unsatiated maws
& freedoms birthright from the weak devours

John Clare

Clare was a poet of the Northamptonshire countryside and no one wrote more movingly about the rural poor, or the struggles of the small farmer and agricultural labourer. The eighteenth century had seen a revolution in farming. Turnips were introduced to allow for crop rotation, and clover was planted to fatten livestock. Drainage became popular, but it required capital and larger holdings. Parliamentary acts promoted the enclosure of land. Clare was an eloquent defender of the old farming methods and the society which they created. Arthur Young, on his travels through England, acted as spokesman for the reformers and for big farming, and he vigorously disparaged the 'Goths and Vandals' of the open-field system.

1825

THE FOUNDATION OF LONDON UNIVERSITY

from **The London University**

Ye Dons and ye doctors, ye Provosts and Proctors,
  Who're paid to monopolize knowledge,
Come make opposition by voice and petition
  To the radical infidel College;
Come put forth your powers in aid of the towers
  Which boast of their Bishops and Martyrs,
And arm all the terrors of privileged errors
  Which live by the wax of their Charters.

Let Mackintosh battle with Canning and Vattel,
  Let Brougham be a friend to the 'niggers,'
Burdett cure the nation's misrepresentations,
  And Hume cut a figure in figures;
But let them not babble of Greek to the rabble.
  Nor teach the mechanics their letters;
The labouring classes were born to be asses,
  And not to be aping their betters.

'Tis a terrible crisis for Cam and for Isis!
  Fat butchers are learning dissection;
And looking-glass makers become Sabbath-breakers
  To study the rules of reflection;
'Sin: φ' and 'sin: θ' what sins can be sweeter?
  Are taught to the poor of both sexes,
And weavers and sinners jump up from their dinners
  To flirt with their Y's and their X's.

Chuckfarthing advances the doctrine of chances
  In spite of the staff of the beadle;
And menders of breeches between the long stitches
  Write books on the laws of the needle;
And chandlers all chatter of luminous matter,
  Who communicate none to their tallows,
And rogues get a notion of the pendulum's motion
  Which is only of use at the gallows.

Winthrop Mackworth Praed

Until 1825 there had been four universities in Scotland, but only two in England, Oxford and Cambridge; and these had excluded Jews, Catholics and Dissenters. The Scottish poet Thomas Campbell and Henry Brougham, a prickly politician – who was later to retire to France and make Cannes a fashionable resort – decided to establish a new university in London, with no clergy on its governing body. They sold shares in it, and representatives of the great liberal families subscribed – J. S. Mill, Macaulay and Goldsmid among them. They founded University College in Gower Street. There, towards the end of the century, J. A. Fleming invented the thermionic valve, without which one could not have had the wireless, television or the computer.

A RETROSPECT

George the First was always reckoned
Vile, but viler George the Second;
And what mortal ever heard
Any good of George the Third?
When from earth the Fourth descended
(God be praised!) the Georges ended.

Walter Savage Landor

King William IV, 1830–7

1832

THE REFORM BILL

from **Pledges, by a Ten-pound Householder**

When a gentleman comes
With his trumpet and drums,
And hangs out a flag at the Dragon,
Some pledges, no doubt,
We must get him to spout
To the shopkeepers, out of a wagon.

For although an MP
May be wiser than we
Till the House is dissolved, in December,
Thenceforth, we're assured,
Since Reform is secured,
We'll be wiser by far than our member.

A pledge must be had
That, since times are so bad
He'll prepare a long speech, to improve them;
And since taxes, at best,
Are a very poor jest,
He'll take infinite pains to remove them.

*

He must solemnly say
That he'll vote no more pay
To the troops, in their ugly red jackets;
And that none may complain
On the banks of the Seine,
He'll dismast all our ships, but the packets.

That the labourer's arm,
May be stout on the farm,
That our commerce may wake from stagnation,
That our trades may revive,
And our looms look alive,
He'll be pledged to all free importation.

*

We must bind him, poor man,
To obey their divan,
However their worships may task him,
To swallow their lies
Without any surprise,
And to vote black is white, when they ask him.

These hints I shall lay,
In a forcible way,
Before an intelligent quorum,
Who meet to debate
Upon matters of State,
Tonight, at the National Forum

Winthrop Mackworth Praed

In 1830 the Tory Government under Wellington was defeated at the polls and a coalition of Whigs, Liberals and Independents, led by the seventy-year-old Earl Grey, took office. Several future PMs – Lord John Russell, Melbourne and Palmerston – were in the Cabinet, and they were determined to bring in a Reform Bill that would abolish the rotten boroughs and widen the franchise to the extent of giving the vote to any male who occupied a house with a rental value of ten pounds or more. There was initial resistance in the Lords, but the Tories were badly led by Wellington and eventually the Bill was forced through. The measure itself had limited scope, being mainly a reform instituted by the middle classes on behalf of the middle classes, but the electorate was increased from 435,000 to 685,000. Revolution was avoided by a classic compromise, and England was set upon a path which was to lead to universal suffrage.

1834

THE TOLPUDDLE MARTYRS

God is our guide! from field, from wave,
From plough, from anvil, and from loom;
We come, our country's rights to save,
And speak a tyrant faction's doom:
We raise the watchword liberty;
We will, we will, we will be free!

God is our guide! no swords we draw,
We kindle not war's battle fires;
By reason, union, justice, law,
We claim the birthright of our sires:
We raise the watchword liberty;
We will, we will, we will be free!!!

George Loveless

George Loveless was the leader of a group of Dorsetshire labourers who had 'combined together' to protect their jobs and their pay. This was an illegal act and the offenders were sentenced to seven years' deportation. After two years of protest, however, they were reprieved and Loveless returned to join the Chartists. He scribbled this poem on a piece of paper as his sentence was passed. He wrote: 'While we were being guarded back to prison, our hands being locked together, I tossed the above lines to some people that we passed; the guard, however, seizing hold of them, they were instantly carried back to the judge; and by some this was considered a crime of no less magnitude than high treason.' Tolpuddle has become the shrine of the Trade Union movement.

1835–41

MELBOURNE'S PREMIERSHIP

To promise, pause, prepare, postpone
And end by letting things alone:
In short, to earn the people's pay
By doing nothing every day.

Winthrop Mackworth Praed

Lord Melbourne told his secretary that being Prime Minister was 'a damned bore'. But he held the office for almost seven years and left it reluctantly in 1841. His behaviour was certainly laid-back, but the march of progress went on: local government was established, the Poor Law was introduced and the first factory acts were passed. From 1837 Melbourne relished the role of guide and mentor to the young Queen Victoria, who was convinced as a result that Whigs were good and Tories bad.

THE VICTORIAN AGE

Queen Victoria, 1837–1901

Welcome now, VICTORIA!
Welcome to the throne!
May all the trades begin to stir,
   Now you are Queen of England;
For your most gracious Majesty,
May see what wretched poverty,
Is to be found on England's ground,
   Now you are Queen of England.

While o'er the country you preside,
Providence will be your guide,
The people then will never chide
   Victoria, Queen of England.
She doth declare it her intent
To extend reform in Parliament,
On doing good she's firmly bent,
   While she is Queen of England.

Says she, I'll try my utmost skill,
That the poor may have their fill;
Forsake them! – no, I never will,
   When I am Queen of England.
For oft my mother said to me,
Let this your study always be,
To see the people blest and free,
   Should you be Queen of England.

Anonymous

Victoria was eighteen years old when she succeeded her uncle, William IV, and during her long reign Britain was to enjoy unparalleled prosperity and power, ruling a vast empire and serving as the workshop of the world. The Queen was a small woman, being less than five feet tall, but she had the strength to bear nine children. In 1840 she married one of her cousins, Albert of Saxe-Coburg, and for the first time in two hundred years the English monarchy enjoyed domestic bliss. Victoria imposed respectability upon the nation: satire dried up and parlour songs became the order of the day.

PRINCE ALBERT

I am a German just arrived,
With you for to be mingling,
My passage it was paid,
From Germany to England;
To wed your blooming Queen.
For better or worse I take her,
My father is a duke,
And I'm a sausage maker.

Here I am in rags and jags,
Come from the land of all dirt,
I married England's Queen.
My name it is young Albert.

I am a cousin to the Queen,
And our mothers they are cronies,
My father lives at home,
And deals in nice polonies:
Lots of sour crout and broom,
For money he'll be giving,
And by working very hard,
He gets a tidy living.

Here I am, &c.

She says now we are wed.
  I must not dare to tease her,
But strive both day and night,
  All e'er I can to please her,
I told her I would do
  For her all I was able,
And when she had a son
  I would sit and rock the cradle.

Here I am, &c.

Anonymous

1838

THE CHARTER

When thrones shall crumble and moulder to dust,
  And sceptres shall fall from the hands of the great,
And all the rich baubles a Monarch might boast,
  Shall vanish before the good sense of a state;
When Lords, (produced by the mandate of Kings),
  So proud and dominant, rampant with power.
Shall be spoken of only as by-gone things
  That shall blast this part of creation no more,
Based firm upon truth, the Charter shall stand
The land-mark of ages – sublimely grand!

When class-distinctions shall wither and die,
  And conscious merit shall modestly bear
The garlands wrought by its own industry,
  The proper rewards of labour and care;
When man shall rise to his station as man,
  To passion or vice no longer a slave;
When the *march of mind* already begun,
  Shall gathering roll like a vast mountain wave,
The Charter shall stand the text of the free,
Of a Nation's rights the sure guarantee.

Anonymous

The Charter was published in 1838 and it called for six reforms, including annual parliaments, the payment of MPs, secret ballots and universal male suffrage. The Chartist cause peaked in 1839, briefly flaring up again in 1848. It failed through the inability of its leaders to suppress their differences, although its spirit survives. Karl Marx, who was living in London at the time, expressed the opinion that England was too placid to encourage a proletarian uprising.

Protest against the Ballot

Forth rushed from Envy sprung and Self-conceit,
A Power misnamed the SPIRIT of REFORM,
And through the astonished Island swept in storm,
Threatening to lay all Orders at her feet
That crossed her way. Now stoops she to entreat
Licence to hide at intervals her head
Where she may work, safe, undisquieted,
In a close Box, covert for Justice meet.
St George of England! keep a watchful eye
Fixed on the Suitor; frustrate her request –
Stifle her hope; for, if the State comply,
From such Pandorian gift may come a Pest
Worse than the Dragon that bowed low his crest,
Pierced by thy spear in glorious victory.

William Wordsworth

1838

Grace Darling

After you had steered your coble out of the storm
And left the smaller islands to break the surface,
Like draughts shaking that colossal backcloth there came
Fifty pounds from the Queen, proposals of marriage.

The daughter of a lighthouse-keeper and the saints
Who once lived there on birds' eggs, rainwater, barley
And built to keep all pilgrims at a safe distance
Circular houses with views only of the sky,

Who set timber burning on the top of a tower
Before each was launched at last in his stone coffin –
You would turn your back on mainland and suitor
To marry, then bereave the waves from Lindisfarne,

A moth against the lamp that shines still and reveals
Many small boats at sea, lifeboats, named after girls.

Michael Longley

When the steamer *Forfarshire* ran aground off the Farne rocks in September 1838, Grace Darling, the twenty-two-year-old daughter of the lighthouse keeper, rowed out with her father in a great storm and helped him save nine people from the wreck. She became an instant heroine: souvenir mugs were produced and admirers offered £5 for a lock of her hair. She continued to live with her father until her death from tuberculosis just four years later. There is a marble effigy of her in Bamburgh churchyard, complete with an oar in her right hand and seaweed carved on the canopy.

1841

THE BIRTH OF EDWARD, PRINCE OF WALES

There's a pretty fuss and bother both in country and in town,
Since we have got a present, and an heir unto the Crown,
A little Prince of Wales so charming and so sly,
And the ladies shout with wonder, What a pretty little boy!

He must have a little musket, a trumpet and a kite,
A little penny rattle, and silver sword so bright,
A little cap and feather with scarlet coat so smart,
And a pretty little hobby horse to ride about the park.

He must have a dandy suit to strut about the town,
John Bull must rake together six or seven thousand pound,
You'd laugh to see his daddy, at night he homewards runs,
With some peppermint or lollipops, sweet cakes and sugar
plums.

Now to get these little niceties the taxes must be rose,
For the little Prince of Wales wants so many suits of clothes,
So they must tax the frying pan, the windows and the doors,
The bedsteads and the tables, kitchen pokers, and the floors.

John Harkness

The Prince had to wait sixty years before ascending the throne as Edward VII, but seems never to have lost his taste for idle and expensive pleasures.

1844

PEEL AND DISRAELI

Young England's Lament

(Young England sitting dolorously before his parlour-fire:
he grievously waileth as follows: –)

I really can't imagine why,
With my confess'd ability –
From the ungrateful Tories, I
Get nothing – but civility.

The 'independent' dodge I've tried,
I've also tried servility; –
It's all the same, – they *won't* provide, –
I only get – civility.

I've flattered PEEL; he smiles back thanks
With Belial's own tranquillity;
But still he keeps me in 'the ranks',
And pays me – with civility.

If not the birth, at least I've now
The *manners* of nobility;
But yet SIR ROBERT scorns to bow
With more than mere civility.

Well, I've been pretty mild as yet,
But now I'll try scurrility;
It's very hard if *that* don't get
Me more than mere civility.

Anonymous

Robert Peel was the son of a Lancashire cotton-spinner and never lost his Lancastrian accent. He was a typical member of the new, thriving and thrusting middle classes, but he led the Tory party, which was principally the party of the old landed interests. He served as Prime Minister from 1841 to 1846 – a remarkable administration, with five future Prime Ministers in the Cabinet. Gladstone said that Peel was the greatest man he had ever known. He was proud and shy, with a propensity to be stiff and stubborn. Disraeli attacked Peel bitterly and once remarked that his smile was like the plate on a coffin. In 1834 he published the first party programme, the Tamworth Manifesto, which set good government and consensus above adherence to party dogma. In 1844 Benjamin Disraeli, who in spite of asking had not been offered any post by Peel, published his novel, *Coningsby*. This argued for a new 'Young England' to arise from the old traditions and customs of the country. Still Disraeli failed to get a job, and he had to wait nearly thirty years before he himself became Prime Minister. By then the romantic dream of a Young England had faded, although Disraeli's eloquent concern for a country which he saw as split into 'Two Nations', rich and poor, was undiminished.

1846

THE REPEAL OF THE CORN LAWS

from Corn Law Rhymes

Child, is thy father dead?
  Father is gone!
Why did they tax his bread?
  God's will be done!
Mother has sold her bed;
Better to die than wed!
Where shall she lay her head?
  Home we have none!

Father clamm'd thrice a week –
  God's will be done!
Long for work did he seek,
  Work he found none.
Tears on his hollow cheek
Told what no tongue could speak:
Why did his master break?
  God's will be done!

Doctor said air was best –
  Food we had none;
Father, with panting breast,
  Groan'd to be gone:
Now he is with the blest –
Mother says death is best!
We have no place of rest –
  Yes, ye have one!

Ebenezer Elliott

The big issue in the 1840s had become whether the Corn Laws, which protected British farmers, should be repealed to allow for cheaper foreign imports. The Anti Corn Law League, which was formed in 1839 and led by John Bright and Richard Cobden, campaigned vigorously across the country. Peel had become a convert to free trade, but what drove him to action was learning of the failure of the Irish potato crop and of the prospect of famine. In 1846 he repealed the Corn Laws, lost office and split the Tory party. Two hundred and thirty-one Tory MPs voted against him. The old party of Pitt, Canning, Liverpool and Wellington broke up. The issue – free trade as against protection – was the same that divided the Tories in 1906, and in both instances disunity was to lead to long periods of government by the opposition.

1848

THE RAILWAYS

'Mr Dombey', *from* Victorian Trains

The whistle blows. The train moves.
Thank God I am pulling away from the conversation
I had on the platform through the hissing of steam
With that man who dares to wear crape for the death of my son.
But I forget. He is coming with us.
He is always ahead of us stocking the engine.
I depend on him to convey me
With my food and my drink and my wraps and my reading
   material
To my first holiday since grief mastered me.
He is the one with the view in front of him
The ash in his whiskers, the speed in his hair.

He is richer now. He refused my tip.
Death and money roll round and round
In my head with the wheels.
I know what a skeleton looks like.
I never think of my dead son
In this connection. I think of wealth.

The railway is like a skeleton,
Alive in a prosperous body,
Reaching up to grasp Yorkshire and Lancashire
Kicking Devon and Kent
Squatting on London.
A diagram of growth
A midwinter leaf.

I am a merchant
With fantasies like all merchants.
Gold, carpets, handsome women come to me
Out of the sea, along these tracks.
I am as rich as England,
As solid as a town hall.

Patricia Beer

The first railway line, running between Stockton and Darlington, was opened in 1825, and the 1830s saw a modest expansion, until by 1838 there were more than 500 miles of track, with London and Birmingham included in the service. The railway boom, whose driving force was George Hudson, the 'Railway King', took off in the 1840s, but burst in 1847, by which time more than 5,000 miles of track had been laid and English industry and society had been transformed. Dickens published *Dombey and Son* in 1848, and the railways play an important part in the book. To Mr Dombey, the cold, proud and stubborn merchant, they represent progress. His sickly son, Paul, has a foster-mother, Polly Toodle, whose husband is a stoker and engine-driver. But Paul is removed from their care and submitted to a wretched and loveless education. Towards the end of the book the villainous Carker dies under an express train. Dickens's description of the railway excavations in North London as an event of seismic consequences is perfectly apt.

1851

THE GREAT EXHIBITION

Fountains, gushing silver light,
  Sculptures, soft and warm and fair,
Gems, that blind the dazzled sight,
  Silken trophies rich and rare,
Wondrous works of cunning skill,
  Precious miracles of art, –
How your crowding memories fill
  Mournfully my musing heart!

Fairy Giant choicest birth
  Of the Beautiful Sublime,
Seeming like the Toy of earth
  Given to the dotard Time, –
Glacier-diamond, Alp of glass,
  Sindbad's cave, Aladdin's hall, –
Must it then be crush'd, alas;
  Must the Crystal Palace fall?

Anonymous

Prince Albert organized the Great Exhibition to celebrate Britain's industrial and commercial leadership of the world. It was housed in an enormous structure of glass and steel, the Crystal Palace, which was erected in Hyde Park and later moved to South London. Disraeli, never at a loss for hyperbole, hailed it as 'an enchanted pile, which the sagacious taste and prescient philanthropy of an accomplished and enlightened Prince have raised for the glory of England and the instruction of two hemispheres'.

It made a profit and on the strength of this, land was bought in South Kensington for Imperial College and the museums that now stand there. The Crystal Palace itself was moved to Sydenham, where it proved a costly embarrassment until it was burnt down in the next century.

The Site of the Crystal Palace

A weed-mobbed terrace; plinths
deserted; an imperial symmetry
partitioned, gone to various bidders.
Down the clogged ghost-promenades

he sees like yesterday, only clearer . . .
Girders wincing, staggering in white glare,
the factory-forged dream, that ordered
brillance, stove in and shrivelling

to mere recorded fact. More real,
his mother's apron, dabbing smoke-
sting back; her grimed ordinary face,
tired then, lost thirty years now,

but flare-lit that night, immutable.

Philip Gross

1852

THE DEATH OF WELLINGTON

from Ode on the Death of the Duke of Wellington

Bury the Great Duke
  With an empire's lamentation,
Let us bury the Great Duke
  To the noise of the mourning of a mighty nation,
Mourning when their leaders fall,
Warriors carry the warrior's pall,
And sorrow darkens hamlet and hall.

*

Lead out the pageant: sad and slow,
As fits an universal woe,
Let the long long procession go,
And let the sorrowing crowd about it grow,
And let the mournful martial music blow;
The last great Englishman is low . . .

Alfred, Lord Tennyson

from **Don Juan**

You are 'the best of cut-throats:' – do not start;
  The phrase is Shakespeare's, and not misapplied: –
War's a brain-spattering, windpipe-slitting art,
  Unless her cause by right be sanctified.
If you have acted *once* a generous part,
  The world, not the world's masters, will decide,
And I shall be delighted to learn who,
Save you and yours, have gain'd by Waterloo?

I am no flatterer – you've supp'd full of flattery:
  They say you like it too –'t is no great wonder.
He whose whole life has been assault and battery,
  At last may get a little tired of thunder;
And swallowing eulogy much more than satire, he
  May like being praised for every lucky blunder,
Call'd 'Saviour of the Nations' – not yet saved,
And 'Europe's Liberator' – still enslaved.

George Gordon, Lord Byron

When he died, Wellington was given a splendid state funeral, as befitted a national hero. Writing forty years earlier, Byron evidently did not share the general adulation, but it is unlikely that Wellington, who once replied to a blackmailing courtesan with the words, 'Publish and be damned!' lost much sleep over this.

THE WEAVING INDUSTRY

from The Hand-loom Weavers' Lament

You gentlemen and tradesmen, that ride about at will,
Look down on these poor people; it's enough to make you crill;
Look down on these poor people, as you ride up and down,
I think there is a God above will bring your pride quite down.
    You tyrants of England, your race may soon be run,
    You may be brought unto account for what you've sorely
      done.

You pull down our wages, shamefully to tell;
You go into the markets, and say you cannot sell;
And when that we do ask you when these bad times will mend,
You quickly give an answer, 'When the wars are at an end.'
    You tyrants of England, &c.

Anonymous

Bury New Loom

As I walked between Bolton and Bury.
  'twas on a moonshiny night,
I met with a buxom young weaver whose
  company gave me delight.
She says: Young fellow, come tell me if your
  level and rule are in tune.
Come give me an answer correct, can you
  get up and square my new loom?

I said: My dear lassie, believe me, I am a
  good joiner by trade,
And many a good loom and shuttle before
  me in my time I have made.

Your short lams and jacks and long lams I
quickly can put in tune.
My rule is in good order to get up and
square a new loom.

She took me and showed me her loom, the
down on her warp did appear.
The lams, jacks and healds put in motion, I
levelled her loom to a hair.
My shuttle run well in her lathe, my treadle
it worked up and down,
My level stood close to her breast-bone, the
time I was reiving her loom.

The cords of my lams, jacks and treadles at
length they began to give way.
The bobbin I had in my shuttle, the weft in
it no longer would stay.
Her lathe it went bang to and fro, my main
treadle still kept in tune,
My pickers went nicketty-nack all the time
I was squaring her loom.

My shuttle it still kept in motion, her lams
she worked well up and down.
The weights in her rods they did tremble;
she said she would weave a new gown.
My strength now began for to fail me. I
said: It's now right to a hair.
She turned up her eyes and said: Tommy,
my loom you have got pretty square.

Anonymous

There were many popular songs of the early nineteenth century that took as their theme the new industrial machinery. Some were in the form of angry denunciations, but as 'Bury New Loom', one of the most famous, indicates, it was also hard to resist an opportunity for humorous sexual innuendo.

1853

A PUBLIC HANGING

A London Fête

All night fell hammers, shock on shock;
With echoes Newgate's granite clanged:
The scaffold built, at eight o'clock
They brought the man out to be hanged.
Then came from all the people there
A single cry, that shook the air;
Mothers held up their babes to see,
Who spread their hands, and crowed for glee;
Here a girl from her vesture tore
A rag to wave with, and joined the roar;
There a man, with yelling tired,
Stopped, and the culprit's crime inquired;
A sot, below the doomed man dumb,
Bawled his health in the world to come;
These blasphemed and fought for places;
Those half-crushed, cast frantic faces,
To windows, where, in freedom sweet,
Others enjoyed the wicked treat.
At last, the show's black crisis pended;
Struggles for better standings ended;
The rabble's lips no longer cursed,
But stood agape with horrid thirst;
Thousands of breasts beat horrid hope;
Thousands of eyeballs, lit with hell,
Burnt one way all, to see the rope
Unslacken as the platform fell.
The rope flew tight; and then the roar
Burst forth afresh; less loud, but more
Confused and affrighting than before.
A few harsh tongues for ever led
The common din, the chaos of noises,
But ear could not catch what they said.
As when the realm of the damned rejoices

At winning a soul to its will,
That clatter and clangour of hateful voices
Sickened and stunned the air, until
The dangling corpse hung straight and still.
The show complete, the pleasure past,
The solid masses loosened fast:
A thief slunk off, with ample spoil,
To ply elsewhere his daily toil;
A baby strung its doll to a stick;
A mother praised the pretty trick;
Two children caught and hanged a cat;
Two friends walked on, in lively chat;
And two, who had disputed places,
Went forth to fight, with murderous faces.

Coventry Patmore

Public executions were not stopped in England until 1868. Thackeray in 1840, and Dickens in a famous letter to *The Times* in 1849, had both tried to bring them to an end. Coventry Patmore denied in later years that he had attacked the imposition of the death penalty, but the last couplet of this poem effectively demolishes the deterrent argument.

1854

The Charge of the Light Brigade

Half a league, half a league,
  Half a league onward,
All in the valley of Death
  Rode the six hundred.
'Forward, the Light Brigade!
Charge for the guns!' he said:
Into the valley of Death
  Rode the six hundred.

'Forward, the Light Brigade!'
Was there a man dismayed?
Not though the soldier knew
 Someone had blundered:
Their's not to make reply,
Their's not to reason why,
Their's but to do and die:
Into the valley of Death
 Rode the six hundred.

Cannon to right of them,
Cannon to left of them,
Cannon in front of them
 Volleyed and thundered;
Stormed at with shot and shell,
Boldly they rode and well,
Into the jaws of Death,
Into the mouth of Hell
 Rode the six hundred.

Flashed all their sabres bare,
Flashed as they turned in air
Sabring the gunners there,
Charging an army, while
 All the world wondered:

Plunged in the battery-smoke
Right through the line they broke;
Cossack and Russian
Reeled from the sabre-stroke
 Shattered and sundered.
Then they rode back, but not
 Not the six hundred.

Cannon to right of them,
Cannon to left of them,
Cannon behind them
  Volleyed and thundered;
Stormed at with shot and shell,
While horse and hero fell,
They that had fought so well
Came through the jaws of Death,
Back from the mouth of Hell,
All that was left of them,
  Left of six hundred.

When can their glory fade?
O the wild charge they made!
  All the world wondered.
Honour the charge they made!
Honour the Light Brigade,
  Noble six hundred!

Alfred, Lord Tennyson

The Crimean War had started in 1854 to prevent Russia from annexing parts of the crumbling Turkish Empire. War fever swept the country, but the British army itself was in a ramshackle state. The soldier's pay of a shilling a day came down, after deductions, to no more than three pence; commissions were for sale; and the organization of supplies and medical care were both scandalously bad. Lord Raglan, the Commander-in-Chief, had not seen service for twenty-five years, and Lord Cardigan, who led the Light Brigade, was a buffoon. Between them they brought about one of the most memorable failures in the history of the British army. The war ended in 1856, and Russia's ambitions had been contained at the cost of 25,000 British dead.

Florence Nightingale

Through your pocket glass you have let disease expand
To remote continents of pain where you go far
With rustling cuff and starched apron, a soft hand:
Beneath the bandage maggots are stitching the scar.

For many of the men who lie there it is late
And you allow them at the edge of consciousness
The halo of your lamp, a brothel's fanlight
Or a nightlight carried in by nanny and nurse.

You know that even with officers and clergy
Moustachioed lips will purse into fundaments
And under sedation all the bad words emerge
To be rinsed in your head like the smell of wounds,

Death's vegetable sweetness at both rind and core –
Name a weed and you find it growing everywhere.

Michael Longley

In 1854 Florence Nightingale was thirty-five years old, a trained nurse, and a friend of the War Minister, Sydney Herbert. Incensed by reports in *The Times* of the way in which soldiers wounded in the Crimean War were being treated, she took it upon herself to lead a small group of volunteer nurses to Scutari, the British military hospital base in Constantinople. The conditions she found there, just ten days after the battle of Balaclava, were appalling. Rats, maggots and lice overran the wards; twenty chamber-pots were shared between 2,000 men; and amid all that filth and indifference typhus, cholera, dysentery, delirium and death flourished. With tremendous vitality and drive she set about cleaning the place up. As she went round the wards with her lamp, wounded soldiers would kiss her passing shadow. Her conduct brought her enemies, principally among the doctors, and when the chief medical officer was awarded the KCB she suggested that it stood for 'Knight of the Crimea Burial-ground.'

On returning to England, she was warmly supported by the Queen and over the next fifty years she became the second most famous woman in the country. By establishing the Nightingale School for

Nurses at St Thomas, she laid the foundations of modern nursing. She lived on until 1907 – a one-woman powerhouse, a relentless reformer and a legend. Characteristically, she once wrote: 'From committees, charity and schism – from the Church of England and all other deadly sins – from philanthropy and all the deceits of the devil – Good Lord deliver us.'

VICTORIANA

Mr Gradgrind's Country

There was a dining-room, there was a drawing-room,
There was a billiard-room, there was a morning-room,
There were bedrooms for guests and bedrooms for sons and
daughters,
In attic and basement there were ample servants' quarters,
There was a modern bathroom, a strong-room, and a
conservatory.
In the days of England's glory.

There were Turkish carpets, there were Axminster carpets,
There were oil paintings of Vesuvius and family portraits,
There were mirrors, ottomans, wash-hand-stands and
tantaluses,
There were port, sherry, claret, liqueur, and champagne
glasses,
There was a solid brass gong, a grand piano, antlers, decanters,
and a gentlemen's lavatory,
In the days of England's glory.

There was marqueterie and there was mahogany,
There was a cast of the Dying Gladiator in his agony,
There was the 'Encyclopaedia Britannica' in a revolving
  bookcase,
There were finger-bowls, asparagus-tongs, and inlets of real
  lace:
They stood in their own grounds and were called Chatsworth,
  Elgin, or Tobermory,
In the days of England's glory.

But now these substantial gentlemen's establishments
Are like a perspective of disused elephants,
And the current Rajahs of industry flash past their wide
  frontages
Far far away to the latest things in labour-saving cottages,
Where with Russell lupins, jade ash-trays, some Sealyham
  terriers, and a migratory
Cook they continue the story.

Sylvia Townsend Warner

Dickens's *Hard Times* appeared in 1854. Mr Gradgrind is one of its characters: a tyrannical patriarch whose views on education are limited to a belief in stuffing children's heads with facts.

THE ENGLISH PUBLIC SCHOOL

from **Rugby Chapel**

Coldly, sadly, descends
The autumn evening. The field
Strewn with its dark yellow drifts
Of withered leaves, and the elms,
Fade into dimness apace,
Silent; hardly a shout
From a few boys late at their play!
The lights come out in the street,
In the schoolroom windows; but cold,
Solemn, unlighted, austere,
Through the gathering darkness, arise
The chapel-walls, in whose bound
Thou, my father! art laid.

There thou dost lie, in the gloom
Of the autumn evening. But ah!
That word, *gloom*, to my mind
Brings thee back, in the light
Of thy radiant vigour, again;
In the gloom of November we passed
Days not dark at thy side;
Seasons impaired not the ray
Of thy buoyant cheerfulness clear.
Such thou wast! and I stand
In the autumn evening, and think
Of bygone autumns with thee.

*

If, in the paths of the world,
Stones might have wounded thy feet,
Toil or dejection have tried,
Thy spirit, of that we saw
Nothing – to us thou wast still
Cheerful, and helpful, and firm!

Therefore to thee it was given
Many to save with thyself;
And, at the end of thy day,
O faithful shepherd! to come,
Bringing thy sheep in thy hand.

And through thee I believe
In the noble and great who are gone;
Pure souls honoured and blest
By former ages, who else –
Such, so soulless, so poor,
Is the race of men whom I see –
Seemed but a dream of the heart,
Seemed but a cry of desire.
Yes! I believe that there lived
Others like thee in the past,
Not like the men of the crowd
Who all round me today
Bluster or cringe, and make life
Hideous, and arid, and vile;
But souls tempered with fire,
Fervent, heroic, and good,
Helpers and friends of mankind.

Servants of God! – or sons
Shall I not call you? because
Not as servants ye knew
Your Father's innermost mind,
His, who unwillingly sees
One of his little ones lost –
Yours is the praise, if mankind
Hath not as yet in its march
Fainted, and fallen, and died!

Matthew Arnold

Matthew Arnold's father, to whose shade this poem is addressed, was the great Dr Thomas Arnold, founder of Rugby School. In that institution, Dr Arnold created the prototype of the English Public School – called 'English', because boys went there to learn Latin and Greek; 'Public', because it was private; and 'School', because so much time was spent playing games. The public schools set out to produce men who would serve God and their country, practitioners of muscular Christianity. Dr Arnold was one of the four 'Eminent Victorians' so vengefully debunked by Lytton Strachey in the next century.

FACTORY CONDITIONS

from **The Cry of the Children**

Do ye hear the children weeping, O my brothers,
    Ere the sorrow comes with years?
They are leaning their young heads against their mothers, –
    And *that* cannot stop their tears.
The young lambs are bleating in the meadows;
  The young birds are chirping in the nest;
The young fawns are playing with the shadows;
  The young flowers are blowing toward the west –
But the young, young children, O my brothers,
    They are weeping bitterly –
They are weeping in the playtime of the others,
    In the country of the free.

*

'For oh,' say the children, 'we are weary,
    And we cannot run or leap –
If we cared for any meadows, it were merely
    To drop down in them and sleep.
Our knees tremble sorely in the stooping –
  We fall upon our faces, trying to go;
And, underneath our heavy eyelids drooping,
  The reddest flower would look as pale as snow.
For, all day, we drag our burden tiring,
    Through the coal-dark, underground –
Or, all day, we drive the wheels of iron.
    In the factories, round and round.

'For, all day, the wheels are droning, turning, –
Their wind comes in our faces, –
Till our hearts turn, – our head, with pulses burning,
And the walls turn in their places –
Turns the sky in the high window blank and reeling –
Turns the long light that droppeth down the wall –
Turn the black flies that crawl along the ceiling –
All are turning, all the day, and we with all –
And all day, the iron wheels are droning;
And sometimes we could pray,
"O ye wheels," (breaking out in a mad moaning)
"Stop! be silent for today!"'

*

They look up, with their pale and sunken faces,
And their look is dread to see,
For they mind you of their angels in their places,
With eyes meant for Deity; –
'How long,' they say, 'how long, O cruel nation,
Will you stand, to move the world, on a child's heart, –
Stifle down with a mail'd heel its palpitation,
And tread onward to your throne amid the mart?
Our blood splashes upward, O our tyrants,
And your purple shows your path;
But the child's sob curseth deeper in the silence
Than the strong man in his wrath!'

Elizabeth Barrett Browning

In most factories of this time conditions were appalling. In 1830 a Tory churchman, Richard Oastler, had started a crusade in Yorkshire against child slavery. In 1834 a law was passed forbidding children under the age of nine to be put to work, while those under thirteen were restricted to a nine-hour day, and those between fourteen and eighteen to a twelve-hour day. Dickens tells of the misery he endured as a young boy employed in a blacking factory. Young girls worked in pits, drawing the wagons. Later, Lord Shaftesbury took up the cause of reform, and in 1850 a maximum ten-and-a-half-hour working day was agreed upon, with seven and a half hours on Saturdays. In 1876 Disraeli fixed a fifty-six-hour week and the Trade Unions were released from criminal liability. Shaftesbury is commemorated by the statue of Eros in Piccadilly Circus – a strange tribute in a strange place for such a good man.

1861

VICTORIA WITHOUT ALBERT

The Widow at Windsor

'Ave you 'eard o' the Widow at Windsor
With a hairy gold crown on 'er 'ead?
She 'as ships on the foam – she 'as millions at 'ome,
An' she pays us poor beggars in red.
(Ow, poor beggars in red!)
There's 'er nick on the cavalry 'orses,
There's 'er mark on the medical stores –
An' 'er troopers you'll find with a fair wind be'ind
That takes us to various wars.
(Poor beggars – barbarious wars!)
Then 'ere 's to the Widow at Windsor,
An' 'ere 's to the stores an' the guns,
The men an' the 'orses what makes up the forces
O' Missis Victorier's sons.
(Poor beggars! Victorier's sons!)

Walk wide o' the Widow at Windsor,
  For 'alf o' Creation she owns:
We 'ave bought 'er the same with the sword an' the flame,
  An' we've salted it down with our bones.
    (Poor beggars – it's blue with our bones!)
Hands off o' the Sons o' the Widow,
  Hands off o' the goods in 'er shop,
For the Kings must come down an' the Emperors frown
  When the Widow at Windsor says 'Stop!'
    (Poor beggars – we're sent to say 'Stop!')
        Then 'ere 's to the Lodge o' the Widow,
          From the Pole to the Tropics it runs –
        To the Lodge that we tile with the rank an' the file,
          An' open in form with the guns.
        (Poor beggars! – it's always they guns!)

We 'ave 'eard o' the Widow at Windsor,
  It's safest to leave 'er alone:
For 'er sentries we stand by the sea an' the land
  Wherever the bugles are blown.
    (Poor beggars! – an' don't we get blown!)
Take 'old o' the Wings o' the Mornin',
  An' flop round the earth till you're dead;
But you won't get away from the tune that they play
  To the bloomin' old rag over'ead.
    (Poor beggars – it 's 'ot over'ead!)
        Then 'ere 's to the Sons of the Widow,
          Wherever, 'owever they roam.
        'Ere 's all they desire, an' if they require
          A speedy return to their 'ome.
        (Poor beggars – they'll never see 'ome!)

Rudyard Kipling

After the death of Albert in 1861 from dysentery caused by the bad drains at Windsor Castle, Victoria entered a prolonged period of mourning. This withdrawal made her a remote and rather unpopular figure. Disraeli, however, coaxed her out of retirement and she continued to reign until 1901. This poem is supposed to have cost Kipling any sign of royal favour during the Queen's lifetime. She was not amused.

1878

TURKEY AND JINGOISM

We don't want to fight, but, by Jingo, if we do,
We've got the ships, we've got the men, we've got the money too.
We've fought the Bear before, and, while Britons shall be true,
The Russians shall not have Constantinople.

G. W. Hunt

In 1877 Russia declared war on Turkey with a view to seizing as much of Turkey's Balkan Empire as it could. Popular feeling in Britain was for the Turks, in spite of the savage massacre they had inflicted upon the Bulgarians in 1876, and a wave of militarism swept the country. The topical music-hall song from which the refrain above is taken led to the coining of a new word, 'jingoism'. Disraeli ordered the fleet to sail to Constantinople, the reserves were called up and Indian troops were moved to the Mediterranean. The last thing Disraeli wanted was a war, but Russia's ambitions had to be checked, especially as its lands bordered on India. Heads of state gathered at the Congress of Berlin, and there, through his diplomacy, Disraeli secured 'peace with honour'. He should have called a general election at that point, but instead he waited until 1880, when he was defeated by Gladstone.

THE ARMY

Tommy

I went into a public-'ouse to get a pint o' beer,
The publican 'e up an' sez, 'We serve no red-coats here.'
The girls be'ind the bar they laughed an' giggled fit to die,
I outs into the street again an' to myself sez I:
O it's Tommy this, an' Tommy that, an' 'Tommy, go away';
But it's 'Thank you, Mister Atkins,' when the band begins to play –
The band begins to play, my boys, the band begins to play,
O it's 'Thank you, Mister Atkins,' when the band begins to play.

I went into a theatre as sober as could be,
They gave a drunk civilian room, but 'adn't none for me;
They sent me to the gallery or round the music-'alls,
But when it comes to fightin', Lord! they'll shove me in the stalls!
For it's Tommy this, an' Tommy that, an' 'Tommy, wait outside';
But it's 'Special train for Atkins' when the trooper's on the tide –
The troopship's on the tide, my boys, the troopship's on the tide,
O it's 'Special train for Atkins' when the trooper's on the tide.

Yes, makin' mock o' uniforms that guard you while you sleep
Is cheaper than them uniforms, an' they're starvation cheap;
An' hustlin' drunken soldiers when they're goin' large a bit
Is five times better business than paradin' in full kit.
Then it's Tommy this, an' Tommy that, an' 'Tommy, 'ow's yer soul?'
But it's 'Thin red line of 'eroes' when the drums begin to roll –
The drums begin to roll, my boys, the drums begin to roll,
O it's 'Thin red line of 'eroes' when the drums begin to roll.

We aren't no thin red 'eroes, nor we aren't no blackguards too,
But single men in barricks, most remarkable like you;
An' if sometimes our conduck isn't all your fancy paints,
Why, single men in barricks don't grow into plaster saints;
While it's Tommy this, an' Tommy that, an' 'Tommy, fall be'ind,'
But it's 'Please to walk in front, sir,' when there's trouble in the wind –
There's trouble in the wind, my boys, there's trouble in the wind,
O it's 'Please to walk in front, sir,' when there's trouble in the wind.

You talk o' better food for us, an' schools, an' fires, an' all:
We'll wait for extry rations if you treat us rational.
Don't mess about the cook-room slops, but prove it to our face
The Widow's Uniform is not the soldier-man's disgrace.
For it's Tommy this, an' Tommy that, an' 'Chuck him out, the brute!'
But it's 'Saviour of 'is country' when the guns begin to shoot;
An' it's Tommy this, an' Tommy that, an' anything you please;
An' Tommy ain't a bloomin' fool – you bet that Tommy sees!

Rudyard Kipling

The army was one of the great institutions of Victorian England. Wellington had the profoundest contempt for most of his soldiers, and the campaign in the Crimea showed what a mess the War Office could make of things. From 1868 Gladstone's minister, Cardwell, brought in the reforms by which county regiments were set up, floggings abolished and modern equipment introduced. The colourful full-dress uniforms of most of today's regiments were the creations of Victorian England. In *Patience*, W. S. Gilbert satirized the Heavy Dragoon:

> When I first put this uniform on,
> I said, as I looked in the glass,
> 'It's one to a million
> That any civilian
> My figure and form will surpass . . .'

But the great national heroes were soldiers – Wolseley, Bobs, Kitchener – and you would be hard pushed to name a Victorian admiral. The highest award for valour was instituted at this time and was called the Victoria Cross. The Queen had only one big war, the Crimean, but there were any number of little ones in China, India, Afghanistan, Zululand, the Sudan, Egypt and West Africa, among other places. The British 'Tommy' held the Empire together: of the 100,000 enlisted men, three quarters served overseas. Kipling became unofficial Poet Laureate to the ordinary soldier, upon whom British pride and power depended, but who otherwise got little thanks. In spite of its honourable record, however, the British army was ill prepared for 1914.

Vitaï Lampada

There's a breathless hush in the Close tonight –
Ten to make and the match to win –
A bumping pitch and a blinding light,
An hour to play and the last man in.
And it's not for the sake of a ribboned coat,
Or the selfish hope of a season's fame,
But his Captain's hand on his shoulder smote –
'Play up! play up! and play the game!'

The sand of the desert is sodden red, –
Red with the wreck of a square that broke; –
The Gatling's jammed and the Colonel dead,
And the regiment blind with dust and smoke.
The river of death has brimmed his banks,
And England's far, and Honour a name,
But the voice of a schoolboy rallies the ranks:
'Play up! play up! and play the game!'

This is the word that year by year,
   While in her place the School is set,
Every one of her sons must hear,
   And none that hears it dare forget.
This they all with a joyful mind
   Bear through life like a torch in flame,
And falling fling to the host behind –
   'Play up! play up! and play the game!'

Henry Newbolt

1885

THE DEATH OF GENERAL GORDON

from **The Hero of Khartoum**

Alas! now o'er the civilized world there hangs a gloom
For brave General Gordon, that was killed in Khartoum;
He was a Christian hero, and a soldier of the Cross,
And to England his death will be a very great loss.

He was very cool in temper, generous and brave,
The friend of the poor, the sick, and the slave;
And many a poor boy he did educate,
And laboured hard to do so early and late.

*

He always took the Bible for his guide,
And he liked little boys to walk by his side;
He preferred their company more so than men,
Because he knew there was less guile in them.

And in his conversation he was modest and plain,
Denouncing all pleasures he considered sinful and vain,
And in battle he carried no weapon but a small cane,
Whilst the bullets fell around him like a shower of rain.

*

In military life his equal couldn't be found,
No! if you were to search the wide world around,
And 'tis pitiful to think he has met with such a doom
By a base *traitor knave* while in Khartoum.

Yes, the black-hearted traitor opened the gates of Khartoum,
And through that the Christian hero has met his doom,
For when the gates were opened the Arabs rushed madly in,
And foully murdered him while they laughingly did grin.

William McGonagall

In 1882, at the instigation of the Prime Minister, William Ewart Gladstone, Britain annexed Egypt with the intention of securing the Suez Canal as the gateway to her Indian Empire. Three years later, a Muslim leader, the Mahdi, raised a revolt in the Sudan, inflicting severe losses on British troops. General Charles Gordon was sent by Gladstone – the Grand Old Man, as he was called – to restore order, but found himself besieged at Khartoum. The Government in London was slow to respond, and when a relief force was sent, it arrived to find that Gordon had been killed two days earlier. The country and the Queen were outraged. Victoria sent an open telegram in which she deplored the 'frightful' delay and spoke of 'the stain left upon England'. Gladstone was called the Murderer of Gordon, and a topical poem went:

The G.O.M., when his life ebbs out,
Will ride in a fiery chariot,
And sit in state
On a red-hot plate
Between Pilate and Judas Iscariot.

The Queen never forgave Gladstone, and it was left to Lytton Strachey in *Eminent Victorians* to challenge the idolatry of Gordon.

EARLY HOPES REVISED

from **Locksley Hall**

Not in vain the distance beacons. Forward, forward let us range,
Let the great world spin for ever down the ringing grooves of
change.
Thro' the shadow of the globe we sweep into the younger day:
Better fifty years of Europe than a cycle of Cathay . . .

Alfred, Lord Tennyson

from **Locksley Hall Sixty Years After**

Chaos, Cosmos! Cosmos, Chaos! who can tell how all will end?
Read the wide world's annals, you, and take their wisdom for
your friend.

Hope the best, but hold the Present fatal daughter of the Past,
Shape your heart to front the hour, but dream not that the hour
will last.

Ay, if dynamite and revolver leave you courage to be wise:
When was age so cramm'd with menace? madness? written,
spoken lies?

Envy wears the mask of Love, and, laughing sober fact to scorn,
Cries to Weakest as to Strongest, 'Ye are equals, equal-born.'

Equal-born? O yes, if yonder hill be level with the flat.
Charm us, Orator, till the Lion look no larger than the Cat,

Till the Cat thro' that mirage of overheated language loom
Larger than the Lion, – Demos end in working its own doom.

Russia bursts our Indian barrier, shall we fight her? shall we
yield?
Pause! before you sound the trumpet, hear the voices from the
field.

Those three hundred millions under one Imperial sceptre now,
Shall we hold them? shall we loose them? take the suffrage of
the plow.

Nay, but these would feel and follow Truth if only you and you,
Rivals of realm-running party, when you speak were wholly
true . . .

Alfred, Lord Tennyson

In the poem published in 1842, Tennyson voices the supreme confidence of early Victorian England. But by 1886 doubts had become apparent: democracy was on the march and party politics threatened to bring down the country and mankind. Later, Chesterton was to characterize the difference between the two times when he wrote that he preferred the fighting of Cobbett to the feasting of Pater.

ASPECTS OF LATE VICTORIAN ENGLAND

The Countryside

from **Why England is Conservative**

Let hound and horn in wintry woods and dells
Make jocund music though the boughs be bare,
And whistling yokel guide his teaming share
Hard by the homes where gentle lordship dwells.
Therefore sit high enthroned on every hill,
Authority! and loved in every vale;
Nor, old Tradition, falter in the tale
Of lowly valour led by lofty will;
And though the throats of envy rage and rail,
Be fair proud England, proud fair England still.

Alfred Austin

The Northern Town

from **Satan Absolved: a Victorian Mystery**

The smoke of their foul dens
Broodeth on Thy Earth as a black pestilence,
Hiding the kind day's eye. No flower, no grass there groweth,
Only their engines' dung which the fierce furnace throweth.
Their presence poisoneth all and maketh all unclean.
Thy streams they have made sewers for their dyes analine.
No fish therein may swim, no frog, no worm, may crawl,
No snail for grime may build her house within their wall.

Wilfrid Scawen Blunt

The Suburbs

from **Thirty Bob a Week**

For like a mole I journey in the dark,
  A-travelling along the underground
From my Pillar'd Halls and broad Suburban Park,
  To come the daily dull official round;
And home again at night with my pipe all alight,
  A-scheming how to count ten bob a pound.

And it's often very cold and very wet,
  And my missus stitches towels for a hunks;
And the Pillar'd Halls is half of it to let –
  Three rooms about the size of travelling trunks.
And we cough, my wife and I, to dislocate a sigh,
  When the noisy little kids are in their bunks.

But you never hear her do a growl or whine,
  For she's made of flint and roses, very odd;
And I've got to cut my meaning rather fine,
  Or I'd blubber, for I'm made of greens and sod:
So p'r'aps we are in Hell for all that I can tell,
  And lost and damn'd and serv'd up hot to God.

John Davidson

1888

JACK THE RIPPER

Eight little whores, with no hope of Heaven,
Gladstone may save one, then there'll be seven.
Seven little whores begging for a shilling,
One stays in Heneage Court, then there's a killing.

Six little whores, glad to be alive,
One sidles up to Jack, then there are five.
Four and whore rhyme aright, so do three and me.
I'll set the town alight, ere there are two.

Two little whores, shivering with fright,
Seek a cosy doorway, in the middle of the night.
Jack's knife flashes, then there's but one.
And the last one's ripest for Jack's idea of fun.

Anonymous

I'm not a butcher,
I'm not a Yid,
Nor yet a foreign skipper,
But I'm your own light-hearted friend,
Yours truly, Jack the Ripper.

Anonymous

Between August and November 1888, a number of prostitutes in Whitechapel were killed in a particularly gruesome way, being ripped open and dismembered. The popular press soon invented the name Jack the Ripper for their unknown assailant – not one of Strachey's 'Eminent Victorians'. Many anonymous letters, and even poems, were sent to the police, purporting to own up. No arrest was made, but over the years an extraordinary variety of candidates has been proposed: a Harley Street surgeon whose son had contracted syphilis from one of the victims; a midwife; a Russian planted by the Tsar's police; a Jewish ritual slaughterman; and a Blackheath schoolteacher – among others. The children of the East End had their own little rhyme about it:

Jack the Ripper's dead,
And lying in his bed.
He cut his throat
With Sunlight Soap.
Jack the Ripper's dead.

1895

FIN DE SIÈCLE

The Arrest of Oscar Wilde at the Cadogan Hotel

He sipped at a weak hock and seltzer
   As he gazed at the London skies
Through the Nottingham lace of the curtains
   Or was it his bees-winged eyes?

To the right and before him Pont Street
   Did tower in her new built red,
As hard as the morning gaslight
   That shone on his unmade bed,

'I want some more hock in my seltzer,
   And Robbie, please give me your hand –
Is this the end or beginning?
   How can I understand?

'So you've brought me the latest *Yellow Book*:
 And Buchan has got in it now:
Approval of what is approved of
 Is as false as a well-kept vow.

'More hock, Robbie – where is the seltzer?
 Dear boy, pull again at the bell!
They are all little better than *cretins*,
 Though this *is* the Cadogan Hotel.

'One astrakhan coat is at Willis's –
 Another one's at the Savoy:
Do fetch my morocco portmanteau,
 And bring them on later, dear boy.'

A thump, and a murmur of voices –
 'Oh why must they make such a din?'
As the door of the bedroom swung open
 And TWO PLAIN CLOTHES POLICEMEN came in:

'Mr Woilde, we 'ave come for tew take yew
 Where felons and criminals dwell:
We must ask yew tew leave with us quoietly
 For this *is* the Cadogan Hotel.'

He rose, and he put down *The Yellow Book*.
 He staggered – and, terrible-eyed,
He brushed past the palms on the staircase
 And was helped to a hansom outside.

John Betjeman

In 1895 Oscar Wilde was the lion of London Society, the arbiter of taste and most celebrated of wits. His plays *The Ideal Husband* and *The Importance of Being Earnest* were being performed to packed houses. So brash and confident was he, that he openly flaunted his passionate affair with Lord Alfred Douglas, son of the Marquis of Queensberry. Incensed, the Marquis left a visiting card at Wilde's club addressed to

'Oscar Wilde posing as a Somdomite' – which was to prove a notorious misspelling. Wilde foolishly started a libel action and, in the course of a two-day cross-examination by Edward Carson, was disastrously compelled to admit that he had engaged in a number of casual homosexual affairs. He was advised to fly to France, but he went instead to the Cadogan Hotel in Sloane Street where he got slightly drunk with Douglas and his friend Robert Ross. Tried for practising 'the love that dare not speak its name', he was found guilty and sentenced to two years' hard labour. It was an appalling humiliation and Victorian society rejoiced in its revenge. From his time in prison, Wilde wrote his finest poem, 'The Ballad of Reading Gaol'. He died in poverty in France in 1900.

On reading Betjeman's poem, Lord Alfred Douglas complained that it was not very accurate.

1895

THE JAMESON RAID

Jameson's Ride

Wrong! Is it wrong? Well, may be:
  But I'm going, boys, all the same.
Do they think me a Burgher's baby,
  To be scared by a scolding name?
They may argue, and prate, and order;
  Go, tell them to save their breath:
Then, over the Transvaal border,
  And gallop for life or death!

Let lawyers and statesmen addle
  Their pates over points of law;
If sound be our sword, and saddle,
  And gun-gear, who cares one straw?
When men of our own blood pray us
  To ride to their kinsfolk's aid,
Not Heaven itself shall stay us
  From the rescue they call a raid.

There are girls in the gold-reef city,
  There are mothers and children too!
And they cry, 'Hurry up! for pity!'
  So what can a brave man do?
If even we win, they'll blame us:
  If we fail, they will howl and hiss.
But there's many a man lives famous
  For daring a wrong like this!

So we forded and galloped forward,
  As hard as our beasts could pelt,
First eastward, then trending northward,
  Right over the rolling veldt;
Till we came on the Burghers lying
  In a hollow with hills behind,
And their bullets came hissing, flying,
  Like hail on an Arctic wind!

Right sweet is the marksman's rattle,
  And sweeter the cannon's roar,
But 'tis bitterly bad to battle,
  Beleaguered, and one to four.
I can tell you it wasn't a trifle
  To swarm over Krugersdorp glen,
As they plied us with round and rifle,
  And ploughed us, again – and again.

Then we made for the gold-reef city,
  Retreating, but not in rout.
They had called to us, 'Quick! for pity!'
  And He said, 'They will sally out,
They will hear us and come. Who doubts it?'
  But how if they don't, what then?
'Well, worry no more about it,
  But fight to the death, like men.'

Not a soul had supped or slumbered
  Since the Borderland stream was cleft,
But we fought, ever more outnumbered,
  Till we had not a cartridge left.
We're not very soft or tender,
  Or given to weep for woe,
But it breaks one to have to render
  One's sword to the strongest foe.

I suppose we were wrong, were madmen,
  Still I think at the Judgment Day,
When God sifts the good from the bad men,
  There'll be something more to say.
We were wrong, but we aren't half sorry,
  And, as one of the baffled band,
I would rather have had that foray,
  Than the crushings of all the Rand.

Alfred Austin

The great wealth of the Transvaal was controlled by the Dutch-descended Boers, whose political leader was Paul Kruger. He stood in the way of Cecil Rhodes's dream of a united South Africa, stretching from the Cape to the Great Lakes and under British sway. The English-speaking inhabitants of the Transvaal had grievances and Rhodes was ready to exploit them if he could thereby overthrow the Boers. On 29 December 1895, Leander Starr Jameson, a close friend of Rhodes's, led a troop of men into Boer territory. They had one field-gun and five Maxims at their disposal, and were supposed to be riding into Johannesburg to help the English population who should have risen. As they rode, messengers from the British Government ordered them to return. Everything went wrong: the guides lost their way; the horses tired and the troopers went hungry; the Boers learned of their coming; and on 2 January they surrendered ignominiously. Jameson was tried in London and sentenced to fifteen months' imprisonment.

The Colonial Secretary, Joseph Chamberlain, was accused of approving the raid. Winston Churchill, then at the beginning of his political career, said of this last, foolish fling in the scramble for Africa: 'I date the beginning of these violent times from the Jameson Raid.' Alfred Austin, however, who had just been appointed Poet Laureate, heedlessly sent this poem off to *The Times*. He never fully recovered from the avalanche of criticism which greeted it, and even Queen Victoria complained about it to the Prime Minister, Lord Salisbury. Mark Twain on a visit to London described the incident as 'a Poet Laureate explosion of coloured fireworks which filled the world's sky with giddy splendours'.

1899–1902

The Boer War

The whip-crack of a Union Jack
In a stiff breeze (the ship will roll),
Deft abracadabra drums
Enchant the patriotic soul –

A grandsire in St James's Street
Sat at the window of his club,
His second son, shot through the throat,
Slid backwards down a slope of scrub,

Gargled his last breaths, one by one by one,
In too much blood, too young to spill,
Died difficultly, drop by drop by drop –
'By your son's courage, sir, we took the hill.'

They took the hill (Whose hill? What for?)
But what a climb they left to do!
Out of that bungled, unwise war
An alp of unforgiveness grew.

William Plomer

In 1886, gold had been discovered in the Witwatersrand and the competition for South Africa started. The Jameson Raid killed whatever hope may have existed that there would be co-operation between Boer settlers and British imperialists. In 1899 the Government in London reluctantly decided to intervene to secure basic rights for the British. At first British troops met with a succession of humiliating defeats, but gradually, under the command of Lord Roberts, Kitchener and Baden-Powell, they won control. The cost, however, was enormous – 20,000 dead – and the greatest imperial power of the day had had to use 200,000 men to fight a mere 60,000 farmers. The Union of South Africa was the immediate result, but the end of the Empire had also moved a step closer.

Following British Failures Exposed by the Boer War

And ye vaunted your fathomless powers, and ye flaunted your
iron pride,
Ere – ye fawned on the Younger Nations for the men who could
shoot and ride!
Then ye returned to your trinkets; then ye contented your souls
With the flannelled fools at the wicket or the muddied oafs at
the goals.

Rudyard Kipling

1901

THE DEATH OF QUEEN VICTORIA

from **1901**

When Queen Victoria died
The whole of England mourned
Not for a so recently breathing old woman
A wife and a mother and a widow,
Not for a staunch upholder of Christendom,
A stickler for etiquette
A vigilant of moral values
But for a symbol.
A symbol of security and prosperity
Of 'My Country Right or Wrong'
Of 'God is good and Bad is bad'
And 'What was good enough for your father
Ought to be good enough for you'
And 'If you don't eat your tapioca pudding
You will be locked in your bedroom
And given nothing but bread and water
Over and over again until you come to your senses
And are weak and pale and famished and say
Breathlessly, hopelessly and with hate in your heart
"Please Papa I would now like some tapioca pudding very much
indeed"'
A symbol too of proper elegance
Not the flaunting, bejewelled kind
That became so popular
But a truly proper elegance,
An elegance of the spirit,
Of withdrawal from unpleasant subjects
Such as Sex and Poverty and Pit Ponies
And Little Children working in the Mines
And Rude Words and Divorce and Socialism
And numberless other inadmissible horrors.

When Queen Victoria died
They brought her little body from the Isle of Wight
Closed up in a black coffin, finished and done for,
With no longer any feelings and regrets and Memories of Albert
And no more blood pumping through the feeble veins
And no more heart beating away
As it had beaten for so many tiring years.
The coffin was placed upon a gun-carriage
And drawn along sadly and slowly by English sailors.

Noël Coward

Victoria had become a symbol in her own lifetime and the term 'Victorian', as well as denoting a period of history, came to stand for styles in furniture, architecture, painting, music and morality. Although Victoria was a constitutional monarch, her longevity and experience enhanced her personal power – she had, after all, survived sixteen different Prime Ministers.

THE HOUSE OF WINDSOR

King Edward VII, 1901–10

There will be bridge and booze 'till after three,
And, after that, a lot of them will grope
Along the corridors in *robes de nuit*,
Pyjamas, or some other kind of dope.

A sturdy matron will be sent to cope
With Lord —, who isn't 'quite the thing',
And give his wife the leisure to elope,
And Mrs James will entertain the King!

Hilaire Belloc

The new King had a lively appreciation of the sensual delights of the world. He smoked twelve large cigars and twenty cigarettes a day. Dinner for him could run to as many as twelve courses. He enjoyed grilled oysters and pheasant stuffed with snipe, all washed down with his favourite champagne. He had several mistresses and lady friends who looked after him during those weekend parties for which Edwardian high society was especially noted. Belloc's poem was never published and owes its survival to the memory of Vita Sackville-West. It dwells on the post-prandial pleasures of a weekend spent with Mrs Willie James at West Dean in Sussex; but Mrs Ronald Greville at Polesden Lacey could just as well have provided the pretext.

TWO PRIME MINISTERS

Balfour, 1902–5

The foundations of Philosophic Doubt
Are based on this single premiss:
'Shall we be able to get out
To Wimbledon in time for tennis?

Rudyard Kipling

Arthur James Balfour was renowned for his indecision, and the title of his first book, *A Defence of Philosophic Doubt*, expresses his whole attitude to life. He was also a keen tennis-player, which led someone to remark: 'His sliced forehand from the base line evoked in him gleams of pale happiness.' Kipling was far harder on him in his prose, describing him as 'arid, aloof, incurious, unthinking, unthanking, gelt'.

Asquith, 1908–16

Mr Asquith says in a manner sweet and calm:
Another little drink wouldn't do us any harm.

George Robey

Lord Oxford and Asquith, a Prime Minister in the Augustan style, was renowned for his drinking and earned the nickname 'Squiffy'. I remember my history master telling us that he had met Asquith at a dinner in Oxford in the 1920s. Brandy was brought round in glasses on a tray. In the time that it would have taken a student to pick a glass off the tray, Asquith snatched up one and drank it, then a second, which he poured into his coffee, and finally a third, to put beside his coffee.

EDWARDIAN IDYLLS

Henley Regatta, 1902

Underneath a light straw boater
In his pink Leander tie
Ev'ry ripple in the water caught the Captain in the eye.
O'er the plenitude of houseboats
Plop of punt-poles, creak of rowlocks,
Many a man of some distinction scanned the reach to Temple Island
As a south wind fluttered by,
Till it shifted, westward drifting, strings of pennants house-boat high,
Where unevenly the outline of the brick-warm town of Henley
Dominated by her church tower and the sheds of Brakspear's Brewery
Lay beneath a summer sky.
Plash of sculls! And pink of ices!
And the inn-yards full of ostlers, and the barrels running dry,
And the baskets of geraniums
Swinging over river-gardens
Led us to the flowering heart of England's willow-cooled July.

John Betjeman

After the long, hard slog to imperial greatness under Victoria, social life under Edward VII appears to have been relaxed, happy and indulgent, with great sporting festivals, idyllic country weekends, groaning tables and a general style of plush opulence. But this is only part of the picture. Elsewhere, we must take note of the industrial unrest that was leading to the growth of the Labour Party; of suffragette militancy; of bitter debate as the power of the House of Lords was broken; and of the increasing threat of civil war in Ireland. Yet the sense of a sunny glow over Edwardian England cannot be entirely effaced, and as late as January 1914 Lloyd George could be quoted by the *Daily Chronicle* as saying: 'Never has the sky been more perfectly blue.'

1905

from Haymaking

In the field sloping down,
Park-like, to where the willows showed the brook,
Haymakers rested. The tosser lay forsook
Out in the sun; and the long waggon stood
Without its team: it seemed it never would
Move from the shadow of that single yew.
The team, as still, until their task was due,
Beside the labourers enjoyed the shade
That three squat oaks mid-field together made
Upon a circle of grass and weed uncut,
And on the hollow, once a chalk-pit, but
Now brimmed with nut and elder-flower so clean.
The men leaned on their rakes, about to begin,
But still. And all were silent. All was old,
This morning time, with a great age untold,
Older than Clare and Cobbett, Morland and Crome,
Than, at the field's far edge, the farmer's home
A white house crouched at the foot of a great tree.

Edward Thomas

1910

THE DEATH OF EDWARD VII

from **The Dead King (Edward VII), 1910**

And since he was Master and Servant in all that we asked him,
We leaned hard on his wisdom in all things, knowing not how
we tasked him,
For on him each new day laid command, every tyrannous hour,
To confront, or confirm, or make smooth some dread issue of
power;
To deliver true judgement aright at the instant, unaided,
In the strict, level, ultimate phrase that allowed or dissuaded;
To foresee, to allay, to avert from us perils unnumbered,
To stand guard on our gates when he guessed that the
watchmen had slumbered;
To win time, to turn hate, to woo folly to service and, mightily
schooling
His strength to the use of his Nations, to rule as not ruling.

Rudyard Kipling

King George V, 1910–36

THE SUFFRAGETTES

In the Same Boat

Here's to the baby of five or fifteen,
    Here's to the widow of fifty,
Here's to the flaunting extravagant queen,
    And here's to the hussy that's thrifty –
Please to take note, they are in the same boat:
They have not a chance of recording the vote.

Here's to the lunatic, helpless and lost,
    Of wits – well, he simply has none, Sir –
Here's to the woman who lives by her brains
    And is treated as though she were one, Sir –
Please to take note, &c.

Here's to the criminal, lodged in the gaol,
    Voteless for what he has done, Sir –
Here's to the man with a dozen of votes,
    If a woman, he would not have one, Sir –
Please to take note, &c.

Here's to the lot of them, murderer, thief,
    Forger and lunatic too, Sir –
Infants, and those who get parish relief,
    And women, it's perfectly true, Sir –
Please to take note, &c.

H. Crawford

In 1903 Emmeline Pankhurst had formed the Woman's Social and Political Union to promote the cause of Votes for Women. The campaign was led and conducted by well-educated, well-dressed, middle-class women – which disconcerted police and politicians alike. Under their purple, white and green colours, they rallied and marched, storming Parliament and Downing Street, smashing shop windows, chaining themselves to railings, mobbing Asquith, attempting to dog-whip Churchill, and interrupting the meetings of Lloyd George who, on one such occasion, said: 'I see some rats have got in; let them squeal, it doesn't matter.' Many protesters were sent to prison, where they resorted to hunger strikes and were forcibly fed. One brave martyr, Emily Davison, threw herself in front of George V's horse at the Derby in 1913.

The Liberal Government wanted to find a positive solution, but was not willing to give in to militancy, which had begun to turn the country against female suffrage. Yet it was this movement that, together with the growing number of industrial strikes and the intractable problem of Ireland, helped to bring to an end the long Indian summer of Edwardian England. In December 1917 an Electoral Reform Bill was passed in the House of Commons by a large majority and this gave women over thirty the right to vote. In 1928 the age was lowered to twenty-one. It has become a commonplace to suggest that the role which women played in the First World War won them the vote, but Mrs Pankhurst and her two formidable daughters paved the way.

from The Female of the Species

When the Himalayan peasant meets the he-bear in his pride,
He shouts to scare the monster, who will often turn aside.
But the she-bear thus accosted rends the peasant tooth and nail.
For the female of the species is more deadly than the male.

*

Man, a bear in most relations – worm and savage otherwise, –
Man propounds negotiations, Man accepts the compromise.
Very rarely will he squarely push the logic of a fact
To its ultimate conclusion in unmitigated act.

Fear, or foolishness, impels him, ere he lay the wicked low,
To concede some form of trial even to his fiercest foe.
Mirth obscene diverts his anger – Doubt and Pity oft perplex
Him in dealing with an issue – to the scandal of The Sex!

But the Woman that God gave him, every fibre of her frame
Proves her launched for one sole issue, armed and engined for
the same;
And to serve that single issue, lest the generation fail,
The female of the species must be deadlier than the male.

*

So it comes that Man, the coward, when he gathers to confer
With his fellow-braves in council, dare not leave a place for her
Where, at war with Life and Conscience, he uplifts his erring
hands
To some God of Abstract Justice – which no woman
understands.

And Man knows it! Knows, moreover, that the Woman that
God gave him
Must command but may not govern – shall enthral but not
enslave him.
And *She* knows, because She warns him, and Her instincts
never fail,
That the Female of Her Species is more deadly than the Male.

Rudyard Kipling

Kipling had little sympathy with the Suffragettes and, when this poem was printed in the *Morning Post*, he fell out with his daughter over it. He should have known better, but perhaps the blustering, saloon-bar style of its argument springs from Kipling's own awkward awareness of the influence two women in particular – his mother and his wife – exerted over him.

1912

THE SINKING OF THE 'TITANIC'

The Convergence of the Twain

In a solitude of the sea
Deep from human vanity,
And the Pride of Life that planned her, stilly couches she.

Steel chambers, late the pyres
Of her salamandrine fires,
Cold currents thrid, and turn to rhythmic tidal lyres.

Over the mirrors meant
To glass the opulent
The sea-worm crawls – grotesque, slimed, dumb, indifferent.

Jewels in joy designed
To ravish the sensuous mind
Lie lightless, all their sparkles bleared and black and blind.

Dim moon-eyed fishes near
Gaze at the gilded gear
And query: 'What does this vaingloriousness down here?' . . .

Well: while was fashioning
This creature of cleaving wing,
The Immanent Will that stirs and urges everything

Prepared a sinister mate
For her – so gaily great –
A Shape of Ice, for the time far and dissociate.

And as the smart ship grew
In stature, grace, and hue,
In shadowy silent distance grew the Iceberg too.

Alien they seemed to be:
No mortal eye could see
The intimate welding of their later history,

Or sign that they were bent
By paths coincident
On being anon twin halves of one august event,

Till the Spinner of the Years
Said 'Now!' And each one hears,
And consummation comes, and jars two hemispheres.

Thomas Hardy

The *Titanic* was the grandest ship ever built. On her maiden voyage she struck an iceberg and sank with a loss of 1,513 lives. She had been the supreme achievement of Victorian engineering, proof positive of man's triumph over nature, and her tragic fate had a suitably Victorian ring to it: women and children were allowed into the lifeboats first, the band struck up as she sank, and that great hymn 'Nearer, My God, to Thee' was sung. Her loss marked the end of an era.

1912

THE MARCONI SCANDAL

Gehazi

Whence comest thou, Gehazi,
   So reverend to behold,
In scarlet and in ermines
   And chain of England's gold?
'From following after Naaman
   To tell him all is well,
Whereby my zeal hath made me
   A Judge in Israel.'

Well done, well done, Gehazi!
  Stretch forth thy ready hand.
Thou barely 'scaped from judgment,
  Take oath to judge the land
Unswayed by gift of money
  Or privy bribe, more base,
Of knowledge which is profit
  In any market-place.

Search out and probe, Gehazi,
  As thou of all canst try.
The truthful, well-weighed answer
  That tells the blacker lie –
The loud, uneasy virtue,
  The answer feigned at will,
To overbear a witness
  And make the Court keep still.

Take order now, Gehazi,
  That no man talk aside
In secret with his judges
  The while his case is tried.
Lest he should show them – reason
  To keep a matter hid,
And subtly lead the questions
  Away from what he did.

Thou mirror of uprightness,
  What ails thee at thy vows?
What means the risen whiteness
  Of the skin between thy brows?
The boils that shine and burrow,
  The sores that slough and bleed –

The leprosy of Naaman
  On thee and all thy seed?
Stand up, stand up, Gehazi,
  Draw close thy robe and go,
Gehazi, Judge in Israel,
  A leper white as snow!

Rudyard Kipling

Rumours had circulated that members of the Government, including Sir Rufus Isaacs, the Attorney General – the Gehazi of this poem – and Lloyd George, had bought shares in Marconi just before the issuing of a large government contract. Although those accused denied it and went to court to clear their names, they were obliged to confess that they had bought shares in the American Marconi company, if not the British one directly concerned. The Government was shaken, but not toppled. Yet feelings ran high, and Kipling expressed the mood of the time, in which a measure of anti-Semitism no doubt helped to fuel the general outrage, when he used the Biblical story of Naaman and Gehazi in this vituperative poem. As the servant of Elisha, Gehazi had dishonestly obtained a reward from Naaman, whom Elisha had cured of leprosy, and was punished by being cursed with the disease himself.

1914–18

THE GREAT WAR

Oh You Young Men

Awake, oh you young men of England,
For if, when your Country's in need,
You do not enlist in your thousands
You truly are cowards indeed.

Eric Blair (George Orwell), aged 11

MCMXIV

Those long uneven lines
Standing as patiently
As if they were stretched outside
The Oval or Villa Park,
The crowns of hats, the sun
On moustached archaic faces
Grinning as if it were all
An August Bank Holiday lark;

And the shut shops, the bleached
Established names on the sunblinds,
The farthings and sovereigns,
And dark-clothed children at play
Called after kings and queens,
The tin advertisements
For cocoa and twist, and the pubs
Wide open all day;

And the countryside not caring:
The place-names all hazed over
With flowering grasses, and fields
Shadowing Domesday lines;
Under wheat's restless silence;
The differently dressed servants
With tiny rooms in huge houses,
The dust behind limousines;

Never such innocence,
Never before or since,
As changed itself to past
Without a word – the men
Leaving the gardens tidy,
The thousands of marriages
Lasting a little while longer:
Never such innocence again.

Philip Larkin

1914

God heard the embattled nations sing and shout
'Gott strafe England!' and 'God save the King!'
God this, God that, and God the other thing –
'Good God', said God,
'I've got my work cut out.'

J. C. Squire

In 1914 the major powers in Europe went to war to contain the military ambitions of Germany. The cause was popular, as the poem by the future George Orwell indicates, and men flocked to the colours encouraged by the famous poster showing the pointing Kitchener and bearing the slogan 'Your Country Needs You'. After the first few months of swift and traditional fighting, prolonged trench warfare took over. Generals on both sides sacrificed men and equipment on a scale unmatched before or since as they attempted to break through the ranks of the enemy, although this often meant gaining no more than a few hundred yards. The whole world was gradually embroiled, with troops pouring in from India, Australia, New Zealand, and eventually America. It was a war that changed global history: kingdoms and empires disappeared, the Bolsheviks assumed power in Russia, and Germany's defeat made the ground fertile for Nazism. If the leaders of Europe in 1914 could have foreseen the state of the continent twenty years later, every one of them would have done all that was possible to avoid war. The catastrophe, however, produced some of the finest poetry of the twentieth century, and the poems can be left to speak for themselves.

The Soldier

If I should die, think only this of me:
That there's some corner of a foreign field
That is for ever England. There shall be
In that rich earth a richer dust concealed;
A dust whom England bore, shaped, made aware,
Gave once her flowers to love, her ways to roam;
A body of England's, breathing English air,
Washed by the rivers, blest by suns of home.

And think, this heart, all evil shed away,
A pulse in the eternal mind, no less
Gives somewhere back the thoughts by England given;
Her sights and sounds; dreams happy as her day;
And laughter, learnt of friends; and gentleness
In hearts at peace, under an English heaven.

Rupert Brooke

Dulce Et Decorum Est

Bent double, like old beggars under sacks,
Knock-kneed, coughing like hags, we cursed through sludge,
Till on the haunting flares we turned our backs,
And towards our distant rest began to trudge.
Men marched asleep. Many had lost their boots,
But limped on, blood-shod. All went lame, all blind;
Drunk with fatigue; deaf even to the hoots
Of gas-shells dropping softly behind.

Gas! Gas! Quick, boys! – An ecstasy of fumbling,
Fitting the clumsy helmets just in time,
But someone still was yelling out and stumbling
And floundering like a man in fire or lime. –
Dim through the misty panes and thick green light,
As under a green sea, I saw him drowning.

In all my dreams, before my helpless sight,
He plunges at me, guttering, choking, drowning.

If in some smothering dreams, you too could pace
Behind the wagon that we flung him in,
And watch the white eyes writhing in his face,
His hanging face, like a devil's sick of sin;
If you could hear, at every jolt, the blood
Come gargling from the froth-corrupted lungs,
Obscene as cancer, bitter as the cud
Of vile, incurable sores on innocent tongues, –
My friend, you would not tell with such high zest
To children ardent for some desperate glory,
The old Lie: Dulce et decorum est
Pro patria mori.

Wilfred Owen

The General

'Good-morning, good-morning!' the General said
When we met him last week on our way to the line.
Now the soldiers he smiled at are most of 'em dead,
And we're cursing his staff for incompetent swine.
'He's a cheery old card,' grunted Harry to Jack
As they slogged up to Arras with rifle and pack.

But he did for them both by his plan of attack.

Siegfried Sassoon

For the Fallen

(1914)

With proud thanksgiving, a mother for her children,
England mourns for her dead across the sea.
Flesh of her flesh they were, spirit of her spirit,
Fallen in the cause of the free.

Solemn the drums thrill: Death august and royal
Sings sorrow up into immortal spheres.
There is music in the midst of desolation
And a glory that shines upon our tears.

They went with songs to the battle, they were young,
Straight of limb, true of eye, steady and aglow.
They were staunch to the end against odds uncounted,
They fell with their faces to the foe.

They shall grow not old, as we that are left grow old:
Age shall not weary them, nor the years condemn.
At the going down of the sun and in the morning
We will remember them.

They mingle not with their laughing comrades again;
They sit no more at familiar tables of home;
They have no lot in our labour of the day-time;
They sleep beyond England's foam.

Laurence Binyon

from Hugh Selwyn Mauberley

IV

These fought in any case,
and some believing,
pro domo, in any case . . .

Some quick to arm,
some for adventure,
some from fear of weakness,
some from fear of censure,
some for love of slaughter, in imagination,
learning later . . .
some in fear, learning love of slaughter;

Died some, pro patria,
                    non 'dulce' non 'et decor' . . .
walked eye-deep in hell
believing in old men's lies, then unbelieving
came home, home to a lie,
home to many deceits,
home to old lies and new infamy;
usury age-old and age-thick
and liars in public places.

Daring as never before, wastage as never before.
Young blood and high blood,
fair cheeks, and fine bodies;

fortitude as never before

frankness as never before,
disillusions as never told in the old days,
hysterias, trench confessions,
laughter out of dead bellies.

V

There died a myriad,
And of the best, among them,
For an old bitch gone in the teeth,
For a botched civilization . . .

Ezra Pound

Elegy in a Country Churchyard

The men that worked for England
They have their graves at home:
And bees and birds of England
About the cross can roam.

But they that fought for England,
Following a falling star,
Alas, alas for England
They have their graves afar.

And they that rule in England,
In stately conclave met,
Alas, alas for England
They have no graves as yet.

G. K. Chesterton

Armistice Day, 1918

What's all this hubbub and yelling,
Commotion and scamper of feet,
With ear-splitting clatter of kettles and cans,
Wild laughter down Mafeking Street?

O, those are the kids whom we fought for
(You might think they'd been scoffing our rum)
With flags that they waved when we marched off to war
In the rapture of bugle and drum.

Now they'll hang Kaiser Bill from a lamp-post,
Von Tirpitz they'll hang from a tree . . .
We've been promised a 'Land Fit for Heroes' –
What heroes we heroes must be!

And the guns that we took from the Fritzes,
That we paid for with rivers of blood,
Look, they're hauling them down to Old Battersea Bridge
Where they'll topple them, souse, in the mud!

But there's old men and women in corners
With tears falling fast on their cheeks,
There's the armless and legless and sightless –
It's seldom that one of them speaks.

And there's flappers gone drunk and indecent
Their skirts kilted up to the thigh,
The constables lifting no hand in reproof
And the chaplain averting his eye . . .

When the days of rejoicing are over,
When the flags are stowed safely away,
They will dream of another wild 'War to End Wars'
And another wild Armistice day.

But the boys who were killed in the trenches,
Who fought with no rage and no rant,
We left them stretched out on their pallets of mud
Low down with the worm and the ant.

Robert Graves

Ode on the Death of Haig's Horse

I

Bury the Great Horse
With all clubdom's lamentation,
Let us bury the Great Horse
To the noise of the mourning of a horsey nation:
Mourning when their darlings fall,
Colonels carry the charger's pall,
And critics gather in smoke-room and stall.

II

Where shall we raise the statue they demand?
One in every home throughout the land.
Only thus shall all who saw him,
All who wrote long letters for him,
Recognize the work their fancy planned.

III

Set up the statue: dull and staid,
As fits an all too common jade,
Lo! our slow, slow decision's made,
And now the carping critics are dismayed
And now the public's piddling taste's displayed;
Another civic statue's made.

Douglas Garman

From the end of the First World War until his death in 1928, Field-Marshal Sir Douglas Haig, from 1915 Commander-in-Chief of British forces on the Western Front, was revered by the nation. Parliament voted him £100,000, he received the Order of Merit, and the ancestral home of the Haigs at Bemersyde was purchased by public subscription and presented to him as a gift. He refused a viscountcy in 1918 and the following year got an earldom. Haig's reputation was first questioned by Lloyd George in his memoirs of the war, and posterity has come to treat him harshly. But to a large extent he had only himself to blame, for, as Lord Beaverbrook said: 'With the publication of his Private Papers in 1952 he committed suicide twenty-five years after his death.' Garman's poem is a parody of Tennyson on Wellington.

SOME PRIME MINISTERS OF THE TWENTIETH CENTURY

David Lloyd George, PM 1916–22

Count not his broken pledges as a crime
He MEANT them, HOW he meant them – at the time.

Kensal Green

Andrew Bonar Law, PM 1922–3

Of all the politicians I ever saw
The least significant was Bonar Law.
Unless it was MacDonald, by the way:
Or Baldwin – it's impossible to say.

Hilaire Belloc

Stanley Baldwin, PM 1923–4, 1924–9, 1935–7

His fame endures; we shall not quite forget
The name of Baldwin till we're out of debt.

Kensal Green

Winston Churchill, PM 1940–5, 1951–5

A sad day this for Alexander
And many another dead commander.
Jealousy's rife in heroes' hall –
Winston Churchill has bluffed them all.

Kensal Green

The lines on Churchill were written in 1927.

the 1920s

A LAND FIT FOR HEROES

Refutation of the Only Too Prevalent Slander that Parliamentary Leaders are Indifferent to the Strict Fulfilment of their Promises and the Preservation of their Reputation for Veracity

They said (when they had dined at Ciro's)
The land would soon be fit for heroes;
And now they've managed to ensure it,
For only heroes could endure it.

G. K. Chesterton

from Cowardice

Do you remember, in the Twenties,
the songs we used to sing,
reading our Westermans and Hentys,
before the days of Bing?
Gramophones were very sharp and tinny,
we could sit there and applaud
shows with stars like Laddie, Sonnie, Binnie,
Jack and Jessie, June and Claude.
We had no truck with opus numbers
or anything called Art –
and fox-trots (long before the rumbas)
gave us our happy start. . . .

This was our taste/ of the future,
we embraced/ that decade,
gleaming in glamour, with our hope not betrayed.
There lay Love – which our ten-year-old scoffing
felt above (girls with men!) – in the offing.

The sight of women set us giggling,
their bottoms broad and fat,
the Charleston and that sexy wriggling,
their bosoms not so flat,
as they jumped and bumped in that gay chorus –
though we watched the dance with scorn,
this was Life cavorting there before us,
and the reason we were born.
Of this we were just dimly conscious,
uneasily we'd sit
and judge, severe, like monks with tonsures –
soon to be part of it. . . .

It was all necks/ with arms round them,
grown-up sex/ on display –
a mystery coming our way.
We weren't too frightened,
we felt partly enlightened
in that faced-by-the-future far decade.

Gavin Ewart

The younger generation of the 1920s wanted to forget the Great War as soon as possible. The war had helped to accelerate social change. In fashion, frock coats were ousted by lounge suits, long skirts by short, and sometimes very short, ones. The radio supplanted the gramophone and the whole country went to the cinema – the first comprehensively popular art form. To be dashing and uninhibited was the thing: ladies smoked in public and contraception was no longer taboo. The chrome and sharp angles of Art Deco provided the blazonry of the times.

1926

THE GENERAL STRIKE

May 4th, 1926

May 4th, 1926 – morning,
East End classroom crowded
With youth and feeling unconfined,
Crimson ties proclaiming oneness
With workers – red flags fluttering
In the corridors of the mind.
To bull-like masters red rags,
Well-worn beyond those cockcrow years,
Beyond betrayals and disasters;
Remembrance that the battering shower
Of time, its storms can never nip.
Among her festivals and bitter tears
Comes home this memory
Like a well-laden, triumphant ship.

Bill Foot

On 1 May 1926, after a prolonged dispute over a miners' wage claim, to which colliery owners had responded by offering a reduction in wages, there was a lock-out. The General Council of the Trade Unions declared a national strike from 3 May, and this was widely supported. Stanley Baldwin, Prime Minister of the day, urged Winston Churchill to bring out a daily paper under the name of the *British Gazette*, in which he called for 'unconditional surrender'. Many people volunteered to keep basic services going. Throughout all this, George V played a moderating role and, when the strike was called off unconditionally, Baldwin resisted any vindictive inclination to turn the affair into a class-war victory.

THE MINERS ON STRIKE

What will you do with your shovel, Dai,
And your pick and your sledge and your spike,
And what will you do with your leisure, man,
Now that you're out on strike?

What will you do for your butter, Dai,
And your bread and your cheese and your fags,
And how will you pay for a dress for the wife,
And shall your children go in rags?

You have been, in your time, a hero, Dai,
And they wrote of your pluck in the press,
And now you have fallen on evil days,
And who will be there to bless?

And how will you stand with your honesty, Dai,
When the land is full of lies,
And how will you curb your anger, man,
When your natural patience dies?

O what will you dream on the mountains, Dai,
When you walk in the summer day,
And gaze on the derelict valleys below,
And the mountains farther away?

And how will the heart within you, Dai,
Respond to the distant sea,
And the dream that is born in the blaze of the sun,
And the vision of victory?

Idris Davies

1929

THE DEPRESSION

Unemployed

Moving through the silent crowd
Who stand behind dull cigarettes,
These men who idle in the road,
I have the sense of falling light.

They lounge at corners of the street
And greet friends with a shrug of shoulder
And turn their empty pockets out,
The cynical gestures of the poor.

Now they've no work, like better men
Who sit at desks and take much pay
They sleep long nights and rise at ten
To watch the hours that drain away.

I'm jealous of the weeping hours
They stare through with such hungry eyes
I'm haunted by these images,
I'm haunted by their emptiness.

Stephen Spender

The 1914–18 war effort had required a strict direction of resources and it proved difficult for many companies, particularly those in heavy engineering, to adapt to the needs of peacetime. The post-war boom soon petered out and unemployment rose to one million, 12 per cent of the British work force. In 1929, particularly as a result of the Wall Street Crash and the collapse of financial institutions in America, unemployment rose sharply to three million. Everyone was at a loss. The Coalition Government under the Labour leader, Ramsay MacDonald, wanted to cut benefits; the influential economist John Maynard Keynes advocated public works; others urged protection. Neville Chamberlain, as Chancellor of the Exchequer, nursed the economy back to health and by 1937 unemployment had been cut by half.

RAMSAY MACDONALD

Allelauder

Ramsay MacDonald to Sir Harry Lauder:
'For fifty years you have been making us happy, and the art you have employed has not had a tinge of the degrading in it. You have dealt with the great fundamental human simplicities, and have taught us to find joy and inspiration in qualities and feelings which belong to the good things in human life.'

The curly nibby has put to flight
The legions of despair.
A flap of Sir Harry Lauder's kilt
And our woes are no longer there.
To God, our help in ages past,
There is no need to pray
When the softest of the family
Presents an easier way.
Most of us may lack the cash
To hear Lauder in person – yet
If we're too poor for the music halls,
Through gramophone disc or radio set,
The little man with the enlarged heart
Can make us wholly forget
All the horrors of war and peace
With which mankind's beset,
Every so-called crisis disappears
– *'He's made us happy for fifty years!'*
Honour to Ramsay MacDonald who
Sees and proclaims this fact,
Knowing that pawky patter does more
Than an Ottawa or O-to-Hell pact.
Dire necessity and foul disease
Are vanquished by a variety act.
Unemployment, poverty, slums
Can be cured by a fatuous song
(If Lauder receives a suitable fee!) –
Then the Government policy's wrong.
Abolish all social services,

Hand Lauder the dough instead,
Give all other public men the sack
And put him alone at the head.
With a waggle here and a wiggle there
The world will soon be rid
Of all its troubles and doubts and fears
– *Happy for good as for fifty years!*
– But even his stupendous powers
May cure life's every loss and want
Save his or MacDonald's brainlessness,
Or stop their ghastly cant.
Oh, Lauder is bad enough, but we
Might have been happier still
If MacDonald every now and again
Hadn't figured too on the bill
– The cross-talk duo, it appears,
Toplining these fifty filthy years.

Hugh MacDiarmid

MacDiarmid kills two birds with one stone. It seems that there was nothing he hated more than the stage Scotsman, whether impersonated by Harry Lauder in the music-hall, or by Ramsay MacDonald at the despatch box of the House of Commons. MacDonald was Prime Minister in 1924, and again from 1929 to 1931. From 1931 to 1935, as leader of the minority party, he headed a coalition government – an act of apostasy for which the Labour Party has never forgiven him. There is no statue in the House of Commons to honour Labour's first PM.

1936

The Death of King George V

'New King arrives in his capital by air . . .'
Daily Newspaper

Spirits of well-shot woodcock, partridge, snipe
   Flutter and bear him up the Norfolk sky:
In that red house in a red mahogany book-case
   The stamp collection waits with mounts long dry.

The big blue eyes are shut which saw wrong clothing
   And favourite fields and coverts from a horse;
Old men in country houses hear clocks ticking
   Over thick carpets with a deadened force;

Old men who never cheated, never doubted,
   Communicated monthly, sit and stare
At the new suburb stretched beyond the run-way
   Where a young man lands hatless from the air.

John Betjeman

At Sandringham on the evening of 20 January 1936 the King's doctor, Lord Dawson of Penn, wrote this last bulletin on a menu card: 'The King's life is moving peacefully to its close.' Three hours later George V was dead. It was only in 1986 that the notes of Dawson were published to reveal that he had administered euthanasia. 'At about 11 o'clock', Dawson wrote, 'it was evident that the last stage might endure for many hours unknown to the patient, but little comporting with that dignity and serenity which he so richly merited and which demanded a brief final scene . . . I therefore decided myself to determine the end and injected myself morphia gr. ¾ and shortly afterwards cocaine gr. 1 into the distended jugular vein.' This meant that the King's death would first be announced 'in the morning papers rather than the less appropriate field of the evening journals'. Dawson had been the doctor of Edward VII and also of Lloyd George, who had insisted on his being made a peer in 1920. He had saved the King's life in 1928, but his treatment during the convalescence led to a good deal of professional jealousy and this piece of doggerel:

Lord Dawson of Penn
Has killed lots of men.
So that's why we sing
God save the King.

King Edward VIII, 1936

The hand that blew the sacred fire has failed,
Laid down the burden in the hour of need,
So brave begun but flinching in the deed.
Nor Mary's power nor Baldwin's word availed,
To curb the beating heart by love assailed.
Vainly did Delhi, Canberra, Capetown plead
The Empire's ruler flouts the Empire's creed
By princes, prelates, people sore bewailed
The triple pillars of the Empire shake
A shock of horror passes o'er the land.
The greatest throne in all the world forsake
To take a favour from a woman's hand?
The hallowed pleasures of a kingly life
Abandoned for a transatlantic wife.

Douglas Reed

This was the shortest reign in English history, if one overlooks that of Lady Jane Grey. Edward had fallen in love with Wallis Simpson, an American, who had been married twice before and was about to divorce her second husband. As head of the Church of England, Edward could not marry Mrs Simpson and remain on the throne. The country was divided. Beaverbook and Churchill supported the King, while Baldwin and Archbishop Lang forced him to the realization that he had to make a choice. He chose to abdicate.

My Lord Archbishop, what a scold you are,
And when a man is down, how bold you are,
Of Christian charity how scant you are
You auld Lang Swine, how full of cant you are!

Anonymous

King George VI, 1936–52

THE BLACKSHIRTS

October 1936

We stood at Gardiner's Corner,
We stood and watched the crowds,
We stood at Gardiner's Corner,
Firm, solid, voices loud.

Came the marching of the blackshirts,
Came the pounding of their feet,
Came the sound of ruffians marching
Where the five roads meet.

We thought of many refugees
Fleeing from the Fascist hordes,
The maimed, the sick,
The young, the old,
Those who had fought the Fascist lords.

So we stopped them there at Gardiner's,
We fought and won our way.
We fought the baton charges,
No Fascist passed that day!

Milly Harris

About 3,000 black-shirted Fascists, under the leadership of Oswald Mosley, were to have marched through the East End of London on 4 October 1936 – a calculated affront to its large Jewish population. The residents, however, blocked the roads at Gardiner's Corner and Cable Street, and Mosley was ignominiously forced to lead his men elsewhere. The following poem, written in the early years of the Second World War, shows the strength of Jewish identification with that part of London.

Whitechapel in Britain

Pumbedita, Cordova, Cracow, Amsterdam,
Vilna, Lublin, Berditchev and Volozhin,
Your names will always be sacred,
Places where Jews have been.

And sacred is Whitechapel,
It is numbered with our Jewish towns.
Holy, holy, holy
Are your bombed stones.

If we ever have to leave Whitechapel,
As other Jewish towns were left,
Its soul will remain a part of us,
Woven into us, woof and weft.

Avram Stencl

In 1938 the Conservative Prime Minister, Neville Chamberlain, came to terms with Adolf Hitler over the German leader's provocative seizing of the Sudetenland. Chamberlain flew back from Munich with the confident boast that he had secured 'peace in our time'. He was the hero of the hour, and all the press supported him, with the exception of the left-wing Sunday newspaper *Reynolds' News*. Duff Cooper was the only Cabinet minister to resign and only thirty Conservative MPs abstained from voting for the agreement. Six months before Munich, Hilaire Belloc had told Duff Cooper that Chamberlain had written this poem:

Dear Czecho-Slovakia,
I don't think they'll attack yer,
But I'm not going to back yer.

1938

THE MUNICH AGREEMENT

from **Autumn Journal**

And the next day begins
  Again with alarm and anxious
Listening to bulletins
  From distant, measured voices
Arguing for peace
  While the zero hour approaches,
While the eagles gather and the petrol and oil and grease
  Have all been applied and the vultures back the eagles.
But once again
  The crisis is put off and things look better
And we feel negotiation is not vain –
  Save my skin and damn my conscience.
And negotiation wins,
  If you can call it winning,
And here we are – just as before – safe in our skins;
  Glory to God for Munich.
And stocks go up and wrecks
  Are salved and politicians' reputations
Go up like Jack-on-the-Beanstalk; only the Czechs
  Go down and without fighting.

Louis MacNeice

England, Autumn 1938

Plush bees above a bed of dahlias;
  Leisurely, timeless garden teas;
Brown bread and honey; scent of mowing;
  The still green light below tall trees.

The ancient custom of deception;
  A Press that seldom stoops to lies –
Merely suppresses truth and twists it,
  Blandly corrupt and slyly wise.

The Common Man; his mask of laughter;
  His back-chat while the roof falls in;
Minorities' long losing battles
  Fought that the sons of sons may win.

The politician's inward snigger
  (Big business on the private phone);
The knack of sitting snug on fences;
  The double face of flesh and stone.

Grape-bloom of distant woods at dusk;
  Storm-crown on Glaramara's head;
The fire-rose over London night;
  An old plough rusting autumn-red.

The 'incurruptible policeman'
  Gaoling the whore whose bribe's run out,
Guarding the rich against the poor man,
  Guarding the Settled Gods from doubt.

The generous smile of music-halls,
  Bars and bank-holidays and queues;
The private peace of public foes;
  The truce of pipe and football news.

The smile of privilege exultant;
  Smile at the 'bloody Red' defeated;
Smile at the striker starved and broken;
  Smile at the 'dirty nigger' cheated.

The old hereditary craftsman;
  The incommunicable skill;
The pride in long-loved tools, refusal
  To do the set job quick or ill.

The greater artist mocked, misflattered;
  The lesser forming clique and team,
Or crouching in his narrow corner,
  Narcissus with his secret dream.

England of rebels – Blake and Shelley;
  England where freedom's sometimes won,
Where Jew and Negro needn't fear yet
  Lynch-law and pogrom, whip and gun.

England of cant and smug discretion;
  England of wagecut-sweatshop-knight,
Of sportsman-churchman-slum-exploiter,
  Of puritan grown sour with spite.

England of clever fool, mad genius,
  Timorous lion and arrogant sheep,
Half-hearted snob and shamefaced bully,
  Of hands that wake and eyes that sleep . . .
England the snail that's shod with lightning . . .
  Shall we laugh or shall we weep?

A. S. J. Tessimond

A LOW DISHONEST DECADE

from **September 1, 1939**

I sit in one of the dives
On Fifty-Second Street
Uncertain and afraid
As the clever hopes expire
Of a low dishonest decade:
Waves of anger and fear
Circulate over the bright
And darkened lands of the earth,
Obsessing our private lives;
The unmentionable odour of death
Offends the September night.

Accurate scholarship can
Unearth the whole offence
From Luther until now
That has driven a culture mad,
Find what occurred at Linz,
What huge imago made
A psychopathic god:
I and the public know
What all schoolchildren learn,
Those to whom evil is done
Do evil in return.

Exiled Thucydides knew
All that a speech can say
About Democracy,
And what dictators do,
The elderly rubbish they talk,
To an apathetic grave;

Analysed all in his book,
The enlightenment driven away,
The habit-forming pain,
Mismanagement and grief:
We must suffer them all again.

*

All I have is a voice
To undo the folded lie,
The romantic lie in the brain
Of the sensual man-in-the-street
And the lie of Authority
Whose buildings grope the sky:
There is no such thing as the State
And no one exists alone;
Hunger allows no choice
To the citizen or the police;
We must love one another or die.

Defenceless under the night
Our world in stupor lies;
Yet, dotted everywhere,
Ironic points of light
Flash out wherever the Just
Exchange their messages:
May I, composed like them
Of Eros and of dust,
Beleaguered by the same
Negation and despair,
Show an affirming flame.

W. H. Auden

1939–45

THE SECOND WORLD WAR

By 1939, attempts to check Hitler's plans of expansion had led nowhere. In August of that year Russia and Germany signed a neutrality pact, both hoping to seize for themselves large parts of Poland; and on 1 September Germany invaded Poland itself. Reluctantly yielding to pressure from a hostile House of Commons – from the Labour Party under its acting leader Arthur Greenwood, and from his own Cabinet – Chamberlain issued an ultimatum demanding German withdrawal by midnight on 2 September. On the following day, when it was clear that this had been ignored, he declared that Britain was at war. It was a justified war, as the Nazi regime in Germany was one of the worst and most cruel tyrannies the world had ever seen.

After the fall of France in June 1940, Britain stood alone in opposing the German offensive. Churchill had by then succeeded Chamberlain as Prime Minister and, in prose as memorable as any poetry, choosing 18 June, the anniversary of the battle of Waterloo, as a suitable moment, he addressed the nation in a speech which included the sentence: 'Let us therefore brace ourselves to our duties, and so bear ourselves that, if the British Empire and its Commonwealth last for a thousand years, men will still say, "This was their finest hour".'

In 1941 Hitler made the decisive mistake of invading Russia, and when the Japanese destroyed an American fleet in Pearl Harbor it became a real world war. From it emerged two pre-eminent global powers, Russia and America. Germany itself was divided in two, and the states of Eastern Europe became Russian satellites. Britain had won a famous victory, but post-war adjustment to a less dominant position in the world was to prove painful.

1940

In Westminster Abbey

Let me take this other glove off
As the *vox humana* swells,
And the beauteous fields of Eden
Bask beneath the Abbey bells.
Here, where England's statesmen lie,
Listen to a lady's cry.

Gracious Lord, oh bomb the Germans.
Spare their women for Thy Sake.
And if that is not too easy
We will pardon Thy Mistake.
But, gracious Lord, whate'er shall be,
Don't let anyone bomb me.

Keep our Empire undismembered
Guide our Forces by Thy Hand,
Gallant blacks from far Jamaica,
Honduras and Togoland;
Protect them Lord in all their fights,
And, even more, protect the whites.

Think of what our Nation stands for,
Books from Boots' and country lanes,
Free speech, free passes, class distinction,
Democracy and proper drains.
Lord, put beneath Thy special care
One-eighty-nine Cadogan Square.

Although dear Lord I am a sinner,
I have done no major crime;
Now I'll come to Evening Service
Whensoever I have the time.
So, Lord, reserve for me a crown;
And do not let my shares go down.

I will labour for Thy Kingdom,
   Help our lads to win the war,
Send white feathers to the cowards
   Join the Women's Army Corps,
Then wash the Steps around Thy Throne
In the Eternal Safety Zone.

Now I feel a little better,
   What a treat to hear Thy Word,
Where the bones of leading statesmen,
   Have so often been interr'd.
And now, dear Lord, I cannot wait
Because I have a luncheon date.

John Betjeman

THE RETREAT FROM DUNKIRK

That night we blew our guns. We placed a shell
Fuze downwards in each muzzle. Then we put
Another in the breech, secured a wire
Fast to the firing lever, crouched, and pulled.
It sounded like a cry of agony,
The crash and clang of splitting, tempered steel.
Thus did our guns, our treasured colours, pass;
And we were left bewildered, weaponless,
And rose and marched, our faces to the sea.

We formed in line beside the water's edge.
The little waves made oddly home-like sounds,
Breaking in half-seen surf upon the strand.
The night was full of noise; the whistling thud
The shells made in the sand, and pattering stones;
The cries cut short, the shouts of units' names;
The crack of distant shots, and bren gun fire;
The sudden clattering crash of masonry.
Steadily, all the time, the marching tramp
Of feet passed by along the shell-torn road,
Under the growling thunder of the guns.

The major said 'The boats cannot get in,
'There is no depth of water. Follow me.'
And so we followed, wading in our ranks
Into the blackness of the sea. And there,
Lit by the burning oil across the swell,
We stood and waited for the unseen boats.

Oars in the darkness, rowlocks, shadowy shapes
Of boats that searched. We heard a seaman's hail.
Then we swam out, and struggled with our gear,
Clutching the looming gunwales. Strong hands pulled,
And we were in and heaving with the rest,
Until at last they turned. The dark oars dipped,
The laden craft crept slowly out to sea,
To where in silence lay the English ships.

B. G. Bonallack

On 10 May 1940 the allied armies advanced into German-occupied Holland, but within five days the Dutch had surrendered and German troops swept through Northern France as far as the outskirts of Paris. The British army of ten divisions had been cut off by this advance and fell back to the coast. The Germans halted their attack on the British on 23 May, allowing an opportunity for evacuation from the port of Dunkirk. On 27 May the British fleet began to pick men up from the beaches, helped by an enormous flotilla of private boats – pleasure steamers, ferries, fishing vessels and so on. In all, 860 boats were able to rescue 338,226 men, 139,000 of them French. Most equipment had been sunk and 474 planes were lost. In immediate military terms, it was a great disaster, but it saved Britain from an even greater one. In his report to the House of Commons on 4 June, Churchill declared: 'We shall defend our Island whatever the cost may be. We shall fight on the beaches, we shall fight on the landing grounds, we shall fight in the fields and in the streets, we shall fight in the hills; we shall never surrender, and even if, which I do not for a moment believe, this Island or a large part of it were subjugated and starving, then our Empire beyond the seas, armed and guarded by the British fleet, would carry on the struggle, until, in God's good time, the New World, with all its power and might, steps forth to the rescue and liberation of the Old.'

THE BATTLE OF BRITAIN

For Johnny

Do not despair
For Johnny-head-in-air;
He sleeps as sound
As Johnny underground.

Fetch out no shroud
For Johnny-in-the-cloud;
And keep your tears
For him in after years.

Better by far
For Johnny-the-bright-star,
To keep your head,
And see his children fed.

John Pudney

After Dunkirk, Hitler prepared to invade Britain. He started by launching Goering's Luftwaffe on a campaign of bombing raids. British pilots, mostly flying Spitfires, took off from the small airfields of southern and eastern England and succeeded in destroying many of the German bombers. In August the Luftwaffe came close to wiping out the airfields of Kent, but on 7 September it switched its attack to London. Dowding's fighter-pilots brought down 1,733 German planes, while the RAF lost 915. In spite of such losses, by September it possessed as many planes as it had had in the previous spring, which says much for the work of Lord Beaverbrook as Minister of Aircraft Production. The bravery of these pilots saved Britain and on 17 September Hitler postponed his invasion. Churchill reported to the House of Commons: 'Never in the field of human conflict was so much owed by so many to so few.' The architect of the victory, Dowding, was removed from his command in November, Churchill having found him too cautious, but history has accorded him due honours.

THE BLITZ

London, 1940

After fourteen hours clearing they came to him
Under the twisted girders and the rubble.
They would not let me see his face.
Now I sit shiftlessly on the tube platforms
Or huddle, a little tipsy, in brick-built shelters.
I can see with an indifferent eye
The red glare over by the docks and hear
Impassively the bomb-thuds in the distance.

For me, a man with not many interests
And no pretensions to fame, that was my world,
My son of fifteen, my only concrete achievement,
Whom they could not protect. Stepping aside
From the Great Crusade, I will play the idiot's part.
You, if you like, may wave your fists and crash
On the wrong doorsteps brash retaliation.

Frank Thompson

On 7 September Goering assumed personal command of the German air offensive and directed his planes against London, which was bombed for fifty-seven consecutive nights. Each night 220 planes dropped incendiary as well as explosive bombs, causing widespread damage. The House of Commons was destroyed, Buckingham Palace was hit, and 30,000 civilians were killed. Londoners slept on the platforms of Underground stations, sandbags were piled around windows, and I remember spending the night under our stairs, which was considered the safest place in the house, and on some occasions being taken out to an air-raid shelter. Other cities besides London were also attacked: Coventry lost 1,236 civilians, Birmingham 2,162, Bristol 1,159, Sheffield 624, and Manchester 1,005. On 29 December the great onslaught on the City of London destroyed eight Wren churches and almost St Paul's Cathedral itself. George VI remained in London throughout the Blitz, as did Churchill, and their example helped stiffen the morale of the people.

Naming Of Parts

Today we have naming of parts. Yesterday,
We had daily cleaning. And tomorrow morning,
We shall have what to do after firing. But today,
Today we have naming of parts. Japonica
Glistens like coral in all of the neighbouring gardens,
  And today we have naming of parts.

This is the lower sling swivel. And this
Is the upper sling swivel, whose use you will see,
When you are given your slings. And this is the piling swivel,
Which in your case you have not got. The branches
Hold in the gardens their silent, eloquent gestures,
  Which in our case we have not got.

This is the safety-catch, which is always released
With an easy flick of the thumb. And please do not let me
See anyone using his finger. You can do it quite easy
If you have any strength in your thumb. The blossoms
Are fragile and motionless, never letting anyone see
  Any of them using their finger.

And this you can see is the bolt. The purpose of this
Is to open the breech, as you see. We can slide it
Rapidly backwards and forwards: we call this
Easing the spring. And rapidly backwards and forwards
The early bees are assaulting and fumbling the flowers:
  They call it easing the Spring.

They call it easing the Spring: it is perfectly easy
If you have any strength in your thumb: like the bolt,
And the breech, and the cocking-piece, and the point of balance,
Which in our case we have not got; and the almond-blossom
Silent in all of the gardens and the bees going backwards and
    forwards,
  For today we have naming of parts.

Henry Reed

1940–2

THE WAR IN THE WESTERN DESERT

Vergissmeinnicht

Three weeks gone and the combatants gone
returning over the nightmare ground
we found the place again, and found
the soldier sprawling in the sun.

The frowning barrel of his gun
overshadowing. As we came on
that day, he hit my tank with one
like the entry of a demon.

Look. Here in the gunpit spoil
the dishonoured picture of his girl
who has put: *Steffi. Vergissmeinnicht*
in a copybook gothic script.

We see him almost with content,
abased, and seeming to have paid
and mocked at by his own equipment
that's hard and good when he's decayed.

But she would weep to see today
how on his skin the swart flies move;
the dust upon the paper eye
and the burst stomach like a cave.

For here the lover and killer are mingled
who had one body and one heart.
And death who had the soldier singled
has done the lover mortal hurt.

Keith Douglas

Britain had a large army in Egypt and in 1940 won spectacular victories when it pushed Germany's Italian allies out of most of modern-day Libya. Germany came to Italy's help and their armies were brilliantly led by Rommel, the 'Desert Fox'. There were wide-ranging battles involving armoured tanks and infantry – just the sort of battles that soldiers of the time had been trained to fight. Rommel pushed the British troops back and in June 1942 Tobruk, on the borders of Egypt, fell to his advance. Montgomery was appointed to command the 8th Army, as Churchill had begun to despair of the defensive strategies of Wavell and Auchinleck. He proved a match for Rommel. He was a great field commander and a charismatic leader who soon won the devotion of his troops. Rommel was forced to evacuate North Africa and his retreat took him through Sicily and Italy.

The German title of Keith Douglas's poem means 'forget-me-not'.

1945

THE END OF THE WAR IN EUROPE

Mr Churchill

Five years of toil and blood and tears and sweat;
  Five years of faith and prophecy and plan!
He spoke our mind before our mind was set;
  He saw our deeds before our deeds began.
He rode the hurricane as none did yet;
  Our Finest Hour revealed our Finest Man.

A. P. Herbert

Germany's surrender on 8 May 1945 was celebrated with a thanksgiving service at St Margaret's, Westminster, and Churchill appeared on the balcony of Buckingham Palace to greet the crowds that had gathered outside. All the Conservative ministers in the coalition government agreed on an early election, so as to capitalize on their leader's great popularity. The result after polling was a huge Labour majority of 180 seats with 47.9 per cent of the popular vote. The nation preserved too many memories of how the Tories had acted in the thirties, and servicemen and their families wanted the assurance of homes, jobs and social security, for which Labour made the more convincing case.

VJ DAY

The Morning After

The fire left to itself might smoulder weeks.
Phone cables melt. Paint peels from off back gates.
Kitchen windows crack; the whole street reeks
of horsehair blazing. Still it celebrates.

Though people weep, their tears dry from the heat.
Faces flush with flame, beer, sheer relief
and such a sense of celebration in our street
for me it still means joy though banked with grief.

And that, now clouded, sense of public joy
with war-worn adults wild in their loud fling
has never come again since as a boy
I saw Leeds people dance and heard them sing.

There's still that dark, scorched circle on the road.
The morning after kids like me helped spray
hissing upholstery spring-wire that still glowed
and cobbles boiling with black gas-tar for VJ.

Tony Harrison

America dropped two atom bombs on Japan – one at Hiroshima on 8 August, and the other at Nagasaki on 29 August. Four days later Japan surrendered and that ended the war. There were parties and street celebrations all over Britain, and I can remember attending a huge bonfire party in Newport which local residents had quickly organized.

1945–51

THE PREMIERSHIP OF CLEMENT ATTLEE

Few thought he was even a starter;
There were many who thought themselves smarter;
But he ended PM,
CH and OM,
An Earl and a Knight of the Garter.

Clement Attlee

from Lest Cowards Flinch

1945

'Though cowards flinch,' the Labour Party trolled,
  'The people's scarlet standard we will raise!'
The Commons blushed beneath that sanguine fold,
  Flag of the revolutionary phase;
The Tories knew for whom the death-bell tolled,
  It tolled for them in Labour's *Marseillaise*,
And in the beat of that triumphant march
Heard tumbrils rumbling up to Marble Arch.

Grim was it in that dawn to be alive,
  Except to those who like their mornings bloody,
The ship of State headlong was seen to dive
  Engulfed in depths unutterly muddy,
As *Jacobins*, like swarms that leave the hive,
  Belched forth from foundry, factory and study,
A cut-throat crew of howling demagogues,
Leading hereditary underdogs.

1947

Two years of Parliamentary civility
  Abate the class, if not the Party, feud;
No Labour Member lacks respectability,
  Although his social background may be rude,
While several have a title to gentility
  Such as the Tory ranks might not exclude,
And manual labourers, if fairly prominent,
On the Front Bench at least are not predominant.

Both birth and intellect are there displayed;
  The Premier is impeccably Oxonian,
A younger son conducts the Board of Trade,
  The Chancellor's a perfect Old Etonian,
The Foreign Secretary, though self-made,
  Is quite magnificently Palmerstonian;
If such as these are Labour mediocrities,
Where is the Tory Cicero, or Socrates?

Sagittarius

In July 1945 the British electorate decisively snubbed its wartime leader, Churchill, by returning 393 Socialist MPs and only 213 Conservatives. Consoled by his wife, Clementine, that the defeat could be interpreted as a blessing disguise, Churchill retorted that the disguise was perfect. Under Attlee, the Socialist Government nationalized the Bank of England and several major industries, and it set up the National Health Service. Its achievements marked the high tide of Socialism in Britain. On the first day of the new Parliament, the Socialist MPs rose and sang 'The Red Flag'. Less than half of their number would have called themselves working-class, and forty-six had been educated at either Oxford or Cambridge.

Sagittarius was the *nom de plume* of the prolific topical poet, Olga Katzin Miller.

1947

THE END OF THE EMPIRE

Partition

Unbiased at least he was when he arrived on his mission.
Having never set eyes on this land he was called to partition
Between two peoples fanatically at odds,
With their different diets and incompatible gods.
'Time,' they had briefed him in London, 'is short. It's too late
For mutual reconciliation or rational debate;
The only solution now lies in separation.
The Viceroy thinks, as you see from his letter,
That the less you are seen in his company the better.
So we've arranged to provide you with other accommodation.
We can give you four judges, two Moslem and two Hindu,
To consult with, but the final decision must rest with you.'

Shut up in a lonely mansion, with police night and day
Patrolling the gardens to keep assassins away,
He got down to work, to the task of settling the fate
Of millions. The maps at his disposal were out of date
And the Census Returns almost certainly incorrect.
But there was no time to check them, no time to inspect
Contested areas. The weather was frightfully hot.
And a bout of dysentery kept him constantly on the trot.
But in seven weeks it was done, the frontiers decided,
A continent for better or worse divided.

The next day he sailed for England, where he quickly forged
The case, as a good lawyer must. Return he would not.
Afraid, as he told his Club, that he might get shot.

W. H. Auden

I Wonder What Happened to Him

The India that one read about
And may have been misled about
In one respect has kept itself intact.
Though 'Pukka Sahib' traditions may have cracked
And thinned
The good old Indian army's still a fact.
That famous monumental man
The Officer and Gentleman
Still lives and breathes and functions from Bombay to
Kathmandu.
At any moment one can glimpse
Matured or embryonic 'Blimps'
Vivaciously speculating as to what became of who.
Though Eastern sounds may fascinate your ear
When West meets West you're always sure to hear –

What became of old Bagot?
I haven't seen him for a year.
Is it true that young Forbes had to marry that Faggot
He met in the Vale of Kashmir?
Have you had any news
Of that chap in the 'Blues',
Was it Prosser or Pyecroft or Pym?
He was stationed in Simla, or was it Bengal?
I know he got tight at a ball in Nepal
And wrote several four-letter words on the wall.
I wonder what happened to him!

Whatever became of old Shelley?
Is it true that young Briggs was cashiered
For riding quite nude on a push-bike through Delhi
The day the new Viceroy appeared?
Have you had any word
Of that bloke in the 'Third',
Was it Southerby, Sedgwick or Sim?
They had him thrown out of the club in Bombay
For, apart from his mess bills exceeding his pay,
He took to pig-sticking in *quite* the wrong way.
I wonder what happened to him!

Whatever became of old Tucker?
Have you heard any word of young Mills
Who ruptured himself at the end of a chukka
And had to be sent to the hills?
They say that young Lees
Had a go of 'DTs'
And his hopes of promotion are slim.
According to Stubbs, who's a bit of a louse,
The silly young blighter went out on a 'souse',
And took two old tarts into Government House.
I wonder what happened to him!

Noël Coward

Britain's rule in India came to an end at midnight on 14 August 1947. As the Indian leader Nehru put it: 'At the stroke of midnight when the world sleeps India will wake to life and freedom.' Mahatma Gandhi, a driving force behind the move towards independence, did not join in the celebrations as he was strongly opposed to the partition of India and Pakistan. The birth of these new states was not accomplished without pain, for hundreds of thousands of Muslims and Hindus were killed in communal violence and there were millions of refugees. Britain left behind a language which was to serve for communication in all parts of that vast sub-continent, an established bureaucracy, now lovingly embellished, and a democratic system of government. The legacy has stood up well. Many former colonial servants and old soldiers 'stayed on', but things were never to be the same for them.

Epilogue To An Empire 1600–1900

An Ode For Trafalgar Day

As I was crossing Trafalgar Square
whose but the Admiral's shadow hand
should tap my shoulder. At my ear:
'You Sir, stay-at-home citizen
poet, here's more use for your pen
than picking scabs. Tell them in England
this: when first I stuck my head in the air,

'winched from a cockpit's tar and blood
to my crow's nest over London, I
looked down on a singular crowd
moving with the confident swell
of the sea. As it rose and fell
every pulse in the estuary
carried them quayward, carried them seaward.

'Box-wallah, missionary, clerk,
lancer, planter, I saw them all
linked like the waves on the waves embark.
Their eyes looked out – as yours look in –
to harbour names on the cabin-
trunks carrying topees to Bengal,
maxims or gospels to lighten a dark

'continent. Blatant as the flag
they went out under were the bright
abstractions nailed to every mast.
Sharpshooters since have riddled most
and buried an empire in their rags –
scrivener, do you dare to write
a little 'e' in the epilogue

'to an empire that spread its wings
wider than Rome? They are folded,
you say, with the maps and flags; awnings
and verandahs overrun
by impis of the ant; sun-
downers sunk, and the planters' blood
turned tea or siphoned into rubber saplings.

'My one eye reports that their roads
remain, their laws, their language
seeding all winds. They were no gods
from harnessed clouds, as the islanders
thought them, nor were they monsters
but men, as you stooped over your page
and you and you and these wind-driven crowds

'are and are not. For you have lost
their rhythm, the pulse of the sea
in their salt blood. Your heart has missed
the beat of centuries, its channels
silted to their source. The muscles
of the will stricken by distrophy
dishonour those that bareback rode the crest

'of untamed seas. Acknowledge
their energy. If you condemn
their violence in a violent age
speak of their courage. Mock their pride
when, having built as well, in as wide
a compass, you have none. Tell them
in England this.'
And a pigeon sealed the page.

Jon Stallworthy

1950

THE GENERAL ELECTION

Parties drilled for the election,
All accoutred to perfection,
March for national inspection,
Parties on parade!
Labour's serried ranks resplendent,
Tories with their aims transcendant,
Liberals , proudly independent,
CP shock brigade.

Attlee in the saddle seated,
With his five year term completed,
Heads his cohorts undefeated,
Near four hundred strong!
All the Party regimented,
Toryism circumvented,
All constituents contented
Cheering loud and long.

Winston on his war-horse bounding,
With the Tory trumpets sounding,
After last election's pounding,
His two hundred leads;
Eden, next in the succession,
Fighting forces of oppression,
With Young Tories, in procession,
Also cheered, proceeds.

Bearers of the Liberal Charter!
Clement Davies is the starter,
Pressed by Lady Bonham Carter
And McFadyean's men.
In the Liberal tradition
All condemn to demolition
Government and Opposition
(Sitting Members, ten).

Gallacher with resolution,
Leads the ranks of revolution,
Hails the day of retribution
With his faithful few;
Champion of the working classes,
Soon to free exploited masses,
When the present order passes
(Sitting Members, two).

Voters, it's no time to dally!
None must shirk or shilly-shally!
To your chosen Party rally
As for power they strive.
If too long you hesitate, or
If the ballot you are late for,
Voters, you will have to wait for
1955.

Sagittarius

The Labour Government had weathered many storms: the devaluation of sterling, a fuel crisis in the severe winter of 1947, and a flourishing black market brought about by rationing. Yet since 1945 they had lost not a single by-election. At the general election of 1950, however, they took office again with a majority of only six over all other parties. Attlee soldiered on for a further eighteen months, until in 1951 he was defeated by Churchill, who was returned with a majority of seventeen. The people were tired of austerity and, under R. A. Butler's guidance, the Tory party presented a more attractive programme attuned to the requirements of post-war Britain.

1951

THE FESTIVAL OF BRITAIN

from **Don't Make Fun of the Fair**

Don't make fun of the festival,
Don't make fun of the fair,
We down-trodden British must learn to be skittish
And give an impression of devil-may-care
To the wide wide world,
We'll sing 'God for Harry',
And if it turns out all right
Knight Gerald Barry,
Clear the national decks, my lads,
Everyone of us counts,
Grab the traveller's cheques, my lads,
And pray that none of them bounce.
Boys and Girls come out to play,
Every day in every way
Help the tourist to defray
All that's underwritten.
Sell your rations and overcharge,
And don't let anyone sabotage
Our own dear Festival of Britain.

Don't make fun of the festival,
Don't make fun of the fair,
We must pull together in spite of the weather
That dampens our spirits and straightens our hair.
Let the people sing
Even though they shiver
Roses red and noses mauve
Over the river.

Though the area's fairly small,
Climb Discovery's Dome,
Take a snooze in the concert hall,
At least it's warmer than home.
March about in funny hats,
Show the foreign diplomats
That our proletariat's
Milder than a kitten.
We believe in the right to strike,
But now we've bloody well got to like
Our own dear festival of Britain.

Noël Coward

The Labour Party, largely at the instigation of Herbert Morrison, decided to try to cheer everyone up by holding a national festival on the South Bank of the Thames, where a brewery had to be pulled down and a tall chimney, once a shot tower, demolished to make room for the site. A celebratory exhibition was held in the Dome of Discovery, erected at the centre alongside a great cigar-shaped construction pointing into the sky and called the Skylon. The one permanent thing to come out of the Festival was the Festival Hall, which looks as if it may last a bit longer than the Crystal Palace. The stone lion which had adorned the brewery now stands at the southern end of Westminster Bridge.

It was typical of the austerity of the time that a huge sculpture of two naked females by one of Britain's leading sculptors, Frank Dobson – also a teacher of Henry Moore – could only be shown as a plaster model, being too expensive to cast in bronze. Later it was put away in a shed, only to be rediscovered in 1987, when £40,000 was found to have it cast in bronze and set up again on the South Bank.

the 1950s

Ancient and Modern

Back in 1950
when Mums did Palais Glides
and girls still got an earful
from dad's short back and sides

and creamy capuccino
overlaid the tongue
with sweet and sexy flavours
and pop was Jimmy Young

and sweets came off the ration
and jazz sprang up in dives
and Comets screamed on newsreels
and Woodbines came in fives

and Tories ruled forever
and Empire meant Free Trade
and intellectuals took their stand
in corduroy and suede

and BBC announcers
said Churchill won applors
and Rank rebuffed Jane Russell
with young Diana Dors

and George gave way to Lizbet
and LPs offered gems
as the Festival of Britain
played sweetly by the Thames

and Compton creamed the bowlers
and Longhurst opened up
and Sunset fell at Beecher's
and Matthews won the Cup

and lady Docker's Daimler
glistened in the mews
and Beaverbrook lost Suez
and Dylan found his muse

and Humph blew infant solos
and Eden made it clear
that only a rich man ever earned
a thousand pounds a year

they brought *you* into being
yes, eyes and nose and chin
all set to smile and play, as if
the past had never been

and parents were for leaving
and history was bunk
and every kind of loving
was money in the bank!

William Scammell

Queen Elizabeth II, 1952–

1953

THE CORONATION OF ELIZABETH II

In a golden coach
There's a heart of gold
  That belongs to you and me.
And one day in June
When the flowers are in bloom
  That day will make history.

Donald Jamieson

The song from which this verse is taken was sung by Dickie Valentine and 200,000 copies of the record were sold. Another popular song of the time included the words:

Everybody's mad about ya
Where would Britain be without ya?
Sailing in the yacht Britannia
Nowhere in the world would ban ya.
Queenie Baby, I'm not foolin',
Only you could do the ruling,
In your own sweet royal way.

from **Little Gidding, Four Quartets**

V

What we call the beginning is often the end
And to make an end is to make a beginning.
The end is where we start from. And every phrase
And sentence that is right (where every word is at home,
Taking its place to support the others,
The word neither diffident nor ostentatious,
An easy commerce of the old and the new,
The common word exact without vulgarity,
The formal word precise but not pedantic,
The complete consort dancing together)
Every phrase and every sentence is an end and a beginning,
Every poem an epitaph. And any action
Is a step to the block, to the fire, down the sea's throat
Or to an illegible stone: and that is where we start.
We die with the dying:
See, they depart, and we go with them.
We are born with the dead:
See, they return, and bring us with them.
The moment of the rose and the moment of the yew-tree
Are of equal duration. A people without history
Is not redeemed from time, for history is a pattern
Of timeless moments. So, while the light fails
On a winter's afternoon, in a secluded chapel
History is now and England.

T. S. Eliot

Index of Titles

Index of First Lines

Acknowledgements

For permission to reprint copyright material the publishers gratefully acknowledge the following:

Faber and Faber Ltd for 'Alas! Poor Queen' from *The Turn of the Day* by Marion Angus; Earl Attlee for 'On Himself' by Clement Attlee; Faber and Faber Ltd for 'September 1, 1939' by W. H. Auden from *The English Auden: Poems, Essays and Dramatic Writings 1927–39* edited by Edward Mendelson (Faber, 1977), and 'Roman Wall Blues' and 'Partition' from *W. H. Auden: Collected Poems* edited by Edward Mendelson (Faber, 1976); Patricia Beer and the Carcanet Press for 'Mr Dombey' in 'Victorian Trains' from *Collected Poems* by Patricia Beer (Carcanet, 1988); A.D. Peters & Co. Ltd for 'On Edward VII' and 'On Bonar Law' by Hilaire Belloc; Oxford University Press for 'Rupert of the Rhine' and 'George III' by E.C. Bentley from *The Complete Clerihews of E. Clerihew Bentley* (Oxford University Press, 1981); John Murray (Publishers) for 'The Arrest of Oscar Wilde', 'Henley Regatta', 'Death of King George V' and 'In Westminster Abbey' from *Collected Poems* by John Betjeman (John Murray, 1958) and *Uncollected Poems* by John Betjeman (John Murray, 1982); Mrs Nicolete Gray and The Society of Authors on behalf of the Laurence Binyon Estate for 'For the Fallen (September 1914)' by Laurence Binyon; Oxford University Press for 'Briggflatts' from *Collected Poems* by Basil Bunting (Oxford University Press, 1978); Macmillan (Publishers) Ltd and David Higham Associates Ltd for 'At the Statue of William the Conqueror' from *Collected Poems* by Charles Causley (Macmillan, 1975); Carcanet Press for 'Kett's Rebellion' by Keith Chandler; Curtis Brown for 'Thus came enclosure – ruin was its guide' from 'The Fallen Elm' by John Clare; the author and Gerald Duckworth for 'After Edgehill, 1642' from *Leafburners: New and Selected Poems* by Gladys Mary Coles (Duckworth 1987); Methuen & Co Ltd for 'The Death of Queen Victoria' from '1901', 'I Wonder What Happened to Him and 'Don't Make Fun of the Fair' from *The Collected Verse of Noël Coward* edited by Martin Payne and Graham Tickner (Methuen, 1984); Kevin Crossley-Holland and Deborah Rogers Ltds for 'Cædmon's Hymn' and 'The Battle of Maldon' taken from *The Anglo-Saxon World: An Anthology* edited and translated by Kevin Crossley-Holland (Oxford University Press, 1984); Punch for 'George I – Star of Brunswick' from 'George Poems' by H. J. Daniel; Oxford University Press for 'Vergissmeinnicht' from *The Complete Poems of Keith Douglas* edited by Desmond Graham (Oxford University Press, 1978) Copyright © Marie J. Douglas; Faber and Faber Ltd. and Harcourt Brace Jovanovich, Inc. for lines from *Murder in the Cathedral* (Faber, 1935), copyright 1935 by Harcourt Brace Jovanovich, Inc., renewed by T. S. Eliot; and for 'Little Gidding' from

Four Quartets by T. S. Eliot (Harcourt Brace Jovanovich, Inc. 1935)/ *Collected Poems 1909–1962* (Faber, 1963) by T. S. Eliot, copyright 1943 by T. S. Eliot, renewed 1971 by Esme Valerie Eliot; Century Hutchinson for 'Cowardice' from *The New Ewart: Poems 1980–82* by Gavin Ewart (Century Hutchinson, 1983); Harry Chambers/Peterloo Poets for 'Portraits of Tudor Statesmen' from *Standing To* by U. A. Fanthorpe (Peterloo Poets 1982); Wishari Press for 'Ode on the Death of Haig's Horse' from *Whips and Scorpions* by Douglas Garman; A. P. Watt Ltd, the Estate of Robert Graves, and Oxford University Press, Inc. for '1805' and 'Armistice Day, 1918' from *The Collected Poems 1975* by Robert Graves, copyright © Robert Graves, 1975; Faber and Faber Ltd for 'The Site of the Crystal Palace' from *The Ice Factory* by Philip Gross (Faber, 1984); Centerprise Publications for 'October 1936' by Milly Harris; Tony Harrison and Fraser & Dunlop Scripts Ltd for 'The Morning After' by Tony Harrison; David Higham Associates for 'Great Black-Backed Gulls' from *A Parliament of Birds* by John Heath-Stubbs (Chatto, 1975); A.P. Watt Ltd on behalf of Lady Herbert for 'Mr Churchill' from *Light the Lights* by A. P. Herbert (Methuen, 1945); André Deutsch Ltd and Oxford University Press, Inc. for 'Requiem for the Plantagenet Kings' from *For the Unfallen: Poems 1952–1958* by Geoffrey Hill (Deutsch, 1959/*Collected Poems* by Geoffrey Hill (Oxford University Press, Inc., 1985), copyright © Geoffrey Hill, 1985; Faber and Faber Ltd and Harper & Row Publishers, Inc. for 'The Martyrdom of Bishop Farrar' from *The Hawk in the Rain* copyright © Ted Hughes, 1957; Faber and Faber Ltd for 'An Arundel Tomb' and 'MCMXIV' from *The Whitsun Weddings* by Philip Larkin (Faber, 1964); Clement (Publishers) Ltd for 'Elizabeth Reflects' from *God Save the Queen: Sonnets of Elizabeth I* by John Loveridge (Clement, 1981); Faber and Faber Ltd and Farrar Straus and Giroux, Inc. for 'Sir Thomas More' from *History* by Robert Lowell (Faber, 1973); Mrs Valda Grieve and Martin Brian and O'Keeffe Ltd for 'Allelauder' by Hugh MacDiarmid; Gerald Duckworth for an extract from 'The Hero of Khartoum' by William McGonagall; Faber and Faber Ltd for lines from 'Autumn Journal' from *The Collected Poems of Louis MacNeice* (Faber, 1966); Peter Newbolt for 'Hawke', 'Drake's Drum' and 'Vitaï Lampada' by Sir Henry Newbolt; the Estate of the Late Sonia Brownell, Secker and Warburg Ltd and A. M. Heath & Co. Ltd for 'Oh You Young Men' by George Orwell; the Estate of William Plomer and Jonathan Cape Ltd for 'The Boer War' from *Collected Poems* by William Plomer (Cape, 1973); Faber and Faber Ltd and New Directions Publishing Corporation for lines from 'Hugh Selwyn Mauberley' from *Collected Shorter Poems* by Ezra Pound (Faber, 1949)/*Personae* by Ezra Pound (New Directions, 1926), copyright © 1926 by Ezra Pound; David Higham Associates Ltd for 'For Johnny' from *Collected Poems* by John Pudney (Putnam 1957); the Estate of Henry Reed and Jonathan Cape Ltd for 'Naming of Parts' from *A Map of Verona* by Henry Reed (Cape, 1946); Jonathan Cape Ltd and the Estate of Olga Katzin Miller for 'Lest Cowards Flinch' by 'Sagittarius'; George Sassoon and Viking Penguin, Inc. for 'The General' from *Collected Poems of Siegfried Sassoon 1908–1956* (Faber, 1947); William Scammell and Harry Chambers/Peterloo Poets for 'Ancient and Modern' from

Jouissance (Harry Chambers/Peterloo Poets, 1985); Carcanet Press Ltd for 'Cranmer' from *Collected Poems* by C.H. Sisson (Carcanet, 1984); Random House, Inc. and Faber and Faber Ltd for 'Unemployed' from *Collected Poems 1928–85* by Stephen Spender (Faber, 1985); Macmillan, London and Basingstoke, for 'God Heard the Embattled Nations' and 'It Did Not Last' from *Collected Poems* by J.C. Squire (Macmillan, 1959); the Director of the Whitechapel Art Gallery for 'Whitechapel in Britain' by Avram Stencl; Hubert Nicholson of Autolycus Publications and the Whiteknights Press for 'England (Autumn 1938)' from *Collected Poems of A.S.J. Tessimond* edited by Hubert Nicholson (1985); Carcanet Press for 'Mr Gradgrind's Country' from *The Collected Poems of Sylvia Townsend Warner* edited by Claire Hanman (Carcanet, 1982); Chatto & Windus Ltd for 'Gloriana Dying' from *12 Poems* by Sylvia Townsend Warner (Chatto, 1980).

Faber and Faber Ltd apologizes for any errors or omissions in the above list and would be grateful to be notified of any corrections that should be incorporated in the next edition of this volume.

Educational Administration

Concepts and Practices

Sixth Edition

Educational Administration

Concepts and Practices

Sixth Edition

Fred C. Lunenburg
Sam Houston State University

Allan C. Ornstein
St. John's University

Australia • Brazil • Japan • Korea • Mexico • Singapore • Spain • United Kingdom • United States

Educational Administration: Concepts and Practices, Sixth Edition
Fred C. Lunenburg and Allan C. Ornstein

Publisher: Linda Schreiber-Ganster

Acquisitions Editor: Mark Kerr

Development Editor: Caitlin Cox

Marketing Manager: Kara Kindstrom Parsons

Marketing Communications Manager: Tami Strang

Art Director: Maria Epes

Manufacturing Manager: Marcia Locke

Senior Manufacturing Buyer: Mary Beth Hennebury

Rights Acquisition Director: Bob Kauser

Rights Acquisition Specialist, Text: Dean Dauphinais

Rights Acquisition Specialist, Image: Dean Dauphinais

Content Project Management: PreMediaGlobal

Production Service: PreMediaGlobal

Cover Designer: Lee Friedman

Production House/Compositor: PreMediaGlobal

Library of Congress Control Number: 2011900768

ISBN-13: 978-1-111-30124-8

ISBN-10: 1-111-30124-7

Wadsworth
20 Davis Dr.
Belmont, CA 94002
USA

Cengage Learning is a leading provider of customized learning solutions with office locations around the globe, including Singapore, the United Kingdom, Australia, Mexico, Brazil, and Japan. Locate your local office at: **international.cengage.com/region**

Cengage Learning products are represented in Canada by Nelson Education, Ltd.

For your course and learning solutions, visit **www.cengage.com**

Purchase any of our products at your local college store or at our preferred online store **www.cengagebrain.com**

Printed in the United States of America
1 2 3 4 5 6 7 15 14 13 12 11

Contents

Administrative Advice

PRO/CON Debates

Administrator Profiles

Foreword

During the past decade, the nation's attention has again been riveted on education. Numerous publications offer a myriad of recommendations focused on what must be done to improve the quality of education in America. This intense desire for a new and restructured education process offers many windows of opportunity for positive change.

When school reform efforts have been directed to and given a sense of direction by those local leaders who are responsible for effective change in our nation's schools, the results have been favorable. *Educational Administration: Concepts and Practices*, Fifth Edition, will serve as a valuable primer for prospective school leaders as they work toward effecting change in an orderly, efficient, and effective manner.

Its authors, Fred Lunenburg and Allan Ornstein, have addressed both the concepts surrounding educational change and the processes they feel are essential for improvement, and they have done it in a forthright and interesting manner. In addition, the authors have discussed the fundamental principles of effective administrative leadership, including the need to effectively manage the process of collaboration and coordinate improvement efforts.

Creative, high quality leadership is essential to the reform and restructuring of American education, as our schools strive to meet the needs and challenges of our society.

Richard D. Miller
Former Executive Director
American Association of
School Administrators

Preface

Educational administrators face a challenging and changing climate in our nation's schools. In the past, textbooks in educational administration have focused mainly on theory and research as a way of providing a knowledge base and preparation for students and professionals. In *Educational Administration: Concepts and Practices*, Sixth Edition, we have attempted to go beyond this tradition by including, in addition to comprehensive coverage of theory and research, a third component: practical applications that help educational administrators make use of the knowledge base they acquire. This practical, applied component makes our book a unique entry to the literature and a resource that we believe will enhance the abilities of future and current educational administrators to become effective leaders in our changing educational climate.

The practical and applied component of *Educational Administration: Concepts and Practices* can be found in many aspects of this text.

- New and unique coverage of topics such as the post–behavioral science era—school improvement, democratic community, and social justice; school accountability and testing; ethics and values; gender, race/ethnicity, and class; critical theory and postmodernism; instructional leadership; site-based decision making; change; curriculum development and implementation; improving teaching and learning; technology; human resources administration; and emergent perspectives are included.
- Chapter openings begin with five to eight focusing questions designed to focus the reader's attention on the major issues within the chapter.
- Administrative Advice sections (about three or four per chapter) demonstrate how significant concepts can be applied to administrative practice.
- PRO/CON Debates (one per chapter) illustrate opposing perspectives on major issues facing educational administrators.
- Summaries at the ends of chapters highlight critical points and especially salient issues in theory, research, and applications.
- Lists of key terms and discussion questions at the end of each chapter stimulate application of concepts and enhance understanding of the chapter.
- Extensive documentation throughout and suggestions for additional readings at the end of each chapter encourage readers to pursue further exploration of significant subject matter.
- "Words of Advice" boxes provide sage suggestions from experienced administrators.
- All chapters have been revised extensively to include the latest in governmental policy, teaching technology, and how the recent economic crisis has impacted public school administration.
- New to this edition is Chapter 10: Excellence, Equality, and Education which deals with the challenges facing school administrators to meet the demands of testing and accountability, close the achievement gap, and provide excellence and equity in our schools and society.

Organization of the Text

This book contains fifteen chapters in four major parts. The introductory chapter defines the field, looks at how it came into existence, and presents a conceptual model that provides a framework for the remainder of the book. The next chapter focuses on several alternative approaches to organizational structure. The last chapter in this opening part provides a cultural context for the study and application of educational administration.

After this foundation is provided, Part II examines the basic administrative processes with chapters on motivation, leadership, decision making, communication, and organizational change. Part III focuses on the structural framework for education. The chapter on the government and education is followed by chapter on excellence, equality, and education; school finance and productivity; and legal considerations in education. Part IV explores the administration of programs and services. Specific chapters deal with curriculum development, teaching strategies, and human resources management.

The four parts and fifteen chapters of the book are relatively self-contained. Thus, an entire part, selected chapters, or even portions of chapters, could be skipped, or studied in a different sequence, without damaging the flow or content of the book.

Companion Website

The book-specific website at www.cengage.com/eduation/lunenburg offers students a variety of study tools and useful resources such as links to related sites, case studies, and an additional chapter on careers in educational administration. For instructors, PowerPoint slides are available for each chapter.

Acknowledgments

This book has been a cooperative effort between scholars and experienced editors and publishers. We wish to express our appreciation to the reviewers and others whose suggestions led to improvements in this and in earlier editions:

Judy A. Alston	Bowling Green State University
Paul Baker	Illinois State University
Edwin D. Bell	East Carolina University
Dale L. Bolton	University of Washington
James Boothe	Xavier University
Norman Boyles	Iowa State University
Fred E. Bradley	University of Missouri, St. Louis
Dennis C. Brennan	University of the Pacific
Jerry Cicchelli	Fordham University
James A. Conway	State University of New York, Buffalo
Philip A. Cusick	Michigan State University
Andrew E. Dubin	San Francisco State University
Martha Ellis	University of Texas, Austin
Janet Fredericks	Northeastern Illinois University
Lloyd E. Frohreich	University of Wisconsin, Madison
Jits Furusawa	California State University, Dominguez Hills
Valeri Helterbran	Indiana University of Pennsylvania
Patricia Hoehner	University of Nebraska, Kearney
Ernest Johnson	University of Texas, Arlington
Franklin B. Jones	Tennessee State University
Lawrence Kajs	University of Houston, Clear Lake
Frank Keane	Fayetteville State University
Donald Layton	State University of New York, Albany
Arthur Lehr	University of Illinois, Urbana-Champaign
Robert B. Lowe	Angelo State University
Betty Jo Monk	Tarleton State University
Robert Morris	State University of West Georgia
Steve Nowlin	Troy State University
Anita M. Pankake	University of Texas, Pan American
Albert Pautler	State University of New York, Buffalo
Lorrie C. Reed	Chicago State University
Glenn B. Schroeder	University of Northern Colorado
Gerald Schumacher	University of Houston, Clear Lake
Linda T. Sheive	State University of New York, Oswego
Roger Shouse	Pennsylvania State University, University Park
Donald W. Smitley	Eastern Illinois University
Carl Steinhoff	University of Nevada, Las Vegas
Rudo Tsesunhu	Pennsylvania State University, University Park
Clark Webb	Brigham Young University
Noelle Witherspoon	Louisiana State University, Baton Rouge

We also wish to gratefully acknowledge the following individuals who contributed boxes for this and prior editions: Henry S. Bangser, Superintendent, New Trier Township High School District, Winnetka/Northfield, IL; Mirabelle Baptiste, Principal, Clifton Middle School, Houston Independent School District, Houston, TX; Richard (Rick) Earl Berry, Superintendent, Cypress-Fairbanks Independent School District, Houston, TX; James F. Causby, Superintendent, Johnson County Schools, Smithfield, NC; Craig L. Elliott,

Superintendent, Maize Unified School District, Maize, KS; Pascal Forgione, Superintendent, Austin Independent School District, Austin, TX; Barry Fried, Principal, John Dewey High School, Brooklyn, NY; Carlos A. Garcia, Superintendent, Clark County School District, Las Vegas, NV; Joe A. Hairston, Superintendent, Baltimore County Public Schools, Towson, MD: David Kazakoff, Principal, Terra Nova High School, Pacifica, CA; William G. Meuer, Principal, Norwood Park School, Chicago Public Schools, Chicago, IL; Joanna Miller, Principal, E. M. Baker Elementary School, Great Neck, NY; Lonnie E. Palmer, Superintendent, City School District of Albany, Albany, NY; Art Rainwater, Superintendent, Madison Metropolitan School District, Madison, WI; Ron Saunders, Superintendent, Barrow County Schools, Winder, GA; Paul Vance, Superintendent, District of Columbia Public Schools, Washington, DC. Your willingness to share your experiences will help to guide and inspire future generations of school administrators.

We wish to thank Marion Czaja for conducting and writing the cases for each chapter of the text that appear on the Wadsworth companion website. We also wish to thank Paula Lester, Long Island University, for her contribution to Chapter 9 of the book and William Owings, Old Dominion University, for his contribution to Chapter 11.

We want to thank the people at Cengage Learning whose contributions made this a much better book: Mark Kerr, Executive Editor; Lisa Kalner Williams, Senior Development Editor; Genevieve Allen, Editorial Assistant; Melena Fenn, Senior Project Manager; Kara Kindstrom, Marketing Manager; Dimitri Hagnere, Marketing Coordinator.

We are grateful to our respective deans Genevieve Brown and Jerry Ross for creating an environment and contributing the resources necessary to complete this book.

Fred C. Lunenburg
Allan C. Ornstein

The Authors

Fred C. Lunenburg is the Jimmy N. Merchant Professor of Education at Sam Houston State University. Prior to moving to the university, he served as a teacher, principal, and superintendent of schools. He has authored or co-authored more than 100 articles and 20 books, including *The Principalship: Vision to Action* (Thomson/Wadsworth, 2006), *Shaping the Future* (Rowman & Littlefield, 2003), *The Changing World of School Administration* (with George Perreault) (Scarecrow Press, 2002), and *High Expectations: An Action Plan for Implementing Goals 2000* (Corwin, 2000). He received the Phi Delta Kappa Research Award in 1986 and was The Distinguished Visiting Professor at the University of Utrecht (The Netherlands) in 1995.

Allan C. Ornstein is Professor of Administrative and Instructional Leadership at St. Johns University. He is the author of 54 books and some 400 articles on education, and has been a consultant for more than 75 government and educational agencies, including the Chicago and New York City school districts. He is a former Fulbright-Hayes Scholar and member of the Fulbright-Hayes screening committee. Among Dr. Ornstein's most recent books are *Foundations of Education,* 10th ed. (Houghton Mifflin, 2008), *Contemporary Issues in Education*, 4th ed. (Allyn and Bacon, 2007), *Pushing the Envelope* (Merrill, 2003), and *Teaching and Schooling in America: Pre and Post September 11* (Allyn and Bacon, 2003). His most recent book, *Class Counts: Education, Inequality and the Shrinking Middle Class* (Rowman and Littlefield, 2007), examines growing inequality, the shrinking middle class, the slow decline of the nation, and the waning influence of education.

Educational Administration

Concepts and Practices

Sixth Edition

1

Development of Administrative Theory

FOCUSING QUESTIONS

1 What is theory?

2 How are theory and research related?

3 What are the uses of theory?

4 What major developments in administrative thought have evolved in the field of educational administration?

5 How have emergent nontraditional perspectives influenced the study and practice of educational administration?

6 How can open systems theory be used to diagnose problems in school operation?

7 How can the learning organization be used to achieve school success?

In this chapter, we attempt to answer these questions concerning theoretical and historical developments in administration. We begin our discussion by exploring the nature of theory. Then we discuss the relationship between theory and research. A discussion of the uses of theory follows. Next, we identify and explain the major developments in administrative thought: classical, human relations, behavioral science, and post-behavioral science approaches. This is followed by a discussion of emergent nontraditional perspectives in the study of educational administration. Next, we examine schools as open systems. We conclude the chapter with a discussion of the learning organization and its impact on the operation of schools.

What Is Theory?

Educational administrators are professionals who have a code of ethics and are licensed by state boards of education.[1] Thus, their behavior is guided by acceptable standards of practice. One of the best criteria of a profession, however, is that it has matured as a science; that is, it has developed a solid theoretical base—a body of organized and tested knowledge. Such is the case with educational administration as a social science.[2] Theory in educational administration has been evolving since the 1950s.[3] To an increasing degree, educational administration is characterized by using theory to explain and predict phenomena in educational organizations.[4]

Fred Kerlinger defines **theory** as "a set of interrelated constructs (concepts), definitions, and propositions that present a systematic view of phenomena by specifying relations among variables with the purpose of explaining and predicting phenomena."[5] Daniel Griffiths includes many of the same ideas in his discussion of theory. He adds that a theory is a deductively connected set of empirical laws and that all statements in a theory are generalizations that explain the empirical laws and unify the areas of subject matter.[6]

A theory, then, is an organized body of interrelated concepts, assumptions, and generalizations that systematically explains and predicts some phenomena. Theories may range from a simple generalization to a complex set of laws, from philosophical to scientific. Some theories deal with simple generalizations, such as results of educational polls or school surveys undertaken by state accrediting associations. Such studies involve measures of the nature of some condition at a particular time. They explain what is. More well-developed theories enable us to make predictions and to control phenomena. For example, meteorologists have well-developed theories. Usually they can make very accurate predictions about the occurrence of hurricanes, tornados, earthquakes, and other atmospheric phenomena. Special education teachers work from a well-developed theory of learning (referred to as *behavioral theory*). Consequently, they can facilitate instructional interventions that typically lead to positive changes in student behavior. Other examples of well-developed theories that enable us to predict phenomena include Albert Einstein's *theory of relativity* and Isaac Newton's *theory of universal gravitation*.

Theory and Research

It is important to note that theory and research are tied together. The theory guides the researcher in what to look for, and the research provides the researcher with what was found. What was found also provides the researcher with an indication of what to look for in the future. It is also important to note that the researcher may not see what he/she does not conceptualize. What the researcher sees must be understood and verified by others. This process of seeing, understanding, and verifying is generally accomplished through the scientific method.

The **scientific method** involves four steps. First, a research problem is specified. Then one or more hypotheses or predictive statements of what the researchers expect to find are formulated. These may come from several sources, including observation, previous experience, and a thorough review of the related literature. Next, a research design is developed to conduct the research and test the hypothesis(ses). Finally, data collection, data analysis, and interpretation of the findings are performed.[7]

Returning to our previous reference to the term hypothesis, we can define a **hypothesis** as a predictive statement about the relationship between two or more variables. A **variable** is a measure used to describe some phenomena. For example, a researcher may count the percentage of students who pass the state mandated achievement test as a measure of a school's productivity. Then a hypothesis might be formulated that increased

---

[1]American Association of School Administrators, *Code of Ethics for School Administrators* (Arlington, VA: The Association, 2012).

[2]It may be more accurate to refer to educational administration as an *applied* science.

[3]Andrew W. Halpin, Administrative Theory in Education (New York: Macmillan, 1958); Daniel E. Griffiths, Administrative Theory (New York: Appleton-Century-Crafts, 1959).

[4]See, for example, Daniel E. Griffiths, "Administrative Theory," in N. J. Boyan (ed.), *Handbook of Research on Educational Administration* (New York: Longman, 1988), pp. 27–51.

[5]Fred N. Kerlinger, *Foundations of Behavioral Research*, 3rd ed. (San Diego, CA: Harcourt Brace, 1986), p. 9.

[6]Griffiths, "Administrative Theory," 1988.

[7]Meredith D. Gall, Joyce P. Gall, and Walter R. Borg, *Educational Research: An Introduction*, 8th ed. (Boston: Pearson/Allyn & Bacon, 2007); L.R. Gay, Geoffrey E. Mills, and Peter Airasian, *Educational Research: Competencies for Analysis and Applications*, 9th ed. (Upper Saddle River, NJ: Pearson/Merrill, 2009).

productivity will result in high job satisfaction for the principal and school faculty. Confirmation of the aforementioned hypothesis would lead to the following implication: If you want to increase the job satisfaction of the principal and school faculty, increase the productivity of the work unit by increasing the passing rates of students on the state mandated achievement test.

Many quantitative research studies are designed to test a theory that has been developed to explain some educational phenomena. However, studies also can be designed so that data are collected first, and then a theory is derived from those data.[8] The resulting theory is called *grounded theory*, because it is "grounded" in the particular set of data the researcher has collected. In this research tradition, hypotheses are the outcome of the study rather than the initiators of it. The usefulness of the theory can be tested in subsequent research. This approach to theory development is more applicable to case studies.

In sum, you will be introduced to many theories in this book. Many of the theories are based on actual studies of organizations. They offer a lens, or way of thinking about how organizations function. You will find that different theories provided in this book will offer you different ways of thinking about the same issue. As you study these theories, think about how they might apply to organizations with which you are familiar: as an employee, a customer, or a graduate student. This is the value of theory; by using different lenses, you will broaden your understanding about how organizations can be structured and managed in more effective ways.

Educational administration as an academic discipline earns credibility by being research driven. Scientific rigor replaces speculation and untested assumptions about employee behavior in the workplace. Behavioral science researchers acquire empirical evidence by using one or more of five different categories of research designs: laboratory studies, field studies, meta-analyses, survey studies, and case studies (see Administrative Advice 1–1).

Uses of Theory

Many school administrators feel uncomfortable with theories. They prefer that social scientists provide them with practical prescriptions for administering their schools. Upon closer examination, however, almost every action a school administrator takes is based to some degree on a theory. For example, a school administrator may include others in a decision involving an issue that is relevant to them and that they have the expertise to make, instead of making the decision unilaterally. Such action is referred to in the research literature as participatory decision making. Participatory decision making, also referred to as shared, collaborative, or group decision making, focuses on decision processes that involve others.

In education, participatory decision making is based on the idea that active involvement of teachers, parents, or community members in school decisions will lead to improved school performance.[9] It is believed that those closest to teaching and learning, namely teachers, and those with the most knowledge about the children, namely parents, should be involved in decisions because they have expertise that is crucial to improving school performance. Furthermore, it is believed that when teachers and parents are involved in decision making, they will be more committed to implementing and supporting the decision, and a sense of ownership in the school will result.[10] Without knowing it, the school administrator made the choice to involve others in the decision-making process on the basis of a theory.

Educational administrators would most likely flounder without theories to guide them in making choices. Thus, theories provide a guiding framework for understanding, predicting, and controlling behavior in organizations. Theories also contribute to the advancement of knowledge in the field.[11] Deobold Van Dalen has suggested six functions of theories, and we follow his categorization in this discussion.[12]

Identifying Relevant Phenomena Theories determine the number and kinds of phenomena that are relevant to a study. A theory tells a social scientist what to observe and to ignore. For example, social scientists may study school administration from the open systems perspective. (Open systems theory is discussed later in this chapter.)

[8] B.G. Glaser, *Theoretical Sensitivity: Advances in the Methodology of Grounded Theory* (Mill Valley, CA: Sociology Press, 1978).

[9] Kristen C. Wilcox and Janet I. Angelis, Best Practices from High-Performing Middle Schools: How Successful Schools Remove Obstacles and Create Pathways to Learning (New York: Teachers College Press, 2010).

[10] Fred C. Lunenburg and Beverly J. Irby, *The Principalship: Vision to Action* (Wadsworth/Cengage, 2006).

[11] Robert Donmoyer, "The Continuing Quest for a Knowledge Base: 1976–1998," in J. Murphy and K. S. Louis (eds.), *Handbook of Research on Educational Administration*, 2nd ed. (San Francisco: Jossey-Bass, 1999), pp. 25–43.

[12] Deobold B. Van Dalen, *Understanding Educational Research*, 4th ed. (New York: McGraw-Hill, 1979).

ADMINISTRATIVE ADVICE 1-1

Methods of Research Used by Behavioral Scientists

Physical scientists have certain methods for obtaining information. So do behavioral scientists. These usually are referred to as research designs. In broad terms, five basic designs are used by behavioral scientists: laboratory studies, field studies, meta-analyses, survey studies, and case studies.[8b]

- *Laboratory studies*. A **laboratory study** is potentially the most rigorous of scientific techniques. The essence of conducting a laboratory study is making sure that the variable being manipulated (the independent variable) influences the results. The independent variable (e.g., a motivational technique) is thought to influence the dependent variable (e.g., productivity). Because laboratory studies are conducted in contrived situations, generalizing the results to practice requires caution.
- *Field studies*. In a **field study**, the investigator attempts to manipulate and control variables in the natural setting rather than in a laboratory. Early field studies in organizations included manipulating physical working conditions such as rest periods, refreshments, and lighting (see, e.g., the classic Hawthorne Studies discussed later in this chapter). Because field studies involve real-life situations, their results often have immediate and practical relevance for school administrators.
- *Meta-analyses*. A **meta-analysis** is an examination of a range of studies for the purpose of reaching an aggregated result. The logic of meta-analysis is that researchers can arrive at a more accurate conclusion regarding a research area by combining the results of many studies in a specific area of inquiry. It is assumed that combining the results of many studies provides a more accurate picture than would be found in any single study. Many of the research findings presented throughout this book are based on meta-analysis rather than the results of a single study.
- *Survey studies*. In a **survey study**, samples of people from specified populations respond to questionnaires. The researchers then draw conclusions about the relevant population. Generalizability of the results depends on the quality of the sampling techniques and the validity and reliability of the questionnaires used.
- *Case studies*. A **case study** is an in-depth analysis of a single individual, group, or organization. Because of their limited scope, results of case studies are not generalizable. Despite this limitation, the case study is widely used as a method of studying organizations. It is extremely valuable in answering exploratory questions.

[8b]Gall, Gall, and Borg, *Educational Research*; Gay, Mills, and Airasian, *Educational Research*.

A relevant component in the open systems approach is the external environment that impacts the organization. Several subsystems exist within this environment. Among the more important are economic, political, productive, distributive, and resource systems. Social scientists may study the external environment from within all these frameworks. Multiple phenomena are associated with each subsystem. Social scientists will not know precisely what phenomena to observe until they construct theoretical solutions for each problem area under investigation.

Classifying Phenomena Scientists rarely work efficiently with masses of phenomena; therefore, they construct theoretical frameworks for classification. The physical sciences have been successful in developing such conceptual schemes. Geologists have developed schemes for classifying rocks, and botanists have devised systems for classifying plants.

An example of a classification scheme in educational administration is the study of organizational climate by Andrew Halpin and DonCroft.[13] Using factor analysis, they developed eight dimensions of organizational climate and classified them into six categories: open, autonomous, controlled, familiar, paternal, and closed. Another example comes from the work of Henry

[13]Andrew W. Halpin and Don B. Croft, *The Organizational Climate of Schools* (Chicago: University of Chicago Press, 1963).

Mintzberg. After extensive, structured observation of five executives (one a school superintendent), Mintzberg classified managerial activities into ten administrative roles: figurehead, leader, liaison (interpersonal); monitor, disseminator, spokesperson (informational); and entrepreneur, disturbance-handler, resource-allocator, negotiator (decisional).[14] If educational administrators fail to develop theoretical frameworks for classifying phenomena, they will limit the advancement of knowledge in the field.

Formulating Constructs Reliable information can be obtained through direct observation and measurement. However, many aspects of behavior cannot be directly observed. Intelligence is not an observable entity; it is inferred from using instruments that sample subject behavior. Affective predispositions such as attitudes, interests, and opinions cannot be observed directly; they are observed indirectly as they manifest themselves in behavior. Consequently, social scientists have developed constructs to explain why certain types of behavior occur. These constructs are often referred to as *hypothetical constructs* to imply that they are a construction of the social scientist's imagination. Kurt Lewin's force-field analysis is an example of a theoretical construct.[15]

Summarizing Phenomena Theories summarize isolated lists of data into a broader conceptual scheme of wider applicability. These summaries can be stated with varying degrees of comprehensiveness and precision. They may range from simple generalizations to complex theoretical relationships. A school superintendent making a generalization about granting certificates of achievement to outstanding teachers in the school district is an example of low-level summarizing; this type of summary is not usually referred to as a theory. But the superintendent might construct a more complex generalization, one that describes the relationship between phenomena. For example, after observing the granting of certificates of achievement to deserving teachers, the superintendent may note a relationship: public recognition is a means of motivating teachers. Summarizing and explaining phenomena permit deeper understanding of data and translate empirical findings into a more comprehensive, theoretical framework.

[14]Henry Mintzberg, *The Nature of Managerial Work* (New York: HarperCollins, 1990).

[15]Kurt Lewin, *Field Theory in Social Science* (New York: Harper & Row, 1951).

In the natural sciences, for instance, the theory of oxidation brings many of the chemical reactions common to everyday life into focus. The more comprehensive the theory, which is supported by verified observations, the more mature the science becomes.

Predicting Phenomena A theory permits social scientists to predict the existence of unobserved instances conforming to it. For example, Abraham Maslow made the following generalization: people at work seek to satisfy sequentially five levels of needs arranged in a prepotency hierarchy.[16] A deprived need dominates the person's attention and determines behavior. Once this deficit is satisfied, the next higher-level need is activated, and the individual progesses up the hierarchy. When the level of self-actualization is reached, progression ceases. The more this need is satisfied, the stronger it grows. On the basis of this theory, one can expect to find a similar pattern of behavior in a variety of work settings where no statistics have been generated. That is, theory enables one to predict what should be observable where no data are available.

Revealing Needed Research Theories generalize about phenomena and predict phenomena. They also pinpoint crucial areas to be investigated and crucial problems to be solved. For example, test theory and development have had a long history in education. Test developers have made significant contributions to the practice of education. Teachers have always used some type of test to measure their students' achievement of academic content. The development of tests of academic achievement relies heavily on test theory and validation. An important problem in educational practice today revolves around the results of testing in our schools. For example, it has been well documented that there is an achievement gap between white students and certain groups of ethnic-minority students.[17] This problem might have gone unnoticed if it were not for the documentation provided by state-mandated achievement tests. The No Child Left Behind (NCLB) Act was enacted primarily to close the achievement gap. Thus, the work of educators at all levels is being shaped by

[16]Abraham Maslow, *Motivation and Personality,* rev. ed. (Reading, MA: Addison-Wesley, 1970).

[17]Tyrone G. Howard, *Why Race and Culture Matter in Schools: Closing the Achievement Gap in America's Classrooms* (New York: Teachers College Press, 2011); Rod Paige, *The Black-White Achievement Gap: Why Closing It Is the Greatest Civil Rights Issue of Our Time* (New York: Amacom, 2011).

national accountability standards designed to improve the performance of *all* students on state-mandated tests. Consequently, tests seem to be driving educational practice.[18]

If one accepts the premise that tests are driving educational practice, perhaps the easiest way to improve practice and increase student achievement is to construct better tests. Critics argue that many state-mandated tests require students to recall obscure factual knowledge, which limits the time teachers have available to focus on critical thinking skills.[19] However, according to Yeh, it is possible to design force-choice items (multiple-choice test items) that test reasoning and critical thinking.[20] Such tests could require students to *use* facts, rather than *recall* them. And test questions could elicit content knowledge that is worth learning. It seems reasonable to say, then, that research is a driving force in educational practice, particularly in the area of student testing. More research is needed in the area of test development and validation.[21]

Development of Administrative Thought

The development of administrative thought can be placed into a loose historical framework. In general, four models emerge: classical organizational theory, the human relations approach, the behavioral science approach, and the post-behavioral science era.

Classical Organizational Theory

Classical organizational theory emerged during the early years of the twentieth century. It includes two different **management perspectives**: scientific management and administrative management. Historically, scientific management focused on the management of work and workers. Administrative management addressed issues concerning how an overall organization should be structured.

Scientific Management

Prior to the turn of the twentieth century, there was almost no systematic study of management. The practice of management was based on experience and common sense. Frederick W. Taylor tried to change that view. An engineer, he pursued the idea that through careful scientific analysis the efficiency of work could be improved. His basic theme was that managers should study work scientifically to identify the "one best way" to perform a task.

Taylor's **scientific management** consists of four principles:[22]

1. *Scientific Job Analysis.* Through observation, data gathering, and careful measurement, management determines the "one best way" of performing each job. Such job analysis replaces the old rule-of-thumb method.
2. *Selection of Personnel.* Once the job is analyzed, the next step is to scientifically select and then train, teach, and develop workers. In the past, workers chose their own work and trained themselves.
3. *Management Cooperation.* Managers should cooperate with workers to ensure that all work being done is in accordance with the principles of the science that has been developed.
4. *Functional Supervising.* Managers assume planning, organizing, and decision-making activities, whereas workers perform their jobs. In the past, almost all work and the greater part of the responsibility were thrust on workers.

Taylor's four principles of scientific management were designed to maximize worker productivity. In his early career as a laborer in the steel industry, he observed firsthand how workers performed well below their capacities. He referred to this activity as *soldiering*. Taylor felt that scientific management—time study for setting standards, separation of managerial and employee duties, and incentive systems—would correct the problem. Rather than relying on past practice or rules of thumb, he provided managers with explicit

[18]Teach for America, *Teaching as Leadership: The Highly Effective Teacher's Guide to Closing the Achievement Gap* (New York: John Wiley & Sons, 2011).

[19]Linda McNeil, *Contradictions of School Reform: Educational Costs of Standardized Testing* (New York: Routledge, 2000).

[20]Stuart S. Yeh, "Tests Worth Teaching To: Constructing State Mandated Tests That Emphasize Critical Thinking," *Educational Researcher*, 30 (2001): 12–17.

[21]W. James Popham, *Educational Assessment: What School Leaders Need to Understand* (Thousand Oaks, CA: Corwin Press, 2010); W. James Popham, *Classroom Assessment: What Teachers Need to Know* (Upper Saddle River, NJ: Prentice Hall, 2011).

[22]Frederick W. Taylor, *Principles of Scientific Management* (New York: Harper, 1911).

Table 1-1 Fayol's Fourteen Principles of Management

Component	Description
Division of work	The object of division of work is improved efficiency through a reduction of waste, increased output, and a simplification of job training.
Authority	Authority is the right to give orders and the power to extract obedience. Responsibility, a corollary of authority, is the obligation to carry out assigned duties.
Discipline	Discipline implies respect for the rules that govern the organization. Clear statements of agreements between the organization and its employees are necessary, and the state of discipline of any group depends on the quality of leadership.
Unity of command	An employee should receive orders from only one superior. Adherence to this principle avoids breakdowns in authority and discipline.
Unity of direction	Similar activities that are directed toward a singular goal should be grouped together under one manager.
Subordination of individual interest	The interests of individuals and groups within an organization should not take precedence over the interests of the organization as a whole.
Remuneration	Compensation should be fair and satisfactory to both employees and the organization.
Centralization	Managers must retain final responsibility, but they should give subordinates enough authority to do the task successfully. The appropriate degree of centralization will vary depending on circumstances. It becomes a question of the proper amount of centralizing to use in each case.
Scalar chain	The scalar chain, or chain of command, is the chain of supervisors ranging from the ultimate authority to the lowest ranks. The exact lines of authority should be clear and followed at all times.
Order	Human and material resources should be coordinated to be in the right place at the right time.
Equity	A desire for equity and equality of treatment are aspirations managers should take into account in dealing with employees.
Stability of personnel	Successful organizations need a stable workforce. Managerial practices should encourage long-term commitment of employees to the organization.
Initiative	Employees should be encouraged to develop and carry out plans for improvement.
Esprit de corps	Managers should foster and maintain teamwork, team spirit, and a sense of unity and togetherness among employees.

Source: Adapted from Henri Fayol, *General and Industrial Administration* (New York: Pitman, 1949), pp. 20–41. (Originally published in French in 1916 with the title *Administration Industrielle et Generale*.)

guidelines for improving production management, based on proven research and experimentation.

Administrative Management

Whereas scientific management focuses on jobs of individual workers, **administrative management** concentrates on the management of an entire organization. The primary contributors to the field of administrative management were Henri Fayol, Luther Gulick, and Max Weber.

Henri Fayol was an engineer and French industrialist. For many years, he served as managing director of a large coal-mining firm in France. He attributed his success as a manager not to any personal qualities he may have possessed but, rather, to a set of management principles that he used. Fayol claimed that all managers perform five basic functions: planning, organizing, commanding, coordinating, and controlling.

Besides the five basic management functions, Fayol identified fourteen principles that he felt should guide the management of organizations and that he found useful during his experience as a manager (Table 1–1).

Fayol's fourteen principles of management emphasize chain of command, allocation of authority, order, efficiency, equity, and stability. Max Weber also recognized the importance of these factors, but Fayol was the first to recognize management as a continuous process.

Luther Gulick, another classical theorist, augmented Fayol's five basic management functions while serving on Franklin D. Roosevelt's Committee on Government Administration. He coined the acronym POSDCoRB, which identified seven functions of management: planning, organizing, staffing, directing, coordinating, reporting, and budgeting.[23]

1. *Planning* involves developing an outline of the things that must be accomplished and the

[23]Luther Gulick and Lyndall Urwick (eds.), *Papers on the Science of Administration* (New York: Columbia University Press, 1937).

methods for accomplishing them. It attempts to forecast future actions and directions of the organization.

2. *Organizing* establishes the formal structure of authority through which work subdivisions are arranged, defined, and coordinated to implement the plan.
3. *Staffing* involves the whole personnel function of selecting, training, and developing the staff and maintaining favorable working conditions.
4. *Directing,* closely related to leading, includes the continuous task of making decisions, communicating and implementing decisions, and evaluating subordinates properly.
5. *Coordinating* involves all activities and efforts needed to bind together the organization in order to achieve a common goal.
6. *Reporting* verifies progress through records, research, and inspection; ensures that things happen according to plan; takes any corrective action when necessary; and keeps those to whom the chief executive is responsible informed.
7. *Budgeting* concerns all activities that accompany budgeting, including fiscal planning, accounting, and control.

One of the most influential contributors to classical organizational theory was German sociologist Max Weber, who first described the concept of bureaucracy. Weber's contributions were not recognized until years after his death.[24] Weber's concept of bureaucracy is based on a comprehensive set of rational guidelines. Similar in concept to many of Fayol's fourteen principles, Weber's guidelines were believed to constitute an ideal structure for organizational effectiveness. Weber's ideal bureaucracy and Fayol's fourteen principles of management laid the foundation for contemporary organizational theory.

Classical organizational theories and their derived principles have many critics. An emphasis on efficiency characterized the classical approach to management. To these theorists, an efficiently designed job and organization were of prime importance. Psychological and social factors in the workplace were ignored. The critics claim that when managers ignore the social and psychological needs of workers, organizations do not provide adequate motivation to their employees. The classicists assumed that financial incentives would ensure worker motivation. In short, the focus of classical organizational theory was on the task, with little attention given to the individual or group in the workplace. This flaw was primarily responsible for the emergence of the second approach to management thought: the human relations approach.

Human Relations Approach

The **human relations approach** is considered to have started with a series of studies conducted at the Hawthorne Plant of Western Electric near Chicago by Elton Mayo and his associates between 1927 and 1933.[25] These studies, widely known as the **Hawthorne studies,** have strongly influenced administrative theory.

The Hawthorne Studies

The Hawthorne studies consisted of several experiments. They included the first Relay Assembly Test Room, the second Relay Assembly Group, the Mica-Splitting Group, the Typewriting Group, and the Bank Wiring Observation Room experiments. In addition, an interview program involving 21,126 employees was conducted to learn what workers liked and disliked about their work environment.

Two experiments in particular are noteworthy. In the Relay Assembly Test Room experiments, the research began with the designation of two groups of female workers. Each group performed the same task, and the groups were located in two separate rooms, each of which was equally lighted. One group, designated the control group, was to have no changes made in lighting or other work-environment factors. The other was the experimental group in which lighting and other environmental factors were varied. Changes in the productivity of the two groups was subsequently measured and analyzed. Regardless of the light level or various changes in rest periods and lengths of workdays and workweeks, productivity in both the control and the experimental groups improved; in fact, the worse things got, the higher the productivity rose.

---

[24]Max Weber, *The Theory of Social and Economic Organization,* trans. Talcott Parsons (New York: Oxford University Press, 1947).

[25]Elton Mayo, *The Human Problems of an Industrial Civilization* (New York: Macmillan, 1933); and Fritz J. Roethlisberger and William J. Dickson, *Management and the Worker* (Cambridge, MA: Harvard University Press, 1939).

In the Bank Wiring Observation Room experiments, a group of nine men were paid on a piecework incentives pay system. That is, their pay increased as their productivity increased. Researchers expected that worker productivity would rise over time. As in the Relay Assembly Test Room experiments, researchers found an unexpected pattern of results. They discovered that the group informally established an acceptable level of output for its members. Most workers, the "regulars," ignored the incentive system and voluntarily conformed to the group's standard level of acceptable output, called a *group norm*. Those who did not conform, the "deviants," were disciplined by the group to bring their output in line with the group's standard output. Workers who produced too much were called "rate-busters" and sometimes were physically threatened to make them conform with the rest of the group. On the other hand, employees who underproduced were labeled "chislers" and were pressured by the group to increase their productivity.

To understand the complex and baffling pattern of results, Mayo and his associates interviewed over 20,000 employees who had participated in the experiments during the six-year study. The interviews and observations during the experiments suggested that a human-social element operated in the workplace. Increases in productivity were more of an outgrowth of group dynamics and effective management than any set of employer demands or physical factors. In the lighting experiment, for example, the results were attributed to the fact that the test group began to be noticed and to feel important. Researchers discovered that the improvement in productivity was due to such human-social factors as morale, a feeling of belonging, and effective management in which such interpersonal skills as motivating, leading, participative decision making, and effective communications were used. Researchers concluded, from the results of the incentive pay-system experiment, that informal work groups emerged with their own norms for the appropriate behavior of group members. In short, the importance of understanding human behavior, especially group behavior, from the perspective of management was firmly established.

Other Contributors to the Human Relations Approach

Mayo and his associates were not the only contributors to the human relations approach. There were several strong intellectual currents which influenced the human relations movement during this period. Kurt Lewin emphasized field theory and research known as group dynamics.[26] Noteworthy is his work on *democratic* and *authoritarian* groups. Lewin and his associates generally concluded that democratic groups, in which members actively participate in decisions, are more productive in terms of both human satisfaction and the achievement of group goals than are authoritarian groups.[27] Furthermore, much of the current work on individual and organizational approaches to change through group dynamics (sensitivity training, team building, Alcoholics Anonymous, and Weight Watchers) and the action-research approach to organizational development is based on Lewin's pioneering work.

Carl Rogers deserves mention here as well. Not only did he develop a procedure for industrial counseling[28] while working with Mayo and his associates at Western Electric, but the metapsychological assumptions on which his client-centered therapy[29] is based also provide the skeletal framework on which the human relations approach is built. For example, according to Rogers, the best vantage point for understanding behavior is from the internal frame of reference of the individual, who exists in a continually changing world of experience; who perceives the field of experience as reality for her; and who strives to actualize, maintain, and enhance her own human condition.[30]

The writings of Jacob Moreno made a substantial contribution to the human relations movement. Like Lewin, Moreno was interested in interpersonal relations within groups. He developed a sociometric technique: people develop selective affinities for other people. Groups composed of individuals with similar affinities for one another will likely perform better than groups lacking such affective preferences.[31]

Additional contributors to the human relations school of thought include William Whyte and George Homans. Using a field study methodology similar to

---

[26]Kurt Lewin, *Field Theory in Social Science*.

[27]Kurt Lewin, Ronald Lippitt, and Robert White, "Patterns of Aggressive Behavior in Experimentally Created 'Social Climates,'" *Journal of Social Psychology,* 10 (1939): 271–299.

[28]Carl R. Rogers, *Counseling and Psychotherapy* (Boston: Houghton Mifflin, 1942).

[29]Carl R. Rogers, *Client-Centered Therapy* (Boston: Houghton Mifflin, 1951).

[30]Ibid., pp. 483–494.

[31]Jacob L. Moreno, *Who Shall Survive?* rev. ed. (New York: Beacon House, 1953).

the one used by Mayo, Whyte studied the nature and functioning of work group behavior in the restaurant industry. He examined intergroup conflict, status within groups, workflow, and the like. Consistent with Moreno's sociometric theory, Whyte found that selective preferences among group members are associated with such factors as similarities in age, sex, and outside interests.[32] His study is significant because the findings are based on observations of real-life situations rather than isolated laboratory conditions. George Homans's general theory of small groups was a major landmark. Homans conceptualized the totality of group structure and functioning that has received wide attention among organizational theorists and practitioners alike.[33]

The major assumptions of the human relations approach include the following ideas:

1. Employees are motivated by social and psychological needs and by economic incentives.
2. These needs, including but not limited to recognition, belongingness, and security, are more important in determining worker morale and productivity than the physical conditions of the work environment.
3. An individual's perceptions, beliefs, motivations, cognition, responses to frustration, values, and similar factors may affect behavior in the work setting.
4. People in all types of organizations tend to develop informal social organizations that work along with the formal organization and can help or hinder management.
5. Informal social groups within the workplace create and enforce their own norms and codes of behavior. Team effort, conflict between groups, social conformity, group loyalty, communication patterns, and emergent leadership are important concepts for determining individual and group behavior.
6. Employees have higher morale and work harder under supportive management. Increased morale results in increased productivity.
7. Communication, power, influence, authority, motivation, and manipulation are all important relationships within an organization, especially between superior and subordinate. Effective communication channels should be developed between the various levels in the hierarchy, emphasizing democratic rather than authoritarian leadership.

The human relationists used field study methods extensively, as well as laboratory experiments, to study the work environment. These social scientists made important contributions to our understanding of employee behavior in the workplace.

Behavioral Science Approach

Behavioral scientists considered both the classicists' rational-economic model and the human relationists' social model to be incomplete representations of employees in the work setting. A number of authors attempted to reconcile or show points of conflict between classical and human relations theory; thus, the **behavioral science approach** was born.

Effectiveness/Efficiency Although a contemporary of many human relationists, Chester Barnard was one of the first authors to take the behavioral science approach. For many years, Barnard served as president of the New Jersey Bell Telephone Company. His executive experience and extensive readings in sociology and organizational psychology resulted in one of management's few classic textbooks.[34]

His best-known idea is the **cooperative system,** an attempt to integrate, in a single framework, human relations and classical management principles. Barnard argues that the executive must meet two conditions if cooperation and financial success are to be attained. First, the executive must emphasize the importance of *effectiveness,* which is the degree to which the common purpose of the organization is achieved. Second, the executive must be aware of *efficiency,* which is the satisfaction of "individual motives" of employees.[35] His main point is that an organization can operate and survive only when both the organization's goals and the goals of the individuals working for it are kept in equilibrium. Thus, managers must have both human and technical skills.

[32]William F. Whyte, *Human Relations in the Restaurant Industry* (London: Pittman, 1949).

[33]George C. Homans, *The Human Group* (New York: Harcourt, Brace & World, 1950).

[34]Chester I. Barnard, *The Functions of the Executive* (Cambridge, MA: Harvard University Press, 1938).

[35]Ibid.

Fusion Process Another major contributor to the behavioral science approach was E. Wight Bakke of the Yale University Labor and Management Center. He views the organization as embodying a **fusion process.**[36] The individual, he argues, attempts to use the organization to further his own goals, whereas the organization uses the individual to further its own goals. In the fusion process, the organization to some degree remakes the individual and the individual to some degree remakes the organization. The fusion of the *personalizing process* of the individual and the *socializing process* of the organization is accomplished through the *bonds of organization,* such as the formal organization, the informal organization, the workflow, the task(s) to be completed, and the system of rewards and punishments.

Individual/Organization Conflict Holding views similar to Bakke's, Chris Argyris argues that there is an inherent conflict between the individual and the organization.[37] This conflict results from the incompatibility between the growth and development of the individual's maturing personality and the repressive nature of the formal organization. Argyris believes that people progress from a state of psychological immaturity and dependence to maturity and independence and that many modern organizations keep their employees in a dependent state, preventing them from achieving their full potential. Further, Argyris believes that some of the basic principles of management are inconsistent with the mature adult personality. The resulting incongruence between individual personality and the organization causes conflict, frustration, and failure for people at work. People learn to adapt to the failure, frustration, and conflict resulting from the incongruency by ascending the organizational hierarchy, by using defense mechanisms, or by developing apathy toward their work that ultimately leads to the dysfunction of the organization's goals. This trend to conformity has been espoused in such popular books as *The Organization Man*[38] and *Life in the Crystal Palace.*[39]

[36]E. Wight Bakke, *The Fusion Process* (New Haven, CT: Yale University Press, 1955).

[37]Chris Argyris, *The Individual and the Organization* (New York: Irvington, 1993).

[38]William H. Whyte, *The Organization Man* (New York: Simon & Schuster, 1956).

[39]Allan Harrington, *Life in the Crystal Palace* (London: Jonathan Cape, 1960).

Nomothetic/Idiographic A useful theoretical formulation for studying administrative behavior is the social systems analysis developed for educators by Jacob Getzels and Egon Guba.[40] Getzels and Guba conceive of the social system as involving two classes of phenomena that are independent and interactive. First are institutions with certain roles and expectations that together constitute the **nomothetic dimension** of activity in the social system. Second are the individuals with certain personalities and need-dispositions inhabiting the system who together constitute the **idiographic dimension** of activity in the social system. Behavior then in any social system can be seen as a function of the interaction between personal needs and institutional goals. Conformity to the institution, its roles, and its expectations results in organizational effectiveness, whereas conformity to individuals, their personalities, and their need-dispositions results in individual efficiency. (Note the similarity between Getzels and Guba's framework and those of Barnard, Bakke, and Argyris.)

Need Hierarchy The behavioral science approach has drawn heavily on the work of Abraham Maslow, who developed a **need hierarchy** that an individual attempts to satisfy.[41] Maslow's theory suggests that an administrator's job is to provide avenues for the satisfaction of an employee's needs that also support organizational goals and to remove impediments that block need satisfaction and cause frustration, negative attitudes, or dysfunctional behavior.

Theory X and Theory Y Based on the work of Maslow, Douglas McGregor formulated two contrasting sets of assumptions about people and the management strategies suggested by each. He called these **Theory X** and **Theory Y.**[42] McGregor believed that the classical approach was based on Theory X assumptions about people. He also thought that a modified version of Theory X was consistent with the human relations perspective. That is, human relations concepts did not go far enough in explaining people's needs and management's strategies to accommodate them. McGregor

[40]Jacob W. Getzels and Egon G. Guba, "Social Behavior and the Administrative Process," *School Review,* 65 (1957): 423–441.

[41]Abraham Maslow, *Motivation and Personality,* rev. ed. (Reading, MA: Addison-Wesley, 1970).

[42]Douglas McGregor, *The Human Side of Enterprise* (New York: McGraw-Hill, 1960).

viewed Theory Y as a more appropriate foundation for guiding management thinking.

Hygiene-Motivation Extending the work of Maslow, Frederick Herzberg developed a two-factor theory of motivation.[43] Herzberg makes a distinction between factors that cause or prevent job dissatisfaction (**hygiene factors**) and factors that cause job satisfaction (**motivation factors**). Only the latter group of factors can lead to motivation. Herzberg's hygiene factors relate closely to Maslow's lower-level needs: physiological, safety, and social; his motivation factors relate to the needs at the top of Maslow's hierarchy: esteem and self-actualization. Recognition of motivation factors calls for a different style of management from that proposed by the classical or human relations advocates.

Systems 1–4 Another writer concerned with the way in which the goals of individuals and those of the organization can coincide is Rensis Likert. Likert conducted extensive empirical research at the Institute for Social Research—University of Michigan to examine the effect of management systems on employees' attitudes and behavior. He developed four management systems, ranging from **System 1**, Exploitive Authoritative, to **System 4**, Participative Group.[44] Each system characterizes an organizational climate based on several key dimensions of effectiveness, including leadership, motivation, communications, interaction/influence, decision making, goal setting, control, and performance goals. Likert posits the participative group system (System 4) as coming closest to the ideal. The essence of System 4 theory is based on three key propositions: supportive relationships, group decision making in an overlapping group structure, which he calls *linking-pins,*[45] and high-performance goals of the leader. (Note the parallel here to McGregor's Theory X and Theory Y dichotomy.) Likert, however, provides more categories and more specificity. His Systems 1–4 represent four different leadership styles.

Managerial Grid In the area of leadership, Robert Blake and Jane Mouton assess managerial behavior on two dimensions: concern for production and concern for people. Managers can plot their scores on an eighty-one-celled **managerial grid.**[46] The grid is designed to help managers identify their own leadership styles, to understand how subordinates are affected by their leadership style, and to explore the use of alternative leadership styles consistent with employees' needs.

Contingency Theory Contingency theories of leadership have come into vogue in recent years. Fred Fiedler developed a contingency theory of leadership effectiveness.[47] The basic premise is that in some situations relationship-motivated leaders perform better, while other conditions make it more likely that task-motivated leaders will be most effective. Three variables determine the situations under which one or the other type of leader will be most effective: leader–member relations (the degree to which leaders feel accepted by their followers), task structure (the degree to which the work to be done is clearly outlined), and position power (the extent to which the leader has control over rewards and punishments the followers receive).

Situational Leadership Another popular leadership theory is situational leadership developed by Paul Hersey and Kenneth Blanchard.[48] **Situational leadership theory** is based primarily on the relationship between follower maturity, leader task behavior, and leader relationship behavior. In general terms, the theory suggests that the style of leadership will be effective only if it is appropriate for the maturity level of the followers. Hersey and Blanchard see two types of maturity as particularly important: job maturity (a person's maturity to perform the job) and psychological maturity (the person's level of motivation as reflected in achievement needs and willingness to accept responsibility).

Transformational Leadership In his examination of the concept of **transformational leadership**, Bernard Bass contrasts two types of leadership behavior: transactional and transformational.[49] According to Bass, transactional leaders determine what subordinates need

---

[43]Frederick Herzberg, *The Motivation to Work* (New Brunswick, NJ: Transaction, 1993).

[44]Rensis Likert, "From Production and Employee-Centeredness to Systems 1–4," *Journal of Management, 5* (1979): 147–156.

[45]Rensis Likert, *New Patterns of Management* (New York: Garland, 1987).

[46]Robert R. Blake and Jane S. Mouton, *The Managerial Grid: Leadership Styles for Achieving Production Through People* (Houston: Gulf, 1994).

[47]Fred E. Fiedler, *A Theory of Leadership Effectiveness* (New York: McGraw-Hill, 1967).

[48]Paul Hersey and Kenneth Blanchard, *Management of Organizational Behavior,* 8th ed. (Paramus, NJ: Prentice Hall, 2007).

[49]Bernard M. Bass and Robert E. Riggio, *Transformational Leadership, 2nd ed.* (Mahwah, NJ: Lawrence Erlbaum, 2006).

to do to achieve their own and the organization's goals, classify those requirements, help subordinates become confident that they can reach their goals by expending the necessary efforts, and reward them according to their accomplishments. Transformational leaders, in contrast, motivate their subordinates to do more than they originally expected to do. They accomplish this in three ways: by raising followers' levels of consciousness about the importance and value of designated outcomes and ways of reaching them; by getting followers to transcend their own self-interest for the sake of the team, organization, or larger polity; and by raising followers' need levels to the higher-order needs, such as self-actualization, or by expanding their portfolio of needs.

Other Important Contributors The great diversity of perspectives in the behavioral science school makes it impossible to discuss all of its contributors here. Social scientists like Victor Vroom,[50] William Reddin,[51] and Amitai Etzioni[52] did much to assist its development. Warren Bennis, in his best-selling book on leadership, identifies bureaucracy and other classical management principles as the "unconscious conspiracy" that prevents leaders from leading.[53]

A key contribution of the contingency perspective may best be summarized in the observation that there is no one best way to administer an organization. There are no motivation strategies, organizational structures, decision-making patterns, communication techniques, change approaches, or leadership styles that will fit all situations. Rather, school administrators must find different ways that fit different situations.

Post–Behavioral Science Era

The behavioral science approach influenced the preparation and practice of school administrators for some time, but it has lost much of its original appeal recently with challenges to modernist views of organizations and leadership. Building on the strengths and short comings of the past, three powerful, interrelated concepts of school improvement, democratic community, and social justice emerge, which form the development of the next era of the profession: the **post–behavioral science era.**[54] This view is reinforced with increased emphasis on emergent nontraditional perspectives (variously labeled neo-Marxist, critical theory, and postmodernism).

School Improvement

Accountability for school improvement is a central theme of state policies. The No Child Left Behind (NCLB) Act of 2001 (Public Law 107-110) sets demanding accountability standards for schools, school districts, and states, including new state testing requirements designed to improve education. For example, the law requires that states develop both content standards in reading and mathematics and tests that are linked to the standards for grades 3 through 8, with science standards and assessments to follow. States must identify adequate yearly progress (AYP) objectives and disaggregate test results for all students and subgroups of students based on socioeconomic status, race/ethnicity, English language proficiency, and disability. Moreover, the law mandates that 100 percent of students must score at the proficient level on state tests by 2014. Furthermore, the NCLB Act requires states to participate every other year in the National Assessment of Educational Progress (NAEP) in reading and mathematics.

Will schools, school districts, and states be able to respond to the demand? In an ideal system, school improvement efforts focus educational policy, administration, and practices directly on teaching and learning. This will require districtwide leadership focused directly on learning. School leaders can accomplish this by (1) clarifying purpose, (2) encouraging collective learning, (3) aligning with state standards, (4) providing support, and (5) making data-driven decisions. Taken together, these five dimensions provide a compelling framework for accomplishing sustained districtwide success for all children.[55]

Clarifying Purpose The school district and the administrators and teachers who work in it are accountable

[50]Victor Vroom and Arthur Jago, *The New Leadership: Managing Participation in Organizations* (Englewood Cliffs, NJ: Prentice Hall, 1988).

[51]William J. Reddin, *Managerial Effectiveness* (New York: McGraw-Hill, 1970).

[52]Amitai Etzioni, *A Comparative Analysis of Complex Organizations,* rev. ed. (New York: Free Press, 1975).

[53]Warren G. Bennis, *Why Leaders Can't Lead: The Unconscious Conspiracy Continues* (San Francisco: Jossey-Bass, 1990).

[54]Joseph Murphy, "Reculturing the Profession of Educational Leadership: New Blueprints," *Educational Administration Quarterly,* 38 (2002): 186.

[55]Fred C. Lunenburg, "The Post-Behavioral Science Era: Excellence, Community, and Justice," in F. C. Lunenburg and Carolyn S. Carr (eds.), *Shaping the Future: Policy, Partnerships, and Emerging Perspectives* (Lanham, MD: Rowman & Littlefield, 2003 pp. 31–55).

for student learning. This assertion has strong economic, political, and social appeal; its logic is clear. What teachers teach and students learn is a matter of public inspection and subject to direct measurement.[56] Superintendents need to develop a practical rationale for school improvement. Clearly and jointly held purposes help give teachers and administrators an increased sense of certainty, security, coherence, and accountability.[57] Purposes cannot remain static for all time, however. They must be constantly adapted to changing circumstances and the needs of the system. Few really successful schools lack purpose.[58]

Encouraging Collective Learning A key task for school administrators is to create a collective expectation among teachers concerning the state's accountability criteria. That is, administrators need to raise teachers' collective sense about state standards. Then administrators must work to ensure that teacher expectations are aligned with the state's accountability criteria.[59] Furthermore, administrators need to eliminate teacher isolation, so that discussions about state standards become a collective mission of the school and school district.

Aligning with State Standards Most states are attempting to align their tests with their standards. States need to consider three principles in this endeavor.[60] First, tests not based on the standards are neither fair nor helpful to parents or students. States that have developed their own tests have done a good job of ensuring that the content of the test can be found in the standards. That is, children will not be tested on knowledge and skills they have not been taught. However, the same is not true when states use generic, off-the-shelf standardized tests. Such tests cannot measure the breadth and depth of each state's standards. Second, when the standards are rich and rigorous, the tests must be as well. Tests must tap both the breadth and depth of the content and skills in the standards. Third, tests must become more challenging in each successive grade. The solid foundation of knowledge and skills developed in the early grades should evolve into more complex skills in the later grades.

Providing Support One of the biggest challenges in advancing state standards and tests, and the accountability provisions tied to them, is providing teachers with the training, teaching tools, and support they need to help all students reach high standards. Specifically, teachers need access to curriculum guides, textbooks, or specific training connected to state standards. They need access to lessons or teaching units that match state standards. They need training on using state test results to diagnose learning gaps.[61] Teachers must know how each student performed on every multiple-choice item or other question on the state test. Schools need to provide additional help to students who lag behind in core subjects. This involves creating an environment that supports school improvement efforts.[62]

Making Data-Driven Decisions How can school districts gauge their progress in achieving high state standards? Three factors can increase a school district's progress in meeting state standards.[63] The primary factor is the availability of performance data connected to each student, broken down by specific objectives and target levels in the state standards. Then schools across the district and across the state are able to connect what is taught to what is learned.

The second factor is the public nature of the measurement system. Assuming the school district has a system of rating schools, the district should publish annually a matrix of schools and honor those schools that have performed at high levels. This provides an impetus for low-performing schools to improve their performance. At the school and classroom levels, it provides a blueprint of those areas where teachers should focus their individual education plans and where grade levels or schools should focus the school's professional development plans.

The third factor is the specifically targeted assistance provided to schools that are performing at low levels.

---

[56]Richard F. Elmore, *School Reform from the Inside Out: Policy, Practice, and Performance* (Cambridge, MA: Harvard Education Publishing Group, 2004).

[57]Roland Barth, *Learning by Heart* (New York: John Wiley, 2004).

[58]Fred C. Lunenburg and Beverly J. Irby, *The Principalship: Vision to Action* (Belmont, CA: Wadsworth/ Thompson, 2006).

[59]Robert Marzano and Timothy Waters, *District Leadership That Works: Striking the Right Balance* (Bloomington, IN: Solution Tree, 2011).

[60]Elizabeth Spalding, *An Introduction to Standard-Based Reflective Practices for Middle and High School Teaching* (New York: Teachers College Press, 2010).

[61]Fred C. Lunenburg and Beverly J. Irby, *High Expectations: An Action Plan for Implementing Goals 2000* (Thousand Oaks, CA: Corwin Press, 2000).

[62]Fred C. Lunenburg, "Improving Student Achievement: Some Structural Incompatibilities," in G. Perreault and Fred C. Lunenburg (eds.), The Changing World of School Administration (Lanham, MD: Rowman & Littlefield, 2002) pp. 5–27.

[63]Susan Sclafani, "Using an Aligned System to Make Real Progress in Texas Students," *Education and Urban Society,* 33(2001): 305–312.

EXEMPLARY EDUCATIONAL ADMINISTRATORS IN ACTION

HENRY S. BANGSER, Ph.D., Superintendent, New Trier Township High School District, Winnetka/Northfield, Illinois.

Words of Advice: As early in your career as possible, hopefully well before you become a superintendent, develop a baseline philosophy and a set of principles around which you will build your management and leadership style. These are standards from which you will not vary. In my opinion, these must embody respect for all individuals within the organization: student to student, student to adult, adult to student, and adult to adult.

Each targeted school is paired with a team of principals, curriculum specialists/instructional coaches, and researchers to observe current practices, discuss student performance data with the staff, and assist in the development and implementation of an improvement plan.

In sum, the new framework for school improvement that we have described here provides a powerful and useful model for achieving school success. Sustained district wide school improvement is not possible without a strong connection across levels of organization (school, school district, community, and state). Internal school development is necessary from principals, teachers, and parents, but school improvement cannot occur unless each school is supported by a strong external infrastructure; stable political environments; and resources outside the school, including leadership from the superintendent and school board as well as leadership from the state.

Democratic Community

The concept of democratic community is not new. Much of the current work is grounded in Dewey's ideas promulgated more than 100 years ago.[64] For example, at the turn of the twentieth century, John Dewey argued that schools should embody the kind of community that combined the best aspects of classic liberalism and communitarianism or, in Dewey's words, of "individualism and socialism"[65]—a place that could prepare people to live within and to maintain a healthy, democratic society. However, Dewey's vision was relatively uninfluential throughout much of the twentieth century. A resurgence of interest in Dewey and his concept of a democratic community as it relates to schooling has emerged in education in recent years.[66]

[64]John Dewey, *The School and Society* (Chicago: University of Chicago Press, 1900).

[65]Dewey, *The School and Society,* p. 7.

[66]See, for example, Patrick M. Jenlink (ed.), Dewey's Democracy and Education Revisited: Contemporary Discourses for Democratic Education and Leadership (Lanham, MD: Rowman & Littlefield, 2009).

At mid-twentieth century, James Contant suggested that the basic tenets of American democracy should be taught in schools, along with language, history, economics, science, mathematics, and the arts.[67] More recently, Wood expanded this theme by suggesting that democratic citizenship should be taught in schools. These include traits such as commitment to community and a desire to participate; values such as justice, liberty, and equality; skills of interpretation, debate, and compromise; and habits of study and reflection.[68] Others concur. Hargreaves suggests that the cultivation of "openness, informality, care, attentiveness, lateral working relationships, reciprocal collaboration, candid and vibrant dialogue, and the willingness to face uncertainty together"[69] is a central purpose of schooling, not merely the production of employable workers.

Critiques concerning the meaning of democracy in our time have proliferated over the last two decades. And a number of publications have addressed the various meanings of community. For example, community is described in multiple ways in the education literature.[70] Community is referred to as "professional

[67]James B. Contant, *Education and Liberty: The Role of the Schools in a Modern Democracy* (New York: Vintage Books, 1953).

[68]George H. Wood, *Schools That Work: America's Most Innovative Public Education Programs* (New York: Dutton, 1992).

[69]Andy Hargreaves, "Rethinking Educational Change: Going Deeper and Wider in the Quest for Success," in A. Hargreaves (ed.), *Rethinking Educational Change with Heart and Mind* (Alexandria, VA: Association for Supervision and Curriculum Development, 1997), p. 22.

[70]Patricia E. Calderwood, *Learning Community: Finding Common Ground in Difference* (New York: Teachers College Press, 2000); Gail C. Furman, *School as Community: From Promise to Practice* (Albany: State University of New York Press, 2003); Karen F. Osterman, "Students' Need for Belonging in the School Community," *Review of Educational Research,* 70 (2001): 323–367; Carolyn M. Shields, "Thinking about Community from a Student Perspective," in G. Furman (ed.), *School as Community: From Promise to Practice* (Albany: State University of New York Press, 2003).

community" among educators, "learning community" among students, "school–community" addressing school–community relations, and "community of difference" in multicultural settings.

Furman and Starratt advocate the definition of community of difference as more compatible with contemporary postmodernism.[71] Thinking about a community of difference requires a reconceptualization of the concept of community itself, moving away from homogeneity toward a new center in which diverse groups negotiate a commitment to the common good. According to Shields, "a *community of difference* begins, not with an assumption of shared norms, beliefs, and values; but with the need for respect, dialogue, and understanding."[72] Educational leaders who want to move toward a community of difference will be informed by research on race and ethnicity.

Similarly, democracy is subject to many interpretations in education. Its most common meaning is usually tied to the idea of the nation-state and the American version of democracy. According to Mitchell, democratic community cannot be limited to such a narrow view of democracy in a world characterized by diversity, fragmentation, and globalization.[73] National boundaries are permeated by regional and global alliances. Children should be educated within an increasingly global context.

Democratic Community and Leadership Our version of democratic community resembles more the ideas promulgated by Gail Furman and Robert Starratt.[74] They extend the emerging work on democratic community through a deeper analysis of the linkages between democratic community and leadership in schools. And Furman and Starratt's model places democratic community in a context of postmodernism, characterized by inclusiveness, interdependence, and transnationalism. In their view and ours, professional community, learning community, school–community, and community of difference, and the American version of democracy, along with Dewey's progressivism, laid much of the groundwork for the concept of democratic community.

Some common themes are beginning to emerge regarding the concept of democratic community derived from Dewey's progressivism and its more contemporary, postmodern interpretations. Furman and Starratt discuss the nature and character of democratic community and how it might be enacted in schools.[75] The central tenets of democratic schools include the following:

1. Democratic community is based on the open flow of ideas that enables people to be as fully informed as possible.
2. Democratic community involves the use of critical reflection and analysis to evaluate ideas, problems, and policies.
3. Democratic community places responsibility on individuals to participate in open inquiry, collective choices, and actions in the interest of the common good.
4. Democratic community involves acting for others as well as with others in the interest of the common good.
5. Democratic community is based on the acceptance and celebration of difference, and focuses on the integral linkages between the school, the surrounding community, and the larger global community.
6. Creating democratic community in schools involves systematic attention to structure, process, and curriculum and instruction.

Social Justice

A concern for social justice is at the core of democracy. The United States prides itself on being a fair and just democracy, a nation in which every citizen is to be treated equally in social, economic, political, and educational arenas. According to its Constitution, the United States seeks to establish "liberty and justice for all." In spite of these goals, U.S. society is composed of many inequities: rich and poor, educated and illiterate, powerful and powerless. Now in the second decade of the twenty-first century, educational leaders must continue

[71]Gail C. Furman and Robert J. Starratt, "Leadership for Democratic Community in Schools," in J. Murphy (ed.), *The Educational Leadership Challenge: Redefining Leadership for the 21st Century* (Chicago: University of Chicago Press, 2002), pp. 105–133.

[72]Carolyn M. Shields, Linda J. Larocque, and Steven L. Oberg, "A Dialogue about Race and Ethnicity in Education: Struggling to Understand Issues in Cross-Cultural Leadership," *Journal of School Leadership,* 12 (2002): 132.

[73]Katheryne Mitchell, "Education for Democratic Citizenship: Transnationalism, Multiculturalism, and the Limits of Liberalism," *Harvard Educational Review,* 71 (2001): 51–78.

[74]Furman and Starratt, "Leadership for Democratic Community in Schools."

[75]Furman and Starratt, "Leadership for Democratic Community in Schools."

to question whether they have an obligation to create a nation whose words are supported by the experiences of its citizens.

The Fourteenth Amendment to the U.S. Constitution addressed the question of equal opportunity, declaring that "no state shall deny to any person within its jurisdiction the equal protection of the laws." The mandate that people receive equal protection extends to equal educational opportunity. While this fundamental affirmation of equal opportunity has been part of American discourse since the inception of this nation and is found in the Declaration of Independence and other documents, inequities in the major social, economic, political, and educational institutions continue to exist in American society.

Inequities in Schooling Among the social injustices with which educational leaders need to be most concerned. Although it has been a stated goal in the United States that all youngsters, regardless of family background, should benefit from their education, many students do not. Most schools do not teach all students at the same academic level. The U.S. educational system to this day is beset with inequities that exacerbate racial and class-based challenges. Differential levels of success in school distributed along race and social-class lines continues to be the most pernicious and prevailing dilemma of schooling. Furthermore, there is considerable empirical evidence that children of color experience negative and inequitable treatment in typical public schools.[76]

Many children of color find themselves marginalized in toxic schools that offer inferior education. These schools affect the opportunities and experiences of students of color in several immediate ways: They tend to have limited resources; textbooks and curricula are outdated; and computers are few and obsolete. Many of the teachers do not have credentials in the subjects they teach. Tracking systems block minority students' access to the more rigorous and challenging classes, which retain these students in non-college-bound destinations. These schools generally offer few (if any) Advanced Placement courses, which are critical for entry into many of the more competitive colleges.

Furthermore, African American students are overrepresented in special education programs, compared with the overall student population. More than a third of African American students (as compared with fewer than a fifth of white students) in special education are labeled with the more stigmatizing labels of "mentally retarded" and "emotionally disturbed." Conversely, four-fifths of the white students (as compared with two-thirds of the African American students) in special education are much more likely to be labeled "learning disabled" or "speech impaired." African American males are more than twice as likely as white males to be suspended or expelled from school or to receive corporal punishment.[77] Jonathan Kozol, in *Savage Inequalities*, described the inferior education received by minority students (particularly African Americans and Hispanic Americans)—fewer resources, inequities in funding, inadequate facilities, tracking systems, low expectations, segregated schools, and hostile learning environments.[78]

These related inequities, the persistent and disproportionate academic underachievement of children of color and their injurious treatment in our schools, are compelling evidence that the United States public education system remains systemically racist.[79] This is not to suggest that racism is consciously intended or even recognized by educators; it is institutional racism that is systemically embedded in assumptions, policies and procedures, practices, and structures of schooling. Nevertheless, every day more than 17 million African American, Hispanic American, Native American, and Asian American children experience the effects of systemic racism in U.S. public schools.[80]

Excellence and Equity Educational leadership for social justice is founded on the belief that schooling must be democratic, and an understanding that schooling is not democratic "unless its practices are excellent and equitable." Educational equity is a precondition for excellence. Gordon linked social justice to excellence and equity by arguing:

> The failure to achieve universally effective education in our society is known to be a correlate of our failure to achieve social justice. By almost any measure, there continue to be serious differences between the level and quality of

---

[76]Linda Skrla, Kathryn Bell McKenzie, and James J. Scheurich, *Using Equity Audits to Create Equitable and Excellent Schools* (Thousand Oaks, CA: Sage, 2010).

[77]Carola Suárez-Orozco and Marcelo M. Suárez-Orozco, *Learning a New Land: Immigrant Students in American Society* (Cambridge, MA: Harvard University Press, 2010).

[78]Jonathan Kozol, *Savage Inequalities: Children in America's Schools* (New York: Crown, 1991).

[79]Skrla, McKenzie, and Scheurich, *Using Equity Audits to Create Equitable and Excellent Schools.*

[80]Linda Skrla, and James J. Scheurich, *Educational Equity and Accountability: Paradigms, Policies, and Politics* (Clifton, NJ: Taylor & Francis, 2004).

> educational achievement for children coming from rich or from poor families, and from ethnic-majority or from some ethnic-minority group families. Low status ethnic-minority groups continue to be overrepresented in the low achievement groups in our schools and are correspondingly underrepresented in high academic achievement groups.[81]

We must achieve equal educational results for all children. Failure to do so will hamper specific groups from attaining the fundamental, primary goods and services distributed by society—rights, liberties, self-respect, power, opportunities, income, and wealth. Education is a social institution, controlling access to important opportunities and resources.

Emergent Nontraditional Perspectives

Positivism was the dominant orthodoxy in educational administration until the late 1970s. Positivism is a view of knowledge as objective, absolutely true, and independent of other conditions such as time, circumstances, societies, cultures, communities, and geography.[82] Another tradition of positivism is *empiricism,* which maintains that knowledge of the world can only be acquired through the senses and through experience. This view of science came to be known as *logical empiricism* or *logical positivism.*[83] From these philosophies there developed positivism—the view that any investigation in the natural or social sciences must be derived from empiricist postulates in order to be considered academically acceptable. Simply stated, positivism is a worldview that all knowledge of the world comes to us from sense experience and observation.

The positivist approach to research consists of several functions: (a) the observation and description of perceptual data coming to us from the world through our senses, (b) the development of theories inferred from such observations and descriptions of perceptual data, (c) the testing of hypotheses derived from theories, and (d) the verification of hypotheses that are then used to verify the theories derived from the observation and description of perceptual data.[84] The approach evolved from an empiricist model of science that involves observation and description, theory building, and hypothesis testing and verification. Quantitative methods using large samples with the objective of statistical inferences was the predominant tool used. The positivist approach to the generation of knowledge dominated research in educational administration until the late 1970s.[85]

At that time, objections began to surface regarding the dominant (positivist) orthodoxy. Alternative paradigms began to appear and continued to be refined through the 1980s. These emerging nontraditional perspectives came under the general heading of *subjectivist* and *interpretivist* approaches. Subjectivist and interpetivist views refer to perspectives that look inward to the mind rather than outward to experience and that connect to philosophical idealism and, more recently, to phenomenology and existentialism.[86] Subjectivist and interpretivist perspectives are illustrated by the early work of scholars such as T.B. Greenfield in Canada; by the work of neo-Marxist and critical theorists such as Richard Bates and others; and by the early work of postmodernists such as Jacques Derrida, Michel Foucault, and Francois Lyotard.[87] The scholars in this tradition have attempted to expand the traditional knowledge domains that define educational administration.

These alternative nontraditional perspectives have spawned scholarship on ethics and values by researchers such as Christopher Hodgkinson, Jackie Stefkovich, Joan Shapiro, Lynn Beck, and Jerry Starratt; gender, race/ethnicity, and class by such scholars as Carol Gilligan, Sonia Nieto, Lisa Delpit, Charol Shakeshaft, Margaret Grogan, Cryss Brunner, Marilyn Tallerico, Beverly Irby, Genevieve Brown, Linda Skrla, Flora Ida Ortiz, Catherine Marshall, Kofi Lomotey, Barbara Jackson, Diana Pounder, Norma Mertz, Cynthia Dillard, and Gretchen Rossman; and critical theory and postmodernism by analysts such as T.B. Greenfield, Henry Giroux, Richard Bates, Peter McLaren, William Foster, Fenwick English, Colleen Capper, Spencer Maxcy, James Scheurich, Michael Dantley, Cornel West, Michelle Young, Colleen Larson, Gary Anderson, Carolyn Shields, Patti Lather, and Paulo Freire.

The subjectivist perspectives led to the increased popularity of qualitative research methods under various labels: qualitative methods, ethnography, participant observation, case studies, fieldwork, and naturalistic inquiry. These approaches are attempts to understand

[81]Edmund W. Gordon, *Education and Justice: A View from the Back of the Bus* (New York: Teachers College Press, 1999), p. XII.

[82]Auguste Comte, *A General View of Positivism* (New York: Cambridge University Press, 2011).

[83]William A. deVries, *Empiricism, Perceptual Knowledge, Normality, and Realism* (New York: Oxford University Press, 2011).

[84]Gall, Gall, & Borg, *Educational Research.*

[85]Lunenburg, "The Post-Behavioral Science Era."

[86]Jon Stewart, *Idealism and Existentialism: Hegel and Nineteenth- and Twentieth-Century Philosophy* (London: Continuum International Publishing Group, Ltd., 2011).

[87]Christopher Butler, Postmodernism (New York: Sterling, 2011); Lynn Fendler, *Michel Foucault* (London: Continuum International Publishing Group, Ltd., 2011).

Table 1–2 Overview of the Four Major Developments in Administrative Thought

Period	Management Elements	Procedures	Contributors and Basic Concepts
Classical organizational theory	Leadership Organization Production Process Authority Administration Reward Structure	Top to bottom Machine Individual Anticipated consequences Rules; coercive Leader separate Economic Formal	Time-and-motion study, functional supervisor, piece rate (Taylor); five basic functions, fourteen principles of management (Fayol); POSDCoRB (Gulick); ideal bureaucracy (Weber)
Human relations approach	Leadership Organization Production Process Authority Administration Reward Structure	All directions Organism Group Unanticipated consequences Group norms Participative Social and psychological Informal	Hawthorne studies (Mayo, Roethlisberger, and Dickson); intellectual undercurrents: group dynamics leadership studies (Lewin, Lippitt, and White); client-centered therapy (Rogers); sociometric technique (Moreno); human relations in the restaurant industry (Whyte); small groups (Homans)
Behavioral science approach	Consideration of all major elements with heavy emphasis on contingency leadership, culture, transformational leadership, and systems theory	Cooperative systems (Barnard); fusion process (Bakke); optimal actualization—organization and individual (Argyris); social systems theory—nomothetic and idiographic (Getzels and Guba); need hierarchy (Maslow); Theory X and Y (McGregor); hygiene-motivation (Herzberg); Systems 1-4 (Likert); open-closed climates (Halpin and Croft); managerial grid (Blake and Mouton); contingency theory (Fiedler); situational leadership (Hersey and Blanchard); expectancy theory (Vroom); 3-D leadership (Reddin); compliance theory (Etzioni); structure of organizations (Mintzberg); leadership-unconscious conspiracy (Bennis)	
Post-behavioral science approach	Interrelated concepts of school improvement, democratic community, and social justice with heavy emphasis on leadership; and emergent nontraditional perspectives	School improvement, democratic community, and social justice (Murphy); transformational leadership (Bass); learning organization (Senge); reframing organizations (Bolman and Deal); TQM (Deming); synergistic leadership theory (Irby, Brown, Duffy, and Trautman); values and ethics (Hodgkinson, Stefkovich, Shapiro, Beck, and Starratt); gender, race/ethnicity, and class (Gilligan, Nieto, Delpit, Shakeshaft, Grogan, Brunner, Tallerico, Irby, Brown, Skrla, Ortiz, Marshall, Lomotey, Jackson, Pounder, Mertz, Dillard, Rossman); critical theory and postmodernism (T. B. Greenfield, Derrida, Foucault, Lyotard, Giroux, Bates, McLaren, Foster, English, Capper, Maxcy, Scheurich, Dantley, West, Young, Larson, Furman, Anderson, Shields, Lather, Freire)	

educational processes within local situations. Societies; cultures; communities; unique circumstances; gender, race, and class; and geography serve as important analytical categories in such inquiry. There seems to be an increasing interest in bringing together positivist and interpretive paradigms that may prove valuable to both the researcher and the practitioner.[88]

In sum, the classical "rational" model evolved around the ideas of scientific and administrative management, including the study of administrative processes and managerial functions. The human relations "social" model was spurred by some early seminal social science research, including experimentation and analysis of the social and psychological aspects of people in the workplace and the study of group behavior. The behavioral science approach was an attempt to reconcile the basic incongruency between the rational-economic model and the social model. The more recent post-behavioral science era includes the interrelated concepts of school improvement, democratic community, and social justice, as well as emergent nontraditional perspectives (variously labeled neo-Marxist, critical theory, and postmodernism). Table 1–2 provides an overview of the four major developments in administrative thought.

[88]Fred C. Lunenburg and Beverly J. Irby, *Writing a Successful Thesis or Dissertation: Tips and Strategies for Students in the Social and Behavioral Sciences* (Thousand Oaks, CA: Corwin Press, 2008).

As shown in Table 1–2, differences in leadership, organization, production, process, power, administration, reward, and structure are important distinguishing characteristics of the four approaches. We can see how organization and administrative theory have evolved from a concern for efficiency and the basic principles of management to an emphasis on human and psychological factors, to social systems and contingency theory, and finally, to a concern for school improvement, democratic community, social justice, and postmodernism. While we have not included all people who have made contributions in the evolution of administrative thought, we have highlighted major contributors and basic concepts and primary eras in the evolution. Furthermore, no attempt is made to date the eras precisely. In fact, if we view the sequence of developments in organizational and administrative theory, we notice a correlational rather than a compensatory tendency.

Traces of the past coexist with modern approaches to administration. For example, while the classical "rational" model has been modified somewhat since its emergence during the 1900s, views of the school as a rational-technical system remain firmly embedded in the minds of policymakers and pervade most educational reforms proposed since the publication of *A Nation at Risk* in 1983[89] and the many reports that followed. Indeed, this view of schooling is in place today with current accountability policy to assess student, teacher, and school performance. Implicit in NCLB[90] is the concomitant expectation that school administrators and teachers will adjust instructional strategies to yield more effective learning outcomes for all children.

Schools as Open Systems

All schools are open systems, although the degree of interaction with the external environment may vary. According to open systems theory, schools constantly interact with their external environment. In fact, they need to structure themselves to deal with forces in the world around them.[91] In contrast, closed systems theory views schools as sufficiently independent to solve most of their problems through their internal forces, without taking into account forces in the external environment. NCLB is a good example of open systems theory and the impact it has had on schools. Since the federal law was passed, states began to focus their policy on standards, accountability, and the improvement of student achievement. Statewide assessment systems were implemented nationwide. Thus was born an era of high-stakes testing complete with rewards and sanctions for low-performing schools. NCLB has impacted local school districts in every state.

A system can be defined as an interrelated set of elements functioning as an operating unit.[92] As depicted in Figure 1–1, an open system consists of five basic elements: inputs, transformation process, outputs, feedback, and the environment.[93]

Inputs

Systems such as schools receive four kinds of inputs from the environment: human, financial, physical, and information resources. Human resources include personnel. Financial resources are the capital used by the school/school district to finance both ongoing and long-term operations. Physical resources include supplies, materials, facilities, and equipment. Information resources are knowledge, curricula, data, and other kinds of information utilized by the school/school district.

Transformation Process

The school administrator's job involves combining and coordinating these various resources to attain the school's/school district's goals, i.e., learning for *all*. Ideally, students are transformed by the school system into educated graduates, who then contribute to the environment. How do school administrators achieve this? Work of some kind is done in the system to produce output. The system *adds value added* to the work in process.[94] This transformation process includes the internal operation of the school/school district and its system of operational management. Some components

[89]National Commission on Excellence in Education, *A Nation at Risk* (Washington, DC: U.S. Government Printing Office, 1983).

[90]No Child Left Behind Act of 2001 (www.ed.gov/nclb/landing.jhtml?src=pb).

[91]Richard W. Scott, *Organizations and Organizing: Rational, Natural and Open Systems Perspectives* (Upper Saddle River, NJ: Prentice Hall, 2007).

[92]Peter M. Senge, *The Fifth Discipline: The Art & Practice of the Learning Organization* (New York: Currency/Doubleday, 2006).

[93]Scott, *Organizations and Organizing.*

[94]Peter Shaw, *The Four Vs of Leadership: Vision, Values, Value Added, Vitality* (New York: John Wiley and Sons, 2006).

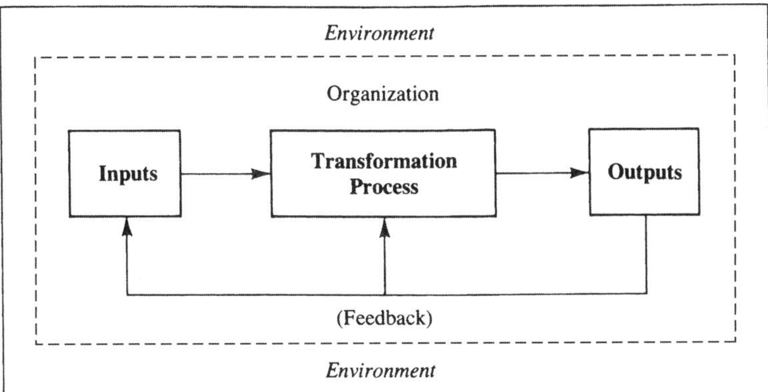

FIGURE 1–1

Open Systems Model

of the system of operational management include the technical competence of school administrators and other personnel, including their decision making and communication skills, their plans of operation, and their ability to cope with change. Activities performed by school administrators and other personnel within the organization's structure will affect the school district's outputs.

Outputs

The school administrator's job is to secure and use inputs from the environment, transform them—while considering external variables—to produce outputs. In school organizations, outputs are the attainment of the *goals* or *objectives* of the school district and are represented by the products, results, outcomes, or accomplishments of the system. Although the kinds of outputs will vary with a specific school, they usually include one or more of the following: student achievement, teacher performance, growth levels of students and teachers, student dropout rates, employee turnover, student and employee absenteeism, employee-management relations, school-community relations, student attitudes toward school, and employee job satisfaction.

Feedback

These outputs provide feedback data to the system. Feedback is crucial to the success of the school operation. Negative feedback, for example, can be used to correct deficiencies in the transformation process or the inputs or both, which in turn will have an effect on the school's future outputs.

Environment

The environment surrounding the school/school district includes the social, political, and economic forces that impinge on the organization. The environment in the open systems model takes on added significance today in a climate of policy accountability. The social, political, and economic contexts in which school administrators work are marked by pressures at the local, state, and federal levels. Thus, school administrators today find it necessary to manage and develop "internal" operations while concurrently monitoring the environment and anticipating and responding to "external" demands.

Since the enactment of the NCLB, education has been near the top of the national political agenda. The federal law nationalized the discussion concerning the well-being of public schooling in America. At the time the report was released and subsequently, there has been concern with an achievement gap in America[95] and our academic competitiveness with other nations,

---

[95]Linda Darling-Hammond, *The Flat World and Education: How America's Commitment to Equity Will Determine Our Future*. New York: Teachers College Press, 2010); Richard DuFour, Rebecca DuFour, Robert Eaker, and Gayle Karhanek, *Raising the Bar and Closing the Gap: Whatever It Takes (Bloomington, IN: Solution Tree*, 2010; Terrence G. Howard, *Why Race and Culture Matter in Schools: Closing the Achievement Gap in America's Classrooms* (New York: Teachers College Press, 2011); Rod Paige, *The Black-White Achievement Gap: Why Closing It is the Greatest Civil Rights Issue of Our Time* (New York: Amacom, 2011).

particularly in mathematics and science.[96] These achievement gaps and academic comparisons have led many people to conclude that the U.S. public school system was underperforming. With recognition of an achievement gap and the rise of international educational comparisons, states began to focus their policy on standards, accountability, and the improvement of student academic achievement.[97]

The social, political, and economic forces that impinge on schools are not all state and national, however. Local school administrators also face a number of challenges that are exclusively local in nature, such as bond referenda, difficult school boards, and teacher unions. These local political issues can at times confound state-mandated policies. Some examples follow. Principals often face mandated programs that do not meet the changing demographics of their student population. Teachers are often bound by union contracts that conflict with the norms of their particular school. Superintendents are expected to respond to federal mandates even though resources are scarce. Zero-tolerance policies may require expelling a student even though it may not be in that student's best interest to miss school for an extended period of time. And education leaders are faced with ongoing pressures to show good results on state-mandated achievement tests, while at the same time dealing with a growing number of management duties, such as budgeting, hiring personnel, labor relations, and site committees resulting from School-Based Management legislation.

The Learning Organization

In recent years, organization theorists have extended the open systems model by adding a "brain" to the "living organization." Today school administrators are reading and hearing a great deal about learning organizations. Peter Senge, a professor at the Massachusetts Institute of Technology, popularized the concept of *learning organization* in his best-selling book *The Fifth Discipline*.[98]

A **learning organization** is a strategic commitment to capture and share learning in the organization for the benefit of individuals, teams, and the organization. It does this through alignment and the collective capacity to sense and interpret a changing environment; to input new knowledge through continuous learning and change; to imbed this knowledge in systems and practices; and to transform this knowledge into outputs.

Senge defines the learning organization as "organizations where people continually expand their capacity to create the results they truly desire, where new and expansive patterns of thinking are nurtured, where collective aspiration is set free and where people are continually learning how to learn together."[99] Senge describes a model of five interdependent disciplines necessary for an organization to seriously pursue learning. He identifies systems thinking as the "fifth discipline" because he believes that thinking systemically is the pivotal lever in the learning and change process. Brief definitions of Senge's principles follow.

- *Systems thinking:* A conceptual framework that sees all parts as interrelated and affecting each other.
- *Personal mastery:* A process of personal commitment to vision, excellence, and lifelong learning.
- *Shared vision:* Sharing an image of the future you want to realize together.
- *Team learning:* The process of learning collectively; the idea that two brains are smarter than one.
- Mental models: Deeply ingrained assumptions that influence personal and organizational views and behaviors.

The five disciplines work together to create the learning organization. A metaphor to describe this systems theory–based model would be DNA or a hologram. Each is a complex system of patterns, and the whole is greater than the sum of its parts.

Senge, author of the best-selling book, *The Fifth Discipline,* has written a companion book directly focused on education. In *Schools That Learn,*[100] Senge argues that teachers, administrators, and other school stakeholders must learn how to build their own capacity; that is, they must develop the capacity to learn. From Senge's perspective, real improvement will occur only if people

[96]U.S. Government Printing Office, *The Condition of Education* (Washington, DC: The Author, 2008).

[97]Clete Bulach, Fred C. Lunenburg, and Les Potter, *Creating a Culture for High-Performing Schools: A Comprehensive Approach to School Reform* (Lanham, MD: Rowman & Littlefield, 2008).

[98]Senge, *The Fifth Discipline*.

[99]Senge, *The Fifth Discipline*, p. 3.

[100]Peter Senge, *Schools That Learn: A Fifth Discipline Fieldbook for Educators, Parents, and Everyone Who Cares about Education* (New York: Doubleday, 2011).

responsible for implementation design the change itself. He argues that schools can be re-created, made vital, and renewed not by fiat or command, and not by regulation, but by embracing the principles of the learning organization.

Senge makes a powerful argument regarding the need for a systems approach and learning orientation. He provides a historical perspective on educational systems. Specifically, he details "industrial age" assumptions about learning: that children are deficient and schools should fix them, that learning is strictly an intellectual enterprise, that everyone should learn in the same way, that classroom learning is distinctly different from that occurring outside of school, and that some kids are smart while others are not. He further asserts that schools are run by specialists who maintain control, that knowledge is inherently fragmented, that schools teach some kind of objective truth, and that learning is primarily individualistic and competition accelerates learning. Senge suggests that these assumptions about learning and the nature and purpose of schooling reflect deeply embedded cultural beliefs that must be considered, and in many cases directly confronted, if schools are to develop the learning orientation necessary for improvement.

Through learning, people make meaning of their experience and of information. Learning helps people to create and manage knowledge that builds a system's intellectual capital. Karen Watkins and Victoria Marsick have developed a model of the learning organization around seven action imperatives that speak to the kind of initiatives that are implemented in learning organizations. (See Administrative Advice 1–2.)

ADMINISTRATIVE ADVICE 1-2

The Seven Action Imperatives of a Learning Organization

The seven action imperatives can be interpreted in terms of what must change to help schools become learning organizations.

- *Create Continuous Learning Opportunities.* This means that learning is ongoing, strategically used, and grows out of the work itself.
- *Promote Inquiry and Dialogue.* The key to this imperative is a culture in which people ask questions freely, are willing to put difficult issues on the table for discussion, and are open to giving and receiving feedback at all levels.
- *Encourage Collaboration and Team Learning.* The relevant action imperative for this level focuses on the spirit of collaboration and the skills that undergird the effective use of teams. People in schools frequently form groups, but they are not always encouraged to bring what they know to the table.
- *Create Systems to Capture and Share Learning.* Technology-based strategies that are used for this purpose focus on the use of software such as Lotus Notes or Microsoft Access to capture ideas across dispersed teams and divisions, and computerized documentation of changes in a particular area.
- *Empower People toward a Collective Vision.* The primary criteria for success with this action imperative are the degree of alignment throughout the organization around the vision, and the degree to which everyone in the organization actively participates in creating and implementing the changes that follow from the vision.
- *Connect the Organization to Its Environment.* Schools must function at both global and local levels. Schools can use benchmarking to see what other schools are doing to achieve excellence and to solve similar problems, and can scan their environment for new trends by using computer databases. Technology enables people in schools to move beyond their walls.
- *Provide Strategic Leadership for Learning.* Leaders who model learning are key to the learning organization. They think strategically about how to use learning to move the organization in new directions.

Source: Adapted from Karen E. Watkins and Victoria J. Marsick, "Sculpting the Learning Community: New Forms of Working and Organizing," *NASSP Bulletin*, 83, no. 604 (1999): 78–87.

PRO CON DEBATE Training School Leaders

Xerox's CEO David Kearns said that schools "are admirably suited to the economy and culture of the 1950s and spectacularly unsuited to the high-tech future of the next century." He believes that education is big business and the same theories that guide industrial executives are the ones school leaders need to solve education's problems.

Question: Is the management training provided by business and industry for their leaders the best source of information and skill development for principals and superintendents?

Arguments PRO

1. Organizational theory is generic. Its essential concepts are applicable in all organizations.
2. Most organizational theory taught in educational administration courses was generated by researchers in the industrial setting. Industrial management thought leads the way. Why not do away with intermediaries?
3. Business and school leaders need to work more closely together. If they share the same training, think about the same ideas, and speak the same language, it will improve the collegial relationship between schools and the communities they serve.
4. Management training is current and tested. Industry has invested heavily in the development of management-training programs. If that resource is being offered to schools, it would be foolish not to take advantage of the offer.
5. Management trainers understand organizational theory well and can teach adult learners in all types of organizations to apply theory to their settings.

Arguments CON

1. Business is private enterprise; schools are public service agencies. It would be a dangerous mistake to borrow management theory wholesale.
2. Many aspects of management theory do not apply in educational settings. It takes several years to adapt management theory into educational administrative theory. Educational researchers play an important role in sifting and applying organizational theory.
3. The scions of industry are one consumer group for schools. Educators' relationship to them is important but no more important than the relationship with the leaders of other consumer groups such as parents, colleges, and civic agencies. While educators should be open to feedback from clients, they should not be co-opted by them.
4. Management training is behaviorist and outcome-driven. It does not consider the social and psychological needs of the teacher as much as the profits of the organization.
5. Management trainers understand profit-driven organizations but do not understand the norms and values of educators.

Summary

1. The practice of educational administration has changed in response to historical conditions and theoretical developments.
2. To an increasing degree, educational administration is characterized by using theory to explain and predict phenomena in educational organizations.
3. The uses of theory include identification of relevant phenomena, classification of phenomena, formulation of constructs, summarization of phenomena, prediction of phenomena, and revelation of needed research.
4. Since the early 1900s, four major perspectives on administration have evolved: classical organization theory, the human relations approach, the behavioral science approach, and the post–behavioral science era.
5. Three contemporary extensions of administrative perspectives are emergent nontraditional perspectives, systems theory, and the learning organization.

6. Emergent nontraditional perspectives have spawned research in ethics and values; gender, race/ethnicity, and class; and critical theory and postmodernism.
7. Systems theory is usually discussed in terms of inputs, a transformation process, outputs, feedback, and environment.
8. The learning organization concept has received much attention since the publication of Peter Senge's book *The Fifth Discipline*. Senge provides five interacting principles that constitute a learning organization: systems thinking, personal mastery, shared vision, team learning, and mental models.

Key Terms

theory
scientific method
hypothesis
variable
laboratory study
field study
meta-analysis
survey study
case study
classical organizational theory
management perspectives
scientific management
administrative management
human relations approach
Hawthorne studies
behavioral science approach
cooperative system
fusion process
nomothetic dimension
idiographic dimension
need hierarchy
Theory X and Theory Y
hygiene factors
motivation factors
Systems 1–4
managerial grid
contingency theories
situational leadership theory
transformational leadership
post-behavioral science era
positivism
open system theory
learning organization

Discussion Questions

1. What is theory?
2. How are theory and research related?
3. What are the uses of theory?
4. What major developments in administrative thought have evolved in the field of educational administration?
5. How have emergent nontraditional perspectives influenced the study and practice of educational administration?
6. How can open systems theory be used to diagnose problems in school operation?
7. How can the learning organization be used to achieve school success?

Suggested Readings

Blankstein, Alan M. *Failure is Not an Option: 6 Principles for Making Student Success the ONLY Option*, 2nd ed. (Thousand Oaks, CA: Sage, 2010). Anchored in the moral purpose of sustaining success for all students, this Second Edition of the bestseller demonstrates how to reshape school cultures to support continuous student success.

Darling-Hammond, Linda. *The Flat World and Education: How America's Commitment to Equity Will Determine Our Future* (New York: Teachers College Press, 2010). *The Flat World and Education* offers an eye-opening wake-up call concerning America's future and vividly illustrates what the United States needs to do to build a system of high-achieving and equitable schools that ensures every child the right to learn.

English, Fenwick W. (ed.). *The SAGE Handbook of Educational Leadership* (Thousand Oaks, CA: Sage, 2005). The *Handbook* reviews how leadership was redefined by management and organizational theory in its quest to become scientific, then looks forward to promising theories, concepts, and practices that show potential for development and application.

Firestone, William A., and Carolyn Riehl (eds.). *A New Agenda for Research in Educational Leadership* (New York: Teachers College Press, 2006). This book, the product of the task force on research co-sponsored by the American Educational Research

Association Division A and the University Council for Educational Administration, sets an ambitious agenda for research in educational leadership. Prominent scholars cover a broad range of topics.

Fullan, Michael. *Leadership & Sustainability: System Thinkers in Action* (Thousand Oaks, CA: Corwin Press, 2005). Fullan asks the question: How do you develop and sustain a greater number of system thinkers in action, or new theoreticians? This groundbreaking work defines an agenda for the new theoretician, including crucial elements of sustainability.

Marzano, Robert J., and Timothy Waters. *District Leadership That Works: Striking the Right Balance* (Bloomington, IN: Solution Tree, 2010). This book introduces a top-down power mechanism called "defined autonomy," a concept that focuses on district-defined, nonnegotiable, common goals and a system of accountability supported by assessment tools.

Skrla, Linda, Kathryn Bell McKenzie, and James J. Scheurich. *Using Equity Audits to Create Equitable and Excellent Schools* (Thousand Oaks, CA: Sage, 2010). This book provides practical strategies for using equity audits to help ensure a high-quality education for all students, regardless of socioeconomic class.

2

Organizational Structure

FOCUSING QUESTIONS

1 What is organizational structure?

2 What are the key elements of organizational structure, and how do they function in schools?

3 How does bureaucracy influence approaches to organizational structure in schools?

4 How do participatory management models influence organizational structure in schools?

5 Can school administrators use alternative models of organizational structure to improve the operation of schools?

6 How can school administrators use social systems theory to better understand how schools function?

In this chapter, we attempt to answer these questions concerning organizational structure in schools. We begin our discussion by examining the key elements of organizational structure. We then discuss the bureaucratic model of organizational structure. Next, we examine the participatory management model, including McGregor's Theory X and Theory Y, Argyris's immaturity–maturity continuum, Likert's system 4 organization, Sergiovanni's moral leadership, school-based management, and Bolman and Deal's four-frame model. We then describe three alternative models of organizational structure: Etzioni's compliance theory, Hage's mechanistic-organic organizations, and Mintzberg's strategy-structure typology. We conclude the chapter with a discussion of the school as a social system using several of Getzel's models.

Table 2-1 Key Design Questions and Answers for Designing an Organization's Structure

Key Design Question	The Answer is Provided by
1. To what degree are activities subdivided into separate jobs?	Job specialization
2. On what basis will jobs be grouped together?	Departmentalization
3. To whom do individuals and groups report?	Chain of command
4. What is the framework for providing direction and control?	Authority and responsibility
5. Where does decision-making authority lie?	Centralization/decentralization
6. What type of authority flows in a direct line in the chain of command, and what type flows to line personnel in the form of advice?	Line & staff authority
7. How many people can an administrator efficiently and effectively direct?	Span of control

What is Organizational Structure?

Organizational structure provides a framework for vertical control and horizontal coordination of the organization. There are seven key elements that school administrators need to address when they design their organization's structure: job specialization, departmentalization, chain of command, authority and responsibility, centralization/decentralization, line and staff authority, and span of control. We present each of these key elements as answers to an important structural question (see Table 2-1).

Job Specialization

A basic concept of organizational structure is to divide the work to be accomplished into specialized tasks and to organize them into distinct units. Examples of **job specialization** are the division of the school into elementary, middle, and high school units; the distinction between administrative and teaching functions; and the variety of position certificates required by the fifty state departments of education, including superintendent, business manager, principal, supervisor, teaching specialties, and the like.

The three most common alternatives to job specialization are job rotation, job enlargement, and job enrichment.[1] *Job rotation* involves systematically moving employees from one job to another. In large school districts, principals are often rotated between schools every five years. *Job enlargement* adds breadth to a job by increasing the number and variety of activities performed by an employee. *Job enrichment* adds depth to a job by adding "administrative" activities (decision making, staffing, budgeting, reporting) to an employee's responsibilities.

Departmentalization

Departmentalization, the organizationwide division of work, permits the organization to realize the benefits of job specialization and to coordinate the activities of the component parts. School districts may be broadly divided into divisions of instruction, business, personnel, and research and development. Further subdividing of a division such as instruction may produce departments responsible for specific subjects, such as English, social studies, mathematics, and science. Departments—frequently labeled divisions, building units, departments, or teams—often indicate hierarchical relationships. Thus, an assistant superintendent may lead a division; a principal, a building unit; a department head, an academic department within a building unit; and a teacher, a grade-level team in a school.

The most common grouping in schools is by function. Functional departmentalization offers a number of advantages. Because people who perform similar functions work together, each department can be staffed by experts in that functional area. Decision making and coordination are easier, because division administrators or department heads need to be familiar with only a relatively narrow set of skills. Functional departments at the central office can use a school district's resources more efficiently because a department's activity does not have to be repeated across several school district divisions. On the other hand, functional departmentalization has certain disadvantages. Personnel can develop overly narrow and technical viewpoints that lose sight

[1]Stephen P. Robbins and Timothy R. Judge, *Organizational Behavior*, 14th ed. (Upper Saddle River, NJ: Pearson/Prentice Hall, 2011).

of the total system perspective, communication and coordination across departments can be difficult, and conflicts often emerge as each department or unit attempts to protect its own area of authority and responsibility.

Chain of Command

Chain of command, concerned with the flow of authority and responsibility within an organization, is associated with two underlying principles. *Unity of command* means that a subordinate is accountable to only one person—the person from whom he receives authority and responsibility. The *scalar principle* means that authority and responsibility should flow in a direct line vertically from top management to the lowest level. It establishes the division of work in the organization in hierarchical form.

Although organizations differ in the degree of their vertical divisions of work and the extent to which it is formalized, they all exhibit aspects of this characteristic. For example, in the military, the vertical specialization is established by specific definitions of roles for the various positions, and there are definite status differences among levels. Within the officer ranks in the Navy, there is a distinct difference of role and status in the hierarchy from ensign to admiral. In the university, there is a hierarchy within the professional ranks: instructor, assistant, associate, and full professor. In the school district organization, there are vertical differentiations of positions ranging from teachers to department heads, principals, directors, and superintendents. These levels are typically well defined, with differences in role and status for the various positions.

Authority and Responsibility

Authority is the right to make decisions and direct the work of others. It is an important concept in organizational structure because administrators and other personnel must be authorized to carry out jobs to which they are assigned. Furthermore, authority and responsibility should be linked; that is, **responsibility** for the execution of work must be accompanied by the authority to accomplish the job.

In a school district, authority stems from the board of education. This body then delegates to the superintendent of schools the authority necessary to administer the district. As authority is delegated further, it becomes narrower in scope. Each succeedingly lower-level occupant has narrower limits on her areas of legitimate authority. This view of authority and responsibility provides the framework for legitimizing organizational hierarchy and provides the basis for direction and control.

Centralization/Decentralization

Delegation of authority between a superior and a subordinate is a way of sharing power. The cumulative effect of all these superordinate-subordinate empowerment practices can have a dramatic impact on the overall organization. If administrators in a school district tend to delegate considerable authority and responsibility, more decisions are made at lower levels in the organization. Subordinates in such districts possess considerable influence in the overall operation of the school district. In these cases, the organization follows an administrative philosophy of **decentralization.** On the other hand, when school administrators retain most of the authority, depending on subordinates to implement decisions only, the organization is practicing **centralization.** Centralization and decentralization represent opposite ends of a continuum. That is, authority is delegated to a relatively small or large degree in the organization.

Should organizations centralize or decentralize? In the United States and Canada, the trend over the last thirty years has been toward greater decentralization of organizations.[2] Decentralization is said to have the following advantages: It makes greater use of human resources, unburdens top-level administrators, ensures that decisions are made close to the firing line by personnel with technical knowledge, and permits more rapid response to external changes.[3]

Line and Staff Authority

Another way to view organizational structure is as line and staff authority. **Line authority** is that relationship in which a superior exercises direct supervision over a subordinate—an authority relationship in a direct line in the chain of command. Line authority relates specifically to the unity of command principle and the scalar principle. For example, line administrators

[2]Richard L. Daft, *Organizational Theory and Design* (Belmont, CA: Cengage South-Western, 2009).

[3]Samuel C. Certo, *Modern Management* (Upper Saddle River, NJ: Prentice Hall, 2009).

such as the superintendent, assistant superintendent, directors of elementary and secondary education, and principals have authority to issue orders to their subordinates. Thus, the superintendent can order the assistant superintendent of instruction to implement a curriculum change, and the assistant superintendent in turn can order the directors of elementary and secondary education to do the same, and so on down the chain of command.

Staff authority is advisory in nature. The function of personnel in a staff position is to create, develop, collect, and analyze information, which flows to line personnel in the form of advice. Staff personnel do not possess the legitimate authority to implement this advice. One familiar example of staff is the "assistant to" in which the person assists the superintendent or other superior in a variety of ways. Another example is the legal counsel who advises the superintendent in legal matters affecting the schools.

Span of Management

Span of management refers to the number of subordinates reporting directly to a supervisor. Is there an ideal span of management? There is no agreement regarding what is the best span of management. The most widely used criteria on this point suggest that spans can be larger at lower levels in an organization than at higher levels.[4] Because subordinates in lower-level positions typically perform much more routine activities, subordinates can be effectively supervised at lower levels. In practice, larger spans are often found at lower levels in organizations. Elementary schools, for example, are characterized by very large spans, with as many as fifty or more teachers reporting to one principal. In such organizations, there is a tendency to assign team leaders within a school. These team leaders (teachers) report to the school principal, and may not be officially legitimized as a layer of administration within the school. The "informal" team leader approach permits a principal to expand the number of teachers he can effectively supervise. At the same time, this unofficial position does not result in another cumbersome layer of administration.

Figure 2–1, highlighting each basic concept of organizational structure, illustrates how these key concepts function in a school setting and are the foundation for most structure decisions. In practice, one can observe these structural dimensions in most organizations. In theory, most scholars recommend a flattening pyramid, but unfortunately, this is not happening in practice in most school districts.

The Bureaucratic Model

Today the term **bureaucracy** has a negative connotation. We tend to associate bureaucracy with rigidity, meaningless rules, red tape, paperwork, and inefficiency. In fact, there is almost no evil that has not, at some point, been attributed to bureaucracy.

The pioneering work on bureaucracy is credited to the famous German sociologist Max Weber, who made a comparative study of many organizations existing at the turn of the twentieth century. From his study, Weber evolved the concept of bureaucracy as an ideal form of organizational structure.

Bureaucratic Characteristics

According to Weber, the ideal bureaucracy possesses the following characteristics.[5]

- *Division of Labor.* Divide all tasks into highly specialized jobs. Give each jobholder the authority necessary to perform these duties.
- *Rules.* Perform each task according to a consistent system of abstract rules. This practice helps ensure that task performance is uniform.
- *Hierarchy of Authority.* Arrange all positions according to the principle of hierarchy. Each lower office is under the control of a higher one, and there is a clear chain of command from the top of the organization to the bottom.
- *Impersonality.* Maintain an impersonal attitude toward subordinates. This social distance between managers and subordinates helps ensure that rational considerations are the basis for decision making, rather than favoritism or prejudices.
- *Competence.* Base employment on qualifications and give promotions based on job-related performance.

---

[4]Robert P. Vecchio, *Organizational Behavior: Core Concepts* (Belmont, CA: Cengage South-Western, 2006).

[5]Max Weber, *The Theory of Social and Economic Organization*, trans. T. Parsons (New York: Oxford University Press, 1947).

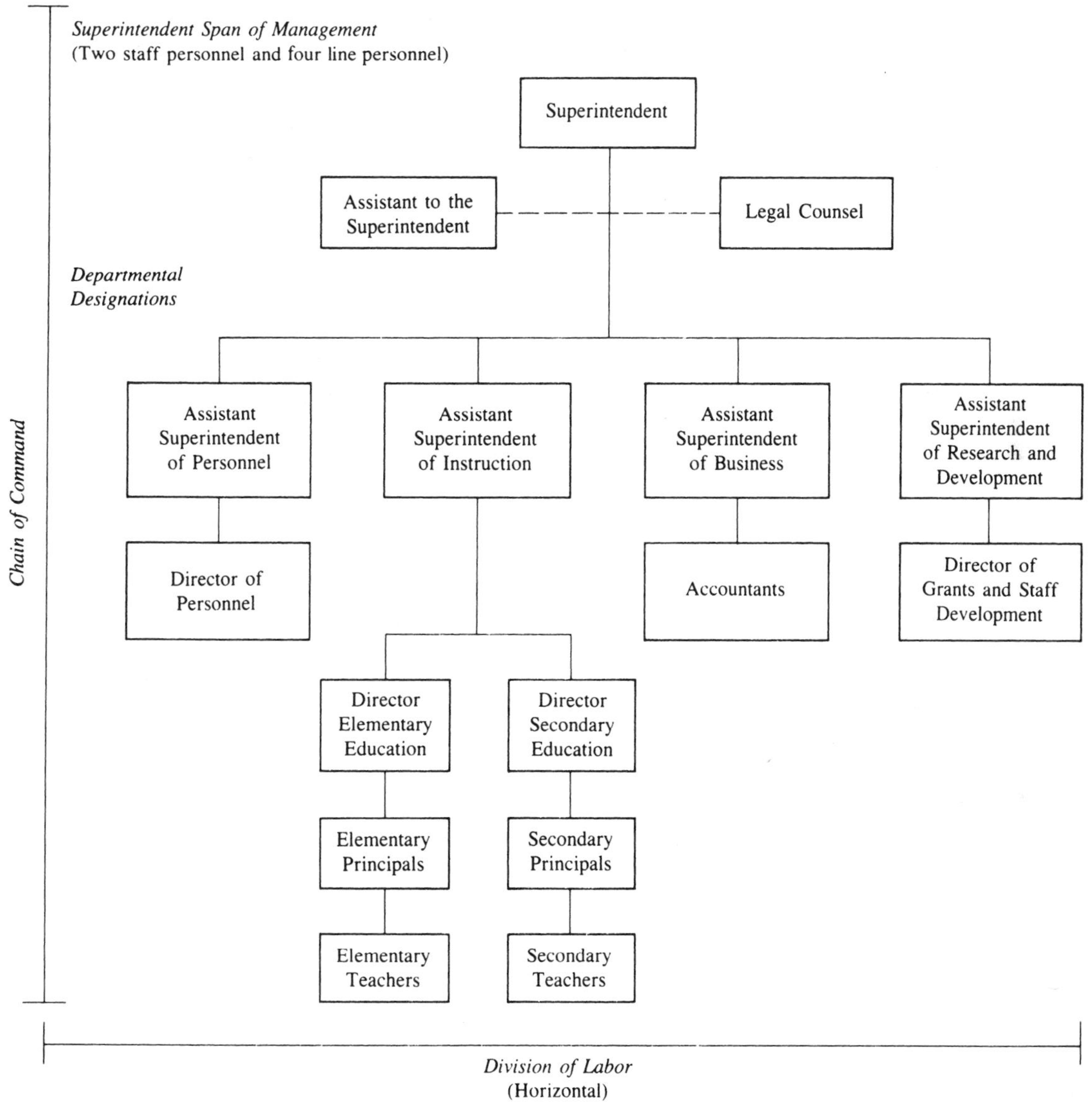

FIGURE 2-1

An Organizational Structure for a Hypothetical School District

As a corollary, protect employees from arbitrary dismissal, which should result in a high level of loyalty.

Weber's characteristics of bureaucracy apply to many large-sized organizations today. General Motors, Xerox, the U.S. military system, the Vatican, most universities, and boards of education are bureaucracies. However, not all characteristics outlined by Weber appear in practice as they were originally intended.[6] Numerous misconceptions in the literature exist regarding Weber's concept of the ideal bureaucracy. Although few "pure" bureaucracies exist today, almost all organizations have some elements of bureaucracy within their structure.

[6]Michael Crozier, *The Bureaucratic Phenomenon* (Edison, NJ: Transaction Publishers, 2010).

Bureaucratic Dysfunctions

Although Weber's intention was based on rational behavior, the bureaucratic characteristics he formulated have some built-in dysfunctions. First, a high degree of division of labor may reduce the challenge and novelty of many jobs, which can eventually result in reduced performance, absenteeism, or turnover. Second, heavy reliance on bureaucratic rules can cause inefficiency or inertia. For example, rules often become ends in themselves rather than the means toward an end. Rules can also lead to excessive red tape and rigidity. Third, Weber advocated that hierarchy of authority helps coordinate activities, maintains authority, and serves a communication function. In theory, the hierarchy has both a downward and an upward communication flow. In practice, however, it typically has only a downward orientation. Many subordinates withhold information from superiors and are frustrated because they do not have an opportunity to participate in decision making. Fourth, Weber proposed that employment and promotion be based on qualifications and performance, which he felt would reduce favoritism and personal prejudices. Because performance is difficult to measure in many professional jobs, the tendency is to base promotions more on seniority and loyalty than on competence and merit. Finally, the impersonal nature of bureaucracy is probably its most serious shortcoming. Recent critics of bureaucracy attack it as emphasizing rigid, control-oriented structures over people.

New viewpoints are leading to a decline in the use of bureaucratic structure in modern organizations.[7] School administrators in the twenty-first century will see a change in some of their duties. One change will be a shift away from simply supervising the work of others to that of contributing directly to the school district's objectives. Instead of shuffling papers and writing reports, the modern administrator may be practicing a craft.[8]

The renowned organization theorist Warren Bennis represents one of the extreme critics of bureaucratic structuring in organizations. Over four decades ago, he forecasted the demise of bureaucracy.[9] In a more recent book, *Reinventing Leadership*,[10] he exposes the hidden obstacles in our organizations—and in society at large—that conspire against good leadership. According to Bennis, within any organization an entrenched bureaucracy with a commitment to the status quo undermines the unwary leader. This creates an unconscious conspiracy in contemporary society, one that prevents leaders—no matter what their original vision—from taking charge and making changes.

In recent years, popular writers have expressed increasing dissatisfaction with bureaucratic structures. This is reflected in the phenomenal appeal of numerous best-selling books such as *In Search of Excellence, The Fifth Discipline, Principle-Centered Leadership,* and *Schools That Learn.*[11] The basic theme permeating these books is that there are viable alternatives to the bureaucratic model. There is a strong implication that warm, nurturing, caring, trusting, challenging organizations produce high productivity in people.

On the surface, school restructuring appears to be worthwhile. It makes good sense to give teachers the power to make important decisions about how their school is run and how teaching occurs—and then hold them accountable for the results. But in practice, giving teachers greater authority is not a simple matter. Most educators embrace stability and accept change cautiously. When we talk about restructuring schools, we're really talking about changing the way the present bureaucracy works—the way we organize, structure, and allocate resources in the schools. (See Administrative Advice 2–1.)

The Participatory Management Model

Participatory management represents an extension of the bureaucratic model. The excessive rigidity and inherent impersonality of the bureaucratic approach stimulated interest in participatory management. These new theories of organization place greater emphasis on employee

[7]Eva Etzioni-Halevy, *Bureaucracy and Democracy* (New York: Routledge, 2010).

[8]Carl D. Glickman, *Leadership for Learning: How to Help Teachers Succeed* (Alexandria, VA: Association for Supervision and Curriculum Development, 2006).

[9]Warren G. Bennis, *Changing Organizations* (New York: McGraw-Hill, 1966).

[10]Warren G. Bennis, *Reinventing Leadership: Strategies to Empower the Organization* (New York: HarperCollins, 2006).

[11]Thomas J. Peters and Robert H. Waterman, *In Search of Excellence,* rev. ed. (New York: Warner Books, 2006); Peter M. Senge, *The Fifth Discipline,* rev. ed. (New York: Doubleday, 2006); Stephen R. Covey, *Principle-Centered Leadership* (New York: Simon & Schuster, 1992); Peter M. Senge, *Schools That Learn* (New York: Knopf Doubleday, 2010).

ADMINISTRATIVE ADVICE 2–1

Restructuring Schools: Changing How the Bureaucracy Works

The wholesale change involved in restructuring the bureaucracy of a school raises a number of questions:

- Can union contracts, board policies, administrative procedures, state mandates, and federal regulations be waived if necessary in order to support restructuring?
- Will there still be school system goals, standards, and expectations?
- What will change mean for the least—and most—successful students?
- What is the role of the school principal, as well as the central office administrators and staff?
- Who will be held accountable for the students' learning, and how will the results be assessed?
- How will the reward and incentive system be changed?
- Will each school develop its own budget?
- Is there a danger that teachers and students in every school will be tempted to be different simply for the sake of being different?
- Are these changes really for the best, and do teachers and parents want them?

Source: Adapted from Thomas W. Payzant, "To Restructure Schools, We've Changed the Way the Bureaucracy Works," *American School Board Journal,* 176 (1989): 19–20. Copyright 1989, the National School Boards Association. Used by permission.

morale and job satisfaction. Participatory management stresses the importance of motivating employees and building an organization for that purpose. The organization is structured to satisfy employees' needs, which will in turn result in high worker productivity.

Theory X and Theory Y

In 1960 Douglas McGregor presented a convincing argument that most managerial actions flow directly from the assumptions managers hold about their subordinates.[12] The idea is that management's views of people control operating practices as well as organizational structure. McGregor referred to these contrasting sets of assumptions as **Theory X** and **Theory Y.**

Managers with Theory X assumptions have the following views of people:

- The average person dislikes work and will avoid it if possible.
- Because people dislike work, they must be coerced, controlled, directed, and threatened.
- The average person prefers to be directed and controlled by someone in authority.

The opposite assumptions characterize the Theory Y manager.

- Work is as natural as play or rest.
- Commitment to objectives is a function of rewards for achievement.
- Under proper conditions, people accept and seek responsibility.

McGregor considers Theory X to be incompatible with democratic or participatory organizations because it conflicts with individual need fulfillment on the job. Therefore, McGregor espouses Theory Y, because people's behavior in modern organizations more nearly matches its set of assumptions.

Theory Y does not concentrate on organizational structure as much as it argues for a general management philosophy that would force reconsideration of structural dimensions. For example, job enrichment would replace highly specialized jobs and departments. Span of control would be wide, not narrow, in order to provide greater freedom and opportunities for growth and fulfillment of employees' needs. Emphasis on hierarchy would be replaced by emphasis on decentralization and delegation of decisions. Formal, rational authority would give way to "empowerment" of subordinates.

[12]Douglas McGregor, *The Human Side of Enterprise* (New York: McGraw-Hill, 1960).

Individual versus Organization

The school administrator's job is to contribute to the achievement of organizational effectiveness. An important part of this effort is to enlist the support of subordinates to this same end. In a school setting, this includes teachers and all other professionals who work with students. Chris Argyris suggests that rigid, impersonal organizations such as those prescribed by the bureaucratic perspective hinder employees from using their full potential. He describes the growth or development of human personality and advocates the premise that organizational structure is often incongruent with the fulfillment of human needs. Argyris asserts that an analysis of the basic properties of relatively mature human beings and the formal organization results in the conclusion that there is an inherent incongruency between the self-actualization of each one.[13] This basic incongruency creates conflict and frustration for the participants.

Argyris proposes that the human personality progresses along an **immaturity–maturity continuum**—from immaturity as an infant to maturity as an adult. He views this progression in psychological rather than in purely physiological terms. That is, at any age, people can have their degree of growth or development plotted according to seven dimensions (see Table 2–2).

According to Argyris's continuum, as individuals mature, they have increasing needs for more activity, a state of relative independence, behaving in many different ways, deeper interests, a long time perspective, occupying a superordinate position in reference to their peers, and more awareness of and control over themselves.

Argyris believes that teachers and other professionals want to be treated as mature people, but modern bureaucratic organizations often treat people as if they fit the immature personality type. Teachers and other professionals react to this treatment by becoming either aggressive or apathetic, which starts a chain reaction. School administrators then impose further restrictions, which turn out to be counterproductive. This hinders optimum organizational effectiveness.

The restraining effects of bureaucratic organizational structure can be alleviated by less rigid rules and operating procedures, a decrease in the division of labor, greater delegation of authority, more participation in decision making, and a more fluid structure throughout the organization. Argyris believes that a more participatory management structure can result in the growth and development of human personality and hence eliminate the incongruency between the individual and the organization.[14]

Table 2-2 The Immaturity-Maturity Continuum

Immaturity Characteristics	Maturity Characteristics
Passivity	Activity
Dependence	Independence
Few ways of behaving	Many ways of behaving
Shallow interests	Deeper interests
Short time perspective	Long time perspective
Subordinate position	Superordinate position
Lack of self-awareness	Self-awareness and control

Source: Adapted from Chris Argyris, *The Individual and the Organization: Some Problems of Mutual Adjustment* (New York: Irvington, 1993).

System 4 Organization

Like McGregor and Argyris, Rensis Likert opposes the kinds of organizations that hew to the bureaucratic model. Likert's theory treats the structural prescriptions for organizational effectiveness more explicitly and completely. He builds his structural recommendations around three key elements that undergird four systems of organization.

Based on many years of research conducted in various organizational settings—industrial, government, health care, and educational—Likert proposed four basic systems of organization.[15] System 1, which Likert originally labeled exploitive authoritative, follows the bureaucratic or classical structure of organization. Characteristics of the classical structure include limited supportive leadership, motivation based on fear and superordinate status, one-way downward communication, centralized decision making, close over-the-shoulder supervision, no cooperative teamwork, and low performance goals of managers.

[13]Chris Argyris, *The Individual and the Organization: Some Problems of Mutual Adjustment* (New York: Irvington, 1993).

[14]Chris Argyris, *Integrating the Individual and the Organization* (New Brunswick, NJ: Transaction Publications, 1990).

[15]Rensis Likert, "From Production and Employee-Centeredness to Systems 1–4," *Journal of Management*, 5 (1979): 147–156.

Table 2-3 Characteristics of System 1 and System 4

Organizational Characteristics	System 1 Organization	System 4 Organization
Leadership	Little confidence and trust between administrators and subordinates	Subordinate ideas are solicited and used by administrators
Motivation	Taps fear, status, and economic motives exclusively	Taps all major motives except fear
Communication	One-way, downward communication	Communication flows freely in all directions
Interaction-influence	Little upward influence; downward influence overestimated	Substantial influence upward, downward, and horizontally
Decision making	Centralized; decisions made at the top	Decentralized; decisions made throughout the organization
Goal setting	Established by top-level administrators and communicated downward	Established by group participation
Control	Close over-the-shoulder supervision	Emphasis on self-control
Performance goals	Low and passively sought by administrators; little commitment to developing human resources	High and actively sought by administrators; full commitment to developing human resources

Source: Adapted from Rensis Likert, *The Human Organization* (New York: McGraw-Hill, 1967), pp. 197–211.

The **System 4 organization,** which Likert calls participative group, is more team-oriented. There is a high level of trust and confidence in the superior; communication flows freely in all directions; decision making occurs throughout the organization; cooperative teamwork is encouraged; and managers actively seek high performance goals. System 2 is less classical than System 1, and System 3 is less supportive than System 4 while coming closer to Likert's ideal model of organization. Table 2–3 shows the characteristics of System 1 and System 4, the extreme ends of Likert's systems continuum.

Key Elements of System 4 According to Likert, System 4 has three key elements: the manager's use of the principle of supportive relationships, the use of group decision making in an overlapping group structure, and the manager's high performance goals for the organization.[16] The underlying theory is that if an organization is to be effective, the leadership and other processes of the organization must ensure that in all interactions between superordinates and subordinates, subordinates will perceive the relationship as enhancing their own sense of personal worth and importance in the organization. Furthermore, Likert argues that "an organization will function best when its personnel function not as individuals but as members of highly effective work groups with high performance goals."[17] In this way, decisions are group decisions, not simply orders from above. And the leader is seen as a "linking-pin"; that is, the leader is the head of one group but a member of another group at the next higher level. For example, the high school principal is the leader of school staff but also a subordinate to an administrator at the central office in another group at the next level in the organization. Thus, the principal serves as an important communication link between two levels of organization—school and school district.

System 4 Variables Likert identifies System 4 as the ideal model of organization. The object of this approach is to move an organization as far as possible toward System 4. To analyze an organization's present system and move it toward System 4, Likert uses an organizational paradigm consisting of three broad classes of variables.

Causal variables are independent variables that affect both the intervening and end-result variables. They include the administrator's assumptions about subordinates, the organization's objectives and how they emerge, administrative behavior and practices, the nature of the authority system that prevails, the

[16] Rensis Likert, *New Patterns of Management* (New York: Garland, 1987).

[17] Ibid.

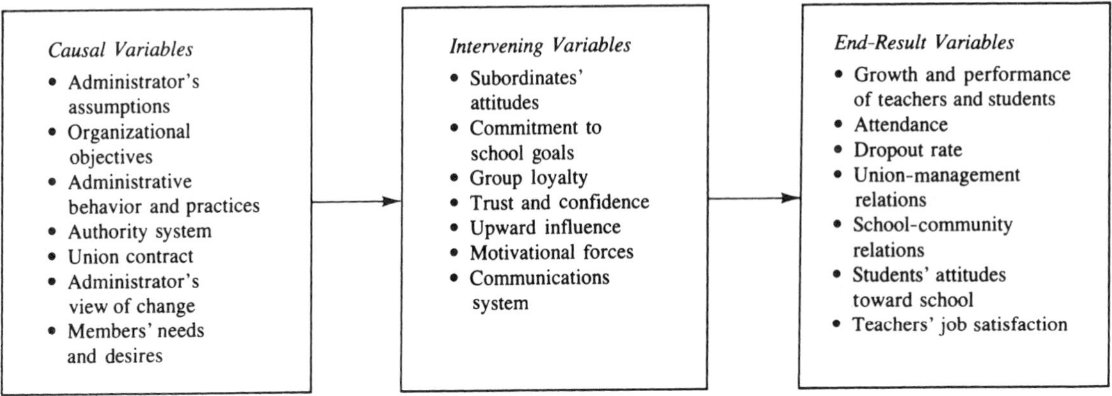

FIGURE 2-2

Relationships Among Casual, Intervening, and End-Result Variables in a System 4 Organization

union contract, the administrator's view of change, and the needs and desires of members of the organization. Causal variables are within the control of administration, and the value that administration places on these variables will determine the organization's management system. Causal variables, then, are the ones administrators should attempt to change in order to move the organization to System 4.

Intervening variables, representing the internal state and health of the organization, are those variables that are subsequently affected by causal variables. They include the attitudes that subordinates have toward their jobs, their superiors, peers, and subordinates; their commitment to organizational goals; their levels of performance goals; their levels of group loyalty and group commitment to the organization; their confidence and trust in themselves and their superiors; their feeling of upward influence in the organization; their motivational forces; and the extent to which communications flow freely and in all directions within the organization.

End-result variables are dependent variables that represent the achievements of the organization. In schools they include performance and growth levels of teachers and students, absence and turnover or dropout rates of employees and students, union-management relations, school-community relations, students' attitudes toward school, and levels of intrinsic job satisfaction of school employees. Figure 2–2 shows the relationship among the variables.

To move an organization to System 4, Likert recommends using the survey-feedback method and leadership training. Using his Profile of Organizational Characteristics instrument, the organization can determine the management system that is currently in place.[18] The survey instrument measures the eight characteristics of organizational systems (see Table 2–3). Respondents are given a range of choices for each item on the questionnaire, through which they indicate whether the organization tends to be exploitive authoritative (System 1), benevolent authoritative (System 2), consultative (System 3), or participative group (System 4). Respondents are also asked where they would like the organization to be on the continuum. Then an organization–systems profile chart is plotted, which visually conveys the organization's present management system and the desired system. Another instrument, the Profile of a School, also measures the organizational systems of schools.[19] It has several versions that can be used with students, teachers, counselors, principals, superintendents, central office administrators, school board members, and parents. By comparing the perceptions of several subgroups within the organization, it is possible to measure the management system of a school or an entire school district.

The profile charts become a basis for discussing and analyzing an organization's management system so that plans for improving it can be made. Because effectiveness and System 4 go together in Likert's theory, the implications for organizational improvement are straightforward: Move the present management style of the organization to System 4 and keep it there. This is accomplished by training all administrators

[18]Ibid.

[19]Additional information on the Profile of a School instrument can be obtained from Rensis Likert Associates, 630 City Center Building, Ann Arbor, Michigan 48104.

throughout the organization to acquire the skills needed for achieving a System 4 structure: manifesting supportive leadership, focusing on high performance goals, and building intact work groups into more effective teams.

Moral Leadership

In a groundbreaking examination of **moral leadership**, Amitai Etzioni provides a case for moral authority as a basis for management.[20] Etzioni acknowledges the importance of basic, extrinsic motivation and higher-order, intrinsic motivation (see Maslow and Herzberg, Chapter 4). But Etzioni goes further. He contends that what means most to people is what they believe, how they feel, and the shared norms, values, and cultural symbols that emerge from the groups with which they identify. He maintains that morality and shared values and commitments are far more important motivators than the basic, extrinsic needs and motives and even some intrinsic concerns.

Thomas Sergiovanni further specifies the concept of moral leadership.[21] He contends that when moral authority transcends bureaucratic leadership in a school, the outcomes in terms of commitment and performance far exceed expectations. His four stages of value-added leadership are the following:

1. *Leadership by Bartering.* The leader and led strike a bargain within which the leader gives to the led something they want in exchange for something the leader wants.
2. *Leadership by Building.* The leader provides the climate and the interpersonal support that enhances the led's opportunities for fulfillment of needs for achievement, responsibility, competence, and esteem.
3. *Leadership by Bonding.* The leader and led develop a set of shared values and commitments that bond them together in a common cause.
4. *Leadership by Banking.* The leader institutionalizes the improvement initiatives as part of the everyday life of the school. This conserves human energy and effort for new projects and initiatives.[22]

A new kind of hierarchy then emerges in the school—one that places purposes, values, and commitments at the apex and teachers, principals, parents, and students below, in service to these purposes. According to Sergiovanni, moral authority is a means to add value to an administrator's leadership practice, and this added value results in extraordinary commitment and performance in schools.

To implement this new kind of hierarchy, Roland Barth views restructuring as learning by heart.[23] In his best-selling book, he examines the adults—parents, teachers, principals, and central office administrators—who help children learn. He describes how these stakeholders can assume responsibility for shaping their own school system. He stresses the importance of collaboration among these stakeholders in promoting learning and promoting schools. He sees transformation as focusing on the fact that the different roles of the major stakeholders serve a common purpose—to improve the education of all children in the school system. According to Barth, change in the classroom is the only change that really matters.

Participatory management proponents have high concern for people in the structuring of organizations. They view people as the most important resource of the organization. Supportiveness, participation, shared decision making, empowerment, flexibility, and employee growth and development are the keys to participatory management.

School-Based Management

School-based management (SBM) represents a change in how a school district is structured, that is, how authority and responsibility are shared between the district and its schools. It changes roles and responsibilities of staff within schools and how the school district's central office staff is organized with respect to its size, roles, and responsibilities.[24] Professional responsibility replaces bureaucratic regulation. School districts accomplish this new structure in two ways: (1) increasing autonomy through some type of relief from constraining rules and regulations and (2) sharing the authority to make decisions with the school's

[20]Amitai Etzioni, *The Moral Dimension* (New York: Macmillan, 1990).

[21]Thomas J. Sergiovanni, *The Lifeworld of Leadership: Creating Culture, Community, and Personal Meaning in Our Schools* (New York: John Wiley and Sons, 2010).

[22]Thomas J. Sergiovanni, *Value-Added Leadership: How to Get Extraordinary Leadership in Schools,* 2nd ed. (New York: Harcourt Brace, 1997).

[23]Roland Barth, *Learning by Heart* (New York: John Wiley, 2005).

[24]Richard F. Elmore, *School Reform from the Inside Out: Policy, Practice, and Performance* (Cambridge, MA: Harvard Education Publishing Group, 2004).

EXEMPLARY EDUCATIONAL ADMINISTRATORS IN ACTION

MIRABELLE BAPTISTE Principal, Clifton Middle School, Houston Independent School District, Texas.

Words of Advice: To the entering student in educational administration, my wisdom word is *believe.* Say it often. The next word is *trust.* The drama of your life each day is greatly enhanced when you believe in the people of your school community and when the sense of trust is present. Your commitment to public education will serve as your guiding beacon. The students believe you can move mountains, and there will be days when you will. Knowing that your school community believes in you and trusts you is the most wonderful feeling you will enjoy each day.

major stakeholder groups, including teachers, parents, students, and other community members.[25]

In practice, authority to make changes at the building level is typically granted by some type of waiver process. Usually, a waiver process is the result of agreements between the school district and teachers' union that expand the scope of authority granted individual school sites. In a few cases, districts may also have agreements with their states that permit waivers from state regulations or laws that mandate school-based decision making.[26]

To increase shared decision making, a school typically forms a school-site council with representatives from the school's major stakeholder groups. The composition of this council, how members are selected, and what their responsibilities are vary considerably between and within school districts. Some councils are composed of teachers elected from the entire faculty or by grade level or department. Others are composed of members from preexisting committees such as the curriculum, staffing, or budget committees. In some schools, the entire faculty constitutes the council.[27]

Numerous states and districts have instituted a variety of school-based management provisions.[28] In Texas, Senate Bill 1 of 1990 and House Bill 2885 of 1991 introduced the term *school-based management* to schools throughout the state of Texas by establishing a legislative decree for school-based management. In the Kentucky Education Reform Act of 1990, House Bill 940 mandated, with few minor exceptions, that all schools in the state employ an SBM model of governance by July 1, 1996. Signed into law in 1989, Act 266 of the Hawaii State Legislature was a major initiative designed to facilitate improved student performance in the public school system through School/Community-Based Management. In Oregon, legislation was passed in 1991 to establish school-based decision-making committees in all public schools in the state by 1995. Related events have unfolded in New York, South Carolina, Tennessee, Washington, and other states.

At the district level, especially in urban areas such as Dade County (FL), Chicago, Los Angeles, and Rochester (NY), similar efforts to move decision-making authority to the school level have been initiated. For example, a provision for the establishment of SBM councils, composed of parents, teachers, citizens, and principals at each school site, was at the heart of legislation passed by the Illinois General Assembly to improve schooling in Chicago.[29] Power was to shift from a large central office to each school site, and a bureaucratic, command-oriented system was to yield to a decentralized and democratic model. The traditional pyramid-shaped organizational structure was to be inverted. The existing insiders, particularly the central administration and the Chicago Teachers Union, found their traditional sources of influence circumscribed.[30] Similar reforms have occurred in Memphis, Detroit, Dallas, Cincinnati, Los Angeles, White Plains (NY), and other school districts.

Frames of Organization

Lee Bolman and Terrence Deal provide a four-frame model (see Table 2–4) with its view of organizations as factories (*structural frame*), families (*human*

[25]Michael Fullan, *All Systems Go: The Change Imperative for Whole System Reform* (Thousand Oaks, CA: Sage, 2010).

[26]Ibid.

[27]Ibid.

[28]Harry A. Patrinos, *Decentralized Decision Making in Schools: The Theory and Evidence on School-Based Management* (New York: World Bank Publications, 2010).

[29]Chicago School Reform Act of 1988; reenacted in 1991.

[30]G. Alfred Hess, *Restructuring Urban Schools: A Chicago Perspective* (Newbury Park, CA: Corwin Press, 1995).

Table 2-4 Overview of the Four-Frame Model

	Frame			
	Structural	**Human Resource**	**Political**	**Symbolic**
Metaphor for organization	Factory or machine	Family	Jungle	Carnival, temple, theater
Central concepts	Rules, roles, goals, policies, technology, environment	Needs, skills, relationships	Power, conflict, competition, organizational politics	Culture, meaning, metaphor, ritual, ceremony, stories, heroes
Image of leadership	Social architecture	Empowerment	Advocacy	Inspiration
Basic leadership challenge	Attune structure to task, technology, environment	Align organizational and human needs	Develop agenda and power base	Create faith, beauty, meaning

Source: Adapted from Lee G. Bolman and Terrence E. Deal, *Reframing Organizations,* 4th ed. (San Francisco: Jossey-Bass, 2008), p. 18.

resource frame), jungles (*political frame*), and temples (*symbolic frame*).[31] Their distillation of ideas about how organizations work has drawn much from the social sciences—particularly from sociology, psychology, political science, and anthropology. They argue that their **four frames** or major perspectives can help leaders make sense of organizations. Bolman and Deal further assert that the ability to *reframe*—to reconceptualize the same situation using multiple perspectives—is a central capacity for leaders of the twenty-first century.[32]

- *Structural Frame.* Drawing from sociology and management science, the structural frame emphasizes goals, specialized roles, and formal relationships. Structures—commonly depicted by organization charts—are designed to fit an organization's environment and technology. Organizations allocate responsibilities to participants ("division of labor") and create rules, policies, procedures, and hierarchies to coordinate diverse activities. Problems arise when the structure does not fit the situation. At that point, some form of reframing is needed to remedy the mismatch.
- *Human Resource Frame.* The human resource frame, based particularly on ideas from psychology, sees an organization as much like an extended family, inhabited by individuals who have needs, feelings, prejudices, skills, and limitations. They have a great capacity to learn and sometimes an even greater capacity to defend old attitudes and beliefs. From a human resource perspective, the key challenge is to tailor organizations to people—to find a way for individuals to get the job done while feeling good about what they are doing.
- *Political Frame.* The political frame is rooted particularly in the work of political scientists. It sees organizations as arenas, contests, or jungles. Different interests compete for power and scarce resources. Conflict is rampant because of enduring differences in needs, perspectives, and lifestyles among individuals and groups. Bargaining, negotiation, coercion, and compromise are part of everyday life. Coalitions form around specific interests and change as issues come and go. Problems arise when power is concentrated in the wrong places or is so broadly dispersed that nothing gets done. Solutions arise from political skill and acumen in reframing the organization.
- *Symbolic Frame.* The symbolic frame, drawing on social and cultural anthropology, treats organizations as tribes, theaters, or carnivals. It abandons the assumptions of rationality more prominent in the other frames. It sees organizations as cultures, propelled more by rituals, ceremonies, stories, heroes, and myths than by rules, policies, and managerial authority. Organization is also theater: Actors play their roles in the organizational drama while audiences

[31] Lee G. Bolman and Terrence E. Deal, *Reframing Organizations: Artistry, Choice, and Leadership,* 4th ed. (San Francisco: Jossey-Bass, 2008).

[32] To preserve the metaphorical content, we have quoted liberally from Bolman and Deal, *Reframing Organizations.*

Types of Power (columns); *Types of Involvement* (rows)

	Coercive	Utilitarian	Normative
Alienative	X		
Calculative		X	
Moral			X

FIGURE 2-3

Etzioni's Compliance Types

form impressions from what they see onstage. Problems arise when actors play their parts badly, when symbols lose their meaning, when ceremonies and rituals lose their potency. Leaders reframe the expressive or spiritual side of organizations through the use of symbol, myth, and magic.

Alternative Models of Organizational Structure

The bureaucratic and participatory management models laid the groundwork for more complex approaches to organizational structure. Top-level school administrators must consider the relative suitability of alternative approaches to organizational structure, based on the problems they face and the environment in which they work. We describe some alternative approaches to organizational structure, including Etzioni's compliance theory, Hage's mechanistic-organic organizations, and Mintzberg's strategy-structure typology.

Compliance Theory

Etzioni developed an innovative approach to the structure of organizations that he calls **compliance theory.**[33] He classifies organizations by the type of power they use to direct the behavior of their members and the type of involvement of the participants. Etzioni identifies three types of organizational power: coercive, utilitarian, and normative, and relates these to three types of involvement: alienative, calculative, and moral (Figure 2–3). This figure, while grossly oversimplifying the relationships, helps to make clear the pattern among the components. It should be noted that life in organizations is much more complicated.

Coercive power uses force and fear to control lower-level participants. Examples of organizations that rely on coercive power include prisons, custodial mental hospitals, and basic training in the military.

Utilitarian power uses remuneration or extrinsic rewards to control lower-level participants. Most business firms emphasize such extrinsic rewards. These rewards include salary, merit pay, fringe benefits, working conditions, and job security. Besides many business firms, utilitarian organizations include unions, farmers' co-ops, and various government agencies.

Normative power controls through allocation of intrinsic rewards, such as interesting work, identification with goals, and making a contribution to society. Management's power in this case rests on its ability to manipulate symbolic rewards, allocate esteem and prestige symbols, administer ritual, and influence the distribution of acceptance and positive response in the organization.

Many professional people work in normative organizations. Examples of such organizations are churches, political organizations, hospitals, universities, and professional associations (such as the American Association of School Administrators, National Association of Secondary School Principals, and National Education Association). Public schools probably fit this category for the most part, although there are vast differences in their use of power to gain member compliance, particularly the control of pupils.

Types of Involvement All three types of power can be useful in obtaining subordinates' cooperation in organizations. However, the relative effectiveness of each approach depends on the organizational participant's involvement. Involvement refers to the orientation of a person to an object, characterized in terms

[33]Amitai Etzioni, *A Comparative Analysis of Complex Organizations,* rev. ed. (New York: Free Press, 1975).

of intensity and direction. Accordingly, people can be placed on an involvement continuum that ranges from highly negative to highly positive. Etzioni suggests that participants' involvement can be broadly categorized as alienative, calculative, or moral.

Alienative involvement designates an intense, negative orientation. Inmates in prisons, patients in custodial mental hospitals, and enlisted personnel in basic training all tend to be alienated from their respective organizations.

Calculative involvement designates either a negative or a positive orientation of low intensity. Calculative orientations are predominant in relationships of merchants who have permanent customers in various types of business associations. Similarly, inmates in prisons ("rats") who have established contact with prison authorities often have predominantly calculative attitudes toward those in power.

Moral involvement designates a positive orientation of high intensity. The involvement of the parishioner in her church or synagogue, the devoted member of his political party, and the loyal follower of her leader are all moral.

Relationship of Power to Involvement According to Etzioni, when an organization employs coercive power, participants usually react to the organization with hostility, which is alienative involvement. Utilitarian power usually results in calculative involvement; that is, participants desire to maximize personal gain. Finally, normative power frequently creates moral involvement; for instance, participants are committed to the socially beneficial features of their organizations.

Some organizations employ all three powers, but most tend to emphasize only one, relying less on the other two. Power specialization occurs because when two types of power are emphasized simultaneously with the same participant group, they tend to neutralize each other.

Applying force, fear, or other coercive measures, for example, usually creates such high-degree alienation that it becomes impossible to apply normative power successfully. This may be one reason why using coercive control in gaining student compliance in schools often leads to a displacement of educational goals.[34] Similarly, it may be why teachers in progressive schools tend to oppose corporal punishment.

In most organizations, types of power and involvement are related in the three combinations depicted in Figure 2–3. Of course, a few organizations combine two or even all three types. For instance, some teachers' unions use both utilitarian and normative power to gain compliance from their members. Nevertheless, school officials who attempt to use types of power that are not appropriate for the environment can reduce organizational effectiveness. Schools tend to be normative organizations. According to this logic, oppressive use of coercive and utilitarian power with teachers and students can be dysfunctional.

Mechanistic-Organic Organizations

Some writers have called attention to the incongruency between bureaucratic and professional norms. Specifically, they argue that occupants of hierarchical positions frequently do not have the technical competence to make decisions about issues that involve professional knowledge. That is, there is a basic conflict in educational organizations between authority based on bureaucracy and authority based on professional norms.[35] Others support the notion that bureaucratic orientations and professional attitudes need not conflict if teachers are provided with sufficient autonomy to carry out their jobs.[36]

We can conclude from this research that most schools have both bureaucratic and professional characteristics that are often incompatible but need not be. Jerald Hage suggests an axiomatic theory of organizations that provides a framework for defining two ideal types of organizations: **mechanistic** (bureaucratic) and **organic** (professional).[37] His theory identifies eight key variables found in schools and other organizations. These key variables are arranged in a means-ends relationship and are interrelated in seven basic propositions.

Eight Organizational Variables Complexity, centralization, formalization, and stratification are the four variables that constitute the organizational *means* by which schools are structured to achieve objectives. Adaptiveness, production, efficiency, and job satisfaction

[34]William Glasser, *The Quality School: Managing Students Without Coercion*, 2nd ed. (New York: HarperCollins, 1992).

[35]Max G. Abbott and Francisco Caracheo, "Power, Authority, and Bureaucracy," in N. J. Boyan (ed.), *Handbook of Research on Educational Administration* (New York: Longman, 1988), pp. 239–257.

[36]Wayne K. Hoy and Scott R. Sweetland, "School Bureaucracies That Work: Enabling, Not Coercive," *Journal of School Leadership*, 10(2000): 525–541.

[37]Jerald Hage, "An Axiomatic Theory of Organizations," *Administrative Science Quarterly*, 10 (1965): 289–320.

are the four variables that represent categories for sorting organizational *ends*. We describe each in turn.

1. *Complexity,* or specialization, refers to the number of occupational specialties included in an organization and the length of training required of each. Person specialization and task specialization distinguish the degree of specialization. A teacher who is an expert in English literature is a person specialist, whereas one who teaches eleventh-grade English is a task specialist. The greater the number of person specialists and the longer the period of training required to achieve person specialization (or degree held), the more complex the organization.
2. *Centralization,* or hierarchy of authority, refers to the number of role incumbents who participate in decision making and the number of areas in which they participate. The lower the proportion of role incumbents who participate and the fewer the decision areas in which they participate, the more centralized the organization.
3. *Formalization,* or standardization, refers to the proportion of codified jobs and the range of variation that is tolerated within the parameters defining the jobs. The higher the proportion of codified jobs in schools and the lesser range of variation allowed, the more formalized the organization.
4. *Stratification,* or status system, refers to the difference in status between higher and lower levels in the school's hierarchy. Differentials in salary, prestige, privileges, and mobility usually measure this status difference. The greater the disparity in rewards between the top and bottom status levels and the lower the rates of mobility between them, the more stratified the organization.
5. *Adaptiveness,* or flexibility, refers to the use of professional knowledge and techniques in the instruction of students and the ability of a school to respond to environmental demands. The more advanced the knowledge base, instructional techniques, and environmental response, the more adaptive the organization.
6. *Production* refers to the quantity and quality of output. Some schools are more concerned with quantity and less concerned with quality, and vice versa. This variable is difficult to measure because of the dichotomy between quantity and quality. For example, some universities are "degree mills"; that is, they award a large number of degrees each year with little concern for quality. Other institutions are less concerned about increasing the quantity of degrees awarded and more concerned about the quality of the product (the degree recipient). The greater the emphasis on quantity, not quality, of output, the more productive the organization.
7. *Efficiency,* or cost, refers to financial as well as human resources and the amount of idle resources. For example, class size ratios of one teacher to thirty students are more efficient than a one-to-ten ratio. The lower the cost per unit of production, the more efficient the organization.
8. *Job satisfaction,* or morale, refers to the amount of importance a school places on its human resources. Measures of job satisfaction include feelings of well-being, absenteeism, turnover, and the like. The higher the morale and the lower the absenteeism and turnover, the higher the job satisfaction in the organization.[38]

Seven Organizational Propositions Central to Hage's axiomatic theory are seven propositions, which have been drawn from the classic works of Weber,[39] Barnard,[40] and Thompson.[41] The major theme permeating Hage's theory is the concept of functional strains, namely that maximizing one organizational-means variable minimizes another. The eight key variables are related in fairly predictable ways. For instance, high centralization results in high production and formalization, high formalization in turn results in high efficiency, high stratification results in low job satisfaction and adaptiveness and high production, and high complexity results in low centralization. These ideas are expressed in seven propositions:

- The higher the centralization, the higher the production.
- The higher the formalization, the higher the efficiency.
- The higher the centralization, the higher the formalization.

[38]Ibid.

[39]Weber, *The Theory of Social and Economic Organization.*

[40]Chester Barnard, "Functions and Pathology of Status Systems in Formal Organizations," in William F. Whyte (ed.), *Industry and Society* (New York: McGraw-Hill, 1964), pp. 46–83.

[41]Victor Thompson, *Modern Organization* (New York: Knopf, 1961).

- The higher the stratification, the higher the production.
- The higher the stratification, the lower the job satisfaction.
- The higher the stratification, the lower the adaptiveness.
- The higher the complexity, the lower the centralization.[42]

Two Ideal Types The interrelationship of the eight key variables in seven basic propositions was used to define two ideal types of organizations, as Table 2–5 shows. Mechanistic and organic concepts are organizational extremes that represent pure types not necessarily found in real life. No school is completely mechanistic (bureaucratic) nor completely organic (professional). Most schools fall somewhere between these two extremes.

Bureaucratic-type schools tend to have a hierarchical structure of control, authority, and communication with little shared decision making (high centralization). Each functional role requires precise definitions of rights and obligations and technical methods (high formalization). These schools emphasize status differences between hierarchical levels in the organization (high stratification); and an emphasis on quantity, not quality, of output at least cost is prevalent (high production, high efficiency). There is little emphasis on professional expertise in both subject-matter knowledge and instructional methodology (low complexity). As well, there is little responsiveness to changing needs of students, society, and subject matter (low adaptiveness); and human resources are of little importance (low job satisfaction).

The ideal professional-type school is characterized by high complexity, adaptiveness, and job satisfaction. That is, school administrators respect the professional knowledge of teachers, respond readily to the changing needs of the school and society, and consider the intrinsic satisfaction of teachers to be an important school outcome. Furthermore, centralization is low because administrators encourage teacher participation in decision making and delegate considerable authority and responsibility to teachers in the operation of the school. A network structure of control, authority, and communication prevails. School administrators adjust and continually redefine tasks and avoid always "going by the book." The organization deemphasizes status differences among the occupants of the many positions in the hierarchy and adopts a collegial, egalitarian orientation. Low efficiency and productivity also characterize the ideal professional school. School administrators in the professional-type school are not as concerned with the quantity of output as they are with the quality of outcomes. Professional-type schools are probably more expensive to operate than bureaucratic-type schools because professional-school administrators tend to deemphasize quantity of output at least cost. Such schools tend to be less efficient but more effective.

Each ideal type of school has advantages and disadvantages. Moreover, there are limits on how much a school administrator can emphasize one variable over another. For example, if there is no codification of jobs (formalization), then a condition of normlessness prevails, which will likely result in low job satisfaction among faculty members. If schools do not respond to the knowledge explosion, technological innovations, and the changing needs of students and society, schools are apt to fail in the face of an ever-changing environment. Conversely, too high a change rate is likely to result in increased costs involved in implementing new programs and techniques. Limits exist on each of the eight variables, beyond which a school dare not move. Hage expresses it this way: "Production imposes limits on complexity, centralization, formalization, stratification, adaptiveness, efficiency, and job satisfaction."[43]

Table 2-5 Characteristics of Mechanistic and Organic Organizational Forms

Mechanistic Organization (Bureaucratic)	Organic Organization (Professional)
Low complexity	High complexity
High centralization	Low centralization
High formalization	Low formalization
High stratification	Low stratification
Low adaptiveness	High adaptiveness
High production	Low production
High efficiency	Low efficiency
Low job satisfaction	High job satisfaction

Source: Adapted from Jerald Hage, "An Axiomatic Theory of Organizations," *Administrative Science Quarterly,* 10 (1965): 305. Used by permission.

[42]Hage, "An Axiomatic Theory of Organizations."

[43]Ibid., p. 307.

ADMINISTRATIVE ADVICE 2–2

Strategic Questions

In structuring a professional-school orientation, school administrators must answer the following strategic questions:

- *In which decisions will professional teachers become involved*? There appears to be general agreement among the major stakeholders that teachers should be more involved in making decisions. However, we need to specify the areas in which teachers will play larger roles in decision making.
- *Who will make what decisions in the school*? How much influence should teachers have with respect to decisions affecting other parties in the school—students, teachers, support staff, principals, central office administrators, school board members? The roles of these stakeholders may need to be clarified or redefined in a professional-school structure.
- *What are the basic tasks of administrators and teachers in the context of a professional-school structure*? Put another way, what is the basis of teachers' expertise and professional identity? The amount of participation in decision making probably should be contingent on whether the issue is relevant to teachers and whether teachers have the expertise to make the decision.
- *What is the role of teacher unions in a professional-school structure*? The involvement of teacher unions is a key strategic issue in structuring a professional-school orientation.

Source: Adapted from Sharon C. Conley and Samuel B. Bacharach, "From School-Site Management to Participatory School-Site Management," *Phi Delta Kappan*, 71 (1990): 539–544.

In other words, extremes in any variable result in the loss of production, even in a school that has the means to maximize this end.

All the relationships specified in the seven propositions are curvilinear. For instance, if centralization becomes too high, production drops; if stratification becomes too low, job satisfaction falls. Therefore, exceeding the limits on any variable results in a reversal of the hypothesized relationships specified in the seven propositions. According to Hage, "These represent important qualifications to the axiomatic theory."[44]

The tension between the mechanistic (bureaucratic) and organic (professional) models is constantly negotiated between teachers and administrators. Sometimes it is resolved in favor of professionals, and sometimes it is resolved in favor of administrators.[45]

Because schools are fragile political coalitions, each decision must be considered strategically, examining its implications for all the major stakeholders.[46] Thus, school administrators must examine several strategic questions before a professional-school orientation can be effectively implemented. (See Administrative Advice 2–2.)

Strategy-Structure Typology

Another alternative approach to organizational structure concerns the relationship between organizational strategy and structure. This approach began with the landmark work of Alfred Chandler, who traced the historical development of such large American corporations as DuPont, Sears, and General Motors.[47] He concluded from his study that an organization's strategy tends to influence its structure. He suggests that strategy indirectly determines such variables as the organization's

[44]Ibid.

[45]Samuel B. Bacharach et al., *Advances in Research and Theories of School Management and Educational Policy* (Greenwich, CT: JAI Press, 2000).

[46]Robert O. Slater and William L. Boyd, "Schools as Polities," in J. Murphy and K. Seashore Louis (eds.), *Handbook of Research on Educational Administration*, 2nd ed. (San Francisco: Jossey-Bass, 1999), pp. 323–335.

[47]Alfred D. Chandler, *Strategy and Structure* (Cambridge, MA: MIT Press, 1962); see also Chandler, *Strategy and Structure: Chapters in the History of the American Industrial Enterprise* (Frederick, MD: Beard Books, 2003).

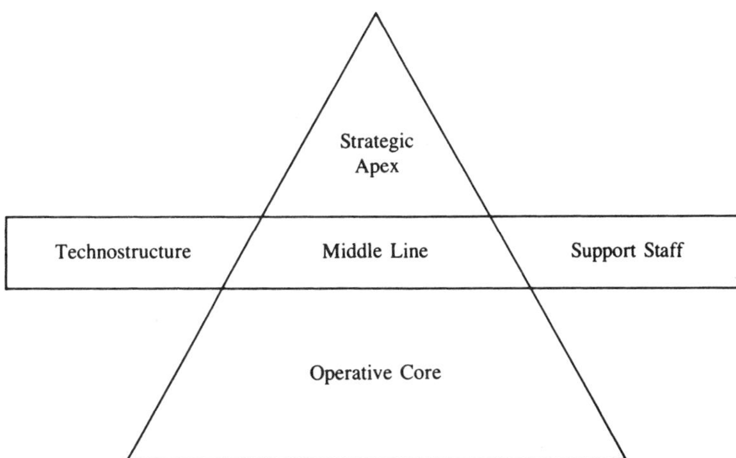

FIGURE 2-4

The Key Parts of an Organization
Source: Adapted from Henry Mintzberg, *Structure in Fives: Designing Effective Organizations*, © 1992, p. 11. Adapted by permission of Prentice Hall, Upper Saddle River, New Jersey. Used with permission.

tasks, technology, and environments, and each of these influences the structure of the organization.

More recently, social scientists have augmented Chandler's thesis by contending that an organization's strategy determines its environment, technology, and tasks. These variables, coupled with growth rates and power distribution, affect organizational structure. Henry Mintzberg suggests that organizations can be differentiated along three basic dimensions: (1) the key part of the organization, that is, the part of the organization that plays the major role in determining its success or failure; (2) the prime coordinating mechanism, that is, the major method the organization uses to coordinate its activities; and (3) the type of decentralization used, that is, the extent to which the organization involves subordinates in the decision-making process.[48] The key parts of an organization are shown in Figure 2–4 and include the following:

- *The strategic apex* is top management and its support staff. In school districts, this is the superintendent of schools and the administrative cabinet.
- *The operative core* are the workers who actually carry out the organization's tasks. Teachers constitute the operative core in school districts.
- *The middle line* is middle- and lower-level management. Principals are the middle-level managers in school districts.
- *The technostructure* are analysts such as engineers, accountants, planners, researchers, and personnel managers. In school districts, divisions such as instruction, business, personnel, research and development, and the like constitute the technostructure.
- *The support staff* are the people who provide indirect services. In school districts, similar services include maintenance, clerical, food service, legal counsel, and consulting to provide support.[49]

The second basic dimension of an organization is its prime coordinating mechanism. This includes the following:

- *Direct supervision* means that one individual is responsible for the work of others. This concept refers to the unity of command and scalar principles discussed earlier.
- *Standardization of work process* exists when the content of work is specified or programmed. In school districts, this refers to job descriptions that govern the work performance of educators.
- *Standardization of skills* exists when the kind of training necessary to do the work is specified. In school systems, this refers to state certificates required for the various occupants of a school district's hierarchy.
- *Standardization of output* exists when the results of the work are specified. Because the "raw material" that is processed by the operative core (teachers) consists of people (students), not

[48]Henry Mintzberg, *Tracking Strategies: Toward a General Theory of Strategy Formation* (New York: Oxford University Press, 2009).

[49]Ibid.

Table 2-6 Mintzberg's Five Organizational Structures

Structural Configuration	Prime Coordinating Mechanism	Key Part of Organization	Type of Decentralization
Simple structure	Direct supervision	Strategic apex	Vertical and horizontal centralization
Machine bureaucracy	Standardization of work processes	Technostructure	Limited horizontal decentralization
Professional bureaucracy	Standardization of skills	Operating core	Vertical and horizontal decentralization
Divisionalized form	Standardization of outputs	Middle line	Limited vertical decentralization
Adhocracy	Mutual adjustment	Support staff	Selective decentralization

Source: Adapted from Henry Mintzberg, *Structure in Fives: Designing Effective Organizations*, 2nd ed. (Upper Saddle River, NJ: Prentice Hall, 1992), p. 153.

things, standardization of output is more difficult to measure in schools than in other nonservice organizations. Nevertheless, a movement toward the standardization of output in schools in recent years has occurred. Examples include competency testing of teachers, state-mandated testing of students, state-mandated curricula, prescriptive learning objectives, and other efforts toward legislated learning.

- *Mutual adjustment* exists when work is co-ordinated through informal communication. Mutual adjustment or coordination is the major thrust of Likert's "linking-pin" concept discussed earlier.[50]

The third basic dimension of an organization is the type of decentralization it employs. The three types of decentralization are the following:

- *Vertical decentralization* is the distribution of power down the chain of command, or shared authority between superordinates and subordinates in any organization.
- *Horizontal decentralization* is the extent to which nonadministrators (including staff) make decisions, or shared authority between line and staff.
- *Selective decentralization* is the extent to which decision-making power is delegated to different units within the organization. In school districts, these units might include instruction, business, personnel, and research and development divisions.[51]

[50]Ibid.

[51]Ibid.

Using the three basic dimensions—key part of the organization, prime coordinating mechanism, and type of decentralization—Mintzberg suggests that the strategy an organization adopts and the extent to which it practices that strategy result in five structural configurations: simple structure, machine bureaucracy, professional bureaucracy, divisionalized form, and adhocracy. Table 2–6 summarizes the three basic dimensions associated with each of the five structural configurations. Each organizational form is discussed in turn.[52]

Simple Structure The **simple structure** has as its key part the strategic apex, uses direct supervision, and employs vertical and horizontal centralization. Examples of simple structures are relatively small corporations, new government departments, medium-sized retail stores, and small elementary school districts. The organization consists of the top manager and a few workers in the operative core. There is no technostructure, and the support staff is small; workers perform overlapping tasks. For example, teachers and administrators in small elementary school districts must assume many of the duties that the technostructure and support staff perform in larger districts. Frequently, however, small elementary school districts are members of cooperatives that provide many services (i.e., counselors, social workers) to a number of small school districts in one region of the county or state.

[52]Henry Mintzberg, *Structure in Fives: Designing Effective Organizations*, 2nd ed. (Upper Saddle River, NJ: Prentice Hall, 1992).

In small school districts, the superintendent may function as both superintendent of the district and principal of a single school. Superintendents in such school districts must be entrepreneurs. Because the organization is small, coordination is informal and maintained through direct supervision. Moreover, this organization can adapt to environmental changes rapidly. Goals stress innovation and long-term survival, although innovation may be difficult for very small rural school districts because of the lack of resources.

Machine Bureaucracy **Machine bureaucracy** has the technostructure as its key part, uses standardization of work processes as its prime coordinating mechanism, and employs limited horizontal decentralization. Machine bureaucracy has many of the characteristics of Weber's ideal bureaucracy and resembles Hage's mechanistic organization. It has a high degree of formalization and work specialization. Decisions are centralized. The span of management is narrow, and the organization is tall—that is, many levels exist in the chain of command from top management to the bottom of the organization. Little horizontal or lateral coordination is needed. Furthermore, machine bureaucracy has a large technostructure and support staff.

Examples of machine bureaucracy are automobile manufacturers, steel companies, and large government organizations. The environment for a machine bureaucracy is typically stable, and the goal is to achieve internal efficiency. Public schools possess many characteristics of machine bureaucracy, but most schools are not machine bureaucracies in the pure sense. However, large urban school districts (New York, Los Angeles, and Chicago) are closer to machine bureaucracies than other medium-sized or small school districts.

Professional Bureaucracy **Professional bureaucracy** has the operating core as its key part, uses standardization of skills as its prime coordinating mechanism, and employs vertical and horizontal decentralization. The organization is relatively formalized but decentralized to provide autonomy to professionals. Highly trained professionals provide nonroutine services to clients. Top management is small; there are few middle managers; and the technostructure is generally small. However, the support staff is typically large to provide clerical and maintenance support for the professional operating core. The goals of professional bureaucracies are to innovate and provide high-quality services. Existing in complex but stable environments, they are generally moderate to large in size. Coordination problems are common. Examples of this form of organization include universities, hospitals, and large law firms.

Some public school districts have many characteristics of the professional bureaucracy, particularly its aspects of professionalism, teacher autonomy, and structural looseness. For example, schools are formal organizations, which provide complex services through highly trained professionals in an atmosphere of structural looseness.[53] These characteristics tend to broaden the limits of individual discretion and performance. Like attorneys, physicians, and university professors, teachers perform in classroom settings in relative isolation from colleagues and superiors, while remaining in close contact with their students. Furthermore, teachers are highly trained professionals who provide information to their students in accordance with their own style, and they are usually flexible in the delivery of content even within the constraints of the state- and district-mandated curriculum. Moreover, like some staff administrators, teachers tend to identify more with their professions than with the organization.

Divisionalized Form The **divisionalized form** has the middle line as its key part, uses standardization of output as its prime coordinating mechanism, and employs limited vertical decentralization. Decision making is decentralized at the divisional level. There is little coordination among the separate divisions. Corporate-level personnel provide some coordination. Thus, each division itself is relatively centralized and tends to resemble a machine bureaucracy. The technostructure is located at corporate headquarters to provide services to all divisions; support staff is located within each division. Large corporations are likely to adopt the divisionalized form.

Most school districts typically do not fit the divisionalized form. The exceptions are those very large school districts that have diversified service divisions distinctly separated into individual units or schools. For example, a school district may resemble the divisionalized form when it has separate schools for the physically handicapped, emotionally disturbed, and learning disabled; a skills center for the potential dropout; a special school for art and music students; and so on. The identifying feature of these school districts is that they

---

[53]Charles E. Bidwell, "The School as a Formal Organization," in J. G. March (ed.), *Handbook of Organizations* (Chicago: Rand McNally, 1965), pp. 972–1022; Karl E. Weick, "Educational Organizations as Loosely Coupled Systems," *Administrative Science Quarterly,* 21 (1976): 1–19.

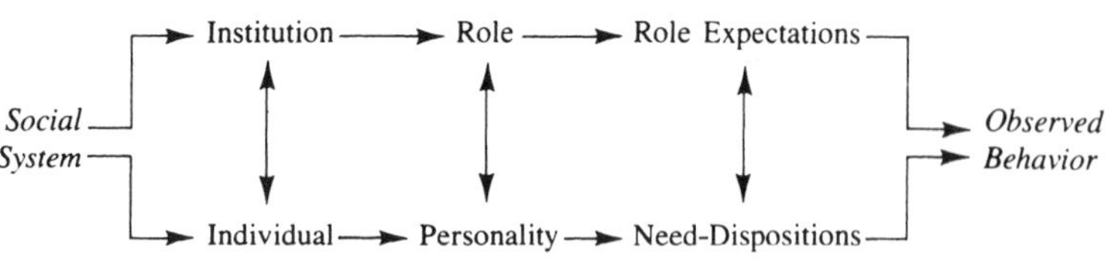

FIGURE 2–5

The Getzels-Guba Model
Source: From Jacob W. Getzels and Egon G. Guba, "Social Behavior and the Administrative Process," *School Review,* 65 (1957), p. 429. Used by permission of the University of Chicago Press.

have separate schools within a single school district, which have separate administrative staffs, budgets, and so on. Elementary and secondary school districts that have consolidated but retained separate administrative structures with one school board are also examples of the divisionalized form. As might be expected, the primary reason for a school district to adopt this form of structure is service diversity while retaining separate administrative structures.

Adhocracy The **adhocracy** has the support staff as its key part, uses mutual adjustment as a means of coordination, and maintains selective patterns of decentralization. The structure tends to be low in formalization and decentralization. The technostructure is small because technical specialists are involved in the organization's operative core. The support staff is large to support the complex structure. Adhocracies engage in nonroutine tasks and use sophisticated technology. The primary goal is innovation and rapid adaptation to changing environments. Adhocracies typically are medium sized, must be adaptable, and use resources efficiently. Examples of adhocracies include aerospace and electronic industries, research and development firms, and very innovative school districts. No school districts are pure adhocracies, but medium-sized school districts in very wealthy communities may have some of the characteristics of an adhocracy. The adhocracy is somewhat similar to Hage's organic organization.

Strategy and Structure The work begun by Chandler and extended by Mintzberg has laid the groundwork for an understanding of the relationship between an organization's strategy and its structure. The link between strategy and structure is still in its infancy stage. Further research in this area, particularly in service organizations like schools, will enhance school administrators' understanding of school organizations. In the meantime, school leaders must recognize that organization strategy and structure are related.

The School as a Social System

We can view the school as a social system. A **social system** refers to activities and interactions of group members brought together for a common purpose.[54] Thus, a school district, a school, and a classroom can all be viewed as social systems. A useful framework for understanding the administrative process within social systems is the Getzels-Guba model (see Figure 2–5).[55]

Dimensions of a Social System

Jacob Getzels and Egon Guba conceive of the social system as involving two dimensions that are independent and interactive. First are institutions with certain roles and expectations that will fulfill the goals of the system. Second are individuals with certain personalities and need-dispositions inhabiting the system, whose interactions comprise observed behavior. Thus, observed behavior can be understood as a function of these major elements: institution, role, and expectations, which together constitute the *nomothetic,* or normative, dimension of activity in a social system; and individual, personality, and need-dispositions, which together constitute the *idiographic,* or personal, dimension of activity in a social system.

Translated into the school setting, this means that an organization is designed to serve one of society's needs—to educate. In this organization, there are positions, or roles, such as the roles of the student, teacher, principal, superintendent, and the like. For each

[54]George C. Homans, *The Human Group* (New York: Harcourt, Brace, & World, 1950).

[55]Jacob W. Getzels and Egon G. Guba, "Social Behavior and the Administrative Process," *School Review,* 65 (1957): 423–441; see also James M. Lipham, "Getzels's Models in Educational Administration," in N. J. Boyan (ed.), *Handbook of Research on Educational Administration* (New York: Longman, 1988), pp. 171–184.

individual who occupies a given role, there are role expectations. Role expectations represent not only the duties and actions expected from each role player but also the expectations concerning the quality of performance. The various roles and role expectations constitute the nomothetic dimension of the social system.

The idiographic dimension includes individuals who occupy the roles and their personal needs. Schools as social systems must be "peopled," and all kinds of individuals who have their own idiosyncrasies "people" them. Thus, individuals chosen to occupy roles are different from one another in action and in reaction, and we can analyze these differences in terms of personality. Personality is determined in part by needs, which predispose a person to behave in a certain way in a given situation. In other words, the individual who occupies a given role has needs he tries to fulfill. These are personalized needs and may not be associated with the needs of the school system.

Behavior can be stated in the form of the equation $B = f(R \times P)$, where B is observed behavior, f is function, R is a given institutional role defined by the expectations attached to it, and P is the personality of the role player defined by his need-dispositions.[56] The proportion of role and personality factors determining behavior varies with the specific act, the specific role, and the specific personality involved.

It is presumed in the military that behavior is influenced more by role than personality, whereas with the freelance artist, behavior is influenced more by personality than by role. Many other examples can illustrate this variation in the influence exerted by role or personality on behavior. In educational organizations, we could hypothesize that the proportion of role and personality might be balanced somewhere between the two. But different educational systems are characterized by different proportions of role and personality.[57]

Expanded Model: Cultural Dimensions

The developers of this early model recognized its oversimplification. In focusing on the sociological dimension with "role" as the central concept and on the psychological dimension with "personality" as the central concept, other dimensions had been omitted, thus giving the model a closed systems orientation. To overcome this deficiency, Getzels and Herbert Thelen expanded the basic model to describe the classroom as a unique social system.[58] According to these social system theorists, the sociological aspects of an institution are mediated by cultural factors—the ethos, mores, and values—in which the institution is embedded. The expectations of the roles must, it seems, be somehow related to the ethos or cultural values. Similarly, the individual's personality functions in a biological organism with certain potentialities and abilities, with the need-dispositions of the personality mediated in some way by these constitutional conditions.

Getzels, James Lipham, and Roald Campbell further extended the model for school administrators. They added a second cultural dimension to interact with the psychological aspects of the individual.[59] The composite model of the school as a social system depicts educational administration as a social process (see Figure 2–6). The bottom line in their model indicates that the culture, ethos, and values held by individuals in schools and school systems explain much social behavior. The model also clearly indicates that any social system (classroom, school, or school district) must operate within a larger environment. The addition of these dimensions gives Getzels's composite model a more open-systems orientation.

Some Derivations Getzels's models suggest three sources of potential conflicts: role conflicts, personality conflicts, and role-personality conflicts.[60] *Role conflicts* refer to situations where a role player is required to conform simultaneously to expectations that are contradictory or inconsistent. Adjustment to one set of expectations makes adjustment to the other difficult or impossible. For example, a teacher may attempt to be a devoted mother and simultaneously a successful career woman. A university professor may be expected by the department head to emphasize teaching and service to students and the community, respectively, while the academic dean expects an emphasis on research and

[56]Jacob W. Getzels, "Administration as a Social Process," in A. W. Halpin (ed.), *Administrative Theory in Education* (New York: Macmillan, 1958), pp. 150–165.

[57]Ibid.

[58]Jacob W. Getzels and Herbert A. Thelen, "The Classroom as a Social System," in N. B. Henry (ed.), *The Dynamics of Instructional Groups,* 59th Yearbook of the National Society for the Study of Education, Part II (Chicago: University of Chicago Press, 1960), pp. 53–83.

[59]Jacob W. Getzels, James M. Lipham, and Roald F. Campbell, *Educational Administration as a Social Process* (New York: Harper & Row, 1968).

[60]Getzels, "Administration as a Social Process."

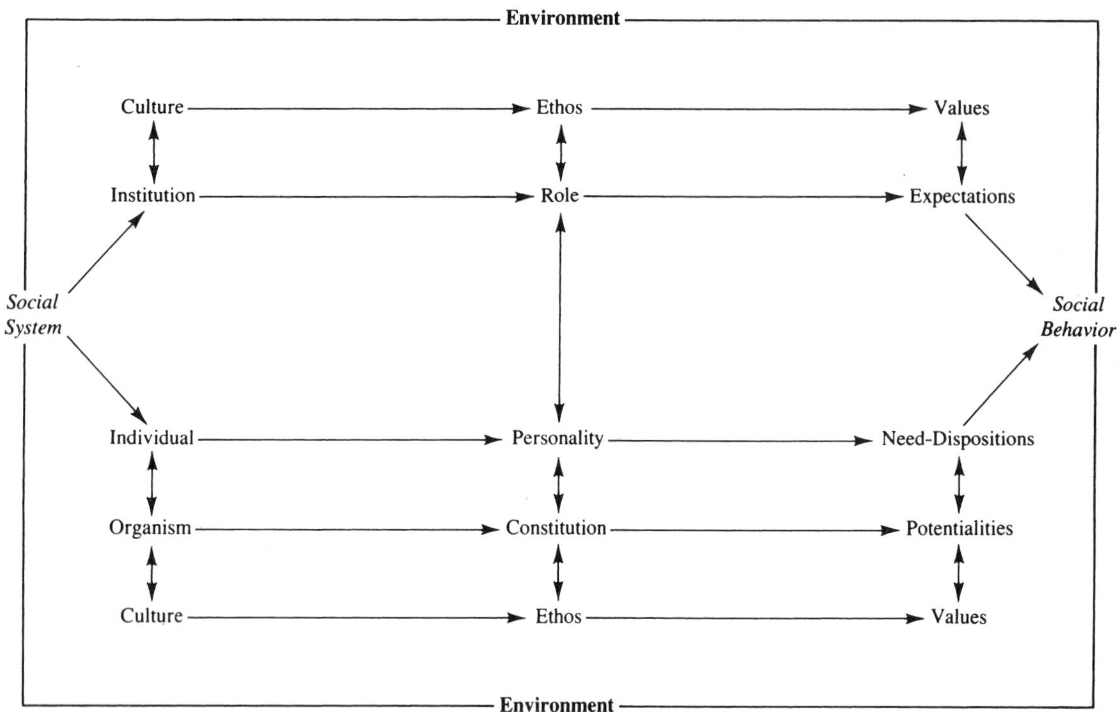

FIGURE 2–6

Composite Model of Behavior in Social Systems
Source: Adapted from Jacob W. Getzels, James M. Lipham, and Roald F. Campbell, *Educational Administration as a Social Process* (New York: Harper & Row, 1968), p. 105. Used with permission.

publication. Role conflicts represent incongruencies in the nomothetic dimension (see Figure 2–6).

Personality conflicts occur as a result of opposing need-dispositions within the personality of the individual role players. For example, a teacher may be expected, as a social norm, to maintain adequate social distance between self and students. However, the teacher may feel the need for more extensive interactions. Personality conflicts represent incongruencies in the idiographic dimension of the social systems model.

Role-personality conflicts occur as a result of discrepancies between the institution's role expectations and the individual's need-dispositions. For example, suppose an introverted school administrator were placed in the role of superintendent in a small- to medium-sized school district. The board of education makes clear its expectation that the newly appointed administrator maintain high visibility and extensive contact with the community. The superintendent, however, has a high need for privacy and anonymity. The superintendent in this school district would experience a role-personality conflict. As shown in Figure 2–6, role-personality conflicts represent incongruencies between the nomothetic and idiographic dimensions of the social systems model.

According to Getzels, incongruencies in the nomothetic and idiographic dimensions, or in their interaction, are symptomatic of administrative failure and lead to a loss in individual and institutional productivity.[61]

Furthermore, Getzels's models suggest three leader-followership styles: normative (nomothetic), personal (idiographic), and transactional.[62] The *normative style* emphasizes the fulfillment of institutional role requirements and obligations rather than the personal needs of individuals. Role definition, authority vested in roles, and organizational goal achievement are stressed. The *personal style* emphasizes the personal activities and propensities of individuals. Minimum role definition, a diffusion of authority, and efforts to maximize each

[61]Ibid.

[62]Getzels, Lipham, and Campbell, *Educational Administration as a Social Process.*

PRO CON DEBATE

School-Based Management

In many school districts, the direction of school reform is away from the bureaucratic patterns of top-down control and toward more autonomy for those who are assigned to the site, that is, the school. Theoretically, the superintendent and central office staff relinquish elements of their authority to a school-based team consisting of the principal, teachers, parents, students, and community members. The expectation is that the school-based team will make better decisions because they better understand the needs of students and teachers at the school.

Question: Does school-based decision making enhance student learning?

Arguments PRO

1. Issues related to the curriculum, resource allocation, and personnel assignments impact classroom instruction. When teachers serve on school-based teams, they are in a position to make decisions that enable student learning.
2. Teachers must be held more accountable. We are increasing teacher certification requirements and teacher salaries in order to secure a more professional workforce. Professionals need a wide sphere of influence. They must have the authority to change whatever needs to be changed to meet standards.
3. School-based teams ensure that everyone with a stake in a matter is consulted. Their decisions are likely to be more workable because all perspectives are considered.

Arguments CON

1. Teachers' expertise is in teaching and learning, not managerial decision making. When teachers serve on school-based teams, their attention and energies are deflected away from ensuring increased student learning.
2. Teachers expect administrators to make school-based decisions. If teachers wished to engage in a wider area of decision making, they would become administrators.
3. Most school-based teams have difficulty because so many different perspectives are on the table. Many points of view are mutually exclusive, so weak compromises are reached.

individual's meaningful contribution to the organization are stressed. The *transactional style* represents a balance of emphasis on the performance of the role requirements of the organization and the expression of personal needs of individuals. The school administrator moves alternately toward the normative style or the personal style depending on the situation.

Getzels's Latest Model: Communities Dimension

In the late 1970s, Getzels expanded his social systems model still further by including a communities dimension.[63] Here Getzels makes much more manifest the cultural setting of the school as a social system and extends its usefulness as an open systems model. He identifies six communities of education and defines communities as groups of people conscious of a collective identity through common cognitive and affective norms, values, and patterns of social relationships. He defines each type of community as follows:

- *Local community* is established in a particular neighborhood or region. Examples include a local neighborhood or school community.
- *Administrative community* is established in a specific, politically determined identity. A country, a city, or a school district are examples.
- *Social community* is established in a particular set of interpersonal relationships not restrained by local or administrative boundaries. An example would be all the people in one's community of friends.
- *Instrumental community* is established through direct or indirect activities and interactions with others who are brought together for a common purpose. Examples include a professional group such as

[63]Jacob W. Getzels, "The Communities of Education," *Teachers College Record, 79* (1978): 659–682.

teachers or professors who make up an educational community, a teachers' union, or a philanthropic community.

- *Ethnic community* is established through affinity with a particular national, racial, or socioeconomic group. Italian, black, or upper-class communities are examples.
- *Ideological community* is established in a particular historic, conceptual, or sociopolitical community that stretches across the local, administrative, social, instrumental, and ethnic communities. Examples include Christian, scholarly, or communist communities.[64]

Getzels's revised and latest models make much more explicit the cultural setting of the school as a social system. The concept of culture, the mainstay of anthropology since its beginnings, is not new. Recently, the concept of organizational culture has enjoyed tremendous appeal in both the popular and professional management literature.

Getzels's models of the school as a social system are widely treated in introductory textbooks in educational administration, textbooks that deal specifically with the school principalship, textbooks on supervision, and references on organizational behavior and theory in educational administration. In addition, the *Handbook of Research on Educational Administration,* a project of the American Educational Research Association, devotes an entire chapter to Getzels's models in educational administration.[65]

Summary

1. Key elements of organizational structure provide a framework for vertical control and horizontal coordination of schools. These key elements include job specialization, departmentalization, chain of command, authority and responsibility, centralization/decentralization, line and staff authority, and span of control.
2. According to this view, division of labor, abstract rules, vertical hierarchy of authority, impersonality in interpersonal relations, and advancement based on competence characterize the ideal bureaucratic structure.
3. The participatory management model is the antithesis of the ideal bureaucracy. Supportiveness, shared leadership, flexibility, and employee growth and development are the keys to participatory management.
4. Compliance theory, mechanistic and organic organizations, and strategy-structure typology are alternative approaches to organizational structure. These approaches integrate several ideas from the classical and participatory management models and the fundamentals of organizational structure.
5. Getzels's models of the school as a social system have proven to have enduring appeal and widespread application in the administration of schools.

Key Terms

job specialization
departmentalization
chain of command
authority and responsibility
centralization and decentralization
line and staff authority
span of management
bureaucracy
Theory X and Theory Y
immaturity–maturity continuum
System 4 organization
moral leadership
school-based management
four frames
compliance theory
mechanistic and organic organizations
simple structure
machine bureaucracy
professional bureaucracy
divisionalized form
adhocracy
social system

Discussion Questions

1. What are the key elements of organizational structure, and how do they function in schools?
2. How does bureaucracy influence approaches to organizational structure, and why are many of the characteristics of Weber's ideal bureaucracy still used in schools today?

---

[64]Ibid.

[65]Lipham, "Getzels's Models in Educational Administration," pp. 171–184.

3. Compare and contrast the participatory management models: Theory X and Theory Y, immaturity–maturity continuum, systems 1–4, moral leadership, school-based management, and frames of organization.
4. Compare and contrast the alternative models of organizational structure: compliance theory, mechanistic-organic organizations, and strategy-structure typology.
5. How can school administrators use social systems theory to better understand how schools function?

Suggested Readings

Bolman, Lee G., and Terrence E. Deal. *Reframing Organizations: Artistry, Choice, and Leadership,* 4th ed. (San Francisco: Jossey-Bass, 2008). In this updated version of their best-selling classic, the authors explain how the powerful tool of "reframing"—appraising situations from diverse perspectives—can be used to build high-performing, responsive organizations.

Fullan, Michael. *All Systems Go: The Change Imperative for Whole System Reform* (Thousand Oaks, CA: Sage, 2010). Changing whole education systems for the better as measured by student achievement requires coordinated leadership at the school, community, district, and government level. Based on Fullan's work with districts and large systems, this resource lays out a comprehensive action plan for achieving whole system reform.

Howley, Aimee, and Craig Howley. *Thinking About Schools: New Theories and Innovative Practices* (Mahwah, NJ: Lawrence Erlbaum Associates, 2006). As its title implies, this book has a deceptively simple mission: to prepare would-be school leaders to draw upon a variety of theoretical perspectives when thinking about schools and schooling. It shows how theories can function as cognitive tools to be mastered, carefully stored in one's intellectual toolbox and used to interpret and resolve real-world problems.

Leithwood, Kenneth, Robert Aitken, and Doris Jantzi. *Making Schools Smarter: Leading with Evidence* (Thousand Oaks, CA: Corwin Press, 2006). Achieve a workable model for effectively reshaping today's school districts for positive outcomes by addressing three of the most central challenges in district and school leadership.

Morgan, Gareth. *Images of Organization* (Thousand Oaks, CA: Sage Publications, 2007). Since its first publication over twenty years ago, *Images of Organization* has become a classic in the canon of management literature. The book is based on a simple premise—that all theories of organization and management are based on implicit images or metaphors that stretch our imagination in a way that can create powerful insights, but at the risk of distortion.

Sarason, Seymour B. *Letters to a Serious Education President,* 2nd ed. (Thousand Oaks, CA: Corwin Press, 2006). In this new edition of his original collection of letters, education luminary Seymour B. Sarason details how school reformers still have difficulty examining the differences between contexts of productive and unproductive learning. Sarason's acute insight into why school reforms fail forces us to ask how we teach all students.

Sergiovanni, Thomas J. *Rethinking Leadership: A Collection of Articles,* 2nd ed. (Thousand Oaks, CA: Corwin Press, 2006). In this innovative approach to reframing leadership, Sergiovanni encourages school leaders to discover the craft of moral leadership while learning how to practice effective instructional leadership and build strong learning communities for today and tomorrow.

3

Organizational Culture

FOCUSING QUESTIONS

1 What is organizational culture?
2 How is an organizational culture created?
3 How is an organizational culture maintained?
4 Can organizational culture be changed?
5 What role does organizational culture play in the life of the school?
6 What is organizational climate?
7 How can organizational climate be conceptualized?

In this chapter, we attempt to answer these questions concerning organizational culture in school settings. We begin our discussion by exploring the nature and characteristics of organizational culture. Next we discuss how organizational cultures are created, maintained, and changed. Then we discuss the features of corporate cultures of excellent firms and their relationship to school organizations. We discuss the similarities between organizational culture and organizational climate. Finally, we present and analyze four well-known organizational climate constructs with implications for improving school effectiveness.

What is Organizational Culture?

The concept of organizational culture was first noted as early as the Hawthorne studies (see Chapter 1), which described work group culture. It was not until the early 1980s, however, that the topic came into its own. Several books on organizational culture were published, including Terrence Deal and Allan Kennedy's *Corporate Cultures*,[1] William Ouchi's *Theory Z*,[2] and Tom Peters and Robert Waterman's *In Search of Excellence*.[3] These books popularized organizational culture, and researchers began in earnest to study the topic.

Organizational theorists indicated that these cultures were real. They acknowledged that organizations have personalities just like people. For example, organizations can be flexible or rigid, supportive or unfriendly, innovative or conservative. Organization theorists documented the important role that culture plays in the lives of organization members.

When you tell people where you work, they will ask you: What is it like there? The description you give likely will have a lot to do with the organization's culture. In calculating your response to the question, you will describe the kinds of people who work at your school/school district. You will describe the work atmosphere on a typical day. Probably you will describe the facilities in your workplace and how you feel people are treated. More than likely, you will describe what it is that defines "success" at your school/school district. These responses give clues that help outsiders understand what your school/school district's culture is really like. To provide you with a more complete understanding of organizational culture, it is necessary to define the concept in more detail.

Definition of Organizational Culture

The culture of an organization is all the beliefs, feelings, behaviors, and symbols that are characteristic of an organization. More specifically, **organizational culture** is defined as shared philosophies, ideologies, beliefs, feelings, assumptions, expectations, attitudes, norms, and values.[4]

While there is considerable variation in the definitions of organizational culture, it appears that most contain the following characteristics:

- *Observed Behavioral Regularities*. When organizational members interact, they use common language, terminology, and rituals and ceremonies related to deference and demeanor.
- *Norms*. Standards of behavior evolve in work groups that are considered acceptable or typical for a group of people. The impact of work-group behavior, sanctioned by group norms, results in standards and yardsticks.
- *Dominant Values*. An organization espouses and expects its members to share major values. Typical examples in schools are high performance levels of faculty and students, low absence and dropout rates of students, and high efficiency.
- *Philosophy*. Policies guide an organization's beliefs about how employees and clients are to be treated. For example, most school districts have statements of philosophy or mission statements.
- *Rules*. Guidelines exist for getting along in the organization, or the "ropes" that a newcomer must learn in order to become an accepted member.
- *Feelings*. This is an overall atmosphere that is conveyed in an organization by the physical layout and the way in which members interact with clients or other outsiders.[5]

None of these characteristics can by itself represent the essence of organizational culture. However, the characteristics taken collectively reflect and give meaning to the concept of organizational culture.

The culture of an organization is interrelated with most other concepts in educational administration, including organizational structures, motivation, leadership, decision making, communications, and change. To better understand this concept, Figure 3–1 depicts organizational culture within the context of social systems theory and more specifically open systems theory, being characterized by inputs, a transformation process, outputs, external environments, and feedback.

Organizations import energy from the environment in the form of information, people, and materials. The imported energy undergoes a transformation designed to channel behavior toward organizational goals and fulfill members' needs. Administrative processes (e.g., motivation, leadership, decision making, communication, and change) and organizational structures (e.g., job descriptions, selection systems, evaluation systems, control systems, and reward systems) have a significant impact on organizational culture and vice versa.

---

[1]Terrence Deal and Allan Kennedy, *Corporate Cultures: The Rites and Rituals of Corporate Life* (Reading, MA: Addison-Wesley, 1984).

[2]William Ouchi, *Theory Z* (Reading, MA: Addison-Wesley, 1981).

[3]Tom Peters and Robert Waterman, *In Search of Excellence* (New York: Harper & Row, 1982).

[4]Edgar H. Schein, *Leadership and Organizational Culture* (New York: John Wiley & Sons, 2011).

[5]Ibid.

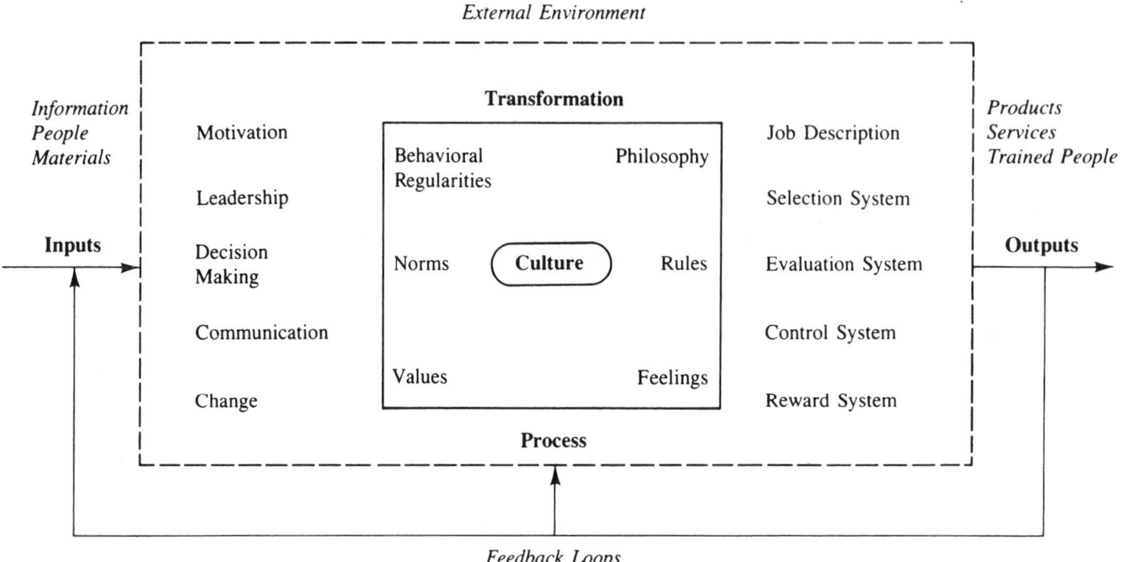

FIGURE 3–1

Dimensions of Organizational Culture

In turn, these administrative processes and organizational structures export a product into the external environment. In a school, the output may be students' knowledge, skills, attitudes, attendance, dropout rates, and more precise performance criteria such as scholastic awards. Figure 3–1 also shows that the organization not only influences but also is influenced by the external environment. And the social system uses feedback in an attempt to examine its present culture or to create a new culture.

Uniformity of Culture

Figure 3–1 shows the interrelationship of organizational culture with most other concepts in educational administration. Thus, culture represents the organization's cumulative learning, as reflected in organizational structures, people, administrative processes, and the external environment. This tends to perpetuate beliefs and behavior and specifies the goals, values, and mission of the organization and the criteria by which the organization's success is measured.

Subcultures Large and complex organizations do not typically manifest single homogeneous beliefs, values, and behavior patterns. In other words, there may be more than one culture in an organization. First, there are differences between the formal culture, which consists of the ideal philosophy of the organization and how organizational members should behave, and the informal culture, which consists of the actual manifestations of the ideal philosophy in the day-to-day behavior of organizational members. Second, there are likely to be different cultures in various functional groups in the organization differences between departments in a school; differences between divisions in a large school district (e.g., divisions of instruction, business, personnel, and research and development); differences between student, teacher, and administrator groups; and differences between elementary, middle school, and high school levels. Put another way, whenever the task requirements have resulted in a unique combination of people, structures, and function, the requirement to fulfill the group's goals will result in a unique culture.[6]

Dominant Culture Besides the subcultures that exist in an organization, the larger organization may also have a culture that distinguishes it from other large systems. For example, one large school district highly

[6]Schein, *Leadership and Organizational Culture.*

favored innovation. This philosophy translated itself into a variety of practices including team teaching, flexible scheduling, teacher-advisor programs, report card conferences, use of speakers' bureaus, collaboration with business firms, and internships. It resulted in values that emphasized good interpersonal relations between students and teachers, teachers and administrators, teachers and parents, and school and community.

Thus, central office administrators created policies and made decisions that perpetuated the overall school district's philosophy of innovation. Most key administrators portrayed the same image. They demonstrated excellent interpersonal and verbal skills and strived to be accessible to students, teachers, parents, and the community. They spent a portion of their time cultivating relations with the business community through membership in the Rotary, Kiwanis, Lions Club, Chamber of Commerce, and so on. This example shows that even large and relatively heterogeneous school districts that are known to have dominant cultures can improve their educational goals.

Creating, Maintaining, and Changing Organizational Culture

Organizational cultures are created, maintained, and changed through similar processes. But the following questions arise: How is an organizational culture created? How is the culture of an organization maintained? Can organizational culture be changed by administrative action? In this section, we explore the answers to these questions.

Creating Organizational Culture

Deal and Kennedy[7] identified four dimensions of organizational culture: values, heroes, rites and rituals, and communication networks. These four dimensions play a key role in creating organizational cultures.

Values

What are values, and how do they affect behavior? **Values** are general criteria, standards, or principles that guide the behavior of organization members.[8] There are two kinds of values: terminal and instrumental. A **terminal value** is a desired outcome that organization members seek to achieve.[9] Schools typically adopt any of the following as terminal values: quality, excellence, and success.[10] An **instrumental value** is a desired mode of behavior.[11] Modes of behavior that most schools advocate include working hard, providing excellent teaching, respecting student diversity, being creative, teamwork, and maintaining high standards.[12]

Thus, an organization's culture consists of outcomes that the organization seeks to achieve (its *terminal values*) and the modes of behavior the organization encourages (its *instrumental values*). Ideally, instrumental values help the organization achieve its terminal values. For example, a school/school district whose culture emphasizes the terminal value of high achievement for all students might attain this outcome by encouraging instrumental values like working hard to reach all students. This combination of terminal and instrumental values leads to school/school district success.

Schools are able to achieve success only when shared values exist among group members.[13] Shared values can provide a strong organizational identity, enhance collective commitment, provide a stable social system, and reduce the need for bureaucratic controls.[14] The following guidelines are recommended to achieve shared values:[15]

- A widely shared understanding of what the school stands for, often embodied in slogans;
- A concern for individuals over rules, policies, procedures, and adherence to job duties;

7Deal and Kennedy, *Corporate Cultures.*

8Gareth R. Jones, *Organizational Theory, Design, and Change*, 5th ed. (Upper Saddle River, NJ: Pearson/Prentice Hall, 2010, p. 178).

9Jennifer M. George and Gareth R. Jones, *Understanding and Managing Organizational Behavior* (Upper Saddle River, NJ: Pearson/Prentice Hall, 2008, p. 568).

10Clete Bulach, Fred C. Lunenburg, and Les Potter, *Creating a Culture for High-Performing Schools* (Lanham, MD: Rowman & Littlefield, 2008).

11George and Jones, *Understanding and Managing Organizational Behavior*, p. 568.

12Bulach, Lunenburg, and Potter, *Creating a Culture for High-Performing Schools.*

13Ibid.

14John R. Schermerhorn, James G. Hunt, and Richard N. Osborn, *Organizational Behavior*, 10th ed. (New York: John Wiley & Sons, 2008, p. 372).

15Schermerhorn, Hunt, and Osborn, *Organizational Behavior*, pp. 372–373.

- A well-understood sense of the informal rules and expectations so that group members and administrators understand what is expected of them;
- A belief that what group members and administrators do is important, and that it is important to share information and ideas;
- A recognition of heroes, whose actions illustrate the organization's shared philosophy and concerns;
- A belief in rites and rituals as important to organization members as well as to building a common identity.

Heroes Most successful organizations have their heroes. Heroes are born and created. The born hero is the visionary institution builder like Henry Ford, founder of the Ford Motor Company, Walt Disney, creator of Disney Studios and theme parks, and Mary Kay Ash, founder of Mary Kay Cosmetics. Created heroes, on the other hand, are those the institution has made by noticing and celebrating memorable moments that occur in the day-to-day life of the organization. Thomas Watson, former head of IBM, is an example of a situation hero. Other well-known heroes include Lee Iacocca at Chrysler, Sam Walton at Wal-Mart, and Vince Lombardi, the legendary coach of the Green Bay Packers. Heroes perpetuate the organization's underlying values, provide role models, symbolize the organization to others, and set performance standards that motivate participant achievement.

In many schools, local heroes and heroines—exemplars of core values—provide models of what everyone should be striving for. These deeply committed staff come in early, are always willing to meet with students, and are constantly upgrading their skills.

Rites and Rituals Another key aspect in creating organizational cultures are the everyday activities and celebrations that characterize the organization. Most successful organizations feel that these rituals and symbolic actions should be managed. Through rites and rituals, recognition of achievement is possible. The Teacher of the Year Award and National Merit Schools are examples. Similarly, a number of ceremonial rituals may accompany the appointment of a new superintendent of schools, including press and other announcements, banquets, meetings, and speeches.

Some organizations have even created their own reward rituals. At Hollibrook Elementary School in Spring Branch, Texas, rites and rituals reinforce student learning. Under the leadership of the principal and faculty, and supported through ties to the Accelerated Schools Model, the school developed numerous traditions to create a powerful professional culture and foster increased student success. For example, faculty meetings became a hotbed of professional dialogue and discussion of practice and published research. "Fabulous Friday" was created to provide students with a wide assortment of courses and activities. A "Parent University" furnishes courses and materials while building trust between the school and the largely Hispanic community. Norms of collegiality, improvement, and connection reinforce and symbolize what the school is about.

Communication Networks Stories or myths of heroes are transmitted by means of the communications network. This network is characterized by various individuals who play a role in the culture of the organization.[16] Each institution has *storytellers* who interpret what is going on in the organization. Their interpretation of the information influences the perceptions of others. *Priests* are the worriers of the organization and the guardians of the culture's values. These individuals always have time to listen and provide alternative solutions to problems. *Whisperers* are the powers behind the throne because they have the boss's ear. Anyone who wants something done will go to the whisperer. *Gossips* carry the trivial day-to-day activities of the organization through the communications network. Gossips are very important in building and maintaining heroes. They embellish the heroes' past feats and exaggerate their latest accomplishments. And, finally, *spies* are buddies in the woodwork. They keep everyone well informed about what is going on in the organization. Each of these individuals plays a key role in building and maintaining an organization's culture. It should be noted that the names used here are those ascribed by Deal and Kennedy to emphasize the importance of communication networks in creating an institution's organizational culture.

How do strong cultures come about? School leaders—including principals, teachers, and often parents and community members—develop and maintain positive values and a shared vision.

School leaders from every level are key to creating school culture. Principals communicate core values in

---

[16]Much of this discussion is based on Deal and Kennedy, *Corporate Cultures*.

ADMINISTRATIVE ADVICE 3–1

How Leaders Influence the Culture of Schools

School leaders do several important things when creating culture. First, they *read the culture*—its history and current condition. Leaders should know the deeper meanings embedded in the school before trying to reshape it. Second, leaders *uncover and articulate core values,* looking for those that reinforce what is best for students and that support student-centered learning. It is important to identify which aspects of the culture are negative and which are positive. Finally, leaders work to *fashion a positive context,* reinforcing cultural elements that are positive and modifying those that are negative and dysfunctional. Positive school cultures are never monolithic or overly conforming, but core values and shared purpose should be pervasive and deep. Some of the specific ways school leaders shape culture follow.

- They communicate core values in what they say and do.
- They honor and recognize those who have worked to serve students and the purpose of the school.
- They observe rituals and traditions to support the school's heart and soul.
- They recognize heroes and heroines and the work these exemplars accomplish.
- They eloquently speak of the deeper mission of the school.
- They celebrate the accomplishments of the staff, the students, and the community.
- They preserve the focus on students by recounting stories of success and achievement.

Source: Adapted from Kent D. Peterson and Terrence E. Deal, "How Leaders Influence the Culture of Schools, *Educational Leadership,* 56(1) (1998): 28–30.

their school buildings. Teachers reinforce values in their words and behavior. Parents enhance spirit when they visit school, participate in governance, and celebrate successes. In the strongest school cultures, leadership comes from many sources. (See Administrative Advice 3–1.)

Maintaining Organizational Culture

Once an organizational culture is created, a number of mechanisms help solidify the acceptance of the values and ensure that the culture is maintained or reinforced (**organizational socialization**). These mechanisms, illustrated in Figure 3–2, are the following steps for socializing employees:[17]

Step 1: Selection of Staff. The socialization process starts with the careful selection of staff. Trained recruiters use standardized procedures and focus on values that are important in the culture. Those candidates whose personal values do not fit with the underlying values of the organization are given ample opportunity to opt out (deselect).

Step 2: Orientation. After the chosen candidate is hired, considerable training ensues to expose the person to the culture. Humility-inducing experiences, which cause employees to question prior beliefs and values, are assigned, thereby making new employees more receptive to the values of the new culture. Many organizations give newly hired employees more work than they can reasonably handle and assign work for which the individual is overqualified. For example, a new faculty member of a university may be assigned undesirable tasks, which senior professors of the department do not wish to perform: teaching the basic courses, off-campus assignments, assignment to several committees, heavy advisement loads, field work, and assignment to an inequitable number of doctoral committees. The message conveyed to the newcomer is, "You must pay your dues."

[17]Richard T. Pascale, "The Paradox of 'Corporate Culture': Reconciling Ourselves to Socialization," *California Management Review*, 27 (1985): 26–41.

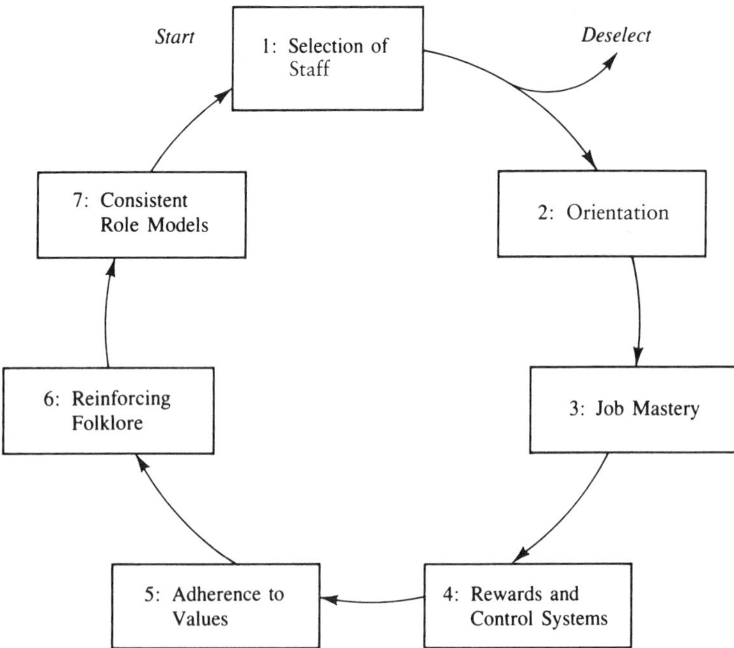

FIGURE 3-2

The Process of Organizational Socialization
Source: Adapted from Richard T. Pascale, "Paradox of 'Corporate Culture': Reconciling Ourselves to Socialization," *California Management Review*, 27 (1985): 38. Copyright 1985 by the Regents of the University of California. Used by permission of the Regents.

Step 3: Job Mastery. Whereas Step 2 is intended to foster cultural learning, Step 3 is designed to develop the employee's technological knowledge. As employees move along a career path, the organization assesses their performance and assigns other responsibilities on the basis of their progress. Frequently, organizations establish a step-by-step approach to this career plan. For example, some states have adopted a three-step career ladder process for teachers: (1) instructors, (2) professional teachers, and (3) career professionals. Another model consists of four steps: (1) licensed teachers, (2) certified teachers, (3) advanced certified teachers, and (4) lead teachers.

Step 4: Reward and Control Systems. The organization pays meticulous attention to measuring operational results and to rewarding individual performance. Reward systems are comprehensive, consistent, and focus on those aspects of the organization that are tied to success and the values of the culture. For example, a school district will specify the factors that are considered important for success. Operational measures are used to assess these factors, and performance appraisals of employees are tied to the accomplishment of these factors. Promotions and merit pay are determined by success on each of the predetermined critical factors. For instance, those school administrators who violate the culture are often transferred or given a relatively innocuous staff position at central office. These administrators are now "off their career tracks," which can inhibit their promotion in the organization. This is the typical pattern used in large bureaucratic school districts as an alternative to firing the administrator.

Step 5: Adherence to Values. As personnel continue to work for the organization, their behavior closely matches the underlying values of the culture. Identification with underlying values helps employees reconcile personal sacrifices caused by their membership in the organization. Personnel learn to accept the organization's values and place their trust in the organization not to hurt them. For instance, school administrators work long hours on a multiplicity of fragmented tasks for which they sometimes receive little recognition from their superiors, subordinates, and the community. They sometimes endure ineffective school board members and supervisors and job assignments that are undesirable and inconvenient. Identification with the common values of the organization allows these administrators to justify such personal sacrifices.

Step 6: Reinforcing Folklore. Throughout the socialization process, the organization exposes its members to rites and rituals, stories or myths, and heroes that

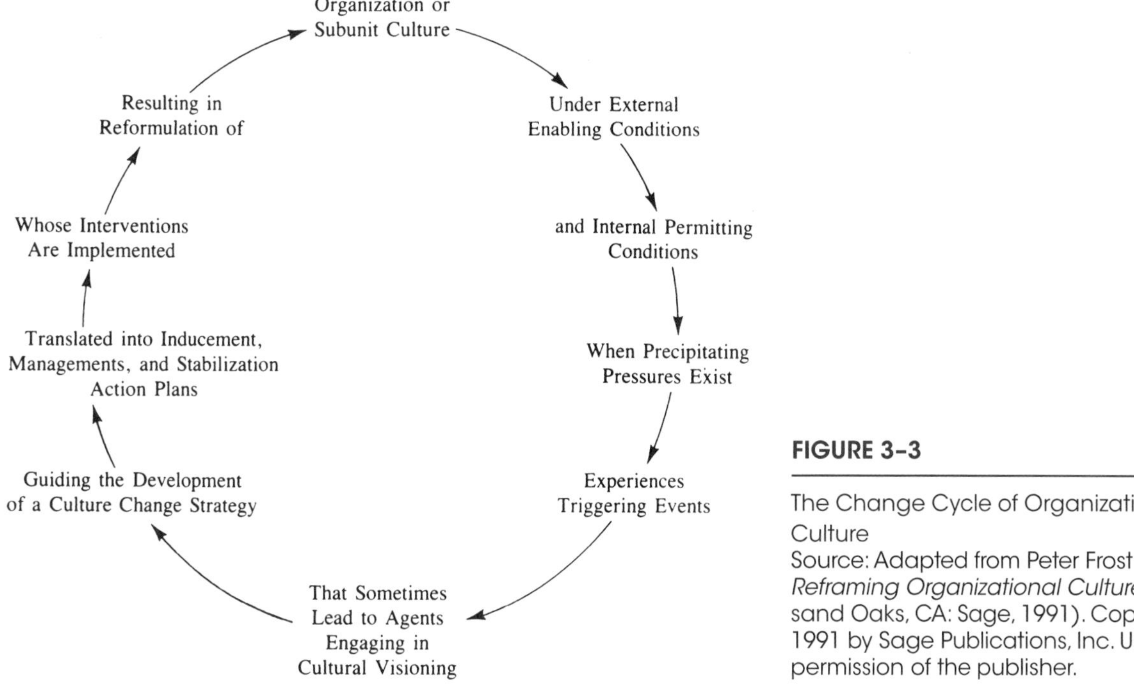

FIGURE 3–3

The Change Cycle of Organizational Culture
Source: Adapted from Peter Frost et al., *Reframing Organizational Culture* (Thousand Oaks, CA: Sage, 1991). Copyright 1991 by Sage Publications, Inc. Used by permission of the publisher.

portray and reinforce the culture. For example, in one educational institution, the story is told of an administrator who was fired because of his harsh handling of subordinates. The administrator had incorrectly believed a myth that being "tough" with his subordinates would enhance himself in the eyes of his superiors. The organization deemed such managerial behavior to be inconsistent with its organizational philosophy of cultivating good interpersonal relationships and high levels of morale and job satisfaction among all its employees.

Step 7: Consistent Role Models. Those individuals who have performed well in the organization serve as role models to newcomers to the organization. By identifying these employees as symbolizing success, the organization encourages others to do likewise. Role models in strong-culture institutions can be thought of as one type of ongoing staff development for all organizational members.

Changing Organizational Culture

To this point, we have discussed how organizational culture is created and maintained. Sometimes an organization determines that its culture needs to be changed. The **change cycle** (see Figure 3–3) has the following components.[18]

External Enabling Conditions. Enabling conditions, if they exist, indicate that the environment will be supportive of culture change. Such conditions are in the external environment and impact the organization. In a school setting, examples include scarcity or abundance of students, stability or instability of the external environment, and resource concentration or dispersion. In combination, these external enabling conditions determine the degree of threat to the organization's input sources (information, people, and materials) (see Figure 3–1).

Internal Permitting Conditions. To increase the likelihood of organizational culture change, four internal permitting conditions must exist: (1) a surplus of change resources (administrative time and energy, financial resources, and the like that are available to the system beyond those needed for normal operating); (2) system readiness (willingness of most members to live with the anxiety that comes with anticipated uncertainty

[18]Schein, *Organizational Culture and Leadership.*

that is characteristic of change); (3) minimal coupling (coordination and integration of system components); and (4) change-agent power and leadership (the ability of administrators to envision alternative organizational futures).

Precipitating Pressures. Four factors that precipitate organizational culture change include (1) atypical performance; (2) pressure exerted by stakeholders; (3) organizational growth or decrement in size, membership heterogeneity, or structural complexity; and (4) real or perceived crises associated with environmental uncertainty.

Triggering Events. Culture change usually begins in response to one or more triggering events. Examples include (1) environmental calamities or opportunities such as natural disasters, economic recession, innovations, or the discovery of new markets; (2) administrative crises such as a major shakeup of top administration, an inappropriate strategic decision, or a foolish expenditure; (3) external revolution such as mandated desegregation, PL101-476, Title IX, or the No Child Left Behind Act of 2001; and (4) internal revolution such as the installation of a new administrative team within the organization.

Cultural Visioning. Creating a vision of a new, more preferred organizational culture is a necessary step toward that culture's formation. Leaders survey the beliefs, values, assumptions, and behaviors of the organization's existing culture. They then seek to anticipate future conditions and create an image of the organization within that future.

Culture Change Strategy. Once a new cultural vision exists, an organization needs a strategy to achieve that culture. Such a strategy outlines the general process of transforming the present culture into the new one.

Culture Change Action Plans. A series of explicit action plans for the inducement, administration, and stabilization of change make a change strategy known. Inducement action planning involves stimulating organizational members to a change or countering resistance to change. Administrative action planning involves outlining interventions and mobilizing change agents. Stabilization action planning focuses on the institutionalization of culture change, that is, establishing the existence of the new culture as an accepted fact.

Implementation of Interventions. An organization selects culture change interventions based on the ecology of a particular organization for each action-plan phase and the change agent's competencies in implementing them.

Reformulation of Culture. When implemented, the intervention plans result in a reformulated culture.

Any comprehensive program of organizational change involves an attempt to change the culture of the organization.

Effects of Organizational Culture

As noted earlier, the culture of an organization affects many administrative processes. Among these are motivation, leadership, decision making, communication, and change. Culture also affects an organization's structural processes. The selection process, evaluation system, control system, and reward system must fit with the organization's culture. In addition, culture has an influence on employee performance and organizational effectiveness. Administrators are evaluated on the basis of the results they achieve; therefore, the organization's culture is an important concept because of the results it produces.

Views of Excellence

Thomas Peters and Robert Waterman, in their search for excellence in America's best-run organizations, found culture to be closely tied to the success of those firms.[19] From their research, they identified the following attributes that characterize excellent companies:

A Bias Toward Action. The organization continually does, experiments, and tries. An example in a school setting might be implementing strategic planning to guide a school district's mission and measure its results.

Close to the Customer. The organization looks to the customer for direction in the formation of new products, quality, and service. School districts that remain tuned-in to their clients' (students') needs while maintaining a close professional relationship with parents remain "close to the customer." Different types of family and community involvement were found to distinguish high-achieving schools from low-achieving schools.[20]

Autonomy and Entrepreneurship. The organization values and fosters risk taking and innovation. School

[19]Peters and Waterman, *In Search of Excellence.*

[20]Bulach, Lunenburg, and Potter, *Creating a Culture for High-Performing Schools.*

districts that encourage innovation and risk taking, while permitting some failure, have a philosophy of "autonomy and entrepreneurship." Such systems can be characterized as dynamic in that they are constantly attempting new ways of accomplishing school district goals.

Productivity Through People. The organization demonstrates a belief in the their employees through shared decision making and encouragement of new ideas. This belief is reflected in the language used by the organization. The organization views the employee as extended family, and there is an absence of rigidity of command. Schools that manifest high levels of trust in subordinates, use participatory decision making, listen to and use members' ideas, and show concern for the welfare of all employees are practicing "productivity through people."

Hands-On, Value-Driven Effort. The organization pays explicit attention to cultural values and devotes substantial effort to promoting and clarifying core values to employees. Strong-culture schools that emphasize high achievement levels for students and high performance and growth for faculty are practicing "hands-on, value-driven effort."

"Sticking to the Knitting." The organization stays in businesses they know how to run. This success attribute can be applied to public schools. The public has thrust upon educators the myth that schools can correct all of society's ills: the breakdown of the family, crime, racial strife, poverty, unemployment, drug abuse, child abuse, teenage pregnancy, and the like. It may be more accurate to say that more responsibility has been thrust upon the schools than they should accept; more results have been expected than they could possibly produce; and in too many cases, schools have assumed more than they should.[21] Put another way, schools have been programmed for failure, just as companies have failed who have expanded beyond their ability to compete in the marketplace.

Simple Form, Lean Staff. The organization does not use complex matrix structures, and keeps corporate staffs small. In the educational setting, this approach resembles somewhat the concept of site-based management.

Simultaneous Loose-Tight Properties. The organization exhibits both tight and loose couplings. It is tight about cultural values and loose or decentralized about autonomy, providing individuals throughout the organization room to perform. By following corporate world goals, schools can promote strong cultural values while providing people with the opportunity to grow and the flexibility to function within the school district's belief system.

Warren Bennis and Burt Nanus found that many organizations are overmanaged and underled. They ascertain that the leader should be concerned with the organization's basic purpose and general direction.[22] Time should be spent on doing the right thing: creating new ideas, new policies, and new methodologies. From the ninety leaders interviewed, they found the following leadership strategies: (1) attention through vision, (2) meaning through communication, (3) trust through positioning, and (4) deployment of self through positive self-regard and positive thinking. In short, effective leaders communicate their vision for the organization and embody this vision by being reliable, persistent, relentless, and dedicated to the implementation of the vision. Effective leaders know their strengths and weaknesses. They build on their strengths and compensate for their weaknesses. Their focus is on success. The word *failure* is rarely used; unsuccessful attempts are considered learning experiences.

Theory Z

William Ouchi examined high-producing companies in order to discover what, if anything, these firms had in common. To explain the success of these companies, Ouchi developed **Theory Z.**[23] Theory Z is an extension of McGregor's Theory X and Theory Y concepts (see Chapter 2). The principal difference is that McGregor's Theory X and Theory Y formulation is an attempt to distinguish between the personal leadership styles of an individual supervisor, whereas Theory Z is concerned with the "culture of the whole organization." That is, Theory Z is not concerned with the attitudes or behavior patterns of an individual supervisor but rather with the difference the organizational culture makes in the way the whole organization is put together and managed. Theory Z culture involves long-term employment, consensual decision making, individual responsibility,

[21]Fred C. Lunenburg and Beverly J. Irby, *The Principalship* (Belmont, CA: Wadsworth, 2006).

[22]Warren Bennis and Burt Nanus, *Leaders: The Strategies for Taking Charge* (New York: HarperCollins, 2007).

[23]William G. Ouchi, *Theory Z: How American Business Can Meet the Japanese Challenge* (New York: Avon Books, 1993).

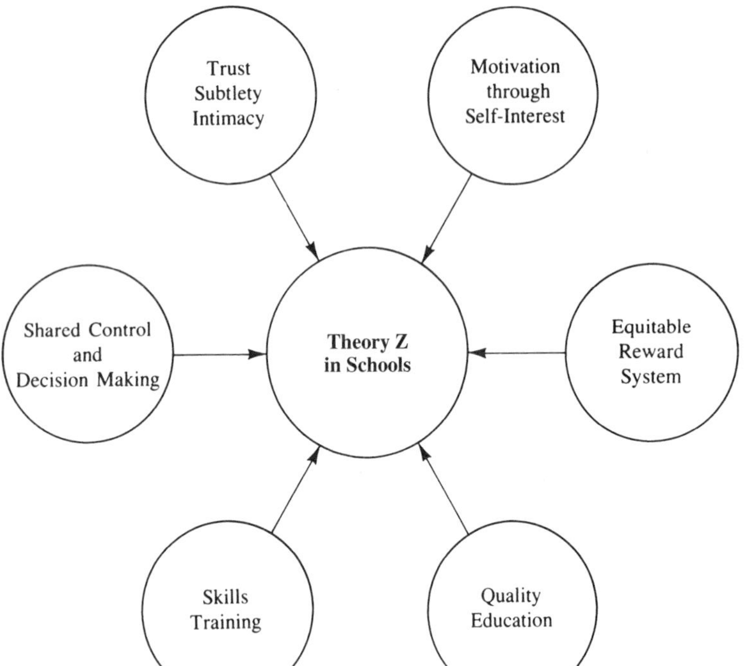

FIGURE 3–4

Major Components of Theory Z as Applied to Schools

slow evaluation and promotion, an informal control system with explicit measures of performance, moderately specialized career paths, and extensive commitment to all aspects of the employee's life, including family.[24]

William Ouchi applied Theory Z to schools in the early 1980s. The features which apply to schools include trust, subtlety, and intimacy; shared control and decision making; training in planning, organizational processes, budgeting systems, and interpersonal skills; motivation through self-interest; rewards over the long run; and the importance of high-quality education.[25] Figure 3–4 depicts these concepts.

Trust, Subtlety, and Intimacy According to Ouchi, no institution can exist without trust, subtlety, and intimacy. Trust in a school can only exist among people who understand that their objectives are compatible in the long run. The concept is based on the assumption that if you don't understand what someone else does, if you don't understand their language, their technology, and their problems, then you can't possibly trust them. Trust can be developed only through intimate, professional experience with someone else, including close interpersonal relations between students and students, teachers and students, teachers and teachers, administrators and teachers, and administrators and students.

Shared Control and Decision Making School administrators must spend adequate time discussing with students, teachers, parents, and the community the objectives of the schools and how the schools are run. School leaders must understand the incentive system available to personnel in their careers and help them to rationalize these incentives so that they can trust them. Then, administrators can invite subordinates to share control, which provides stakeholders with input into decisions that will affect the way they perform their responsibilities.

Skills Training The concept of *quality circles,* also called learning teams or cooperative learning groups, is advocated. Quality circles consist of small groups of employees who meet regularly to discuss the way they do their jobs and to recommend changes. The purpose

[24]Ibid.

[25]William Ouchi, "Theory Z and the Schools," *School Administrator,* 39 (1982): 12–19.

is to yield a group-based suggestion system for solving problems and improving the quality of the system.[26] This requires a period of training to increase participation, consensus in decisions, and shared control. The training is directed toward getting to know the organization: its objectives, problems, and overall resources. Specifically, teachers and other nonadministrative personnel are trained in planning, organizational processes (motivation, leadership, decision making, communication, and change), the system's budgetary process, group dynamics, and many of the school administrator's day-to-day activities to which teachers are rarely exposed. The training is designed to create a culture that lends itself to openness, trust, and employee involvement.

Motivation Through Self-Interest Ouchi believes that there is only one form of interest—self-interest. If you cannot create a setting in which people are permitted to naturally do what seems desirable to them—to satisfy their self-interest—then you are always fighting, constraining, holding back, and can never have high commitment nor high productivity. In the Theory Z organization, because people have participated in shaping the goals and objectives of the system, you can say to people, "Do what comes naturally; do what you prefer to do, because we have agreed that those things you choose to do are simultaneously good for the institution."[27]

Equitable Reward System An organizational memory is essential. Some key person must remember who has gone the extra mile, who is committed, and who has put in extra time; this person must ensure that those efforts are recognized and rewarded. According to Ouchi, if there is that kind of organizational memory, then people will have confidence that as long as they do what is right, there will be equity in the end. They therefore lose whatever incentives they might have to be selfish, narrow-minded, or short-sighted. What does Ouchi say about the lockstep salary schedules prevalent in most school districts? He deems it necessary that schools disassemble the currently bureaucratical approach to evaluation, promotion, and pay.

Quality Education One of the greatest assets any country has in developing its social health and its economic health is its school systems. High-quality education leads to an educated workforce, thereby increasing economic capital in the improved country. An enlightened citizenry is important to the welfare of a nation.

[26]John J. Bonstingl, *Schools of Quality* (Thousand Oaks, CA: Corwin Press, 2001).

[27]Ouchi, "Theory Z and the Schools," p. 14.

A Typology of Organizational Culture

Carl Steinhoff and Robert Owens developed a framework that suggests four distinctive **culture phenotypes** likely to be found in public schools.[28] These phenotypes are clearly describable and differentiated from one another in terms of the metaphorical language elicited from school participants.

Unlike most students of organizational culture, the researchers examined the culture of schools by survey methods rather than by using the more typical ethnographic approach. To support this methodology, Owens found in conducting a long-term ethnographic study of a senior high school that a culture assessment instrument could have been valuable in that study.[29]

Consistent with survey research methods, the researchers drew upon the literature to develop a theory of organizational culture.[30] As discussed earlier, the theory posits that organizational culture is the *root metaphor* of an organization. That is, "the culture of an organization does not merely describe what an organization is like, it describes the essence of the organization itself."[31] With this concept as an organizer, the researchers developed a taxonomic structure of organizational culture. The resulting taxonomy has six interlocking dimensions that define the culture of a school: (1) the history of the organization; (2) values and beliefs of the organization; (3) myths and stories that explain the organization; (4) cultural norms of the organization; (5) traditions, rituals, and ceremonies characteristic of the organization; and (6) heroes and heroines of the organization.

[28]Carl R. Steinhoff and Robert G. Owens, "The Organizational Culture Assessment Inventory: A Metaphorical Analysis in Educational Settings," *Journal of Educational Administration,* 27 (1989): 17–23.

[29]Robert G. Owens, "The Leadership of Educational Clans," in L. T. Sheive and M. B. Schoenheit (eds.), *Leadership: Examining the Elusive* (Alexandria, VA: Association for Supervision and Curriculum Development, 1987).

[30]Steinhoff and Owens, "The Organizational Culture Assessment Inventory."

[31]Steinhoff and Owens, "The Organizational Culture Assessment Inventory," p. 18.

Based on the taxonomy of organizational culture, Steinhoff and Owens constructed the Organizational Culture Assessment Inventory (OCAI) that, when taken as a whole, represents the consensual press, that is, the root metaphor perceived by organizational participants. "Culture as root metaphor promotes a view of organizations as expressive forms, manifestations of human consciousness."[32] These metaphors serve to illuminate the perceptual reality of the respondents and therefore serve as the basis on which they set goals, make commitments, and execute plans.

School Culture Phenotypes After several revisions of the initial form of the OCAI, the final version was validated in pilot studies of teachers, principals, and central office administrators in forty-seven elementary and secondary schools. The responses were sorted on the basis of school metaphor to establish metaphorical themes prevalent among the three groups. Data analysis produced four distinctive phenotypes of school culture, each of which can be described in terms of its metaphorical content.[33]

Family Culture This school can be described using metaphors such as family, home, or team. The principal in this school can be described as a *parent* (strong or weak), *nurturer, friend, sibling,* or *coach*. In this school, "concern for each other is important as well as having a commitment to students above and beyond the call of duty." Everyone should be willing to be a part of the family and pull their own weight. The school as family then is nurturing and friendly, often cooperative and protective, to which members are alternately submissive and rebellious—leaning on the shoulders, or bosom, of someone who has their best interests at heart.

Machine Culture This school can be described using the metaphor of the machine. Metaphors for the school include *well-oiled machines, political machines, beehives of activity,* or *rusty machines*. Metaphors for the principal range from *workaholic, Paul Bunyan,* and *The General* to *Charlie Brown* and the *slug*. The school as machine then is viewed purely in instrumental terms. The driving force appears to come from the structure of the organization itself, and administrators are described in terms of their varying ability to provide maintenance inputs. The social structure of these schools is tightly woven; however, unlike those of the family culture, its mission is protection rather than warmth. The school is a machine teachers *use* to accomplish work.

Cabaret Culture Metaphors such as a *circus,* a *Broadway show,* a *banquet,* or a *well-choreographed ballet* performed by well-appreciated *artists* describe this school. The principal is seen as a *master of ceremonies,* a *tightrope walker,* and a *ring master.* Teachers in these schools experience many of the same group-binding social activities as do their colleagues in the family culture school. The essential difference is that, in this culture, relationships center on performances and the reactions of the audience. There is great pride in the artistic and intellectual quality of one's teaching, which is carried out under the watchful eye of the maestro. At the cabaret the show must go on!

"Little Shop of Horrors" Culture This school can be described as an unpredictable, tension-filled *nightmare* having the characteristics of a war zone or revolution. "One never knows whose head will roll next." Teachers report their schools as *closed boxes* or *prisons*. The principal is a *self-cleansing statue* ready to offer up a sacrifice if it will maintain his position. In general, administrators in this school are seen as individuals whose main function is to keep things smoothed over. Others have a Napoleon complex that promotes dominance and control or Jekyll-Hyde personalities that promote a *walking-on-eggs* style of adaptive behavior among faculty. Unlike the family and cabaret cultures, teachers in this school lead isolated lives; there is little social activity. For example, written requests are often needed to hold any social activity—even for special occasions like Thanksgiving. One is expected to conform and to smile when appropriate. Verbal abuse among faculty is common, and closeness seems to be melting away. This culture is cold, hostile, and paranoid. "Almost anything can get you—and it often does."

Steinhoff and Owens's school culture phenotypes resemble somewhat the cultures delineated by Peters and Waterman.[34] With increasing emphasis in the literature for school administrators to become managers of culture, typologies such as these can be useful in examining the culture of school organizations. Moreover,

[32]Ibid.

[33]To preserve the metaphorical content used to describe the four culture phenotypes, we have quoted liberally from Steinhoff and Owens, "The Organizational Culture Assessment Inventory."

[34]Peters and Waterman, *In Search of Excellence.*

EXEMPLARY EDUCATIONAL ADMINISTRATORS IN ACTION

RICHARD (RICK) EARL BERRY Superintendent, Cypress-Fairbanks Independent School District, Houston, Texas.

Words of Advice: The advice that I would like to share with others includes several ideas that have served me well:

- Practice the golden rule.
- Seek out mentors.
- Keep balance in your life.
- Build trusting relationships with those around you.
- Surround yourself with intelligent, talented, creative, and caring people.
- Work hard and work smart.
- Be a problem solver, but before there is a problem, plan ahead.
- Strive not to make permanent enemies.

Steinhoff and Owens's OCAI appears to be a valid and reliable device to provide researchers and practitioners with a rich source of imagery not found in conventional instruments designed to measure organizational environments.

Organizational Climate

Organizational climate is the total environmental quality within an organization. It may refer to the environment within a school department, a school building, or a school district. Organizational climate can be expressed by such adjectives as *open, bustling, warm, easygoing, informal, cold, impersonal, hostile, rigid,* and *closed.*

Theorists refer to organizational culture and climate as overlapping concepts.[35] Organizational culture has its roots in sociology and anthropology, whereas organizational climate is rooted in psychology. Recent attention to school effectiveness and organizational cultures has reemphasized the importance of organizational climate. Organizational climate has been studied with a multitude of variables, methodologies, theories, and models, resulting in a substantial body of research. Studies of organizational climate have been shown to contain elements of leadership, motivation, and job satisfaction.[36] For example, in one comprehensive review of organizational climate studies, these elements have been linked with climate.[37]

We discuss four well-known constructs for conceptualizing organizational climate in schools: Halpin and Croft's concept of open and closed climates; Hoy and Tarter's organizational health construct; NASSP's Comprehensive Assessment of School Environments; and Willower, Eidell, and Hoy's concepts of pupil control ideology.

Open and Closed Climates

Andrew Halpin and Don Croft postulate a conceptual continuum that extends from **open** to **closed climates.** Their observations of how schools differ provided the major impetus for their research into organizational climate.[38] Halpin notes: "Anyone who visits more than a few schools notes quickly how schools differ from each other in their 'feel.'" And as one moves from school to school, "one finds that each appears to have a 'personality' that we describe here as the 'organizational climate' of the school. Analogously, personality is to the individual what organizational climate is to the organization."[39]

[35]John B. Miner, *Organizational Behavior 3: Historical Origins, Theoretical Foundations, and the Future* (New York: M. E. Sharpe, 2006).

[36]Cecil G. Miskel and Rodney Ogawa, "Work Motivation, Job Satisfaction, and Climate," N. J. Boyan (ed.), *Handbook of Research on Educational Administration* (New York: Longman, 1988), pp. 278–304.

[37]Wayne K. Hoy and Cecil G. Miskel, *Educational Administration: Theory, Research, and Practice,* 8th ed. (Boston: McGraw-Hill, 2008).

[38]Andrew W. Halpin and Don B. Croft, *The Organizational Climate of Schools* (Chicago: University of Chicago Press, 1963).

[39]Andrew W. Halpin, *Theory and Research in Administration* (New York: Macmillan, 1966), p. 131.

Table 3-1 The OCDQ Subtests

Characteristics	Intensity Scale[a]	
	Open	Closed
Teacher's Behavior		
Disengagement indicates that teachers do not work well together. They pull in different directions with respect to the task; they gripe and bicker among themselves.	–	++
Hindrance refers to teachers' feelings that the principal burdens them with routine duties, committee demands, and other requirements, which teachers construe as unnecessary busywork.	–	+
Esprit refers to morale. Teachers feel that their social needs are being satisfied while enjoying a sense of accomplishment in their job.	++	—
Intimacy refers to teachers' enjoyment of friendly social relations with each other.	+	+
Principal's Behavior		
Aloofness refers to formal and impersonal principal behavior; the principal goes by the book and maintains social distance from the teachers.	–	+
Production emphasis refers to behavior that is characterized by close supervision of the staff. The principal is highly directive and task oriented.	–	+
Thrust refers to behavior in which an attempt to "move the school" is made through the example that the principal sets for teachers.	++	–
Consideration refers to behavior that is characterized by an inclination to treat teachers "humanly," to try to do a little something extra for them in human terms.	+	–

[a]++ Very high emphasis; + high emphasis; – low emphasis; — very low emphasis.

Source: Adapted from Andrew W. Halpin, *Theory and Research in Administration* (New York: Macmillan, 1966), pp. 150–151.

The instrument that Halpin and Croft constructed is the Organizational Climate Description Questionnaire (OCDQ). It contains sixty-four Likert-type items that are assigned to eight subtests delineated by factor-analytic methods. Four subtests pertain primarily to characteristics of the group, as a group, and the other four to characteristics of the principal as a leader. From the scores of these eight subtests, they then constructed for each school a profile, which determines the relative position of the school on the open-to-closed continuum.[40] Table 3–1 presents the eight subtests together with the open-to-closed intensity scale.

As Table 3–1 shows, the open-climate school is low in disengagement, low in hindrance, very high in esprit, high in intimacy, low in aloofness, low in production emphasis, very high in thrust, and high in consideration. The closed-climate school is depicted as very high in disengagement, high in hindrance, very low in esprit, high in intimacy, high in aloofness, high in production emphasis, low in thrust, and low in consideration.

Using this information, we can sketch a behavioral picture of each climate. Composites for the two extremes of the climate continuum, the open and closed climates, are described next.

Open Climate An energetic, lively organization that is moving toward its goals and that provides satisfaction for group members' social needs describes the open climate. Leadership acts emerge easily and appropriately from both the group and the leader. Members are preoccupied disproportionately with neither task-achievement nor social-needs satisfaction; satisfaction on both counts seems to be obtained easily and almost effortlessly. The main characteristic of this climate is the "authenticity" of the behavior that occurs among all members.

Closed Climate A high degree of apathy on the part of all members of the organization characterizes the

[40]Halpin and Croft, *The Organizational Climate of Schools.*

closed climate. The organization is not "moving"; esprit is low because group members secure neither social-needs satisfaction nor task-achievement satisfaction. Members' behavior can be construed as inauthentic; indeed, the organization seems to be stagnant.

The OCDQ has had tremendous heuristic value and has promoted a broad-based interest in school climate within elementary and secondary schools.[41] Two revised versions of the OCDQ were developed recently: one for elementary schools—the OCDQ–RE—and one for secondary schools—the OCDQ–RS.[42]

The overwhelming majority of studies on school climate focus on adults in the form of teachers and principal-teacher relations. However, in recent years, the emphasis in climate has shifted from a management orientation to a focus on students.[43] The three school climate constructs, which we now discuss, are examples of avenues of research in this tradition.

Healthy and Sick Schools

Another instrument to assess the climate of the school is the Organizational Health Inventory (OHI) developed by Wayne Hoy and John Tarter.[44] Whereas the OCDQ examines the openness/closedness of teacher-teacher and principal-teacher interactions, the OHI describes the health of the interpersonal relations in schools among students, teachers, administrators, and community members.

Hoy and Tarter conceptualize organizational health at three levels: institutional, administrative, and teacher. The institutional level connects the school with its environment. The administrative level controls the internal managerial function of the organization. The teacher level is concerned with the teaching and learning process. A healthy school is one that keeps the institutional, administrative, and teacher levels in harmony, meets functional needs and successfully copes with disruptive external forces, and directs its energies toward school goals.

Three versions of the instrument were developed: one for elementary schools (the OHI–E), one for middle schools (the OHI–M), and one for secondary schools (the OHI–S). The elementary, middle, and secondary school versions of the OHI contain five, six, and seven subtests and thirty-seven, forty-five, and forty-four items, respectively, in a four-point, Likert-type format.[45] The subtests of the OHI–M are summarized in Table 3–2. Brief descriptions of the healthy and sick school follow.[46]

Healthy School A *healthy school* is characterized by student, teacher, and principal behavior that is harmonious and works toward instructional success. Teachers like their colleagues, their school, their job, and their students (high teacher affiliation), and they are driven by a quest for academic excellence. Teachers believe in themselves and their students; consequently, they set high but achievable goals. The learning environment is serious and orderly, and students work hard and respect others who do well academically (high academic emphasis). Principal behavior is also healthy—that is, friendly, open, egalitarian, and supportive. Such principals expect the best from teachers (high collegial leadership). Principals get teachers the resources they need to do the job (high resource support) and are also influential with superiors (high principal influence); they go to bat for their teachers. Finally, a healthy school has high institutional integrity; teachers are protected from unreasonable and hostile outside forces.

Sick School A *sick school* is vulnerable to destructive outside forces. Teachers and administrators are bombarded by unreasonable parental demands, and the school is buffeted by the whims of the public (low institutional integrity). The school lacks an effective principal. The principal provides little direction or structure, exhibits scant encouragement for teachers

[41]Miskel and Ogawa, "Work Motivation, Job Satisfaction, and Climate."

[42]Wayne K. Hoy and Sharon I. Clover, "Elementary School Climate: A Revision of the OCDQ," *Educational Administration Quarterly*, 22 (1986): 93–110; Robert B. Kottkamp, John A. Mulhern, and Wayne K. Hoy, "Secondary School Climate: A Revision of the OCDQ," *Educational Administration Quarterly*, 23 (1987): 31–48.

[43]Thomas J. Sergiovanni and Robert J. Starratt, *Supervision: A Redefinition*, 8th ed. (New York: McGraw-Hill, 2006).

[44]Wayne K. Hoy and C. John Tarter, *The Road to Open and Healthy Schools: A Handbook for Change, Elementary and Middle School Edition* (Thousand Oaks, CA: Corwin Press, 1997); *The Road to Open and Healthy Schools: A Handbook for Change, Middle and Secondary School Edition* (Thousand Oaks, CA: Corwin Press, 1997).

[45]Ibid.

[46]Wayne K. Hoy and C. John Tarter, *The Road to Open and Healthy Schools: A Handbook for Change, Elementary and Middle School Edition* (Thousand Oaks, CA: Corwin Press, 1997).

Table 3-2 The OHI-M Subtests

Characteristics
Institutional Level
Institutional integrity is the degree to which the school can cope with its environment in a way that maintains the educational integrity of its programs. Teachers are protected from unreasonable community and parental demands.
Administrative Level
Collegial leadership is principal behavior that is friendly, supportive, open, and guided by norms of equality. At the same time, the principal sets the tone for high performance by letting people know what is expected of them.
Principal influence is the principal's ability to influence the actions of superiors. Influential principals are persuasive with superiors, get additional consideration, and proceed relatively unimpeded by the hierarchy.
Resource support is the extent to which classroom supplies and instructional materials are readily available; in fact, even extra materials are supplied if requested.
Teacher Level
Teacher affiliation is a sense of friendliness and strong affiliation with the school. Teachers feel good about each other, their job, and their students. They are committed to both their students and their colleagues and accomplish their jobs with enthusiasm.
Academic emphasis is the extent to which the school is driven by a quest for academic excellence. High but achievable academic goals are set for students, the learning environment is orderly and serious, teachers believe in their students' ability to achieve, and students work hard and respect those who do well academically.

Source: Adapted from Wayne K. Hoy and C. John Tarter, *The Road to Open and Healthy Schools: A Handbook for Change, Elementary and Middle School Edition* (Thousand Oaks, CA: Corwin Press, 1997), pp. 58–59.

(low collegial leadership), and has negligible clout with superiors (low influence). Teachers don't like their colleagues or their jobs. They act aloof, suspicious, and defensive (low teacher affiliation). Instructional materials, supplies, and supplementary materials are not available when needed (low resource support). Finally, there is minimal press for academic excellence. Neither teachers nor students take academic life seriously; in fact, academically oriented students are ridiculed by their peers and viewed by their teachers as threats (low academic emphasis).

Comprehensive Assessment of School Environments (CASE)

The National Association of Secondary School Principals (NASSP) named a task force to investigate the current literature and measures of school climate. After an extensive review of the literature, the task force found that most existing definitions of climate were unclear, that many climate studies were based on one stakeholder group (usually teachers), that climate and satisfaction measures were frequently confused, and that measures with good psychometric properties were scarce and rarely used by practitioners.

The task force formulated a general model depicting the contextual, input, mediating, and outcome variables of school environments (see Figure 3–5). Assumptions accepted in the formulation of the model were as follows:

- Climate and satisfaction are distinct but related concepts.
- Climate does not define effectiveness; it only predicts it.
- Student outcomes (cognitive, affective, and psychomotor) and efficiency data (cost) are the most appropriate measures of school effectiveness.

The model of the school environment developed by the NASSP task force goes beyond a simple consideration of school climate to encompass a full range of inputs and outputs to the process of school improvement. As Figure 3–5 shows, perceptions of climate held by stakeholder groups (students, teachers, parents) are mediating variables—influencing factors—not outcome measures. Teacher and parent satisfaction are input variables. Student satisfaction is both a mediating variable and an outcome measure; it both influences school success and corroborates it.

The Instruments The Comprehensive Assessment of School Environments (CASE) battery consists of four survey instruments: the NASSP School Climate Survey,

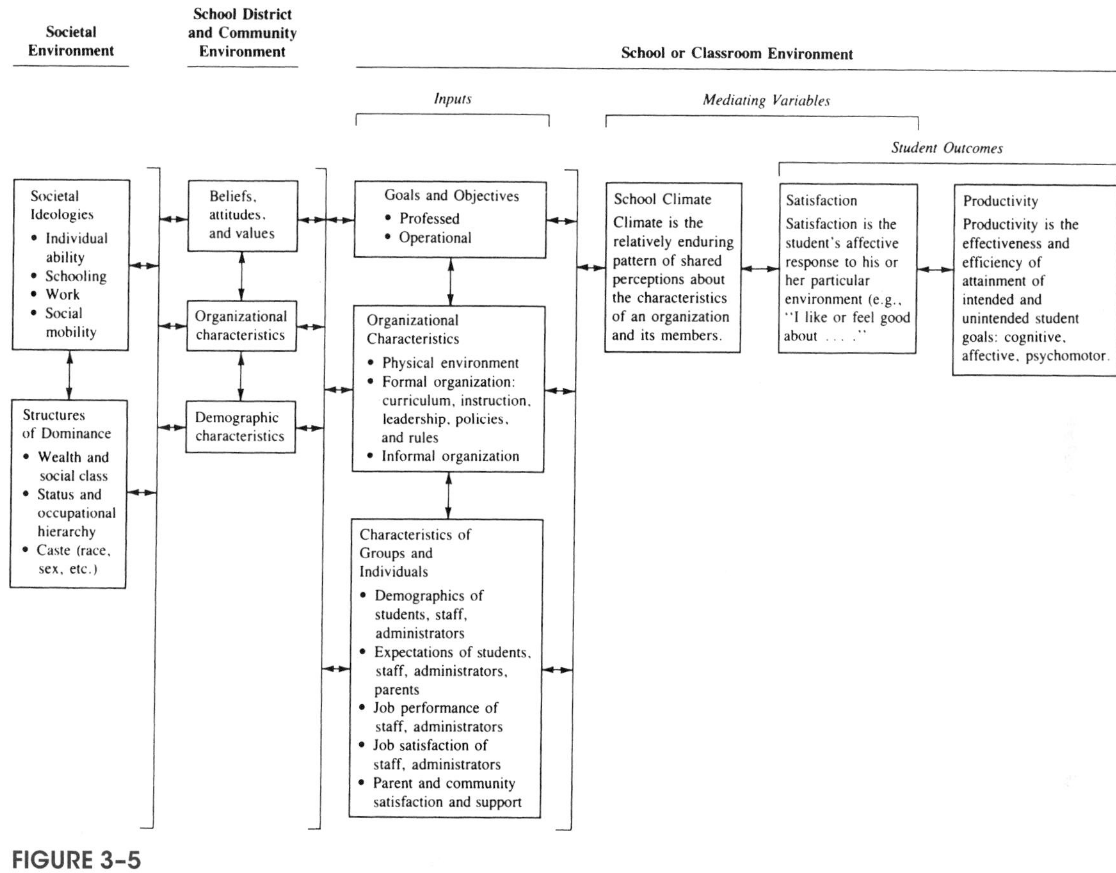

FIGURE 3–5

An Interactive Model of the School Environment
Source: James W. Keefe and Eugene R. Howard, "Redesigning Schools for the New Century: A Systems Approach," NASSP, 1997. Used by permission.

which is designed to elicit responses from all major stakeholder groups (students, teachers, parents), and three separate NASSP Satisfaction Surveys, one for each of the three major stakeholder groups.

The NASSP survey instruments were validated in national pilot and normative studies of 1500 teachers, 14,600 students, and 4400 parents. Each survey has eight to ten subscales touching on all important aspects of the school environment. Computer scoring programs provide separate climate and satisfaction profiles for each school.[47]

[47]NASSP Task Force, *Comprehensive Assessment of School Environments: Examiner's Manual* (Reston, VA: National Association of Secondary School Principals, 1987).

The NASSP School Climate Survey collects and measures data about perceptions on the following subscales:

- *Teacher-student relationships:* The quality of the interpersonal and professional relationships between teachers and students.
- *Security and maintenance:* The quality of maintenance and the degree of security people feel at the school.
- *Administration:* The degree to which school administrators are effective in communicating with different role groups and in setting high performance expectations for teachers and students.
- *Student academic orientation:* Student attention to task and concern for achievement at school.
- *Student behavioral values:* Student self-discipline and tolerance for others.

- *Guidance:* The quality of academic and career guidance and personal counseling services available to students.
- *Student-peer relationships:* Students' care and respect for one another and their mutual cooperation.
- *Parent and community school relationships:* The amount and quality of involvement in the school of parents and other community members.
- *Instructional management:* The efficiency and effectiveness of teacher classroom organization and use of classroom time.
- *Student activities:* Opportunities for and actual participation of students in school-sponsored activities.

The NASSP survey instruments have been developed as measures within a CASE battery based on the task-force model (see Figure 3–5). The instruments can be used singly or in any combination, but the task force encourages their use within the context of the entire model. The principal aim of the measures and procedures of the CASE model is to foster school improvement. The CASE data may also be useful in preparing school reports required by state or regional accrediting agencies. Outcomes-based evaluation for school accreditation is gaining support and acceptance from several accrediting bodies.[48] The CASE battery permits the organization and monitoring of outcomes-based data.

The CASE organizational climate variables imply that most schools are not as effective as they might be. Because effectiveness is a continuum, schools can always improve their performance. Unfortunately, schools are not easy to change. Schools that somehow manage to produce achievement levels higher than that predicted by the socioeconomic composition of the school and community are by definition exceptions. If becoming an effective school were easy, such schools would be the rule rather than the atypical extreme. Nevertheless, there are a number of other identifiable characteristics that can be used to measure school quality. (See Administrative Advice 3–2.)

Pupil Control Ideology

Another method of conceptualizing organizational climate is in terms of the attitudes toward students and the behavior faculty use to control them. Willard Waller was one of the first to underscore the saliency of pupil control in the organizational life of public schools.[49] Moreover, according to nearly four decades of annual Gallup polls, pupil control remains a key concern of teachers, administrators, and citizens.[50] In fact, a teacher's inability to control students effectively is a major source of dissatisfaction for many of today's teachers.[51]

The importance of pupil control in schools is not surprising. Schools are people-developing or people-changing institutions. The objective of the school as a social institution is to achieve major changes in the child. These changes are not restricted to cognitive behavior (learning) but include a wide range of social, emotional, physical, and, in some cases, moral behavior.[52] Organizations that achieve or attempt to achieve the most thoroughgoing change are performing functions crucial to the maintenance of social control.

Furthermore, schools accept as conscripted clients all those who legally must attend. That is, neither the organization (school) nor the client (student) exercises choice concerning participation in the relationship.[53] The mandatory nature of the pupil's participation suggests that schools are dealing with clients whose motivations and desires for the school's services cannot be assumed. It seems reasonable that pupil control would be a major concern.

Evidence to support the prominence of pupil control in schools is provided by a field study of a junior high school in which the researchers indicated that pupil control was the "integrative theme" that pervaded the culture of the school.[54] This study eventually led to the

48Ibid.

49Willard Waller, *The Sociology of Teaching* (New York: Wiley, 1932).

50Alex Gallup, *The Gallup Poll Cumulative Index: Public Opinion, 1968–2008* (Lanham, MD: Rowman & Littlefield, 2009).

51Lunenburg and Irby, *The Principalship*.

52Charles E. Bidwell, "The School as a Formal Organization," in J. G. March (ed.), *Handbook of Organizations* (Chicago: Rand McNally, 1965), pp. 972–1022.

53Richard O. Carlson, "Environmental Constraints and Organizational Consequences: The Public School and Its Clients," in D. E. Griffiths (ed.), *Behavioral Science and Educational Administration* (Chicago: University of Chicago Press, 1964), pp. 262–276.

54Donald Willower and Ronald Jones, "Control in an Educational Organization," in J. Raths, J. Pancella, and J. Van Ness (eds.), *Studying Teaching* (Englewood Cliffs, NJ: Prentice Hall, 1967), pp. 424–428.

ADMINISTRATIVE ADVICE 3–2

Characteristics to Measure School Quality

The quality of a school is the result of a number of factors, many of which are listed here. Any school possessing a majority of these characteristics can be called a high-quality school.

- *High Expectations for All.* The school adopts the philosophy that all students, if motivated and provided adequate opportunities, can learn important, challenging, and interesting content. Important knowledge is no longer for an elite. It is for all students, regardless of their social circumstances or career aspirations.
- *Responsiveness to Student Diversity.* Educators view the increasing cultural, linguistic, and socio-economic diversity of the student population as an opportunity as well as a challenge. Curriculum content and pedagogical approaches are built on and are respectful of this diversity.
- *Emphasis on Active Learning.* Students spend far less time passively receiving knowledge. They spend far more time—sometimes individually, often in groups—doing, experimenting, and discovering knowledge and understanding for themselves.
- *Essential Curriculum.* Schools select the most important concepts and skills to emphasize, so that they can concentrate on the quality of understanding rather than on the quantity of information presented. Students acquire the tools to add to their knowledge independently.
- *Diverse Pedagogy.* Educators employ more diverse and more balanced kinds of teaching and learning experiences to implement curricula. This will require new kinds of teacher training and staff development for teachers and administrators.
- *Time as a Learning Resource.* School time is organized around learning, instead of the other way around. Teacher and administrator needs are secondary to the needs of learners. The typical fifty-minute, seven period day may need to be restructured to fit the curricula content.
- *Authentic Assessment:* The type of assessment employed means there will be increased use of performance as a means of assessment. Educators as well as students are held accountable for what students can do instead of relying solely on standardized test results.
- *Heterogeneous Grouping.* Schools have ended tracking and have reduced ability grouping.
- *Cooperative Learning.* Students engage in far less competitive learning. In heterogeneous groups, they work democratically and collaboratively.
- *Technology as a Tool.* Computers, videodiscs, satellite TV, and other technologies are viewed as resources to enhance learning, not as symbols of excellence or innovation.

Source: Adapted from Fred C. Lunenburg, "The Urban Superintendent's Role in School Reform," *Education and Urban Society*, 25 (1992): 37–38. Used by permission.

development of the construct of **pupil control ideology** as a school climate descriptor. The conceptualization of pupil control and the research initiated by Donald Willower, Terry Eidell, and Wayne Hoy at Pennsylvania State University have permitted some of the first steps toward a systematic analysis of pupil control in the school.[55]

[55]Donald J. Willower, Terry L. Eidell, and Wayne K. Hoy, *The School and Pupil Control Ideology*, rev. ed. (University Park: Pennsylvania State University Studies Monograph No. 24, 1973).

Willower and his colleagues postulate pupil control along a humanistic to custodial continuum. These terms refer to contrasting types of individual ideology and the types of school organization that they seek to rationalize and justify. Prototypes of humanistic and custodial schools are presented next.[56]

The Humanistic School The model for humanistic control orientation is an educational community in which students learn through cooperative interaction

[56]Ibid.

and experience. In this model, learning and behavior are viewed in psychological and sociological terms rather than moralistic ones. Learning is viewed as an engagement in worthwhile activity rather than the passive absorption of facts. The withdrawn student is seen as a problem equal to that of the troublesome one. Self-discipline is substituted for strict teacher control. The humanistic orientation leads teachers to desire a democratic atmosphere with its attendant flexibility in status and rules, sensitivity to others, open communication, and increased student self-determination. Both teachers and pupils are willing to act on their own volition and to accept responsibility for their actions.

The Custodial School The prototype of custodial control orientation is the traditional school that often provides a rigid and highly controlled setting concerned with the maintenance of order. Students are generally stereotyped in terms of their appearance, their behavior, and their parents' social status. Teachers who have a custodial orientation tend to conceive of the school as an autocratic organization with a well-defined pupil–teacher status hierarchy. Furthermore, teachers are predisposed to view the flow of power and communication as unilateral and as downward where students must accept the decisions of teachers without question. Teachers do not attempt to understand student behavior but, instead, view it in moralistic terms. Student misbehavior is taken as a personal affront; students are perceived as irresponsible and undisciplined persons who must be controlled through punitive sanctions. Impersonality, pessimism, and "watchful mistrust" imbue the atmosphere of the custodial school.

To operationalize pupil control ideology along a humanistic-custodial continuum, the Pupil Control Ideology form (PCI) was developed and field tested.[57] The PCI consists of twenty Likert-type items. Examples of items are: "Beginning teachers are not likely to maintain strict enough control over their pupils," "Pupils can be trusted to work together without supervision," and "It is often necessary to remind pupils that their status in school differs from that of teachers." Responses are made on a five-point scale in a strongly agree to strongly disagree format. The scoring range is 20 to 100; the higher the score, the more custodial the ideology of the respondent. Pooled scores represent the pupil control ideology of the school. The reliability and validity of the instrument have been reported in numerous studies.[58]

Pupil Control Ideology: A School Climate Descriptor Each school appears to have a prevailing pupil control ideology that influences its members. For instance, pupil control ideology is a school characteristic that affects the values of new teachers coming into a school. They are heavily influenced by the prevailing climate. Studies show how student teachers and neophyte teachers gradually shift from very humanistic values proselytized by teacher education staffs to more prevalent values held by teachers in the schools.[59]

One study found that pupil control ideology was a fruitful measure of the climate of the school; humanism in school pupil control ideology was associated with openness in organizational climate.[60] Another study tested further the utility of the humanistic-custodial construct as a predictor of school climate. To determine the openness of the climate of the fifty-three-school sample, Fred Lunenburg used three organizational climate subtests of the OCDQ (esprit, thrust, and disengagement) to compare the most humanistic schools and the most custodial schools in terms of their climate-openness scores.[61] There were no surprises. Schools with custodial pupil control ideologies had significantly lower esprit and thrust scores and significantly higher disengagement scores. That is, custodial schools as compared to humanistic schools appear to have (1) teachers who have low morale, reflecting low job satisfaction with respect to both task achievement and social needs satisfaction; (2) principals who are ineffective in directing the activities of teachers through personal example; and (3) teachers who do not work well together, resulting in minimal group achievement.

[57] Ibid.

[58] John S. Packard, "The Pupil Control Studies," in N. J. Boyan (ed.), *Handbook of Research on Educational Administration* (New York: Longman, 1988), pp. 185–207.

[59] Fred C. Lunenburg, "The Influence of Experience on the Student Teacher," *High School Journal*, 69 (1986): 214–217; Wayne K. Hoy and Richard Rees, "The Bureaucratic Socialization of Student Teachers," *Journal of Teacher Education*, 28 (1977): 23–26.

[60] Fred C. Lunenburg and Robert R. O'Reilly, "Personal and Organizational Influence on Pupil Control Ideology," *Journal of Experimental Education*, 42 (1974): 31–35.

[61] Fred C. Lunenburg, *Pupil Control in Schools: Individual and Organizational Correlates* (Lexington, MA: Ginn, 1984).

Recognizing Excellent Schools

In the past decade, more and more attention has been given to informing the public about the state of the schools. Schools are rated nationally, statewide, and locally. Poor schools receive attention, and, frequently, additional resources to spur their development. Excellent schools receive recognition through such awards as the National merit Schools, which are recognized annually at a ceremony in the Rose Garden of the White House.

Question: When excellent schools are recognized, is it an incentive for those schools to maintain excellence and for other schools to strive for excellence?

Arguments PRO

1. When an outstanding school is recognized by the President of the United States, it receives the recognition it deserves. Communities, parents, children, and educators are proud. Everyone wins.
2. The possibility of national recognition for excellence will spur mediocre schools to positive action.
3. Competition is part of U.S. culture. We recognize outstanding athletes, actors, musicians, poets, car salespersons, and school superintendents. Why not excellent schools?
4. Although we know excellence when we see it, we have not developed yet a national image of excellent public schooling. An award will force us to identify more and better indicators of excellence. Excellence will be pursued more easily by all schools when a clearer picture of it emerges.
5. Principals are key figures in school effectiveness. Excellent schools do not happen by accident. They are led by strong leaders with clear vision. Such principals deserve rewards and career advancement.

Arguments CON

1. Those who are recognized as excellent are not necessarily the best. The application process is so demanding and redundant that many have chosen to put their energies into other efforts.
2. The majority of schools do not have the resources to achieve excellence. The recognition that a few receive will be a disincentive for the many.
3. Competition among schools can have negative effects. People in the winning schools develop an unrealistic sense of worth; once they are recognized, some people will rest on their laurels.
4. Principals and teachers will put their energies into meeting the criteria identified by the award rather than dealing with other areas that need improvement. The arbitrary parameters established by the award rather than the clear pursuit of excellence will guide action.
5. Superintendents will expect principals to apply for awards and receive them. Principals whose school won an award will have an advantage when they apply for new principalships. Principals, rather than schools, will be the real winners.

Two researchers developed and tested hypotheses concerning relationships among pupil control ideology, pupil control behavior, and the quality of school life. The hypotheses, tested in 239 elementary and secondary school classrooms in five school districts, were confirmed.[62] Custodialism in pupil control ideology and in pupil control behavior (another climate construct) were associated with students' negative reactions to the quality of school life. In addition, differences in pupil control ideology, pupil control behavior, and the quality of school life were found among urban, suburban, and rural schools. Urban schools were significantly more custodial in both pupil control ideology and behavior and had lower quality of school life scores than did either suburban or rural schools.

In a comprehensive study of school climate and alienation of high school students, one study reported that the more custodial and closed the school climate,

[62]Fred C. Lunenburg and Linda J. Schmidt, "Pupil Control Ideology, Pupil Control Behavior, and the Quality of School Life," *Journal of Research and Development in Education*, 22 (1989): 36–44.

the greater the students' sense of alienation.[63] Another inquiry involving high school students found a relationship between a humanistic school climate and high levels of self-actualization among the student body.[64] Moreover, humanistic pupil control ideology and pupil control behavior (a companion construct) were associated with environmental robustness (a positive school climate).[65]

Yet another study, involving nearly 3000 students in thirty-five elementary schools, found that the humanistic school, not the custodial one, was associated with high student self-concept as a learner. In addition, students' perceptions of a humanistic school climate were positively related to their motivation, task orientation, problem solving, and seriousness about learning.[66]

Do teachers' pupil control ideologies influence students' feelings toward teachers? Researchers explored this question in a comprehensive study involving over 3000 students and teachers in 131 elementary school classrooms. As predicted, custodialism in teacher pupil control ideology was directly related to students' projections of rejection and hostility toward teachers. The hypothesis was supported in the overall sample of 131 teachers ($r = .60$) and in subsamples of male ($r = .71$) and female ($r = .54$) teachers.[67]

In another study, the more custodial the pupil control ideology of the teacher, the more severe were his reported reactions to specific incidents of pupil disruptive behavior.[68] Further research indicated that teacher burnout was related to both custodial pupil control ideology and external locus of control. Additional analysis revealed that external, custodial teachers were found more often to experience depersonalized feelings and to frequently and intensely experience a lack of personal accomplishment (or self-efficacy).[69]

Summary

1. Organizational culture is the pattern of beliefs and assumptions shared by organizational members. Some important characteristics of organizational culture include observed behavioral regularities, norms, dominant values, philosophy, rules, and feelings.
2. Shared values, organizational heroes, rites and rituals, and communication networks play key roles in creating organizational cultures.
3. In maintaining a culture, institutions carry out several steps including careful selection of staff, orientation, job mastery, implementation of reward and control systems, careful adherence to values, reinforcing folklore, and the consistent use of role models.
4. Changing organizational culture involves the following steps: external enabling conditions; internal permitting conditions; precipitating pressures; triggering events; cultural visioning; culture-change strategy; culture-change action plans; implementation of interventions; and reformulation of the culture.
5. Organizational culture has effects on administrative processes (e.g., motivation, leadership, decision making, communication, and change) and organizational structures (e.g., the selection process, evaluation system, control system, and reward system).
6. Certain types of cultures characterize excellent enterprises. Peters and Waterman offer a generalized concept of excellence. Ouchi postulates Theory Z as an approach to excellence, with specific application to schools.
7. Organizational climate is the total environmental quality within an organization. Four climate constructs were discussed: the open and closed climates, healthy and sick schools, CASE, and pupil control ideology.

[63] Wayne K. Hoy, "Dimensions of Student Alienation and Pupil Control Orientations of High Schools," *Interchange*, 3 (1972): 38–52.

[64] John Deibert and Wayne Hoy, "Custodial High Schools and Self-Actualization of Students," *Educational Research Quarterly*, 2 (1977): 24–31.

[65] Fred C. Lunenburg, "Pupil Control Ideology and Behavior as Predictors of Environmental Robustness: Public and Private Schools Compared," *Journal of Research and Development in Education*, 24 (1991): 15–19.

[66] Fred C. Lunenburg, "Pupil Control Ideology and Self- Concept as a Learner," *Educational Research Quarterly*, 8 (1983): 33–39.

[67] Fred C. Lunenburg and Jack W. Stouten, "Teacher Pupil Control Ideology and Pupils Projected Feelings Toward Teachers," *Psychology in the Schools*, 20 (1983): 528–533.

[68] Fred C. Lunenburg, "Educators' Pupil Control Ideology as a Predictor of Educators' Reactions to Pupil Disruptive Behavior," *High School Journal*, 74 (1991): 81–87.

[69] Fred C. Lunenburg and Victoria Cadavid, "Locus of Control, Pupil Control Ideology, and Dimensions of Teacher Burnout," *Journal of Instructional Psychology*, 19 (1992): 13–22.

Key Terms

organizational culture
values
terminal value
instrumental value
heroes
rites and rituals
communications network
organizational socialization
change cycle
Theory Z
culture phenotype
family culture
machine culture
cabaret culture
"little shop of horrors" culture
organizational climate
open and closed climates
healthy and sick schools
Comprehensive Assessment of School Environments (CASE)
pupil control ideology

Discussion Questions

1. Describe several important characteristics of organizational culture and give some examples of each operating in your school/school district.
2. How are organizational cultures developed, maintained, and changed?
3. Describe some of the features of the cultures of excellent firms as elaborated by Thomas Peters and Robert Waterman and apply these to your school or school district.
4. Discuss the tenets of Theory Z as described by William Ouchi. What are its applications to schools?
5. Discuss the four culture phenotypes developed by Carl Steinhoff and Robert Owens. What are their application to schools?
6. How do each of the four organizational climate constructs relate to school effectiveness? Analyze these in relation to your school or school district.

Suggested Readings

Bulach, Cletus R., Fred C. Lunenburg, and Les Potter. *Creating a Culture for High-Performing Schools* (Lanham, MD: Rowman & Littlefield, 2008). The authors offer an extensive look at comprehensive school reform. They emphasize how an organizational approach to school reform creates a distinctly different school culture that addresses the needs of school administrators, teachers, and students. The book provides excellent guidance and practical suggestions for educators who want to change school dynamics and improve students' academic achievement.

Deal, Terrence E., and Kent D. Peterson. *Shaping School Culture: The Heart of Leadership* (New York: John Wiley, 2003). The authors draw from over twenty years of research and work to show how leaders can harness the power of school culture to build a lively, cooperative spirit and a sense of school identity. They describe the critical elements of culture—the purposes, traditions, norms, and values that guide and glue the community together—and show how a positive culture can make school reforms work.

Gerstner, Louis V. *Who Says Elephants Can't Dance* (New York: Harper Business, 2002). Louis Gerstner, seen by many as one of the greatest CEOs of all time, sums up his view of what is important for success in organizations: Culture! Gerstner clearly demonstrates in the book that he understands how culture is created, how it is valuable, how it can become an impediment to change, and how to go about changing it. Espoused values and underlying assumptions are not the same. Most organizations say their cultures are about the same things-outstanding customer service, excellence, teamwork, stakeholder value, responsible organizational behavior, and integrity. These kinds of values do not necessarily translate into the same kind of behavior in all organizations. Culture is how people actually go about their work, how they interact with one another, and what motivates them.

Ouchi, William G. *Theory Z: How American Business Can Meet the Japanese Challenge* (New York: Avon Books, 1993). To explain the success of high-producing Japanese companies, Ouchi developed Theory Z, which becomes the basis for describing and understanding the cultural mindset of an organization and the manner in which its members think, feel, and behave.

Peters, Thomas J., and Robert H. Waterman. *In Search of Excellence,* rev. ed. (New York: DIANE Publishing Company, 2006). The authors point out that the culture of an organization affects many administrative processes (motivation, leadership, decision making, communication, and change), structural processes (selection process, evaluation system, control system, and reward system), and has an influence on employee performance and organizational effectiveness.

Sarason, Seymour B. *Revisiting the Culture of the School and the Problem of Change* (New York: Teachers College Press, 1996). Part I reproduces the second edition of Sarason's ground-breaking work, *The Culture of the School and the Problem of Change,* in which he detailed how change can affect a school's culturally diverse environment—either through the implementation of new programs or as a result of federally imposed regulations. In Part II, Sarason "revisits" the text and the issues twenty-five years after the original publication.

Sashkin, Marshall, and Herbert J. Walberg (eds.). *Educational Leadership and School Cultures* (Berkeley, CA: McCutchan, 1993). Recognized experts explore pieces of the puzzle of educational leadership and culture: the nature of educational leadership, the nature of culture in schools and school systems, and the way leaders construct high-performance cultures.

4

Motivation

FOCUSING QUESTIONS

1 Why are some employees highly motivated, while others lack drive and commitment?

2 Which motivation theory is most practical for school administrators: need hierarchy, existence related growth, motivation-hygiene, or learned needs theory?

3 What can school administrators learn from self-efficacy theory to improve their effectiveness in motivating organization members?

4 How can school administrators determine employees' paths toward outcomes that will satisfy their needs in expectancy theory?

5 How might school administrators improve equity to avoid dysfunctional consequences?

6 What are the key elements of goal-setting theory? How do they pertain to employee motivation?

In this chapter, we attempt to answer these questions concerning work motivation in school organization. We begin our discussion with some brief definitions of motivation, and we examine the concepts of effort, persistence, and direction of employee motives as a foundation of work motivation. Next, we describe and contrast several popular content theories of motivation: need hierarchy, existence related growth, motivation-hygiene, and learned needs approaches. Finally, we examine four process theories of motivation: self-efficacy, expectancy, equity, and goal-setting approaches.

Defining Motivation

School administrators widely agree that **motivation** is a critical determinant of performance in organizations, but there is less agreement on the definition of the word *motivation*. Derived from the Latin word *movere* (which means "to move"),

Table 4-1 Types of Motivation Theories

Type	Characteristics	Theories	Examples
Content	Concerned with identifying specific factors that motivate people	Need hierarchy Existence relatedness growth Motivation-hygiene Learned needs	Satisfying people's needs for pay, promotion, recognition
Process	Concerned with the process by which motivational factors interact to produce motivation	Self-efficacy Expectancy Equity Goal setting	Clarifying people's perception of work inputs, performance requirements, and rewards

this definition is far too narrow in scope, from an organizational perspective. Motivation has been defined as "those processes within an individual that stimulate behavior and channel it in ways that should benefit the organization as a whole";[1] "the forces acting on and coming from within a person that account, in part, for the willful direction of one's efforts toward the achievement of specific goals";[2] and "motivation means three things: the person works hard; the person keeps at his or her work; and the person directs his or her behavior toward appropriate goals."[3] In general, these definitions seem to contain three common aspects of motivation: effort, persistence, and direction.[4]

Effort Effort concerns the magnitude, or intensity, of the employee's work-related behavior. For example, a superintendent of schools might manifest greater effort by implementing a districtwide program to decrease school dropouts in his school district. A building principal might exhibit greater effort by examining several strategies to increase student attendance in the school. And a teacher might show greater effort by developing various types of media and other supplementary materials to accompany the text used in a social studies course. All are exerting effort in a manner appropriate to their specific jobs.

[1]John B. Miner, *Organizational Behavior 5: From Unconscious Motivation to Role-Motivated Leadership* (New York: M. E. Sharpe, 2008).

[2]Jerald Greenberg, *Behavior in Organizations,* 10th ed. (Upper Saddle River, NJ: Prentice Hall, 2011, p. 214).

[3]Jennifer M. George and Gareth R. Jones, *Understanding and Managing Organizational Behavior* 5th ed. (Upper Saddle River, NJ: Prentice Hall, 2008, pp. 181–182).

[4]Ibid.

Persistence Persistence concerns the sustained effort employees manifest in their work-related activities. For example, school superintendents who make many important contributions to the district early in their tenure and then rest on their laurels for several years prior to retirement would not be considered highly motivated. Likewise, building principals who work very hard in the morning each day and then leave the job to play golf in the afternoon would not be considered highly motivated. Neither school employee has been persistent in applying effort on the job.

Direction Whereas effort and persistence concern the quantity of work performed, **direction** refers to the quality of an employee's work—that is, the investment of sustained effort in a direction that benefits the employer. From an employer's perspective, a high school counselor is expected to provide sound advice concerning available and suitable career opportunities or appropriate college placements to her group of graduating seniors. To the extent that correct decisions are made by the counselor, persistent effort is translated into desired school outcomes.

These three aspects of motivation serve as the basis for our discussion of the most prominent theories of motivation. Most theories can be separated into two major categories, according to whether they are concerned with the content or process of motivation. Table 4–1 summarizes these approaches.

Content Theories

Content theories of motivation focus on the question: what energizes human behavior? The four most popular content theories of motivation are Maslow's

Table 4–2 Maslow's Need Hierarchy

	General Factors	Need Levels	Organizational Factors
Complex Needs ↑	Growth Achievement Advancement	Self-actualization (5)	Challenging job Advancement in organization Achievement in work
	Self-esteem Esteem from others Recognition	Esteem (4)	Titles Status symbols Promotions
	Affection Acceptance Friendship	Social (3)	Quality of supervision Compatible work group Professional friendships
	Safety Security Stability	Safety (2)	Safe working conditions Fringe benefits Job security
↓ Basic Needs	Water Food Shelter	Physiological (1)	Heat and air conditioning Base salary Working conditions

need hierarchy theory, Alderfer's existence relatedness growth (ERG) theory, Herzberg's motivation-hygiene theory, and McClelland's learned needs theory. These theories have received considerable attention both in research exploration and in organizational application.

Need Hierarchy Theory

Abraham Maslow's **need hierarchy theory** is probably one of the best known and most widely used theories for the study of motivation in organizations.[5] Maslow identified five basic groups of human needs that emerge in a specific sequence or pattern—that is, in a hierarchy of importance. In this scheme, once one need is satisfied, another emerges and demands satisfaction, and so on through the hierarchy. The five levels of needs, which represent the order of importance to the individual, are physiological, safety, social, esteem, and self-actualization (see Table 4–2).

Physiological needs include the need for food, water, and shelter. Once these needs are sufficiently satisfied, other levels of needs become prominent and provide motivation for an individual's behavior. Organizations might satisfy these needs by providing a base salary and basic working conditions such as heat, air conditioning, and cafeteria services.

Safety needs include protection against danger, threat, and deprivation, including avoidance of anxiety. Organizations can provide these needs with safe working conditions, fair rules and regulations, job security, pension and insurance plans, salary increases, and freedom to unionize.

Social needs include affection, affiliation, friendship, and love. People who reach this third level in the hierarchy have primarily satisfied physiological and safety needs. Organizations might meet these needs by including employee-centered supervision, providing opportunities for teamwork, following group norms, and sponsoring group activities such as organized sports programs and school or distinctwide picnics.

Esteem needs focus on self-respect and include recognition and respect from others. Fulfilling esteem needs produces feelings of self-confidence, prestige, power, and control. Organizations can satisfy this need through recognition and award programs, articles in the district newsletter, promotions, and prestigious job titles (e.g., Team Leader, Director of Computer Services, or Senior Researcher).

Self-actualization needs focus on the attainment of one's full potential for continued self-development; in Maslow's words, the desire to become "more and more

[5]Abraham H. Maslow, *Motivation and Personality*, 2nd ed. (Reading, MA: Addison-Wesley, 1970).

ADMINISTRATIVE ADVICE 

Practical Motivational Strategies

Applying the concepts of motivation theory is sometimes difficult to achieve. However, if this is done effectively, school administrators can help teachers become more effective and more fulfilled instructors. Below are some practical motivational strategies to enhance teacher performance and growth.

Personal Regard. To show personal regard, personally follow up on all faculty concerns, affirm the inquiry, and appropriately question to determine a common understanding; each day, discuss informally—with a set number of faculty members—what can be done to assist them; and be sensitive to faculty members' feelings when implementing new policies and procedures.

Communication. To enhance communication, develop, publish, and model clear and consistent educational goals; seek opinions and viewpoints on changes that affect the faculty; listen to understand, not to respond or to defend; and listen, listen, listen.

Recognition. To recognize teachers, start each faculty meeting or memo with words of appreciation for a job well done; promote teacher successes when talking to students, parents, central office personnel, the community, and other teachers; inform teachers of professional opportunities that might appeal to them; and frequently give teachers specific praise face-to-face.

Participation. To allow participation in the decision-making process, use cooperative goal setting in formative evaluation; elect an administrative advisory committee; allow faculty to have a major voice in staff development, evaluation, and in-service programs; and create ad hoc, small groups to brainstorm problems.

Source: Adapted from Lynn E. Lehman, "Practical Motivational Strategies for Teacher Performance and Growth," *NASSP Bulletin*, 73 (1989): 76–80. Used by permission.

what one idiosyncratically is, to become everything one is capable of becoming."[6] Unlike the other needs, self-actualization is manifested differently in different people. For example, to achieve ultimate satisfaction, a musician must create music, an artist must paint, a teacher must teach students, and an administrator must lead people. Organizations might provide self-actualization by involving employees in planning job designs, making assignments that capitalize on employees' unique skills, and relaxing structure to permit employees' personal growth and self-development.

Implications for Practice Maslow's hierarchy of needs theory is easy to understand and quite popular with practitioners. Research evidence fails to support the existence of a precise five-step, pre-potency hierarchy of needs. The needs are more likely to operate in a flexible rather than in a strict step-by-step hierarchy. However, there is some evidence that unless the two lower-order needs (physiological and security) are basically satisfied, organization members will not be greatly concerned with higher-order needs.[7]

Maslow considered his most important contribution to be his work on self-actualization, which he considered far more important than the needs hierarchy theory.[8] Maslow suggested that people are motivated to reach their highest potential once lower needs are satisfied. He argued that organizations need to be structured to help people reach their potential. Maslow opposes oppressive bureaucratic structures that prevent group members from fulfilling higher-order needs.[9]

Outstanding schools require leaders who have the ability to motivate people to maximize their performances, to grow professionally, and to change. To achieve these goals, school administrators must know and be able to apply the basic theories of motivation. (See Administrative Advice 4–1).

[6]Ibid., p. 46.

[7]Ellen L. Betz, "Two Tests of Maslow's Theory of Need Fulfillment," *Journal of Vocational Behavior*, 24 (1984): 204–220.

[8]Abraham H. Maslow, *Maslow on Management* (New York: John Wiley & Sons, 1998).

[9]Ibid.

EXEMPLARY EDUCATIONAL ADMINISTRATORS IN ACTION

JAMES F. CAUSBY, Ed.D., Superintendent, Johnston County Schools, North Carolina.

Words of Advice: Students who aspire to become educational administrators should be aware of what a rewarding career they can have in educational administration if they approach it with the right attitude and the right priorities. There has never been a more exciting time in our profession than the present. There are so many changes and challenges that one is never bored, and opportunities to do good things for students come in abundance.

Career opportunities for educational administrators have never been better. As the student population in our nation grows, and as those of us who are baby boomers retire, there will be a tremendous demand for school administrators at all levels and in all parts of our nation. An individual who is a good teacher, who is willing to complete a quality school administrator program, and who enjoys working with people will find many opportunities to advance his or her career. And school administrator salaries have vastly improved over recent years.

Aspiring school administrators must understand that they will live in a glass house. They will be admired and looked up to, but they will constantly be in the public eye. They must learn, and be able to accept, the fact that their friendships and personal relations will be limited to others who share their profession because there is no one else who can truly understand their job and their concerns. Everyone in the community will either work for them or have children in their schools.

They should understand that high quality and strong leadership will enable them to achieve wonderful things for their employees and the children in their care. Educational administration is the very best career in the world!

Existence Relatedness Growth Theory

Clayton Alderfer's existence relatedness growth theory is an extension Maslow's need hierarchy theory.[10] Like Maslow, Alderfer feels that people do have needs, that these needs can be arranged in a hierarchy, that there is a basic distinction between lower-level needs and higher-level needs, and that needs are important determinants of employee motivation in organizations. Alderfer suggests three broad categories of needs: existence (E), relatedness (R), and growth (G)—hence, the **ERG theory:**

1. *Existence needs* comprise all forms of physiological and material desires, such as food, clothing, and shelter. In organizational settings, specific examples include salary, fringe benefits, job security, and work conditions. This category corresponds roughly to Maslow's physiological and safety needs.
2. *Relatedness needs* include all those that involve interpersonal relationships with others—supervisors, colleagues, subordinates, family, friends, and so on. Alderfer stresses that relatedness needs can be satisfied by expressing anger and hostility as well as by developing close, warm, and personal relationships with others. This need category corresponds approximately to Maslow's social needs and to those esteem needs involving feedback from others.
3. *Growth needs* concern the individual's intrinsic desire to grow, develop, and fulfill one's potential. In the workplace, satisfaction of growth needs results when an employee engages in tasks that involve not only the full use of his skills and abilities but also tasks that may require the creative development of new skills and abilities. This category of ERG needs corresponds to Maslow's self-actualization needs and certain aspects of his esteem needs.

ERG theory differs from Maslow's need hierarchy theory in two important ways. First, Maslow's theory proposes that a lower-level need must be gratified before other needs become operative. ERG theory, on the other hand, proposes that people may experience several needs simultaneously. Existence needs do not necessarily have to be satisfied before a person can become concerned about the satisfaction of his relatedness or growth needs. Hence, ERG theory is more flexible than is need hierarchy theory and accounts for a wide variety of individual differences in need structure. Second, Maslow's theory proposes that a satisfied need is no longer a motivator. According to Alderfer, however,

[10]Clayton P. Alderfer, *Existence, Relatedness, and Growth* (New York: Free Press, 1972).

the continual frustration of higher-order needs will lead employees to regress to a lower-need category.

Implications for Practice To see how this process works, let us examine the case of an elementary school principal whose existence and relatedness needs (lower-level needs) are relatively satisfied. Currently, the principal is motivated to try to satisfy her growth needs but finds this difficult to accomplish because she has been in the same position for the past ten years. She is very skilled and knowledgeable about all aspects of her current position, but the demands of the job leave her little time to pursue anything new or exciting. Essentially, the principal's motivation to satisfy her growth needs is being frustrated because of the nature of her job. According to Alderfer, this frustration will increase the principal's motivation to satisfy a lower-level need such as relatedness. As a result of this motivation, the principal becomes more concerned about interpersonal relationships at work.

There has not been much research on ERG theory. However, there are two key administrative implications associated with ERG. The first deals with the frustration-regression aspect of the theory discussed above. School administrators should bear in mind that organization members may be motivated to pursue lower-level needs because they are frustrated with a higher-level need. This suggests the importance of meeting certain group members' needs on the job. This would include providing enough financial remuneration so that members can meet basic needs and have some sense of security (existence needs). Provisions for health insurance and retirement plans reassure group members concerning other aspects of life. The increasing use of teams and committees in today's schools enhances socialization on the job, as do programs such as "casual Fridays" (relatedness needs). Furthermore, Alderfer suggests that administrators share responsibility and empower group members in addition to recognizing their achievements.

Second, ERG theory is consistent with the finding that cultural differences influence needs, needs are influenced by each individual's personal values, and people are motivated by different needs at different times in their lives.[11] This implies that school administrators should customize their reward and recognition programs to meet organization members' varying needs.

Motivation-Hygiene Theory

Frederick Herzberg developed a unique and exciting motivation theory that builds on Maslow's and Alderfer's earlier work. The theory has been called the **motivation-hygiene theory,** the two-factor theory, and the dual-factor theory.[12] Like Maslow's need hierarchy theory and Alderfer's ERG theory, the motivation-hygiene theory seeks to determine factors that cause motivation. Rather than looking for needs energized within the individual, Herzberg focused attention on the work environment to identify factors that arouse in people either positive or negative attitudes toward their work.

The original research used to develop the theory was conducted with 203 accountants and engineers employed in nine manufacturing firms in the Pittsburgh area. Herzberg used the critical incident technique to obtain data for analysis. The subjects in the study were asked to think of times when they felt good about their jobs. Each subject was then asked to describe the conditions that led to those feelings. Herzberg repeated this same approach with a wide variety of other employees. Results obtained from the critical incident method were fairly consistent across the various subjects. Reported good feelings were generally associated with the job itself—content, intrinsic, or psychological factors. These included achievement, recognition, the work itself, responsibility, advancement, and growth. Herzberg named these content factors "job satisfiers," or *motivators*, because they fulfill an individual's need for psychological growth. Reported bad feelings, on the other hand, were generally associated with the environment surrounding the job—context, extrinsic, or physical factors. These included company policies, supervision, interpersonal relations, working conditions, and salary. Herzberg named these context factors "job dissatisfiers," or *hygiene factors*, because they are preventative and environmental. Figure 4–1 illustrates these findings.

The motivation-hygiene theory is related to the need hierarchy theory. Herzberg has reduced Maslow's

[11]B. Verplanken and Robert W. Holland, "Motivated Decision Making: Effects of Activation and Self-Centrality of Values and Choices and Behavior," *Journal of Personality and Social Psychology*, 82 (2002): 434–437; Steven Hitlin and Jane Allyn Pilavin, "Values: Reviving a Dormant Concept," *Annual Review of Sociology*, 30 (2004): 359–393.

[12]Frederick Herzberg, Bernard Mausner, and Barbara S. Snyderman, *The Motivation to Work* (New Brunswick, NJ: Transaction, 1993).

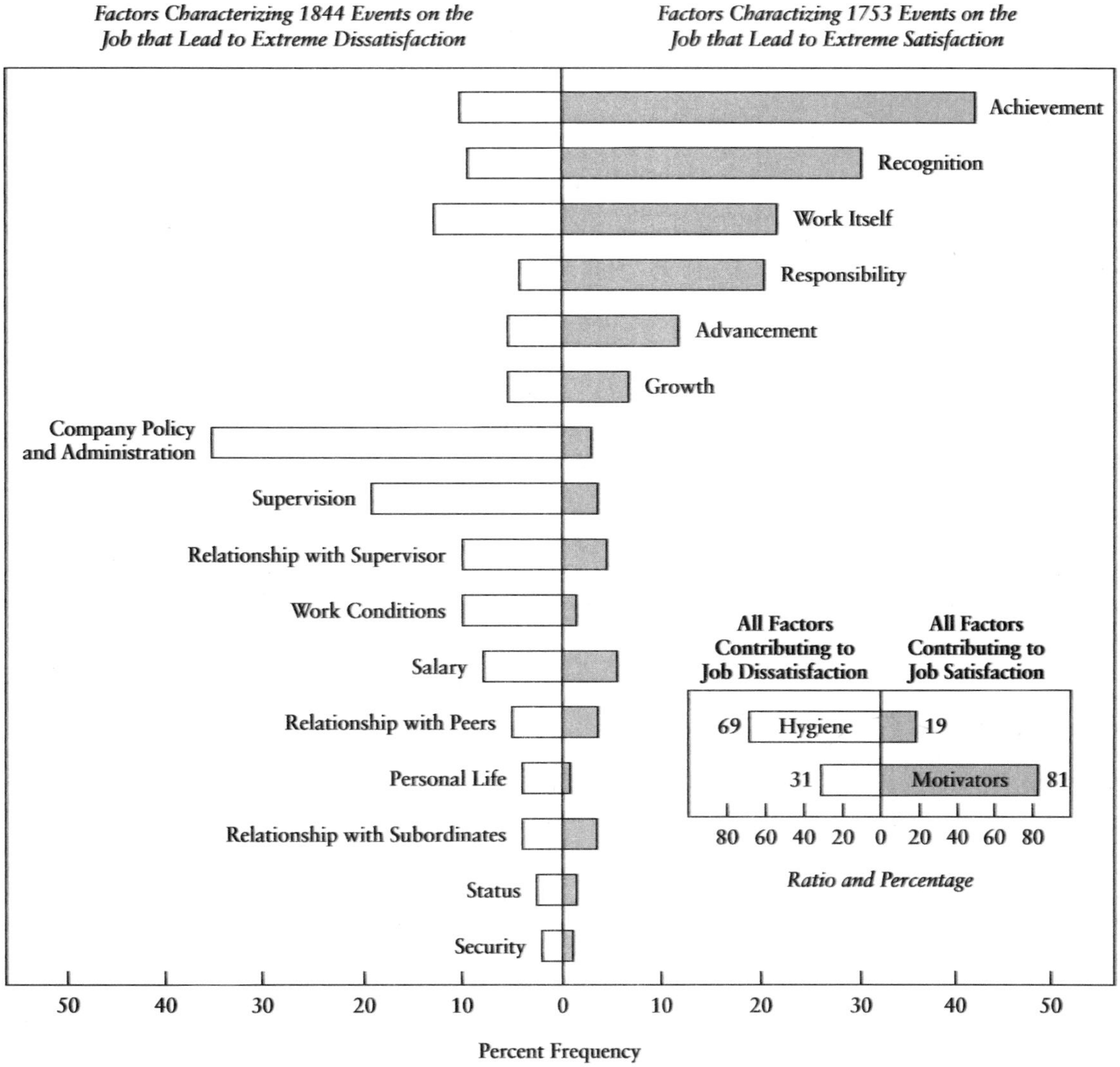

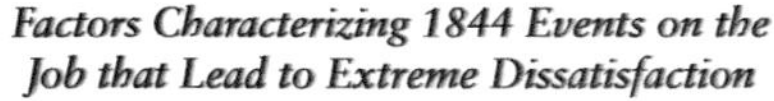

FIGURE 4–1

Comparison of Satisfiers and Dissatisfiers
Source: Reprinted by permission of *Harvard Business Review.* Adapted from "One More Time: How Do You Motivate Employees?" by Frederick Herzberg, issue 65 (1987): 112. Copyright © 1987 by the Harvard Business School Publishing Corporation. All rights reserved.

five-level need system to a two-level system—hygiene needs and motivation needs. Hygiene factors (dissatisfiers) are roughly equivalent to Maslow's lower-level needs, because they serve to reduce dissatisfaction but do not lead to satisfaction. Motivators (satisfiers) are roughly equivalent to Maslow's higher-level needs. According to Herzberg, dissatisfiers may ensure that employees will perform at minimum levels, but motivation, which contributes to superior performance, is possible only through satisfiers. That is, only the work itself and recognition, advancement, personal growth, and development stemming from this work will provide a situation for motivated behavior in the workplace.

ADMINISTRATIVE ADVICE 4–2

Improving Teacher Job Satisfaction

The following are some tips that can help school administrators improve teacher job satisfaction.

Use Praise to Recognize Exemplary Behavior. Catch your faculty members doing something right and tell them. Often, the only contact teachers have with administrators is when they do something wrong, and then they are "zapped"! Moreover, tell parents about staff accomplishments through the school newsletter.

Rotate Faculty Meeting Locations. Conduct faculty meetings in different classrooms to give your teachers an opportunity to tell their colleagues about the things they are doing.

Institute a "5–10 Report" from Teachers. Promote "quick and easy" communication. A 5–10 report takes no more than five minutes to read and ten to write. Each report is divided into three parts: a quick update of job-related activities; a description of the teacher's morale; and an idea for improving the efficiency or effectiveness of the school.

Empower Teachers. Establish a school leadership team consisting of yourself, teachers you select, and teachers selected by faculty members. Have the team participate in decisions concerning budget preparations, school improvement projects, and the like.

Recognize Group Accomplishments. Work with your PTA or other support groups to recognize schoolwide accomplishments, perhaps over morning doughnuts or with a staff appreciation banquet or afternoon cake and ice cream.

Don't Overlook the Little Things. Design inexpensive birthday or holiday cards that can be produced on duplicating machines or by computer. Before the school year begins, have the school secretary preaddress and stamp each card and arrange for them to be mailed at the appropriate times.

Create a "Bragging Wall" in the Faculty Lounge. Use an area of the faculty lounge to post "smile-a-grams," articles faculty members have published, newspaper clippings, letters from parents, and other examples of good things that are going on in your school.

Follow Up on Requests. Get back quickly to faculty members who make requests for a decision or status report. Such behavior demonstrates that you are concerned about their needs.

Select a Faculty Member of the Month. Make the selection yourself or ask the staff leadership team to help with the decision.

Institute a Teacher-for-a-Day Program. Select one day a year and recruit key community members to come to your school to teach for the entire day or for a period. Teachers will benefit from a new sense of community participation (especially if the local press covers the story).

Source: Adapted from Terry B. Grier, "15 Ways to Keep Staff Members Happy and Productive," *Executive Educator,* 10 (1988): 26–27. Copyright 1988, the National School Boards Association. Used by permission.

Implications for Practice Herzberg has contributed substantially to the study of work motivation. He extended Maslow's needs hierarchy theory and Alderfer's ERG theory and made them more applicable to work motivation. Herzberg also drew attention to the importance of job content factors in work motivation by making a distinction between hygiene and motivation factors. Prior to Herzberg, school administrators had generally concentrated on the hygiene factors. When faced with a morale problem, the typical solution was higher pay, more fringe benefits, and better working conditions. However, this simplistic solution did not really work. By concentrating only on the hygiene factors, school administrators were not really motivating their personnel.[13] Thus, the motivation-hygiene theory broadened administrators' perspectives by showing the potentially powerful role of intrinsic rewards that evolve from the work itself.

Job satisfaction and job dissatisfaction are important concepts of Herzberg's motivation-hygiene theory. School administrators may neglect to consider that dissatisfied teachers may weaken the educational program. Basic motivational principles and techniques can help administrators meet teacher needs. (See Administrative Advice 4–2.)

[13]Frederick Herzberg, *One More Time: How Do You Motivate Employees?* (Boston: Harvard Business School Press, 2009).

Learned Needs Theory

David C. McClelland has proposed a **learned needs theory** of motivation.[14] The theory is based on the premise that people acquire or learn certain needs from their culture. Among the cultural influences are family, personal and occupational experiences, and the type of organization for which a person works. Three of these *learned needs* are the need for achievement (nAch), the need for affiliation (nAff), and the need for power (nPow). McClelland suggested that when a need is strong in a person, its effect is to motivate the person to use behavior to satisfy the need.

Need for Achievement (nAch) People with a strong **need for achievement (nAch)** want to accomplish reasonably challenging but attainable goals through their own effort. They prefer working alone rather than in teams. They choose tasks with a moderate degree of difficulty. High nAch people also desire specific feedback and recognition for their accomplishments. Accomplishment is seen as important primarily for its own sake, not just for the rewards that accompany it. Therefore, money is a weak motivator, except when it provides feedback and recognition.[15]

As school administrators, high nAch people tend to expect that their organization members will also be oriented toward high achievement. These high expectations sometimes make it difficult for high nAch school administrators to delegate effectively and for "average" group members to satisfy their administrator's demands. Furthermore, school administrators who set unreasonably high standards or goals are not motivating high nAch members effectively, because the high nAch person's satisfaction is strongest when the goal is attainable. Nor do goals that are set too low motivate the high nAch member.

However, a shift has occurred in achievement motivation research. Its focus has moved from the high nAch individual to the organizational climate and opportunity structure of the organization that encourage and reward high achievement.[16] McClelland and David Winter indicated that this phenomenon is contingent on organizational variables; the less bureaucratic the organization, the more favorable the organizational context for high-achievement behavior.[17] You may recall that Maslow also advocated a less bureaucratic organizational structure.[18] And in a large-scale study of 45 high schools in Chicago, two researchers found a strong relationship between bureaucratic structure and custodialism in control orientation and behavior.[19]

Need for Affiliation (nAff) People with a high **need for affiliation (nAff)** have the desire for friendly and close interpersonal relationships. They prefer to spend more time maintaining social relationships, joining groups, and wanting to be loved. High nAff people tend to be helpful and supportive. They can contribute greatly to the school and committees through their efforts to promote positive interpersonal relations. Conflict can be diffused through their attempts to reduce tension. The relationships they have with others are close and personal, emphasizing friendship and companionship.

High nAff school administrators may have difficulty being effective leaders. A high concern for positive social relationships usually results in a cooperative work environment. However, overemphasis on the social dimension may interfere with the accomplishment of tasks. High nAff school administrators may have difficulty assigning challenging tasks, directing work activities, and monitoring work effectiveness without worrying about being disliked. However, whether high affiliation needs of school administrators are functional or dysfunctional for attaining school goals depends on the congruence between the informal group norms and goals and those of the school district.[20]

Need for Power (nPow) People with a high **need for power (nPow)** want to influence others, take control, and change people and situations. They frequently rely

[14]David C. McClelland, *The Achieving Society* (New York: Irvington Publishers, 1976).

[15]Ibid.

[16]Fred C. Lunenburg, *Conceptualizing School Climate: Measures, Research, and Effects* (Berkeley, CA: McCutchan, 1983); Harold F. Gortner, Kenneth L. Nichols, and Carolyn Ball, *Organization Theory*, 3rd ed. (Belmont, CA: Wadsworth, 2007).

[17]David C. McClelland and David G. Winter, *Motivating Economic Achievement* (New York: Free Press, 1971).

[18]Maslow, *Maslow on Management.*

[19]Fred C. Lunenburg and Scarlett A. Mankowsky, "School Bureaucratization, Pupil Control Ideology, and Pupil Control Behavior," Paper presented at the Annual Meeting of the American Educational Research Association, April, 2000).

[20]Fred C. Lunenburg, *Conceptualizing School Climate;* Rensis Likert, *New Patterns of Management* (New York: Garland, 1987).

on persuasive communication and make more suggestions in meetings. McClelland suggested that there are two types of power: personalized power and socialized power. Those who have a high need for *personalized power* enjoy their power for its own sake, use it to advance personal interests, and display it as a status symbol. Those who have a high need for *socialized power* are concerned for others, have an interest in organizational goals, and have a desire to be useful to the organization and society.

McClelland proposed that the more effective administrators have a high need for socialized rather than personalized power. Because socialized power is exercised for the benefit of others—the accomplishment of group goals—it engenders confidence in followers; they feel better able to accomplish whatever goals they share. Followers feel more rather than less powerful.

Implications for Practice McClelland suggested that administrators should learn how to identify the presence of nAch, nAff, and nPow in themselves and in others, since each need can be linked with a set of job preferences. People with a high need for achievement will prefer individual responsibilities, challenging goals, and performance feedback. People with a high need for affiliation are drawn to interpersonal relationships and opportunities for communication. People with a high need for power seek influence over others and like attention and recognition.

McClelland found that high needs for power and achievement are critical for high-performing administrators. People with these high needs are particularly good at increasing morale, creating clear expectations for performance, and getting others to work for the good of the organization. However, the need for power is more important for administrative success than the need for achievement. People high in need for achievement tend to be reluctant to delegate work to others and tend to be impatient when working toward long-range goals, behaviors that are necessary for effective administrators. Finally, McClelland found that senior executives (in a school setting: superintendents and principals in large schools) are high in power needs but low in affiliation needs. Why? Senior executives need to make difficult decisions and cannot worry about being disliked by followers.[21]

[21]David C. McClelland and David C. Burnham, "Power is the Great Motivator," *Harvard Business Review*, 54, March/April, 1976: 100–111.

The following guidelines are recommended for school administrators in fostering achievement motivation of followers: [22]

- *Provide good role models of achievement.* Organization members should be encouraged to have heroes to emulate.
- *Guide members' aspirations.* Organization members should think about setting realistic goals and the ways in which they can attain them.
- *Provide periodic feedback on members' performance.* Feedback enables members to modify their behavior as needed.
- *Help followers modify their self-images.* High-achievement people accept themselves and seek job challenges and responsibilities.
- *Successful school administrators are high in power motivation.* Administrators who have been successful are higher in power motivation than in affiliation motivation.

Content Motivation Theories: Similarities and Conclusions

The four content theories of motivation are compared in Figure 4–2. McClelland proposed no lower-order needs. Moreover, his needs for achievement and power are not identical to Herzberg's motivators, Maslow's higher-order needs, or Alderfer's growth needs; however, there are some similarities. A major difference between the four content theories of motivation is McClelland's emphasis on socially learned needs. Furthermore, Maslow's theory provides a static need hierarchy system; Alderfer offers a more flexible three-need classification; and Herzberg presents motivators and hygiene factors.

Each of the content theories is an attempt to provide the clearest, most meaningful, and most accurate explanation of motivation. Each of the theories has strengths and limitations that practicing school administrators need to consider; none of the theories is clearly inferior or superior to the others, considering today's diverse workplace. Adept school administrators will consider all of these approaches to provide insights in leading their schools.

[22]Fred C. Lunenburg and Carolyn S. Carr, *Shaping the Future: Policy, Partnerships, and Emerging Perspectives* (Lanham, MD: Rowman & Littlefield, 2003); John Hellriegel and John W. Slocum, *Organizational Behavior*, 13th ed. (Mason, OH: South-Western/Cengage Learning, 2011, p. 168).

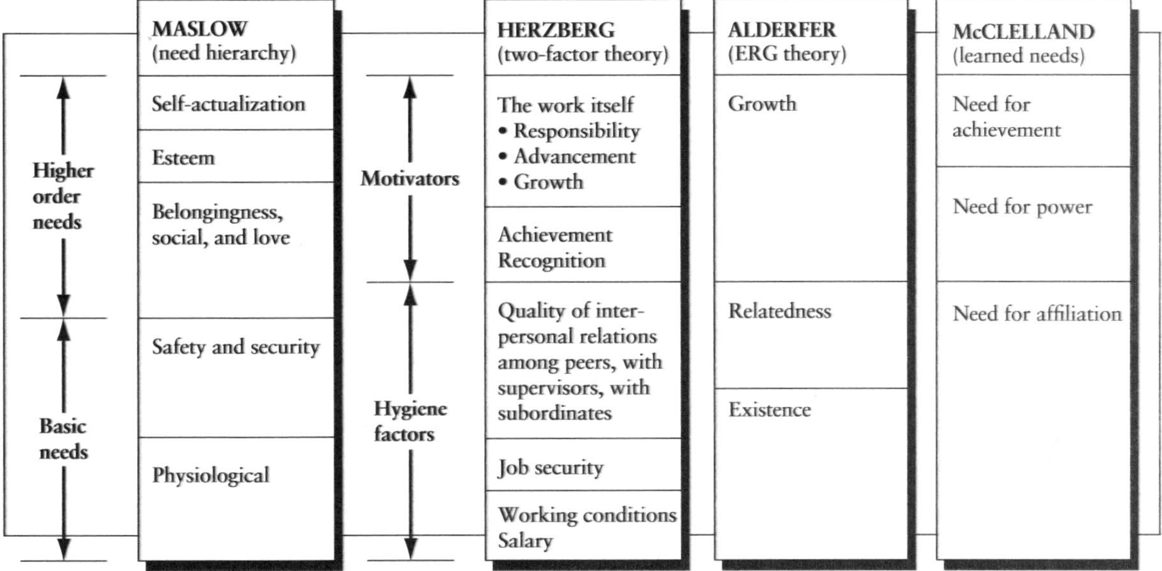

FIGURE 4–2

A Comparison of Four Content Theories of Motivation

Process Theories

The content theories of motivation attempt to identify *what* motivates employees in the workplace (e.g., advancement, self-actualization, and growth). The **process theories,** on the other hand, are more concerned with *how* motivation occurs—in other words, they explain the process of motivation. Self-efficacy theory, expectancy theory, equity theory, and goal-setting theory are the four major process theories that concern this approach to motivation in organizational settings.

Self-Efficacy Theory

Mainly due to the work of Albert Bandura, self-efficacy has a widely acclaimed theoretical foundation,[23] an extensive knowledge base,[24] and a proven record of application in the workplace.[25] Nine large-scale meta-analyses consistently demonstrate that the efficacy beliefs of organization members contribute significantly to their level of motivation and performance.[26]

Self-efficacy (also known as *social cognitive theory* or *social learning theory*) is a person's belief that she is capable of performing a particular task successfully.[27] Self-efficacy has three dimensions: *magnitude*, the level of task difficulty a person believes she can attain; *strength*, the conviction regarding magnitude as strong or weak; and *generality*, the degree to which the expectation is generalized across situations. An employee's sense of capability influences his perception, motivation, and performance.[28] We rarely attempt to perform a task when we expect to be unsuccessful.

Following is an example. One professor may believe that she can learn how to teach graduate courses online on her own. Another professor may have strong doubts about his ability to learn how to teach graduate courses online without taking some formal training. Self-efficacy has powerful effects on learning, motivation, and performance, because people try to learn and perform only those tasks that they believe they will be able

[23]Albert Bandura, *Social Foundations of Thought and Action* (Upper Saddle River, NJ: Prentice Hall, 1986).

[24]Albert Bandura, *Self-Efficacy: The Exercise of Control* (New York: W.H. Freeman, 1997).

[25]Alexander D. Stajkovic and Fred Luthans, "Self-Efficacy and Work-Related Performance," *Psychological Bulletin*, 24 (1998): 240–261.

[26]Albert Bandura and Edwin A. Locke, "Negative Self-Efficacy and Goal Effects Revisited," *Journal of Applied Psychology*, 88 (2003): 87–99.

[27]Bandura, *Self-Efficacy: The Exercise of Control.*

[28]Ibid.

to perform successfully. Self-efficacy affects learning and performance in the following ways:[29]

Self-efficacy influences the goals that employees choose for themselves. Employees with low levels of self-efficacy tend to set relatively low goals for themselves. Conversely, an individual with high self-efficacy is likely to set high personal goals. Research indicates that people not only learn but also perform at levels consistent with their self-efficacy beliefs.

Self-efficacy influences learning as well as the effort that people exert on the job. Employees with high self-efficacy generally work hard to learn how to perform new tasks, because they are confident that their efforts will be successful. Employees with low self-efficacy may exert less effort when learning and performing complex tasks, because they are not sure the effort will lead to success.

Self-efficacy influences the persistence with which people attempt new and difficult tasks. Employees with high self-efficacy are confident that they can learn and perform a specific task. Thus, they are likely to persist in their efforts even when problems surface. Conversely, employees with low self-efficacy, who believe they are incapable of learning and performing a difficult task, are likely to give up when problems surface. In an extensive literature review on self-efficacy, Albert Bandura and Edwin Locke concluded that self-efficacy is a powerful determinant of job performance.[30]

Sources of Self-Efficacy

Since self-efficacy can have powerful effects on schools, it is important to identify its origin. Bandura has identified four principal sources of self-efficacy: past performance, vicarious experience, verbal persuasion, and emotional cues.[31] These four sources of self-efficacy are shown in Figure 4–3.

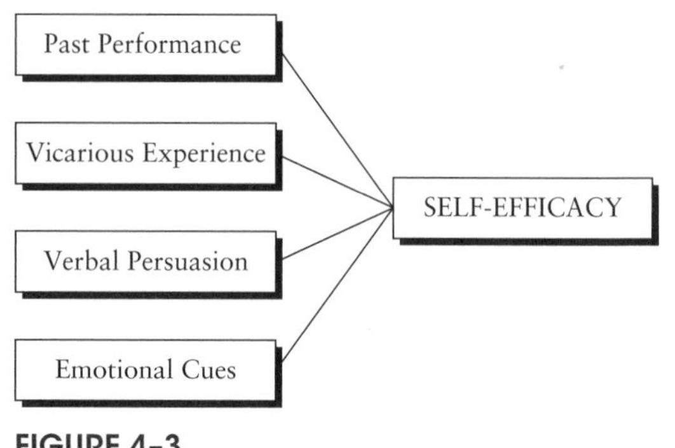

FIGURE 4–3

Sources of Self-Efficacy

Past Performance According to Bandura, the most important source of self-efficacy is past performance. Employees who have succeeded on job-related tasks are likely to have more confidence to complete similar tasks in the future (high self-efficacy) than employees who have been unsuccessful (low self-efficacy). School administrators can boost self-efficacy through careful hiring, providing challenging assignments, professional development and coaching, goal setting, supportive leadership, and rewards for improvement.

Vicarious Experience A second source of self-efficacy is through vicarious experience. Seeing a co-worker succeed at a particular task may boost your self-efficacy. For example, if your co-worker loses weight, this may increase your confidence that you can lose weight as well. Vicarious experience is most effective when you see yourself as similar to the person you are modeling. Watching LeBron James dunk a basketball might not increase your confidence in being able to dunk the basketball yourself if you are 5 feet, 6 inches tall. But if you observe a basketball player with physical characteristics similar to yourself, it can be persuasive.

Verbal Persuasion The third source of self-efficacy is through verbal persuasion. Essentially this involves convincing people that they have the ability to succeed at a particular task. The best way for a leader to use verbal persuasion is through the *Pygmalion effect*. The Pygmalion effect is a form of a self-fulfilling prophesy in which believing something to be true can make it true.

Most educators are familiar with Rosenthal and Jacobson's classic study in which teachers were told that one group of students had very high IQ scores (when in fact they had average to low IQ scores), and the same teacher was told that another group of students had low IQ scores (when in fact they had high IQ scores). Consistent with the Pygmalion effect, the teachers spent more time with the students they *thought* were smart, gave them more challenging assignments, and expected more of them—all of which led to higher student self-efficacy and better student

[29]Albert Bandura, "Self-Efficacy Mechanism in Human Agency," *American Psychologist*, 37 (1982): 122–147.

[30]Bandura and Locke, "Negative Self-Efficacy and Goals Effects Revisited."

[31]Bandura, *Self-Efficacy: The Exercise of Control.*

grades.[32] The leader's expectations about job performance might be viewed as an important input to the employees' perceptions of their own levels of self-efficacy. The power of the persuasion would be contingent on the leader's credibility, previous relationship with the employees, and the leader's influence in the organization.[33]

Emotional Cues Finally, Bandura argues that emotional cues dictate self-efficacy. A person who expects to fail at some task or finds something too demanding is likely to experience certain physiological symptoms: a pounding heart, feeling flushed, sweaty palms, headaches, and so on. The symptoms vary from individual to individual, but if they persist may become associated with poor performance.

Implications for Practice Self-efficacy has been related to other motivation theories. Edwin Locke and Gary Latham suggested that goal-setting theory and self-efficacy theory complement each other. When a leader sets difficult goals for employees, this leads employees to have a higher level of self-efficacy and also leads them to set higher goals for their own performance. Why does this happen? Research has shown that setting difficult goals for people communicates confidence.[34] For example, suppose that your supervisor sets a high goal for you. You learn that it is higher than the goal she has set for your colleagues. How would you interpret this? You would probably think that your supervisor believes you are capable of performing better than others. This sets in motion a psychological process in which you are more confident in yourself (higher self-efficacy) and then you set higher personal goals for yourself, causing you to perform better. Self-efficacy may also be related to effort-performance relationships in expectancy theory. Both goal-setting theory and expectancy theory will be discussed later in this chapter.

Expectancy Theory

Victor Vroom is usually credited with developing the first complete version of the **expectancy theory** with application to organizational settings.[35] Expectancy theory is based on four assumptions. One assumption is that people join organizations with expectations about their needs, motivations, and past experiences. These influence how individuals react to the organization. A second assumption is that an individual's behavior is a result of conscious choice. That is, people are free to choose those behaviors suggested by their own expectancy calculations. A third assumption is that people want different things from the organization (e.g., good salary, job security, advancement, and challenge). A fourth assumption is that people will choose among alternatives so as to optimize outcomes for them personally.

Basic Expectancy Model

The expectancy theory based on these assumptions has four key elements: outcomes, expectancy, instrumentality, and valence (see Figure 4–4).

Outcomes, classified as first or second level, are the end results of certain work behaviors. *First-level outcomes* refer to some aspect of performance and are the direct result of expending some effort on the job. *Second-level outcomes* are viewed as consequences to which first-level outcomes are expected to lead. That is, the end result of performance (first-level outcome) is some type of reward (second-level outcome) for work goal accomplishment. Examples include salary increases, promotion, peer acceptance, recognition by the supervisor, or a sense of accomplishment.

Expectancy is the strength of belief that job-related effort will result in a certain performance level. Expectancy is based on probabilities and ranges from 0 to 1. If an employee sees no chance that effort will lead to the desired performance level, the expectancy is 0. On the other hand, if the employee is completely certain that the task will be completed, the expectancy has a value of 1. Generally, employee estimates of expectancy lie somewhere between these two extremes.

Instrumentality is the relationship between performance (first-level outcomes) and rewards (second-level outcomes). As with expectancy, instrumentality ranges from 0 to 1. If an employee sees that a good performance rating will always result in a salary increase, the instrumentality has a value of 1. If there is no perceived relationship between the first-level outcome (good

---

[32]Robert Rosenthal and Lenore Jacobson, *Pygmalion in the Classroom* (New York: Holt, Rinehart, and Winston, 1968).

[33]Dov Eden, "Self-Fulfilling Prophesies in Organizations, in J. Greenberg (ed.), *Organizational Behavior: The State of the Science*, 2nd ed. (Mahwah, NJ: Lawrence Erlbaum, 2004), pp. 91–122.

[34]Edwin A. Locke and Gary P. Latham, "Building a Practically Useful Theory of Goal Setting and Task Motivation: A 35-Year Odyssey," *American Psychologist*, 57, No. 9 (2002): 705–717.

[35]Victor H. Vroom, *Work and Motivation* (San Francisco: Jossey-Bass, 1994).

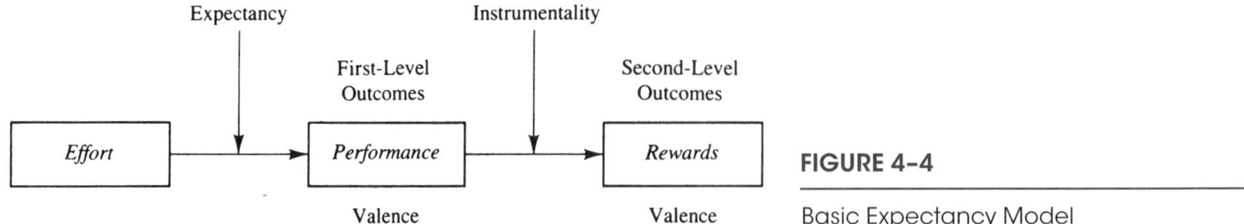

FIGURE 4-4

Basic Expectancy Model

performance rating) and the second-level outcome (salary increase), then the instrumentality is 0.

Valence is the strength of an employee's preference for a particular outcome or reward. Thus, salary increases, promotion, peer acceptance, recognition by supervisors, or any other second-level outcome might have more or less value to individual employees. The valence of first-level outcomes is the sum of the product of the associated second-level outcomes and their instrumentalities. That is, the valence of a first-level outcome depends on the extent to which it results in valuable second-level outcomes. Unlike expectancy and instrumentality, valences can be either positive or negative. If an employee has a strong preference for attaining an outcome, valence is positive. At the other extreme, valence is negative. And if an employee is indifferent to an outcome, valence is 0. The total range is from -1 to $+1$. Theoretically, an outcome has a valence because it is related to an employee's needs. Valence, then, provides a link to the content theories of motivation.

In sum, the basic expectancy model shows that the motivational force that an employee exerts on the job is a function of (1) the perceived expectancy that a certain level of performance will result from expending effort and (2) the perceived instrumentality that rewards will result from a certain level of performance, both of which are moderated by the valences attached to these outcomes by the employee. The combination of these three factors that produces the strongest motivation is high positive valence, high expectancy, and high instrumentality. If any key element is low, then motivation will be moderate. If all three elements are low, weak motivation will result.

Implications for Practice Vroom's expectancy theory differs from the content theories of Maslow, Alderfer, Herzberg, and McClelland in that Vroom's expectancy theory does not provide specific suggestions on what motivates organization members. Instead, Vroom's theory provides a process of cognitive variables that reflects individual differences in work motivation. The logic of expectancy theory is that school administrators should intervene in work situations to maximize work expectancies, instrumentalities, and valences that support organizational goals. To influence expectancies, school administrators need to select people with appropriate skills and abilities, provide them with continuous professional development, support them with needed resources, and identify clear performance goals. To accomplish this, school administrators should make the desired performance goals attainable. Effective school administrators not only make it clear to people what is expected of them but also help them attain that level of performance.[36] To influence instrumentality, school administrators need to clarify performance–reward relationships, and then follow through on rewards for good performance. To influence valences, school administrators should identify the needs that are important to each individual and then try to adjust rewards to match these needs.

Equity Theory

Earlier, Herzberg found that feelings of inequity were a frequently reported source of dissatisfaction among employees. Although Herzberg did not pay much attention to this finding, a number of theorists have examined the concept of equity to explain employee motivation. Among them, Stacy Adams has developed the most detailed and organizationally relevant equity theory.[37]

[36]Fred C. Lunenburg and Beverly J. Irby, *The Principalship: Vision to Action* (Belmont, CA: Wadsworth/Cengage Learning, 2006).

[37]J. Stacy Adams, "Inequity in Social Exchange," in L. Berkowitz (ed.), *Advances in Experimental Social Psychology*, vol. 2 (New York: Academic Press, 1965): 267–299.

Equity theory asserts that employees hold certain beliefs about the outputs they receive from their work and the inputs they invest to obtain these outcomes. The outcomes of employment refer to all things the employee receives as a result of performing the job, such as salary, promotions, fringe benefits, job security, working conditions, job prerequisites, recognition, responsibility, and so on. **Inputs** cover all things that the employee contributes to performing the job and include education, experience, ability, training, personality traits, job efforts, attitude, and so on. Employees expect that the ratio of their outcomes to inputs will be fair or equitable. But how do employees judge fairness?

General Model Simply put, equity theory argues that employees evaluate the equity, or fairness, of their outcomes by a process of social comparison. Employees compare the ratio of their outcomes to inputs with the ratio of outcomes to inputs for some comparison other. The **comparison other** may be a colleague or a group average (such as prevailing standards in a school, school district, or job role). For example, superintendents often use other superintendents as the comparison others rather than corporate executives. The equity relationship can be diagrammed as follows:

$$\frac{\text{Outcomes (employee)}}{\text{Inputs (employee)}} \quad \text{versus} \quad \frac{\text{Outcomes (comparison others)}}{\text{Inputs (comparison others)}}$$

When these ratios are equal, the employee should feel that a fair and equitable exchange exists with the employer. Such equitable exchange should contribute to employee–job satisfaction. Conversely, when ratios are unequal, inequity is perceived by the employee, which should contribute to job dissatisfaction. Obviously, the ideal ratio between outcomes and inputs is perfect equity. Schematically, perfect equity is

$$\frac{\text{Outcomes (employee)}}{\text{Inputs (employee)}} = \frac{\text{Outcomes (comparison others)}}{\text{Inputs (comparison others)}}$$

Inequity can occur in either direction: (1) when employees feel their ratio of outcomes to inputs is less than that of the comparison other and (2) when employees feel their ratio of outcomes to inputs is greater than that of the comparison other. The first situation, in which the employee's perceived outcomes-to-inputs ratio is less than the comparison other, can be diagrammed as follows:

$$\frac{\text{Outcomes (employee)}}{\text{Inputs (employee)}} < \frac{\text{Outcomes (comparison others)}}{\text{Inputs (comparison others)}}$$

The second situation, in which the employee's perceived ratio of outcomes to inputs is greater than that of the comparison other, can be diagrammed as follows:

$$\frac{\text{Outcomes (employee)}}{\text{Inputs (employee)}} > \frac{\text{Outcomes (comparison others)}}{\text{Inputs (comparison others)}}$$

This prediction is less straightforward than the former because the employee is at an advantage vis-à-vis the comparison other. Nevertheless, the theory argues that employees will feel uncomfortable about the inequity of their outcome-to-input ratio compared to the outcome-to-input ratio of their comparison other.

Comparisons of the inputs and outputs of the employee and comparison other are similar to those judgments made by employees according to expectancy theory. They are based on the employee's perceptions, which may or may not be valid. Inequity in either direction creates discomfort and tension, and the employee is motivated to reduce the tension and restore equity.

Methods of Restoring Equity An employee may engage in any of the following behaviors to restore equity:[38]

Alter Inputs. An employee who feels underpaid may contribute less time and effort to the job or demand a salary increase. An employee who feels overpaid may increase the quantity and quality of his work, expend extra hours without pay, and so on.

Alter Outcomes. Unions attract members by pledging to improve salary, working conditions, and hours without any increase in employee effort or input. For example, many teacher unions have managed to negotiate a decrease in calendar days while increasing teacher salaries, fringe benefits, and working conditions.

---

[38]Lyman W. Porter et al. *Motivation and Work Behavior* (New York: McGraw-Hill, 2003).

Cognitively Distort Inputs or Outcomes. According to the theory of cognitive dissonance, the individual tries to modify one of the incompatible perceptions so as to reduce the tension or dissonance. In a sense, that person engages in coping behavior to regain a condition of consonance or equilibrium. For example, if a colleague (comparison other) were receiving disproportionately high outcomes in comparison with another employee, that fact could make the employee tense. As a coping strategy, the employee could distort his perception by reasoning that the comparison other possesses more job knowledge or intelligence than the employee does. Conversely, an employee can justify the disproportionately high outcomes he receives by convincing himself that he possesses more experience or ability than the comparison other does.

Change the Inputs or Outcomes of the Compari-son Other. Behaviors designed to change the actual or perceived inputs or outcomes of the comparison other can take many forms. A colleague (comparison other) may be forced to reduce his inputs, or a colleague may be pressured into leaving the organization. Or the comparison other's inputs or outputs may come to be viewed differently. For example, an employee may come to believe that the comparison other actually works harder than he does and therefore deserves greater outcomes or rewards.

Change the Comparison Other. If the input-to-outcome ratio of an employee to a comparison other results in feelings of inequity, the employee can switch his comparison other to restore equity. For example, a very ambitious superintendent, who has been comparing herself to the state's top superintendents, may decide instead to use his colleagues in smaller school districts who are paid less than he is as his comparison others.

Leave the Organization. An employee can request a transfer or leave the organization entirely.

Implications for Practice Recent development in equity theory can be extended into what is now commonly referred to as organizational justice.[39] **Organizational justice** is the extent to which organization members perceive that they are treated fairly at work. This led to the emergence of three dimensions of organizational justice: distributive, procedural, and interactional.[40] **Distributive justice** is the perceived fairness of how rewards are distributed. **Procedural justice** is the perceived fairness of the procedures used to make decisions. Research indicates that positive perceptions of distributive and procedural justice are enhanced when organization members are given input in decisions that affect them.[41]

Interactional justice is the perceived quality of the treatment organization members receive when rewards are distributed and procedures are implemented. For example, a merit raise in a university may be based on the number of publications the faculty member produces in a given year. Faculty member A produces 10 publications consisting of 4 printed pages each = 40 pages. Faculty member B produces a book (single author) consisting of 550 pages = 550 pages. The university considers a book as one publication. Faculty member B may consider this procedure to be unfair, believing the university administration should instead base merit pay raises on page production. A 40-page production (Faculty Member A) is not equivalent to producing 550 pages (Faculty Member B). In this case, it is both the outcome (distributive justice) and the procedure (procedural justice) which is in dispute.

Among the many implications of equity theory, those dealing with organizational justice must be considered. The way organization members perceive they are treated in the workplace with respect to distributive, procedural, and interactional justice is likely to affect their motivation. It is their perceptions of these justice dimensions made in the context of equity comparisons that influence organization members' level of motivation.

Goal-Setting Theory

Goals have a pervasive influence on behavior in school organizations and administrative practice. Nearly every modern school organization has some form of goal setting in operation. Programs such as campus improvement plans (CIP), planning programming budgeting systems (PPBS), management information systems (MIS), as well as systems thinking and strategic planning, include the development of specific goals.

[39] Jerald Greenberg and Russell Cropanzano (eds.), *Advances in Organizational Justice* (Palo Alto, CA: Stanford University Press, 2001).

[40] Jason A. Colquitt, "On the Dimensionality of Organizational Justice: A Construct Validation of a Measure," *Journal of Applied Psychology*, 86 (2001): 386–400.

[41] Ibid.

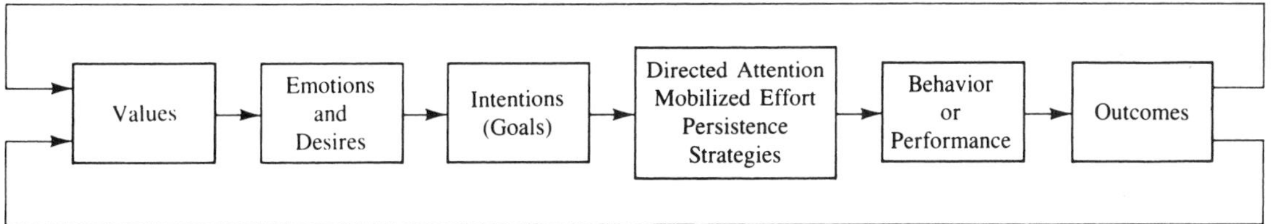

FIGURE 4–5

General Model of Goal-Setting Theory

There has been considerable development of **goal-setting theory** initiated primarily by the work of Edwin Locke. Locke's contributions to goal-setting theory are the following.[42]

1. Difficult goals lead to higher task performance than do easier goals.
2. Specific goals lead to higher performance than do vague goals such as "do your best."
3. The mechanisms by which goals affect performance are directing attention and action, mobilizing effort, increasing persistence, and motivating a search for appropriate performance strategies.
4. Feedback appears necessary for goal setting to work because it allows people to compare their performance against their goals.
5. Goal commitment is necessary if goals are to affect performance, and expectation of success and degree of success affect goal commitment.
6. Individual differences in factors like personality and education are not generally related to goal-setting performance.

General Model Figure 4–5 depicts a simplified view of goal-setting theory. According to the theory, there appear to be two cognitive determinants of behavior: values and intentions (goals). A goal is defined simply as what the individual is consciously trying to do. Locke postulates that the form in which one experiences one's value judgments is emotional. That is, one's values create a desire to do things consistent with them. Goals also affect behavior (job performance) through other mechanisms. For Locke, goals therefore direct attention and action. Furthermore, challenging goals mobilize energy, lead to higher effort, and increase persistent effort. Goals motivate people to develop strategies that will enable them to perform at the required goal levels. Finally, accomplishing the goal can lead to satisfaction and further motivation, or frustration and lower motivation if the goal is not accomplished.[43]

Implications for Practice Under the right conditions, goal setting can be a powerful technique for motivating organization members. The following are practical suggestions for school administrators to consider when attempting to use goal setting to enhance motivation.[44]

Goals need to be specific. Organization members perform at higher levels when asked to meet a specific high-performance goal. Asking organization members to improve, to work harder, or to do your best is not helpful, because that kind of goal does not give them a focused target. Specific goals (often quantified) let organization members know what to reach for and allow them to measure their own progress. Research indicates that specific goals help bring about other desirable organizational goals, such as reducing absenteeism, tardiness, and turnover.[45]

---

[42]Edwin A. Locke and Gary P. Latham "Building a Practically Useful Theory of Goal Setting and Task Motivation." *The American Psychologist*, 57, No. 9 (2002): 705–717.

[43]Ibid.

[44]Jerald Greenberg, *Behavior in Organizations*, 10th ed. (Upper Saddle River, NJ: Prentice Hall, 2011); John W. Newstrom, *Human Behavior at Work* (New York: McGraw-Hill, 2011).

[45]Locke and Latham, "Building a Practically Useful Theory of Goal Setting and Task Motivation."

PRO CON DEBATE

Merit Pay

In many workplaces financial incentives are offered to motivate performance. For example, salespeople frequently operate on commission—the more they sell, the more they earn. In the educational realm, many administrators receive annual salary increments based on some form of merit pay system. A merit pay system allows those whose performance is judged as superior to earn more than those whose work is deemed to be average.

Question: Would merit pay increase teacher performance?

Arguments PRO

1. Teachers receive little or no external recognition for the important work they do. Merit pay would justly reward truly superior teachers and motivate them to continue their fine work.
2. Unlike thirty years ago, we now know what good teaching is. We can ensure that it occurs in classrooms by measuring it and awarding salary proportionally.
3. With a merit pay system, average teachers would be motivated to excel. Competition works for students, why not for teachers? Our society functions on the basis of competition.

Arguments CON

1. Excellent teachers are born, not made. The work itself motivates them, not some external reward.
2. While we can recognize good teaching when we see it, it is difficult to develop a system that recognizes excellence in all its forms. Most attempts at merit pay in education have failed because of this measurement problem.
3. A norm of the teaching profession is cooperation, so teachers avoid situations where the actions of a few are singled out as either good or bad. Merit pay does not fit this norm of cooperation.

Goals must be difficult but attainable. A goal that is too easily attained will not bring about the desired increments in performance. The key point is that a goal must be difficult as well as specific for it to raise performance. However, there is a limit to this effect. Although organization members will work hard to reach challenging goals, they will only do so when the goals are within their capability. As goals become too difficult, performance suffers because organization members reject the goals as unreasonable and unattainable.

Goals must be accepted. Goals need to be accepted. Simply assigning goals to organization members may not result in their commitment to those goals, especially if the goal will be difficult to accomplish. A powerful method of obtaining acceptance is to allow organization members to participate in the goal-setting process. In other words, participation in the goal-setting process tends to enhance goal commitment. Participation helps organization members better understand the goals, ensure that the goals are not unreasonable, and helps them achieve the goal.

Feedback must be provided on goal attainment. Feedback helps organization members attain their performance goals. Feedback helps in two important ways. First, it helps people determine how well they are doing. For example, sports teams need to know the score of the game; a sharpshooter needs to see the target; a golfer needs to know his score. The same can be said for a work team, department, school, or school district. Performance feedback tends to encourage better performance. Second, feedback also helps people determine the nature of the adjustments to their performance that are required to improve. For example, sports teams watch video reproductions of a game and adjust their play; a sharpshooter can adjust his shot; a golfer can adjust her swing; and a school can do an item analysis of the state-mandated achievement test and remedy gaps in performance.

Despite the benefits of goal setting, there are a few limitations of the goal-setting process.[46] First, combining goals with monetary rewards motivates many organization members to establish easy rather than difficult goals. In some cases, organization members have negotiated goals with their supervisor that they have already completed. Second, goal setting focuses organization members on a narrow subset of measurable performance indicators while ignoring aspects of job performance that are difficult to measure. The adage "What gets measured is what gets done" applies here. Third, setting performance goals is effective in established jobs, but it may not be effective when organization members are learning a new, complex job.

Summary

1. Motivation is the extent to which persistent effort is directed toward organizational goals.
2. Content theories of motivation are concerned with identifying the specific factors that motivate employees. The four content theories discussed were Maslow's need hierarchy theory, Alderfer's ERG theory, Herzberg's motivation-hygiene theory, and McClelland's learned needs theory.
3. Maslow's need hierarchy theory proposes five levels of needs (physiological, safety, social, esteem, and self-actualization). These needs are arranged in a prepotency hierarchy. School administrators often use it when analyzing motivational problems in schools.
4. Alderfer's ERG theory is similar to Maslow's need hierarchy theory, but it is not as rigid concerning prepotency of needs. ERG theory makes a distinction between intrinsic and extrinsic motivation. The theory is easily understood and useful to school administrators.
5. Herzberg's motivation-hygiene theory proposes that two distinct factors influence motivation: hygienes, which merely prevent dissatisfaction, and motivators, which are the source of satisfaction and motivation of employees.
6. McClelland's learned needs theory of motivation is based on the premise that people acquire or learn certain needs from their culture. Among the cultural influences are family, personal, and occupational experiences, and the type of organization for which a person works. Three of these learned needs are the need for achievement, the need for affiliation, and the need for power.
7. Process theories of motivation focus on how various factors interact to affect employee motivation. The four process theories discussed were Bandura's self-efficacy theory, Vroom's expectancy theory, Adams' equity theory, and Locke and Latham's goal-setting theory.
8. Self-efficacy theory (also known as *social cognitive theory* or *social learning theory*) is a person's belief that she is capable of performing a particular task successfully. Self-efficacy has three dimensions: *magnitude*, the level of difficulty a person believes she can attain; *strength*, the conviction regarding magnitude as strong or weak; and *generality*, the degree to which the expectation is generalized across situations.
9. Expectancy theory helps school administrators explain how behavior is directed. It is concerned with why employees choose certain paths toward obtaining outcomes that will satisfy their needs.
10. Equity theory helps school administrators understand how employees calculate what they put into the job and what they receive for their performance, and compare that with what they perceive others are contributing and receiving as rewards for performance. Inequitable relationships resulting from such calculations cause the equity-sensitive employee to restore equity.
11. Goal setting helps channel an employee's persistent effort toward organizationally relevant outcomes. Goals can be a powerful motivational device, providing they are specific, attainable, accepted, and accompanied by feedback.

Key Terms

motivation
effort
persistence
direction
content theories
need hierarchy theory
ERG theory
motivation-hygiene theory
learned needs theory
need for achievement
need for affiliation

[46]Ibid.

need for power
process theories
self-efficacy theory
past performance
vicarious experience
verbal persuasion
emotional cues
expectancy theory
outcomes
expectancy
instrumentality
valence
equity theory
inputs
comparison other
organizational justice
distributive justice
procedural justice
interactional justice
goal-setting theory

Discussion Questions

1. Describe how a school administrator would assess the individual needs of employees.
2. Once needs are assessed, discuss how the school administrator could use the needs hierarchy theory, ERG theory, motivation-hygiene theory, and learned needs theory to motivate employees.
3. Of what practical value is the expectancy theory to school administrators? What can school administrators learn from the theory to improve their effectiveness in motivating employees at work?
4. Of what practical value is self-efficacy theory to school administrators? What can school administrators learn from the theory to improve their effectiveness in motivating employees at work?
5. How might a school employee's perceived inequity be dysfunctional to the school system?
6. What are the four key elements of goal-setting theory, and how do they pertain to employee motivation?

Suggested Readings

Annenberg Institute for School Reform. *Human Capital* (Providence, RI: The Author, 2010). This text provides readers with a comprehensive treatment of how school systems and their partners can improve educator quality.

Carlson, Richard. *Don't Sweat the Small Stuff* (New York: Hyperion, 1998). If you can learn to treat the smaller hassles with more perspective, wisdom, patience, and with a better sense of humor, you will begin to bring out the best in yourself as well as in others.

Darling-Hammond, Linda. *The Flat World and Education: How America's Commitment to Equity Will Determine Our Future* (New York: Teachers College Press, 2010). The *Flat World and Education* offers an eye-opening wakeup call concerning America's future and vividly illustrates what the United States needs to do to build a system of high-achieving and equitable schools that ensures the right to learn for every child.

DuFour, Richard, Rebecca DuFour, Robert Eaker, and Gayle Karhanek. *Raising the Bar and Closing the Gap: Whatever It Takes* (Bloomington, IN: Solution Tree, 2010). The authors examine schools and districts in North America to illustrate how PLC at Work is a sustainable and transferable model that ensures struggling students get the support they need to achieve.

Glickman, Carl. *Those Who Dared: Five Visionaries Who Changed American Education* (New York: Teachers College Press, 2008). Deborah Meier, John Goodlad, James Comer, Ted Sizer, and Henry Levin share their personal stories in this inspirational call to action.

Grubb, W. Norton. *The Money Myth: School Resources, Outcomes, and Equity* (New York: Russell Sage Foundation, 2010). The Money Myth is an analysis to determine what factors impact student performance. It is these kinds of micro-analyses that will move our knowledge forward about what resources matter to student school performance.

Welch, Jack, with John Byrne. *Jack: Straight from the Gut* (New York: Warner Books, 2001). Jack Welch, *Fortune's* Manager of the 20th century and possibly the most influential CEO of the second half of the twentieth century, reveals the key to his managerial philosophy. In reflecting on his career at General Electric, beginning with his first job in the GE plastics division in 1960 to his rise to CEO in 1981 and then to his appointment of his successor in 2000, Welch reports that GE was all about finding and building great people.

5

Leadership

FOCUSING QUESTIONS

1 What is leadership?

2 What is the difference between leadership and management?

3 Are there traits that differentiate leaders from nonleaders and effective leaders from ineffective ones?

4 What kinds of leadership behaviors are more effective than others?

5 What role does the situation play in whether a leader is effective or ineffective?

6 What are some key situational factors that are significant in determining which leadership style to use in a given situation?

7 What contribution have other contemporary perspectives made in the study and practice of leadership?

In this chapter, we attempt to answer these questions concerning leadership in school organizations. We begin our discussion by exploring the nature of leadership in organizations, in which we define leadership and contrast leadership from management. Next we examine trait, behavior, and contingency theories of leadership. Then we present and analyze various styles of leadership. We conclude the chapter with a discussion of other contemporary perspectives of leadership.

The Nature of Leadership

There is perhaps no subject that has received more attention than the topic of leadership. Because of the importance of leadership in our society, it has been the subject of thousands of studies, books, and films all designed to say something about what leadership is, and how to become a better leader. Despite all this, there is still a great deal we do not know about leadership. In this chapter, we will examine some of what we do know.

Are people born to be leaders? Can people learn to become leaders? Or does leadership depend entirely on the situation? What personal characteristics distinguish leaders from nonleaders? What leadership behaviors distinguish effective leaders from ineffective leaders? What role do followers play in leadership? Is each leader equally suited to influence all types of followers? What role does the context or situation play with respect to leadership? Do all situations involving group effort require leadership? These questions constitute some of the ideas that we will pursue in subsequent pages.

Leadership Defined

The study of leadership has a long history, dating back to Plato's *Republic* in 400 B.C. Many attempts have been made to define leadership. Unfortunately, almost everyone who studies or writes about leadership defines it differently. However, three extensive reviews of the leadership literature by Bernard Bass,[1] Gary Yukl,[2] and Warren Bennis[3] have provided a clearer understanding of the phenomenon. While some conceptual disagreements prevail, one definition of leadership accepted by many experts is the following: **leadership** is the process whereby one individual influences other group members toward the attainment of defined or organizational goals.[4] This definition contains three important aspects: (a) leadership involves influence; (b) leadership involves goal attainments; and (c) leadership requires followers.

Leadership Involves Influence Leadership is an influence process. The influence process is one in which a leader changes the actions or attitudes of several group members or subordinates. Leaders influence many aspects of behavior in organizations that we have discussed in previous chapters: organizational structure (Chapter 2), organizational culture (Chapter 3), motivation (Chapter 4), and that we will discuss in subsequent chapters: decision making (Chapter 6), communication (Chapter 7), change (Chapter 8), curriculum (Chapter 13), teaching and learning (Chapter 14), and human resource management (Chapter 15). Research has shown, for example, that leaders influence the organization's structure, followers' group culture; levels of motivation; performance, absenteeism and turnover; and the quality of their decision making; communication patterns; and their receptivity to change; curriculum implementation; and group learning.

Leadership Involves Goal Attainments Leadership involves the exercise of influence for a purpose—to attain defined group or organizational goals. That is, leaders focus on changing the actions or attitudes of group members that are related to specific goals. The leaders of a group or organization are the individuals who exert such influence. An *effective* leader helps a group or organization to achieve its goals; an *ineffective* leader does not.[5]

Leadership Requires Followers The influence process implies that leadership is reciprocal. In other words, leaders influence followers in various ways, and leaders also are influenced by their followers (e.g., see the reciprocal influence theory discussed later in this chapter). Furthermore, it may be safe to say that leadership exists only in relation to followers: one cannot lead without followers. As Chester Barnard, author of the classic text *The Functions of the Executive*, stated "... leadership implies that followers must consent to being influenced."[6]

All leaders exert influence over group members or the organization. However, some leaders have formal authority to influence, while others do not. **Formal leaders** are those individuals who are given the authority (position power) to influence other members in the organization to achieve its goals.[7] **Informal leaders** have no formal authority to influence others but sometimes can exert just as much influence in an organization as formal leaders do—because of some special skills or talents they possess that organization members realize will help them achieve their goals.[8] Although we realize

---

[1]Bernard Bass, *The Bass Handbook of Leadership: Theory, Research, and Managerial Applications* (New York: Simon & Schuster, 2010).

[2]Gary Yukl, *Leadership in Organizations*, 7th ed. (Upper Saddle River, NJ: Prentice Hall, 2010).

[3]Warren Bennis, *Learning to Lead* (New York: Basic Books, 2010).

[4]Yukl, *Leadership in Organizations.*

[5]Peter F. Drucker, *Management: Tasks, Responsibilities, Practices* (New York: Transaction Publishers, 2008).

[6]Chester Barnard, *The Functions of the Executive* (Cambridge, MA: Harvard University Press, 1938, p. 165).

[7]Yukl, *Leadership in Organizations.*

[8]Ibid.

the impact informal leaders can have on a group or organization, the focus of this chapter is on formal leadership.

Leadership and Management

To fully understand what leadership is all about, it is important to examine the difference between leadership and management. The terms leadership and management tend to be used interchangeably in everyday speech. However, the two terms, although overlapping at times, are not identical and need to be clearly distinguished.

The first scholar to take a stand on this issue was Abraham Zaleznik, with his landmark article published in the *Harvard Business Review* in 1977.[9] Zaleznik argues that both leaders and managers make a valuable contribution to an organization and that each one's contribution is different. Whereas **leaders** advocate change and new approaches, **managers** advocate stability and the status quo. Furthermore, whereas leaders are concerned with understanding people's beliefs and gaining their commitment, managers carry out responsibilities, exercise authority, and worry about how things get accomplished.

More recently, John Kotter argues that leadership and management are two distinct, yet complementary, systems of action in organizations.[10] Specifically, he states that leadership is about coping with change, whereas management is about coping with complexity.[11] For Kotter, the leadership process involves (a) developing a vision for the organization; (b) aligning people with that vision through communication; and (c) motivating people to action through empowerment and through basic need fulfillment. The leadership process creates uncertainty and change in the organization.

In contrast, the management process involves (a) planning and budgeting, (b) organizing and staffing, and (c) controlling and problem solving. The management process reduces uncertainty and stabilizes the organization. Robert House concurs when he says that management consists of implementing the vision and direction provided by leaders, coordinating and staffing the organization, and handling day-to-day problems.[12]

In emphasizing the difference between leaders and managers, Warren Bennis notes: "To survive in the twenty-first century, we are going to need a new generation of leaders—leaders, not managers. The distinction is an important one. Leaders conquer the context—the volatile, turbulent, ambiguous surroundings that sometimes seem to conspire against us and will surely suffocate us if we let them—while managers surrender to it."[13] More recently, Bennis summarized his previous quotation as follows: "Managers do things right, while leaders do the right things."[14]

From a comprehensive review of the literature on this issue, we provide specific differences between leadership and management (see Table 5–1). The pairs of attributes, shown in Table 5–1, are presented as the extremes of a continuum. Most school administrators do not function at these extremes. However, patterns that tend toward leadership on the one hand or management on the other hand are likely to emerge as school administrators develop and use their skills in the workplace.

As you examine Table 5–1, mark the point on each continuum item that reflects the relative emphasis on leadership or management by a person for whom you have worked. School administrators may lean more heavily toward either leadership or management at various times depending on the situation. However, most tend to operate primarily in terms of either the leadership or the management profile.[15]

There are several conclusions that can be drawn from the information presented in Table 5–1. First, good leaders are not necessarily good managers, and good managers are not necessarily good leaders. Second, good management skills transform a leader's vision into action and successful implementation. Some scholars believe that effective implementation is the driving force

---

[9]Abraham Zaleznik, "Managers and Leaders: Are They Different," *Harvard Business Review*, 55 (1977): 67–78.

[10]John P. Kotter, "What Leaders Really Do," *Harvard Business Review*, 68 (1990): 103–111; and John P. Kotter, *A Force for Change: How Leadership Differs from Management* (New York: Free Press, 1990).

[11]John P. Kotter, *The Leadership Factor* (New York: Free Press, 1987).

[12]Robert J. House and Robert N. Aditya, "The Social Scientific Study of Leadership: Quo Vadis?" *Journal of Management*, 23 (1997): 445–456.

[13]Warren G. Bennis, "Managing the Dream: Leadership in the 21st Century," *Journal of Organizational Change Management*, 2 (1989): 7.

[14]Warren G. Bennis and Burt Nanus, *Leaders: The Strategies for Taking Charge* (New York: HarperCollins, 2007).

[15]Fred C. Lunenburg, "Leadership versus Management: A Key Distinction—in Theory and Practice," in F. L. Dembowski (ed.), *Educational Administration: The Roles of Leadership and Management* (Houston, TX: The NCPEA Press/Rice University, 2007), pp. 142–166.

Table 5-1 Comparisons between Leadership and Management

Category	Leadership		Management
Thinking Process	Focuses on people	-----	Focuses on things
	Looks outward	-----	Looks inward
Goal Setting	Articulates a vision	-----	Executes plans
	Creates the future	-----	Improves the present
	Sees the forest	-----	Sees the trees
Employee Relations	Empowers	-----	Controls
	Colleagues	-----	Subordinates
	Trusts & develops	-----	Directs & coordinates
Operation	Does the right things	-----	Does things right
	Creates change	-----	Manages change
	Serves subordinates	-----	Serves superordinates
Governance	Uses influence	-----	Uses authority
	Uses conflict	-----	Avoids conflict
	Acts decisively	-----	Acts responsibly

Table 5-2 Traits of Effective Leaders

Trait	Description
Drive	Inner motivation to pursue goals.
Integrity	The will to translate words into deeds
Leadership motivation	The need to exercise influence over others to reach shared goals
Self-confidence	Belief in his or her own leadership skills and ability to achieve goals
Intelligence	Above-average cognitive ability to integrate and interpret large amounts of information
Task-relevant knowledge	Tacit and explicit knowledge about the organization, profession, and technical matters
Emotional maturity	The ability to control his or her feelings and accept criticism
Flexibility	Ability to respond appropriately to changes in the setting

of organizational success, especially in relatively stable, "domesticated," organizations like public schools.[16] Third, organizational success requires a combination of effective leadership and management.[17] Furthermore, team-based organizational structures are extending leadership functions to work groups and cross-department teams in most modern school organizations. Thus, there is greater opportunity for more input from group members at all levels of the organization.[18]

[16]Fred C. Lunenburg, Barbara Thompson, and Dana Pagani, *The Multifactor Leadership Questionnaire (MLQ): Factor Structure of an Operational Measure*, paper presented at the annual meeting of the American Educational Research Association, Denver, CO, May 4, 2010.

[17]Lunenburg, "Leadership versus Management."

[18]Clete Bulach, Fred C. Lunenburg, and Les Potter, *Creating a Culture for High-Performing Schools: A Comprehensive Approach to School Reform* (Lanham, MD: Rowman & Littlefield, 2008).

Trait Theories

The scientific study of leadership began by concentrating on **personal traits** that distinguish leaders from non-leaders and effective leaders from ineffective ones. Researchers have identified several such traits. These are listed in Table 5–2.[19]

Leaders have a high need for achievement. This drive represents the inner motivation that leaders possess to pursue their goals and encourage others to pursue theirs. Leaders have a strong need to influence others to accomplish goals that benefit the team or organization. They demonstrate confidence in their leadership skills and the ability to achieve team or organization goals. They must be trustworthy. To be trusted, they must have authenticity. Without trust, they cannot maintain the

[19]Bass, *The Bass Handbook of Leadership*; Yukl, *Leadership in Organizations.*

ADMINISTRATIVE ADVICE 5–1

The Big Five Dimensions of Personality Traits

The Big Five model of personality structure can provide a common vocabulary for interpreting the results of leadership trait research.

- *Surgency.* Surgency measures the degree to which an individual is sociable, gregarious, assertive, and leaderlike, versus quiet, reserved, mannerly, and withdrawn. Some of the more common personality traits associated with this dimension include dominance, capacity for status or social presence, the need for power, sociability, or assertiveness.
- *Agreeableness.* Agreeableness measures the degree to which individuals are sympathetic, cooperative, good natured, and warm, versus grumpy, unpleasant, disagreeable, and cold. Personality traits associated with this dimension include likeability, friendly compliance, need for affiliation, and openness to love.
- *Conscientiousness.* Conscientiousness differentiates individuals who are hardworking, persevering, organized, and responsible from those who are impulsive, irresponsive, undependable, and lazy. Personality traits categorized under this dimension include prudence and ambition, will to achieve, need for achievement, dependability, constraint, and willingness to work.
- *Emotional Stability.* This dimension of personality concerns the extent to which individuals are calm, steady, cool, and self-confident, versus anxious, insecure, worried, and emotional. Some of the personality traits associated with emotional stability include composure, self-awareness and acceptance, and affect.
- *Intellectance.* This dimension of personality concerns the extent to which an individuals is imaginative, cultured, broad minded, and curious, versus concrete minded, practical, and having narrow interests. Personality traits associated with this dimension include curiosity, broad-mindedness, tolerance, and openness to experience.

Adapted from Robert Hogan, Gordon J. Curphy, and Joyce Hogan, "What We Know About Leadership: Effectiveness and Personality," *American Psychologist*, 49 (1994): 503–504.

loyalty of their followers. At the same time, they have to be emotionally mature enough to recognize their own strengths and weaknesses. Moreover, leaders must have above-average intelligence in order to process enormous amounts of information. They do not have to be the smartest in the group, but they must be smart enough to analyze a variety of complex alternatives and opportunities. In addition, leaders must have tacit and explicit knowledge of their social setting. This knowledge and experience help the leader to recognize opportunities and understand the organization's capacity to capture opportunities and the requirements of the situation. Finally, leaders must have the ability to adapt to the needs of followers and the requirements of the situation.

The leadership traits identified in Bass's and Yukl's review[20] (see Table 5–2) easily map onto the Big Five model of personality structure endorsed by many modern psychologists.[21] This model holds that leadership traits as perceived by supervisors and subordinates can be described in terms of five broad dimensions: surgency, agreeableness, conscientiousness, emotional stability, and intellectance. (See Administrative Advice 5–1.)

A study of personality traits and leadership effectiveness in education[22] is consistent with the Big Five

[20]Ibid.

[21]Pierce J. Howard, *The Owner's Manual for Personality at Work: How the "Big Five" Personality Traits Affect Performance, Communication, Teamwork, and Leadership* (Austin, TX: Bard Press, 2001); Gerald Matthews, *Personality Traits* (New York: Cambridge University Press, 2010); John P. Villanueva, *Personality Traits: Classifications, Effects, and Changes* (New York: Nova Science Publishers, 2011).

[22]Fred C. Lunenburg and Lynn Columba, "The 16PF as a Predictor of Principal Performance: An Integration of Quantitative and Qualitative Research Methods," *Education*, 113 (1992): 68–73.

personality model, as well as the meta-analyses of Bass and Yukl. The purpose of the study was to examine the validity of the Sixteen Personality Factor Questionnaire (16PF) as a predictor of principal performance. One hundred seventy-nine elementary and secondary school principals from two large urban school districts were administered the 16PF. Four independent criteria were used to measure principal effectiveness: supervisor's ratings, paired comparison ratings, peer nomination ratings, and teacher ratings, resulting in an overall effectiveness score. The results of the study revealed that Factors E (dominant), M (imaginative), Q2 (self-sufficient), and A (warm) were consistent predictors of superior performance.

Factor E characterizes individuals as assertive, self-confident, and independent. Factor M individuals prefer to deal with dynamic, essential matters rather than with superfluous, marginal issues. Moreover, persons high in this factor are more open to interaction with those different from themselves, not necessarily out of friendliness but because of curiosity coupled with self-confidence, which reduces fear and suspicion of the unfamiliar. Factor Q2 characterizes individuals who prefer their own decisions, are self-sufficient, and show resourcefulness. And finally, those individuals high in Factor A are good-natured, easygoing, emotionally expressive, ready to cooperate, attentive to people, softhearted, kindly, and adaptable.[23] These personality traits appear to fit the demands of an urban principal to deal with a diverse school population in a collaborative manner.

Emotional Intelligence

Recent studies are indicating that another trait that may indicate effective leadership is emotional intelligence (EI). Building on Howard Gardner's concept of multiple intelligences,[24] Daniel Goleman and colleagues criticize the traditional model of intelligence (IQ) for being too narrow, thus failing to consider interpersonal competence. Goleman's broader regime includes abilities such as being able to motivate oneself, to persist in the face of difficulties, to control impulse and delay gratification, to keep distress from interfering with the ability to think, and to empathize with others.[25]

Research conducted by Daniel Goleman and colleagues is bringing scientific data to the question of leadership. They have been tracking the science of outstanding performance for the last three decades. In order to identify the essential ingredients of outstanding leadership, they reviewed data ranging from neurology to measures of the emotional climate that the leader creates. Hundreds of studies in organizations of all kinds—from small family businesses to the largest companies, from religious groups to schools and hospitals—have yielded a dozen or so abilities that distinguish the best leaders. (See Table 5–3 to rate yourself on some of these essentials of leadership.)

Just what are the essentials of leadership? Goleman's work and that of hundreds of other researchers make clear that what sets beloved leaders apart from those we hate is excellence at things like "motivating power," "empathy," "integrity," and "intuitive ability." These abilities fall within the domain of **emotional intelligence**—an adeptness at managing ourselves and our interactions with others—not school smarts. For instance, why do Phil Jackson, Oprah Winfrey, the Dalai Lama, and Colin Powell have what it takes to be effective leaders? Phil Jackson, LA Lakers coach, winner of eleven NBA championships, has "motivating power." His skill in bringing out the best from his players helps to make the team a winner. Oprah Winfrey has "empathy." Her capacity to listen, to relate, and to communicate the pain and resolve of millions has given her enormous authority. The Dalai Lama has "integrity." His consistent stance of tolerance, nonviolence, and humility has made him a great moral leader and a voice of conscience. Former Secretary of State Colin Powell has "intuitive ability." His ability to connect with others makes him a superior diplomat.

According to Daniel Goleman and colleagues, new findings in brain science reveal that this kind of intelligence uses different parts of the brain than does the academic kind. Cognitive abilities such as verbal fluency or mathematics skills reside in the neocortex, the wrinkled topmost layers, which are the most recent evolutionary addition to the human brain. But emotional intelligence relies largely on the ancient emotional centers deep in the midbrain between the ears, with links to the

[23]Robert R. Cattell, Harold Eber, and Michael Tatsuoka, *Handbook for the Sixteen Personality Questionnaire (16PF)* (Champaign, IL: Institute for Personality and Ability Testing, 1986).

[24]Howard Gardner, *Frames of Mind: The Theory of Multiple Intelligences* (New York: Basic Books, 2005); Gardner, *Multiple Intelligences: New Horizons* (New York: Basic Books, 2007).

[25]Daniel Goleman, Richard Boyzatzis, and Annie McKee, *Primal Leadership: Realizing the Power of Emotional Intelligence* (Boston: Harvard University Press, 2002).

Table 5-3 Leadership Skills: Rate Yourself

The best leaders have strengths in at least a half-dozen key emotional-intelligence competencies out of 20 or so. To see how you rate on some of these abilities, assess how the statements below apply to you. While getting a precise profile of your strengths and weaknesses requires a more rigorous assessment, this quiz can give you a rough rating. More important, we hope it will get you thinking about how well you use leadership skills—and how you might get better at it.

Statement	Seldom	Occasionally	Often	Frequently
1. I am aware of what I am feeling.	☐	☐	☐	☐
2. I know my strengths and weaknesses.	☐	☐	☐	☐
3. I deal calmly with stress.	☐	☐	☐	☐
4. I believe the future will be better than the past.	☐	☐	☐	☐
5. I deal with changes easily.	☐	☐	☐	☐
6. I set measurable goals when I have a project.	☐	☐	☐	☐
7. Others say I understand and am sensitive to them.	☐	☐	☐	☐
8. Others say I resolve conflicts.	☐	☐	☐	☐
9. Others say I build and maintain relationships.	☐	☐	☐	☐
10. Others say I inspire them.	☐	☐	☐	☐
11. Others say I am a team player.	☐	☐	☐	☐
12. Others say I helped to develop their abilities.	☐	☐	☐	☐
Total the number of checks in each column:	___	___	___	___
Multiply this number by:	×1	×2	×3	×4
To get your score, add these four numbers: =	___ +	___ +	___ +	___

Interpretation: **Total:** ___

36+: An overall score of 36 or higher suggests you are using key leadership abilities well—but ask a coworker or partner for his opinions, to be more certain. **30–35:** Suggests some strengths but also some underused leadership abilities. **29 or less:** Suggests unused leadership abilities and room for improvement.

Leaders are unique, and they can show their talent in different ways. To further explore your leadership strengths, you might ask people whose opinions you value: "When you have seen me do really well as a leader, which of these abilities am I using?" If a number of people tell you that you use the same quality when doing well, you have likely identified a leadership strength that should be appreciated and nurtured.

Source: Daniel Goleman, "Could You Be a Leader?" Sunday Star Ledger, *Parade Magazine*, June 16, 2002, p. 5.

prefrontal cortex—the brain's executive center, just behind the forehead.[26]

According to Goleman and colleagues, this may explain the fact that IQ and emotional intelligence are surprisingly independent. Of course, to be a great leader, you need enough intelligence to understand the issues at hand, but you need not be supersmart. By the same token, people who are intellectually gifted can be disasters as leaders. Such situations are all too common in organizations everywhere. It happens when people are promoted for the wrong set of skills: IQ abilities rather than the emotional intelligence abilities that good leaders display.

[26]Ibid; See also, Fred C. Lunenburg, *The Fitness Movement: Exercise, Nutrition, and the Brain* (New York: Harmony Books, in Press).

According to Goleman and colleagues, the aptitudes of leadership, unlike academic or technical skills, are learned in life. That's good news for all of us. If you are weak in leadership, you can get better at virtually any point in life with the right effort. But it takes motivation, a clear idea of what you need to improve, and consistent practice. For example, good leaders are excellent listeners. Let's assume that you need to become a better listener. Perhaps you cut people off and take over the conversation without hearing them out. The first step: become aware of the moments you do this and stop yourself. Instead, let the other people speak their minds. Ask questions to be sure you understand their viewpoints. Then—and only then—give your own opinion. With practice, you can become a better listener.

Another skill that good leaders possess is helping others stay in a positive emotional state. Research shows that leaders who achieve the best results get people to laugh three times more often than do mediocre leaders.[27] Laughter signals that people are not caught up in, say, anger or fear, but rather are relaxed and enjoying what they do—and so they are more likely to be creative, focused, and productive. In sum, leaders are made, not born.

Behavior Theories

Another way of understanding leadership is to compare the behaviors of effective and ineffective leaders to see how successful leaders behave. The focus shifts from trying to determine what effective leaders *are* to trying to determine what effective leaders *do*. The issues to be explored include: in what way do leaders lead? How hard do leaders push their subordinates? How much do they listen and use their subordinates' ideas? The dichotomy between the trait and behavioral approach is not as sharp a division as one might suspect. A leader's personal traits and characteristics probably influence his leadership behavior or style. For example, an individual who feels adequate and feels comfortable with people will ordinarily adopt a people-oriented behavior style. On the contrary, a person who feels inadequate and feels threatened by people will probably adopt a production-oriented behavior style.

Three widely known studies of classic behavioral theories of leadership were conducted at the University of Iowa, Ohio State University, and the University of Michigan. Each theory is closely identified with the sponsoring university. We examine these theories by describing and classifying the leader behavior constructs developed in each. Then we examine some of the subsequent research associated with each theory; that is, the effects of leader behaviors on organizational outcomes such as job satisfaction, morale, and productivity.

The Iowa Studies: Authoritarian, Democratic, and Laissez-Faire Leadership

An early attempt to classify and study the effects of different styles of leader behavior on the group was conducted at the University of Iowa.[28] In a series of experiments, the Iowa researchers manipulated three leadership styles to determine their effects on the attitudes and productivity of subordinates. Leadership was classified into three different types, according to the leader's style of handling several decision-making situations during the experiments:

Authoritarian Leadership. Leaders were very directive and allowed no participation in decisions. They structured the complete work situation for their subordinates. Leaders took full authority and assumed full responsibility from initiation to task completion.

Democratic Leadership. Leaders encouraged group discussion and decision making. Subordinates were informed about conditions affecting their jobs and encouraged to express their ideas and make suggestions.

Laissez-Faire Leadership. Leaders gave complete freedom to the group and left it up to subordinates to make individual decisions on their own. Essentially, leaders provided no leadership.

Table 5–4 describes the three leadership styles. The table summarizes typical behaviors exhibited by leaders using the three different leadership styles in a variety of dimensions of leadership behavior.

Some of the results of the Iowa leadership studies include the following:[29]

1. Of the three styles of leadership, subordinates preferred the democratic style the best, which makes intuitive sense. The general trend today is toward wider use of participatory management practices because they are consistent with the supportive and collegial models of modern organization.
2. Subordinates preferred the laissez-faire leadership style over the authoritarian one. For subordinates, even chaos was preferable to rigidity.
3. Authoritarian leaders elicited either aggressive or apathetic behavior that was deemed to be reactions to the frustration caused by the authoritarian leader.
4. Apathetic behavior changed to aggressive behavior when the leadership style changed from authoritarian to laissez-faire; the laissez-faire leader produced the greatest amount of aggressive behavior.

[27]Goleman, Boyzatzis, and McKee, *Primal Leadership: Realizing the Power of Emotional Intelligence*.

[28]Kurt Lewin, Ronald Lippitt, and Robert K. White, "Patterns of Aggressive Behavior in Experimentally Created 'Social Climates,'" *Journal of Social Psychology*, 10 (1939): 271–299.

[29]Ibid.

Table 5-4 Differences in Leader Behavior Style as Identified by the Iowa Researchers

Behavior	Authoritarian	Democratic	Laissez-Faire
Policy determination	Solely by leader	By group's decision	No policy—complete freedom for group or individual decision
Establishment of job techniques and activities	Solely by leader	Leader suggests—group chooses	Up to individual
Planning	Solely by leader	Group receives sufficient information to obtain perspective needed to plan	No systematic planning
Establishment of division of labor and job assignments	Dictated by leader	Left to group decision	Leader uninvolved
Evaluation	Leader personal in praise and criticism	Evaluation against objective standards	No appraisal—spontaneous evaluation by other group members

Source: Adapted from Kurt Lewin, Ronald Lippitt, and Robert K. White, "Patterns of Aggressive Behavior in Experimentally Created 'Social Climates,'" *Journal of Social Psychology*, 10(1939): 271–299. Copyright 1939 by Heldref Publications. Used by permission of the Helen Dwight Reid Educational Foundation.

5. Productivity was slightly higher under the authoritarian leader than under the democratic one, but it was lowest under the laissez-faire leader.

Later studies done at the University of Michigan, however, indicate a sharp increase in productivity initially under authoritarian leadership, but this was followed by drastic decreases in productivity over the long run for authoritarian-led groups; and these groups ultimately reached levels well below democratically led groups in productivity.[30]

Implications for Practice The Iowa studies were important in that they helped focus attention on the investigation of leadership *behavior*. Furthermore, they provided a useful basis for describing and classifying alternative leader behavior styles. In fact, today the three styles identified by the Iowa researchers more than seventy years ago are commonplace in the literature and in parlance among practitioners in the field of educational administration.

The Ohio State Studies: Initiating Structure and Consideration

The research at Ohio State University aimed to identify leader behaviors that were important for the attainment of group and organizational goals. Specifically, researchers sought to answer the following questions: What types of behavior do leaders display? What effect do these leader behaviors have on work group performance and satisfaction?

During these studies, researchers from the disciplines of psychology, sociology, and economics developed and used the Leader Behavior Description Questionnaire (**LBDQ**) to study leadership in different types of groups and situations.[31] Studies were made of Air Force commanders and members of bomber crews; officers, noncommissioned personnel, and civilian administrators in the Department of the Navy; executives of regional cooperatives; manufacturing supervisors; leaders of various student and civilian groups; and teachers, principals, and school superintendents.

[30]David G. Bowers, *Systems of Organization: Management of the Human Resource* (Ann Arbor: University of Michigan Press, 1977).

[31]Ralph M. Stogdill and Alvin E. Coons (eds.), *Leader Behavior: Its Description and Measurement* (Columbus: Bureau of Business Research, Ohio State University, 1957).

Group responses to the **LBDQ** were then subjected to factor analysis, a mathematical technique that permits identification of a smaller set of common dimensions undergirding a large set of questionnaire responses. From the factor analysis came two dimensions that characterized the behavior of leaders in the numerous groups and situations investigated: initiating structure and consideration.

Initiating Structure **Initiating structure** refers to the extent to which a leader focuses directly on organizational performance goals, organizes and defines tasks, assigns work, establishes channels of communication, delineates relationships with subordinates, and evaluates work group performance. Leaders who initiate structure assign staff members to particular tasks, maintain definite standards of performance, emphasize meeting deadlines, encourage the use of uniform procedures, let staff members know what is expected of them, and see to it that staff members are working up to capacity.

Consideration **Consideration** refers to the extent to which a leader exhibits trust, respect, warmth, support, and concern for the welfare of subordinates. Leaders who manifest consideration listen to staff members' ideas, are friendly and approachable, treat all staff members as equals, and frequently use employee ideas. A high consideration score indicates psychological closeness between leader and subordinate; a low consideration score indicates a more psychologically distant and impersonal approach on the part of the leader.

The result was a two-dimensional leadership model. These dimensions are seen as being independent, thus resulting in four leadership behaviors as depicted in Figure 5–1.

Implications for Practice Over the years, the usefulness of the high initiating structure/high consideration style has been tested many times.[32] Overall, results have been mixed. There has been very little research about these leader behaviors until recently. Findings from a meta-analysis of 130 studies involving more than 20,000 participants indicated that initiating structure and consideration had a moderately strong, significant relationship with leadership outcomes. For example, consideration had a strong positive relationship with perceived leader effectiveness, employee motivation, and employee job satisfaction. Initiating structure had a strong positive relationship with employee motivation and moderate positive relationships with perceived leader effectiveness, employee job satisfaction, and overall unit performance.[33]

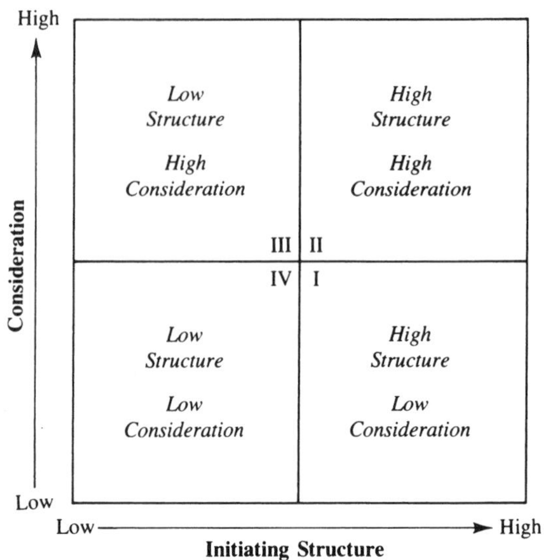

FIGURE 5–1

Ohio State Leadership Grid

The Michigan Studies: Production Centered and Employee Centered

Around the time that the Ohio State leadership studies were being conducted, a series of leadership studies were in progress at the University of Michigan's Institute for Social Research. The Michigan researchers used an approach to identify leaders who were rated as either effective or ineffective and then studied the behavior of these leaders in an attempt to develop consistent patterns of behavior that differentiated effective from ineffective leaders.

The Michigan studies identified two distinct leadership behaviors that were very similar to the initiating structure and consideration dimensions which evolved from the Ohio State studies. The two dimensions identified were

[32]Edwin A. Fleishman, "Consideration and Structure: Another Look at Their Role in Leadership Research," in F. Dansereau and F.J. Yammarino (eds.), *Leadership: The Multilevel Approaches* (Stamford, CT: JAI Press, 1998), pp. 51–60.

[33]Timothy A. Judge, Robert F. Piccolo, and Richard Ilies, "The Forgotten Ones? The Validity of Consideration and Initiating Structure in Leadership Research," *Journal of Applied Psychology*, 89 (2004): 36–51.

EXEMPLARY EDUCATIONAL ADMINISTRATORS IN ACTION

CRAIG L. ELLIOTT, Ed. D., Superintendent, Maize Unified School District, Kansas.

Words of Advice: There are two words that are very important to our profession, and to the superintendency: *patience* and *compassion*. Both words are necessary for survival as a superintendent. As I have watched and mentored building principals that move into central office positions, I have observed that the aspect of the job they have the most difficult time with is understanding that many decisions do not need to be made quickly. As a building principal, one often needs to make quick decisions. The fear is being known as a leader who cannot make a decision. As a central office administrator, we often are not the ones to be making the decision in the first place; rather, we should facilitate the process of decision making. And we should do this by asking questions.

When moving into central office work, one must adjust to a larger environment (arena may be the more fitting term, because we all know that we have many publics to please). I have witnessed all too often the quicker a decision, the sooner the decision has to be "adjusted." Many times, inexperienced central office administrators have to correct a situation because they were making their decision as an administrator responsible for a select group of children and adults, not as an administrator whose decision affects all of the district's children and adults.

Compassion, I've found, is necessary in understanding others. Teaching requires a deep understanding of why certain things are not understood by select individuals. Our natural instinct as educators is to try to help. Compassion means that you have put yourself in the other person's shoes, whether that be an employee, parent, or student. In so doing, you are understanding all points of view and, therefore, have an opportunity to look at the big picture rather than have a narrow focus. Knowing when to use patience and how to use compassion is the key to an effective and successful administration.

called production-centered leadership and employee-centered leadership.

Production-centered leader behavior is very similar to high initiating structure leader behavior. The **production-centered leader** emphasizes employee tasks and the methods used to accomplish them. Leaders who are production centered set tight work standards, organize tasks carefully, prescribe work methods to be followed, and closely supervise their subordinates' work.

Employee-centered leader behavior is very similar to high consideration leader behavior. An **employee-centered leader** emphasizes the employee's personal needs and the development of interpersonal relationships. Leaders who are employee centered tend to be supportive of their subordinates, use group rather than individual decision making, encourage subordinates to set and achieve high performance goals, and endeavor to treat subordinates in a sensitive, considerate way.

Implications for Practice Hundreds of studies in a wide variety of business, hospital, government, and other organizations were conducted. Thousands of employees, performing tasks ranging from unskilled to highly professional and scientific, completed a variety of questionnaires developed by the Michigan researchers. The initial research indicated that the most productive work groups tended to have leaders who were employee centered rather than production centered.[34] Subsequent research, however, concluded that leaders with the best production records were both production centered and employee centered.[35] However, the Michigan research findings have not been totally consistent. In comparison, the Ohio State leadership studies appear to have become more famous, at least in the educational setting, because of the number of studies that were generated by the initiating structure and consideration dimensions. And because many of these studies were done in school organizations.

Leadership Grid: A Contemporary Extension

Robert Blake and Jane Mouton developed the **Leadership Grid** (formerly the *Managerial* Grid) as a tool for identifying a leader's style.[36] They define two dimensions

[34]Rensis Likert, *The Human Organization: Its Management and Value* (New York: McGraw-Hill, 1967); Likert, *New Patterns of Management* (New York: Garland, 1987).

[35]Bowers, *Systems of Organization: Management of Human Resource*.

[36]Robert R. Blake and Jane S. Mouton, *The Managerial Grid: Leadership Styles for Achieving Production Through People* (Houston: Gulf, 1994).

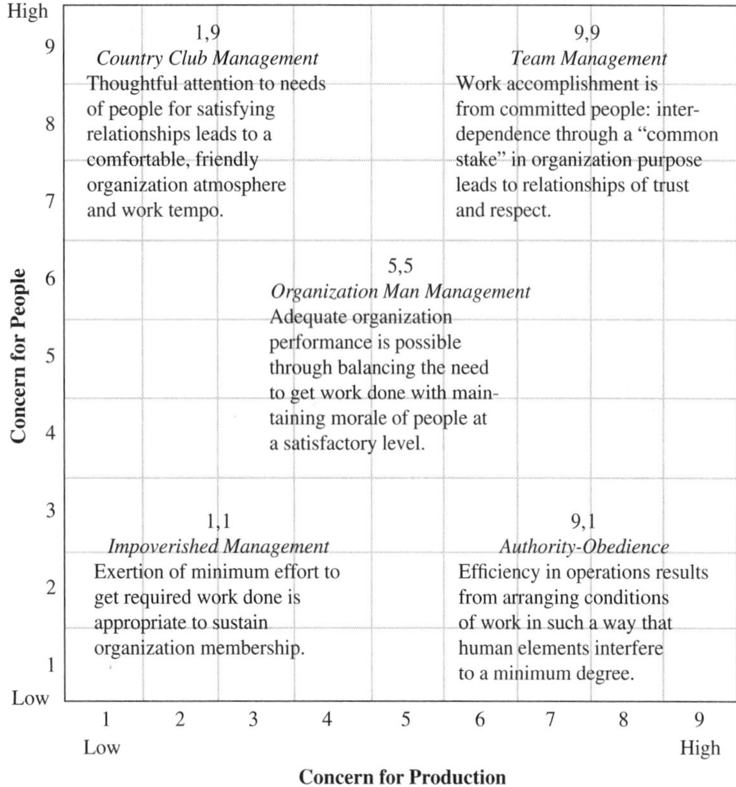

FIGURE 5–2

The Leadership Grid® Figure
Source: The Leadership Grid® figure, Paternalism Figure and Opportunism, from *Leadership Dilemmas—Grid Solutions*, by Robert R. Blake and Anne Adams McCanse (formerly the Managerial Grid by Robert R. Blake and Jane S. Mouton). Houston: Gulf Publishing Company, P. 29. Copyright © 1991 by Scientific Methods, Inc. Reproduced by permission of the owners.

of leader style as concern for production and concern for people, which essentially mirrors the Ohio State studies' dimensions of initiating structure and consideration.

The Grid portrays five key leadership styles. Concern for production is rated on a 1 to 9 scale on the horizontal axis, while concern for people is rated similarly on the vertical axis (see Figure 5–2). The Grid identifies a range of leader orientations based on the various ways in which task-oriented and people-oriented styles can interact with each other.

Leadership Styles Although there are eighty-one possible styles in the Grid, the five styles noted in Figure 5–2 and discussed below are treated as benchmarks in the theory. Blake and Mouton view leaders as being capable of selecting from among them.

- *9,1 Authority-Obedience.* Leaders concentrate on maximizing production through the use of power, authority, and control.
- *1,9 Country Club Management.* Leaders place primary emphasis on good feelings among colleagues and subordinates even if production suffers as a result.
- *1,1 Impoverished Management.* Leaders do the minimum required to remain employed in the organization.
- *5,5 Organization Man Management.* Leaders concentrate on conforming to the status quo and maintaining middle-of-the-road or "go-along-to-get-along" assumptions.
- *9,9 Team Management.* Leaders use a goal-centered approach to gain high-quantity and high-quality results through broad involvement of group members: participation, commitment, and conflict resolution.

Implications for Practice The Leadership Grid can be distinguished from the Ohio State studies discussed earlier. The Ohio State studies are fundamentally descriptive and nonevaluative, whereas the Grid is normative and prescriptive. Specifically, according to the Grid, team management (9,9) is the best style of leader behavior. This is the basis on which the grid has been used for leadership training in an organization's professional development program. Blake and Mouton have developed instruments that are designed to stimulate feedback from colleagues, associates, subordinates, and

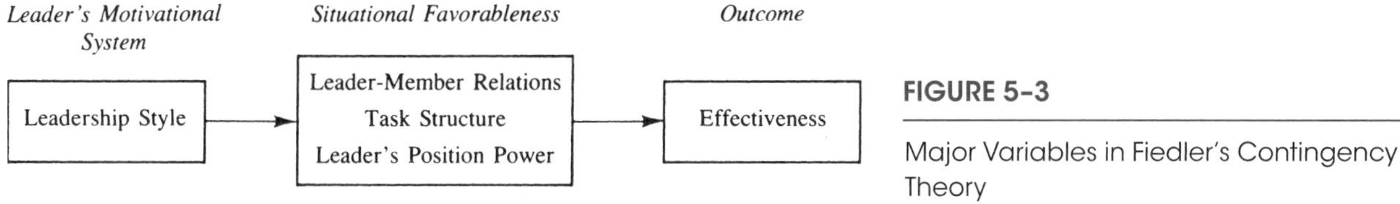

FIGURE 5–3

Major Variables in Fiedler's Contingency Theory

the like, which enable the targeted person to learn from others how they experience his or her leadership, that is, as 1,9-oriented, 9,1-oriented, 9,9-oriented, and so on. Therefore, the Grid is used to help people analyze different possibilities and likely results to be achieved by each of the Grid styles. As an organizational development technique, trainers aim to transform the leader in the organization to lead in the "one best way," which according to Blake and Mouton's Grid is the (9,9) team management style. The team management approach is one that combines optimal concern for production and optimal concern for people.

Contingency Theories

Efforts to discover the one best set of leader traits and the one best set of leader behaviors in *all situations* have failed. Contemporary researchers and school administrators are more likely to believe that the practice of leadership is too complex to be represented by a single set of traits or behaviors. Instead, the idea that effective leadership behavior is "contingent" on the situation is more prevalent today.

The contingency approach to leadership is considerably more complex than either the trait or the behavioral approach. According to **contingency theory**, effective leadership depends on the interaction of the leader's personal traits, the leader's behavior, and factors in the leadership situation. At the same time, the contingency approach is based on the proposition that effective leadership cannot be explained by any one factor. Instead, it proposes that all factors must be considered in the context of the situation in which the leader must lead. We discuss two contingency theories of leadership that have received a great deal of attention. The questions we ask regarding contingency leadership shift from: "Is authoritarian, initiating structure, production-centered leadership more effective than democratic, consideration, employee-centered leadership?" to a different question: "In what situations will production-centered leadership be effective, and under what set of circumstances will employee-centered leadership be effective?"

Fiedler's Contingency Theory

Fred Fiedler and his associates have spent more than two decades developing and refining a contingency theory of leadership.[37] According to the theory, the effectiveness of a leader in achieving high group performance is contingent on the leader's motivational system and the degree to which the leader controls and influences the situation. The three situational factors include leader-member relations, task structure, and the leader's position power. Figure 5–3 depicts the interrelationship among these variables. We discuss the three components of Fiedler's theory—leadership style, situational favorableness, and the contingency model—and the empirical evidence concerning the validity of the theory.

Leadership Style Fiedler developed a unique technique to measure leadership style. Measurement is obtained from scores on the *least preferred co-worker* (LPC) scale. Table 5–5 presents an example of an LPC scale. The scale usually contains twenty-four pairs of adjectives, written as a bipolar list, each of which could be used to describe a person. The leader completing the LPC scale is asked to describe the person with whom he worked least well in accomplishing some task, by placing Xs at the appropriate points between each of the adjective pairs. The most positive response for each pair of adjectives is assigned a score of 8 and the least positive response a score of 1. Summing all item scores on the instrument gives a leader's LPC score. A high score indicates that the leader views the least preferred co-worker in relatively favorable terms. A low score means that the least preferred co-worker is described in a very negative, rejecting manner.

How can the leader's LPC score be interpreted? Fiedler interprets a leader's LPC score to be a personality trait that reflects the leader's motivational system or behavioral preferences. High LPC leaders (those who

[37]Fred E. Fiedler and Martin M. Chemers, *Improving Leadership Effectiveness: The Leader Match Concept*, 2nd ed. (New York: Wiley, 1984).

Table 5-5 Sample of Items from the LPC Scale

										Scoring
Pleasant	8	7	6	5	4	3	2	1	Unpleasant	______
Friendly	8	7	6	5	4	3	2	1	Unfriendly	______
Rejecting	8	7	6	5	4	3	2	1	Accepting	______
Tense	8	7	6	5	4	3	2	1	Relaxed	______
Distant	8	7	6	5	4	3	2	1	Close	______
Cold	8	7	6	5	4	3	2	1	Warm	______
Supportive	8	7	6	5	4	3	2	1	Hostile	______
Boring	8	7	6	5	4	3	2	1	Interesting	______

Source: Adapted from Fred E. Fiedler and Martin M. Chemers, *Improving Leadership Effectiveness: The Leader Match Concept*, 2nd ed., © 1984, p. 19. Used by permission of John Wiley & Sons, Inc., New York.

perceive their least preferred co-workers positively) have as their basic goal the desire to maintain close interpersonal relationships with subordinates and behave in a considerate and supportive manner toward them. If the leader reaches this goal, he will be able to attain such secondary goals as status and esteem. In return, these leaders want their subordinates to admire and recognize them. Low LPC leaders have a different motivational structure: Task accomplishment is their primary goal. Needs such as esteem and status are fulfilled through the accomplishment of tasks, not directly through relationships with subordinates. Hence, a high LPC score indicates a relationship-motivated (employee-centered) leader whose interpersonal relationship needs have first priority, and a low LPC score indicates a task-motivated (production-centered) leader whose task achievement needs have first priority.

Situational Favorableness After classifying leaders according to their LPC scores, Fiedler set out to discover what type of leader is most effective. The basic premise of his contingency theory is that in some situations high LPC (relationship-motivated) leaders will be more effective, whereas other circumstances make it more likely that low LPC (task-motivated) leaders will be most effective. Fiedler concludes therefore that the relationship between leadership style and effectiveness depends on several factors in the situation. He identified three: leader-member relations, task structure, and position power.

Leader-member relations refer to the quality of the relationship between the leader and the group. The degree of confidence, trust, and respect subordinates have in the leader assesses it. Good or bad classifies leader-member relations. The assumption is that if subordinates respect and trust the leader, it will be easier for the leader to exercise *influence* in accomplishing tasks. For example, if subordinates are willing to follow a leader because of her referent power, they are following the leader because of personality, trustworthiness, and so on. On the other hand, when the relationship between leader and subordinates is not good, the leader may have to resort to special favors (reward power) to get good performance from subordinates.

Task structure refers to the nature of the subordinate's task—whether it is routine (structured) or complex (unstructured). Task structure can be operationally defined by (1) the extent of goal clarity (i.e., the degree to which the task requirements are known by subordinates), (2) the multiplicity of goal paths (i.e., whether there are many or few procedures for solving the problem), (3) the extent of decision verifiability (i.e., whether performance can be easily evaluated), and (4) the solution specificity (i.e., whether there are one or many correct solutions). When the task to be performed is highly structured, the leader should be able

Leader Member Relations	*Good*				*Poor*			
Task Structure	Structured		Unstructured		Structured		Unstructured	
Position Power	Strong	Weak	Strong	Weak	Strong	Weak	Strong	Weak
Situations	I	II	III	IV	V	VI	VII	VIII

Favorable ◄——————► **Unfavorable**

FIGURE 5–4

Fiedler's Contingency Model
Source: Adapted from Fred E. Fiedler, *A Theory of Leadership Effectiveness*, © 1967, p. 37. Used by permission.

to exert considerable influence on subordinates. Clear goals, clear procedures to achieve goals, and objective performance measures enable the leader to set performance standards and hold subordinates accountable (for example, "Type ten error-free manuscript pages per hour"). On the other hand, when the task is unstructured, the leader may be in a poor position to evaluate subordinate performance because the goals are unclear, there are multiple paths to achieve them, and the leader may possess no more knowledge about the task than the subordinates (for example, "Devise a plan to improve the quality of life in our school").

Position power refers to the extent to which the leader possesses the ability to influence the behavior of subordinates through legitimate, reward, and coercive powers. Examples are the power to hire and fire, to give pay raises and promotions, and to direct subordinates to task completion. The more position power held by the leader, the more favorable the leadership situation. In general, committee chairpersons and leaders in voluntary organizations have weak position power. School boards, superintendents, and principals of school organizations have strong position power.

Contingency Model Leader-member relations, task structure, and position power determine the situational favorableness for the leader. To combine these factors in the simplest way, Fiedler simply split each into two categories and thus produced eight possible combinations (see Figure 5–4). The eight situations vary in terms of their overall favorableness for the exercise of leadership. As Figure 5–4 shows, the most favorable situation (greater leader influence) is one in which leader-member relations are good, the task is highly structured, and the leader has strong position power. The least favorable situation (least leader influence) is one in which leader-member relations are poor, tasks are unstructured, and leader position power is weak.

Fiedler hypothesized that the favorableness of the situation with the leadership style determines effectiveness. He reviewed studies conducted in over 800 groups to investigate which type of leader was most effective in each situation.[38] Among the groups studied were Air Force bomber crews, combat tank crews, basketball teams, fraternity members, surveying teams, open-hearth steel employees, form-supply service employees, and educational administrators. The general conclusion reached, as shown in Figure 5–5, is that task-motivated leaders were most effective in extreme situations where the leader either had a great deal of influence or very little power and influence. Relationship-motivated (high LPC) leaders were most effective where the leader had moderate power and influence.

Why is the task-motivated leader successful in very favorable situations? Fiedler provided the following explanation:

> In the very favorable conditions in which the leader has power, informal backing, and a relatively well-structured task, the group is ready to be directed and the group expects to be told what to do. Consider the captain of an airliner in its final landing approach. We would hardly want him to turn to his crew for a discussion on how to land.[39]

To explain why the task-motivated leader is successful in a highly unfavorable situation, Fiedler cites the following example:

> . . . [T]he disliked chairman of a volunteer committee . . . is asked to plan the office picnic on a beautiful Sunday. If the leader asks too many questions about what the group ought to do or how he should proceed, he is likely to be told that "we ought to go home."[40]

As Figure 5–5 shows, the relationship-motivated (high LPC) leader is effective in the intermediate range

---

[38]Fred E. Fiedler, *A Theory of Leadership Effectiveness* (New York: McGraw-Hill, 1967).

[39]Ibid. p. 147.

[40]Ibid.

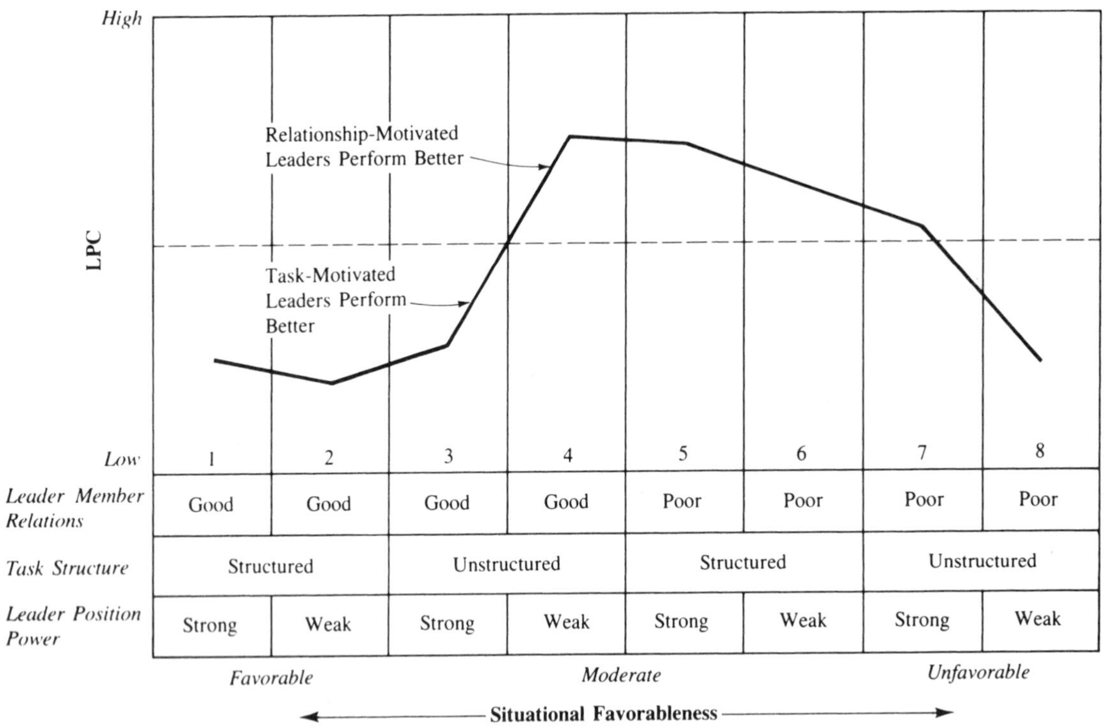

FIGURE 5–5

Summary of Contingency Model Research
Source: Adapted from Fred E. Fiedler and Martin M. Chemers, *Leadership and Effective Management*, © 1974, p. 80. Used by permission of Fred E. Fiedler.

of favorableness (octants 4, 5, 6, and 7). An example of such situations is the typical university committee staffed by professionals. In these situations, the leader may not be completely accepted by the group, the task may be ambiguous, and little power may be vested in the leader. Under such circumstances, Fiedler's theory predicts that relationship-motivated leaders will be most effective.

Implications for Practice Fiedler considers leadership styles to be relatively fixed or enduring. That is, a leader cannot alter her leadership style according to the situation. A practical implication of Fiedler's theory would be for the leader to be assigned to situations in which they will be more effective. A second alternative would be for the leader to make the situation more favorable. This can be accomplished by (a) improving relationships with organization members, (b) clarifying task structure by providing more guidelines and instructions to organization members, and (c) requesting more position power from the organization.

Path-Goal Theory

Another widely known contingency theory of leadership is the path-goal theory of leadership effectiveness. **Path-goal theory** is based on the expectancy theory of motivation and emphasizes the leader's effect on subordinates' goals and the paths to achieve the goals. Leaders have influence over subordinates' ability to reach goals, the rewards associated with reaching goals, and the importance of the goals.

The modern development of path-goal theory is usually attributed to Martin Evans and to Robert House and his colleagues.[41] Essentially, the path-goal theory

[41]Martin G. Evans, "The Effects of Supervisory Behavior on the Path-Goal Relationship," *Organizational Behavior and Human Performance*, 5 (1970): 277–298; Robert J. House, "A Path-Goal Theory of Leader Effectiveness," *Administrative Science Quarterly*, 16 (1971): 321–339.

attempts to explain the impact of leadership behavior on subordinate motivation, satisfaction, effort, and performance as moderated by situational factors of the subordinates and the work environment. House's general model and each of its parts are examined in the following sections.

Leader Behavior Four distinct types of leader behavior comprise House's path-goal model:

Directive Leadership. A **directive leader** lets subordinates know what is expected of them, provides specific guidance concerning what is to be done and how to do it, sets performance standards, requests that subordinates follow standard rules and regulations, schedules and coordinates work, and explains his role as leader of the group. Directive leadership is similar to the Ohio State researchers' initiating structure.

Supportive Leadership. A **supportive leader** is friendly, approachable, and concerned with the needs, status, and well-being of subordinates. A supportive leader treats subordinates as equals and frequently goes out of his way to make the work environment more pleasant and enjoyable. This leadership style is similar to what the Ohio State researchers call consideration.

Participative Leadership. A **participative leader** consults with subordinates concerning work-related matters, solicits their opinions, and frequently attempts to use subordinates' ideas in making decisions.

Achievement-Oriented Leadership. An **achievement-oriented leader** sets challenging goals for subordinates, emphasizes excellence in performance, and shows confidence in subordinates' ability to achieve high standards of performance.

Numerous research studies in path-goal theory suggest that the same leader can manifest these four styles of leadership in various situations. Unlike Fiedler's contingency model, which considers leadership behavior as unidimensional, path-goal theory views leadership behavior as relatively adaptable.

Situational Factors Each type of leader behavior works well in some situations but not in others. Two situational factors moderate the relationship between leader behavior and subordinate outcomes. The two situational variables are subordinate characteristics and environmental forces.

With respect to subordinate characteristics, the theory asserts that leadership behavior will be acceptable to subordinates to the extent that subordinates see such behavior as either an immediate source of satisfaction or as instrumental to future satisfaction.[42] Subordinate characteristics are seen to partially determine the extent to which subordinates perceive a leader's behavior as acceptable and satisfying. House and Baetz identified three subordinate characteristics:

Ability. An important personal characteristic of subordinates is their perception of their ability to perform a task. For example, subordinates who feel they have low task ability should appreciate directive leadership, whereas subordinates who feel quite capable of performing the task will find directive leadership unnecessary and perhaps irritating.

Locus of Control. Locus of control refers to the degree to which an individual sees the environment as systematically responding to his behavior.[43] Individuals with an internal locus of control believe outcomes are a function of their own behavior. Individuals with an external locus of control believe outcomes are a function of luck or chance. Research suggests that "internals" are more satisfied with participative leadership and "externals" are more satisfied with a directive leadership style.[44]

Needs and Motives. The dominant needs, motives, and personality characteristics of subordinates may influence their acceptance of and satisfaction with alternative leadership styles. For example, subordinates who have a high need for esteem and affiliation should be more satisfied with a supportive leader. Those with a high need for security will be more satisfied with a directive leader. Furthermore, subordinates with a high need for autonomy, responsibility, and self-actualization will probably be more motivated by a participative leader, and those who are high-need achievers should be more satisfied with achievement-oriented leaders.

With respect to the second situational factor, environmental forces, path-goal theory states: leadership behavior will be motivational to the extent that (1) it makes

---

[42]Robert House and Mary L. Baetz, "Leadership: Some Empirical Generalizations and New Research Directions," *Research in Organizational Behavior*, vol. 12 (Greenwich, CT: JAI Press, 1990).

[43]J. B. Rotter, "Generalized Expectancies for Internal versus External Control of Reinforcement," *Psychological Monographs*, 80 (1966), whole issue.

[44]Avis L. Johnson, Fred Luthans, and Harry W. Hennessey, "The Role of Locus of Control in Leader Influence Behavior," *Personnel Psychology*, 37 (1984): 61–75.

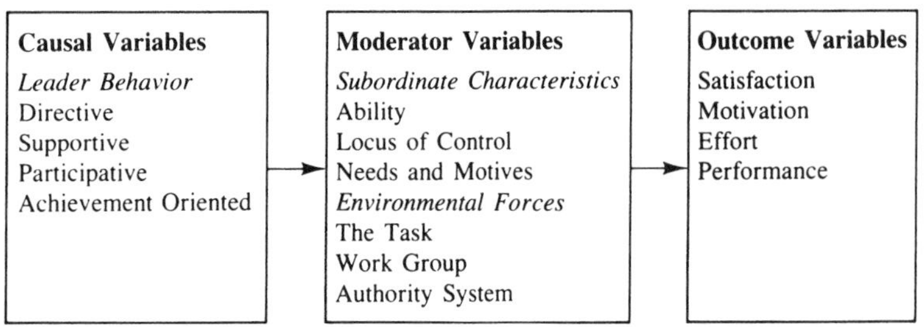

FIGURE 5–6

Relationship of Variables in the Path-Goal Theory

satisfaction of subordinate needs contingent on effective performance, and (2) it complements the environment of subordinates by providing the coaching, guidance, support, and rewards that are necessary for effective performance and that may otherwise be lacking in subordinates or in their environment.[45] Environmental forces include three broad aspects of situational factors: subordinates' tasks, the primary work group, and the formal authority system.

Tasks. An important environmental force that moderates the effects of leader behavior on subordinate outcomes is subordinates' tasks. Generally, researchers have classified tasks as highly structured or highly unstructured. Research has provided some evidence that supportive and participative leadership is more likely to increase subordinate satisfaction on highly structured tasks. This is because the tasks are routine and no further direction is necessary. Subordinates should be more satisfied with directive leadership on unstructured tasks because directive behavior can help clarify an ambiguous task.[46]

Work Group. The characteristics of work groups may also influence subordinate acceptance of a particular leadership style. For example, the path-goal theory asserts that "when goals and paths to desired goals are apparent because of . . . clear group norms . . . , attempts by the leader to clarify paths and goals would be redundant and would be seen by subordinates as an imposition of unnecessarily close control."[47]

Formal Authority System. The final environmental force concerns such matters as (1) the degree of emphasis on rules, regulations, policies, and procedures governing the performance of tasks; (2) situations of high stress; and (3) situations of great uncertainty. Some examples follow: with tasks (e.g., typing manuscripts) that are self-evident due to mechanization, standards, and procedures, directive leadership may lead to subordinate dissatisfaction. Research suggests that directive and supportive leadership will increase subordinate satisfaction in some stressful situations. In environments of uncertainty, leaders may initially use a participatory leadership style to solicit ideas in reaching a decision but later may resort to directive leadership once the final decision is made.

Figure 5–6 summarizes the path-goal theory of leadership effectiveness. As the figure shows, leader behavior moderated by subordinate characteristics and environmental forces results in subordinate motivation, satisfaction, effort, and performance.

Implications for Practice Testing path-goal theory has been difficult due to its complexity. The theory does correlate employee satisfaction with leadership, but its impact on performance has not yet been confirmed. Thus, the validity of the entire path-goal theory is yet to be determined.[48] Nevertheless, the path-goal theory is an improvement over the trait and behavior theories for at least three reasons. First, the theory is an attempt to indicate which factors affect motivation to perform. Second, the theory broadens the range of leadership behaviors a leader can choose from. Third, the path-goal theory introduces both subordinate characteristics (i.e., ability, experience, and need for independence) and environmental factors (task, work group, and authority system) when examining leader behavior and

[45]House and Baetz, "Leadership: Some Empirical Generalizations and New Research Directions."

[46]House and Dessler, "The Path-Goal Theory of Leadership."

[47]Ibid., pp. 29–62.

[48]John R. Villa, John P. Howell, & Peter W. Dorfman, "Problems with Detecting Moderators in Leadership Research Using Moderated Multiple Regression," *Leadership Quarterly*, 14 (2003): 3–23.

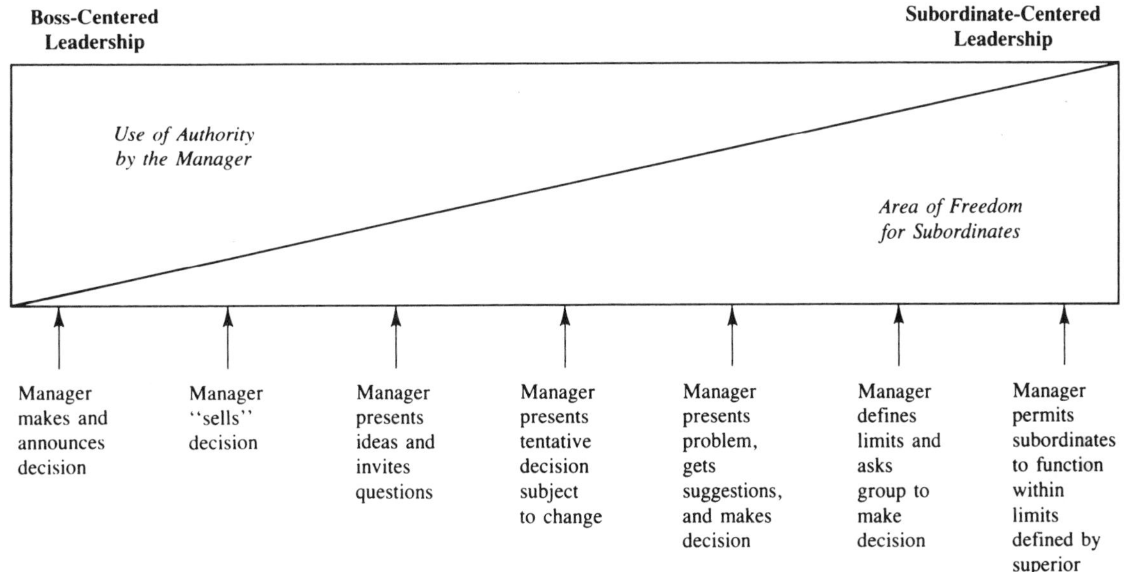

FIGURE 5–7

Leadership Style Continuum
Source: Adapted from Robert Tannenbaum and Warren Schmidt, "How to Choose a Leadership Patern," *Harvard Business Review*, 51 (1973): 167. Copyright © 1973 by the President and Fellows of Harvard College. Used by permission.

outcomes such as satisfaction and performance. School administrators are advised to modify their leadership behaviors to fit these subordinate characteristics and environmental factors.

Leadership Styles

The classic leadership studies (trait and behavioral approaches) and the contingency theories of leadership all have direct implications for what style the leader uses in managing human resources. The term *style* is roughly equivalent to the manner in which the leader *influences* subordinates. In the following sections, we present the most recent approaches that deal directly with style.

Leadership Style Continuum

Robert Tannenbaum and Warren Schmidt[49] elaborated on two styles identified in the earlier trait and behavioral studies of leadership. They conceive of a continuum that runs between *boss-centered leadership* at one extreme and *subordinate-centered leadership* at the other. Between these extremes are five points representing various combinations of managerial authority and subordinate freedom. Figure 5–7 depicts their concept of a **leadership style continuum.**

Leadership Behaviors The authors identify five typical patterns of leadership behavior from their model:

1. *Telling.* The leader identifies a problem, considers alternative solutions, chooses one of them, and then tells subordinates what they are to do. They may be considered but do not participate directly in the decision making. Coercion may or may not be used or implied.
2. *Selling.* The leader makes the decision but tries to persuade the group members to accept it. The leader points out how she has considered organizational goals and the interests of group members, and she states how the members will benefit from carrying out the decision.
3. *Testing.* The leader identifies a problem and proposes a tentative solution, asking for the reaction of

[49]Robert Tannenbaum and Warren Schmidt, "How to Choose a Leadership Pattern," *Harvard Business Review*, 51 (1973): 162–180.

those who will implement it, but making the final decision.

4. *Consulting.* The group members have a chance to influence the decision from the beginning. The leader presents a problem and relevant background information. The group is invited to increase the number of alternative actions to be considered. The leader then selects the solution she regards as most promising.
5. *Joining.* The leader participates in the discussion as a member and agrees in advance to carry out whatever decision the group makes.

Influences on the Leader Tannenbaum and Schmidt assert that a wide range of factors determines whether superordinate-centered leadership, subordinate-centered leadership, or something in between is best. These factors fall into four broad categories: forces in the leader, forces in the group, forces in the situation, and long-run objectives and strategy.

Forces in the Leader.

Value system: How strongly does the leader feel that individuals should have a share in making the decisions that affect them? Or, how convinced is the leader that the official who is paid or chosen to assume responsibility should personally carry the burden of decision making? Also, what is the relative importance that the leader attaches to organizational efficiency and personal growth of subordinates?

Confidence in the group members: Leaders differ in the amount of trust they have in other people. After considering the knowledge and competence of a group with respect to a problem, a leader may (justifiably or not) have more confidence in his own capabilities than in those of the group members.

Personal leadership inclinations: Leaders differ in the manner (e.g., telling or team role) in which they seem to function more comfortably and naturally.

Feelings of security in an uncertain situation: The leader who releases control over the decision-making process reduces the predictability of the outcome. Leaders who have a greater need than others for predictability and stability are more likely to "tell" or "sell" than to "join."

Forces in the Group Members. Before deciding how to lead a certain group, the leader will also want to remember that each member is influenced by many personality variables and expectations. Generally speaking, the leader can permit the group greater freedom if the following essential conditions exist:

Members have relatively high needs for independence.

Members have readiness to assume responsibility.

Members have a relatively high tolerance for ambiguity.

Members are interested in the problem and feel that it is important.

Members understand and identify with the goals of the organization.

Members have the necessary knowledge and experience to deal with the problem.

Members expect to share in decision making.

Forces in the Situation. Some of the critical environmental pressures on the leader are as follows:

The problem itself: Do the members have the kind of knowledge that is needed? Does the complexity of the problem require special experience or a one-person solution?

The pressure of time: The more the leader feels the need for an immediate decision, the more difficult it is to involve other people.

Long-Run Objectives and Strategy. As leaders work on daily problems, their choice of a leadership pattern is usually limited. But they may also begin to regard some of the forces mentioned as variables over which they have some control and to consider such long-range objectives as

Raising the level of member motivation.

Improving the quality of all decisions.

Developing teamwork and morale.

Furthering the individual development of members.

Increasing the readiness to accept change.

Generally, a high degree of member-centered behavior is more likely to achieve these long-range purposes. But the successful administrator can be characterized as neither a strong leader nor a permissive one. Rather, a successful leader is sensitive to the forces that influence her in a given situation and can accurately assess those forces.

Implications for Practice The Tannenbaum-Schmidt model has not generated any empirical research, probably because there are no instruments associated with

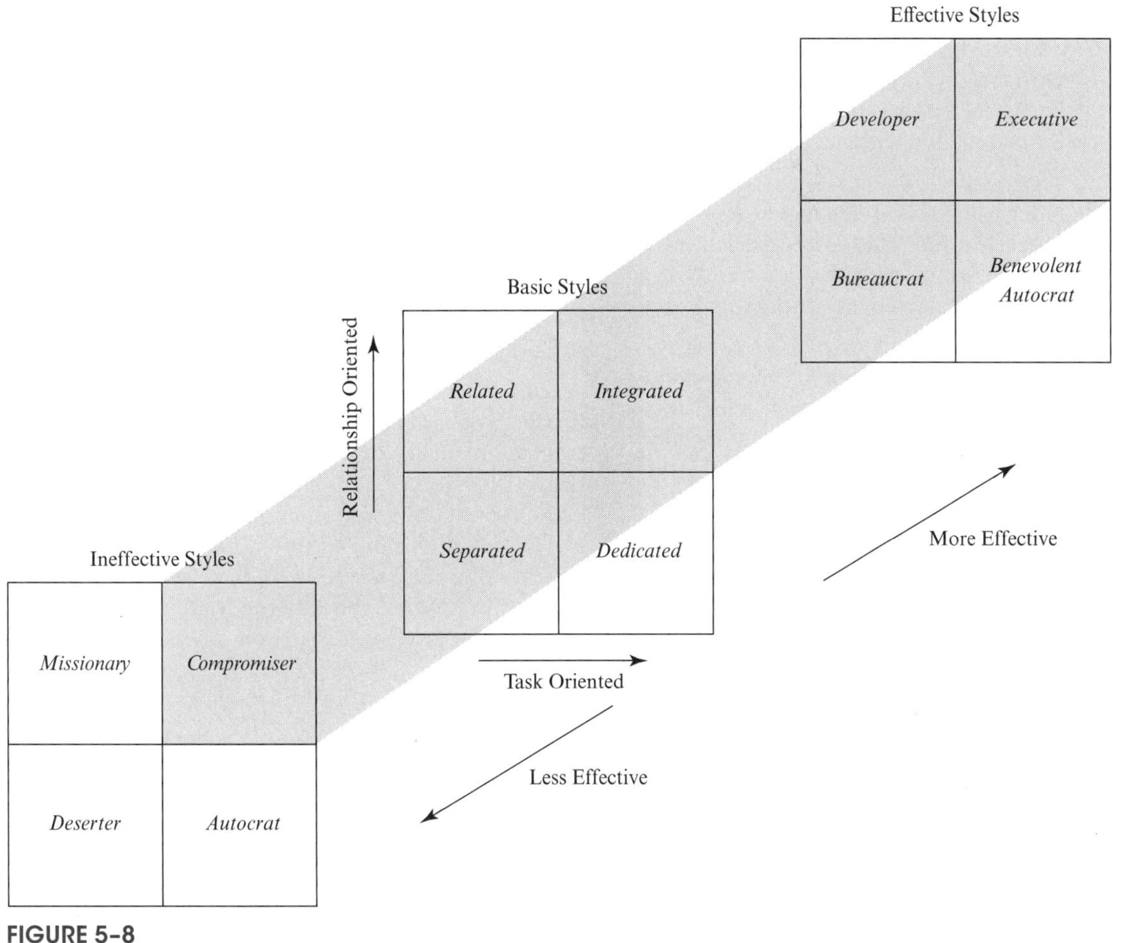

FIGURE 5–8

Reddin's Three-Dimensional Model of Leadership Effectiveness
Source: Adapted from William J. Reddin, *Managerial Effectiveness*, © 1970, p. 230.

the formulation. However, the model makes intuitive sense and can be used to identify alternative leadership behaviors available to a school administrator and the general classes of factors (influences on the leader) that are relevant in selecting an appropriate leadership style to fit a given situation.

Three-Dimensional Leadership Styles

William Reddin developed another useful model for identifying the leadership styles of practicing school administrators.[50] Figure 5–8 shows his **three-dimensional model.** By adding an effectiveness dimension to the task behavior and relationship behavior dimensions of the earlier Ohio State leadership models, Reddin has attempted to integrate the concepts of leadership style with the situational demands of a specific environment. As Figure 5–8 shows, when the style of a leader is appropriate to a given situation, it is termed *effective*; when the style is inappropriate to a given situation, it is termed *ineffective*. In the center grid, the four basic leadership styles in the model are related, integrated, separated, and dedicated. Reddin proposes that any of the four basic leadership styles may be effective or ineffective depending on the situation. These effective and ineffective equivalents result in eight operational leadership styles, which we briefly summarize.

[50]William J. Reddin, *Managerial Effectiveness* (New York: McGraw-Hill, 1970).

Effective Styles

Developer. A leader using this style gives maximum concern to relationships and minimum concern to tasks. The leader is seen as having implicit trust in people and concerned mainly with developing them as individuals.

Executive. A leader using this style gives a great deal of concern to both tasks and relationships. The leader is seen as a good motivator, setting high standards, recognizing individual differences, and using team management.

Bureaucrat. A leader using this style gives minimum concern to both tasks and relationships. The leader is seen as conscientious and is interested mainly in rules and wants to maintain and control the situation by the use of rules.

Benevolent Autocrat. A leader using this style gives maximum concern to tasks and minimum concern to relationships. The leader is seen as knowing exactly what she wants and how to get it without causing resentment.

Ineffective Styles

Missionary. A leader using this style gives maximum concern to people and relationships and minimum concern to tasks in a situation in which such behavior is inappropriate. The leader is seen as a "do-gooder" who values harmony as an end in itself.

Compromiser. A leader using this style gives a great deal of concern to both tasks and relationships in a situation that requires emphasis on only one or on neither. The leader is seen as a poor decision maker, easily affected by pressure.

Deserter. A leader using this style gives minimum concern to tasks and relationships in a situation where such behavior is inappropriate. The leader is seen as uninvolved and passive.

Autocrat. A leader using this style gives minimum concern to tasks and minimum concern to relationships in a situation in which such behavior is inappropriate. The leader is seen as having no confidence in others, as unpleasant, and as interested only in the immediate job.

Implications for Practice Reddin's model incorporates three theoretical bases discussed previously, namely leader traits and behaviors, groups, and situational factors. Reddin's model has not been the object of much empirical research. Instead, it has become a popular technique for use in training administrators in numerous organizational contexts. Using Reddin's sixty-four-item questionnaire, administrators can identify their leadership styles. Primarily, executive development seminars conducted by Reddin and his colleagues are designed to make participants cognizant of a variety of leadership styles and train leaders to adapt styles to particular situations in order to achieve maximum effectiveness.

Situational Leadership Styles

Another well-known and useful framework for analyzing leadership behavior is Paul Hersey and Kenneth Blanchard's **situational leadership theory.**[51] It is an extension of Tannenbaum and Schmidt's leadership-style continuum, Blake and Mouton's managerial grid, and Reddin's three-dimensional leadership styles. Following the lead of the earlier Ohio State leadership studies, and like the leadership-style continuum, the grid, and the three-dimensional frameworks, situational leadership theory identifies two key leadership behaviors: task behavior and relationship behavior.

- *Task Behavior.* The leader engages in one-way communication by explaining what each subordinate is to do, as well as when, where, and how tasks are to be performed.
- *Relationship Behavior.* The leader engages in two-way communication by providing socio-emotional support, "psychological strokes," and "facilitating behaviors."

Situational Factor: Readiness of Followers Taking the lead from Fiedler's contingency factors, Hersey and Blanchard incorporated the readiness of followers as a key situational variable in their model. Hersey and Blanchard see two types of readiness as particularly important: willingness and ability.

- *Willingness* is a combination of the varying degrees of confidence, commitment, and motivation. Any one of these variables can be prepotent; that is, a person may be completely committed to the job, quality,

---

[51]Paul Hersey and Kenneth H. Blanchard, *Management of Organizational Behavior*: International Edition (Upper Saddle River, NJ: Prentice Hall, 2008).

and the organization. The person may be motivated with a strong desire to do well and at the same time be insecure about their ability to do the job. Even though the person's commitment and motivation are strong, their insecurity will have to be addressed before they can move forward into Readiness. Someone or something will have to help then over this hurdle. The number one error in diagnosing willingness is to view someone who is insecure or apprehensive as unmotivated.

- *Ability* is determined by the amount of knowledge, experience, and demonstrated skill the follower brings to the task. A diagnosis based on the actual display of ability. The caution here is not to diagnose Readiness based on the leader's beliefs of what the follower should know. A frequent leadership error is to assume knowledge and hold the follower accountable for skills he or she has not had an opportunity to demonstrate.

Leadership Styles The key for leadership effectiveness in Hersey and Blanchard's model is to match the situation with the appropriate leadership style. Four basic leadership styles are in the model: telling, selling, participating, and delegating.

- *Telling Style.* This is a high-task, low-relationship style and is effective when subordinates are low in motivation and ability.
- *Selling Style.* This is a high-task, high-relationship style and is effective when subordinates have adequate motivation but low ability.
- *Participating Style.* This is a low-task, high-relationship style and is effective when subordinates have adequate ability but low motivation.
- *Delegating Style.* This is a low-task, low-relationship style and is effective when subordinates are very high in ability and motivation.

Figure 5–9 summarizes the situational leadership theory.

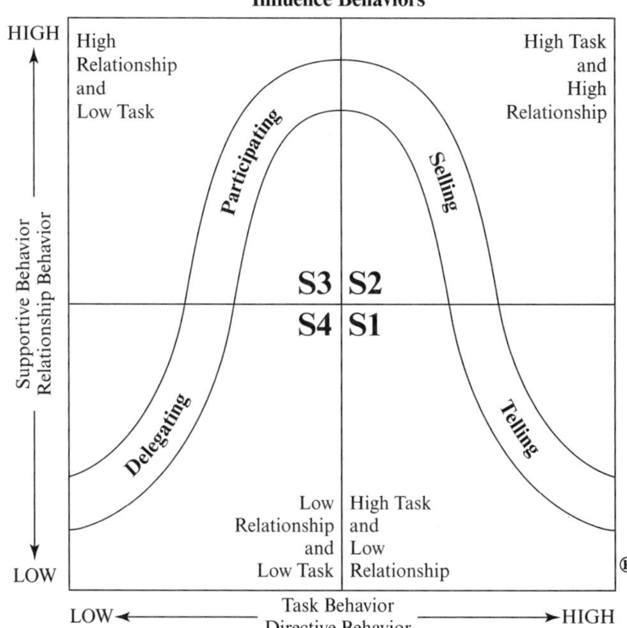

Performance Readiness®

HIGH	MODERATE		LOW
R4	**R3**	**R2**	**R1**
Able and Confident and Willing	Able but Insecure or Unwilling	Unable but Confident or Willing	Unable and Insecure or Unwilling

FIGURE 5–9

The Hersey-Situational Leadership®Model
Source: © Copyright 2006 Reprinted with permission of the Center for Leadership Studies, Inc., Escondido, CA 92025.

ADMINISTRATIVE ADVICE 5–2

Applying Situational Leadership

School administrators should consider situational leadership styles systematically, and decide under what circumstances each is appropriate. School administrators can apply the four leadership styles in the following manner:

- *Telling Style.* Give specific instructions and supervise staff members closely. This leadership style is primarily for first-year teachers who need a lot of instruction and supervision.
- *Selling Style.* Explain decisions and solicit suggestions from followers but continue to direct tasks. This leadership style works especially well with non-tenured teachers, who are in their second or third year on the job. They're gaining confidence and competence, but they're still getting their feet on the ground.
- *Participating Style.* Make decisions together with staff members and support their efforts toward performing tasks. This leadership style works with highly creative teachers. Applying this style can take the form of supporting teachers when they come up with excellent ideas and helping them to bring those ideas to fruition.
- *Delegating Style.* Turn over decisions and responsibility for implementing them to staff members. This leadership style works with people who go above and beyond their instructions.

Source: Adapted from Bob Webb, "Situational Leadership: The Key Is Knowing When to Do What," *Executive Educator,* 12 (1990): 29–30. Copyright 1990, the National School Boards Association. Used by permission.

As Figure 5–9 shows, when subordinates have very low readiness, leaders should define roles and direct the behavior of group members. When subordinates have moderately low readiness, leaders should provide some direction, but they can attempt to persuade subordinates to accept decisions and directions. When subordinates have moderately high readiness, initial direction is not needed, but group members should share in decision making. Finally, when subordinates have high readiness, leaders should demonstrate confidence in group members by delegating tasks to them. Successful leadership is achieved by selecting the right leadership style, which Hersey argues is contingent on the level of followers' readiness. To use the model, identify a point on the readiness continuum that represents follower readiness to perform a specific task. Then construct a perpendicular line from that point to a point where it intersects with the curved line representing leader behavior. This point indicates the most appropriate amount of task behavior and relationship behavior for that specific situation.

Note that the curved line never goes to either the lower left or the lower right corner. In both quadrants 1 and 4, there are combinations of both task and relationship behavior. Style 1 always has some relationship behavior and style 4 always has some task behavior. It should be noted that the Hersey Situational Leadership ® Model is both a developmental and a regression model.

The key to the success of situational leadership is matching leadership styles to the appropriate people and situations. (See Administrative Advice 5–2.)

Implications for Practice The Hersey-Situational Leadership® Model is useful because it builds on other explanations of leadership that emphasize the role of task and relationship behaviors. As a result, it is widely used for leadership training and development in a wide variety of organizational settings. The situational leadership model has intuitive appeal as well. School administrators can benefit from this model by attempting to diagnose the readiness of followers before choosing the right leadership style.

Until recently, there was almost no empirical research evidence to support the validity of the Hersey-Blanchard model. However, one study in a school setting provides partial support for this model. The study was a field test of Hersey and Blanchard's situational leadership theory in a school setting. Elementary school principals from one large, urban school district received training using Hersey and Blanchard's framework. Pretests and posttests were administered to the principals and a sample of their teachers before and after training to determine the effects of training on principals' leadership effectiveness and style range. The study provided only partial support for the Hersey-Blanchard theory. Principals were perceived as more effective three years after training than before training. However, no significant differences were found in principals' effectiveness immediately following training, nor in principals' leadership style range before and after training.[52]

Other Contemporary Perspectives

Given the importance of leadership, researchers devote attention to studying new and insightful perspectives. Five other contemporary perspectives of recent interest are the synergistic leadership theory, leader-member exchange theory, reciprocal influence theory, substitutes for leadership, and transformational leadership.

Synergistic Leadership Theory

Modernist theories in leadership were traditionally dominated by masculine incorporation and lacked feminine presence in development and language. The **synergistic leadership theory** (SLT), developed by Irby and colleagues, seeks to explicate the need for a postmodernist leadership theory by providing an alternative to, and not a replacement for, traditional theories.[53] The SLT includes issues concerning diversity and the inclusion of the female voice in the theory. In a tetrahedron model, the theory uses four factors to demonstrate aspects not only of leadership but its effects on various institutions and positions (see Figure 5–10). The factors are beliefs, attitudes, and values; leadership behavior; external forces; and organizational structure.

Factor 1: Beliefs, Attitudes, and Values As shown in Figure 5–10, beliefs, attitudes, and values are depicted as dichotomous, as an individual or group would either adhere or not adhere to specific beliefs, attitudes, or values at a certain point in time. Some dichotomous examples include the following: (a) believes in the importance of professional growth for all individuals including self; does not believe that professional development is important; (b) has an openness to change; does not have an openness to change; (c) values diversity; does not value diversity; or (d) believes that integrity is important for all involved in schooling; does not value integrity.

Factor 2: Leadership Behavior The second factor of the theory, leadership behavior, derives directly from the literature on male and female leadership behaviors and is depicted as a range of behaviors from autocratic to nurturer. The range of behaviors includes those ascribed to female leaders, such as interdependence, cooperation, receptivity, merging acceptance, and being aware of patterns, wholes, and context; as well as those ascribed to male leaders, including self-assertion, separation, independence, control, and competition.

Factor 3: External Forces External forces, as depicted in the model, are those influencers outside the control of the organization or the leader that interact with them and that inherently embody a set of beliefs, attitudes, and values. Significant external influencers or forces relate to local, national, and international community and conditions, governmental regulations, laws, demographics, cultural climate, technological advances, economic situations, political climate, family conditions, and geography. These examples of external forces, as well as others, including those listed in the model, interact in significant ways with the other factors in the synergistic leadership theory.

Factor 4: Organizational Structure Organizational structure refers to characteristics of the organizations and how they operate. The synergistic leadership theory model (Figure 5–10) depicts organizational structures as ranging from open, feminist organizations to tightly bureaucratic ones. Bureaucratic organizations include division of labor, rules, hierarchy of authority, impersonality, and competence, whereas feminist organizations are characterized by practices such as participative decision making, systems of rotating leadership, promotion of community and cooperation, and power sharing.

Implications for Practice The synergistic leadership theory provides a framework for describing interactions and dynamic tensions among beliefs, attitudes, and values; leadership behaviors; external forces; and organizational structure. As a result, a leader can analyze and describe particular interactions that may account for tension, conflict, or harmony at specific points in time or over time. If it is discovered that

---

[52] Salvatore V. Pascarella and Fred C. Lunenburg, "A Field Test of Hersey and Blanchard's Situational Leadership Theory in a School Setting," *College Student Journal*, 21 (1988): 33–37.

[53] Beverly J. Irby, Genevieve Brown, Jo Ann Duffy, and Diane Trautman, "The Synergistic Leadership Theory," *Journal of Educational Administration*, 40 (2002): 304–322.

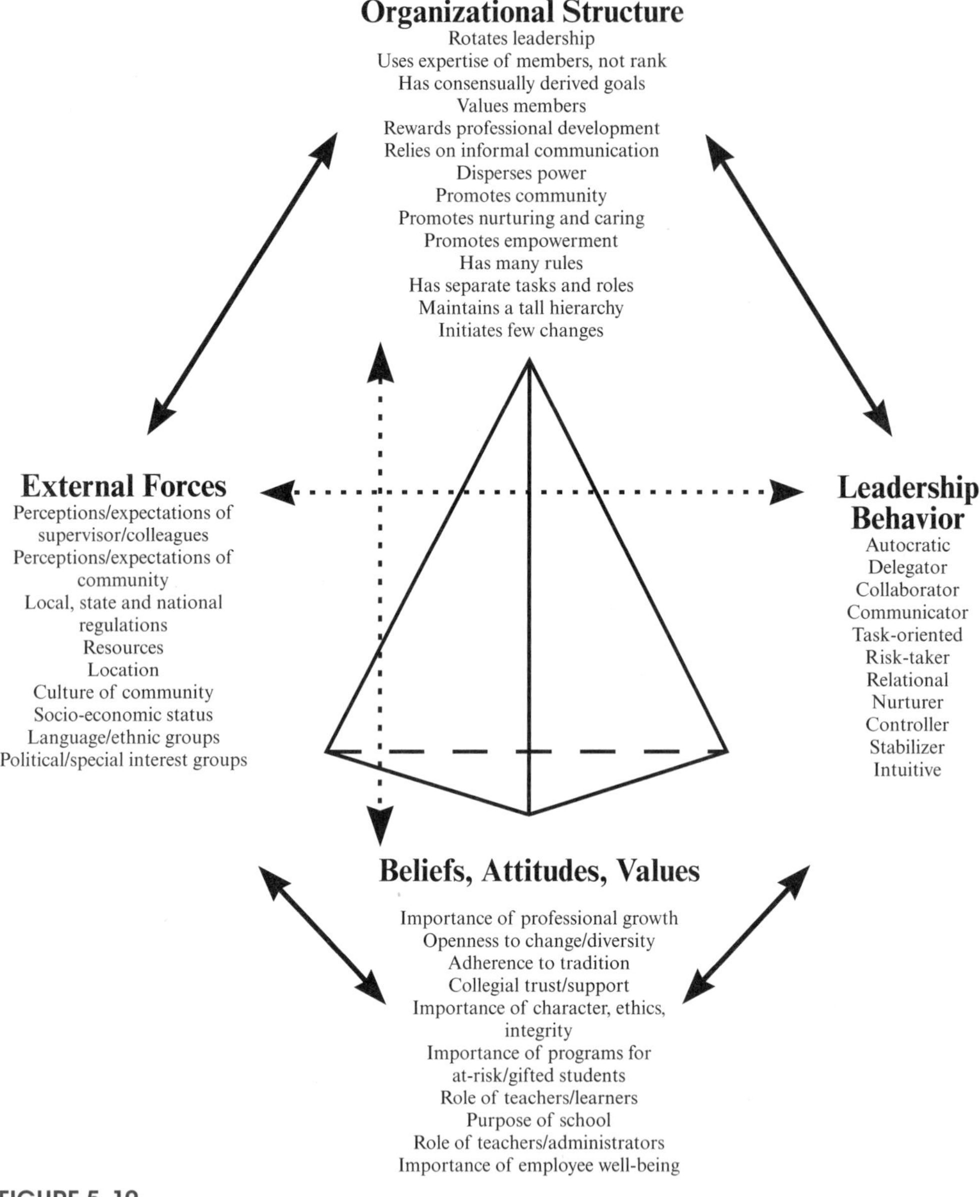

FIGURE 5–10

Irby, Brown, Duffy, and Trautman's Synergistic Leadership Model
Source: Adapted from Beverly. J. Irby, Genevieve Brown, Jo Ann Duffy, and Diane Trautman, "The Synergistic Leadership Theory," *Journal of Educational Administration*, 40 (2002): 313.

tension exists between even two of the factors, then the effectiveness of the leader or the organization itself can be negatively impacted. Not only is the SLT beneficial in determining "fit" while a leader is employed in an organization, but also it can be of assistance in job selection. Moreover, the SLT can serve to build an understanding of the environment to aid in decisions made by the leader. And SLT fosters a reflective practice approach, as it encourages the leader to engage in self-assessment.

Numerous validation studies of the SLT theory have been conducted to date. These empirical tests of the theory have included national and international samples and non-majority populations.[54]

Leader-Member Exchange Theory

Many theories of leadership assume that the superior behaves in essentially the same manner toward all members of his work group. In fact, however, leaders often act very differently toward different subordinates, and develop contrasting kinds of relationships with them. This perspective on the leadership process is provided by the **Leader-Member Exchange Theory (LMX)**.[55]

The LMX theory focuses on a dyad, that is, the relationship between a leader and each subordinate considered independently, rather than on the relationship between the superior and the group. Each linkage, or relationship, is likely to differ in quality. Thus, the same administrator may have poor interpersonal relations with some subordinates and open and trusting relations with others. The relationships within these pairings, or dyads, may be of a predominantly in-group or out-group nature.

A leader initiates either an in-group or an out-group exchange with a member of the organization early in the life of the dyadic relationship. Members of the in-group are invited to participate in decision making and are given added responsibility. The leader allows these members some latitude in their roles; in effect, the leader and key subordinates negotiate the latter's responsibilities in a noncontractual exchange relationship. In essence, an in-group member is elevated to the unofficial role of "trusted lieutenant." In-group members, in many respects, enjoy the benefits of job latitude (influence in decision making, open communications, and confidence in and consideration for the member). The subordinate typically reciprocates with greater than required expenditures of time and effort, the assumption of greater responsibility, and commitment to the success of the organization.

In contrast, members of the out-group are supervised within the narrow limits of their formal employment contract. Authority is legitimated by the implicit contract between the member and the organization. The leader will provide the support, consideration, and assistance mandated by duty but will not go beyond such limits. In effect, the leader is practicing a contractual exchange with such members; they are "hired hands," who are being influenced by legitimate authority rather than true leadership. In return, out-group members will do what they have to do and little beyond that.

Implications for Practice An important implication of the leader-member exchange theory is that the quality of the relationship between the leader and each group member has important job consequences. Specifically, the research supporting the LMX theory indicates that subordinates with in-group status with their leaders will have higher productivity and job satisfaction, improved motivation, and engage in more citizenship behaviors at work.[56] These findings are not surprising, considering the self-fulfilling prophesy (see Chapter 4). Leaders invest more resources in those they expect to perform well (i.e., those they have designated as in-group members); and they treat them differently than they do out-group members. Therefore, it is suggested that school administrators develop high-quality relationships with as many subordinates as possible. They should have as large an in-group and as small an out-group as possible.

Reciprocal Influence Theory

The trait theories of leadership, leadership behavior approaches, and contingency theories of leadership share one underlying assumption: Leader behavior affects subordinate behavior. Particularly in correlational studies, any association between leader behavior and group effectiveness has been interpreted as measuring

[54]Beverly J. Irby, Genevieve Brown, and LingLing Yang, "The Synergistic Leadership Theory: A 21st Century Leadership Theory," in C.M. Achilles, B.J. Irby, B. Alford, & G. Perreault (eds.), *Remember Our Mission: Making Education and Schools Better for Students* (Lancaster, PA: Pro-Active Publications, 2009), pp. 93–105.

[55]George B. Graen and Mary Uhl-Bien, "Relationship-Based Approach to Leadership: Development of Leader-Member Exchange (LMX) Theory of Leadership over 25 Years: Applying a Multi-Level Multi-Domain Perspective," *Leadership Quarterly*, 6 (1995): 219–247.

[56]Remus Ilies, Jennifer D. Nahrgang, and Frederick. P. Morgeson, "Leader-Member Exchange and Citizenship Behaviors: A Meta-Analysis," *Journal of Applied Psychology*, 92 (2007): 269–277; Ziguong Chen, Wing Lam, and Jian An Zhong, "Leader-Member Exchange and Member Performance: A Look at Individual-Level Negative Feedback-Seeking Behavior and Team-Level Empowerment Culture," *Journal of Applied Psychology*, 92 (2007): 202–212.

the impact of the leader's action on subordinate satisfaction, motivation, or performance. More recently, however, it has been recognized that in any complex organization the flow of influence or authority is not unilateral and downward—from leader to subordinate—but also upward from subordinate to leader. **Reciprocal influence theory** states that certain leader behaviors cause subordinate behaviors, and certain acts of subordinates (for example, low performance) can cause the leader to modify behavior.[57]

The reciprocal influence theory is a reality in most organizations. For example, consider the principal of a school who is dedicated to the mission of improving student achievement scores in the building. How is this principal's behavior influenced by subordinates? One obvious response is that the leader will closely supervise teachers who are not performing well and will loosely supervise others who are fulfilling their mission of improving instruction. Thus, by their performance, subordinates are influencing the leader. Of course, the leader is influencing them as well. As another example, consider a university dean who has a tenured professor who is very hot tempered. Although the dean has authority over this faculty member and can order the individual to perform many job-related activities, the dean may be fearful of the subordinate's temper and will modify her leadership style to accommodate this individual. In this case, the professor is probably exerting more influence on the university dean than the leader is influencing the subordinate.

Implications for Practice Several studies support the notion of reciprocal influence between leaders and subordinates. The results to date suggest the following:

1. Leader consideration or employee-centered behavior and leader positive reinforcement both can lead to employee job satisfaction.
2. High initiating structure or production-centered leadership sometimes leads to lower employee job satisfaction.
3. Low-performing subordinates tend to cause leaders to use more initiating structure/production-centered leadership and punitive reward behavior (that is, punishment).
4. High leader positive reward behavior tends to lead to improved subordinate performance. However, few studies have shown any direct evidence that leader initiating structure or leader consideration causes increases or decreases in subordinate performance. These findings emphasize the importance of rewards as an influence factor in determining subordinate behavior.[58]

In short, it is realistic to view organizations as places where leaders and subordinates interact in a complex way, each exerting reciprocal influence on the other. Research efforts examining the reciprocal influence process will continue to be of interest to school administrators and researchers and will be used to emphasize the dynamics of leadership in schools.

Substitutes for Leadership

The concept of substitutes for leadership has evolved in response to dissatisfaction with the progress of leadership theory in explaining the effects of leader behavior on performance outcomes. Research studies demonstrate that, in many situations, leadership may be unimportant or redundant. Certain subordinate, task, and organizational factors can act as **substitutes for leadership** or neutralize the leader's influence on subordinates.[59] Table 5–6 lists some possible leadership substitutes and neutralizers for supportive/relationship leadership and instrumental/task leadership.

As shown in Table 5–6, subordinate experience, ability, and training may substitute for instrumental leadership. For example, professionals such as teachers may have so much experience, ability, and training that they do not need instrumental leadership to perform well and be satisfied. Such leadership acts would be redundant and might be resented, and could even lead to reduced performance. Similarly, subordinates who have a strong professional orientation (like teachers) might not require instrumental or supportive leadership.

---

[57]Frederick A. Starke, *Management: Leading People and Organizations in the 21st Century* (Upper Saddle River, NJ: Prentice Hall, 2001).

[58]Andrew D. Szilagi, *Management and Performance* (Upper Saddle River, NJ: Addison Wesley, 2010).

[59]Steven Kerr and John M. Jermier, "Substitutes for Leadership: Their Meaning and Measurement," *Organizational Behavior and Human Performance*, 22 (1978): 375–403; John P. Hovell and Peter W. Dorfman, "Leadership and Substitutes for Leadership among Professional and Nonprofessional Workers," *Journal of Applied Behavioral Science*, 22 (1986): 29–46.

Table 5-6 Substitutes and Neutralizers for Supportive and Instrumental Leadership

Factor	Supportive Leadership*	Instrumental Leadership*
Subordinate Characteristics		
1. Experience, ability, training		Substitute
2. "Professional" orientation	Substitute	Substitute
3. Indifference toward organizational rewards	Neutralizer	Neutralizer
Task Characteristics		
1. Structured, routine task		Substitute
2. Task feedback		Substitute
3. Intrinsically satisfying task	Substitute	
Organizational Characteristics		
1. Cohesive work group	Substitute	Substitute
2. Leader lacks position power	Neutralizer	Neutralizer
3. Formalization of goals and plans		Substitute
4. Rigid rules and procedures		Neutralizer
5. Physical distance between leader and subordinates	Neutralizer	Neutralizer

*Supportive and instrumental leadership are analogous to leader consideration and leader initiating structuring.

Source: Gary A. Yukl, *Leadership in Organizations*, 7th ed. (Upper Saddle River, NJ: Prentice Hall, 2010), p. 237. © 2010. Reprinted by permission of Prentice Hall, Upper Saddle River, NJ.

When subordinates do not desire the rewards a leader can provide, this would neutralize almost any behavior on the part of the leader.

Certain types of work (for example, teaching) are highly structured and automatically provide feedback (through students' oral and written responses) and, therefore, substitute for instrumental leadership. Furthermore, when the task is intrinsically satisfying (like teaching), there will be little need for supportive behavior on the part of the leader to make up for poor design. Finally, when the organization is structured in a way that makes clear the paths to goals—for example, through plans, rules, policies, and standard operating procedures—such structure reduces the need for instrumental leadership. This is particularly apparent in sociotechnical and autonomous work groups found in schools. Sometimes a strong union has the same effect, if it has a collective bargaining agreement that severely constrains the administrator's position power.

Implications for Practice It appears that leadership matters most when substitutes are not present in subordinates' skills, task design, or the organization's structure. When substitutes are present, the impact of leadership is neutralized.

Transformational Leadership

Building on the work of James McGregor Burns,[60] Bernard Bass[61] has developed an approach that focuses on both transformational and transactional leadership. Recent research has focused on differentiating transformational leaders from transactional leaders.[62] The more traditional **transactional leadership** involves

[60]James McGregor Burns, *Leadership* (New York: Harper & Row, 1978).

[61]Bernard M. Bass, *Leadership and Performance Beyond Expectations* (New York: Free Press, 1985); Bernard M. Bass and Ronald E. Riggio, *Transformational Leadership*, 2nd ed. (Mahwah, NJ: Lawrence Erlbaum, 2006).

[62]Bernard M. Bass, Bruce J. Avolio, D.I. Jung, and Y. Berson, "Predicting Unit Performance by Assessing Transformational and Transactional Leadership," *Journal of Applied Psychology*, 88 (2003): 207–218; U.R. Dumdum, Kevin B. Lowe, and Bruce J. Avolio, "A Meta-Analysis of Transformational Leadership Correlates of Effectiveness and Satisfaction: An Update and Extension," in B. J. Avolio and F. J. Yammarino (eds.), *Transactional and Charismatic Leadership: The Road Ahead* (New York: JAI Press, 2002), pp. 35–66; Timothy A. Judge and Robert F. Piccolo, "Transformational and Transactional Leadership: A Meta-Analytic Test of Their Relative Validity," *Journal of Applied Psychology*, 89 (2004): 755–768.

leader-follower exchanges necessary for achieving agreed-upon performance goals between leaders and followers. These exchanges involve four dimensions: contingent reward, management by exception (active), management by exception (passive), and laissez faire.[63]

- *Contingent Reward:* contracts the exchange of rewards for effort; promises rewards for good performance; recognizes accomplishments.
- *Management by Exception (active):* watches for deviations from rules and standards; takes corrective action.
- *Management by Exception (passive):* intervenes only if standards are not met.
- *Laissez-Faire:* abdicates responsibilities; avoids making decisions.

Transformational leadership is based on leaders shifting the values, beliefs, and needs of their followers in three important ways: (a) increasing followers' awareness of the importance of their tasks and the importance of performing them well; (b) making followers aware of their needs for personal growth, development, and accomplishment; and (c) inspiring followers to transcend their own self-interests for the good of the organization.[64] Transformational leadership has four dimensions: idealized influence, inspirational motivation, intellectual stimulation, and individualized consideration. These four dimensions are often called "the Four I's."[65]

Idealized Influence: involves behaving in ways that earn the admiration, trust, and respect of followers, causing followers to want to identify with and emulate the leader. Idealized influence is synonymous with *charisma*. For example, Steve Jobs, who founded Apple Computer, showed idealized influence by emphasizing the importance of creating the Macintosh as a radical new computer. He has since followed up with products like the iPod.

Inspirational Motivation: involves behaving in ways that foster enthusiasm for and commitment to a shared vision of the future. Frequently, that vision is transmitted through the use of symbols to focus efforts. As an example, in the movie *Patton*, George C. Scott stood on a stage in front of his troops with a wall-sized American flag in the background and ivory-handled revolvers in holsters at his sides.

Intellectual Stimulation: involves behaving in ways that challenge followers to be innovative and creative by questioning assumptions and reframing old situations in new ways. For example, your boss encourages you to "think out of the box," that is, to look at a difficult problem in a new way.

Individualized Consideration: involves behaving in ways that help followers achieve their potential through coaching, professional development, and mentoring. For example, your boss stops by your office and makes comments which reinforce your feeling of personal worth and importance in the organization.

The full range of leadership model (transactional and transformational leadership) is depicted in Figure 5–11. As shown in Figure 5–11, laissez-faire is the least effective of the leader behaviors. Leaders using this style are rarely viewed as effective. Management by exception (active or passive) is slightly better than laissez-faire, but it is still considered ineffective leadership. Leaders who practice management by exception leadership either search for deviations from standards and take corrective action or tend to intervene only when there is a problem, which is usually too late. Contingent reward leadership can be an effective style of leadership. The leader attains follower agreement on what needs to be accomplished using promised or actual rewards in exchange for actual performance. Leaders are generally most effective when they regularly use each of the four transformational leadership behaviors: idealized influence, inspirational motivation, intellectual stimulation, and individualized consideration.[66]

How Transformational Leadership Works A great deal of research has been done to explain how transformational leadership works. Generally four elements emerge: creativity, goals, vision, and commitment.

Creativity Transformational leaders are more effective because they are more creative themselves. They are also more effective because they encourage their followers to be more creative as well.[67] Transformational leaders are

[63]Bass and Riggio, *Transformational Leadership*.

[64]Bernard M. Bass, *The Bass Handbook of Leadership: Theory, Research, and Management Applications*, 5th ed. (New York: Simon & Schuster, 2010).

[65]Bass and Riggio, *Transformational Leadership*.

[66]Ibid.

[67]D.I. Jung, "Transformational and Transactional Leadership and Their Effects on Creativity in Groups," *Creativity Research Journal*, 13 (2001): 185–195; D.I. Jung, C. Chow, and A. Wu, "The Role of Transformational Leadership in Enhancing Innovation: Hypotheses and Some Preliminary Findings," *Leadership Quarterly*, 14 (2003): 525–544.

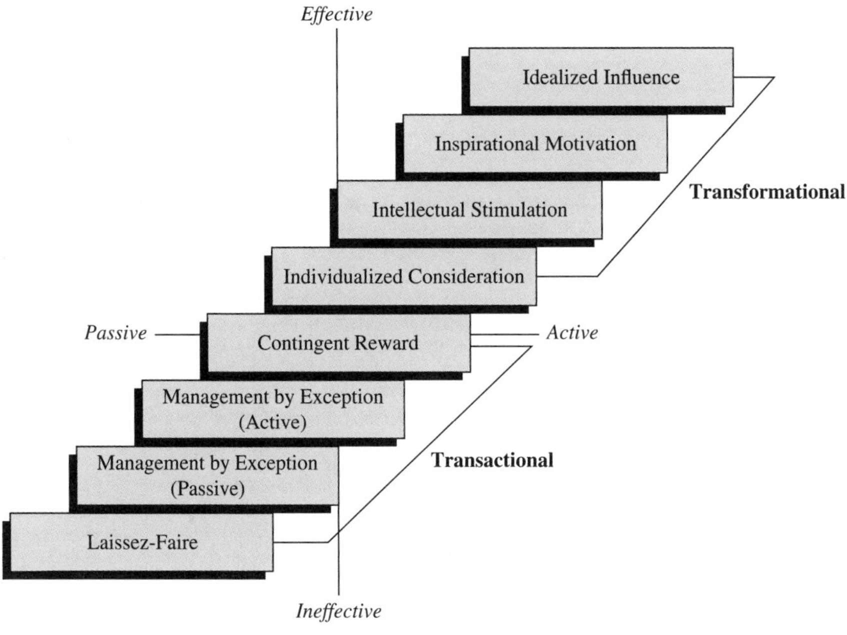

FIGURE 5–11

Full Range Leadership Model

proactive rather than reactive; creative rather than compliant; and audacious rather than adherent.[68]

Goals Goals are another key element in how transformational leadership works. Followers of transformational leaders are more likely to pursue ambitious goals, understand and agree with the formal goals of the organization, and believe that the goals they are pursuing will lead to their own self-fulfillment.[69]

Vision Transformational leaders create a strategic vision that energizes and unifies followers.[70] They communicate the vision with emotional appeal that captivates followers and other stakeholders.[71] Not only do transformational leaders communicate a vision, they also model the vision. In other words, they "walk the talk" by doing things that enact the vision.[72] For example, leaders in higher education (deans, associate deans, department heads) walk the talk by doing research, acquiring grants, and publishing extensively in the research and professional literature alongside the faculty members they lead.

Commitment Making a vision a reality requires followers' commitment. Transformational leaders build commitment to the vision through enthusiasm for every project they tackle; by being persistent in their follow-through on all projects; and by involving followers in the creation of the vision.[73]

Research Findings Transformational leadership is currently the most popular leadership approach. The

[68]Clete Bulach, Fred C. Lunenburg, and Les Potter, *Creating a Culture for High-Performing Schools: A Comprehensive Approach to School Reform* (Lanham, MD: Rowman & Littlefield, 2008).

[69]Yair Berson and Bruce J. Avolio, "Transformational Leadership and the Dissemination of Organizational Goals: A Case Study of a Telecommunications Firm," *Leadership Quarterly*, 15 (2004): 625–646.

[70]Warren G. Bennis, *Learning to Lead* (New York: Basic Books, 2011).

[71]Gary A. Yukl, *Leadership in Organizations*, 4th ed. (Upper Saddle River, NJ: Prentice Hall, 2010).

[72]Peter G. Northouse, *Leadership: Theory and Practice*, 5th ed. (Thousand Oaks, CA: Sage, 2010).

[73]Michael J. Fullan, *All Systems Go: The Change Imperative for Whole School Reform* (Thousand Oaks, CA: Sage, 2010).

evidence supporting transformational leadership is impressive. Transformational leadership has been supported in various occupations (for example, school superintendents, school principals, college presidents, naval commanders, military cadets, ministers, shop stewards, sales personnel, and school teachers) and at various job levels.

A meta-analysis of 49 studies indicated that transformational leadership was positively associated with measures of leadership effectiveness and followers' job satisfaction.[74] A second meta-analysis of 87 studies indicated that transformational leadership was positively related to leader effectiveness ratings, group or organizational performance, and followers' job satisfaction and motivation.[75] A third meta-analysis of 39 studies revealed that the transformational leadership dimensions of inspirational motivation, individualized consideration, and intellectual stimulation were related to leadership effectiveness in most studies, as well as idealized influence when an organization was in crisis. Moreover, except for the contingent reward dimension, the transactional leadership styles did not result in leadership effectiveness ratings.[76]

These results were reinforced by findings from two large-scale studies of transformational leadership in public school settings. The first study involved 317 school superintendents and their followers (564 principals). The second study included 275 principals and their followers (397 teachers). In both studies (n = 1553 participants), three of the four transformational leadership dimensions (inspirational motivation, intellectual stimulation, and individualized consideration) were related to leader effectiveness ratings.[77] The authors concluded that idealized influence, or charisma, may not be a significant factor in stable public school environments. Furthermore, none of the transactional leadership behaviors, except contingent reward, were related to leader effectiveness ratings.

Most of the research on transformational leadership to date has relied on Bass and Avolio's[78] Multifactor Leadership Questionnaire (MLQ) or qualitative research that describes leaders through interviews. A confirmatory factor analysis of the MLQ using data from the two aforementioned public school studies (n = 1553) supported a three-factor model of transformational leadership.[79] The three factors supported by the confirmatory factor analysis appear to be consistent with three of the "Four I's" proposed by Bass.

Implications for Practice There are several important leadership implications that can be derived from the studies of transformational leadership. Previous research has found transformational leadership to be positively related to leader effectiveness ratings, group or organizational performance, and follower job satisfaction and motivation. However, idealized influence, or charisma, may not be relevant for leaders in stable public school environments. Some researchers have begun to explore the idea that idealized influence, or charisma, may be more appropriate in some situations than in others.[80] For instance, idealized influence is probably more appropriate when organizations are in crisis and need to adapt than when environmental conditions are stable—that is, when dissatisfaction is high and value congruence and unquestioned obedience are needed to ensure organizational survival.[81] This line of thinking is consistent with several contingency theories

---

[74]Dumdum, Lowe, and Avolio, "A Meta-Analysis of Transformational and Transactional Leadership Correlates of Effectiveness and Satisfaction."

[75]Judge and Piccolo, "Transformational and Transactional Leadership: A Meta-analytic Test of their Relative Validity."

[76]Kevin B. Lowe, K. Galen Kroeck, and Nagaraj Sivasubramanium, "Effectiveness Correlates of Transformational and Transactional Leadership: A Meta-Analytic Review of the MLQ Literature," *Leadership Quarterly*, 7 (1996): 385–425.

[77]Barbara Thompson and Fred C. Lunenburg, *Superintendents' Transformational and Transactional Leadership Styles, School Accountability Ratings, and School District Financial and Demographic Factors*, Paper Presented at the Annual Meeting of the American Educational Research Association, Chicago, IL, April 2003; Dana Pagani and Fred C. Lunenburg, *Principals' Transformational and Transactional Leadership Styles, School Accountability Ratings, and School District Financial and Demographic Factors*, Paper Presented at the Annual Meeting of the American Educational Research Association, Chicago, IL, April 2003.

[78]Bernard M. Bass and Bruce J. Avolio, *Full Range Leadership Development: Manual for the Multifactor Leadership Questionnaire* (Palo Alto, CA: Mindgarden, 1997).

[79]Fred C. Lunenburg, Barbara Thompson, and Dana Pagani, *Transformational Leadership: Factor Structure of the Multifactor Leadership Questionnaire*, Paper Presented at the Annual Meeting of the American Educational Research Association, Denver, CO, May 4, 2010.

[80]Caralyn P. Egri and Susan Herman, "Leadership in the North American Environmental Sector: Values, Leadership Styles, and Contexts of Environmental Leaders and Their Organizations," *Academy of Management Journal*, 43 (2000): 457–604; Badrinarayan. S. Pawar and Kenneth K. Eastman, "The Nature and Implications of Contextual Influences on Transformational Leadership: A Conceptual Examination," *Academy of Management Review*, 22 (1997): 80–109.

[81]Bulach, Lunenburg, and Potter, *Creating a Culture for High-Performing Schools*.

PRO CON DEBATE Leadership Style

The contemporary heroes of education are people like Joe Clark who revitalized an inner-city high school, Jaime Escalante who taught calculus to Hispanic youth, and Madeline Hunter who brought research to classroom teachers. These are people with common characteristics: a vision and the perseverance to actualize it. Their styles of interaction with others as they pursue their visions are relatively constant although different.

Question: Is a person's leadership style really important?

Arguments PRO

1. Leaders have followers. The ways leaders work with their followers is important. In the worst possible scenario, followers rebel or withdraw, and the leader's vision remains a dream.
2. An understanding of leadership style and the ability to flex one's style are important for school administrators. The context of administration changes, and situations differ. Able leaders are always open to new ways of thinking about how to work better with people in a variety of situations.
3. Researchers investigating leadership style have identified several models that practicing administrators find useful. The value of this work is evident: Journal articles on the topic are widely read; conference sessions on leadership style are well attended; and books on leadership are on nonfiction best-seller lists.
4. Principals and superintendents lose their jobs because their styles are incompatible with the values and/or norms of organizations. When the loss of high-visibility leaders is analyzed in the popular press, leadership style invariably surfaces as the problem.

Arguments CON

1. Style is a means to achieve an end. Time spent thinking about style is better invested in the development of good substantial ideas. People will follow leaders with good ideas.
2. School administrators are identified because they have effective styles of working with people to accomplish organizational goals. In most instances, their styles remain the same over their careers.
3. The research on leadership style has not made the impact on education that other areas of inquiry have made. Research and development funds are better spent on areas such as effective schools where the impact is clear or ethics where the impact is needed.
4. There is an old adage about success in administration: the right person in the right job at the right time. As contexts change, career administrators change their jobs but not their styles.

of leadership, which propose that individuals must modify their behavior to fit the situation or find a situation that fits their leadership style.[82] Clearly, studying transformational leadership in turbulent environments might lead to a better understanding of idealized influence, or charisma.

[82]Martin G. Evans, "The Effects of Supervisory Behavior on the Path-Goal Relationship," *Organizational Behavior and Human Performance*, 5 (1970): 277–298; Fred E. Fiedler and Martin M. Chemers, Improving Leadership Effectiveness: The Leader Match Concept, 2nd ed. (New York: Wiley, 1884); Robert J. House, "A Path-Goal Theory of Leadership Effectiveness: *Administrative Science Quarterly*, 16 (1971): 321–339); Beverly J. Irby, Genevieve Brown, Jo Ann Duffy, and Diane Trautmenn, "The Synergistic Leadership Theory," *Journal of Educational Administration*, 40 (2002): 304–322.

However, the other three dimensions of transformational leadership (inspirational motivation, intellectual stimulation, and individualized consideration) may be very important in achieving leader effectiveness. This approach would be in agreement with Bennis and Nanus,[83] who studied 90 innovative leaders in industry and the public sector and found that articulating a vision of the future, emphasis on organizational and individual learning, and the development of commitment and trust were the factors that characterized transformational leaders. These results are consistent with the three public school studies reported earlier. Similarly, Yukl[84] describes

[83]Warren G. Bennis and Burt Nanus, *Leaders: The Strategies for Taking Charge* (New York: HarperCollins, 2007).

[84]Yukl, *Leadership in Organizations.*

transformational leadership as influencing major changes in organization members and building commitment for the organization's goals. Thus, educational leaders should communicate a sense of where the organization is going, develop the skills and abilities of followers, and encourage innovative problem solving.

Summary

1. The study of leadership has a long history, dating back to Plato's *Republic* in 400 B.C. Many attempts have been made to define leadership. One definition of leadership accepted by many experts is the following: leadership is the process whereby one individual influences other group members toward the attainment of defined or organizational goals.
2. To fully understand what leadership is all about, it is important to examine the difference between leadership and management. The terms leadership and management tend to be used interchangeably. However, the two terms, although overlapping at times, are not identical and need to be clearly distinguished.
3. The scientific study of leadership began by concentrating on personal traits that distinguish leaders from non-leaders and effective leaders from ineffective ones. Researchers have identified several such traits: drive, integrity, leadership motivation, self-confidence, intelligence, task-relevant knowledge, emotional maturity, and flexibility.
4. The Big Five personality traits correlate highly with Bass and Yukl's meta-analyses of leadership traits. The Big Five model includes: surgency, agreeableness, conscientiousness, emotional stability, and intellectance.
5. Recent studies are indicating that another trait that may indicate effective leadership is emotional intelligence. Daniel Goleman's emotional intelligence dimensions include: self-motivation, persistence, impulse control, stress resistance, and empathy.
6. Another way of understanding leadership is to compare the behaviors of effective and ineffective leaders to see how successful leaders behave. The focus shifts from trying to determine what effective leaders *are* to trying to determine what effective leaders *do*. The Iowa studies, Ohio State studies, and Michigan studies identified distinct leader behaviors.
7. Efforts to discover the one best set of leader traits and the one best set of leader behaviors has its limitations. The idea that effective leadership behavior is contingent on the situation is more prevalent today. Fiedler's contingency theory, Evans and House's path-goal theory, Tannenbaum and Schmidt's leadership style continuum, Reddin's three-dimensional leadership styles, and Hersey and Blanchard's situational leadership theory has been useful in this regard.
8. Other contemporary perspectives include the synergistic leadership theory, leader-member exchange theory, reciprocal influence theory, substitutes for leadership, and transformational leadership.

Key Terms

leadership
formal leaders
informal leaders
leaders
managers
personal traits
emotional intelligence
authoritarian leadership
democratic leadership
laissez-faire leadership
initiating structure
consideration
production-centered leader
employee-centered leader
Leadership Grid
contingency theory
path-goal theory
directive leader
supportive leader
participative leader
achievement-oriented leader
three-dimensional model
situational leadership theory
synergistic leadership theory
leader-member exchange theory
reciprocal influence theory
substitutes for leadership
transactional leadership
transformational leadership

Discussion Questions

1. Evaluate your boss using Table 5–1, Comparisons between Leadership and Management. What can you conclude from the profile derived?

2. Using Table 5–2, what specific personal traits do you possess? What can you conclude from this exercise about your readiness to assume a leadership position?
3. Evaluate yourself on emotional intelligence using Table 5–3 developed by Daniel Goleman. What can you conclude about your readiness to assume a leadership role from this exercise?
4. Where do you place yourself on The Leadership Grid (Figure 5–2)? What can you conclude about your readiness to assume a leadership position from this exercise?
5. What function does the situation or context play in the use of one or another style of leadership? Discuss each one of the contingency and style theories of leadership to determine the role that situation plays in choosing an appropriate leadership style for a given situation.
6. Examine the other contemporary theories of leadership: synergistic leadership theory, leader-member exchange theory, reciprocal influence theory, substitutes for leadership, and transformational leadership. As a leader, how could you apply each of these theories in a work setting?

Suggested Readings

Collins, Jim. *Good to Great: Why Some Companies Make the Leap . . . and Others Don't* (New York: HarperCollins, 2001). Although *Good to Great* is geared more toward business, its concepts can be applied to any field. The research identified seven characteristics of companies that successfully moved from mediocrity to greatness and sustained that level of performance for fifteen years. Those characteristics included the involvement of "level 5" leaders; the importance of getting the right people "on the bus"; confronting the brutal facts as a basis for improvement; identification of what an organization does better than any other organization; the existence of a culture of discipline; and the understanding that technology is an accelerator, not a cause, of improvement. All these qualities of good-to-great companies were undergirded by what is called the flywheel concept—the idea that there is no single defining action that leads to success. Rather, the study showed that consistent, day-to-day actions aligned with the organization's basic and unifying idea—its hedgehog concept—guided it to success. With each push of the flywheel, the organization gathered momentum on its journey toward greatness.

Covey, Stephen R. *The 7 Habits of Highly Effective People: Powerful Lessons in Personal Change* (New York: Simon & Schuster, 2004). This book conveys a "principle-centered, character-based, inside-out approach to personal and interpersonal effectiveness." Covey's habits are based on principles—deep, fundamental truths that become guidelines for behavior. His discussion of behavior is almost biblical as he speaks to the importance of honesty, integrity, courage, and compassion. One of the most influential segments of his book addresses the value of a personal mission statement. He entices the reader to "begin with the end in mind" and to live life accordingly.

Freiberg, Kevin, and Jackie Freiberg. *Nuts! Southwest Airlines' Crazy Recipe for Business and Personal Success* (Belmont, CA: Thomson South-Western, 2001). As you read the book, you begin to get a sense of the learning community that exists within the company. This is built upon a system of trust, risk taking, passion for the work, and celebration of individual and team contributions. It is easy to make the connection to the work in public education in which we are engaged. For strong believers in the power of relationships in our work, this book reinforces the conviction that it is the people in the organization that make the difference.

Gladwell, Malcolm. *The Tipping Point: How Little Things Can Make a Difference* (New York: Little, Brown, 2006). Gladwell begins by introducing the concept of "The Law of the Few," or (more specifically) how social epidemics are often driven by a few exceptional people—people with unique and powerful communications skills, people with a rare set of social gifts. In his treatise on "tipping points," Gladwell identifies three specific types of exceptional people or messengers who make "The Law of the Few" work: Connectors, Mavens, and Persuaders. He also notes that in creating epidemics, the messenger is critical; it is only through outstanding messengers that an epidemic spreads. Identifying and cultivating those who are not only Mavens and Connectors but also Persuaders can be of amazing value in moving forward the agenda of a district.

Gladwell, Malcolm. *Blink: The Power of Thinking without Thinking* (New York: Little, Brown, 2007). In *Blink*, Malcolm Gladwell proposes a new name for an old concept of decision making—intuition—and provides psychological explanations for how it happens and why it often works, even in high-stakes decisions. "Blinking" occurs when a person filters out all but the most critical information related to an issue and reaches a split-second conclusion or impression, instead of applying a logical thinking process. Gladwell calls this "thin slicing": a rapid cognition process that draws upon a person's alternate consciousness and can occur as quickly as within two seconds of being confronted with a dilemma. The "blink" ability is not a gift but rather is developed through storing the associated outcomes and consequences of past experiences and then generalizing the lessons learned in a new but similar context; it is related to Thorndike's theory of transfer and is a product of *wisdom*—the synergy of education and experience.

Lencioni, Patrick M. *The Five Temptations of a CEO: A Leadership Fable* (New York: John Wiley, 1998). According to Lencioni, the secret to success comes down to resisting the following five temptations: (1) choosing status over results, (2) choosing popularity over accountability, (3) choosing certainty over clarity, (4) choosing harmony over conflict, and (5) choosing invulnerability over trust. The underlying premise of the book, which resonates throughout, is that chief executives who fail have given in to one or more of the five temptations. This concept is hard for us to accept. Knowing that these temptations are ever-present, we must be willing to engage in ongoing behavioral self-examination. If life at the top of an organization is to be productive, we must be true to ourselves, morally and ethically.

Phillips, Donald T. *Lincoln on Leadership: Executive Strategies for Tough Times* (New York: Warner Books, 2001). Phillips has compiled an impressive body of research, quotations, and stories that serve as parables for how a person can provide truly great leadership. He examines leadership through Abraham Lincoln's interactions, both oral and written, as an aspiring country attorney, a senate candidate, and ultimately president and commander in chief during the Civil War. "Lincoln Principles" appear at the end of each chapter, serving as practical tips to be used by leaders at all levels. Leadership attributes are divided into four broad categories: people, character, endeavor, and communication. Within each category, Phillips provides several chapters that explore "modern management theory," which (in his opinion) Lincoln mastered long ago. The discussion includes management by walking around, alliance building, use of persuasion, need for integrity in all dealings, and the power of a clear and well-communicated vision.

6

Decision Making

FOCUSING QUESTIONS

1 Why is decision making such an important activity for school administrators?
2 What types of decisions do school administrators make?
3 How are decisions made?
4 Why is it virtually impossible for school administrators to make optimum decisions?
5 How can decision-making models help school administrators improve their decisions?
6 What are the benefits of group decision making?
7 What are some problems with group decision making?
8 What are some decision-making techniques that can be used to improve decision making?

In this chapter, we attempt to answer these questions concerning decision making in school organizations. We begin our discussion by exploring the nature of decision making. Then we discuss the types of decisions school administrators make. We examine two important models of decision making: the rational model and the bounded rationality model. Next, we discuss the benefits of group decision making. This is followed by a discussion of some problems with group decision making. We conclude the chapter by examining some group decision-making techniques that can be used to improve decision making.

The Nature of Decision Making

Decision making, universally defined as the process of choosing from among alternatives, is important to an understanding of educational administration because choice processes play a key role in motivation, leadership, communication, and organizational change. Decision making pervades all other administrative functions as well. Planning, organizing, staffing, directing, coordinating, and controlling all involve decision making.

School administrators at all levels make decisions. These decisions may ultimately influence the school's clients—the students. All decisions, however, have some influence, whether large or small, on the performance of both faculty and students. Therefore, school administrators must develop decision-making skills because they make many decisions that will affect the organization. Furthermore, because school administrators are evaluated on the results of their decisions, the quality of the decisions is one criterion in judging administrators' effectiveness. Consider the following scenarios:

1. You are the principal of a small, rural high school, and it is one week away from the beginning of the state basketball tournament. The basketball team has a record of 20–0 for the season and is the favorite to win the Class A State Championship. You have just caught the star player of the basketball team, an all-state candidate, drinking an alcoholic beverage at a local restaurant. This is the player's second offense. According to board of education policy, a second offense carries a penalty of a four-week suspension from the team. The policy has not been consistently enforced by the various athletic coaches.
2. You are the assistant superintendent for business of a large, urban school district. The district operates its budgetary procedures on a variation of program planning budgeting systems (PPBS). There is a $200,000 surplus in this year's research and development account that you must spend before the end of the fiscal year. Three program priorities for the current school year are expansion of the vocational education facilities and curriculum, initiation of a new special education curriculum for the hearing impaired, and a districtwide remediation program for students who fall below the national average on the state-administered standardized tests in the basic skills.
3. You are the superintendent of a wealthy, suburban school district. Student enrollment, increased by 20 percent during the past five years, has occurred primarily in grades 1–5. The current facilities of the school district can no longer accommodate the increased student population. The board of education has discussed several options: Merge with an adjacent urban school district, which has experienced a decline in enrollment; change the grade structure in the district from (K–5, 6–8, 9–12) to (K–4, 5–8, 9–12); build another elementary school; go on double sessions in the elementary schools; or rent one of the buildings from the nearby parochial school.

School administrators at different hierarchical levels and career stages face these problems or variations thereof every day. The elements of each problem differ—for example, athletic disciplinary action, allocation of funds from the research and development unit, and expansion of school facilities. Nevertheless, there is similarity among the scenarios; all require that a decision be made. The quality of the decision reached not only will have an impact on the school's clients but also will determine the school administrator's perceived value to the school district.

Types of Decisions

Routine and nonroutine problems in the modern school call for different types of decisions. Routine problems arise on a regular basis and can be addressed through standard operating procedures, called **programmed decisions.** These decisions simply trigger solutions that have already been determined by past experience as appropriate for the problem in question. Examples of programmed decisions include: periodic reordering of inventory; maintaining a necessary grade point average for academic standing; and disciplining a student who violates the school district's no tolerance policy of bringing a weapon to school.

Nonroutine problems are novel and unstructured. There is no established procedure for handling the problem, either because it involves issues that have never been encountered before or because it is complex or extremely important. Such decisions are called **nonprogrammed decisions** and deserve special treatment. Examples of nonprogrammed decisions include: construction of a new school or classroom facilities; consolidation of two school districts; and the purchase of experimental equipment.

Certain types of nonprogrammed decisions are known as **strategic decisions.**[1] These decisions are typically made by committees of upper-level administrators (school superintendents, college presidents) and have important long-term implications for the organization. Strategic decisions reflect a consistent pattern for directing the organization according to an underlying organizational philosophy or mission. For example,

[1]David J. Hunger, *Essentials of Strategic Management* (Upper Saddle River, NJ: Prentice Hall, 2011).

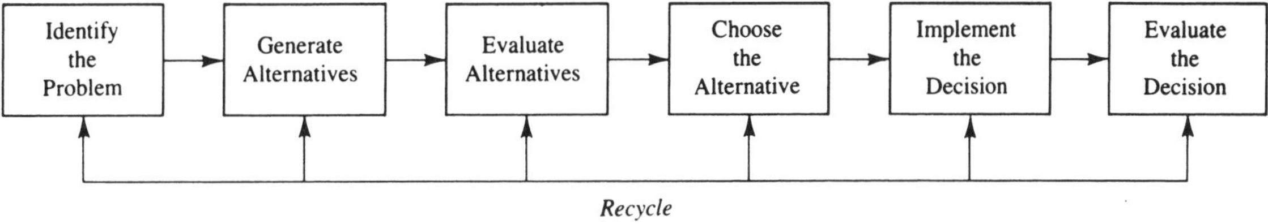

FIGURE 6–1

The Decision-Making Process

a university may make a strategic decision to grow in enrollment at a specified annual rate, or be guided by a certain code of ethics. Both decisions may be considered "strategic" because they guide the future direction of the organization. Some examples of strategic decisions include: the initiation of on line courses; distance learning; the creation of school and department web pages; installation of electronic schedules of events (marquees) placed in front of the school; the introduction of electronic meeting systems. Another successful strategic decision that has had national impact was the launching of Amazon.com in 1994. It provided university students with the opportunity to purchase textbooks through the internet quickly and at a reduced price.

Generally, top-level administrators (school superintendents, university presidents) typically are concerned with nonprogrammed decisions, while middle-level administrators (principals, college deans) and first-level administrators (department heads) in most organizations are concerned with programmed decisions, although in some cases they will participate in nonprogrammed decisions as well. In other words, the nature, frequency, and degree of certainty surrounding a problem usually dictates at what level of administration the decision should be made. Regardless of the type of decision made, it is important to understand how individuals and groups make decisions.

How Are Decisions Made?

Now that we have identified the types of decisions administrators make in organizations, we will now consider the matter of how people go about making decisions. Scientists have considered several different approaches to how individuals make decisions. Here, we will discuss two of the most important models of decision making: the rational model and the bounded rationality model.[2]

[2]James G. March, *Primer on Decision Making: How Decisions Happen* (New York: Simon & Schuster, 2010).

The Rational Model

The **rational model** of decision making assumes that decision making is a rational process whereby decision makers seek to maximize the chances of achieving their desired objectives by considering all possible alternatives, exploring all conceivable consequences from among the alternatives, and then making a decision. The rational model of decision making is based on the concept of complete **rationality**. According to the rational model, the decision-making process can be broken down into six steps: identifying the problems, generating alternatives, evaluating alternatives, choosing an alternative, implementing the decision, and evaluating the decision (see Figure 6–1).

Identifying the Problem The first step in the decision-making process is **identifying the problem.** If there is no problem, there is no need to make a decision. A warning of a possible problem is a discrepancy between existing and desired conditions. For example, if a school district establishes an objective that 70 percent of the students will be reading on grade level and if only 30 percent of students are reading on grade level at the end of the period, there is a gap between actual performance and the desired level of achievement. If the student dropout rate increases 25 percent over the preceding year, if students and parents file numerous complaints about the schools, if faculty grievances significantly increase, if new book and classroom supply deliveries are twelve months past due, and if the local newspaper runs a series of articles about deficiencies in school district operations, there are problems that require decisions.

Identifying problems is more difficult than one might suspect. One writer proposes four steps in problem identification: measure results, compare results to objectives, determine the significance of the difference, and communicate threshold differences to administration.[3]

[3]Scott G. Isaksen, *Creative Approaches to Problem Solving: A Framework for Innovation and Change* (Thousand Oaks, CA: Sage, 2011).

Another acknowledges similar steps in problem formulation: An administrator (1) must be alert to recognize a problem, (2) must determine a level of performance so that actual performance can be measured against it, (3) must divide complex problems into sub-problems and set priorities based on the seriousness of the problem, and (4) must specify the problem in terms of what, where, when, and how big the deviations are from the performance standards previously set.[4]

Generating Alternatives After identifying and defining the problem, the school administrator should **generate** but not evaluate a list of **alternatives**. That is, all possible alternatives should be included no matter how ridiculous they may first appear; a choice will be made later. Eliminating alternatives from the list too early decreases the options for the best solution. The administrator must then seek information regarding each alternative and its various consequences that will contribute to solving the problem.

Evaluating Alternatives In **evaluating alternatives**, an additional search for information should be done. Three steps are recommended in the process.[5]

1. The decision maker must recognize all possible outcomes from each alternative solution, both positive and negative.
2. The decision maker must assess the value of each outcome, both positive and negative.
3. The decision maker must assess the likelihood of each possible outcome to each alternative.

Estimating the likelihood of each outcome prepares the decision maker to evaluate and compare alternatives, which is done under one of three conditions: certainty, risk, or uncertainty. These conditions force the school administrator into the area of quantitative decision making. An in-depth quantitative analysis of alternatives and their outcomes is beyond the scope of this book. However, we give a brief definition of each term to clarify the process.

Certainty exists when the decision maker knows exactly what the probabilities of the outcome of each alternative will be. Thus, he must estimate the probabilities of the occurrence of the various outcomes.[6] *Risk* exists when the decision maker estimates the probabilities of the outcome of each alternative and determines that success is not 100 percent assured. Thus, predictions can be made, but risk is associated with the various alternatives.[7] *Uncertainty* exists when the decision maker does not know what the probabilities of the outcome of each alternative will be; that is, the likelihood of success or failure associated with alternatives is not clear.[8] In working through the three conditions of certainty, risk, and uncertainty, the decision maker should rank all alternatives from best to worst according to their likelihood of providing the greatest payoffs to the school district.

Choosing an Alternative The next step in the decision-making process involves **choosing an alternative** that the school administrator considers most effective, that is, the one that allows the administrator to solve the problem and accomplish the school district's objectives. The choice can be difficult even when outcomes have been evaluated based on some comparable criteria. James March, a leading decision theorist, has proposed five types of alternatives:[9]

1. A *good alternative* has a high probability of positively valued outcomes and a low probability of negatively valued outcomes.
2. A *bland alternative* has a low probability of both positively and negatively valued outcomes.
3. A *mixed alternative* has a high probability of both positively and negatively valued outcomes.
4. A *poor alternative* has a low probability of positively valued outcomes and a high probability of negatively valued outcomes.
5. An *uncertain alternative* is one for which the decision maker cannot assess the relative probabilities of outcomes. (This alternative was discussed earlier.)

Some combinations of these types of alternatives will result in more difficult choices than will other combinations. Consider a school administrator who is faced with two alternatives. If one alternative is good and the other is bland, mixed, poor, or uncertain, then choosing an alternative is easy. Now consider the choice between

---

[4]Alan H. Schoenfeld, *A Theory of Goal-Oriented Decision Making and Its Educational Implications* (New York: Routledge, 2011).

[5]Franz Eisenfuhr, *Decision Making* (New York: Springer, 2011).

[6]Craig Friedman, *Decision-Theoretic Methods for Learning Probabilistic Models* (Boca Raton, FL: CRC Press, 2011).

[7]Ibid.

[8]Ibid.

[9]March, *Primer on Decision Making*.

any other combination of two alternatives, excluding the good alternative. It is difficult to choose between a bland and a mixed alternative, a bland and a poor alternative, and so on.

For instance, consider the decision of an athletic director of a major university to hire an interim basketball coach to complete the season because the existing coach suddenly died just prior to the opening of the season. One alternative (uncertain) is to hire a former high school basketball coach with an outstanding record but no experience at the college level. Thus, the coach is virtually untested at the university level. Another alternative (poor) is to hire a mediocre coach from a nearby small college or junior college. A third alternative (mixed) is to hire an outstanding coach who won several NCAA championships but who was fired by his school administration for manifesting erratic and irrational behavior during games and for striking a player. While one would expect a good season, there is also the chance of alienating the school administration and a repeat of the irrational behavior and player abuse. The final alternative (bland) is to select one of the assistant coaches to assume the head coaching position. Though skilled in other areas, neither assistant coach possesses the technical court skills nor the personality to motivate players. Such a decision is likely to produce an average season in terms of record and relations with the school's administration and players.

Implementing the Decision Once a decision is made to choose a solution, it must be **implemented.** The decision maker will have already considered all conceivable problems that may be associated with the implementation of the solution during the previous step in the decision-making process. However, in school organizations, administrators depend on others to implement decisions, so they must have skills not only for problem solving but also for "selling" the decision to those affected by it.[10]

Evaluating the Decision The decision-making process does not end when the decision is implemented. The school administrator must **evaluate the decision**—that is, determine the extent to which the solution achieved the school district's objectives. Measuring actual performance against performance specified in the objectives is one way of evaluating success. If a discrepancy exists between actual and expected results, then the decision-making process must be recycled. Changes in the alternative chosen, how it was implemented, or the determination of objectives are necessary.

For example, it is possible that the objectives established are unrealistic and that no reasonable alternative could result in a successful decision. Such a situation stresses the importance of determining measurable objectives. Unless specific objectives are set, mutually agreed on, and met at all levels of operation, there will be relatively little value or basis for measuring the effectiveness of the school district's decisions.

The Bounded Rationality Model

The rational decision-making model, discussed earlier, characterizes the decision maker as completely rational. More specifically, he is assumed to (1) recognize all possible alternative solutions to the problem, (2) be aware of all possible consequences of each alternative, (3) be able to evaluate the consequences against his value system, (4) be able to rank the alternatives in the order in which they are likely to meet his objectives, and (5) select the alternative that maximizes his objectives. The rational model assumes that the decision maker has perfect information (i.e., is aware of a problem, knows all alternatives and their possible consequences, and possesses a criterion for making the decision) and seeks to maximize some expected objective.

Frequently, school administrators are not aware that problems exist. Even when they are, they do not systematically search for all possible alternative solutions. They are limited by time constraints, cost, and the ability to process information. So they generate a partial list of alternative solutions to the problem based on their experience, intuition, advice from others, and perhaps even some creative thought. Rationality is, therefore, limited. Herbert Simon coined the term **bounded rationality** to describe the perspective of the decision maker who would like to make the best decisions but normally settles for less than the optimal. Simon won the Nobel Prize in 1978 for his bounded rationality theory.[11]

The bounded rationality model, also referred to as the administrative model, explains how people *actually* make decisions in organizations.[12] The model has five assumptions:

1. Decisions will always be based on an incomplete and, to some degree, inadequate comprehension of the true nature of the problem being faced.

---

[10]Gerald Corey, *Group Techniques* (Belmont, CA: Brooks/Cole, 2011).

[11]Herbert A. Simon, *Economics, Bounded Rationality and the Cognitive Revolution* (Northampton, MA: Edward Elgar Publishing, 2009).

[12]Helle Nielsen, *Bounded Rationality in Decision Making* (Dobbs Ferry, NY: Manchester University Press, 2011).

EXEMPLARY EDUCATIONAL ADMINISTRATORS IN ACTION

PASCAL D. FORGIONE, JR., Ph.D., Superintendent, Austin Independent School District, Austin, Texas, and Adjunct Professor, Department of Educational Administration, College of Education, University of Texas at Austin.

Words of Advice: One of the greatest inventions of American democracy is the American public school. Today, we must recommit ourselves to the efficacy and centrality of its mission and recruit a new generation of skillful and dedicated leaders who can build the education systems that will produce positive academic success for all students and manage the complex urban systems with efficiency and effectiveness.

2. Decision makers will never succeed in generating all possible alternative solutions for consideration.
3. Alternatives are always evaluated incompletely because it is impossible to predict accurately all consequences associated with each alternative.
4. The ultimate decision regarding which alternative to choose must be based on some criterion other than maximization or optimization because it is impossible ever to determine which alternative is optimal.
5. Conflicting goals of different stakeholders (e.g., students, teachers and support staff, administrators, parents, community members, and school board) can restrict decisions, forcing a compromising solution.

Satisficing One version of bounded rationality is the principle of **satisficing.** This approach to decision making involves choosing the first alternative that satisfies minimal standards of acceptability without exploring all possibilities. This is the usual approach taken by decision makers. Simon expresses it this way: most human decision making, whether individual or organizational, is concerned with the discovery and selection of satisfactory alternatives; only in exceptional cases is it concerned with the discovery and selection of optimal alternatives.[13]

A practical example of satisficing is finding a radio station to listen to in your car. You cannot optimize because it is impossible to listen to all the stations simultaneously. Thus, you stop searching for a station when you find one playing a song you like. Another example of satisficing frequently occurs in schools when hiring personnel. Schools begin by listing criteria that an acceptable candidate should meet (such as having an appropriate degree from an accredited college or university, job-related experience, and good references). Then the school will select a candidate who meets the criteria. If schools were to make the optimal hiring decision rather than a satisfactory one, they would have to select the best candidate—the person with the best educational background, prior experience, and references. It would be virtually impossible to do this. The best person may not have applied for the position, so you select a satisfactory candidate from among those who applied for the position.

[13]Simon, Economics, *Bounded Rationality and the Cognitive Revolution.*

Contextual Rationality and Procedural Rationality

Simon later proposed two other forms of bounded rationality: contextual rationality and procedural rationality. Contextual rationality suggests that a decision maker is embedded in a network of environmental influences that constrain purely rational decision making.[14] Although the school administrator wants to make optimal decisions, these are mediated by such realities of organizational life as internal and external politics, conflict resolution requirements, distribution of power and authority, and limits of human rationality. Furthermore, schools have vague and ambiguous goals. This, coupled with the lack of a clearly defined success criterion, leads to policies and procedures designed to maintain stability and control, and the objectives of the school as a social institution are to achieve major changes in the student. These changes are not restricted to cognitive behavior (learning), but include a wide range of social, emotional, physical, and, in some cases, moral behavior. Thus, school administrators must pursue multiple and often conflicting goals, within a network of environmental constraints, that restrict the maximization of goal achievement.[15]

[14]Ibid.

[15]Fred C. Lunenburg, "The Post-Behavioral Science Era: Excellence, Community, and Justice," in F.C. Lunenburg and C. S. Carr (eds.), *Shaping the Future: Policy, Partnerships, and Emerging Perspectives* (Lanham, MD: Rowman & Littlefield, 2003), pp. 36–55.

We noted that bounded rationality, satisficing, and contextual rationality limit perfectly rational decision making. This results in the inability of decision makers to "maximize" outcomes. What, then, can school administrators do to improve their decisions in view of the constraints on complete rationality implied by the classical decision-making model? Simon proposes the principle of **procedural rationality**. Instead of focusing on generating and evaluating all possible **alternative solutions** to a problem and their consequences, decision makers focus on the procedures used in making decisions. Thus, techniques are perfected and used to make the best possible decisions, including operations research, systems analysis, strategic planning, program planning budgeting systems (PPBS), management information systems (MIS), and so on, each prescribed to improve the reliability of decisions. Rational procedures are not designed to focus on generating and evaluating all available information to solve problems, but they are aimed at adequate acquisition and processing of relevant information.

Intuition Throughout most of the twentieth century, social scientists believed that administrators' use of intuition was ineffective. That is no longer the case. There is growing evidence that administrators use their intuition to make decisions.[16] Henry Mintzberg, in his study of the nature of managerial work, found that in many instances executives do not appear to use a rational systematic, step-by-step approach to decision making. Rather, Mintzberg argued that executives make decisions based on "hunches."[17]

Gary Klein, a renowned cognitive psychologist, writes in his book *The Power of Intuition*, that skilled decision makers rely on deeply held patterns of learned experience in making quick and efficient decisions.[18] According to Klein, these deeply held patterns of learned experience (templates) represent tacit knowledge that has been implicitly acquired over time. When a template fits or does not fit the current situation, emotions are produced that motivate us to act.

Lee Iacocca, who saved Chrysler from bankruptcy in the 1980s and brought it to profitability, writes in his autobiography: "To a certain extent, I've always operated by gut feelings."[19] Other researchers have found that intuition was used extensively as a mechanism to evaluate decisions made more rationally.[20]

Intuition has been described variously as follows:[21]

- The ability to know when a problem exists and to select the best course of action quickly without conscious reasoning
- The smooth automatic performance of deeply held patterns of learned experience
- Reliance on mental models—internal representations of the external environment that allow us to anticipate future events from current observations.

These definitions share several common assumptions. First, there seems to be an indication that intuition is fast. Second, intuition is an automatic unconscious analytic process. Third, there seems to be agreement that intuition is based on experience and usually engages emotions. Fourth, intuition offers potential for creativity and innovation.

When relying on intuition, the school administrator arrives at a decision without using a rational step-by-step logical process. The fact that experience contributes to intuition means that school administrators can learn to become more intuitive in solving many difficult problems. Furthermore, intuition does not necessarily operate in opposition to rational decision making. Rather, the two can complement each other. School administrators should attempt to use both when making decisions. For example, rational decision making can be used to verify intuition.

Incrementalizing Another approach to decision making, sometimes referred to as "muddling through," involves making small changes (increments) in the existing situation. Charles Lindblom, its author, distinguishes between completely rational decision making based on the

[16]Martin Heidegger, *Phenomenology of Intuition and Expression* (New York: Continuum International Publishing Group, 2011); Bartoli Ruelas, *Psychology of Intuition* (New York: Nova Science Publishers, 2011).

[17]Henry Mintzberg, *The Nature of Managerial Work* (Reading, MA: Addison-Wesley, 1998); see also Mintzberg, *Strategy Safari: A Guided Tour through the Wilds of Strategic Management* (New York: Simon & Schuster, 2011).

[18]Gary Klein, *The Power of Intuition: How to Use Your Gut Feelings to Make Better Decisions at Work* (New York: Knopf Doubleday, 2005).

[19]Lee Iacocca, Iacocca: An Autobiography (Darby, PA: DIANA Publishing Company, 1999); see also Iacocca, *Where Have All the Leaders Gone?* (New York: Simon & Schuster, 2009).

[20]Matthias Ehrgott, *Trends in Multiple Criteria Decision Analysis* (New York: Springer, 2011); Jerry Mendel, *Perceptual Computing: Aiding People in Making Subjective Decisions* (New York: Wiley, 2011); Constantin Zopounidis, *Multiple Criteria Decision Aiding* (New York: Nova Science Publishers, 2011).

[21]Klein, *The Power of Intuition*.

rational model and **incrementalizing**, which is based on successive limited comparisons.[22] The rational approach to decision making involves determining objectives, considering all possible alternative solutions, exploring all conceivable consequences of the alternative solutions, and finally choosing the optimal alternative solution that will maximize the achievement of the agreed-on objectives. Incrementalizing, on the other hand, does not require agreement on objectives, an exhaustive search of all possible alternatives and their consequences, or selection of the optimal alternative. Instead, Lindblom argues that no more than small or incremental steps—no more than muddling through—is ordinarily possible. In other words, incrementalizing is a process of successive limited comparisons of alternative courses of action with one another until decision makers arrive at an alternative on which they agree.

The Garbage Can Model Earlier we noted that while the school administrator wants to make optimal decisions, the realities of organizational life—including politics, time constraints, finances, and the inability to process information—limit purely rational decision making. Applying the rational decision-making model is particularly troublesome for schools. The technologies of teaching are varied and not well understood. Moreover, schools have multiple and conflicting goals that are vague and ambiguous. And schools lack clearly defined success criteria. Thus, problems and solutions cannot be translated easily into a logical sequence of steps (rational decision-making model).[23] In accordance with this view, David Cohen and his associates conceptualized this decision making process as a **garbage can model.**[24] As members of a school or school district generate problems and alternative solutions to problems, they deposit them into the garbage can. The mixture is seen as a collection of solutions that must be matched to problems. Participants are also deposited into the garbage can. Mixing problems, solutions, and decision participants results in interaction patterns leading to decisions that often do not follow the rational decision-making model sequence.

[22]Charles E. Lindblom, *The Science of "Muddling Through"* (New York: Irvington, 1993).

[23]Fred C. Lunenburg, "Improving Student Achievement: Some Structural Incompatibilities," in G. Perreoult and F. C. Lunenburg (eds.), *The Changing World of School Administration* (Lanham, MD: Scarecrow Press, 2002), pp. 5–27.

[24]David M. Cohen, James G. March, and Johan D. Olsen, "A Garbage Can Model of Organizational Choice," *Administrative Science Quarterly*, 17 (1972): 1–25.

A number of studies in educational administration have specified and tested comparative models of decision making, using the rational and bounded rationality models as one of several. For example, one study found that high schools were more likely to resemble the bounded rationality model than were elementary schools, which more closely resembled the rational model.[25] According to the researchers, because high schools were typically departmentalized and had more diverse goals, they could be characterized as more loosely coupled than elementary schools.

Several other studies address some of the assumptions of bounded rationality. Research on administrative behavior in schools is consistent in identifying the demands on the administrator as fragmented, rapid fire, and difficult to prioritize.[26] For example, one study noted that the fragmented and unpredictable workday of principals was not conducive to rational decision making.[27]

Road Map to Decision Making: The Decision Tree

Victor Vroom and Philip Yetton have devised a sophisticated model of decision making that involves a clear statement of what the decision maker is supposed to accomplish: (1) decision quality, (2) decision acceptance, and (3) timeliness.[28] The model first identifies five decision-making styles. Second, it identifies criteria for choosing among the decision-making styles. Third, it describes attributes of decision problems that determine which levels of subordinate participation are feasible. Finally, it offers the school administrator rules for making the final choice from among an array of feasible alternatives.

Decision Effectiveness As noted, three critical aspects influence overall effectiveness, or **decision feasibility:** quality, acceptance, and timeliness.

[25]William A. Firestone and Robert E. Herriott, "Images of Organization and the Promotion of Change," in R.G. Corwin (ed.), *Research in Sociology of Education and Socialization*, vol. 2 (Greenwich, CT: JAI Press, 1981), pp. 221–260.

[26]Fred C. Lunenburg and Beverly J. Irby, *The Principalship: Vision to Action* (Belmont, CA: Wadsworth/Cengage, 2006).

[27]Fred C. Lunenburg and Lynn Columba, "The 16PF as a Predictor of Principal Performance: An Integration of Quantitative and Qualitative Research Methods," *Education*, 113 (1992): 68–73.

[28]Victor H. Vroom and Philip W. Yetton, *Leadership and Decision Making* (Pittsburgh: University of Pittsburgh Press, 1973).

Decision Quality Decision quality refers to the extent to which a decision is effective. Different problems have different quality requirements. For example, decisions such as a technique to evaluate teacher competence, the assignment of teachers to specific tasks, the selection of textbooks and other instructional materials, and the development of policies and procedures for operating a school require high decision quality. Conversely, a decision on what brand of milk to place in the school cafeteria or which teacher to put on a school committee when all are equally qualified requires low decision quality. Generally, when decision quality is important and subordinates have the expertise to make the decision, a participatory decision-making style leads to more effective decisions than does a more autocratic style.

Decision Acceptance Decision acceptance refers to the extent to which decisions are accepted by those subordinates who must implement them. Even if a leader's decision is high in decision quality, the decision will not be effective if it is not implemented. Thus, school administrators need to consider acceptance just as important as quality in arriving at effective decisions. Research demonstrates that subordinate involvement in decision making is advantageous for arriving at better-quality decisions and for promoting acceptance. House's path-goal model (see Chapter 5) also shows that if subordinates have influence in decision making, they tend to perceive decisions as their own and are motivated to implement them successfully.

Timeliness Timeliness refers to the amount of time available to the decision maker to arrive at a decision. Participatory decision making is very costly in terms of time. If time is an important factor, the leader may need to choose a more autocratic leadership style. If, however, a long-term development of the skills and competencies of the group is the most important criterion, then choosing a more participative style may be more productive.

Decision-Making Styles Vroom and Yetton identify and describe five alternative decision-making styles that can be placed on a continuum from highly autocratic to highly participatory (see Table 6–1). The styles labeled A are basically autocratic, those labeled C are consultative, and those labeled G are group styles. Roman

Table 6-1 Five Decision-Making Styles of the Vroom-Yetton Model

Style	Method
Autocratic	
AI	Solve the problem or make the decision yourself using the information available to you at the present time.
AII	Obtain any necessary information from subordinates, then decide on a solution to the problem yourself. You may or may not tell subordinates the purpose of your questions or give information about the problem or decision on which you are working. The input provided by them is clearly in response to your request for specific information. They do not play a role in the definition of the problem or in generating or evaluating alternative solutions.
Consultative	
CI	Share the problem with the relevant subordinates individually, getting their ideas and suggestions without bringing them together as a group. Then *you* make the decision. This decision may or may not reflect your subordinates' influence.
CII	Share the problem with your subordinates in a group meeting where you obtain their ideas and suggestions. Then, *you* make the decision, which may or may not reflect your subordinates' influence.
Group	
GII	Share the problem with your subordinates as a group. Together you generate and evaluate alternatives and attempt to reach agreement (consensus) on a solution. Your role is much like that of chairman, coordinating the discussion, keeping it focused on the problem, and ensuring that the critical issues are discussed. You can provide the group with information or ideas that you have but you do not try to press them to adopt your solution and are willing to accept and implement any solution that has the support of the entire group.

Source: Adapted and reprinted from Victor H. Vroom and Philip W. Yetton, *Leadership and Decision Making,* by permission of the University of Pittsburgh Press. © 1973, The University of Pittsburgh Press.

numerals identify variants of each style. As you study each style in Table 6–1, try to determine which of these styles you used in a given situation. Test this by thinking of leadership situations you have encountered on your job and see if you can classify your styles in terms of the Vroom-Yetton taxonomy.

Choosing the Correct Decision-Making Style

According to Vroom and Yetton, one leader can use all five styles as listed in Table 6–1, depending on the situation. As a decision maker, the leader may be autocratic in one situation and participatory in the next. Thus, different types of situations require different styles. The key to effective administration is the ability to correctly diagnose the situation and then choose an appropriate decision-making style.

The Vroom-Yetton normative model contains a set of seven diagnostic questions that an administrator can use in determining which decision-making style to choose in any given situation. These diagnostic questions are based on a set of seven rules aimed at simplifying the selection of the appropriate decision-making style. The first three rules focus on the quality of the decision, and the remaining four deal with decision acceptance (see Table 6–2).

Vroom and Yetton use a decision tree to relate the seven diagnostic questions, listed at the bottom of the decision tree, to the appropriate decision-making style (see Figure 6–2). Starting at the left, the administrator answers each question along the path. At the end of each path is a list of acceptable decision-making styles. Some paths end with one acceptable style; others end with five acceptable styles. To be acceptable, the style must meet the criteria of the seven decision rules that protect quality and acceptance. If more than one style remains after the test of both quality and acceptance, the third most important aspect of a decision—timeliness—determines the single best style that should be used in a given situation.

Table 6–2 Rules for Decision-Making Selection

Rules to protect the quality of the decision

1. *Leader information rule.* If decision quality is important and the leader does not possess enough information or expertise to solve the problem by himself, then eliminate AI from the feasible set.
2. *Goal congruence rule.* If decision quality is important and subordinates are not likely to pursue the organization goals in their efforts to solve this problem, then eliminate GII from the feasible set.
3. *Unstructured problem rule.* In decisions in which decision quality is important, if the leader lacks the necessary information or expertise to solve the problem alone, and if the problem is unstructured, the problem-solving method should provide for interaction among subordinates likely to possess relevant information. Accordingly, eliminate AI, AII, and CI from the feasible set.

Rules to protect the quality of the decision

4. *Acceptance rule.* If decision acceptance by subordinates is critical to effective implementation and if it is not certain that an autocratic decision will be accepted, eliminate AI and AII from the feasible set.
5. *Conflict rule.* If decision acceptance is critical and if an autocratic decision is not certain to be accepted and disagreement among subordinates in methods of attaining the organizational goal is likely, the problem-solving methods should enable those in disagreement to resolve their differences with full knowledge of the problem. Accordingly, under these conditions, eliminate AI, AII, and CI, which permit no interaction among subordinates and therefore provide no opportunity for those in conflict to resolve their differences, from the feasible set. Their use runs the risk of leaving some of the subordinates with less than the needed commitment to the final decision.
6. *Fairness rule.* If decision quality is unimportant but acceptance of the decision is critical and not certain to result from an autocratic decision, the decision process must generate the needed acceptance. The decision process should permit subordinates to interact with one another and negotiate over the fair method of resolving any differences with the full responsibility on them for determining what is fair and equitable. Accordingly, under these circumstances, eliminate AI, AII, CI, and CII from the feasible set.
7. *Acceptance priority rule.* If acceptance is critical, but not certain to result from an autocratic decision, and if subordinates are motivated to pursue the organizational goals represented in the problem, then methods that provide equal partnership in the decision-making process can provide greater acceptance without risking decision quality. Accordingly, eliminate AI, AII, CI, and CII from the feasible set.

Source: Adapted and reprinted from Victor H. Vroom and Philip W. Yetton, *Leadership and Decision Making,* by permission of the University of Pittsburgh Press. © 1973, The University of Pittsburgh Press.

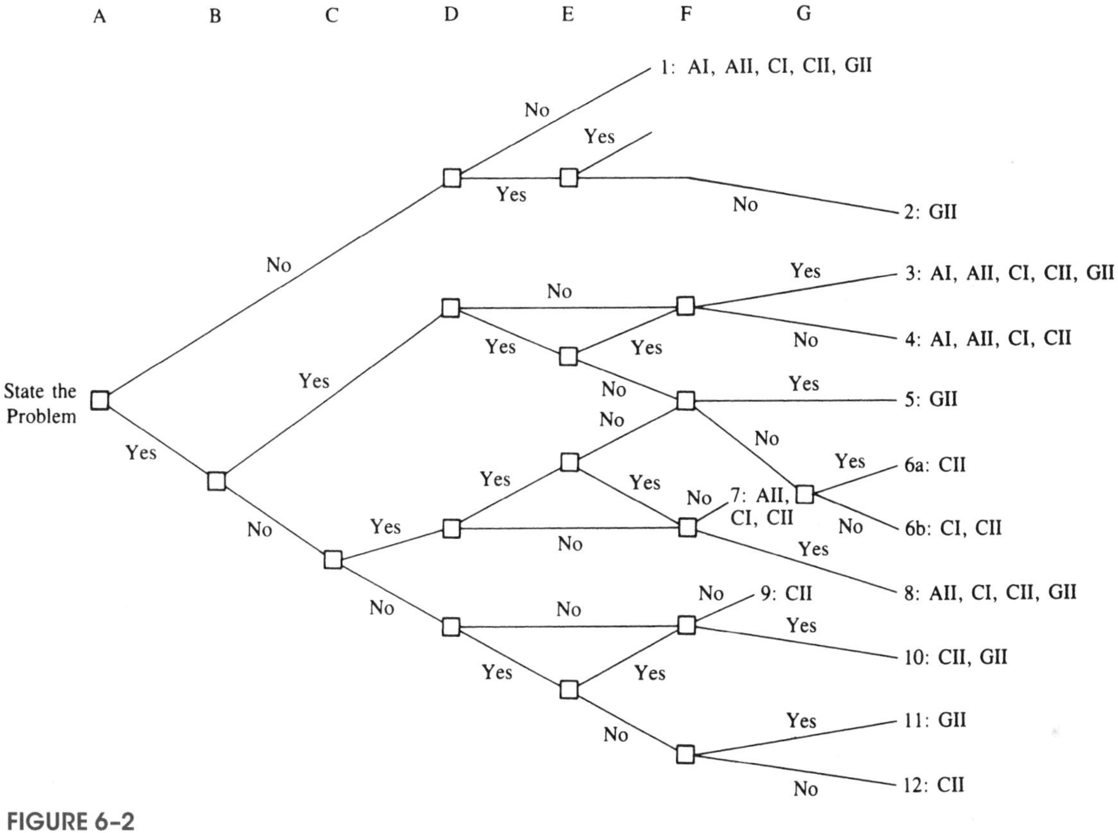

FIGURE 6–2

The Decision Tree
Source: Adapted and reprinted from Victor H. Vroom and Philip W. Yetton, *Leadership and Decision Making,* by permission of the University of Pittsburgh Press. © 1973, The University of Pittsburgh Press.

Benefits of Group Decision Making

Up to this point, we have been discussing decision making as an individual activity. We pictured a school administrator working at a hectic pace and making decisions under pressure with little time for reflective planning. But more often than not, a number of people participate in important decisions in schools, and they come together to solve school problems. Whether decision making involves individual or group activity, the process requires the individual or group to go through the typical decision-making steps: identifying the problem, generating alternatives, evaluating alternatives, choosing an alternative, implementing the decision, and evaluating the decision. We pointed out, however, that this description of decision making is limited by various forms of bounded rationality and thus misrepresents how decisions are actually made in school organizations.

In the group decision-making process, decisions are the product of interpersonal decision processes and group dynamics.[29] Thus, the school administrator must be concerned with leading the group from a collection of individuals to a collaborative decision-making unit. This implies that school administrators must develop group decision-making skills as well as skills in individual decision making.

---

[29]Magnus Gunnarsson, *Group Decision Making* (Frederick, MD: Verlag, 2010); see also, Gerald Corey, *Group Techniques* (Belmont, CA: Brooks/Cole, 2011).

School administrators and faculty alike spend large amounts of time participating in committees that are attempting to make decisions. Superintendents are usually chosen by boards of education. Principals are selected by committees consisting of a variety of organizational participants including administrators, teachers, students, and sometimes community members. Faculty committees usually decide on which textbooks to adopt. Formal review committees normally process curriculum modifications. These activities are intended to bring school participants into the organization's decision-making process.

It is believed that group decision making results in a number of benefits over individual decision making, including increased decision quality, creativity, acceptance, understanding, judgment, and accuracy. Experts advise school districts that a proven method to increase school effectiveness is to involve school employees in the decision-making process.[30] With these generalizations in mind, the benefits of group decision making include the following.[31]

Decision Quality. A greater sum of knowledge and information is accessible in a group than in any of its members. Members can often fill in each other's information gaps. Groups are more vigilant, can generate more ideas, and can evaluate ideas better than individuals.

Decision Creativity. Groups provide a greater number of approaches to a problem because individuals are more likely to be close minded in their thinking. Because group members do not have identical approaches, each can contribute by getting people to become more open minded in their thinking. Group participation increases performance. More participation leads to more creative thinking, which often results in more feasible solutions to problems.

Decision Acceptance. Participation in decision making increases acceptance of the decision or the solution to the problem. This idea is exemplified in the movement toward site-based decision making. Site-based decision making, however, is not viable in school districts that are highly centralized.

Decision Understanding. Group participation increases understanding of the decision. When group members have been involved in the decision-making process, further information about the decision does not have to be provided to them. Moreover, members comprehend the decision better because they were involved in the developmental stages of the decision process.

Decision Judgment. Groups are more effective at establishing objectives, identifying alternatives, and evaluating alternatives because of the increased knowledge and viewpoints available to them.

Decision Accuracy. Because group members evaluate each other's thinking, major errors, bloopers, and glitches tend to be avoided. Poor or nonfeasible alternatives are more likely to be spotted.

Do groups actually make better decisions than individuals? The discussion here suggests that they do. Reviews of research on the benefits of shared decision making, however, are inconsistent. Research related specifically to the relationship between participative decision making and decision outcomes reveals ambiguity or nonsupport for the relationship.[32] Most research in this area assumes the benefits of teacher participation as a given.[33] The benefits of group decision making are probably not directly related to decision outcomes but instead are more associated with morale and job satisfaction.[34] One review of research concludes that groups usually produce more and better solutions to problems than do individuals working alone.[35] The conclusions of the latter two works are qualified by the exact nature of the problem being solved and the composition of the group making the decision. More specifically, groups should perform better than individuals when (1) group members differ in relevant skills and abilities, as long as they don't differ so much that conflict occurs; (2) some division of labor can occur; (3) memory of facts is an

---

30Alan H. Schoenfeld, *How We Think: A Theory of Goal-Oriented Decision Making and Its Educational Applications* (New York: Routledge, 2011).

31Joseph Bonito, *Interaction and Influence in Small Group Decision Making* (New York: Routledge, 2011).

32James A. Conway, "The Myth, Mystery and Mastery of Participative Decision Making in Education," *Educational Administration Quarterly,* 20 (1984): 11–40.

33Schoenfeld, *How We Think.*

34Pascale Zarate, *Collaborative Decision Making: Perspectives and Challenges* (Amsterdam, The Netherlands: IOS Press, 2009).

35Dorothy Norris-Tirrell, *The Practice of Strategic Collaboration: From Silos to Action* (Boca Raton, FL: CRC Press, 2010).

ADMINISTRATIVE ADVICE 6–1

Premises of Group Decision Making

While group decision making (GDM) takes many forms, it emphasizes several common beliefs or premises.

- Those closest to the students and "where the action is" will make the best decisions about the students' education.
- Teachers, parents, and school staff should have more to say about policies and programs affecting their schools and children.
- Those responsible for carrying out decisions should have a voice in determining those decisions.
- Change is most likely to be effective and lasting when those who implement it feel a sense of ownership and responsibility for the process.

Source: Adapted from Lynn Balster Liontos, "Shared Decision Making," *ERIC Digest*, 87 (1994) (ED 368034), p. 1.

important issue; and (4) individual judgments can be averaged to arrive at a group position.[36]

Group decision making, seems destined to be one of the major reforms of the twenty-first century. The American Association of School Administrators and the National Education Association are pushing for adoption of GDM practices. And some states and school districts have mandated a variant of GDM called site-based decision making (SBDM). Therefore, school administrators need to learn as much as possible about SBDM. One of the first steps to success with SBDM is understanding what it is. (See Administrative Advice 6–1.)

Problems with Group Decision Making

We have pointed out the potential benefits of group decision making over individual decisions; however, the social nature of group processes can negatively affect performance. More specifically, three tendencies in particular can damage group decision processes: groupthink, risky shift, and escalation of commitment.

Groupthink

Irving Janis coined the term **groupthink**, which happens when in-group pressures lead to a deterioration in mental efficiency, poor testing of reality, and lax moral judgment.[37] It tends to occur in highly cohesive groups in which the group members' desire for consensus becomes more important than evaluating problems and solutions realistically.

Janis observed that sometimes groups of highly qualified and experienced people make very poor decisions.[38] The decision made by President John F. Kennedy and his advisers to launch the Bay of Pigs invasion of Cuba in 1960; the decision made by President Lyndon B. Johnson and his advisers between 1964 and 1967 to escalate the war in Vietnam; the decision made by President Richard M. Nixon and his advisers to cover up the Watergate break-in in 1972; the decision made by NASA in 1986 to launch the *Challenger* space shuttle (which exploded after takeoff, killing all seven crew members); the decision made by NASA in 2003 to launch the space shuttle *Columbia* (which exploded over Texas upon reentering the earth's atmosphere, killing all seven crew members)—all these decisions were influenced by groupthink.

Janis's analyses of groupthink focused primarily on political and military decisions, but the potential for groupthink in school organizations is likely as well. For example, when a group of teachers collectively decides to go on strike, the decision may be a product of groupthink.

[36]Scott G. Isaksen, *Creative Approaches to Problem Solving: A Framework for Innovation and Change* (Thousand Oaks, CA: Sage, 2011); David Jonassen, *Learning to Solve Problems: A Handbook* (New York: Routledge, 2011).

[37]Irving L. Janis, *Groupthink: Psychological Studies of Policy Decisions and Fiascoes*, 2nd ed. (Boston: Houghton Mifflin, 1982).

[38]Ibid.

Janis identified several symptoms of groupthink:[39]

Invulnerability. Most or all group members develop an illusion of invulnerability, which causes them to become overly optimistic and take extreme risks.

Rationalization. Group members collectively rationalize in order to discount warnings that might lead them to reconcile their assumptions before they recommit themselves to their past policy decisions.

Morality. Group members develop an unquestioned belief in the group's inherent morality, inclining the members to ignore ethical or moral consequences of their decisions.

Stereotyping. Group members develop stereotyped views of opposition leaders as too evil to warrant genuine attempts to negotiate or as too weak and stupid to counter whatever risky attempts are made to defeat their purposes.

Pressure. Group members apply direct pressure on any member who expresses strong arguments against any of the group's stereotypes, illusions, or commitments, making clear that this type of dissent is contrary to what is expected of all loyal members.

Self-Censorship. Group members censor themselves from any deviations from the apparent group consensus, reflecting each member's inclination to minimize the importance of his doubts and counterarguments.

Unanimity. Group members perceive a shared illusion of unanimity concerning judgments conforming to the majority view (partly resulting from self-censorship of deviations, augmented by the false assumption that silence means consent).

Mindguards. Some group members appoint themselves to protect the group from adverse information that might shatter their shared complacency about the effectiveness and morality of their decisions.

The likelihood that groupthink will emerge is greatest when: (1) the group is cohesive, (2) the group becomes insulated from qualified outsiders, and (3) the leader promotes his own favored solution.[40] In suggesting ways of avoiding groupthink, Janis hopes to reduce cohesiveness and open up decision activity in various ways. One way is to select ad hoc groups to solve problems; in this way, the members do not already belong to a cohesive group. Another approach is to have higher-level administrators set the parameters of the decision. Still another method is to assign different groups to work on the same problem.[41] And, finally, different group decision-making techniques can be used to limit the effects of groupthink and other problems inherent in shared decision making. Nine suggestions for avoiding groupthink are as follows:[42]

1. The leader of a policy-forming group should assign the role of critical evaluator to each member, encouraging the group to give high priority to airing objections and doubts.
2. The leaders in an organization's hierarchy, when assigning a policy-planning mission to a group, should be impartial instead of stating their preferences and expectations at the outset.
3. The organization should routinely follow the administrative practice of setting up several independent policy-planning and evaluation groups to work on the same policy question, each carrying out its deliberations under a different leader.
4. Through the period when the feasibility and effectiveness of policy alternatives are being surveyed, the policy-making group should from time to time divide into two or more subgroups to meet separately, under different chairpersons, and then come together to reconcile their differences.
5. Each member of the policy-making group should periodically discuss the group's deliberations with trusted associates in her own unit of the organization and report their transactions back to the group.
6. One or more outside experts or qualified colleagues within the organization who are not core members of the policy-making group should be invited to each meeting on a staggered basis and should be encouraged to challenge the views of the core members.
7. At each meeting devoted to evaluating policy alternatives, at least one member should be assigned the role of devil's advocate, expressing as many objections to each policy alternative as possible.

[39]Ibid.

[40]Ibid.

[41]Isaksen, *Creative Approaches to Problem Solving;* Jonassen, *Learning to Solve Problems.*

[42]Janis, *Groupthink.*

8. Whenever the policy issue involves relations with a rival organization, a sizable block of time should be spent surveying all warning signals from the rivals and constructing alternative scenarios of the rivals' intentions.
9. After reaching a preliminary consensus about what seems to be the best policy alternative, the policy-making group should hold a second-chance meeting at which the members are expected to express as vividly as they can all their residual doubts and to rethink the entire issue before making a definitive choice.

Risky Shift

Problem solving in groups always involves some degree of risk. One can never be certain whether a decision made in a group would be the same as a decision made by an individual. This raises an interesting question: Do groups make decisions that are more or less risky than individual decisions? Or is a group decision simply the average of the individuals in the group?

In the 1960s, James Stoner initiated research on the amount of risk taken by groups in making decisions. Stoner tested the hypothesis that group decisions would be more cautious than individual decisions. He compared individual and group decisions using a series of hypothetical cases developed to measure an individual's propensity for risk taking. The alternative choices provided in each case ranged from relatively cautious with moderate payoffs to relatively risky with higher payoffs. For example, situations ranged from a football team playing cautiously for a tie or riskily for a win to a graduate student choosing to pursue a Ph.D. degree in chemistry at one of two universities. Contrary to Stoner's prediction, the group decisions were consistently riskier than individual decisions.[43] This finding has been called the **risky shift** in group decision making.

Several explanations have been proposed for this risky shift phenomenon:

- Making a decision in a group produces a diffusion of responsibility. Because no single person is held accountable for a bad decision, the group takes greater risks. Blame for a bad decision can then be shared with others; in fact, individuals may shift the blame entirely to others.
- Leaders of groups are greater risk takers than other members and so are more likely to persuade others to become more risky.
- Group discussion leads to a more thorough examination of the pros and cons of a particular decision than individual decision making. Consequently, greater familiarization with all aspects of a problem leads to higher risk levels.
- Risk taking is socially desirable in our culture, and socially desirable qualities are likely to be expressed in a group rather than individually.[44]

Subsequent research refutes the conclusion that groups consistently take greater risk than individuals. For some groups and some decisions, cautious shifts were observed; that is, groups arrived at decisions that were less risky than those of individuals. Thus, both risky and cautious decisions are possible in groups. A key factor in determining which kind of shift occurs—more risky or more cautious—is the position assumed by the members before group interaction occurs. If the members lean initially toward risk, group discussion results in a shift toward greater risk; and if members lean initially toward caution, discussion leads to a cautious shift. Group discussion tends to polarize the initial position of the group.[45] This phenomenon, called *group polarization*, is a reality in group decision making, but risky shift is more prevalent. Risky shift and group polarization are aspects of group decision making worth the attention of school administrators. In both cases, variance in individual decisions is reduced in groups.

Escalation of Commitment

Escalation of commitment deals with the tendency of groups to escalate commitment to a course of action in order to justify their original decision. There are many classic examples of escalation around the world. The Shoreham Nuclear Power Plant in Long Island, New York is one example. The project was initiated in 1966

[43]James A. Stoner, "Risky and Cautious Shifts in Group Decisions: The Influence of Widely Held Values," *Journal of Experimental Social Psychology*, 4 (1968): 442–459.

[44]James L. Bowditch, *A Primer on Organizational Behavior* (New York: Wiley, 2008).

[45]Robert F. Bordley, "A Bayesian Model of Group Polarization," *Organizational Behavior and Human Performance*, 32 (1983): 262–274.

at an estimated cost of $75 million with a completion date by 1973. Due to a strong antinuclear movement by Suffolk County residents, the project took 23 years to complete at a cost of more than $5 billion. The plant was never opened.[46] Escalation also occurred when the Metropolitan Transport Bureau of Tokyo proposed to build a 20-mile, high-speed subway system under the city at a tremendous profit. The multibillion-dollar project was well over budget and more than three years overdue. Experts estimate that the massive subway system will not be profitable until 2040.[47] The savings and loan crisis of the 1980s resulted from decisions made by loan officers to make riskier loans in an escalating effort to recoup losses resulting from earlier poor loan decisions.[48] A similar near crisis occurred in 2009, resulting in near record-breaking home foreclosures.

Other examples of escalation follow. Denver's International Airport set out to add a state-of-the-art automated baggage handling system to its airport construction. The project was never completed, which caused a delay in the opening of the airport by nearly two years and $2 billion over budget.[49] Despite many years of *investment* costing millions of dollars, Henry Ford was never able to produce sufficient quantities of rubber in the Amazon.[50] The decision made by the Bureau of Alcohol, Tobacco, and Firearms agents to raid the heavily armed Branch Dividian compound outside Waco, Texas is another example of escalation of commitment.[51] Escalation also occurred when the British government continued to fund the Concorde supersonic jet long beyond its economic feasibility. After three decades, the Concorde fleet was eventually retired in 2003. Industry experts estimate that it cost British Airways $1,200 in profits per customer who took the Concorde supersonic jet instead of a 747.[52]

Several theories have been proposed to explain the escalation of commitment phenomenon. Self-justification theory has received considerable attention.[53] According to self-justification theory, decision makers will escalate their commitment to a course of action because they do not want to admit, to themselves or others, that prior resources were not allocated properly. In other words, they are inclined to protect their beliefs about themselves as rational, competent decision makers by convincing themselves and others that they made the right decision in the first place.

We have focused on several classic escalation examples from business, but the potential for escalation of commitment in schools is just as likely. For example, a school board makes a decision to renovate a high school building rather than build a new one. As the project progresses, the board soon becomes aware that the renovation will cost considerably more money than it would have cost to build an entirely new structure. The decision makers continue to commit additional resources into what obviously was a poor decision. It is important for school administrators to recognize that groups making decisions face problems similar to those faced by individuals making decisions.

Group Decision-Making Techniques

Because decision making in schools is frequently based on group participation, several techniques have been developed to improve the process. Five important techniques for group decision making are brainstorming, nominal group technique, the Delphi technique, devil's advocacy, and dialectical inquiry.

Brainstorming

Brainstorming, developed by Alex Osborn more than fifty years ago, is a technique for creatively generating

[46]Jerry Ross and Barry M. Staw, "Organizational Escalation and Exit: Lessons from the Shoreham Nuclear Power Plant," *Academy of Management Journal*, 36 (1993): 701–732.

[47]M. Fackler, "Tokyo's Newest Subway Line: A Saga of Hubris, Humiliation," *Associated Press Newswires* (20 July, 1999).

[48]Henry Moon, "Looking Forward and Looking Back: Integrating Completion and Sunk-Cost Effects within an Escalation of Commitment Progress Decision," *Journal of Applied Psychology*, 86 (2001): 104–113.

[49]Kin Fai Ellick Wong and Jessica Y.Y. Kwong, "The Role of Anticipated Regret in Escalation of Commitment," *Journal of Applied Psychology*, 92 (2007): 545–553.

[50]Barry M. Staw, "Knee-Deep in the Big Muddy—A Study of Escalating Commitment to a Chosen Course of Action," *Organizational Behavior and Human Performance*, 16 (1976): 27–44.

[51]Xin He and Vikas Mittal, "The Effect of Decision Risk and Project Stage on Escalation of Commitment," *Organizational Behavior and Human Decision Processes*, 103 (2007): 225–237.

[52]I. Swanson, "British Airways Face Grilling over Costs," *Evening News*, (6 June 2003), p. 2.

[53]George Whyte, "Escalating Commitment in Individual and Group Decision Making: A Prospect Theory Approach," *Organizational Behavior and Human Decision Processes*, 54 (1993): 430–455.

alternative solutions to a problem.[54] The unique feature of brainstorming is the separation of ideas from evaluation. Earlier, we noted the importance of generating a wide variety of new ideas during the generating alternatives step of the decision-making process (see Figure 6–1). This increases the number of alternatives from which school administrators can choose when evaluating alternatives and making their decisions. People tend to evaluate solutions to problems when they are proposed, which often eliminates many creative and feasible ideas from further consideration. The following rules are central to brainstorming:[55]

1. *Do Not Evaluate or Discuss Alternatives.* Evaluation comes later. Avoid criticism of your own or others' ideas.
2. *Encourage "Freewheeling."* Do not consider any idea outlandish. An unusual idea may point the way to a truly creative decision.
3. *Encourage and Welcome Quantities of Ideas.* The greater the number of ideas generated, the greater the number of useful ideas will remain after evaluation.
4. *Encourage "Piggybacking."* Group members should try to combine, embellish, or improve on an idea. Consequently, most of the ideas produced will belong to the group and not to a single individual.

As an idea-generating technique, group brainstorming may not be any more effective than individual brainstorming. However, the technique is in widespread use today in all types of organizations, including schools.

Nominal Group Technique

Another technique that can be used in group decision making, which incorporates some of the features of brainstorming, is the **nominal group technique.**[56] As in brainstorming, individuals are brought together to develop a solution to a problem. Unlike brainstorming, the nominal group technique is concerned with both the generation of ideas and the evaluation of these ideas. The process of decision making in nominal groups has several steps:[57]

Silent Generation of Ideas. Allow five to ten minutes for this phase. The problem should be posted on a flip chart in the front of the room. Group members are asked to solve the problem on the chart. They are cautioned not to talk to or look at the worksheets of other participants.

Round-Robin Recording of Ideas. The leader circulates around the room eliciting one idea from each group member and recording it on the flip chart. This continues, round-robin fashion, until all ideas are exhausted. The chief objective of this step is to place before the group an accurate list of ideas that can serve as a compilation of group ideas.

Discussion of Ideas. Each idea on the flip chart is discussed in the order it appears on the chart. The leader reads each item and asks the group if there are any questions, needs for clarification, agreement, or disagreement.

Preliminary Vote on Item Importance. Each participant makes an independent judgment about the alternatives by rank ordering them secretly on 3 × 5 inch cards. The average of these judgments is used as the group's decision. The nominal group process may end here, or the decision may be further refined through discussion and revoting.

Additional Discussion. The voting patterns are analyzed and reasons examined to determine if a more accurate decision can be made.

Final Vote. The final voting occurs in the same manner as the preliminary vote, by secret rankings. This action completes the decision process and provides closure.

As noted, the nominal group technique separates ideation from evaluation. Ideas are generated nominally (without verbal communication). This prevents inhibition and conformity, which we noted in the phenomenon of groupthink. Evaluation occurs in a structured manner that allows each idea to get adequate attention.

---

[54]Alex Osborn, *Applied Imagination* (New York: Scribner, 1957).

[55]Osborn, *Applied Imagination.*

[56]André L. Delbecq, Andrew H. Van de Ven, and David H. Gustafsen, *Group Techniques for Program Planning: A Guide to Nominal Group and Delphi Processes* (Middleton, WI: Green Briar Press, 1986).

[57]Ibid.

The research on the effectiveness of the nominal group technique is encouraging. In terms of the number and quality of ideas generated, studies indicate that nominal group technique is superior to both ordinary group decision making and brainstorming.[58] Furthermore, nominal group techniques often facilitate the implementation of decisions.[59] In any event, the nominal group technique provides for both greater expression and evaluation of creative ideas by group members than either brainstorming or ordinary group decisions. Despite the research support for the nominal group technique, many school administrators still do not take advantage of its benefits in group decisions.

Delphi Technique

Researchers at the Rand Corporation developed the **Delphi technique** in the 1960s.[60] Unlike brainstorming and the nominal group technique, the Delphi approach relies completely on a nominal group; that is, participants do not engage in face-to-face discussions. Instead their input is solicited by mail at their various home bases, thus allowing the polling of large numbers of experts, clients, administrators, or constituencies who are removed from the organization by distance and scheduling problems. For example, suppose the superintendent of schools of a large urban school district wishes to evaluate the curriculum in the basic skills areas. Selected members of the student body, administration, faculty, community, and nationally renowned experts could participate in the various phases of the Delphi process.

The Delphi technique has many variations, but generally it works as follows.[61]

1. The organization identifies a panel of experts, both inside and outside the organization, and solicits their cooperation.
2. Each member of the panel receives the basic problem.
3. Each individual expert independently and anonymously writes comments, suggestions, and solutions to the problem.
4. A central location compiles, transcribes, and reproduces the experts' comments.
5. Each panelist receives a copy of all the other experts' comments and solutions.
6. Each expert provides feedback on the others' comments, writes new ideas stimulated by their comments, and forwards these to the central location.
7. The organization repeats Steps 5 and 6 as often as necessary until consensus is reached or until some kind of voting procedure is imposed to reach a decision.

Success of the Delphi technique depends on the expertise, communication skills, and motivation of the participants and the amount of time the organization has available to make a decision.

There are several benefits of the Delphi approach. First, it eliminates many of the interpersonal problems associated with other group decision-making approaches. Second, it enlists the assistance of experts and provides for the efficient use of their time. Third, it allows adequate time for reflection and analysis of a problem. Fourth, it provides for a wide diversity and quantity of ideas. And, finally, it facilitates the accurate prediction and forecasting of future events.[62] The major objectives of the Delphi technique include the following[63]

- To determine or develop a range of possible program alternatives.
- To explore or expose underlying assumptions or information leading to different judgments.
- To seek out information that may generate a consensus among the group members.
- To correlate informed judgments on a subject that spans a wide range of disciplines.
- To educate group members concerning the diverse and interrelated aspects of the subject.

Today, numerous organizations in business, government, the military, health care agencies, and schools are

---

[58]Gerald Corey, *Group Techniques* (Belmont, CA: Brooks/Cole, 2011).

[59]Ibid.

[60]Norman Dalkey, *The Delphi Method: An Experimental Study of Group Opinion* (Santa Monica, CA: Rand Corporation, 1969).

[61]Ibid.

[62]Ibid.

[63]Delbecq, Van de Ven, and Gustafsen, *Group Techniques for Program Planning.*

using the Delphi technique. Research shows that the technique is superior to ordinary group decision making in terms of the number and quality of ideas generated and group members' overall satisfaction.[64] The major disadvantage of the Delphi technique is the amount of time involved in going through the questionnaire phases of the process. Variations of the Delphi technique have been used to overcome this problem.

One special type of Delphi approach is a procedure called *ringi* used by the Japanese. This version of the Delphi technique involves the circulation of a written document from member to member, in nominal group fashion, for sequential editing until no more changes are required and each participant has signed off the final document. Another Japanese variation of the Delphi technique is assigning parts of the problem to each of several subgroups who prepare responses for their assignments. This version differs from the pure Delphi approach in that the written mini-reports are then circulated among the group members before face-to-face discussion starts. In essence, the latter Japanese version of the Delphi technique combines with simple group decision making.

Devil's Advocacy

Devil's advocacy, another technique for improving the quality of group decisions, introduces conflict into the decision-making process. Janis suggests that this concept is an antidote for groupthink. Earlier, we noted that groupthink results in inhibitions and premature conformity to group norms. Devil's advocacy can nullify these and other group phenomena to which group members are subjected. After a planning group has developed alternative solutions to a problem, the plan is given to one or more staff members, with instructions to find fault with it. If the plan withstands the scrutiny of the devil's advocates, it can be presumed to be free of the effects of groupthink . . . and thus viable.[65] Although devil's advocacy can be used as a critiquing technique after alternative solutions to a problem have been developed, it can also be used during the early stages of the decision-making process. For example, during a decision-making session one member could be assigned the role of devil's advocate, expressing as many objections to each alternative solution to a problem as possible.[66]

[64]Corey, *Group Techniques.*

[65]Ibid.

Dialectical Inquiry

Like devil's advocacy, **dialectical inquiry** is an alternative approach for controlling group phenomena such as groupthink in decision making. The process can be described as follows:[67]

1. The process begins with the formation of two or more divergent groups to represent the full range of views on a specific problem. Each group is made as internally homogeneous as possible; the groups, however, are as different from one another as possible. Collectively they cover all positions that might have an impact on the ultimate solution to a problem.
2. Each group meets separately, identifies the assumptions behind its position, and rates them on their importance and feasibility. Each group then presents a "for" and an "against" position to the other groups.
3. Each group debates the other groups' position and defends its own. The goal is not to convince others but to confirm that what each group expresses as its position is not necessarily accepted by others.
4. Information, provided by all groups, is analyzed. This results in the identification of information gaps and establishes guidelines for further research on the problem.
5. An attempt to achieve consensus among the positions occurs. Strategies are sought that will best meet the requirements of all positions that remain viable. This final step permits further refinement of information needed to solve the problem.

Although agreement on an administrative plan is a goal of this approach, a full consensus does not always follow. Nevertheless, the procedure can produce useful indicators of the organization's planning needs.

[66]David M. Schweiger and Phyllis A. Finger, "The Comparative Effectiveness of Dialectical Inquiry and Devil's Advocacy: The Impact of Task Biases on Previous Research Findings," *Strategic Management Journal*, 5 (1984): 335–350.

[67]Vincent P. Barabba, "Making Use of Methodologies Developed in Academia: Lessons from One Practitioner's Experience," in R. H. Kilmann et al. (eds.), *Producing Useful Knowledge for Organizations* (New York: Praeger, 1983), pp. 147–166.

PRO CON DEBATE

Principal Power

With the introduction of collective negotiations into most educational workplaces in the late 1960s, principals' roles changed. For over forty years, principals have administered the negotiated contract in their buildings. Many principals who have served both before and after collective negotiations indicate that their decision-making discretion was limited by the constraints of union contracts. In the 2000s, the school as a workplace will be altered again in the area of principal decision making. Employee participation in decision making is evident in the most innovative recent contracts.

Question: Does teacher participation in decision making enhance principals' power?

Arguments PRO

1. Power increases when it is shared. When principals share decisions with other stakeholders in the system (teachers, parents, students), all become more responsible for outcomes.
2. By becoming facilitators of the decision-making process, principals enhance their personal power as well as their role power.
3. Principals who are experienced in shared decision making point out that, like the students who participate in establishing rules of behavior in the classroom, teachers are tougher on themselves than are principals.
4. As teachers assume greater responsibility for improving the educational environment of the school, principals become the leaders of leaders. The principal leads rather than manages.
5. Principals' roles will change for the better. For example, most articles in professional journals on shared decision making are written by administrators or administrator-teacher teams.
6. The national reform literature is filled with recommendations that teachers assume more responsibility and accountability for schooling. Principals who accommodate this call will increase their stature in the community.

Arguments CON

1. If principals are accountable for everything that happens in their buildings, they should have the power to control people, resources, events, and plans.
2. Principals can only effect desired outcomes if they have the role power to do so.
3. Teacher tenure puts serious limits on principals' power to deal with weak teachers. If principals' power to supervise teachers diminishes, the quality of classroom instruction will decrease.
4. If teachers are responsible for school decisions, principals will act less as instructional leaders and more as managers.
5. Few teachers are willing to make school decisions. They expect principals to support their work in the classroom by dealing with the traditional tasks of budgeting, hiring, firing, disciplining, and monitoring.
6. Parents expect someone to be in charge of the school. When they have concerns about their children, they want someone to make immediate decisions. Parents will view principals as weak if principals must share in decision making.

Summary

1. Decision making is a process of choosing from among alternatives. All decision-making models include the concept of rational activity. Decision-making models can be thought of as ranging on a continuum from perfect rationality (rational model) to nonrationality (bounded rationality model).
2. Rational decision making consists of several steps: identifying problems, generating alternatives, evaluating alternatives, choosing the optimum alternative, implementing the decision, and evaluating the decision.
3. Although school administrators want to make optimum decisions, the realities of school life affect

rational decision making. These include internal and external politics, conflict resolution techniques, distribution of power and authority, time constraints, cost, the inability to process information, and other limits of human rationality.

4. There are advantages of group decision making in schools. Groups have the potential to generate and evaluate more ideas, and once a decision is made, acceptance will be easier.
5. The disadvantages of group decision making include groupthink, risky shift, and escalation of commitment.
6. Techniques to improve group decision making include brainstorming, the nominal group technique, the Delphi technique, devil's advocacy, and dialectical inquiry.

Key Terms

decision making
programmed decisions
nonprogrammed decisions
strategic decisions
rational model
rationality
identifying the problem
generating alternatives
evaluating alternatives
choosing an alternative
implementing the decision
evaluating the decision
bounded rationality
behavioral model
satisficing
contextual rationality
procedural rationality
intuition
incrementalizing
garbage can model
decision feasibility
groupthink
risky shift
escalation of commitment
brainstorming
nominal group technique
Delphi technique
devil's advocacy
dialectical inquiry

Discussion Questions

1. Give an example of a decision-making situation with which you are familiar and illustrate how the problem was solved.
2. What are the basic assumptions of the rational model of decision making? Describe the steps that occur in the decision-making process.
3. Should school administrators attempt to make decisions according to the rational model? Why or why not?
4. What are the major benefits and problems of group decision making?
5. What group techniques can be used to improve group decision making?

Suggested Readings

Conzemius, Anne, and Jan O'Neill. *Building Shared Responsibility for Student Learning* (Baltimore: Association for Supervision and Curriculum Development, 2001). Learn how schools reach "success" by creating shared responsibility for student learning among educators, administrators, students, and parents. Examples from winning schools and numerous tools and strategies help you focus diverse constituents on common goals, encourage reflection, and promote collaboration.

Epstein, Joyce L., Mavis G. Sanders, Beth S. Simon, Karen Clark Salinas, Natalie Rodriguez Jansorn, and Frances L. Van Voorhis. *School, Family, and Community Partnerships: Your Handbook for Action,* 3rd ed. (Thousand Oaks, CA: Corwin Press, 2009). This book offers a research-based framework that guides state and district leaders, school principals, teachers, parents, and community partners to form Action Teams for Partnerships, and to plan, implement, evaluate, and continually improve family and community involvement.

Glickman, Carl D. *Leadership for Learning: How to Help Teachers Succeed* (Baltimore: Association for Supervision and Curriculum Development, 2002). School leaders can't improve education all by themselves. In fact, they don't have to. Because with the right plans and systems in place, you can get your entire faculty focused on continuous improvement and committed to advancing student learning.

Distinguished educator and author Carl D. Glickman explains how and provides all of the guidelines and components you need.

Hargreaves, Andy, Lorna Earl, Shawn Moore, and Susan Manning. *Learning to Change: Teaching Beyond Subjects and Standards* (San Francisco: Jossey-Bass, 2001). "In a compelling highly readable book the reader learns what supports and hinders teachers' struggle to create higher standards for their students. The authors go beyond the technical and intellectual work of teaching recognizing the highly emotional cultural aspects of change."—Ann Lieberman, senior scholar, The Carnegie Foundation for the Advancement of Teaching.

Murphy, Joseph. *The Educator's Handbook for Understanding and Closing Achievement Gaps* (Thousand Oaks, CA: Corwin Press, 2010). Comprehensive School Reform (CSR) is proving to be one of the most promising avenues for improving student achievement. The authors have found that leadership is frequently acknowledged to be a prime factor in the successful implementation of comprehensive school reform. Murphy and Datnow have gathered together a group of CSR insiders and researchers to examine the issue of leadership in CSR for the first time.

Rubin, Hank. *Collaborative Leadership: Developing Effective Partnerships in Communities and Schools,* 2nd ed. (Thousand Oaks, CA: Corwin Press, 2009). In his provocative book, visionary Hank Rubin empowers school, community, and government leaders with usable, successful models of collaboration that can boost their performance and capacity to propel their missions forward. He illustrates how to cultivate mutually beneficial relationships, including 24 specific attributes that foster successful collaboration, 12 phases of collaboration, and the 7 essential characteristics of effective collaborative leaders.

Sergiovanni, Thomas J. *The Lifeworld of Leadership: Creating Culture, Community, and Personal Meaning in Our Schools* (New York: Wiley, 2009). Sergiovanni gets to the heart of school reform and renewal in this book. He shows how local school communities can construct standards that support serious learning and effective caring for students.

7

Communication

FOCUSING QUESTIONS

1. Why is communication important in school organizations?
2. What are the steps in the communication process?
3. Why is it important for school administrators to become familiar with nonverbal cues?
4. In what directions do communications flow in schools?
5. What is the significance of the grapevine in organizational communication?
6. What functions do network patterns and network analysis play in understanding communication in schools?
7. What advances in technology have influenced the quantity and quality of communications in schools?
8. What are the barriers to effective communication? What are some techniques for overcoming these barriers?

In this chapter, we attempt to answer these questions concerning communication in school organizations. We begin our discussion with a brief treatment of the importance of communication in schools. Then we examine the process of verbal and nonverbal communication. Next, we describe direction of communication flows in school organizations. This is followed by a discussion of communication networks, including network patterns and network analysis. Then we examine the most recent advances in communication technology and its impact on the quantity and quality of communication in schools. We identify and describe some common barriers to communication. Finally, we discuss some useful techniques for overcoming these communication barriers.

The Importance of Communication

Anyone who walks through a school will observe numerous communication activities taking place. Secretaries type letters, memoranda, and reports; others talk on the telephone; a parent conference is under way in the assistant principal's office; the principal is in an evaluation conference with a teacher; other meetings are in session; teachers and students exchange information in classrooms; other students use the computer terminals in another part of the building; the library buzzes with activity; and a number of other communication activities, using a variety of media, can be observed.

Communication, the lifeblood of every school organization, is the process that links the individual, the group, and the organization.[1] To be sure, communication mediates inputs to the organization from the environment and outputs from the organization to the environment. Communication occupies a central place in organizations, because the structure, extensiveness, and scope of organizations are almost entirely determined by communication techniques.[2] Put another way, communication is the "essence of organizations."[3]

The administrator of today's school organization has a multifaceted job, which includes setting objectives, organizing tasks, motivating employees, reviewing results, and making decisions. School administrators plan, organize, staff, direct, coordinate, and review. Tasks cannot be accomplished, objectives cannot be met, and decisions cannot be implemented without adequate communication.[4]

The centrality of communication to the overall job of the administrator is evident when we consider how much time administrators spend communicating in organizations. The results of two separate studies of executives across a spectrum of organizational types and administrative levels indicate that administrators spend 80 percent of their time in interpersonal communication.[5] Similar findings, ranging from 70 to 80 percent, have been reported for elementary and high school principals.[6] School administrators, therefore, need a clear understanding of the process of communication.

The Communication Process

The **communication process** involves the exchange of information between a sender and a receiver. Figure 7–1 depicts the key components of the communication process, which involves a sequence of eight steps.[7] Barriers to communication can occur at any step in the process but most frequently occur between transmission and reception.

Develop an Idea

Senders in a school district can be central office administrators, building administrators, faculty members, departments within a school, a school, or the school district itself. Administrators communicate with other administrators, subordinates, students, the board of education, and members of the community. Faculty members communicate with administrators, staff, students, parents, and the community. Communications within the school district are important ways of coordinating the tasks of superintendents, assistant superintendents, directors, coordinators, supervisors, principals, and teachers. Communications within school buildings help coordinate the work of faculty and staff. School districts communicate with employees at all levels: unions, the community, the school board, and local, state, and federal governments. The first step is to develop an **idea** that the sender wishes to transmit.

---

[1]Joann Keyton, *Communication and Organizational Culture: A Key to Understanding Work Experiences* (Thousand Oaks, CA: Sage, 2011).

[2]Heather Canary, *Communication and Organizational Knowledge: Contemporary Issues for Theory and Practice* (New York: Taylor & Francis, 2011).

[3]George Cheney, *Organizational Communication in an Age of Globalization: Issues, Reflections, Practices* (Long Grove, IL: Waveland Press, 2011).

[4]Judith A. Pauley, *Communication: The Key to Effective Leadership* (Milwaukee, WI: ASQ Quality Press, 2010).

[5]Henry Mintzberg, *Mintzberg on Management: Inside Our Strange World of Organizations* (New York: Simon & Schuster, 2008).

[6]Reginald L. Green, *The Four Dimensions of Principal Leadership: A Framework for 21st Century Schools* (Boston: Pearson, 2010; Fred C. Lunenburg and Beverly J. Irby, *The Principalship: Vision to Action* (Wadsworth/Cengage, 2007); L. Joseph Matthews and Gary M. Crow, *The Principalship: New Roles in a Professional Learning Community* (Boston: Pearson, 2010); Thomas J. Sergiovanni, *The Principalship: A Reflective Practice Perspective* (Boston: Allyn & Bacon, 2009).

[7]Cheney, *Organizational Communication in an Age of Globalization.*

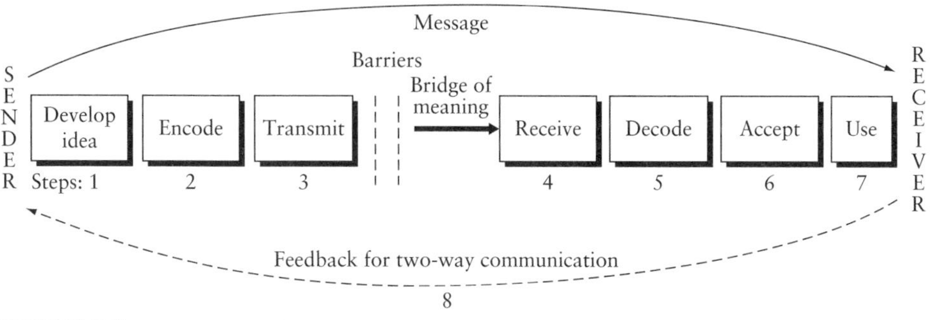

FIGURE 7–1

The Communication Process

Encode

Step 2 is to **encode** (convert) the idea into words, nonverbal cues, diagrams, or other symbols of transmission. Meaning cannot be transmitted because it lies in the significance that the encoder attributes to the symbol. The receiver of the message will also assign meaning to that symbol. The greater the agreement between the sender and the receiver regarding the meaning of the symbols, the greater the probability of understanding between the two parties. It is important, therefore, that school administrators select symbols that have mutual meaning for them and their intended receivers.

Transmit

Once the message is developed, step 3 is to **transmit** it by one of several methods including memoranda, telephone, closed-circuit television, computers, board policy statements, and face-to-face communication. Unintended messages such as silence or inaction on particular issues are not as obvious. And such nonverbal cues as hand gestures, body position, facial expression, and voice intonation also communicate messages.

Receive

The transmission allows another person to **receive** a message, which is step 4. The receiver needs to be a good listener if the message is oral. If the message is written, the receiver must be attentive to its stated and implied meaning.

Decode

Step 5 is to **decode** the message so that it can be understood. Because meaning cannot be transmitted, it cannot be received. Therefore, receivers must take transmitted messages and give meaning to them. Barriers to communication can occur at any stage of the communication process, and sometimes they can occur during the decoding step.

Accept

When the receiver has obtained and decoded the message, that individual has a choice to **accept** or reject it, which is step 6. Some factors affecting acceptance or rejection of the message involve the authority and credibility of the sender, the sender's persuasive skills, the implications for the receiver, and the receiver's perception of the accuracy of the message.

Use

Step 7 in the communication process is for the receiver to **use** the information. The receiver can ignore the communication, store it for possible action later, or do something with it.

Feedback

The receiver should give **feedback** to the sender that the message was received and understood. Feedback completes the communication cycle (step 8). See the feedback arrow at the bottom of Figure 7–1.

The most obvious modes of communication are speaking and writing. Words are the main communication symbol used when speaking and writing. A major difficulty is that nearly every common word has several meanings. This difficulty is compounded when people from diverse backgrounds—such as different educational levels, ethnicity, or cultures—attempt to communicate. It is no wonder that we have trouble communicating with one another. If words could be simplified, the receiver would understand them more

ADMINISTRATIVE ADVICE 

Guidelines for Readable Writing

Following are some suggestions for making your writing more readable.

Use simple and familiar words. This makes comprehension more likely.

Use personal pronouns such as "you" and "I," as if you were speaking directly to the reader.

Use illustrations (figures, tables), and examples. "A picture is worth a thousand words."

Use short sentences and paragraphs.

Use active verbs. Active words have impact.

Use only necessary words.

Use a structure that resembles an outline, including ample headings and subheadings.

Use chunking (i.e., lists of key points, accented by numbers or bullets).

Use techniques of emphasis (e.g., boldface, italics) to accent important ideas.

easily. This assumption underlies the idea of **readability**, which is the process of making speech and writing more understandable.[8] (See Administrative Advice 7–1: Guidelines for Readable Writing.)

Nonverbal Communication

We communicate as many messages nonverbally as we do verbally. **Nonverbal communication**—the way we stand, the distance we maintain from another person, the way we walk, the way we fold our arms and wrinkle our brow, our eye contact, being late for a meeting—conveys messages to others. However, we need not perform an act for nonverbal communication to occur. We communicate by our manner of dress and appearance, the automobile we drive, and the office we occupy.[9]

The four kinds of nonverbal communication are kinesics, proxemics, paralanguage, and chronemics. They are important topics for school administrators attempting to understand the meanings of nonverbal signals from organization members.[10]

Kinesics

Kinesics is the study of body movements, including posture.[11] Body movements or kinesics includes gestures, facial expressions, eye behavior, touching, and any other movement of the limbs and body. Body shape, physique, posture, height, weight, hair, and skin color are the physical characteristics associated with kinesics.

Gestures reveal how people are feeling. People tend to gesture more when they are enthusiastic, excited, and energized. People tend to gesture less when they are demoralized, nervous, or concerned about the impression they are making. Hand gestures, such as frequent movements to express approval and palms spread outward to indicate perplexity, provide meaningful hints to communication.

Facial expressions convey a wealth of information. The particular look on a person's face and movements of the person's head provide reliable cues as to approval, disapproval, or disbelief. When people begin to experience an emotion, their facial muscles are triggered. The six universal expressions that most cultures recognize are happiness, sadness, anger, fear, surprise, and disgust.

---

[8]Fred C. Lunenburg and Beverly J. Irby, *Writing a Successful Thesis or Dissertation: Tips and Strategies for Students in the Social and Behavioral Sciences* (Thousand Oaks, CA: Corwin Press, 2008).

[9]Mark L. Knapp and Judith Hall, *Nonverbal Communication in Human Interaction* (Belmont, CA: Wadsworth/Cengage, 2010).

[10]Adrian Furnham. *Body Language in Business: Decoding the Signals* (New York: Palgrave Macmillan, 2011).

[11]Mark Bowden, *Winning Body Language: Control the Conversation, Command Attention, and Convey the Right Message without Saying a Word* (New York: McGraw-Hill, 2011); Mark Hickson, *Nonverbal Communication: Studies and Applications* (New York: Oxford University Press, 2010); Stan B. Walters, *Principles of Kinesic Interview and Interrogation* (Boca Raton, FL: CRC Press, 2011).

Smiling, for example, typically represents warmth, happiness, or friendship, whereas frowning conveys dissatisfaction or anger. However, smiling can be real or false, interpreted by differences in the strength and length of the smile, the openness of the eyes, and the symmetry of expression.

Eye contact is a strong nonverbal cue that serves four functions in communication. First, eye contact regulates the flow of communication by signaling the beginning and end of conversation. Second, eye contact facilitates and monitors feedback, because it reflects interest and attention. Third, eye contact conveys emotion. Fourth, eye contact relates to the type of relationship between communicators. One can gauge liking and interest by the frequency and duration of time spent looking. Eye and face contact displays one's willingness to listen and acknowledgement of the other person's worth. Eye contact does not necessarily indicate truthfulness, as some people believe. It does show interest in the other person's point of view. Prolonged and intense eye contact usually indicates feelings of hostility, defensiveness, or romantic interest. Lack of interest may be indicated through contractions of the pupils or wandering eyes.

Touching is a powerful vehicle for conveying such emotions as warmth, comfort, agreement, approval, reassurance, and physical attraction. Generally, the amount and frequency of touching demonstrate closeness, familiarity, and degree of liking. A lot of touching usually indicates strong liking for another person. It should be noted that men and women interpret touching differently. Concerns about sexual harassment and sexism have greatly limited the use of touching in the workplace.

Posture is another widely used cue as to a person's attitude. Leaning toward another person suggests a favorable attitude toward the message one is trying to communicate. Leaning backward communicates the opposite. Standing erect is generally interpreted as an indicator of self-confidence, while slouching conveys the opposite. Posture and other nonverbal cues can also affect the impressions we make on others. Interviewers, for example, tend to respond more favorably to job applicants whose nonverbal cues, such as eye contact and erect posture, are positive than to those who display negative nonverbal cues, such as looking down or slouching.

Another nonverbal cue is mode of dress. Much of what we say about ourselves to others comes from the way we dress. Despite the general trend toward casual clothing in the workplace, higher-status people tend to dress more formally than lower-ranking organization members. For example, suppose you joined a new organization (school district, community college, university) and on your first day, you entered a room full of employees. How would you know which person was the leader? Increasingly, people who specialize in recruiting top executives (such as superintendents and college presidents) are coming to the conclusion that the old adage "clothes make the man or woman" is a particularly good nonverbal clue as to who is in charge. Somehow, the leader is the person who always seems to wear the best tailored suit that flatters his or her physique, or the nicest shirt or blouse, or the shiniest shoes, and the best-looking briefcase. Top executive, Donald Trump, admits that he learned the hard way the importance of wearing the right clothes.[12] The payoff is that when you look like a leader, people will often treat you like one and so over time this increases your chances of promotion and success.[13]

Proxemics

Proxemics is the way people perceive and use space, including seating arrangements, physical space, and conversational distance (personal space).[14a] For example, how close do you stand to someone in normal conversation?

Edward Hall, an anthropologist, suggests that in the United States there are definable *personal space zones*.[14b]

1. *Intimate Zone (0 to 2 Feet)*. To be this close, we must have an intimate association with the other person or be socially domineering.
2. *Personal Zone (2 to 4 Feet)*. Within this zone, we should be fairly well acquainted with the other individual.

---

[12]Donald J. Trump, *Think Like a Champion: An Informal Education in Business and Life* (New York: Vanguard Press, 2011).

[13]Joe Navarro, *Louder Than Words: Take Your Career from Average to Exceptional with the Hidden Power of Nonverbal Intelligence* (New York: HarperCollins, 2011).

[14a]Edward T. Hall, "Proxemics," in A.M. Katz and V.T. Katz (eds.), *Foundations of Nonverbal Communication* (Carbondale, IL: Southern Illinois University Press, 1983); see also Jinni Harrigan, *New Handbook of Methods in Nonverbal Behavior Research* (New York: Oxford University Press, 2009).

[14b]Hall, "Proxemics."

3. *Social Zone (4 to 12 Feet).* In this zone, we are at least minimally acquainted with the other person and have a definite purpose for seeking to communicate. Most behavior in the business world occurs in this zone.
4. *Public Zone (Beyond 12 Feet).* When people are more than 12 feet away, we treat them as if they did not exist. We may look at others from this distance, provided our gaze does not develop into a stare.

Related to the notion of personal space zones is the concept of physical space. For example, employees of higher status have better offices (more spacious, finer carpets and furniture, and more windows) than do employees of lower status. Furthermore, the offices of higher-status employees are better protected than those of lower-status employees. Top executive areas are typically sealed off from intruders by several doors, assistants, and secretaries. Moreover, the higher the employee's status, the easier they find it to invade the physical space of lower-status employees. A superior typically feels free to walk right in on subordinates, whereas subordinates are more cautious and ask permission or make an appointment before visiting a superior.

Seating arrangements is another aspect of proxemics. You can seat people in certain positions according to your purpose in communication. To encourage cooperation, you should seat the other person beside you, facing the same direction. To facilitate direct and open communication, seat the other person at right angles from you. This allows for more honest disclosure. When taking a competitive position with someone, seat the person directly across from you. Furthermore, high-ranking people assert their higher status by sitting at the head of rectangular tables, a position that has become associated with importance. It also enables high-ranking organization members to maintain eye contact with those over whom they are responsible.

Paralanguage

Paralanguage consists of variations in speech, such as voice quality, volume, tempo, pitch, nonfluencies (for example, uh, um, ah), or laughing.[15] People make attributions about the sender by deciphering paralanguage cues. Aspects of speech such as pitch, volume, voice quality, and speech rate may communicate confidence, nervousness, anger, or enthusiasm. Intelligence is often judged by how people speak.

Chronemics

Chronemics is concerned with the use of time, such as being late or early, keeping others waiting, and other relationships between time and status.[16] For example, being late for a meeting may convey any number of different messages including carelessness, lack of involvement, and lack of ambition. Yet, at the same time, the late arrival of high-status persons reaffirms their superiority relative to subordinates. Their tardiness symbolizes power or having a busy schedule.

In sum, despite the implications of the information about nonverbal communication, be aware that many nonverbal messages are ambiguous. For example, a smile usually indicates agreement and warmth, but it can also indicate nervousness, contempt, deceit, fear, compliance, resignation—even, on occasion, anger. Nevertheless, nonverbal messages are a rich source of information. Your own nonverbal behavior can be useful in responding to others, making stronger connections with others, and conveying certain impressions about yourself.

As you read this material ask yourself, "What can I do to present myself more favorably to those around me in the workplace? Specifically, what can I do nonverbally to cultivate the impression that I have the qualities to be a good leader?" As we have seen, speaking and writing can enhance your image as a strong leader. Also, there are several things you can do nonverbally that will enhance your leadership image. (See Administrative Advice 7–2.)

Direction of Communication

Communication is interlinked with most of the processes that take place in school districts, such as planning, organizing, staffing, directing, coordinating, and reporting. The purpose of organizational communication is to provide the means for transmitting information essential to goal achievement. Much of this **communication flow** is carried in four distinct directions

[15]Jeffrey Jacobi, *How to Say It with Your Voice* (Upper Saddle River, NJ: Prentice Hall, 2009); Kathryn S. Young, *Communicating Nonverbally: A Practical Guide to Presenting Yourself More Effectively* (Long Grove, IL: Waveland Press, 2008).

[16]Hickson, *Nonverbal Communication.*

ADMINISTRATIVE ADVICE 7–2

Nonverbal Behaviors to Enhance Your Leadership Image

People who are self-confident speak and write with assurance. They also project their leadership image through various nonverbal cues. Following are some suggestions.

Maintain eye contact and smile at those with whom you speak.

Nod your head to indicate that you are listening when someone is speaking to you.

Use hand gestures in a relaxed, nontechnical manner.

Stand and sit erect. Do not slouch.

Do not cower when confronted. Stand up straight.

Be neat, well groomed, and wear clean, well-tailored clothes.

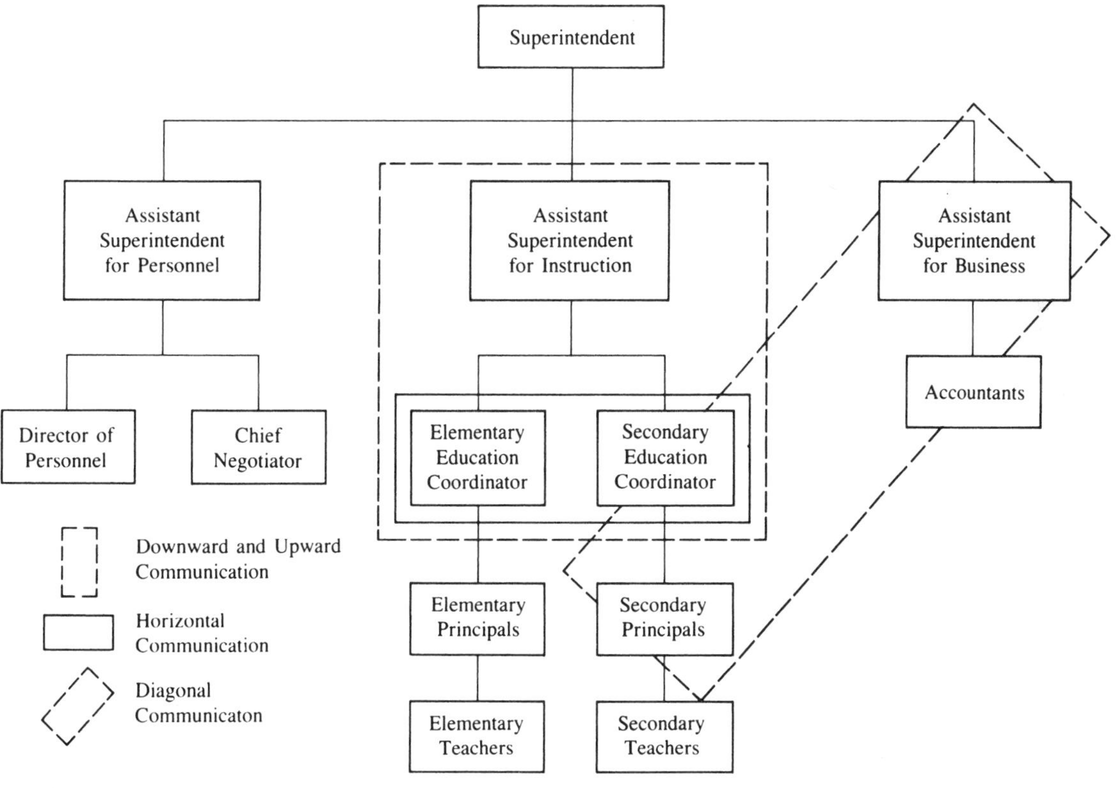

FIGURE 7–2

School District Communication Flows

(see Figure 7–2): downward, upward, horizontally, and diagonally.[17] The other major communication flow is the grapevine.

[17]George Cheney, *Organizational Communication in an Age of Globalization: Issues, Reflections, Practices* (Long Grove, IL: Waveland Press, 2011).

Downward Communication

Hierarchical systems like large school districts tend to use downward communication, in which people at higher levels transmit information to people at lower levels. The communication can take place among different groups of senders and receivers, including superintendent to assistant superintendents, assistant superintendents to principals, principals to department heads, department heads to teachers, or any other combination of superior to subordinate.

For example, the school district's superintendent might instruct the assistant superintendent of instruction to prepare for a new personnel evaluation system mandated by the state. In turn, the assistant superintendent would provide specific instructions to the principals, who would inform the teachers accordingly. Downward communication is necessary to help clarify the school district's goals, provide a sense of mission, assist in indoctrinating new employees into the system, inform employees about educational changes impacting the district, and provide subordinates with data concerning their performance.

Downward communication occurs easily, but it is frequently deficient. One problem is that subordinates select from among the various directives transmitted from above those most in keeping with their perceptions of their boss's character, personality, motivation, and style and give them priority. Another problem is that not enough time and effort are devoted to learning whether messages sent from above have been received and understood. A third problem is that those at the top of the hierarchy may shut off this channel at times and on certain subjects, that is, withhold information on a need-to-know basis.[18] And, finally, downward communication tends to dominate in mechanistic organizations as opposed to organic systems, which are characterized by more open and unidirectional flows of information.[19]

One author has identified three ways for administrators to improve downward communication.[20]

1. School districts should adopt communication training programs for all administrative personnel. Most school administrators could benefit greatly from learning better ways of communicating, as well as developing more effective listening skills.
2. School administrators should get out of their offices and talk to employees on the "firing line." One author refers to this technique as management by wandering around (MBWA).[21] It allows administrators to become more aware of the needs of their subordinates.
3. School administrators should conduct regular supervisory-subordinate discussions. Such participative interactions will help administrators identify, analyze, and solve problems collaboratively with subordinates.

Upward Communication

Upward communication also follows the hierarchical chart and transmits information from lower to higher levels in the organization. For example, a teacher might conceive of a new course in social studies. The teacher would pass this information upward to the department head, who would in turn pass the information to her immediate supervisor, who would then inform the superintendent. Upward communication is necessary to provide administrators with feedback on downward communication, monitor decision-making effectiveness, gauge organizational climate, deal with problem areas quickly, and provide needed information to administrators.

For several reasons, upward communication is difficult to achieve.[22] Upward communication is usually subject to filtering and distortion because subordinates do not want their superiors to learn anything that may be potentially damaging to subordinates' careers. This tendency is likely to increase when subordinates do not trust supervisors. Furthermore, highly cohesive groups tend to withhold information from superiors that might be damaging to the group as a whole. However, all subordinates tend to distort upward communication somewhat less under a participatory management system than under an authoritative system. Other research shows that lower-level subordinates perceive much less openness to upward communication than is perceived at higher levels in the organization. In fact, "higher-level managers involve their subordinates more in the decision-making process and thus expect upward communication more than do lower-level managers." Similar findings have been reported in educational settings.

---

[18]Dennis Tourish, *Auditing Organizational Communication: A Handbook of Research, Theory and Practice* (New York: Routledge, 2010).

[19]Jay M. Shafritz, *Classics of Organization Theory* (Belmont, CA: Wadsworth/Cengage, 2011); see also Gareth Morgan, *Images of Organization* (Thousand Oaks, CA: Sage, 2007).

[20]Pamela S. Shockley-Zalabak, *Fundamentals of Organizational Communication: Knowledge, Sensitivity, Skills, Values* (Boston: Allyn & Bacon, 2009).

[21]Larry Frase, *School Management by Wandering Around* (Lanham, MD: ScarecrowEducation, 2003).

[22]Tourish, *Auditing Organizational Communication.*

Other research recommends four practices to improve upward communication: employee meetings, open door policy, employee letters, and participation in social groups.[23]

Employee Meetings These meetings attempt to probe job problems, needs, and administrative practices that help and hinder subordinate job performance. These meetings, sometimes referred to as *quality circles,* provide feedback to administrators and encourage subordinates to submit ideas to supervisors. As a consequence, subordinates feel a sense of personal worth and importance because administrators listen to them. By opening channels upward, administrators help the flow and acceptance of communication downward. Also, subordinates' attitudes improve, and turnover declines.

Open Door Policy An open door policy is a statement that encourages subordinates to walk in and talk to administrators many levels up the hierarchy. Generally, however, subordinates are encouraged to see their immediate supervisors first. Then, if their problem is not resolved at that level, they are free to approach higher-level administrators. Bringing a problem to one's immediate supervisor first should alleviate resentment among administrators who are bypassed when subordinates skip several administrative levels in the hierarchy. The goal of an open door policy—to facilitate upward communication—has merit but is often difficult to implement because psychological barriers often exist between superiors and subordinates. Some subordinates do not want to be identified as having a problem or lacking information. A more effective open door procedure is for administrators to get out of their offices and observe firsthand what is happening in the organization. This was referred to earlier as "management by wandering around."

Employee Letters Programs that use employee letters or suggestions serve as a type of written open door policy. This direct and personal method provides subordinates with the opportunity to present their ideas to administrators. To increase the effectiveness of this procedure, submissions can be anonymous, all submissions must be answered, and replies must be delivered without delay. Replies can be directed to the appropriate lower-level administrator or, in cases where the communicator is anonymous, responses can be deposited in an "answer box," similar to a suggestion box in which employees communicate with superiors.

Participation in Social Groups This method provides excellent opportunities for unplanned upward communication. Information at these activities is shared informally between subordinates and superiors. Examples include departmental parties, sports events, picnics, golf outings, and other employer-sponsored activities. The major barrier to such activities is lack of attendance; that is, those who need to share information the most may not attend the activities. Although upward communication is not the primary goal of these activities, it is certainly an important by-product. It is also a means of enhancing employee morale. Other approaches are job satisfaction surveys, grievance or complaint procedures, counseling programs, exit interviews, discussions with union representatives, consultative supervision, and suggestion systems.

Horizontal Communication

Horizontal communication takes place between employees at the same hierarchical level. This type of communication is frequently overlooked in the design of most organizations. Integration and coordination between units in an organization is facilitated by horizontal communication. At the upper levels of a school district, for example, the assistant superintendents for instruction, business, and personnel will coordinate their efforts in arriving at an integrated strategic plan for the district. In a high school, meanwhile, the department chairpersons will work together in developing a curriculum for the entire school. Likewise, in a school of education of a large university, it is common to observe departments coordinating their efforts for the purpose of ensuring that all units of the school are working toward the same general goals. This horizontal communication is frequently achieved through cross-functional committees or council meetings, groups or liaison positions that tie together units horizontally, and informal interpersonal communication.

Besides providing task coordination, horizontal communication furnishes emotional and social support among peers. In effect, it serves as a socialization process for the organization. The more interdependent the various functions in the organization, the greater the need to formalize horizontal communication.

---

[23]Heather Canary, *Communication and Organizational Knowledge: Contemporary Issues for Theory and Practice* (New York: Taylor & Francis, 2011).

Diagonal Communication

Diagonal communication is important in situations in which participants cannot communicate effectively through other channels. For example, the assistant superintendent for business of a large, urban school district may wish to conduct an instructional program cost analysis for each high school. One part of the analysis involves having each high school principal send a special report directly to the assistant superintendent for business, rather than go through the traditional circuitous channels of assistant superintendent for instruction to the coordinator of secondary education to the high school principals and back again. Thus, the flow of communication would be diagonal rather than vertical (downward and upward). In this instance, diagonal communication minimizes the time lag in securing the needed data. The four directions of organizational communication flows are shown in Figure 7–2.

The Grapevine

When the shortcomings of the four types of organizational communication become apparent, employees build their own channels of communication, **grapevines.** Grapevines exist in all large organizations regardless of communication flow. This type of communication flow does not appear on any organizational chart, but it carries much of the communication in the organization. The term *grapevine* applies to all informal communication, including institutional information that is communicated verbally between employees and people in the community. It coexists with the administration's formal communication system. Therefore, school administrators should learn to integrate grapevine communication with formal communication.

Because the grapevine is flexible and usually involves face-to-face communication, it transmits information rapidly. Moreover, nearly five out of every six messages are carried by the grapevine rather than through official channels.[24] And in normal work situations, well over 75 percent of grapevine information is accurate.[25]

The grapevine has both positive and negative features. Its positive features include the following:[26]

- Keeps subordinates informed about important organizational matters.
- Gives school administrators insights into subordinates' attitudes.
- Provides subordinates with a safety valve for their emotions.
- Provides a test of subordinates' reactions to a new policy or procedural change without making formal commitments. (School administrators have been known to "feed" ideas into the grapevine in order to probe their potential acceptance by subordinates.)
- Helps build morale by carrying the positive comments people make about the school district.

One of the negative features of the grapevine, the one that gives the grapevine its poor reputation, is rumor. A rumor is an unverified belief that is in general circulation. Because the information cannot be verified, rumors are susceptible to severe distortion as they are passed from person to person within the organization. One way to minimize the spread of rumors is to improve other forms of communication. If school administrators provide information on issues relevant to subordinates, then damaging rumors are less likely to develop.

Joseph Licata and Walter Hack examined grapevine structures among principals and report that grapevine linkages differed between elementary and secondary school principals. In elementary schools, where relationships are closer, principals tended to communicate informally; in high schools, where the structure is more formal, principals built the grapevine around professional survival and development.[27]

Communication Networks

As noted, organizational communication can be transmitted in a number of directions: downward, upward, horizontally, diagonally, and through the grapevine. These communications can be formal or informal; in

[24]John M. Ivancevich, Robert Konopaske, and Michael Matteson, *Organization Behavior and Management* (New York: McGraw-Hill, 2011).

[25]John W. Newstrom, *Human Behavior at Work* (New York: McGraw-Hill, 2011).

[26]Terrence E. Deal and Kent D. Peterson, *Shaping School Culture: Pitfalls, Paradoxes, and Promises* (New York: Wiley, 2011).

[27]Joseph W. Licata and Walter G. Hack, "School Administrator Grapevine Structure," *Educational Administration Quarterly*, 16 (1980): 82–99.

EXEMPLARY EDUCATIONAL ADMINISTRATORS IN ACTION

BARRY FRIED Principal, John Dewey High School, Brooklyn, New York.

Words of Advice: An effective leader must set clearly defined goals and expectations for all staff and students. Resources and support systems are integral attributes for any successful organization, primarily when student achievement is the benchmark for success. Employ the experiences of your personnel to help in effective management of a school. You cannot do it alone! Accepting this responsibility and accountability is inherent for all members of the school community to be able to succeed. You need to be accessible and involved in all facets of the learning and management process. Objective observation, monitoring, evaluation and reevaluation of programs, instructional strategies, and performance are crucial to improve the quality of education in addressing individual student needs. Take risks, encourage teachers to explore, experiment, and experience new programs and methodologies. Support these experiences and prepare leaders of tomorrow. Offering gestures of "thank-you" and "signs of appreciation" bolsters self-esteem and encourages staff to continue these efforts. Speak with your students. Let them know who you are, and listen to their concerns. They are attuned to the school and can provide valuable insights. Establish meaningful relationships among all constituencies of the school community. It is essential to shape, foster, and nurture the students through "experiential learning."

either case, the actual pattern and flow of communication connecting senders and receivers are called communication networks. Because this system contains all the communication of the organization, these networks have a pervasive influence on the behavior of individuals functioning within them.

Network Patterns

Network patterns are derived from laboratory experiments in which the structure of the groupings can be manipulated by the experimenter. Figure 7–3 depicts five of the more frequently used networks (wheel, chain, Y, circle, and star). The major difference among the networks is the degree to which they are centralized or decentralized.[28] Each network pattern is discussed in turn.

The *wheel network,* a two-level hierarchy, is the most structured and centralized of the patterns because each member can communicate with only one other person. For example, a superintendent of schools and those who are his immediate subordinates (assistant superintendent for business, instruction, personnel, and assistant to the superintendent), probably form a wheel network. The superintendent is A and his assistant superintendents are B, C, D, and E, respectively. The four subordinates send information to the superintendent, and the superintendent sends that information back to them, usually in the form of decisions.

The *chain network* ranks next highest in centralization. Only two people communicate with one another, and they in turn have only one person to whom they communicate. Information is generally sent through such a network in relay fashion. A typical chain network would be one in which a teacher (B) reports to the department head (C), who in turn reports to the principal (A), who reports to the assistant superintendent for instruction (D), who reports to the superintendent (E). Another example is the grapevine through which information passes throughout a school building or district between different departments and organizational levels.

The *Y network* is similar to the chain except that two members fall outside the chain. In the Y network, for example, members A and B can send information to C, but they can receive information from no one. C and D can exchange information; E can receive information from D but cannot send any information. For example, two assistant principals (A and B) report to the principal (C). The principal, in turn, reports to the assistant superintendent (D), who reports to the superintendent (E).

The *circle network,* a three-level hierarchy, is very different from the wheel, chain, and Y networks. It is

[28]Shockley-Zalabak, *Fundamentals of Organizational Communication.*

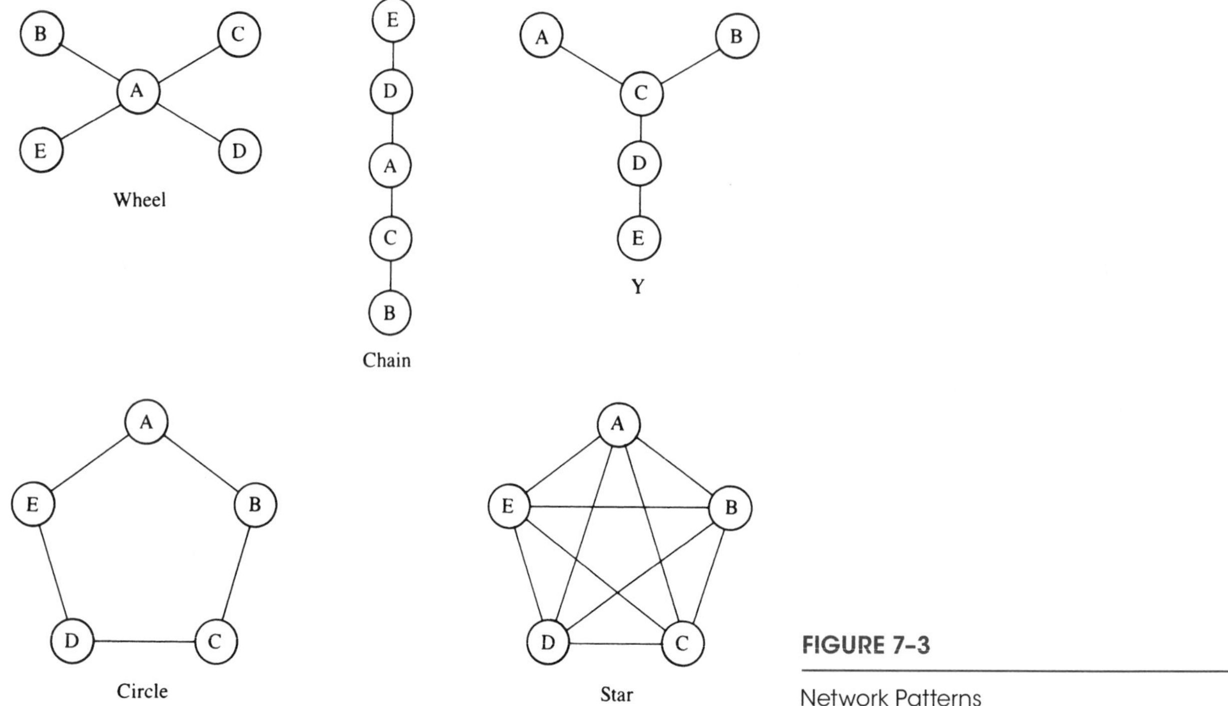

FIGURE 7-3

Network Patterns

symbolic of horizontal and decentralized communication. The circle gives every member equal communication opportunities. Each member can communicate with persons to their right and left. Members have identical restrictions, but the circle is a less restricted condition than the wheel, chain, or Y networks. For example, the circle network has more two-way channels open for problem solving (i.e., five) than the four channels of the aforementioned networks. In the circle network, everyone becomes a decision maker.

The *star network* is an extension of the circle network. By connecting everyone in the circle network, the result is a star, or all-channel, network. The star network permits each member to communicate freely with all other persons (decentralized communication). The star network has no central position, and no communication restrictions are placed on any member. A committee in which no member either formally or informally assumes a leadership position is a good example of a star network.

Effectiveness of Different Networks The importance of a communication network lies in its potential effects on such variables as speed, accuracy, morale, leadership, stability, organization, and flexibility. Studies in communication networks show that the network effectiveness depends on situational factors.[29] For example, centralized networks are more effective in accomplishing simple tasks, whereas decentralized patterns are more effective on complex tasks. In addition, the overall morale of members of decentralized networks is higher than those of centralized networks. This finding makes sense in view of the research indicating that employees are most satisfied with their jobs when they have participated in decision making about them. Moreover, research shows that a member's position in the network can affect personal satisfaction. Members in more central positions in the network tend to be more satisfied.[30]

Network Analysis

Besides network patterns, another method to help school administrators analyze communication flows and patterns is network analysis. In **network analysis,**

[29]Peter J. Schulz, *Communication Theory* (Thousand Oaks, CA: Sage, 2011).

[30]Ibid.

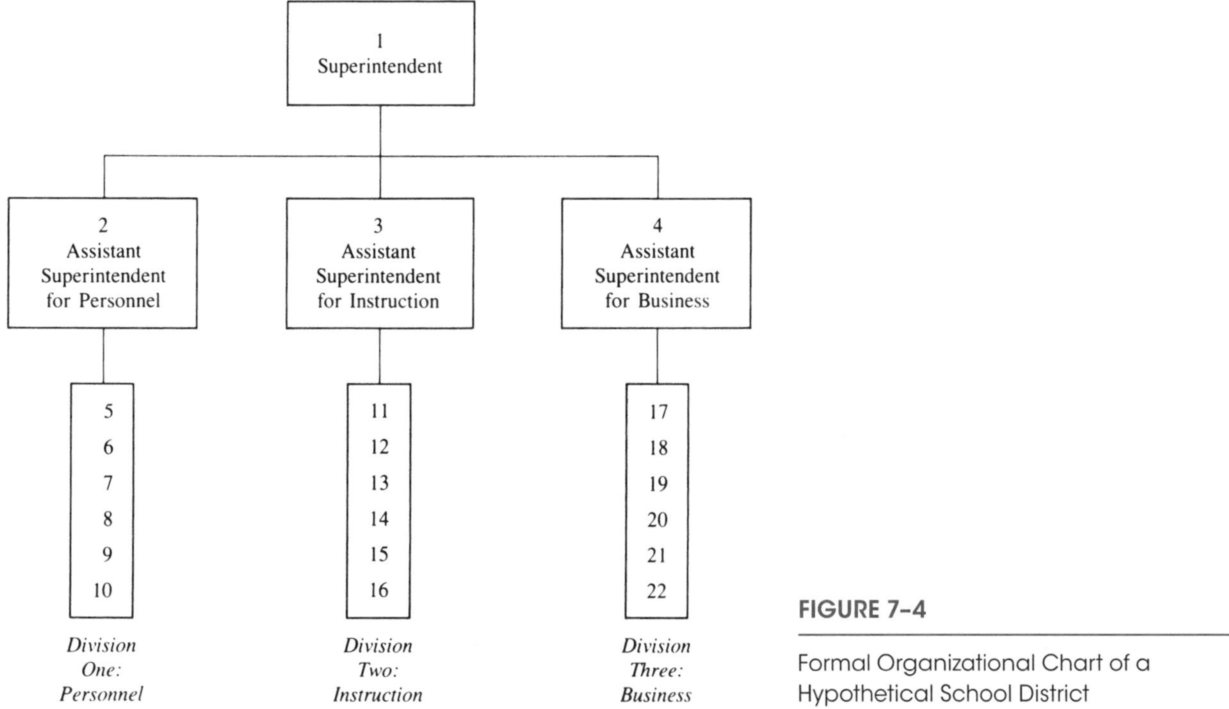

FIGURE 7–4

Formal Organizational Chart of a Hypothetical School District

communication flows and patterns are analyzed between units and across hierarchical positions. Network analysis uses survey sociometry rather than controlled laboratory experiments to identify cliques and certain specialized roles of members in the communication structure of real-life organizations.

To illustrate, consider the communication network for a hypothetical school district.[31] Figure 7–4 presents a formal organizational chart showing the hierarchical positions occupied by twenty-two people in three divisions of the school district. The numbers within the boxes represent individuals in the school district. Person 1 at the top of the hierarchy is the superintendent of schools. The three people immediately below him are the assistant superintendents of the three divisions: personnel, instruction, and business. The remaining individuals are employees in each division. This chart represents the formal structure of communications within the school district. Through network analysis, Figure 7–5 shows a communication network and contrasts it with the school district's formal structure (Figure 7–4). As Figure 7–5 shows, Person 1 (the superintendent) frequently communicates with Persons 2, 3, and 4, the assistant superintendents for personnel, instruction, and business, respectively. His communications with other lower-level members are less frequent or nonexistent. Figure 7–5 also identifies cliques in the communication network of the twenty-two members on the basis of intercommunication patterns among them. The lines indicate patterned communication contacts. Some communication contacts are two way (↔), and some are one-way (→). Two-way arrows connect Persons 1 and 4, 1 and 2, 1 and 3, and 2 and 4, while one-way communications exist between Persons 2 and 3, 4 and 17, and so on.

There are four cliques in the school district: A, B, C, and D. "A clique is a subsystem whose elements interact with each other relatively more frequently than with other members of the communication system."[32]

[31]Our hypothetical illustration is similar to the data provided in the description of the network analysis by Everett M. Rogers and Rekha Agarwala Rogers, *Communication in Organizations* (New York: Free Press, 1976).

[32]Ibid., p. 130.

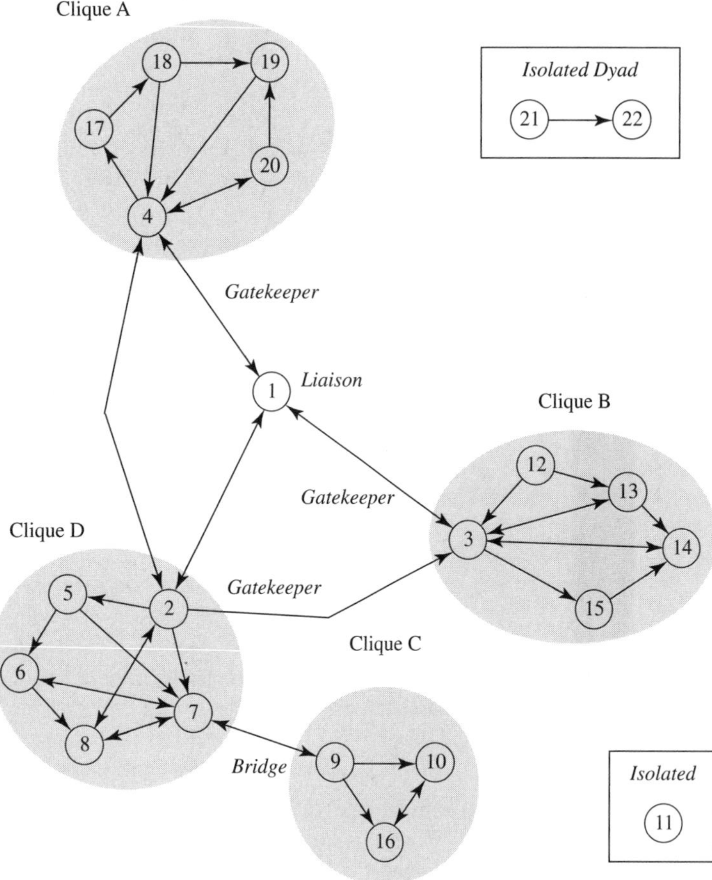

FIGURE 7–5

Communication Network of a Hypothetical School District

Clique A is composed of Persons 4, 17, 18, 19, 20; Clique B is composed of Persons 3, 12, 13, 14, and 15; and so on. Most clique members in a network are usually relatively close to each other in the formal hierarchy of the organization. However, a school district's actual communication network can be very different from the pattern of communication established by its formal organizational structure. Four main communication roles have emerged in network analysis: gatekeepers, liaisons, bridges, and isolates.

Person 1, the superintendent, is dependent on Persons 2, 3, and 4, the three assistant superintendents, for access to communication flows. The three superintendents are also *gatekeepers,* having the capacity to control information moving in either direction between the superintendent and the rest of the school district. Person 1 also serves as a *liaison* (an individual who interpersonally connects two or more cliques within the system without himself belonging to any clique) who connects Clique A, Clique B, and Clique D. If this liaison were removed from the network, it would be a much less interconnected system. Person 7 is a *bridge,* a person who is a member of one communication clique and links it, via a communication dyad, with another clique. Thus, Person 7 is a member of Clique D and communicates with Person 9, who is a member of Clique C. Person 11 is an *isolate* (an individual who has few communication contacts with the rest of the system) and is virtually cut off from communication. Person 21 has an in-group relationship in an isolated dyad with Person 22.

Patrick Forsyth and Wayne Hoy studied communication isolates in five secondary schools. Results indicated that communication isolates tend to be separated from perceived control, the school's control structure, respected colleagues, and sometimes friends.[33] A subsequent study of communication isolates in elementary schools reports similar findings, except that isolation from friends was not related to isolation from formal authority.[34] In another study of communication networks in one high school and five elementary schools, using sociometry and frequency surveys of communication, results indicate more frequent communication contacts in elementary schools as compared with high schools. According to this study, three factors affect horizontal communication patterns in schools: level and size of school, specialization, and proximity.[35]

In sum, we have identified and described individuals who have potential influence in the informal communication network and their roles in interpersonal communication in school districts. School administrators entering a school district would be well advised to establish good interpersonal relationships with gatekeepers, liaisons, and bridges. Furthermore, it is vital to be cognizant of the potentially destructive aspect of isolates who often become alienated and exhibit detrimental behaviors dysfunctional to the school district. Knowledge of communication networks can serve as useful interpersonal communication sources. More important, such knowledge can determine the success or failure of a school administrator on the job.

Communication and Technology

Advances in technology have influenced the quantity and quality of communications in the workplace. Six developments that illustrate the impact of technology on communication are e-mail, instant messaging, social networking, internet or Web logs (blogs), computer slide presentations, and video conferencing.[36]

[33]Patrick B. Forsyth and Wayne K. Hoy, "Isolation and Alienation in Educational Organizations," *Educational Administration Quarterly*, 14 (1978): 80–96.

[34]Arlene E. Zielinski and Wayne K. Hoy, "Isolation and Alienation in Elementary Schools," *Educational Administration Quarterly*, 19 (1983): 27–45.

[35]W. W. Charters, "Stability and Change in the Communication Structure of School Facilities," *Educational Administration Quarterly*, 3 (1967): 15–38.

[36]Rich Ling, *New Technology, New Ties: How Mobile Communication Is Reshaping Social Cohesion* (Cambridge, MA: MIT Press, 2011).

Electronic Mail (e-mail)

E-mail uses the internet to send and receive computer-generated text and documents. As a communication tool, e-mail has a number of benefits. E-mail messages can be written quickly, edited, and stored. They can be distributed to one person or thousands of people with a click of a mouse. They can be read at any time by the receiver. The cost of sending e-mail messages to organization members is much less than the cost of printing, duplicating, and distributing a comparable letter or other document.[37] There are some drawbacks to using e-mail: misinterpreting the message, communicating negative messages, sending emotionally-charged e-mails, privacy concerns, and overuse of e-mail.[38]

Instant Messaging

Instant messaging (IM) allows people who are online to share messages with one another instantaneously, without having to go through an e-mail system. Sending an instant message opens up a small onscreen window into which each party can type messages for the other to read. This makes it possible to exchange written notes in real time, as well as share Web links and files of all types. The use of IM is expected to grow rapidly, because IM is an inexpensive alternative to multiple telephone calls and travel, creates a document trail for future reference; offers integration with voice and video; and provides the capability of carrying on several IM conversations at the same time.

Text messaging is a variant of IM. Text messaging (also called SMS for Short Message Service), like e-mail but unlike IM, uses portable communication devices. IM is usually sent via desktop or laptop computer, whereas SMS is transmitted via cellphones or handheld devices such as Blackberrys.[39] IM and SMS are not likely to replace e-mail. E-mail is still a superior device for sending long messages that need to be saved.

[37]Kenneth Zeigler, *Organizing for Success*, 2nd ed. (New York: McGraw-Hill, 2011).

[38]John Freeman, *The Tyranny of E-mail: The Four-Thousand Year Journey to Your Inbox* (New York: Simon & Schuster, 2012).

[39]Friedhelm F. Hillebrand, *Short Message Service (SMS): The Creation of Personal Global Text Messaging* (New York: Wiley, 2011).

Social Networking

Social Networking is another emerging form of information technology. Two well-known social networking platforms are Facebook and MySpace. **Facebook** is composed of separate networks based on schools, companies, or regions.[40] **MySpace** profiles contain two sections: "About Me" and "Who I'd Like to Meet." Profiles can also contain "Interests" and "Details" sections, photographs, blogs, and other information.[41]

MySpace, compared to Facebook, is more likely to be used for personal reasons.[42] In addition to Facebook and MySpace, professional networking sites have entered the marketplace. Companies such as IBM and Microsoft have their own social networks. Public schools and universities are also entering the social networking arena.

Web Logs (Blogs)

Web logs (or blogs) are online diaries or journals created by people to express their personal thoughts and to comment on topics of interest to them. The benefits of blogs include the opportunity for people to discuss issues in a casual format. These discussions serve much like chat groups and thus can provide administrators with insights from a wide segment of school stakeholders. The two major pitfalls of blogs are the lack of legal guidelines regarding what can be posted online and the potential for employees to say negative things about their employer and the organization, as well as to leak confidential information.[43]

Some employees believe that the First Amendment gives them the right to say whatever they want on their personal blogs.[44] Thus, many employers now monitor employees' Web sites at work. Some organizations have instituted policies restricting employee blogging activities. If you plan on maintaining a personal blog, be sure to install a work-personal firewall.

Presentation Technology

Computer-generated slide software, such as **PowerPoint,** is a mode of communication currently being used in classrooms, professional conferences, and faculty meetings. Speakers supplement their talk with computer-generated slides and typically organize their presentations around their slides. Audiences have become accustomed to watching presentations accompanied by an assortment of eye-catching graphics.[45]

The communication challenge is that during these presentations, the predominant means of connection between sender and receiver should be eye contact, not the screen. The implication for presenters is to find a way to integrate speaking skills with the technology. In Administrative Advice 7–3, we provide some suggestions for improving multi-media presentations.[46]

Videoconferencing

Videoconferencing uses video and audio links together with computers to enable individuals in different locations to conduct meetings without getting together face to face.

In the late 1990s, videoconferencing was conducted from special rooms equipped with television cameras. More recently, cameras and microphones are being attached to an individual's computer monitor, allowing them to participate in long-distance meetings and training sessions without leaving their offices.[47]

In sum, some of the electronic communication devices omit many verbal and most nonverbal cues that

---

[40]Leah Perlman, Facebook (New York: Wiley, 2011); Clara Shih, *The Facebook Era: Tapping Online Social Networks to Market, Sell, and Innovate on the Web* (Upper Saddle River, NJ: Prentice Hall, 2011).

[41]Chris Cole, *Building Open Social Apps: A Field Guide to Working with MySpace Platform* (New York: Addison Wesley, 2010).

[42]Ibid.

[43]Susan Getgood, *Professional Blogging* (New York: Wiley, 2011).

[44]Kern Alexander and M. David Alexander, *American Public School Law*, 8th ed. (Belmont, CA: Wadsworth/Cengage, 2011).

[45]Linda I. O'Leary, *Microsoft Powerpoint 2010: A Case Approach, Complete* (New York: McGraw-Hill, 2011); see also Granville Toogood, *The Articulate Executive: Look, Act, and Sound Like a Leader* (New York: McGraw-Hill, 2011).

[46]Lunenburg and Irby, *Writing a Successful Thesis or Dissertation*.

[47]Adam C. Raylor, *Videoconferencing: Technology, Impact, and Applications* (Hauppauge, NY: Nova Science Publishers, 2011); see also Camille Cole, *Videoconferencing for K-12 Classrooms: A Program Development Guide* (Eugene, OR: International Society for Technology in Education, 2010).

ADMINISTRATIVE ADVICE 7–3

Multi-Media Presentations

Following are some suggestions for improving multi-media presentations.

Talk to the audience, not the screen. A problem with computer-generated PowerPoint slides is that the speaker as well as the audience tend to focus on the slide. Minimize looking at the slide and spend time looking at the audience. This will make it easier to make eye contact with them.

Provide your audience with your PowerPoint slides. Make 3–6 slides per page. Some people like to follow the PowerPoint slides on screen. Others prefer to follow the hard copy and take notes. The hard copy also provides the audience with a "take away" from the meeting.

Reduce your PowerPoint slides to bulleted items. A rule of thumb is: include no more than 24 words per slide. Use a large enough font size for the slide to be viewed at a distance of at least 20 feet.

Keep the slide in view long enough for the audience to comprehend its meaning. All too often, slide presentations deteriorate into a continual array of flashings on the screen. Synchronize the slides with meaningful comments.

Practice learning the content of your talk (or presentation). If you cannot memorize the content, practice reading the presentation with as much enthusiasm—variation in pitch, tone, and modulation of your voice, as well as periodic eye contact with your audience—as possible. The trick to reading a talk (or presentation) is to appear not to be reading it.

During the question portion of your presentation, answer questions completely and succinctly. When answering the question, maintain eye contact with the questioner while periodically scanning the entire audience. In a large meeting, you might repeat the question for all to hear using a microphone.

people use to acquire feedback. Preventing visibility and depersonalization in the workplace are concerns when using information technologies such as e-mail, instant messaging, text messaging, and videoconferencing.

Barriers to Communication

Effective communication plays a vital role in accomplishing the goals of the school district. However, barriers may interfere with effective communication and include frames of reference, filtering, structure, information overload, semantics, and status differences.

Frames of Reference

People can interpret the same communication differently, depending on their learning, culture, and experience. This type of communication barrier is related to the encoding and decoding components of the communication process discussed earlier. If the sender and receiver have a common **frame of reference**—that is, when the encoding and decoding of a message are similar—communication is likely to be effective. If, on the other hand, the communicators have different frames of reference, communication is likely to become distorted.[48] For example, people raised in different cultures may react quite differently to the same message. Other examples of different frames of reference in a school district may include those of superintendent and principal, principal and teacher, teacher and student, and management and union. While neither of these groups is right or wrong, each group has unique experiences, and each plays a different role, which often results in unintentional distortions of the communication between them in the school district.

---

[48]John D. Hatfield and Richard C. Huseman, "Perceptual Congruence About Communication as Related to Satisfaction: Moderating Effects of Individual Characteristics," *Academy of Management Journal*, 25 (1982): 349–358.

Filtering

Another barrier to effective communication is **filtering,** a process that occurs as information is transmitted from one level to another. It involves the transmittal of partial information by the sender. Filtering can occur in either downward or upward flows of communication.

During downward communication flows, unintentional filtering can occur because of errors in encoding and decoding messages. Differences in learning, culture, and experiences may account for unintentional filtering. Intentional filtering occurs when a sender assumes that parts of a message are not needed by the receiver. This can result in distortions of the original meaning of the message. Research shows that administrators may be reluctant to transmit negative information downward. For example, subordinates who had good performance ratings were more likely to be informed of those ratings than subordinates who had poor ratings.[49] Administrators may also be reluctant to communicate positive information if they feel the subordinate will use it to support a claim against the organization or to oppose the administration sometime in the future.

Given this finding, it is not surprising that administrators and their subordinates sometimes have differing perceptions concerning subordinate performance ratings. Filtering by school administrators can also be a constructive means of uncertainty absorption, according to James March and Herbert Simon.[50] Administrators may intentionally withhold information that they feel might create anxiety in subordinates and thus result in a decrease in subordinates' productivity.

In school districts, filtering problems occur more often in upward communication than in downward communication. Because administrators are in a position to withhold rewards, subordinates manipulate unfavorable information flowing upward in the school district. The reason for such filtering should be obvious. Administrators make merit evaluations, give salary increases, and promote employees based on information they receive from subordinates. Research indicates that subordinates with strong aspirations for upward mobility are especially likely to filter information in upward communication. Moreover, subordinates who distrust their superiors and lack security will filter their messages. And those who desire to impress their superiors to achieve a promotion will manipulate unfavorable information about themselves.[51]

Structure

The **structure** of the school district can affect the quality of communications within it. A tall structure is one in which there are many hierarchical levels of authority. Generally, communication efficiency decreases with the number of levels through which information must pass before reaching its intended receiver. The reason is fairly simple: the more levels of administration through which a message must be transmitted, the greater the danger that it will be changed, modified, shortened, amended, or misinterpreted or will totally fail to reach its receiver.[52] The tall structure is very useful for horizontal communication flow. Individuals tend to communicate more at their own level than to attempt to circumvent levels and converse with others at the top and bottom of the hierarchy. Thus, communication among colleagues is good, but upward and downward communication is frequently poor and distorted.[53]

A flat structure, which has few levels between the top and bottom of the hierarchy, has many people at the bottom. It is relatively easy to get a message from the bottom to the top of the hierarchy in a flat structure. This provides a partial explanation of why face-to-face communication works more effectively in small rather than in large school districts. Direct channels can be used more readily because fewer levels of administration have to be penetrated.[54] For example, in very small school districts, board members often speak directly to building principals or teachers, bypassing the superintendent. Similarly, in small school districts, teachers often communicate directly with board members, violating the formal hierarchy. Furthermore, in a flat structure, there is less gatekeeping, and vertical (upward and downward) communication between superior and subordinate is better.

An example of a tall structure might be the New York City public schools, and an example of a flat structure

---

[49]Gary Johns, *Organizational Behavior: Understanding and Managing Life at Work* (Upper Saddle River, NJ: Prentice Hall, 2008).

[50]James G. March and Herbert A. Simon, *Organizations*, 3rd ed. (Cambridge, MA: Blackwell, 2004).

[51]Shockley-Zalabak, *Fundamentals of Communication.*

[52]Cheney, *Organizational Communication in an Age of Globalization.*

[53]Ibid.

[54]Andrew J. DuBrin, *Essentials of Management* (Belmont, CA: Thomson South-Western, 2009).

might be a small, rural elementary school. The New York City public school system has many levels of authority, with smaller units under each; the typical small, rural elementary school has a principal and several teachers. One disadvantage of the flat structure is that the head administrator might suffer from information overload because the span of control in a flat structure is generally greater than in a tall structure.[55]

Information Overload

In today's complex school organizations, school administrators are frequently overloaded with more information than they can handle effectively. This **information overload** occurs for several reasons. First, school districts face higher levels of uncertainty today because of increasing turbulence in the external environment.[56] School districts respond by obtaining more information to reduce the uncertainty. Second, increased role specialization and task complexity create a need for more information. For example, school districts employ counselors, social workers, school psychologists, business managers, personnel directors, professional negotiators, and curriculum directors, to name only a few. In the curriculum area of special education alone, there are teacher specialists in emotionally disturbed (ED), learning disabilities (LD), educable mentally handicapped (EMH), physically handicapped and other health impairments (PHOHI), multiply handicapped (MH), orthopedically handicapped (OH), and severely and profoundly handicapped (SPH).[57] The wide variety of specialists provide needed information to accomplish a complexity of tasks. This specialization results in additional demands to process the increased amount of information. Third, advances in communication technology, such as the use of computers, increases the quantity of information and data available. As a result, administrators are deluged with information; they cannot absorb or adequately respond to all of it. Thus, they select parts of it, which often results in incomplete or inaccurate information on which to make decisions. The problem today is not a scarcity but an overabundance of information that can be processed effectively.

One research team identifies seven categories of response to communication overload: *omitting* (failing to process some of the information); *erroring* (processing information incorrectly); *queueing* (leveling the peak loads by delaying until a lull occurs); *filtering* (separating out less relevant information); *approximating* (categorizing input and using a general response for each category); *employing multiple channels* (introducing alternative channels for information flow); and *escaping* (avoiding the information).[58]

Semantics

The same words may have different meanings to different people. Thus, it is possible for a school administrator and subordinates to speak the same language but still not transmit understanding. As defined previously, communication is the transmission of information from a sender to a receiver through the use of common symbols. However, one cannot transmit understanding; one can only transmit information in the form of words, which are the common symbols conveying ideas, facts, and feelings. **Semantics** can be a communication barrier because of the misinterpretation of words. Meanings are not in the words but in the minds of the people who receive them.

Meanings of concrete words do not differ much from sender to receiver. Little misunderstanding arises when we speak of typewriter, computer, paper, or book. Because words such as love, happiness, and virtue are more abstract, more misunderstandings are likely to occur. Similarly, words that evoke emotional responses, like liberal and conservative, are prime candidates for greater misunderstandings.

One reason for semantic differences relates to the use of numerous specialists who tend to develop their own professional jargon. This special language can provide in-group members with feelings of belongingness, cohesiveness, and even self-esteem. And it can enhance effective communication within the group. However, the use of in-group language can often result in barriers to communication for outsiders. For example, special education teachers use abbreviations like LD (learning disabilities), ED (emotionally disturbed), EMH (educable mentally handicapped), and IEP (individualized education plan),

[55]David D. Van Fleet, "Span of Management Research and Issues," *Academy of Management Journal*, 26 (1983): 546–552.

[56]Catherine A. Lugg et al., "The Contextual Terrain Facing Educational Leaders," in J. Murphy (ed.), *The Leadership Challenge: Redefining Leadership for the 21st Century* (Chicago: University of Chicago Press, 2002), pp. 20–41.

[57]Special education nomenclature varies from state to state.

[58]Jerald Greenberg, *Behavior in Organizations*, 10th ed. (Upper Saddle River, NJ: Prentice Hall, 2011).

which is common terminology among these professionals. Such abbreviations or terms will probably have little meaning to people outside this specialized group.

Status Differences

Another barrier to communication is **status difference,** which exists within every school district. School districts create status differences through titles, size of office, carpeting, office furnishings, stationery, private secretary, a reserved parking space, salary, and the formal organizational chart. Regardless of the symbols, status interferes with effective communication between personnel at different levels of the hierarchy. The status of superordinate-subordinate relationships, for example, inhibits the free flow of information vertically (upward and downward).

The higher one's status in the school district, the less likely the person will have effective communications with personnel a few levels removed. In general, individuals who have higher status also receive more communication demands on them. Out of necessity, they must limit their communications to those who have direct influence on them—that is, their direct supervisors and subordinates. For example, the superintendent needs to be concerned with establishing communications with the assistant superintendents directly under him as well as with the board of education, who is directly above the superintendent. Such a communication pattern was outlined previously. Recall that the superintendent communicated frequently with the assistant superintendents. However, the superintendent's communication with other lower-level personnel was less frequent or nonexistent (see Figure 7–5).

Thus, as shown in network analysis, communication between higher-status personnel and lower-status personnel tends to be limited, and the messages that subordinates send upward in the hierarchy tend to be positive (filtering). Moreover, subordinates may be reluctant to express an opinion that is contrary to their supervisor's. One reason for this behavior is that the administration has the power to grant and withhold rewards such as merit evaluations, salary increases, promotions, and better work assignments. School administrators, because of time constraints, indifference, or arrogance, may actually strengthen status differentials by not being open to feedback or other forms of upward communication. However, when the status differences become too great, communications decrease, and subordinates initiate less communication with superiors.

Overcoming Barriers to Communication

Effective communication requires a sustained effort by both school administrators and employees to overcome communication barriers and arrive at mutual understandings. Although there should be some responsibilities on both sides, successful communication seems to lie primarily with school administrators because they are the ones to develop a two-way communicative climate. In an attempt to overcome some of the communication barriers, we examine five communication skills—repetition, empathy, understanding, feedback, and listening—that are a means of improving school district communications.

Repetition

One of the most frequently used techniques of effective communication is repetition. **Repetition** involves sending the same message over and over again, using multiple channels (e.g., telephone call, face-to-face discussion, memorandum, or letter). Most communication is subject to some distortion. By using two or more channels to transmit a message, communication failure is less likely to occur. For example, a personal discussion can be followed up with a memorandum or letter. Here both written and oral channels are used. The sender has gained the attention of the receiver as a result of face-to-face communication. The sender and receiver also have written records of the conversation for future reference and to stipulate all details of the conversation. Similarly, sending minutes of a meeting to participants is using repetition and multiple channels of communication to ensure understanding.

It is customary in large school districts for school administrators to use multiple channels to communicate the results of a subordinate's performance evaluation. The subordinate first receives a verbal explanation of the results that is accompanied or followed by a written statement, which the superior and subordinate sign as an indication that each has read and understands its content.

Empathy

Effective communication means that the sender can make predictions about how the receiver will respond to a message. The sender can accomplish this by visualizing the receiver's frame of reference into the transmission of the message. In other words, a school administrator should figuratively walk in the shoes of the subordinate and attempt to anticipate personal and situational factors that might influence the subordinate's interpretation of the message. For superintendents to communicate effectively with assistant superintendents, for assistant superintendents to communicate effectively with principals, for principals to communicate effectively with faculty, and for faculty to communicate effectively with students, empathy is an important ingredient and can reduce many of the aforementioned barriers to communication.

Empathy is a technique for understanding the other person's frame of reference. The greater the gap between the learning, the culture, and the experiences of the sender and the receiver, the greater the effort that must be made to find a common ground of understanding.

Understanding

Earlier we said that communication is effective to the extent that both the sender and the receiver have high agreement in their understanding of a transmitted message. School administrators must remember that effective communication involves transmitting **understanding** as well as messages. Regardless of the communication channel used, messages should contain simple, understandable language. School administrators must encode messages in words and symbols that are understandable to the receiver.

As noted, understanding cannot be communicated; only messages can. This is the idea behind the concept of readability popularized by several authors. [59] Readability seeks to make writing and speech more understandable. Flesch and others developed readability formulas that can be applied to written and oral communication alike. Some research has found that much written communication that is transmitted to employees is rated as beyond the level of satisfactory reading for typical adults.[60]

Feedback

Feedback ensures effective communication and determines the degree to which a message has been received and understood. This two-way communication, in which the sender and the receiver arrive at mutual understanding, contrasts with one-way communication of the kind that occurs in most downward communication. In downward communication, for example, distortions often occur because of insufficient opportunity for feedback from receivers. For example, when the superintendent distributes a memorandum on an important board policy to all professional personnel in the school district, this act alone does not guarantee that communication has taken place.

One might expect feedback in the form of upward communication to be encouraged more in school districts that use participatory management, site-based management, and site-based decision-making practices. School districts need effective upward communications if their downward communications are to be effective. Some studies report numerous benefits of two-way communication (feedback) over one-way communication. For example, although two-way communication is more time-consuming than is one-way communication, it provides increased satisfaction and is recommended in all but the simplest and routine transmission of information.[61]

Written messages provide much less opportunity for feedback than does face-to-face communication. When possible, school administrators should use face-to-face communication because this approach allows the individuals communicating with each other to receive both verbal and nonverbal feedback. Brief, straightforward questions such as the following can be helpful in eliciting feedback from subordinates about the reception of a message: How do you feel about my statement? What do you think? What did you hear me say? Do you see any problems with what we have talked about?[62] Such attempts to elicit feedback from a receiver of a message can avoid misunderstandings between a sender and a receiver.

Some guidelines that school administrators can use to elicit feedback from subordinates include the following:[63]

- Promote and cultivate feedback, but don't try to force it.
- Reward those who provide feedback and use feedback received.
- Whenever possible, go straight to the source and observe the results—don't wait for feedback.

[59]Lunenburg and Irby, *Writing a Successful Thesis or Dissertation*; see also Rudolf Flesch, *The Art of Readable Writing* (NewYork: Macmillan, 1994).

[60]Jeff Butterfield, *Written Communication, Oral Communication, and Presentation Skills* (Belmont, CA: South-Western/ Cengage Learning, 2010).

[61]Eric M. Eisenberg et al., *Organizational Communication: Balancing Creativity and Constraint* (New York: Bedford/ St. Martin's Press, 2010).

[62]DuBrin, *Essentials of Management*.

[63]Greenberg, *Behavior in Organizations*.

ADMINISTRATIVE ADVICE 7–4

Listening Styles

One way of viewing listening is to look at listening styles. Six listening styles which have been developed by Performax Systems International can help school administrators improve their listening skills.

Leisure Listener. This listener is very relaxed and tunes in primarily to what is pleasant. To be more effective, a leisure listener needs to avoid wandering off on tangents and to focus on the task at hand. This listener should also be willing to listen to important information, even if it is unpleasant and makes her uncomfortable.

Inclusive Listener. This listener takes in everything, wanting to understand the main ideas of the speaker in order to be comfortable. To be more effective, an inclusive listener needs to avoid getting impatient with ramblers, to stop trying to take in everything, and to concentrate more on analyzing and evaluating the message.

Stylistic Listener. This listener tunes in to the mannerisms and dress of the speaker and wants to know the speaker's background and credentials. This listener also tends to place the speaker in a favorable or unfavorable category. To be more effective, a stylistic listener needs to avoid stereotyping and to pay more attention to the content that is being presented.

Technical Listener. This listener is very tuned in to processing information and is listening or gathering specific data within a narrow but in-depth listening range. To be more effective, a technical listener needs to avoid tunnel listening and to become more inclusive. This listener would also profit by paying more attention to nonverbal cues and being more open to the emotions of the speaker.

Empathic Listener. This listener is looking for the unstated message and needs to understand the emotions of the speaker before becoming comfortable with the interpersonal communications. To be more effective, an empathic listener needs to focus on the task at hand, realizing that the content of the message is important as well as the emotions.

Nonconforming Listener. This listener analyzes, evaluates, and has a tendency to agree or disagree quickly. This listener also tends to challenge the speaker and listens for supporting data to use in agreement or disagreement. (This is different from the technical listener who gathers supporting data to apply to a specific task situation.) To be more effective, a nonconforming listener needs to avoid hasty judgments and to look for points of agreement early in the speaker's message. This person also has a tendency to overprotect stimuli and assign a deeper meaning than was intended.

Source: Adapted from Frank W. Freshour, "Listening Power: Key to Effective Leadership," *Illinois School Research and Development,* 26 (1989): 17–23.

- Give feedback to subordinates on the outcome of the feedback received. Thus, the school administrator elicits feedback, uses it, and feeds back its results to subordinates.

Listening

Earlier, we noted that school administrators spend over 70 percent of their time communicating. Moreover, estimates indicate that over 30 percent of an administrator's day is devoted to listening. More important, tests of listening comprehension suggest that these individuals listen at only 25 percent efficiency.[64] Listening skills affect the quality of colleague and superordinate-subordinate relationships in schools. (See Administrative Advice 7–4).

Successful communication therefore requires effective **listening** on the part of both the sender and the receiver. The receiver must listen to receive and understand the sender's messages; and the sender must listen to

[64] Ibid.

Parent Involvement

Parent-teacher organizations and booster clubs provide many schools with volunteer assistance in classrooms, school libraries, and school offices. In some communities, their fundraising abilities supply instructional, athletic, and musical equipment beyond the scope of the school budget. These resources provide visible support for schools, but they are not intended to impact directly on school policy or curriculum. Recently, the literature recommends parent involvement on school and district committees so that parents can influence decisions about schooling.

Question: When parents sit on district and school committees, does this communication channel enhance the relationship between school and community?

Arguments PRO

1. Parents and educators are partners in the child's development. A partnership suggests separate but equal contributions and shared responsibility. Parents deserve greater access to the inner workings of schools. The relationship between school and community will only improve when schools provide vehicles for access.
2. Parents, especially the urban poor who were themselves not successful in school, are disenfranchised stakeholders in the educational system. They have a vested interest in the welfare of their own children but are intimidated by school policies and procedures. These parents need nonthreatening interactions with educators. Service on committees provides an arena for work on mutual goals and the development of positive attitudes.
3. Through involvement on district and school committees, parents provide the client's view of the educational system. Traditionally, this viewpoint has been sought only rarely. The relationship between school and community is enhanced because the client's perspective is valued.
4. When parents are oriented to their role in governance, they develop the knowledge and skills they need to operate well in committee structures. A period of orientation and training increases mutual understanding between parents and teachers.
5. Parents have too few opportunities to interact with schools in a positive, professional manner. Through involvement such as service on committees, parents will observe that teachers are skilled problem solvers.

Arguments CON

1. The school acts *in loco parentis,* in place of the parent. School personnel have the responsibility for providing educational service and are certified to do so by the state. Frequently, parents are the problem, not the solution. Their access to school matters should be limited.
2. Most parents are concerned about their child's education, but, with changes in families (mothers working outside the home, single parents, etc.), many are too busy. In some settings, parents ignore or are hostile toward educators. They do not participate voluntarily in school-sponsored events such as open house. Those who need to volunteer won't.
3. Most of what parents know about the school they learn from their own children. They overgeneralize on the basis of that limited data. Their motivation is to improve conditions for only their child. They have little interest in supporting procedures that benefit the general welfare. Because committees act for the general good, parents are thwarted in their efforts. In the long run, the school-community relationship worsens.
4. Parents lack the educational expertise to understand the complex issues raised on committees. School-community relations will worsen because parents cannot participate on an equal footing with professional educators.
5. Parents have ample opportunity to observe and interact with teachers on matters related to their children's instruction. However, parents are often intimidated by teachers' knowledge. In working together on committees, they will see teachers as formal and distant.

receive and understand the receiver's feedback. Often listening is the weak link in the chain of two-way communication. Many people do not work actively at listening well. One author emphasizes that listening is an active process that demands a great deal of concentration and effort.[65] Recently, some organizations have designed training programs that explore techniques for improving listening skills.[66] For example, the following guidelines can be helpful to school administrators:[67]

- *Stop talking.*
- Put the talker at ease.
- Show the talker you want to listen.
- Remove distractions.
- Empathize with the talker.
- Be patient.
- Hold your temper.
- Go easy on argument and criticism.
- Ask questions.
- *Stop talking.*

Note that the first and last rule for good listening is to "stop talking." Some researchers estimate that administrators spend as much as 85 percent of time devoted to communicating—in talking.[68] This does not leave much time for listening and feedback. School administrators must realize that effective communication involves understanding as well as being understood.

Lee Iacocca stresses the importance of listening, Tom Peters and Robert Waterman suggest that service to clients is the foundation of listening, and Paul Hersey and Kenneth Blanchard make numerous references to listening in their situational leadership theory.[69] And numerous reform reports—including *A Nation at Risk,* the Holmes Group, the Carnegie Task Force on Teaching as a Profession, and the Governor's Report—all recommend formal instruction in listening skills in schools.

[65]Bruce Benward and Timothy J. Kolosick, *Ear Training: Revised* (New York: McGraw-Hill, 2010).

[66]Larry Barker, *Listen Up: How to Improve Relationships, Reduce Stress and Be More Productive by Using the Power of Listening* (New York: St. Martin's Press, 2000).

[67]Kay Dans, *Human Behavior at Work* (New York: McGraw-Hill, 1972).

[68]Greenberg, *Behavior in Organizations.*

[69]Lee Iacocca, *Iacocca* (New York: Random House, 2009); Thomas J. Peters and Robert H. Waterman, *In Search of Excellence* (New York: Collins Business Essentials, 2006); Paul Hersey and Kenneth Blanchard, *Management of Organizational Behavior*, 9th ed. (Upper Saddle River, NJ: Prentice Hall, 2010).

Summary

1. Communication is an important skill because school administrators spend over 70 percent of their time communicating.
2. The communication process is continuous and involves eight steps: ideating, encoding, transmitting, receiving, decoding, acting, using, and feedback. Nonverbal communication involves encoding and decoding body language, vocal cues, use of time, and spatial relationships to more effectively understand verbal messages.
3. Communications within school organizations flow in four primary directions: downward, upward, horizontally, and diagonally. These communication flows are more likely to occur in open than in closed organizational climates.
4. The major informal communication flow in school organizations is called the grapevine. The grapevine carries both accurate information and rumors.
5. Whether formal or informal, the actual pattern of communication connecting people within school organizations is called a network. A school organization's network is often quite different from the pattern of relationships established by its formal structure.
6. Advances in technology have influenced the quantity and quality of communications in the workplace. Six developments that illustrate the impact of technology on communication are the following: e-mail, instant messaging, social networking, internet or Web logs (blogs), computer slide presentations, and videoconferencing.
7. The barriers to effective communication include differing frames of reference, filtering, structure, information overload, semantics, and status differences. Techniques for overcoming barriers to effective communication include repetition, empathy, understanding, feedback, and listening.

Key Terms

communication process
idea
encode

transmit
receive
decode
act
feedback
readability
nonverbal communication
kinesics
proxemics
paralanguage
chronemics
communication flow
grapevine
network pattern
network analysis
e-mail
instant messaging
text messaging
social networking
Facebook
Myspace
Web logs (blogs)
PowerPoint
videoconferencing
frame of reference
filtering
structure
information overload
semantics
status differences
repetition
empathy
understanding
feedback
listening

Discussion Questions

1. Select a communication you have had recently and analyze it using the model shown in Figure 7–1.
2. Using network analysis, develop a communication network for your school. Compare your communication network with the formal structure of the school.
3. Why is it difficult to obtain accurate information from upward and downward communication flows?
4. What are six barriers to effective communication in school organizations? And what are some techniques for overcoming these barriers?
5. Observe the nonverbal communication behavior of organizational participants for fifteen minutes. Explain the nonverbal behavior you observe. Is there any inconsistency between nonverbal and verbal behaviors?
6. Discuss the six different advances in technology presented in this textbook. How is your school organization using any or all of these communication devices?

Suggested Readings

Bagin, Don, Donald R. Gallagher, and Leslie W. Kindred. *The School and Community Relations* (Needham Heights, MA: Allyn and Bacon, 1994). The authors clarify the present situation of the field and combine both theory and practice in charting a course toward the steady improvement of public education with programs for better school-community communication.

Brislin, Richard, and Tomoko Yoshida. *Intercultural Communication Training: An Introduction* (Thousand Oaks, CA: Sage, 1994). The approaches this volume covers—such as assessing needs, establishing goals, and building positive attitudes—apply to any situation where good personal relations and effective communication need to be established with people from different cultural backgrounds.

Burleson, Brant, Terrance L. Albrecht, and Irwin G. Sarason (eds.). *Communication of Social Support: Messages, Interactions, Relationships, and Community* (Thousand Oaks, CA: Sage, 1994). Chapters examine functional and dysfunctional patterns involved in the communication of support, and offer both scholarly and applied audiences an understanding of social support as a communication process grounded in ongoing relationships.

Gudykunst, William B. *Bridging Differences: Effective Intergroup Communication*, 3rd ed. (Thousand Oaks, CA: Sage, 1999). This volume includes culture and ethnicity; intergroup attitudes and stereotyping; managing intergroup attitudes; community building; exchanging messages with other groups; and the knowledge, motivation, and skills necessary for intergroup communication.

Gumbrecht, Hans U., and Ludwig K. Pfeiffer (eds.). *Materialities of Communication* (Stanford, CA: Stanford University Press, 1994). This volume describes the whole process of communication from ideation to activity, including barriers and methods of overcoming them.

Knapp, Mark L., and Gerald R. Miller (eds.). *Handbook of Interpersonal Communication,* 3rd ed. (Thousand Oaks, CA: Sage, 1998). The handbook lays out the key theoretical and methodological issues; focuses on component parts or growth processes, verbal and nonverbal behavior, situational and cultural influences, the characteristics each communicator brings to an encounter; and examines mutual influence and temporal processes and interpersonal processes in four important relational contexts.

Warner, Carolyn. *Promoting Your School: Going Beyond PR* (Thousand Oaks, CA: Corwin, Press, 1994). Smart school leaders have learned from corporate America that marketing is a potent tool that can help forge a partnership among educators, parents, community, and the private sector to meet the ever-increasing demands on schools.

8

Organizational Change

FOCUSING QUESTIONS

1 What are the major forces for change facing schools?

2 Why do school employees resist change?

3 What strategies can school administrators use to overcome resistance to change?

4 What models can school administrators use to manage change?

5 Are there organizational development techniques or interventions school administrators (or change agents) can use to plan and implement change? What are they?

In this chapter, we attempt to answer these questions concerning change in school organizations. We begin our discussion by examining the major forces for change facing schools. Then we discuss the major sources of resistance to change. This is followed by strategies school administrators can use to overcome resistance to change. Next, we examine three models school administrators can use to manage change: Kurt Lewin's force-field analysis, John Kotter's eight-step plan, and Ben Harris's five-phase model. Finally, we present and analyze six organizational development techniques or interventions designed to plan and implement change in school settings. The first set of techniques includes group approaches to change: total quality management, strategic planning, and survey feedback. The next set of interventions includes individual approaches to change: job enrichment, laboratory training, and behavioral performance management.

Forces for Change

Change has become the norm in most schools. *Adaptiveness, flexibility*, and *responsiveness* are characteristics of the schools that will succeed. In the past, schools could claim success by adhering to managerial-type indicators, such as financial stability, clean buildings, and well-behaved students. This is not the case today. The current accountability environment in which schools operate demands excellence of all students on state-mandated tests, as well as competent school administrators. We discuss five specific forces that are acting as stimulants for change in schools: accountability, changing demographics, staffing shortages, technological changes and knowledge explosion, and processes and people.

Accountability

School administrators have always had to deal with bureaucratic accountability, that is, accountability with respect to superordinate-subordinate relationships. For example, the teacher is accountable to the principal; the principal is accountable to the superintendent; the superintendent is accountable to the school board. However, accountability to constituencies external to the local school board increasingly drives accountability frameworks today. The business community pressures schools to graduate skilled workers for today's economy. Governors and state legislators play key roles in designing accountability plans. The national education plan, titled *No Child Left Behind* (NCLB), stipulates specific requirements that states must follow regarding student accountability.

As accountability has become more prominent at the state and national levels, the focus has shifted from accountability for inputs or transformation processes to outputs. This is reflected in state standards and testing. Presently, all 50 states have statewide assessment systems in place, and in nearly half of the states the stakes attached to these outcomes have been gradually increased.[1] Furthermore, with the reauthorization of NCLB, each state will be required to implement a statewide system of assessment in reading and mathematics for grades 3 through 8.[2]

Another new form of accountability is market accountability. Open enrollment policies, which allow students to choose public schools within and outside their home districts, have become popular. In addition, there has been growing political support for nontraditional methods of funding public schools, such as the expansion of home schooling, charter schools, and school vouchers. Such an expansion of public school choice frameworks has forced some school administrators to reallocate their time from internal to external functions, such as marketing and fundraising.

Changing Demographics

Currently, enrollment in public schools is growing. Higher enrollment is generally associated with greater ethnic, racial, and linguistic diversity, a school population that has the greatest level of needs. The United States Census in 2000 reported that out of the nation's 49 million students, 62.9 percent were white, 17.1 percent were African American, 15 percent were Hispanic, 3.9 percent were Asian or Pacific Islander, and 1.1 percent were American Indian or Alaskan Native.[3] Ethnicity is closely related to poverty and the dropout rate. For example, 36.5 percent of African American and 33.6 percent of Hispanic families with children lived in poverty in 2000 compared to only 14.5 percent of white families.[4] And African American and Hispanic students are much more likely to drop out of school than white students.[5]

Immigration is also creating demographic changes in public schools. According to estimates, nearly one million legal and illegal immigrants come to the United States every year. Many of these immigrants and their children are poor and have limited English proficiency, which places greater demands on educating these students and has increased political debates about bilingual education and testing.[6]

---

[1] W. James Popham, *Everything School Leaders Need to Know About Assessment* (Thousand Oaks, CA: Corwin Press, 2010).

[2] *No Child Left Behind Act of 2001.*

[3] U.S. Census Bureau, United States Department of Commerce, *School Enrollment* (Washington, DC: U.S. Census Bureau, 2000).

[4] National Center for Education Statistics, *School-Age Children Living in Poverty in the United States: 2000–2001* (Washington, DC: Author, 2003).

[5] National Center for Education Statistics, *Dropouts in Public Schools in the United States: 2000–2002* (Washington, DC: Author, 2003).

[6] Carola Suárez-Orozco and Marcelo Suárez-Orozco, *Learning a New Land: Immigration Students in American Society* (Cambridge, MA: Harvard University Press, 2011).

Staffing Shortages

After many years of having a steady stream of qualified teachers and principals, many school districts are facing severe shortages.[7] Shortages of teachers and administrators are due largely to retirements, an expanding student population, career changes, and increasing teacher and administrator turnover. Expanding student enrollment in general and a growing population of students with special needs may further exacerbate these shortages, especially in areas such as special education and bilingual education.

Another issue facing school administrators is increasing the racial and ethnic diversity of personnel. Although the student population is growing racially and ethnically more diverse, similar demographic shifts have not occurred in the teaching ranks. The teaching force is predominantly white (87.2%), with the remainder coming from minority groups (12.8%).[8] This student-teacher mismatch often results in considerable cultural and social distance between middle-class white teachers and students of color. It have been suggested that white educators and school administrators do not have a thorough enough understanding of how to deal with students from different cultural backgrounds. This mismatch may have learning consequences for students of color.[9] Teacher preparation programs rarely train teacher candidates in strategies for teaching culturally diverse students. The lack of familiarity with students' cultures, learning styles, and communication patterns translates into some teachers holding negative expectations for students. And, often, inappropriate curricula, instructional materials, and assessments are used with these students.[10]

Technological Changes and Knowledge Explosion

Another source of external pressure for change is the technological explosion all organizations are experiencing. This pressure is due in part to research and development efforts within organizations. For example, many large, urban school districts now have research and development departments as part of their organizational structures. However, a great deal of technological development occurs outside the organization. This development is the result of government-sponsored research efforts and the efforts of numerous educational organizations including the American Association of School Administrators (AASA), National Association of Secondary School Principals (NASSP), National Association of Elementary School Principals (NAESP), Cooperative Program in Educational Administration (CPEA), University Council for Educational Administration (UCEA), National Council of Professors of Educational Administration (NCPEA), National Academy for School Executives (NASE), Association for Supervision and Curriculum Development (ASCD), National Society for the Study of Education (NSSE), and the American Educational Research Association (AERA).

Concurrent with the development of new technologies is an explosion of knowledge. More people than ever before are attending college, and a large percentage of the population is receiving graduate degrees. Higher education is no longer reserved for the elite few. There is also a growing emphasis on continuing education courses offered on university campuses across the country, and nontraditional students (older students) are returning to junior colleges and four-year institutions. New technologies require the development of knowledge to implement the technology. Thus, the interaction of new technology and the knowledge required to generate the technology into the organization compounds the rate of technological change exponentially.

Processes and People

Pressures in the internal environment of the organization can also stimulate change. The two most significant internal pressures come from processes and people. Processes that act as forces for change include communications, decision making, leadership, and motivational strategies, to name only a few. Breakdowns or problems in any of these processes can create pressures for change. Communications may be inadequate; decisions may be of poor quality; leadership may be inappropriate for the situation; and employee motivation may be nonexistent.

Some symptoms of people problems are poor performance levels of teachers and students, high absenteeism of teachers or students, high dropout rates of students, high teacher turnover, poor school-community relations, poor management-union relations, and low levels of teacher morale and job satisfaction. A teachers' strike, numerous employee complaints, and the filing of

[7]National Center for Education Statistics, *Digest of Educational Statistics, 2002* (Washington, DC: Author, 2003).

[8]National Education Association, *Status of the American Public School Teacher, 2000–2001* (Washington, DC: Author, 2004).

[9]Fred C. Lunenburg, "Cocking Lecture: Improving Student Achievement: Some Structural Incompatibilities," in G. Perreault and F.C. Lunenburg (eds.) *The Changing World of School Administration* (Lanham, MD: Scarecrow Press, 2002, pp. 5–27.)

[10]Joseph Murphy, *The Educator's Handbook for Understanding and Closing Achievement Gaps* (Thousand Oaks, CA: Corwin Press, 2010).

ADMINISTRATIVE ADVICE 8–1

Making Change Work

Four conditions that help facilitate change are the following:

Condition 1: Participant Involvement. Recent management theory, including W. Edwards Deming's popular Total Quality Management (TQM) model, speaks directly to involvement of participants in decisions that affect their work life. Many authors make a strong case for using consensus when introducing changes in the schools.

Condition 2: Senior Administrator Support. The superintendent is not typically the change agent at the local level, but her or his support is critical to the success of a change effort. Financial support, comments about the initiative at school board meetings, and visits to the school will have a positive influence on staff members.

Condition 3: No Escalation of Teacher Workload. Teachers typically have overburdened work schedules and have little time for extra duties. Ideally, a change should not add to an already overburdened work assignment. Changes that require greater time commitment should include a plan to lighten other responsibilities.

Condition 4: Change Agent's Active Involvement. The change agent may be anyone in the school or school district. The person with direct line responsibility for the change must take an active and supportive role in overseeing the change at the local level. This will assure the day-to-day progress of change and provide an informational resource for those involved.

Source: Adapted from Richard L. Bucko, "Making Change Work," *School Administrator,* 6 (1994): 32.

grievances are some tangible signs of problems in the internal environment. These factors provide a signal to school administrators that change is necessary. In addition, internal pressures for change occur in response to organizational changes that are designed to deal with forces for change exerted by the external environment.

Today, planning for change is essential as many school administrators move to one of the forms of site-based decision making (SBDM) or seek improvements in curriculum and instruction. Drawing from the related research, we can identify the primary conditions that greatly enhance the success of any change effort. (See Administrative Advice 8–1.)

Resistance to Change

A well-documented finding from studies of organizations of all kinds is that their members resist change.[11] Even when organization members are shown data that suggests that change is necessary, they resist it. Most employees see change as threatening.[12]

One example of such resistance to change that received world-wide media coverage a few years ago was the firing of Lawrence Summers, former president of Harvard University. Lawrence Summers accepted the presidency of Harvard in 2001. He immediately began to make massive changes in the somewhat complacent institution. These changes included revamping the undergraduate curriculum, proposing that the university become more directly involved in the problems of education and public health, and revamping the existing organizational structure in order to place more power in the president's office.[13] In 2006, Summers commented publicly that women were less capable of excelling in math and science than men. The faculty revolted. Within a few weeks, Summers was forced to resign. According to reports, Summers demise was not about gender

[11]Bert Spector, *Implementing Organizational Change: Theory into Practice, International Edition* (Upper Saddle River, NJ: Prentice Hall, 2011); Michael Fullan, *The Challenge of Change* (Thousand Oaks, CA: Corwin Press, 2009); Andy Hargreaves and Michael Fullan, *Second International Handbook of Educational Change* (New York: Springer, 2011).

[12]Alan M Blankstein, Paul D. Houston, and Robert W. Cole, *Data-Enhanced Leadership* (Thousand Oaks, CA: Corwin Press, 2010).

[13]James Taub, "Harvard Radical," *The New York Times Magazine*, August 24, 2003, pp. 28–45.

differences and the ability of women to succeed in math and science. The bigger concern of the Harvard faculty was Summer's management style and his aggressive approach to change. In 2007, Summers was replaced by Drew Gilpin Faust, Harvard University's first female president. She promised to be less aggressive in making changes.[14]

Summer's case illustrates that many change agents fail because organization members resist change. We discuss seven causes of resistance to change: interference with need fulfillment, fear of the unknown, threats to power and influence, knowledge and skill obsolescence, organizational structure, limited resources, and collective bargaining agreements.

Interference with Need Fulfillment

Changes that interfere with a person's economic, social, esteem, or other needs are likely to meet with resistance. People usually resist changes that could lower their income or job status, such as termination or a demotion. Besides the fulfillment of economic and esteem needs, people work for social reasons. The social relationships that develop in the organization are often more important to its members than is commonly realized. For example, even such seemingly minor changes as relocating employees within the same building or school district may affect social-status relationships and result in resistance.

Fear of the Unknown

People like stability. They may have invested a great deal of time and effort in the current system. They have established a normal routine in performing their jobs. They have learned their range of duties and what their supervisor's expectations are for performing these duties. They have some idea of the routine problems that may surface in the performance of their jobs. In other words, they have learned how to perform their jobs successfully, how to get good performance ratings from their supervisors, how to interact with their work group, and so on. Put another way, the present system offers a high degree of certainty.

Changes in established work routines or job duties create potential unknowns. For example, organization members may fear that they will not be able to perform up to their previous standards. They may have to learn a new job. They may have to learn to adjust to a new supervisor's expectations. They may have to adjust to a new work group. They may have to make new friends. When a change occurs, the normal routine is disrupted, and the organization member must begin to find new and different ways to function within the environment.

Threats to Power and Influence

Resistance can also occur because the proposed changes may reduce one's power and influence in the organization. One source of power in organizations is the control of something that other people need, such as information or resources. Individuals or groups who have established a power position in an organization will resist changes that are felt to reduce their power and influence. For example, a superintendent of schools whose school district is threatened with consolidation with another school district will resist the merger in order to maintain his current position. Similarly, the trend toward management information systems (MIS) in today's school districts, which makes more information available to more school district members, is likely to be resisted by top-level administrators. These administrators would lose this source of influence and power if MIS were implemented.

Knowledge and Skill Obsolescence

Somewhat related to threats to power and influence is knowledge and skill obsolescence. While the former usually applies to administration, the latter can apply to any member of the organization's hierarchy. Organization members will resist changes that make their knowledge and skills obsolete. For example, consider the school bookkeeper who has mastered a complex accounting system over a long period of time. The superintendent of schools announces the implementation of a new computerized accounting system that is reputed to be easier and more efficient. The bookkeeper is threatened by a change to a new computerized system and will likely resist the change because her identity is based on the mastery of the old and more complex accounting system.

---

[14]Alan Finder, Patrick D. Healy, and Kate Zernike, "President of Harvard Resigns, Ending Stormy 5-Year Tenure," *The New York Times*, February 22, 2006, pp. A1, A19.

Organizational Structure

In Chapter 2, we characterized the school district as a bureaucratic organizational structure. Like all modern organizations, schools have many of the characteristics of an ideal bureaucracy—a hierarchy of authority, a division of labor and specialization, rules and regulations, impersonality in interpersonal relationships, and a career orientation. In fact, the very meaning of organization implies that some degree of structure must be given to groups so that they can fulfill the organization's goals. However, this legitimate need for structure can be dysfunctional to the organization and serve as a major resistance to change. For example, schools typically have narrowly defined roles; clearly spelled out lines of authority, responsibility, and accountability; and limited flows of information from the top to the bottom of the hierarchy.

Recall from Chapter 7 that an emphasis on the hierarchy of authority causes employees to feed back only positive information to superiors concerning their jobs. The avoidance of negative feedback by subordinates hampers school administrators from identifying subordinates' concerns and needed changes in the organization. Also recall that the taller the organizational structure is, the more numerous the levels through which a message must travel. This increases the probability that any new idea will be filtered as it travels upward through the hierarchy because it violates the status quo in the school or school district.

Limited Resources

Some school districts prefer to maintain the status quo, whereas others would change if they had the available resources. Generally, change requires resources: capital and people with the appropriate skills and time. A school district may have identified a number of innovations that could improve the effectiveness of the district operation. However, the district may have to abandon the desired changes because of inadequate resources. We are certain that you can identify a number of local school district innovations, as well as those initiated by the federal and state governments, that have been deferred or completely abandoned due to resource limitations.

Collective Bargaining Agreements

The most pervasive changes in educational policy matters have been brought about by the practice of negotiating formally with the teachers' union and other employee unions in a school district. Agreements between management and union usually impose obligations on participants that can restrain their behaviors. Collective bargaining agreements are a good example. That is, ways of doing things that were once considered management prerogatives may become subject to negotiation and be fixed in the collective bargaining agreement. Some examples include salaries, cost-of-living adjustments (COLA), class size, teacher transfer, school calendar, class hours, evaluations, and promotions. Such agreements restrain the behavior of school administrators from implementing desired changes in the system.

Overcoming Resistance to Change

Six strategies have been suggested for overcoming resistance to change: participation, communication, support, rewards, planning, and coercion.[15] We will discuss each one briefly.

Participation

One of the best methods for overcoming resistance to change is to invite those who will be affected by the change to participate in planning, design, and implementation. There are at least three explanations for the effect of participation in reducing resistance to change: (1) As those affected by the change plan, design, and implement it, new ideas and information can be generated. The increased information is likely to result in a more effective change; (2) participation builds ownership for the change, thus leading to a commitment to see the change successfully implemented; and (3) by providing information about the nature and consequences of the change, anxiety about the unknown is reduced, and rumors are stifled.[16]

Communication

Another method for overcoming resistance to change involves communicating and explaining to organization members the nature of and need for the change.

[15]Fullan, *The Challenge of Change*; Hargreaves and Fullan, *Second International Handbook of Educational Change*; Spector, *Implementing Organizational Change*.

[16]Chris Argyris, *Reasons and Rationalizations: The Limits to Organizational Knowledge* (New York: Oxford University Press, 2007).

EXEMPLARY EDUCATIONAL ADMINISTRATORS IN ACTION

CARLOS A. GARCIA Superintendent, Clark County School District, Nevada.

Words of Advice: The current trend that allows norm-referenced tests to guide educational standards is very misleading. To improve education in the United States, school districts should be able to use and emphasize diagnostic testing to improve student achievement. Norm-referenced testing does little to improve student achievement because it does not allow us to pinpoint exactly where educational weaknesses exist. Because of the politics that surround norm-referenced testing in public education, I am not sure the United States will ever be bold enough to change the way we test our students.

Another trend I find disturbing is the criticism of public education. Public education is the greatest invention of all time—where would our country be without public education? One way we can stop this trend is for educators to take the lead in problem solving and not wait for others to fix the problems within the system.

In explaining the need, administrators are advised to explain the effects the change will have on organization members. This too will lessen employees' fear of the unknown. Organization members who are informed about the logic behind administrative decisions are more likely to support new ideas.[17]

Support

Effective implementation of a change requires support from top-level administrators such as the superintendent of schools and his cabinet. Support from the superintendent usually means that administrators lower in the organization's hierarchy, such as building principals, will be committed to the change. It is particularly important for building principals to manifest *supportive* and *considerate* leadership behaviors when change is being implemented. This type of leader behavior includes listening to subordinates' ideas, being approachable, and using employee ideas that have merit. Supportive leaders go out of their way to make the work environment more pleasant and enjoyable. For example, difficult changes may require training to acquire new skills necessary to implement the change. Administrators need to provide such training.[18] In short, when procedures are established to implement changes smoothly, less resistance is likely to be encountered.

Rewards

When change is imminent, most people say, "What's in it for me?" Subordinates are less likely to resist changes that will benefit them directly.[19] For example, during collective bargaining between the board of education and the teachers' union, certain concessions can be given to teachers in exchange for support of a new program desired by management. Such concessions may include salary increases, bonuses, or more union representation in decision making. Administrators can also use standard rewards such as recognition, increased responsibility, praise, and status symbols. Thus, building in rewards may help reduce subordinates' resistance to change.

Planning

Prospective changes should be well planned in advance. Change inevitably leads to subordinate anxiety about new expectations and fear of the unknown. The proposed change may require new performance levels. Therefore, performance levels need to be given careful consideration by administrators when planning a change. Performance levels that are set too low can negatively affect performance. Conversely, performance levels that are set too high can result in frustration and low performance.[20] Moreover, introducing change incrementally can lessen the impact of change

[17]Jim Grieves, *Organizational Change: Themes and Issues* (New York: Oxford University Press, 2011).

[18]Richard Schmuck, *Action Research for Higher Educators: Collaborative Principles and Practices for Positive Change* (Maryland Heights, MO: Elsevier, 2011).

[19]Jay Conger, *The Leader's Change Handbook: An Essential Guide to Setting Direction and Taking Action* (New York: Wiley, 2010).

[20]Spector, *Implementing Organizational Change.*

ADMINISTRATIVE ADVICE 8–2

Addressing Resistance to Change

Adhere to the following principles when initiating change.

Make key teachers, parents, board members, and community leaders feel that the project is their own.

Get support for the change effort from the top.

Engage in site-based management. Encourage consensual decision making.

Be willing to delegate leadership of the change effort. As a change facilitator, you may not always be the most effective leader in all change efforts.

Adhere to the following principles when implementing change.

Let participants in the change effort see that it reduces rather than increases workloads.

Reassure participants that the change is in accordance with longstanding values.

Present the change effort as attractive and interesting to those who will be most involved.

Be flexible. Be open to different ways of handling the issue to be addressed by the change effort.

Clarify any misconceptions about the change as soon as they occur. Help participants understand that change is a process, not an event.

Build trust and rapport among participants.

Source: Adapted from John Chamley, Ellen Caprio, and Russell Young, "The Principal as a Catalyst and Facilitator of Planned Change," *NASSP Bulletin,* 78 (1994): 1–7. Used by permission.

on subordinates and allow them time to adjust to new expectations and conditions.[21]

Coercion

When other methods have failed, coercion can be used as a last resort. Some changes require immediate implementation. And top-level administrators may have considerable power. Such instances lend themselves more readily to administrators using coercion to gain compliance to changes. Subordinates can be threatened with job loss, decreased promotional opportunities, no salary increases (this technique is used infrequently in public schools), or a job transfer to achieve compliance with a change. There are, however, negative effects of using coercion, including frustration, fear, revenge, and alienation. This in turn may lead to poor performance, dissatisfaction, and turnover.[22]

[21]Robert E. Hoskisson and Craig S. Galbraith, "The Effect of Quantum versus Incremental M-Form Reorganization on Performance: A Time-Series Exploration of Intervention Dynamics," *Journal of Management,* 11 (1985): 55–70.

[22]William A. Pasmore, *Research in Organizational Change and Development* (Bingley, UK: Emerald Group Publishing, 2011).

Two questions should be asked in preparing to manage staff resistance to change: Who is initiating the change? How will the change be implemented? These questions will help change agents identify the source, type, and method of change. (See Administrative Advice 8–2.)

Managing Change

Now we will examine several approaches to managing change: Lewin's three-step model, Kotter's eight-step plan, Harris's five-phase model, followed by organizational development.

Lewin's Three-Step Model

To better understand resistance to change, Kurt Lewin developed the concept of **force-field analysis.**[23] He looks upon a level of behavior within an organization not

[23]Kurt Lewin, *Field Theory in Social Sciences* (New York: Harper & Row, 1951).

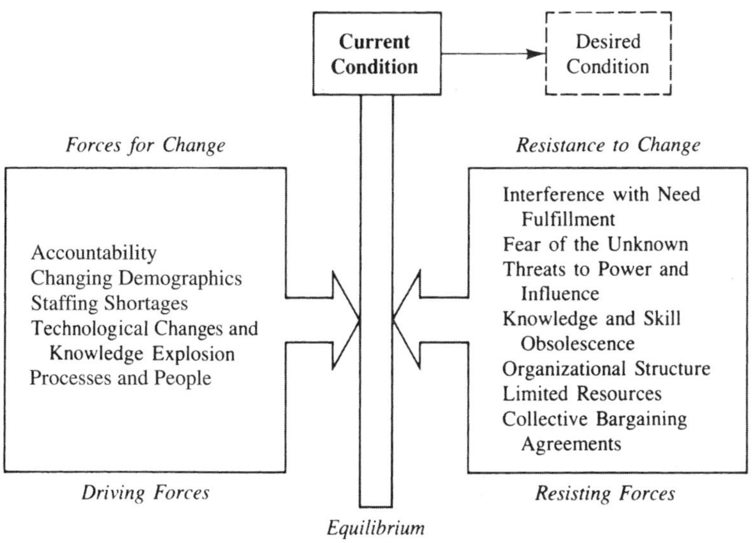

FIGURE 8–1

Forces for Change and Resistance to Change

as a static custom but as a dynamic balance of forces working in opposite directions within the organization. He believes that we should think about any change situation in terms of driving forces or factors acting to change the current condition (forces for change) and resisting forces or factors acting to inhibit change (resistance to change). These forces may originate in the internal or external environment of the organization or in the behavior of the change agent.

School administrators must play an active role in initiating change and in attempting to reduce resistance to change. School administrators can think of the current condition in an organization as an equilibrium that is the result of driving forces and resisting forces working against each other. Change agents must assess the change potential and resistance and attempt to change the balance of forces so that there will be movement toward a desired condition. There are three ways of doing this: increasing the driving forces, reducing the resisting forces, or considering new driving forces.

Lewin points out that increasing one set of forces without decreasing the other set of forces will increase tension and conflict in the organization. Reducing the other set of forces may reduce the amount of tension. While increasing driving forces is sometimes effective, it is usually better to reduce the resisting forces because increasing driving forces often tend to be offset by increased resistance. Put another way, when we push people, they are likely to push back. Figure 8–1 illustrates the two sets of forces—forces for change and resistance to change. This is the type of situation that school administrators face and must work with on a daily basis when attempting to effect change.

As Figure 8–1 shows, change results when an imbalance occurs between the ratio of driving forces and resisting forces, Such an imbalance alters the existing condition—one hopes in the direction planned by the school administrator—into a new and desired condition. Once the new, desired condition is reached, the opposing forces are again brought into equilibrium. An imbalance may occur through a change in the velocity of any force, a change in the direction of a force, or the introduction of a new force.

Moreover, change involves a sequence of organizational processes that occurs over time. Lewin suggests this process typically requires the following steps: unfreezing, moving, and refreezing.[24]

Unfreezing. This step usually means reducing the forces acting to keep the organization in its current condition. Unfreezing might be accomplished by introducing new information that points out inadequacies

[24]Ibid.

Table 8-1 Steps in Managing Organizational Change

Step	Description
1. Establish a sense of urgency	Unfreeze the organization by creating a compelling reason for why change is needed.
2. Create the guiding coalition	Create a cross-functional, cross-level group of people with enough power to lead the change.
3. Develop a vision and strategy	Create a vision and strategic plan to guide the change process.
4. Communicate the change vision	Create and implement a communication strategy that consistently communicates the new vision and strategic plan.
5. Empower broad-based action	Eliminate barriers to change, and use target elements of change to transform the organization. Encourage risk taking and creative problem solving.
6. Generate short-term wins	Plan for and create short-term "wins" or improvements. Recognize and reward people who contribute to the wins.
7. Consolidate gains and produce more change	The guiding coalition uses credibility from short-term wins to create more change. Additional people are brought into the change process as change cascades throughout the organization. Attempts are made to reinvigorate the change process.
8. Anchor new approaches in the culture	Reinforce the changes by highlighting connections between new behaviors and processes and organizational success. Develop methods to ensure leadership development and succession.

Source: Adapted from John P. Kotter, *Leading Change* (Boston: Harvard Business School Press, 1996).

in the current state or by decreasing the strength of current values, attitudes, and behaviors. Crises often stimulate unfreezing. Examples of crises are significant increases in the student dropout rate, dramatic enrollment declines, shifts in population within a school district, a sudden increase in teacher or middle management turnover, a costly lawsuit, and an unexpected teacher strike. Unfreezing may occur without crises as well. Climate surveys, financial data, and enrollment projections can be used to determine problem areas in a school district and initiate change to alleviate problems before crises erupt.

Moving. Once the organization is unfrozen, it can be changed. This step usually involves the development of new values, attitudes, and behaviors through internalization, identification, or change in structure. Some changes may be minor and involve a few members—such as changes in recruitment and selection procedures—and others may be major, involving many participants. Examples of the latter include a new evaluation system, restructuring of jobs and duties performed by employees, or restructuring the school district, which necessitates relocating faculty to different school sites within the system.

Refreezing. The final step in the change process involves stabilizing the change at a new quasistationary equilibrium. Changes in organizational culture, changes in group norms, changes in organizational policy, or modifications in organizational structure often accomplish this.

Figure 8–1 illustrates force-field analysis that shows both the pressures for change and resistance to change within a school setting.

Kotter's Eight-Step Plan

Building on Lewin's three-step model, John Kotter of Harvard University developed a more detailed approach for managing change.[25] Kotter began by listing common errors that administrators make when attempting to initiate change. These included the inability to create a sense of urgency about the need for change; failure to create a coalition for managing the change process; the absence of a vision for change; failure to effectively communicate that vision; failure to remove obstacles that could impede the achievement of the vision; failure to provide short-term achievable goals; the tendency to declare victory too soon; and failure to anchor the changes into the organization's culture. Based on these errors, Kotter proposed an eight-step process for managing change (see Table 8–1).

[25]John P. Kotter, *Leading Change* (Boston: Harvard Business School Press, 1996).

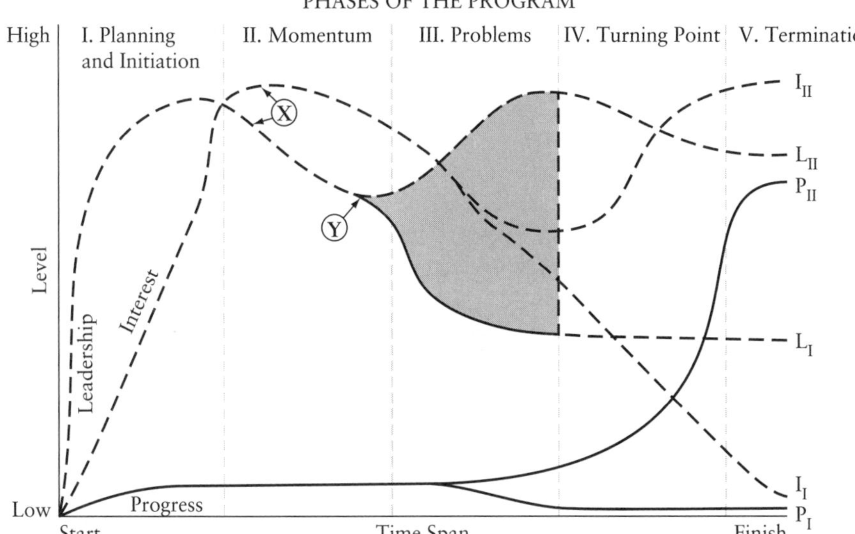

FIGURE 8–2

Harris's Five-Phase Change Model

Note how Kotter's steps build on Lewin's model. Kotter's first four steps represent Lewin's "unfreezing" stage. Steps 5 through 7 represent Lewin's "movement" stage. The final step corresponds to Lewin's "refreezing" stage. Thus, Kotter's contribution provides school administrators and change agents with a more detailed guide for managing change successfully.

Harris's Five-Phase Model

Ben Harris, formerly of The University of Texas, created a five-stage model for managing change.[26] (See Figure 8–2.) He stated that these phases come in a sequential order, but they often overlap one another. Each phase will be discussed briefly.

Phase I: Planning and Initiation. The purpose of the change is considered, goals are clarified, activities are selected, and resources needed are considered. Interest mounts as individuals involved sense the relationships between the change and its goals and their needs.

Phase II: Momentum. Goal-directed activities get underway. Resources begin to be used. Interest continues to be high and mounts. Feelings of involvement and personal worth grow. The activities are recognized as potentially satisfying. Leading and organizing processes are most heavily employed in this phase.

Phase III: Problems. Activities lead to unexpected problems. The plans become increasingly complex. Initial activities lead to a proliferation of still more activities. Certain resources are not readily available. Differences in goal perception among group members become apparent. The demands of other responsibilities produce conflicts. The goal seems more remote and more difficult to attain than before. Some participants fail to live up to expectations. Interest levels out and begins a steep decline. A leadership investment is crucial during this phase.

[26]Ben M. Harris, *Supervisory Behavior in Education*, 2nd ed. (Englewood Cliffs, NJ: Prentice Hall).

Phase IV: Turning Point. The problem trends described in the previous phase either continue to grow or are overcome and minimized. The momentum the change has gained, the effectiveness of initial planning, and the individuals in the operation are all quite important during this phase. Above all, the amount and quality of leadership continues to be crucial.

Phase V: Termination. There can be such expected problems as: the task is too complex; there is a lack of resources; there is pressure of other responsibilities; and interest is waning, and consensus to proceed has still not been reached. This will result in termination of efforts because goal-directed activities will rapidly deteriorate and come to a halt. If, on the other hand, problems are dealt with promptly; the task is analyzed and simplified; new resources are made available; and goals are clarified, then interest gradually mounts again and goal directed activities proceed at an increasing pace. Interest is now based on a sense of anticipated accomplishment and personal worth.

This sequence of events points out the importance of leadership at various phases of the change process. Undoubtedly, this sequence of events will have variations and exceptions depending on the change, activities, and the participants involved.

Organizational Development

Organizational development (OD) is a set of social science techniques or interventions designed to plan and implement change in work settings for the purposes of enhancing the personal development of individuals (individual approaches) and improving the effectiveness of the organization (group approaches).[27] What are some of the OD techniques or interventions for implementing change? We present six interventions that change agents might use. The first set of OD techniques we discuss are group approaches to change. The aim of group approaches to change is to improve the performance of groups or the organization. We will discuss the following group approaches to change: TQM, strategic planning, and survey feedback.

[27]William Rothwell, *Practicing Organization Development: A Guide for Leading Change* (New York: Wiley, 2010); see also Thomas G. Cummings, *Handbook of Organizational Development* (Thousand Oaks, CA: Sage, 2008).

Total Quality Management

Total Quality Management (TQM) is based on the assumption that people want to do their best and that it is management's job to enable them to do so by constantly improving the *system* in which they work.[28] TQM is not new. It resembles Douglas McGregor's Theory Y[29] and William Ouchi's Theory Z.[30] What is new is that large corporations are taking Theory Y and Theory Z seriously by assigning more authority and responsibility to frontline workers. However, like Theory Y and Theory Z, TQM is more than delegation. It requires teamwork, training, and extensive collection and analysis of data.

When educators look at TQM principles they assume that the model applies only to profit-making organizations. Actually, TQM applies as well to corporations, service organizations, universities, and elementary and secondary schools.

Indeed, the concepts formulated by TQM founder W. Edwards Deming have proved so powerful that educators want to apply TQM to schools. Deming's philosophy provides a framework that can integrate many positive developments in education, such as team teaching, site-based management, cooperative learning, and outcomes-based education.

The problem is that words like *learning* and *curriculum* are not found in Deming's fourteen points. Some of Deming's terminology needs to be translated to schools as well. For example, superintendents and principals can be considered *management.* Teachers are *employers* or *managers* of students. Students are *employees,* and the knowledge they acquire is the *product.* Parents and society are the *customers.* With these translations made, we can see many applications to schools.

The framework for transforming schools using Deming's principles follows.

Create Constancy of Purpose for Improvement of Product and Service. For schools, the purpose of the system must be clear and shared by all stakeholder groups. Customer needs must be the focus in establishing educational aims. The aims of the system must be to improve the quality of education for all students.

[28]W. Edwards Deming, *Out of the Crisis* (Cambridge, MA: MIT Press, 2000).

[29]Douglas McGregor, *The Human Side of Enterprise* (New York: McGraw-Hill, 1960).

[30]William G. Ouchi, *Theory Z: How American Business Can Meet the Japanese Challenge* (New York: Avon Books, 1993).

Adopt the New Philosophy. Implementation of Deming's second principle requires a rethinking of the school's mission and priorities, with every one in agreement on them. Existing methods, materials, and environments may be replaced by new teaching and learning strategies where success for every student is the goal. Individual differences among students are addressed. Ultimately, what may be required is a total transformation of the American system of education as we know it.

Cease Dependence on Inspection to Achieve Quality. The field of education has recently entered an era that many American corporations have abandoned: inspection at the end of the line.[31] In industry this was called "product inspection." According to Deming, it always costs more to fix a problem than to prevent one. Reliance on remediation can be avoided if proper intervention occurs during initial instruction. Furthermore, preventive approaches such as Head Start, Follow Through, and preschool programs can help students to avoid learning problems later.

End the Practice of Awarding Business on the Basis of Price Alone. The lowest bid is rarely the most cost efficient. Schools need to move toward a single supplier for any one time and develop long-term relationships of loyalty and trust with that supplier.

Improve Constantly and Forever Every Activity in the Company, to Improve Quality and Productivity. The focus of improvement efforts in education, under Deming's approach, are on teaching and learning processes. Based on the latest research findings, the best strategies must be attempted, evaluated, and refined as needed. And, consistent with learning style theories[32] and Howard Gardner's multiple intelligences,[33] educators must redesign the system to provide for a broad range of people—handicapped, learning-disabled, at-risk, special needs students—and find ways to make them all successful in school.

Institute Training on the Job. Training of educators is needed in three areas. First, there must be training in the new teaching and learning processes that are developed. Second, training must be provided in the use of new assessment strategies. Third, there must be training in the principles of the new management system.

Institute Leadership. Deming's seventh principle resembles Peter Senge's systems thinking.[34] According to both Senge and Deming, improvement of a stable system comes from altering the system itself, and this is primarily the job of management and not those who work within the system. Deming asserts that the primary task of leaderships is to narrow the amount of variation within the system, bringing everyone toward the goal of perfection. In schools, this means closing the achievement gap among student subgroups.

Drive Out Fear. A basic assumption of TQM is that people want to do their best. The focus of improvement efforts then must be on the processes and on the outcomes, not on trying to blame individuals for failures. If quality is absent, the fault is in the system, says Deming. It is management's job to enable people to do their best by constantly improving the system in which they work.

Break Down Barriers Among Staff Areas. Deming's ninth principle is somewhat related to the first principle: Create constancy of purpose for improvement of product and service. In the classroom this principle applies to interdisciplinary instruction, team teaching, writing across the curriculum, and transfer of learning. Collaboration needs to exist among members of the learning organization so that total quality can be maximized.

Eliminate Slogans, Exhortations, and Targets That Demand Zero Defects and New Levels of Productivity. Implicit in most slogans, exhortations, and targets is the supposition that staff could do better if they tried harder. This offends rather than inspires the team. It creates adversarial relationships because the many causes of low-quality and low productivity in schools are due

---

[31]John J. Bonstingl, *Schools of Quality,* 3rd. ed. (Thousand Oaks, CA: Corwin Press, 2001).

[32]Rita Dunn and Kenneth Dunn, *Teaching Students Through Their Individual Learning Styles,* 2 vols.: *Practical Approaches for Grades 3–12* (Needham Heights, MA: Allyn and Bacon, 1992); Rita Dunn, Kenneth Dunn, and Janet Perrin, *Teaching Young Children Through Their Individual Learning Styles: Practical Approaches for Grades K–2* (Needham Heights, MA: Allyn and Bacon, 1994).

[33]Howard Gardner, *Frames of Mind,* rev. ed. (New York: Basic Books, 1994).

[34]Peter M. Senge, *The Fifth Discipline,* rev. ed. (New York: Doubleday, 2006).

to the system and not the staff. The system itself may need to be changed.[35]

Eliminate Numerical Quotas for the Staff and Goals for Management. There are many practices in education that constrain our ability to tap intrinsic motivation and falsely assume the benefits of extrinsic rewards. They include rigorous and systematic teacher evaluation systems, merit pay, management by objectives, grades, and quantitative goals and quotas. These Deming refers to as forces of destruction. Such approaches are counterproductive for several reasons: setting goals leads to marginal performance; merit pay destroys teamwork; and appraisal of individual performance nourishes fear and increases variability in desired performance.

Remove Barriers That Rob People of Pride of Workmanship. Most people want to do a good job. Effective communication and the elimination of "demotivators"—such as lack of involvement, poor information, the annual or merit rating, and supervisors who don't care—are critical.

Institute a Vigorous Program of Education and Retraining for Everyone. The principal and staff must be retrained in new methods of school management, including group dynamics, consensus building, and collaborative styles of decision making. All stakeholders on the school's team must realize that improvements in student productivity will create higher levels of responsibility, not less responsibility.

Put Everyone in the Organization to Work to Accomplish the Transformation. The school board and superintendent must have a clear plan of action to carry out the quality mission. The quality mission must be internalized by all members of the school organization. The transformation is everybody's job.[36]

As educational leaders begin to adopt TQM as their operational philosophy, they are discovering that Total Quality Management cannot be successful if it is viewed as a school district's project for *this* school year. The real rewards begin to emerge when TQM ideas and practices become embedded in the culture of the organization. Its greatest benefits come about as a natural part of the evolutionary process of implementing a program of continuous improvement in a consistent manner. (See Administrative Advice 8–3)

[35]The authors are not in total agreement with this item. Educators tend to use numerous slogans as a general practice.

[36]Deming, *Out of the Crisis*, pp. 23–24.

Strategic Planning

The process of **strategic planning** typically follows seven steps.[37] Although these steps are not always followed in the exact order specified, they do resemble the way most school districts go about planning strategically.[38] As we describe these steps, you may find it useful to follow along with the steps shown in Figure 8–3.

A. Develop a Mission A strategic plan must begin with a stated goal. Typically, goals involve a school district's outcomes (e.g., to improve student achievement on standardized tests) and/or to improve its organizational culture (e.g., to make the work environment more pleasant). It is important to note that a school district's overall goals must be translated into corresponding goals to be achieved by various organizational units. In large school districts, this would include Divisions of Instruction, Finance, Research and Development, Public Relations, etc. and individual school buildings and departments within them.

B. Conduct a Critical Analysis of Internal Environment By "internal environment," we are referring to the nature of the organization itself as identified by the characteristics described in previous chapters of this book. For example, does the organizational structure stimulate or inhibit goal achievement (Chapter 2)? Does the culture of the school district (or individual school) encourage personnel to be innovative and to make positive changes, or does it encourage organization members to maintain the status quo (Chapter 3)? Are organization members motivated sufficiently to strive for the realization of school district goals (Chapter 4)? Is there adequate, effective leadership to move the school

[37]Simon Wootton, *Strategic Thinking: A Step-by-Step Approach to Strategy and Leadership* (London: Kogan Page, 2011); see also Leonard Goodstein, *Strategic Planning: A Leadership Imperative* (Alexandria, VA: American Society for Training and Development, 2011).

[38]Robert Ewy, *Stakeholder-Driven Strategic Planning in Education: A Practical Guide for Developing and Deploying Successful Long Range Plans* (Milwaukee, WI: ASQ Press, 2010).

ADMINISTRATIVE ADVICE 8–3

The Four Pillars of Total Quality

Total Quality Management, viewed through Deming's fourteen points, can best be understood as an integral set of fundamental tenets.

The organization must focus, first and foremost, on its suppliers and customers. In schools, the student is the teacher's customer, the recipient of educational services. The teacher and the school are suppliers of effective learning to the student, who is the school's *primary customer.* The school's stakeholders and *secondary customers*—including parents, businesses, community, taxpayers—have a legitimate right to expect progress in students' competencies. Administrators work collaboratively with *their* customers: teachers.

Everyone in the organization must be dedicated to continual improvement, personally and collectively. The Japanese call this ethos *kaizen,* a societywide covenant of mutual help in the process of continual improvement. If schools are to be true learning organizations, they must be afforded the resources, especially time and money, needed for training, quality circles, research, and communication with the school's stakeholders.

The organization must be viewed as a system, and the work people do within the system must be seen as ongoing processes. A system consists of the seemingly immutable patterns of expectations, activities, perceptions, resource allocations, power structures, values, and the traditional school culture in general. Every system is made up of processes, and improvements made in the quality of those processes in large part determine the quality of the resulting products. In the new paradigm of education, continual improvement of learning processes will replace the outdated "teach and test" mode of instruction.

The success of Total Quality Management is the responsibility of top management. Educational leaders must provide concerted, visible, and constant dedication to making TQM principles and practices part of the culture of the organization. School leaders must focus on establishing the context in which students can best achieve their potential through the continual improvement of teachers' and students' work together.

Source: Adapted from John J. Bonstingl, "The Quality Revolution in Education," *Educational Leadership,* 50 (1992): 5–7.

district forward (Chapter 5)? Do decision making practices encourage goal accomplishment (Chapter 6)? Do people communicate with each other clearly enough to accomplish their goals (Chapter 7)? Are organization members willing to change in order to improve school district performance (Chapter 8)?

B. Conduct a Critical Analysis of External Environment As we discussed in Chapter 1 of this book, school districts (and schools) do not operate in a vacuum. Rather, they function within external environments (see Figure 1–1 Open Systems Model). For example, local, state, and federal laws impact the internal operation of school districts (and schools). For instance, consider the impact of the NCLB legislation on the internal operation of public schools throughout the United States.

C. Prepare Planning Assumptions To clearly understand the nature of your strategic plan, it is important to highlight the assumptions underlying the plan: (a) Is the planning process based on deliberate analyses or based on intuition and informal knowledge? (b) Is the strategic plan based on the assumption that radical change is not only possible, but desirable; or instead, will the plan involve only minor incremental adjustments to the current ways of operating? (c) The strategic plan will be made primarily in the interest of which stakeholder groups (community, school board, administrators, teachers, support staff, or students)? Furthermore, What resources does the school district (or school) have available to plan and implement its strategy? The resources include financial, physical, and human resources. The assumptions underlying the strategic planning process are important to the ultimate success of the strategic plan.

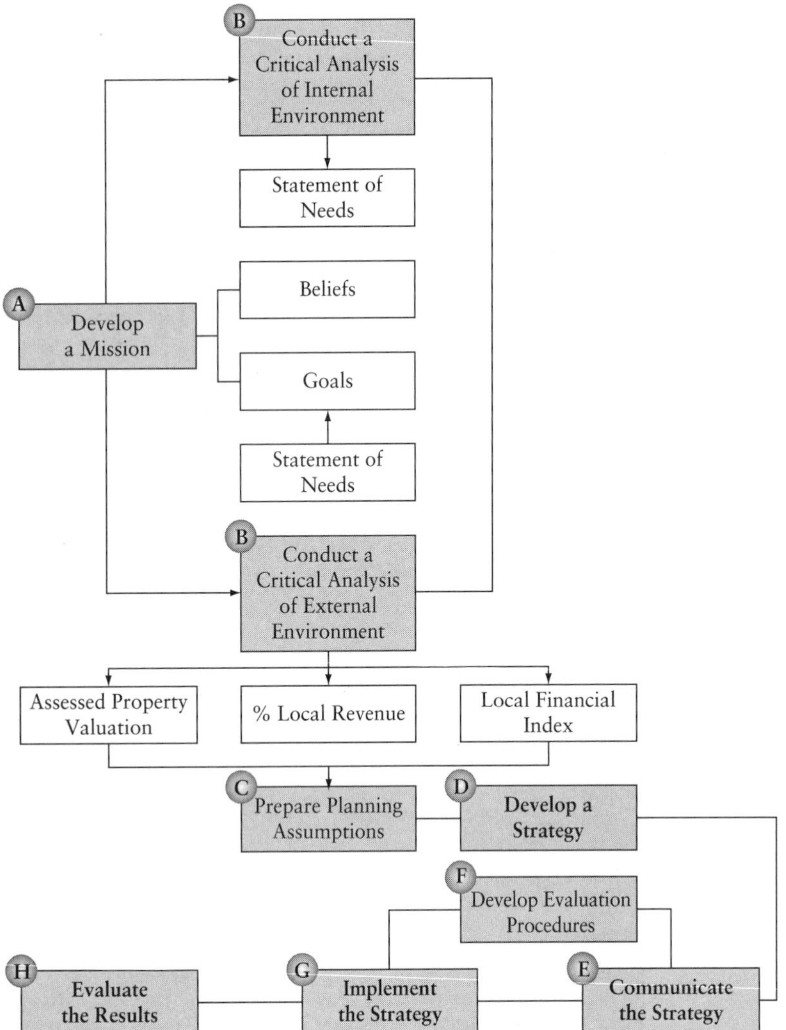

FIGURE 8–3

Strategic Planning: An Eight-Step Process

D. Develop a Strategy A strategy is the means by which a school district achieves its goal. Based on a careful assessment of the school district's position on the aforementioned factors or characteristics (e.g., the school district's organizational structure, its culture, motivation of its members, leadership, decision making strategies used, communication, inclination toward change, and available resources), a decision is made about how to go about achieving its goal.

E. Communicate the Strategy The strategy must be communicated to stakeholders–individuals or groups in whose interest a school district is run. These are individuals who have a stake in the school district. The most important stakeholders include students, teachers, support staff, administrators, school board, and community members. It is essential to communicate a school district's strategic plan to stakeholders very clearly, so they can contribute to its success, either directly (e.g., organization members who help achieve goals) or indirectly (e.g., school board who set policy, taxpayers who provide local funds, as well as the state and federal government). Unless stakeholders fully understand and accept a school district's strategic plan, it is unlikely to receive the full support it needs to meet its goals.

F. Develop Evaluation Procedures Evaluation procedures need to be developed prior to *Evaluating the Results*. These procedures will serve to guide the implementation of the strategy and evaluation of the outcome.

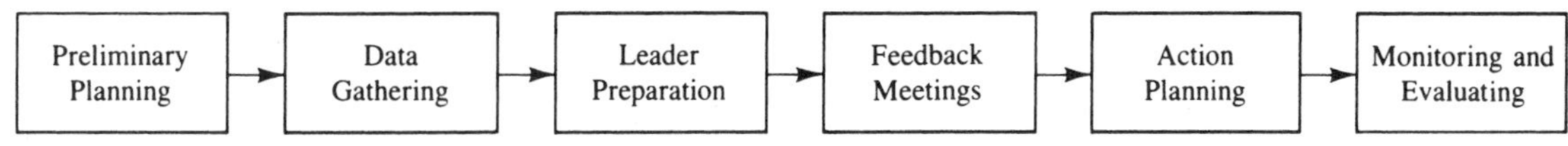

FIGURE 8–4

Steps Involved in Survey Feedback

G. Implement the Strategy Once a strategy has been developed and communicated, the strategy is implemented. When this occurs, there may be some resistance. As we discussed previously, people tend to resist change. School administrators need to apply various techniques to overcome resistance to change, which were discussed earlier in the chapter.

H. Evaluate the Results Finally, after a strategy has been implemented, it is important to determine if the goals have been achieved. If so, then new goals are developed. If not, then different goals may be defined, or different strategies for accomplishing the goals may be attempted.

Business has devoted a great deal of attention to strategic planning.[39] Only recently has any emphasis been placed on the study of strategic planning in school settings. In a study of 127 school districts in Kentucky, researchers found relationships between strategic planning and student achievement in reading, language arts, and mathematics at several grade levels. None of the relationships was strong, however. In addition, the researchers found a direct relationship between strategic planning and both school district wealth and per-pupil expenditures. That is, the higher the assessed property value per child and the greater the percentage of revenue from local sources supporting education, the more likely the school district is engaged in strategic planning efforts.[40]

Survey Feedback

Survey feedback is an organizational approach to change that involves collecting data (usually by means of a survey questionnaire) from members of a work group or whole organization, analyzing and summarizing the data into an understandable form, feeding back the data to those who generated it, and using the data to diagnose problems and develop action plans for problem solving.[41]

Similar to process consultation in some respects, survey feedback places greater emphasis on the collection of valid data and less emphasis on the interpersonal processes of individual work groups. Instead, survey feedback focuses on the relationships between administrative personnel and their subordinates at all levels of hierarchy.

If used properly, attitude surveys can be a powerful tool in school-improvement efforts. Change agents who use survey feedback point out that most attitude surveys are not used properly. At best, most give higher-level administrators some data for changing practices or provide a benchmark against which to compare trends. At worst, they are filed away with little consequence for school improvement.

Survey feedback has two major phases. Collecting data is only part of the process; providing appropriate feedback to the organization's members is equally significant. Figure 8–4 outlines the six steps involved in survey feedback, which are described next.[42]

Step 1: Preliminary Planning Organizational members at the top of the hierarchy are involved in the preliminary planning. Surveys used in organizational change efforts are usually constructed around a theoretical model. This allows the user to rate himself or the organization in terms of the theory. When the approach involves a theoretical model, commitment to the model must be obtained. If top management does not accept

---

39David Campbell, *Business Strategy: An Introduction* (New York: Palgrave Macmillan, 2012).

40Vicki Basham and Fred C. Lunenburg, "Strategic Planning, Student Achievement, and School District Financial and Demographic Factors," *Planning and Changing*, 20 (1989): 158–171.

41Edward J. Conlon and Lawrence O. Short, "Survey Feedback as a Large-Scale Change Device: An Empirical Examination," *Group and Organization Studies,* 9 (1984): 399–416.

42David G. Bowers and Jerome L. Franklin, *Survey-Guided Development: Data-Based Organizational Change* (La Jolla, CA: University Associates, 1977).

the theoretical model undergirding the survey, the approach will likely fail no matter how effective the effort is toward gathering data.

Step 2: Data Gathering A questionnaire is administered to all organizational members. The best-known survey-feedback instrument is the one developed by the Institute for Social Research (ISR) at the University of Michigan.[43] The questionnaire generally asks the respondents' perceptions on such organizational areas as communications, goal emphasis, leadership styles, decision making, coordination between departments, and employee attitudes. The ISR instrument, a standardized questionnaire, permits the additions of questions that may be of interest to the organization under study. However, many organizations, including schools, develop their own questionnaires that are specific to their individual needs rather than relying on a standardized instrument.

Step 3: Leader Preparation Once the data have been obtained from the questionnaire, an external or internal change agent helps school administrators understand the data and instructs them on how to present the data to the work group. Data are then fed back to the top administrative team and down through the hierarchy in functional teams.

Step 4: Feedback Meetings Each superior conducts group feedback meetings with his subordinates in which the data are discussed and in which subordinates are asked to help interpret the data, plans are made for making constructive changes, and plans are made for introducing the information at the next lower level of subordinates.

For example, the superintendent of schools and the major divisional assistant superintendents meet and compare the survey findings for each of the district's functional areas—such as personnel, business, instruction, and research and development. Each assistant superintendent can see the summary data for her division and for the total school district. Problems unique to each division, the implications of the findings, and themes common to the total organization are discussed.

The next feedback meetings occur as each assistant superintendent meets with building principals or other subordinates to discuss survey data specific to each. The process continues until department heads discuss with teachers or other school personnel the issues raised in each work group by the survey data.

Step 5: Action Planning The fact that a discrepancy exists between the actual state of the organization and the ideal theoretical model does not in and of itself provide sufficient motivation to change. Organizational members must be made aware of how the change can be effected. Thus, resources are allocated to implement the changes in accordance with the needs indicated by the group feedback meetings and the systematic diagnosis of the data by the change agent and top-level administrators.

Step 6: Monitoring and Evaluating The change agent helps organizational members develop skills that are necessary to move the organization toward their goals. Some of these skills include listening, giving and receiving personal feedback, general leadership techniques, problem solving, goal setting, and diagnosing group processes. Additional questionnaires are administered and analyzed to monitor the change process. Finally, the school district is formally reassessed to evaluate change, again using questionnaire data.

We have examined three group OD change techniques or interventions (TQM, strategic planning, and survey feedback). Our focus now shifts to individual OD change techniques. This involves two basic types of approaches. The first type is aimed at changing the job or the person's perception of the job. The objective is to make the job more intrinsically satisfying to the organization member. The second type is aimed at changing the person. The individual approaches to change we discuss are job enrichment, laboratory training, and behavioral performance management.

Job Enrichment

Frederick Herzberg's motivation-hygiene theory has stimulated programs in job enrichment in many organizations. Herzberg feels that the challenge to

---

[43] James C. Taylor and David G. Bowers, *Survey of Organizations: A Machine Scored Standardized Questionnaire Instrument* (Ann Arbor: Institute for Social Research, University of Michigan, 1972).

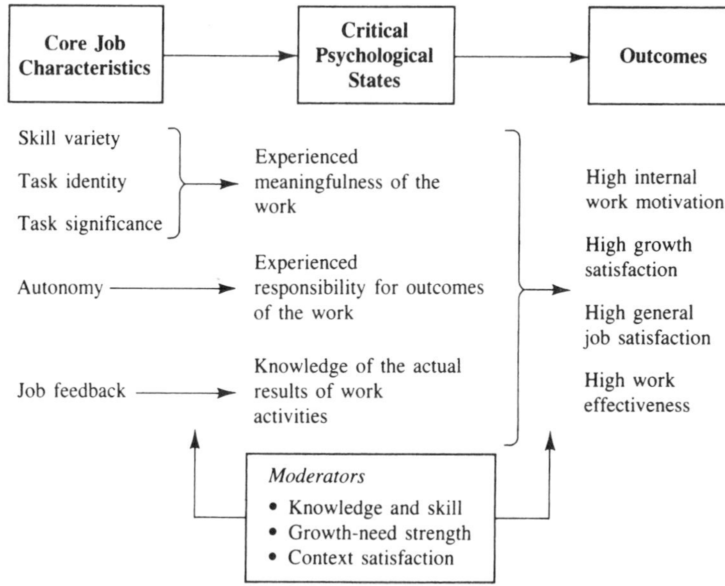

FIGURE 8–5

Job Enrichment Model
Source: Adapted from J. Richard Hackman and Greg R. Oldham, *Work Redesign*, © 1980, p. 90. Reprinted by permission of Pearson Education, Inc., Upper Saddle River, N.J.

organizations is to emphasize motivation factors while ensuring that the hygiene factors are present. He refers to job enrichment as the method for achieving such a condition.[44] **Job enrichment** focuses on achieving organizational change by making jobs more meaningful, interesting, and challenging.

Expanding on the earlier work of Herzberg, Richard Hackman and Greg Oldham provide an explicit framework for enriching jobs.[45] Based on their own research and the work of others, they developed a job-characteristics model (see Figure 8–5). As the figure shows, five core job characteristics create three critical psychological states that in turn lead to a number of employee outcomes. The employee's knowledge and skills, growth-need strength, and satisfaction with context factors moderate the linkage among the job characteristics, the psychological states, and the outcomes.

The five job characteristics that are essential to job enrichment are the following:

1. *Skill variety* is the degree to which a job requires a variety of different activities in carrying out the work, which involves the use of a number of different skills and talents of the employee.
2. *Task identity* is the degree to which a job requires completion of a "whole" and identifiable piece of work—that is, doing a job from beginning to end with a visible outcome.
3. *Task significance* is the degree to which the job has a substantial impact on the lives of other people, whether those people are in the immediate organization or in the external environment.
4. *Autonomy* is the degree to which the job provides substantial freedom, independence, and discretion to the individual in scheduling the work and in determining the procedures to be used in doing the work.
5. *Job feedback* is the degree to which carrying out the work activities required by the job provides the individual with direction and clear information about the effectiveness of his performance.[46]

As shown in Figure 8–3, skill variety, task identity, and task significance together affect "experienced meaningfulness of the work." Autonomy and feedback independently affect the other two psychological

[44]Frederick Herzberg, *One More Time: How Do You Motivate Employees?* (Boston: Harvard Business School Press, 2009).

[45]J. Richard Hackman and Greg R. Oldham, *Work Redesign* (Reading, MA: Addison-Wesley, 1980).

[46]Ibid.

states, respectively, "experienced responsibility for outcomes of the work" and "knowledge of the actual results of the work activities." And according to Hackman and Oldham, only employees who have job-related knowledge and skills, high growth-need strength, and high satisfaction with context factors (Herzberg's hygienes) are likely to be affected in the manner specified in the model.

Hackman and Oldham have developed the job diagnostic survey (JDS) to diagnose the job dimensions in their model (see Figure 8–5) and to determine the effect of job changes on employees.[47] Thus, the job dimensions in the job enrichment model can be combined into the following mathematic expression, which explains the relative impact of change in each dimension of the Hackman-Oldham model:

$$\text{MPS} = \frac{\text{Skill variety} + \text{Task identity} + \text{Task significance}}{3} \times \text{Autonomy} \times \text{Feedback}$$

The motivation potential score (MPS) formula sums the scores for skill variety, task identity, and task significance and divides the total by three. The combination of these three job characteristics is equally weighted, with autonomy and feedback considered separately. The result is an overall measure of job enrichment.

Laboratory Training

Lewin was instrumental in the development of **laboratory training,** also known as sensitivity training or T-groups.[48] The National Training Laboratories (NTL) developed and refined laboratory training in 1946. From this beginning, training has emerged as a widely used organizational strategy aimed at individual change, which generally takes place in small groups.

[47]J. Richard Hackman and Greg R. Oldham, "Development of the Job Diagnostic Survey," *Journal of Applied Psychology,* 60 (1975): 159–170.

[48]For a discussion of laboratory training, see Donald L. Anderson, *Organization Development: The Process of Leading Change* (Thousand Oaks, CA: Sage, 2010).

Goals of Laboratory Training Based on an extensive review of the literature, two researchers have outlined six basic objectives common to most laboratory training sessions:

1. To increase understanding, insight, and self-awareness about one's own behavior and its impact on others, including the ways in which others interpret one's behavior.
2. To increase understanding and sensitivity about the behavior of others, including better interpretation of both verbal and nonverbal cues, which increases awareness and understanding of what the other person is thinking and feeling.
3. To improve understanding and awareness of group and intergroup processes, both those that facilitate and those that inhibit group functioning.
4. To improve diagnostic skills in interpersonal and intergroup situations, which is attained by accomplishing the first three objectives.
5. To increase the ability to transform learning into action, so that real-life interventions will be more successful in increasing member effectiveness, satisfaction, or output.
6. To improve an individual's ability to analyze her own interpersonal behavior, as well as to learn how to help self and others with whom she comes in contact to achieve more satisfying, rewarding, and effective interpersonal relationships.[49]

These objectives point out that laboratory training can be a useful strategy for bringing about organizational change. School districts that are experiencing problems with communications, coordination, or excessive and continuing conflict in interpersonal relationships may benefit from laboratory training as a means of improving individual and organizational effectiveness.

Design of Laboratory Training Laboratory training groups (T-groups) typically consist of ten to fifteen members and a professional trainer. The duration of T-group sessions ranges from a few days to several weeks. The sessions are usually conducted away from

[49]John P. Campbell and Marvin D. Dunnette, "Effectiveness of T-Group Experience in Managerial Training and Development," *Psychological Bulletin,* 70 (1968): 73–104.

the organization, but some occur on university campuses or on the premises of large business organizations. Laboratory training stresses the process rather than the context of training and focuses on attitudinal rather than conceptual training.

The four basic types of training groups are stranger, cousin, brother, and family laboratories. In *stranger* T-groups, members are from different organizations and therefore are unknown to each other before training. An example would be several superintendents from different districts. *Cousin* laboratories consist of members taken from a diagonal slice of an organization, which cuts across two or three vertical hierarchical levels without a superior and subordinate being in the same group. An example would be the coordinator of secondary education and elementary school principals from the same district. *Brother* laboratories include members who occupy similar horizontal roles in an organization but without superiors and subordinates in the same group. For example, a group of principals from the same district would be brothers. In the *family* laboratory, all members belong to the same subunit of an organization. The superintendent of a school district and his administrative cabinet or the principal of a school and its department heads are examples of a family training group.

The trainer may structure the content of the laboratory training by using a number of exercises or management games or follow an unstructured format in which the group develops its own agenda. Robert Blake and Jane Mouton were among the first trainers to modify the unstructured format into an instrumental one.[50]

Stranger laboratory groups with an unstructured format were the classic form of T-groups used during the early beginnings of laboratory training. However, the difficulty encountered in applying interpersonal skills acquired away from the organization to the home-base organization when participants returned has led to the use of cousin and family groups in recent years. In fact, there has been a movement recently away from laboratory training groups and toward team building. This more recent application of T-groups has been exemplified in the work of Chris Argyris, an early proponent of laboratory training.[51] Thus, laboratory training is often used today as part of more complex organizational change strategies.

Behavioral Performance Management

Behavioral performance management has its roots in B. F. Skinner's theory of operant conditioning, which emphasizes the effect of environmental influences on behavior.[52] More recently, a social learning approach has been suggested as a more comprehensive theoretical foundation for applying behavior modification in organizations.[53] Thus, organizational behavior modification is the process of changing the behavior of an employee by managing the consequences that follow his work behavior.

Fred Luthans's S-O-B-C model provides a useful way of viewing the behavior modification process.[54] Based on a social learning approach, the behavior modification process recognizes the interaction of four parts: *S* (stimulus), *O* (organism or employee), *B* (behavior), and *C* (consequences) (see Figure 8–6).

Stimulus The *S* in the model refers to stimulus, which includes internal and external factors, mediated by learning, that determine employee behavior. External factors include organizational structure and organizational and administrative processes interacting with the structure: decision making, control, communication, power, and

[50]Robert R. Blake and Jane S. Mouton, *The Managerial Grid: Leadership Styles for Achieving Production Through People* (Houston: Gulf, 1994).

[51]Chris Argyris, *Learning in Organizations* (Alexandria,VA: American Society for Training and Development, 2009).

[52]B. F. Skinner, *About Behaviorism* (New York: Knopf, 1974); see also Alyce M. Dickenson, "The Historical Roots of Organizational Behavior Management in the Private Sector," *Journal of Organizational Behavior Management*, 20 (2000): 9–58.

[53]Alexander D. Stajkovic and Fred Luthans, "A Meta-Analysis of the Effects of Organizational Behavior Modification on Task Performance, 1975–95," *Academy of Management Journal*, 40 (1997): 1122–1149; Alexander D. Stajkovic and Fred Luthans, "Behavioral Management and Task Performance in Organizations: Conceptual Background, Meta-Analysis, and Test of Alternative Models," *Personnel Psychology*, 56 (2003): 155–194.

[54]Fred Luthans and Robert Kreitner, *Organizational Behavior Modification and Beyond: An Operant and Social Learning Approach* (Glenview, IL: Scott, Foresman, 1985).

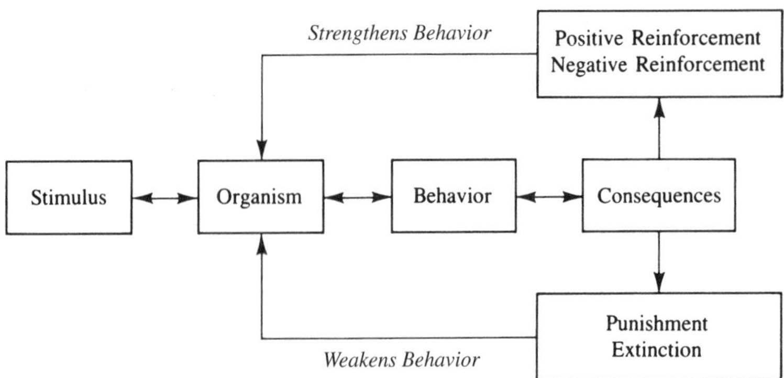

FIGURE 8–6

S-O-B-C Model
Source: Adapted from Fred Luthans, *Organizational Behavior*, 5th ed., © 1989, p. 15. Used by permission of McGraw-Hill, Inc., New York.

goal setting. Internal factors include planning, personal goals, self-observation data, stimulus removal, selective stimulus exposure, and self-contracts.[55]

Organism The *O* in the model refers to the organism, or school employee. The internal and external factors in the situation constitute the organizational environment in which the school employee operates. School employees can be thought of as consisting of cognitive and psychological processes. For example, much of what we discussed about motivating behavior with need theories, expectancy theory, equity theory, goal setting, and management by objectives applies to this part of the model.

Behavior The *B* in the model represents employee behavior. The study of the organizational environment (*S*) and the school employee (*O*) leads to a better understanding of the school employee's behavior—the overt and covert responses to the organizational environment. Behavior includes verbal and nonverbal communication, actions, and the like. In schools we are specifically interested in work behaviors such as performance, attendance, promptness, participation in committees, superordinate-subordinate relations, interaction among colleagues, or leaving the organization.

Consequences The *C* part of the model represents the consequences that result from employee behavior. The study of behavioral consequences can help improve the prediction and control of employee behavior, but this is a very simplified generalization. Social learning theorists place more emphasis on internal states and processes when explaining job behavior than the so-called radical behaviorists.[56] However, approaches such as self-management are insufficient in producing a coordinated organizational behavior modification effort. As shown in the model, behavior is a function of internal and external cues and consequences that follow a given behavior. Some types of consequences strengthen behavior while others weaken it.

Contingencies of Reinforcement Changing the interrelationships among organizational environment (*S*), employee (*O*), behavior (*B*), and consequences (*C*) is referred to as managing the *contingencies of reinforcement*.[57] As Figure 8–6 shows, the consequences that strengthen behavior are positive reinforcement and negative reinforcement. The consequences that weaken behavior are extinction and punishment.

Positive reinforcement involves following a desired behavior with the application of a pleasant stimulus, which should increase the probability of the desired behavior. Examples of positive reinforcement in a school setting include promotions, salary increases, merit raises, praise, more desirable work assignments, awards, or simply smiles. All reinforcement

[55]Luthans and Kreitner, *Organizational Behavior Modification and Beyond*.

[56]Robert Kreitner and Fred Luthans, "A Social Learning Approach to Behavioral Management: Radical Behaviorists' Mellowing Out," *Organizational Dynamics*, 13 (1984): 47–65.

[57]B. F. Skinner, *The Behavior of Organisms* (Acton, MA: Copley, 1991).

strategies, however, are specific to a given individual or situation.

Negative reinforcement involves the removal of an unpleasant stimulus on the appearance of a desired behavior, which should increase the probability of that behavior. For example, a football coach of a major university requires all football players to attend an early Sunday morning practice whenever their performance in a game falls below a minimum level. The players strive for a high performance level in the next game to avoid the unpleasant early Sunday morning practice.

Extinction involves removing a reinforcer that is maintaining some undesired behavior. If the behavior is not reinforced, it should gradually be extinguished. For instance, suppose you have an assistant who enjoys talking about her personal life for fifteen or twenty minutes every time you come into the office. In the past, you have been polite and have listened attentively as she related her personal experiences. In essence, you have been positively reinforcing her behavior. To stop her undesired behavior, you must ignore all conversations after exchanging some brief courtesies, turn around, and walk out of the office. This should dissipate the undesired behavior that is interfering with the performance of her work.

Punishment involves following an unwanted behavior with the application of some unpleasant stimulus. In theory, this should reduce the probability of the undesired behavior. Examples of punishment include oral reprimands, written warnings, suspensions, demotions, and discharge. While punishment may eliminate undesirable employee behavior in the short run, long-term, sustained use of punishment is dysfunctional to the organization.[58]

Steps in Organizational Behavior Modification

Luthans and Kreitner suggest five steps for using organizational behavior modification to change employee-behavior patterns:[59]

Step 1: Identify Significant Performance-Related Behaviors The principal and the teachers begin by identifying and describing the changes they desire to make. The analysis includes identification of significant performance-related behaviors that can be observed, counted, and specified precisely. The teacher or the principal can do the identification process. In either case, it requires training to identify behaviors for which reinforcement strategies can be used.

Step 2: Measure Performance-Related Behaviors Obtain, prior to learning, baseline measurements of the frequency of the desired target behaviors. Use tally sheets and time sampling to gather the data. In a school setting, select for assessment observed classroom performance, work-assignment completions, participation in committees, student achievement, advisement, publications, absences, service to the community, curriculum writing, and complaints. Establish some preliminary period of assessment as a baseline.

Step 3: Analyze the Antecedents and Consequences of Behaviors The behavior to be changed is often influenced by prior occurrences (antecedents) and has some identifiable consequences. For example, a particularly ineffective teacher may be a case for study. The teacher lacks effective instructional techniques, has poor rapport with students, complains incessantly about administrative policies and procedures, and adversely affects the performance and attitudes of colleagues. During this step, the principal identifies existing contingencies of reinforcement to determine when the behaviors occur, what causes them, and what their consequences are. Effective behavior change in the teacher requires replacement or removal of these reinforcing consequences.

Step 4: Implement the Change Approach Use positive reinforcement, negative reinforcement, extinction, and punishment to change significant performance-related behaviors of teachers or other employees. In other words, develop an intervention strategy, then apply the strategy using suitable contingencies of reinforcement. Finally, maintain the behaviors with appropriate schedules of reinforcement, including variable ratio, fixed ratio, variable interval, and fixed interval.[60]

---

[58] Janice M. Beyer and Harrison M. Trice, "A Field Study of the Use and Perceived Effects of Discipline in Controlling Work Performance," *Academy of Management Journal*, 27 (1984): 743–764.

[59] Luthans and Kreitner, *Organizational Behavior Modification and Beyond.*

[60] For more information on schedules of reinforcement, see Fred Luthans, *Organizational Behavior*, 12th ed. (New York: McGraw-Hill, 2011).

PRO CON DEBATE: Mandated Staff Development

Staff development proponents argue that change begins with people. Many planned change efforts include provisions for intense, long-term staff development. In some states, practicing educators must participate in ongoing professional development to earn and/or keep their licenses to teach or administer.

Question: Does mandated staff development enhance organizational change?

Arguments PRO

1. Mandates are the best way to cause change to occur because the power of the legal system is harnessed. New laws or regulations guarantee that people conform to changes that they might not like.
2. Teachers may not choose to learn what they need to learn. A teacher's knowledge base, like that of all professionals, eventually becomes obsolete. The organization must guarantee that teachers' professional knowledge is current if appropriate change is to occur.
3. In a factory, it is cost-effective to maintain equipment. In a home, it is cost-effective to make repairs. In education, which is labor-intensive, it is cost-effective to require ongoing, continual professional development just to maintain the basic unit, the teacher.

Arguments CON

1. Mandates are only as strong as the compliance system behind them. While people can be forced to attend staff development sessions, there is no cost-effective way to insist that the people perform differently when they return to their classrooms or schools.
2. Educators are highly trained professionals. Most have many degrees and licenses. When teachers need more professional knowledge, they will identify and address that need. Teachers are lifelong learners who model learning for their students.
3. Staff development is expensive. Not only must districts bear the training costs, they must also pay for substitute teachers who replace teachers in classrooms and administrators in offices. The government should not mandate unreimbursed expenses.

Step 5: Evaluate Behavior Change. Evaluate the effectiveness of behavior modification in four areas: reaction of the teachers to the approach, learning of the concepts programmed, degree of behavior change that occurs, and impact of behavior change on actual performance. In evaluating the success or failure of the behavior modification program, compare the original baseline measurements with outcome measurements of behavior. If it becomes apparent at Step 5 that the intervention strategy implemented in Step 4 has not resulted in the desired impact, start the process over again at Step 1.

Summary

1. Schools face the following forces for change: accountability, changing demographics, staffing shortages, changing technology and knowledge explosion, and processes and people.
2. School employees frequently resist change. Resistance can stem from several sources, including interference with need fulfillment, fear of the unknown, threats to power and influence, knowledge and skill obsolescence, organizational structure, limited resources, and collective bargaining agreements.

3. Methods school administrators can use to overcome resistance to change include participation, communication, support, rewards, planning, and coercion.
4. Several models have been developed to manage change. The most popular models are Kurt Lewin's force-field analysis, John Kotter's eight-step plan, and Ben Harris's five-phase model.
5. There are numerous organizational development (OD) techniques or interventions designed to plan and implement change. Some OD techniques are designed to improve the performance of groups or the organization (group approaches). These include TQM, strategic planning, and survey feedback.
6. Another type of OD techniques is aimed at changing the individual (individual approaches). These include job enrichment, laboratory training, and behavioral performance management. In practice, the approaches generally are used in combination to effect organizational change in school districts.

Key Terms

force-field analysis
organizational development
total quality management
strategic planning
survey feedback
job enrichment
laboratory training
behavioral performance management

Discussion Questions

1. Using Kurt Lewin's force-field analysis model, diagnose your school district, school, university, or other educational institution. Place the driving forces for change on the left portion of the model and the resisting forces on the right side of the model. What will it take to implement positive change in your institution?
2. Organization members typically resist change. Why do employees resist change? What can school administrators do to overcome resistance to change?
3. What models can school administrators use to manage change?
4. Describe an organization that needs change. Which of the OD techniques presented in this chapter would you use to make the organization more effective?
5. Explain why school administrators typically need to use a combination of approaches (i.e., group and individual approaches) to effect change. Cite examples.

Suggested Readings

Darling-Hammond, Linda. *The Flat World and Education* (New York: Teachers College Press, 2010). Linda Darling-Hammond offers an eye-opening wake-up call concerning America's future and vividly illustrates what the United States needs to do to build a system of high-achieving and equitable schools that ensures every child the right to learn.

DuFour, Richard, Rebecca DuFour, Robert Eaker, and Gayle Karhanek. *Raising the Bar and Closing the Gap: Whatever It Takes* (Bloomington, IN: Solution Tree, 2010). The authors examine schools and districts across North America to illustrate how (Professional Learning Communities) is a sustainable and transferable model that ensures struggling students get the support they need to achieve.

Fullan, Michael (Ed.). *The Challenge of Change* (Thousand Oaks, CA: Corwin Press, 2009). This collection addresses the concerns behind the school change movement, examines theories and implementation strategies, and provides practical examples for tri-level reform—school, district, and state educators collaborating to strengthen the capacity for change.

Fullan, Michael. *All Systems Go: The Change Imperative for Whole System Reform* (Thousand Oaks, CA: Sage, 2010). Based on Fullan's work with districts and large systems, this resource lays out a comprehensive action plan for achieving whole system reform.

Hargreaves, Andy and Dennis Shirley. *The Fourth Way: The Inspiring Future for Educational Change* (Thousand Oaks, CA: Corwin Press, 2009). The authors offer a reform framework that integrates teacher professionalism, community engagement, government policy, and accountability.

Rotberg, Iris C. (Ed.). *Balancing Change and Tradition in Global Education Reform* (Lanham, MD: Rowman & Littlefield, 2010). Rotberg brings together examples of current education reforms in 16 countries, written by "insiders."

Smylie, Mark A. *Continuous School Improvement* (Thousand Oaks, CA: Corwin Press, 2010). Providing a powerful synthesis of change theory and research on continuous improvement, Smylie offers a succinct overview of organizational change and provides school leaders an exceptional foundation for sustaining reform initiatives.

9

Government and Education

FOCUSING QUESTIONS

1. How has the federal role in education changed in recent years?
2. How has the national reform movement in education affected local schools?
3. What are the different roles and responsibilities of the governor, state legislature, and state courts in deciding school policy?
4. What are the major functions of the state board of education, state department of education, and chief state school officer?
5. How can the state reform movement be improved?
6. What is the ideal size of a school district? Why?
7. What are the major responsibilities of the school board?
8. What are the major problem areas faced by superintendents?

We attempt to answer these questions by first exploring the relationship between the federal government and education, and then that between state government and education. We examine congressional influence on education and the various federal programs designed to enhance learning. We consider the role of the federal courts and also discuss the national reform movement in education. We discuss the roles that state officials—the governor, legislature, and courts—have in determining policy. Next, we examine the structure of state boards, departments of education, and chief executive officers. We explore the state reform movement in education.

Then we examine school districts, in particular their size and structure. We discuss the structure and duties of the local school board, the responsibilities of the superintendent, and the relationship between the board and the superintendent. Finally, we explore the role of the central office staff and its obligations to the district and the superintendent.

The Federal Role in Education

A national system of education does not exist in the United States in the same sense that it does in England, France, Germany, Japan, India, or Russia. Education in the United States is considered both a state and a local function; there are fifty different state systems, and many differences exist among local school systems within the same state. In total, there are some 15,000 different local school districts—each with its own philosophy and goals.

The U.S. Constitution makes no mention of public education, but the Tenth Amendment to the Constitution reserves to the states all powers not specifically delegated to the federal government or prohibited to the states by the Constitution. This amendment is the basis for allocating primary legal responsibility for public education to the states. However, the states have delegated to the local districts the responsibility of the practical day-to-day operation of school districts.

The schools have always been a provincial domain of the towns and cities of the United States, rooted in the colonial tradition of the nation, but the federal government has always had some say in public education. Beginning with the land grants that antedated the U.S. Constitution and highlighted by the welfare clause of the Constitution (Article I, Section 8), which gives Congress the power to tax for the general good and for broad social purposes, education has always been the federal government's concern. Although education is not specifically identified in Article I, the language is general enough for the government to use public tax monies to support the nation's schools and school programs and to enact educational laws for the welfare of the people.

Changing Roles in the Federal Government and Education

To fully understand the federal government and its relations with the schools, one must understand that there has been a gradual shift from the historical **separation of powers** between the federal government and states toward the federal government's playing a greater role in education and social areas. Recently, there has been a trend toward greater decentralization at the federal level and sharing of educational responsibilities and functions between the federal government and states. At the same time, there is a countertrend to develop national goals, standards, and high-stake testing—a shift toward greater nationalization of the curriculum, as part of the reform movement to upgrade education.[1]

The first 150 years of U.S. education can be considered the period of **dual federalism,** whereby the founding fathers' majority view to limit the federal government at all levels and most functions prevailed. During this period, federal programs and activities in education were passive and uncoordinated. Sometime around the Great Depression and the Roosevelt administration the next period, called **national federalism,**[2] evolved. Economic and social circumstances of the day called for greater federal intervention, first in the area of labor legislation and relief acts in education and public works; followed by educational legislation for the Cold War and Sputnik period of the late 1940s and 1950s; and then the War on Poverty and civil rights movement that affected schools and society in the 1960s and 1970s. What became apparent during this national federalism period was that national action and national coordination of programs and activities were needed to resolve many problems that extended beyond the boundaries of state and local governments. National identity and national welfare were at stake, and there were dramatic increases in federal commitment to education.

---

[1]Phillip C. Schlechty, *Inventing Better Schools* (San Francisco: Jossey-Bass, 2001); Marc S. Tucker and Judy B. Codding, *Standards for Our Schools* (San Francisco: Jossey-Bass, 1998).

[2]Roald F. Campbell et al., *The Organization of American Schools,* 6th ed. (Columbus, OH: Merrill, 1990). (It should be noted, however, that Campbell and his associates put the beginning of this second period at the time of the Civil War and the "due process" clause of the Fourteenth Amendment.) Also see Kenneth Leithwood et al., *Making Schools Smarter,* 3rd ed. (Thousand Oaks, CA: Corwin, 2006); Kenneth A. Strike et al., *The Ethics of School Administration* (New York: Teachers College Press, Columbia University, 2005).

Current Period: 1980s to 2010

Starting in the 1980s under President Ronald Reagan and continued by President George Bush, a **new federalism** evolved, which called for a dramatic shift in federal policy and programs. Driven by a belief that the federal government was too meddlesome and involved in too many activities and regulations, Reagan and Bush reduced federal funds (vis-à-vis inflation), activities, and regulations in education as well as in other social sectors of the economy.[3] In addition, monetary and program responsibilities were shifted to state (and local) agencies. Federal rules and regulations governing education were revoked or more loosely enforced. President Bill Clinton acknowledged, at least implicitly, the limits of federal activity in education, although he believed that government could solve social and economic problems.[4]

The new federalism showed up in the Reagan-Bush I and II administrations despite the rhetoric about the need to bolster education and human capital. First, there was a shift in priorities from human, social, and educational concerns to big business and military interests. This shift showed up in their lack of formal policy regarding education and in the belief that the federal government should be involved less, not more, in the education of the nation's children and youth. It also showed up in the Clinton administration with Clinton's support of choice and voucher programs, in his belief, as well as his predecessor's, in the private sector to improve education.

During the Clinton administration, new philanthropists and donors—corporate leaders such as Jim Barksdale, Michael Dell, Bill Gates, Mike Milken, and the Walton family—began to fill a vacuum in federal funding and provided discretionary money for school reform. Under the Bush II administration, the private donor trend was accelerated. By 2009, according to the Chronicle of Philanthropy, the three top philanthropists were Stanley and Fiona Druckenmiller, John M. Templeton, and Bill and Melinda Gates. The Gates Foundation donates over $350 million annually to education. New to the list were Louise Nippert and J. Ronald and Frances Terwilliger.[5]

The Clinton administration sought to align federal programs with state reform and accountability plans, and to enhance the idea of a federal–state partnership,[6] contrary to the thinking of the Reagan and Bush I administrations, which sought to *deregulate* or reduce the federal enforcement of rules and regulations and *decentralize* or reduce federal intrusion into what should be a state or local responsibility.

With the Clinton administration, the emphasis was on accountability and testing, smaller class sizes, improving teaching and increasing the teaching force, connecting classrooms to the Internet, preparing teachers to use technology, improving reading programs, and upgrading science and math programs. By the time the Clinton administration came to an end, forty-nine states had established state standards and/or testing programs.[7]

During the Reagan and Bush I administrations, the big-city school districts were shortchanged. Federal monies were shifted to the states to dispense to local schools, under the guise of *deemphasizing* the federal role in education and shifting more responsibility to the states. For example, by the mid-1990s, only 20 percent of block grant monies (funds earmarked by the federal government for the states) were being dedicated to compensatory and basic skills programs.[8] The Clinton administration was unable to change this shift in federal funding, and Title I schools continued to be underfunded.

---

[3]Norman Amaker, "Reagan Record on Civil Rights," *Urban Institute Policy and Research Report,* 18 (1988): 15–16; Dennis P. Doyle, "The White House and School House," *Phi Delta Kappan,* 74 (1992): 129; Allan C. Ornstein, "The Changing Federal Role in Education," *Kappa Delta Pi Record,* 21 (1985): 85–88.

[4]Evans Clinchy, "The Educationally Challenged American School District," *Phi Delta Kappan,* 80 (1998): 272–277; Dorothy Rich, "What Educators Need to Explain to the Public," *Phi Delta Kappan,* 87 (2005): 154.

[5]*Wall Street Journal* (February 8, 2010), "America's Top 50 Philanthropists Gave Less in 2009"; *New York Times* (March 8, 2008), "How Many Billionaires Does It Take to Fix a School System?"; Also see Erik W. Robelen, "Spending by Education Philanthropies Drops," *Education Week* (January 20, 2010): 1, 12.

[6]Richard W. Riley, "Education Reform Through Standards and Partnerships, 1993–2000," *Phi Delta Kappan,* 83 (2002): 700–707.

[7]Riley, "Education Reform Through Standards and Partnerships, 1993–2000"; Michael S. Trevisan, "The States' Role in Ensuring Assessment Competence," *Phi Delta Kappan,* 83 (2002): 766–771.

[8]*Digest of Education Statistics 1998* (Washington, DC: U.S. Government Printing Office, 1999), table 365, p. 416; Also see Susan B. Neuman, *Changing the Odds for Children at Risk* (New York: Teachers College Press, Columbia University 2009); Richard Rothstein, *Class and Schools: Using Social, Economic, and Educational Reform to Close the Black–White Achievement Gap* (New York: Teachers College Press, Columbia University, 2004).

Table 9-1 Federal Funds (in billions) from Department of Education, and All Federal Departments, 1970–2009

	1970	1980	1990	2000	2009
Department Education					
K–12	$2,719	$6,629	$9,681	$20,758	$38,900
Higher education	1,187	5,682	11,175	15,834	30,267
All other programs, all departments	12,526	13,137	23,198	33,985	75,081

Source: *Digest of Education Statistics, 1993* (Washington, DC: U.S. Government Printing Office, 1993), tables 348, 349, 350, pp. 363–368; *Digest of Education Statistics 2000* (Washington, DC: U.S. Government Printing Office, 2001), tables 364–365, pp. 416–417. *Digest of Education Statistics, 2009* (Washington, DC: U.S. Government Printing Office, 2010), table 377, p. 547.

The Bush II administration adopted a national accountability and testing program. As a result, the reauthorization in 2001 of the Elementary and Secondary School Act required a series of annual tests for each state in grades 3 through 8, with timetables for improvement. Federal funding now comes with some leverage to expect improvement, along with penalties for not achieving target benchmarks (see Table 9–1).

As a part of this new federalism, beginning with the Clinton administration and accelerated by the Bush II administration, the **national standards movement** has been gaining momentum. This movement shows a deepening concern for declining student scores on national and international achievement tests and for the declining quality of the teaching workforce as evidenced by the difficulty of a large percentage of entry teachers in passing basic skill tests.[9] A new consensus is developing—one that promotes national needs and goals as more important than local or pluralistic needs and goals, supports more rigorous teacher training and national testing and professional standards for teachers, and seeks a common and traditional core of subjects, content, and values in the traditional mode of the arts and sciences.

George W. Bush continued the idea by requiring statewide goals and adequate improvement over time, along with corrective action for school districts that are unable to meet state standards. Teachers and principals are able to use test data to make informed decisions for improving student performance under the new federal guidelines. Schools identified for improvement or corrective action must provide parents with the option of enrolling their children in another public school, including an alternative or charter school, and the school district must provide transportation funds, as well as funds for tutoring low-income students who fail to meet standards.[10]

Within the context of nationalization of standards, some critics ask: Why raise standards if students cannot meet them? Why talk about a nationalized set of goals or curriculum when the focus has always been on local control of the schools and when there is little agreement on goals, standards, or requirements among the fifty states and some 14,000 school districts?

It appears as though the Obama administration is expanding the role of the federal government in educational reform efforts. Specifically, the federal government is allocating funds for innovation and is not prescribing how states should spend the money. Some reform efforts include pay for performance, charter schools, and data systems. According to Anne Bryant, the executive director of the National School Boards Association, "Obama's legacy is already being fashioned in the unprecedented amount of funds devoted to education, in the energy of his Secretary of Education, and in the potential for change that new programs have given the administration."[11]

The president's 2011 budget calls for a 6.2 percent increase in the budget of the Department of Education. This includes an additional $4 billion in grants

[9]Linda Darling-Hammond, *The Flat World and Education* (New York: Teachers College Press, Columbia University, 2010); James H. Stronge, *Teacher Pay and Teacher Quality* (Thousand Oaks, CA: Corwin, 2006); and Tucker and Codding, *Standards for Our Schools.*

[10]Daniel L. Duke, "What We Know and Don't Know About Improving Low-Performing Schools," *Phi Delta Kappan,* 87 (2006): 728–734; Margaret E. Goertz, "Redefining Government Roles in an Era of Standards-Based Reform," *Phi Delta Kappan,* 83 (2001): 62. Also see James P. Comer et al., *Six Pathways to Healthy Child Development and Academic Success* (Thousand Oaks, CA: Corwin, 2004).

[11]Lawrence Hardy, "Year One," *American School Board Journal,* 197 (2009): 15–19.

for K-12 education. In 2010, the discretionary budget for the Department was approximately $63.7 billion. The 2011 budget is expected to merge 38 Education Department programs into 11 and do away with six other programs.[12]

Clarifying the Federal Role in Education

The federal government's role in education is compelling because how we educate our children and youth will determine the kind of nation we become. The issue is not whether we do or do not reduce the federal role or nationalize standards in education; the issue is to clarify and determine how the federal government can and should use its resources and dollars to effectively promote schools and other social institutions. Federal leadership should support and work with state and local agencies, not for the purpose of promoting the needs of one group versus another but for our shared priorities as a people or nation.

Federal leadership can work hand in hand with local school districts, and the focus should be on enhancing academic achievement of all students and ensuring that students with special needs have equal opportunity to succeed. In no way should our goals or priorities suggest that schools be nationalized or that the federal government establish national standards of educational performance.

The federal role in education should be based on helping local schools and school districts build consensus and confidence in educating their clients. Many educational problems are both national and local. The problem is national because it occurs in many parts of the country and because world and national events help construct it. It is also local in the sense that the composition and needs of the student population differ from place to place and that local efforts and resources are needed to resolve the problem. If local efforts and resources are not funded, then the services or personnel will not be provided. A federal strategy is needed—one that stimulates state and local school planning and reform and supplements state and local efforts and resources.

The Department of Education

Although many different federal agencies (thirteen departments and about fifteen other agencies or units) are involved in some type of educational program or activity, the U.S. Department of Education is the major agency through which the federal government demonstrates its commitment to education. Of the thirteen departments, it receives 45 percent of all federal funds for education.

Table 9–1 shows an increase in federal funding in actual and real dollars (after inflation) for the Department of Education since 1980, reflecting its new role with full department status (starting in 1979) alongside thirteen other federal departments. However, federal funding for all programs (K–college) and federal departments decreased in real dollars in the 1980s when the new federalism movement first surfaced. After increasing 30 percent in real dollars between 1970 and 1980, it declined 5 percent between 1980 and 1990. Elementary and secondary education slightly declined in real dollars between 1980 and 1990, whereas higher education increased in real dollars (almost 25 percent). Many educators have criticized this shift in federal education priorities—from K–12 schooling to higher education—given the fact that the eventual outcomes of human capital are rooted or primarily formed in the children's early years of schooling. As a result of the criticism, since 1995 the DOE has funded more money for K–12 programs than for higher education.[13] Whereas the public often criticizes public schools for being inefficient or wasteful, perhaps there is greater need to scrutinize the budgets of colleges and universities since they are receiving increased federal dollars.

When the Department of Education was formed in 1867, its commissioner had a staff of three clerks and a total of $18,600 to spend. From these humble beginnings, the department has grown to more than 4525 employees and annual expenditures of $57 billion in 2003. The department presently administers over 200 separate programs.[14] The original purpose of the department was to collect and disseminate statistics and facts and to promote the goals of education throughout the country. Even though it was known as the Department of Education, the commissioner was not a member of the president's cabinet. In fact, the department

[12]Alyson Klein, "Obama to Seek up to $4 Billion Boost for Education," *Education Week* (January 27, 2010): 17, 21.

[13]Daniel U. Levine and Allan C. Ornstein, "Assessment of Student Achievement: National and International Perspectives," *NASSP Bulletin*, 77 (1993): 46–59, *Digest of Education Statistics*, 2003 (Washington, DC: U.S. Government Printing Office, 2004), tables 171, 247, pp. 210–211, 402–403.

[14]*Digest of Education Statistics, 1989* (Washington, DC: U.S. Government Printing Office, 1989), fig. 20, p. 333; *Digest of Education Statistics, 1993*, table 351, p. 371; *Digest of Education Statistics, 2005*, table 367, p. 436.

was attached to the Department of the Interior in 1868 and given the status and name of a bureau.

In 1929, the title Office of Education was adopted; ten years later, the office was transferred to the Federal Security Agency. In 1953, the Office of Education was transferred again, this time to the newly formed Department of Health, Education, and Welfare (HEW). The Office of Education continued to perform its original functions and assumed new responsibilities of (1) administering grant funds and contracting with state departments of education, school districts, colleges, and universities; (2) engaging in educational innovation, research, and development; and (3) providing leadership, consultative, and clearinghouse services related to education.

In 1979, after much congressional debate, a Department of Education (DOE) was signed into law by President Carter who declared that education was the "biggest single national investment" and that the creation of the department was the "best move for the quality of life in America for the future." A secretary of education, Shirley Hufstedler, was named with full cabinet-level status, and the department officially opened in 1980.

In theory, there now exists a person (the Secretary of Education) with potentially widespread influence and with cabinet status, who can exert persuasion and pressure in political and educational circles and who is in charge of educational policy at the federal level and the promotion of programs to carry out these policies.

Although President Reagan almost eliminated the Department of Education and reduced its staff by one-third between 1980 and 1985,[15] it was during his administration that the department gained in stature and visibility because of the outspoken and controversial William Bennett, Secretary of Education between 1985 and 1988. Bennett stated forceful positions on several educational issues, including but not limited to academic standards, moral education, school discipline, computer literacy, school prayer, drug education and getting drugs out of schools, teacher accountability and teacher testing, and teaching essential knowledge for a democratic society and national pride. His critics, in fact, labeled Bennett as a "bully" and charged that he used his office as a "bully pulpit."

The secretary during the later Bush II administration, Margaret Spellings, was much less visible and controversial. Spellings focused on achieving the goals of No Child Left Behind, disseminating test information and tracking student progress, holding school districts accountable and using government leverage to demand results, and creating better partnerships among educators, parents, business people, labor, and the community.[16] Although few people can quarrel with such lofty goals, achieving them is another story. (See the Pro/Con Debate at the end of this chapter.)

Secretary of Education Arne Duncan states that the United States "is on the cusp of a new era in public education." Empowered by hundreds of millions in economic stimulus aid for education to offset cutbacks in state funding, as well as the support of President Obama, whom he knew when Duncan was Chicago Superintendent, Duncan has enormous power and is moving quickly to push reform in charter schools, teacher evaluations, teacher performance pay, academic standards, and assisting low-performing schools.[17]

Federal Programs and Activities in Education

Although the framers of the Constitution gave the states primary responsibility to maintain and operate schools through the Tenth Amendment, they also provided another important provision—that Congress could "provide for the . . . general welfare of the United States."

Congress remained in the background for the first 150 years, at least in terms of supporting and enacting educational legislation. But a sense of national need, starting in the mid-1930s with the Great Depression, moved Congress to strengthen school support and enact laws. Between 1787 and 1937, for example, Congress enacted only fourteen major educational laws. During the last seventy years, however, more than 175 major laws were passed.[18]

[15]Thomas Skelly, director of Budget Systems Division, Department of Education, personal communication, February 23, 1989.

[16]William A. Proefriedt, *High Expectations: The Cultural Roots of Standards Reform in American Education* (New York: Teachers College Press, Columbia University, 2008); Seymour B. Sarason, *Letters to a Serious Education President* (Thousand Oaks, CA: Corwin, 2006).

[17]Lawrence Hardy, "Year One," *American School Board Journal,* 197 (2009): 15–19; McNeil, "Duncan Carving Deep Mark on Policy."

[18]*Digest of Educational Statistics, 2006* (Washington, DC: U.S. Government Printing Office, 2006).

Until the mid-twentieth century, the federal government gave very little financial assistance to the states (or local schools) for the education of students. This attitude was in line with the majority belief that the federal government should have little to do with education and that education is a state responsibility. Federal programs and activities might be characterized as passive and uncoordinated during this period. This is not to say that the federal government had no influence on education. National laws and federal programs had a significant impact on the way education developed in the United States. But we must remember that these programs and acts were not part of a broadly conceived national plan for education. After Sputnik in 1957, however, as national policy became more closely linked to education, federal funding dramatically increased, steadily involving specific educational targets. This growth was curbed in the 1980s (with the Reagan and Bush I administrations) but restored in the 1990s with Clinton. Although federal funding in real dollars has decreased with Bush II, federal involvement remains significant.

Grants for Schools

The **Northwest Ordinances** of 1785 and 1787 were the first instances of federal assistance to education. The Northwest Ordinance of 1785 divided the Northwest Territory into townships and each township into thirty-six sections; it reserved the sixteenth section "of every township for the maintenance of public schools within the said township." The Ordinance of 1787 stated that "schools and the means of education shall forever be encouraged" by the states. The federal government thus demonstrated its commitment to education while ensuring the autonomy of state and local schools. As a result of these ordinances, thirty-nine states received over 154 million acres of land for schools from the federal government.[19]

Grants for Colleges

Seventy-five years passed before another major federal educational program was enacted. This program involved institutions of higher learning, not elementary and secondary schools. In the **Morrill Act** of 1862, federally owned lands totaling 30,000 acres were set aside for each state, with the provision that the income from the sale or rental of these lands was to be used to establish colleges for the study of agriculture and mechanical arts. A total of 6 million acres of federal lands was given to the states. These "people's colleges," or land grant institutions, were to become the great multipurpose state universities that now enroll students from all segments of society. The Morrill Act demonstrated that the federal government would take action in education for the good and welfare of the nation; it also marked the beginning of meaningful federal influence on higher education.

Vocational Education Acts

The third phase of federal activity in public education came with the conditional grants for highly specific purposes in public secondary schools. The **Smith-Hughes Act** of 1917 provided money grants for vocational education, home economics, and agricultural subjects. The original act called for federal appropriations to be matched by state or local educational agencies. It was extended by various acts between 1929 and 1984; the 1984 legislation, called the Perkins Vocational Education Act, extended funding into the 1990s through various job training amendments and included people with handicaps, single parents, homemakers, and the incarcerated among its beneficiaries.

The 1917 federal vocational act marked the federal government's first annual appropriation for public secondary education. The 1963 federal vocational act appropriated $235 million for vocational training, quadruple the annual appropriations of the original Smith-Hughes Act;[20] by 1998, the annual federal funding for vocational programs had reached $1.5 billion, and the average vocational program (Carnegie) units completed by public high school students was 3.8 (including consumer and homemaker education and labor-market preparation) with rural students averaging 4.5 course units. In 2009, vocational funding increased to $2.2 billion.[21]

Unquestionably, some educators are alarmed at the vocational budget. They would not only increase monies but also establish a national apprenticeship program, as in Europe, that would encourage non-college-bound students to stay in school two years longer in order to

[19]Ellwood P. Cubberly, *Public Education in the United States*, rev. ed. (Boston: Houghton Mifflin, 1934).

[20]*The Condition of Education, 1983* (Washington, DC: U.S. Government Printing Office, 1983), table 3.8, p. 152.

[21]*Digest of Education Statistics 2009* (Washington, DC: U.S. Government Printing Office, 2010), table 375, p. 540.

get further training and be better prepared to move into the workforce. In fact, Clinton had once proposed that all employers invest up to 1.5 percent of their payroll in retraining their workforce so as to keep it competitive.[22]

In order for the U.S. to remain competitive on a global basis, some business pundits are urging that more funds be allocated to technology education (which is a federal component of vocational and adult education appropriations). Bill Gates addressed the National Governors Association education summit in 2003 and asserted, "When I compare our high schools to what I see when traveling, I am terrified for our work force of tomorrow."[23] Given the fact that approximately 90 percent of current engineers and scientists are being graduated from China, India, and Japan, Gates's observation about America's future is cause for concern.[24]

Relief Acts

The fourth phase of federal activity emerged during the Great Depression. Federal interest in schools at that time was only incidental to greater concerns for the welfare of unemployed youth from ages sixteen to twenty-five. The Civilian Conservation Corps (CCC) was organized in 1933 for unemployed males ages seventeen to twenty-three. More than half of the youth who joined had never finished grade school, and a substantial number were practically illiterate. The act provided federal appropriations for the education and vocational training of more than 3 million youth until it was abolished in 1943. Almost a generation passed before the CCC idea was brought back as part of the Job Corps in the mid-1960s.

Other federal programs of the Depression era included the National Youth Administration (1933), which provided welfare and training programs for unemployed youth ages sixteen to twenty-five as well as financial aid for needy students attending secondary schools and colleges; the Federal Emergency Relief Administration (1933), which allocated funds for the employment of unemployed rural teachers; the Public Works Administration (1933) and Works Progress Administration (1935), both of which provided federal money for school construction and repairs, amounting to 30 to 45 percent of the national allocation of funding of new schools from 1933 to 1938. All federal relief agencies were terminated by the mid-1940s. Although some educators were concerned about possible federal domination of public schooling during the 1930s, these fears subsided; the communities that had participated in these programs were in a better position to meet the classroom shortage that occurred after World War II.[25]

War Acts

The fifth phase of federal activity took place during World War II and the immediate postwar period. Three major bills were passed at this time.

1. The Lanham Act (1941) provided aid for construction and maintenance of local schools in areas where military personnel resided or where there were extensive federal projects.
2. The Occupational Rehabilitation Act (1943) provided educational and occupational assistance to disabled veterans.
3. The Serviceman's Readjustment Act (1944), commonly called the **GI bill**, provided funds for the education of veterans and enabled hundreds of thousands of Americans to attend institutions of higher learning or special training schools.

The benefits of the GI bill were extended to the Korean and Vietnam conflicts. Direct aid, totaling more than $10 billion, has helped more than 7.5 million veterans to attend institutions of higher learning or special training schools. The GI bill, along with the baby boom, was a major factor in the growth and expansion of American colleges, including community colleges.

Since 1990, the GI education benefits have been extended by four bills and amendments, including the "Veterans" Educational Assistance Amendments (PL 102–127), which restored benefits to reserve and active duty personnel, and amended Title 38, which increased veterans' education and employment programs. In

[22]Bill Clinton, "The Clinton Plan for Excellence in Education," *Phi Delta Kappan,* 74 (1992): 131–138.

[23]"Gates 'Appalled' by High Schools," *Seattle Times,* February 27, 2005, p. 27.

[24]Allan C. Ornstein, *Class Counts: Education, Inequality and the Shrinking Middle Class* (Lanham, MD: Rowman & Littlefield, 2007).

[25]Roland S. Barth, *Lessons Learned* (Thousand Oaks, CA: Corwin, 2003); Marvin Lazerson and W. Norton Grubb, *The Education Gospel: The Economic Power of Schooling* (Cambridge, MA: Harvard University Press, 2004).

2003 as much as $2.6 billion in tuition assistance was granted to Iraq veterans, an increase of only 10 percent since 1980.[26] By 2009, about $680 million in tuition assistance was provided for military personnel.

National Defense Education Act

The Cold War and the Soviet launching of Sputnik in 1957 increased pressure for better schools and federal funding. This led to the sixth phase of federal education legislation, particularly the **National Defense Education Act** (NDEA) of 1958. The act stressed the importance of education to the national defense, and funding was earmarked for educational programs that enhanced "the security of the nation . . . and [developed] the mental resources and technical skills of its young men and women."

This broad act emphasized improvement of instruction in science, mathematics, foreign languages, and other critical subjects; provided college and university students loans and scholarships; funded numerous teacher training programs, including those for teaching the disadvantaged; stimulated guidance and counseling programs; and promoted curriculum reform and programs in vocational and technical education. By 1960, the federal government was spending nearly $240 million annually on NDEA programs; in the mid-1960s, the act was extended to include history, geography, English, and reading as critical subjects.[27]

Compensatory Education Acts

The 1960s and 1970s brought a new emphasis on equality in education and represents the seventh stage of federal programs. With the War on Poverty and the spread of the civil rights movement, national policy became linked to education, as the government targeted specific groups—namely, minorities and the poor—and created specific policies to improve their educational opportunities. The federal government took on an active and coordinated posture with reference to education as it substantially increased its contributions to a variety of targeted programs and increased its regulations over specific policies.

The most important act of this period was the **Elementary and Secondary Education Act** (ESEA) of 1965, part of President Johnson's Great Society. It focused on compensatory programs for the disadvantaged students, immediately providing $1 billion for the first year. In 1980, at the height of its popularity, monies totaled $3.5 billion, or about $300 per disadvantaged child; from 1965 to 1980, $30 billion had been appropriated. (Appropriations for the disadvantaged fluctuated between $3.2 billion and $4.5 billion per year from 1980 to 1990.)[28] Considering inflation, this was a slight drop in real dollars that reflected the general cutbacks in education by the federal government during this period. However, by 2008 funding had increased to $14 billion or an additional $1,000 per disadvantaged child, reflecting the nation's emphasis on social and educational spending. By 2009, $15.9 billion was allocated for disadvantage of children:[29] This dollar amount was amid increased military and home security spending and consolidation of many federal programs, reflecting the elements of President George W. Bush's prized Reading First Program and Leave No Child Behind plan.[30]

During this forty-four-year period (1965–2008), the Consumer Price Index increased about five times, but compensatory funding soared about 14 times.[31] Funding for **Title I**, or disadvantaged students, has become big business—with a host of bureaucratic layers and jobs and subsequent advocates for compensatory funding. In the name of a variety of environmental and behavioral theories, as well as President Johnson's dream of the Great Society, compensatory programs proliferated as educators and social designers rushed to make claims to federal monies, spending billions of dollars based on hunches and sometimes sloppy program designs. Although compensatory programs from

[26] *Digest of Education Statistics, 1989*, table 304, p. 337; *Digest of Education Statistics, 2003*, table 367, p. 436; *Digest of Education Statistics, 2009*, table 575, p. 541.

[27] Allan C. Ornstein, *Education and Social Inquiry* (Itasca, IL: Peacock, 1978); S. Alexander Rippa, *Education in a Free Society*, 8th ed. (New York: Longman, 1997).

[28] *Digest of Education Statistics, 1983–84* (Washington, DC: U.S. Government Printing Office, 1983), table 144, p. 174; *Digest of Education Statistics, 1989*, table 307, p. 344.

[29] *Digest of Education Statistics, 1993*, tables 3, 21, 350, pp. 12, 29, 365–368; *Digest of Education Statistics, 2003*, table 368, p. 437; *Digest of Education Statistics, 2009*, table 375, p. 540.

[30] Erik W. Robelen, "Amid Crisis, Outlook for ESEA Overhaul Unclear," *Education Week* (September 26, 2001): 25–26; Robelen, "Congress Refocuses on ESEA," *Education Week* (October 3, 2001): 27, 31. Also see Stuart Yeh, *Raising Student Achievement Through Test Reform* (New York: Teachers College Press, 2006).

[31] *Digest of Educational Statistics, 2009*, tables 32, 375, pp. 53, 540.

the Johnson era to the George W. Bush administration had a great deal in common, the latter was the first president to raise the difficult issue of how to define *failing schools;* how to resolve the problem, however, has always remained unclear during these four decades.

It should also be noted that most grants for compensatory education are earmarked for urban disadvantaged students, now called at-risk students, and tend to fall in early childhood programs (such as Head Start and Follow-Through) and reading, language, and basic skills development (nearly half deal directly with the improvement of basic skills in reading, language, and communication).

Title

Title IX (PL 92-318) of the 1972 Education Amendments to the **Civil Rights Act** prohibits discrimination against women in educational programs receiving federal assistance. Part of the movement toward equality of opportunity (and later acts such as the Women's Educational Equity Act of 1974) and a host of affirmative action rulings enforced by the Office of Civil Rights (which is also under the jurisdiction of the Department of Labor) evolved out of the Civil Rights Act of 1964 to include women's rights and concerns.

Federal control over these school matters is implicitly stated by the regulations governing Title IX and outline in detail what schools and colleges must do in terms of making available female sports programs and facilities and in the hiring of women to prevent sex discrimination and possible loss of federal funds. Individuals and organizations can challenge any discriminatory practice by contacting the local agency of the Office of Civil Rights or Department of Labor. Moreover, Title VII of the Civil Rights Act of 1964 covers all educational institutions regardless of whether they receive federal funds or not. The latter condition reflects the fact that the U.S. Supreme Court has ruled that education is a right, guaranteed by the Constitution, and therefore it extends federal influence over schools and colleges.[32]

The law, which marked its thirtieth anniversary in 2002, mandates gender equality at the K–12 and college levels not only in sports (the original goal) but also in math and science classes. Even as proponents celebrate this law, opponents behind the scenes still exist. The other side of the coin is that Title IX "robs Peter to pay for Pauline," and a number of second-tier male sports such as wrestling, gymnastics, rowing, and volleyball have been dramatically cut, in some cases eliminated.

The debate is influenced by recent trends in higher education. From 2000 to 2007, more females (13 percent) than males (8 percent) enrolled in 2-year institutions. Based on current projections, by 2018, this trend will continue as approximately 4.5 million females and 3.0 million males enroll in 2-year institutions. From 2000 to 2007, more females (26 percent) than males (23 percent) enrolled in 4-year institutions. Based on current projections, by 2018, this trend will continue as approximately 5.8 million females and 4.2 million males enroll in 4-year institutions.[33] Between the mid-1970s to 2007, more females (approximately 1.4 million) than males (910,000) enrolled in graduate programs; current projections for 2018 show that this gap will continue.[34]

Bilingual Education

Bilingual education, which provides instruction in the native language of non-English-proficient students, has been expanding in U.S. public schools—in part due to federal policy. In 1968, Congress passed the **Bilingual Education Act** and amended it in 1974 to ensure that instruction be given in English or the native language of the child, whichever is more suitable, "to allow the child to progress effectively through the educational system."

Much of bilingual educational expansion is based on the 1974 U.S. Supreme Court ruling in *Lau v. Nichols* that requires schools to help students who "are certain to find their classroom experiences wholly incomprehensible" because they do not understand English. Congressional appropriations for bilingual education increased from $36.4 million in 1974 to $496 million in 1999. In 2009, the budget for English language acquisition was $730 million.[35] Although the federal and state governments fund bilingual projects for more than sixty language groups speaking various Asian, Indo-European, and Native American languages, the

[32]Kern Alexander and M. David Alexander, *American Public School Law,* 8th ed. (Belmont, CA: Wadsworth, 2010).

[33]*The Condition of Education 2009* (Washington, DC: U.S. Government Printing Offices, 2010), Indicator 10, p. 22.

[34]Ibid, Indicator 11, p. 24.

[35]*Digest of Education Statistics, 1976* (Washington, DC: U.S. Government Printing Office, 1976), table 157, p. 173; *Digest of Education Statistics, 2000,* table 361, p. 407; *The Fiscal Year 2000 Budget,* Appendix, p. 8; *Digest of Education Statistics, 2009*, table 375, p. 540.

Table 9-2 Total U.S. and Minority Population, Based on Current Immigration Rates and Fertility, 1980–2020 (in millions)

	1980		2000		2020 (est.)	
	Number	%	Number	%	Number	%
White (non-Hispanic)	181.0	79.9	200.3	71.7	205.6	64.9
Black	26.5	11.7	36.4	13.0	44.4	14.0
Hispanic	14.6	6.5	30.3	10.8	46.6	14.7
Asian	4.4	2.0	12.1	4.3	20.3	6.3
Total:	226.5	100.0	279.1	100.0	316.9	100.0

Source: Adapted from Allan C. Ornstein, "Urban Demographics for the 1980s: Educational Implications," *Education and Urban Society*, 16 (1984), table 2, p. 486. Used by permission.

large majority (about 70 percent) of children in these projects are Hispanic.

Although this country continues to attract hundreds of thousands of immigrants from around the world each year, Hispanics represent the fastest growing ethnic population in the country. Based on current immigration and fertility trends as shown in Table 9–2, the Hispanic population reached 30 million in the year 2000 (10.8 percent of the total population) and is projected to be 47 million in 2020 (14.7 percent), surpassing the U.S. black population (14 percent) as the largest minority group. On the heels of the Hispanic population is the Asian group—the next fastest growing minority group. It reached 12 million in 2000 (4.3 percent) and is expected to reach 20 million in 2020 (6.3 percent) compared to 4 million (2 percent) in 1980.[36] The composition of the United States is undergoing considerable ethnic change—largely because of immigration trends—and the federal government is responding in the schools by requiring that the states and local educational agencies meet the needs of these children.

Bilingual education has been expanding partly because the federal Office of Civil Rights (OCR) has been insisting that special educational opportunities be improved for limited-English-proficient (LEP) and non-English-proficient (NEP) students. Controversies over bilingual education have become somewhat embittered as federal and state actions have led to the establishment of various bilingual programs. There are arguments between those who would "immerse" children in an English-language environment and those who believe initial instruction will be more effective in the native language. On one side are those who favor maintenance because they believe this would help build a constructive sense of identity, and on the other are those who believe that cultural maintenance is harmful because it separates groups from one another or discourages students from mastering English well enough to function successfully in the larger society.[37]

Education for the Handicapped

Federal legislation focusing on the rights of handicapped people and governing much of the subsequent activity in educating handicapped students was spelled out in three major laws: the Rehabilitation Act of 1973, Public Law 93-380 in 1974, and **Public Law 94-142** (the **Education for All Handicapped Children Act**) in 1975.

The Rehabilitation Act provided that no "program" or "activity" receiving federal assistance can exclude or discriminate against persons solely because of their handicaps. Public Law 93-380 authorized increased levels of aid to states for the implementation of special education services and set forth due process requirements to protect the rights of affected children and their families. Public Law 94-142 set forth as national policy the goal that "free appropriate public education . . . must be extended to handicapped children as their fundamental right."

36L. F. Bouvier and C. B. Davis, *The Future Racial Composition of the United States* (Washington, DC: Population Reference Bureau, 1982); Allan C. Ornstein, "Enrollment Trends in Big-City Schools," *Peabody Journal of Education*, 66 (1989): 64–71; Ornstein, "Curriculum Trends Revisited," *Peabody Journal of Education*, 69 (1994), pp. 4–20. Also see Harold Hodgkinson, "Educational Demographics: What Teachers Should Know," *Educational Leadership*, 58 (2000): 6–11.

37James A. Banks, and Cherry A. Banks, *Multicultural Education: Issues and Perspectives*, 7th ed. (Boston: Allyn & Bacon, 2010); Jean Oakes and Marisa Saunders, *Beyond Tracking* (Cambridge, MA: Harvard Education Press, 2007).

Table 9-3 Number of Students Receiving Public Educational Services by Type of Disability, 1980-2007

Handicap	1980	1990	2000	2007
Learning disabled	1,462,000	2,129,000	2,789,000	2,573,000
Speech impaired	1,168,000	985,000	1,068,000	1,456,000
Mentally retarded	830,000	535,000	597,000	500,000
Emotionally disturbed	347,000	390,000	462,000	442,000
Hard of hearing/deaf	79,000	58,000	70,000	79,000
Orthopedically impaired	59,000	49,000	69,000	67,000
Other health impaired	98,000	55,000	221,000	641,000
Visually impaired	31,000	23,000	26,000	29,000
Multiple disabilities	68,000	96,000	106,000	138,000
Deaf-blind	3,000	1,000	2,000	2,000
Autism	a	a	67,000	296,000
Developmentally delayed	a	a	12,000	358,000
Preschool disabled (three to five years old)	231,000	441,000	568,000	NA
Total: (all conditions)	4,144,000	4,761,000	6,055,000	6,606,000
Percentage of public school enrollment	10.1	11.4	13.0	13.4

Note: a = no information.

Source: *Digest of Education Statistics, 1987* (Washington, DC: U.S. Government Printing Office, 1987), table 38, p. 49; *Digest of Education Statistics 2003* (Washington, DC: U.S. Government Printing Office, 2004), table 53, p. 73; *Digest of Education Statistics 2009* (Washington, DC: U.S. Government Printing Office, 2010), table 50, p. 84.

The 1975 Act has been rewritten several times and was renamed the Individuals with Disabilities Education Act (IDEA) in 1990. IDEA requires that states have "an approved plan meeting certain specified guidelines assuring all disabled children education benefits." The plan is known as the Individualized Education Plan (IEP) and requires a document explaining what and how education services will be provided to special needs students, particularly disabled ones, so they can benefit from their schooling.

The IEP must include (1) an assessment of the student's present performance, (2) the effects of the disability on the student's involvement and progress in the school curriculum, (3) measurable annual goals related to meeting the student's needs and involvement in the school curriculum, (4) the provision for services and personnel to meet the student's needs, and (5) assurance that the disabled student will participate in curricular activities and other experiences with nondisabled students.

As indicated in Table 9–3, the total number of special education students served by public funds has increased over twenty-seven years, from 4.1 million to 6.6 million (or 13.4 percent of the public school enrollment), with 57 percent being served in regular classes (part time or full time), 15 percent in self-contained classes, and the remaining in special schools or facilities.[38]

The rising number of handicapped students has been associated with the civil rights movement and its concern with making equal educational opportunity available to all students—not that more of our students have become handicapped. The numbers also include a somewhat large and fuzzy category, "learning disabled," in which many slow learners, underachievers, and precocious students are hastily slotted—in part because of an overemphasis on the testing and labeling students and the influence of special education advocates as a lobby and advocate group. Although *Brown v. Board of Education* in 1954 addressed the segregation of black students, it also served as a precedent in establishing the rights of students with special needs to be provided with equal educational opportunity under the umbrella notion of **mainstreaming.**

[38] *Digest of Education Statistics, 1994* (Washington, DC: U.S. Government Printing Office, 1994), table 53, p. 66; *Digest of Education Statistics 2003*, table 53, p. 73; *Digest of Education Statistics 2009*, table 51, p. 85.

EXEMPLARY EDUCATIONAL ADMINISTRATORS IN ACTION

JOE A. HAIRSTON Superintendent, Baltimore County Public Schools, Towson, Maryland.

Latest Degree and Affiliation: Ed.D., Virginia Polytechnic Institute and State University.

Words of Advice: There is an urgency that we cannot deny any longer for educators to embrace the phrase "quality education for all children." If any school system in America can find the way to make a difference for children, my school district must be the one. If anyone can take the negative energy that is out there and turn it into opportunities for children to have a meaningful educational experience, my staff will be the ones to do it.

I have an uncompromising belief in the possibilities created when the right people are in the right positions that together we can bring dignity, caring, and integrity back to the business of teaching and learning.

This is not about stifling the human spirit; rather, it is about enabling teachers to be all they can be. It is about making their work and the students' work more engaging and therefore making both groups able to know more and do more. It is a simple fact that all children can learn more than they are currently learning if they are provided with schoolwork they find to be engaging.

In terms of costs, special education expenditures rose steadily in the 1970s and 1980s. The average cost of educating a child with handicaps is much higher than the national average for a nonhandicapped child—almost double the national average of $8100 in 2002 and $9700 in 2006.[39] Although federal law requires local school districts to provide free appropriate education, the federal government, which originally contributed relatively few dollars to this effort, has dramatically increased its funding in the 1990s, largely corresponding with the Clinton administration. Federal expenditures for special education increased from $79 million in 1970 to $1.5 billion in 1980 to $3.5 billion in 1990 to $5.4 billion in 2000, and it more than doubled to $11.7 billion in 2009.[40] In real dollars, after inflation, this amounts to an increase of about 50 percent since 1980. Still, special education mandates place a heavy financial burden on the states and local educational agencies.

The Call for Excellence

Since the mid-1980s, national attention has turned to the need for higher academic standards: tougher subjects, rigorous testing, and stiffer high school graduation and college admission requirements. The educational dimensions of and reasons for this new movement were documented in a number of policy reports released between 1983 and 2010. Many of these (including the most famous *A Nation at Risk*) were written and distributed by the federal government, and all called for reforms to improve the quality of education in the United States. The background data to these reports show a low performance standard that must be addressed:

1. Schools and colleges have shifted away from requiring students to take what had been the standard academic core curriculum for graduation thirty years ago: foreign language, mathematics, science, English, and history. Elective courses and remedial courses have replaced many standard academic courses.
2. Grade inflation continues to be on the rise, and students are required to complete less homework (in 2008, 27 percent of twelfth-grade high school students completed less than one hour of homework a night, and 28 percent claim they have no homework). In addition, 24 percent never or hardly ever read for fun. Thirty percent read five or fewer pages daily in school and for homework.[41]
3. Although National Assessment of Educational Progress (NAEP) indicates that math proficiency improved for all age groups between 1973 and 2008, with nine-year olds making the greatest gains, among twelfth-grade students only 59 percent were

[39]*Digest of Education Statistics, 2003,* figure 11, p. 53. *Twenty-fifth Annual Report to Congress on the Implementation of the Education of the Handicapped Act* (Washington, DC: U.S. Government Printing Office, 2005); *Digest of Education Statistics, 2009,* table 182, p. 261.

[40]*Digest of Education Statistics, 1993,* table 350, pp. 365–368; *Digest of Education Statistics, 2000,* table 361, p. 407; *Digest of Education Statistics, 2009,* table 375, p. 540.

[41]*The Digest of Education Statistics, 2009*, table 118, p. 179.

capable of performing at grade level (61 percent in 1999), and only 6.2 percent were capable of advanced work such as calculus or statistics (8.4 percent in 1999).[42]

4. The NAEP continues to show an achievement gap in reading and math between white and black students. In 2008, there was a gap in reading of: 24 points among nine-year-olds; 21 points among thirteen-year-olds; and 29 points among seventeen-year-olds. Between 1999 and 2008, black nine-year-olds gained 18 points in reading; black thirteen-year-olds gained 9 points; and seventeen-year-olds gained 2 points. In 2008, there was a gap in math of: 26 points among nine-year-olds; 28 points among thirteen-year-olds; and 27 points among seventeen-year-olds. Between 1999 and 2008, black nine-year-olds gained 13 points in math, black thirteen-year-olds gained 11 points; and black seventeen-year-olds gained 4 points.[43]
5. Overall, in reading, twelfth graders scored 6 points lower in 2005 (which was the year that they were tested in reading) than in 1992. However, their scores were only 1 point lower in 2005 than in 2002. The gap in reading between white and black students was 26 points. The gap between white and Hispanic students was 21 points. The minority–white gap continues to remain constant in all social class levels or when measured by parents' education.[44]
6. Between 1992 and 2007, reading scores were slightly higher for both fourth and eighth graders. Students eligible for free or reduced-price lunch also made small improvements. However, the gap between students in schools with 10 percent or less eligible for free or reduced-price lunch and students in schools with more than 75 percent eligible showed a gap of 40 points in fourth and eighth grade. The greater the student body receiving free or reduced-priced lunch, the greater the gap.[45]
7. Average achievement scores on the Scholastic Aptitude Test (SAT) demonstrate a virtually unbroken decline from 1963 to 1994. Average verbal scores fell over 40 points (466 to 423), and mathematics scores dropped 13 points (492 to 479). In the next thirteen years (1995–2008) there was an increase of 49 points total (verbal and math combined), mainly because the mean scores were adjusted downward in 1995, thus masking the continual decline.[46]
8. For white students, compared to black students, the critical reading score (formerly known as the verbal section) was 96 points higher in 1987, 92 points higher in 1997, 99 points higher in 2008 and 2010. In math, white students scored 103 points higher than black students in 1987 and 1997, 103 points higher in 2008, and 108 points higher in 2010. In writing (first administered in 2005), white students scored 91 points higher than black students in 2005, 96 points higher in 2008, and 86 points higher in 2010. The Hispanic-white gap was about 50 points in reading and math in 1997 and 2005. However in 2008 and 2010, the differences spiked to as high as 99 points in reading and 78 points in math. The difference in writing was 69 points in 2005, 65 points in 2008, and 69 points in 2010.[47] The education picture is bleak, since an increasing number of school enrollments are minorities who exhibit this achievement gap. Approximately one-third drop out and never even get to take the SATs.
9. In 2010 President Obama revealed the latest international test scores, a grim picture, with the U.S. ranked 21st in science and 25th in math. President Obama recommended federal money to hire 10,000 new science and math teachers in order to stay economically competitive.[48] On another dismal note, U.S. students graduating from college have dropped from the highest international percentage in 2000 to ninth place ten years later.[49]
10. Some 23 to 25 million U.S. adults are functionally illiterate by the simplest tests of everyday reading and writing. Moreover, about 13 percent of

---

[42]Ibid., table 133, p.196.

[43]*The Condition of Education, 2009* (Washington, DC: U.S. Government Printing Office, 2010), Indicator 14, p. 34, 160–161; *The Digest of Education Statistics, 2009,* table 133, p. 196.

[44]*The Condition of Education, 2009*, Indicator 12, p. 30, 153; Indicator 14, p. 34, 160–161.

[45]Ibid., Indicator 13, p. 32, 157–159.

[46]*Digest of Education Statistics 1998* (Washington, DC: U.S. Government Printing Office 1998), table 131, p. 146; *Digest of Education Statistics, 2009*, table 143, p. 208.

[47]*Digest of Education Statistics, 2009*, table 143, p. 208; "Students' SAT Scores Stay in Rut," *Wall Street Journal*, September 14, 2010.

[48]President Obama, discussion on the TODAY show, NBC (September 27, 2010.)

[49]Karl Weber, *Waiting for "Superman": How We Can Save America's Falling Public Schools* (Beverly Hills, CA: Participant Media, 2010).

all seventeen-year-olds in the United States are considered functionally illiterate, and this rate jumps to 35 percent among minority youth. The percentage of adults age 25 or older who reported reading any literature (novel, short story, poem, play, news-magazine article) in the past year declined from 1982 to 2005, from 50 to 45 percent. It dropped to 38 percent among those with a high school diploma and 17 percent for those with less than a high school diploma.[50]

11. The percentage of public high school students who graduated on time with a regular diploma in 2005–2006 was 73.4 percent. In 2007, the U.S. dropout rate for 16- through 24-year-olds was 9 percent. Foreign-born Hispanics had a dropout rate of 34 percent, while native-born Hispanics had a dropout rate of 11 percent. For blacks the dropout rate approaches 25 percent. In some large cities such as New York and Chicago, the dropout rate for minority students ranges from 33 to 40 percent.[51]
12. Business and military leaders complain that they are required to spend millions of dollars annually on remedial education and training programs in the basic skills or the Three Rs. Between 1980 and 2010, remedial mathematics courses in four-year colleges increased by 75 percent and constituted one-fourth of all mathematics courses taught in these institutions. As many as 24 percent of college students have taken a remedial reading course, and 16 percent have taken three or more remedial courses. As many as 25 percent of the recruits in the armed forces cannot read at the ninth-grade level.[52]
13. All these figures pile up and stare at us, despite the fact that our student–teacher ratios were 16.5:1 in 2000, which put us seventh lowest in the world (whereas such countries as Japan and Korea have higher student-teacher ratios—18:1 and 28:1, respectively). Yet our pupil expenditures for education K–12 were the second highest in the world (about $500 less than first-ranked Switzerland).[53]

[50]*The Condition of Education, 2007* (Washington, DC: U.S. Government Printing Office, 2007), Indicator 18, p. 45, 154.

[51]*The Condition of Education, 2009*, Indicator 19, p. 48, 178–181; Indicator 20, p. 50, 182.

[52]*The Condition of Education, 2001,* Indicator 28, p. 49; "Hurdles Emerge in Rising Effort to Rate Teachers," *New York Times*, December 27th, 2010, p. A1, A15.

[53]*Digest of Education Statistics, 2009*, tables 401, 416, pp. 587, 602.

Racial and Class Implications

How we interpret these trends largely depends on our social lens and political motives, what side of the ideological aisle we sit on, and to what extent and how we balance issues related to excellence, equality, and equity. It also depends on whether we want to focus on class or caste. For example, we can talk about *cultural inversion,* a concept introduced by black social scientists such as John Ogbu or John McWhorter.[54] Their thesis is that poor academic achievement among blacks has more to do with their own negative attitudes than the effects of prejudice or poor schools; and that negativism is rooted in slave history and segregation, but dramatically worsened by a "cult of separation," which makes blacks think that whatever whites do, they should do the opposite. As well, they identify a "cult of anti-intellectualism," which holds that academic excellence is a white thing, and "cult of victimization" in which black youth adapt and act out the labels or stereotypes foisted on them by the majority population—"dumb," "lazy," or "delinquent."

This negativism is also supported by prejudicial attitudes of teachers and their low expectations of minority students, compounded by years of unequal schooling and institutional racism. Roland Fryer, a black Harvard economist, looked at 90,000 minority students from grades 7 to 12 and concluded that acting white and getting good grades is a problem in integrated schools but not in all-black schools or private schools. He concludes that black and Hispanic students with good grades end up with fewer friends at integrated public schools, but it is more a *class* issue than a racial problem. In any society where inequality exists, members of the disadvantaged group have torn loyalties—wanting to excel in the larger society but maintaining kinship and loyalty to one's own subgroup.[55]

Class is an important idea, particularly now, when race and class vie for the reformer's eye and seem to be competing for popularity in the reform literature. In fact, President Roosevelt's New Deal and President Johnson's Great Society used a poverty index or economic need in lieu of race to determine how additional resources would be allocated. The concept of welfare rights, affirmative action, entitlements, and reparations have only been tied to race since the late 1960s,

[54]John N. Ogbu, *Minority Education and Caste* (New York: Academic Press, 1978); John H. McWhorter, *Losing the Race* (New York: Simon & Schuster, 2000).

[55]Roland Fryer, "Acting White" *Education Next,* Winter 2006: 52–59.

coinciding with the civil rights movement. Some scholars advocate a return to the poverty index and funneling resources and services based on need or *class,* not for a particular racial/ethnic group or *caste.* It's a matter of focusing on *all* low-performing students, not just minority students. Until recently most policymakers and educators have been afraid to publically discuss this issue or to suggest that school integration or government funding be based on class and not race.[56]

Reform Reports on Excellence

From 1980 to 2010 about 25 major education policy reports were published. The reports highlight deficiencies that have come to light at a time when the demand for highly skilled military personnel and workers in labor and industry is accelerating rapidly and amidst growing concern that the United States is being overtaken by other nations in commerce, industry, science, and technology.

The two most influential reports were *A Nation at Risk*, published in 1983 under the Reagan Administration, and No Child Left Behind, published in 2002 under the Bush II administration. *A Nation at Risk* stated that the "Federal Government has the primary responsibility to identify the national 'interest of education.'"[57] This report highlighted the need for school reform, specifically for the development of national standards. The findings that schools were not "adequately preparing students to compete with other nations,"[58] supported the need to improve high school graduation rates. From now on, the minimum standard would include at least four years of English; three years of mathematics, science and social studies; and one-half year of computer science. Two years of a foreign language were recommended for students who wanted to go to college. Other recommendations included extending the school calendar (school day and/or the school year), paying teachers in relationship to their performance, and developing and approving measurable standards. In addition, attendance and discipline codes needed to be tightened. More homework, more rigorous grading and periodic testing, improved attendance and discipline were also recommended, along with the need to provide more money and programs for disadvantaged as well as gifted and talented students.

The No Child Left Behind Act, enacted in 2002, was a reauthorization of the Elementary and Secondary Education Act of 1965. Accountability was a key ingredient. All states were required: to have accountability plans (they were allowed to have different academic goals); to test students in grades 3 and 8 and once in high school each year to see if they improved (achieving adequate yearly progress in areas such as basic reading, literacy, and math by 2014); to disaggregate data in order to examine the progress of all students; and to take part in the Nation's Report Card. It basically focused on turning around the educational experiences of poor and minority children.[59] One purpose of this law was to put an end to the achievement gap between students from middle-class, affluent backgrounds and "underserved students" (students with special needs, limited English proficient students, minority students, and students from low socioeconomic backgrounds). Students were given the choice to transfer to another school within their district if thier school failed to show progress two years in a row. In addition, students were given additional services such as afterschool (or private) tutoring if their school failed to show progress three years in a row.

The other major policy reports emphasize the need to strengthen the curriculum on the core subjects of English, math, science, social studies, and foreign language. The focus is thus on a common curriculum. Technology and computer courses are mentioned often, either as components of science or math or as a separate subject area (sometimes referred to as the Fourth R). High-level cognitive and thinking skills are also stressed. Most of the reports are also concerned with programs and personnel for disadvantaged students and students with learning disabilities, although this message is not always loud and clear.

Reports emphasize tougher standards and tougher courses, and seven out of the twelve propose that colleges raise their admission requirements. Many of the reports also mention increasing homework, time for learning, and time in school, as well as instituting more rigorous grading, testing, homework, and discipline. They mention upgrading teacher certification,

[56]See Richard D. Kahlenberg, "The New Integration," *Educational Leadership,* 63 (2006): 22–26; Ornstein, *Class Counts: Education, Inequality, and the Shrinking Middle Class;* and Rothstein, *Class and Schools.*

[57]Thomas A. Kissenger, "Efforts Toward National Educational Reform: An Essentialist Political Agenda," *Mid-Western Educational Researcher,* 20 (2007): 16–23.

[58]David J. Hoff and Kathleen Kennedy Manzo, "Risk Report's Anniversary Prompts Reflection," *Education Week,* April 30, 2008, p. 24. Also see *Great Expectations: Holding Ourselves and Our Schools Accountable for Results* (Washington, D.C.: U.S. Government Printing Office, 2009).

[59]*Great Expectations: Holding Ourselves and Our Schools Accountable for Results.*

increasing teacher salaries, increasing the number of and paying higher salaries for science and math teachers, and providing merit pay for outstanding teachers. Overall, most stress academic achievement (not the whole child) and increased productivity (not valuing or humanism).

Most of the reports express concern that the schools are pressed to play too many social roles, that the schools cannot meet all these expectations, and that the schools are in danger of losing sight of their key role—teaching basic skills and core academic subjects, new skills for computer use, and higher-level cognitive skills for the world of work, technology, and military defense. Many of the recent reports, concerned not only with academic productivity but also with national productivity, link human capital with economic capital. Investment in schools, this argument runs, is an investment in the economy and in the nation's future stability. If education fails, so do our workforce and nation. Hence, it behooves business, labor, and government to work with educators to help educate and train the U.S. populace.

Despite criticisms by some members of the educational community that the reports are too idealistic and unrealistic, that they put too much emphasis on excellence at the expense of equality and equity, and that they are enormously expensive to implement,[60] the reports have captured national attention, spotlighted nationwide concern for the quality of education, and upgraded nationwide school standards.

Many of the reports have come under severe criticism as being unrealistic, and *No Child Left Behind* is criticized as a "simple" and "stupid" phrase that has minimal monetary backing.[61] In addition, James Popham has raised many concerns about the testing process involved with NCLB, reporting on a monthly basis in *Educational Leadership* and writing a recent book dealing with reliability validity, and useability problems of high-stake tests.[62]

[60]Carl D. Glickman, "Dichotomizing School Reform," *Phi Delta Kappan,* 83 (2001): 147–152; Allan Odden, "The New School Finance," *Phi Delta Kappan,* 83 (2001): 85–91; Robert Hess, *Excellence, Equity, and Efficiency* (New York: Rowman & Littlefield, 2005).

[61]M. Donald Thomas and William L. Bainridge, "No Child Left Behind: Facts and Fallacies," *Phi Delta Kappan,* 83 (2002): 781–782; Christopher A. Tracey et al., *Changing NCLB District Accountability Standards* (Cambridge, MA: Harvard University Press, 2005); Gerald W. Bracey, "No Child Left Behind: Where Does the Money Go?" Educational Policy Studies Laboratory, Arizona State University, Tempe, June 2005.

[62]See W. James Popham, *What Every Teacher Should Know about Educational Assessment,* 2nd ed. (Boston: Allyn & Bacon, 2007).

In 2009, President Barack Obama signed the American Recovery and Reinvestment Act of 2009, which provided almost $91 billion for education. Two major programs are the State Fiscal Stabilization Fund and Race to the Top. Through the State Fiscal Stabilization Fund, approximately $49 billion was set aside to assist states in minimizing the effects of budget cuts. The Race to the Top Fund focuses on four major areas: increasing teacher effectiveness (merit pay); collecting and utilizing student and classroom **level data**; turning around poorly performing schools; and improving academic standards and student and teacher assessments. The Act also provides funds for special education, Head Start, childcare service, educational technology, teacher salaries, education of homeless children, support for working college students, Pell grants, low-income public school children, and to states to analyze student performance.[63]

Need for Caution

Administrators must understand the broad cycles of change and improvement, which come and go like a pendulum, and the fact that schools have been burdened by the rest of society with roles and responsibilities that other agencies and institutions no longer do well or, for that matter, want to do.[64] The schools are seen as ideal agencies to solve the nation's problems and to reform or change what ails us. With this perspective, many people refuse to admit their own responsibilities in helping children and youth develop their individual capacities and adjust to society. Similarly, parents and policymakers alike often expect administrators and teachers to be solely responsible for carrying out reform.

Seasoned administrators have learned that there are no "magic bullets" for reforming schools; there is no one policy or single combination of policies that will automatically lead to answers or transform ineffective schools into effective ones. School life, like human life itself, is much more complicated. Over and over, reform measures that have been imposed on school officials by

[63]Michele McNeil, "Report Calculates Stimulus Saved 329,000 School Jobs Last Fall," *Education Week* (February 10, 2010): 4. Sabrina Laine, Amy Potemski, and Cortney Rowland, "Compensation Reform in the Schools," *School Administrator,* 67 (March 2010): 10–14. Alyson Klein, "Race to Top Sets Stage for ESEA," *Education Week* (February 10, 2010), S18.

[64]John Chubb, *Within Our Reach* (New York: Rowman & Littlefield, 2005); Leithwood, *Making Schools Smarter;* and Diane Ravitch (ed.), *Brookings Papers on Education Policy: 2005* (Washington, DC: Brookings Institute, 2005).

the federal government and other groups have failed. As one author notes, "The freeway of American education is cluttered with the wrecks of famous bandwagons."[65]

Some critics conclude that we have been spending too much on school reform and compensatory programs and not getting enough in return. What often occurs is a marginal improvement in the beginning—then, gradually, diminishment until input (time and money) is wasted because there is virtually no increase in output.[66] A "flat area"—less output in relation to input—is eventually reached or, even worse, there is no return. According to critics, demand for money has created a cottage industry for reformers and lawyers to exploit the legal system and to point the finger of blame at teachers and administrators, while ignoring students and parents—and their role in academic output.[67] The same kind of criticism has been leveled at school reform in general, although the reasons and responsibilities vary according to the critics' politics and view of the social world.

Administrators need to remember to go slow in the beginning of reform, to weigh the risks and rewards before making decisions, and to search for a balance—where there is no extreme emphasis on subject matter or students' sociopsychological needs, no extreme emphasis on one or two subjects at the expense of others, or no extreme emphasis on excellence or equality. What we need is a prudent social policy, one that is politically and economically feasible and that serves the needs of all students and society. Implicit in this view of education is that too much emphasis on any one policy, sometimes at the expense of another, may do harm and cause conflict. How much we emphasize one policy is critical because no society can give itself over to extreme "isms" or political views and still remain a democracy. The kind of society into which we evolve is in part reflected in our educational system, which is influenced by the policies that we eventually define and develop.

[65]Ron Brandt, keynote address to Washington State Association for Curriculum Development and Supervision, Seattle, February 11, 1983.

[66]Allan C. Ornstein, "In Pursuit of Cost-Effective Schools," *Principal*, 70 (1990): 28–30; Herbert J. Walberg et al., "Productive Curriculum Time," *Peabody Journal of Education*, 69 (1994): 86–100; Walberg, "Productive Teachers," in A. C. Ornstein et al., *Contemporary Issues in Curriculum*, 4th ed. (Boston: Allyn & Bacon, 2007), pp. 99–112.

[67]Eric A. Hanushek (ed.), *Courting Failure: How School Financing Lawsuits Exploit Judges' Good Intentions and Harm Our Children* (Stanford, CA: Education Next Books, 2006).

State Government and Education

Every state, today, by constitution, statute, and practice, assumes that education is the function of the state, and federal and state courts have supported this interpretation. The federal government's powers related to education have been delegated to the states through the Tenth Amendment of the Constitution. This is a dramatic difference from what exists in most parts of the world, including almost every industrialized nation, where the schools are centralized and controlled by the federal government, usually through a ministry of education.

Each state in the United States has legal responsibility for the support and maintenance of the public schools within its borders. Local school boards, as we will see in the next chapter, are considered creatures of the state and have been devised for the purpose of running a system of schools. Being responsible for the schools, the state enacts legislation; determines school taxes and financial aid to local school districts; sets minimum standards for training, certification, and salaries of personnel; decides on curriculum (some states establish minimum requirements, others establish recommendations); provides special services (such as transportation and free textbooks); and provides funding through monetary grants and various aid formulas.

The state school code is a collection of laws that establish ways and means of operating schools and conducting education in the state. The state, of course, cannot enact legislation that is contrary to or conflicts with the federal Constitution. State statutes can be divided into two groups: (1) mandatory laws that establish a minimum criterion or program of education and (2) permissive laws that define the functions that are delegated to the school district under appropriate conditions.

State Hierarchy of Education

Although state constitutions and statutes provide for the establishment of a uniform system of schools, provisions in most states are detailed concerning state and local powers and authority and methods of school operation. The typical state hierarchy, as with the federal government, consists of three branches: (1) executive or governor, (2) legislative or state legislature, and (3) judicial or state courts.

The governor usually depends on a group of advisors and consultants to report on educational matters. The state legislatures have created a **state education agency** consisting of a state board of education, chief state officer, and state department of education. The relationship between the state education agency and local school districts has changed over time to reflect new problems and concerns. Since the 1980s, for example, with the new federalism, the state legislature and its education agency have taken on a more active role in educational reform. The state courts have also become increasingly active in educational matters.

The Governor

Although the powers of governors vary widely, their authority on educational matters is spelled out in law. Usually, the governor is charged with the responsibility of formulating educational budget recommendations to the legislature. In many states, the governor has legal access to any accumulated balances in the state treasury, and these monies can be used for school or college purposes.

The governor (and state legislature) has available staff members and agencies to help analyze and interpret data and can obtain additional information on matters of educational concern as needed. The governor can appoint or remove administrative school personnel at the state level. These powers often carry restrictions, such as approval by the legislature. In a majority of states, the governor can appoint members to the state board of education and, in a few states, the chief state officer. Except in North Carolina, a governor can "kill" educational measures through his veto powers or threaten to use the veto to discourage the legislature from enacting laws he opposes—or at least encourage the legislature to modify a pending bill.

The governor in today's political arena will invariably have an educational platform during the election campaign. Thus, all candidates will make specific commitments and promises for education. These platforms vary widely—from a promise to reduce educational spending or to increase it, a pledge for increasing educational equality such as increased prekindergarten programs or college scholarships for minority and needy students on one hand to increased quality and productivity in math, science, and technical education on the other.

The successful gubernatorial candidate must listen to different lobby groups, and the various educational administrative associations recognize the importance of gaining the ear of each candidate. In recent years, the National School Boards Association, National Chief States School Organization, and American Association of School Administrators have increased their lobby efforts and funding to help elect candidates who support their political views on education.[68] In most states, however, the lobby efforts are focused on state legislative officials—at least once the governor is elected.

State Legislatures

With the exception of Nebraska (which has a unicameral arrangement), every state has a two-house legislative body. There is much variation in size and resources, however. Membership in the state Senate ranges from a low of 21 in Nevada to a high of 67 in Minnesota, with most states electing 30 to 40 state senators. Membership in the state House ranges from 40 in Alaska to 400 in New Hampshire, with most states electing 100 to 125 state House members.[69] Nationwide, the state legislative staff size has grown from 27,000 state workers (average size of 519) in 1979 to 40,000 (average size of 800) in 2004, despite the fact that financial conditions of most states worsened during this period. Vermont and South Dakota are the only states with fewer than 100 staff members, whereas California and New York have 3000 or more staff members. The typical state legislator is a white male (about 30 percent are female and another 25 percent are minority) who is an attorney or businessperson by profession.[70]

In most states, the legislature is responsible for establishing and maintaining the public schools and has broad powers to enact laws pertaining to education. These powers are not unlimited; there are restrictions in the form of federal and state constitutions and court decisions. But within these parameters, the legislature has the full power to decide basic school policy in the state.

The state legislature usually determines how the state boards of education will be selected, what their responsibilities will be, how the chief state officer will be selected, what the duties of this office will be, what the functions of the state department of education will be, what types of local and regional school districts there will be, and what the methods of selection and powers of local school boards will be. The legislature

---

[68] Kathy Christie, "Stateline: Exploring New Possibilities," *Phi Delta Kappan*, 87 (2006): 421–422; Marc Tucker, "Changing the System is Only One Solution," *Phi Delta Kappan*, 91 (2010): 28–30.

[69] "2005 Elections," *State Legislature*, 31 (2005): 19.

[70] *Directory of Legislative Leaders 2005* (Denver: National Conference of State Legislatures, 2005); *State Legislative Directory 2006* (Denver: National Conference of State Legislatures, 2006).

usually decides on the nature of state taxes for schools, the level of financial support for education, and the taxing power for schools to be allocated on a local or municipal level. The legislature may determine what may or may not be taught, how many years of compulsory education will be required, the length of the school day and school year, and whether there will be state community colleges and adult and vocational schools. The legislature may also determine staff and student policies and testing and evaluation procedures, authorize school programs, set standards for building construction, and provide various auxiliary services (e.g., student transportation and school lunches). Where the legislature does not enact these policies, they are usually the responsibility of the state board of education.

The system tends to operate much more effectively when the legislature focuses on broad policies such as financing and organization of schools, thus delegating enforcement of specific criteria and operation of schools to the various state education agencies. The legislature only establishes the minimums in public education, with the proviso that local school districts may exceed these minimum yardsticks. There should be a partnership concept between those who establish legal requirements and basic policies for a state educational system—that is, the legislature—and those who are responsible for implementing the will of the legislature: the state agencies (state board of education, state department of education, and state chief officer).

State Interest and Lobby Groups State legislative officials respect the prevailing political climate and wishes of the people with respect to education and other policy issues. In effect, the people elect state legislatures and speak through the laws enacted by the officials they have elected. All representatives in the state legislatures understand the necessity of listening and responding to the wishes of the people in their district if they wish to be reelected.

The role of educational groups in the state political process usually evolves into a basic form: **political action committees** (PACs) to financially support, volunteer time for, or endorse candidates for election and educational groups—including administrative associations, teacher associations, parent associations, and special interest groups (such as those concerned with bilingual education, special education, and vocational education). All recognize the need for coalition building and working toward as well as challenging or spearheading policies that affect education.

Another important function of interest groups is their lobbying efforts—both direct, face-to-face presentations and indirect contacts by mail and telephone.[71] Because education is a state responsibility, rather than a federal one, education lobbyists—whether groups of people or associations—focus on state legislatures. And because education is usually the largest expenditure item in the state budget (about 60 percent on a total state-by-state basis when transportation is omitted),[72] it makes the existence of educational interest groups and their lobby efforts an important element of the political arena and policymaking process at the state level.

State Courts

All states have constitutional provisions pertaining to education but leave the details, policies, and provisions to legislative bodies. There is no national uniformity in the state court organization. At the lowest level, most states have a court of original jurisdiction, often referred to as a *municipal* or *superior court,* where cases are tried. Adverse decisions can be appealed to the next level, usually called the *appellate court,* by the losing side. This court reviews the trial record from the lower court and additional materials submitted by both sides; it assumes that appropriate laws were properly applied at the lower court level. Should any one side still not be satisfied, another appeal can be made to the state's highest court, often called the *state supreme court.* The decision of this court is final unless an issue involving the U.S. Constitution has been raised. The U.S. Supreme Court can be petitioned to consider such an issue; this is a growing trend in issues involving education.

State court decisions have force only in the area served by that court. For this reason, it is possible to find conflicting rules in different circuits. Judges often look to previous law, and to surrounding court circuits,

[71]Susan H. Fuhrman, ed., *From the Capitol to the Classrom* (Chicago: National Society for the Study of Education, 2001); Charles De Pascale, *Education Reform Restructuring Network* (Quincy, MA: Department of Education, 1997); and Rita Schweitz et al., *Future Search in School District Change* (New York: Rowman & Littlefield, 2006).

[72]Julie Bell, director of education affairs, National Conference of State Legislatures, personal communication, May 17, 1994; Agnes G. Case, *How to Get the Most Reform for Your Reform Money* (New York: Rowman & Littlefield, 2004); Jacqueline P. Danzberger, Michael W. Kirst, and Michael P. Usdan, *Governing Public Schools* (Washington, DC: Institute for Educational Leadership, 1992); Susan Moore Johnson, *Leading to Change* (San Francisco: Jossey-Bass, 1996); and Schweitz et al., *Future Search in School District Change.*

in rendering decisions. Similarly, a state supreme court decision in one state may conflict with a decision of the court in another state; decisions rendered in one state are not binding in another state. Nevertheless, there is a good deal of consistency among the states in matters dealing with education.

In all cases, the authority of the state to prescribe policies is upheld so long as these policies do not conflict with federal or state constitutional provisions.

In many relationships between officials of the state and those at the school district level, differences evolve that are carried into court—such as matters dealing with school desegregation, school finance, school prayer and Bible reading, teacher and student rights, affirmative action, and school safety. Often these cases have gone beyond the state supreme courts to the federal courts. Many other issues end up in state courts because they have little to do with the U.S. Constitution. These issues mainly deal with compulsory attendance, administrator or teacher fitness, teacher strikes, teacher gay rights, school negligence, child abuse, educational malpractice, copyright laws, computer ethics, and a school AIDS policy.

State Education Agencies

All states recognize the importance of establishing a state education agency or what is sometimes called a state system of education. The idea of a *state education agency* is based on the Northwest Ordinances of 1785 and 1787, which enabled territories to transform into states, subject to many conditions including a system of public education to be implemented through the state.

Until the mid-twentieth century, the role of the state education agency was limited, and leadership in public education was mainly expressed at the local level. We illustrate this with two historical examples: (1) Horace Mann's idea of a system of public education supported by public money and controlled by the state was slow to be accepted beyond Massachusetts and Connecticut in the 1820s; (2) as late as 1930, only 17 percent of total school revenues came from state sources compared with 83 percent from the local level.

The state education agency is a system comprising the state board of education, chief state school officer, and state department of education. In most cases, the governor appoints the state board of education, and the latter usually appoints the chief state school officer. In a few states, voters elect members of the state board of education and chief state school officer. The state department of education usually consists of career educators, and a few leadership and directorship posts are filled by the chief state school officer.

The State Board of Education

The *state board of education* is usually the most influential and important state education agency. Almost all states have some sort of state board of education, which is dependent on the state legislature for appropriations and authority and serves an advisory function for the legislature. (New York's Board of Regents is perhaps the strongest and most respected state board of education.) In addition, most states have a separate governing board for the public schools for grades K–12 and for state colleges and universities; thus, there are often two separate state boards, one for elementary and secondary education and another for higher education.

With the exceptions of Minnesota and Wisconsin, all states have boards of education. As of 2009, thirty-two were appointed by the governor of the state, ten were elected by popular vote (this method has increased during the last twenty years), two (New York and South Carolina) were appointed by state legislatures, one (Mississippi) was appointed by the governor and the legislature, and three (Louisiana, Ohio, and Washington) were elected and appointed by the governor. The number of members of state boards ranges from seven to twenty-one, with a nine-member board occurring most frequently. (An odd number of members eliminates tie votes.) The term of appointment or election ranges from three to nine years, with most states at the four- to five-year range.[73]

There is some controversy involving the method by which the state board of education members acquire their position. The controversy centers on the merits of election versus gubernatorial appointment. The rationales for election are the following: It provides the people with a direct voice in educational policy; the governor tends to appoint people who agree with her views; it enhances political representation of the people; and gubernatorial appointments concentrate too much power in the hands of one official, whereas elections provide for a system of checks and balances.[74]

---

[73]*State Education Governance at a Glance* (Alexandria, VA: National Association of State Boards of Education).

[74]Richard Rothstein, et al., *Grading Educations* (New York: Teachers College Press, Columbia University 2008); Thomas J. Sergiovanni, *Rethinking Leadership* (Thousand Oaks, CA: Corwin, 2006).

One recent survey of state boards shows that most members tend to be older (88 percent were age forty or older) and well educated (99 percent have at least some postsecondary education, and 67 percent have a degree beyond the bachelor's). The voluntary nature of service on a state board means that the members must have the time and resources to participate. As a result, the survey found that most board members who were in the workforce described their occupation as managerial (24 percent) or professional (55 percent); those not in the paid workforce were either retired (16 percent) or homemakers (5 percent) with a history of voluntary service.[75]

The precise duties and functions of state boards of education vary, but generally the boards are charged with the following functions.

1. Setting statewide curriculum standards.
2. Establishing qualifications and appointing personnel to the state department of education.
3. Setting standards for teacher and administrative certificates.
4. Establishing standards for accrediting schools.
5. Managing federal and state funds earmarked for education.
6. Keeping records and collecting data needed for reporting and evaluating.
7. Adopting long-range plans for the development and improvement of schools.
8. Creating advisory bodies as required by law.
9. Advising the governor or legislature on educational matters.
10. Appointing the chief state school officer, setting minimum salary schedules for teachers and administrators, and adopting policies for the operation of institutions of higher learning.[76]

Chief State School Officer

The *chief state school officer* (sometimes known as the *state superintendent* or commissioner of education) serves as the head of the state department of education and, in most cases, is also the chief executive of the state school board. He or she is usually a professional educator.

The first chief state officer's position was established in New York in 1812, with the title "superintendent of common schools," and the duties of this position revolved around coordination and management. Perhaps the two most famous chief state officers were Horace Mann, the first Massachusetts "commissioner of education," who spearheaded the common school movement in the mid-1820s, and Henry Barnard, the first Connecticut state commissioner in 1838, who adopted many of Mann's progressive ideas and later became the first U.S. commissioner of education from 1867 to 1870.[77] After Mann popularized the role of state commissioner, the position increased rapidly that by 1859 this post was found in twenty-four states.[78] To be sure, the role of state school officer came into being many decades after local school districts within the states were in operation.

The office is filled in one of three ways: In 2009, twelve states filled the position through appointment by the governor, twenty-four states through appointment by the state board of education, and twelve states by popular election.[79] The duties of the chief state school officer and the relationship between that position and the state board and state department vary from state to state. They usually depend on whether the official was appointed or voted into office. When the chief officer is elected, he tends to have more independence.

As of 2009, five chief state school officers were minority; moreover, there were nineteen female chief officers. The increasing number of women as chief state school officers (two in 1985, nine in 1994, nineteen in 2009) represents a

[75]*Membership Directory 2009* (Alexandria, VA: National Association of State Boards of Education, 2009).

[76]National Association of State Boards of Education, *Annual Report 1999* (Alexandria, VA: National Association of State Boards of Education, 1999); *State Boards of Education in an Era of Reform, Final Report of the National Association of State Boards of Education* (Alexandria, VA: National Association of State Boards of Education, 1987). Also see Allan C. Ornstein and Daniel U. Levine, *Foundations of Education,* 11th ed. (Boston: Houghton Mifflin, 2011).

[77]Lawrence A. Cremin, *The Republic and the School* (New York: Teachers College Press, 1957); E. P. Cubberly, *The History of Education* (Boston: Houghton Mifflin, 1920).

[78]Richard Gorton and Judy A. Alston, *School Leadership and Administration,* 8th ed.; Stephen J. Knezevich, *Administration of Public Education,* 4th ed. (New York: Harper & Row, 1984); Theodore J. Kowalski, *Contemporary School Administration,* 3rd ed. (Boston: Allyn & Bacon, 2007).

[79]*Chief State School Officers 2009* (Washington, DC: Council of Chief State School Officers, 2009). *State Education Governance at a Glance* (Alexandria, VA: National Association of State Boards of Education, 2009).

noticeable change[80] and a departure from the "old boy network" that is common in school administration.

Because of differences in method of selection and in legal relationship between the state board of education and the chief state officer, the responsibilities of the chief state officer vary widely. However, the major responsibilities associated with the office are likely to include the following duties:

1. Serving as the chief administrator of the state department of education.
2. Selecting personnel for the state department of education.
3. Recommending and administering an educational budget for the state department of education.
4. Ensuring compliance with state educational laws and regulations.
5. Explaining and interpreting the state's school laws.
6. Deciding controversies involving the administration of the schools within the state.
7. Arranging the studies, committees, and task forces necessary to identify problems and recommend solutions.
8. Reporting on the status of education within the state to the governor, legislature, state board of education, and public.
9. Recommending improvements in educational legislation and policies to the governor and state legislature.
10. Working with local school boards and administrators to improve education within the state.[81]

State Departments of Education

Another major state education agency is the *state department of education,* which usually operates under the direction of the state board of education and is administered by the chief state school officer. Traditionally, the primary function of state departments of education was to collect and disseminate statistics about the status of education within the state. Since the 1950s, they have enlarged their services and functions to include (1) accrediting schools; (2) certifying teachers; (3) apportioning funds; (4) overseeing student transportation and safety; (5) monitoring state regulations; (6) conducting research, evaluating programs, and issuing reports; and (7) monitoring federally funded programs to ensure compliance with regulations.[82]

During recent decades, state departments have had to grapple with controversial issues such as desegregation, compensatory education, bilingual and special education, student rights and unrest, school finance reform and school choice, aid to minority groups, increasing enrollments, collective bargaining, accountability, assessment and standards, and certification for teachers and principals. The federal government, the courts, and active interest groups have wrestled with many educational or school issues—forcing governors and legislators to increase the staff budget and functions of state departments of education.

State departments of education, once innocuous and invisible, have doubled and tripled in size and have assumed new responsibilities in administering complex programs. In 1900, there were a total of 177 staff department employees nationwide, and 47 were chief state school officers.[83] By 1982, only six states (Delaware, Idaho, Nevada, South Dakota, North Dakota, and Wyoming) had professional staffs of fewer than 100, and six states (California, Connecticut, Michigan, New Jersey, New York, and Texas) had staffs of more than 1000. Twenty years later (2002), five states (omit Connecticut) had staffs of more than 1000.[84]

---

[80]Ibid. Also see James W. Guthrie and Patrick J. Schuermann, *Successful School Leadership* (Boston: Allyn & Bacon, 2010).

[81]Roland Campbell et al., *The Organization of American Schools;* Walter G. Hack, J. Carl Candoli, and John R. Ray, *School Business Administration,* 6th ed. (Needham Heights, MA: Allyn & Bacon, 1998); Allan C. Ornstein, *Education and Social Inquiry* (Itasca, IL: Peacock, 1978); Ronald W. Rebore and Angela Walmsley, *Genuine School Leadership* (Thousand Oaks, CA: Corwin Press, 2008).

[82]Joseph Murphy and Karen Seashore Louis (eds.) *Handbook of Research on Educational Administration,* 2nd ed. (San Francisco: Jossey-Bass, 2000); Ornstein, *Education and Social Inquiry*; Richard Owens and Thomas Valesky, *Organizational Behavior in Education,* 10th ed. (Boston: Allyn & Bacon, 2011).

[83]Fred F. Beach and Andrew H. Gibbs, *Personnel of State Department of Education* (Washington, DC: U.S. Government Printing Office, 1952); Knezevich, *Administration of Public Education;* Ronald W. Rebore, *Human Resources Administration in Education,* 9th ed. (Boston: Allyn and Bacon, 2011).

[84]Dinah Wiley, *State Boards of Education* (Arlington, VA: National Association of State Boards of Education, 1983). Telephone conversation with David Griffiths, Director of Public Affairs, National Association of State Boards of Education, February 5, 2003.

As a general rule, the more populated the state and/or the larger the number of local school districts in the state, the higher the degree of centralization and the larger the state department staff. Less-populated states and states with fewer school districts have smaller and decentralized staffs. Although some divisional administrators of these departments change with changes of political party control or with a change in the chief officer, the professional staff—such as researchers and statisticians, curriculum and supervisory specialists, and clerks and secretaries—are usually career or civil service employees. By and large, staff members of the state departments of education are recruited from public school personnel and from local school districts and colleges of education.

Recent federal funding policies and mounting state deficits have put additional pressure on state departments to spend educational money wisely, to administer the state programs effectively, and to think about the bottom line. Competition over school choice, voucher programs, and charter schools have increased this pressure on state departments. In addition, controversial issues in education will not go away, and public groups are becoming more aggressive and astute in making their demands felt at the state level, including tougher academic standards, high-stake testing, and teacher/school accountability. In short, state departments of education must now provide increased leadership and technical assistance to local school districts as well as to state boards of education, state legislators, and governors.

State Reform Movements

Not since the wave of school reform that followed Sputnik has education been so prominently on stage at the national and state level, on television, and in local newspapers. Presidential candidates, governors, state legislators, and chief state school officers have all gotten involved, indicating the high priority of education, the desire to reform it, and the need to allocate more resources for it. Businesses such as Microsoft, IBM, and Motorola have recently taken active roles in helping to shape education policy, in part because jobs are becoming more demanding and complex and the school products (students) are becoming "dumber." Teachers' unions have shifted their focus from the welfare of teacher members to the need to cooperate with school administrators and school board members for purposes of reform; in making this transition, they have shifted the image of union-based organizations to professional organizations and are now willing to work with (not against) administrative associations for institutional welfare.[85]

Nationwide, more than 1500 state statutes affecting some aspect of school reform were enacted between 1985 and 1990. During the next twenty years, 1991 to 2010, approximately 3500 state statutes dealing with reform were enacted.[86] They came as "waves" with tremendous fanfare, publicity, and controversy attached to the reform measures. These waves can be classified into four reform-type packages: (1) academic standards, (2) professional policy, (3) curriculum development, and (4) assessment and accountability. In general, all four waves stressed productivity and efficiency as well as education excellence.

The first wave, dealing with student achievement, focused on *academic standards;* graduation and college admission requirements; more frequent exit tests; time on task, attendance, and homework; reduced class size; and early childhood education. The second wave, dealing with *professionalism,* focused on competency-based training, certification and testing requirements, accountability, salary increases, merit pay and career ladders, differential roles and salaries, evaluation, and staff development. The third wave focused on the *curriculum*—the need to emphasize the basics, computers, and technology; a common core (academic) high school curriculum, especially increased science, math, and foreign language; and business–university–school partnerships. The fourth wave focused on *school improvement;* standard-based education; accountability and high-stake testing. The latest Bracey Report examines three assumptions related to the current educational situation regarding the issues of standards and testing. They are: "high-quality schools can eliminate the achievement gap between whites and minorities; mayoral control of public schools is an improvement over the more common elected board governance systems;

---

[85]Tom Loveless (ed.), *Conflicting Missions: Teacher Unions and Education Reform* (Washington, DC: Brookings Institution, 2000); Albert Shanker, "School Boards Are Being Massacred," *American School Board Journal,* 176 (1989), pp. 29–30. Also see James P. Spillane et al., *Distributed Leadership in Practice* (New York: Teachers College Press, Columbia University, 2008).

[86]Jay P. Greene, *Education Myths: What Special Interest Groups Want You to Believe About Our Schools* (New York: Rowman & Littlefield, 2006); Thomas Hatch, *Managing to Change* (New York: Teachers College Press, Columbia University, 2009); Josephy Murphy and Amanda Datnow, *Leadership Lessons from Comprehensive School Reforms* (Thousand Oaks, CA: Corwin, 2003).

Table 9-4 Average Number of Carnegie Units Earned by Public High School Graduates in Academic Subjects, 1982, 1994, 1998, 2000, and 2005

	Total	English	Social Studies	Math	Science	Foreign Language	Computer Science
1982	21.6	3.9	3.2	2.6	2.2	1.0	0.14
1994	24.2	4.2	3.6	3.4	3.0	1.8	0.65
1998	25.1	4.3	3.7	3.4	3.1	1.9	0.74
2000	26.0	4.4	3.8	3.6	3.2	1.9	0.83
2005	26.7	4.4	4.0	3.7	3.3	2.0	

Source: *The Condition of Education 1998* (Washington, DC: U.S. Government Printing Office, 1998), indicator 26, p. 88; *Digest of Education Statistics, 2000* (Washington, DC: U.S. Government Printing Office, 2001), table 138, p. 154; *Digest of Education Statistics, 2004* (Washington, DC: U.S. Government Printing Office, 2005), table 135, p. 152. *Digest of Education Statistics, 2009* (Washington, DC: U.S. Government Printing Office, 2010), table 149, p. 215.

and higher standards will improve the performance of public schools."[87]

By 2005, a series of actions had been taken at the state level, largely to improve the quality of education. All states had undertaken academic and curriculum reform (categories 1 and 3), forty-seven states had undertaken items dealing with professional reform (category 2) and/or school improvement (category 4), and all states had implemented some form of standards, accountability, and/or testing, also category 4.[88]

Especially dramatic increases of students' enrollment in academic programs, core academic subjects, and advanced placement examinations occurred after the 1983 publication of *A Nation at Risk*. The concerns voiced today parallel those voiced after Sputnik and during the Cold War. Although military concerns have been replaced by economic concerns, the threat of foreign competition still forms the basis of our educational debates. What was unimaginable began to occur in the 1970s and 1980s—other nations were surpassing our educational attainments and industrial output. Even though our population is increasing, our human capital is being depleted. This decline is linked to the foundations of our educational institutions and a growing underclass, which is spilling over into the workplace and other sectors of society.

The states have responded. Between 1985 and 2005, forty-nine states increased or introduced student assessment programs, twenty-eight states required competency tests for high school graduation, all fifty introduced or raised requirements for high school graduation in terms of Carnegie units (see Table 9–4), and forty-three states raised college entrance requirements. Twelve states increased the length of the school year, and thirteen states introduced additional instructional time. Twenty states reduced class sizes, and twenty-four states started students at a younger age.[89] Surprisingly, however, the U.S. high school graduate rate has leveled off, from 72 percent in 1985 to 74 percent in 2007—suggesting a flat outcome or fade-out factor despite increased reform efforts.[90]

By 2005, all fifty states had introduced changes in teacher preparation, thirty-four required testing for admission to teacher-education programs, thirty-five required exit tests from teacher-education programs, thirty-nine required testing for initial certification of teachers, and twelve introduced career ladders for teachers.[91] In thirty-nine states, higher teacher salaries were attributed, in part, to the national reform

[87]Gerald Bracey, *The Bracey Report on the Condition of Public Education, 2009* (Boulder, CO: Education and Public Interest Center, 2009).

[88]Paul Hill and James Harvey, *Making School Reform Work* (Washington, DC: Brookings Institution, 2005); Sharon L. Nichols and David C. Berliner, "Why Has High-Stakes Testing Slipped into Contemporary American Life," *Phi Delta Kappan*, 89 (2008): 672–676; Vicki Phillips and Carina Wong, "Tying Together the Common core of Standards, Instruction and Assessments," *Phi Delta Kappan*, 91(2010): 37–42.

[89]Bruce J. Biddle and David C. Berliner, "Small Class Size and Its Effects," *Educational Leadership*, 59 (2002): 12–23; *The Condition of Education 2006* (Washington, DC: U.S. Government Printing Office, 2006), Indicators, 28, 35, pp. 65, 78; *Digest of Education Statistics 2009*, table 6, p. 8; and Rick Stiggins, "Assessment for Learning," *Phi Delta Kappan*, 90 (2009): 419–421.

[90]*Digest of Education Statistics, 2003*, table 102, p. 134; *Digest of Education Statistics, 2009*, table 105, p. 166.

[91]*The Condition of Education, 2006*, Indicator 37, p. 80, and Linda Darling-Hammond and J. Bransford, *Preparing Teachers for a Changing World* (San Francisco: Jossey-Bass, 2005).

movement. As many as thirty-five states have upgraded the educational and testing requirements for principals between 1985 and 2005, and others have demanded stricter evaluation and accountability of principals.[92] More than twenty-five states have already introduced centers or academies for principals, to help them improve their leadership and managerial skills.

Lessons to Be Learned

Recent efforts show that education reform, if it is to be successful, cannot come from only one group—politicians, state officials, taxpayers, administrators, or teachers—but needs cooperation among all groups. Moreover, responsibility is needed at all levels. For example, regardless of how much money is earmarked for increased salaries or merit pay, we need responsible teachers and administrators at the school level; no one can reform dedication and hard work. Regardless of number or type of student tests, or how much homework is assigned, students (and parents) must make a concerted effort in academic input and performance. Regardless of the motivation or incentives we provide, no student can be compelled to learn; enthusiasm for learning cannot be coerced. Learning involves delayed gratification and sweat; it does not come easy and cannot be regulated by a clause, resolution, or mandate.

The second lesson to be learned is that education reform—more precisely, the success of reform—depends in large measure on the features of the local school: the school organization, school culture, and school ethos. In effect, school as a whole and school as a process are interlinked, with a changing and dynamic environment. A broader construct in education that represents this concept of school organization, culture, and ethos is referred to as school climate (see Chapter 3). The idea of a corporation's culture as used by Thomas Peters and Robert Waterman's analysis of the best-run American companies comes near to capturing this concept.[93] A more precise term is **subjective culture**—that is, the way the organizational environment or social system operates, its belief systems, structures, stereotype formations, norms, roles, values, rules, and task definitions.[94] The values, beliefs, and behaviors of the school's players—administrators, teachers, students (even parents)—all play a role in determining reform and what will be accomplished at the school level.

The third lesson, although somewhat over-simplified, is that the reform measures that states adopt are not likely to make a difference or lead to serious improvement unless the policies are responsive to local needs and pressures and unless the local school environment, including the people, is willing to adopt those measures.

Although states generally control funding, curriculum requirements, teacher and administrative certification, high school graduation requirements, and even textbook selection (in twenty-two states), they still have limited control over the daily operation of schools. State efforts to reform education may be visible and vocal and may take on many political and economic dimensions, but the dynamics of local schools and school administrators can torpedo authorized reform policies. State reform, then, must be sensitive to and include the local interpretation and responses to the official version of reform. Educational change must be played out in the classrooms and schools of America, and state-initiated reforms should conform—at least be modified—to local politics, processes, and perceptions.

Organization of School Districts

The organization of school districts permits several grade plans and combinations of elementary and secondary schools. Figure 9–1 shows 10 common organizational plans; a description for each follows.

1. Plan A shows the traditional 8–4 organizational plan consisting of an eight-year elementary school and a four-year high school.
2. Plan B exemplifies a 4–4–4 district plan, where the first four grades are elementary schools, the next four are middle schools, and the final four are high schools.

[92]John C. Daresh, *Beginning the Principalship* (Thousand Oaks, CA: Corwin Press, 2006); Dennis Sparks, "What I Believe About Leadership Development," *Phi Delta Kappan* and Marc Tucker and Judy B. Codding, *The Principal Challenge* (San Francisco: Jossey-Bass, 2002).

[93]Thomas Peters and Robert Waterman, *In Search of Excellence: Lessons Learned from America's Best-Run Companies* (New York: Harper & Row, 1982).

[94]Terrance E. Deal and Kent D. Peterson, *Shaping School Culture* (San Francisco: Jossey-Bass, 1998); Michael Fullan, *The New Meaning of Educational Change,* 4th ed. (New York: Teachers College Press, Columbia University, 2007).

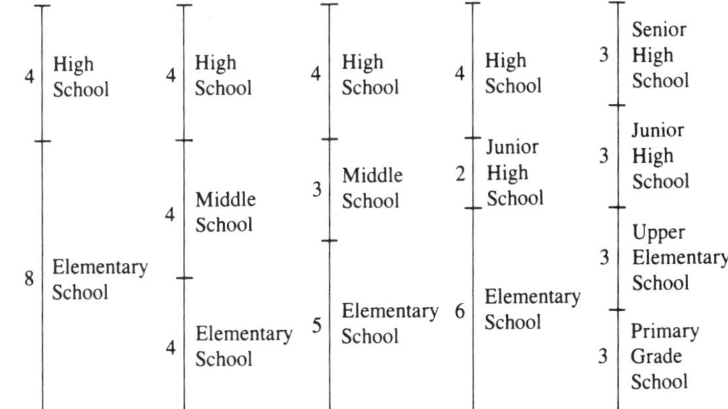

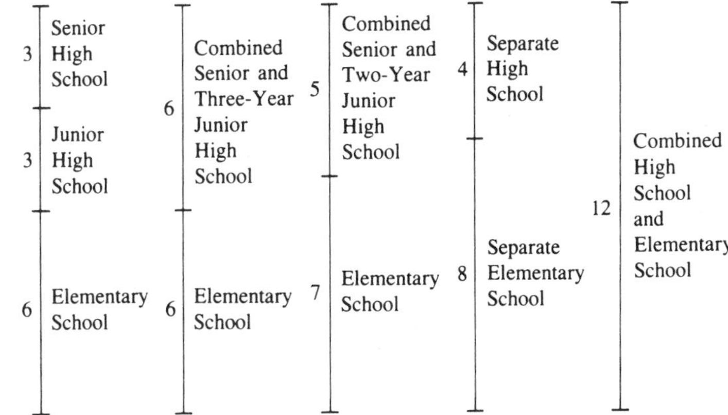

FIGURE 9-1

School District Organization by Grades
Source: Adapted from *Digest of Education Statistics, 2005* (Washington, DC: U.S. Government Printing Office, 2006, fig. 1, p. 9).

3. Plan C illustrates the 5–3–4 plan, providing a five-year elementary school, a three-year middle school, and a four-year high school. Both Plans B and C are growing in popularity because of the middle-school movement.
4. Plan D shows a 6–2–4 district plan, where grades 1 to 6 comprise the elementary school, grades 7 to 8 comprise the junior high school, and grades 9 to 12 comprise the high school.
5. Plan E is the 3–3–3–3 plan, used in parts of the country that wish to promote school integration at the elementary school level or in rural areas that need to consolidate school facilities. There is also a three-year junior high school and a three-year senior high school.
6. Plan F represents a typical 6–3–3 elementary, junior high, and senior high school plan. Plans D, E, and F illustrate the junior high school in relation to elementary school and either high school or senior high school.
7. Plan G is the 6–6 organizational plan consisting of an elementary school for grades 1 to 6 and a combined three-year junior high school and a three-year senior high school.
8. Plan H illustrates the 7–5 grade pattern, where the elementary school goes to grade 7, and there is a combined two-year junior high school and three-year senior high school. Plans G and H show the elementary school with a combined junior and senior high school, representative of a small number of U.S. schools.
9. Plan I shows two separate, usually adjacent, districts, where the elementary school grades K to 8 represent one district and the high school grades 9 to 12 represent the other district.

10. Plan J is the 1–12 plan, representative of even a smaller number of schools, usually special schools, alternative schools, one-room schoolhouses, or schools not classified by grade level.

It is difficult to say which plan is better or worse; it varies with educational philosophy and the conditions in the school district. Most progressive educators or communities prefer a middle-grade or junior high school as a means of putting preadolescent students (who are usually undergoing rapid physical and social changes) under one roof for a number of years to facilitate their growth and development.

Size of School Districts

What is the ideal size for a school district? In terms of minimum size, how many students must be enrolled to justify offering diversified programs, services, and personnel needed to meet modern educational requirements? The studies that suggest optimal size, over the last seventy years, have focused on cost analysis, curriculum offerings, staffing, and student achievement as the most important variables. During this period, the minimum ideal size tends to be 10,000 to 12,000 students, and the maximum size tends to be 40,000 to 50,000 students.[95] One classic study considered the maximally effective school district to comprise 100,000 students.[96]

Today small is considered better; the idea is to scale down the school enterprise, whereas in the past big was considered better. Advocates of small school districts and rural schools point out that 5000-student maximums are more cost effective, have fewer student dropouts (in percentages), higher student SAT and ACT scores, and higher graduation and college entry rates than do school districts with more than 5000 students.[97] Although social class was not controlled in these studies, educational expenditures were. Small school districts, 5000 or fewer students, cluster in the 14th to 30th percentile in per-pupil expenditures but rank in the top 10 percent on nationwide achievement scores and other indicators of student performance (fewer dropouts, more high school graduates).[98]

Other advocates maintain that school districts with 20,000 or fewer students have a significant positive relationship with SAT scores, high school graduation rates, and slightly more favorable pupil–teacher ratios than do districts with more than 20,000 students. Smaller school districts have significantly lower levels of parental income and spend about $250 less per student.[99] In short, "smaller districts . . . appear to achieve better results for students at equal [or less] cost."[100]

Studies of hundreds of school districts nationwide also confirm the relationship between inverse district

[95]Howard A. Dawson, *Satisfactory Local School Units,* Field Study no. 7 (Nashville, TN: George Peabody College for Teachers, 1934); Mario D. Fantini, Marilyn Gittell, and Richard Magat, *Community Control and the Urban School* (New York: Praeger, 1970); A. Harry Passow, *Toward Creating a Model Urban School System* (New York: Teachers College Press, 1967); and *Summary of Research on Size of Schools and School Districts* rev. ed. (Arlington, VA: Educational Research Service, 1994). Also see William L. Boyd et al. The *Transformation of Great American School Districts* (Cambridge, MA: Harvard Education Press, 2008).

[96]Paul R. Mort and Francis G. Cornell, *American Schools in Transition* (New York: Teachers College Press, 1941); Paul R. Mort, William S. Vincent, and Clarence Newell, *The Growing Edge: An Instrument for Measuring the Adaptability of School Systems,* 2 vols. (New York: Teachers College Press, 1955).

[97]*A Critique of North Carolina Department of Public Instruction's Plan to Mandate School District Mergers Throughout the State* (Raleigh: North Carolina Boards Association, 1986); Jacqueline P. Danzberger, Michael W. Kirst, and Michael P. Usdan, *Governing Public Schools: New Times, New Requirements* (Washington, DC: Institute for Educational Leadership, 1992); Kenneth A. Strive, *Small Schools and Strong Communities* (New York: Teachers College Press, Columbia University, 2010).

[98]Allan C. Ornstein, "School District and School Size: An Evolving Controversy," *High School Journal,* 76 (1993): 240–244; Ornstein, "School Size and Effectiveness: Policy Implications," *Urban Review,* 22 (1990): 239–245; and Diane M. Truscott and Stephen D. Truscott, "Differing Circumstances: Finding Common Ground Between Urban and Rural Schools," *Phi Delta Kappan,* 87 (2005): 123–130.

[99]Robert W. Jewell, "School and School District Size Relationships," *Education and Urban Society,* 21 (1989): 140–153; Jean Johnson, "Do Communities Want Smaller Schools?" *Educational Leadership,* 59 (2002): 42–46; Johnson "Will Parents and Teachers . . . Reduce School Size?" *Phi Delta Kappan,* 83 (2002): 353–356.

[100]Jewell, "School and School District Size Relationships," p. 151. Also see Kari Artstrom, "Overlooked Too Long, Small Schools Deserve Our Attention," *School Administrator,* 56 (1999): 50; Kenneth Leithwood et al., *Making Schools Smarter,* 3rd ed. (Thousand Oaks, CA: Corwin Press, 2006).

Table 9-5 Distribution of School Districts by Size, 2007-2008

Size of District (Number of Pupils)	Public School Districts		Public School Students	
	Number	Percent	Number[a]	Percent
Total operating districts	13,924	100.0	48,184	100.0
25,000 or more	281	2.0	16,670	34.6
10,000–24,999	590	4.2	8957	18.6
5000–9999	1064	7.6	7423	15.4
2500–4999	2012	14.4	7124	14.8
1000–2499	3364	23.8	5384	11.2
600–999	1762	12.7	1388	2.9
300–599	1903	13.7	840	1.7
1–299	2724	19.6	398	0.8
Size not reported	279	2.0	—	—

[a] in millions, based on Fall 2007.

Source: *Digest of Education Statistics, 2009* (Washington, DC: Department of Education, 2010), table 87, p. 126.

size and student achievement, after controlling for per-pupil expenditures and social class.[101] Although larger school districts may be more efficient when it comes to spending—that is, per-unit costs decline with a greater number of students served because districts usually purchase more units cheaper and employ fewer teachers and administrators per student—the economies of scale enjoyed by large school districts come at the expense of educational outcomes. Moreover, there are some data to suggest that large school districts are actually inefficient and wasteful.[102] The dependence on costs seems U-shaped, with very small and very large school districts spending more per student than moderate-sized districts.

Number of School Districts

Historically, 10,000 students is a large number for a school district. Our schools, we must remember, are an outgrowth of one-room schoolhouses and school districts in the rural United States. With the exception of a few urban areas, even as late as the turn of the twentieth century, most school districts consisted of three, four, or five schools and a few hundred students. As late as 1930, nearly 50 percent of U.S. school districts had fewer than 300 students. By 2007, as many as 20 percent of the school districts (enrolling only 1 percent of the nation's students) had fewer than 300 students. Inversely, 4.2 percent of public school districts had 10,000 or more students. There were only 281, or 2.0 percent, school districts with 25,000 or more students, but they accounted for 16.7 million students, or 35 percent, of the nation's public school enrollment.[103] Table 9–5 shows how school districts today are distributed.

Most of the larger school districts (25,000 or more students) are in California, Florida, Texas, and Maryland, but the states with the largest district averages are Hawaii, Maryland, Florida, and Louisiana. The states with the smallest district averages—that is, less than 1000 students per district—are Maine, Vermont, Nebraska, and Montana.[104]

---

[101]Tom V. Ark, "The Case for Small High Schools," *Educational Leadership,* 59 (2002): 55–59; David H. Monk, "Secondary School Size and Curriculum Comprehensiveness," *Economics of Education Review,* 6 (1987): 137–150; William J. Fowler and Herbert J. Walberg, "School Size, Characteristics, and Outcomes," *Educational Evaluation and Policy Analysis,* 13 (1991): 189–202; and Joe Nathan and Karen Febey, *Smaller, Safer, Saner, Successful Schools* (Minneapolis: Center for School Change, 2001).

[102]Rick Allen, "Big Schools: The Way We Were," *Educational Leadership,* 59 (2002): 36–41; Donna Driscoll, Dennis Halcoussis, and Shirley Svorny, "School District Size and Student Performance," *Economics of Education Review,* 22 (2003): 193–201; Joyce Epstein et al., *School, Family and Community Partnerships,* 3rd ed. (Thousand Oaks CA: Corwin Press, 2008).

[103]*Digest of Education Statistics, 2009* (Washington, DC: U.S. Government Printing Office, 2010), table 87, p. 126.

[104]Ibid., table 90, pp. 130–140.

As many as twenty-seven school districts have enrollments that exceed 100,000 students. In most cases, the larger school districts are located in or near cities, the largest being the New York City system with approximately 989,990 students, followed by Los Angeles with 693,680 students, Chicago with 407, 500 students, and Dade County, Florida, with 348,128 students.[105] Reflecting both national enrollment trends and immigration trends to the larger cities, six of the ten largest school districts (in the Sunbelt) have experienced increased enrollments in the last ten years. The four cities (New York City, Baltimore, Detroit, and Philadelphia) that have experienced minus growth are located in the North (sometimes called the Frostbelt). The medium-sized and smaller school districts have followed metropolitan sprawl and tend to be located in the outer ring of the suburbs or in rural areas.

Students and Schools

Across the nation, public school enrollments show a 23 percent projected increase from 1989 to 2014, from 41 million to 50 million, and it is anticipated to reach a new high in 2018 of 53.9 million students (an increase of 9 percent) between 2006 and 2018. The public school elementary school enrollment (grades PK–8) is expected to grow from 34.2 million to 38.2 million in 2018; the public high school enrollment (grades 9–12) is expected to grow from 14.6 million to 15.8 million in 2018.[106] Based on geographic region, public school enrollments are expected to grow by 18 percent in the South, 15 percent in the West, less than 1 percent in the Midwest and to drop by 5 percent in the Northeast.[107]

The number of public elementary schools grew from 61,340 in 1990 to 73,254 in 2007. The number of public secondary schools grew from 23,460 in 1990 to 30,648 in 2007. In total, there were 82,475 public schools in 1990 and in 2007 there were 97,680—an 18 percent increase.[108]

The growth in student enrollments has affected school size in two ways: increasing the average school size at the elementary level from 449 in 1990 to 469 in 2007 and at the secondary level from 663 in 1990 to 816 in 2007. It also correlates with a reduction of small school districts (fewer than 300 students), from 3816 in 1990 to 2724 in 2007, a reduction of nearly 29 percent.[109]

Demographics and Diversity In 1970, minority students comprised 20 percent of student enrollments. By 1995, it was 32 percent. In 2003, 42 percent of all students were minority. From 1972 to 2007, the percentage of white students dropped from 78 percent to 56 percent, while the percentage of minority students grew from 22 percent (1972) to 44 percent (2007). The biggest increase occurred within the Hispanic population. The percentage of Hispanic students grew from 11 percent in 1987 to 21 percent in 2007, making them the largest minority group in American schools. The percentage of black students dropped from 17 percent in 1987 to 15 percent in 2007; the percentage of Asian Americans was approximately 4 percent in 2007. It is also interesting to note that the percentage of minority students varies based on geographic region. From 1972 to 2007, there were more minority students due largely to Hispanic increases in the West and the South than in the Midwest and the Northeast.[110]

The U.S. Census predicts that by 2050 race in America will be turned upside down. It is estimated that by 2050, 50.5 percent of the population will be white; 25.7 percent will be Hispanic; 13.8 percent will be black; and 9.2 percent will be Asian Americans.[111] Today's school enrollments exemplify the future; it is the most racial mix of students this country has experienced. Today's cities like New York, Miami, Houston, Dallas, Detroit, Chicago, and Los Angeles are already mostly comprised of minorities, and the public school student population in these cities comprises 85 percent minority or more.

By 2010, whites will account for only 9 percent of the world's population, compared to 17 percent in 1997—making them the world's smallest ethnic minority. Only 12 percent of our current immigration is from Europe; almost all the rest is from Latin America

---

[105]Ibid., table 92, p.181.

[106]*The Condition of Education, 2009* (Washington, DC: U.S. Government Printing Office, 2009), Indicator 4, tables A-4-1, A-4-2, pp. 10, 126, 128.

[107]*Projections of Education Statistics to 2018* (Washington, DC: U.S. Government Printing Office, 2009), tables A, B, 4–9, pp. 5–7, 45–53.

[108]*Digest of Education Statistics, 2009,* table 86, p. 125.

[109]Ibid., table 94, p. 155.

[110]*The Condition of Education, 2009* (Washington, DC: U.S. Government Printing Office, 2009), Indicator 7, tables A-7-1, A-7-2, p. 16, 136–137.

[111]*Population Projections of the United States by Age, Sex, Race, and Hispanic Origin: 1995 to 2050* (Washington, DC: U.S. Department of Commerce, Economics and Statistics Administration, Bureau of the Census, 2006), p. 13.

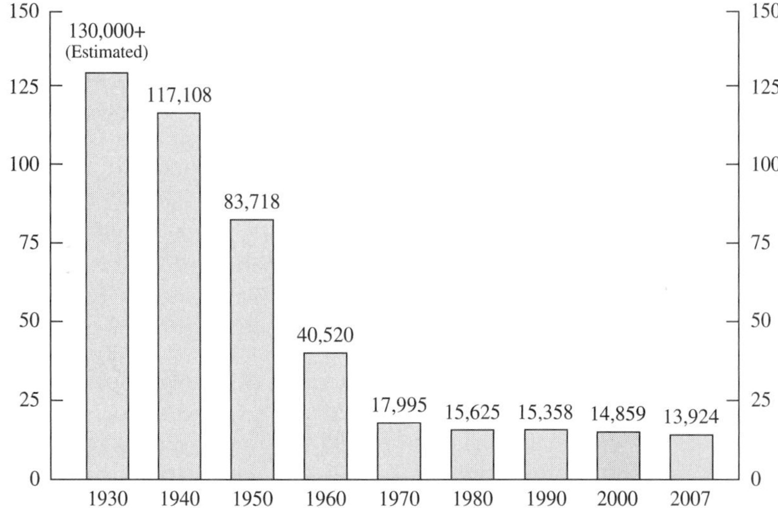

FIGURE 9–2

Declining Number of School Districts, 1930–2007
Source: *Digest of Education Statistics, 1972* (Washington, DC: U.S. Government Printing Office, 1973), fig. 7, p. 53; *Digest of Education Statistics, 2009* (Washington, DC: U.S. Government Printing Office, 2010), table 86, p. 125.

and Asia.[112] The children of these immigrants represent the new immigrant students enrolling in schools across the nation. The successful administrator of the twenty-first century will have to deal with ethnic, religious, and linguistic diversity. The issue for schools is the same as it was one hundred years ago—to socialize immigrant children as soon as possible, but with understanding and respect for group and individual differences.

Consolidation of School Districts

The number of school districts in the United States continues to decline. In 1930, there were more than 130,000 school districts. By 1980, the number had shrunk to 15,625; and by 2007, to 13,924—suggesting a leveling process (see Figure 9–2).

The reduced number of school districts is a result of **consolidation**, the combination of a number of smaller school districts into one or two larger ones. Consolidation is thought to bring about more effective schools by increasing the tax base, quality of professional personnel, breadth of educational programs, special services, and transportation facilities and by reducing overall educational costs per student.[113]

The data on consolidation, however, remain inconclusive. Moreover, consolidating districts usually means closing some schools, and this has proved to be a serious and emotional matter, especially in small and rural school districts where the local school may be a focal point of the community's identity. In many cases state school officials, operating under the assumption that consolidation is cost-effective and enhances student opportunity, have clashed with local townspeople who resent the interference of distant bureaucrats. The process can be demoralizing to students, parents, and the community at large. Local taxpayers, who might normally support plans for saving money, have often refused to endorse consolidation.[114]

Because of this opposition, officials in many states have begun looking for ways to obtain the benefits of consolidation without eliminating schools or districts. One method is for neighboring districts to share programs and personnel. Minnesota, for example, encourages this trend by providing up to 75 percent of the cost of shared secondary school facilities and programs. Wisconsin provides additional Title I support for sharing facilities.[115] Iowa provides between 5 and 50 percent extra funding to local school districts that share course offerings, teachers, administrators, and school buildings.[116] In Illinois, Montana, and Nebraska, there is a hold on new

[112]Tyrone C. Howard, *Why Race and Culture Matter in Schools* (New York: Teachers College Press, Columbia University,). Allan C. Ornstein, *Teaching and Schooling in America: Pre- and Post-September 11* (Boston: Allyn & Bacon, 2003).

[113]William Howell (ed.), *Besieged: School Boards and the Future of Education Politics* (Washington, DC: Brookings Institution Press, 2005): 56–80; Jewell, "School and School District Size Relationships"; Deborah Meier, "Just Let Us Be: the Genesis of a Small Public School," *Educational Leadership, 59* (2002): 76–80; Strike, *Small Schools and Small Communities*.

[114]Ornstein, "School District and School Size."

[115]Jeremy D. Finn, "Small Classes in American Schools," *Phi Delta Kappan,* 83, (2002): 551–560; Chris Pipho, "Rural Education," *Phi Delta Kappan,* 69 (1987): 6–7.

[116]*Annual School District Reorganization Report* (Des Moines: Iowa Department of Education, 1999).

consolidation plans, and there are school committees organized to restructure school district sizes.[117]

Some educators contend that consolidation has served its major purpose—eliminating many one-room schools and inefficient small districts—and that this trend will soon pass. But it remains a controversial issue that affects many school districts across the country.

Decentralization of School Districts

Changes in the urban population after 1950 gave rise to changes in the composition of urban schools. As middle-class and white populations fled to the suburbs—in what became known as the "white flight movement"—the percentages of low-income and minority residents increased in the cities. As a result, city schools became multiethnic, and many schools in the suburbs became more homogeneous in terms of income and race. By the 1960s, many inner-city ethnic groups, especially blacks, began to feel that the schools did not serve their needs. They began to call for decentralization as a means to greater community involvement in the schools.

By definition, **decentralization** divides the school system into smaller units, but the focus of power and authority remains in a single central administration and board of education. There is usually little controversy over decentralization as long as jobs are not consolidated or expanded on the basis of racial or ethnic patterns. Even professional educators today see a need to reduce school bureaucracy and to accept decentralization because it allows the professional educators to retain power. At the same time, school critics and minority spokespersons believe that decentralization will give the people greater access to the schools.

The concept of decentralization now seems to be on the decline for two reasons: (1) there has been a drop in the percentage of decentralized school districts, from 67 percent (forty-two out of sixty-six) in 1980 to 31 percent (sixteen out of fifty-one) in 1988, and (2) the majority of districts currently claiming to be decentralized seems more committed to centralization. There is also research suggesting that increased administrative layers leads to bureaucracy, extra costs, and slower decision making at the central office. Thus, in an effort to enhance fiscal management and consolidate power and authority at the central office, the biggest governance change for New York City's schools in the last four decades was enacted in 2003: The thirty-two community school districts were abolished and replaced with 10 regional divisions, each headed by a superintendent, ranging in number of students from 67,700 to 137,200.[118] By 2007, the 10 regions were dissolved, and all schools had the opportunity to select one of three school support organizations (empowerment support, learning support, or partnership support).[119]

Other data also suggest that, despite apparent decentralization, the large, urban school districts in fact remain highly centralized. Decisions regarding curriculum, instruction, staffing and teacher evaluation, student testing, graduation requirements, and budgeting are still made at the central level or at what is sometimes referred to as the "downtown" office. Furthermore, the central office is increasingly involved in negotiations with teachers' unions, compliance with court-ordered busing requirements, affirmative action, and allocation of state monies and special programs for the local district. All these trends tend to expand the authority of the main district office and reduce the effect of decentralization.[120] See Administrative Advice 9–1.

Local School Boards

The local school boards of education have been delegated powers and duties by the state for the purpose of ensuring that their schools are operated properly. Despite the fact that their prerogatives are limited by the state, school boards have assumed significant decision-making responsibility. School boards have the power for the most part to raise money through taxes. They exercise

[117]Evans Clinchy, "The Educationally Challenged American School District," *Phi Delta Kappan*, 80 (1998): 272–277; Allan C. Ornstein, "Controversy Over Size Continues," *School Administrator,* 46 (1989): 42–43; Pipho, "Rural Education"; Michael Salmonowicz, "Meeting the Challenge of School Turnaround," *Phi Delta Kappan*, 91(2010): 19–24.

[118]John Gehring, "New York: Schools Get New Aid," *Education Week,* November 27, 2002, p. 18. New York City Department of Education, Press Release, "Map of Instructional Divisions," January 23, 2003.

[119]Courasatun with Robert Brasco, Farmer District Superintendent, New York City May 2010.

[120]Ronald E. Everett et al., *Financial and Managerial Accounting for School Administrators,* 2nd (Lanham, MD: Rowman & Littlefield, 2008); Michael Fine and Janis Somerville (eds.), *Small Schools: Big Imaginations* (Chicago: Campaign for Urban School Reform, 1998); Debra Viadero, "Big-City Majors' Control of Schools Yield Mixed Results," *Education Week,* September 11, 2002, p. 8.

ADMINISTRATIVE ADVICE 9–1

Questions to Consider When Your School District Contemplates Consolidation or Decentralization

Both school consolidation and school decentralization often involve emotional issues—where some groups are perceived as "winners" and others as "losers." Often the issues become highly vocalized at school meetings and in the local press, and so-called solutions are often slogans rather than carefully worked-out concepts understood and accounted for in the rhetoric or press. We assume the "community voice" is the most visible or vocal, and yet we sometimes fail to consider the silent parents who have their own views of reform for their children's education. Thus, there is good reason to proceed with caution. As an administrator, ask yourself the questions below. Be candid and analytic in your answers.

- Who are the advocates?
- What are their motivations? What are their political-economic reasons? Do they have hidden agendas?
- Does the majority of the community want to consolidate (decentralize)? Or is a small, well-organized group behind the plan?
- Do students, parents, teachers, and community residents gain under the plan? How?
- Which parents or community residents lose, or feel they lose, under the plan?
- How do various interest groups feel about the plan? Is there considerable conflict or emotion? Is it really worthwhile to proceed, given the conflict or emotion? Why?
- How do the various interest groups want to be represented under the plan? Are there differences among groups based on race, ethnicity, social class, or residents with and without children?
- How do community agencies and local business groups fit into the plan? Have their concerns or interests been considered?
- As a result of the plan, will teaching jobs or administrative positions be affected? Is there current concern among the professional staff?
- What administrative levels (central office, decentralized, or field office) should be consolidated (decentralized)? Why?
- How does the plan affect student performance? Are there data to indicate that the plan will have a positive impact on student performance?
- What unit size is most effective? Most efficient? Is there past history in adjacent (or similar) communities or school districts to verify these assumptions?
- When does bigness lead to increased bureaucracy? When does smallness lead to reduced range of educational services?
- What is the projected cost of the plan? Is it realistic? Is it worthwhile in terms of assumed outcomes?
- Does the plan consider future population growth? Student enrollments? School construction sites? School integration?
- Who really benefits from the plan? Students? (Remember, they are the real consumers and the reason for the schools.)

power over personnel and school property. Some states leave curriculum and student policy in the hands of the school board, but others, by law, impose specific requirements. In general, the school board must conform to state guidelines to qualify for state aid, as well as conform to federal guidelines where federal monies are involved.

Methods of selecting board members are prescribed by state law. The two basic methods are election and appointment. Election is thought to make for greater accountability to the public, but some people argue that appointment leads to greater competence and less politics. (See the Pro/Con Debate at the end of this chapter.) Election is the most common practice. In 2009, 90 percent of school board members nationwide were elected and 10 percent were appointed.[121]

[121]Selection of Local School Boards (Alexandria, VA: National School Boards Association, 2009).

Appointment is more common in large urban districts than in suburban or small-town districts; between 1988 and 2008, 11 to 15 percent of urban board members were appointed. A few states specify a standard number of board members, still others specify a permissible range, and a few have no requirements. Most school boards (80 percent) comprise a seven- to nine-member range, with the largest school board having nineteen members; the average size is seven members.[122]

A recent nationwide survey of school board members indicates that the percentage of women on school boards is 39 percent and minority representation is 14 percent. (Southern states show a higher minority representation on school boards: 16 percent black and 3 percent Hispanic.)[123] School board members tend to be older than the general population (94 percent are over age forty); more educated (67 percent have had four or more years of college); wealthier (59 percent have family incomes of $75,000 or more, and 37 percent earn more than $100,000 annually); and more likely to be professionals or businesspeople (45 percent) or homemakers or retired persons (26 percent).[124] Interestingly, 51 percent have no children in school right now, and 41 percent are relative neophytes, having served on the boards for five or fewer years.[125]

The largest school systems (those enrolling 50,000 or more students) tend to have more heterogeneous boards. One survey indicates that minority members constitute 29 percent of the school board in these systems; women make up 36 percent, but family income and educational levels are more diversified.[126] In another survey of the 100 largest school districts in the country, as many as 27.5 percent of the board members were classified as minority, including 21 percent who were black.[127] As for urban school boards, comprising the Council of the Great City Schools (consisting of 66 school districts), about 81 percent in 2008 served four-year terms, 10 served three-year terms, 5 percent served five-year terms, and 2 percent did not have a term limit. As many as 52 percent were white, 33 percent were black, 9 percent were Latino, and 4 percent were Asian. Approximately 55 percent were female.[128]

School Board–Public Problems

The top five problems of school board members are school finance, student achievement, special education, educational technology, and teacher quality (see Table 9–6). Budget issues held the top spot on board members' worry lists for the last eighteen out of twenty years. Academic issues have been in the top five because of the media and state mandates.[129] Since 2000, the public ranked finances as a top concern. The second to fifth concerns of school board members reflect state and local pressures to improve what goes on in schools and classrooms. Infrastructure problems and student enrollments, which have often been among the top concerns of school boards, have now been replaced by drug, discipline, and gang problems, which have always been top concerns of the public.

In the eyes of the public, drug abuse, school violence, and lack of discipline consistently ranked as three of the five most important problems throughout the 1980s, 1990s and 2000s.[130] These rankings were related to a perceived breakdown of student behavior, including their moral standards, lack of interest and truancy, drinking and alcoholism, crime and vandalism, disrespect for teachers, and fighting. Historically, school board members did not have such strong feelings about

---

[122]Thomas A. Shannon, former executive publisher of the *American School Board Journal*, personal communication, July 14, 1999; "Twenty-first Annual Survey of School Board Members," *American School Board Journal,* 186 (1999): 34–37; Michael D. Usdan, "School Boards: A Neglected Institution in an Era of School Reform," *Phi Delta Kappan,* 91 (2010): 8–10.

[123]"School Board Members," *American School Board Journal,* 185 (1998): A-15; Kathleen Vail, "The Changing Face of Education," *American School Board Journal,* 188 (2001): 39–42; Gene I. Maeroff, "School Boards in America," *Phi Delta Kappan,* 91 (2010): 31–34.

[124]Frederick M. Hess, *School Boards at the Dawn of the 21st Century* (Alexandria, VA: National School Boards Association, 2002), Tables 24–27, pp. 26–28. Hess, "Weighing the Case for School Boards," *Phi Delta Kappan,* 91 (2010): 15–19.

[125]Ibid.

[126]Allan C. Ornstein, "Composition of Boards of Education of Public School Systems Enrolling 50,000 or More Students," *Urban Education,* 16 (1981): 232–234.

[127]Allan C. Ornstein, "School Superintendents and School Board Members: Who They Are," *Contemporary Education,* 63 (1992): 157–159.

[128]*Urban School Board Survey: Characteristics, Structure, and Benefits* (Washington, DC: Council of the Great City Schools, 2009), pp. 2, 4–5.

[129]Hess, *School Boards at the Dawn of the 21st Century;* "Money and Other Worries," *American School Board Journal,* 177 (1990): 34–35.

[130]"Board Members' Worries," *American School Board Journal,* 185 (1998): A-15; "Money and Other Worries"; "The Public's Attitude Toward Public Schools," *Phi Delta Kappan,* 80 (1998): 51.

Table 9-6 Problems in Rank Order Facing Schools: Boards versus Public[a]

As Seen by the School Board	As Seen by the Public
School finance	Lack of financial support
Student achievement	Lack of discipline
Special education	Overcrowded schools
Educational technology	Use of drugs
Teacher quality	Fighting/violence/gangs
Parental support	Lack of good teachers
Federal/state regulations	Lack of standards
Drug/alcohol use	
Discipline	

[a]Respondents to the school board survey were asked to indicate "significant" or "moderate" concerns. Respondents to the public poll, on the other hand, were asked to name the biggest problems facing their public schools. In both surveys, percentages total more than 100 because of multiple responses.

Source: Frederick M. Hess, *School Boards at the Dawn of the 21st Century* (Alexandria, VA: National School Boards Association, 2002); "41st Annual Phi Delta Kappan/Gallup Poll of Public Schools," *Phi Delta Kappan,* 91 (2009): 10.

Table 9-7 Public's Attitude toward School, 2005–2009

	Grade the Public Schools in Your Community		Grade the Public Schools Nationally	
	2005	2009	2005	2009
A, B	48%	51%	24%	19%
A	12	10	2	1
B	36	41	22	18
C	29	32	46	55
D	9	11	13	19
F	5	3	4	6
Don't know	9	3	13	1

Source: "The 41st Annual Phi Delta Kappa/Gallup Poll of . . . Public Schools," *Phi Delta Kappan,* 91 (2009): 11.

the breakdown of school discipline, moral standards, or the law. Interestingly, both school boards and the public are not too concerned about school integration or busing, which was one of the most controversial issues in the sixties and seventies. Since the year 2000, lack of financial support has topped the list of school problems as purported by the public, with overcrowded schools and lack of discipline mentioned second or third in the years 2000, through 2002 and 2006 through 2009.

Since the mid-1970s, respondents to the Phi Delta Kappa/Gallup education polls have been asked to grade the public schools in their communities and the nation as a whole on a scale of A to F. Table 9–7 shows that when people are asked about the schools they know, the grades they assign go up. The percentage of respondents who award schools an A or B increases when respondents are asked about the schools in their own community rather than the nation's schools. However, based on a study conducted in Michigan in 2003, "African Americans and urban residents are far less likely than other citizens to award their local schools an A or a B."[131]

When the public is asked how much confidence they have in American institutions, respondents give the highest ratings to churches (57%) and schools (42%). Local government, state government, big business, national government, the justice/legal system, and organized labor, in descending order, receive lower ratings.[132] In the nationwide Hart survey, 66 percent of adults believe we are asking our schools to do too many things that really should be handled by parents at home.[133]

Over a five-year period (2005–2009), the percentage of the public that favors the idea of charter schools has grown from 49 percent to 64 percent. From 1984 to 2009, the percentage of the public that favors merit pay has grown from 65 percent to 72 percent. From 1984 to 2009, the percentage of the public that favors national standards for certifying teachers has grown from 68 percent to 73 percent.[134]

School Board Meetings

There are three general types of board meeting: regular, special, and executive. The first two are usually open meetings, and the public is invited. The third type is

131"The 41st Annual Phi Delta Kappa/Gallup Poll of Public Schools," *Phi Delta Kappan,* 91 (2009): 1–23;

132"The 41st Annual . . . Poll."

133"News and Notes: Survey Roundup," *Thrust for Educational Leadership,* 28 (1998): 4. See Shell Oil Survey Conducted by Peter D. Hart Research Associates, 1998.

134"The 41st Annual Phi Delta Kappa/Gallup Poll of Public Schools," *Phi Delta Kappan,* 91 (2009): 13, 15, 16.

usually closed to the public and deals with managerial issues or serious problems. Open or **public board meetings** obviously enhance school–community relations and allow parents to understand the problems of education as well as air their concerns; however, they can also degenerate into gripe sessions or conflict if someone in charge is not skilled in guiding large-group discussions and building consensus.[135] If a skilled leader is not available, it is best to limit the number of public meetings.

Holding closed or **executive board meetings** to reach major policy decisions is generally discouraged, but school boards occasionally use this tactic if conflict and tension arise. Many school districts, however, have mandated open meetings except under certain specified conditions. However, the executive meeting, if properly organized, produces the best results in terms of time management and outcomes.[136]

School board meetings are actually control systems that bring school resources into line with school policies. One way to ensure that organizational work is directed toward the appropriate mission statements or goals is to make school board meetings more focused in terms of resources and policies. Board members spend about twenty-five hours a month on board business, and roughly one-third of that time in board meetings. In large school districts (25,000+ students), 35 percent of the members claim they spend more than fifty hours a month.[137]

School board meetings, just as with meetings involving school administrators, are rarely one-time events; they are usually part of an ongoing cycle. According to one administrator, "Effective board meetings are the first prerequisite for an effective board. There's no one pattern for effective board meetings. Boards have traditions. What works for one school board may not work for another."[138]

Managers in private industry contend they spend 25 to 60 percent of their time in meeting rooms, and much of that time is wasted. "Meetings are where you keep the minutes and throw away the hours."[139] Thousands of school administrators would most likely nod in agreement—school meetings are places where participants learn to doodle, look attentive, nod politely, and pinch themselves to keep awake. Most people agree that school meetings, including board meetings and staff meetings, should be trimmed and that shorter meetings (no more than one to one and a half hours) are more productive than longer meetings. Generally, one meeting a month is enough.[140] (See Administrative Advice 9–2.) Board meetings (or meetings in general) with too many people—or people from too many bureaucratic layers—with many different interests or agendas will cause bog-down.

The use of a consent agenda "can help boards streamline meetings so they can spend more time on important matters." By using a consent agenda, boards are able to include routine items under a broad category (curriculum, personnel) and vote on each category with a single motion.[141] However, data suggest that strong superintendents conduct longer meetings (two to three hours per session), more meetings, and more board functions than do weak superintendents. In school districts controlled by the board, members make quick decisions and board meetings average less than one hour, with the superintendent simply carrying out board mandates.

School Board Responsibilities

The administration and management of schools is big business, and school board members must have or acquire knowledge of good business practices. Overall, school boards have fiscal responsibility for more than $611 billion each year and employ over 6.3 million individuals; this makes them the largest nationwide employer.[142] Board members must also be fair and mindful of the law when dealing with students, teachers, administrators, parents, and other community residents. Board members are public servants and represent the community and are expected to govern the school

---

[135]Renzue S. Townsend et al., *Effective Superintendent-School Board Practices* (Thousand Oaks: Corwin Press, 2007).

[136]John Eller and Howard C. Carlson, So *Now You're the Superintendent* (Thousand Oaks, CA: Corwin Press, 2008); Roger Soder, *The Language of Leadership* (San Francisco: Jossey-Bass, 2001).

[137]Hess, *School Boards at the Dawn of the 21st Century,* table 11, p. 17.

[138]Donald McAdams, "The Short, Productive Board Meeting," *School Administrator,* 62 (2005): 6.

[139]Lynn Oppenheim, "Why Meetings Sometimes Fail, *Executive Educator,* 11 (1989): 6.

[140]Michael R. Weber, "A Balancing Act of Demands and Needs," *School Administrator,* 56 (1999): 38–41.

[141]Judith A. Zimmerman, "Free to Focus," *American School Board Journal,* 191 (2004): 39–41.

[142]*Digest of Education Statistics, 2009,* tables 1, 27, 79, pp. 15, 48.

ADMINISTRATIVE ADVICE 9–2

Making Board Meetings More Meaningful

Most school board members spend too much time at meetings (usually without compensation) and are unable to devote sufficient time to important policy issues; alternately, they find the meetings mired in controversy. Here are some suggestions from two board presidents (Arcement and Rude) and two superintendents (Chopra and Kleinsmith) from different parts of the country (Louisiana, California, Pennsylvania, and Missouri) to make meetings more productive.

A. *Board members need to:*

1. *Understand* their own roles and duties, especially the relationship between the superintendent and board president.
2. Understand the importance of *teamwork,* trust, and exchange of ideas at meetings.
3. Exhibit *positive attitudes* in the way they conduct themselves at meetings, including support for the district's programs, professional staff, and other members of the school board.
4. *Communicate* with lay and professional people at meetings in an honest and open way, *listening* to others when they are talking.
5. Learn *committee structure*—how to present information in committees, how to follow standard procedures, how to avoid airing dirty laundry at meetings, and how to avoid prolonged meetings that often result in conflict.
6. Exhibit *professional behavior* at meetings and control their emotions; if board members show up at meetings to demand action, they should do so as individual citizens.
7. Ask good *questions,* seek clarification of issues, and follow parliamentary procedures.

B. *Board presidents need to:*

1. Ask themselves whether the meeting is *necessary*—or can the task be accomplished without a meeting, say with a memo or a telephone call.
2. State the *purpose* or agenda of the meeting in advance, or at a previous meeting, in the form of written communication.
3. Be *punctual*—come on time to meetings and begin promptly. Others will get the message.
4. Direct the flow of *discussion,* ask *questions,* encourage democratic or balanced *participation,* and be aware of *time.*
5. *Summarize* frequently, follow parliamentary *procedures,* maintain necessary *control,* and bring discussions to a satisfactory *close.*
6. Keep and publish *minutes* to ensure follow-up, monitor progress, and use as a reference.
7. Make the *superintendent* feel comfortable at meetings by not surprising her or him, not undercutting the person, and not probing too much in front of others (the latter can be done in private).

Source: Raj K. Chopra, "Making Your Meetings Matter," *Executive Educator,* 11 (1989): 23; Ron Rude, "Administration: Lessons from the Top," *American School Board Journal,* 186 (1999): 41–42; Stephen L. Kleinsmith, "What Comprises an Award-Winning Board," *School Administrator,* 62 (2005): 8; Elaine L. Wilmore, *Superintendent Leadership* (Thousand Oaks, CA: Corwin Press, 2008).

system without encroaching on the authority of the superintendent. Members have no legal authority except during a board meeting and while acting as a collective group or board.[143] Board members must be politically prudent because someone will eventually ask for a favor—a friend, a friend of a friend, or a special interest group—and this pressure should be resisted.

According to a survey of sixty-six Illinois school superintendents, school boards have become more political and divisive in recent years; board members are less willing to compromise on major issues, and there is a greater tendency among candidates to represent coalitions or special interest groups when running for election.[144] In short, new board members seem more

[143]Davis W. Campbell and Diane Greene, "Defining the Leadership Role of School Boards in the 21st Century," *Phi Delta Kappan,* 75 (1994): 391–395; Howard Good, "Governance: Then and Now," *American School Board Journal,* 185 (1998): 50–51.

[144]David Elsner, "School Boards More Political," *Chicago Tribune,* January 22, section 2, p. 4. Also see Penny Bender Sebring and Anthony S. Bryk, "School Leadership and the Bottom Line in Chicago," *Phi Delta Kappan,* 81 (2000): 440–443.

interested in the views of their electors than in the views of other board members or professional educators.

Some board members run because they have an ax to grind, a hidden agenda, or a specific educational view. Overall, fewer people want to serve on school boards. In 2005, on Long Island, New York, board members ran unopposed in about one-third of the elections. This is not uncommon in other areas.[145]

In addition, many board members do not attend training sessions. Part of the problem is that only eighteen states, mostly in the South, require training for new school board members. In these states, and in the others where training is voluntary, training sources include state school boards, state departments of education, regional service units, and universities. Superintendents feel the focus on training should be the following: (1) conducting a superintendent's search, (2) dealing with school sports, (3) dealing with members of the community, (4) resisting pressure to hire family members or firing employees they don't like, (5) understanding their roles and responsibilities, and (6) understanding legal and ethical obligations.[146]

In districts where the school board is elected, board members are subject to the same laws as other elected officials; in many states, each member must file a statement of ethics. In the final analysis, the quality of the local schools is an important factor in determining the community's reputation, the value of property, and the willingness of businesses to locate in the vicinity. Board members represent the public at large; and they must be willing to work with businesses, government, and community organizations to promote the community's schools and students' welfare.[147]

[145]Carol Chmelynski, "In Some Communities, Fewer People Are Willing to Run for the School Board," *School Board News*, 23 (2003): 7; Mark Grossman, "Wanted—School Board Candidates," *American School Board Journal*, 192 (2005): 47–53; Jack McKay and Mark Peterson, "Recruiting Board Members: Should Superintendents Have a Role in the Process? A Survey Finds Divided Results," *School Administrator*, 61 (2004): 27–29.

[146]Nicholas D. Caruso, Jr., "Teach the Board Its Proper Role," *School Administrator*, 62 (2005): 8; Gloria L. Johnston, *The Superintendent's Planner* (Thousand Oaks, CA: Corwin Press, 2008).

[147]Kathleen Vail, "The Changing Face of Education: Portrait of a School Board," *American School Board Journal*, 188 (2001): 39–42; Malia Villegas, "Leading in Difficult Times: Are Urban School Boards up to the Task?" *Policy Trends* (San Francisco, CA: WestEd, 2003).

In general, the most efficient school boards pull together as a team and get along with the superintendent. They are characterized by effectively using the strengths of each other, having confidence in each other's abilities, giving one another honest feedback about each other's performance in board matters, and generally supporting one another, especially when the "chips are down."

School Board Views on School Reform

These days it is hard to find anyone—inside or outside of education—who doesn't believe that schools need to be reformed.

Superintendents and principals are the most likely leaders of school reform, according to school board members, followed closely by school board members themselves and state departments of education. Most other players (teachers, professors, social reformers) or groups (federal agencies, community groups, or teacher associations) are not perceived as having much impact or interest in reform.

As many as 10 percent of board members characterize their own school district as "moderately" or "greatly" involved in reform—and on a grassroots basis or from local initiatives (superintendent or the board)—not from state or federal directives. More than half (58%) maintain that reform is improving the quality of education.[148]

Curriculum and instruction reforms are most prevalent in school districts: involving computer instruction (91%), programs for at-risk students (84%), foreign language instruction (84%), adoption of a common core curriculum (75%), and whole language instruction (73%). Given the current emphasis on standards and high-stake testing, we would expect more emphasis today on aligning the curriculum with state standards and tests. This is highlighted by the public's response to support a standardized national curriculum both in 1991 (69% in favor) and again when asked in 2002 (66% in favor).[149] In 2006, 47 percent of the public responded

[148]Thomas H. Gaul, Kenneth E. Underwood, and Jim C. Fortune, "Reform at the Grass Roots," *American School Board Journal*, 181 (1994): 35–38, 40; Susan Penny Gray et al., *From Good Schools to Great Schools* (Thousand Oaks, CA: Corwin Press, 2008).

[149]"The 38th Annual Phi Delta Kappa/Gallup Poll of . . . Public Schools," 47. Also see Thomas R. Guskey, "Helping Standards Make the Grade," *Educational Leadership*, 59 (2001): 20–27; Deborah Meier, "Standardization Versus Standards," *Phi Delta Kappan*, 84 (2002): 190–198.

that the current curriculum should be changed in order to meet the challenges of today. As many as 40 percent of respondents believe that every high school student should take at least one course online while in school.[150]

By 2009, more Americans had an unfavorable attitude to NCLB (48 percent) when compared to their attitude in 2007 (40 percent). Two-thirds (66 percent) were in favor of annual testing of students in grades three to eight. This number has remained constant since 2002 (67 percent). In addition, 66 percent were in favor of letting each state use its own test instead of a single, national standardized test. This number has remained fairly consistent since 2002 (68 percent).[151]

Another common reform strategy among school districts, according to board members, involves school time. Two-thirds of the school districts have modified the school calendar or clock: offering summer school (68%), offering before- and after-school study sessions (48%), extending the school day (42%), introducing flexible scheduling options (40%), and extending the school year (38%). Perhaps the only radical change is that 16 percent say their schools are on a year-round calendar.

When it comes to less traditional, more fashionable changes, only a small percentage of board members say they are embarking on reforms that involve (1) alternative assessment, (2) parental training programs, (3) student work apprenticeships, (4) school choices, (5) charter schools, (6) magnet schools, and (7) voucher systems.[152]

Budget limitations have proven to be the biggest obstacle to reform. Some 48 percent of school board members claim they don't have sufficient revenues to do what they think needs to be done. A second obstacle, as perceived by board members, are teachers and teacher associations. Not surprisingly, teacher associations perceive school board members as adversaries—hindering improved salaries and working conditions.[153]

According to the public, the top four reasons that prevent the schools in their community from "moving in the right direction" include in descending order: lack of money (71 percent); lack of community support (58 percent); lack of teacher support (53 percent); and the belief that school education is good enough already (51 percent).[154]

The irony is that while school board members perceive themselves, their superintendents, and state departments of education as vanguards of reform, they perceive teachers, scholars, and social reformers as having almost no role, responsibility, or influence in school reform. However, these latter people see school board members as an obstacle to school reform, especially in urban school districts where political and ethnic rivalries dominate board meetings and where serious questions about disbursement of funds and nepotism concerning contracts and jobs have surfaced.[155] Urban school boards are viewed as constantly being in flux and turmoil, exhibiting "a lack of skill among members in resolving conflicts and tensions both within the board and with superintendents."[156] They are also perceived as "reactive [and emotional] and for having poor relationships with state policy members" and units of general local government.[157]

Suburban, and especially rural and small-town, school boards are viewed as maintaining tradition and spending too much time dealing with administrative trivia. The suburban/rural boards generally operate in less-contentious political environments and govern with more cohesive community values; and although the board members usually have leadership experience, they are seen as representing entrenched power groups or special interests and "defending the status quo"—sometimes having as much interest in athletic and social events as in academic outcomes—or more.

---

[150]Ibid. Also see "The 37th Annual Phi Delta/Gallup Poll of . . . Public Schools," 53.

[151]The 41st Annual Phi Delta Kappa/Gallup Poll of Public Schools," *Phi Delta Kappan,* 91 (2009): 12.

[152]"The 37th [and 38th] Annual Phi Delta/Gallup Poll[s]."

[153]Lawrence Hardy, "Building Blocks of Reform," *American School Board Journal,* 186 (1999): 16–21; Donna Harrington-Lueker, "AFT Goes in Quest of School Reform," *American School Board Journal,* 178 (1991): 49; Jo Anna Natale, "NEA: Toward a More Perfect Union," *American School Board Journal,* 178 (1991): 49; Allan Odden, "The Costs of Sustaining Educational Change Through Comprehensive Reform," *Phi Delta Kappan,* 81 (2000): 433–439.

[154]The 41st Annual Phi Delta Kappa/Gallup Poll of Public Schools," *Phi Delta Kappan,* 91 (2009): 20.

[155]Larry Cuban and Michael Usdan (eds.), *Powerful Reforms With Shallow Roots* (New York: Teachers College Press, Columbia University, 2001); Frederick M. Hess, "The Urban Reform Paradox," *American School Board Journal,* 185 (1998): 24–29; Diane Ravitch, "Why Public Schools Need Democratic Governance." *Phi Delta Kappan,* 91 (2010): 24–27.

[156]Linda J. Dawson, "Coherent Governance: A Board-Superintendent Relationship Based on Defined Goals Can Raise Achievement," *School Administrator,* 61 (2004): 4; Villegas, *Leading in Difficult Times.*

[157]Frederick M. Hess, *Spinning Wheels: The Politics of Urban School Reform* (Washington, DC: Brookings Institution, 1999); Ron A. Zimbalist, *The Human Factor in Change* (Lanham, MD: Rowman & Littlefield, 2005).

According to 2008 survey data, 50 percent of the urban school board members have served up to four years; 28 percent have served between 4 and 8 years; 12 percent between 8 and 12 years; and 10 percent more than 12 years. In addition, the average urban superintendent worked in the district for 3.5 years (this is an increase from 3.1 years in 2006); 18 percent have worked in the district for 5 or more years (this is a decrease from 2006); 49 percent have worked in the district between 1 and 5 years (this is an increase from 2006); and 33 percent have worked in the district for 1 year or less (this is the same as in 2006).[158]

The outcome is that many school boards are viewed as giving lip service to reform. Without consensus and saddled by gridlock and mistrust, school boards are perceived as focusing on short-term management problems, committee intrigue, and rules of order, and responding to special-interest factions. As Philip Schlechty remarks, "Perhaps the greatest barrier to revitalizing America's schools is that too many board members view themselves as educational leaders and too few [view] themselves as moral and cultural leaders."[159]

Effective School Reform

Reformers have developed a literature on **more effective schools,** which purports that inner-city schools can successfully educate poor and minority students. Advocates in this camp pay attention to schools as an institution and the environment in which they operate, usually defined in terms of student achievement and usually focused on primary and elementary school. This emphasis corresponds with environmental research data indicating that intervention is most critical in the early stages of human development, because that is the period of most rapid cognitive growth (50 percent by age 4, another 25 percent by age 9 according to Bloom).[160]

Given that the early years are so formative, it would be wise for the nation to commit to the care and education of its young and to make it compulsory, especially for "at-risk" and poor children, in order to prepare them for or catch them up to grade level when they enter school. A few states such as Massachusetts, Vermont, and West Virginia are providing comprehensive programs for infants and toddlers, and the federal government in 2000 provided $3.5 billion in block grants to states to provide some child-care services and assist working women with children (73 percent of women between ages 25 and 34 are in the workforce.)[161] The outcomes are piecemeal and inadequate; we need more like $12 billion, twice the appropriations for Head Start, to ensure that all our nation's poor or at-risk children are receiving appropriate services and education.

The advent of school nutrition programs; extended-day, weekend, and required preschool programs; required summer school for primary students (grades 1–3); to neutralize cognitive deficits as opposed to allowing them to increase; reading and tutoring programs, and parenting education, as well as making class size and schools smaller, are all considered crucial.[162] The instruction that is recommended is prescriptive and diagnostic; emphasis is on basic-skill acquisition, review and guided practice, monitoring of student programs, providing prompt feedback and reinforcement to students, and mastery-learning opportunities.[163] All of these instructional methods suggest a behaviorist, direct, convergent,

[158] *Urban School Board Survey: Characteristics, Structure, and Benefits* (Washington, DC: Council of the Great City Schools 2009), pp. 5–6.

[159] Philip C. Schlechty, "Deciding the Fate of Local Control," *American School Board Journal,* 179 (1992): 28. Also see Philip C. Schlechty, *Shaking Up the Schoolhouse* (San Francisco: Jossey-Bass, 2000).

[160] Benjamin S. Bloom, *Stability and Change in Human Characters* (New York: Wiley, 1964).

[161] Elena Bodrova and Deborah J. Leong, "Uniquely Preschool," *Educational Leadership,* 63 (2005): 44–47; Sharon L. Kagan and Lynda G. Hallmark, "Early Care and Education Policies in Sweden: Implications for the United States," *Phi Delta Kappan,* 83 (2001): 237–245, 254; Sally Lubeck, "Early Childhood Education and Care in Cross National Perspective," *Phi Delta Kappan,* 83 (2001): 213–215.

[162] Lorin Anderson and Leonard O. Pellicer, "Synthesis of Research Compensatory and Remedial Education," *Education Leadership,* 48 (1990): 10–16; Allan C. Ornstein and Daniel U. Levine, "School Effectiveness and Reform: Guidelines for Action," *Clearing House,* 63 (1990): 115–118; William C. Symonds, "How to Fix America's Schools," *Business Week,* 19 March 2001, pp. 68–80. Also see Donald L. Rollie, *The Keys to Effective Schools* (Thousand Oaks, CA: Corwin Press, 2002). Georgia was the first state to require pre-K programs for all four-year-olds in the state. The authors would start with toddler programs at age three.

[163] Linda Darling-Hammond and Olivia Ifill-Lynch, "If They'd Only Do Their Work," *Educational Leadership,* 63 (2006): 8–13; Daniel U. Levine and Allan C. Ornstein, "Research on Classroom and School Effectiveness and Its Implications for Improving Big-City Schools," *Urban Review,* 21 (1989): 81–95; Allan C. Ornstein and Daniel U. Levine, "Urban School Effectiveness and Improvement," *Illinois School and Research Development,* 71 (1991): 111–117.

systematic, and low cognitive level of instruction as opposed to a problem-solving, abstract, divergent, inquiry-based, and high level of instruction. (Some critics would argue this type of instruction is second-rate and reflects our low expectations of low-achieving students.)

The fact is that schools with high concentrations of poor students are usually overloaded with enormous problems, ranging from (1) inexperienced and uncertified teachers, poor morale, and working conditions; (2) children who cannot read at grade level or control themselves in class; (3) children deprived of sleep, food, and basic health care; and (4) children victimized by drugs, gangs, crime, and teenage pregnancy. All that is needed is a critical mass of poor students, about 25 to 30 percent, and the values and behaviors of this group will take over and prevail in the school.[164] There is a threshold where the climate or ethos of a school deteriorates due to the attitudes and behavior of students. There is also a point when schools cannot have much positive impact (i.e., Coleman, Jencks, Duncan, Moynihan, Hanushek thesis), and other social or psychological factors (i.e., family, peer group, community, socioeconomic status, students' motivation, personality, and prior achievement) become more critical in determining academic outcomes. Indeed the "rags to riches" story has real significance for many immigrant groups, but it remains largely a fable for those immersed in the "culture of poverty."

The United States provides real potential for upward mobility that is unusual by international standards,[165] but the advantages to the middle class and upper class are more numerous and noticeable. This will always be the case unless we wish to socialize society and redistribute income. Depending on whose figures you accept, 21 to 25 percent of American students live in poverty[166]—most of them in a "culture of poverty," from one generation to the next. Writes one author, "We have put great faith in public schools to enhance social mobility and equality. Suggestions or evidence that this part of the American dream is at risk or in decline is at best disquieting to Americans and often produces controversial debates among intellectuals and policymakers. But those who live on the downside of advantage are more often destined to remain at the bottom of the heap."[167]

In order to neutralize skeptical and conservative attitudes about the minimal influence of schooling, reformers have developed a literature on more effective schools, which claims that inner-city schools successfully educate poor and minority students. Advocates in their camp pay attention to the school environment, teacher attitudes and behaviors, principal leadership—and usually define "success" in terms of student achievement and usually focus on preschool and elementary schools. In a review of six cities, for example, Paul Hill concludes that for schools to become more effective, they need to (1) define and use a consistent plan based on a particular philosophy or pedagogy so that teachers are clear on aims, goals, and strategies, (2) encourage parental and family engagement in their children's schooling, and (3) increase teacher responsibility for improving their own teaching practices and engagement in innovation. On a more theoretical level, Hill recommends that staff members from effective schools be permitted "to charge for help and advice given to other schools" in the district,[168] thus enhancing performance incentives and professionalism.

With the exception of **compensatory programs** such as reading or tutoring, the more effective school approach suggests very little additional cost and depends more on leadership of the principal, as well as the attitudes, motivation, and responsibility of the teachers, parents, and students. Money does not seem to be the answer; in fact, failure becomes a rationale to demand more money. The approach is not piecemeal, or perceived as part of the compensatory movement (which costs billions of dollars). The focus is on a macro level—the entire school, not a specific program or specific teacher. The need is to analyze, modify, and improve the roles, values, and beliefs of all those concerned with

---

[164]This tipping point is rooted in the studies of social class by Allison Davis, Robert Havinghurst, and Lloyd Warner in the 1940s and 1950s; in the studies of equality by Samuel Bowles, Herbert Gans, and Frederick Mosteller in the 1960s and 1970s; and in the ethnographic studies of Phillip Cusick, Elizabeth Eddy, and Sara Lawrence Lightfoot in the 1980s and 1990s.

[165]Richard C. Leone, "Forward." In R.D. Kahlenberg (ed.), *A Nation at Risk: Preserving Public Education as an Engine for Social Mobility* (New York: Century Foundation, 2000), pp. v–viii.

[166]Harold Hodgkinson, "Educational Demographics: What Teachers Should Know," *Educational Leadership* (January 2001): pp. 6–11; Lynn Olson and Greg F. Orlofsky, "2000 and Beyond: The Changing Face of American Schools," *Education Week,* September 28, 2000, pp. 30–38. Also see Richard Rothstein, *Class and Schools* (New York: Teachers College Press, 2004).

[167]Allan C. Ornstein, *Teaching and Schooling in America: Pre- and Post-September 11* (Boston: Allyn & Bacon, 2003): 459.

[168]Paul Hill, "Good Schools for Big-City Children," Research Paper published by the Brookings Institution, Washington, DC, November 2000.

the teaching and learning process. According to the current education secretary, Arne Duncan, "the success of school reform still depends on the vision, commitment, and resources that a mayor can bring to bear, working in tandem with the superintendent and appointees to the board. It takes more than a school to educate a student."[169]

Probably the most important factor in more effective schools is a strong *principal* with conviction, zeal, and a clear mission who can stretch budgets and get more out of people than might be expected. Second, there is a need for hardworking and dedicated *teachers* who expect students to learn. Next, *parents* must accept their responsibilities in providing support structures and a home environment that is conducive to proper socialization, personal growth, and learning. Finally, *students* must be held responsible for their actions and must accept that it takes self-control, self-reliance, no excuses, no laying blame on others, and not expecting a free ride to achieve academic success. It needs to be reemphasized that time-on-task, completing homework, review and practice, and studying are basic ingredients for academic success. This simply translates into Thomas Sowell's concept of hard work, or what Admiral Rickover, fifty years ago, and Thomas Edison, some seventy-five years ago, called "perspiration."

The School Superintendent

One of the board's most important responsibilities is to appoint a competent superintendent of schools. The superintendent is the executive officer of the school system, whereas the board is the legislative policymaking body. Because the school board consists of laypeople who are not experts in school affairs, it is their responsibility to see that the work of the school is properly performed by professional personnel. The board of education often delegates many of its own legal powers to the superintendent and his staff, although the superintendent's policies are subject to board approval.

The Superintendent's Job

One of the major functions of the school superintendent is to gather and present data so that school board members can make intelligent policy decisions. Increasing board reliance on the superintendent and staff is evident as school districts grow. The superintendent advises the school board and keeps members abreast of problems; generally, the school board will refuse to make policy without the recommendation of the school superintendent. However, it is common knowledge that when there is continued disagreement or a major conflict over policy between the school board and the superintendent, the latter is usually replaced.

According to survey data, the average tenure of superintendents is approximately 5.5 years. The average tenure for a superintendent in a small district is 6 years, while the average tenure of a superintendent in a large district is 4 years;[170] for Great City Superintendents (66 big-city schools/districts), the average tenure increased from 2.5 years in 2001 to 3.5 years in 2008. According to school board members, the ideal superintendent's contract should last two to three years (and then be open for renewal). The majority of superintendents move around every few years seeking "greener pastures." More than 50 percent of the 13,800 superintendents were expected to retire between 1998 and 2008;[171] hence, the opportunity to become a chief school executive is increasing as we move forward into the twenty-first century. In fact, in a recent survey it was found that 33 percent of Great City superintendents were freshmen superintendents.[172]

Although a wealth of data exists on what makes a school principal effective, there is little information on what makes a superintendent effective and to what extent, if any, the superintendent contributes to teacher effectiveness or student performance. This dearth of information is probably related to the fact that the superintendent is considered a manager of the entire district, not a direct leader of curriculum, instruction, teaching, or learning.

---

[169] Arne Duncan, "Education Secretary Arne Duncan: The Importance of Board and Mayor Partnerships," *American School Board Journal*, 196 (2009): 30–31.

[170] "Highlights of Administrators' Survey," *Education Week*, 20 January 1988, p. 23; *Tenure of Urban School Superintendents Almost Five Years* (Alexandria, VA: National School Boards Association, 2002).

[171] Council of the Great City Schools, *Urban School Superintendents: Characteristics, Tenure, and Salary* (Washington, DC: The Council, 2009); *Professional Standards for the Superintendency* (Arlington, VA: American Association of School Administrators, 2009).

[172] Allan C. Ornstein, "School Superintendents and School Board Members: Who They Are," *Education Week*, November 1990, p. 5. Also see John R. Hoyle et al., *The Superintendent as CEO* (Thousand Oaks, CA: Corwin Press, 2005); Council of the Great City Schools, *Urban School Superintendents*.

The superintendent's powers are broad, and duties are many and varied. Besides being an advisor to the board of education, the superintendent is usually responsible for certain functions:

1. Serves as supervisor and organizer of professional and nonteaching personnel (e.g., janitors and engineers).
2. Makes recommendations regarding the employment, promotion, and dismissal of personnel.
3. Ensures compliance with directives of higher authority.
4. Prepares the school budget for board review and administers the adopted budget.
5. Serves as leader of long-range planning.
6. Develops and evaluates curriculum and instructional program.
7. Determines internal organization of the school district.
8. Makes recommendations regarding school building needs and maintenance.[173]

In addition, the superintendent is responsible for the day-to-day operation of the schools within the district and serves as the major public spokesperson for the schools.

Superintendents are often under strong pressure from various segments of the community, and much of the superintendent's effectiveness will depend on his ability to deal with such pressure groups. In large, urban school districts, for example, demands may be made for better facilities for students with handicaps or learning disabilities, more bilingual programs, improved vocational education, and school desegregation. In middle-class suburbs, parents may be especially sensitive to student achievement scores, demanding upgraded academic programs if they feel the education is not as superior as their children deserve. Such students are often overprogrammed and overstressed, and a confident school leader is needed to balance the demands and expectations of the parents with the sociopsychological needs of the students. In small or rural districts where enrollments are declining, the superintendent may be pressured, on one hand, to save money by closing schools and, on the other hand, to keep all schools open to preserve the pride and identity of the community. Given the politics, policies, and pressures of the job at the community and state levels, "the superintendent must never lose sight that the ultimate client is the student," asserts former New York deputy superintendent Robert Brasco.[174] Educational administration courses fall short in this area because the emphasis is on leadership, management, organizational theory, school finance and law—not on the needs or interests of the students.

Up the Professional Ladder

Although it takes a mixture of hard work, luck, and political savvy, moving from district to district is usually the quickest way to move up the career ladder—especially if the district is small and the superintendency is your goal. Otherwise, you will sit in the same place for years waiting for someone to retire or die, with the possibility of being passed over because of a new boss or school board. Of course, there are more openings in larger school districts, and in a recent report 39 percent of new superintendents in districts with more than 25,000 students said they had come up from within the district, compared to 29 percent in smaller districts.[175]

The path to the superintendency usually consists of two major roads: 49 percent take the teacher–principal–central office route and 31 percent travel the teacher–principal route (43 states require superintendents to have education training and be former educators). All other roads to the top are secondary, as shown in Table 9–8, although 61 percent stopped off at the central office for a while before becoming superintendents. Most associate superintendents or superintendents land their first administrative job before age thirty (assistant principal or principal), and most make

[173]William E. Eaton, *Shaping the Superintendency* (New York: Teachers College Press, Columbia University, 1990); John R. Hoyle et al. *The Superintendent as CEO* (Thousand Oaks, CA: Corwin Press, 2005); and Rene S. Townsend et al., *Effective Superintendent-School Board Practices* (Thousand Oaks, CA: Corwin Press, 2006).

[174]Robert Brasco, former Deputy Superintendent, Community District #32, New York City; personal communication, March 16, 2007.

[175]Thomas E. Glass, et al., *The Study of American School Superintendents* (Arlington, VA: American Association of School Administrators, 2000); Hess, *School Boards at the Dawn of the 21st Century*, table 17, p. 22; Lance D. Fusarelli and Barbara L. Jackson, "How Do We Find and Retain Superintendents?" *School Administrator*, 61 (2004): 56.

Table 9-8 Paths to the Superintendency

49%	Teacher, Principal, Central Office
31%	Teacher, Principal
9%	Teacher, Central Office
2%	Teacher only
2%	Principal, Central Office
2%	Principal only
1%	Central Office only
4%	Not reported

Source: Thomas E. Glass, et al., *The Study of the American School Superintendency* (Alexandria, VA: American Association of School Administrators, 2000), table 6.20, p. 86.

the decision to become superintendent while serving as a school principal.[176]

The first superintendent job is considered the hardest. It involves many job searches, interviewing skills, and matching personal experience and style with school district needs and expectations, to compensate for lack of experience as a superintendent. The more mobility someone has, the better the chances. The number-one barrier limiting administrative opportunities relates to lack of mobility of family members (21% for males; 41% for females.)[177] Perhaps for this reason, 80 percent of the superintendents report remaining in one state for their entire career.[178] Female superintendents are making the most progress, up from 2.8 percent in 1984, 4.5 percent in 1990, and 16.5 percent in 1998, and 21.7 percent is 2006. They still have a way to go until they are equitably represented.[179]

Having a doctorate is important: 41 percent of the nation's superintendents possess this degree, and today there are more women than men enrolled in educational administration doctoral programs. Because of burnout, retirement, and the usual turnover among experienced superintendents, the demand for new superintendents is expected to increase. And because of the gender breakdown among administrative doctoral candidates, we expect a continued increase in female superintendents, especially black females in big-city school districts. As of 2008, 34 percent of big-city superintendents (Great City Schools) were female (20% were black, 12% were white, and 2% were Hispanic or Asian).[180]

For 2015, the projections are 50 to 55 percent female big-city superintendents. The "old boy network" has been eroding since the 1990s; just count the number of female superintendents profiled by Jay Goldman, editor of *School Administrator.*[181] And although 10 percent of the nation's superintendents are minority, within the larger 100 school districts the percentage is more than 35 percent, and within the sixty-six Great City School districts the minority percentage is 52.[182]

Each school district is unique, as is each superintendent. But once you have landed the job, your challenges begin! Peter Negroni, former superintendent of the Springfield public schools, Massachusetts, recommends several job strategies:

1. *Watch Your Image.* Be aware of how the board and the public perceive you. The image you create the first three to six months will most likely stick with you.
2. *Find Out About Your Predecessor.* The former superintendent's attitudes and behaviors left a mark on the office. Find out what the people didn't like about him or her, and make it a point not to repeat those mistakes.

176Glass et al., *The Study of American School Superintendents,* tables 6.20, 6.23, pp. 85–86; Frederick M. Hess, *Common Sense School Reform* (Gordonville, VA: Palgrave, 2006); Yong-Lynn Kun and C. Cryss Brunner, "School Administrators' Career Mobility to the Superintendency.' *Journal of Educational Administration,* 47(2009): 75–107.

177Glass et al., *The Study of American School Superintendents,* table 6.28, p. 88.

178Thomas E. Glass, "Superintendent Leaders Look at the Superintendency," Paper issued by the Education *Commission of the States,* Denver, July 2001.

179Joyce A. Dana and Diana M. Bourisaw, *Women in the Superintendency* (Lanham, MD: Rowman & Littlefield, 2006); "Memo to Women: You're Making Progress," *Executive Educator,* 14 (1992): 18; Hess, *School Boards at the Dawn of the 21st Century,* p. 22; Marilyn Tallerico and Joan N. Burstyn, "Retaining Women in the Superintendency," *Educational Administration Quarterly,* 56 (1999): 642–664. *The Study of the American School Superintendency: A Mid-Decade Study* (Alexandria, VA: American Association of School administrators, 2006).

180*Urban Indicator* (Washington, DC: Council of Great City Schools, 2008), p. 5.

181See Jay Goldman's "Profile" series. Between 2000 and 2003, 35 percent of the profiles were women superintendents. Also see Robert R. Spillane and Paul Regnier, *The Superintendent of the Future* (Annapolis, MD: Aspen, 1998).

182Jay Mathews, "On the Job Training of Nontraditional Superintendents," *School Administrator,* 56 (1999): 28–33; Rosemary Henze et al., *Leading for Diversity* (Thousand Oaks, CA: Corwin Press, 2002); Ornstein, "School Superintendents and School Board Members: Who They Are"; Council of the Great City Schools, *Urban School Superintendents; Urban Indicator.*

3. *Don't Bite Off More Than You Can Chew.* Don't take the job if you find it is too stressful or full of political minefields that you feel you cannot navigate.
4. *Keep Focused.* Keep track of your progress toward certain goals.
5. *Build a Positive Relationship with the School Board.* This requires constant attention and communication, knowledge of changing issues and hidden agendas, and familiarity with the personalities of the board members.
6. *Improve Your Relations with the Public and the Media.* The local press can vilify or champion your cause. Learn to define an issue in public in 30 seconds or less.
7. *Don't Be a Loner.* You cannot run a school district locked in your office. Get out to the schools and community.[183]

One board member in Newbury, Massachusetts, links the superintendent's success with the school budget. Despite previous increases in state aid, board members everywhere are now struggling with spiraling costs, painful cutbacks, and the need to streamline programs and staff. As superintendent, you must deal with fiscal reality and recommend cuts without major harm to the basic educational program. Cutting sports programs is an emotional issue; avoid it if possible. Trimming the transportation and maintenance budgets is easier and more common. Unessential programs such as elective courses, extracurricular activities, and special services are more acceptable than the academic basics. Rather than reducing or freezing teachers' salaries, it is better to cut teacher preparation periods, classroom aides, and professional travel or in-service programs; to increase student–teacher ratios by 1 or 2; and to let attrition and retirement take its course without hiring as many teacher replacements. Most important, involve the community in budget priorities and fundraising to pick up some of the slack.[184]

[183]Peter J. Negroni, "Landing the Big Job," *Executive Educator,* 14 (1992): 21–23; Negroni, "The Right Badge of Courage," *School Administrator,* 56 (1999): 14–17; Priscilla Pardini, "Ethics in the Superintendency," *School Administrator,* 61 (2004): 10–19.

[184]Don Davies, "The 10th School Revisited: Are School/Family/Community Partnerships on the Reform Agenda Now?" *Phi Delta Kappan,* 83 (2002): 388–392; Joyce L. Epstein, "Creating School, Family, Community Partnerships," in A. C. Ornstein et al., *Contemporary Issues in Curriculum,* 3rd ed. (Boston: Allyn & Bacon, 2003): 354–373.

Politics influence the superintendent's leadership role. Some superintendents are hired to implement change: "reform," "restructure," "innovate." And others are hired to maintain the status quo. In still other cases, reform is "tolerated," such as responses to state or court mandates, but the underlining or private order is to go slow. The turnover rate among superintendents is high. In one study by Thomas Glass, 64 percent of school districts reported having three or more superintendents in the last ten years. And 23 percent of the districts indicated asking the previous superintendent to leave, not renewing or buying out the person's contract.[185] The turnover among big-city superintendents is well known and largely associated with politics and ethnic controversy. As many as 82 percent of the superintendents in the largest school districts have held the job for five years or less, in comparison to 64 percent in 2001.[186] Not only must superintendents have administrative experience, they must also be politically savvy in their responses to board members and the public, as well as to various pressure groups. You must understand the community and treat most educational issues in a political context.

Former successful urban superintendents offer the following advice: "(1) The main thing is to maintain student achievement as the primary objective, (2) if what you are doing does not improve what happens in classrooms between teachers and students, it is probably not worth doing, (3) conflict is the price you pay for leadership, (4) listen to the people around you, and (5) making permanent change means changing the things that are permanent."[187]

Probably the only saving grace of the job is that the superintendent has the luxury of time and the option to consult with others before making most critical decisions. This is quite different from the situation of the school principal, who is always on the firing line and must make decisions on the spot, often without consulting with the next level of the bureaucratic hierarchy.

[185]Thomas E. Glass, "School Board Presidents and Their View of the Superintendency." Paper issued by the Education Commission of the States, Denver, CO: May 2002. Also see David E. Lee, "Landmines in the Pathway of the Superintendency," *School Administrator,* 63 (2006): 47.

[186]Council of the Great City Schools, *Urban School Superintendents,* 2009.

[187]Council of the Great City Schools, *The Urban Superintendent: Creating Great Schools While Surviving on the Job* (Washington, DC: The Council, 2003).

Eventually, the job comes down to "management of our schools," asserts Franklin Smith, the former superintendent of the Washington, DC, schools, and "learning from the experience of others, exploring various options," and integrating new ideas into a system of management. "We must look to the vast resources of community"—its people, businesses, and institutions—to contribute to the education of our students. The school cannot do the job alone. "We are out of tricks," adds Smith.[188] All superintendents, new and experienced, need to rethink education and to look for outside help and partnerships with groups that have a vested interest in education.

Robert Brasco, who was New York City deputy superintendent for eleven years, believes in teamwork, but the ultimate decision rests with the superintendent, "the person at the top is going to take the 'rap,' if the decision is wrong. Michael Corleone, of the *Godfather*, would agree with this perspective, and so would General Patton."[189] Shared decision making is nice, but it has its limitations for the person who is ultimately responsible for the school district.

Superintendents' Problems and Performance

Major reasons why superintendents ultimately come under attack or resign can be classified into ten problem areas:

1. Too many board members who want to run the show; that is, too many people think they are "presidents."
2. Budget cuts, accompanied by a shrinking tax base.
3. Increasing amounts of reports and paperwork to meet government or legal requirements.
4. Dissension among school board members.
5. Declining enrollments matched with increasing expenditures.
6. Taxpayers' resistance to supporting education.
7. Teacher strikes and militancy.
8. Special interest groups that persistently promote their own causes.
9. Student crime and vandalism as well as discipline problems.
10. News media reportage that is erroneous or controversial.[190]

Although only two reasons (1 and 4) are directly linked to the school board, two others are related to community factors (2 and 6), which in turn have a ripple effect on board members who represent the community.

The typical conflict between superintendents and school board members usually involves political agendas and different philosophies or values. Typically, the stage is set when two or more school board incumbents are challenged and unseated; this is an indicator of community dissatisfaction that can be easily transferred to the superintendent's office.[191] Increasingly, new board members are being elected on a single-issue platform or by a special interest group—a situation that is likely to cause conflict with the superintendent. When community demographics rapidly change and are accompanied by a new advocacy group or by demands for a change in the superintendent—one who is more relevant, more sensitive, or more in line with new demands—it's time to look at other options. The situation boils down to politics and has nothing to do with performance or ability.[192]

The idea is to control the conditions under which the superintendent leaves, not to fight a losing battle or try to enlist a special interest group and split the community. When a superintendent does battle with the school board, students, parents, and community members lose as frustrations, emotions, and charges run rampant.

---

[188]Franklin L. Smith, "The Outside Opinion," *American School Board Journal,* 181 (1994): 42.

[189]Robert Brasco, former deputy superintendent, Community District #32, New York City; personal communication, January 29, 2007; May 18, 2010.

[190]Dale Brubaker, *The Charismatic Leader* (Thousand Oaks, CA: Corwin Press, 2005); Sidney A. Freund, "Superintendent: Here's How I Stay Friends with the Board President," *American School Board Journal,* 175 (1998), 39–40; Jack Kaufhold, "Lessons not Taught in Superintendents' School," *School Administrator,* 60 (2003): 36.

[191]Alan K. Gaynor, *Analyzing Problems in Schools and School Systems* (Mahwah, NJ: Erlbaum, 1998); John R. Hoyle, *Leadership and Factoring,* 2nd ed. (Thousand Oaks, CH: Corwin Press, 2007); Frank W. Lutz and Carol Merz, *The Politics of School/Community Relations* (New York: Teachers College Press, Columbia University, 1992).

[192]Andrew K. Davis, "The Politics of Barking and the State of Our Schools," *Phi Delta Kappan,* 82 (2001): 786–789; Priscilla Pardini, "When Termination's in the Air," *School Administrator,* 55 (1998): 6–12; Michael Rist, "Race and Politics Rip into the Urban Superintendency," *Executive Educator,* 47 (1990): 23–25. Also see Kenneth A. Strike, *Ethical Leadership in Schools* (Thousand Oaks, CA: Corwin Press, 2006).

And when a superintendent leaves a district, whether by quitting or being fired, the school and community, the students, teachers, and staff lose considerable continuity and progress toward sustainable reform.[193]

Although school boards have stated procedures for evaluating superintendents, too often the procedure is not technically valid, reliable, or useful, and it may result in turning the evaluation process into whatever board members decide to make of it. In theory, the superintendent's evaluation is not complicated; it should be based on precise *criteria* (agreed-on behaviors or competencies) and a method of *measurement* (such as a rating scale, observations, letters, or self-appraisal reports).

Board members, working with or independent of the superintendent, can determine the priorities, behaviors, or responsibilities they wish to stress. Nine major areas of responsibility, with equal weight, were originally adopted by the American Association of School Administrators (AASA) in 1980. They were (1) board relations, (2) community relations, (3) staff personnel management, (4) fiscal management, (5) facilities management, (6) curriculum and instruction, (7) student services, (8) planning, and (9) professional development. The nine categories, each with several subcategories, remained major criteria for evaluating superintendents for twenty years. In fact, Marion Hunt, who was in charge of disseminating the instrument for the AASA, contended that the demand for the instrument was high among school board members and school superintendents throughout the 1990s.[194]

According to Hess, the relationship with the school board, the morale of system teachers and administrators, and the safety of district students are the top three factors that school boards examine in evaluating the superintendent.[195] School districts also have adopted superintendent evaluation systems that coincide with or include (1) state standards for improving student achievement, (2) the direction and goals of the school board, (3) the superintendent's personal/professional goals for the year, (4) a collaborative goal-setting arrangement between the superintendent and school board, and (5) merit pay or performance bonuses. Board members are divided almost evenly between whether pay for performance of superintendents is likely to increase student achievement.[196]

The key to the evaluation process is to collect data from several sources, including major client groups within the school district: board members, central administrators, community leaders, and parents (or parent groups). The advantage of a client-based or stakeholder-based evaluation instrument is that it has public relations value among board members, staff, and community members because they have been included in the process. Not only does it help head off potential problems because of its openness and inclusion, but also a hostile board would have difficulty building a case by itself for dismissal because the superintendent is being judged by many more people besides the board members.

Of course, when termination is around the corner, the evaluation instrument will most likely be used as a paper trail to accelerate the dismissal process. These days, being forced out as superintendent rarely carries a stigma or spells the end of a professional career, because dismissal is an occupational hazard of the position.[197] It is prudent, however, to leave on a voluntary basis, before the bell sounds: to move on to a larger or better-financed school district, with bigger challenges and a bigger salary and benefit package. Of course, happy endings do not always occur.

The Central Staff

The superintendent is assisted by a **central office staff.** In large districts of 25,000 or more students, there may be many levels in the staff hierarchy: a deputy superintendent, associate superintendents, assistant superintendents, directors, department heads, and a number of coordinators and supervisors, each with supporting staff members. The picture is further complicated when a large school district decentralizes its operation into several areas or subdistricts; there may be a "field"

---

[193]Negroni, "The Right Badge of Courage"; Larry Nyland, "The Shortcut Search: What to Do When You Need to Hire a Superintendent—Now," *American School Board Journal,* 185 (1998): 48–49.

[194]Marion Hunt, AASA Director of Membership Services, personal communication, June 24, 1999; December 1, 2002.

[195]Hess, *School Boards at the Dawn of the 21st Century,* p. 23.

[196]Larry Lashway, "Instruments for Evaluation," *School Administrator,* 55 (1998): 14–20; Scott Lafee, "Pay for Performance," *School Administrator,* 56 (1999); 18–23; Sharon Rallis et al. "Superintendents in Classrooms: From Collegial Conversation to Collaborative Action," *Phi Delta Kappan,* 87 (2006): 537–545; Don Senti and Linda A. Smith, "A Client-Based System for Superintendent Evaluations," *School Administrator,* 55 (1998): 44–45.

[197]Gordon Ambach "Leadership Education for the 'Fortune 300' of Education," *Phi Delta Kappan,* 87 (2006): 519–520; Linda Chion-Kenny, "The Perils of Pension Partiality," *School Administrator,* 55 (1998): 24–27; Pardini, "When Termination's in the Air."

ADMINISTRATIVE ADVICE 9–3

Considering a Promotion to the Central Office?

Many successful principals are lured into central office positions and view the move as a promotion in terms of status and salary. Before considering the move, especially if you are successful and happy as principal, read between the lines in the job description, visit the central office, and speak to trusted central office colleagues. Some important questions to consider are the following:

- What does the word *coordinate* or *direct* actually mean?
- Does the word *supervise* ever appear in the job description? What are the ramifications?
- What is the superintendent's perception of my job?
- Will I have line authority for decision making, or will I be only a facilitator?
- Will I provide a genuine professional service to the educational process, or is the job best defined as a district "gofer"?
- Will I be directly involved in budget preparation and budget allocations?
- What are my roles and responsibilities involving the community, staff, curriculum, and planning?
- Will my leadership role make a difference in school improvement, reform, or restructuring of the schools within the district?
- What does the statement "other duties as assigned by the superintendent" really mean?
- What is the overall mission or objective of the position? Does it have ongoing tasks and responsibilities included, or are many of them short-term or terminal tasks?
- Are there other benefits beyond those enjoyed by the principalship in the new job?

superintendent, with his or her own staff (as well as other administrators) in each area who in turn reports to an associate superintendent in the central office. Although the idea of decentralization and on-site management is to reform and streamline the system, what often happens is that the school district gets a new bureaucratic layer.

Most large school districts are highly centralized. The key issue is power and control. Central staff matrices are often built on top of other matrices, each with its own functions that are jealously guarded. (See Administrative Advice 9–3.) Decisions that should take days or weeks often take months or even years, as each department conducts its own review and adds its own recommendations to be considered by the next level. This phenomenon is typical not only of large school districts but also of large corporations, which have had to learn some tough lessons about inefficiency and have recently trimmed and streamlined top layers to save money.[198] In an era of retrenchment, school administrators may have to learn the same lesson. To be sure, there is a recent trend to push decisions closer to the school site and level of implementation.

Large Districts: Increased Central Offices

Large, urban districts have tended to expand their centralized staff and activities over recent years in order to administer court-ordered policies and state and federal guidelines, programs, and funds and to cope with union-style teacher associations. All these trends, according to one recent study, lead to elaborate bureaucratic efforts, in which central office personnel are hired to oversee these efforts.[199] In addition, when there is a changing of the guard at the top level in large school districts, new managers are sometimes brought in from outside and/or others are promoted from within. The old guard or outgroup often are career administrators with tenure. They are not replaced but reassigned; thus,

[198] Dale L. Brubaker and Larry D. Coble, *The Hidden Leader* (Thousand Oaks, CA: Corwin Press, 2005); Thomas Moore, "Goodbye, Corporate Staff," *Fortune*, December 21, 1987, pp. 65, 68, 76; Robert R. Spillane and Paul Regnier, "A World Apart: Decision Making in the Public and Private Sectors," *School Administrator*, 55 (1998): 20–23.

[199] Peter Flynn, "Ready, Set, Decide!" *School Administrator*, 55 (1998): 14–18; Jack Frymier, "Bureaucracy and the Neutering of Teachers," *Phi Delta Kappan*, 69 (1987): 9–14; Elizabeth A. Herbert, *The Boss of the Whole School* (New York Teachers College Press, Columbia University, 2006).

the central staff continues to grow. Similarly, school principals who are displaced because of community politics or pressures often find refuge at the central office in a new quasi-administrative clerical position, and their seniority and tenure are protected.[200]

Economics or efficiency is not always the key issue in large, urban districts; rather, school politics and ethnic considerations often affect who gets hired or fired. To support the bloated bureaucracy, school districts sometimes waste money and hire consulting firms to claim that the bureaucracy is needed and that administrator-teacher or administrator–student ratios are within tolerant ranges, by selecting and comparing school districts elsewhere that are just as top heavy or more so at the central level. In short, the central administration gets the results it wants, since it is paying the consultant; it's a matter of spelling out the particulars.[201]

Only when the money runs out, enrollments are drastically down, and the community is looking to put a lid on spending will school board officials look to topple school administrators or take other saving measures. However, many school districts will consolidate facilities, close down schools, and/or cut teaching positions before they trim down the central office staff.[202] New York City's budget trimming for 2003 represents the most dramatic reduction of central administrators in the nation's school history: in one year some 550 central administrators' jobs were eliminated as part of a $200 million budget cut for the school district. The 550 administrators who were laid off represent 21 percent of the district's central administrators.[203]

A centralized authority is characteristic of school districts that have a tall hierarchy and an increased specialization of professional tasks. In a centralized system, important decisions can be made quickly with few personnel involved. A decentralized authority suggests a flat hierarchy and/or several school sites that are considered part of a particular subdistrict or area. Upper management must be willing to work through subordinates in a decentralized system. However, subordinate power is only temporary, as long as the person has the title or until the job or task is completed. Many superintendents (as well as associates or assistants) are turf-conscious and are reluctant to part with their authority.

Small Districts: Understaffed Central Offices

Small school districts, and especially rural ones, face almost the opposite dilemma. They tend to be understaffed at the central level to the extent that superintendents, and whatever assistant superintendents or directors there are, often seem overworked and involved in many areas of responsibility, which they lack time to adequately perform. As one superintendent (twenty years experience) of a small school district in Pennsylvania stated: "Owing to skimpy staffing in central offices, many school chiefs do the work of several administrators. Eventually, they are unable to distance themselves from day-to-day tasks [and lose sight of] the big picture." The problem of not enough time for small school superintendents and their central staff "is real," and some of these administrators become "isolated and frustrated" by all their chores.[204]

Jack Lortz wound up at the end of the world—Fossil, Oregon, population 430, student enrollment 100. As superintendent, his tasks included grading English papers, proofreading the student newspaper, supervising the lunchroom and schoolyard, making coffee, putting up bulletin boards in the hall, and filling the soda machine. He classified some of his tasks as "menial, sometimes quirky," but as a good trooper he also felt they were "necessary . . . and bread and butter [for] running school districts in rural America."[205]

Some districts are so small (almost 20 percent have fewer than 300 students and another 26 percent have between 300 and 1000 students)[206] that the superintendent is allotted only one or two assistants (sometimes on a part-time level). In still other cases, the

---

[200]Priscilla Ahlgren, "An Overabundance of Decision Makers?" *Milwaukee Journal,* July 30, 1990, pp. 1, 5; Fred Hess, "Who'll Replace Retiring School Leaders," *American School Board Journal,* 175 (1988): 43–48; John R. Hoyle and Robert O. Slater, "The Role of Educational Leadership in the 21st Century," *Phi Delta Kappan,* 82 (2001): 790–794.

[201]Vickie Bane and Kay Pride, "The $325 Million Bargain," *American School Board Journal,* 180 (1993): 24–28; Carol Peek and Dee Ann Spencer, "Getting the Results You Want," *School Administrator,* 55 (1998): 17–23; Garnett J. Smith, "The Consultant from Oz Syndrome," *School Administrator,* 55 (1998): 30–35.

[202]Allan C. Ornstein, "Trimming the Fat, Stretching the Meat for School Budgets," *School Administrator,* 46 (1989): 20–21; Ornstein, "School Budgets for the 1990s," *Educational Digest,* 55 (1990): 15–16; Randi Weingarten, "Pink Hearts, Not Pink Slips," *New York Times,* May 16, 2010, Sect 4, p. 51.

[203]Abby Goodnough, "Jobs Are First of 550 Central Staff Will Lose," *New York Times,* November 23, 2002, p. B1.

[204]Kathleen Grove, "The Invisible Role of the Central Office," *Educational Leadership,* 59 (2002): 45–47. Also see Kate Beem, "In the Name of Survival: The Dual Superintendency," *School Administrator,* 63 (2006): 18.

[205]Jack Lortz, "School Daze: The Life of a Rural Administrator," *School Administrator,* 55 (1998): 36.

[206]*Digest of Education Statistics,* 2009, table 87, p. 126.

superintendent is expected to manage two adjacent districts in an effort for both districts to save money.[207] Obviously, there is no central office to speak about in these small school districts, and the superintendent relies on the school principals (and teachers) to carry out many activities that are otherwise delegated to the central office personnel in large school districts.

It is common for school principals and teachers in large school districts (25,000 or more students) to be sometimes disfranchised from decisions involving specific areas such as curriculum, instruction, teaching, testing, and learning, and they become distant from the top administration.[208] In small school districts (1000 or fewer students), teachers and principals are often overburdened with these types of responsibilities. In large districts, teacher empowerment is the issue; in small districts, administrative and teacher overload is the issue.

Organizational Hierarchy

In small school districts, the operation of the central office is less bureaucratic simply because there are fewer layers. The organizational hierarchy of larger school districts would be cumbersome, and those with 100,000 or more students (.02 percent of all school districts) would extend off the page. Most readers would have difficulty understanding these latter charts, organizational charts of latter, not because they are incomprehensible but because of the nature of bureaucratic and hierarchical complexity in big school districts.

Efficiency Ratios

Just because large school districts have more hierarchical layers at the central office, and their organizational charts are taller and more difficult to understand, does not mean they have better or worse manager–student ratios or are more or less efficient in running the schools within the district. For example, in a survey of fifty-one school districts with 50,000 or more students, the manager–student ratio at the central office averaged one manager per 569 students and the median was 578. The ranges were as high or efficient as one manager per 1650 students and as low or inefficient as one manager per 161 students.[209]

Eleven school districts out of fifty-one had one central administrator per 750 students. The researcher concluded that school districts should aim for one central manager per 1200 or more students. Only six of the fifty-one surveyed school districts achieved this level of efficiency (Los Angeles 1343:1, Indianapolis 1401:1, Mesa, AZ 1446:1, West Jordon, UT 1512:1, Clark County, NV 1539:1, and Granite, UT 1650:1).[210]

Nationwide, as of 2007, there was one district administrator for 830 students, and for principals and assistant principals combined the ratio is 1 to 313 students, but the teacher-student ratio is 1:15.5.[211] As budget-minded school officials look at administrative jobs, there probably will be improved manager–student ratios (what William Bennett, the former Secretary of Education, some fifteen years ago termed the "blob"—or bloated bureaucracy). In school districts with declining student enrollments, the target of one manager to 1200 students ratio will be difficult to achieve without changes at the central administrative level. It will be up to moderate voices and rational groups to prevent this degree of change. In school districts with increasing student enrollments, this target is feasible, and what may be needed is to wait for administrative attrition to take its effect.

Finally, we need to ask the following: To what extent do administrator–student ratios represent cost-effectiveness and efficiency, and to what extent to do the ratios connote budget restraints and limited education spending? At what point do administrative numbers become costly, laborious, and a drag on decision making? What is the optimal number of school administrators in relation to the number of students? How many associate and assistant superintendents are necessary? How many directors and coordinators are needed? How big should be their support staffs? A reduction program may be directly related to economic factors—that is, budget problems (and not efficiency)—but who gets eliminated is a political consideration and can have legal implications.

It can also be argued, however, that the size and cost of school administration is a manufactured issue. The American Association of School Administrators (AASA) argues that central administrators represent 1.0 percent of the total staff and 4.5 percent of the total budget

---

[207]Guy Gahn, Research Consultant, Iowa Department of Education, personal communication, March 12, 1999.

[208]Roland S. Barth, "Improving Relationships Within the Schoolhouse," *Educational Leadership,* 63 (2006): 8–13; Tom Corcoran, Susan H. Fuhrman, and Catherine L. Belcher, "The District Role in Instructional Improvement," *Phi Delta Kappan,* 83 (2001): 78–84; Allan C. Ornstein, "Leaders and Losers," *Executive Educator,* 15 (1993): 28–30.

[209]Allan C. Ornstein, "Administrator/Student Ratios in Large School Districts," *Phi Delta Kappan,* 70 (1989): 806–808.

[210]Ibid.

[211]*Digest of Education Statistics, 2009*, table 80, p. 119.

of public school districts nationwide. All principals and assistant principals add another 2.4 percent to the staff and 5.6 percent to the budget, whereas teaching and instructional services comprise about 70 percent.[212] Diverting *all* salaries of central administrators to teacher salaries would theoretically increase the average pay 5 percent; diverting it all to reducing class size would amount to a reduction of only one student per class. The AASA argues there is no "blob" or bloated bureaucracy at the central level; moreover, the percentage of overhead for central and school site administration has changed very little over the years—about 10 percent.[213] The popular assertion that school administrators are overpaid or have erected an overweight bureaucracy diverts attention from real educational issues.

The Principal and the School

Usually, each school has a single administrative officer, a principal, who is responsible for the operation of the school. In small schools, the person may teach part-time as well. In large schools, there also may be one or more assistant or vice principals. The administrative hierarchy may also consist of a number of department chairpersons, a discipline officer (e.g., dean of boys, dean of girls), a director of guidance, and so on.

Although functions vary by locality and size, the principal is primarily responsible for administering all aspects of a school's operations. It is common practice for the principal to work with some type of community group for the improvement of the school; this group is often a PTA or advisory school community committee. Increased teacher militancy and the movement toward teacher empowerment have also led many principals to share decision-making responsibilities with teachers. This new role for teachers is seen by school authorities, including many principals, as essential if schools are to improve.

Conditions, Employment, and Trends

On the average, grades K to 8 principals work 51 hours a week on school-related activities, while the number of hours a day ranges from 8 to 10 hours, including an additional 8 hours at home.[214] High school principals average about 53 hours a week on the job and 11 hours in the evening.[215] In theory, the work of high school principals can be categorized into 149 specific tasks in which unscheduled meetings account for 27.5 percent of their time, scheduled meetings for 17.3 percent, desk work 16 percent, personal exchanges (and conversations) 14.1 percent, hallway-classroom tours 7.7 percent, and phone calls 5.8 percent.[216] In total, face-to-face contacts involve 59 percent of the principal's time on the job, and they tend to occur in their offices (usually in meetings); thus, skills in verbal communication is an important part of the principal's job. Similar percentages are reported in two separate studies of elementary principals' task performance by time.[217]

Bureaucracy and politics are at the top of the list of school administrators' complaints. Fifty-seven percent of the principals reported that "even good administrators in their district are so overwhelmed by day-to-day activities that their ability to provide vision and leadership is stymied."[218]

Researchers have asked principals to specify how they spend time and how they would prefer to spend time. Five general categories of work activities were developed: administrative operations, staff and curriculum development, community relationships, student services, and evaluation. Detailed logs were kept for several weeks. Discrepancies exist between actual and ideal use of time, where both elementary and secondary level principals would prefer to spend more time on staff and curriculum development and staff evaluation. On the other hand, they would prefer to spend less time on administrative operations (that is, daily

---

[212]Nancy Protheroe, "The Blob Revisited," *School Administrator, 55* (1998): 26–29.

[213]See Allan Odden and Sarah Archibald, *Reallocating Resources* (Thousand Oaks, CA: Corwin Press, 2001); Frederick M. Hess, *The Future of Educational Enterpreneurship* (Cambridge, MA: Harvard University Press).

[214]James L. Doud, "The K–8 Principal in 1988," *Principal,* 68 (1989): 6–12; James L. Doud and Edward P. Keller, "The K–8 Principal in 1998," *Principal,* 78 (1998): 5–12. Also see Vincent Ferrandino, "Challenges for 21st-Century Elementary School Principals," *Phi Delta Kappan,* 82 (2001): 440–442.

[215]Gay Fawcett et al., "Principals and Beliefs-Driven Change," *Phi Delta Kappan,* 82 (2001): 405–410; Gerald C. Ubben, Larry W. Hughes, and Cynthia J. Norris, *The Principal: Creative Leadership for Effective Schools,* 5th ed. (Boston: Allyn & Bacon, 2006).

[216]Ibid.

[217]Doud and Keller, "The K–8 Principal in 1998"; Ronald H. Heck, "Conceptual Issues in Investigating Principal Leadership," *Peabody Journal of Education,* 73 (1998): 51–80.

[218]Jean Johnson, "Staying Ahead of the Game," *Educational Leadership, 59* (2002): 26–30.

tasks, meetings, and paperwork) and student services (primarily discipline and record-keeping functions).[219]

Two independent views of principals suggest the principal occupies a role with contradictory demands. They are expected to work to transform, reform, and restructure schools while they hold positions historically committed to controlling change and maintaining stability.[220] Researchers from the University of Washington identified seven leadership functions that exist in schools: "instructional, cultural, managerial, human resources, strategic, external development, and micropolitical."[221]

Typically, superintendents interview three to six candidates from a pool of applicants for principal. In a recent study of 725 superintendents, the mean number of interviews was 4.6. Larger schools tend to draw the most applicants and the superintendents interview more candidates. In 5 percent of the cases, superintendents interviewed only one candidate, usually an insider. Ironically, however, 52 percent of the superintendents rated candidates to be "average" or "below average." On a five-point scale, the mean rating given to all applicants by the superintendents was average (2.6%).[222]

Nationwide, the pool of candidates for qualified principals (K to 12) is shrinking, and some estimates show that the pool is only half of what it was ten years ago. Interestingly, more people are earning administrative certificates and doctorates in educational administration, but fewer are actually applying for available positions.[223] School districts, in response to the undersupply of qualified principals, are grooming their own teachers in university-sponsored programs.

The decline in the supply of qualified candidates can be explained in terms of lack of financial incentives vis-à-vis the increased complexity of the job, time demands, and accountability for results—which all amount to more stress. The added job commitment, compared to a typical teacher's job, also affects the decision of some women with children not to apply. Another factor is that twenty-five years ago, the principal was the master of the ship. Changes over the last decade have enhanced the power and influence of students, teachers, and parents. The legal issues are more complex, and demands for accountability for student performance by the states and public have dramatically increased. These trends lead some principals to frustration and burnout and others not to apply because of quality of life and family concerns.

Despite all these concerns, principals feel positive about their career choice: 90 percent report high morale, and 60 percent indicate that the principalship is their final professional goal. Job security is not an issue. About 85 percent report that they are pleased with their relationships with superintendents and school board members. Principals with fewer than five years of experience report more positive experiences working with their superintendent, probably because the boss selected them. The most pervasive concerns among principals are the fragmentation of their time (72%), the need for additional resources (56%), and students not performing to their potential (32%).[224]

To attract qualified principals, the authors believe that the average base salary should be $200,000 as of the year 2010. Based on years of experience, education, and the number of teachers they supervise, these leaders should have the potential to earn $250,000 to $300,000. Big-city principals have a tougher job than suburban and rural principals and an extra stipend (10 to 20 percent) should be provided—possibly linked to improving student achievement. Leadership needs to be properly recognized and rewarded. As the old axiom says: You get what you pay for.

Evaluation of Principals Principals generally lack expertise in assessment. They are not effective in conducting school-level assessment or classroom assessment (of their own teachers), according to authorities, because they lack evaluation and assessment training. Even when such courses are offered in their preparation programs,

[219]James L. Hager and L. E. Scarr, "Effective Schools—Effective Principals: How to Develop Both," *Educational Leadership,* 40 (1983), 37–41; Janice L. Herman and Jerry J. Herman, "Deferring Administrative Tasks, Escalating Performance," *NASSP Bulletin,* 79 (1995): 16–21; Peggie J. Robertson, "How Principals Manage Their Time," *Principal,* 86 (2006): 12–16.

[220]Michael Fullan, *What's Worth Fighting For in the Principalship* (New York: Teachers College Press, Columbia University, 1997); Lynda Lyman, *How Do They Know You Care? The Principal's Challenge* (New York: Teachers College Press, Columbia University, 2000).

[221]Bradley Portin, "The Roles That Principals Play," *Educational Leadership,* 61 (2004): 14–18.

[222]Thomas E. Glass and Amy L. Bearman, "Criteria and Processes Used by Superintendents to Select and Hire Secondary Principals." Paper commissioned by the Education Commission of the States (Denver, CO: 2001).

[223]Robin Ray Field and Thomas Diamantes, "Task Analysis of the Duties Performed in Secondary School Administration," *Education,* 124 (2004): 709–712; John H. Holloway, "A Defense of the Test for School Leaders," *Educational Leadership,* 59 (2002): 71–75; *Is There a Shortage of Qualified Candidates for Openings in the Principalship?*; Richard P. McAdams, "Who'll Run the Schools?" *American School Board Journal,* 185 (1998): 37–39.

[224]Doud and Keller, "The K–8 Principal in 1998"; "Education Vital Signs 1998," *American School Board Journal,* 185 (1998): A–15.

PRO CON DEBATE

The Politics of School Elections

Although people in the United States value the democratic process, for many people the term *politics* carries a negative connotation. Politics implies tradeoff, compromise, less-than-perfect solutions and, perhaps, secret deals that benefit those in power. Given this perception, the practice of electing to office those who set policy for schools is debatable.

Question: Considering the political ramifications of elections, should school board members be elected?

Arguments PRO

1. Service on the school board requires little political experience. Concerned citizens can assume office and contribute to the general welfare in important and meaningful ways without major changes in their personal or professional lives. They need not be or become career politicians.
2. Election is effective and sacred. The electoral process guarantees that issues are discussed in an open forum. Voters choose candidates who are most conversant with the issues and most able to act upon them.
3. Single-issue candidates are rarely elected to office because their constituents are a small portion of the community. If elected, their perspective broadens as they learn about other issues and the board's responsibilities.
4. An appointed board vests power in the person making the appointments. It leads to rule by an elite or specific pressure group rather than rule by the people.
5. As chief executive officers, school superintendents are accountable to the community for the state of the schools. It is right and proper for local citizens to express their concerns to their elected board members and for board members to carry these concerns to the superintendent. Board members protect superintendents from capricious expectations.

Arguments CON

1. A seat on the school board is sometimes an entry-level political office. Board members who are striving for more prestigious offices use the board seat to attract the attention of the media and the public, thereby bringing undue stress to the superintendent and the school district.
2. Election is inefficient. For example, many school board members are elected to three-year terms. It takes them at least two years to learn boardsmanship. Then they begin running for reelection.
3. Single-issue candidates may be elected to the board. Their narrow focus prevails, regardless of the needs of the community or the schools. They are more concerned about representing special interest groups than representing the larger community.
4. Appointed board members are selected on the basis of their unique skills at policy development. Those making appointments ensure that a board is balanced so that all interests are represented.
5. Some of the most competent school superintendents lose their positions because they are unable or unwilling to appease elected board members. This is especially apparent in small towns where local citizens often want to run the schools. They are more concerned about administrative details than large policy issues.

those courses are usually optional and bypassed because competence in assessment does not appear to affect certification or employability.[225] Nonetheless, principals are required to conduct formal assessments in their roles as instructional leaders, managers, and change agents—to obtain information for making decisions about the school, particularly with regard to students and staff.

Evaluation of principals' contractual obligations has taken on new importance, coinciding with the general frenzy of testing and evaluation; today, more and more superintendents are insisting on clarifying the evaluation process involving principals. According to the AASA, indicators of a good evaluation are that: (1) the evaluation

[225] Gary L. Anderson, "A Critique of the Test for School Leaders," *Educational Leadership*, 59 (2002): 67–70; Ronald W. Rebore, *A Human Relations Approach to the Practice of Education Leadership* (Boston: Allyn & Bacon, 2003); David Squires, *Aligning and Balancing the Standards-Based Curriculum* (Thousand Oaks, CA: Corwin Press, 2004).

is conducted in a positive climate; (2) the superintendent is familiar with the principal's goals and/or has communicated expectations to the principal early in the process; (3) the superintendent gives the principal frequent and timely feedback; (4) the superintendent's judgments are supported with specific examples; (5) the evaluation focuses on performance results, not personalities; (6) the principal is afforded an opportunity to respond to the evaluation; and (7) the evaluation is limited to those matters over which the principal has responsibility.[226]

Given the fact that the school principal has been cited as the most influential person in promoting school reform, change, and innovation, and given the public's concern about student achievement, the evaluation of principals has changed from a static or matter-of-fact process to a hot issue. Many administrators welcome new evaluation options because they believe traditional evaluation forms are outmoded and irrelevant to the performance of the school and the demands of the public.

The reform movement in education, followed by the state standards movement and the public's interest in school choices and alternative education, has stimulated the age of accountability for all educational players—teachers, principals, and superintendents.

Whether we call it accountability to the public (as educators call it), better management (as business, government, and a few school administrators would say), or improving test scores (as parents and school boards would have it), the challenge is to get better results with no increase in cost.[227] Across the country, superintendents now receive annual bonuses for meeting new standards of learning and/or district goals. There is no reason why principals will not move in the same direction in the near future.

For example, New York City's contract in 2007 with school principals not only holds them accountable for students' progress but also provides for them to be rated by teachers. Several district superintendent positions will be eliminated, and principals will gain power and become "field commanders."[228] To be sure, evaluation systems of school principals will be further developed to reward academic improvement, as well as other goals, and to penalize poor performance.

Summary

1. The federal role in education dramatically increased through the twentieth century, especially between the Roosevelt and Carter years. Since the 1980s, however, federal involvement in education has been reduced, highlighted by the new federalism.
2. The Department of Education (DOE) was established in 1980 with full cabinet status. Secretary William Bennett added visibility and prestige to the department even though many of his views on education were considered controversial.
3. Federal programs and activities in education were uncoordinated until the enactment of the relief acts during the Depression and the War Act during World War II. After Sputnik and with the War on Poverty and civil rights movement, national policy became linked to education, and federal funding dramatically increased.
4. The national reform movement in education shifted educational policy from equality to excellence. The current demand for excellence is highlighted by a series of policy reports for national consumption. Of all the reports, *A Nation at Risk,* the best-known one, started the movement.
5. The state hierarchy of education includes the governor, state legislature, and courts. In recent years, all three groups have taken a more active role in education.
6. With the exception of Wisconsin, all states have state boards of education. State departments of education operate under the direction of the state boards and are headed by the chief state school officer.
7. Schools are organized into school districts, and today there are nearly 14,000 public school systems operating under a widely accepted system of laws, regulations, and customs.

[226]Jack McCurdy, *Building Better Board-Administrator Relations* (Arlington, VA: American Association of School Administrators, 1992).

[227]John L. Herman, "The State of Performance Assessments," *School Administrator,* 55 (1998): 17–23; Richard J. Stiggins, "Assessment Crisis: The Absence of Assessment for Learning," *Phi Delta Kappan,* 83 (2002): 758–765; Stiggins, "From Formative Assessment to Assessment For Learning," *Phi Delta Kappan,* 87 (2005): 324–328.

[228]David M. Herszenhorn, "Respect Is Nice, But Principals Want A Raise," *New York Times*, January 29, 2007, p. B1.

8. Board members are the official link between the public and school administration. Board members reflect the public will and have managerial responsibilities that are crucial to the operation of schools.
9. Superintendents spend most of their time as managers, not as leaders. The average workday is largely desk work, phone calls, and meetings. Superintendents interpret school board policy and carry it out in connection with contemporary events; there is little time for them to initiate reform.
10. The central administrative staff, usually consisting of an associate superintendent, a number of assistant superintendents, department heads, and coordinators, are given responsibility by the superintendent to help run the schools. The central staff is usually top heavy in large districts and streamlined in small districts.

Key Terms

separation of powers
dual federalism
level data
national federalism
new federalism
national standards movement
Northwest Ordinances
Morrill Act
Smith-Hughes Act
GI bill
National Defense Education Act
Elementary and Secondary Education Act
Title I
Title IX
Civil Rights Act
Bilingual Education Act
Education for All Handicapped Children Act (Public Law 94-142)
mainstreaming
Scholastic Aptitude Test
state education agency
political action committees
subjective culture
consolidation
decentralization
public board meeting
executive board meeting
more effective schools
compensatory programs

Discussion Questions

1. What are the arguments for and against shifting educational responsibility from the federal government to the states?
2. What are the arguments for and against Title IX, special education legislation, bilingual education legislation, and No Child Left Behind?
3. What are the major responsibilities and functions of the state boards of education and state departments of education?
4. What are the advantages and disadvantages of an elected or appointed local board of education?
5. How would you describe an effective superintendent? How do you see the superintendent's role in context with effective schools?

Suggested Readings

Alexander, Kern, and M. David Alexander. *American Public School Law,* 7th ed. (Belmont, CA: Wadsworth, 2009). The authors provide a comprehensive overview of the laws governing the state and local school systems.

Deal, Terrence E., and Kent D. Peterson. *Shaping School Culture,* rev. ed. (New York: John Wiley, 2009). The book provides an action blueprint for school leaders.

English, Fenwick W. *Encyclopedia of Educational Leadership and Administration* (Thousand Oaks, CA: Sage Publications, 2006). The book contains over 600 entries on theories, research, and concepts in education.

Murphy, Joseph, and Coby V. Meyers, *Turning Around Failing Schools: Leadership Lessons from the Organizational Sciences* (Thousand Oaks, CA: Corwin, 2008). The authors provide a model for preventing organizational deterioration and restructuring schools.

Ornstein, Allan C. *Teaching and Schooling in America: Pre- and Post-September 11* (Boston: Allyn & Bacon, 2003). The author discusses inequality and equality, injustice and justice, immorality and morality, and a host of reform issues.

Owens, Robert G. *Organizational Behavior in Education,* 10th ed. (Boston: Allyn & Bacon, 2011). The author emphasizes organization, behavior and culture, school leadership, and decision making.

Sergiovanni, Thomas J. *Rethinking Leadership* (Thousand Oaks, CA: Corwin Press, 2006). The author examines the concept of leadership and its relation to learning.

10

Excellence, Equality, and Education

FOCUSING QUESTIONS

1 What is the role of the school in a democratic society? In providing economic opportunity? In socializing youth? In enhancing a national identity?

2 How would you describe the relationship between schooling and equal opportunity?

3 Can schools overcome the effects of class? What other social conditions effect economic outcomes? How are less fortunate students supposed to overcome money, power, privilege, and political connections that more fortunate students posses?

4 Why might some people argue that schools are no longer the great social or economic equalizer?

5 How did William Harris and Charles Eliot influence American education? How would you describe their economic philosophy and principles of competition?

6 Why were most social reformers unconcerned about extremely low percentages of students graduating from high school and entering college at the turn of the twentieth century?

7 Why did some early twentieth-century critics link immigration to civil strife and the downfall of the country?

8 What is the modern or current view of inequality of educational opportunity?

9 What is the relationship between excellence and education? Excellence and luck? Education credentials and performance?

10 How should we define excellence and equality? How should society balance excellence and equality?

No country has taken the idea of *equality* more seriously than the United States. Politically, the idea is rooted in the Declaration of Independence and the Constitution. We have fought two wars over the definition of equality: the American Revolution and the Civil War. Starting in the 1960s, first with the War on Poverty and then the civil rights movement, the language of progressive thought and protest became associated with inequality. The concern focused on rights for the poor and minorities, including women.

Inequality in today's world deals with the growing gap in income and wealth between the rich and the rest of us. The notion of *excellence* is a recent concept, first introduced by the British sociologist Michael Young in 1958 in his book, *The Rise of the Meritocracy*, in which the process of advancement by **merit** is outlined.[1] The best and highest paid positions in society are obtained on the basis of individual performance, rather than positions being allocated at random, by group characteristics such as race or gender, or by political and social networking, patronage or nepotism. Of course, such a society does not exist and the book is a utopian concept.

In the United States, John Gardner, the founder of Common Cause, wrote a small pocket-sized book in 1961 called *Excellence: Can We Be Equal Too?* In this book, he points out the need for a democratic society to balance excellence and equality.[2] It must reward people for their abilities, but it also needs to make provision for the less able person. In both books, the authors remind us that family origins should not count as an advantage or handicap in determining economic outcomes. The key to economic success should be attributable to the person's abilities and education (or training) that should make the person more valuable to society.

[1]Michael Young, *The Rise of the Meritocracy, 1870–2033* (London: Thames and Hudson, 1958).

[2]John W. Gardner, *Excellence: Can We Be Equal Too?* (New York: Harper and Row, 1961).

Definitions and Labels

Every modern society must deal with the relationship between excellence, equality, and education. When society considers *excellence*, it must deal with the division of labor and what it will pay for certain jobs. When 95 percent of jobs in the U.S. pay less than $100,000 per year, we need to ask why certain other jobs pay a million dollars or more—and whether the benefits and importance (or responsibilities) of the high-paying jobs are worth the cost. If merit is defined in terms of performance, we need to distinguish between performance and credentials. (Having appropriate education credentials doesn't guarantee a good performance.) We must also work out definitions or criteria for performance (good, average, poor, etc.), and testing and evaluation procedures in school and in the work place for determining merit and performance—and then what are appropriate rewards.

Society must consider *equality* in terms of power and wealth—which people or groups have more or less political muscle and earn more or less (and by how much more or less) than the average income—and why. The more egalitarian or progressive the society, the more safety nets it will provide to help ordinary, slow, unqualified, and disabled workers obtain and pay for essential human goods (such as food and shelter) and services (such as health, education, and transportation). The exact benefits and standards for obtaining the benefits must be worked out politically. Hence, it depends on what political group (liberal or conservative) controls the process. The more the benefits available—unemployment insurance, health insurance, pensions and social security for the poor, disabled and aged—the more egalitarian the society.

From its birth in 1776 to the turn of the twentieth century, the United States moved from an agrarian to an industrial society. Education and training were important but not crucial factors for increasing opportunity. Farm and industrial societies are primarily based on muscle power and not brain power, so that a good deal of mobility could be achieved without a high school or college diploma. Apprenticeships, training, and learning on the job were more important than a formal education for the masses to live a decent life.

As society became more complex and bureaucratic, education became more important. With the coming of the information age and knowledge-based society at the mid-twentieth century, formal education took on even greater importance for opportunity and mobility. Brain power now substituted muscle power as the crucial factor for economic advancement. The female liberation movement which started in the 1950s, with its demand for more equality, coincided with the coming information/knowledge revolution, and provided a much easier vehicle for women to obtain middle-class jobs, economic independence, and greater equality in just a few decades.

Education, today, is the link between excellence and equality. It is considered essential for promoting a person's opportunity and mobility and for improving the productivity of society. In a society dedicated to the pursuit of social justice, intensive efforts should be devoted to providing the best education for all its citizens and to close the education gaps that exist between the "haves" and "have nots." It must not write off its disadvantaged populations as "uneducable" or slot them into poorly funded schools and second rate programs.

Our Founding Fathers understood the notion of social justice, although they called it by names such as "freedom," "liberty," and "natural rights" of man. They wanted the children of the common people to have a fair chance to grow up as equal as possible. Equal opportunity, regardless of parentage, combined with the need for civic responsibility, were the driving forces for schooling in America.

The Role of the Schools

The origins of American public schools are demonstrated by the concept of equal opportunity and the notion of universal and free education. Thomas Jefferson understood that the full development of talent among all classes could and should be developed in the New World, and especially among the common classes. "Geniuses will be raked from the rubbish," he wrote in his *Notes on the State of Virginia* in 1782. He added that the common people of America had **natural rights** for a decent life, for opportunity and success, and to participate in the social progress of the nation—denied to them in the Old World.

Horace Mann also understood the need for schooling and argued that education was the chief avenue where the "humble and ambitious youth" could expect to rise. The rise of the **"common school"** was spearheaded by Mann in the 1820s. In the words of Columbia University's Lawrence Cremin, in *The Republic and the School*, Mann envisioned the schools as "the great equalizer of the condition of men—the balance wheel of the social machinery."

Mann also established a stewardship theory, aimed as at the upper class, that the public good would be enhanced by public education. Schools for all children would create a stable society in which people would obey the laws and add to the nation's political and economic well being. To the workers and farmers, Mann asserted that the common school would be a means of social mobility for their children. To the Protestant community, he argued that the common school would assimilate ethnic and religious groups, promote a common culture, and help immigrant children learn English and the customs and laws of the land.[3] He was convinced that the common school was crucial for the American system of equality and opportunity, for a sense of community to be shared by all Americans, and for the promotion of a national identity.

Equality of opportunity in the late nineteenth and early twentieth centuries meant an equal start for all children, but the assumption was that some would go farther than others. Differences in backgrounds and abilities, as well as motivation and personality, would create differences in outcomes among individuals, but the school would assure that children born into any class would have the opportunity to achieve wealth and status as persons born into other classes. Implicit in the view was that the "schools represented the means of achieving the goal . . . of equal chance of success" relative to children of all strata.[4]

The connection with schooling and society was symbolized by the "little red school house" on the prairie and idealized by **Horatio Alger's themes** in his sentimental books on the self-made man, vision of the American dream, and power of the individual to rise above his social class. The goal of schooling fit into the popular biographies of Andrew Jackson and Abe Lincoln, how they rose from their log cabins on the frontier to become president, and it fit with the words of poet Russell Lowell, that the essence of the American promise was "to lift artificial weights from all shoulders [and] afford all an unfettered start, a fair chance, in the race of life."

---

[3]Lawrence A. Cremin, *The Republic and the School: Horace Mann on the Education of the Free Man* (New York: Teachers College Press, Columbia University, 1957); Jonathan Messerlie, *Horace Mann: A Biography* (New York: Knopf, 1972).

[4]Henry M. Levin, "Equal Educational Opportunity and the Distribution of Educational Expenditures," in A. Kopan and H.J. Walberg, eds. *Rethinking Educational Equality* (Berkeley, CA: McCutchan, 1974). Also see Marvin Lazerson, *The Education Gospel: The Economic Power of Schooling* (Cambridge, MA: Harvard University Press, 2004).

In retrospect, the schools did not fully achieve the goal of equal opportunity, because school achievement and economic outcomes are highly related to social class and family background. Had the schools not existed, however, social mobility would have been further reduced. The failure of the common school to provide social mobility raises the question of the role of school in achieving equality—and the question of just what the school can and cannot do to affect cognitive and economic outcomes. Can schooling overcome the effects of class?

Class is a matter of culture—what educators now call "**social capital,**" the kind of family and community resources available to children. The difference in capital leads to a system of inequality in terms of how students perform in schools and what kinds of jobs they eventually obtain. The question of fairness or equality is how we interpret this inequality. Do middle-class children simply "outcompete" their poor and working-class counterparts in school and therefore land better jobs (a conservative perspective). Or is it discrimination and exploitation that ensures the latter group performs poorly in school and their parents, who clean up offices or hotels or work on assembly plants, earn significantly less than their bosses (a liberal perspective)?

The notion of differences in class and the relationship to heredity have remained in the background in American thought, an idea rooted in the Old World to help explain the success of the nobility class—and later used by conservative Americans to explain the rise of the plantation, merchant, and banking class in colonial America, and then the capitalist class in the late nineteenth century during the Gilded Age. By the 1880s, Herbert Spencer, the English philosopher, maintained that the poor were "unfit" and should be eliminated through competition and the "**survival of the fittest.**" Because the evolutionary process involved long periods of time, according to laws independent of human behavior, education could never serve as an important factor in social and economic progress. The best schools could do was to provide basic knowledge that enabled people to adapt and survive within their environment. What Spencer failed to grasp is that with an educated mind, the character and speed of evolution for humans change, moving from a traditional and static society to a dynamic and rapid changing society.

From 1873 (when the **Kalamazoo, Michigan court decision** provided for free public high schools) to 1900 questions revolved around the school curriculum: What should be taught at the elementary and secondary school? What courses should the curriculum comprise? Who should attend high school? Should there be separate tracks or programs for smart and slow students? Should the same education be available for all students? Should high school be considered preparatory for college? What curriculum provisions should be made for terminal students? Who should attend college? See Table 10–1.

Table 10-1 Percentage of Students Enrolled in Secondary School and College, 1900-2010

	14- to 17-Year-Olds Enrolled in Secondary School by Percent	17-Year-Olds Graduating High School by Percent	18- to 21-Year-Olds Enrolled in College by Percent
1900	11.5	6.5	3.9
1910	15.4	8.8	5.0
1920	32.3	16.8	7.9
1930	51.4	29.0	11.9
1940	73.3	50.8	14.5
1950	76.8	59.0	26.9
1960	86.1	65.1	31.3
1970	93.4	76.5	45.2
1980	93.7	74.4	46.2
1990	95.8	85.4	48.5
2000	97.9	87.5	53.7
2010	96.5	86.0	60.0

Source: Allan C. Ornstein, *Teaching and Schooling in America: Pre- and Post-September 11* (Boston: Allyn and Bacon, 2003), Table 5–1, p. 249. Original data from *Digest of Educational Statistics 1982, 1985, 1989, 1998, 2000, 2007* and *Projections of Educational Statistics to 2008, 2011, 2015.*

The Conservative Slant

William Harris (1834–1926), the former St. Louis Commissioner of Education from 1861 to 1881 and U.S. Commissioner of Education from 1889 to 1906, and Charles Eliot (1835–1909), president of Harvard University from 1869 to 1909, dominated the reform movement during this period. Both educators were traditionalists and moralists. Harris had Mann's faith in free public schools.

Harris wrote in 1871, "If the rising generation does not grow up with democratic principles, the fault will lie in the system of popular education."[5] He thought that the common schools should teach morality and citizenship, "lift all classes of people into a participation in civilized life [and] instill social order."[6] Whereas Mann saw the common school as a great equalizer and force for social morality, Harris saw it as an instrument to preserve society's customs and norms. Mann saw schools as a key to a child's growth and development, whereas Harris saw schools as an extension of society, not as an agent of change.

At the high school level, Harris emphasized the classics, Greek, Latin, and mathematics. His curriculum was rigorously academic, and it discouraged working-class and ordinary children from attending high school. Harris resisted the idea of a vocational or practical curriculum, arguing that all children should follow the same curriculum. Lawrence Cremin, the education historian, summed it up in *The Transformation of the School:* Harris consolidated the revolution Mann had wrought "[but was] patiently conservative." Harris's emphasis was "on order rather that freedom, on work rather than play, on effort rather than interest, on prescription rather than election or regularity [and] silence" and on preserving the civil order.[7] Harris stressed rules, testing and grading, and failed to recognize that the poor and average student could not compete, simply because the academic track he delineated was too rigorous and there was no compensatory assistance for them.

Harris believed in the natural (Hegelian) laws of history and the (Darwinist) laws of nature, reinforced by the economic doctrines of Herbert Spencer—and that the free market was the great regulator of the economy. In this context, he argued that American prosperity was due to the principles of self-help, competition, and the sanctity of private property. The U.S. represented the culmination of the world spirit, which he linked to *laissez-faire* economics and the self-realization of the individual. Socialism was a primitive form of economics, rooted in the Old World and its feudal economy, which hindered individual achievement and a nation-state's development. Harris not only refuted all doctrines of social and progressive reform, but also maintained that such reform would destroy all American civilization and throw it back to primitive stages.[8]

Eliot was even more conservative. He saw "civilized society" as comprising four layers: (1) the upper one, "thin" in numbers and consisting of "the managing, leading and guiding class—the intellectuals, discovers, the inventors, the organizers, and the managers"; (2) a "much more numerous class, namely, the highly trained hard-workers who functioned as "skilled manual labor"; (3) a populous "commercial class" consisting of those who engage in "buying, selling and distributing"; and (4) a large class engaged in "household work, agriculture, mining, quarrying, and forestry."[9] Schools, Eliot argued, must offer programs to all four classes, but the content and instruction would reflect the abilities, what he referred to as the "capacity," of the child. The more progressive and democratic reformers of the era saw Eliot's class system as elitist and biased.[10]

The resulting influence of Harris and Eliot was that the curriculum reform committees of the 1890s and early 1900s emphasized training of the mind, tough subject matter, and the evolutionary thesis of Darwinism and Spencerism. The development of

[5]*Sixteenth Annual Report of the Board of Education* (St. Louis, MO: Board of Education, 1871), p. 28.

[6]William T. Harris, *Psychologic Foundations of Education* (New York: Appleton, 1898), p. 20.

[7]Lawrence A. Cremin, *The Transformation of the School* (New York: Random House, 1961), p. 20.

[8]One hundred years later Ayn Rand would write her 1957 novel *Atlas Shrugged*—similar to Harris' philosophy—about the virtues of self-interest, competition, unfettered capitalism, and limited government. As social and progressive measures are introduced the economy collapses—sought of today's reality-based conservative economy, as perceived by the followers of Ayn Rand and the preview and early warnings of Harris.

[9]Charles Eliot, cited in R.H. Bremmer, ed. *Children and Youth in America: A Documentary History, 1866–1932* (Cambridge, MA: Harvard University Press, 1971) p. 114.

[10]For a more liberal and kinder view of Harris and Eliot, see Diane Ravitch, *Left Behind: A Century of Failed School Reform* (New York: Simon and Schuster, 2000).

mind and nature of academic work in the high school coincided with the so called "laws of nature," and that only a very small percentage of students were expected to succeed in high school or go on to college. Most people accepted this argument and social and economic improvement for the masses based on educational opportunities was exasperatingly slow. As evidenced by Table 10–1, the outcome was that by 1900, only 11.5 percent of 14–17 year olds were enrolled in high school, 6.5 percent graduated, and just 4 percent of 18–21 year olds were enrolled in college. Not too many people were concerned about these figures, since America was still a farm and factory-based society with plenty of "manly" jobs available for working people—who worked with their hands not their minds. To this extent, it might be argued that class and custom trumped education equality and opportunity.

Thus at the turn of the century, in his book *The Future America*, English author H.G. Wells linked peasant immigration to the country as the downfall of America. "I believe that if things go as they are going, the great mass of them will remain a very low lower class" and the U.S. population "will remain largely illiterate industrial peasants."[11] Today, the debate is couched in terms like "human capital," "brain-drain," and "illegal immigration." Many Americans contend we are attracting low-wage, low-educated agricultural workers, hotel staff, and landscapers while discouraging the foreign-educated students, scientists, and engineers on which the American economy depends.

Ellwood Cubberly, a former school superintendent and professor of education at Stanford University, and one of the most influential education voices at the turn of the twentieth century, feared the arrival of immigrants from Southern and Eastern Europe. In *Changing Conceptions of Education*, he argued that they were slow-witted and stupid compared to the Anglo-Teutonic stock of immigrants. The new immigrants were "illiterate, docile, lacking in self-reliance and initiative, and not possessing the Anglo-Teutonic concepts of law, national stock, and government." The new immigrant and working-class children had little need for an academic curriculum, according to Cubberly, as they were lacking in mental ability and character; in fact, he insisted the common man demanded vocational training for their children. It was foolhardy to saturate these immigrants and working-class children "with a mass knowledge that can have little application for their lives."[12]

Although progressive educators were concerned about the education of the poor, working-class, and immigrant children, the fact remains that the great change in school enrollment did not occur until just prior to and during the Great Depression. Adolescent students were encouraged to attend high school so as not to compete with adults for jobs. Once more we refer to Table 10–1. By 1930, as many as 50 percent of 14–17 year olds were attending high school, 29 percent of 17 year olds had graduated, and 12 percent of 18–21 year olds were enrolled in college. The concept of mass education was just beginning to take shape—as America moved from a farm-based to industrial-based country.

Sputnik and Post-Sputnik

Enrollment in high school continued to increase so that by 1950 as many as three quarters of eligible students were attending high school. During the **Sputnik** and Cold War era, Harvard University President James Conant wrote two books, *The American High School Today* in 1959 and *Slums and Suburbs* in 1961. In the first book, he argued that in order to stay competitive with the Soviets the schools had to pay special attention to the gifted and talented students (top 3 or 4 percent) as well as the above-average or top 20 percent, and to encourage them to attend college and major in science, math, and foreign languages. The curriculum had to be beefed up with more homework, more testing, and more honors and advanced study courses. The average and below average student was considered more or less as a "postscript" or "nonstudent," someone who could always get a job in the labor force and contribute to society.[13]

As for the second book, the civil rights movement was in its infancy and Conant sensed the need for greater education and employment opportunities for minority youth. He warned that the "social dynamic" was building in the cities because of massive unemployment among black youth and adults. He compared suburban and city schools, citing vast differences in resources, classroom size, and teaching experience, and

---

[11]H.G. Wells, *The Future of America* (New York: Harper and Bros., 1906), pp. 142–43.

[12]Ellwood Cubberly, "Does the Present Trend Toward Vocational Education Threaten Liberal Culture," *School Review* (September 1911), p. 461.

[13]James B. Conant, *The American High School Today* (New York: McGraw-Hill, 1959).

advocated a vocational curriculum for nonacademic students attending slum schools as a method for providing them with future jobs.[14] Although his reform ideas were accepted by the Establishment, the minority and reform community in later years condemned his views as racist; it was argued that blacks would be slotted in a second rate curriculum and limited to vocational and blue collar jobs. Conant never responded to his critics.

From the 1950s through the 1990s, conservative psychologists such as William Shockley, Arthur Jensen, and Richard Herrnstein, placed heavy emphasis on heredity as the main factor for intelligence—and the reason why the poor remained poor from one generation to the next. Although the arguments were written in educational terms, the implications were political and implied class warfare, and most disturbing, it resulted in a stereotype for explaining mental inferiority among the lower class, especially blacks, thereby explaining the need for vocational programs and putting blacks on the defensive.

According to Richard Herrnstein, in *IQ in the Meritocracy*, **intelligence tests** measure both heritable and socially significant factors. Although the exact percentages are unknown, the genetic factor is estimated between 45 and 80 percent, depending on the research cited. But as society succeeds in equalizing opportunity, "the genetic factors likely become relatively more important, simply because the non-genetic factors having been equalized, no longer contribute to the differences in people."[15] To make matters worse, in western societies there are no arranged marriages, and in a democracy, smart people tend to intermarry—making genetic factors more important and contributing to class differences among future generations, These outcomes, Herrnstein claimed, are "lethal to all forms of egalitarianism."[16] However, he failed to understand that more Americans believe human nature is plastic and capable of improvement through improved social environment and opportunity.

Depending on whether someone is for or against intelligence testing, IQ partially explains class differences. In fact, Herrnstein contends that wherever equal opportunity exists, in Anglo-speaking countries, supposedly income distribution correlates with IQ distribution. Most thoughtful people would rather not hear or accept this analysis because the policy implications reject the values of a democratic society and coincide with the outmoded belief that lower-class people and blacks are intellectually inferior. Generally speaking, today, the vast majority of liberals and minorities reject the IQ thesis and schools rarely use IQ tests.

Barring drastic egalitarian policies, the gifted and talented will move to the top of the totem pole and earn the most money. Most of us accept this type of mobility and it is the kind of society that leads to the most productivity in today's world. What Herrnstein and other conservative pundits fails to recognize is that capable people are often held back and prevented from realizing their potential because of discrimination or finances. In fact, throughout the ages, societies have often wasted human talent by denying them social and education opportunities. In today's scientific and technological world, this spells disaster for such a society—and is an important factor why the vast majority of nations remain undeveloped.

Not until post-World War II, with the **G.I. Bill**, were large numbers of capable students attending college. Even then, occupational choices and opportunities did not always reflect IQ potential—rather social circumstances and family and personal expectations. Nevertheless, by the year 2000, more than 15.3 million students enrolled in degree granting institutions of higher learning. Five years later, the number totaled 17.5 million,[17] a 16 percent increase, illustrating the current need for a college education in order to economically succeed. The fact is, mass education is a major reason for why the U.S. is the leading economic engine of the world (although today its power, status, and influence are being challenged by emerging countries such as China, India, and Brazil).

However, one might also make the argument, which some conservative educators do, that half of all children are statistically below the average in IQ and basic achievement, and many just do not belong in college. According to Charles Murray, the co-author of *The Bell Curve,* "if you don't have a lot of g," that is general intelligence, "when you enter kindergarten, you are never going to have a lot of it. No change in the educational system will change that hard fact."[18] Now that is a tough pill to swallow, especially in a society that prides

[14]James B. Conant, *Slums and Suburbs* (New York: McGraw-Hill, 1961).

[15]Richard J. Herrnstein, *IQ in the Meritocracy* (Boston: Little Brown, 1971) , p. 45.

[16]Ibid. p. 54.

[17]*Digest of Education Statistics, 2007* (Washington, DC: U.S. Government Printing Office, 2008), Tables 183, 187, pp. 274, pp. 278.

[18]Charles Murray, "Intelligence in the Classroom," *Wall Street Journal*, January 16, 2007, p. A21.

itself in being egalitarian or among school people who are reform oriented and believe in the power of education and the opportunities that go along with it.

For Murray, the top 25 percent of high school graduates have the abilities to make good use of a college education, and the remaining youth would do better in vocational training. Combine those who are unqualified because of lack of intelligence and those who are unqualified as well as unmotivated, and the majority of college students today are putting a false premium on attending college and looking for something that college was not designed to provide. The outcome is, according to some observers, an overeducated American workforce. This is one reason why more than one third the graduating class of 2010 were unable to find jobs after college. Another consideration is that college tuition has increased twice as rapidly as the Consumer Price Index in the last 20 years. Few working and middle-class parents, who are spending thousands of dollars a year on their child's college education, want to hear this analysis—or even worse, that perhaps their children should become plumbers or electricians.

Now, it may also be too frightening for the rich and well-born to suppose that the reason for their fortunes has little to do with intelligence, but in a longitudinal study of 7,400 Americans between 1979 and 2004, Ohio State's Professor Jay Zagorsky found no meaningful correlation between wealth and high IQ scores. "Those with low intelligence should not believe they are handicapped and those with high intelligence should not believe they have an advantage." There was a slight correlation between IQ scores and income; each point in IQ scores was associated with about $400 of income a year.[19] Assuming a 10-point spread in IQ and 40 years of work, the difference is only $160,000, which can evaporate in one or two bad financial decisions. The IQ link breaks down with wealth, that is the accumulation of assets, because smart people are just as likely as others to make bad financial choices over their lifetime. (Someone earning $100,000 a year and saving $20,000 will accumulate more wealth than someone earning $1,000,000 and spending $1.2 million per year.) One very bad decision can wipe out a lifetime savings. More important, wealth often takes generations to accumulate and to pass from one generation to the next.

What all this seems to mean is that the sorting out process between IQ, education, and economic outcomes are not easy to separate or pigeon hole into neat predictions. Not only do Americans have multiple chances to succeed, but also you don't have to be an intellectual whiz-kid or a college graduate to succeed. Bill Gates, Steve Jobs, Evan Williams (of Twitter) and Mark Zuckerberg (of Facebook) never finished college. We would like to think that the American education system is designed, at least in theory, to enable every youngster to fulfill his human potential, regardless of race, ethnicity, gender, or class, and regardless of intelligence or creativity. But education, although important, is only one factor to consider in explaining economic mobility and social stratification.

Educational and Economic Opportunity

The modern view of educational equality, which emerged in the 1950s, goes much further than the old view that was concerned with **equal opportunity**. In light of this, James Coleman, when he was a professor of education at Johns Hopkins University, outlined in the *Harvard Educational Review* five views of inequality of educational opportunity, paralleling liberal philosophy: (1) inequality defined by the same curriculum for all children, with the intent that school facilities be equal; (2) inequality defined in terms of social and racial compositions of schools; (3) inequality defined in terms such intangible characteristics as teacher morale and teacher expectation of students; (4) inequality based on school consequences or outcomes for students with equal backgrounds and abilities; and (5) inequality based on school consequences for students with unequal backgrounds and abilities.[20]

The first two definitions deal with race and social class; the next definition deals with concepts that are hard to define and hard to change; and the fourth definition deals with school finances and expenditures. The fifth definition is an extreme revisionist interpretation: Equality is reached only when the outcomes of schooling are similar for all students—those who are lower class and minority as well as middle class and majority. All these definitions and nuances may be hard for the reader to follow. So let's sum up: The easiest and most explicit way is to rely on *New York Times* OP writer David Brooks's ditty: "Liberals emphasize inequality. . . .

[19]Robert Frank, "Not Being Smart Makes You Rich?" *Wall Street Journal*, May 5, 2007, p. B4.

[20]James S. Coleman, "The Concept of Equality of Educational Opportunity," *Harvard Educational Review* (Winter 1968), pp. 7–22.

Conservatives believe inequality is acceptable so long as there is opportunity."[21]

When inequality is defined in terms of unequal outcomes (both cognitive and economic), we start comparing racial, ethnic, and religious groups. In a heterogeneous society like ours, this results in some hotly debated issues, including how much to invest in human capital, how to determine the cost effectiveness of social and educational programs, who should be taxed and by how much, to what extent we are to handicap our brightest and talented minds (the swift runners) to enable those who are slow to catch up, and whether affirmative action policies lead to reverse discrimination. Indeed, we cannot treat these issues lightly, because they affect most of us in one way or another and lead to questions over wars which have been fought in the past.

In a more homogenous society such as Japan, South Korea, Norway, or Germany, the discussion of race, ethnicity, or religion would not deserve special attention nor require judicial measures. Although it is doubtful if increased spending in big-city schools (where poor and minority students are concentrated) would dramatically effect educational outcomes, poor and minority students still deserve equal education spending—better paid teachers, small class sizes, high-tech resources, new textbooks, and clean bathrooms—as in affluent suburbs where expenditures often are twice or more the amount in adjacent cities.

Students deserve equality of expenditures simply on the basis that schools are public institutions, not private. In a democracy, citizens and their children are entitled to similar treatment, especially because intellectual capital is a national concern, not designed for the benefit of one class or group of students nor the exclusion of another group. It can also be argued that the poor are entitled to special treatment because in the long run the health and vitality of the nation are at stake. Sadly, in comparison to other industrialized nations, the U.S. enrolls the largest percentage of poor students, approximately 24 to 25 percent.[22] Since school performance reflects the social and economic system, this high percentage of poverty explains why, among other factors, the U.S. students consistently fall behind their counterparts from other industrialized nations on international tests.

There is no question that other factors arise to prevent equal school spending that are not simply symptoms of racism or class prejudice. They deal with the notion of values and the rights of people: The preservation of neighborhood schools, concern about big government and state-imposed policies at the local level, fear of increased taxation and why someone should have to pay for someone else's child's education, and the inability of politicians to curtail well-to-do parents from supporting their own neighborhood schools and property values. The question is, how much education equality should we strive for? We can have greater equality by lowering standards or by pulling down bright students (as in affirmative action) or by providing an enormous amount of additional resources for low-performing students (as in compensatory funding). But eventually we come to slippery slope and ask: how much money? Who is to pay for it?

In his classic book on *Excellence*, John Gardner, who we have already mentioned, points out that, in a democracy, the difference among groups cannot be dwelled on and we go out of the way to ignore them. He describes the dilemma: "Extreme equalitarianism . . . which ignores differences in native capacity and achievement, has not served democracy well. Carried far enough, it means. . . . the end of that striving for excellence which has produced mankind's greatest achievement." Gardner contends that if a society cannot pursue excellence "the consequences will be felt in everything it undertakes. The resulting debility will be felt in all parts of the system." Gardner also asserts that "no democracy can give itself over to emphasize extreme individual performance and retain its democratic principles—or extreme equalitarianism and retain its vitality." Our society should seek to develop "all potentialities at all levels. It takes more than educated elite to run a complex, technological society."[23] Every modern society, as well as every ancient society, has learned this hard lesson, some only after tremendous bloodshed and loss of life.

Every efficient and innovative society has also learned to recognize and reward various abilities, talents, and creative endeavors. In school, and other aspects of American society, the chief instrument for identifying ability and talent is a standardized test. It is not surprising, according to Gardner, that such tests are the object of criticism and hostility, because they encourage the sorting ad selecting of students into

---

[21]David Brooks, "A Human Capital Agenda," *New York Times,* May 15, 2007, p. A19.

[22]Allan C. Ornstein, *Class Counts: Education Inequality, and the Shrinking Middle Class* (Lanham, MD: Rowman & Littlefield, 2007).

[23]Gardner, *Excellence: Can We Be Equal Too?,* pp. 17–18, 83–90.

special tracks and programs. The fact is, "the tests are designed to do an unpopular job." They are designed to measure what a person knows or how well a person can perform particular tasks. The data can be used to compare people and make decisions—such as who gets into what college and who gets selected for various jobs. Tests are also used for applying standards to determine quality—and who gets ahead in schools and society. Although in our society, unlike other societies, we are given multiple chances to succeed, Gardner is still concerned that the search for talent and the importance of education in our high-tech and knowledge based society will lead to increasing inequality among educated and uneducated individuals.

While considerations of efficiency and objectivity are good reasons for relying on standardized tests, they should not be allowed to distort or limit our notion of talent. There are many different forms of talent—creative, artistic, athletic, etc.—that don't rely on heavy academic emphasis nor are measured by standardized tests. The demand for talent is crucial in a bureaucratic and complex society, but the importance of formal education is not always paramount for higher order and special kinds of talent. There are not only talented physicians and engineers to nurture, but we need also to recognize talented plumbers and talented chefs. While we need to reward different forms and types of talent, society needs to be realistic and discourage negative talents like the ability to pick pockets or deemphasize esoteric talents such as the ability to stand on your head. A democratic society must recognize multiple talents, and not only talents based on cognitive intelligence. That is the genius of a progressive democratic society.

The question of talent and rewards go hand-in-hand and lead to results related to inequality—and the values of society. What rewards should highly talented individuals earn? In 2008, the mean salary for American wage workers was approximately $36,000.[24] When someone is paid tens of millions of dollars because of a special talent related to entrepreneurial risk, acting, or sports, we need to consider how these earnings contribute to inequality, as well as the emotional consequences felt by middle-income and professional people who have college degrees and play by the book and can barely keep up with the payment of their bills. We need to consider whether the rewards, especially if excessive, contribute to the common good and needs of society, to what extent these extraordinary salaries or earnings lead to inequality, and how they affect the standard of living of the ordinary working people that comprise the foundation of American democracy. Since services and goods are limited, people with vast amounts of income drive up the prices of homes, autos, college tuition, and even baseball tickets.

Do Schools Make a Difference? Large-Scale Studies

The mid-1960s and early 1970s produced a series of large-scale studies, the biggest in education history, which basically showed that teachers and schools have minimal effect on student achievement. Over the years, the data have been ignored or buried by the liberal/minority community, because it lets teachers and schools off the hook, and implies that there is little educators (or society) can do to overcome the effects of poverty on education. In startling contrast to conventional wisdom, the studies by James Coleman, Christopher Jencks, and Otis Duncan concluded that schools have little influence on children's academic achievement. The results of these studies are difficult to present concisely, since the analysis include a host of variables and a large number of subgroups.

The Coleman Report

The Coleman survey deals with 625,000 children and 4,000 schools, and the report is about 1,300 pages long, including 548 pages of statistics.[25] It is the largest educational research enterprise conducted in the United States, and almost everyone of whatever political persuasion can find something in it to quote. Coleman found that the effects of the **home environment** far outweighed the effects that the school program or the teacher had on achievement. The report analyzed the results of testing at the beginning of grades 1,3,6,9, and 12. Achievement of the average Mexican American, Puerto Rican, American Indian, and black student was much lower that the average Asian American and white student at all grade levels. Moreover, the differences widened at higher grades. The characteristics of teachers and schools had the least impact on black students among all other minority groups; teachers and school characteristics could not account for all the reasons blacks, who started only six months behind in reading at the first grade, ended up 3½ years behind whites in reading at the twelfth grade.

[24]Ornstein, *Class Counts, Education, Inequality and the Shrinking Middle Class.*

[25]James S. Coleman et al., *Equality of Educational Opportunity* (Washington, DC: U.S. Government Printing Office, 1966).

Table 10-2 Coleman Report: Conditions of Student Achievements, Grades 6 and 9

	Total Group of Students (Maximum 8)
Student Body Characteristics	
1. Mean nonverbal test score.	8
2. Mean verbal test score	8
3. Preparation in college prep curriculum	6
4. Preparation of pupils with encyclopedia in home	5
5. Preparation of pupils who are white	3
6. Average number of white pupils in preceding year	3
7. Average attendance as a percentage of enrollment	2
8. Preparation of pupils who think teacher expects their best work	2
9. Preparation of pupils where mother went to college	2
10. Preparation of school's graduates in college	1
School Characteristics	
11. Teacher's verbal score	5
12. Teacher's race	4
13. Teacher's estimate of quality of own college	3
14. Teacher's attitude towards integration	3
15. Teacher's salary	3
16. Teacher's preference for teaching middle class pupils	2
Finances and Programs	
17. Comprehensiveness of curriculum	2
18. Mathematics offering	2
19. Per-pupil expenditure	1

Source: Adapted from *Supplemental Appendix to the Survey on Equality of Education Opportunity* (Washington, DC: U.S. Government Printing Office, 1966), pp. 143ff.

The general approach used by Coleman sorts 45 school characteristics or variables into correlates and noncorrelates of student achievement (see Table 10–2 and Table 10–3). For this purpose, a *correlate* was loosely defined as any school characteristic that correlates 0.2 or better with any one of three achievement measures (reading, mathematics, and general information) and any one of eight groups of students (Mexican-Americans, Puerto Ricans, American Indians, Asian Americans, Northern blacks, Southern blacks, Northern whites, and Southern whites. Of the 45 variables, 19 showed some relationship with at least one of three achievements tests, and 26 failed to do so.

The 19 correlates that tend to be associated with student achievement cluster around *student* and *teacher* characteristics, and especially around students; these are *hard-to-change* variables. Those that are unassociated with student achievement are by and large *school* characteristics and *easy-to-change* variables. In effect, the Coleman Report says that schools in general have little impact on learning, and the variables associated with learning, such as the students' or teachers' mean verbal test scores, are difficult to change. Changes effected by spending more money—such as teachers' experience, teacher turnover, student-teacher ratios, books and materials, tracking, and length of school day—are easier to bring about but have little relation to achievement. In fact, the correlation between expenditures per student and learning was essentially zero at each grade level examined.

Coleman's findings raise difficult policy questions for the nation's educators. If increases in student expenditures, higher teacher salaries, reduced classroom sizes, and other conventional remedies for low achievement have virtually no effect, what grounds are there to seek increased funds for education? Compensatory education advocates were being told that extra spending

Table 10-3 Coleman Report: Noncorrelates of Student Achievements, Grades 6 and 9

Student Body Characteristics

1. Number of twelfth grade pupils
2. Pupil mobility (transfers in and out)
3. Average hours pupils spend on homework
4. Proportion of students who read over 16 books the preceding summer
5. Teacher's perception of the quality of the student body
6. Proportion of the students whose mothers expect the best work

Characteristics of Instructional Personnel

7. Teacher's socioeconomic status
8. Teacher's experience
9. Teacher's localism
10. Teacher's highest degree received
11. Teacher's absences
12. Amount of teacher turnover
13. Availability of guidance counselors
14. Pupil-teacher ratio

Programs, Facilities, Other

15. Extracurricular offerings
16. Tracking
17. Movement between tracks
18. Accelerated curriculum
19. Policy on promotion of slow learners
20. Foreign language offerings
21. Number of days in session
22. Length of school day
23. Number of science labs
24. Volumes per pupil in school library
25. School location (urban/rural)
26. Teacher's perception of quality of school

Source: Adapted from *Supplemental Appendix to the Survey on Equality of Education Opportunity* (Washington, DC: U.S. Government Printing Office, 1966), pp.143 ff.

makes no difference in outcomes because it does not correlate with student achievement. Reform advocates generally are being told they need to come up with a better idea than increased spending.

Even worse, the data led to the conclusion that schools and teachers can do very little to effect changes in student achievement; rather, home characteristics and peer group influences are, in that order, the two major variables associated with achievement. In a subsequent interview, Coleman put it this way: "All factors considered, the most important variable—in or out of school—in a child's performance remains his family background. The second most important factor is the social-class background of the families of the children in the school, that is the **peer group**." Those two elements are much more important than any physical attributes for the school.[26]

An important qualification of this conclusion is that schools seem to have greater impact on some minority children, namely Hispanics and Native Americans. (See Table 10–2) Nevertheless, Coleman's findings of

[26]James S. Coleman, "Class Integration—A Fundamental Break with the Past," *Saturday Review* (May 27, 1972), p. 59.

a small relationship between school facilities and student achievement, a conclusion that contradicts the opinions and ideology of reform advocates, has inspired a searching analysis of the topic and arguments for and against the report since its publication.

The major criticism leveled against the Coleman Report is that the criterion of academic achievement is almost exclusively a measure of verbal abilities, which are more likely to be the product of the child's home than his or her school experience.[27] Another criticism is that it is difficult to find circumstances where one can measure and account for all the factors that result in student achievement.[28] However, most other studies rely on the same test measurements (reading and math tests) and use similar subgroups (including class or ethnicity); when the results appear more positive, these so called bias factors are not mentioned. If Coleman can be criticized for this bias, it follows that almost all other studies on school achievement are also misleading.

Still another criticism pertains to Coleman's method of analysis, in particular his heavy dependence on **regression analysis**, which unavoidably leads to an underestimate of the effects of school investment.[29] When independent variables in a multiple regression analysis are related, controlling for the first will reduce the correlation of the second. For example, controlling for the social class of the student indirectly controls also for part of the variation of school resources. The additional predictive powers associated with the addition of school resources to the analysis thus represents a downward estimate of the real relationship between school resources and achievement. These statistical problems were recognized by Coleman; it is for this reason that he permitted a low correlation of 0.2 to represent the level of acceptance, whereas most other studies would require a much higher correlation.[30] Moreover, Coleman accepted relationships on any one of three tests for any one of two grade levels as significant; each of the 45 variables had six opportunities to show a correlation with achievement. Had he required a higher correlation, or had he used only one test with only one grade level, there would have been almost zero correlates—a major factor to consider.

Most important, the reanalysis of the Coleman data by other investigators,[31] as well as other large-scale statistical studies of the determinants of student achievement, show similar results. A large fraction of the variation in student achievement is accounted for in out-of-school variables, such as the students' community and home characteristics. Another large fraction is attributable to the so-called peer group effect—that is, the characteristics of the students' classmates. The blunt fact is that most student output is directly related to the student input: High ability yields high achievement; low ability yields low achievement. Of the variation that is explained by school factors (usually no more than 17 to 20 percent), only part of this percent can be attributed to teachers (no more than 10 percent).[32] We will return to these percents later in our discussion.

The Jencks Study

Whereas Coleman showed that there was not much schools could do to improve the achievement levels of students, Christopher Jencks went one step further and indicated that the differences in school achievement as well as economic attainment are related more to socioeconomic origin than schooling. In his four-year study of the reanalysis of the U.S. Census, the Coleman Report, Project Talent (a study of more than 100 high schools), and several smaller studies, Jencks concluded

1. The schools do almost nothing to close the gap between the rich and the poor, the disadvantaged or advantaged learner.

[27]Henry S. Dryer, "School Factors and Equal Educational Opportunity," *Harvard Educational Review* (Winter 1968), pp. 33–56.

[28]Sarah E. Turner, "A Comment of 'Poor School' Funding, Child Poverty, and Mathematics Achievement," *Educational Researcher* (June-July 2000), pp. 15–20.

[29]Samuel Bowles, "Towards Equality of Educational Opportunity," *Harvard Educational Review* (Winter 1968), pp. 89–99.

[30]A perfect correlation is 1.0. Most studies try to obtain 0.5 or higher correlations. The smaller the number of variables being considered, usually the higher the correlation because there is less noise and/or overlapping variables; the greater number of variables being controlled usually the smaller the correlation.

[31]George W. Mayeske et al., *A Study of Our Nation's Schools* (Washington, DC: U.S. Government Printing Office, 1966); Fredrick Mosteller and Daniel P. Moynihan, eds., *On Equality of Educational Opportunity* (New York: Random House, 1972).

[32]Harvey Averch et al., *How Effective Is Schooling? A Critical Review and Synthesis of Research Findings* (Santa Monica, CA: Rand Corporation, 1972); Raymond Boudon, *Education Opportunity and Social Inequality* (New York: John Wiley & Sons, 1973); and Herbet J. Kiesling, *The Relationship of School Inputs to Public School Performance in New York State* (Washington, DC: Rand Corporation, 1966).

EXEMPLARY EDUCATIONAL ADMINISTRATORS IN ACTION

DAVID A. KAZAKOFF Principal, Terra Nova High School, Pacifica, California.

Latest Degree and Affiliation: Ed. D., Organization and Leadership, University of San Francisco; M.A., Educational Administration; B.A., Industrial Education.

Words of Advice: If the funding for education, federal and state, continues to dwindle, there will be no public education as we know it. A two-class education system will begin to exist. In some cases, it probably already exists. The Bush administration continued to push school vouchers and private education by increasing student accountability and trying to relax the church-school separation system that had been in place since the Founding Fathers had envisioned its necessity. Teacher and student accountability is a good thing, but it seems as though the federal government and the states are pushing accountability too fast and too soon without proper research and proper funding. As usual, the powers that be start the ball rolling, fund it, and then reduce funding but still expect schools to raise performance with less qualified teachers, loss of funding, and a system of testing that changes at the whim of the budget analyst of each state. You will never get quality teachers without giving them adequate compensation. Most states and counties (with very few exceptions) in this nation are compensating teachers at just above the subsistence level.

Anyone who wants to become an administrator needs to be trained as an intern in all areas of administration before being given a responsible position. Most administrators I know have all been put into a position and told "Go for it" without proper training. The colleges and universities cannot come close to real-life situations that administrators handle on a daily basis.

2. The quality of education has little effect on what happens to the students (with regard to future income) after they graduate.
3. School achievement depends largely on a single input—that is, the family characteristics of the students—and all other variables are either secondary or irrelevant.
4. About 45 percent of IQ is determined by heredity, 35 percent by environment, and 20 percent by a covariance or interaction factor.
5. There is no evidence that school reform (such as compensatory spending or integration) can substantially reduce the cognitive inequality that exists among students. [33]

Jencks maintained that it would require actual **redistribution of income** to achieve complete economic equality regardless of ability. Considering the historical period, it was a major shift in thinking—from equal opportunity to equal results. Given the world we live and believe in, that is, "capitalist utopia," it is hard to talk about increased or progressive taxation, or any other "Robin Hood" theory that takes from the rich and gives to the poor.

[33]Christopher Jencks et al., *Inequality: A Reassessment of the Effect of Family and Schooling in America* (New York: Basic Books, 1972).

The main policy implications of the findings are that schools cannot contribute significantly to equality. Jencks maintains that educators at all levels of instruction are not improving the lives of their students, but this is not really their fault; rather, the problem lies with the children's social class and other home characteristics. Economic equality in U.S. society will have to be achieved by changing not the schools but the economic institutions. School reforms fail because educators try to effect changes that are not feasible under normal conditions.

Jencks' positions on hereditary and environment, his support of standardized tests for predicting school success and academic skills, his belief that schooling is without significant value, and his espousal of income redistribution, regardless of differences between those who are smart and ambitious or dumb and lazy, aroused criticism from the political Left and Right alike. The *Harvard Educational Review* devoted an issue to the study. In trying to answer his critics, Jencks strongly responded that those who are politically oriented or are advocating a specific position will "deplore anything that undercuts [their] arguments." He said that sufficient criticism had been leveled at the book, so that educators, lay people, and policymakers could "feel free to accept or reject its conclusions according to their prejudices" The critics arguments were unconvincing, he said: "Most of the ideas they raise [were originally] covered in the text . . . or appendices." This does not necessarily mean that the study's conclusions were correct, but "the assumptions are plausible" and those who reject the data are under obligation to offer an alternative view of how the world works, along with some empirical evidence that their view is more accurate than ours."[34]

In a related study, Jencks and Marsha Brown found few relationships between high school characteristics and measures of school effectiveness. Using portions of the Project Talent study (an extensive survey conducted during the 1960s for purposes or estimating the range and levels of ability among American high school students), they concluded that changes in high school characteristics are unlikely to change academic outcomes. Characteristics such as student expenditures, teacher salaries, teacher experience, and socioeconomic composition have little impact on cognitive growth between ninth and twelfth grades and on college plans and occupational success.[35]

The Jencks and Brown study pre-tested and post-tested some 4,900 students on six different reading and math tests in the ninth and twelfth grades in 98 high schools across the country. The researchers estimated the contribution of various high school characteristics to the variation of these test scores, and estimated how high school quality affected high school graduation, college plans, and career plans five years after high school. The findings indicate that high schools (and teachers) can teach toward a specific test, but they are generally unable to raise test scores across the board. Moreover, the increased test scores have nothing to do with students finishing their education, implying that inflating one test score by cramming or teaching to the test will not have a long-term effect on the students' education. In the present era of testing and performance standards, Jencks's concepts and conclusions are classic: We can fool some of the people some of the time, by gearing our instructional time and review practices toward a specific test, but this will not modify student learning over long periods of time. Teaching toward the test (as opposed to integrating new learning experiences with prior experiences) almost guarantees that students will graduate school forgetting what they have supposedly learned.

The fact that socioeconomic composition does not seem to affect student achievement scores is at odds with Coleman's conclusions, but the rest of the findings tend to coincide with the Coleman Report and the earlier Jencks Study. The implications of this study by Jencks and Brown are that more money, smaller classrooms, more graduate work for teachers, higher salaries for teachers, socioeconomic desegregation, and possibly other traditional remedies do not have much effect on educational attainment. In effect, it mainly boils down to the fact that student input (not process) accounts for student output. Obviously, some people would argue that the idea is mean-spirited and contradicts the themes and dreams of what America is all about.

The Duncan Model

Coleman and Jencks challenge both traditional and revisionist theorists who put more stock on the influence of education. Whereas the traditionalists argue that education is the main avenue of opportunity, the revisionists criticize it as a vehicle by which inequality is perpetuated by a "dominant" group that discriminates against and imposes tracking and testing barriers against the "subordinate" group. Both theorist groups probably overstate their cases as to the influence of education.

The correlations among occupation, income, and education are based on averages. The spread around the mean is considerable, which reduces the real predictability for each occupational and income group. In a classic study, on occupational mobility of over 20,000 male Americans, Peter Blau and Otis Duncan show that the direct correlation between schooling and occupational status is a modest 0.32, but that when all variables are considered, education accounts for only 10 percent of the variation in occupational status.[36]

Blau and Duncan further explain the relationship. A high school graduate, on average, has a lower occupational status than a man who has attended college. However, a considerable number of high school graduates have better jobs than those who leave college before graduating as well as those who finish, and one-third do as well as those who do graduate work. At the other end of the scale, half the men who did not complete high school are doing as well as those who did

[34]Christopher Jencks et al., "Inequality in Retrospect," *Harvard Educational Review* (February 1973), pp. 104–105, 113.

[35]Christopher Jencks and Marsha D. Brown, "Effects of High Schools on their Students," *Harvard Educational Review* (August 1975), pp. 273–324.

[36]Peter M. Blau and Otis D. Duncan, *The American Occupational Structure* (New York: John Wiley and Sons, 1967).

complete high school, although as an entire group the high school graduate earns more than the high school dropout.

In a related research project, Duncan found that education is only one of several variables influencing a person's occupational status and income later in life.[37] What accounts for the assumed relationship between education and occupation and income are a number of underlying variables related to education, such as family origin, family education, inherited IQ, and socioeconomic class. For example, parents with high incomes are able to provide more education for their children, just as they spend more on food and housing, and therefore the children of the affluent obtain more education and go on to higher-paying jobs. Parents with high educational levels themselves are more likely to expect and to motivate their children to continue further in schooling. There is also a relationship between social class and intelligence of parents and, in turn, the inherited IQ and education of children; thus those with higher measured IQ scores are more likely to attain higher levels of education.

The data on which the research are based on leads to the following conclusions:

1. Family origin or socioeconomic class is correlated with IQ, but the correlation is low, indicating that IQ is a result of other non-measured environmental or hereditary variables.
2. A person's IQ has a direct influence on how much education he or she gets. Independent of education, IQ also has some direct influence on the status of occupation and income.
3. The socioeconomic status of a family has its main influence in education; it has some direct influence on occupational status and it has virtually no direct influence in income.
4. Education is highly correlated with occupational status (or type of job) and therefore has an indirect influence on income.
5. The main determinant of how much money a person earns leads to the status of his or her occupation. Education and IQ have less important direct effects on income; family origin has a greater impact. (Not too many educators want to hear this last point.)

[37]Otis D. Duncan, David S, Featherman, and Beverly Duncan, *Socioeconomic Background and Achievement* (New York: Seminar Press, 1982).

Unaccounted Factors: Luck

A large body of sophisticated research on social mobility within the past twenty years generally supports the preceding conclusions. Of this research, the most controversial and well known is Christopher Jencks, who studied the effect on income for the following variables: (1) father's educational status, (2) father's years of schooling, (3) father's IQ, (4) respondent's IQ at age 11, (5) respondent's Armed Forces aptitude test, (6) respondent's years of schooling, (7) respondent's occupational status, and (8) respondent's income.[38] Jencks found that the number of years of school does not significantly predict income. For white males with the same family background and initial ability, an additional year of elementary or secondary education increases future income by about 4 percent; an additional year of college, about 7 percent; and additional year of graduate school, 4 percent. Controlling for IQ, the top fifth of the population earns seven times as much as the bottom fifth, where as it should only account for 1.4 times as much; this suggests that other factors are related to inequality of income.

All eight variables (including education and IQ) combined explain only 23 percent of the existing differences in income. This means that if everyone had the same family origin, if everyone had the same IQ and education, and if everyone had the same occupational status most of the existing differences would remain. Jencks calls this ***luck***. If by "luck," one means all those variables not accounted for by Jencks, then Jencks is correct.

To call all these variables *luck,* however, is not a very good choice of words, because it implies that people have little control over their economic fates. Moreover, most of us in the business of education find it hard to accept that luck, or factors unrelated to schooling, has much influence (actually more influence than in schooling) in the outcomes of life. To believe such a thought would mean that our professional jobs and efforts are somewhat meaningless. But Jencks argues that two brothers who are brought up in the same family and who have approximately the same IQ and years of schooling may earn considerably different incomes. One becomes a surgeon who earns $500,000 a year; the other becomes a college professor who earns $100,000 a year (the author's example and figures). There is considerable difference in their incomes, but this difference, may not

[38]Jencks et al. *Inequality: Reassessment of the Effect of Family and Schooling.*

be a result of luck. It could be the result of their decisions, of which both brothers had full control. Indeed, choices are important and often lead to other choices which over years add up and have major impact on the lives of people—and their income and wealth.

Rather than conclude that the individual success is largely based on luck, it might make more sense to say that economic success is only partially related to family origin, ability, or education, and there are many other **intangible factors**—such as motivation, disposition, drive, knowing people or networking, and overall personality and people skills—influencing income differences among individuals. The list of unaccounted factors is endless, and it goes way beyond schooling. It is important for educators to understand and accept that there are limitations to what schools can do to bring about equality, despite the philosophy of Jefferson, Mann, and Dewey, and despite the faith all of us have in schools as the instrument of equality.

Although many may disagree with Jencks's reference to the unexplained variation of income as luck, he may be right in concluding that equalizing opportunity or equalizing opportunity of education will not reduce inequality. Jencks, who is a revisionist, argues for the redistribution of income—taxing the upper-middle class and the upper classes and distributing the revenues to the poor.

International Achievement Gaps in Education

While we all seem to recognize the importance of information and knowledge in a global economy, and that a country's human capital and potential for innovation is tied to their systems of higher education, we cannot overlook that the foundation for this talent is rooted in the K-12 education system. The key question is whether a nation's teaching and learning is "dumbed down" or promotes it's "best and brightest." The answer is clear. Despite hundreds of task force reports and attempts for school reform, and despite thousands of compensatory programs and tens of billions of dollars spent annually on low-income and low-achieving students, our education system for the past fifty years has been in a state of depression. Although we can point to individual schools and school districts that are successful, our system as a whole has not improved.

Achievement gaps between Asian and white students compared to Hispanic and black students remain alarmingly high, and by 2015 the latter group of students will represent the majority of enrollment. Comparatively, U.S. students consistently score below students in other industrialized nations on achievement tests, despite the fact we spend more money per student on education than all the countries except Switzerland. The numbers of U.S. college students majoring in science, math and engineering are flat, and the percentage of graduates in these two essential areas in Western European and especially Asian countries have increasingly outpaced our nation.

The state of American education can be summed up by the report, *A Nation at Risk*, published more than twenty-five years ago, which indicated that a "rising tide of mediocrity" is eroding the well-being of the nation.[39] This mediocrity is linked to the foundations of our educational institutions and is spilling over into the workplace and other sectors of society. The report listed several aspects of educational decline that were evident to educators and citizens alike: lower achievement scores, lower testing requirements, lower graduation requirements, lower teacher expectations, fewer academic courses, more remedial courses, and higher illiteracy rates. It noted that the schools have attempted to tackle too many social problems that the home and other agencies of society either will not or cannot resolve. The report called for tougher standards for graduation, more courses in science, mathematics and foreign language, a longer school day and school year, more homework, improved and updated textbooks, more rigorous testing and higher expectations for student achievement, teacher accountability, higher salaries for teachers, and more rigorous certification standards for teachers.

The report was hailed by school administrators, policy makers, and business people as the most important government document published for and about education and as the prescription for reform. The report could have been written in 2013 (30 years later) because almost nothing has changed; in fact, disappointingly it can be argued that conditions have worsened.

Although we can present a cascading number of facts and figures about our failure to achieve significant education progress, the idea in this book is to focus on the big picture and avoid scores of data. That said, after spending nearly half a trillion dollars on **compensatory programs** for low-income and low-achieving students since the early 1960s, educators are still unable to

[39] *A Nation At Risk* (Washington, DC: National Commission on Excellence in Education, 1983).

ADMINISTRATIVE ADVICE 10–1

Principles for Improving Schools

A number of important principles result in school effectiveness and excellence. School leaders can adapt these principles to help improve their own schools.

- The school has a clearly stated mission or set of goals.
- Students are achieving at a level commensurate with their abilities.
- School achievement is closely monitored.
- Provisions are made for *all* students, including tutoring for low achievers and enrichment programs for the talented and gifted.
- Teachers and administrators agree on what is "good" teaching and learning.
- Emphasis on cognition is balanced with concerns for students' personal, social, and moral growth; students are taught to be responsible for their actions and behaviors; every student has a "home base" where teachers advise and provide guidance.
- Teachers and administrators are up to date on the knowledge of teaching and learning, as well as knowledge in their specific area or specialty.
- Teachers and administrators expect students to learn and convey their expectations to students and parents.
- Teachers are expected to make significant contributions to school improvement.
- Administrators provide ample support, information, and time for teacher enrichment.
- A sense of teamwork prevails; the staff works together in teams, and there is interdisciplinary and interdepartmental communication.
- Incentives, recognition, and rewards are conveyed to teachers and administrators for their efforts on behalf of the team and school mission.
- The interests and needs of the individual staff members are matched with the expectations of the institution (or school).
- New professional roles are created and others are redefined; the staff has the opportunity to be challenged and creative; there is a sense of professional enrichment and renewal.
- Staff development programs provide teachers with the latest instructional techniques, including how to teach students how to learn so they can eventually learn without the teacher.
- The school environment is safe and healthy; there is a sense of order (not control) in classrooms and hallways.
- Parents and community members are supportive of the school and are involved in school activities.
- The school has a structure and identity of its own that students, teachers, parents, and community members understand and share.
- The school is a learning center for the larger community, for the young and old, for students and parents alike; it reflects the norms and values of the community, and the community sees the school as an extension of the community.

determine which programs work and whether more spending affects educational outcomes.

The International Report Card

Moving on to the demands of knowledge and technology, the data are not impressive when comparisons in math and science are made between U.S. students and students in advanced technological countries. European and Asian students consistently outperform American students on international tests in science and mathematics, and the gaps consistently increase in the higher grades.

The international comparisons started in the mid 1960s, with the International Association for the Evaluation of Educational Achievement (IEA) and the publication of Torsten Husen's study, in the area of mathematics, involving 133,000 elementary and secondary students and 5,450 schools in twelve technologically advanced countries.[40] Especially noticeable were the overall good showings of Japan and Israel and the poor showings of the United States. The range of difference between high- and low-performing countries decreased when the most able students were compared, indicating that the "cream of mathematics talent" is distributed equally over various countries. Student characteristics highly correlated with achievement, and the child's social class accounted for the greatest share of variation in learning. The study also showed that at every age level, and in most countries, boys outperformed girls.

In the next group of studies, the researchers embarked on a six subject survey, including science. In this study, 258,000 elementary and secondary students and 9,700 schools in nineteen countries (four of them undeveloped) were involved. U.S. students never finished first or second in any of the six subject areas and were last seven times; in science, they scored below the international average. Student characteristics highly correlated with achievement, and a child's social class accounted for the greatest share in variation related to learning, thus corresponding with the Coleman, Jencks, and Duncan analysis. Although the impact of the home was considerably greater than the direct effect of school variables, the impact of schooling was shown to be generally more important for science and foreign language than for other areas. The suggestion that certain subjects might be more amenable to school influences is encouraging to those who feel that schools should have a significant effect on learning.

As a matter of common knowledge among text experts, there are unique limitations with large-scale international studies, including common content across countries, translation of content and selection or representation of students to be tested. Nevertheless, international test comparisons have continued for the last thirty-five years. For this policy agenda, the **international report card** for U.S. students would be around a "D."

Fast forwarding to the most recent and famous international tests in mathematics and science are the Trends in International Mathematics and Science Study (**TIMSS**), administered three times in grades 4, 8, and 12 in 1995, 1999, and 2003. In the first two studies, published between 1998 and 2001, U.S. fourth grade students in math ranked eighth out of eighteen among industrialized countries that participated, and in science tied for third place. In eighth grade, U.S. students ranked slightly below average in math (twenty-three out of thirty-eight industrialized countries) and slightly above average in science (below 14 countries). By the twelfth grade, American students scored last in math among twenty industrialized countries, and in science they scored below 16 countries. While the international average math/science scores were 500, the U.S. average in math was 461 and in science 480.[41]

International test comparisons were so bleak that for the third study, the U.S. government decided to compare U.S. scores and relative ranking with all countries, including those from the third world and poorest parts of the world. Not surprisingly, U.S. math and science scores were reported average or above average by *Newsweek*, *Time* and the *Wall Street Journal*. In 2003 science scores of fourth graders were seventh highest among 25 countries and eighth graders were twelfth highest among 44 other participating countries such as Armenia, Cyprus, Iran, Moldova, and Tunisia. What this proves is nothing of substance, since a high-tech nation (U.S.) is being compared with low-tech nations. In mathematics the results were similar.[42]

America's decline in human capital continues beyond the TIMSS studies. The Program for International Student Assessment (**PISA**) reported in 2003 the mathematical literacy and scientific literacy skills of 15-year olds among 28 other industrialized countries and 10 non-industrialized countries. U.S. students scored lower than twenty of the industrialized countries and three of the non-industrialized countries in math and lower than nineteen of the industrialized countries and three of the non-industrialized countries in science. The average U.S. *math* score was lower (483) than the average student performance of the 28 other industrialized countries (500). For *science* the average U.S. score was 491 compared to the average score (500).[43] Further analysis of the data revealed that a greater percentage of U.S. students than the industrialized average scored at the lowest levels of performance in mathematics literacy and all four broad areas of problem solving. (No information on specific science topics was available in PISA 2003.)

In the more recent PISA test, administered in 2006, U.S. 15-year olds ranked 25th lowest out of 30 in math

[40]Torsten Husen, *International Study of Achievement in Mathematics: A Comparison of Twelve Countries*, Vols 1 and 2. (New York: Wiley, 1967).

[41]*The Condition of Education, 2005* (Washington, DC: U.S. Government Printing Office, 2005), Indicators 11–13, pp. 45–47; *The Condition of Education, 2006* (Washington, DC: U.S. Government Printing Office, 2006), Indicators 13, 18, pp. 45, 50.

[42]*The Condition of Education, 2006*, Table 8, p. 18.

[43]Ibid Tables 9, 10, pp. 20–21, Appendix Notes, pp. 240–241.

and 24th lowest out of 30 in science among other industrialized countries. That put our average on the same level as Portugal and Slovakia, rather than with other industrialized countries such as Australia, Canada, or South Korea. Of all the industrialized countries, the U.S. had the greatest percentages of students at or below the lowest level of proficiency in math and science, called level 1, "limited knowledge."[44] This statement is true not only for science and math, but also for reading.[45]

The International Adult Literacy and Lifeskills Survey (ALL) analyzed the degree to which the adult population could perform mathematical tasks in daily life and the work place. Specific areas of measurement included the ability to apply math skills to number sense, estimation, measurement and statistics. Six countries participated, including Switzerland, Norway, Canada, and Bermuda—all which scored higher than the U.S.—and Italy.[46] Moreover, the Educational Testing Service has concluded that better educated people are leaving the workforce and being replaced by people with less education and skill. This trend reflects U.S. demographic changes—an increase in the minority population and a shift in the immigration policy.

For example, Hispanics scored 75 points lower than whites, and blacks score 63 points lower. Native-born whites and Asian Americans were tied for second place in the international ranking in literacy. Immigrants account for 40 percent of the U.S. labor force, but they rank 74 points behind native-born workers. In short, American productivity is partially based on the G.I. Bill and pre-1960 immigrants who were largely from Europe and were more skilled than today's immigrants who hail from non-European and non-industrialized nations. Soon the more skilled workers will be retiring and replaced by a less literate workforce. The effect on productivity and global competition, and the subsequent economic decline of the country, can be predicted by referring to the trends in our demographic outcomes.

The Economics of Schooling

As the U.S. falls further behind in achievement, the McKinsey consulting firm released a report, *The Economic Impact of the Achievement Gap in America's Schools* in 2009. The implications of the report revealed our national decline in productivity and jobs. Had America been able to close the gap in science and math achievement between 1983 and 1998 and raised its performance to the level of such nations as Canada, Finland and South Korea, the U.S. **Gross Domestic Product** in 1998 would have been approximately $2 trillion higher. If the achievement gap had been closed between black and Hispanic students and white and Asian students by 1998, the Gross Domestic Product in 2008 would have been about $400 to $500 billion higher. If the gap between America's low-income students (25 percent) and the remaining students (75 percent) had been similarly narrowed, GDP in 2008 would have been $400 to $670 billion higher. In terms of PISA math and science output and the amount of money we spend on each student, which is among the highest in the world, the report concludes that "we get 60 percent less for our education dollars in terms of average test score results than do other wealthy [industrialized] nations."[47]

Classroom size or teacher-student ratios of a group contribute to student learning and ultimately to test outcomes. Obviously, one-to-one learning (a coach and student) is ideal and more effective than a ten-to-one ratio of students to teacher, and this small group is more beneficial than a classroom size of thirty students. But the fact is that social-class difference and ethnic difference (even when class is controlled) contribute to attitudes and behaviors related to learning. The U.S. average classroom size is 15 to 1 compared to Japan, South Korea, and Hong Kong where ratios are 19:1 to 28:1, yet the latter countries always outscore U.S. students in math and science tests.[48]

Pulling It Together

The picture worsens when education spending is compared on an international level. Among industrialized countries reporting education spending, the United States spends more than 4.5 of its GDP on education, ranking us mid range among industrialized countries. But our expenditures per student is high—as indicated earlier, second only to Switzerland.[49] In other words,

[44]*The Condition of Education 2008,* (Washington, DC: U.S. Printing Office, 2008).

[45]See Gerald W. Bracey, "PISA: Not Leaning Hard on U.S. Economy," *Phi Delta Kappa.* 90 (2009): 450–451.

[46]*The Condition of Education 2008.*

[47]*The Economic Impact of the Achievement Gap in America's Schools* (Washington, DC: McKinsey & Company, 2009).

[48]*Digest of Education Statistics 2009* (Washington, DC: U.S. Government Printing Office, 2009), table 401, p. 587.

[49]Ibid.

other countries do not have same resources as we do, yet they make a greater effort by spending more of their GDP on education. The inference is that we do not get our money's worth in education spending—and money alone is not going to solve our education problems. To be sure, education is big business—and about $600 billion is annually spent on K-12 education. However, there is little indication that spending more on schools will improve student achievement. The issue involves human capital—the values, motivation and work and study ethic of the nation and its youth.

There is a wealth of data over a 40-year period, from the 1966 Coleman report entitled *Equal Educational Opportunity* to the 2008 National Mathematics Advisory Panel report, *Foundations for Success*, showing that the most important variable related to student achievement is the child's family background and the second most important factor is the peer group. Other variables, including what the schools or teachers do, "are secondary or irrelevant" in the words of Harvard's Christopher Jencks. In fact, as reported earlier there is data from the Rand Corporation and other studies suggesting that no more than 17 to 20 percent of the variance related to student learning is associated with schooling and teaching.[50] People with political motives would prefer to bury this data and hold teachers and school accountable.

The point is, no person alive can say what education and social programs in schools have been consistently successful. Chapter by chapter, we have learned about the failure of one government program after another, including compensatory education, job training, urban renewal, and welfare—each of which cost tax payers billions of dollars a year.[51] The analysis has suggested that with respect to school financing, we are already spending too much in terms of what we are getting in return. In the early stages of school and related compensatory programs, input increments have a high marginal return, but they gradually diminish as they are extended to large numbers of low-achieving children. Early gains fade out and there is virtually no increase in output; in fact, in many areas of education we reach a "**flat area**," of less output in relation to input, or worse, no return.

Sadly, nearly half its nation's students who graduate high school test at the seventh grade level in math and eighth grade in science, and one-third below ninth grade in reading. Today's high school students are tomorrow's workforce. The effects of school achievement is seen in the erosion of America's global competitiveness—and future jobs which require skills that build on math and science literacy and reading. Business and military leaders complain that they are required to spend billions of dollars annually on costly remedial education and training programs in the basic skills, or the three Rs. Between 1980 and 2000, remedial mathematics courses in four-year colleges increased by 75 percent, and by 2005, constituted one-fourth of all mathematic courses taught in these institutions.[52] That year, more than 1.8 million, or 20 percent, of college students in two-and four-year colleges were enrolled in "learning strategies," and "study skills." These courses have become a cottage industry at the high school, college, and armed service levels.

Excuses and More Excuses

So what excuse can U.S. educators muster to explain the consistently low scores of American students, despite concerted federal, state, and local efforts since the post-Sputnik era to increase math and science achievement scores? Here's a short list:

1. About 20 to 33 percent of American middle school and high school science and math teachers are teaching out of license; furthermore, nearly half of those certified to teach science and math teach subjects they are not qualified to teach. (For example, a biology teacher may not be qualified to teach chemistry or physics and a math teacher may not be qualified to teach calculus (only algebra and geometry).
2. Since the mid 1950s there has been a slight average increase in science and math coursework among graduating U.S. high school students, leveling at 2.5 and 2.9 years respectively. But the data is not impressive when comparisons are made with high school seniors in other advanced countries. Japanese, South Korean, and Hong Kong high school students, for example, average 1¼ science courses per year and 1½ math courses per year, including calculus and statistics. The result is that Japanese, South Korean,

[50]Averch, *How Effective is Schooling?*; Frederick Mosteller and Daniel P. Moynihan, *On Equality of Educational Opportunity*. (New York: Random House, 1972).

[51]For the Opposite view, see Stanley Pogrow Teaching Content Outrageously: *How to Capitivate All Students and Accelerate Learning, Grades 4-12* (San Francisco: Jossey-Bass, 2008).

[52]*The Coming Crisis in Citizenship* (Wilmington, DE: Intercollegiate Studies Institute, 2006); *Failing Out Students: Failing America* (Wilmington, DE: Intercollegiate Studies Institute, 2007).

and Hong Kong students consistently outperform American students on international tests.

3. Measuring the cumulative achievement on a short test may not sufficiently cover what students have learned. About 25 percent of the test items in math and science reflect topics not studied by American test takers.
4. American science and math textbooks are numerous—some above average, some average, and some below average in quality—whereas textbooks in other countries are approved by the ministry of education so there is consistency of coverage.
5. American high school students have less homework (23 percent of eleventh graders report having no assigned homework, 14 percent do not do their homework, and 26 percent do less than one hour per day of homework), and engage in more social activities, out-of-school activities, and part-time jobs than their international counterparts who often have four to five hours of homework daily.
6. American students average 3.5 hours per day of TV viewing, not to mention Internet surfing and texting, and we know there is an inverse relationship between TV viewing and student achievement, especially after the second or third grade. (The positive effects of watching Sesame Street and other language-skill programs become increasingly irrelevant after age seven or eight.)
7. European and Asian students have a longer school day and school year, with European countries averaging 200 days and Asian countries averaging 220 days, compared to the United States, which has about a 180-day school calendar. The American school day is approximately six hours, compared to the European school day which is seven hours and the Asian school day which is nearly eight hours. Over 12 years, the difference equates to two to three years of extra school time.
8. Student poverty among American students is the highest, about 21 to 25 percent. It is nearly 50 percent higher than any other industrialized country; next is Australia with 14 percent and Canada with 13.5 percent. Moreover, we know poverty correlates in an inverse relationship with student achievement. In addition, the United States has among the highest student drug addiction, student violence, gang activity, and teenage pregnancy among industrialized nations.
9. The breakdown of the American family is well documented. More than 50 percent of American students live with a single head of household; it approaches 75 percent in our big cities, where student achievement is the lowest compared to other parts of the country.
10. Finally, it should not be assumed that students taking the test in all countries are drawn from a normal bell curve or ability distribution. Some countries—such as China, Japan, and Russia—may have certain political agendas, or sensitivity about "saving face," and are more selective in determining which students will take the test.[53]

Although all of these reasons help explain the low scores in math and science achievement among American students on international tests, part of the problem lies in the limited amount of course work in these twin subject areas. By way of example, if you want to learn how to drive, play tennis or chess, or read, you need to devote time to the endeavor—the more *instructional time*, the more proficient you should become. Thus, if Americans are concerned about math and science, (and we should be because of the information-technology age we live in), then we need to increase instructional time to allow for proficiency in these subjects. This consideration must be weighed against a belief among many educators that schools need to emphasize the whole child and the liberal arts, and that teachers should be paid on the basis of qualifications and experience with no differential for specific subjects, such as math and science. Based on supply and demand, as well as the needs for the nation, free marketers would support higher pay for math and science teachers. In fact, in an era of high-stake testing, with most school districts focusing on reading and math achievement, there is concern among policy makers that science is getting shortchanged in the elementary and junior high schools.

While most of us recognize that spending money on education is an investment in the nation's future, pouring more money in schools scratches the surface of the larger problem of family structure and culture—which in turn deal with stratification and inequality. A liberal view is that society prepares the achievement gap

[53]For a more detailed analysis, with supporting citations, see Ornstein, *Teaching and Schooling in America: Pre- and Post-September 11th* (Boston: Allyn and Bacon, 2003), pp. 404–407.

before the students enter school; the poor and minority populations are the victims and the test results are the evidence that society is unfair and unjust. A conservative view emphasizes personal responsibility and fingers the family as the source of the education problem.

A few disenfranchised children will succeed in school, but the majority face major obstacles because the so-called solution is isolated from the larger social and economic issues—basically inequality. According to Richard Wilkinson and Kate Pickett, British social scientists, in rich countries where incomes are more evenly distributed, the citizens have higher educational achievement, live longer, and have fewer rates of obesity and delinquency. In their book, *The Spirit Level*, higher taxes on the rich and smaller difference in pay lead to a better quality of life for all citizens of that country. Where inequality is greatest, the lower classes and those who feel discriminated perform worse on cognitive tests than in countries where there are fewer differences in socio-economic status.[54] But in a society (like ours) that rewards individual achievement and innovation, it is argued that lower taxes cause people to work harder and the argument for more equality breaks down.

Brain Drain Counts

The new wave of scientific and technological knowledge will come from Asia, given existing education and economic trends. There is a reset or shift in brain power from the East to the West, commonly called "**brain drain**," as foreign students are beginning to leave, or decline to attend, first-rate U.S. institutions of higher learning and follow the lure of economic opportunity, slowing down in the West and routed back to the East.

Not only has the number of foreign student enrollments in U.S colleges and universities dropped since 9/11, down from 583,000 to 565,000, fewer students are opting to come to the United States, even after being accepted. In the meantime, between 2003 and 2008, the number of students from China and India enrolled in Australian and Canadian universities increased three- to four-fold because of an immigration "point system" that puts a premium on education, and the European Union is in the process of issuing "blue cards" that will give talented people in science and technology a "fast track" to EU citizenship. And, here is the latest brain-drain score. As many as 10 percent of Australia's employed population are highly qualified foreigners. For Canada, it is 7 percent; for the U.S. it is 3 percent; and for the EU it's 1.7 percent.[55]

As for the U.S., the number of Chinese and Indian students—totaling 25 percent of all foreign students in 2008—has declined because of improved economies and opportunities in these two countries. The booming economies of emerging nations around the world are welcoming the return of their own talent that was once taken for granted would get educated and then remain in the U.S. The world is opening up to ambitious and educated foreigners at precisely the same time the U.S. is closing down. The outcome is that we are beginning to lose our competitive edge, as most of these students were enrolled in science, math, and technological fields and then remained in the United States.

The more graduate students in science and engineering we attract from Asia, the larger our pool of human capital that may wind up in Silicon Valley, North Carolina's Golden Triangle, and other high-tech and innovative centers. "Brain workers" migrate to "brain working" centers. Given the rapid increase in globalization and the internet, brain-based jobs are highly mobile. U.S. immigration policies must attract innovative and technological talent, not repel it by making it difficult to obtain student visas or science/engineering job visas. But Congress has not revised the visa rules for the last twenty years, and have added more restrictions since 9/11. Hence, there are many brilliant minds who try to get into the U.S. and now go elsewhere. Most disturbing, the nation's competitiveness and wealth is tied to brain drain, which is now being reversed. In making immigration laws, the U.S. Congress tends to cater to big business' demand for cheap labor to fill the ranks of agribusiness, hotel, and restaurant industries, and sweatshop manufacturing, while short-changing high-tech, high-wage industries and ignoring the economic advantages of human capital. For example, an estimated 75 percent of the agricultural work force is here illegally.[56]

The fact is, foreign student graduates earn a significant percentage of the nation's degrees in science and engineering. For example, in 2007, the U.S. Department of Education reported that 27 percent of the science/technology and 39 percent of the engineering masters and 44 percent of the science/technology and 63 percent

[54]Richard Wilkinson and Kate Pickett, *The Spirit Level*, (New York: Penguin Books, 2009).

[55]"Not the Ace in the Pack" *Economist,* October 27 2007, p. 60; Allan C. Ornstein, *Wealth versus Work*, in progress.

[56]Jason DeParle, "Rising Breed of Migrant Workers," *New York Times,* August 20, 2007, p. 1A.

Balancing Excellence and Equality

Most societies over the centuries have been efficient in keeping the vast majority of people down. The terms "slave", "serf," "peasant," "indentured servant," and even "factory worker" are good examples of how a person's status was determined not by intelligence or other talents but by membership in a family or class.

Question: Can a democratic society provide for both excellence and equality? To what extent?

Arguments PRO

1. Every student should "shoot" for the moon and have sufficient ambition to achieve the American Dream.
2. Except in extreme cases of retardation, everyone should have the right to a college education; that is, to work with one's mind and not to be limited to work with one's hands or muscles.
3. Individuals of great capacities and great energies help create a dynamic and innovative society; such people should be nurtured, supported, and rewarded according to their ability and levels of achievement.
4. Those who display special intelligence must be provided with incentives for their performance.
5. An environment that provides freedom and rewards is conducive for a society that fosters excellence and creativity; and, in turn productivity, economic vitality, and high standards of living for its members.
6. When democracies remove the ceilings and expectations, nothing is more beneficial for those who are smarter or stronger than their peers.
7. The notion of the self-made person often combines with upper-class and aristocratic sentiments in order to combat equalitarian ideas and movements. This has led to American conservatism in politics.

Arguments CON

1. Obsessive ambition leads to emotional breakdown and bitter defeats; youth must realize room at the top is limited.
2. Educating everyone to the limits of their potential does not mean sending everyone to college; the top 30% should benefit from a college education and everyone else should be encouraged to vocational education or learning on the job.
3. No one should be regarded as better than anyone else in a democratic society; in the important matters of life and death, all people are equally worthy of society's care and concerns.
4. Not everyone can hit homeruns, but everyone is entitled to get up at bat.
5. A fair society needs floors and ceilings to protect the average person and to restrict those who's obsessive drive for great power and wealth could lead to exploiting the public and conquering others.
6. A democratic society must balance extreme emphasis on individual performance with safety nets and social programs, for those who run a slow race or are weaker than their peers.
7. The titans of industry and banking often need to be regulated by government in order to protect working and middle-class people. This has led to American liberalism in politics.

of the engineering doctorate degrees were granted to foreign students. Immigrants make up two thirds of the nation's supply of such workers (science, technology, and engineers), and it is estimated to be 75 percent by 2015.[57]

[57]"Give Us your Scientists." *Economist*, March 7, 2009, p.84; "Made in America," *New York Daily News*, August 3, 2008, p.24. Also see Ajay Agrawal, et al. "Brain Drain or Brain Bank" NBER Working Paper No. 14592, December 2008.

Their role in innovation and economic growth is obvious, and the more we attract talented immigrants the more likely new ideas will flourish and turn into future jobs and national wealth. Congress is supposed to revise the student visa rules, currently capped at 85,000 per year and requiring foreigners to wait six years or more for a green card. In the meantime many of these students are being lost to the United States—the nation that educated them. What the U.S. needs to do to maintain the flow of "brain drain" from other countries is to create an immigration policy that slashes the influx of unskilled immigrants and rewards human capital with a point system modeled after Canada and Australia.

Economists think of knowledge professionals, unlike physical goods, as nonrival. Ideas and innovation by one person do not preclude use by others. The knowledge industry is not a zero sum game, and in fact the common argument is that one good innovation leads to another; knowledge builds on knowledge. All well and good, but directing a talented mathematician into engineering or Wall Street is a zero sum game, since the number of skilled mathematicians are limited in the U.S. For every mathematician or potential engineer that chooses a career in finance, the nation loses about five other knowledge and technological jobs. We need to rethink paying "rookie" Wall Street players $250,000 to $350,000 (including bonuses) and "freshman" scientists and engineers $50,000 to $60,000. Eventually, this kind of thinking—where a company considers a Wall Street person a "profit" item or money maker and scientist or engineer as a "cost" item—is going to lead us into an economic hole and hobble us into decline.

Centers of Creativity

Now, the U.S. is in a fortunate position. Its universities are highly regarded, its national character welcomes immigrants and its economy is still dynamic, inventive and tech-driven. Hence, it does not have to advertise or make special efforts to attract talented foreigners. To keep competitive, all it needs to do is to expand the supply of visas and make it easier for talented foreigners to obtain citizenship. What we need to understand is that migration today is not only about poor people moving to rich countries for opportunities. People from rich countries are now moving all over the world, chasing jobs that are being outsourced from rich to emerging countries. More important, skilled and educated immigrants have come to the realization that emerging countries are growing faster than the U.S. and the European Union; they are following jobs where there are opportunities. As a result, "brain drain" is being reversed—away from the U.S. These new shifts in world population need to be recognized if we are to retain American knowledge, innovation, and wealth. The U.S. is still considered the top country in generating new ideas and adopting them quickly, according to a major European business school, INSEAD, based near Paris. But other studies by the World Bank rated the U.S. third in terms of innovation, behind Singapore and New Zealand.[58]

Summary

Normally we would end the chapter by highlighting the main points. For this new chapter, the authors thought it would be appropriate to focus on growing inequality in America. In this connection, one of the authors published *Class Counts* in 2007 and started the book with 14 points entitled "What this Book is About." The same points are being used to sum up this chapter, but keep in mind, the gap between the rich and the rest of us has worsened since the original points were published. In short, the balance between excellence and equality, rich and the rest of us, is tilting to the extent that the middle class is struggling and shrinking; inequality is growing and the U.S. is heading for a financial oligarchy, much worse than the aristocratic Old World–class structure that our Founding Fathers feared and tried to avoid.

1. Class Counts. Class differences and class warfare have existed since the beginning of Western Civilization, with the Greeks and Romans, and since our nation was founded. It was reflected in the different philosophies of Thomas Jefferson and Alexander Hamilton and presently between liberals and conservatives. It is keenly expressed in who gets admitted to Harvard or Yale and who attends second- or third-tier colleges; only 3 percent of students at the nation's top 146 colleges come from families in the bottom economic quartile (or lowest 25 percent).
2. The gap in income and wealth between the rich (the top 10 percent) and the rest (the bottom 90 percent) has increased steadily in the last twenty-five years. In 2005, the average top worker in the United States earned $43,506. Among Fortune 500 companies, the average top executive was paid $11.3 million, not including stock options, which have the potential effect of doubling or tripling the earnings of a CEO.
3. In 2005 the bottom 90 percent of the population earned $117,000 or less, while the top 0.1 percent earned $16 million or more. From 1950 to 1970 for every additional dollar earned by the lower 90 percent—what I like to call the "new struggling class"—those on the top 0.1 earned $162. From

[58]Robert Guy Matthews, "U.S. Leads the Way in Innovation." *Wall Street Journal,* January 16, 2007.

1990 to 2002, for every dollar earned by the lower 90 percent, these top taxpayers earned an additional $18,000. This kind of gap is eventually going to shred the middle class and then the democratic process.

4. For the last twenty-five years, real wages of the working class have remained flat at about $15 to $16 per hour. Job loss and job insecurity are at an all time high in the United States, as reflected in the loss of high-paying jobs and the outsourcing of white-collar jobs, as well as the reduction or elimination of company-funded pensions and health insurance. Replacement jobs result in a one-third reduction in wages, regardless of retraining and education.
5. Despite continuous growth in the economy from the 2000 stock market bubble (to 2007), nearly two-thirds of new jobs—more than 5 million in total—pay less than $35,000 a year. The largest U.S. employer is Walmart, where the average worker earns about $7.50 per hour and has minimal health insurance coverage.
6. As many as 85 percent of American families remain in the same class or move up or down one quintile three decades later. During a twenty-five-year period ending in 2004, 61 percent of families in the lowest income quintile were stuck at the same level. In reverse, 59 percent of the highest income quintile remained at the same level.
7. The middle class is struggling and shrinking. The average consumer debt was more than $9,300 in 2005; the savings rate was a negative 0.4 percent, the first time since the Depression in 1933 that Americans' spending exceeded disposable income. Educated young Americans are in worse shape. The average debt from student loans among college students was more than $18,000 and among graduate students was approximately $45,000 in 2005.
8. Tuition at private colleges has increased 110 percent in the last decade, compared to 60 percent for four-year state colleges; however, income for the bottom 50 percentile increased 35 percent and, after considering inflation, there was no gain. Measures designed to create tax free savings accounts for college disproportionately benefit families in the top 40 percentile.
9. Today, 23 percent of all people sixty-five to seventy-four years old hold jobs, compared to 16 percent just two decades ago. The number of workers in the sixty-five to seventy-four group grew three times the rate as the overall workforce in 2004 and 10 million previously retired people were forced back into work in order to make ends meet. Although most seniors want to keep their homes, 44 percent of home-owners at age seventy will have sold their house by age eighty-five to pay for living costs and basic needs.
10. The Medicare trust is expected to start running a deficit in 2013 and Social Security is expected to go bust by 2044. Looming deficits in both social programs are forcing the government to curtail benefits. Some 50 percent of the American populace are without pensions and are relying on Social Security for retirement. While hundreds of billions of dollars are passed on yearly to the offspring of the rich (the top 10 percent) and super-rich (the top 1 percent), 86 percent of U.S. households will receive less than $1,000 in cash value or no inheritance at all.
11. Education is no longer the great equalizer. Schools and colleges cannot overcome the difference between those born on third base and those who are struggling to get up to bat. The American dream is slowly evaporating and becoming more unattainable for the under-thirty generation.
12. So long as Americans have the view that the Michael Eisners, Michael Dells, and Michael Jordans of the world, and all their descendents, are entitled to all their wealth because they worked hard, founded highly successful companies, or could shoot a ball through a hoop, then the millions that they make will continue to create economic imbalance and doom the rest of us to a bleak future characterized by vast inequality.
13. A democratic society requires some kind of balance between achievement and equality. Endpoints or benchmarks are needed to establish economic ceilings and floors. A moral society, one that is fair and just, sets limits on the accumulation of wealth and inherited privilege and also guarantees a safety net for the less fortunate. Without such limits, social mobility and opportunity become abstract and unachievable ideals representing nothing more that propaganda derived from a sham notion of a mobile society driven by the notion of equality, the Protestant work ethic and American dream.
14. Cultural and social differences and religious views, reflected in red and blue voting patterns, mask important economic and safety net issues such as jobs, pensions, Social Security, and health-care and college tuition costs. New laws and policies are required, including government regulation of Wall Street and the financial and banking industries, as well as increased safety nets for American people.

15. There needs to be a redistribution of wealth in order to make U.S. society more democratic, fair, and just. Recommended are a host of taxes, including, but not limited to, luxury taxes, windfall profit taxes, estate taxes, and fuel taxes. Other recommendations include eliminating taxes on food, drugs, and low-cost clothing, free state-college tuition for above-average students, and zero tax on the first $50,000 earned in annual wages for all Americans.
16. A strategy is outlined in order to restore the social contract that is supposed to exist between the government and the people. The U.S. standard of living and quality of life for the bottom 90 percent of the economic scale is at stake. The idea is for people to vote for their pocketbook, and not be derailed by secondary or side cultural issues.[59]

Key Terms

Merit
Natural rights
Common school
Horatio Alger's themes
Social capital
Survival of the fittest
Kalamazoo, Michigan court decision
Sputnik
Intelligence tests
G.I. Bill
Equal opportunity
Home environment
Peer group
Regression analysis
Redistribution of income
Luck
Intangible factors
Compensatory programs
International report card
TIMSS
PISA
Gross Domestic Product
Flat area
Brain drain

[59]Allan C. Ornstein, *Class Counts: Education Inequality and the Shrinking Middle Class* (Lanham, MD: Rowman & Littlefield, 2007), pp. VII–IX.

Discussion Questions

1. How would you describe the relationship between excellence, equality, and education?
2. In what way did our Founding Fathers and early educational pioneers embrace the idea of equal education opportunity?
3. In what ways do conservative (liberal) educators define excellence and equality in education?
4. What important conclusions do you reach after reading the Coleman-Duncan-Jencks studies?
5. What important factors are associated with U.S. student performance on international math and science tests?

Suggested Readings

Duke , Daniel. *The Challenges of School District Leadership* (Clifton, N.J.: Routledge, 2010). In order to prepare future generations, school leaders need to meet the demands of testing and accountability.

Gardner, John. *Excellence: Can We Be Equal and Excellent Too,* rev ed. (New York: Norton, 1984). Originally published in 1961, the book is still relevant today, describing the conditions under which excellence and equality can coexist in our society.

Hammond, Linda Darling. *The Flat World and Education* (New York: Teachers College Press, Columbia University, 2009). How equality and equity at all levels of education are essential for the nation's future prosperity.

Murphy, Joseph and Coby V. Meyers. *Turning Around Failing Schools* (Thousand Oaks, CA: Corwin Press, 2007). Diagnosing failing schools and turning them around.

Profriedt, William A. *High Expectations: The Cultural Roots of Standards Reform in American Education* (New York: Teachers College Press, Columbia University, 2008). Educational reforms are placed in historical and cultural perspective, with the emphasis on closing the achievement gap.

Ornstein, Allan C. *Class Counts: Education, Inequality, and the Shrinking Middle Class* (Lanham, MD: Rowman & Littlefield, 2007). The relationship between class, education, and mobility, and growing inequality between the rich and the rest of us.

Spring, Joel. *Pedagogies of Globalization* (Mahwah, NJ: Erlbaum, 2006). The role of globalization and its influences on excellence, equality, and economics.

11

School Finance and Productivity

FOCUSING QUESTIONS

1. What are the three major sources of revenue for public schools, and what proportion of school revenues do they contribute?
2. Why are many local school authorities increasingly looking to the states for educational revenues?
3. What is wrong with solely relying on property taxes as revenue sources for schools?
4. What fiscal problems characterize urban schools?
5. Given the task to reduce your school budget 10 percent, what three or four items would you cut? Why?
6. How can school productivity be increased without changing expenditures?
7. What financial trends will most likely affect school management in the twenty-first century?
8. What is the average age of the schools in your district? What school infrastructure problems are most costly in your district?
9. Why is there such resistance to closing schools? What is the best economic solution to take in dealing with closed schools?

In this chapter, we attempt to answer these questions about education financing and productivity by first examining the funding sources and distribution. Next we explore the methods of school funding and the advantages and disadvantages of each. Then we discuss developing budgets and the correlation between expenditures and student productivity. We examine how aging school buildings and environmental hazards can affect expenditures. Finally, we explore international and U.S. spending for education.

Education and Economics

Education is big business. In 2009, the grades K-12 operating school budget was more than $600 billion, an increase from $127 billion expended six years ago.[1] The estimated middle range expenditures for K-12 education in America should increase another $50 billion by 2018.[2]

The operating school budget of K-12 public schools is equivalent to 3.7 percent of the nation's gross domestic product. (The **gross domestic product**, GDP, is the market value of all goods and services produced within a specified period—in practice, one year.) When institutions of higher education are included, that amount increases to 7.4 percent of GDP.[3] In terms of people involved, more than 6.2 million individuals are employed nationally by public schools—about one in four of every American is engaged in some aspect of education as a student, teacher, administrator, counselor, aide, or support staff.[4] The estimated school clientele served in 2009 included 49.8 million K-12 public school students; 5.2 million private school students; 3.2 million public school teachers; and approximately 3.2 million public school administrators, counselors, and support staff.[5] What we spend on services to develop human capital in schools is likely to determine the quality of life for our children and grandchildren.

Education expenditures have generally increased more rapidly than inflation. As a result of the so-called Great Recession which officially began in late 2007, education is experiencing severe financial difficulty. As of 2010, state revenues had declined in 44 states for which comparable earlier data were available. With tax revenues declining and budget reserves largely drained, 29 states and the District of Columbia cut education spending. State revenue shortfalls for fiscal year 2011 totaled $350 to $375 billion, depending on the source. Thus, in the 2009–2010 year, states decreased education spending an average of 4.8 percent to help alleviate budget problems.[6] The National Conference of State Legislatures estimates that cuts to education in fiscal 2011 (school year 2010–2011) could total $55 billion, or about 15 percent of the states' total shortfall.[7]

Examples of where K-12 budget cuts have been made in the 2009–2010 school year can be seen in the percentage of school districts that have (1) increased class size (44%), (2) laid off school personnel (44%), (3) deferred maintenance (33%), (4) cut extracurricular activities (28%), and (5) eliminated academic programs (22%).[8] Amid growing signs of taxpayer resistance, school districts from New York to California are biting into teachers' and administrators' salaries and benefits. Across the country school districts are freezing teacher salaries, implementing teachers' and administrators' givebacks (temporary pay cuts), requiring professional furlough days (that is shortening the school year and reducing pay accordingly), laying off teachers and administrators, and lowering contributions for pensions and health programs.

Ah, welcome to the new world of school board bargaining sessions, where corporate-style accountability, cost-cutting measures and layoffs threaten to implode. As New York Governor David Paterson asserted, "It's all about keeping taxes where they are and shrinking the budget." Or as New Jersey Governor Chris Christie said, "Today, we are fulfilling the promise of a smaller government that lives within its means."[9] The states simply do not have the money; the collapse of state tax revenues caused by the recession is the sharpest on record.

Contrast this picture with that of about a decade ago, in 1998, when state government budget surpluses totaled $40 billion.[10] Part of the problem is that professional hires are determined by money available instead of projected needs. In good times, school districts become bloated, and union pressure makes it difficult to cut slots when there are revenue shortfalls. For example, New York City added 15,000 new teachers between 2000 and 2009, even though enrollment fell 121,000 during the same period. In Florida, student enrollment increased 6 percent and the number of teachers rose

[1]*Digest of Education Statistics 2009* (Washington, DC: U.S. Department of Education, 2009), p. 118.

[2]*Projections of Education Statistics to 2018* (Washington, DC: U.S. Department of Education, 2009), p. 20.

[3]Ibid, p. 45.

[4]Ibid, p. 117.

[5]Ibid.

[6]*An Update on State Budget Cuts* (Washington, DC: Center on Budget and Policy Priorities, 2010), p. 6; Bob Herbert, "Invitation to Disaster," *New York Times,* January 8, 2010, p. A19.

[7]"School Funding on Block Again as States' Fiscal Pain Continues," *Education Week,* March 3, 2010, pp. 15, 18.

[8]"By the Numbers: Budget Cut Impacts," *American School Board Journal,* 197 (2010): 54.

[9]James T. Madore, "Pain in the Budget," *Newsday,* March 17, 2010, p. A2; David M. Halbfinger, "Christie Calls for Sharp Cuts in State Budget," *New York Times,* March 17, 2010, pp. A1, A25.

[10]"NCSL Tracks Link Between State Surpluses, Education Spending," *Education Week,* August 5, 1998, p. 24.

Table 11-1 Revenues for Public Elementary and Secondary Schools, by Source of Funds, 1919-2007

Year	Federal %	State %	Local %	Total %
1919–1920	0.3	16.5	83.2	100
1929–1930	0.4	16.9	82.7	100
1939–1940	1.8	30.3	68.0	100
1949–1950	2.9	39.8	57.3	100
1959–1960	4.4	39.1	56.5	100
1969–1970	8.0	39.9	52.1	100
1979–1980	9.8	46.8	43.4	100
1989–1990	6.1	47.1	46.8	100
1999–2000	7.3	49.5	43.2	100
2006–2007	8.5	47.6	43.9	100

*Totals may not equal 100% due to rounding errors.

Source: *Biennial Survey of Education in the United States, 1919–20 through 1955–56* (Washington, DC: U.S. Government Printing Office, 1957); *Revenues and Expenditures for Public Elementary and Secondary Education 1970–71 Through 1986–87* (Washington, DC: U.S. Government and Printing Office, 1988); *Digest of Education Statistics 2009* (Washington, DC: U.S. Government Printing Office, 2010), Table 172, p. 194.

20 percent. In North Carolina, student enrollment was up 9 percent and teacher hires were up 22 percent.[11]

The three major sources of revenue or financial support for public schools are the local, state, and federal governments. As Table 11–1 depicts, state and local monies remain the basic sources of revenue while the federal contribution remains a distant third, relatively steady at about 6 to 10 percent. State contributions for public education have increased from 16.5 percent in 1920 to a high of 49.5 percent in 2000; lately, the state share has begun to slowly decrease. The local share has decreased from 83 percent in 1920 to 44 percent in 2007. The federal share has increased from less then 1 percent in the 1920s and 1930s to as high as 10 percent in 1980 and is currently 8.5 percent. It began to sharply increase since the 1970s to help compensate for local school shortfalls. It is appropriate that the local share has decreased and the state share has increased, since the Tenth Amendment to the U.S. Constitution names education as a state and not a local function.

Tax Sources of School Revenues

Public schools' operation relies primarily on revenues generated from taxes, especially the local property tax, state sales and income taxes, and indirectly on the national individual income tax. Certain types of taxes are considered superior to others. Most people today accept several criteria for evaluating various forms of taxes including:

1. *A Tax Should Not Cause Unintended Economic Distortions.* It should not alter economic behavior, change consumer spending patterns in favor of one good or service over another, negatively affect a taxpayer's willingness to work, or cause the relocation of business, industry, or people.
2. *A Tax Should Provide Economic Neutrality.* Ideally, taxes should leave individuals in the same relative position after taxes as before paying taxes. As taxes are diversified through income, property, sales, and similar taxes, the impact of any one tax lessens.
3. *A Tax Should be Collected Easily.* This requires that the tax be collected with minimum costs to the taxpayer or government; it also means that it should be difficult to evade and should have minimal or no loopholes.
4. *A Tax Should Be Responsive to Changing Economic Conditions.* During times of inflation when government costs and expenditures rise, the tax revenue should also rise. In a recession, the tax revenue should remain constant or decrease. Responsive taxes are **elastic** to economic conditions while those that are not responsive are **inelastic.**

[11]"Fewer Students, More Teachers," *Wall Street Journal*, April 12, 2010, p. 23.

5. *A Tax Should Provide Adequacy of Yield.* There is no logic in having a tax with little potential for yield revenue in substantial amounts. Nuisance taxes that provide small amounts of monies should be avoided as they often result in added bureaucracy and a frustrated public.
6. *A Tax Should Have Low Administration Costs.* When the administrative costs of collecting taxes are low, it is considered to be more efficient and less bureaucratic.
7. *A Tax Should be Equitable.* A tax should be based on the taxpayer's ability to pay. Those with greater incomes or with property worth more money should pay more in taxes than those who earn less income or own less desirable property. Basically, a fair tax places a greater burden on the rich than the poor. Taxes that are not equitable and require lower-income groups to pay a higher proportion of their income than higher-income groups are called **regressive taxes.** In contrast, taxes that require high-income groups to pay higher percentages of their income are called **progressive taxes.**
8. *A Tax Should Have Visibility of Benefit.* A publically visible benefit of taxes provides taxpayers with a tangible reminder of their tax dollars at work. A well-maintained and functioning new school reminds the community of their tax benefit.
9. *A Tax Should Have Convenience of Payment.* A good tax is convenient for citizens to pay. If taxpayers must stand in line for hours, shuffle from office to office, or take time from work, the tax loses its utility. Taxes are more convenient when they can be paid by mail or electronically.[12]

Local Financing of Public Schools

Although education is the states' responsibility, they have traditionally delegated much of this responsibility to the local school districts. As indicated earlier, the local contribution to school financing has decreased over the last decades, whereas the state contribution has increased. Nevertheless, local funding remains a crucial part of public school funding.

[12]Allan C. Ornstein and Daniel U. Levine, *Foundations of Education, 11th ed.* (Boston: Houghton Mifflin, 2010); William Owings and Leslie Kaplan, *American Public School Finance* (Belmont, CA: Wadsworth, 2006).

Property Tax

The **property tax** is the main source of local revenue for school districts. It is the most important tax structure supporting education. It has a long history in this country, dating back to the Massachusetts Law of 1642, which required settlements of 100 or more households to tax property owners to provide education services.

Today, property taxes are determined by first determining a property's **market value**—the price the property would likely bring if it were sold. Sometimes, the market value is converted to an **assessed value** using a predetermined index or ratio, such as one-fourth or one-third. For example, a property with a market value of $100,000 might have an assessed value of only $25,000. The assessed value is nearly always less than the market value in order to protect the owner and to avoid controversies and appeals, an expensive process with high financial and public relations costs. Finally, the local tax rate, expressed in mills, is applied to the assessed value. A **mill** represents one-thousandth of a dollar ($.001); thus, a tax rate of 10 mills amounts to $10 for each $1,000 of assessed value.

The property tax does not rate well on the equity criterion. Because of differing assessment practices and lack of uniform valuation, people owning equivalent properties may pay different taxes. This results in unequal treatment of equal property. Additionally, the property tax does not always distribute the tax burden according to the ability to pay. For instance, a retired couple may have a home whose market value has increased substantially, but because they live on a fixed income, they cannot afford the increasing taxes. In this respect, it can be argued that sometimes property taxes may have a regressive impact.

In addition, the property tax is not immediately responsive to changing economic conditions. In some states, properties are assessed each year, while others reassess property every two, three, or four years. Thus, a property's assessed value and actual tax are often based on old market conditions. If property values have risen since the last reassessment, then the school district is losing potential tax income; if property values have declined, property taxes may be over burdensome, thereby causing a declining neighborhood to deteriorate further.

The property tax is not always easy to administer or collect. Administratively, an inventory of all properties in the locality must be maintained and assessed with a mechanism to handle appeals. Collection depends on the local tax collection department's efficiency. Wealthy individuals and businesses that contest their property

EXEMPLARY EDUCATIONAL ADMINISTRATORS IN ACTION

WILLIAM G. MEUER Principal, Norwood Park School, Chicago, Illinois.

Words of Advice: While school administration can be stressful and exhausting, it can be enormously rewarding. I have enjoyed and continue to enjoy it every day.

First, determine the age range of students you wish to work with. Develop an expertise for specific areas of the curriculum and a thorough understanding of the psychology for the age group you select.

Seek out a school community that supports your philosophy or one that is open to or desires change. Communicate your philosophy, goals, and beliefs.

Limit the number of goals on the "front burner." Where are these goals coming from? Are they coming down from the central office? The parent community? How does each impact the teaching/learning process? Has the staff had input into the decisions and is there a feeling of ownership?

Celebrate your successes! Everyone needs to know when the task is completed—the goal met, the objective accomplished.

Recognize that children need some fun! Plan and celebrate student successes. Individual and group recognition is essential.

Recognize that staff have out-of-school responsibilities, needs, and interests. Some may be in a degree program that occupies untold hours of study and schoolwork. For another, it may be the responsibility of an aging parent, a health issue, or a second job. Listen! Listen! Listen! Don't be afraid to ask a question.

Finally, I communicate to the staff that I am not above doing what I am requesting of them. Model organization and hard work. Always keep a sense of humor! It has served me well!

taxes often receive abatements. Most states specify the basic minimum property tax rate that localities can levy. An increase in the tax rate often requires local voter approval. Since the mid-1970s, local school districts have had difficulty getting voter approval for raising taxes. Now into the twenty-first century, the school funding pendulum is shifting from reliance on the property tax to reliance on other sources of revenue such as user fees, state sales taxes, and personal property taxes.

User Fees

Besides the property tax, some school districts gather revenue through user fees, special income taxes, and revenue-sharing monies. **User fees**—that is, fees charged specifically to people who use a certain facility or service—are becoming increasingly popular (both with state and local governments) for supporting, partially or wholly, specific services or functions. Usually, income from user fees is earmarked for a particular agency fund supporting the activity that justifies imposing the fee. In cases where the fees do not cover the entire cost of the service, the legislature may pick up the difference by appropriating general revenues. For example, if a state or locality needs funds for a transportation project, it may place a toll on the particular project and make other funds available for education.

User fees are attractive because the public helps pay for the service's provision and only those using the service are "taxed." A few school districts (mostly affluent) already levy user fees on bus services, textbooks, athletic and recreational activities, nursery classes, and after-school centers (where it is legal to do so). To maintain balanced budgets in difficult financial times, schools will probably increase these fees, just as colleges and universities are increasing tuition and other charges. But as college and university tuitions are regressive because they are not based on ability to pay, so are user fees (unless such fees are reduced or waived for low-income or elderly residents).

Tobacco Settlement

Educators want their fair share of the $246 billion tobacco settlement (available from 2000 through 2024) from the states that won this amount in a successful lawsuit against the largest tobacco companies. At the same time, other state agencies raise concerns about the wisdom of shifting these funds from health-related programs, maintaining that tobacco monies should be used for health-related needs.[13] Poor school districts have

[13]Eric Lichtblau, "US Lawsuit Seeks Tobacco Profits," *New York Times*, March 18, 2003, p. A1, A29. Also see http://www.tobaccofreekids.org/reports/settlements/.

considerably fewer opportunities than do wealthier districts to generate additional funds. Hopefully, these tobacco funds will be allocated equitably, with poorer districts receiving a larger portion of the tobacco settlement monies as opposed to a proportional share or an amount based on student enrollments.

Since 2002, states and local governments across the country have been turning to tobacco money to "plug" their deficits at a time when the states are experiencing the worst fiscal crisis in decades. As of 2010, only nine states (Alaska, Delaware, Hawaii, Maine, Montana, North Dakota, South Dakota, Vermont, and Wyoming) spent 50 percent or more of the tobacco settlement monies on tobacco prevention programs.[14] Fourteen states (Alabama, Georgia, Illinois, Kansas, Kentucky, Massachusetts, Michigan, Missouri, New Hampshire, New Jersey, Ohio, South Carolina, Tennessee, and Texas) spent less than 10 percent on tobacco prevention programs.[15]

Many states' credit ratings have been lowered or been placed on alert by the major credit rating agencies. When credit ratings are lowered, states have to pay higher interest rates on bonds to compensate investors for increased risk, raising the capital costs for projects from school construction to roads by hundreds of millions of dollars. Credit rating agencies are concerned that opting to use large sums of tobacco settlement money to reduce budget deficits is a signal of fiscal crisis, although other causes of a downgraded credit rating may exist.[16]

Credit agencies are also worried that states are borrowing money over longer periods of time, such as twenty years or more. In the past, state and city bonds have been sold for shorter time periods. Borrowing over a longer period raises the cost and the potential that the state or local government may be under fiscal stress for a more extended period than usual.

Urban/Suburban Disparities

As helpful as state and federal aid is to most school districts (See Table 11–1), the differential ability of school districts to support education persists. A school district located in a wealthy area or even an area with a broad tax base can generate more local revenue than can poor school districts. As a consequence, total expenditures per student in many states may be three to five times greater in the five wealthiest school districts than in the five poorest school districts. Between big cities and surrounding suburbs the difference is often two to three times greater. For example, in 2009–2010 spending per student for the New York City Schools was $19,500, compared to the Nassau County school districts of Great Neck ($39,900), Manhasset ($28,600) and Roslyn ($26,500) and the Westchester County school districts of Bronxville ($36,300), Scarsdale ($26,900) and Tarrytown ($36,400).

Variations in per pupil spending exist among communities in every state. Disparities in per pupil expenditures between urban areas and their adjacent suburban areas tend to be growing wider. This trend is more apparent in the Northeast and Midwest, owing to the relocation of urban populations and businesses to the suburbs and the Sunbelt states (which in turn further depletes the tax base and increases disparities between rich and poor school districts).

Most urban property taxes (and those of certain poor suburbs) are alarmingly high, about 33 to 100 percent higher per capita than taxes in wealthy adjoining suburbs. High property taxes make it difficult to attract middle-income residents and new jobs to broaden the tax base. The loss of cities' middle-class population and businesses further undermines their tax base. Cities are forced to cut their services, including education, to balance their budgets; these cuts drive away more middle-class citizens and businesses and their potential tax revenues. This negative cycle reinforces itself, exacerbating and partially explaining the decline of many urban schools. Financing has become the major problem for many city schools, and cutting costs and reducing wasteful programs have become important issues.

This phenomenon exists despite federal government attempts to favor poorer and urban school districts through Title 1 and compensatory funding and despite the various states' attempts to equalize funding—to redistribute school revenues through funding formulas and court-ordered reforms. For example, in 2006, federal revenues for schools averaged 9.1 percent nationwide. Among the ten largest school districts (with 50,000 or more students) with the highest poverty indices, the average federal share of revenue was 15.3 percent (See Table 11–2). Detroit has the distinction of having the highest percentage of students in poverty, 39.4 percent, followed by El Paso (37.6%), Fresno (32.4%), and Milwaukee (32.4%). Also included is Brownsville, Texas, to show that high levels of poverty do not end in school systems with 50,000 or more students.

[14]http://www.tobaccofreekids.org/reports/settlements/.

[15]Ibid.

[16]Jonathan Fuerbringer, "Tobacco Money Could Harm Credit Rating of Some States," *New York Times*, November 29, 2002, pp. C1, C5.

Table 11-2 Highest Poverty Rates Among Ten Large School Districts (and Brownsville) and Federal Revenues as a Percent of District Budget

School District	Number of Students	Poverty Rate	% of Federal Revenue
Detroit, MI	107,874	39.4	17.9
El Paso, TX	62,123	37.6	15.3
Fresno, CA	76,460	32.4	14.7
Milwaukee, WI	86,819	32.4	13.9
Philadelphia, PA	172,704	31.7	12.8
Columbus, OH	55,269	31.4	11.1
Memphis, TN	115,342	31.3	13.4
San Antonio, TX	54,779	31.0	18.0
Dallas, TX	157,804	29.4	13.4
Houston, TX	199,534	27.6	13.3
Mean of Above	**108,871**	**32.4**	**14.4**
Brownsville, TX	43,272	44.5	16.8

Source: *Digest of Education Statistics 2009* (Washington, DC: U.S. Government Printing Office, 2010), Table 92, p. 117.

Brownsville (with 43,000 students) has a student poverty rate of 44.5 percent. The fact remains that U.S. school funding is largely based on a local community's ability to fund education through property taxes, in contrast to most other industrialized countries where funding is relatively equal among students throughout the nation, state, province, or municipality.[17]

Municipal and Educational Overburden

Cities are overwhelmed by what is commonly called **municipal overburden,** or severe financing demands for public functions because of high population density and the high proportion of disadvantaged and low-income groups. Therefore, large cities cannot devote as great a percentage of their total tax revenues to the schools as can suburban and rural districts. For instance, in the 1990s Cleveland, Detroit, Gary (Indiana), Newark (New Jersey), and New York City spent less than 30 to 35 percent of all local tax revenues for school purposes, whereas the rest of their respective states were able to spend 45 to 50 percent of local taxes for schools.[18]

Education overburden is another critical issue. A large percentage of the student population in city schools is in technical and vocational programs; these programs cost more per student to operate than the regular academic high school program. Similarly, city schools enroll a greater proportion of special needs students—children living in poverty, students with learning disabilities, English language learners—than do suburban or rural schools. These students require special services and programs that may cost up to twice as much per student as basic academic programs. Similarly, the need for additional services tends to increase geometrically with the concentration of immigrant children and poverty.[19] City schools, therefore, have to spend more educational resources per student than a similar-size school district or group of school districts enrolling middle-class students. One recent study estimates that students in poverty and Limited English Proficient (LEP) students should have a pupil weighting factor of up to 215 percent of regular education students, and special education students of at least 185 percent.[20]

[17]Allan C. Ornstein, *Teaching and Schooling in America: Pre- and Post-September 11* (Boston: Allyn and Bacon, 2003).

[18]Allan Ornstein, "Regional Population Shifts: Implications for Educators," *Clearing House*, 59 (1986): 284–290; George C. Galster and Ronald Mincy, "Poverty in Urban Neighborhoods," *Urban Institute*, 23 (1993): 11–13. Also see Joseph Cordes, Robert D. Ebel, and Jane Gravelle, *Encyclopedia of Taxation and Tax Policy* (Washington, DC: Urban Institute, 1999).

[19]See Milton Schwebel, *Remaking America's Three School Systems: Now Separate and Unequal,* (Lanham, MD: Rowman and Littlefield, 2003); Bruce Katz and Robert Lang, *Redefining Urban and Suburban America* (Washington, DC: Brookings Institution, 2003).

[20]William Duncombe and John Yinger, "How Much More Does a Disadvantaged Student Cost?" *Economics of Education Review,* 24 (2005): 513–532.

Finally, cities have higher facility costs than do their suburban and urban counterparts. Vandalism, increased insurance costs, and higher maintenance expenses raise city schools' facilities outlays, especially since urban schools are typically older than suburban schools. Many suburban districts have as a matter of policy replaced experienced teachers (before receiving tenure) with new teachers to save money. Both city and rural school districts spend more than suburban districts on transportation.

Spending versus Outcomes

Scholars disagree about whether a direct relationship exists between school spending and student performance. In a classic study, Paul Mort summarized his research by stating that "empirical study of the relationship between expenditure level and quality of education . . . is that the relationship is strong."[21] In other classic studies of equality and opportunity, however, Jerome Coleman[22] and Christopher Jencks[23] maintained that "costs . . . have only a minor effect on achievement of students when compared with the much larger effect of their local community's values, family background, peer group, and IQ scores." Jencks took the analysis one step further by arguing that "luck," or the unaccounted for variance related to economic outcomes, was more important than school factors in producing student achievement, further confusing the issue.

John Coons summed up the situation: "There are similar studies suggesting stronger positive consequences from dollar increments; there are others suggesting only trivial consequences, and still others suggesting no effect."[24] And Eric Hanushek declared that "there is no strong or systematic relationship between school expenditures and student performance."[25]

[21]Paul Mort, *Problems and Issues in Public School Finance* (Washington, DC: National Conference of Professors of Educational Administration, 1952), p. 9.

[22]Jerome Coleman, et al. *Equality of Educational Opportunity* (Washington, DC: U.S. Government Printing Office, 1966).

[23]Christopher Jencks, et al. *Inequality: A Reassessment of the Effect of Family and Schooling in America* (New York: Basic Books, 1972).

[24]John Coons, William Clune, and Stephen Sugarman, *Private Wealth and Public Education* (Cambridge, MA: Belknap Press of Harvard University Press, 1970), p. 36.

[25]Eric A. Hanushek, "The Impact of Differential Expenditures on School Performance," *Educational Researcher*, 18 (1989): 47.

A fifteen-year analysis of studies by the National Institute of Education noted that the school makes a difference if it emphasizes (1) a safe, secure environment, (2) instructional leadership from its principal, (3) personnel who have high expectations of the students, (4) a careful monitoring system, (5) a schoolwide emphasis on basis skill instruction, and (6) classroom time on task.[26] Moreover, "value added" studies in Texas indicate that teacher quality makes a significant difference in student achievement. The Texas study indicates that when students are assigned to effective teachers for three consecutive years, reading scores rise from the 59th percentile to the 76th percentile in grades 4 through 6. Conversely, scores for students assigned to ineffective teachers for three consecutive years drop from the 60th percentile in grade 4 to the 42nd percentile in grade 6. This reflects a 35 percentile point decline for students who started out at the same achievement level three years earlier.[27]

But it has also been found that higher per pupil expenditures, new schools, smaller classes, higher teacher salaries, and increased instructional expenditures have little to do with student performance. Money might make a difference if it was spent properly and under the right circumstances.[28] Debate continues about the relationship between money and student achievement. Looking more broadly, a variety of factors affect student performance—money, intelligence, student motivation and prior achievement, family background, school culture, and teachers' effectiveness. If we really want to increase student performance, then we have to look at some other sensitive issues: financial adequacy and equity, student and family responsibilities, peer group influences in and outside of school, teacher and administrator preparation programs, and meaningful teacher evaluation systems to ensure that high levels of teacher quality is the norm for all students.

State Financing of Public Schools

The Tenth Amendment to the U.S. Constitution makes education a state function. Over the years, states have delegated many powers and responsibilities to local

[26]Michael Cohen, "Effective Schools: Accumulating Research Findings," *American Education* (January/February 1982): 13–16.

[27]H. Jordan, R. Mendro, D. Weerasinge, "Teacher Effects on Longitudinal Student Achievement." Paper presented at the *Create* Annual Meeting, Indianapolis, IN, July 1997.

[28]Mano Singham, *The Achievement Gap in U.S. Education* (Lanham, MD: Rowman & Littlefield, 2005).

school districts. Nevertheless, each state remains legally responsible for educating its children and youth. Because many local districts are now having problems financing their schools through property taxes, states are expected to assume greater responsibility and control over schools. Moreover, courts have ruled that since education is a state function, the level of resources available to students should not be a function of the district's wealth, but rather the wealth of the state as a whole. This concept is known as **fiscal neutrality.**

The sales tax and personal income tax are the two major sources of state revenue. Because states pay a bit less than half of the cost of education, these two taxes are important elements in public education's overall support. Since sales and personal income tax receipts vary with economic conditions, schools sometimes experience a revenue roller coaster. This is especially true during an economic recession. When people are concerned about their jobs and finances, they tend to spend fewer dollars, and these potential sales tax dollars are lost to the state. Likewise, when people lose their jobs, their income tax dollars are lost to the state. Conversely, in the 1990s, most states experienced "economic boom times" and stood on the receiving end of robust sales and personal income levels.

Sales Tax

State sales tax is now their second largest revenue source, contributing 31.9 percent of states' revenue.[29] Forty five states have state-wide sales taxes. Only Alaska, Delaware, Montana, New Hampshire, and Oregon lack sales tax provisions. Sales taxes generate significant income for states. In 2009, state tax collections totaled $715.2 billion in revenue. That figure was down 8.6 percent, or $66.9 billion from the previous year.[30]

Although the sales tax is a viable means for generating education revenue, it may cause some economic distortions. For example, the difference in the tax rates may make it worthwhile for consumers to travel to a low-tax or no-tax state to purchase expensive items; this practice has generated a *use tax* among states. For example, if a consumer purchases an automobile out of state, in order to *use* it the owner must pay what the sales tax would have been to register and license the car in his/her own state.

[29]http://www.taxadmin.org/fta/rate/09taxdis.html.

[30]http://www2.census.gov/govs/statetax/2009stcreport.pdf.

The sales tax meets the equity criterion if food and medical prescriptions are removed from the tax base. A sales tax placed on all goods, however, penalizes low-income groups because they spend a larger portion of their incomes on basic goods such as food and drugs. Federal and state assistance available to low-income individuals through food stamp programs and through Medicaid has moderated this penalty to a degree.

The sales tax is elastic because the revenue derived from it tends to parallel the economy. The trouble is, when a state is in a recession, sales tax revenues can decrease sufficiently to reduce the state's income. But a relatively small change in the sales tax rate can result in significant revenue, which can reduce or eliminate deficits. According to the National Conference of State Legislators, in fiscal year 2010 states increased sales tax rates and removed many exemptions (food and drugs), which generated an additional $7.2 billion in revenue.[31]

In 1970, the median sales tax was 3 percent, and only one state had a rate as high as 6 percent. By 1987, the median rate was 4.75 percent, and seven states had rates of 6 percent or higher. By 2010, the median sales tax rate had increased to 6 percent; twenty-four states had rates that were 6 percent or higher.[32] Since 1985, states enacted rate increases to offset both the erosion of the sales tax base (especially in farm and energy states) and to make up for the states increasingly exemption of food (40 states) and drug (49 states) purchases from the tax base.[33]

Nearly every state was in financial crisis, as a result of the 2007–2010 recession, forcing governors to take unpopular trimming measures. The recovery reduced state revenues so that the amount of money states had on hand at the end of fiscal year 2010 was less than 1 percent, the smallest cushion since the Depression of the 1930s. Total state collections declined 5 percent from 2005 to 2010, even as spending grew by 1.5 percent per year.[34] The recession represented a dramatic shift from years of robust growth that produced revenue windfalls that encouraged increased spending and healthy increases in teacher and administrative salaries. While most of this recession officially occurred in 2008 and 2009, state revenue shortfalls were not realized

[31]http://ncsl.org/?tabid=2010.

[32]http://www.taxadmin.org/fta/rate/sales.pdf.

[33]Ibid.

[34]*State Tax Actions 2010* (Denver: National Conference on State Legislators, 2010).

until the end of 2009, when state budgets began to address the shortfalls.

Personal Income Tax

The personal income tax is the now the largest source of tax revenue to the states, contributing 34.4 percent of all state revenue.[35] Only seven states do not levy a personal income tax (Alabama, Florida, Nevada, South Dakota, Texas, Washington, and Wyoming). New Hampshire and Tennessee limit state income tax to dividends and interest income. Just as sales tax rates vary, so do income taxes. While most states increase tax rates as income increases, some states tax income at a flat rate. As of 2010, depending on income level, the state income tax rates in Arkansas varied from 1 percent to 7 percent with six-figure bracket earners. Hawaii's income tax rates varied from 1.4 percent of income to 11 percent for the highest 1 percent of tax brackets. Illinois, on the other hand, had a flat tax rate of 3 percent.[36]

A properly designed income tax should cause no economic distortions. Assuming no loopholes, a personal income tax rates very high in equity. In theory, the personal income tax is supposed to reflect the taxpayer's income and ability to pay. The income tax is also more equitable than other taxes because it considers special taxpayer circumstances—such as the number of dependents, medical expenses, and moving expenses—and uses tax deductions or credits to account for these individual variations. It becomes less equitable only if the taxpayer has many items that can be deducted to minimize the tax.

The personal income tax is very elastic; it allows the state government to vary rates (if it wishes) according to the economy. On the other hand, the income tax's elasticity makes it vulnerable to recession, because the revenue derived from it declines at a faster rate than revenue from other sources.

As a result of the 1986 Tax Reform Act, personal state taxes have become more progressive than they were formerly, as a result of decreased property write-offs, standard deductions, and personal exemptions. The following year, 1987, 11 states that formerly imposed taxes on poor families eliminated those taxes, and in the 1990s several other states lightened taxes on poor and middle-class families.[37] However, by 2009, state personal income tax revenues were down 12.8 percent from the previous year due to a downturn in the economy. In mid-FY 2010, 10 states revised their budget revenue estimates downward as state revenues failed to match forecasts. Twenty-eight states reported that personal income tax collections were below the revised, lower estimates. Most states do not forecast a significant turnaround in economic conditions until 2015.[38] Since education is one of the largest expense items for states, usually second to health care, teachers and administrators will have to learn to deal with less in terms of student expenditures, academic programs and salaries.

Lotteries and Other State Taxes

Other state taxes contribute limited amounts to education. These taxes include excise taxes on liquor and tobacco products; motor vehicle license taxes; estate and gift taxes; real estate transfer taxes; insurance premium taxes; hotel taxes (from the last edition of this text to this current edition, the New York City hotel tax rate rose from 13.3 percent to 18.75 percent plus $3.50 per day in fees); and severance taxes (on the output of minerals and oils).

Establishing state lotteries to support education is a growing trend. Currently 42 states and the District of Columbia have lotteries that raise a total of $53.8 billion in revenue. The national average in pay out for winning tickets is 64.5 percent; administration costs average 4 percent, leaving 31.5 percent, or just under $17 billion in net proceeds to the states.[39] Some states earmark lottery funds for education, while other states allocate lottery monies to the general fund.

Critics challenge lotteries for two reasons. First, many educators see the lottery funds actually reducing the general fund for education. Some report that bond issues and other traditional revenue sources for education are diminished because the electorate has been led to believe the lottery revenues are paying for education. In reality, however, lottery monies do not grow education funding. After money for prizes, marketing, and administrative costs are subtracted, the net proceeds to public schools are only 10 to 15 percent of the money

[35]http://www.taxadmin.org/fta/rate/09taxdis.html.

[36]Ibid.

[37]*State Deficit Management Strategies* (Denver: National Conference of State Legislatures, 1987).

[38]http://www.ncsl.org/default.aspx?tabid=19579.

[39]http://www.ncsl.org/?TabId=12747.

Table 11-3 Per Pupil Expenditures in Selected States, Highest and Lowest, 2008

State	Per-Pupil Expenditure	% Federal Revenue	% State Revenue	% Local Revenue	% Private
New Jersey	$16,587	4.4	43.5	50.0	2.2
New York	$15,837	7.3	43.0	48.9	0.8
Connecticut	$15,219	5.3	38.2	54.9	1.5
Mississippi	$7,800	15.8	54.0	27.3	2.9
Arizona	$7,749	11.7	47.8	38.0	2.6
Tennessee	$7,742	11.4	43.2	39.0	6.4
Oklahoma	$7,623	13.7	53.4	28.2	4.7
Idaho	$7,343	10.8	57.5	30.1	1.7
Utah	$6,629	10.1	55.0	32.7	2.2

Source: *Digest of Education Statistics 2009* (Washington, DC: U.S. Government Printing Office, 2010), Table 182, p. 162.

generated[40]—a fraction of the billions that were promised to voters.

Others disagree with the lottery on moral grounds. Lotteries tend to be a voluntary type of tax; however, they are also regressive. A greater proportion of lower-income individuals play the lottery and spend a larger percentage of their income on tickets than do higher-income individuals. The National Gambling Impact Study Commission's report stated, ". . . that lottery players with incomes below $10,000 spend more than any other income group, an estimated $597 per year. Further, high school dropouts spend four times as much as college graduates. Blacks spend five times as much as whites. In addition, the lotteries rely on a small group of heavy players who are disproportionately poor, black, and have failed to complete a high school education."[41]

The States' Ability to Finance Education

By geographic accident, some students are more fortunate than others. State residence has much to do with the quality of education received. In 2008, as Table 11–3 shows, three states (New Jersey, New York, Connecticut) spent more than $15,000 per student. Six states spent less than $8,000 per pupil: Mississippi, Arizona, Tennessee, Oklahoma, Idaho, and Utah. The difference between the highest and lowest state spending is more than twofold or 100 percent. Over a twelve-year period, the accumulative effect (of geographical accident) takes its toll.

Based on dollars alone, it is incorrect to assume that some states value education more than others. We must ask about the states' relative wealth to make those types of comparisons. Also, we must ask what the states spend on all other services and functions—such as social safety net programs, housing, transportation, and Medicare. In the first case, we are able to obtain a good idea of the states' **fiscal capacity**—or their level of wealth to fund programs such as education. In the second case, we can determine the states' priorities.

For example, the six states with the per pupil expenditures less than $8,000 (Table 11–3) received on average 51.8 percent of their revenues from the state, whereas the three states with per pupil expenditures above $15,000 received on average 41.6 percent of their revenues from the state. Calculating those percentages of local revenue shows that the six states with the lowest expenditures receive on average 32.5 percent of their revenue from local sources while the three states with the highest expenditures receive 51.3 percent of their revenue from local sources. Examining federal revenue shows that the less wealthy states receive a greater percentage of their revenue from federal dollars. This suggests that states with lower capacity may rely more on state and federal revenue to operate the schools while wealthier states rely more on local revenue for their budgets. In other words,

40 *Earmarking State Taxes, 8th ed.* (Denver: National Conference of State Legislators, 2008).

41 *National Gambling Impact Study Commission Final Report* (Washington, DC: U.S. Government Printing Office, 1999), pp. 7–10.

wealthier states can boost their spending by tapping local revenues while poorer states cannot.

Regional attitudes toward education also impact the ability to finance schooling. For example, nine out of 12 states in the Southeast, three of the four states in the Southwest, and five of the six states in the Rocky Mountains spent less money per pupil than the national average ($10,506) in the 2009–2010 school year. The Southeast and Southwest states tend to be politically conservative and spend less money per capita in human services than the states in the New England and Mid East region. In contrast, all six New England and six Mid East region states spent more money per student than the national average.[42]

Historically, the Northeast and Mid East regions have been the net losers of education dollars in the tax burden borne as compared with the monies received back from the federal government in terms of programs, contracts and assistance. This is the federal government's attempt to shift tax dollars from high fiscal capacity states to low fiscal capacity states.

State Financial Responsibility

State funding of education is largely based on a mixture of **discretionary funding** (subjective criteria based on need or eligibility requirements) and **formula funding** whereby all recipients are treated equally and the role of the administrator is merely ministerial. Over the years, states have used a variety of funding patterns. Many states have established a policy that individual students will be given an authorized amount of financial support regardless of where they live within the state. States have different procedures by which that authorized amount is collected.

State Funding Methods

States use one of six basic methods or some combination to finance public education. They include:

1. *Flat Grant Model.* This is the oldest, simplest, and most unequal method of financing public schools. State aid to local school districts is based on a fixed per pupil amount multiplied by the number of students in attendance. It does not consider the students' special needs (bilingual students are more expensive to educate than native English-speaking students), special programs (vocational programs are more expensive than regular programs), or school district wealth (wealthy school districts have more money to spend on students or schools than do less-wealthy districts).

   In most states, the distribution of funds is based on a type of equalization formula designed to provide extra funds for less wealthy school districts. The remaining methods (except #6) seek to bring about greater equity and equality of educational opportunity by allocating more funds to the school districts in greatest need of assistance. No state uses the flat grant model solely to fund its schools. Since education is a state function, courts have made the case for fiscal neutrality—that is, the level of resources available to students should not be a function of the district's wealth, but rather of the wealth of the state as a whole.

2. *Foundation Plan.* This is the most common state approach to school funding. Its purpose is to guarantee a minimum annual expenditure per student (the foundation) for all students in the state, regardless of the local taxable wealth. A foundation program establishes a foundation level of pupil spending that localities must meet with a combination of state and local funding. By law, no locality can fall below that funding level. Wealthier localities receive less state funding to meet this foundation level, and poorer localities receive more state funding to meet this level. Reformers usually consider the minimum level too low while wealthy school districts far exceed the minimum levels.

3. *Power-Equalizing Plan.* A relatively more recent plan which many states have adopted, the state pays a percentage of the local district expenditures in an inverse ratio to the school district's wealth. Although the district has the right to establish its own expenditure levels, wealthier school districts are given fewer matching state dollars. The program is constrained by lower and upper fiscal limits, and the matching dollars are insufficient for poor school districts. In the end, the equalization effect is usually insufficient.

4. *Guaranteed-Tax Base Plan.* The guaranteed-tax base plan has the same economic philosophy as the power-equalizing plan, equalizing fiscal capacity and expenditures as much as possible. This is

[42] *Rankings and Estimates: Rankings of the States 2009 and Estimates of School Statistics 2010* (Washington, DC: NEA, 2010), p. 96.

accomplished by determining an assessed valuation per student, which the state guarantees to the local school district. State aid becomes the difference between what the district raises per student and what the state guarantees per student.

5. *Weighted-Student Plan.* In this model, students are weighted in proportion to their special characteristics (i.e., students with disabilities) or special programs (e.g., vocational or bilingual) to determine the instructional cost per student. For example, a state may provide $10,000 as the base cost per student. A vocational program may be weighted at 1.1, which would provide $11,000 for vocational students. A specific type of special education program may be weighted at 1.5, or $15,000. Most weighted-student plans have been scaled back over the last decade or so.
6. *Choice and Voucher Plans.* Some states allow parents more choice in selecting their children's school, even using a financial voucher to permit attendance at a non-public school. These actions are controversial and court decisions are varied but seem to allow the practice depending on the state's constitutional language. Low-performing schools have been the center of voucher discussions where private companies "take over" management of failed schools.

School Budgeting

Budgeting is both an executive and legislative function. The executive entity (superintendent and district staff, school principal and/or assistant) proposes, and the legislative entity (Board of Education or School Board) enacts. On formal adoption by the school board, the budget becomes a legal document that serves as the basis for annual expenditures, accounting, and auditing. According to school finance experts, budgeting involves five major steps: preparation, submission, adoption, execution, and evaluation. The third step, adoption, involves the school board, which appropriates specific amounts for specific categories. The other four steps involve the superintendent, business manager, and/or principal.

Typically, the budget is organized around four major categories: objects (e.g. salaries, supplies, travel), functions (e.g. instruction, transportation, plant), programs (e.g., English, math, gifted education), and location (school, groups of schools, or district). The state usually mandates the items for objects and functions whereas the school district usually develops the items for programs and locations. The budget may also include other features such as a list of goals, objectives or criteria; projected revenues from all local, state, and federal sources; comparison of expenditures for last year by categories; the amount needed to pay the principal and interest for the school bonds maturing during the fiscal year; and a budget summary (See Administrative Advice 10–1).

Although the superintendent (with staff assistance) holds the major responsibility for submitting the budget, the principal's role in budgeting may either be limited or substantial. A superintendent who maintains a high centralized administration will most likely limit the principal's responsibilities to filling out requisitions, receipts, and disbursements. A decentralized administration will delegate more fiscal decision-making responsibilities to the principal.

Regardless of professional empowerment, the school staff must understand that only 5 to 10 percent of the district's budget is available for modification. About 65 to 70 percent is earmarked for salaries and benefits; around 20 to 25 percent goes for operating expenses such as utilities, insurance, repairs, and maintenance; and some monies should be committed for reserves and replacement. Although the principal (and staff) may be permitted to make budget recommendations, the school board finalizes the budget.

The principal's budgeting roles can be classified into four major activities: (1) *budget planning,* assisting the superintendent in identifying budget priorities and focusing on school needs at the planning stage; (2) *budget analysis*, dealing with the goals, objectives, and evaluative criteria, suggestions for curriculum materials and instructional equipment, and communicating concerns of the students, parents, teachers, and community about specific expenditures or special purposes; (3) *budget requesting,* involving a review of requests by different groups such as teachers or parents, establishing program priorities, submitting a total budget, and negotiating specific items; and (4) *budget controls,* dealing with inventory expenses, receipts and disbursements, monthly reporting, and balancing the books at the building level.[43] The fourth activity deals with the regular school operation, which involves ongoing paperwork and record keeping.

---

[43]L. Joseph Matthews and Gary M. Crow, *Being and Becoming a Principal* (Boston: Allyn and Bacon, 2003); Anthony G. Picciano, *Data-Driven Decision Making for Effective School Leadership* (Columbus, OH: Merrill, 2006).

ADMINISTRATIVE ADVICE 11–1

Checklist for Developing a School Budget

A budget is a financial plan that reflects the local needs of the school (or school district), its history, and its fiscal health. A number of state and local factors such as past practices, state/local codes and regulations, and board policies influence the process, format, and contents. Below is a general checklist for administrators to adapt and use when organizing their own budget.

Process: Conducting the Hearings	**Yes**	**No**
1. Roles of board and superintendent clearly defined	☐	☐
2. Board financial policies updated regularly	☐	☐
3. Accuracy and timeliness of all financial data	☐	☐
4. Adequate staff involvement in budget request	☐	☐
5. Adequate public hearings and citizen participation	☐	☐
6. Budget document (or summary) widely distributed	☐	☐
7. Compliance with legal requirements	☐	☐
8. Community/political support generated for budget	☐	☐
9. Contingency strategy for cuts (budget options)	☐	☐
10. Efficient accounting/financial reporting system	☐	☐
Format: Organizing the Document		
11. Attractive cover, title page, overall appearance	☐	☐
12. Table of contents or index; numbered pages	☐	☐
13. Names of board members, officers listed	☐	☐
14. Table of organization, administrators listed	☐	☐
15. Budget message or letter of transmittal	☐	☐
16. Graphics—artwork, charts, figures, tables	☐	☐
17. Clarity of style; avoidance of technical jargon	☐	☐
18. Manageable size and shape of document	☐	☐
19. Glossary of key terms	☐	☐
20. Concise executive summary ("budget-in-brief")	☐	☐
Contents: Compiling the Data	**Yes**	**No**
21. Political feasibility of bottom-line request	☐	☐
22. School system goals and objectives	☐	☐
23. Budget assumptions, guidelines, or priorities	☐	☐
24. Object budget summary (e.g., salaries, supplies)	☐	☐
25. Program budget summary (e.g., reading, math)	☐	☐
26. Site budget summary (e.g., individual schools)	☐	☐
27. Budget history (expenditures for past five years)	☐	☐
28. Unit-cost analysis (per-pupil expenditures)	☐	☐
29. Summary of estimated revenues (all sources)	☐	☐
30. Explanation of impact on tax rates	☐	☐

31. Explanation of major cost factors (contracts, inflation)	☐	☐
32. Budget coding system explained (chart of accounts)	☐	☐
33. Performance measures program outcomes; test data	☐	☐
34. Pupil enrolment projections by grade	☐	☐
35. Staffing history and projections	☐	☐
36. Long-range plans (five years) for the school system	☐	☐
37. Justification for major decisions (layoffs, school closing)	☐	☐
38. Comparisons with other districts (or with state averages)	☐	☐
39. Capital budget summary (capital improvement projects)	☐	☐
40. Budget detail (line-item expenditure data)	☐	☐

Source: Adapted from Harry J. Hartley, "Checklist for Evaluating Local School Budgets," *American School Board Journal*, 46 (1989): 36. Copyright 1989, the National School Boards Association. Used by permission.

In large elementary schools, a person (perhaps the assistant principal or a teacher) representing a program area or grade level, and in secondary schools a department head, is usually asked to list and prioritize needs. If cutbacks make it necessary to reduce school budgets, the trimming process usually begins with the low-priority programs or items. Ultimately the principal submits the budget to the central office. There, it is either approved or modified, with or without negotiation with the principal. Eventually, an approved budget is returned to the principal. Each month, a person at the program or department level may be required to fill out requisitions and purchase orders; each month a budget summary to date may be returned by the school district business manager or financial officer to the principal and/or school department or program, indicating the amount of money remaining in each account item.

Usually, the principal is required to submit a monthly budget to the central office, which includes several income and expense categories. Depending on the school district's accounting system, the budget items may include receipts, vouchers, bank statements, a method for authorizing expenditures, expenditures paid only by check, a regular audit, and monthly and annual reporting.[44]

A word of caution is needed. Whether the budget is prepared at the school district or school, school leaders must be responsible money managers and guard against spending on educational fads or unproven programs or methods that have an inadequate research base or limited history of empirical success. Too many educational programs and concepts expand based on anecdotal data or on ideas considered "innovative" or "reform-oriented" after appearing in the popular educational journals without credible research support.

Why some educational leaders jump onto popular programs and spend large sums of money in the absence of hard data is difficult to answer. One possible explanation involves "pressure" for reform, as pendulums swing and impulses take on a life of their own. Common sense affirms that before administrators adopt a program on a large scale, well-designed pilot testing and evaluation in school settings are needed.[45] The emphasis should shift from what is *new* to what *works*.

School Effectiveness and Productivity

There are few agreed-on indicators to determine the ideal (or most efficient) school size or to determine whether a school is effective. Just what is a productive, or well-run, school? When do local or state decision makers know that they are getting their money's worth in a school? The indicators are extremely fuzzy, but research evidence can help clarify the data.

[44]Richard D. Sorenson and Lloyd M. Goldsmith, *The Principal's Guide to School Budgeting* (Thousand Oaks, CA: Corwin Press, 2006).

[45]See Lee G. Bolman and Terrance E. Deal, *Reframing the Path to School Leadership* (Thousand Oaks, CA: Corwin Press, 2002).

Size of Schools

Educators have long debated the optimal school size that produces maximum efficiency and positive student outcomes. A school is considered too small where underutilization of staff and curriculum occurs and when the operating unit cost per student exceeds the state's average cost. In contrast, a school is considered too large when students lose a sense of personal or school identity. Students are unable to fully participate in social and athletic activities, have difficulty interacting among themselves, or feel they do not belong to the student body or school in general.[46] An overlarge school causes a sense of aimlessness, isolation, even despair among many students—which in turn causes other more overt social and psychological problems (such as delinquency and drugs).

In terms of numbers, 9 percent of public elementary schools are considered too small (fewer than 200 students), and 11 percent are too large (over 800 students). As many as 37 percent of the public secondary schools are too small (under 300 students) and as many as 14 percent are too large (over 1500 students). Moreover, 1.3 percent of the secondary schools enroll 3000 or more students.[47]

Conventional wisdom has maintained that large schools are more efficient and offer more diversified opportunities for students. Raymond Callahan's "cult of efficiency" influenced this thinking, associating bigness with growth, productive efficiency, and greater opportunity to specialize. James Conant's description of the American high school during a period of school consolidation also prompted this perspective, as he promulgated the need for large "comprehensive" high schools (comprising graduating classes of 100 students or more) and considered small high schools problematic and economically wasteful in terms of lack of special facilities and subjects.[48]

In addition, large schools were considered well organized, offering something for everyone, and a means for advancing integration and democratic values among diverse students under one roof. Small schools' strengths—a sense of community, minimum bureaucracy, and the "core curriculum" (four years of English and history; three years of science and math; and two or three years of a foreign language)—were overlooked.[49]

In sparsely populated areas, technological innovations can partially equalize small schools' educational opportunities as two-way interactive television, cable and satellite networks, the internet, and various regional networks can provide high quality and rigorous course offerings over vast portions of a state. Teacher professional development is needed to make these technology resources meaningful, however. Data suggest that it takes three to five weeks for teachers to make the necessary adjustment in "electronic education" while it takes high school students two or three days.[50]

Sociological data strongly suggest that small schools (K–12) are often considered part, even the hub, of a homogeneous neighborhood where parental involvement and school-community relations are high. Parental pressure has impact in the school, teacher expectations have influence in the home, and school and civic cooperation are widespread. In fact, social life often centers on school and community activities.

As larger schools are divided into smaller and smaller unit sizes, students have the potential to play an increased role in school-community functions. Students in small schools have more opportunities to participate in leadership roles and extracurricular activities, especially the high-status activities including student government, student newspaper, school band, and athletics. With fewer students on a district-wide or school-wide basis, they also have a better chance for academic recognition.[51] Moreover, the socio-psychological benefits of recognition and affiliation and the result for

---

[46]Allan C. Ornstein, "Private and Public School Comparisons," *Education and Urban Society*, 21 (1989): 192–206; Ornstein, "School Size and Effectiveness: Policy Implications," *Urban Review*, 22 (1990): 239–245.

[47]*Digest of Education Statistics 2007* (Washington, DC: U.S. Government Printing Office, 2008), Table 95, p. 155.

[48]Raymond Callahan, *Education and the Cult of Efficiency* (Chicago: University of Chicago Press, 1962); James B. Conant, *The American High School Today* (New York: McGraw-Hill, 1959).

[49]See Deborah Meier, "As Though They Owned the Place: Small Schools as Membership Communities," *Phi Delta Kappan*, 87 (2006): 657–662; Nel Noddings, "What Does it Mean to Educate the Whole Child?" *Educational Leadership*, 63 (2005): 8–13; Mary Raywid, "Small Schools: Themes That Serve Schools Well," *Phi Delta Kappan*, 87 (2006): 654–656.

[50]Mary Burns, "From Compliance to Commitment: Technology as a Catalyst for Learning," *Phi Delta Kappan*, 84 (2002): 295–302; Selma Wasserman, "Growing Teachers: Some Important Principles for Professional Development," *Phi Delta Kappan*, 90 (2009): 485–489.

[51]Alfie Kohn, *Unconditional Parenting* (New York: Altria, 2005); Kenneth A. Strike, *Small Schools and Strong Communities* (New York: Teachers College Press, Columbia University, 2010).

self-concept and motivation for achievement are well documented in the social and educational literature.

According to the authors, large schools exclude students, teachers, parents, and community members from curriculum development, and the administrative hierarchy centralizes and standardizes the curriculum. Large high schools win state sports championships and academic scholarships; they also have impressive bands and student newspapers. Yet with the exception of a few talented ball players, scholars, and social elites, most students don't participate or receive recognition from their teachers or counselors. Thus, the costs for these extra facilities and activities are high (and dysfunctional) per student.

In this connection, Gregory and Smith argue that school size, school structure, and community life are interrelated and should be seriously considered in the school reform literature. After reviewing several studies, they recommend a high school size of no more than 250 students because larger enrollments result in a counterproductive and administrative preoccupation with control and order; moreover, and anonymity works against students sharing ideas and working together in learning. Structurally, these authors are concerned with large schools' governance and how space, time, and people are organized; in small schools these kinds of arrangements are more supportive and positive to human functioning. By *community*, Gregory and Smith express concern with interpersonal bonding—generating commitment and morale among students, teachers, and parents—increasing the feeling of ownership and pride in the school and the community. This sense of community is more easily obtained in small schools that are located in the small towns and villages of America.[52]

With the exception of Richard and Patricia Schmuck's study (they visited eighty small schools in twenty-five small districts) which characterizes small schools as "regimented and authoritarian" and run by few well-educated board members,[53] most other studies find that small schools are effective in terms of management, spending, and achievement. Small schools get better results than big schools (and school districts) for less money. When attached to schools, the characteristics of "large" appear to consistently connote negative descriptors, at least a "less satisfying" school experience.[54] All things considered, children have a better chance of being recognized as individuals and for their accomplishments when the enrollment numbers are fewer and the surroundings are familiar. Actually, large schools tend to be more expensive per student than smaller ones because of increased bureaucracy, staff support, and extra curriculum and instructional offerings, but student outcomes (even when social class is held constant) appear to be higher in small schools.

Research now shows that oversized schools are actually a detriment to student achievement, especially for poor children. Even assuming that larger schools did bring more fiscal efficiency, diverse curriculum, and extracurricular activities, those factors have rarely translated into better student achievement. In fact, the research is pretty clear on this point: Smaller schools help promote learning.[55] And, contrary to the prevailing wisdom, research shows that small schools are able to offer a strong core curriculum and, except in extremely small schools, a nearly comparable level of academically advanced courses. Additional research has shown that students from smaller schools have better attendance, and that when students move from large schools to smaller ones their attendance improves. Smaller schools also have lower dropout rates and fewer discipline problems.[56]

Not only are larger schools less safe, they are also less efficient and more expensive because their sheer size requires more administrative support. More importantly, additional bureaucracy translates into less flexibility and innovation.[57] Research shows that

[52]Thomas Gregory and Gerald Smith, *High Schools as Communities: The Small School Reconsidered* (Bloomington, IN: Phi Delta Kappan Educational Foundation, 1987).

[53]Richard A. Schmuck and Patricia A. Schmuck, *Small Districts, Big Problems* (Newbury, CA: Corwin Press, 1992).

[54]John I. Goodlad, *A Place Called School* (San Francisco, CA: Jossey-Bass, 1984); Goodlad, *Educational Renewal* (San Francisco, CA: Jossey-Bass, 1998). Also see Arthur Levine and Laura Scheiber, *Unequal Fortunes* (New York: Teachers College Press, Columbia University, 2010).

[55]Jerry D. Johnson et al., *Size, Excellence and Equity* (Athens, OH: Ohio University College of Education, 2002); Stephen W. Raudenbush, *Schooling, Statistics and Poverty* (Princeton, NJ: Educational Testing Service, 2004).

[56]Anderew Rotherham, "When it Comes to School Size, Smaller is Better," *Education Week*, February 24, 1999, pp. 76–77.

[57]See Tom Vander Ark, "The Case for Small High Schools," *Educational Leadership*, 59 (2002): 55–59; Mary Raywid, "The Policy Environments of Small School and Schools Within Schools," *Educational Leadership*, 59 (2002): 47–54; Marc Tucker, "Changing the System Is the Only Solution," *Phi Delta Kappan*, 91 (2010): 28–30.

economically advantaged students can achieve in larger schools. Paradoxically, it is underprivileged students who are likely to be concentrated in oversized schools.

Effective Schools

A powerful and long-term commitment is required to bring about substantial, widespread, and enduring gains in student performance. Attention must be paid to the school as an institution and to the larger context of the school district and the social/political/economic environment in which schools operate. The effectiveness of the whole school helps determine what happens in each classroom. In the words of one observer, "School performance is unlikely to be significantly improved by any measure or set of measures that fails to recognize that schools are institutions"—complex organizations composed of interdependent parts, "governed by well-established rules and norms of behavior, and adapted for stability."[58] Money does not seem to be the key ingredient; rather, a number of intangible items that promote school effectiveness and productivity appear to coincide with school climate or culture.

Most of the recent **effective schools** research has focused on elementary education. Various studies have identified specific characteristics of effective elementary schools and have usually defined effectiveness at least partly in terms of outstanding student achievement. Ronald Edmonds and his colleagues conducted some of the best known studies. He defined an effective school as one in which lower-class students score as high as middle-class students on basic skills tests. After analyzing such schools, Edmonds identified an effective school as one in which there is strong leadership, an orderly, humane climate, frequent monitoring of students' progress, high expectations and requirements for all students, and focus on teaching important skills to all students.[59]

Additional observers and groups frequently extend this list to include one or more additional characteristics. A good example is the analysis used by the Connecticut School Effectiveness Project, which describes an effective school as having the following characteristics:

1. *A safe and orderly environment* that is not oppressive and is conducive to teaching and learning.
2. *A clear school mission* through which the staff shares a commitment to instructional goals, priorities, assessment procedures, and accountability.
3. *Instructional leadership* by a principal who understands and applies the characteristics of instructional effectiveness.
4. *A climate of high expectations* in which the staff demonstrates that all students can attain mastery of basic skills.
5. *Time on task* brought about when a high percentage of students' time is spent "engaged" in planned activities to master basic skills.
6. *Frequent monitoring of student progress,* using the results to improve individual performance and the instructional program.
7. *Positive home-school relations* in which parents support the school's basic mission and play an important part in helping to achieve it.[60]

Several individuals and agencies have gone even further in refining and modifying research to identify characteristics of unusually effective schools. In addition to the characteristics highlighted by earlier studies, Lawrence Stedman's research has emphasized other key features of effective schools, including (1) attention to goals involving cultural pluralism and multicultural education, and (2) emphasis on responding to students' personal problems and developing their social skills.[61] Educators have stressed cooperation between educators and parents and parental participation in school decision making. These theories and policies are guiding educational projects in New Haven, Connecticut, and Baltimore, Maryland, among other school districts.[62]

[58]John Chubb, "Why the Current Wave of School Reform will Fail," *Public Interest,* 90 (1988): 29. Also see Chubb, *Within Our Reach: How America Can Educate Every Child* (Lanham, MD: Rowman and Littlefield, 2005).

[59]Ronald E. Edmonds, "Programs of School Improvement," *Educational Leadership*, 40 (1982): 4–11; Edmonds, "Characteristics of Effective Schools," in U. Neiser (ed.), *The School Achievement of Minority Children* (Hillsdale, NJ: Erlbaum, 1986), pp. 89–111.

[60]Ornstein, *Teaching and Schooling in America: Pre- and Post-September 11.*

[61]Lawrence Stedman, "The Effective Schools Formula Still Needs Changing," *Phi Delta Kappan,* 69 (1988): 22–27.

[62]James P. Comer, *Child by Child* (New York: Teachers College Press, Columbia University, 1999); Robert E. Slavin, "Putting the School Back in School Reform," *Educational Leadership*, 58 (2000): 22–27.

Among the actions and changes that appear to help at-risk students, other researchers propose the following:

1. Emphasis on reading and language development programs and willingness to remediate reading failure as soon as possible, since reading and academic success are linked.
2. Remedial and tutoring programs in all subject areas—before school starts, after school, and even Saturday sessions.
3. Daily homework assignments that are monitored by teachers.
4. Strict discipline enforced.
5. Teachers required to participate in staff development programs that help them diagnose student problems and modify instruction according to student needs.
6. Teachers required to visit the home of absentees and students receiving a D or an F.
7. Teachers and schools that enforce discipline, encourage civility, foster responsibility, and build character—what some might call "old-fashioned" values.[63]

And, when we consider teacher input in school year 2009–2010, 74 percent of teachers surveyed in *Primary Sources* contend that clear standards have a strong or very strong effect on student achievement; 92 percent believe ongoing classroom assessments are important for bolstering achievement; but only 27 percent say state-required tests are important. In *Supporting Teacher Talent*, 71 percent of Gen Y teachers (32 years old and under) favor financial incentives for teachers who work harder and put in more time than other teachers, but 72 percent of Gen Y teachers maintain tying teacher pay to student performance is unfair (because other factors contribute to academic outcomes) and only 10 percent rate standardized testing as successful.[64]

Effective School Indicators

Criteria of school effectiveness typically emphasize student achievement scores. Some of the indicators commonly assessed include (1) a comparison of expected levels of student achievement with current levels of achievement; (2) analysis of levels of student achievement in a prior grade compared with that in the present grade; (3) a comparison of achievement scores between similar schools, sometimes after controlling for family income or social class; (4) a comparison of subgroups of students by gender, race, and social class; and (5) an analysis of grade inflation and how it skews achievement levels. High schools can also analyze or compare student participation and achievement in advanced placement courses or honors classes, student achievement by programs or courses, high school graduation, and college acceptance.[65]

Additional indicators might include attitudes and levels of satisfaction among students, staff, parents, and community residents as well as clear academic goals, order and discipline, focus on academic learning time, remedial and tutoring programs, teacher morale, staff development, administrative leadership, and community support. Almost all these effectiveness criteria involve little or no extra money; rather, they require changes in school climate or school culture that school leadership can induce.

Table 11–4 illustrates indicators for judging school effectiveness at the elementary, junior high school, and high school levels. The elementary indicators are based on the North Central Association's guide for self-study and team visits in evaluating successful schools. The junior high and high school indicators are based on the U.S. Department of Education's Secondary School Recognition Program, which identifies 202 effective secondary schools. While the elementary school indicators tend to mix cognitive and affective outcomes, the secondary school indicators are more achievement and social oriented. The elementary school indicators go beyond students and also look at staff, parents, and the community; the secondary school indicators focus on students and their performance.

---

[63]Richard L. Allington and Patricia M. Cunningham, *Schools That Work* (Bloomington, IN: Phi Delta Kappan Educational Foundation, 2002); Roland S. Barth, *Lessons Learned* (Thousand Oaks, CA: Corwin Press, 2003); Linda Darling-Hammond, *The Right to Learn* (San Francisco: Jossey-Bass, 2001).

[64]*Primary Sources: America's Teachers on America's Schools* (Seattle, WA: Bill and Melinda Gates Foundation, 2010); *Supporting Teacher Talent: A View from Generation Y* (New York: Public Agenda, 2009); Also See "Listening to American Teachers," *Phi Delta Kappan,* 91 (2010):6.

[65]Larry Cuban, *How Can I Fix It?* (New York: Teachers College Press, Columbia University, 2001); Richard Rothstein, et al., *Grading Education: Getting Accountability Right* (New York: Teachers College Press, Columbia University, 2008).

Table 11-4 Indicators for Judging School Effectiveness

Elementary School Indicators	Junior High/Middle School Indicators	High School Indicators
1. Scores on norm-reference tests	1. Student performance on standard achievement tests	1. Student performance on standard achievement tests
2. Scores on criterion-reference tests	2. Student performance on minimum-competency tests	2. Student performance on minimum-competency tests
3. Scores on teacher-made tests, writing samples, and other nonstandardized measures	3. Student success in high school	3. Numbers of students who go on to postsecondary education, enlist in the military, or find employment
4. Valid measures of affective outcomes such as self-concept	4. Daily student and teacher attendance rates	4. Daily student and teacher attendance rates
5. Teacher (and administrator) opinions of student goal attainment	5. Rates of student suspensions and other exclusions	5. Rates of suspensions and other exclusions
6. Opinions of students, parents, and community residents	6. Awards for outstanding school programs and teaching	6. Student awards in academic or vocational competition
7. Participation of students in extracurricular activities	7. Student awards in academic or vocational competitions	7. Awards for outstanding school programs
8. Student awards and distinctions		8. Percentage of students enrolled in advanced education subjects and/or scored above 3 on placement exams
9. Attendance		
10. Amount of material borrowed from media center or library		
11. Quality of student performance in programs such as art, music, and drama		
12. Community support organizations devoted to school programs		

Source: Adapted from Allan C. Ornstein, *Teaching and Schooling in America: Pre- and Post-September 11* (Boston: Allyn and Bacon, 2003), p. 474.

School Finance Trends

Several monetary trends are affecting schools. As we examine those trends, we should note that the concepts of "equal educational opportunity" and "egalitarianism" are no longer the focus of attention as they were from the 1970s to the early 2000s. Today's monetary trends stress "excellence," "efficiency," "accountability," and "productivity." Budgets today are leaner, with less actual money (after accounting for inflation) earmarked for schools. Despite increased national productivity, fewer actual dollars are apportioned among all public groups and sectors of the economy. Moreover, the growing elderly population is demanding more of the economic pie—at the expense of children and youth. For example, since 1980 the economic well-being of the elderly has improved while that of children has deteriorated. This reflects the increased tax burdens on parents to accomplish the tax transfers to Social Security and health benefits for the aging population.[66] It also reflects the increasing school conflicts over religion and values, as well as over vouchers and school choice—in short, disenchantment with our public schools and the breakdown of the American family.[67] Fewer than 25 percent of U.S. families consist of a mom and dad, what some of us call a "nuclear family." The number of latchkey children is around 70 percent.[68]

[66]Laurence J. Kotlikoff and Scott Burns, *The Coming Generation Storm* (Cambridge, MA: MIT Press, 2004).

[67]Richard F. Elmore, "Breaking the Cartel," *Phi Delta Kappan*, 87 (2006): 517–518; Tyrone L. Howard, *Why Race and Culture Matter in Schools* (New York: Teachers College Press, Columbia University, 2010).

[68]"Nearly 20.5 Million Children of Employed Parents in Child Care," *Urban Institute Policy and Research Report*, 15 (2002): 1–2; Ornstein, *Teaching and Schooling in America*.

Streamlining Budgets

In an era of taxpayer weariness, school boards have been pressed to reduce spending like never before. Not only must school outcomes meet expected standards, but the budget must withstand reduced resources and close scrutiny. Although the taxpayer's resistance to increased property tax for schools crested in the 1990s, schools today are expected to prune budgets and save money. Given competing demands for public money, especially from our "graying population," coupled with the reduced percentage of households with children in school and the current budget deficits, school districts are forced to downsize school expenditures and do more with less money per student.

Businesses and corporations have many ways to slim down—by selling off unprofitable enterprises, closing old plants, and cutting corporate and regional staff. In some respects, life in the "minimalist" corporation is tougher but simpler. With smaller staffs, decisions can be made more quickly, accountability is clearer, and many people seem to work harder. Not surprisingly, the same principles are being applied to the public schools. Corporate leaders often serve on school boards, and the gospels of "streamlining" and "cost efficiency" have spilled over to U.S. education. We should continue to see the following cost-reducing trends:

1. *Class size.* Class size, in the interest of economy, levelled off to 15 students per teacher in 2010. The data on class size and student achievement are somewhat complex and contradictory, and most studies show only small differences between achievement in small classes and in large classes.[69] However, research affirms that class size appears to matter most for reading and math at the early elementary years for all students and especially for at-risk students.[70]

2. *Modernization of Older Buildings.* In the era of declining enrollments, many older school buildings were closed. Often these facilities were rented to other social service agencies such as churches and community centers or sold to private developers, who converted them into shopping malls and condominiums.

   In an era of increasing enrollments, for the last twenty-five years, more schools are clearly needed. But the funds to build them are hard to find. This is especially true in the major Frostbelt cities where the land and labor costs and the need to enclose and insulate space makes the total expense of new construction much higher than what it would be in the rural South or Southwest.

   In the hope of avoiding extensive, new construction and to minimize costs, many districts choose to maintain and modernize their old buildings, especially in the Northeast and Midwest. Although properly maintaining older buildings is expensive, it is often less costly than starting from blueprints and bricks. Frequently, older buildings were better constructed than recent ones. Moreover, older buildings per se are not detrimental to student learning. A government report found in 1995 that $112 billion was needed to repair or upgrade America's schools to a "good overall condition."[71] By the year 2005, the figure was more than $320 billion to repair and modernize America's public schools and provide necessary technology.[72]

3. *Smaller Schools.* Emphasis will be placed on smaller schools because they are cheaper to operate (per square foot) than larger schools, especially if they are well insulated and stress optimal space utilization. Big expensive cafeterias, auditoriums, and gymnasiums may become expendable because they come with major fuel, lighting, insurance, and maintenance expenses. These facilities add to construction costs, remain unoccupied for a large portion of the day and year, and cost a great deal to operate and maintain. Smaller schools usually mean

[69]William Ayers and Michael Klonsky, "The Small School Movement Meets the Ownership Society," *Phi Delta Kappan*, 87 (2006): 453–456; Robert Marzano, Debra Pickering and Jane Pollack, *Classroom Instruction That Works: Research-Based Practices for Increasing Student Achievement* (Alexandria, VA: ASCD, 2001).

[70]Michael F. Addonizio and James L. Phelps, "Class Size and Student Performance: A Framework for Policy Analysis," *Journal of Education Finance*, 26 (2000): 135–156; ERIC Digest "Class size reduction and urban students," *ERIC Clearinghouse on Urban Education*, 182 (2003); Research Points "Class size: Counting students can count," *American Educational Research Association* (2003): www.aera.net/pubs/rp/RPFall03ClassSize-PDF2.pdf.

[71]James C. Moulton, "Structurally Sound?" *American School Board Journal* (1999): 38–40. To view the original report, see http://nces.ed.gov/surveys/frss/publications/2000032/index.asp?sectionID=3.

[72]See Charles M. Payne, *So Much Reform, So Little Change* (Cambridge, MA: Harvard Education Press, 2008).

not only more efficient use of space but also fewer administrators, which lower costs.[73]

Rather than replace or build new schools, approximately 20 percent of the nation's public schools planned to build permanent additions between 2000 and 2005. This was more a response to overcrowded conditions (increasing enrollments) than the need to repair or replace schools. As of 2005, 22 percent of the nation's public schools were considered overcrowded and another 26 percent were operating within 95 percent of capacity.[74]

4. *Energy Economies.* Between 1973 and 1980, the total bill for heating schools in the United States tripled despite reduced fuel consumption.[75] Despite school officials discovering several ways to reduce energy use, energy prices continued to rise, doubling again in most parts of the country by 1984.[76] However, post-1984 consumption-cutting techniques paid off when coupled with sharply declining fuel prices. For example, the bill for heating Midwest schools in 1988 returned to 1980 price levels. Between 1988 and 1996, the average Midwest school heating bill increased less than 5 percent per year.[77] Between 1996 and 2006, however, the heating bill (especially in the Northeast where oil is still used on a large scale) increased between 50 to 125 percent, depending on the region and energy source.[78] Between 2006 and 2010 heating oil increased another 35 to 50 percent, as heating oil cost ranged from $70 to $140 per barrel.[79]

   The next energy crisis has arrived, however, as emerging world economies vie with established economies for fossil fuels. Some schools are forced to dial down classroom temperatures, delay warming up the school before classes each morning, or reduce heat in the hallways. Other schools continue to save money by insulating pipes, walls, and windows and installing energy-saving devices. An increasing number of school districts are bypassing utility companies and buying directly from gas and oil distributors. Future-oriented school officials have invested money in upgraded equipment for more energy-efficiency and by training personnel to operate in an energy-efficient manner. Those schools slow to take precautionary energy-related steps in the recent past are paying dearly. And, as auto gasoline hovers around $3 to $4 plus per gallon, hybrid, electric, and hydrogen vehicles are becoming more commonplace.

   As of 2008, utility bills (including gas, electric, and water) have become the second largest operating expense (next to salaries) for most school districts, and the cost of lighting and air conditioning accounts for 40 percent. Turning off lights in the hallway or dimming security lights after 10 P.M., using energy efficient bulbs, and turning the cooling system up to 75°F or 76°F yields enormous savings. Watch those utility bills, also: about one out of twenty schools is overcharged $50,000 to $150,000 a year.[80]

5. *Reduction in Force (Layoffs).* Reports from around the country, from Seattle to Savannah and from Mississippi to Minnesota, have announced education cutbacks in terms of hiring freezes, furloughs, and layoffs during the 2009–2010 academic year. The streamlining focus has begun to shift away from teachers to administrators. While effective teachers are essential to student learning, the teacher ranks have suffered the most cuts because they comprise the largest numbers of employees. "But the times they are a-changing," to quote an old folk song by Bob Dylan. When a school district needs to downsize, those being identified are also school counselors, curriculum specialists, coordinators, directors, managers, and assistant superintendents.

   While school administrators may also be cut, little evidence suggests that an "administrative blob" exists in education. Administrators' responsibilities have increased substantially over the last two decades. They supervise and evaluate teachers

[73]Rick Allen, "Big Schools: The Way We Were," *Educational Leadership,* 59 (2002): 36–41.

[74]*Digest of Education Statistics 2008,* Table 113, p 163.

[75]John Mulholland, "How to Save Fuel in School," *Phi Delta Kappan,* 62 (1980): 639.

[76]Allan C. Ornstein, "Frostbelt-Sunbelt Energy Policies," *High School Journal,* 67 (1984): 92-103.

[77]Brian Quirk, Public Affairs Specialist, U.S. Department of Energy, personal communication, May 15, 1997.

[78]Lou Dobbs, "Money Line," CNN News, June 30, 2006.

[79]http://www.eia.doe.gov/emeu/international/prices.html#Distillate.

[80]*Digest of Education Statistics 2008,* Table 174, p. 250; http://ase.org/uploaded_files/greenschools/School%20Energy%20Guidebook_9-04.pdf.

and staff; oversee instructional testing and disaggregating data; supervise building security, budgets, transportation, and food service; participate in and monitor special education policies; as well as discipline disruptive students and meet with parents. Many of these responsibilities did not exist or did not exist to this level just a generation ago.[81]

But there is another side to the coin. Critics claim that administrators often sit in big central offices away from schools and generate their own layers of bureaucracy within their departments—additional supervisors, consultants, and support staff—all of whom, no doubt, are good to have and are useful on frequent occasions. But they do bloat the school district payroll, and in tough times they are unneeded. Obviously, not too many people studying for an administrative certificate want to hear this news.

A school district's organizational chart should be something that a parent can understand, yet most of the charts depicting large school districts cannot be understood by many professional educators. In an age of downsizing, the time has come to clear out the crowd at central offices. Profitable corporations have learned this lesson, in some cases the hard way. Some large companies operate with as few as 1 headquarters manager to 500 employees.[82] Now is the time for wise decision makers to slowly eliminate staff matrices built on top of other matrices; doing so through attrition will be far less painful than waiting for financial problems to force school officials to cut needed staff.

Environmental Hazards

A number of environmental hazards, including asbestos, toxic waste, landfill and chemical dump sites, ground water contamination, lake and river pollution, air pollution, and ozone depletion threaten America's health and economy and dominate the headlines. Moreover, in the 1990s these hazards moved indoors and now threaten the schools and workplace.

Asbestos For the last 35 years, the U.S. Environmental Protection Agency (EPA) has ordered government and commercial property owners to clean up **asbestos-laden buildings**; likewise, the agency has ordered local schools to inspect for building material containing asbestos and prepare management plans to prevent or reduce asbestos hazards. Asbestos is a naturally occurring mineral fiber, once widely used in buildings for its insulating properties and fire resistance. While removal of asbestos from schools is an option for schools, many local education agencies have elected to manage some asbestos-containing buildings by containing or encapsulating the material in place. Intact, undisturbed asbestos materials do not usually pose a health risk. It is only when asbestos becomes friable (where asbestos fibers are disturbed or deteriorated and leak into the air by simple hand pressure) that a health risk is posed. Asbestos exposure can lead to diseases such as lung cancer, asbestosis (lung scarring), and mesothelioma (cancer of the lung cavity lining). Symptoms may not appear until 30 years after exposure.

Estimated costs to clean up these buildings are difficult to find, although one estimate suggests $100 billion for government and commercial buildings and $3.5 billion for 45,000 schools in 31,000 school districts.[83] Another nationwide study puts the estimate at $1.2 billion, or $22,858 per school and $31 per student. In 1990, the cost exceeded $150 per student in 10 percent of the schools. The Oklahoma City School District had the greatest expenditures: $65 million, or $1688 per student.[84] One 132-year old school in Cortland, Ohio was demolished in 2010, but $800,000 had to be allocated for asbestos removal.[85]

During the 1980s and 1990s, the federal government imposed many environmental requirements and regulations on schools but did not provide funds for compliance. Many school districts delayed removing the asbestos, while others used funds from their school maintenance budget to comply with federal regulations. However, one EPA study reports that as much as 75 percent of all school cleanup work up to 1985 was

[81]Owings and Kaplan, *American Public School Finance*.

[82]Thomas Moore, "Goodbye, Corporate Staff," *Fortune*, December, 21, 1987, pp. 65, 68, 76; Allan C. Ornstein, "School Finance in the 90s," *American School Board Journal*, 177 (1990): 36–39; and Nancy Protheroe, "The Blob Revisited," *School Administrator*, 55 (1998): 26–29.

[83]Louis S. Richman, "Why Throw Money at Asbestos?" *Fortune*, June 6, 1988, pp. 155–170.

[84]Allan C. Ornstein and Robert C. Cienkus, "The Nation's School Repair Bill," *American School Board Journal*, 177 (1990): 2A–4A.

[85]http://www.mesotheliomanews.com/2010/02/26/asbestos-removal-would-cost/.

done improperly.[86] Rather than mitigating the problem, the problem was exacerbated in many cases; indeed the "cure" was worse than the "disease," especially with a lot of "sip and skip" companies. If court cases in the 2010 news are any indication, that trend still continues. Today, while the cleanup efforts are better, around half are still done improperly.[87]

Removal is not the only form of asbestos abatement, although the great majority of school districts have chosen this option. Encapsulation, if done properly, can last for ten or more years, depending on what and how the materials are applied, at an average cost of 10 percent of the removal bill. The savings may appear obvious, but in cases where asbestos is loose or crumbling, removal is the best solution. In still other cases, encapsulation is only a stopgap measure until a school district can raise sufficient money for removal when costs are likely to be much higher (see Administrative Advice 11–2).

Radon Gas Asbestos in schools is not the only cancer threat. **Radon gas** is also a cancer threat, considered the second leading cause of lung cancer among adults. A naturally occurring radioactive gas that comes from the decay of uranium which is found in nearly all soils, this gas is found most frequently in New England, since much of the geographic area is build on granite, which can contain higher levels of the uranium that causes the gas.[88] The gas seeps into buildings through the foundation from soil and rocks. In some cases well water may be a source of radon gas. A 2010 Environmental Protection Agency (EPA) report ranks the health risk of radon gas as equivalent to smoking approximately one pack of cigarettes a day.[89] A 2008 EPA report states that one in five schools nationwide has classrooms with unacceptably high levels of radon gas.[90]

Average corrective costs per school run from as low as $1000 if ventilation adjustment works, to more than $10,000 if subventilation is needed. Some observers contend that the cost for decontaminating the nation's schools runs into billions of dollars. Since the connection between radon and illness has not been firmly proven, it may not be worth the cost to ventilate schools. If this problem is suspected in a school, it would be wise to work with the local health department in determining exact levels of contamination and ask for recommendations.

Electromagnetic Fields **Electromagnetic fields** (EMF) are everywhere. They are part of our complicated and growing technology: radio, television, copy machines, computers, microwave, and fluorescent lights. The most controversial and visible electromagnetic fields are produced by transmission lines running through our communities—often near our schools, playgrounds, and homes. Only six states set limits on the strength of EMF around transmission lines. New York State, for example, requires a 350-yard corridor around their lines. The fear seems to coincide with mixed research data: Children exposed to EMF greater than 0.4 microteslas (a measure of magnetic induction) suffer from childhood cancer two to three times more (depending on years of exposure) than children who are not exposed to such levels.

The EMF issue is complex. Some of us work at a computer for hours; some only rarely. A number of us have older appliances; others have newer appliances. Basic objects with electric motors such as electric clocks, hairdryers, televisions and even telephones present a possible risk to people. These household objects may be more dangerous than transmission lines because our bodies are often a few inches or feet away. Certain individuals have complicating factors—cigarette smoke exposure, for example. In general, the research on EMF is highly complicated and tentative. Scientists are unsure what to measure to determine exposure. Right now, the best precaution is to have children keep their distance from all EMF emitters at home and in school, especially microwaves, televisions, and computers. Schools need to enforce this concept of distance and purchase computers and electronic equipment with screens or filters. Since there is little public pressure to spend money on computer or electronic equipment screens or filters, and no legislation requires schools to take corrective steps, few schools are actively considering these precautions.

School Lead "Water, water everywhere, and not a good drop to drink" is a play on words reflecting a real possibly of a contaminated water supply. The water our children are drinking at home and school may be

[86]Telephone conversation with Robert Garratt, Staff Specialist, Environmental Protection Agency, Region 5, personal communication, June 7, 1990.

[87]Telephone conversation with Glen I. Earthman, Virginia Tech professor emeritus and facilities expert, personal communication, April 9, 2010.

[88]Ibid.

[89]http://www.epa.gov/radon/pubs/physic.html#HealthRisk.

[90]http://www.epa.gov/ne/children/pdfs/healthy_schools.pdf, p. 2.

ADMINISTRATIVE ADVICE 11–2

Dealing with Asbestos Abatement Contractors

Most school districts, especially the larger ones, are still involved in asbestos abatement. Some still need time extensions, some have an abatement plan in place, others are involved with contract bids, and others are in the process of removing or encapsulating this "wonder fiber." Here are some questions that school districts might consider when selecting an asbestos contractor.

- How many companies are bidding for the job? (Permit at least three to bid each job.)
- Has the company performed other jobs for your district?
- How long has the company been in business?
- What are the company's assets? What jobs has the company performed? For whom? Is the company willing to provide references?
- Has someone in the district called the regional or state EPA and local regulatory agency to ensure that the company has not been cited for health or work violations?
- Are the contractor's workers fully certified? Is the company licensed or certified by the state or local regulatory agency?
- Is the company bonded for performance? Do the workers have adequate liability insurance?
- Does the company carry adequate liability insurance? From an A or A1 rated insurance company? At least a $5 million umbrella policy for each occurrence (not cumulative)?
- Does the company employ a state-licensed health (or air quality) engineer? If not, will an engineer supervise the health aspects of the job?
- Are the health safeguards clearly outlined in the proposal and contract? Will the contaminated areas be properly sealed off?
- Will the company test the air quality before the job, hourly on the job, and after the job? Who will ensure that the readings are accurate? (Preferably an independent or third party should inspect the quality of the air and conduct appropriate tests.)
- Is a timetable clearly established? Are penalties provided for unusual delays?
- Will the public be properly notified when the job is to commence? Will students be in the surrounding area? What about vacation or summer time?
- Besides removal, what other options has the asbestos company suggested? Will guarantees be included with the other options?
- How viable are the options? Have you considered the cost for removal versus the cost for the other options?
- Does the district's contract with the company include a save harmless agreement? Does the district have an escape clause (and right to hire another company) in the event that legal, health, or governmental problems arise?

tainted with lead. Lead accumulates in their brains, blood, and bones. As the lead bonds with the oxygen in the blood's hemoglobin molecules, it eventually dulls the mind and causes severe behavior problems and learning disorders.

According to a 2009 Center for Disease Control and Prevention (CDC), blood lead levels (BLL) in school-aged children have decreased 89 percent between 1980 and 2004, mainly due to phasing out leaded gasoline and lead paint remediation in building codes.[91] Elevated BLL in some school-aged children is still problematic in older, poor, inner-city areas where lead paint has not been remediated. The report cites special concern for New York State, where almost half of the 3.3 million children live in housing units built before 1950.

The CDC maintains that lead poisoning is the nation's number-one preventable child health problem, and proper lead abatement would eventually reduce the cost of child medical care and special education as much as $45 billion annually.[92] The CDC has revised its

[91] http://www.cdc.gov/mmwr/preview/mmwrhtml/mm5803a3.htm.

[92] Ibid.

definition of lead poisoning, lowering the level at which lead is now considered dangerous, from 25 micrograms per deciliter in 1974 to 10 micrograms in 1991. The last revision resulted in a tenfold increase in the number of children now considered poisoned—about 1.5 percent (affecting 15 percent of all U.S. preschoolers).[93] Many of these cases are the result of home repairs involving lead paint.[94] Moreover, at least twenty recent U.S. and international studies from industrialized nations show that lead levels in children are associated with measures of low IQ, language and reading incompetency, limited attention span, inability to follow instructions, behavioral impairment, and 40 additional cognitive, social, psychological, and health problems.[95]

Dangerous traces of lead are sometimes found in the municipal water we drink. Even worse, lead gets into water from lead lines in our older water coolers, faucets (unless made from plastic, which most people feel is inferior in quality), copper pipes (because of the lead solder on the joints), and the old plumbing in cities and villages that connects the water main to our schools and homes. Allowing water to run for a couple of minutes before drinking it or using it for cleaning foods can flush out the lead that has collected—but that idea does not always sit well with budget-minded people who pay utility bills.

It costs about $50 to $75 for a laboratory to test each water faucet and cooler in our schools; however this is not going to happen on a large scale unless schools are forced to budget this item. The estimates are that $30 million per year is needed for paint and water testing in our schools, a tiny sum for such an important safety measure.[96] Since the problem is odorless and invisible, and since most parents are not aware the problem even exists, school officials are not under pressure to take appropriate measures.

Few if any testing and reporting procedures are required for lead, and school authorities have been remiss in dealing with the problem. The cost of lead abatement is estimated between $5,000 and $15,000 per 1000 square feet of lead paint coverage. Most school boards (and property owners) find the price tag too expensive and simply leave the problem as is, gambling that their insurance will pay for any lead-injury claim. Verdicts in such cases run as high as $10 million, though most are settled for around $500,000.[97]

In short, childhood poisoning may be one of the most important and least acknowledged causes of school failure and learning disorders. Given the rhetoric, urgency, and funding for school reform, which focuses on curriculum, instruction, teaching, and testing, it may be seriously myopic not to recognize the serious environmental contributions to school failure.

Indoor Air Quality **Sick building syndrome** (SBS) and other indoor air-quality shortcomings have come to notice as energy economy measures prompt schools to increase insulation and tighten facilities (and office buildings) to save fuel and utility costs. In extreme cases, the outcome is virtually no outside air infiltration into the school.

Almost everything in a building generates some form of toxic emission. The human body exhales carbon dioxide, and it emits body odors, gases, and other bioeffluents. Carbon monoxide, a colorless and highly poisonous gas, results from incomplete fuel combustion. For instance, when auto engines are left running in school parking lots near open windows when parents pick up or drop off their children, carbon monoxide levels grow. Diesel exhaust from parked buses is also common as drivers wait for students or warm the bus in winter before students board. Likewise, carpets, plastics (most furniture and bathroom fixtures contain plastics), and pressed wood emit formaldehyde and other gases. Room dividers and window blinds emit a host of carbon chemicals. Copy machines give off ozone, and fluorescent lights give off ultraviolet rays.

Then too, the dilemma of doing battle with pests—fleas, cockroaches, termites, wasps, and rodents—creates additional problems. Although chemical pesticides are a critical component of successful pest control, they are inconsistent with our concern to limit or rid schools of pesticides.[98] More than half the states have school pesticide policies that are considered "inadequate" or "unsatisfactory" for protecting children from pesticides

---

[93] Susan Black, "Heavy Metal," *American School Board Journal,* 188 (2001): 62.

[94] Telephone conversation with Glen Earthman, April 9, 2010.

[95] *Lead Action News,* 8 (2001): 6–8; Harry L. Needleman, "Childhood Exposure to Lead," *Phi Delta Kappan,* 74 (1992): 35–37.

[96] *Legislative Guidance for Comprehensive State Groundwater Protection Program, rev ed.* (Denver: National Conference of State Legislatures, 2009).

[97] Russ Banham, "Lead Paint Poisoning: Who's Liable? Who Pays?," *Independent Agent,* 24 (2004): 22–30.

[98] Robert Krieger, "Policing Pests," *American School Board Journal,* 187 (2000): 52–54.

that are harmful to their central nervous system and have profound consequences for learning. A 2009 EPA document calls for schools to use integrated pest management (IPM) practices as children are more sensitive than adults to pesticides.[99] IPM is called a "common sense" approach to pest management, including the judicious use of pesticides. Regular cleaning of food-contaminated areas and dumpsters, tight fitting trash can lids, sealing cracks in walls and floors, and routine cleaning of lockers and desks are a few ideas associated with IPM.

Even drywall, paints, and cleaning fluids have **volatile organic compounds** (**VOCs**) that are dangerous if present in sufficient quantities. Long-term exposure to chemicals and VOCs from art supplies, science labs, shop facilities, and indoor pools is potentially dangerous. It affects all students because the vapors and dusts enter the heating and cooling systems. Excessive humidity—found in locker rooms, pool areas, and school basements—can lead to mold and fungus growths that multiply to potentially harmful levels, often without school authorities recognizing it.

As schools become more insulated, the toxins from cigarette smoke, chalk dusts, science labs, art rooms, and shop facilities cannot escape and become circulated through the air-filtering system. In addition, the entire duct system usually contains dust or mold that spreads germs throughout the building. Few schools regularly clean their vents. Legionnaires' disease is an example of illness caused by germs in the duct system's vents and return lines.

Roughly one-third of the nation's schools (and offices) are considered to be afflicted with sick building syndrome, and roughly two-thirds have concentrations of one or more toxic chemicals serious enough to exceed commonly accepted levels of health risk. The problem is highlighted by the fact that the EPA does not check the air at schools, and only 125 out of 128,000 public and private schools monitor for air pollution. No one really knows for sure how severe is the problem at the national level, even in big cities where schools are often one or two miles from factories or industrial plants.[100]

The human symptoms of poor indoor air quality are eye, nose, throat, or lung irritations. Students (and teachers) are drowsy, exhibit shorter attention spans, or become out of breath when walking up stairs or playing in the gym. In identifying indoor air quality problems, it is important to determine whether people's symptoms disappear a few hours after school ends. Parents whose children suffer from respiratory problems often suspect that their children are being infected by classmates—not considering the strong possibility that the school air may be the culprit.

The EPA suggests twelve ways to make schools healthier. Here are the top 6 recommendations.

1. **Rid the school building of radon.** Schools should test the level of radon gas in their buildings with a radon test kit. If the test results are above healthy levels, remedial steps should be taken.
2. **Use toxics with caution.** Schools should look for alternatives to toxic pesticides and cleaning chemicals. Products should be used only as directed, and stored in high, locked cabinets in original containers. Remove sources of lead, mercury, asbestos, and PCBs from the school environment when possible.
3. **Buy chemicals carefully.** Health, safety, and environmental implications should be considered before chemicals are purchased for use in schools. Proper chemical use and management (storage, labeling, and disposal) is critical for reducing chemical exposures and costly accidents.
4. **Test the water.** School districts should know the quality of the drinking water in their school buildings and should have it tested regularly.
5. **Get the lead out.** Schools built before 1978 should be tested for lead paint. Renovations and repairs should be done in a manner that does not create lead dust.
6. **Have a "safe school" plan.** School districts should identify hazards, evaluate safety planning, and prepare for emergencies. [101]

School Infrastructure Costs

The nation's **school infrastructure** is in a state of critical disrepair. By *infrastructure* we mean the physical facilities that underpin the school plant (plumbing,

[99]http://www.epa.gov/opp00001/ipm/.

[100]*Legislative Requirements Under the Clean Act Amendment,* rev. ed. (Denver: National Conference of State Legislatures, 2003); "Students Choke as EPA Sighs," *USA Today,* December 11, 2008, p. 10A.

[101]*Healthy Schools: Lessons for a Clean Educational Environment* (Washington, DC: U.S. Environmental Protection Agency, 2008).

sewer, heat, electric, roof, masonry, carpentry). Schools seem to be deteriorating at a faster rate than they can be repaired and faster than new schools can be built or renovated.

According to a 2008 American Federation of Teachers report, the total school infrastructure need across all 50 states stands at $254.6 billion, with the average state funding need at almost $5.1 billion.[102] According to Lawrence Summers, the President's former chief economic advisor, 75 percent of the nation's schools have structural deficiencies, particularly ventilation, sewage, and roof systems problems.[103] Table 11–5 shows the ten states with the most funding needs.

Although not shown in the table, Vermont has the lowest estimate of infrastructure needs at $325.7 million: California has the highest need at $25.4 billion. Between 1995 and 2010, U.S. school districts spent just over $270 billion for school construction. Between 1995 and 2001, more than half the construction dollars went towards additions and renovations. Since 2002, spending has shifted to almost 75 percent allocated towards new school construction, leaving leaking roofs, faulty wiring, and other deferred expenditures on hold.[104]

And it is pretty safe to conclude, as does the AFT report, that "the burden for the funding of school infrastructure . . . will likely . . . result in a zero sum game whereby existing state and local tax dollars are redirected away from other critical needs. The capacity of states and local communities to fully redress public schools' infrastructure deficiencies, particularly under current economic conditions, is almost certainly insufficient in light of an estimated funding need of $254.6 billion."[105]

Getting the nation's schools up to par is an enormous problem and part of the overall infrastructure challenge facing the nation as it tries to modernize or replace schools, highways, dams, bridges, and sewers built for the twentieth century. If the United States is to remain a first-class nation with a first-class economy and education system, we will need to figure out ways to raise enormous amounts of money to rebuild our educational system and other structures.

Table 11-5 Selected State Estimates of School Infrastructure Funding Need

State	Funding in Billions
California	$25.4
New York	21.2
Texas	12.6
New Jersey	10.4
North Carolina	9.8
Ohio	9.3
Pennsylvania	9.2
Florida	8.9
Michigan	8.9
Missouri	8.8
Nationwide Total	$254.6

Source: Faith E. Crampton and David C. Thompson, *Building Minds, Minding Buildings: School Infrastructure Funding Need* (Washington, DC: AFT, 2008), p. 13.

A school building has five stages. It has lived its normal life the first twenty to twenty-five years, especially in the Sunbelt where construction is cheaper. When it is twenty-five to thirty years old, frequent equipment replacement is needed. When it is thirty to forty years old, most of the original equipment and materials should have been replaced—especially roofs, lighting fixtures, and heating equipment. Accelerated deterioration takes place when it is forty to fifty years old. A fifty-year-old building is sometimes too new to abandon, especially in the Frostbelt, where construction is usually good; but after sixty years, a number of buildings are usually abandoned, reconstructed, or replaced.[106] That said, a significant number of buildings in big cities, especially in Chicago, Detroit, St. Louis, and Houston are at least 75 years old.

Government estimates for the condition of the nation's schools are grim. The top items rated as "inadequate" and in need of repair or replacement in the year 2000 were as follows: (1) heating, air, and ventilation (29%);

---

[102]Faith E. Crampton, and David E. Thompson, *Building Minds, Minding Buildings: School Infrastructure Funding Need* (Washington, DC: AFT, 2008), p. 60.

[103]Bob Herbert, "Falling Further Behind," *New York Times,* February 10, 2010, p. A17.

[104]Paul Abramson, "Fifteenth Annual School Construction Report," *School Planning and Management* (Dayton, OH: Peter Li Education Group, 2010): 2.

[105]Crampton and Thompson, *Building Minds, Minding Buildings,* p. 62.

[106]Ann Lewis, *Wolves at the Schoolhouse Door* (Washington, DC: Education Writers Association, 1989); Ornstein and Cienkus, "The Nation's School Repair Bill"; and Paul Theobald, "Urban and Rural Schools: Lingering Obstales," *Phi Delta Kappan,* 67 (2006): 116–122.

(2) plumbing (25%); (3) exterior walls, windows or doors (24%); (4) roofs (22%); and (5) electricity (22%). As much as 50 percent of the nation's schools had at least one inadequate feature.[107]

Nationwide, 29 percent of all public schools are considered in "inadequate condition," built before 1970. Sixty-one percent have been built after 1970 but renovated since 1980, and these are considered in "adequate" condition. Ten percent are considered in "good" condition, built after 1984. A larger percentage of schools in the Midwest (36 percent) and Northeast (33 percent) are considered inadequate and in need of major repair or renovation, compared to the Southeast (21 percent) and West (25 percent). Only 6 percent of schools in the Midwest and 5 percent in the Northeast are in the "new" category ("good" condition) compared to 11 percent in the Southeast and 15 percent in the West.[108] The differences among regions reflect, in part, stagnant enrollments in the Midwest and Northeast and growing enrollments in the Southeast and West.

Small schools (fewer than 300 students) have an average age of 48 years compared to large schools (1000 or more students) with an average age of 39 years. City schools have a mean age of 46 years compared to suburban (40 years) and rural schools (42 years).[109] Nationwide, 26 percent of schools were built before 1950. Schools in poorer areas have a greater percentage of newer schools than those in middle-class areas. For example, for schools with less than 20 percent of students eligible for free or reduced-price lunch, 48 percent were built before 1950. In contrast, for schools where 50 percent or more students are eligible for free or reduced-price lunch, 42 percent were built before 1950.[110]

Several factors other than age contribute to the deterioration of school buildings and the costs for repairs and renovation.

1. *Energy Prices.* Although energy prices stabilized in the 1990s, they have dramatically increased since 2000. K–12 schools spend more than $7 billion a year on energy costs—or more than $125 per student per year. Most schools, particularly in old, Frostbelt communities, continue to be heated by inefficient boilers. Electrical costs are higher because the school design rarely takes advantage of sunlight. The operating funds devoted to increased energy costs and energy-saving devices have redirected schools monies away from repairs and maintenance.
2. *Weather Conditions.* In certain parts of the country, the weather is severe, especially in the Frostbelt where the 100- to 120-degree annual temperature range causes considerable contraction and expansion of school buildings, roofs, and pavements. The intense cold makes the water and sewer systems and exterior brick vulnerable to cracks and leaks. In addition, acid rain, common in heavily industrialized or polluted areas, causes deterioration of all structural surfaces.
3. *Density and Vandalism.* Big-city schools are usually located in densely populated areas, resulting in concentrated use of and greater demand for facilities. Moreover, many of these schools are located in areas of highly-concentrated poverty and service youth populations that are more often involved in property destruction and theft than youth from more affluent areas. All this results not only in higher costs and more frequent repairs but also in higher budgets for security measures. These expenses deplete a system's financial resources and operating funds for repairs and maintenance.
4. *Newer Buildings.* Many new schools were constructed during the last 25 years, especially in the Sunbelt and suburbs. Many of these schools were constructed hastily to accommodate expanding enrollments. Construction quality suffered, and these buildings are now approaching the end of their life spans. In contrast, the problems with older buildings involve not only their quality but also their energy efficiency, their failure to meet health and safety codes, and the results of accumulated neglect.
5. *A Ticking Time Bomb.* For the most part, educators and the public alike prefer not to discuss the time bomb that is ticking in U.S. schools. What catches our attention is student test scores and the need to reform or upgrade the curriculum; the safety and operating efficiency of the schools are not on the minds of the public unless there is a call for new taxes.

Many school board officials are aware of our schools' environmental and structural problems, but have left them for the next generation. Ignoring our inadequate school facilities has enormous costs—fiscally and physically—and potentially will lead to inadequate education.

[107] *Digest of Education Statistics 2005* (Washington, DC: U.S. Government Printing Office, 2006), Table 110, p. 176.

[108] *The Condition of Education, 2000* (Washington, DC: US Government Printing Office, 2001), Indicator 49, p. 75.

[109] Ibid, Table 49-1, p. 168.

[110] Ibid.

The longer the wait, the greater the school districts' costs for future educational services and the more difficult it becomes to sustain long-term educational growth and financial solvency.

Financing School Construction

Public investment in new schools, compared to other public sectors, has been minimal in the last fifteen to twenty years because of prior taxpayer resistance and student-enrolment declines. Where will the money to build new schools come from? Although the states fund about 50 percent of the revenues for school maintenance and operation, they only contribute about 23 percent for construction. According to one study, 27 states use grant programs (equalized, flat, or matching) to finance new schools, 12 states rely on state or local bonds, two states use fully funded capital programs, but 16 states provide no state financial assistance.[111]

Building a new school is no simple task. The construction rules are complex, the stakes are high, and the considerations are political. Try these questions: How many students will the school accommodate? Where will the building site be located? How will attendance boundaries be drawn? Have environmental concerns been fully addressed? How will the cost be funded? How will voters react? Which companies will get the contracts? How many minority contractors will be hired? The list of questions, with the potential for vague or controversial answers, is endless.

Is it possible for one school serving the same number of students to be three or four times more expensive than another? Absolutely! Consider different building requirements (local construction codes, insulation factors, space requirements), building designs (open-air or enclosed, horizontal or vertical), land prices, professional fees, labor and material expenses, ease of access to the building site, and a host of other factors.

Where you build is important. The cost of a school building can run from $100 to $150 a square foot in rural southern areas to $200 to $300 per square foot in the major cities (and adjacent metropolitan areas).[112]

[111]*Projection of Population by States, 2009–2019* (Washington, DC: National Association of State Directors of Education Plant Services, 2008).

[112]See Ornstein, "School Finance Trends for the Year 2000," Projections for 2010 were estimated based on the 2000 data.

Square footage is another factor to consider. High schools need about 1½ times more square footage than do elementary schools to adequately serve their clientele. Older students require specialization and additional facilities—larger auditoriums, pools, theatres, cafeterias, indoor gyms, outdoor ball fields, and student parking lots. Schools in cold climates cannot use outdoor areas as effectively as schools in warm climates. In 2010 a typical high school serving 1000 students might comprise 100 square feet per student (at $150 per square foot) in the rural South. Another high school serving the same number of students might comprise 200 square feet per student (at $250–$300 per square foot) in the urban Northeast or Midwest. On a national level, the median cost for an elementary school (in 2010) was $185 per square foot and for a high school was $203 per square foot. The school's total cost in the urban Northeast or Midwest can run two to three times as high as in rural sites: One school costs $15,000 per student, and the other costs $30,000 per student.[113] To be sure, these differences in school construction costs have ramification for property tax assessments and what taxpayers wind up paying.

A political firestorm erupted over the construction of the Robert F. Kennedy K-12 School in Los Angeles in 2010, which costs $578 million—the nation's most expensive public school ever built.[*] That price tag averaged a whopping $135,000 per student. It's true that construction costs in L.A. are the second-highest in the nation. But no matter how educators try to defend the cost, it turns into a political firestorm: It's outlandish to talk about marble or murals in hallways, olympic-sized pools, or high-tech installations in an era when teachers are being fired, education budgets are being trimmed, and school bonds are being scrutinized by voters around the country. It is hard to defend the idea that children will flourish in a pleasant environment when they are run by the same

[113]Abramson, *School Planning and Management*; Ornstein, "School Finance Trends."

*"'Taj Manal' a High-Class School" *Boston Herald*, August 2010; Howard Blume, "It's a New School Year and There Are 17 New Campuses, including RFK Complex, L.A.'s Most Expensive", *L.A. Times*, September 2010. Two other L.A. schools were among the nation's most expensive—the Royal Learning Center, opened in 2008, a $377 million price tag, and the Visual and Performing Arts High School debuted in 2009, costing $232 million.

people who have given us a 50 percent dropout rate in big cities like L.A.

Schools in the future will cost more than current prices because the designs will be more complex and built for varied functions using more sophisticated components and materials. There will probably be more (1) technological equipment, such as computers, videos and satellite dishes; (2) school laboratories; (3) places for small-group and independent study; (4) flexible spaces, module classrooms, and adaptable walls; (5) contrasting or great spaces such as common rooms, atriums and open courtyards; (6) innovative spaces and materials such as underground structures and new plastic and prefabricated materials; (7) expensive and high-efficient lighting, heating, and communications equipment; (8) energy-conservation controls, solar features, heat pumps and geothermal heating and cooling systems; (9) earth berms and high clerestory windows; (10) curved corners and curved furniture, (11) pitched roofs and arches; and (12) centers or wings to house child care, elder care, and community services.[114] Yesterday's "boxy" classrooms and rectangular buildings will increasingly be replaced by flexible spaces and a variety of exterior designs. "Going green" is now the "in" word and new design feature, despite the additional cost.

International Comparisons of Education Spending

There is a growing interest in obtaining international comparisons of expenditures and other aspects of educational information. Because it is unreasonable to make comparisons with Third World or developing nations, most of the international comparisons are made with countries similar to ours. As shown in Figure 11–1, the United States spends 4.8 percent (down from 5.3 percent less than ten years ago) of its GDP on education; such expenditure ranks the country sixteenth among the 27 industrialized countries listed with data.

One way to view these patterns is to conclude that the United States makes a less than average effort to finance education. Because its capacity for funding education is high, our less than average effort is embarrassing. But our nation devotes resources to many different public areas, especially social security, health, and medicine; therefore, it might be argued we are actually doing very well in our social and education funding patterns.[115]

When we look at what we spend and what we produce, we learn sadly that our output, as measured in the form of international achievement test scores, is low compared to that of other industrialized nations. Japan and South Korea, for example, rank low in education spending compared to gross domestic product, (3.4% and 4.3% respectively), yet they usually have the highest math and science achievement test scores.[116] One could infer that school expenditures do not correlate directly with academic output; other variables are more important (see Chapter 10).

Regardless of all the reasons, we are living in the midst of a workforce time bomb—growing illiteracy among U.S. workers will subsequently influence our economic output. Not only are our junior and senior high school students outperformed by their international counterparts, but the same holds true for American adults under age forty. For example, at the 55 to 65 age bracket, American adults rank fifth in literacy among seventeen industrialized nations; in the 36 to 45 age bracket, Americans rank eighth; in the 16 to 25 bracket, they rank fourteenth. Overall, U.S. adult literacy ranks tenth out of seventeen.[117] It appears, then, that we need to depend (and have depended) on "brain drain" from other countries, especially from Asia, to prop up American science and technology, and economic output in general.

As shown in Figure 11–1, examining the GDP is perhaps the best indicator of spending comparisons. GDP comparisons allow us to factor in expenditures relative to various nations' ability to finance education. According to the Organization for Economic Cooperation and Development (OECD), a positive correlation exists between GDP per capita and levels of education. Wealthier countries tend to spend more per primary, secondary, and post-secondary students than do

[114]Ornstein, "School Finance and the Condition of Schools"; Marla C. Rist, "Schools by Design," *American School Board Journal*, 176 (1989): 42–43, 48; Also see Anthony S. Bryk, "Organizing Schools for Improvement," *Phi Delta Kappan*, 91 (2010): 23–30.

[115]Allan C. Ornstein, *Wealth Vs. Work*, in progress.

[116]Ibid

[117]Aaron Bernstein, "The Time Bomb in the Work Force: Illiteracy," *Business Week*, February 25, 2002, p. 122.

[118]*Education at a Glance 2008* (Paris: OECD, 2009).

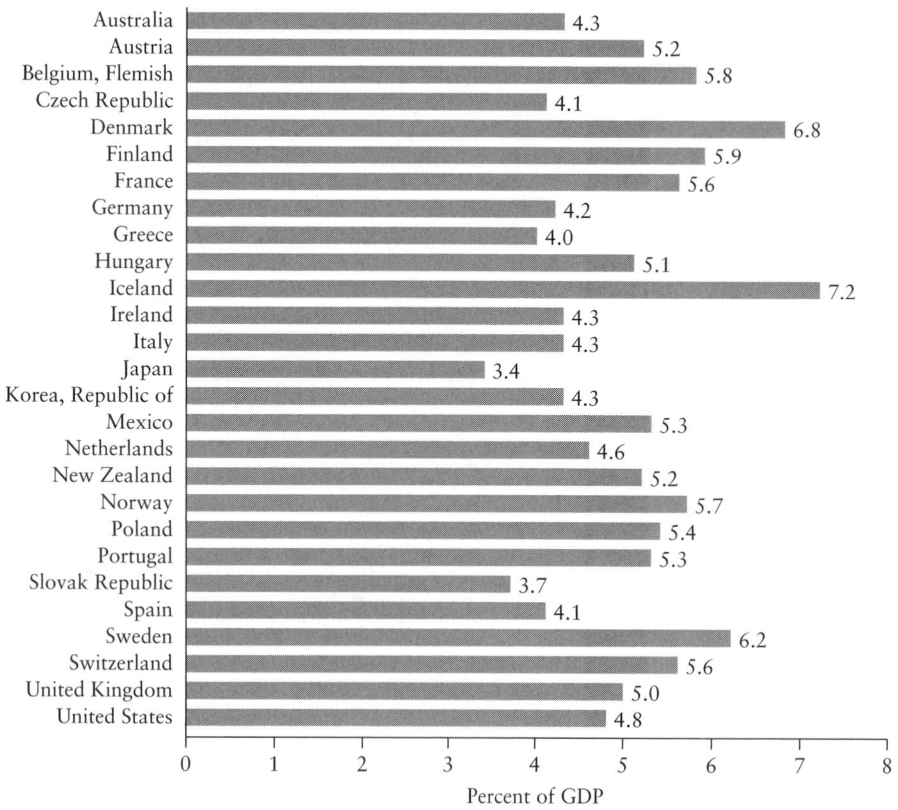

FIGURE 11–1

Expenditures for Education as a Percentage of Gross Domestic Product (GDP) by OECD Country
Note: Includes all OECD countries for which comparable data are available. Includes all government expenditures for education institutions, plus public subsidies to living costs that are not spent at education institutions.
Source: *Education at a Glance 2008* (Paris: Organization for Economic Cooperation and Development [OECD], 2009).

less wealthy countries. Among OECD countries, U.S. spending (not shown in Figure 11–1) in actual dollars per student is higher—second only to Switzerland.[118]

Similarly, the United States averaged 14.6 students per class at the elementary school level, eleventh lowest among thirty industrialized countries, and 14.7 at the junior high school level, eighteenth lowest among thirty industrialized countries.[119] Nonetheless, U.S. achievement on international tests in reading, math, and science remains among the lowest compared to other industrialized nations; financial input does not correlate with academic output.

There are enough explanations to choose from to explain the input/output (money/achievement) factors for funding American schools. Although educators have improved their methods for analyzing and comparing international expenditures on education, it is still difficult to make precise comparisons that account for differences in operation of schools, money exchange rates, and social/political variables. At present, the data should be viewed with some reservations; however, it is difficult to have a frank discussion on policy issues involving different groups of students within the United States, and the cause-effect relations involving student achievement.

[119]*Digest of Education Statistics 2009*, Table 401, p. 62.

Financing Education

Since colonial times, education in America has flourished at the local level. Over time most state governments have accepted primary responsibility. This acceptance is in accordance with the 10th Amendment to the U.S. Constitution, state constitutional obligations, and the U.S. Supreme Court's judicial review. Federal aid has affected the states' responsibility. Currently the generally accepted educational practice (NAEP) is one of federalism: a partnership of local control, state responsibility, federal interest.

Question: Should state government bear the primary responsibility for financing education?

Arguments PRO

1. The Tenth Amendment to the U.S. Constitution implicitly suggests (since education is not mentioned in the Constitution) that education is the responsibility of individual states.
2. State constitutions, statutes, and practice affirm that education is the function of the state.
3. In *San Antonio Independent School District v. Rodriguez* (1973), the U.S. Supreme Court declared that "education was not among the rights protected by the U.S. Constitution."
4. The U.S. Supreme Court has refused to hear any case dealing with educational finance since the *Rodriguez* case. Since *Rodriguez,* forty-one states have been involved in litigation concerning the financing of education. Financing education is primarily a state responsibility.
5. State educational leaders know better the conditions in a state than people in Washington, DC; there are many differences between Pennsylvania and Montana, for example. Pennsylvanians and Montanans should be able to solve those educational differences as they see fit.
6. The practice of the federal government to spend about 7 percent of the educational funding has resulted in the federal government wanting significant control—instituting national standards, national tests, national promotion policies, etc. Based on their financial commitment, their controlling actions are far in excess of what they deserve or merit.
7. States still have the right, if they choose, to institute support programs for nonpublic schools.

Arguments CON

1. Article 1, Section 8, of the U.S. Constitution gives Congress the power to "lay and collect taxes . . . to provide for the . . . general welfare of the United States." Education is part of the general welfare.
2. The U.S. Constitution's Fourteenth Amendment provides that "no state shall deny any person . . . equal protection of the law."
3. In *Brown v. Board of Education* (1954), the U.S. Supreme Court stated that "where the state has undertaken to provide it, [education] is a right which must be made available to all on equal terms."
4. The Supreme Court justices can change their collective mind. There are many examples of that in our history. Contrast, for example, the Dred Scott decision that stated "a slave was property" to the civil rights cases of the Warren and subsequent courts. The courts are influenced by social change.
5. Because the federal government sends billions of dollars to states to solve nationwide needs, the federal government has the right to be assured that the money is being used efficiently, and for the purpose it was intended to be used.
6. Education is a national need and deserves national leadership. Almost all industrialized countries in the world have stronger central or federal control over schools than the United States. Implementing national standards and a national curriculum might very well improve our international test results.
7. There are serious constitutional questions generated when such aid is implemented.

Summary

1. Schools are supported by local, state, and federal revenues, with the greatest share derived from state sources and the smallest share from federal sources. Since the early twentieth century, state support has increased dramatically, and local support has been reduced; federal support grew until the early 1990s and then leveled off.
2. School finance is based on the principle of equality of opportunity; nevertheless, wide variation exists in the financial ability among states and within states (at the local school district level) to support education. Not all states or school districts can finance education equally well.
3. Poorer school districts tend to receive more money from their respective states than do wealthier school districts. Poorer states, especially those in the South and Southwest, tend to receive more money from the federal government than do wealthier states and states in the Northeast and Midwest. The additional amount of revenue received, however, rarely makes up for the total difference in expenditures.
4. There are six basic methods the states use to finance public education. The flat grant model is the oldest and most unequal method because it is based on a fixed amount multiplied by the number of students in attendance. The most common methods of finance are based on some type of equalization plan to supplement less wealthy school districts. The power-equalizing plan (which deals with inverse ratios of wealth) and weighted-student plan (which deals with special characteristics of students and special programs) are the most common methods. Another method is using choice as an option.
5. Developing a budget can be classified into four major activities: planning or identifying priorities; analysis, dealing with goals or evaluative criteria; establishing priorities and negotiating; and controls, dealing with inventory, receipts, and disbursements.
6. Education costs per student tend to be higher in larger schools.
7. Most research indicates that specific items related to school effectiveness are not cost-related; rather, they deal with organizational climate and culture.
8. Because of the current economy, significant pressure remains to trim school budgets and save money. Competing demands for public revenues, especially from the aging population, and the fact there are fewer households with children attending school, are some reasons why taxpayers are not interested in spending more money for schools.
9. Controversy over school infrastructure costs and environmental hazards such as asbestos and radon gas are likely to affect school expenditures in the future.
10. Although Americans have high expenditures for public education, the results are not impressive when compared to other nations in our financial commitment to education and our academic achievement.

Key Terms

gross domestic product
regressive taxes
progressive taxes
elastic taxes
inelastic taxes
property tax
market value
assessed value
mill
user fees
municipal overburden
educational overburden
fiscal neutrality
fiscal capacity
discretionary funding
formula funding
effective schools
asbestos-laden buildings
radon gas
electromagnetic fields
sick building syndrome
volatile organic compounds (VOCs)
school infrastructure

Discussion Questions

1. Why do city schools have more fiscal problems than suburban or rural schools?
2. What state taxes are used to provide school revenues? Which ones are progressive? Regressive?

3. What are the primary indicators for judging effective schools? Which ones are most important, based on your own experiences?
4. What are the primary reasons for closing schools? What options do school administrators have when they must close down schools?
5. What factors or financial considerations must school administrators deal with when building schools?

Suggested Readings

Bracey, Gerald. *The War Against America's Public Schools: Privatizing Schools, Commercializing Education* (Boston: Allyn and Bacon, 2002). The author describes the influence of corporate America on education.

Cooper, Bruce et al. *Handbook of Education Politics and Policy* (Clifton, NJ: Routledge, 2008). The authors examine the politics of finance and school reform.

Hess, Frederick M. *Educational Entrepreneurship* (Cambridge, MA: Harvard Education Press, 2008). Examines the relationship of creative, productive and financial policies in education.

Moe, Terry M. *Schools, Vouchers, and the American Public* (Washington, DC: Brookings Institution, 2002). The author gives an analysis of school choice and public opinion.

Odden, Allan, and Sarah Archibald. *Doubling Student Performance* (Thousand Oaks, CA: Corwin Press, 2009). The authors explain how schools can better plan and allocate resources to boost student achievement.

Owings, William, and Leslie Kaplan. *American Public School Finance* (Belmont, CA: Wadsworth, 2006). The authors provide a complete overview of school finance, including debunking myths about spending on public education.

Sergiovanni, Thomas J. *Rethinking Leadership,* 2nd ed. (Thousand Oaks, CA: Corwin Press, 2006). The focus is on moral leadership, school change, and financial policy.

12

Legal Considerations and Education

FOCUSING QUESTIONS

1 Why is it important for school administrators to be knowledgeable about the law?

2 What is the legal framework for public education?

3 What are the legal issues pertaining to school personnel?

4 What are the legal issues pertaining to students?

5 What are the legal issues pertaining to schools and the state?

In this chapter, we attempt to answer these questions concerning the law as it applies to public schools. We begin our discussion by exploring the legal framework for public education. We examine the federal and state roles in education, including the major provisions of the U.S. Constitution affecting education, the American judicial system, and state constitutions and statutes. Then we discuss such personnel issues as certification, contracts, termination of employment, discrimination in employment, and tort liability. Next, we examine the law as it pertains to students, including school improvement efforts, school attendance, student discipline, freedom of expression, classification practices, and students with disabilities. Finally, we discuss such school-state issues as school desegregation, church-state relations, and financing education.

We emphasize decisions of the United States Supreme Court and those decisions of the highest state courts. The cases cited were selected for their precedent-setting value on substantive legal principles of school law rather than their recency.

Legal Framework for Public Education

All three units of government—federal, state, and local—exercise some degree of authority and control over U.S. public education. Educational governance of public schools is the result of constitutional and statutory provisions of the federal government, the fifty state governments, and case law. The degree of authority and control that local school boards have over school operations depends on the constitutional and statutory provisions of their state.

Federal Role in Education

Education is not a function specifically delegated to the federal government. This is recognized in the Tenth Amendment to the U.S. Constitution, which provides that "the powers not delegated to the United States by the Constitution, nor prohibited by it to the States, are reserved to the States respectively, or to the people." Although education is not specifically delegated to the federal government, it has exercised considerable influence in educational matters, primarily through the provisions of the federal Constitution, decisions of the U.S. Supreme Court, and congressional acts.

United States Constitution The Constitution established three separate branches of government: legislative, the Congress (Article I); executive, the president (Article II); and judicial, a Supreme Court and necessary inferior courts (Article III).[1] These three branches of government provide a system of checks and balances to ensure that the intent of the Constitution is upheld.

The federal Constitution is the supreme law of the land. All statutes passed by Congress, state constitutions and statutes, and policies of local boards of education are subject to the provisions of the U.S. Constitution. The provisions of the Constitution that have had the greatest impact on the operation of public schools are the general welfare clause, commerce clause, Article I, Section 10, and the First, Fourth, Fifth, Ninth and Fourteenth Amendments.

General Welfare Clause The **General Welfare Clause** of Article I, Section 8 of the U.S. Constitution provides, "The Congress shall have Power to lay and collect Taxes, Duties, Imposts and Excises, to pay the Debts and provide for the common Defence and general welfare of the United States . . ."[2] Federal involvement in education has emanated principally from the General Welfare Clause.

Some of the areas of legislation Congress has enacted over the years, emanating from the general welfare rationale, include defense (National Defense Education Act of 1958); vocational education (Vocational Education Act of 1963); civil rights (Civil Rights Act of 1964); elementary and secondary education (Elementary and Secondary Education Act of 1965); bilingual education (Bilingual Education Act of 1968); sex discrimination (Title IX of the Education Amendments of 1972); protecting information concerning students (Family Educational Rights and Privacy Act of 1974); pregnancy bias (Pregnancy Discrimination Act of 1978); children with disabilities (Section 504 of the Rehabilitation Act of 1973, the Education for All Handicapped Children Act of 1975, renamed the Individuals with Disabilities Act of 1990, the Individuals with Disabilities Education Act of 1997 and 2004); national health and safety concerns (Asbestos School Hazard Detection and Control Act of 1980 and Indoor Radon Abatement Act of 1988); and protecting the welfare of minors concerning the suitability of materials made available through the Internet (Children's Internet Protection Act of 2002).

The No Child Left Behind (NCLB) Act of 2001 (Public Law 107-110) represents the latest major federal enactment. Federal expenditure of tax dollars for NCLB is justified under the General Welfare Clause. NCLB was signed into law by George W. Bush on January 8, 2002. The central thesis of NCLB is three fold: increasing the performance of public schools, requiring accountability of states and local school districts, and promoting parental choice.

Commerce Clause Beyond the limitations governing general welfare, Congress is empowered under the **Commerce Clause** to "regulate Commerce with foreign Nations, and among the several States, and with the

[1]U.S. Constitution, Articles I, II, III, ratified 1789.

[2]Article I, § 8, cl. 1.

Indian Tribes."[3] Safety, transportation, and labor regulations enacted pursuant to this clause have affected education.

One would naturally assume that the term "commerce" included commercial activity–buying, selling, and trading goods among the states. However, the Supreme Court has favored a broad interpretation of "commerce" and an expanded federal role in regulating commercial activity to ensure national prosperity. In *Gibbons v. Ogden*, Chief Justice Marshall maintained that commerce was defined not merely as an exchange of goods but also as a means for "advancement of society, labor, transportation, intelligence, care, and various mediums of exchange. . . ."[4] The *Gibbons* case reinforced the importance of literacy as a necessity, and a right, of every human being. In this broad context, the constitutional assertion of education and knowledge as an aspect of commerce is vital to the growth and prosperity of the nation.

Obligation of Contracts Article I, Section 10, provides in part that "no state shall . . . pass any . . . law impairing the obligation of contracts." This article guaranteeing the **obligation of contracts** has been litigated in numerous public school cases. Court decisions have verified that contracts entered into by school districts (including personnel contracts and other contracted services) are fully protected under Article I, Section 10. The provision also applies when a state legislature seeks to alter a teacher tenure or retirement statute in which contractual status prevails under the law.[5]

First Amendment The **First Amendment** provides that "Congress shall make no law respecting the establishment of religion, or prohibiting the free exercise thereof; or abridging the freedom of speech, or of press; or of the right of the people peaceably to assemble, and to petition the Government for a redress of grievances." The first part of the amendment dealing with religious freedoms precipitated litigation challenging government aid to parochial schools and public school policies objected to on religious grounds. The *freedom of speech* portion has evoked numerous court cases involving students' and teachers' rights to freedom of expression. The *rights of assembly* part has precipitated litigation involving students' organizations and employees' rights to organize and bargain collectively.

Fourth Amendment The **Fourth Amendment** provides in part that "the right of the people to be secure . . . against unreasonable searches and seizures . . . and no Warrants shall issue, but upon probable cause. . . ." This amendment has been the subject of litigation involving searches of students' lockers and person and, in some cases, teachers' rights to privacy.

Fifth Amendment The **Fifth Amendment** reads in part that "no person . . . shall be compelled in any criminal case to be a witness against himself, nor deprived of life, liberty, or property without due process of law; nor shall private property be taken for public use, without just compensation." The first clause is relevant to cases where teachers have been questioned by superiors about their alleged activities with subversive organizations. The **due process clause** pertains specifically to acts of the federal government. The last clause is germane in instances where states or school boards acquire property for school building purposes.

Ninth Amendment The **Ninth Amendment** stipulates, "The enumeration in the Constitution of certain rights, shall not be construed to deny or disparage others retained by the people." Essentially, the Ninth Amendment assures that rights not enumerated in the other clauses of the Bill of Rights are retained by the people. The Ninth Amendment was brought forth in educational litigation in which teachers have asserted that their right to personal privacy outside the classroom is protected as an unenumerated right. Furthermore, teachers and students have challenged dress and grooming regulations as infringing on their individual liberties and freedoms under this amendment. We will examine some Supreme Court cases pertaining to these issues later in the chapter.

Fourteenth Amendment The **Fourteenth Amendment** provides in part that no state shall "deprive any person of life, liberty or property without due process of law. . . ." Numerous education cases involving this provision have come to the courts. Compulsory school attendance laws give students a property right to attend school. Teachers with **tenure** have a property right to continued employment. Liberty rights include interests in one's reputation and the right to personal privacy.

---

[3]Article I, § 8, cl. 3.

[4]*Gibbons v. Ogden*, 22 U.S. (9 Wheat) 1 (1824).

[5]*Ball v. Board of Trustees of Teachers Retirement Fund*, 58 Atl. 111 (N.J. 1904).

The Fourteenth Amendment also provides that no state shall "deny to any person within its jurisdiction the equal protection of the law." The **equal protection clause** of the Fourteenth Amendment has been involved in a wide variety of education cases in recent years. Among them are cases involving alleged discrimination based on race, sex, ethnic background, age, and handicaps and state financing of public schools.

State Role in Education

At no point does the federal Constitution refer to education. This, coupled with the language of the Tenth Amendment (". . . powers not delegated to the United States by the Constitution, nor prohibited by it to the States, are reserved to the States respectively, or to the people"), vested in state government the legal responsibility for the control and direction of public education. Thus, while federal authority is restrictive concerning education, the state has complete authority to provide a public education system.

State Constitutions The United States is organized into two streams of government activity: a federal legal system and fifty separate state legal systems. Each state has its own constitution that forms its basic laws. The primary function of state constitutions is to restrict the powers of state legislatures to exact laws that are at variance with federal law or the provisions of state constitutions.[6] Generally, state constitutions contain a mandate for the establishment of public education systems. Frequently, state constitutions deal with the same subjects as the federal Constitution does, but, on some issues, such as separation of church and state, state constitutions may be more stringent.

State Statutes Every state legislature enacts, amends, and repeals laws. These laws affecting public schools form the statutes of the fifty U.S. states. Recall that the Tenth Amendment of the U.S. Constitution is a plenary, absolute, power grant to the state legislatures over public education. However, the laws enacted cannot contravene federal law or the state constitution.

For example, over the years, the federal government has limited state authority over public education as school operation matters have been challenged in the courts. Decisions on such state issues as racial desegregation of public schools, teachers' free speech, students' symbolic protest, students' procedural due process, constitutionality of corporal punishment, search and seizure, and nontort liability of school board members have placed state authority over public school operations within the legal boundaries of the federal Constitution. Courts resolved these conflicts, and those decisions became part of **case law**, that is, principles of law derived from court decisions.

Local Boards of Education Obviously, state legislatures cannot assume supervisory responsibility for public schools. In keeping with the framework of decentralization of educational operation, the general supervision and administration of each state's public school system is delegated to state and local boards of education who in turn are responsible for hiring school administrators and classroom teachers. These groups have the authority to enforce policies and procedures for the operation and management of public schools. Their actions must be within the legal boundaries of federal and state constitutions and statutes. For example, building principals and classroom teachers rely on this authority in dealing with such issues as administering student punishment, suspensions and expulsions, searching a student's locker, and the like.

American Judicial System

The provisions of federal and state constitutions, statutes, and policies of local boards of education do not guarantee proper execution of the law. A mechanism exists in our legal system for allowing an individual or group whose constitutional rights may have been violated to seek adjudication in the courts. Courts, however, do not act on their own initiative. Instead, courts settle only those disputes referred to them for decision.[7]

The U.S. judicial system is complex and multifaceted. As noted earlier, it is organized into one federal court system and fifty state court systems.

Federal Court System Article III, Section 1, of the U.S. Constitution provides that "(t)he judicial power of the United States shall be vested in one Supreme Court, and in such inferior courts as the Congress may from

[6]Kern Alexander and M. David Alexander, *American Public School Law*, 8th ed. (Belmont, CA: Wadsworth/Cengage, 2011).

[7]Ibid.

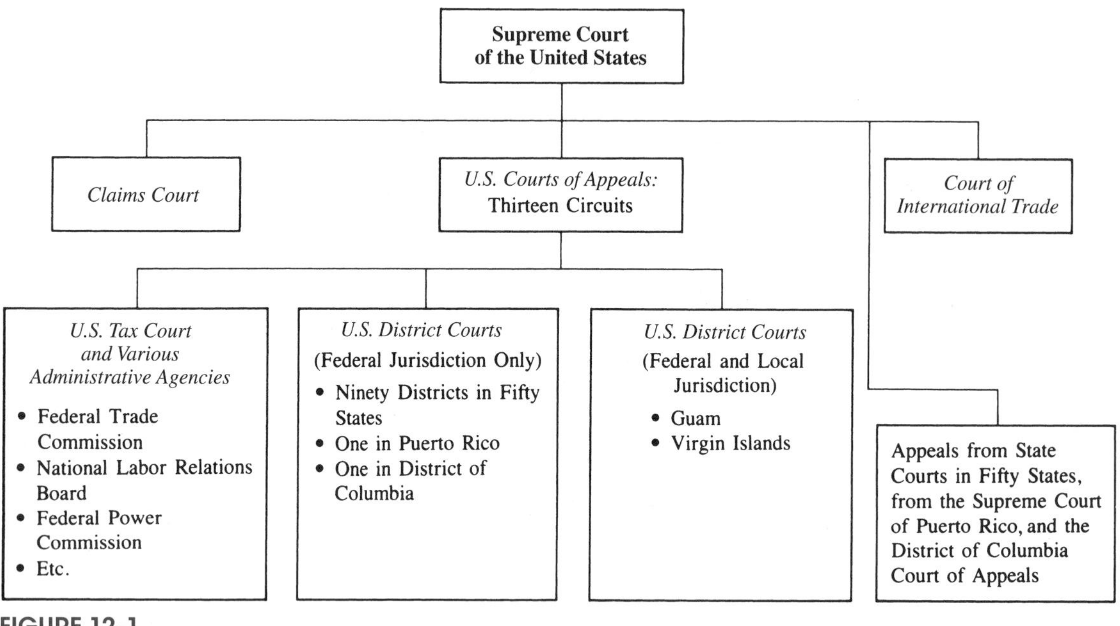

FIGURE 12–1

The Federal Court System
Source: Adapted from *A Guide to the Federal Courts,* rev. ed. (Washington, DC: WANT Publishing, 1984).

time to time ordain and establish."[8] These courts have the authority to adjudicate cases dealing with a provision of the federal Constitution or a federal statute. For example, a federal court might decide an alleged breach of contract between a board of education and a private contractor under Article I, Section 10, of the U.S. Constitution or the nonrenewal of a tenured teacher's employment contract under the same article or the due process clause of the Fourteenth Amendment.

The federal court system contains three levels of general jurisdiction: district courts, courts of appeals, and the U.S. Supreme Court. In addition, there are some courts of special jurisdiction such as the claims court, tax court, and court of international trade. Figure 12–1 depicts the federal court system.

The federal court system contains ninety federal district courts. These are designated as courts of original jurisdiction or trial courts and serve as the first level in the federal court structure. Each state has at least one district court, and many states have between two and four districts. For example, California, New York, and Texas have four district courts each. In addition, separate districts exist with federal jurisdiction only in Puerto Rico and the District of Columbia and with federal and local jurisdictions in Guam and the Virgin Islands.

Appeals from the federal district courts can go to the U.S. Courts of Appeals, the next level in the federal court system. There are twelve federal circuits, with an appeals court for each. A thirteenth federal circuit court has jurisdiction to hear special claims such as customs, patents and copyrights, taxes, and international trade. (See the map in Figure 12–2.) Decisions rendered in each appeals court are binding only in the states within its circuit, but such decisions often influence other federal appeals courts dealing with similar issues.

The U.S. Supreme Court, the highest court in the system, is the court of final appeal on federal law questions. Of the education-related questions that eventually reach the Court, petitioners claim that a state's statutes or the policies of a local board of education have violated their constitutional rights or some provisions of federal law. In cases directly involving educational

[8]U.S. Constitution, Art. III, Sec. 1, ratified 1789.

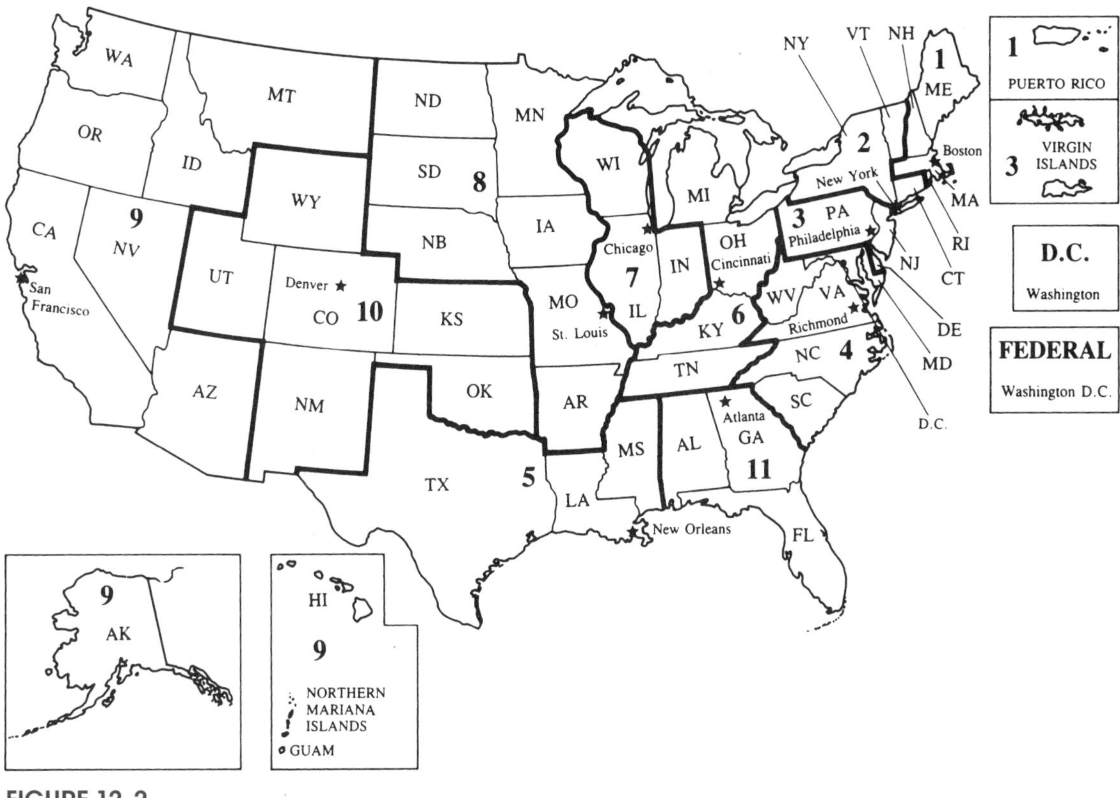

FIGURE 12–2

The Federal Judicial Circuits

matters, certain provisions of the U.S. Constitution are involved more often than others. These provisions, noted previously, are Article I, Section 10, and the First, Fourth, Fifth, and Fourteenth Amendments, especially the due process and equal protection clauses of the Fourteenth Amendment.

State Court Systems Because education is a state function, state courts decide most cases involving educational matters. Each state has its own unique court structure, but similarities exist. Many states have a three-level structure similar to the federal court system. Typically, there are courts of original jurisdiction (trial courts), courts of appeal (appellate courts), and the state's highest court (Supreme Court), often referred to generally as the "court of last resort." Names assigned to these courts at each of the three levels are not uniform among the states. Decisions rendered by the state's highest court can be appealed to the U.S. Supreme Court only if a question of federal law is involved.

The Law and Professional Personnel

The federal Constitution vested in state government the legal responsibility for the control and direction of public education through the fifty state legislatures. However, the actual administration of public school systems is delegated to state boards of education, state departments of education, and local boards of education. These agencies adopt and enforce reasonable rules and regulations emanating from statutes enacted by state legislatures for the operation of public school systems. In this section, we discuss the following issues related to professional personnel: certification, contracts, termination of employment, discrimination in employment, and tort liability.

Certification

The schools employ several categories of professional personnel: superintendents, principals, curriculum specialists, business managers, school psychologists, social workers, counselors, classroom teachers, and the like. To be eligible for employment in a professional position, the individual should possess a valid certificate issued according to statutory provisions of a given state. These statutes, varying from state to state, concern requirements and procedures for obtaining the different certificates. Generally, the legislature delegates the legal authority to issue and process certification to state boards and departments of education. In some states, however, the legislature delegates that authority to a local school district as is the case in New York City and more recently in Chicago.

The preparation standards for each type of certificate are similar from state to state, with only a few exceptions. For example, every state requires applicants to have a college degree with a minimum number of credit hours in a prescribed curriculum. Besides educational requirements, other prerequisites may include evidence of good moral character, a minimum age, U.S. citizenship, and satisfactory performance on a state-administered examination.

The initial certification is usually issued for a specified period of time, including various designations such as temporary, emergency, conditional, standard, life, or permanent. It is the certificate holder's responsibility to keep it renewed. This may require evidence of additional coursework, professional experience in a public school, or passage of a standardized examination such as the National Teachers Examination (NTE). Certificates also include specific endorsements (e.g., superintendent, principal, counselor, teacher), subject areas (e.g., English, social studies, mathematics, sciences), and grade levels (e.g., elementary, middle or junior high school, high school). A school board's failure to assign professional personnel to positions for which they are certified can result in loss of state accreditation and federal funding.[9]

The state also has the power to revoke certification. Certification revocation is different from dismissal from employment by a local board of education. A local school board can legally dismiss a superintendent, principal, teacher, or other professional employee, but the state is generally the only government body that can revoke a certificate. Moreover, state statutes usually specify the grounds and procedures for certification revocation. For example, under the Kentucky statute, it is provided that "any certification . . . may be revoked by the Education Professional Standards Board for immorality, misconduct in office, in competency or willful neglect of **duty**. . . . Before the certification is revoked the defendant shall be given a copy of the charges against him and given an opportunity, upon not less than twenty (20) days' notice, to be heard in person or by counsel."[10]

Contracts

A certificate renders the holder eligible for employment in a state; it does not guarantee employment. Statutory law provides that local boards of education have the legal authority to enter into contracts with professional personnel. The relationship between a school board and its professional employees is contractual. The general legal principles governing contracts—offer and acceptance, competent parties, consideration, legal subject matter, and proper form—apply to this contractual relationship.

Offer and acceptance pertains to the job description, compensation level, and time of performance to which both parties have agreed. In most states, because only the board of education has the power to employ personnel, it must exercise that function itself. It cannot delegate the employment duty to the superintendent of schools or to individual members of the school board. Further, a local board of education is considered to be a legal body only as a corporate unit; therefore, for a board to enter into a valid contract with a teacher or other professional personnel, there must be a meeting of the board.

Competent parties means that, for a valid contract to exist, the parties must be authorized by law to enter into a contractual relationship. By law the school board possesses the legal authority to enter into contracts. A teacher or other professional employee is legally competent to contract providing she possesses the necessary certification and meets other state requirements. An application of this element of contracts is found in a Kentucky case. A teacher lacked a certificate when she began teaching and was ineligible for one because she was under the state's minimum-age requirement for certification. Consequently, the contract between the parties was void, and the teacher was not entitled to receive a salary for the work she performed while a minor.[11]

---

[9]Stephen B. Thomas, Nelda H. Cambron-McCabe, and Martha M. McCarthy, *Public School Law*, 6th ed. (Boston: Pearson, 2009).

[10]*Kentucky Rev. Stat.*, Ch. 161.120 (1992).

[11]*Floyd County Bd. of Educ. v. Slone*, 307 S.W. 2d 912 (Ky. 1957).

Consideration pertains to the promises bargained for and exchanged between the parties. Consideration is something of value—usually money or the equivalent. Promises to perform services gratuitously are not contracts because they are not supported by consideration. To have valid consideration, each party must give up something of value. In the case of an employment contract, consideration consists of the exchange of promises between the employee and the school district. The employee promises to perform specified services, and the school board promises to pay a specified salary.

Legal subject matter refers to mutual assurance between the parties that the job and its performance would not be a violation of the law. Finally, *proper form* means that all legal requirements, as stipulated in the state's statutes, must be followed in order for a contract to be valid. The precise form for contracts may vary from one state to another, but in most states, the statute requires that contracts with professional personnel be written.[12]

The policies and procedures of the local board of education, provisions of the state constitution and its statutes, and the collective bargaining agreement, if there is one, are considered part of the contract between the school district and the teacher or other professional employee. It is recommended therefore that the aforementioned inclusions to an employee's contract be referenced either in the body or on the face of the contract; they then become expressly part of the individual employment contract.

Termination of Employment

Local boards of education possess the legal authority to terminate the employment of school personnel. The U.S. Supreme Court bestowed on school boards this authority when it held that ". . . school authorities have the right and the duty to screen the officials, teachers, and employees as to their fitness to maintain the integrity of the schools as part of ordered society. . . ."[13] However, despite the legal authority of a board of education to terminate the employment, it cannot arbitrarily discharge personnel at any time.

Tenure Law Tenure statutes protect teachers (and other school district personnel specifically enumerated in state statutes) from arbitrary actions by local boards of education. The courts have sustained the constitutionality of such statutes. Teachers' Tenure Act cases[14] have concluded that tenure exists to protect competent teachers and other members of the teaching profession against unlawful and arbitrary board actions and to provide orderly procedures for the dismissal of unsatisfactory teachers and other professional personnel.

Tenure is attained by complying with specific provisions prescribed by state statutes. The nature of these provisions varies from state to state, but certain conditions are included in most legislation. Nearly all statutes require that teachers serve a probationary period before tenure becomes effective. Generally, the probationary period ranges from three to five years, during which time a teacher is employed on a term contract. On completion of the probation period, personnel acquire tenure either automatically or by school board action. Texas law is an exception and permits the local school board to choose between adopting continuing contracts and remaining under term contracts, in which case teachers do not have tenure.[15]

Which positions are to be covered under tenure laws is within the prerogative of state legislatures. In some jurisdictions, tenure legislation extends to selected administrative positions, but rarely to superintendents. Others afford tenure only to teachers. For example, in South Carolina, South Dakota, and Missouri, a school administrator possessing a teacher's certificate is a "teacher" within the meaning of tenure laws.[16] In Kentucky, "(t)he term 'administrator' for the purpose of (tenure) shall mean a certified employee, below the rank of superintendent. . . ."[17]

Although principals and certain other supervisory personnel can acquire tenure either as teachers or as principals in states having tenure laws, superintendents are not generally covered by tenure in that position unless the statute specifically indicates such inclusions. For example, the Illinois Supreme Court ruled that, because they are district employees who require certification, superintendents are covered by the tenure law, but that the tenure protection extended only to a teaching

[12]*Gordon v. Board of Directors of West Side Area Vocational Tech. School,* 347 A. 2d 347 (Pa. 1975).

[13]*Adler v. Bd. of Educ.,* 342 U.S. 485 (1952).

[14]*Teachers' Tenure Act Cases,* 329 Pa. 213, 197 A. 344 (1938).

[15]*White v. South Park,* I.S.D., 693 F. 2d 1163 (5 Cir. 1983).

[16]*Snipes v. McAndrew,* 313 S.E. 2d 294 (S.C. 1984); *Waltz v. Bd. of Educ.,* 329 N.W. 2d 131 (S.D. 1983); *Fuller v. N. Kansas City,* S.D., 629 S.W. 2d 404 (Mo. 1982).

[17]*Ky. Rev. Stat.,* Ch. 161.720, Sec. 8 (1992).

position and not to an administrative one.[18] On the other hand, tenure can be acquired by superintendents in New Jersey.[19]

In discussing the termination of employment of teachers and supervisory personnel, the terms *nonrenewal* and *dismissal* are often used interchangeably. There is a substantial difference, however, in the manner in which the termination operates in each case. If not protected by tenure, a school employee may be nonrenewed for no reason or for any reason whatsoever, providing it does not violate an employee's substantive constitutional rights (e.g., free speech, protection against racial discrimination). Courts have reasoned in these cases that the contract has simply terminated and there is no "expectancy of continued employment." Dismissal, on the other hand, whether under tenure status or during an unexpired contract, is permissible only "for cause." Consequently, a dismissal of a tenured employee or a nontenured professional during a contract year is entitled to a due process hearing embodying all the statutory and constitutional safeguards.

Dismissal Procedures Most tenure laws provide specific procedures for dismissing tenured employees. The procedure typically includes three elements: notice by a specific date, specification of charges against the employee, and a hearing at which the charges are discussed. When state law describes a specific procedure for dismissal, it must be followed exactly to make the action legal.

Besides the procedures required under state law, tenure rights qualify for constitutional procedural protections encompassed within the concepts of **property** and **liberty interests** under the due process clause of the Fourteenth Amendment. The holding of a teaching position qualifies as a property right if the employee has an unexpired contract or has acquired tenure. The aforementioned protections of the Fourteenth Amendment do not normally extend to nontenured employees. The Supreme Court has affirmed the view of the courts that nontenured employees have no property or liberty interests in continued employment.[20] In exceptional situations, courts have recognized "de facto tenure" where there was no tenure law, but tenure was acquired by custom and precedent.[21] However, de facto tenure is not possible where there is a well-established statewide system.

A liberty interest would be an issue in dismissal, and due process required, when evidence exists that a charge has been made that places a stigma on an employee's reputation, thus foreclosing future employment opportunities or seriously damaging his standing in the community.[22] A liberty interest would not be a constitutional safeguard when school board members and school administrators refrain from making public statements or releasing information that is derogatory to the employee. Even when statements are made, if they simply describe unsatisfactory performance in general, normally they do not constitute a constitutional violation of the employee's Fourteenth Amendment rights.

Examples of charges against employees not involving stigma include ineffective teaching methods, inability to maintain classroom discipline, and inability to get along with administrators and colleagues. Failure to award tenure does not automatically create a stigma. Examples of stigmas that qualify for constitutional due process protection include manifest racism, immoral conduct, serious mental disorder, a drinking or drug problem, willful neglect of duty, and responsibility for the deterioration of a school.[23]

When a liberty or **property interest** is involved, the Fourteenth Amendment requires that the employee be notified of charges, provided with an opportunity for a hearing and representation by counsel, examine and cross-examine witnesses, and have an official record of the hearing. (See Figure 12–3.)

Causes for dismissal are generally specified in state statutes and differ from one state to another; however, there are similarities. For example, in Kentucky tenured employees can be dismissed for insubordination; immoral character or conduct; physical or mental disability; or inefficiency, incompetency, or neglect of duty.[24] In Illinois cause for dismissal is specified as incompetency, cruelty, negligence, immorality or other sufficient cause and whenever in the board's opinion a teacher is not qualified to teach or the best interests of the school require it.[25] In Connecticut cause is enumerated

---

[18] *Lester v. Bd. of Educ. of S.D.*, No. 119, 230 N.E. 2d 893 (Ill. 1967).

[19] *N.J. Stat. Ann.*, Sec. 18A:28–5(4) (1999).

[20] *Roth v. Bd. of Regents*, 408 U.S. 564 (1972).

[21] *Perry v. Sinderman*, 408 U.S. 593 (1972).

[22] *Roth v. Bd. of Regents.*

[23] Alexander and Alexander, *American Public School Law.*

[24] *Ky. Rev. Stat.*, Ch. 161.790 (1998).

[25] *Ill. Ann. Stat.*, Ch. 122, Sec. 10–22.4 (1998).

1. Notice of the charges
2. Opportunity for a prompt hearing
3. Opportunity to prepare for the hearing
4. Access to evidence and names of all witnesses
5. Hearing before an impartial tribunal
6. Representation by legal counsel
7. Opportunity to present evidence and cross-examine adverse witnesses
8. Decision based on the evidence and findings of the hearing
9. Official record of the hearing
10. Opportunity to appeal the decision to higher authority

FIGURE 12–3

Procedural Due Process Elements in Employee Dismissal Proceedings

as inefficiency, incompetency, insubordination, moral misconduct, disability as shown by competent medical evidence, elimination of position, or for other due and sufficient cause.[26]

Discrimination in Employment

Recent federal laws intended to remove discrimination in employment have had a direct impact on school board employment practices. Such legislation includes Title VII of the Civil Rights Act of 1964, Title IX of the Education Amendments of 1972, the Rehabilitation Act of 1973, the Equal Pay Act of 1963, the Age Discrimination Act of 1986, the Pregnancy Discrimination Act of 1978, and the Americans with Disabilities Act of 1990 (ADA). In addition, guidelines and policies from such federal agencies as the Equal Employment Opportunity Commission (EEOC), the Office of Economic Opportunity (OEO), and 42 U.S.C. Section 1983, in particular, have been applied in claims of employment discrimination. This section briefly discusses race and gender discrimination, sexual harassment, discrimination based on disabilities, age, religious, and maternity discrimination.

Race and Gender Discrimination Beginning in the early 1970s, the federal courts heard several cases challenging discrimination. In 1971 the U.S. Supreme Court, in *Griggs v. Duke Power Company*, determined that Title VII of the Civil Rights Act of 1964 (pertaining to hiring, promotion, salary, and retention) covered not only overt discrimination but also practices that are discriminatory in operation.[27] The Court held that an employment practice is prohibited if the exclusion of minorities cannot be shown to be related to job performance. The case involved requiring job applicants to possess a high school diploma and make a satisfactory score on a general intelligence test as criteria for employment. The practice was shown to discriminate against black applicants. during the same year, the Court, in *Phillips v. Martin Marietta Corporation*, handed down a decision relative to the disparate treatment of the sexes in the workplace. The Court ruled that discriminatory treatment of the sexes, by employment practices not necessary to the efficient and purposeful operation of an organization, is prohibited by the same federal legislation.[28]

The effect of these two landmark decisions was to force employers to remove "artificial, arbitrary, and unnecessary" barriers to employment that discriminate on the basis of race and gender classification. In 1972, the

[26]*Conn. Gen. Stat. Ann.*, Tit. 5A, Sec. 10–151 (1999).

[27]*Griggs v. Duke Power Co.*, 401 U.S. 424 (1971).

[28]*Phillips v. Martin Marietta Corp.*, 400 U.S. 542 (1971).

coverage of these provisions of Title VII, which previously had applied only to private employment, were extended to discriminatory employment practices in educational institutions. Subsequent to *Griggs* and *Phillips*, lower courts have applied these same legal standards to Fourteenth Amendment, Section 1983, and Title VII equal protection cases.

To establish a constitutional violation of equal protection, aggrieved individuals must prove that they have been victims of discrimination. In 1981, the Supreme Court set forth the procedural steps to file a Title VII suit.[29] The plaintiff has the initial burden of establishing a prima facie case of discrimination by showing the existence of five factors: (1) member in a protected group (e.g., minorities, women, aged, handicapped), (2) application for the position, (3) qualification for the position, (4) rejection for the position, and (5) employer's continued pursuit of applicants with the plaintiff's qualifications for the position. These factors constitute an initial, or prima facie, case of discrimination in any type of personnel decision. Once a prima facie case of discrimination is established, the defendant (employer) must articulate a nondiscriminatory reason for the action. If this is accomplished, the plaintiff (employee or applicant) then must prove that the explanation is a pretext for discrimination, the real reason for the personnel decision being based on the consideration of "impermissible factors" in employment.[30] In 1993, the Supreme Court reiterated that the ultimate burden of proof in a discrimination suit lies with the plaintiff.[31] The legal standards emanating from *Griggs, Phillips,* and *Hicks* in claims of discriminatory employment practices under Title VII have been applied also under civil rights legislation barring discrimination based on age. Title VII does not cover discrimination based on disabilities. Employees with disabilities in public schools must look to the Rehabilitation Act of 1973 (Section 504) and the Americans with Disabilities Act of 1990 (ADA).

Sexual Harassment Charges of sexual harassment in the workplace have been litigated under Title VII of the Civil Rights Act of 1964 and Title IX of the Education Amendments of 1972. The regulations implementing Title VII define sexual harassment as follows:

> Unwelcome sexual advances, requests for sexual favors, and other verbal or physical conduct of a sexual nature constitute sexual harassment when (i) submission to such conduct is made either explicitly or implicitly a term or condition of an individual's employment, (ii) submission to or rejection of such conduct by an individual is used as the basis for employment decisions affecting such individual, or (iii) such conduct has the purpose or effect of unreasonably interfering with an individual's work performance or creating an intimidating, hostile, or offensive working environment.[32]

In *Meritor Savings Bank v. Vinson,*[33] the Supreme Court initiated this definition by identifying two different forms of sexual harassment: *quid pro quo* harassment and hostile environment harassment. **Quid pro quo sexual harassment** involves conditioning tangible employment benefits (e.g., promotion, demotion, termination) on sexual favors. **Hostile environment sexual harassment** involves a pattern of unwelcome and offensive conduct that unreasonably interferes with an individual's work performance or creates an intimidating or offensive work environment. The Court warned that "for sexual harassment to be actionable, it must be sufficiently severe or pervasive to alter the conditions of (the victim's) employment and create an abusive working environment."[34] In 1993, the Supreme Court elaborated further on the concept of the hostile environment form of sexual harassment,[35] which creates a more difficult task for the courts to interpret than quid pro quo. In reaffirming the standard set in *Meritor,* the Court said that for sexual harassment to be actionable the conduct must cause "tangible psychological injury" rather than conduct that is "merely offensive." Courts determine this by examining such factors as frequency of the conduct, severity of the conduct, whether it is physically threatening or humiliating, and whether it unreasonably interferes with the employee's work performance.

Five kinds of sexual harassment include sexual bribery, sexual imposition, gender harassment, sexual coercion, and sexual behavior.

---

[29] *Texas Department of Community Affairs v. Burdine,* 450 U.S. 248 (1981).

[30] *McDonnell Douglas Corp. v. Green,* 411 U.S. 792 (1973).

[31] *St. Mary's Honor Center v. Hicks,* 113 S. Ct. 2742, 125 L. Ed. 2d 407 (1993).

[32] 29 C.F.R., Sec. 1604.11(a) (1991).

[33] 477 U.S. 57 (1986).

[34] *Meritor Savings Bank, id.* at 67.

[35] *Harris v. Forklift Systems, Inc.,* 114 S. Ct. 367, 126 L. Ed. 2d 295 (1993).

EXEMPLARY EDUCATIONAL ADMINISTRATORS IN ACTION

JOANNA MILLER, Ed. D., Principal, E. M. Baker Elementary School, Great Neck, New York.

Words of Advice: State standards and concomitant testing at specific grade levels have had a tremendous effect on education at the local level. Requiring youngsters as early as age 10 to communicate effectively in writing, to use data and information from documents, and to listen to a passage, take notes, and then respond to questions has raised the bar in New York State elementary schools and created great angst among children, teachers, administrators, and parents. Our teachers and children have risen to the occasion, and student writing has improved. Is there carryover after The Test? That remains to be seen. No one would argue that the skills being tested are not essential if one is to succeed as a student and productive adult. One might also argue that high-stakes testing for fourth graders is excessive and occurs too early in one's life.

What can you as an educational administrator do? You can set the tone for achieving state standards in a manner that is rational, grounded in good educational theory and practice, supportive of teachers, and cognizant of individual student needs. A tall order—and it can be done. Rely on your staff—you will probably have a lot of teacher talent. Use their ideas and expertise; support your teacher leaders. Encourage creativity, flexibility, and compassion. Don't become hysterical about results—if teachers have done their job in preparing children, then the results are what they are, and you can use them to help kids and improve instruction. Do your best to educate parents, which is not easy, as many parents are convinced that elementary school test results will affect college admission.

Sexual Bribery **Sexual bribery** is solicitation of sexual activity or other sex-linked behaviors by promise of rewards; the proposition may be either overt or subtle.

Sexual Imposition Examples of gross **sexual imposition** are forceful touching, feeling, grabbing, or sexual assault.

Gender Harassment **Gender harassment** means generalized sexist statements and behaviors that convey insulting or degrading attitudes about the opposite sex. Examples include insulting remarks, offensive graffiti, obscene jokes, or humor about sex or women in general.

Sexual Coercion **Sexual coercion** means coercion of sexual activity or other sex-linked behavior by threat of punishment; examples include negative performance evaluations, withholding of promotions, threat of termination.

Sexual Behavior **Sexual behavior** means unwanted, inappropriate, and offensive sexual advances. Examples include repeated unwanted sexual invitations, insistent requests for dinner, drinks, or dates, persistent letters, phone calls, and other invitations.[36]

School administrators are strictly liable for quid pro quo sexual harassment under both Title VII of the Civil Rights Act of 1964 and Title IX of the Education Amendments of 1972. Therefore, school leaders need to take positive steps to prevent sexual harassment in the workplace. (See Administrative Advice 12–1.)

Discrimination Based on Disabilities The principal federal statutes that affect people with disabilities are the Rehabilitation Act of 1973 (Section 504) and the Americans with Disabilities Act of 1990 (ADA). These statutes prohibit discrimination based on disabilities against persons who are "otherwise qualified" for employment. These laws extend to all stages of employment, from recruiting and screening to hiring, promotion, and dismissal.

Section 504 and the ADA define a disabled person as one who has a physical or mental impairment that substantially limits one or more of such person's major life activities, has a record of such impairment, or is regarded as having such an impairment.[37] The ADA and Section 504, as recently amended, specifically exclude from the coverage of either law persons currently using illegal drugs and alcoholics, whose use of

[36]Jerry Lowe and Kelly Strnadel, "Sexual Harassment: Approaches to a More Positive Work Environment," unpublished paper, Sam Houston State University, Huntsville, Texas, January 12, 1999.

[37]29 U.S.C. Sec. 706 (8) (B) (i) (1988); 42 U.S.C.A., Sec. 12102(2) (West Supp. 1992).

ADMINISTRATIVE ADVICE 12–1

Positive Approaches to Sexual Harassment for the Workplace

There are several positive approaches to sexual harassment that school leaders can take to maintain a positive work environment.

Establish a No Tolerance Policy. Declare that the employer will not stand for sexual harassment, discrimination, or retaliation in the workplace. Under the law, the employer has the affirmative duty to rid the workplace of sexual harassment and discrimination. All employees should know their employer's policy that forbids sexual harassment, discrimination, and retaliation.

Widely Disseminate the Policy. Everyone should have the policy readily available. This is important for both employer and employee.

Make It Easy for Employees to File Complaints. Employees should be able to complain to someone other than their immediate superior. Someone outside the employee's chain of command, such as a human resource staff member, should be available to hear the complaint.

Investigate Complaints Promptly and Objectively. Promptness and objectivity should be the standard response. If management has knowledge of discrimination or sexual harassment happening, an investigation should be conducted. Prompt and objective investigation says to everyone that the complaint is serious.

Take Appropriate Remedial Action to Prevent a Reoccurrence. Actions might include informal resolution between parties and disciplinary action against harassers. Offer the victim free counseling, if appropriate. Most importantly, provide training to all employees periodically.

Source: Adapted from Jerry Lowe and Kelly Strnadel, "Sexual Harassment: Approaches to a More Positive Work Environment," unpublished paper, Sam Houston State University, Huntsville, Texas, January 12, 1999.

alcohol interferes with job performance. But those in drug rehabilitation programs or who have successfully completed a program may be considered disabled.

The statutory definitions of a disabled person seem to include those with communicable diseases who are qualified to perform the job and whose condition does not threaten the health and safety of others. For example, the Supreme Court has ruled that the definition of a disabled person includes those with an infectious disease such as tuberculosis;[38] and a lower court has extended coverage to teachers with AIDS.[39]

The Supreme Court has said that an otherwise qualified disabled person is one who can meet all of the essential requirements of a job in spite of the disability. In determining whether a person with a disability is qualified to do a job, the central factors to consider are the nature of the disability in relation to the demands of the job. However, when a disabled person cannot meet all of the requirements of a job, an employer must provide "reasonable accommodation" that permit a qualified individual with a disability to perform the "essential functions" of a position.[40] Furthermore, courts have ruled that Section 504 and the ADA protect otherwise qualified disabled individuals but do not require accommodations for persons who are not qualified for the positions sought.[41]

Age Discrimination The Age Discrimination in Employment Act (ADEA) was enacted to promote employment of older persons based on their ability and to prohibit arbitrary age discrimination in the terms and conditions of employment.[42] The law covers public employees, including teachers and school administrators. Thus mandatory retirement for teachers is prohibited by law.[43]

[38]*Sch. Bd. of Nassau Cty, FL v. Arline,* 480 U.S. 273 (1987).

[39]*Chalk v. U.S. District Court,* 840 F. 2d 701 (9th Cir., Cal., 1988).

[40]42 U.S.C.A., Sec 12101 (West Supp. 1992).

[41]*Southeastern Community College v. Davis,* 442 U.S. 397 (1979); *Beck v. James,* 793 S.W. 2d 416 (MO Ct. App. 1990); *DeVargas v. Mason & Hanger-Silas Mason Co.,* 911 F. 2d 1377 (10th Circ. 1990, *cert. denied,* 111 S. Ct. 799 (1991).

[42]29 U.S.C.A., Sec. 621–634 (1990) and (West Supp. 1992).

[43]29 U.S.C.A., Sec. 631 (West Supp. 1992).

The act parallels Title VII in its application and operation. Thus, litigation under ADEA follows the disparate treatment standard used for race and gender discrimination cases. A school district charged with age discrimination may defend itself by articulating nondiscriminatory reasons for the adverse employment decision, such as inferior qualifications or poor performance rather than age.

Religious Discrimination Citizens' free exercise of religion is protected under the religion clauses of the First Amendment and the Equal Protection Clause of the Fourteenth Amendment. These clauses prohibit discrimination against any public school employee on the basis of religious beliefs. In addition to constitutional safeguards, public school employees are protected from religious discrimination under Title VII. In Title VII, as amended, Congress requires accommodation of "all aspects of religious observances and practices as well as belief, unless an employer demonstrates that he is unable to accommodate an employee's or prospective employee's religious observance or practice without undue hardship on the conduct of the employer's business."[44] The Equal Employment Opportunity Commission (EEOC) has developed guidelines with suggested accommodations for religious observance, such as assignment exchanges, flexible scheduling, job assignment changes, and using voluntary substitutes.

Maternity Discrimination Mandatory maternity leave policies have been the subject of litigation. In *Cleveland Board of Education v. LaFleur*,[45] the Supreme Court held that a school board policy that required all pregnant teachers regardless of circumstances to take mandatory maternity leave for specified periods before and after childbirth was unconstitutional. The Court stated that it had long recognized that freedom of personal choice in matters of marriage and family life is one of the liberties protected under the due process clause of the Fourteenth Amendment. "By acting to penalize the pregnant teacher for deciding to bear a child . . . can constitute a heavy burden on the exercise of these protected freedoms."

The Constitution still permits school boards to implement maternity leave policies that are not arbitrary and fulfill a legitimate goal of maintaining continuity of instruction in a school system. For example, a mandatory maternity leave beginning date for teachers set at the beginning of the ninth month of pregnancy was upheld on "business necessity" grounds by the Court of Appeals, Ninth Circuit.[46] A New Jersey court has sustained a period of child-bearing disability of four weeks before expected birth and four weeks following the actual date of birth for purposes of sick leave benefits.[47] A court found a male teacher not entitled to paid maternity leave for the purpose of caring for his disabled pregnant wife.[48] However, child-rearing leave must not be made available only to females. Such a provision in a collective bargaining agreement was declared to violate Title VII.[49]

A federal law, the Family and Medical Leave Act (FMLA) of 1993,[50] requires state and local government employers to provide up to twelve work weeks of unpaid leave during any twelve-month period for the birth or adoption of a child. Upon return from FMLA leave, an employee must be restored to his or her original job, or to an equivalent job with equivalent pay and benefits. Other provisions of the act are requirements to provide thirty days' notice of leave, medical certifications supporting the need for leave, and reports regarding the employee's intention to return to work. Employees can bring civil action for employer violations of the provisions of the act.

Tort Liability

A **tort** is a civil wrong, not including contracts, for which a court will award damages. The three major categories of torts are intentional interference, strict liability, and negligence. Instances of intentional interference and strict liability in school-related injuries are rare and will not be pursued in this section. Accordingly, we examine the elements of negligence and the defenses against negligence. Liability under Section 1983 of the Civil Rights Act is also addressed.

Elements of Negligence To establish a legal cause for action in tort, four essential elements must exist: The individual has a duty to protect others against unreasonable risks; the individual failed to exercise an appropriate standard of care; the negligent act is the proximate cause

[44]42 U.S.C., Sec 2000e (j) (1988).

[45]414 U.S. 632 (1974).

[46]*deLaurier v. San Diego Unified Sch. Dist.*, 588 F. 2d 674 (9 Cir. 1978).

[47]*Hynes v. Bd. of Educ. of Tp. of Bloomfield, Essex County*, 190 NJ Super. 36, 461 A. 2d 1184 (1983).

[48]*Ackerman v. Bd. of Educ.*, 287 F. Supp. 76 (S.D. NY 1974).

[49]*Shafer v. Bd. of Educ. of Sch. Dist. of Pittsburgh, PA*, 903 F. 2d 243 (3 Cir. 1990).

[50]PL 103-3 (1993).

of the injury; and a physical or mental injury, resulting in actual loss or damage to the person, exists.[51]

Duty School employees have a duty to protect students entrusted to their care from being injured. Specifically, these duties include adequate supervision and instruction, maintenance of premises and equipment, and foreseeability. The test of foreseeability is whether under all circumstances the possibility of injury should have been reasonably foreseen and that supervision likely would have prevented the injury. For example, a teacher was found guilty of negligence when an eighth-grade pupil was injured from pebble throwing that continued for almost ten minutes during a morning recess.[52] Similarly, in a New Jersey suit, an elementary school principal was held liable for injuries suffered when a pupil was struck by paperclips shot from a rubber band by another child before the classrooms opened. The court found the principal had acted improperly by announcing no rules on the conduct of students before entering classrooms, by not assigning teachers to assist him in supervising the pupils before school, and by engaging in activities other than overseeing the activities of the pupils.[53]

Standard of Care Failure of a school employee to act in a manner that conforms to an appropriate **standard of care** can render said employee negligent. The standard of care is that which a reasonable and prudent person would have exercised under similar circumstances. For example, the Oregon Supreme Court said "Negligence . . . is . . . the doing of that thing which a reasonably prudent person would not have done, in like or similar circumstances. . . ."[54] The model for the reasonable and prudent person has been described as one who possesses "(1) the physical attributes of the defendant himself, (2) normal intelligence, (3) normal perception and memory with a minimum level of information and experience common to the community, and (4) such superior skill and knowledge as the actor has or holds himself out to the public as having."[55]

The standard of care required would depend on such circumstances as the age, maturity, and experience of students; the type of activity; the environment; and the potential for danger. The amount of care owed to children increases with the immaturity of the child. A higher standard of care is required in shop, physical education, and laboratory classes and in situations and environments that pose a greater threat of danger (e.g., school field trips).

Proximate Cause There must be a connection between the action of school personnel and the resultant **injury** sustained by the pupil. Courts will ask, Was the failure to exercise a reasonable standard of care the **proximate cause** of the injury? The cause of the injury first must be established. Then it must be shown that there was some connection between the injury and the employee's failure to exercise a reasonable standard of care.

As in determining whether an appropriate standard of care has been exercised, the test of foreseeability is used in establishing proximate cause. It is not necessary that a particular injury was foreseen for proximate cause to be established. If reasonable precautions are taken and an intervening injury not foreseen occurs, no negligence exists. Such was the case when a student returned to his desk and sat on a sharpened pencil placed there by another student. School authorities were not held liable for the injury.[56]

Injury There must be proof of actual loss or damage to the plaintiff resulting from the injury. If the injury suffered is caused by more than one individual, damages will be apportioned among the defendants.[57] A school district may be required to compensate an injured party for negligent conduct of an officer, agent, or employee of the district. Individual school board members or employees (superintendents, principals, teachers) may also be liable personally for torts that they commit in the course of their duties. (See Administrative Advice 12–2.)

Defenses against Negligence Several defenses can be invoked by a defendant (school board, superintendent, principal, teacher) in a tort action. These defenses include **contributory negligence**, assumption of risk, comparative negligence, and government immunity.

[51]William Prosser, John Wade, and Victor Schwartz, *Cases and Materials on Torts,* 7th ed. (St. Paul, MN: West, 1982).

[52]*Sheehan v. St. Peter's Catholic School,* 291 Minn. 1, 188 N.W. 2d 868 (1971).

[53]*Titus v. Lindberg,* 49 N.J. 66, A. 2d 65 (1967).

[54]*Biddle v. Mazzocco,* 284 P. 2d 364 (Ore. 1955).

[55]Kern Alexander and M. David Alexander, *American Public School Law,* 7th ed. (Belmont, CA: Wadsworth, 2009), p. 646.

[56]*Swaitkowski v. Bd. of Educ. of City of Buffalo,* 36 A.D. 2d 685 (N.Y. 1971).

[57]Thomas, Cambron-McCabe, and McCarthy, *Public School Law.*

ADMINISTRATIVE ADVICE 12–2

Guidelines for Safer Playgrounds

You risk a lawsuit every time a child sets foot on your school playground. A child falls from a slide or ladder; a child is injured on the swings or seesaws. To protect students from injury—and schools from liability—the enlightened school administrator learns to identify and eliminate these dangers. To help make your playgrounds better and safer, the following principles of design, maintenance, and supervision are suggested:

Avoid Steep Slopes. Ramps, slides, or climbing nets should not be installed at angles of greater than 45 degrees and preferably closer to 35 degrees. The steeper the slope, the greater the risk a child will suffer injury.

Limit Falls to 24 Inches. A playground structure should follow a multilevel design—a series of constantly rising platforms. The distance between levels should vary from 18 to 24 inches, depending on the age of the children using the equipment. If a play structure is designed properly, no child should be able to fall more than two feet.

Consider Accessibility. Playground design must take the "flow of play" into account. Injuries often occur when children who become impatient waiting their turn look for unsafe paths to their destination. The principle here: Give children room to play together and avoid waiting in line.

Provide Safe Clearances. Place play equipment at least 20 feet away from trees, fences, or other playground structures.

Consider Exposure to the Sun. Installing playground equipment under the shade of trees or buildings allows children to play longer and more actively. Shade also reduces the risk of sunburn or burns caused by hot metal slides.

Provide Enclosed Spaces. Providing partially enclosed tube slides or tunnels makes playground equipment more versatile. Enclosures must be large enough for children to move freely through them and to permit teachers to supervise visually.

Use Interconnective Play Components. An interconnective play structure connects ramps, climbing nets, stairs, slides, platforms, and pathways to provide easy movement throughout the play structure.

Use Good-Quality Materials. Safe playground equipment requires strong, durable, and nontoxic material. The equipment must be structurally sound to support the weight of many children and adults at the same time. All edges must be rounded, smooth, and free of splinters.

Inspect Equipment Regularly. Regular inspections are essential to ensure the safety of playground equipment.

Source: Adapted from Louis Bowers, "Follow These Guidelines for Better—and Safer—Playgrounds," *Executive Educator,* 11 (1989): 27–28.

Contributory Negligence If it is shown that a student's own negligence contributed to the injury, the law in many states would charge the student with contributory negligence. However, a student cannot be charged with contributory negligence if he is too immature to recognize the risks: a standard of care that is adequate when dealing with adults generally will not be adequate when dealing with children. For example, in about a dozen states, courts have ruled that students under seven years of age cannot be prohibited from recovery damages because of negligence. In other states, the age has been set at four, five, or six years. And for older children up to the age of fourteen, there is a "rebuttable presumption" that they are incapable of contributory negligence.[58]

Assumption of Risk Another commonly used defense in tort actions is the doctrine of **assumption of risk.** It is based on the theory that one who knowingly and willingly exposes oneself to a known danger may be denied tort recovery for injuries sustained. An essential requisite to invoking a defense of assumption of risk is that there be knowledge and appreciation of the

[58]Alexander and Alexander, *American Public School Law.*

danger. Thus, it was held that a child who was cut by submerged broken glass while playing in a high school sandpit did not assume the risk of injury because he did not know the glass was in the sandpit.[59] On the other hand, the Oregon Supreme Court found an assumption of risk in the injury of a high school football player when he was injured in a scheduled football game.[60] Like contributory negligence, courts will consider the age and maturity level of students when assessing a defense of assumption of risk in tort.

Comparative Negligence Where the common law rule of contributory negligence and assumption of risk is followed, plaintiffs whose own negligence contributed to an injury are barred completely from recovery. This harsh rule has been modified. A number of states have adopted the doctrine of **comparative negligence.** Under the comparative negligence doctrine, a plaintiff can obtain a proportionate recovery for injury depending on the amount of negligence she contributed to the injury. Specific statutory provisions vary from state to state.[61]

Government Immunity The origin of the doctrine of **government immunity** from tort liability can be traced to two early cases, one in England in 1788 and the other in Massachusetts in 1812.[62] The courts held that the government could not be sued for negligence. Thus, the precedent of the immunity of school districts from tort liability was established and remained in effect until the passage of the Federal Tort Claims Act of 1946. Subsequently, the doctrine of state immunity in tort has been abrogated or modified by state legislatures. However, tort law does extend certain immunity to teachers and administrators in the scope and performance of their duties. One example is administering corporal punishment in schools.[63]

School board members also have some degree of immunity in the scope and performance of their duties. However, Section 1983 of the Civil Rights Act rooted in 1871 changed the status of the immunity of school board members for their activities. This section provides that every person who subjects any citizen of the United States to the deprivation of any rights secured by the Constitution be liable to the (injured) party in an action at law.[64] A plethora of court cases have been litigated under the act, primarily dealing with First and Fourteenth Amendment rights. The tort liability of school board members was further extended under Section 1983 to students by the Supreme Court decision in *Wood v. Strickland*.[65] The Court held that school board members could be sued individually by students whose constitutional rights were denied. The case involved a denial of due process of students in a suspension hearing.

The Law and Students

Schools exist for the purpose of educating the citizenry. Throughout its history, education has served as the backbone of the U.S. democratic system. This view is based on the premise that the country is best served by an educated, enlightened citizenry. With this mandate, the states have enacted legislation pertaining to the education of the nation's youth. These statutes provide regulations pertaining to school improvement, school attendance, student discipline, freedom of expression, and classification practices.

School Improvement

Accountability for school improvement is a central theme of state policies. The NCLB Act of 2001 (Public Law 107-110) sets demanding accountability standards for schools, school districts, and states, including new state testing requirements designed to improve education. For example, the law requires that states develop both content standards in reading and mathematics and tests that are linked to the standards for grades 3 through 8, with science standards and assessments to follow. States must identify adequate yearly progress (AYP) objectives and disaggregate test results for all students and subgroups of students based on socioeconomic status, race/ethnicity, English language proficiency, and disability. Moreover, the law mandates that 100 percent of students must score at the proficient level on state tests by 2014. Furthermore, the NCLB Act requires states to participate every other year in the

[59] *Brown v. Oakland,* 124 P. 2d 369 (Cal. 1942).

[60] *Vandrell v. S.D.* No. 26C Malheur Cty., 233 Ore. 1, 376 P. 2d 406 (1962).

[61] Alexander and Alexander, *American Public School Law.*

[62] *Russell v. Men of Devon,* 100 Eng. Rep. 359, 2 T. R. 667 (1788); *Mower v. Leicester,* 9 Mass. 237 (1812).

[63] *Ingraham v. Wright,* 430 U.S. 651 (1977).

[64] 42 U.S.C., Section 1983 (1871).

[65] 420 U.S. 308 (1975).

National Assessment of Educational Progress (NAEP) in reading and mathematics.[66]

School Attendance

All fifty states have some form of compulsory school attendance law. These statutes provide the right of children residing in a district to receive a free public education up to a certain age and exact penalties for noncompliance on parents or guardians.

Compulsory Attendance Laws The courts have sustained compulsory attendance laws on the basis of the legal doctrine of **parens patriae.** Under this doctrine, the state has the legal authority to provide for the welfare of its children. In turn, the welfare of the state is served by the development of an enlightened citizenry.

Attendance at a public school is not the only way to satisfy the compulsory attendance law. Over eighty years ago, the U.S. Supreme Court in *Pierce v. Society of Sisters* invalidated an Oregon statute requiring children between the ages of eight and sixteen to attend public schools.[67] The Court concluded that by restricting attendance to public schools, the state violated both the property rights of the school and the liberty interests of parents in choosing the place of education for their children, protected by the Fourteenth Amendment to the Constitution.

Subsequent to *Pierce*, states have expanded the options available to parents (guardians) for meeting the compulsory attendance law. For example, currently in the state of Kentucky, parents are in compliance with that state's statute by selecting from the following options: enrolling their children, who must regularly attend, in a private, parochial, or church-related day school; enrolling their children, who must regularly attend, in a private, parochial, church- or state-supported program for exceptional children; or providing home, hospital, institutional, or other regularly scheduled, suitable, equivalent instruction that meets standards of the state board of education.[68]

Parents or guardians who select one of the options to public school instruction must obtain equivalent instruction. For example, the Washington Supreme Court held that home instruction did not satisfy that state's compulsory attendance law, for the parents who were teaching the children did not hold a valid teaching certificate.[69] In its decision, the court described four essential elements of a school: a certified teacher, pupils of school age, an institution established to instruct school-age children, and a required program of studies (curriculum) engaged in for the full school term and approved by the state board of education. Subsequently, statutes establishing requirements for equivalent instruction (such as certified teachers, program of studies, time devoted to instruction, school-age children, and place or institution) generally have been sustained by the courts.[70]

Exceptions to Compulsory Attendance The prevailing view of the courts is that religious beliefs cannot abrogate a state's compulsory attendance law. An exception is the U.S. Supreme Court ruling in *Wisconsin v. Yoder*, which prevented that state from requiring Amish children to submit to compulsory formal education requirements beyond the eighth grade.[71] The Court found that this was a violation of the free exercise of religion clause of the First Amendment. However, most other attempts to exempt students from school based on religious beliefs have failed.

It is commonly held that married pupils, regardless of age, are exempt from compulsory attendance laws. The rationale is that married persons assume adult status, and consequently the doctrine of parens patriae no longer applies. The precedent in this area is based on two Louisiana cases in which fifteen- and fourteen-year-old married women were considered not "children" under the compulsory attendance law.[72] A later New York case followed the rationale of the two Louisiana cases in declaring that the obligations of a married woman were inconsistent with school attendance.[73] It should be noted, however, that a state cannot deny married minors the right to attend school if they wish.

Some parents have used illness as an exemption from compulsory school attendance. In such situations, the school has the right to require proof of illness through medical certification of a physician. For example, in an

---

[66] *No Child Left Behind Act of 2001* (www.ed.gov/legislation/ESEA02/).

[67] *Pierce v. Society of Sisters*, 268 U.S. 510 (1925).

[68] *Ky. Rev. Stat.*, Ch. 159.030 (1992).

[69] *State ex. rel. Shoreline S.D. No. 412 v. Superior Court*, 55 Wash. 2d 177, 346 P. 2d 999 (1959).

[70] *State ex. rel. Douglas v. Faith Baptist Church of Louisville*, 454 U.S. 803 (1981).

[71] *Wisconsin v. Yoder*, 406 U.S. 205 (1972).

[72] *State v. Priest*, 210 La. 389, 27 So. 2d 173 (1946); *in re State*, 214 La. 1062, 39 So. 2d 731 (1949).

[73] *In re Rogers*, 36 Misc. 2d 680, 234 N.Y.S. 2d 179 (1962).

Illinois case, parents were charged with truancy when their school-age child was absent from school for 339½ days during a two-year period. As a defense, the parents claimed illness of the child as a reason for nonschool attendance. The pupil's physician testified that the child suffered from allergies but not sufficient to warrant excessive absence from school. The charge of truancy against the parents was upheld by the Illinois court.[74]

Vaccinations In an effort to protect the health and welfare of all students, states have required students to be vaccinated. The precedents in this area are derived from two U.S. Supreme Court cases decided nearly a century ago.[75] A more recent case struck down a challenge to a state's mandatory vaccination on religious grounds, even though there was no epidemic imminent.[76] Other courts have upheld religious exemptions against vaccination when such practices are prohibited in official church doctrine.[77] A Kentucky federal district court rejected a parent's attempt to use statutory religious exemptions merely because he was "philosophically opposed" to immunization.[78]

Students with AIDS Recent controversy has focused on school attendance of pupils with acquired immunodeficiency syndrome (AIDS). Medical research indicates that AIDS cannot be transmitted through casual contact.[79] An AIDS-infected child poses negligible risk for transmission to classmates or to other school personnel and thus does not threaten their health and safety. Therefore, having AIDS is not grounds to exclude a child automatically from school. In fact, courts have ruled that children have a right to attend school, and, barring complications, AIDS does not diminish that right, provided that the AIDS-infected child is "not a significant health risk" to others.[80]

Some states have adopted policies governing school attendance of students with AIDS, modeled after guidelines issued by the National Centers for Disease Control and Prevention (CDC). The CDC stipulates that students with AIDS who are under medical care may continue regular school attendance unless they have skin eruptions, exhibit inappropriate behavior such as biting, or are unable to control bodily secretions. The CDC further suggests that decisions concerning school attendance for AIDS-infected students be made on a case-by-case basis. Continuing research on the nature and prevention of this dreaded disease will undoubtedly yield further legal guidelines for its prevention and control. (See Administrative Advice 12–3.)

Curriculum The state legislature has the authority to prescribe the curriculum of the public schools. Such authority is based on the premise that the course of study in the public schools includes those subjects that are essential to good citizenship. All states require teaching of the federal Constitution, and most mandate instruction in U.S. history. Other subjects commonly required include English, mathematics, science, family life and sex education, drug education, and health and physical education.

All state-mandated courses must be offered, but local school boards have great latitude in supplementing the curriculum required by the state legislature. The precedent-setting case in this area was the landmark 1874 decision of the Michigan Supreme Court, which held that the local board of education had the authority to maintain a high school.[81] This landmark decision and subsequent cases established the implied powers of local school boards in curricular matters. These implied powers apply not only to additions of specific curricular elements, such as sex education, drug education, competitive sports, and vocational education programs, but also the determination of methods of carrying out state-mandated curriculum. Generally, the courts have sustained such local board activities, providing they do not contravene the state constitution and the federal Constitution.

The implied powers of local school boards in curriculum matters has led to the teaching of controversial topics such as abortion, contraception, venereal disease, and AIDS. In some situations, parents have objected that such instruction violates their privacy rights or

[74]*People v. Berger,* 65 Ill. Dec. 600, 441 N.E. 2d 915 (1982).

[75]*Jacobsen v. Commonwealth of Mass.,* 197 U.S. 11 (1905); *Zucht v. King,* 260 U.S. 174 (1922).

[76]*Bd. of Educ. of Mt. Lakes v. Maas,* 56 N.J. Super. 245, 152 A 2d 394 (1959).

[77]*State v. Miday,* 140 S.E. 2d 325 (N.C. 1965); *Maier v. Besser,* 341 N.Y.S. 2d 411 (N.Y. Sup. Ct. 1972).

[78]*Kleid v. Bd. of Educ. of Fulton, Kentucky Indep. Sch. Dist.,* 406 F. Supp. 902 (W.D.KY 1976).

[79]Rothstein, *Children with AIDS,* 12 Nova L. Rev. 1259 (1988).

[80]*Martinez v. Sch. Bd. of Hillsborough Cty,* 861 F. 2d 1502 (11th Cir. 1988); *Doe v. Dolton Elem. Sch. Dist.,* 694 F. Supp. 440 (N.D. IL 1988); *Phipps v. Saddleback Valley Unified Sch. Dist.,* 251 Cal. Rptr. 720 (Cal. Ct. App. 1988); *Parents of Child, Code No. 870901w v. Coker,* 676 F. Supp. 1072 (E.D. OK 1987).

[81]*Stuart v. S.D. No. 1 of Village of Kalamazoo,* 30 Mich. 69 (1874).

ADMINISTRATIVE ADVICE 12–3

CDC Guidelines for AIDS Education Programs

Guidelines for AIDS education have been developed to help school personnel and others plan, implement, and evaluate educational efforts to prevent unnecessary mortality associated with AIDS. The guidelines incorporate principles for AIDS education that were developed by the president's Domestic Policy Council and approved by the president in 1987. You can assess the extent to which your district program measures up with the guidelines by answering each question below:

- To what extent are parents, teachers, students, and appropriate community representatives involved in developing, implementing, and assessing AIDS education policies and programs?
- To what extent is the program included as an important part of a more comprehensive school health education program?
- To what extent is the program taught by regular classroom teachers in elementary grades and by qualified health education teachers or other similarly trained personnel in secondary grades?
- To what extent is the program designed to help students acquire essential knowledge to prevent HIV infection at each appropriate grade?
- To what extent does the program describe the benefits of abstinence for young people and mutually monogamous relationships within the context of marriage for adults?
- To what extent is the program designed to help teenage students avoid specific types of behavior that increase the risk of becoming infected with HIV?
- To what extent is adequate training about AIDS provided for school administrators, teachers, nurses, and counselors—especially those who teach about AIDS?
- To what extent are sufficient program development time, classroom time, and educational materials provided for education about AIDS?
- To what extent are the processes and outcomes of AIDS education being monitored and periodically assessed?

Source: Adapted from Centers for Disease Control, "Halt the AIDS Rampage," *School Administrator,* 10 (1988): 53–55. Used by permission.

their protected religious freedom. A New York appellate court asserted that the state had a compelling interest in the issue because the purpose of the educational requirement was the protection of the health and safety of students.[82] However, a decision by one state court, that compulsory courses in AIDS for all public school students does not violate parents' constitutionally protected religious freedom, does not require courts of other jurisdictions to arrive at the same conclusion.[83] As new courses dealing with controversial topics (e.g., abortion, contraception, venereal disease, AIDS) are developed, the legality of teaching them will be judged on their content, manner of delivery, and whether they are elective or compulsory in nature.[84]

Residency Requirements Generally, eligibility to attend tuition free the public schools of a district is extended by statute to school-age children who have a domicile in the district or who are residents of the district. To understand the decision of the courts in this area, it is necessary to define the residence and domicile of pupils and their parents. These terms are legally defined as follows:[85]

- **Domicile** is a place where one intends to remain indefinitely, and each person may have only one domicile. A minor child's legal domicile is that of the father

[82] *Ware v. Valley Stream H.S. Dist.,* 545 N.Y.S. 316 (A.D. 1989).

[83] *Ware v. Valley Stream H.S. Dist.,* 550 N.E. 2d 420 (N.Y. 1989) (burden on the state to deny the exemption from AIDS course).

[84] Alexander and Alexander, *American Public School Law.*

[85] Henry Black, *Black's Law Dictionary,* 8th ed. (Belmont, CA: Wadsworth, 1998).

except in special circumstances, such as the father's death or parental separation or divorce where custody of the child has been awarded to the mother or another custodial guardian.

- **Residence** is the place where one is actually, physically living.

Generally, it is held that a child has the right to attend the public school of a district in which he or she is living—unless the child is living in that district solely for the purpose of attending school there, in which case the child is not entitled to education without the payment of tuition.[86]

Student Discipline

It is expected that schools will be operated according to the rules and regulations of local boards of education. However, teachers and other school personnel are granted wide discretion in disciplining students. The legal doctrine that defines the relationship of educator to pupil is **in loco parentis** ("in place of the parent"). The doctrine is well stated in a precedent-setting Wisconsin case:

> While the principal or teacher in charge of a public school is subordinate to the school board . . . and must enforce rules and regulations adopted by the board . . . he does not derive all his power and authority in the school and over his pupils from affirmative action of the board. He stands for the time being in loco parentis to his pupils, and because of that relation he must necessarily exercise authority over them in many things concerning which the board may have remained silent.[87]

In this section, we examine students' rights pertaining to corporal punishment, expulsions and suspensions, and search and seizure.

Corporal Punishment Under common law, teachers and other school personnel have the right to administer reasonable corporal punishment, which is the infliction of physical pain on a student for misconduct. State statutes deal with corporal punishment in different ways. Some states authorize it; others forbid it. Still others are silent on the matter but by implication allow it.[88] Massachusetts and New Jersey prohibit corporal punishment by statute. In Maryland state board of education policy bans corporal punishment. New York permits corporal punishment unless local boards of education prohibit it. Kentucky allows a teacher to use physical force to maintain reasonable discipline in a school, class, or other group.[89]

In the landmark Supreme Court decision *Ingraham v. Wright,* the Court held that corporal punishment of students does not violate the Eighth Amendment nor the due process guarantees of the Fourteenth Amendment. The Court said that the Eighth Amendment's prohibition of cruel and unusual punishment applies to criminals only and is not applicable to the disciplining of students in public schools. The Court noted that "at common law a single principle has governed the use of corporal punishment since before the American Revolution: Teachers may impose reasonable but not excessive force to discipline a child." Regarding due process, the Court held that a student is not entitled to notice and a hearing prior to the imposition of corporal punishment.[90]

Although the Supreme Court has held that the federal Constitution does not prohibit corporal punishment in schools, its use may conflict with state constitutions, state statutes, or local school board policies.

Expulsions and Suspensions Expelling and suspending students from school are among the most widely used measures of disciplining students. From a practical standpoint, expulsion is the exclusion of a student from school for a period of time exceeding ten days or more. Under common law, the power of expulsion is vested exclusively in the board of education. Professional personnel may not expel students unless authorized by state statute.

Generally, courts have held that expulsion of students from school jeopardizes a student's property interests in an education. Thus, students are guaranteed at least minimum due process under the Fourteenth Amendment. (See Figure 12–4 for procedural elements.)[91]

Suspensions generally involve exclusion of a student from school for a brief, definite period of time, usually not exceeding ten days. In contrast to detailed procedures related to expulsion, state statutes have been less specific regarding the procedures that should be followed when suspending students from schools.

---

[86] *Turner v. Bd. of Educ.*, N. Chicago Community H.S. Dist. 123, 54 Ill. 2d 68, 294 N.E. 2d 264 (1973).

[87] *State ex. rel. Burpee v. Burton*, 45 Wis. 150, 30 Am. Rep. 706 (1878).

[88] Alexander and Alexander, *American Public School Law.*

[89] *Ky. Rev. Stat.*, Ch. 503.110 (1992).

[90] *Ingraham v. Wright*, 430 U.S. 651 (1977).

[91] Alexander and Alexander, *American Public School Law.*

- Notification of the charges
- Opportunity to answer the charges
- Time to prepare an adequate defense
- Hearing conducted by an impartial tribunal
- Right to representation by legal counsel
- Names of adverse witnesses, access to evidence, right to introduce evidence
- Opportunity to cross-examine adverse witnesses and introduce defense witnesses
- Decision based on evidence adduced at the hearing
- Written record of the proceedings
- Opportunity to appeal an adverse decision

FIGURE 12–4

Procedural Due Process for Student Expulsions

Prior to 1975, procedural due process accorded to suspended students was poorly defined. Lower courts differed widely in their interpretation of the Fourteenth Amendment guarantees in suspension cases.

In 1975, in *Goss v. Lopez,* the U.S. Supreme Court prescribed the minimum constitutional requirements in cases involving student suspensions of ten days or less.[92] The Court concluded that oral notice to the student of the reason for short suspensions, followed by an immediate, informal hearing by a local school official, would fulfill the due process requirement in brief suspensions. The Court specifically rejected the usual trial-type format including the involvement of attorneys and the presentation and cross-examination of adverse witnesses typical in criminal cases.

The Rehabilitation Act (Section 504), the Individuals with Disabilities Education Act (IDEA), and the Americans with Disabilities Act (ADA) provide special safeguards in the suspension and expulsion of children with disabilities. IDEA, in particular, assures all children with disabilities a free appropriate public education in the least restrictive environment. Federal courts have regarded expulsion and long-term suspension as a change in placement when children with disabilities are involved.[93]

A crucial issue when suspending or expelling a disabled child is whether the misbehavior is related to the disability. Disabled students may be suspended for ten days or fewer without inquiry into whether the student's misbehavior was caused by the disability.[94] Courts reasoned that short-term suspension is not a change of placement and therefore does not trigger the procedures of IDEA. Expulsions and suspensions of more than ten days are changes of placement. They may not be used if there is a relationship between the misbehavior and the child's disability.[95] In these cases, transferring the child to a more restrictive environment is an option, after following change-of-placement procedures. If the misbehavior is not related to the disability, then expulsion and long-term suspension are permissible; but all educational services cannot be terminated.[96] These special safeguards for the disciplining of disabled children do not apply to pupils who use illegal drugs or alcohol as stipulated in the ADA.[97]

Search and Seizure The Fourth Amendment provides that "the right of people to be secure in their persons, houses, papers, and effects, against unreasonable

[92] *Goss v. Lopez,* 419 U.S. 565 (1975).

[93] *S-1 v. Turlington,* 635 F. 2d 342 (5th Cir. 1981), *cert. denied,* 454 U.S. 1030 (1981); *Honig v. Doe,* 484 U.S. 305 (1988).

[94] *Bd. of Educ. of Peoria v. IL State Bd. of Educ.,* 531 F. Supp. 148 (C.D. IL 1982).

[95] *S-1 v. Turlington.*

[96] Ibid.

[97] 29 U.S.C.A., Sec. 706 (8) (West Supp. 1992).

Probable Cause Standard

- Police officers must secure a warrant prior to conducting a search.
- Facts or evidence must indicate that a person has committed, is committing, or will be committing a crime.
- A judge issues a warrant describing the place to be searched and the person or items to be seized.

Reasonable Suspicion Standard

- School officials are not required to obtain a warrant to search a student.
- The legality of a search of a student depends on the "reasonableness" of the search.[99]
- Two tests are used to determine reasonableness.

1. Is the search justified at its inception?
   Was the motivation for the search reasonable in light of the information obtained by the school official?
2. Is the scope of the search reasonable?
   Were the measures adopted for the search reasonably related to the objectives of the search (e.g., lockers, cars, personal possessions, etc.) and not excessively intrusive in light of the age and sex of the student and the nature of the infraction?

FIGURE 12–5

Probable Cause and Reasonable Suspicion for Searches

searches and seizures shall not be violated, and no warrants shall issue, but upon probable cause. . . ." The clause has been involved in numerous criminal cases. Evidence obtained in violation of the amendment is inadmissible in court.

The introduction of drugs and other contraband in schools has placed school officials in the position of searching students' person or lockers, and students claim that such acts are a violation of their Fourth Amendment guarantees. A student's right to the Fourth Amendment's protection from unreasonable search and seizure must be balanced against the need for school officials to maintain discipline and to provide a safe environment conducive to learning. State and federal courts generally have relied on the doctrine of in loco parentis, reasoning that school officials stand in the place of a parent and are not subject to the constraints of the Fourth Amendment.

However, in 1985 in *New Jersey v. T.L.O.*, the U.S. Supreme Court held that searches by school officials in schools come within the constraints of the Fourteenth Amendment.[98] The Court concluded that the special needs of the school environment justified easing the warrant and probable cause requirement imposed in criminal cases, provided that school searches are based on "reasonable suspicion." (See Figure 12–5.)

In 1995, the United States Supreme Court rendered its decision in *Vernonia School District 47J v. Acton,*[100] holding that a school district's random suspicionless drug testing of student athletes as a condition for participation in interscholastic athletics did not violate the Fourth Amendment's prohibition against unreasonable searches and seizures. In this particular case, however, the Court noted specific features including student athletes' decreased expectations of privacy, the relative unobtrusiveness of the search procedures, and the seriousness of the need met by this search. Regardless of the procedures, however, this case clearly lowered schools' previous legal search standard of "reasonable suspicion," set forth by *New Jersey v. T.L.O.* in 1985.

The Supreme Court ruled on the issue of random suspicionless drug testing of students in June 2002

[98] *New Jersey v. T.L.O.* 469 U.S. 325 (1985).

[99] Ibid.

[100] *Vernonia School District 47J v.* 515 U.S. 466 (1995).

with its decision in *Board of Education v. Earls,*[101] a 10th Circuit case from Oklahoma in which drug testing of students in any extracurricular activities was determined to be unconstitutional. In a 5–4 decision, the Supreme Court upheld the school district's policy of random suspicionless drug testing of all students who participated in any extracurricular activities, not just athletics. Using *Vernonia* as a guideline, the 10th Circuit in *Earls* held that "before imposing a suspicionless drug testing program a school must demonstrate some identifiable drug abuse problem among a sufficient number of those to be tested, such that testing that group will actually redress its drug problem." In overturning the 10th Circuit's decision, the Supreme Court's majority in *Earls* stated that "a demonstrated drug abuse problem is not always necessary to the validity of a testing regime." Furthermore, the Court defends this stance by adding that "the need to prevent and deter the substantial harm of childhood drug use provides the necessary immediacy for a school testing policy." Thus, based on the *Earls* decision, random suspicionless drug testing of students does not violate the Fourth Amendment's protection from unreasonable searches and seizures.

Freedom of Expression

Of all the freedoms guaranteed in this country, none is more protected than the right of freedom of speech and the press and the right to peaceable assembly as set forth in the First Amendment. Specifically, it provides that "Congress shall make no law . . . abridging the freedom of speech, or of press; or the right of the people peaceably to assemble. . . ." The gamut of protected expression litigated in state and federal courts includes symbolic expression, dress and grooming, oral and written expression, and group associations and assembly. These categories of expression have received differential treatment in the courts.

Personal Expression Historically, students generally played a submissive role in relation to freedom of expression within the public schools. In 1969, the landmark case of the U.S. Supreme Court *Tinker v. Des Moines Independent School District*[102] marked the emergence of a new era in students' protected expression in the public schools. The Court invalidated a rule prohibiting students from wearing black arm bands in school as a protest against the Vietnam War. The Court stated that "undifferentiated fear or apprehension of disturbance is not enough to overcome the right to freedom of expression." Furthermore, the Court declared that the prohibition of the wearing of symbols can be sustained only if such activity would "materially and substantially disrupt the work and discipline of the school."

Thus, the *Tinker* test of "material and substantial disruption" emerged as a determinant in subsequent student expression litigation. The Court made it clear that school authorities would not be permitted to deny a student her fundamental First Amendment rights simply because of a "mere desire to avoid discomfort and unpleasantness that always accompany an unpopular viewpoint."

Freedom of Speech and Press Courts commonly extend broad-based protection to freedom of speech and press. Nevertheless, they recognize that free expression rights can be restricted. For example, freedom of speech does not allow an individual to yell "Fire!" in a crowded theater when there is no fire because of the tremendous potential for harm to people and property.[103] Although public school students enjoy free speech rights, the Supreme Court has recognized that "the constitutional rights of students in public school are not automatically coextensive with the rights of adults in other settings."[104] In other words, the First Amendment rights of students may be restricted by the operational needs of the schools.

Not all student expression receives the same level of First Amendment protection. Obscene, defamatory, and inflammatory expression are not protected by the First Amendment. To be legally obscene, material must violate three tests developed by the U.S. Supreme Court: (1) It must appeal to the prurient or lustful interest of minors, (2) it must describe sexual conduct in a way that is "potently offensive" to community standards, and (3) taken as a whole, it "must lack serious literary, artistic, political, or scientific value."[105] *Defamation* may be defined as a false statement made to a third party that subjects a person to public shame or ridicule. *Inflammatory expression,* or "fighting words," refers to face-to-face communication that is likely to incite violence.[106]

---

[101]*Bd. of Educ. of Independent School District No. 92 of Pottawatomie County v. Earls,* 536 U.S. 822 (2002).

[102]393 U.S. 503 (1969).

[103]*Schenck v. United States,* 249 U.S. 47, 52 (1919).

[104]*Bethel Sch. Dist. No. 403 v. Fraser,* 478 U.S. 675 (1986).

[105]*Miller v. California,* 413 U.S. 15 (1973).

[106]*Chaplinsky v. New Hampshire,* 315 U.S. 568 (1942).

Nonetheless, school authorities retain the burden of justifying restraints on student expression. In this regard, the Supreme Court has relied primarily on the "material and substantial disruption" standard derived from the *Tinker* decision. More recently, in *Bethel School District No. 403 v. Fraser,*[107] the Supreme Court expanded the rationale for schools to restrict students' freedom of speech when obscenity is involved. The case arose when Matthew Fraser delivered a speech at a required assembly of about 600 high school students that featured sexual innuendo. He was subsequently suspended from school and later brought suit on First and Fourteenth Amendment grounds. The U.S. Supreme Court ruled that no constitutional rights had been abrogated. In its decision the Court made a distinction between the silent political speech in *Tinker* and the lewd, vulgar, and offensive speech of Fraser. The Court said that ". . . the determination of what manner of speech in the classroom or in a school assembly is appropriate properly rests with the school board." The Court added that while students have the right to advocate controversial rules in school, ". . . that right must be balanced against the school's interest in teaching socially appropriate behavior."[108]

During the 1970s, a number of courts considered school-sponsored publications as forums for student expression. Accordingly, courts held that school newspaper articles on controversial topics such as abortion, the Vietnam War, and contraception could not be barred from these publications.[109] Courts scrutinized policies requiring prior administrative review and placed the burden on school officials to justify such review procedures.

In 1988, the U.S. Supreme Court heard the case of *Hazelwood School District v. Kyhlmeier*[110] involving a high school student newspaper. The case arose when a principal deleted certain stories that had been scheduled for release in the school newspaper. One story recounted personal experiences of three pregnant girls in the school. The other related personal accounts of siblings whose parents were going through a divorce proceeding and was strongly accusative of the father. The Court differentiated the case from *Tinker* in that here the issue was not personal speech, which is still protected by a strict scrutiny under the "material and substantial disruption" standard, but rather the right of school authorities not to promote particular speech. In other words, the Supreme Court drew a distinction between speech occurring in school-sponsored (curriculum-related) and nonschool-sponsored contexts. The Court reasoned that school authorities have much greater leeway in regulating speech that has the imprimatur of the school, provided that restrictions are based on "legitimate pedagogical concerns."

Based on the *Bethel* and *Hazelwood* decisions, the school's authority to prohibit "lewd, vulgar, and offensive" speech in the context of school-sponsored activities is well established. Recent courts have followed these precedents by allowing censorship of student speeches at school assemblies provided that the decision was based on "legitimate pedagogical concerns."[111]

Student Appearance School boards may enact reasonable regulations concerning student appearance in school. Appearance regulations have focused on male hairstyles and pupil attire. Student challenges to these regulations have relied on First Amendment constitutional freedoms to determine one's appearance. The U.S. Supreme Court has consistently refused to review the decisions of lower courts on these matters. In one case involving male hairstyle, Court Justice Hugo Black commented that he did not believe "the federal Constitution imposed on the United States courts the burden of supervising the length of hair that public school students should wear."[112]

Pupil Hairstyle Five of the federal circuit courts of appeal (third, fifth, sixth, ninth, and tenth) have sustained the authority of public schools to regulate hairstyles of male students. Four federal circuit courts (first, fourth, seventh, and eighth) have overturned such regulations, finding that hair-length regulations impinge student's constitutional rights. Significantly, all circuit courts refused to treat hairstyle as a form of symbolic speech, which would implicate the test of the *Tinker* case.[113]

Pupil Attire Generally, courts tend to provide less protection to some forms of expression (e.g., pupil

---

[107]478 U.S. 675 (1986).

[108]Ibid.

[109]*Gambino v. Fairfax Cty. Sch. Bd.*, 564 F. 2d 157 (4th Cir. 1977); *Shanley v. Northeast Indep. Sch. Dist.*, 462 F. 2d 960 (5th Cir. 1972); *Koppell v. Levine*, 347 F. Supp. 456 (E.D. NY 1972).

[110]484 U.S. 260 (1988).

[111]*Poling v. Murphy*, 872 F. 2d 757 (6th Cir. 1989), *cert. denied*, 493 U.S. 1021 (1990).

[112]*Karr v. Schmidt*, 401 U.S. 1201 (1972).

[113]Alexander and Alexander, *American Public School Law.*

hairstyle and attire) than to others (e.g., symbolic expression and student publications). Nonetheless, awareness of constitutional freedoms places limits on school officials to regulate student dress, excluding special situations (e.g., graduation and physical education classes). Pupil attire can always be regulated to protect student health, safety, and school discipline. In short, the extent to which school officials may control student appearance depends more on different community mores and on "the times" than on strict principles of law.

Freedom of Association and Assembly Under the First Amendment, students have a constitutional right to freedom of association and to peaceable assembly. Public schools are places where student associations and clubs are part of the daily routine of the school, some of which have been formally designated as cocurricular activities. However, most schools prohibit secret societies, associations, clubs, fraternities and sororities, and satanic cults. Courts have reasoned that such organizations have a detrimental influence on schools by tending to perpetuate antidemocratic values such as elitism, discrimination, and divisiveness. Various pleas of an abrogation of students' First and Fourteenth Amendment rights in these situations have not prevailed.[114] An Oregon court ruled that any nonschool-affiliated organization could associate in any manner it wished.[115]

Classification Practices

The courts have evaluated classification practices to determine their legitimacy under the equal protection clause of the Fourteenth Amendment, state constitutions, and state and federal statutes. In this section, we explore student classification practices based on gender, marriage and pregnancy, age, and ability.

Gender Litigants claiming sex discrimination can seek relief under the equal protection clause of the Fourteenth Amendment, Title VII of the Civil Rights Act of 1964, Title IX of the Education Amendments of 1972, Section 1983, the Equal Educational Opportunities Act of 1974, equal rights amendments to state constitutions, and new and evolving sex discrimination statutes.

To receive affirmation from the courts, defendants in sex discrimination cases must present a preponderance of evidence that gender-based classifications are completely related to a legitimate government purpose. One public school case to reach the Supreme court, *Vorchheimer v. School District of Philadelphia,* involved a challenge brought by a female student who had been denied admission to an all-male academic high school. The school district maintained among its high schools two sex-segregated schools for high-achievement students. The Court, equally divided, affirmed an earlier Third Circuit Court of Appeals decision that had ruled in favor of the school district.[116]

On the other hand, sex discrimination was held to violate the equal protection clause in two public school districts in which the schools set higher standards for girls than for boys.[117] In another case, the exclusion of male students from participation in a sex-segregated girls' program in a coeducational public high school was held to violate the state constitution's provision against sex discrimination.[118] In a more recent and famous university case, the Court held that the denial of admission to a male registered nurse to a state-supported university for women was unconstitutional discrimination based on gender classification.[119]

An area that has received much publicity concerning gender-based classifications is high school athletics. A precedent-setting eighth circuit court case invalidated a school policy that restricted participation to only male athletes on several noncontact sports' teams.[120] Generally, most courts have followed suit. The general proposition that female athletes must be provided the opportunity to participate in contact sports either through single-sex or coeducational teams has been sustained in federal district courts in Wisconsin, Missouri, and New York and the Pennsylvania Supreme Court. The converse is not true, however; male athletes can be barred from all-female teams if their participation impedes the athletic opportunities of the females.[121]

---

[114] *Passel v. Fort Worth I.S.D.*, 453 S.W. 2d 888 (Tex. Civ. App. 1970); *Robinson v. Sacramento U.S.D.*, 53 Calif. Reptr. 781, 788–789 (1966).

[115] *Burkitt v. S.D. No. 1, Multnomah Cty.*, 195 Ore. 471, 246 P. 2d 566 (1952).

[116] *Vorchheimer v. S.D. of Philadelphia,* 532 F. 2d 880 (3 Cir. 1976), aff. 430 U.S. 703 (1977).

[117] *Bray v. Lee,* 337 F. Supp. 934 (D. Mass. 1972); *Berkelman v. San Francisco U.S.D.*, 501 F. 2d 1264 (9 Cir. 1974).

[118] *Opinion of the Justices to the Senate,* 373 Mass. 883, 366 N.E. 2d 733 (1977).

[119] *Mississippi University for Women v. Hogan,* 458 U.S. 718 (1982).

[120] *Brenden v. Independent School District,* 477 F. 2d 1292 (8 Cir. 1973).

[121] Thomas, Cambron-McCabe, and McCarthy, *Public School Law.*

Marriage and Pregnancy Historically, public school districts have generally discouraged, and in some cases even barred, students from school attendance or participation in school-sponsored activities for reason of marriage or pregnancy. In more recent years, courts have invalidated school district policies for differential treatment of married or pregnant students. Federal district courts in Massachusetts, Mississippi, Montana, Ohio, Tennessee, and Texas have held that exclusion from school attendance and from participation in various school-sponsored activities could not be made solely on the basis of marital status or pregnancy.[122]

It is apparent from federal district court decisions in various states that students within the age limits of statutorily permitted school attendance are entitled to a free public school education. As such, they may not be excluded because of marriage or pregnancy from school activities nor isolated from contact with other students within the school environment.

Age School boards have used age as a criterion for public school admission, compulsory education, and participation in some cocurricular activities. Courts have generally sustained school board policy and state statutes specifying minimum age requirements used in operating school systems. For example, a Wisconsin court and a federal district court in Maine supported a local school board policy and the state's minimum-age law, respectively, as a valid criterion for admission to its public schools. And a New York court upheld a school board policy restricting entry into a special accelerated junior high school program solely on the basis of an age requirement.[123] The Age Discrimination Act of 1975 has had little effect on public school students.

Ability Generally, courts have supported ability grouping in theory unless racial or cultural bias is shown. In a famous case, *Hobson v. Hansen*, a federal district court in Washington, D.C., invalidated an ability-grouping plan based on the use of standardized test scores because it was shown to discriminate against minority students.[124] Subsequently, the fifth and ninth circuit courts struck down ability-grouping practices based on the use of standardized achievement tests for the same reason. Later, the eleventh, another fifth circuit court, and an Illinois federal district court upheld grouping as free of cultural bias and contributing to the instruction and achievement of minority students.[125]

Students with Disabilities

Historically, the attitude that prevailed concerning the education of disabled students was that retarded, learning disabled, emotionally disturbed, deaf, blind, or otherwise disabled children were not the responsibility of the public schools. Consequently, many disabled children were exempted from compulsory school attendance laws either by parental choice or by school district design. Nationally, services for the disabled were either nonexistent or nonextensive. Very few school districts provided services; where such services existed, they were inadequate to meet even the minimal needs of this vulnerable minority group.

In recent years, substantial changes in the attitude toward the disabled have occurred. Although disabled students do not comprise any "protected group" (such as race or gender) that is entitled to constitutional guarantees, federal statutes and state special education statutes were enacted to satisfy their constitutional rights. Lower court decisions and federal and state legislative enactments of the past three decades have mandated that all children, including the disabled, are entitled to admission to a school and placement in a program that meets their special needs. As summarized in the landmark Supreme Court school desegregation case, *Brown v. Board of Education of Topeka,* "education . . . is a right which must be made available to all on equal terms."[126] Although the Brown decision dealt with the constitutional protections afforded minority children, its consent agreement implied a mandate that all students of legal school age must be provided with appropriate school and classroom placement.

Two key court decisions outlined the legal framework for the constitutional protections of disabled children. In *Pennsylvania Association for Retarded Children (PARC) v. Commonwealth,*[127] a federal district court held that retarded children in Pennsylvania were entitled to a free public education and that,

[122] Alexander and Alexander, *American Public School Law.*

[123] Thomas, Cambron-McCabe, and McCarthy, *Public School Law.*

[124] *Hobson v. Hansen,* 269 F. Supp. 401 (D.C.C. 1967), aff. *Smuck v. Hobson,* 408 F. 2d 175 (D.C. Cir. 1969).

[125] Thomas, Cambron-McCabe, and McCarthy, *Public School Law.*

[126] 347 U.S. 483 (1954).

[127] 334 F. Supp. 279 (E.D. Pa. 1972).

whenever possible, disabled children must be educated in regular classrooms and not segregated from other students. In *Mills v. Board of Education of the District of Columbia,*[128] another federal district court expanded the PARC decision to include all school-age disabled children.

Subsequent to the *PARC* and *Mills* decisions, Congress passed two landmark pieces of legislation that led to the rapid development of comprehensive, nationwide educational programs for the disabled. Section 504 of the Rehabilitation Act of 1973 is a broad-based federal law that addresses discrimination against the disabled both in the workplace and in schools. The statute, as amended, stipulates:

> No otherwise qualified individual with handicaps . . . shall solely by reason of her or his handicap, be excluded from participation in, be denied the benefits of, or be subjected to discrimination under any programs or activity receiving Federal financial assistance.[129]

Thus Section 504 would cut off all federal funds from schools that discriminate against the disabled. The statute also provides that all newly constructed public facilities be equipped to allow free access by disabled individuals.

The Education for All Handicapped Children Act (EAHCA) of 1975 and the IDEA provide federal funds to school districts that comply with its requirements. The major thrust of these acts was to ensure the right of all disabled children to a public education. Major provisions include a free appropriate public education, an individualized education program, special education services, related services, due process procedures, and the least restrictive learning environment.[130]

According to IDEA, all disabled children have the right to a "free appropriate public education." An appropriate education for the disabled is defined as special education and related services. Special education refers to specially designed instruction at public expense, including a variety of opportunities on a spectrum from regular classroom instruction and special classes to placement in a private facility. Related services include transportation, physical and occupational therapy, recreation, and counseling and medical diagnosis. A written **individualized education program** (**IEP**) is another key element in a free appropriate public education. An IEP includes an assessment of the child's needs, specification of annual goals, strategies (methods, materials, interventions) to achieve the goals, and periodic evaluations of the child's progress. And, finally, a disabled child must be educated in the least restrictive environment. That is, the placement must be tailored to the special needs of the disabled student. In combination with related state laws, these federal statutes provide the guidelines for the education of the disabled.

In addition to the Rehabilitation Act, the disabled are now protected by the Americans with Disabilities Act (ADA) of 1990.[131] This law prohibits discrimination in employment (and other situations) against any "qualified individual with a disability." Essentially it amplifies and extends prohibitions of Section 504 of the Rehabilitation Act of 1973. Coverage is not dependent on involvement of federal funds. A "reasonable accommodation" that would permit a qualified individual with a disability to perform the "essential functions" of a position (or other activity) must be provided.

The definition of a disabled person under the ADA is somewhat different from the Rehabilitation Act. Under the newer law, a "qualified individual with a disability" means "an individual with a disability who, with or without reasonable modifications . . . meets the essential eligibility requirements for the receipt of services or the participation in programs or activities provided by a public entity."[132] To prevent conflict between the Rehabilitation Act and ADA, legislation requires that ADA be interpreted consistently with the older law. Thus, court decisions interpreting Section 504 are not affected by the later law. Furthermore, the Rehabilitation Act looks to the terms of the IDEA for resolution of most disputes concerning the education of the disabled; and compliance with IDEA will usually meet the requirements of ADA. Of these three laws, IDEA has had the most significant impact on public schools.

IDEA 2004 On November 19, 2004, Congress passed legislation reauthorizing IDEA and replacing it with the Individuals with Disabilities Education Improvement Act (Public Law 108-446), known as IDEA 2004.[133]

---

[128]348 F. Supp. 866 D.D.C. (1972).

[129]29 U.S.C. Sec. 794 (a) (1988).

[130]20 U.S.C.A. Sec. 1400 (a) (West Supp. 1992).

[131]42 U.S.C.A., Secs. 12101-12213 (1990 & West Supp. 1992).

[132]42 U.S.C.A., Sec. 12131 (2) (West Supp. 1992).

[133]Council for Exceptional Children, http://www.cec.sped.org/pp/IDEA_120204.pdf; Congressional Research Service, http://www.nasponline.org/advocacy/IDEACRSAnalysis.pdf.

Table 12-1 Summary of Requirements to Be a Highly Qualified Special Education Teacher

Category of Special Education Teachers	Requirements Under P.L. 108-446 (IDEA)
All special education teachers	*General Requirements* Hold at least a bachelor's degree Must obtain full state special education certification or equivalent licensure Cannot hold an emergency or temporary certificate
New or veteran *elementary school* teachers teaching one or more core academic subjects only to children with disabilities held to alternative academic standards (most severely cognitively disabled)	In addition to the General Requirements above, may demonstrate academic subject competence through "a high objective uniform state standard of evaluation" (HOUSSE) process
New or veteran *middle or high school* teachers teaching one or more core academic subjects only to children with disabilities held to alternative academic standards (most severely cognitively disabled)	In addition to the General Requirements above, may demonstrate "subject matter knowledge appropriate to the level of instruction being provided, as determined by the State, needed to effectively teach to those standards"
New teachers of *two or more academic subjects* who are highly qualified in either mathematics, language arts, or science	In addition to the General Requirements above, has two-year window in which to become highly qualified in the other core academic subjects and may do this through the HOUSSE process
Veteran teachers who teach *two or more core academic subjects* only to children with disabilities	In addition to the General Requirements above, may demonstrate academic subject competence through the HOUSSE process (including a single evaluation for all core academic subjects)
Consultative teachers and other special education teachers who do not teach core academic subjects	Must only meet the General Requirements above
Other special education teachers teaching core academic subjects	In addition to the General Requirements above, meet relevant NCLB requirements for new elementary school teachers, new middle/high school teachers, or veteran teachers

President George W. Bush signed this bill into law on December 3, 2004. IDEA 2004 has significantly affected the professional lives of general education teachers and special educators as well as parents of children with disabilities, all of whom encountered new roles and responsibilities as a result of the law.

> The Individuals with Disabilities Education Improvement Act of 2004 (New IDEA) increased the focus of special education from simply ensuring access to education to improving the educational performance of students with disabilities and aligning special education services with the larger national school improvement efforts that include standards, assessments, and accountability.[134]

Following are highlights of some significant issues addressed in this historic document. These provisions provide a framework for individual states to develop their own standards and procedures.

Highly Qualified Special Education Teachers The language contained in IDEA 2004 concerning who is considered a "highly qualified" special educator is complementary to the standards promulgated in the NCLB. (See Table 12–1.)

Individualized Education Program (IEP) Process

- Short-term objectives and benchmarks will no longer be required except for those pupils who are evaluated via alternate assessments aligned to alternate achievement standards.
- Assessment of the progress that a student is making toward meeting annual goals, which must be written in measurable terms, is still required. Reference, however, to the current requirement of reporting the "extent to which progress is sufficient to enable the child to achieve goals by the end of the year" is eliminated. The IEP will now need to describe how

---

[134]Victor Nolet and Margaret J. McLaughlin, *Accessing the General Curriculum: Including Students with Disabilities in Standards-Based Reform*, 2nd ed. (Thousand Oaks, CA: Corwin Press, 2005), pp. 2–3.

the individual's progress toward achieving annual goals will be measured and when these progress reports will be made.

- A new provision of the legislation allows for members of the IEP team to be excused from participating in all or part of the meeting if the parents and school district agree that attendance is not necessary because the individual's area of curriculum or related service is not being reviewed or modified. The team member will be required, however, to submit written input into the development of the IEP prior to the meeting.
- PL 108-446 allows for alternatives to physical IEP meetings such as video conferencing and conference telephone calls.
- Once an IEP is established, IDEA 2004 will allow for changes to be made via a written plan to modify the document without convening the entire team and redrafting the whole IEP.
- The new legislation deletes references to transition services beginning at age fourteen. Now, transition services are to begin no later than the first IEP in effect when the student turns sixteen (and updated annually). It also establishes a new requirement for postsecondary goals pertaining to appropriate education, training, employment, and independent living skills.
- School districts will be allowed, with parental consent, to develop multiyear IEPs (not to exceed three years).
- The U. S. Department of Education is charged with developing and disseminating model IEP forms and model IFSP (individualized family service plan) forms.

Identifying Students with Specific Learning Disabilities Under IDEA 1997, when identifying an individual for a possible learning disability, educators typically looked to see if the student exhibited a severe discrepancy between achievement and intellectual ability. This discrepancy provision was removed from IDEA 2004. School districts will now be able, if they so choose, to use a process that determines if the pupil responds to empirically validated, scientifically based interventions—a procedure known as Response-To-Intervention. Under the new guidelines, rather than comparing IQ with performance on standardized achievement tests, general education teachers can offer intensive programs of instructional interventions. If the child fails to make adequate progress, a learning disability is assumed to be present and additional assessment is warranted.

Discipline

- PL 108-446 stipulates that when a student is removed from his current educational setting, the pupil is to continue to receive those services that enable participation in the general education curriculum and ensure progress toward meeting IEP goals.
- IDEA 1997 allowed school authorities to unilaterally remove a student to an interim alternative educational setting (IASE) for up to forty-five days for offenses involving weapons or drugs. IDEA 2004 now permits school officials to remove any pupil (including those with and without disabilities) to an IASE for up to forty-five days for inflicting "serious bodily injury."
- Removal to an IASE will now be for forty-five *school* days rather than forty-five calendar days.
- Behavior resulting in disciplinary action still requires a manifestation review; however, language requiring the IEP team to consider whether the pupil's disability impaired his ability to control behavior or comprehend the consequences of his actions has been eliminated. IEP teams now need to ask only two questions: (1) Did the disability cause or have a direct and substantial relationship to the offense? (2) Was the violation a direct result of the school's failure to implement the IEP?
- IDEA 2004 modifies the "stay put" provision enacted during an appeals process. When either the LEA (local education agency) or parent requests an appeal of a manifestation determination or placement decision, the pupil is required to remain in the current IASE until a decision is rendered by the hearing officer or until the time period for the disciplinary violation concludes. A hearing must be held within twenty school days of the date of the appeal.

Due Process

- Parents will encounter a two-year statute of limitations for filing a due process complaint from the time they knew or should have known that a violation occurred. Alleged violations might involve identification, assessment, or placement issues or the failure to provide an appropriate education.
- A mandatory "resolution session" is now required prior to proceeding with a due process hearing.

(The parents and school district may waive this requirement and proceed to mediation.) School districts must convene a meeting with the parents and IEP team members within fifteen days of receiving a due process complaint. If the complaint is not satisfactorily resolved within thirty days of the filing date, the due process hearing may proceed.

- Under provisions of IDEA 1997, parents who prevailed in due process hearings and/or court cases could seek attorney's fees from the school district. IDEA 2004 now permits school districts to seek attorney's fees from the parents' attorney (or the parents themselves) if the due process complaint or lawsuit is deemed frivolous, unreasonable, or without foundation or the attorney continues to litigate despite these circumstances. Reasonable attorney fees can also be awarded by the court if the complaint or lawsuit was filed for an improper purpose such as to harass, cause unnecessary delay, or needlessly increase the cost of litigation.

Funding IDEA 2004 continues to be a discretionary program allowing Congress to fund it at whatever level it chooses. When IDEA was initially enacted in 1975 as PL 94-142, Congress authorized the federal government to pay 40 percent of the "excess cost" of educating pupils with disabilities (commonly referred to as "full funding"). Although mandatory full funding was not accomplished with this reauthorization, a six-year plan or "glide path" for achieving this goal was enacted. Interestingly, only two days after passing this law, Congress appropriated significantly less ($1.7 billion) than it had just promised. While considerable, the federal government currently provides only about 18 percent of the cost of educating students with disabilities.

Evaluation of Students

- School districts will be required to determine the eligibility of a student to receive a special education and the educational needs of the child within a sixty-day time frame. (This provision does not apply if the state has already established a timeline for accomplishing this task.) The sixty-day rule commences upon receipt of parental permission for evaluation.
- Reevaluation of eligibility for a special education may not occur more than once per year (unless agreed to by the school district and parent); and it must occur at least once every three years unless the parent and school district agree that such a reevaluation is unnecessary.
- IDEA 2004 modifies the provision pertaining to native language and preferred mode of communication. New language in the bill requires that evaluations are to be "provided and administered in the language and form most likely to yield accurate information on what the child knows and can do academically, developmentally, and functionally, unless it is not feasible to so provide or administer."
- School districts are not allowed to seek dispute resolution when parents refuse to give their consent for special education services. If parents refuse to give consent, then the school district is not responsible for providing a free and appropriate public education.

Assessment Participation PL 108-446 requires that all students participate in all state- and district-wide assessments (including those required under the NCLB Act), with accommodations or alternative assessments, if necessary, as stipulated in the pupil's IEP. States are permitted to assess up to 1 percent of students with disabilities (generally those pupils with significant cognitive deficits) with alternative assessments aligned with alternative achievement standards. This legislation further requires that assessments adhere to the principles of universal design when feasible.

The Law and State Issues

This section focuses on major legal issues pertaining to school desegregation, church-state relations, and school finance schemes.

School Desegregation

A U.S. Supreme Court decision, *Plessy v. Ferguson*, established the "**separate but equal**" doctrine regarding the use of public railroad facilities by blacks and whites in 1896.[135] Subsequently, this doctrine was used as the basis for public school segregation of black and white students for the next fifty years in many states. Under dual school systems, black students attended all-black schools staffed predominantly by black teachers, and white children attended all-white schools. Such de jure

[135] *Plessy v. Ferguson*, 163 U.S. 537 (1896).

segregation was rendered constitutional because the separate-but-equal rationale served as a national standard satisfying the equal protection clause of the Fourteenth Amendment.

In 1954 the landmark decision of *Brown v. Board of Education of Topeka* repudiated the Plessy doctrine.[136] The Court stated that "in the field of public education the doctrine of 'separate but equal' has no place. Separate educational facilities are inherently unequal." Because of the significant impact of this decision, the Court postponed for one year the issuance of an enforcement decree. The decision, known as *Brown II,* directed lower federal courts to enforce remedies "with all deliberate speed."[137]

Following *Brown,* southern school districts attempted numerous strategies to avoid desegregation—including transfer provisions; closing the public schools and maintaining state-supported, private, segregated white schools; integrating schools on a one-grade-a-year plan and freedom-of-choice plans; rezoning school districts; and the like—all of which perpetuated segregated dual school systems. Fourteen years after *Brown II,* the Court discarded the "all deliberate speed" criterion for complying with its desegregation enforcement decree. It stated that ". . . every school district is to terminate dual school systems at once and to operate now and hereafter only unitary schools."[138]

This ultimatum affected only those states with **de jure segregation**—segregation that is derived from the influence of the law and is unconstitutional. Southern school districts were quick to point out that there was plenty of segregation in the North created by special forces (such as housing patterns), independent of state sponsorship, which is called **de facto segregation** and is not unconstitutional. for de jure segregation to exist, three factors must be present: (1) Segregation must be initiated and supported by government action; (2) the action must have been taken with the intent to segregate; and (3) the action must have created or increased segregation.[139]

After the *Alexander* decision, many types of remedies of de jure segregation were ordered by lower federal courts. The famous *Swann v. Charlotte-Mecklenburg Board of Education* busing case served as a model remedy for school desegregation. The Court concluded: "In these circumstances, we find no basis for holding that the local school authorities may not be required to employ bus transportation as a tool of school desegregation. Desegregation plans cannot be limited to the walk-in school."[140] This case launched busing as an effective tool to remedy school desegregation.

The courts have used interdistrict desegregation as another remedy for de jure segregation in some situations. In what has become known as the "Detroit case," the Supreme Court affirmed de jure segregation in Detroit because it was shown that racially discriminatory acts of one or more school districts caused racial segregation in an adjacent district and that district lines were deliberately drawn on the basis of race.[141] Three years later, the Detroit case was heard by the Supreme Court once again.[142]

The Court ordered several curriculum programs to eradicate the vestiges of de jure segregation, including remedial reading, teacher in-service training in human relations, expanded counseling and career guidance services for minority students, and a nondiscriminatory testing program. Also ordered was state support of one-half the cost to implement these programs. Subsequent interdistrict remedies were ordered in numerous school districts including Jefferson County, Kentucky, which has served as a model of interdistrict desegregation for many years.[143]

Church-State Relations

Issues concerning church-state relations have provided a steady stream of litigation since World War II. No other area in school law, except school desegregation, has received more attention in the courts than issues involving religion in the public schools. In this section, we examine legal developments concerning church-state-education relationships. Our discussion is limited to school prayer and Bible reading, religion in the curriculum, released time for religious instruction, and use of facilities.

Contained in the U.S. Constitution is a separation of church and state provision, which guarantees religious

[136]*Brown v. Bd. of Educ. of Topeka,* 347 U.S. 483 (1954).

[137]*Brown v. Bd. of Educ. of Topeka,* 349 U.S. 294 (1955).

[138]*Alexander v. Holmes Cty. Bd. of Educ.,* 396 U.S. 19 (1969).

[139]Alexander and Alexander, *American Public School Law.*

[140]*Swann v. Charlotte-Mecklenburg Bd. of Educ.,* 402 U.S. 1 (1971).

[141]*Milliken v. Bradley,* 418 U.S. 717 (1974).

[142]*Milliken v. Bradley,* 433 U.S. 267 (1977).

[143]*Newburg Area Council, Inc., v. Bd. of Educ. of Jefferson County, Ky.,* 510 F. 2d 1358 (6 Cir. 1974), cert. den. 421 U.S. 931 (1975).

freedom and forbids the establishment of religion by the government. The First Amendment provides in part that "Congress shall make no law respecting the establishment of religion, or prohibiting the free exercise thereof." These two religious clauses, the *establishment clause* and the *free exercise clause,* protect a person's religious liberty. The two combined prevent religious indoctrination in the public schools and prohibit the use of public funds to support religion.

It should be noted that this provision restricts only the federal government from making such laws. However, through numerous Supreme Court decisions, justices have incorporated clauses in the U.S. Constitution as applicable to the states by means of the Fourteenth Amendment. This has been effected primarily through two Court cases. The free exercise clause was incorporated in *Cantwell v. Connecticut* and the establishment clause in *Everson v. Board of Education.*[144]

Vouchers On June 27, 2002, the U.S. Supreme Court ruled in favor of a Clevelend program that allows public money to be used to send children to private schools, including religious schools. The 5–4 ruling, which overturned a lower court ruling, was seen as a victory for "school voucher" programs that have been established in some parts of the country with the goal of providing more options to students who would otherwise be sent to underperforming public schools. The decision sparked more debate in the controversy over separation of church and state, especially after an appeals court ruled the Pledge of Allegiance unconstitutional because it mentions "under God."[145]

School Prayer and Bible Reading Historically, many public schools began each day with a prayer and/or Bible reading. Three significant Court decisions established the precedent concerning Bible reading in the public schools. In *Engel v. Vitale*, the Court struck down a New York statute requiring the recitation of a prayer as a violation of the establishment clause of the First Amendment.[146] One year later, in *School District of Abington v. Schempp*, the Court declared unconstitutional a Pennsylvania statute requiring Bible reading and recitation of the Lord's Prayer ". . . when it is part of the school curriculum and conducted under the supervision of teachers employed in the schools."[147] The *Lemon v. Kurtzman* decision established a three-factor test of constitutionality under the establishment clause. The Court declared that to withstand constitutional challenge, the statute must pass three tests: (1) It must have a secular purpose, (2) have a primary effect that neither advances nor inhibits religion, and (3) not foster excessive government entanglement with religion.[148] This three-factor test has been applied in most establishment clause cases.

Persistent litigation concerning prayer and Bible reading in the public schools continued in the lower courts, but it was not until 1985 that a similar challenge reached the Supreme Court in *Wallace v. Jaffree.*[149] In this case, the issue was whether setting aside class time for silent prayer was constitutional. The Court held that such activity was unconstitutional. Although the Court applied the three-factor ***Lemon* test,** a minority of justices objected to its rigidity in assessing individual situations.

In 1992, in *Lee v. Weisman,* the Supreme Court declared that opening prayers at graduation ceremonies are unconstitutional.[150] The question addressed by the Court was "whether including clerical members who offer prayers as part of the official school graduation ceremony is consistent with the Religions Clauses of the First Amendment." The Court followed the standard set in *Engel* and *Abington:* "The principle that government may accommodate the free exercise of religion does not supersede the fundamental limitations imposed by the Establishment Clause."

Three post–*Lee v. Weisman* decisions of the Fifth Circuit Court of Appeals illustrate distinctions that courts may make for different school events. After ruling that student-led prayer at commencements were valid under the *Lee* guidelines,[151] the court struck down as unconstitutional school practices that allowed school employees to participate in or supervise student-led prayers

---

[144]*Cantwell v. Connecticut,* 310 U.S. 296 (1940); *Everson v. Board of Education,* 330 U.S. 1 (1947).

[145]ABC News Internet Ventures, June 27, 2002. http://abcnews.go.com/section/us/DailyNews/scotus_vouchers020627.html

[146]*Engel v. Vitale,* 370 U.S. 421 (1962).

[147]*S.D. of Abington Twp., Pa. v. Schempp,* 374 U.S. 203 (1963).

[148]*Lemon v. Kurtzman,* 403 U.S. 602 (1971).

[149]472 U.S., 105 (1985).

[150]*Lee v. Weisman,* 60 U.S.L.W. 4723 (1992).

[151]*Jones v. Clear Creek Indep. School Dist.,* 977 F. 2d 963 (5th Cir. 1992). But see, *contra: ACLU v. Black Horse Pike Regional Bd. of Educ.,* 84 F. 3d 1471 (3d Cir. 1996) (refusing to follow Jones and overturning student-initiated prayers at high school graduation).

at athletic team games and practices, while upholding school permission for the school choir to adopt a Christian religious song as its theme song.[152] Still later, the same court struck down a Mississippi statute that authorized student-initiated prayer at sporting events, student assemblies, and other school-related student events.[153]

Released Time for Religious Instruction Two Supreme Court cases have addressed the issue of released time for religious instruction. In the first case, *McCollum v. Board of Education*, the Court invalidated a program in which religion classes were taught in the public schools.[154] The Court declared that the use of tax-supported school facilities to promote religious instruction was clearly a violation of the First Amendment. In the second case, *Zorach v. Clausen*, the Court upheld a program whereby students were permitted to leave the school premises during the school day to receive religious instruction at various religious centers.[155] The significant difference between *Zorach* and *McCollum* was that the latter program did not involve the use of public school buildings or the direct use of public funds. Such released-time religious instruction is used in many school communities throughout the country. The arrangement does not violate the federal Constitution as long as the established program is not held on school grounds and is not conducted by teachers or religion instructors affiliated with the school and as long as these instructors are not paid by the school district.

Religion in the Curriculum The *Lemon* test was used in two cases to assess the permissibility of offering Bible study courses in the public schools. In earlier decisions dealing with the constitutionality of school-sponsored prayer and Bible reading, the courts noted that the teaching of the Bible and religion as an aspect of our culture and our history and as a nonbiased academic subject is permissible. In *Wiley v. Franklin* and four years later in *Crockett v. Sorenson*, the courts ruled such practices unconstitutional.[156] Study of the Bible in both jurisdictions when scrutinized by the courts failed one or more prongs of the *Lemon* tripartite test. In a related case, a third circuit court held that a course on Transcendental Meditation (TM) violated the First Amendment.[157] In applying the *Lemon* test, the court concluded that the objectives of TM may have been secular but the means used were religious.

A recent development in this area involves state statutes requiring the teaching of creationism in courses that also teach about the theory of evolution. State statutes in Arkansas and Louisiana that required balanced treatment of the two perspectives were struck down as efforts to advance religion and in violation of the First Amendment.[158]

Equal Access Act It is common practice in public schools to permit student organizations to use school buildings during noninstructional time. Local boards of education have implied powers to regulate such use. In such situations, the question arises concerning the constitutionality of meetings involving religious groups. In 1984, Congress passed the Equal Access Act (EAA), which has since been amended, in an attempt to clarify the unsettled area of law where students' free speech rights compete with the rights of public schools to control access to the school as a forum for public discourse. (See Figure 12–6.)[159]

In 1990, the Supreme Court resolved some of the legal questions when it rendered a decision in *Board of Education of Westside Community Schools v. Mergens*.[160] The case arose when a group of high school students sought permission to form a club that would meet at the public school on noninstructional time and engage in Bible discussions, prayer, and fellowship. The Court held that the school could not bar the religious club from non-curriculum-related student group meetings during noninstructional time. The Court reasoned that denial of recognition to a student-initiated religious

[152]*Doe v. Duncanville Ind. School Dist.*, 70 F. 3d 402 (5th Cir. 1995). See also *Bauchmann v. West High School*, 900 F. Supp. 254 (Utah 1995), which held that singing Christian songs at Christian places of worship by a high school choir did not violate the religious freedom of a Jewish choir member. A contrary view was taken by another court for a student-organized gospel choir that a school secretary supervised. *Sease v. School Dist. of Phila.*, 811 F. Supp. 183 (E.D. Pa. 1993).

[153]*Ingebretson v. Jackson Public School Dist.*, 88 F. 3d 274 (5th Cir. 1996).

[154]333 U.S. 203 (1948).

[155]*Zorach v. Clausen*, 343 U.S. 306 (1952).

[156]*Wiley v. Franklin*, 474 F. Supp. 525 (Tenn. 1979); *Crockett v. Sorenson*, 568 F. Supp. 1422 (Va. 1983).

[157]*Malnak v. Yogi*, 592 F. 2d 197 (3 Cir. 1979).

[158]*McLean v. Arkansas Board of Education*, 529 F. Supp. 1255 (Ak. 1982); *Aguillard v. Edwards*, 765 F. 2d 1251 (5 Cir. 1985).

[159]20 U.S.C., Sec. 4071–4074 (2008).

[160]496 U.S. 226 (1990).

Sec. 801 (a) of the **Equal Access Act, 20 U.S.C. §§ 4070–4074 (2008)** stipulates: It shall be unlawful for any public secondary school which receives federal financial assistance and which has a limited open forum to deny equal access or a fair opportunity to, or discriminate against, any students who wish to conduct a meeting within that limited open forum on the basis of the religious, political, philosophical, or other content of the speech at such meetings.

(b) A public secondary school has a limited open forum whenever such school grants an offering to or opportunity for one or more noncurriculum related student groups to meet on school premises during noninstructional time.

(c) Schools shall be deemed to offer a fair opportunity to students who wish to conduct a meeting within its limited open forum if such school uniformly provides that the meetings:

(1) are voluntary and student-initiated

(2) involve no school or government sponsor

(3) allow the presence of school employees only in a nonparticipatory capacity

(4) do not materially and substantially interfere with the orderly conduct of educational activities within the school; and

(5) are not directed, controlled, or regularly attended by nonschool persons

FIGURE 12–6

The Equal Access Act

club by a public school that recognized a variety of other non-curriculum-related student groups violated the EAA.

Financing Education

Throughout the history of public education in the United States the property tax has served as the major source of financing for public schools at the local level. The use of the property tax to finance public education has received much attention recently and has led to a steady stream of litigation in state and federal courts. Challenges have been advanced on the issue of equality of educational opportunity for all people. Dependence on local property tax revenues to support public education has caused wide inequities in interdistrict funding of educational programs in various states. The equal protection clause of the Fourteenth Amendment and specific state statutes have been the primary vehicles under which litigants have sought relief. This section focuses on levying taxes and challenges to state finance schemes.

School Taxes The Tenth Amendment to the U.S. Constitution provides: "The powers not delegated to the United States by the Constitution nor prohibited by it to the states, are reserved to the states respectively, or to the people." This clause confers on the state the authority not only to regulate and control education but also to devise and implement its own system of taxation. Congress was reminded of the sovereignty of the state over public education in an early Supreme Court case. The Court concluded that "all powers not expressly granted to the United States by the Constitution or reasonably implied therefrom were reserved to the states."[161] This statement provided a case law basis for the state's power to tax and to appropriate funds for public schools.

The authority of school districts to raise and collect taxes for schools is a power that must be conferred on them by the legislature. Furthermore, not all districts have the same taxing power. The legislature can classify school districts and delegate varied financial powers to them depending on their classification.[162]

There are two broad classifications of school districts with respect to their power to tax and raise funds

[161] *U.S. v. Butler,* 297 U.S. 1 (1936).

[162] *Pirrone v. City of Boston,* 364 Mass. 403, N.E. 2d 96 (1973).

for public schools: fiscally independent and fiscally dependent school districts. The vast majority of the more than 15,000 public school districts in the nation are fiscally independent.

Fiscally Independent School Districts These school districts are granted legal authority by the state legislature to set the tax rate on real property, within state constitutional and legislative limits; to levy and collect taxes for the support of local schools; and to approve the expenditure of the funds collected. States require local school boards to prepare budgets of proposed expenditures. In fiscally independent school districts, then, boards of education have a relatively free hand in determining how and where expenditures are to be made, subject to limitations on the total amount by the state's constitution or statute. For example, in Florida local school authorities levy and collect taxes for school purposes, independent of the local county or city governments. However, Florida state law sets a legal limit on the tax rates that can be established by local boards of education.[163] Similarly, in Kentucky state statutes grant local school boards authority to tax property for the support of public schools.[164]

Fiscally Dependent School Districts In this configuration, the board of education prepares and adopts a budget specifying the anticipated expenditures and projected revenue needs. Then a different municipal government may reduce the total budget or eliminate items not required by state law and apportion the school taxes. For example, in Chicago statutory language authorized the school tax levy to be a cooperative endeavor, joining the board of education and city officials. While the local board performed all the preliminary steps in the budget process—preparation, review, and adoption—no school taxes could be forthcoming without the adoption by the city council of an ordinance levying the tax.[165] In a more recent case in Chicago, a two-year collective bargaining agreement was held unenforceable regarding the second year's salary provisions. The state statute stipulated that the local board of education could not incur a contractual liability without an apportionment of funds, and apportionments were made annually by the city council.[166] Similarly in Alaska, Maryland, Massachusetts, New Hampshire, New York, and Pennsylvania, school districts are fiscally dependent on the municipal government to apportion taxes for school purposes.[167]

Challenges to State Finance Schemes Beginning in the late 1960s and continuing to the present, litigation has addressed the issue of inequality of educational opportunity resulting from public school finance schemes. Rooted in the famous landmark desegregation case, *Brown v. Board of Education of Topeka*, courts initially invoked equal protection rights as a means of forcing redistribution of state funds for public education. A key paragraph of *Brown*, often used by plaintiffs in school finance litigation, recognizes the importance of education in contemporary American society:

> Today, education is perhaps the most important function of state and local governments . . . [and] the great expenditures for education . . . demonstrate our recognition of the importance of education to our democratic society. . . . In these days, it is doubtful that any child may reasonably be expected to succeed in life if he is denied the opportunity of an education.

The Court went on to say, "Such an opportunity, where the state has undertaken to provide it, is a right which must be made available to all on equal terms."[168]

Educational Needs Standard Two 1968 Supreme Court cases challenged the constitutionality of state finance schemes in Illinois and Virginia under the equal protection clause of the Fourteenth Amendment. The first case, *McInnis v. Shapiro*, was a class action suit brought on behalf of elementary and secondary public school students and their parents in four Cook County school districts in Illinois.[169] The plaintiffs claimed that the Illinois system of public school finance violated the equal protection guarantees of the Fourteenth Amendment. Additionally, they claimed that there were markedly inequitable per-pupil expenditures among Illinois school districts.

In rejecting their contention, the court cited the following points: (1) The Fourteenth Amendment did not

---

[163]*Gulesian v. Dade Cty. School Board,* 281 So. 2d 325 (Fla. 1973).

[164]*Ky. Rev. Stat.,* Ch. 160.593 (1992).

[165]*Latham v. Bd. of Educ. of the City of Chicago,* 31 Ill. 2d 178, 201 N.E. 2d 111 (1964).

[166]*Bd. of Educ. v. Chicago Teachers Union,* Local 1, A.F.T., 26 Ill. App. 3d 806 N.E. 2d 158 (1975).

[167]Alexander and Alexander, *American Public School Law.*

[168]*Brown v. Bd. of Educ. of Topeka,* 347 U.S. 483 (1954).

[169]*McInnis v. Shapiro,* 293 F. Supp. 327 (N.D. Ill. 1968), aff., *McInnis v. Ogilvie,* 394 U.S. 322 (1969).

require that public school expenditures be made solely on the basis of "educational needs"; (2) "educational expenses" were not the "exclusive yardstick" for measuring the quality of a child's educational opportunity; and (3) there were no "judicially manageable standards" by which a federal court could determine if and when the equal protection clause is satisfied or violated. The court further stated, "The General Assembly's delegation of authority to school districts appears designed to allow individual localities to determine their own tax burden according to the importance which they place upon public schools." The U.S. Supreme Court affirmed the judgment. In the same year, the Court rejected a second challenge in Virginia, *Burruss v. Wilkerson*, advanced on the **educational needs standard.**[170]

Fiscal Neutrality Standard In 1971 the California Supreme Court, in *Serrano v. Priest (Serrano I)*, contradicted the stance taken by the U.S. Supreme Court two years earlier.[171] In both *McInnis* and *Burruss*, the U.S. Supreme Court rejected the federal constitutional theory that education is a right under the Constitution. The Court left in the hands of state legislatures the responsibility to remedy any existing inequities in state funding systems. *Serrano v. Priest*, then, represents an evolutionary step in judicial expansion of equal rights protection under the federal Constitution regarding public school finance. This case generated more reaction than any decision rendered in a state court, for it restricted the state's plenary power to devise and implement its own system of funding public schools.

The plaintiffs in *Serrano*, a group of elementary and high school pupils and their parents, brought a class action suit against the state of California and the county of Los Angeles pertaining to the financing of the public schools. The plaintiffs argued that the California school finance scheme, which relied heavily on local property taxes, caused wide interdistrict disparities in per-pupil expenditures. Such a system was not fiscally neutral, according to the court, because it made the quality of a child's education dependent on the wealth of the school district and therefore invidiously discriminated against the poor in violation of the equal protection clause of the Fourteenth Amendment and similar provisions in the California constitution. The California Supreme Court concluded that under the **fiscal neutrality standard,** the quality of a child's education could not be a function of the wealth of the child's local school district but rather must be based on the wealth of the state as a whole.

The California Supreme Court in *Serrano v. Priest (Serrano II)* reaffirmed its position in *Serrano I* and provided remedies available to the legislature to rectify the wide disparities in the state-funding formula in California. Included among the remedies were the following proposals: full state funding to be supported by a statewide property tax; district consolidation with boundary realignments to equalize assessed valuations of real property among school districts; retention of present school district boundaries with removal of commercial and industrial property from tax warrant rolls for school purposes and placement on state-tax warrant rolls for school purposes; and implementation of a voucher system.[172] One decade later, *Serrano v. Priest (Serrano III)* held that there had been full compliance with the original *Serrano* order to improve the inequities in state financing of public schools in California.[173]

The Rodriguez Case Another major case that has had significant impact on public school finance is *San Antonio Independent School District v. Rodriguez*. The U.S. Supreme Court altered the Serrano attitude that public education is a fundamental right protected by the Constitution. Further, it struck down the fiscal neutrality standard that the equality of public education cannot be a function of wealth, other than the wealth of the state as a whole. *San Antonio v. Rodriguez* marked a return to the view that education is a plenary power granted to the states and not directly a federal matter.

Rodriguez was originally heard by a three-judge federal district court in Texas in which the state's school finance system was challenged. The plaintiffs alleged that the Texas system of financing its public schools, which relied heavily on the local property tax base, tolerated inequitable per-pupil expenditures among local school districts and discriminated against poor families. The rationale of fiscal neutrality and precedents of *Serrano* fashioned their plea. The district court concluded that the Texas system of financing public schools was a violation of the Fourteenth Amendment.[174]

---

[170] *Burruss v. Wilkerson*, 301 F. Supp. 1237 (W.D. Va. 1968), 310 F. Supp. 372 (W.D. Va. 1969), aff., 397 U.S. 44 (1970).

[171] *Serrano v. Priest*, 5 Calif. 3d 584, 96 Calif. Rptr. 601, 487 P. 2d 1241 (1971).

[172] *Serrano v. Priest*, 18 Calif. 3d 728, 135 Calif. Rptr. 345 (1976), *cert. den.* 432 U.S. 907 (1977).

[173] *Serrano v. Priest*, 226 Calif. Rptr. 584 (1986).

[174] *Rodriguez v. San Antonio I.S.D.*, 337 F. Supp. 280 (W.D. Tex. 1971).

Upon appeal of the state of Texas, the U.S. Supreme Court reversed the lower court.[175] The appellees' rationale was rejected on two fundamental points. First, the Court commented that the evidence did not support the contention that the Texas finance system was discriminatory against the poor. The Court stated that the suit involved "a large, diverse, and amorphous class, unified only by the common factor of residence in districts." Further, the fiscal neutrality standard was struck down by the Court because the Texas school finance system was based on a statewide minimum foundation program financed by state and local revenue. The program was designed to provide at least a basic education to each student in the state. Local school districts contributed a portion to the state's foundation program reflective of the assessed property valuation in the district. The Court concluded that no child was completely deprived of educational opportunity in Texas.

Second, concerning the issue of whether education is a "fundamental" constitutional right under the equal protection clause, the Court concluded that there was no such right "explicitly or implicitly guaranteed by the Constitution." In so ruling, the Court reverted to the traditional attitude of leaving the financing of public schools in the hands of state legislatures. The Court concluded: "The . . . complexity of the problems of financing . . . a state-wide public school system suggests that there will be more than one constitutionally permissible method of solving them, and that, within the limits of rationality, the legislature's efforts should be entitled to respect.[176]

Post-*Rodriguez* Litigation Subsequent to *Rodriguez*, litigation in school finance issues continued to flourish. The federal courts were abandoned, however, as an arena for such litigation. The Supreme Court's position in *Rodriguez* made it clear that successful challenges to state finance systems must be pursued on state constitutional grounds rather than on the provisions of the U.S. Constitution. Plaintiffs continued to pattern their arguments on the *Serrano* and *Rodriguez* cases. Because of individual differences in each state's constitution, decisions have been inconsistent.

The highest courts in eleven states (Arizona, Colorado, Georgia, Idaho, Illinois, Maryland, Michigan, New York, Oklahoma, Oregon, and Pennsylvania) have upheld the state's system of financing public schools as constitutional. Most of these decisions were rendered by the court using the *Rodriguez* rationale and precedents. On the other hand, decisions by the highest courts in other states (Arkansas, California, Connecticut, Kentucky, Montana, New Jersey, Texas, Washington, West Virginia, Wisconsin, and Wyoming) have struck down the constitutionality of the state's public school finance system. Most of these decisions were rejected primarily on the legal principles forwarded by the California Supreme Court in *Serrano*.[177]

Summary

1. All three units of government—federal, state, and local—exercise some degree of authority and control over public education.
2. The state was given plenary power over public education through the Tenth Amendment to the U.S. Constitution.
3. Nevertheless, the federal government has exercised and continues to exercise profound influence in educational matters, primarily through the provisions of the federal Constitution, decisions of the U.S. Supreme Court, and congressional enactments.
4. The provisions of the Constitution that have had the greatest impact on the public schools are Article I, Section 10, and the First, Fourth, Fifth, Ninth, and Fourteenth Amendments.
5. Litigation has reached both federal and state courts primarily in the areas of school desegregation, religion in the schools, and, more recently, challenges to state school finance schemes and sexual harassment.
6. U.S. Supreme Court decisions have been prevalent also in such student-related issues as corporal punishment, search and seizure, freedom of expression, and various classification practices related to sex, marriage and pregnancy, ability grouping, and handicaps.

---

[175] *San Antonio I.S.D. v. Rodriguez,* 411 U.S. 1 (1973).

[176] Ibid.

[177] Michael Imber and Tyll Van Geel, *Education Law,* 4th ed. (New York: Routledge, 2010).

PRO CON DEBATE

Equal Access

Congress passed the 1984 Equal Access Act in an attempt to clarify the unsettled area of law wherein the free-speech rights of students compete with the right of schools to control access to schools as a forum for public discourse. Since that time, lawsuits and court decisions have only added to the confusion and uncertainty.

Question: Should student religious clubs be allowed to meet in public school facilities?

Arguments PRO

1. Young people should be encouraged to engage in wide-ranging discussions on any issue. The developmental stage of adolescence is one where young adults are interested in religion.
2. Students do not leave their constitutional rights to freedom of speech at the schoolhouse door. They have the right to express their views in the classroom during class time. Why should they not be allowed to express them in after-school activities that are tied to religious groups?
3. Student religious clubs should have the same access to school facilities as is routinely granted to secular groups. Frequently, religious clubs have church or synagogue sponsors, and adults are present to supervise the students.
4. Under the federal equal access law, it is unlawful for a public secondary school that has created a limited open forum to deny access to student-initiated groups on the basis of the religious, political, or philosophical content of the group's speech.

Arguments CON

1. The U.S. Constitution provides for the separation of church and state. No religious events of any kind should be allowed in public school buildings.
2. Opening the schools to one student-initiated group opens the doors to all student-initiated groups. School administrators need clear restraints on the use of school buildings so that they do not have to decide on the basis of the desirability of one religious group over another. Without a limitation, students may request that an undesirable club, such as a cult or paramilitary group, meet in the school.
3. The current law restricts the amount of supervision that can be exercised over religious clubs. For purposes of safety, school administrators must have the latitude to supervise any student group that meets in the building.
4. The right way to guarantee freedom of religion is to keep the state out of the religious process altogether. To require the schools to allow access to religious groups is to get the schools involved, not to keep church and state separate.

Key Terms

General Welfare Clause
Commerce Clause
obligation of contracts
First Amendment
Fourth Amendment
Fifth Amendment
Ninth Amendment
due process clause
Fourteenth Amendment
equal protection clause
case law
tenure
property interest
liberty interest
quid pro quo sexual harassment
hostile environment sexual harassment
sexual bribery
sexual imposition
gender harassment
sexual coercion
sexual behavior
tort
duty
standard of care
proximate cause
injury
contributory negligence
assumption of risk

comparative negligence
government immunity
parens patriae
domicile
residence
in loco parentis
individualized education program (IEP)
"separate but equal"
de jure segregation
de facto segregation
Lemon test
educational needs standard
fiscal neutrality standard

Discussion Questions

1. What are the roles of the federal, state, and local governments in the operation of schools?
2. What is the basic structure of the federal and state judicial systems?
3. Which provisions of the U.S. Constitution have had the greatest impact on litigation involving public schools? Discuss the major Supreme Court cases applicable to each provision enumerated, and evaluate the principles of law derived from these court decisions.
4. What can school administrators hope to gain from a knowledge of the sources of law that impact schools?
5. Which case (or cases) has had the greatest impact on your role as a professional educator, or which has changed your attitude toward the operation of schools?

Suggested Readings

Alexander, Kern, and M. David Alexander. *American Public School Law*, 8th ed. (Belmont, CA: Wadsworth/Cengage Learning, 2011). The text is designed to inform the practicing educator of the current and rapidly evolving nature of the law as it affects public schools.

Fischer, Louis, David Schimmel, and Cynthia Kelly. *Teachers and the Law*, 7th ed. (Boston: Allyn and Bacon, 2006). This book covers those issues most central to the daily lives of teachers, using a question-answer format.

Imber, Michael, and Tyll van Geel. *Education Law*, 4th ed. (New York: Routledge, 2010). This textbook is approximately two-thirds cases, with the cases integrated throughout.

LaMorte, Michael W. *School Law: Cases and Concepts*, 9th ed. (Boston: Pearson Education, 2008). The author examines the sources of law under which educators operate, the legal constraints to state action in the educational arena, the legal rights and restrictions applicable to students' behavior, the historical and legal foundations of both desegregation and recent school finance reform, and the application of tort law to public education.

Reutter, E. Edmond. *The Law of Public Education*, 6th ed. (Westbury, NY: Foundation Press, 2003). This textbook-casebook is designed to provide basic knowledge of the law directly affecting public education in the United States, including hundreds of cases and judicial decisions.

Thomas, Stephen P., Nelda H. Cambron McCabe, and Martha M. McCarthy. *Public School Law*, 6th ed. (Boston: Pearson Education, 2009). The text provides a comprehensive treatment of the evolution and current status of the law governing public schools.

Valente, William D. and Christina M. Valente. *Law in Schools*, 5th ed. (Upper Saddle River, NJ: Prentice Hall, 2004). The text thoroughly addresses the legal principles governing American schools, discusses the origin and development of laws pertaining to schools, and explores the many ways in which laws influence specific educational policies, practices, and goals.

13

Curriculum Development and Implementation

FOCUSING QUESTIONS

1 How can we define curriculum?
2 What approach to curriculum do most administrators adopt?
3 How do philosophy of education and psychology of learning influence curriculum and instruction?
4 Why are curriculum development models usually behaviorist in nature? Can humanistic educators rely on such models?
5 What are good criteria to use in selecting content and experiences for planning curriculum?
6 How are content, experiences, and environment related in the planning of curriculum?
7 Why is change difficult to implement in schools?
8 What strategies or methods of change are important for a school environment?

In this chapter, we attempt to answer these questions about curriculum development and implementation by first defining curriculum and examining the four basic approaches to develop it. Then we list the criteria for and define the administrator's role in planning and implementation. Finally, we look at ways to implement a new curriculum and to urge staff to accept the change it may bring about.

Much of the professional literature currently stresses the need for supervisors and administrators to become more involved in curriculum development and implementation. The need to plan effective curricula is obvious because curriculum is often considered the heart of schooling. The difficulty, however, is there are various definitions of curriculum development and implementation. Not everyone agrees what curriculum is or what is involved in curriculum development and implementation. We present a definition that allows different views and interpretations to exist—and which permits school administrators to become more involved in curriculum matters.

Curriculum Definitions and Approaches

What is curriculum? What is its purpose? How does it affect students, teachers, and administrators? The way we define curriculum in part reflects our approach to it. A curriculum can be defined as a *plan* for action, or a written document, which includes strategies for achieving desired goals or ends. Most educators agree with this definition, as do most administrators who approach curriculum in terms of a behavioral or managerial outlook.

Curriculum can also be defined broadly, as dealing with the *experiences* of the learner. This view considers almost anything in school, even outside of school (as long as it is planned) as part of the curriculum. It is rooted in John Dewey's definition of experience and education, as well as Hollis Caswell and Doak Campbell's view, from the 1930s, that curriculum was "all the experiences children have under the guidance of the teacher."[1] Humanistic curricularists and elementary school administrators subscribe to this definition, at least more so than traditional curricularists and secondary school administrators.

Curriculum can be viewed as a *field of study*, that is, as an intellectual or an academic subject that attempts to analyze and synthesize major positions, trends, and concepts of curriculum. The approach tends to be historical and philosophical and, to a lesser extent, social and psychological in nature. The discussion of curriculum making is usually scholarly and theoretical, not practical, and concerned with broad issues of curriculum. Many administrators would reject this approach as lacking in practical value; administrators who might appreciate this approach as providing a worthwhile framework to help explain curriculum are those with advanced degrees and/or with several courses in curriculum. Those who might have faith in curriculum as a field of study would appreciate the functions of theory and theory building. They might also view curriculum as a *system* with its own definitions, operational constructs, assumptions, postulates, generalizations, laws, and specialists to interpret this knowledge.[2]

Finally, curriculum can be viewed in terms of specific *subject matter* (mathematics, science, English, history, etc.) and *grade levels*. This viewpoint emphasizes knowledge, concepts, and generalizations of a particular subject or group of subjects (such as the core curriculum, which combines two separate subjects such as history and English, or the broad fields curriculum, which combines many similar subjects into new courses such as social studies, language arts, or general science). All classroom and school approaches have elements of this definition—that is, there is recognition of subjects and grades.

Behavioral Approach

Rooted in the University of Chicago school, the behavioral approach is the oldest and most popular approach to curriculum. As a means-ends approach, it is logical and prescriptive. It relies on technical and scientific principles and includes models, prescriptions,

[1]John Dewey, *Experience and Education* (New York: Macmillan, 1938); Hollis L. Caswell and Doak S. Campbell, *Curriculum Development* (New York: American Books, 1935), p. 69. Also see Thomas Fallace, "Repeating the Race Experience: John Dewey and the History Curriculum at the University of Chicago Lab School," *Curriculum Inquiry,* 39 (2009): 381–405.

[2]Herbert M. Kliebard, "What Is a Knowledge Base?" *Review of Educational Research,* 63 (1993): 295–304; Allan C. Ornstein and Francis P. Hunkins, "Theorizing about Curriculum Theory," *High School Journal,* 72 (1989): 77–82; James T. Sears and Dan Marshall, "General Influences on Contemporary Curriculum," *Journal of Curriculum Studies,* 32 (2000): 199–214.

and step-by-step strategies for formulating curriculum.[3] Usually based on a plan, sometimes called a *blueprint,* it specifies goals and objectives, sequences content and experiences to coincide with the objectives, and evaluates learning outcomes in relation to the goals and objectives.

This curriculum approach, which has been applied to all subjects for the last 90 years (since the Bobbitt era), constitutes a frame of reference against which other approaches to curriculum are compared and criticized.[4] Other names have been used to identify this approach—including logical/positivist, conceptual/empiricist, experimentalist, rational/scientific, and technocrat.[5]

The behavioral approach started with the idea of efficiency, promoted by business and industry, and the scientific management theories of Frederick Taylor, who analyzed factory efficiency in terms of time-and-motion studies and concluded that each worker should be paid on the basis of individual output, as measured by the number of units produced in a specified period of time. Efficient operation of the schools (and other social systems), sometimes called **machine theory** by its critics, became a major goal in the 1920s and 1930s.

Often, ensuring efficiency in schools meant eliminating small classes, increasing student-teacher ratios, hiring few administrators, cutting costs in teacher salaries, maintaining or reducing operational costs, and so on, and then preparing charts and graphs to show the resultant lower costs. Raymond Callahan later branded this idea the "cult of efficiency."[6] The effects were to make administration in general and curriculum making more scientific, at least more precise, and to reduce teaching and learning to precise behaviors with corresponding activities that could be measured.

Franklin Bobbitt described the problems as he set out to organize a course of studies for the elementary grades. "We need principles of curriculum making. We did not know that we should first determine objectives from a study of social needs . . . [and] we had not learned that [plans] are means, not ends."[7]

Bobbitt further developed his objectives and activities approach in the early 1920s in *How to Make a Curriculum.* He outlined more than 800 objectives and related activities to coincide with student needs. These activities ranged from the "ability to care for [one's] teeth . . . eyes . . . nose, and throat; . . . to keep home appliances in good working condition; . . . to spelling and grammar."[8] Bobbitt's methods were sophisticated for the day; but taken out of context, his list of hundreds of objectives and activities, along with the machine or factory analogy that he advocated, was easy to criticize.

It was left to Ralph Tyler, a graduate student of Bobbitt's, to recognize the need for behavioral objectives that were not as tiny or lockstep, whereby basic techniques of curriculum, instruction, and evaluation were combined in a simple plan. He outlined four broad questions that he believed should be answered by anyone involved in planning or writing a curriculum for any subject or grade level:

1. What educational purposes should the school seek to attain?
2. What educational experiences can be provided that are likely to attain these purposes?
3. How can these educational experiences be effectively organized?
4. How can we determine whether these principles are being attained?[9]

Although Tyler's questions were not new when he wrote them, rather a condensed version of the *Twenty-Sixth Yearbook* of the National Society for the Study of Education (NSSE), he put forth the ideas in easy-to-read

---

[3]Linda Behar and Allan C. Ornstein, "An Overview of Curriculum: The Theory and Practice," *NASSP Bulletin,* 76 (1992): 1–10; Allan C. Ornstein, "The Field of Curriculum: What Approach? What Definition?" *High School Journal,* 70 (1987): 208–216; Allan C. Ornstein, Edward Pajak, and Stacey B. Ornstein, *Contemporary Issues in Curriculum,* 5th ed. (Needham Heights, MA: Allyn and Bacon, 2010).

[4]Herbert M. Kliebard, *The Struggle of the American Curriculum: 1893–1958* (New York: Routledge & Kegan Paul, 1987); Kliebard, *Changing Course: American Curriculum Reform in the 20th Century* (New York: Teachers College Press, Columbia University, 2002); William H. Schubert, "*Currere* and Disciplinarity in Curriculum Studies," *Educational Researcher,* 38 (2009): 136–140.

[5]Michael W. Apple, *Official Knowledge* (New York: Routledge, 1993); Elliot Eisner, *The Educational Imagination,* 3rd ed. (Columbus, OH: Merrill, 2002).

[6]Raymond Callahan, *Education and the Cult of Efficiency* (Chicago: University of Chicago Press, 1962).

[7]Franklin Bobbitt, *The Curriculum* (Boston: Houghton Mifflin, 1918), p. 283.

[8]Franklin Bobbitt, *How to Make a Curriculum* (Boston: Houghton Mifflin, 1924), pp. 14, 28.

[9]Ralph W. Tyler, *Basic Principles of Curriculum and Instruction* (Chicago: University of Chicago Press, 1949), p. 1.

and brief form (128 pages). His approach, considered today a classic method and read by curriculum specialists and school administrators, combines behaviorism (objectives are an important consideration) with progressivism (the emphasis is on the needs of the learner); the procedures outlined are still applicable in varying school situations today.

Managerial Approach

The managerial approach considers the school as a social system, reminiscent of organizational theory, in which groups of people such as students, teachers, curriculum specialists, and administrators interact according to certain norms and behaviors. Administrators who rely on this approach plan the curriculum in terms of programs, schedules, space, resources and equipment, and personnel and departments. This approach advocates, among other things, the need for selecting, organizing, communicating with, and supervising people involved in curriculum decisions. It considers committee and group processes, human relations, leadership styles and methods, and decision making.

An offshoot of the behavioral approach, the managerial approach also relies on a plan, rational principles, and logical steps, but not necessarily behavioral approaches. The managerial aspect tends to zero in on supervisory and administrative aspects of curriculum, especially the organizational and implementation process.[10]

Advocates of this approach are interested in change and innovation and in how curriculum specialists, supervisors, and administrators can facilitate these processes. The curriculum specialist and supervisor are considered to be practitioners—change agents, resource people, and facilitators—not theoreticians. They report to an administrator and follow the mission and goals of the school. If the school does not appreciate change, then the change role of the job is minimized. If the school is progressive, then changes are expected to be child centered. If the school emphasizes the three Rs, then the curriculum specialist introduces plans accordingly.

The managerial approach is rooted in the organizational and administrative school models of the early 1900s—a period that combined a host of innovative plans involving curriculum and instruction that centered on individualization, departmentalization, nongrading, classroom grouping, homeroom, and work-study activities. It was an era when various school district plans were introduced by their respective superintendents in an attempt to modify the horizontal and/or vertical organization of the schools. The names of the plans were usually based on either the school district's name or organizational concept—such as the Batavia (New York) Plan, Denver Plan, Elizabeth (New Jersey) Plan, Pueblo (Colorado) Plan, Platoon (Gary, Indiana) Plan, Portland (Oregon) Plan, Santa Barbara (California) Plan, Study Hall (New York City) Plan, and Winnetka (Illinois) Plan. Superintendents and associate superintendents were very much involved in curriculum leadership, often developing a plan in one school district and being hired by another one to implement the plan there. Hence, there was a good deal of hopscotching around of administrators, based on a combination of their managerial and curriculum skills.

The managerial approach became dominant in the 1950s and 1960s among school principals and superintendents. During this era, Midwest school administrators and professors (with administrative backgrounds) dominated the field of curriculum in terms of setting policies and priorities, establishing the direction of change and innovation, and planning and organizing curriculum and instruction.

The pacesetters for this era were such school superintendents as Robert Anderson (Park Forest, Illinois), Leslee Bishop (Livonia, Michigan), William Cornog (New Trier Township, Winnetka, Illinois), Robert Gilchrist (University City, Missouri), Arthur Lewis (Minneapolis), Sidney Marland (Winnetka, Illinois), Lloyd Michael (Evanston, Illinois), Stuart Rankin (Detroit), and J. Lloyd Trump (Waukegan, Illinois). Other superintendents (or associate superintendents) from outside the Midwest were also influential, such as Chester Babcock (Seattle), Muriel Crosby (Wilmington, Delaware), Gerald Firth (Roslyn, New York), and John McNeil (San Diego).[11]

These superintendents were very active politically, at both the local and national levels. They used the professional associations and their respective journals

[10]Michael Fullan, *Leadership and Sustainability: System Thinkers in Action* (Thousand Oaks, CA: Corwin Press, 2005); John R. Hoyle, Leadership and Futuring, 2nd ed. (Thousand Oaks, CA: Corwin Press, 2007); Jon Wiles and Joseph Bondi, *Curriculum Development: A Guide to Practice*, 8th ed. (Boston: Allyn and Bacon, 2010).

[11]Allan C. Ornstein and Francis P. Hunkins, *Curriculum: Foundations, Principles, and Issues,* 5th ed. (Boston: Allyn and Bacon, 2009).

and yearbooks as platforms to publicize their ideas. In particular, they were frequently published by the Association for Supervision and Curriculum Development, American Association of School Administrators, and National Association of Secondary School Principals. Many like Anderson (Harvard), Firth (University of Georgia), Lewis (University of Florida), McNeil (UCLA), and Trump (University of Illinois, Urbana) became professors at major universities; others became active as board directors and executive committee members of professional and administrative organizations that have had major impact on curriculum, supervision, and administration.

Most of these administrators tended to be less concerned about teaching and learning than about organization and implementation. Similarly, they were less concerned about subject matter, methods, or materials than improving curriculum in light of policies, plans, and people on a school-wide or school district basis. They envisioned curriculum change and innovation as they administered the resources and restructured the schools. Most of their innovative practices can be grouped into five categories—personnel, instructional media, instructional groups, grading, and schools—according to how they were to be organized or modified:

1. Personnel changes focused on the way staff was to be used in the classroom, involving team teaching, differential staffing, and teacher aides (or paraprofessionals).
2. Media changes focused on instructional technology, including programmed instruction, language laboratories, and educational television.
3. Grouping practices involved individualized instruction, independent instruction, small-group instruction, and various homogeneous and heterogeneous groups.
4. Grading practices included nongraded plans, continuous progress plans, and pass-fail.
5. School plans were numerous and included various options such as flexible scheduling and module scheduling, as well as open schools, schools without walls, community schools, street academies, special service schools (for the emotionally disturbed or mentally retarded), and specialized schools (music, art, engineering, science, etc.).

Most of the curriculum innovations developed during this period are still considered viable today and often discussed in the literature and implemented as new or innovative. Indeed, these administrators had good theoretical insight, and their practices would prove lasting; their plans were usually well thought out and developed.

Systems Approach

It was not far to leap from organizing people and policies, a managerial view, to organizing curriculum into a system. The systems aspect tends to view various units and subunits of the organization in relation to the whole, and organizational units, flowcharts, and committee structures are often diagrammed as the curriculum plan is introduced and monitored.[12]

Sometimes referred to as **curriculum engineering**, the approach includes processes necessary to plan the curriculum by *engineers*—superintendents, directors, coordinators, and principals; *stages*—development, design, implementation, and evaluation; and *structures*—subjects, courses, unit plans, and lesson plans. The systems approach to curriculum was influenced by systems theory, systems analysis, and systems engineering. These principles, originally developed by social scientists in the 1950s and 1960s, continue to be used or at least discussed widely by school managers as part of administrative and organizational theory.

In the systems approach to curriculum, the "parts" of the total school district or school are closely examined in terms of their interrelatedness and influence on each other. Components like departments, personnel, equipment, and schedules are planned to create changes in people's behavior and expectations. In general, information is communicated to administrators who consider alternatives and choices.

One application of the systems approach was developed by the Rand Corporation and has rapidly spread from government to business and school agencies. It is called a *planning, programming, budgeting system* (PPBS), and it brings together those components with the system's structure, functions, and capabilities. In this case, the system is the curriculum.

Another well-known systems approach is the *program evaluation and review technique* (PERT), which was introduced by the Department of Defense and

[12] Madeleine R. Grumet, "Curriculum Inquiry, Theory and Politics," *Curriculum Inquiry*, 14 (2009): 221–234. Allan C. Ornstein, "Analyzing the Curriculum," *NASSP Bulletin*, 77 (1993): 58–64; Ornstein, "The Field of Curriculum: What Approach? What Definition?"

subsequently spread to business and industry in the 1960s; like PPBS, it has been introduced into education. Progress and interruptions of various facets of the program, in this case the curriculum, are computed, analyzed, and made available to administrators. Progress reports are continually updated, reflecting changes in schedule, possible difficulties, and achievement rates. In both systems' approaches, the curriculum is closely monitored by administrators; revisions and corrective action are introduced on a continual basis.

It was George Beauchamp (a former school administrator and professor of curriculum) who developed the first systems theory of curriculum. He divided theories of education into five major theories of equal importance: administrative, counseling, curriculum, instructional, and evaluation.[13] Many school administrators do not accept this notion of equal theories, for they view administration as their major system or field of study and curriculum as a component or subsystem of the major system. In fact, they often delegate supervisors to take care of curriculum matters, especially if they view their leadership role chiefly in terms of management. On the other hand, curriculum specialists usually view curriculum as the major system and related fields such as supervision, teaching, instruction, and evalution as subsystems, which help implement the curriculum.[14]

However, what Beauchamp was trying to convey is that the five theories of education are applied realms of knowledge that draw their ideas from the foundations of education: psychology, sociology, history, philosophy, and so on. Rather than disputing what the major systems or subsystems are, it is more important to design procedures that are applicable to the real world and use whatever theory that can be helpful.

Administrators who value the systems approach take a macro, or broad, view of curriculum and are concerned with curriculum issues and questions that relate to the entire school or school system, not only in terms of subjects or grades. They ask theoretical questions, often referred to as the "fundamental" or "basic" questions of curriculum, listed in Table 13–1. These questions do not have simple or linear answers, and they evoke philosophical and political debates among respondents.

These types of questions were first raised in 1930, when a famous twelve-person committee on curriculum, headed by Harold Rugg, presented a general statement on curriculum making and raised eighteen "fundamental questions" for the National Society for the Study of Education (see Table 13–1). They were raised again in the 1983 Yearbook of the Association for Supervision and Curriculum Development,[15] and still later on by other curriculum specialists.[16] They are generic questions that have stood the test of time.

The posture one takes in answering the questions in Table 13–1 will greatly influence the planning of curriculum; the place and function of subject matter; the types of subjects offered; the methods and materials for facilitating instruction; the role of curriculum specialists and supervisors, as well as teachers; and how the school (or school district) is organized to carry out curricula functions. It will determine in part how curriculum is to be developed and implemented, as well as the policies and processes involved in administering the curriculum.

Humanistic Approach

Some administrators and curriculum leaders reflect on the field and contend that the above approaches are too technocratic and rigid. They contend that in our attempt to be scientific and rational, administrators (or supervisors) in charge of curriculum miss the personal and social aspects of curriculum and instruction; ignore the artistic, physical, and cultural aspects of subject matter; rarely consider the need for self-reflection and self-actualization among learners; and, finally, overlook the sociopsychological dynamics of classrooms and schools.

---

[13]George A. Beauchamp, *Curriculum Theory,* 4th ed. (Itasca, IL: Peacock, 1981).

[14]Allan C. Ornstein, "Curriculum, Instruction, and Supervision—Their Relationship and the Role of the Principal," *NASSP Bulletin,* 70 (1986): 74–81; Edward Pajak, "Clinical Supervision and Psychological Functions," *Journal of Curriculum and Supervision,* 17 (2002): 189–205; Thomas Popkewitz, "Curriculum Study, Curriculum History and Curriculum Theory," *Journal of Curriculum Studies,* 41 (2009): 301–319.

[15]Elizabeth Vallence, "Curriculum as a Field of Practice," in F. W. English (ed.), *Fundamental Curriculum Decisions,* 1983 Yearbook (Washington, DC: Association for Supervision and Curriculum Development, 1983), pp. 154–164.

[16]Jon W. Wiles, *Curriculum Essentials: A Resource for Educators,* 2nd ed. (Boston: Allyn and Bacon, 2005); Decker F. Walker, Jonas F. Soltis, and Frances Schoonmaker, *Curriculum and Aims* 5th ed. (New York: Teachers College Press, Columbia University, 2009).

Table 13-1 Fundamental Questions of Curriculum

Eighteen Questions (1930)

1. What period of life does schooling primarily contemplate as its end?
2. How can the curriculum prepare one for effective participation in adult life?
3. Are the curriculum makers of the schools obliged to formulate a point of view concerning the merits or deficiencies of American civilization?
4. Should the school be regarded as a conscious agency for social improvement?
5. How shall the content of the curriculum be conceived and stated?
6. What is the place and function of subject matter in the education process?
7. What portion of education should be classified as "general" and what portions as "specialized" or "vocational" or purely "optional"? To what extent is general education to run parallel with vocational education and to what extent is the latter to follow on the completion of the former?
8. Is the curriculum to be made in advance?
9. To what extent is the "organization" of subject matter a matter of pupil thinking and construction of, or planning by, the professional curriculum maker as a result of experimentation?
10. From the point of view of the educator, when has "learning" taken place?
11. To what extent should traits be learned in their "natural" setting (i.e., in a "life situation")?
12. To what degree should the curriculum provide for individual differences?
13. To what degree is the concept of "minimal essentials" to be used in curriculum construction?
14. What should be the form of organization of the curriculum? Shall it be one of the following or will you adopt others?
    (a) A flexibly graded series of suggested activities with reference to subject matter that may be used in connection with the activities? Or,
    (b) A rigidly graded series of activities with subject matter included with each respective activity? Or,
    (c) A graded sequence of subject matter with suggestion for activities to which the subject matter is related? Or,
    (d) A statement of achievements expected for each grade, a list of suggested activities, and an outline of related subject matter, through the use of which the grade object may be achieved? Or,
    (e) A statement of grade objectives in terms of subject matter and textual and reference materials?
15. What use, if any, shall be made of the spontaneous interests of children?
16. What types of materials [or activities] should the curriculum maker [provide] for students?
17. How far shall methods of learning be standardized?
18. For what time units [and] what geographic units shall the curriculum be made [national, state, school district, local school]? What is the optimal form in which to publish the course of study?

Source: Adapted from Harold Rugg et al., "List of Fundamental Questions on Curriculum Making," in G. M. Whipple (ed.), *The Foundations of Curriculum Making*, Twenty-Sixth Yearbook of the National Society for the Study of Education, Part II (Bloomington, IL: Public School Publishing, 1930), p. 8.

This view is rooted in progressive philosophy and the child-centered movement of the early 1900s (first spearheaded at the University of Chicago when John Dewey, Charles Judd, and Francis Parker developed progressive methods of teaching, based on the student's natural development and curiosity). In the 1920s and 1930s, the progressive movement moved east and was dominated by Teachers College, Columbia University, and by such professors as Frederick Bosner, Hollis Caswell, L. Thomas Hopkins, William Kilpatrick, Harold Rugg, and John Dewey (who had changed professional affiliations to Columbia). This progressive view gained further impetus in the 1940s and 1950s with the growth of child psychology (which deals with the needs and interests of children) and humanistic psychology (which deals with valuing, ego identity, psychological health, freedom to learn, and personal fulfillment).

From this approach, a host of curriculum activities have emerged, mainly at the elementary school level, including lessons based on life experiences, group games, group projects, artistic endeavors, dramatizations, field trips, social enterprises, learning and interest centers, and child and adolescent needs. These activities include creative problem solving and active student participation; they emphasize socialization and life adjustment for students, as well as stronger family and school-community ties. They are representative of Parker, Dewey, and Washburne's (Parker and Washburn were superintendents) ideal school, and the kinds of curriculum activities they put into practice are still practiced in many private and university lab schools and suburban school districts across the United States.

The humanistic curriculum seems more suitable for middle- and upper middle-class students, as well as high achievers. Evidence suggests that these students exhibit high independence in learning and are better off in low-structured situations in which they can exercise their own initiative. Lower-class students often lack inner controls necessary for self-discipline, and low-achieving students often lack cognitive skills necessary for independent learning. These students need stricter rules, highly structured activities in class, and more opportunities at all education levels.[17]

This does not necessarily mean that inner-city schools cannot be humanistic. What counts is that teachers and administrators have faith in and high expectations for students, attempt to form meaningful and honest relationships between teachers and students (not coercive or controlling relationships), and that teachers try to foster individuality, self-direction, and self-confidence. Without a humanistic principal, a person who is more concerned about people than tasks, it is almost impossible for inner-city schools (or for that matter suburban or rural schools) to exhibit a humanistic atmosphere.[18] Inner-city schools tend to be characterized not only by the regular bureaucratic tasks (which many schools exhibit) but also by basic tasks dealing with classroom discipline, reading and language problems, and lack of parental support for learning. Without involved parents and better childhoods, it is difficult to expect lasting reform or humanistic programs, on a large scale, that work.

Curriculum leaders who believe in the humanistic approach tend to put faith in cooperative learning, independent learning, small-group learning, and social activities, as opposed to competitive, teacher-dominated, large-group learning, and only cognitive instruction. Each child, according to the humanistic approach, has some input in curriculum and shares responsibility with teachers in planning classroom instruction. Administrators tend to permit teachers more input in curriculum decisions. Curriculum committees are bottom up instead of top down, and students are often invited into curriculum meetings to express their views on content and experiences related to curriculum development.

The humanistic approach became popular again in the 1970s, as relevancy, radical school reform, open education, and alternative education became part of the reform movement in education. Today, demands for educational excellence and academic productivity have resulted in emphasis on cognition, not humanism, and on subjects such as science and math, not art or music. The humanistic approach has always represented a minority view among administrators, who are usually more concerned with the "nuts and bolts" of curriculum—that is, the three Rs in elementary school and the basic academic subjects in secondary school. The humanistic approach has now been relegated almost to a fringe view, overshadowed by a return to "back to basics," tougher academic standards, and high-stake testing.

Curriculum Development

The need to develop curriculum is obvious; however, there are various ways to define and proceed with **curriculum development.** Ideally, those who are affected by curriculum should be involved in the process of *planning* and then in the process of *implementation* and *evaluation.* Table 13–2 raises important questions pertaining to these three phases of curriculum. Administrators and supervisors involved in curriculum making should be willing to discuss these questions with their respective board members and professional staff. But like many aspects of education, there is some debate about the formula to follow in order to achieve the particular educational goal. Although there are many developmental models of curriculum to choose from, we focus on one representative model for each approach previously mentioned. (See Administrative Advice 13–1.)

Tyler: Behavioral Model

Ralph Tyler is often considered the bridge between the first and second half-century of the field of curriculum, whereby he fused the best ideas of curriculum making

---

[17]Larry Cuban, *How Can I Fix It?* (New York: Teachers College Press, Columbia University, 2001); Carolyn Evertson, et al., *Classroom Management for Elementary Teachers,* 8th ed. (Boston: Allyn and Bacon, 2008); Linda Darling-Hammond *the Flat World and Education* (New York: Teachers College Press, Columbia University, 2009).

[18]Richard F. Elmore, "Breaking the Cartel," *Phi Delta Kappan,* 87 (2006): 517–518; Andy Hargreaves and Dean Fink, "The Ripple Effect," *Educational Leadership,* 63 (2006): 16–21; and Mary Anne Raywid, "Themes That Serve Schools Well," *Phi Delta Kappan,* 87 (2006): 654–656.

Table 13–2 Steps in Curriculum Development

I. Planning the Curriculum

1. Who assigns committee members?
2. What groups are represented within the committee?
3. Who determines priorities, standards, competencies, etc.?
4. How do we identify needs, problems, issues, etc.?
5. Who formulates goals and objectives? What type of goals, objectives?

II. Implementing the Curriculum

1. Who defines what knowledge is most important?
2. Who decides on instructional materials and media?
3. Who evaluates teachers? What measurement criteria are used?
4. Who decides how teachers will be prepared and trained for the program?
5. Who determines how much money/resources will be made available?

III. Evaluating the Curriculum

1. Who decides how the curriculum will be evaluated?
2. Who decides on assessment procedures? Tests? And how are they to be used?
3. Have our goals and objectives been addressed in the evaluation?
4. Does the program work? To what extent? How can it be improved?
5. Who is responsible for reporting the results? To whom?
6. Do we wish to make comparisons or judgments about the program? Why? Why not?

during the early period and set the stage for the modern period.[19] Tyler proposed a number of steps in planning a curriculum, outlined in Figure 13–1, starting with the goals of the school. These goals would be selected on the basis of what he called **sources of information** about important aspects of contemporary life, subject matter, and the needs and interests of learners. By analyzing changing society, at the local, state, or national level, it could be determined what goals (and also what subject matter) were most important. By consulting with subject specialists (as well as teachers), helpful decisions could be determined about concepts, skills, and tasks to be taught in the various subjects (reading, math, science, etc.). By identifying the needs and interests of students, a beginning point in content, methods, and materials could be determined. (Hence, Tyler helped popularize the concept of a needs assessment study.)

Tyler then suggested that the school staff, possibly organized as a curriculum committee, **screen** the recommended **goals** according to the school's (or school district's) *philosophy* and beliefs about *psychology* of learning (or what some might call learning theory). What resulted from this screening process would be *instructional objectives,* more specific than the school's goals and designed for classroom use.

Tyler then proceeded to the *selection of learning experiences* that would allow the attainment of objectives. Learning experiences would take into account the developmental stage of the learners, such as their age and abilities, and consider the learners' background (present attainments), external environment (classroom and school), and what the learners did (their behavior) when learning. Tyler next talked about *organizing learning experiences* in a systematic way to produce a maximum, positive effect. Here he elaborated on the vertical (recurring subject matter such as social studies from grade to grade) relationship and horizontal (integration of different subjects at the same grade level) relationship of curriculum.

Tyler elaborated on the need for *evaluation* to determine whether the objectives were achieved or the learning experiences actually produced the intended results. Also, it was necessary to determine whether

[19]Tyler, *Basic Principles of Curriculum and Instruction.*

ADMINISTRATIVE ADVICE 13–1

Guidelines for Curriculum Development

Below are some guiding statements to help clarify the steps involved in curriculum development. These statements are based on school practice and apply to all curriculum models.

- The curriculum-design committee should include teachers, parents, and administrators; some schools might include students, too.
- The committee should establish a sense of mission or purpose in the early stages or meetings.
- Needs and priorities should be addressed in relation to students and society.
- School goals and objectives should be reviewed, but they should not serve as the only guiding criteria on which to develop the curriculum. Such criteria should connote a broad educational philosophy to guide curriculum development.
- Alternative curriculum designs should be contrasted in terms of advantages and disadvantages such as cost, scheduling, class size, facilities and personnel required, existing relationship to present programs, and so on.
- To help teachers gain insight into a new or modified design, it should reveal expected cognitive and affective skills, concepts, and outcomes.
- Principals have significant impact on curriculum development through their influence on school climate and their support of the curriculum process.
- District administrators, especially the superintendent, have only a peripheral impact on curriculum development because their outlook and concerns center on managerial activities. Their curriculum role is minor, but their support and approval are essential.
- State education officials have even less impact on curriculum development, although various departments publish guides, bulletins, and reports that can be informative. However, these educators establish policies, rules, and regulations that affect curriculum and instruction.
- The influence of special interest groups and local politics should not be underestimated. Polarization or conflict has frequently obscured reasonable efforts for reform and meaningful dialogue between educators and parents in regard to educational matters.

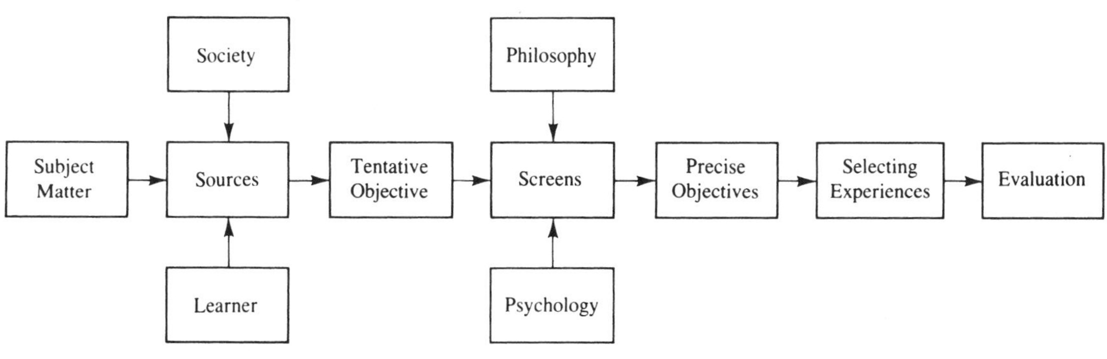

FIGURE 13–1

Organizing the Curriculum—A Behavioral Approach, Based on the Tyler Model

the curriculum was effective or ineffective and whether changes should be made or a new curriculum was warranted.

Although Tyler never introduced his model of curriculum development in a graphic manner, Figure 13–1 helps interpret what he was hoping to achieve. Because Tyler did not clarify at what level his model could be used, school district or school level, or whether it was a top-down (line staff) model or bottom-up (teacher empowerment) model, it can be applied to both

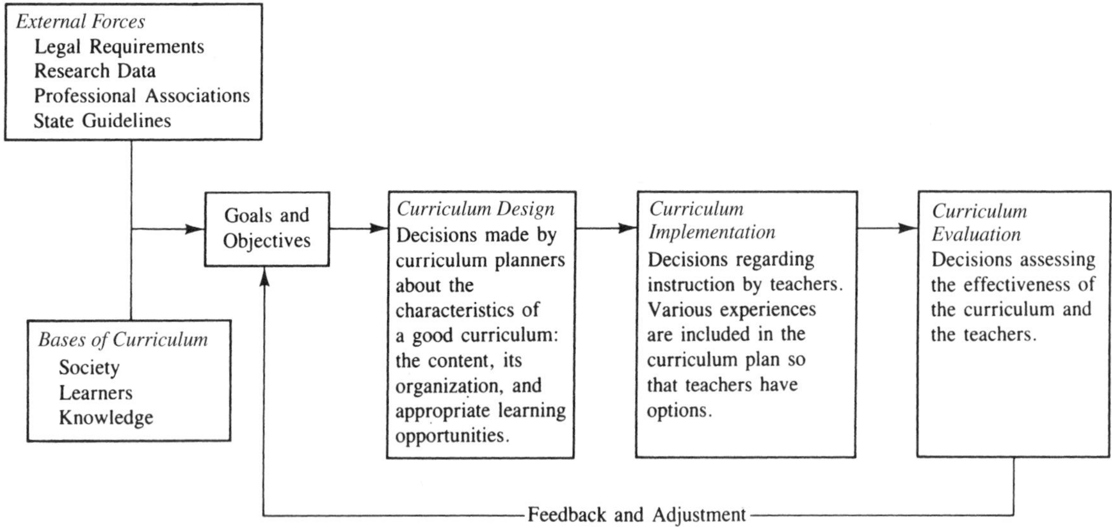

FIGURE 13–2

Managing the Curriculum
Source: Adapted from J. Galen Saylor, William M. Alexander, and Arthur J. Lewis, *Curriculum Planning for Better Teaching and Learning,* 4th ed (New York: Holt, Rinehart, 1981), pp. 29–30.

orientations. However, at the period of his writings, the top-down model prevailed in schools: Curriculum experts usually presented ideas for teachers to develop, and administrators either supervised or delegated supervisors to ensure that the ideas were implemented in the classroom.

Saylor, Alexander, and Lewis: Managerial Model

Galen Saylor and his colleagues belong to the managerial school. As former administrators, they were very clear about the lines of authority and the need for supervisors and administrators to be in charge of the curriculum at the state and local district levels, in terms of curriculum guidelines and textbook selection, as well as at the school level, in terms of subjects for study on the basis of grade levels.[20] Saylor saw curriculum as a general plan, through which particular plans for individual programs of studies, courses of study, syllabi, unit plans, policy statements, handbooks, and learning packages were used in different parts of the school and school district by many groups of people and individuals. Curriculum had to be put together or incorporated as a total package, or *curriculum plan,* by those in charge of running the schools.

As Figure 13–2 indicates, a number of considerations enter into the development of curriculum. *Goals and objectives* are largely influenced (1) by external forces such as legal requirements, current research, professional knowledge, interest groups, and state agencies and (2) by the bases of curriculum such as society, learners, and knowledge. (These bases were similar to Tyler's sources, which had originally been elaborated on by Boyd Bode and John Dewey.)

Agreed on goals and objectives then provide a basis for **curriculum design,** that is, a view of teaching and learning. Five different designs are examined: (1) subject matter/disciplines, (2) competencies, (3) human traits and processes, (4) social functions and activities, and (5) individual needs and interests. A subject matter design emphasizes the role of knowledge and problem-solving activities. Specific competencies emphasize performance objectives, task analysis, and measurable outcomes. Human traits and processes are concerned with the learners' feelings, emotions, and values, as well as the affective domain of learning. A design that focuses on social functions and activities emphasizes the needs of society and, to a lesser extent,

[20] J. Galen Saylor, William M. Alexander, and Arthur J. Lewis, *Curriculum Planning for Better Teaching and Learning,* 4th ed. (New York: Holt, Rinehart & Winston, 1981).

the needs of students. The individual needs and interests design is concerned with what is relevant to and motivates learners and what learning experiences lead to their full potential. Depending on the nature of management, the design can be optional and chosen by the classroom teacher, or it can be recommended by a school curriculum committee (administrators, supervisors, and/or teachers) or required by the central school district. School authorities, however, rarely require a particular design because curriculum matters involve teachers as well as possibly students and parents.

Curriculum implementation is mainly concerned with instructional activities that facilitate or put in practice the design. It includes instructional methods, materials, and resources, often listed in courses of study, unit plans, and lesson plans and often observed in classrooms as the teaching and learning process unfolds. Curriculum implementation includes supervision of instruction, teacher-supervisor planning and meetings, as well as staff development programs. The help teachers receive from resource personnel, supervisors, and administrators is the basis of implementation.

Curriculum evaluation involves the procedures for evaluating student outcomes and the curriculum plan. Evaluative data become the basis for decision making and planning among administrators. Administrators rarely engage in this type of evaluation; rather, they often delegate it to supervisors or outside consultants who report their findings to administrators, who in turn have the option of communicating the findings to teachers, parents, or the community.

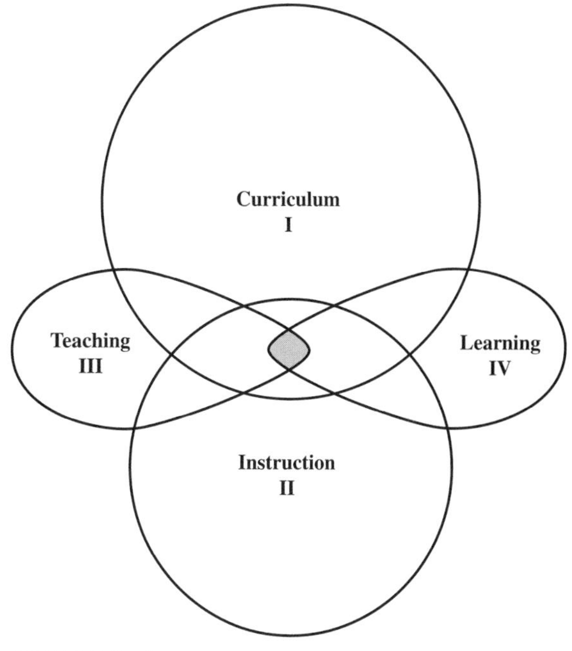

FIGURE 13–3

Systematizing the Curriculum
Source: Adapted from James B. Macdonald, "Educational Models for Instruction," in J. B. Macdonald (ed.), *Theories of Instruction* (Washington, DC: Association for Supervision and Curriculum Development, 1965), p. 5.

Macdonald: Systems Model

Theory development prior to the 1960s tended to separate curriculum and instruction from teaching and learning. The classic model by James Macdonald showed the relationship between these four systems, as illustrated in Figure 13–3. He defined curriculum as a plan *for* instruction as the plan is *put into* action. Teaching was defined as the *broad behavior* of the teacher and learning as the *change* in learner.

Another way of explaining the Macdonald model is the following: *Curriculum* is planning endeavors that take place prior to instruction; *instruction* deals with teacher-student interaction (usually taking place in the classroom, library, or laboratory); *teaching* is the act of presenting stimuli or cues; and *learning* involves student responses. When appropriate instruction and teaching take place, desired responses will occur. When instruction or teaching is inappropriate, dysfunctional or unintended responses will take place.

Most curriculum leaders today agree with the Macdonald model: Curriculum is viewed as planning; instruction is seen as implementation; teaching involves behavior, methods, and/or pedagogy; and learning connotes desired responses or student actions. Macdonald's view was easy to understand, a reason for the classic status of the model, and it helped show the relationship among the four systems. Breaking from the previous generation of linear models by interrelating his systems, Macdonald contended that curriculum was the heart of the educational enterprise (note that it represents the largest component in his system, as per Figure 13–3) in part because everything that followed was based on this plan and in part because he was a curriculum theorist—not a professor of pedagogy or philosophy. Had he been a professor of educational psychology, Macdonald probably would have seen teaching and learning as the most important

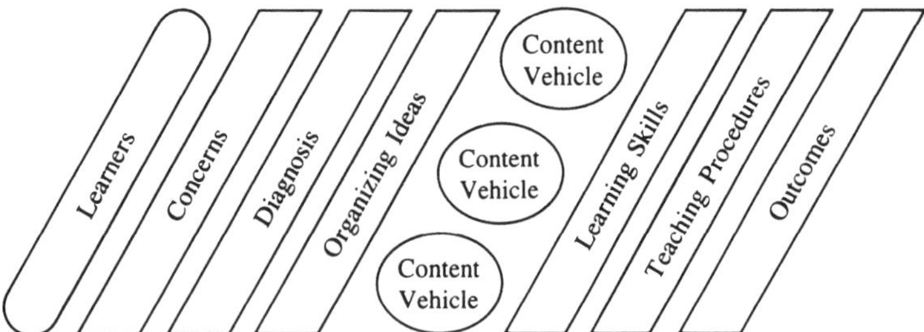

FIGURE 13–4

Curriculum of Affect
Source: Gerald Weinstein and Mario D. Fantini, *Toward Humanistic Education,* p. 35. Copyright © 1970 by the Ford Foundation.

component. Similarly, had he been a professor of supervision or administration, he might have viewed supervision (or supervision of instruction) as more important than curriculum, or curriculum as a subcomponent or one aspect of the larger field of educational leadership. Indeed, a person's professional background and knowledge base determines his or her view of what is essential or secondary in education, what is a macrosystem and a microsystem.

Weinstein and Fantini: Humanistic Model

Gerald Weinstein and Mario Fantini link sociopsychological factors with cognition so learners can deal with their problems and concerns. For this reason, these authors consider their model a "curriculum of affect." In viewing the model, some readers might consider it part of the behavioral or managerial approach, but the model shifts from a deductive organization of curriculum to an inductive orientation and from traditional content to relevant content.[21]

The first step, shown in Figure 13–4, is to identify the *learners,* their age, grade level, and common cultural and ethnic characteristics. Weinstein and Fantini are concerned with the group, as opposed to individuals, because most students are taught in groups. Therefore, knowledge of common characteristics and interests is considered prerequisite to differentiating and diagnosing individual problems.

In the second step, the school determines the learners' *concerns* and assesses the reasons for these concerns. Student concerns include the needs and interests of the learners, self-concept, and self-image. Because concerns center on broad and persistent issues, they give the curriculum some consistency over time. Through *diagnosis,* the teacher attempts to develop strategies for instruction to meet learners' concerns. Emphasis is on how students can gain greater control over their lives and feel more at ease with themselves. In *organizing ideas,* the next step, the teacher should select themes and topics around learners' concerns rather than on the demands of subject matter. The concepts and skills to be taught should help the learners cope with their concerns.

The *content* is organized around three major principles, or what Weinstein and Fantini call *vehicles:* life experiences of the learners, attitudes and feelings of the learners, and the social context in which they live. These three types of content influence the concepts, skills, and values that are taught in the classroom, and they form the basis of the "curriculum of affect."

According to the authors, *learning skills* include the basic skill of learning how to learn which in turn increases learners' coping activity and power over their environment. Learning skills also help students deal with the content vehicles and problem solve in different subject areas. Self-awareness skills and personal skills are recommended, too, to help students deal with their own feelings and how they relate to other people.

Teaching procedures are developed for learning skills, content vehicles, and organizing ideas. Teaching procedures should match the learning styles of students, which in turn are partially based on their common characteristics and concerns (the first two steps). In the last step, the teacher evaluates the *outcomes* of the curriculum: cognitive and affective objectives. This evaluation component is similar to the evaluation components of the previous models (Tyler and Saylor); however, there is more emphasis on the needs, interests, and self-concept of learners—that is, affective outcomes.

[21]Gerald Weinstein and Mario D. Fantini, *Toward Humanistic Education* (New York: Praeger, 1970).

Scientific-Aesthetic Model

Elliot Eisner combines scientific and behavioral principles with aesthetic components to form a curriculum planning model. It is more rational and measurable than one might expect from Eisner who tends to stress artistic and qualitative forms of education. His model comprises four major areas of planning: (1) aims and objectives, (2) curriculum planning, (3) teaching, and (4) evaluation. Each contains numerous categories, as shown in Figure 13–5.

Aims and Objectives (Category 1) include (a) behavioral objectives that can be easily observed and measured; (b) problem-solving objectives that involve broader concepts and various forms and solutions that cannot be easily measured; and (c) expressive outcomes—that is, results or qualities (intended or unintended, attitudinal or artistic) that are not always rational, predictable, or easy to measure.

Curriculum Planning (Category 2) includes the input and influence of the (a) federal and (b) state agencies, which provide direction, policies, and money; (c) the school district, which appoints curriculum committees and personnel for planning content and developing materials; (d) the teacher's role in planning, such as choosing topics, textbooks, and other materials to meet objectives; (e) research centers, which develop materials, methods, and pilot programs; (f) commercial publishers, which provide textbooks, materials, and (if the authors may add) tests; and (g) curriculum developers, groups, and professional associations, which prescribe content in particular subject areas.

Teaching (Category 3) involves (a) the art of teaching as expressive and qualitative forms and behaviors; (b) the difference between teaching and instruction, the latter of which is more technical and controls content and classroom activities; and (c) the difference between teaching and curriculum—in simple Eisner terms, "curriculum is the content that is taught and teaching is how the content is taught."

Evaluation (Category 4) is divided into five areas: (a) diagnose student learning and prescribe treatment; (b) revise, that is, modify and/or improve the curriculum; (c) compare programs to determine which is more effective for specific students; (d) identify education needs by employing interviews, questionnaires, and tests in order to justify programs and content; and (e) determine if objectives have been achieved—to what extent and whether revisions are needed, or possibly new objectives are needed.

While Eisner touches on the role of the artist in curriculum and teaching, it is important to note there is little discussion today on the contributions of the artist, musician and filmmaker in shaping curriculum, despite the fact that the media plays such an important role in shaping society worldwide. Artists are expected to inspire people and challenge public thinking, but their role is often underrated and undervalued in schools, especially with regard to curriculum making. Reading, math, and science take preference, partially due to the emphasis on high-stake testing, the traditional notion that reading is the key to academic success, and the current notion that math and science are essential for a high-tech and innovative society.

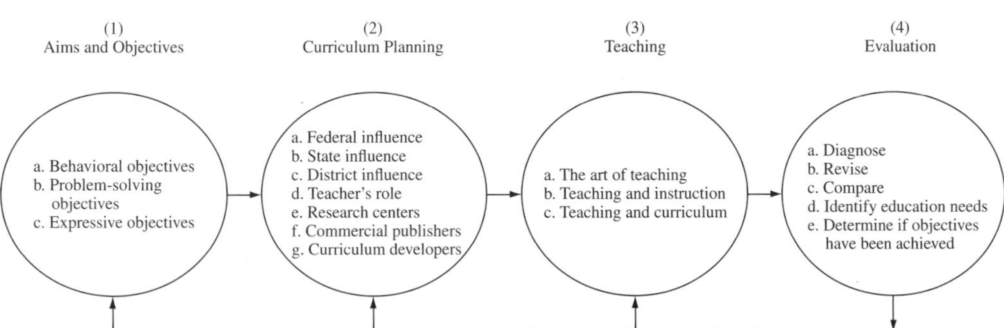

FIGURE 13–5

Eisner's Curriculum Planning Model
Source: Adapted from Elliot W. Eisner, *The Educational Imagination,* 3rd ed. (Columbus, OH: Merril, 2002), chs. 6–7, 9–10. Diagram and sequencing have been interpreted by the authors.

Curriculum Overview

Figure 13–6 presents an overview of the procedures and steps to consider for planning, developing, and evaluating the curriculum. The model is based on a behavioral/managerial model, rooted in the Tyler-Taba (behavioral) and Saylor-Alexander (managerial) approaches.

Overall, the model reflects a *traditional* approach because decisions and actions take place within a formal organization that has a prescribed and expected way of doing things. In joining the school (or school district), participants accept an authority relationship and understand certain roles, limits, and expectations of behavior,

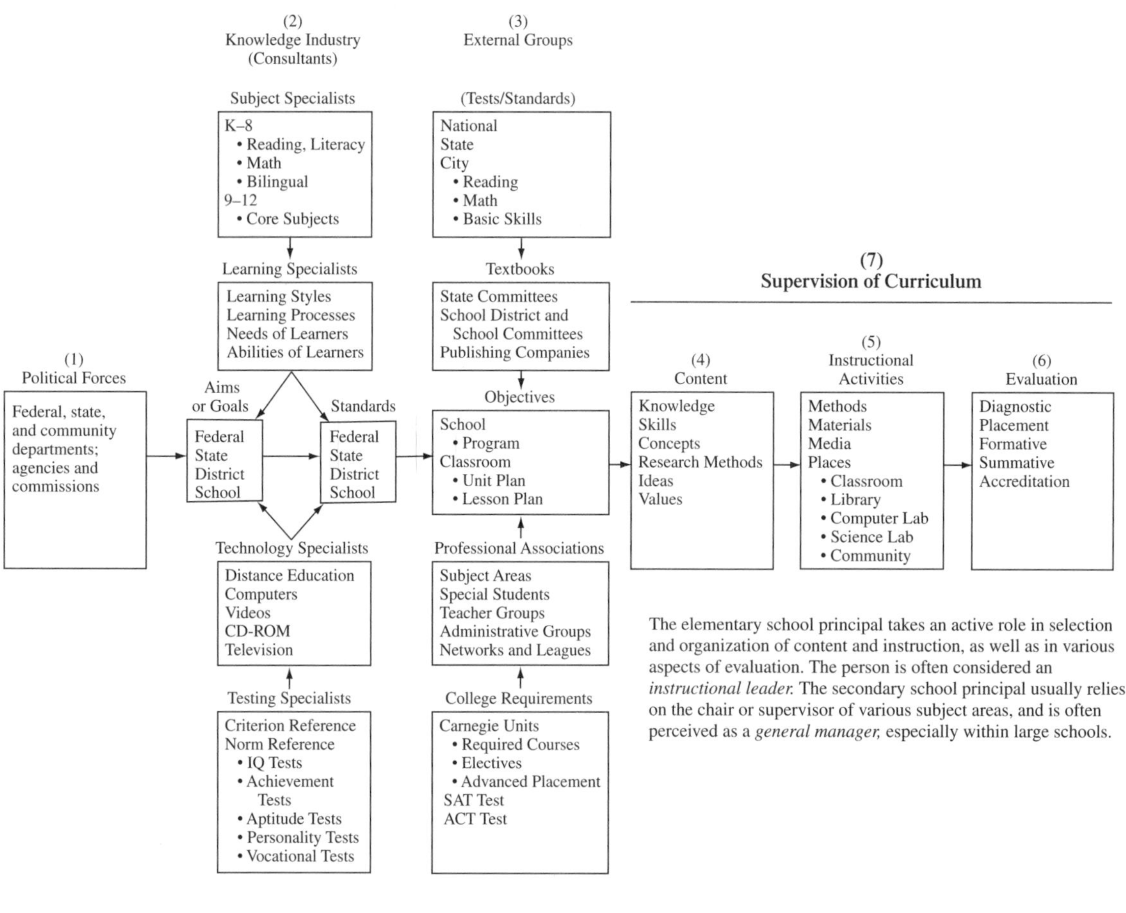

FIGURE 13–6

Planning and Developing the Curriculum
Source: Allan C. Ornstein, "Curriculum Planning and Development," in Fred Lunenburg and Allan Ornstein, *Educational Administration: Concepts and Practices,* 4th ed. (Belmont, CA: Wadsworth, 2004). Copyright © by Allan Ornstein, 2003. Revised by Allan Ornstein, 2007, 2011.

and certain policies and procedures for communication, collegiality, and change (the three Cs).

As part of *curriculum planning,* the political forces (category 1) are considered, the situation as it "really is"—or, more precisely, as it appears to the participants. National, state, and local issues and opinion in general will reflect in the aims, goals,[22] and objectives of the curriculum, but they will change over time. Standards are expressed at the federal and state level—and imposed on the local or district/school level. Specialists, consultants, and experts can provide knowledge or expertise (category 2) for modifying the school district's or school's goals and objectives. These people will most likely be subject, learning, technological, or testing specialists. In determining what to teach, external groups (category 3) play a major role in influencing curriculum participants, organizational norms and policies, and criteria for the selection of content. Major external groups are from the testing industry, textbook companies, professional associations, and colleges. The connection between the external forces and individual participants is virtually "one way"; that is, external groups influence participants' decisions and actions, but the reverse influence is almost nonexistent or slight. Viewed as "experts," those involved in determining the content of tests (and now standards), the content of textbooks, college requirements (or Carnegie units), and/or establishing standards and policies of professional associations transmit, from one generation to the next, many of the major ideas of objectives and subsequent content.

"Experts" from external groups may see the world quite differently than teachers and principals, but the latter have little influence in determining the content domain (category 4); basically, their job is to implement the curriculum. *Curriculum implementation* involves the what and how of curriculum. The content is the *what,* sometimes called the heart of the curriculum, and the instructional activities represent the *how.* Content is divided into knowledge, skills, concepts, research methods, ideas, and values. (Knowledge and skills have been delineated elsewhere by Adler, Taba, and Tyler; concepts and relationships are best represented by the theories of Bruner, Dewey, and Ausubel; research methods are expressed by Bruner, Dewey, and Tyler; ideas are described by Adler, Bruner, and Taba; and values are delineated by Adler, Dewey, and Tyler).

[22]Aims and goals are sometimes used interchangeably at the federal and state level. Ralph Tyler also used them interchangeably, in his book *Basic Principles of Curriculum and Instruction,* referring to them as "purposes."

Instructional activities (category 5)—methods, materials and media—usually take place in the classroom (although they can take place in the local and larger community) and represent the processes through which the teacher delivers the content. Activities are part of the implementation process. Although most activities are well entrenched by tradition, different methods, materials, and media evolve and replace traditional modes of instruction. The tension between traditional and progressive ideas of education is clearly depicted in Dewey's compact book, *Education and Experience* (1938). The term *instructional activities* (category 5) closely resembles what Dewey called "techniques and practices," what Kilpatrick called "purposeful methods," what Taba and Tyler referred to as "experiences," and what Bruner termed "processes." In short, instruction deals with ways in which content (subject matter) is taught by the teacher and learned by the student—that is the *how* of implementation.

Curriculum evaluation provides information for the purpose of making judgments and decisions about students, teachers, and programs—or whether to postpone, modify, continue, or maintain the curriculum. Such decisions can be made at the classroom, school, and school district level. The role of the curriculum leader—resource teacher, program director, supervisor or chair, principal or superintendent in charge of curriculum—is crucial at this stage. The person in charge, the curriculum leader, provides direction, oversees content and instruction, and then based on some form of evaluation makes recommendations and decisions for maintaining, improving, or terminating the program. Five purposes and forms of evaluation (category 6) are listed: diagnosing problems; placement of students; formative, that is, during the implementation stage; summative, or at the end of the program; and accreditation, the whole program is assessed.

Finally, curriculum leaders at the school level include program directors, coordinators, chairs, and principals. They are responsible for overseeing curriculum, instruction, and evaluation. In Figure 13–6, this is represented by the term *supervision of curriculum* (category 7). At the district level, the curriculum leader is usually called a director or an assistant or associate superintendent.

Nontechnical Model

The danger in noting that one model is systematic, rational, or technical and another is nonsystematic, irrational, or nontechnical is that the latter will be considered as fluff, watered down, or disorderly by most administrators, who rely on an orderly and rational world. Advocates of the latter model take issue with the assumption and consequences of traditional models. They reject the high degree of objectivity, order, and logic; they also reject the assumption that reality can be defined and represented by symbolic forms—by boxes, arrows, or graphs. Finally, they feel that aims and goals of education cannot always be known in advance, stated precisely, or addressed in a linear or step-by-step approach.

It may not make practical sense for administrators who need to plan and who have only so much time in the day, but the world is much more complex, involving subjective, personal, aesthetic, heuristic, transactional, and intuitive forms of thinking and behavior. The argument is that curriculum cannot be precisely planned—it evolves as a living organism as opposed to a machine which is precise and orderly.

Common among advocates of the **nontechnical model,** sometimes called naturalistics, conversationalists, critical pedagogists, and postpositivists, is the belief that the focus should be on the student, not the content or subject matter. Subject matter has importance only to the degree that students can find meaning in it for themselves. Subject matter should provide opportunities for reflection and personal growth.[23]

In contrast to the majority of teachers and administrators who consider curriculum as a plan, blueprint, or product—consisting of a series of rational steps and outcomes—people in the nontechnical camp often view curriculum more as a drama or conversation. People don't develop conversation or plan it; they create opportunities for it to evolve. If we accept that curriculum involves conversation, then it makes sense to reflect on the social, political, and moral thoughts and voices involved in curriculum making. Such consideration brings into focus concepts that are ignored in technical approaches, such as ideology, values, beliefs, and power. Communication, collegiality, and consensus are necessary processes or social activities to consider. Creating curricula through conversation relies on dialogue, debate, and deliberation—the ebb and flow of ideas and ideology.

The contemporary, nontraditional paradigm of curriculum questions the scientific paradigm of sound logical thought that rests on Newtonian logic. In a theoretical sense, these nontraditional people advocate that we detach ourselves from rational or scientific models of accepted procedures that follow preestablished rules. They suggest that our actions in creating curricula cannot be judged according to predetermined criteria, generalized findings, or rational or empirical judgment; moreover, what appears objective or rational is frequently selective, incomplete, or reflective of a political agenda.[24]

According to this model, old criteria cannot be used to critique new curricula. It challenges the technical rationality of viewing the world as a machine that we can study, observe, and objectively evaluate as bystanders. It questions assumptions about facts as well as about cause and effect. The data we obtain through tests and evaluative procedures are also questioned. In short, all the old assumptions about curriculum development that administrators rely on are challenged by many who call themselves postmodern thinkers.

Nontechnical contemporary educators believe that curriculum making represents an uncertain system and an uncertain set of procedures. People like James Macdonald, Elliot Eisner, Peter McLaren, and William Pinar argue that aesthetic rationality and artistic forms complement our technical rationality. What we are asked to do as education leaders is to transform images and aspirations about education into curriculum programs.[25]

The nontechnical process evolves in an open, unexpected, free-flowing way. It even permits chaos to occur so that some unplanned system may result. In the same vein, artistry is considered a special way of knowing and constructing reality. Reality, according to Peter Senge, exists in circles and is constructed of overlapping and interacting systems, not neat little boxes or flowcharts. Reality involves circularity, confusion, and interrelatedness of

[23]Gary D. Fenstermacher, et al. *Approaches to Teaching,* rev. ed. (New York: Teachers College Press Columbia University, 2009); Herbert Kohl, *Beyond the Silence* (Westport, CT: Heinemann, 1998); Nel Noddings, *The Challenge to Care,* 2nd ed. (New York: Teachers College Press, Columbia University, 2005).

[24]Tom Barone, "Science, Art, and the Predispositions of Educational Researchers," *Educational Researcher,* 30 (2001): 24–28; Gerald W. Bracey, "How to Avoid Statistical Traps," *Phi Delta Kappan,* 63 (2006): 78–82; Elliot Eisner, "Back to Whole," *Educational Leadership,* 63 (2005): 14–19; and William A. Reid, "Reconceptualist and Dominant Perspectives in Curriculum Theory," *Journal of Curriculum and Supervision,* 13 (1998): 287–298.

[25]Elliot W. Eisner, *The Kind of School We Need* (Westport, CT: Heinemann, 1998); Peter McLaren, *Life in Schools,* 5th ed. (Boston: Allyn and Bacon, 2007); William F. Pinar, *Contemporary Curriculum Discourses* (New York: Peter Lang, 1999).

EXEMPLARY EDUCATIONAL ADMINISTRATORS IN ACTION

LONNIE E. PALMER Superintendent, City School District of Albany, New York.

Words of Advice: One current trend in education is to test students extensively and to use these results to drive decision making. While the analytical part of my background agrees that such an approach will provide the best research for measured, productive, positive change, I'm also concerned that in the process we'll lose what truly makes learning a lifelong, exciting quest for knowledge and opportunity. The assumption that somehow we can teacher-proof the curriculum with research-tested, instructional methods and thereby help children from poverty to achieve test success, ignores some basic facts.

Teaching is as much an art as a science. And while the science can help us with strategies and tactics to overcome the obstacles that children face as they learn, nothing can replace the love of learning, the love of children, and the understanding of those factors in children's backgrounds that inhibit their success.

While the pendulum swings far to the right with federal No Child Left Behind policies and programs and New York State–mandated testing and prescriptive academic intervention services, little attention is being paid to the hearts, souls, and values of those entering the education profession. Educators must not only be smarter, more attuned to research and data, and cognizant of the best research-based strategies for student learning; they must also care deeply for their students, their parents, and their communities.

decisions and actions.[26] Goals (objectives) and outcomes (products) are no longer perceived so much as ends but as beginnings, a view advocated by Dewey that is now part of the new literature on change and curriculum reform. Of course, all this new dialogue is hard to sell to a school principal or superintendent who is responsible for meeting goals and achieving certain products and must deal with social, political, and educational reality—high-stake tests, state standards, and students who are entering the workforce or applying to college.

The nontechnical model maintains that curriculum specialists have lost their visionary, moral, and social purposes, their sense of reform and innovation. This argument dates back to George Counts, in his famous speech to the Progressive Education Association published a year later under the title *Dare the Schools Build a New Social Order?*[27] Actually, Joseph Schwab's concern with theory and practice represents a benchmark or transition period between the traditional and new models. An advocate of scientific methods and rational planning, a person who appreciated the need for technical experts, Schwab also had a clear moral vision of schooling, an awareness of social and cultural forces influencing curriculum, and a concern for relations of people involved in curriculum making. He argued that "the field of curriculum [had become] moribund,"[28] that it had ceased to flourish and offer anything new, and that it needed to be "resurrected to include alternative perspectives and systems as viable solutions to varying problems."[29] This rejection of the traditional curriculum by a traditionalist, and the need to revise or remake the curriculum in terms of alternative ways, is a prelude to the nontechnical interpretation of the field of curriculum today.[30]

A wider conception of curriculum—nontechnical and more philosophical, personal, and interesting methods—includes numerous theories and ideas that are artistic and aesthetic (Elliot Eisner), gay (James Sears) and feminist (Madeline Grumet), pluralistic and diverse (James Banks), political/social (Henry Giroux and Peter McLaren), moral/ethical (William Reid), visionary and imaginative (Maxine Greene), and even spiritual (William Pinar). These new theories and ideas represent a rejection of traditional curriculum planning,

[26]Peter M. Senge, *The Fifth Discipline* (New York: Doubleday, 1990).

[27]George S. Counts, *Dare the Schools Build a New Social Order?* (New York: John Day, 1932).

[28]Joseph J. Schwab, "Education and the State: Learning Community," in R. M. Hutchins and M. J. Adler (eds.), *The Great Ideas Today* (Chicago: Encyclopedia Britannica, 1976), p. 238.

[29]Ibid, p. 271.

[30]See William F. Pinar (ed.), *Contemporary Curriculum Discourses* (New York: Peter Lang, 1999); William A. Reid, "Rethinking Schwab: Curriculum Theorizing as a Visionary Activity," *Journal of Curriculum and Supervision,* 17 (2001): 29–41; Leonard J. Waks, "Reid's Theory of Curriculum as Institutionalized Practice," *Journal of Curriculum Studies,* 32 (2000): 589–598.

a rethinking of curriculum, but not necessarily a "practical" interpretation (a term used by Schwab and later Reid) that assists teachers and curriculum leaders (directors, chairs, supervisors, principals, etc.) in the organization and operation of classrooms and schools. Although some of these new concepts may be considered dysfunctional and divisive, as well as impractical for practitioners, among theorists and academics they are considered relevant—or at least interesting. Much of the new "new" curriculum is considered more speculative, expressive, emotional, argumentative, and political—based on heated controversy and crisis, far different from the rational, logical, behaviorist, and technocratic ideas that have characterized mainstream curriculum making.

Components of Curriculum Development

Curriculum leaders must always be concerned with *what* should be included and *how* to present or arrange what is selected. In other words, they must first deal with content or subject matter and then learning experiences. Regardless of the curriculum approach or development model used, curriculum leaders cannot ignore these two components.

Groups charged with curriculum planning have options in selection of **content and experiences**—to be determined in part by the philosophical and psychological views of the committee members and school. Unquestionably, there are too much content and too many learning experiences to include, and committee members (or those in charge of curriculum) must decide what content and experiences to include.

Criteria for Selecting Content

Curriculum planners should apply criteria in choosing curriculum content. Although the following criteria are neutral and can fit into any curriculum approach or model, various philosophical camps might place greater emphasis on particular criteria. For example, Hilda Taba, in a classic text on curriculum, maintains that content should include the following functions.

1. *Four Levels of Knowledge.* These include specific facts, skills, and processes; basic ideas such as generalizations, principles, and causal relationships within the subject matter; concepts dealing with abstract ideas, complex systems, multiple causations, and interdependence; and thought systems or methods of problem solving, inquiry, and discovery.
2. *New Fundamentals to Master.* The content in many subjects becomes increasingly obsolete, especially in light of the explosion of knowledge. The curriculum must be periodically updated to include new content to be learned.
3. *Scope.* Scope is the breadth, depth, and variety of the content and includes the coverage of boundaries of the subject.
4. *Sequence.* By sequencing, there is recognition of and need for differentiating levels of knowledge, that learning is based on prior knowledge, and that the curriculum should be cumulative and continuous.[31]
5. *Integration.* Integration emphasizes the relationships among various content themes, topics, or units; it helps explain how content in one subject is related to content in another subject.[32]

A more recent text established seven additional criteria to consider when selecting and organizing content. Whereas Taba stresses cognitive learning theory for her five criteria, these seven combine cognitive and humanistic psychology:

1. *Self-Sufficiency.* A guiding principle for content selection is that it helps learners attain learning skills and self-sufficiency in learning (economy of the teacher's effort and time in instruction and economy of students' efforts and time in learning).
2. *Significance.* Content should contribute to learning particular concepts, skills, or values; it should be significant in terms of what knowledge needs to be transmitted to students.
3. *Validity.* As new knowledge is discovered, old knowledge that is less relevant, misleading, or incorrect must be pruned. Only relevant and accurate knowledge should be a part of the curriculum content. The content should also be sound in relation to stated goals and objectives.

---

[31]This concept is similar to Jerome Bruner's idea of a "spiral curriculum". Previous learning is the basis of subsequent learning; learning should be continuous, and the content (or subject matter) is built on a foundation (from grade to grade).

[32]Hilda Taba, *Curriculum Development: Theory and Practice* (New York: Harcourt, Brace & World, 1962).

4. *Interest.* Content is easier to learn when it is meaningful. The interest criterion is a progressive concept, but all content should be selected in part on the basis of students' interests.
5. *Utility.* Content should be useful in and out of school. What is considered useful will also reflect philosophy.
6. *Learnability.* The content must be within the experiences and understanding of the learner; content should be selected and arranged on the basis that it makes learning easy, at least less difficult, for students.
7. *Feasibility.* The content must be considered in terms of time allotted, personnel and resources available, and sometimes existing legislation, political climate, and money. Although some educators may like to think that they have an entire world of content from which to choose, they do have limitations on their actions. (Consider content related to sex education, race relations, morality, and religion, for starters.)[33]

Criteria for Selecting Learning Experiences

Tyler, in his classic text on curriculum, outlined five general principles in selecting learning experiences. These experiences can take place in the classroom, outside the classroom (say, in the schoolyard, auditorium, or laboratory), or outside the school (on a field trip, in the library or a museum, etc.).

1. *Learners Must Have Experiences That Give Them Opportunity to Practice the Behavior(s) Implied by the Objective(s).* If the objective is to develop problem-solving skills, then students must have ample opportunity to solve problems. In other words, there must be experiences for students to practice what they are required to learn.
2. *Students Must Obtain Satisfaction in Carrying Out or Performing the Learning Experiences.* Students need satisfying experiences to develop and maintain interest in learning; unsatisfying experiences hinder learning.
3. *Learning Experiences Must Be Appropriate to the Student's Present Attainments.* This basically means that the teacher must begin where the student is and that prior knowledge is the starting point in learning new knowledge.
4. *Several Experiences Can Attain the Same Objective.* There are many ways for learning the same thing; as long as they are effective and meaningful, a wide range of experiences is better for learning than a limited range. Capitalize on the various interests of students.
5. *The Same Learning Experience Usually Results in Several Outcomes.* While students are acquiring knowledge of one subject or idea, they often develop ideas and attitudes in other subjects and certain attitudes toward the original subject.[34]

More recently, the criteria for selecting experiences have been stated in the form of a question: Will the learning experience do what we wish it to do in light of the overall aims and goals of the program and specific objectives of the curriculum? The following are specific extensions of this questions. Are the experiences

1. Valid in light of the ways in which knowledge and skills will be applied in out-of-school situations?
2. Feasible in terms of time, staff expertise, facilities available within and outside of the school, and community expectations?
3. Optimal in terms of students' learning the content?
4. Capable of allowing students to develop their thinking and problem-solving skills?
5. Capable of stimulating in students greater understanding of their own existence as individuals and as members of groups?
6. Capable of fostering an openness to new experiences and a tolerance for diversity?
7. Such that they will facilitate learning and motivate students to continue learning?
8. Capable of allowing students to address their needs?
9. Such that students can broaden their interests?
10. Such that they will foster the total development of students in cognitive, affective, psychomotor, social, and spiritual domains?[35]

---

[33]Ornstein and Hunkins, *Curriculum: Foundations, Principles, and Issues;* Allan C. Ornstein and Richard Sinatra, *K-8 Instructional Methods* (Boston: Allyn and Bacon, 2005).

[34]Tyler, *Basic Principles of Curriculum and Instruction.*

[35]Ronald C. Doll, *Curriculum Improvement: Decision Making and Process,* 9th ed. (Needham Heights, MA: Allyn and Bacon, 1996).

What educators need to remember is that content and experiences are interrelated. If students are engaged in some experience in classrooms, such as reading a book, they are combining that experience with content. Students cannot engage in learning without experiencing some activity and content. Likewise, students cannot deal with content without being engaged in some experience or some activity. Content and experience comprise curriculum unity.

The story of curriculum, according to this view, is a "grand narrative" or "collective story" that forms the framework for structuring knowledge. The curriculum that evolves in the classroom and school is based on lived *experiences* and an arrangement of subject matter or *content*. It filters through a cultural and contextual lens that is acceptable to the norms and institutions of society and helps us understand our place in society.[36]

Balance in Determining the Curriculum

The need for a **balanced curriculum** with appropriate emphasis on content and experiences to ensure a proper weight and broad range to each aspect of the curriculum is obvious, but not easy to achieve given competing philosophies, ideologies, and views of teaching and learning. John Goodlad maintains that the curriculum should be balanced in terms of subject matter and learner; however, he comments that "the interested observer has little difficulty finding school practices emphasizing one component to the impoverishment of the other." He further points out that balance needs to be incorporated into the curriculum to "impose floors and ceilings," a proper range of required knowledge, skills, concepts, and learning experiences that considers the "interests, abilities, and backgrounds" of students,[37] as well as the educational space and environment. (See Administrative Advice 13–2.)

For Doll, a balanced curriculum fits the learner in terms of educational needs, abilities, and growth pertaining to the learner's development. Within the classroom and school, the student should receive content and experiences of two sorts: those suitable for the whole group and those specifically designed for the individual student—his or her personal needs and abilities.[38] This is easier said than done, since it takes a highly effective teacher to meet the needs, abilities, and interests of the whole group while serving the needs, abilities, and interests of individuals. It is much easier to teach toward the average, some "mystical mean"; sadly, high-achieving students are often bored, and low-achieving students are often frustrated as the teacher teaches toward the "average" student in the class.

Adding to the complexity of attaining balance in the curriculum is that what might be considered balanced today might be considered imbalanced tomorrow. What might be considered balanced in one school district might not be considered balanced in an adjacent school district. The times in which schools find themselves are always changing. As we strive for balanced content and experiences, we must always consider the pulls and tugs of traditional and contemporary philosophies, conservative and liberal politics, and changing state standards. It behooves curriculum leaders to consider the elements of balance—the mix of philosophy and politics, as well as the various schools of thought on teaching and learning—in developing curriculum. The question arises, what should be an appropriate emphasis? To be sure, the concept of balance invokes several competing forces and variables, and a great deal of controversy in some schools and very little controversy in other schools. On a practical level, supervisors and administrators need to compromise on differences and reach consensus on the following program concerns, philosophical and social issues, and moral questions:

1. Needs of society vs. learner
2. Excellence vs. equality
3. Standard-based vs. individualized education
4. Cognitive, affective, psychomotor, and moral domains of learning
5. Behavioral vs. nonbehavioral objectives
6. Technological/computerized vs. humanistic/artistic focus
7. Subject-centered vs. student-centered curriculum
8. General vs. specialized content
9. Breadth vs. depth in content

[36]Maxine Greene, "Curriculum and Consciousness," in D. Flinders and S. J. Thornton, eds. *The Curriculum Studies Reader,* 2nd ed. New York: Routledge, 2004); Angelina Weenie, "Curricular Theorizing From the Periphery," *Curriculum Inquiry* 38 (2008); 545–557.

[37]John I. Goodlad, *Planning and Organizing for Teaching* (Washington, DC: National Education Association, 1963), p. 29.

[38]Doll, *Curriculum Improvement: Decision Making and Process.*

ADMINISTRATIVE ADVICE 13–2

Dealing with the Physical and Health Factors of the Environment

Until recently curriculum leaders did not give much attention to the curriculum environment. One way of viewing this environment is to look at the physical and health factors that affect student learning. The factors considered below represent a "nuts and bolts" view, typical of a supervisor or practitioner who deals in the real world of classrooms and schools as opposed to the theoretical world.

- **Arrangements.** Identify the activities that will take place and the best way to combine or arrange the physical layout or setting. Different configurations must be evaluated on the basis of how they will accommodate lectures, demonstrations, experiments, etc. Other factors include storage space, electrical/telephone outlets, teacher work space, student learning space (open/closed) and grouping patterns (whole group, small group, and independent learning) or spaces.
- **Floors, Ceilings, Windows.** Consider carpeting versus tile in terms of cost, durability, and esthetics. Electrostatic charges are important, too, in terms of human sensitivity and technical equipment (especially computers). Ceiling materials and window treatments affect acoustics and lighting.
- **Temperature.** The research data suggest that students learn best when the temperature is 70° to 74° Fahrenheit, since they are seated and somewhat inactive in most classroom situations. They also learn best when the relative humidity is between 40 and 60 percent.
- **Electrical.** Electrical wires should run parallel to the walls, and when they run across floors they should be taped down to prevent accidents. Equipment and adapter plugs should be stored when not in use, and in no one's way when in use. There should be more than one circuit in a classroom to guard against possible line failure, and surge suppressers need to be installed in schools/classrooms that cannot risk data loss in the event of a power surge.
- **Lighting.** In most cases windows are suitable for providing adequate light, coupled with the standard fluorescent lighting to save money. In small learning areas, recessed lighting is more effective than fluorescent light.
- **Acoustics.** Room noise can be a problem, especially when students are active or involved in an open classroom setting and are permitted to talk or engage in multiple activities at the same time. Neutralizing noise with appropriate floor, ceiling, and window treatments are basic considerations; some schools are experimenting with soft background music, and in other schools special window panes have been installed to reduce outside noise.
- **Security.** Physical security is a consideration in entryways, hallways, and schoolyards, especially in terms of unwarranted intruders. It is also a factor when storing office and instructional equipment, as well as with student lockers and teacher closets. Schools are increasingly installing special locks and bolts, steel plates with locking cables, electronic trackers, closed circuit television, and alarm systems connected to police departments.
- **Dust.** Elimination of dust has always been a concern. When remodeling or designing a new school, all chalkboards should be replaced with dry marker boards. Special consideration should also be given to paper and disk storage.
- **Safety.** To protect students (or teachers) from injury and the school from liability, the smart administrator learns to identify and eliminate as many hazards as possible. Science labs, gyms, cafeterias, and schoolyards are major places where accidents take place, but injuries also occur in classrooms, hallways, and auditoriums.

Source: Allan C. Ornstein, "Components of Curriculum Development," *Illinois School Research and Development*, 26 (1990): 208–209. Used by permission.

10. Content vs. process
11. Essential (core) knowledge vs. abstract (problem-solving) methods
12. Traditional vs. progressive ideas (and authors)
13. National vs. global (Western vs. non-Western and Industrialized vs. Emerging Notions) history and culture
14. Academic, business, vocational, and technical tracks
15. Gifted, talented, average, and slow learners

16. Advanced placement, required, and elective subjects
17. Whole language vs. phonetics
18. Classroom, lab activities vs. community, field-based activities
19. Homogenous vs. heterogeneous grouping
20. Whole-group, small-group, and individualized instruction.

Leadership Considerations

Regardless of how we view the relationship among content, experience, and environment, the center of curriculum development continues to be the local school, which in turn is related to the abilities and performance of the school principal and her assistants. The key to curriculum leadership is not the school superintendent, who should be more concerned about political and managerial decisions; it is the school principal.

The problem is, however, that many school superintendents are not clear about delegating authority over curriculum matters to the school principal. The superintendent is usually much clearer about delegating responsibility at the centralized level—say, to the business manager or director of public information—than about delegating it to the principal. In these cases, it seems that the superintendent is more concerned about business or community affairs—that is, how the school district appears—than curriculum for students the district serves.

Another problem seems to involve a conflict between local school personnel (teachers, chairpersons, and principals) and supervisors from the central office—and that the latter sometimes bypass or ignore the prerogatives of curriculum leaders in their own schools. On the other hand, principals who are zealots are sometimes known to operate their schools as little fiefdoms or empires, ignoring the advice and help of the supervisors from the central office. Certainly, the roles and responsibilities of the various school personnel, as they relate to curriculum matters, need to be clear to avoid conflict.

In large school districts (50,000 or more students), the central office usually houses a curriculum department whose responsibility is to develop curriculum materials and guides while minimizing the role of the teacher and school principal. Curriculum development is centralized and usually rubber-stamped at the school level; what ideas people have at the local level are passed upward but often lost in the paper shuffle at the centralized level.

In small school districts, however, teachers, principals, and even parents are expected to spend substantial time and effort in curriculum making. Under the leadership of the principal, schools are often expected to develop mission statements, a clear understanding of what constitutes learning, the content and experiences to be included in the curriculum, how the curriculum is to be implemented and evaluated, and how the community is to be included.[39] Many teachers and principals become involved in curriculum development as a matter of professional routine; but they are rarely, if ever, paid for their time after 3 P.M.

Differences also exist between elementary and secondary school principals. Most elementary principals devote more time to curriculum and instructional matters than do their secondary counterparts, and they view themselves more often as curriculum or instructional leaders rather than managers. Secondary school principals usually complain they have little time for curriculum and instruction (although they recognize the importance of such matters) and see themselves more often as general managers.[40] Most school principals have been taught to accept some bureaucratic, scientific, or rational model of management, but elementary principals have been forced to throw away their managerial theories and deal with the needs and concerns of the students at the school door, as well as their parents and the community.

Part of the difference is related to school size. Within the same school district, high schools are usually two to four times the size of elementary schools. In high schools that house more than 1000 students (24 percent of U.S. high schools), principals are often engaged with a continual stream of problems that make it difficult for them to leave the office, and they are more concerned about administrative detail and formal structures than with people.[41] Another reason for the difference is that in medium-sized secondary schools (750 to 1000 students) and large secondary schools (1000+ students), there are usually chairpersons responsible for particular

[39]Jeffrey Glanz, *What Every Principal Should Know About School-Community Leadership* (Thousand Oaks, CA: Corwin Press, 2006); Thomas J. Sergiovanni, *The Principalship: A Reflective Practice Perspective,* 6th ed. (Needham Heights, MA: Allyn and Bacon, 2006).

[40]Dale L. Brubaker and Lawrence H. Simon, "How Do Principals View Themselves, Others?" *NASSP Bulletin,* 71 (1987): 72–78; Fenwick W. English, "The Battle for the Principalship," *NASSP Bulletin,* 78 (1994): 18–25; and Frederick M. Hess, "Looking Beyond the Schoolhouse Door," *Phi Delta Kappan,* 87 (2006): 513–514.

[41]Deborah Meier, "As Though They Owned the Place: Small Schools as Membership Communities," *Phi Delta Kappan,* 87 (2006): 657–662; Allan C. Ornstein, "School Size and Effectiveness: Policy Implications," *Urban Review,* 22 (1990): 34–45.

subject areas who plan with teachers and supervise curriculum and instruction. Elementary schools do not have chairpersons as part of their staff, and the focus is on the three Rs (not particular subjects). The principal is supposed to provide the curriculum and instructional leadership in this general area of study.

Some balance is needed. In large school districts, curriculum leaders at the central level should make it easier for school personnel to become involved in curriculum opportunities. In small school districts, teachers involved in curriculum should be paid for their services or relieved from other duties, so they can devote time to curriculum. Without being made to feel guilty, school authorities should recognize that teachers are already performing important responsibilities other than curriculum development and teachers should have the option to reject new responsibilities.

What Knowledge Is of Most Worth?

Some 150 years ago, Herbert Spencer in his famous essay, "What Knowledge Is of Most Worth?" argued that science was the most practical subject for the survival of the individual and society, yet it occupied minimal space in the curriculum because impractical and ignorant traditions prevailed. Spencer also maintained that students should be taught how to think (and problem solve) and not what to think.[42] Spencer's ideas were to influence John Dewey some fifty years later.

Although many of Spencer's ideas about evolution and social progress (less intelligent, lazy, and weak people would slowly disappear, and heredity was the key to intelligence) created a furor—and they still do among observers today—his ideas fit well with many thinkers of the second half of the nineteenth century, a period that was characterized by industrial growth, manifest destiny, and colonial expansion of European countries and the United States.

Spencer's original question about the worth of subject matter is more relevant today because of the increased complexity of society. Actually, the question dates back to ancient Greece, when Plato and Aristotle questioned the value of knowledge in relation to citizenship and government affairs, and to ancient Rome, when Quintilian (influenced by Plato)[43] set forth the seven liberal arts—grammar, rhetoric, logic, arithmetic, geometry, astronomy, and music—as the ideal curriculum for educated citizens of public life: senators, lawyers, teachers, civil servants, and politicians. During the modern school period, these seven liberal arts have expanded to include many other subjects.

One must understand that Greek and Roman education (the latter influenced by the Greeks) cultivated contemplative knowledge, metaphysics, and rationality for the purpose of nurturing the mind, body, and soul. The truly educated person had the power to think, to exercise reason, and to judge moral and ethical behavior. (This separates us from lower animals.) The good life was one of balance and moderation. This interpretation of knowledge and intellectual thought, promoted by Aristotle and Plato, was adopted by the medieval universities and by humanistic philosophers. It is the opposite type of knowledge—concerned with utility, function, vocational education, and relevant education—that is trendy and becomes obsolete in a few years.

Knowledge as Facts

Spencer also advocated a curriculum appropriate for an industrialized and scientific society, characterized by problem solving and specialized professions. But facts, more facts, and still more facts was the ideal method of teaching and learning, keenly expressed by Charles Dickens in his novel *Hard Times*. Mr. Gradgrind, the school patron, demonstrates model teaching for the school-teacher: "Now what I want is Facts. Facts alone are wanted in life. Plant nothing else, and root out everything else, this is the principle on which I bring up children. Stick to the facts, Sir!!"

There is little difference between facts and some aspects of knowledge, but more than one hundred years after the publication of *Hard Times* the issues are still being discussed. In a well-accepted classification of thinking and problem solving by Benjamin Bloom, knowledge was ranked as the lowest form of cognitive learning. However, he pointed out that the acquisition of knowledge is the most common educational objective, that teachers tend to emphasize it in the classroom, and test makers tend to emphasize it on tests.[44] To help clarify Bloom: knowledge by itself has limited value and should be used as a basis or foundation for more advanced thinking, what he calls "problem solving."

---

[42]Herbert Spencer, *Education: Intellectual, Moral, and Physical* (New York, Appleton, 1860).

[43]Plato also advocated several subject areas in his *Republic*, although there was greater emphasis on mastering reading, being involved in gymnastics, and displaying good rules of diet and hygiene.

[44]Benjamin S. Bloom et al., *Taxonomy of Educational Objectives, Handbook I: Cognitive Domain* (New York: McKay, 1956).

Of course, basic knowledge has some practical or functional value, but it only serves as the rudiment of more theoretical or abstract thinking.[45]

Knowledge is often construed as an index of intelligence and level of education attained by a person: Witness the popularity of the "$64,000 Question" and forty years later "Who Wants to Be a Millionaire?" Facts drive the shows, and listeners often comment how "smart" someone is who answers several fact-oriented or knowledge-based questions. The point is, however, that knowledge of facts is of little value if it cannot be used in new situations and for more complex learning; the learner (and teacher) need to make use of knowledge—as a base or tool for the pursuit of higher forms of cognition—often called problem solving by progressive educators (Dewey and Tyler), inquiry-based or discovery learning (Ausubel and Bruner), formal operations (Piaget and Vygotsky), and/or critical thinking (Marzano or Sternberg).

Explosion of Knowledge

Since the 1950s, many educators have continued to call attention to the explosion of knowledge. Every fifteen years or so, our significant knowledge doubles. Although it cannot continue indefinitely to double in the future, the explosion of knowledge—especially in health, science, and technology—makes it important to continuously reappraise and revise existing curricula. "It can be affirmed unequivocally," says Bently Glass, "that the amount of scientific knowledge available at the end of one's life will be almost one hundred times what it was when he was born." Moreover, 95 percent of all scientists who ever lived are alive today.[46]

Although Glass published these remarks more than thirty years ago, they still ring true; in fact, it can be inferred that half of what a graduate engineer or computer specialist studies today will be obsolete in ten years; half the pills dispensed today at your local pharmacist will also be replaced or improved. The authors venture to guess that half or more of what we need to know to function in scientific or technical jobs by the year 2025 is not even known today, by anyone.

The idea that knowledge is increasing exponentially or geometrically obscures the fact that the development of knowledge in many fields—especially science, technology and medicine—is more typically related to "branching"—that is, the creation of several subdivisions or specialties within fields, not just simple growth. Each advance in a particular field has the potential for creating another branch. (In education, one can find some indicators of proliferation of several fields of study or branches, sometimes identified by departments, programs, and core courses or minors), and within each field or branch several specializations of knowledge and job titles.

With this increase of knowledge come new professional journals, papers, and speeches, all adding to the proliferation of knowledge. The almost incredible explosion of knowledge threatens to overwhelm us unless we can find ways to deal with the new and growing wealth of information; new knowledge must be constantly introduced into each field of study while less important material is pruned away. In assessing the ongoing rush of knowledge, Alvin Toffler once asserted that knowledge taught should be related to the future. "Nothing should be included in the required curriculum unless it can be strongly justified in terms of the future. If this means scrapping a substantial part of the formal curriculum, so be it."[47]

The question arises whether teachers are readily keeping up with the explosion of knowledge, at least the knowledge in pedagogy or the content they teach. A harsh portrait of the teacher was made by one of the authors as it relates to change and the explosion of knowledge when he was younger and more feisty: "Had Rip Van Winkle been a teacher and slept for *fifty years* he could return to the classroom and perform relatively well; the chalk, eraser, blackboard, textbook, and pen and paper are still the main tools for most teachers, as they were a half a century ago—or longer. If Mr. Van Winkle's occupation had been related to one of three fields . . . science, technology, and medicine . . . and had he dozed off for five years, he would be unable to function effectively, for his knowledge and skills would be drastically dated."[48]

---

[45]The goal is to encourage advanced thinking—what the Greeks called "contemplation," John Dewey called "rational" and "reflective thinking," what Jerome Bruner and Joseph Schwab called "structure," what Mortimer Adler and Ted Sizer called "ideas," what Jeanne Chall and E. D. Hirsch called "deep understanding," what learning theorists today call "critical thinking" and "high-order thinking," and what the authors simply call old-fashioned, "analysis and problem solving."

[46]Bentley Glass, *The Timely and Timeless* (New York: Basic Books, 1980). Also see Edward Teller, *A Twentieth-Century Journey in Science and Politics* (Cambridge, MA: Perseus Press, 2001). Cornering scientific knowledge, not sharing it with others, was a crucial factor in the outcomes of World War II and the Cold War.

[47]Alvin Toffler, *Future Shock* (New York: Random House, 1970), p. 132. Also see Alvin Toffler, *The Third Wave* (New York: Morrow, 1980).

[48]Allan C. Ornstein, *Urban Education* (Columbus, OH: Merrill, 1972), p. 50.

The above statement was made nearly *forty years* ago, before the proliferation of the computer. No question, the computer represents a significant change in the classroom, and is essential for teachers to be competent. Yet, we all know that most classrooms don't have computers; the pen or pencil still makes the point, and a goodly percentage of older teachers (fifty years or more) are computer illiterate. To update matters, had Rip Van Winkle gone to sleep for ninety years (the original 50 + 40), he would still be able to bluff his way in the classroom. If he taught at the middle school or high school level, he would most likely need to do some last-minute preparation in his content area. But we all know teachers who teach out of license, and others who lack depth of knowledge in their content area, and prepare by reading the homework assignment or textbook the night before teaching the lesson.

Essential Knowledge

If you will welcome or support E. D. Hirsch's idea of **cultural literacy,** then Mr. Van Winkle's content or subject preparation is basically intact because more than 80 percent of the 5000 items Hirsch recommends as important refer to events, people, or places in use for more than a hundred years; in facts, 25 percent of his essential knowledge deals with the classics. The inference is that Hirsch is against large-scale pruning and updating of the curriculum; as a modern-day essentialist, he maintains there is a body of knowledge essential to learn for cultural literacy (what he calls "functional literacy") and "effective communication for our nation's populace. . . . Shared information is necessary for true literacy," and it has nothing to do with white or middle-class culture (or the metaphors of domination) nor specific job-related tasks, but with the imperatives of a broad grasp and understanding of mainstream culture.[49] This argument, of course, omits pop culture and the contributions of media that influence our changing culture, as well as all ethnic and folk references.

Complementing his narrative is a compilation of "essential items from history, geography, literature, and science," not to be memorized as Mr. Gradgrind might have us do, but for students to know something about in context with their thoughts and discussion. We don't have to know the fine details, but there should be some minimum level of understanding and competence, depending on the subject area and topic, for effective communication.

Hirsch maintains that students who are unable to master the common knowledge cannot become intelligent readers and cannot speak properly (or formally).[50] He also stresses the importance of scientific information at all levels of schooling; moreover, he has written a series of follow-up books on essential knowledge for every grade level. Knowing the facts, for him and a growing number of present-day essentialists (Lynne Cheney, William Bennett, Chester Finn, Diane Ravitch, et al.) increases the students' capacity to comprehend what they read, see, hear, and discuss. The need for background knowledge is judged important for future communication and specialization. Finally, Hirsch argues that we have overlooked content and have stressed process—or thinking skills—with little regard for subject matter. The outcome has been a decline in national literacy.

The need is to transmit the shared knowledge and values of adult society to youth. Without the transmission of a shared cultural core to the young, conservative educators argue, our society will become fragmented and our ability to accumulate and communicate information across the nation and to various segments of the populace will diminish, especially among immigrants and ethnic groups. We may all subscribe to multicultural education and recognize we are a nation of many nations, but this only increases the need for a knowledge base and an academic core, to be taught to all students.

What knowledge is essential for the workforce in an increasingly global and high-tech society? For many business and government leaders, this usually boils down to more math and science and deeper understanding of problem-solving and computer skills. Measuring such subjects and skills will require assessment instruments more sophisticated than multiple-choice tests. This is no easy task, given the high-stake testing and standards movement which puts emphasis on short-answer items. Concern among other critics is the growing indifference toward the liberal arts, or even worse that the virtues and value of the arts (and social studies, history, geography, etc.) will be dismissed as irrelevant or reactionary.[51]

[49]E. D. Hirsch, *Cultural Literacy: What Every American Needs to Know,* rev. ed. (Boston: Houghton Mifflin, 1987), p. 10.

[50]E. D. Hirsch, *The Knowledge Deficit* (Boston: Houghton Mifflin, 2006).

[51]See Paul Basken, "Spellings Term Fought over Emphasizing Liberal Arts," *Chronicle of Higher of Education,* July 11, 2008: pp. 1, 12; David Brooks, "Lord of the Memes," *New York Times,* August 8, 2008, p. A19; Richard Newmann, "American Democracy at Risk," *Phi Delta Kappan,* 89 (2008): 328–339.

Returning to the Liberal Arts

A few years ago, Allan Bloom, in *The Closing of the American Mind,* voiced concern about education being relative to particular times and places instead of being consistent with universal standards and subjects.[52] Bloom asserts that cultural relativism—with its emphasis on trivial pursuits, quick fixes, relevancy, and self-esteem—has eroded the quality of American education. Our media and educational institutions are marked by an easygoing, flippant indifference to critical thoughts. Deprived of a serious liberal arts and science education, avoiding an engagement with great works and great ideas of the past, our youth lack educational depth.

Harry Lewis, a former dean at Harvard, finds American institutions "soulless," deprived of high ideals and moral virtues for future American leaders: where students are more concerned about well-paying jobs and making money.[53] In a multicultural and global world, the universities need to educate students about liberal and democratic ideals. With the absence of a core curriculum, based on common values, anything goes. Even worse, grade inflation is common, professors teach what they want—based on their own interests (not on the needs of students), and the curriculum consists of a hodge podge—a group of "a la carte" courses—that lack coherence and democratic ideals.

If we want to ask ourselves how and where we went wrong, why we are in social and moral decline, Bloom and Lewis offer a conservative analysis and sense of fundamental reform and what is crucial to the well-being of the nation. To remedy American education and to neutralize the problems caused by cultural relativism, Bloom and Lewis, as did Robert Hutchins and Mortimer Adler over thirty-five years ago, seek to reestablish the idea of an educated person along the line of the great books and great thinkers and to reestablish the virtues of a liberal education.

Now it is somewhat mind-boggling, even foolhardy, to downplay the importance of Western culture (our own civilization) or the **great books** that purport our heritage and illustrate the great ideas, principles, and values that have evolved and shaped our culture over the last 2500 to 5500 years. (Where we trace our historical roots and culture depends largely on whether we start with the Hebrews or the Greeks.) It is fashionable to criticize the great books as white, male, and Eurocentric, but Western civilization is rooted in European history, philosophy, and literature—and with the exception of the ancient Greeks, past civilizations rarely gave women equal education or equal status. (Athena is perched at the top of the Acropolis as a reminder that the ancient Greeks believed in equal opportunity. "Imagine" all the major civilizations believing in equality among people. I guess you can say John Lennon was not the only dreamer.)

The great-book approach, along with serious thinking and meritocracy, is disfavored partially because of matters of political correctness. Many educators would like to stress what Robert Hutchins (former president of the University of Chicago) called the *liberal arts,* what Jeanne Chall (Harvard reading specialist) calls *world knowledge,* what E. D. Hirsch calls *essential knowledge* and *cultural literacy,* and what Allan Bloom (and also Mortimer Adler) call the *great books.* But educators are afraid of being labeled as antiminority and not sensitive to multiculturalism and diversity. It is this fear that makes it easy to substitute works by women, minority and Third World authors for Plato, Locke, Kant, or Ibsen.[54]

Western civilization as perceived by postmodernists has come at a price, according to Shelby Steele, that is, the exploitation and victimization of people of color[55] (and, if we may add, women). Therefore, a revisionary list of great books and liberal arts courses is needed to balance the literature of the dominant group. The cultural capital of women and minorities, their voices and stories, must be heard to "educate" those who need to be educated and to learn the "truth." It is this war in academia that holds hostage many educators and prevents them from advancing the great ideas and great literature of Western civilization, and leads, we are sad to say, to cultural relativism and the decline of liberal arts, reiterated by Bloom and Hutchins.

Modern Languages

Once more—what knowledge is worth learning? The number-one primary language in the world is Mandarin, followed by English, Hindi, and Spanish. Japanese

[52]Allan Bloom, *The Closing of the American Mind* (New York: Simon and Schuster, 1987).

[53]Harry Lewis, *Excellence without a Soul* (New York: Public Affairs, 2006).

[54]Allan C. Ornstein, *Teaching and Schooling in America: Pre- and Post-September 11* (Boston: Allyn and Bacon, 2003). The gender/race/class argument is keenly depicted in the writings of Michael Apple, James Banks, and especially Henry Giroux and Peter McLaren (the latter two often labeled as neomarxists).

[55]Shelby Steele, "War of the Worlds," *Wall Street Journal,* September 17, 2001, p. 18.

ranks tenth and German and French rank lower. Nearly all foreign language programs in American schools offer Spanish, French, and Italian, and some offer German and Latin. Only 41 percent (or 5 million) of all high school students (grades 9–12) are enrolled in foreign language courses. As many as 58 percent of secondary students enrolled in a foreign language study Spanish, but only 0.3 percent of U.S. high school students enrolled in a foreign language course study Japanese, and about 0.2 percent attempt Mandarin.[56]

Failure to train students in Mandarin, the official language of China, is representative of our attitude toward the non-Western world, a dysfunctional foreign policy, and the closed-mindedness of ignoring the largest country in the world—stemming from the Cold War thinking of the Eisenhower-Dulles administration. What percentage of American high school students study Hindi, the official language of the second-largest country? None. What percentage of American high school students, except those in Islamic private schools, study Arabic and Farsi, the two major languages of the Muslim world? Next to none (less than 0.05 percent for Arabic and possibly zero for Farsi).[57] Do high schools offer these languages? Yes. About one-half of one percent in the country have a community education program, usually meeting once or twice a week in the evening, serving adults and not children or youth.

During the Cold War, there were increased enrollments in Russian language courses and other "security related" courses such as math, science, and engineering at the college level. A sense of relaxation surfaced, coinciding with the reduced threat of war with the Soviet Union. Thus, over the last decade many schools of international relations shifted their emphasis from security to human rights, global economics, and environmental issues.[58]

As we begin the twenty-first century, it would be a shame if any modifications in foreign language courses—from European or Western languages to Mandarin, Hindi, Arabic, or Farsi—were to be based on an international crisis, a reaction to the new economic enemy being China or India, or the Muslim world. This type of thinking only creates new polarities: the United States versus China or the West versus Islam. Instead of modifying the curriculum because of a new understanding of economic markets, respect for other cultures and people, or the fact that the world is more interconnected, the curriculum may be changed because of perceived threats or fear. If so, that would be counterproductive—almost as counterproductive as framing the Chinese, Indian, or Islamic world in sweeping generalizations. One billion Chinese, one billion Indians, and one billion Muslims are very diverse. Although history does not change (it only gets revised or rewritten), political leaders and economic conditions do change, and, subsequently, so do foreign policy and the need to communicate with, understand, and respect other cultures.

In an age of multiculturalism, pluralism, and diversity, why is it that foreign language requirements for four-year college graduation have decreased from 34 percent in 1965 to less than 20 percent today?[59] Is it simply because the increasing worldwide use of English dictates that we no longer have to learn other languages? Is it because the Cold War spurred the growth of foreign languages and now there is no Soviet threat? (If so, why didn't we offer Russian classes in high school when the Cold War was hot?) Is it based on difficulty of the language or lack of willingness to break from Western tradition? Why is it that in a world in which Western countries represent less than 10 percent of the population, Spanish, French, Italian, German, and Latin (Western and European languages) dominate almost 99 percent of all high school foreign language study? Given a shrinking Western world and the declining role of Spain, France, Italy, and Germany on the world stage, why do we cling to an outdated ethnocentric view of the world?

Many Americans have no interest in learning difficult languages and languages other than those of Western nations. We seem to need some foreign stimulant, some vague feeling that we should expand our horizons—something like a wartime concern, an economic imperative, or even some missionary calling. "Multiculturalism may not have prodded us to study cultures fundamentally different from our own," writes one observer,

[56]Ornstein, Pajak, and Ornstein, *Contemporary Issues in Curriculum;* Ornstein, *Teaching and Schooling in America: Pre- and Post-September 11.*

[57]Dora Johnson of the Center for Applied Linguistics in Washington, DC claims that only two public high schools—one in Dearborn, Michigan, and the other in Houston—offer two or more years in Arabic. None offer Farsi. Personal conversation, July 23, 2002.

[58]Eyal Press, "It's a Volatile, Complex World," *New York Times Education Life,* November 11, 2001, pp. 20–22, 35. Terrance R. Carson, "Internationalizing Curriculum: Globalization and the Wordliness of Curriculum Studies," *Curriculum Inquiry*: 39 (2009): 145–158.

[59]Telephone conversation with Laura Siaya, American Council on Education, July 24, 2002.

but the "war on terrorism" may be the catalyst.[60] For the last 100 years or more, the door has been closed to studying other cultures, despite the fact that about 700,000 immigrants from non-Western countries have come to our shores each year since 1970. Given the shrinking global village we live in, and the need to understand the world's inhabitants (so we won't kill each other or blow ourselves off the map), we need to expand global education and foreign language studies.

Computer Knowledge and Technology

Certainly, technology has changed the curriculum in terms of new skills and ideas to learn, but many students and teachers have superficial knowledge and some have limited exposure due to lack of opportunity or choice. A number of states are now requiring proficiency in using technology in order to be certified to teach, and several school districts are offering online courses for middle school and high school students. At the college level the day has come when it is now easier to sit in bed or on a couch at home than to go to class, as reading assignments and notes become available online. The biggest problem is the lack of socialization, and creating a passive recipient knowledge that does little to improve problem-solving skills.

Do students learn more with computers? Of hundreds of studies involving computers and students, grades K–12, few have focused on learning outcomes. Several problems have been reported, however, including dropped computers and broken monitors; misplaced accessories such as cards, discs, and batteries; technical problems like freezing, crashing, and misaligned printing (requiring the addition of an extra technician); physical strains among laptop users (back and neck); and the lack of proper teacher training.[61] Thus, one child's great new organizational learning tool can be another child's electronic headache. Being wired up and having access to unlimited information doesn't necessarily improve students' thinking or increasing their reading of important books or their understanding of important ideas.

After wading through the hype about the potential of computers, the research suggests there is no academic improvement among most students who use computers.[62] A computer can make it easier for students to retrieve information, process words for a report, and communicate with people around the world, but it doesn't motivate them to learn or improve their learning. Increased time on the computer or smart phone often means spending time e-mailing, chatting, or browsing at the expense of schoolwork and reading books.

Actually, there are too many students nestled in their respective time zones chatting with people online in Boston, Chicago, and LA, exchanging intimacies and pictures and spending hours of "E-life" time that otherwise might be spent engaged in homework and related academics. It is a world of instant messaging, a world that inadvertently pulls children into a web of people, boys and girls, men and women, whom they don't know; yet, they converse sometimes for hours with these "virtual" strangers. Increasingly, parents will have to take responsibility and free their children from this escapism, and help them rejoin the world of reality—even if it means communicating occasionally with Luddites. Teachers and schools will have to find ways to (1) help parents restrict the use of computers for children so they stay in touch with friends and family, (2) adopt age-appropriate guidelines for children's computer use, (3) educate children to make good choices about their computer use, and (4) equalize access to computers for rich and poor students.

The new technology has changed the reading habits of students (and their parents), as electronic book readers such as Kindle, Nook, and iPad saturate the market place. The new hybrids add pictures, videos and dialogue to the text, as well as demonstrations on how–to, perform exercises, or tell a story. Textbook authors and publishers can no longer think linear with their books. As information becomes increasingly digital, **textbooks** will become customized to fit the particular needs and interests of teachers and schools. Authors will be expected to establish Web sites and blogs, even engage in conversations and text message with readers. Reader comments will be incorporated into the texts or subplots of stories. Authors will be expected to pick and choose from suggestions or comments from readers and incorporate those ideas in designated places of the book. Book-reading software for phone, computer

---

[60]Margaret Talbot, "Other Woes," *New York Times Magazine,* November 18, 2001, p. 24.

[61]Daniel J. Rocha, "The Emperor's New Laptop," *Education Week,* September 27, 2001, pp. 42, 46–47.

[62]William M. Bulkeley, "Hard Lessons," *Wall Street Journal,* Technology section, November 17, 1997, pp. 1, 4, 6; Rocha, "The Emperor's New Laptop." Also see Donna Deconnaro "Sociotechnical Cultural Activity: Expanding an Understanding of Emergent Technology Practices," *Journal of Curriculum Studies,* 40 (2008): 329–351.

tablets and other mobile devices will also be released by publishing companies for students who prefer electronic books.

Moral Knowledge

It is possible to give instruction in *moral knowledge* and ethics. We can discuss philosophers such as Socrates, Plato, and Aristotle who examined the good society and the good person; the more controversial works of Immanuel Kant, Franz Kafka, and Jean-Paul Sartre; religious leaders such as Moses, Jesus, and Confucius; and political leaders such as Abraham Lincoln, Mohandas Gandhi, and Martin Luther King. Through the study of the writings and principles of these moral people, students can learn about moral knowledge. Teaching Johnny or Jane to read by assigning "Dick and Jane" workbooks or "cat and mouse" readers alone is inadequate; the idea is to encourage good reading (which has social and moral messages) at an early age—and which teaches self-respect, tolerance of others, and social good.

The teaching of morality starts at the first grade with folktales such as "Aesop's Fables," "Jack and the Beanstalk," "Guinea Fowl and Rabbit Get Justice," and the stories and fables of the Grimm Brothers, Robert Louis Stevenson, and Langston Hughes. For older children, there are *Sadako and the Thousand Paper Cranes, Up from Slavery,* and *The Diary of Anne Frank.* And for adolescents, there are *Of Mice and Men, A Man for all Seasons, Lord of the Flies,* and *Death of a Salesman.* By the eighth (and surely the ninth) grade, assuming average or above average reading ability, students should be up to reading the authors (and books) listed in Table 13–3. This list of twenty-five recommended titles exemplifies literature rich in social and moral messages.

As students move up the grade levels and their reading improves, greater variety and options among authors are available to them. Of course, community mores will influence the book selection process. Here we are dealing with issues of whose morality? Whose values? The assumption is that there are agreed-upon virtues such as hard work, honesty, patriotism, integrity, civility, and caring that represent local consensus, if not an American consensus. All we as educators need is sufficient conviction to find core commonalities.

The works suggested in Table 13–3 can be read in traditional history and English courses or in an integrated course such as Junior Great Books, World Studies, or American Studies. Harry Broudy refers to this type of content as a *broad fields approach* to curriculum; he organizes the high school curriculum into five categories, including "moral problems" that address social and moral issues.[63] Florence Stratemeyer and her coauthors developed a curriculum based on ten "life situations," comprising the ability to deal with social, political, and economic forces.[64] Mortimer Adler divided the curriculum into organized knowledge, intellectual skills, and understanding of ideas and values. The latter deals with discussion of "good books" (his

Table 13–3 Twenty-five Recommended Works to Be Read by Eighth Grade

1. Maya Angelou, "The Graduation"
2. Pearl Buck, *The Good Earth*
3. Truman Capote, "Miriam"
4. James Fenimore Cooper, *The Last of the Mohicans*
5. Charles Dickens, *Great Expectations*
6. Anne Frank, *The Diary of a Young Girl*
7. William Faulkner, *Brer Tiger and the Big Wind*
8. William Golding, *Lord of the Flies*
9. John Kennedy, *Profiles in Courage*
10. Martin Luther King, *Why We Can't Wait*
11. Rudyard Kipling, "Letting in the Jungle"
12. Harper Lee, *To Kill a Mockingbird*
13. Jack London, *The Call of the Wild*
14. Herman Melville, *Billy Budd*
15. George Orwell, *Animal Farm*
16. Tomas Rivera, "Zoo Island"
17. William Saroyan, "The Summer of the Beautiful White Horse"
18. John Steinbeck, *Of Mice and Men*
19. Robert Louis Stevenson, *Dr. Jekyll and Mr. Hyde*
20. William Still, *The Underground Railroad*
21. Ivan Turgenev, *The Watch*
22. Mark Twain, *The Adventures of Huckleberry Finn*
23. John Updike, *The Alligators*
24. H. G. Wells, *The Time Machine*
25. Elie Wiesel, *Night*

Note: List, compiled by Allan Ornstein, of works that address moral and social issues. Originally published in Allan C. Ornstein, *Teaching and Schooling in America* (Boston: Allyn and Bacon, 2003).

[63]Harry S. Broudy, B.O. Smith, and Joe R. Bunnett, *Democracy and Excellence in American Secondary Education* (Chicago: Rand McNally, 1964).

[64]Florence B. Stratemeyer et al., *Developing a Curriculum for Modern Living* (New York: Teachers College Press, Columbia University, 1947).

term), and not textbooks, and the Socratic method of questioning.[65] Ted Sizer has organized the high school curriculum into four broad areas, including "History and Philosophy" and "Literature and the Arts."[66]

The content of moral knowledge, according to Phillip Phenix, covers five main areas: (1) *human rights,* involving conditions of life that ought to prevail, (2) *ethics,* concerning family relations and sex, (3) *social relationships,* dealing with class, racial, ethnic, and religious groups, (4) *economic life,* involving wealth and poverty, and (5) *political life,* involving justice, equity, and power.[67] The way we translate moral content into moral conduct defines the kind of people we are. It is not our moral knowledge that counts; rather, it is our moral behavior in everyday affairs that is important.

Moral Character

A person can have moral knowledge and obey secular and religious laws but still lack moral character. *Moral character* is difficult to teach because it involves patterns of attitudes and behavior that result from stages of growth, distinctive qualities of personality, and experiences. It involves a coherent philosophy and the will to act in a way consistent with that philosophy; it also means to help people, to accept their weaknesses without exploiting them, to see the best in people and to build on their strengths, to act civilly and courteously in relations with classmates, friends, or colleagues, to express humility, and to act as an individual (and accept individual responsibility) even if it means being different from the crowd.

Perhaps the real test of moral character is to cope with crisis or setback, deal with adversity, and be willing to take risks (that is, possible loss of a job, even life itself) because of one's convictions. Courage, conviction, and compassion are the ingredients of character. What kind of person do we want to emerge as a result of our efforts as teachers or principals? We can engage in moral education and teach moral knowledge, but can we teach moral character? In general, the morally mature person understands moral principles and accepts responsibility for applying these principles in real-life situations.

The world is full of people who understand the notion of morality but take the expedient way out or follow the crowd. Who among us possesses moral character? Who among the students in our schools will develop into morally mature individuals? To be sure, moral character cannot be taught by one teacher; rather, it involves the leadership of the principal and takes a concerted effort by the entire school, cooperation among a critical mass of supervisors and teachers within the school, and the nurturing of children and youth over many years. Ted and Nancy Sizer ask teachers to confront students with moral questions and moral issues about their own actions or inactions in ways that may be unsettling or difficult; teachers need to address things that threaten the self-concept and self-esteem of students.[68] We need to deal with issues of inequity and social injustice, while promoting cooperative behaviors and intergroup relations among children and youth.

The authors believe that schools should adopt moral character as priority or policy, adopted in turn by all teachers. One or two teachers by themselves cannot have real impact—relevant and long term. It takes the leadership of the principal, as well as a school-community, to implement a program cultivating moral character, through which students are taught responsibility for their actions and the worth of values such as honesty, respect, tolerance, compassion, and a sense of justice.

As education leaders, we have an obligation to promote character development while recognizing that there is a broad range of opinion on what this means or whether it is even possible. Amy Gutman represents one extreme in her belief that moral issues are inappropriate in public schools because of the diverse backgrounds and biases of students. At the other extreme is Nel Nodding's notion that caring for strangers is more important than shaping minds and attitudes of students.[69]

In spite of the controversy, school leaders must not be afraid to take moral positions. There are certain events that are horrifying and represent the most evil aspects of human behavior. Students who laugh at pictures of the rape of Nanking, the Holocaust, the Killing Fields—or

---

[65] Mortimer J. Adler, *The Paideia Program* (New York: Macmillan, 1984).

[66] Theodore Sizer, *Horace's Compromise* (Boston: Houghton Mifflin, 1987).

[67] Phillip Phenix, *Realms of Meaning* (New York: McGraw-Hill, 1964).

[68] Theodore R. Sizer and Nancy Faust Sizer, *The Students Are Watching: Schools and the Moral Context* (Boston: Beacon Press, 1999).

[69] Amy Gutman, *Democratic Education,* rev. ed. (Princeton: Princeton University Press, 1999); Nel Noddings, *Educating Moral People: A Caring Alternative to Character Education* (New York: Teachers College Press, Columbia University, 2002).

incineration of the World Trade Center—should not be excused because of their ignorance, or religious, racial, or ethnic background; nor should they be permitted to voice their "justification" or to get into a historical debate about racial superiority or the decadent values of Western civilization. They are wrong on all moral grounds. Here the schools are not being asked to impose Western or Christian values on the nation's student population. Rather, schools can help teach the understanding that accentuating visible differences under the banner of religious freedom, or tolerating hate groups under the guise of free speech or free press, does not prepare students for a diverse world.

The Roles of the Curriculum Worker

Much has been written about the roles and responsibilities of the curriculum worker. *Curriculum worker* is a general term that includes a variety of educators from teacher to superintendent. Any person involved in some form of curriculum development, implementation, or evaluation is a curriculum worker. A *curriculum supervisor* is usually a chairperson, assistant principal, or principal; he or she usually works at the school level. A *curriculum leader* can be a supervisor or administrator—not only a chairperson or principal but also a director or associate superintendent of curriculum. A *curriculum coordinator* usually heads a program at the school district, regional, or state level; it may be a special government-funded program or a traditional subject area involving math or English. A *curriculum specialist* is a technical consultant from the district level, regional or state department of education, or university. The person provides advice or in-service assistance, sometimes in the classroom but usually at meetings, conferences, or staff sessions. Most of the terms, as well as the related responsibilities and functions of these people, depend on the philosophy and organization of the school district (or state education agency) and the personal preferences and views of the administration.

Confusion exists about whether curriculum planning or development should take place at the local, state, or national level. In the past, emphasis on curriculum development was at the school or school district level. (Bear in mind that most other nations have a national ministry of education with major curriculum responsibilities.)

Curriculum roles in the past were defined at the local level, and decisions were made to develop curriculum leaders at the chair and principal's level. The majority of school districts depend on school people (teachers and supervisors) to develop curriculum—and usually without pay, unless they meet in the summer; parents are also included in many curriculum committees at the school level. Staff limitations make unlikely the provision of curriculum specialists from the central office, and if such a person exists it is one person (possibly two) whose time is limited because of other responsibilities. Only large school districts can afford to have a curriculum department with a full staff of specialists. In such school districts, most curriculum development takes place at the central level and teachers often complain that their professional input is minimal, relegated to implementing predetermined and prepackaged materials from the district office.

Responsibilities of the Curriculum Worker

What are the responsibilities of the curriculum worker? Assigned responsibilities within the school structure are important but unclear, because a variety of people (teachers, supervisors, principals, district personnel, and others) are expected to serve in the role of curriculum worker. Each position holder has different professional responsibilities, needs, and expectations. Adjustments must be made by each holder of a position. For example, teachers are usually expected (among other things) to provide instruction, but principals are expected to manage a school and provide assistance to teachers.

The curriculum worker has many different titles; nonetheless, the teacher is a member of the curriculum team and works with supervisors and administrators as part the team. Early identification of teachers to serve in the capacity of curriculum workers is essential for the growth of teachers and the vitality of a school (and school district). Where there is need or attention for clarifying the responsibilities of curriculum workers, consider the following:

1. Blend theory building with practice; obtain curriculum knowledge and apply it to the real world of classrooms and schools.
2. Agree on what is involved in curriculum development and design, including the relationships that exist among the elements of curriculum.
3. Agree on the relationship among curriculum, instruction, and supervision, including the explicit language of each area and how each aids the work of the other.
4. Act as a change agent who considers schools in context with society; balance the demands and views of the local community with state and national goals and interests.

5. Create a mission or goal statement to provide direction and focused behavior within the organization.
6. Be open to new curriculum trends and thoughts; examine various proposals and suggest modifications, while not falling victim to fads and frills of a particular pressure group.
7. Confer with various parental, community, and professional groups; have skills in human relations and in working with groups and individuals.
8. Encourage colleagues and other professionals to innovate, solve professional problems, and adopt new programs and ideas.
9. Develop a process for continual curriculum development, implementation, and evaluation.
10. Balance and integrate subject areas and grade levels into the total curriculum; pay close attention to scope and sequence by subject and grade level.

Other theorists identify other responsibilities and duties of curriculum leaders. For example, Ronald Doll tends to see the curriculum leader involved in coordinating instructional activities, facilities, materials, and special personnel (such as librarians, resource personnel, and program coordinators) and working with and interpreting the curriculum to the public. The focus is on *process*.[70] Allan Glatthorn is more task oriented and *product based*. He envisions the curriculum leader aligning school goals with curricular subjects, organizing and monitoring curriculum committees and projects, and using assessment data to implement and improve curriculum.[71] Finally, John McNeil focuses on the teacher's role in developing curriculum and encourages teachers to develop postmodernist ideas and see the implications of these ideas for their own practice. His recommendation for the curriculum leader is to adapt to and foment social change.[72]

The authors' list of responsibilities tends to be more theoretical than the responsibilities advocated by Doll and Glatthorn—the latter of which tend to be more practical. However, McNeil is the most theoretical of all of us. Our view implies that curriculum workers may be teachers, supervisors (chairs or assistant principals), coordinators, or directors employed at the school, school district, or state level. Doll and Glatthorn examine the activities of curriculum leaders and connote a narrower view, which suggests a chair or principal operating at the school level. McNeil is even more restrictive and views the curriculum leader as a teacher who makes decisions in consultation with the assistant principal or principal. Finally, the authors' concept of the curriculum worker frames the person in terms of broad responsibilities and the whole organization. The others focus on explicit responsibilities or activities that are considered important for explicit personnel, such as the school principal with Doll and Glatthorn or the teacher with McNeil—and thus consider a limited or particular part of the school organization.

Leadership Role of the Principal

In recent decades, the terms *climate, ethos,* and *culture* have been used to capture or describe the norms, values, behaviors, and rituals of the school organization, what can simply be called the significant features or personality of the organization. Here we are talking about everything that goes on in school: how teachers interact and dress, what they talk about, what goes on at meetings, their expectations of students, how students behave, how parents interact with the staff, and what type of leadership behavior is exhibited by the principal.

Peterson and Deal contend that many schools have **toxic cultures**—that is, over time the staff becomes fragmented and demoralized. The purpose of serving students has been lost; negativism and criticism dominate. A disgruntled staff attacks new ideas, criticizes dedicated teachers, makes fun of colleagues who attend conferences or workshops, and recounts past failures. In contrast, other schools have **positive cultures,** where the staff shares a sense of purpose, and is dedicated to teaching and school improvement. Student successes are highlighted and collegiality permeates the atmosphere. High morale, caring, and commitment abound.[73]

According to Peterson and Deal, the school leader is key in shaping school culture. Principals communicate core values, behaviors, and expectations in their

---

[70]Doll, *Curriculum Improvement: Decision Making and Process.*

[71]Allan A. Glatthorn, *Curriculum Leadership* (Glenview, IL: Scott, Foresman, 1987); Glatthorn and Jailall, *The Principal as Curriculum Leader,* 3rd ed. (Thousand Oaks, CA: Corwin Press, 2009).

[72]John D. McNeil, *Curriculum: The Teacher's Initiative,* 3rd ed. (Upper Saddle, NJ: Prentice Hall, 2002).

[73]Kent D. Peterson and Terrance E. Deal, "How Leaders Influence the Culture of the Schools," *Educational Leadership,* 56 (1998): 28–30. Also see Terrance Deal and Kent D. Peterson, *Shaping School Culture: The School Leader's Role* (San Francisco: Jossey-Bass, 1999).

everyday work and interaction with staff. Their actions, words, memos, and even nonverbal behavior send messages and over time shape culture. Either they encourage and reward effective teachers and accomplished students, or they ignore them and bury themselves in micromanagement or politics.

Leadership has been described as a balancing act between self and others, and people's competing and overlapping perceptions, expectations, and concerns. Not all leaders face this conflict well, and having technical skills is no substitute for the ability to deal with people and subsequently to lead. People skills are just as important as, possibly more important than, technical skills. Although there is agreement in the literature on the need to improve the leadership role of the principal, there is disagreement on what behaviors or practices principals should pursue—and to what extent a principal should be a **general manager** or **curriculum-instructional leader.**

When given the opportunity to categorize their professional colleagues into one of five leadership roles (principal/teacher, scientific manager, instructional leader, curriculum leader, or general manager), 60 percent of secondary school principals in a North Carolina sample of 370 choose general manager.[74] Female principals and principals with more formal education (doctorate degree), however, prefer the role of curriculum or instructional leader compared with male principals and principals with less education (masters degree, sixth-year certificate), who prefer the role of general manager.

In a study of 149 successful elementary school principals in Massachusetts, selected on the basis of being strong leaders and because of their schools' student achievement levels, more than 75 percent described themselves as "instructional leaders" who devoted most of their own professional development time and resources to curriculum, instruction, and school improvement.[75]

Other data suggest that suburban school principals and elementary school principals spend more time on curriculum and instructional matters than do urban and secondary school principals, but still not enough time, given the fact they must still deal with leaking roofs, shrinking budgets, and personnel squabbles. Secondary school principals, especially those in large schools, devote more time to managerial concerns. The latter group of principals rely on their assistant principals and chairpersons in various subject areas to deal with curriculum and instructional activities.[76]

Elementary schools are smaller than high schools and are often cornerstones of homogeneous neighborhoods, whereas secondary schools often cut across and include many neighborhoods. Because of neighborhood size and homogeneity, elementary principals must be more sensitive to the needs, views, and priorities of parents and community members, which often center around curriculum and instructional leadership. However, a point is reached, when a school is very small (fewer than 100 students) or rural, where the principal is given other duties that take away time from curriculum matters. These might deal with central office tasks, teaching, or the shared principalship of another site.[77]

Managerial Role of the Principal

The role of manager is essential for the principal and is probably the most important aspect of school leadership. In their classic text on organizational behavior, Daniel Katz and Robert Kahn divide management skills into three major areas: *technical,* involving good planning, organizing, coordinating, supervising, and controlling techniques; *human,* dealing with human relations and people skills, good motivating and morale-building skills; and *conceptual,* emphasizing knowledge and technical skills related to the service (or product) of the organization.[78] (For principals, conceptual leadership connotes knowledge or curriculum, instruction, teaching, and learning.) Thomas Sergiovanni has added three other areas of management for school administrators, including *symbolic leadership,* those actions the principal emphasizes and

---

[74]Dale L. Brubaker and Lawrence H. Simon, "How Do Principals View Themselves, Others?" *NASSP Bulletin,* 71 (1987): 72–78. Also see Lee G. Bolman and Terrance E. Deal, *Reframing the Path to School Leadership* (Thousand Oaks, CA: Corwin Press, 2002).

[75]Laura A. Cooper, "The Principal as Instructional Leader," *Principal,* 68 (1989): 13–16; Jean Johnson, "The Principal's Priority 1," *Educational Leadership*: 66 (2008): 72–76.

[76]William L. Boyd, "What School Administrators Do and Don't Do," *Canadian Administrator,* 22 (1983): 1–4; Brett D. Jones and Robert J. Egley, "Looking Through Different Lenses: Teachers' and Administrators' Views of Accountability," *Phi Delta Kappan,* 87 (2006): 767–771; Dennis Sparks, "What I Believe in Leadership Development," *Phi Delta Kappan,* 90 (2009): 514–517.

[77]Jonathan Hill, "The Rural School Principalship: Unique Challenges, Opportunities," *NASSP Bulletin,* 77 (1993): 77–81; Ernestine C. Riggs and Ana G. Serafin, "The Principal as Instructional Leader," *NASSP Bulletin,* 82 (1998): 78–85.

[78]Daniel Katz and Robert L. Kahn, *The Social Psychology of Organizations* (New York: Wiley, 1966).

wishes to model to the staff; *cultural leadership,* those values and beliefs the principal believes are important;[79] and *moral leadership,* behavior built around purpose, ethics, and beliefs—which can help transform a school from a formal organization to a "community" and inspire commitment, loyalty, and service.[80] Michael Fullan and Seymour Sarason add a seventh dimension of school management—the principal as a *change agent* and facilitator.[81] Finally, Deal and Peterson refer to an eighth characteristic, based on *cooperative leadership,* that is, building collegiality, a sense of school identity, and a democratic and inspiring school culture.[82]

In general, there seems to be agreement that principals must "lead from the center," that is, be more democratic, delegate responsibilities, share decision-making powers, and develop collaborative efforts that bond students, teachers, and parents. In an era of reform and restructuring of schools, with increased legal consideration and government regulations, the principal's duties and tasks have increased to an overload level.[83] Principals are almost forced to share responsibilities with and empower others in order to manage schools on a day-to-day basis. But if they give away power selectively to individuals and groups, they can retain and enhance their span of control and subsequent influence.

Curriculum-Instructional Role of the Principal

Although the literature generally agrees on the need for the principal to be a leader in the areas of curriculum and instruction, it sometimes disagrees on what specific roles and behaviors should be exhibited and how much time should be devoted to these twin areas of leadership. When principals are surveyed, they often report that the curriculum and instruction aspects of the job are top-priority work areas and that they need to spend more time on the job related to these two technical areas of development.[84]

Given the national and state standards movement, and the need to upgrade the curriculum to meet these standards, school principals' attention has increasingly focused on curriculum. Most national standards have been greeted with approval by business groups but not by all state education agencies or education administrative groups. The standards emphasize specific knowledge, modes of inquiry and thinking, and consider certain subjects more important than others. Through legislation and assessment, they impact school practice, leadership behavior, and teaching practices.[85]

But a significant discrepancy exists between statements and actions. Data suggest that teachers do not view curriculum-instructional leadership as a major responsibility of principals, do not see much evidence of such leadership on the part of principals, and are reluctant to accept principals in this leadership capacity.[86] Often teachers feel that principals are not capable of providing such leadership, and don't always want the principal's assistance in these technical areas that teachers consider to be more appropriate for peer coaching and collegial staff development.[87]

---

[79]Thomas J. Sergiovanni, *The Principalship: A Reflective Practice Perspective,* 3rd ed. (Needham Heights, MA: Allyn and Bacon, 1995); Sergiovanni, *Moral Leadership* (San Francisco: Jossey-Bass, 1996); Sergiovanni, *Rethinking Leadership,* 2nd ed. (Thousand Oaks, CA: Corwin Press, 2006).

[80]Thomas J. Sergiovanni, *Building Community in Schools* (San Francisco: Jossey-Bass, 1999); Sergiovanni, *Leadership for the Schoolhouse* (San Francisco: Jossey-Bass, 2000).

[81]Michael G. Fullan and Suzanne M. Stiegelbauer, *The New Meaning of Educational Change,* 3rd ed. (New York: Teachers College Press, Columbia University, 2001); Seymour B. Sarason, *Barometers of Social Change* (San Francisco: Jossey-Bass, 1996); Sarason, *Educational Reform* (New York: Teachers College Press, Columbia University, 2002).

[82]Terrance E. Deal and Kent D. Peterson, *Shaping School Culture* (San Francisco: Jossey-Bass, 1998); Deal and Peterson, *The Leadership Paradox* (San Francisco: Jossey-Bass, 2000).

[83]Judith Chapman, *Creating and Managing the Democratic School* (New York: Falmer Press, 1964).

[84]Lynn Beck and Joseph Murphy, *Understanding the Principalship* (New York: Teachers College Press, Columbia University, 1992); L. Joseph Matthews and Gary M. Crow, *Being and Becoming a Principal* (Boston: Allyn and Bacon, 2003); James P. Spillane and John B. Diamond, *Distributed Leadership in Practice* (New York: Teachers College Press, Columbia University, 2007).

[85]O. L. Davis, "National and State Curriculum Standards," *Journal of Curriculum and Supervision,* 13 (1998): 297–299; Allan A. Glatthorn, *Performance Assessment and Standards-Based Curricula* (Larchmont, NY: Eye on Education, 1998); David A. Squires, *Curriculum Alignment* (Thousand Oaks, CA: Corwin Press, 2009).

[86]Michael Fullan, Barrie Bennett, and Carol R. Bennett, "Linking Classroom and School Improvement," *Educational Leadership,* 47 (1990): 13–19; Robert Hess, *Excellence, Equity, and Efficiency* (Lanham, MD: Rowman & Littlefield, 2005); Anita Woolfolk-Hoy and Wayne K. Hoy, *Instructional Leadership: A Learner Centered Guide* (Boston: Allyn and Bacon, 2003).

[87]Bruce J. Biddle and Lawrence J. Saha, "How Principals Use Research," *Educational Leadership,* 63 (2006): 72–78; Robert J. Garmston, "How Administrators Support Peer Coaching," *Educational Leadership,* 44 (1987): 18–26; Pete Hall, "Building Bridges: Strengthening the Principal Induction Process," *Phi Delta Kappan,* 89 (2008): 449–452.

Principals have historically spent little time (15 to 20 percent)[88] coordinating activities in curriculum and instruction, and spend much less time (3 to 7 percent) observing teachers in the classroom, complaining that managerial activities take up most of their time.[89] Dealing with the daily operation of the school and attending meetings tend to take up most of their time. Although the major principal associations (NAEP and NASSP) overwhelmingly envision the principal as a curriculum-instructional leader, and this theme continually appears in their respective journals (which principals read), the realities of the job do not permit emphasis in these twin leadership areas.

In this connection, Joseph Murphy has developed six curriculum and instructional roles for the principal:

1. *Promoting Quality Instruction.* Ensuring consistency and coordination of instructional programs and defining recommended methods of instruction.
2. *Supervising and Evaluating Instruction.* Ensuring that school goals are translated into practice at the classroom level and monitoring classroom instruction through numerous classroom observations.
3. *Allocating and Protecting Instructional Time.* Providing teachers with uninterrupted blocks of instructional time and ensuring that basic skills and academic subjects are taught.
4. *Coordinating the Curriculum.* Translating curriculum knowledge into meaningful curriculum programs, matching instructional objectives with curriculum materials and standardized tests, and ensuring curriculum continuity vertically and across grade levels.
5. *Promoting Content Coverage.* Ensuring that content of specific courses is covered in class and extended outside of class by developing and enforcing homework policies.
6. *Monitoring Student Progress.* Using both criterion- and standardized-reference tests to diagnose student problems and evaluate their progress, as well as using test results to set or modify school goals.[90]

Based on a review of the research, according to Murphy, the six major dimensions or roles exemplify an effective principal; moreover, Murphy's research supports the assumption that the distinguishing reason for effective schools is a school principal who exhibits strong curriculum-instructional leadership.

The Teacher and the Curriculum

Although Ronald Doll views the curriculum expert primarily as a chair or principal, he is concerned with the teacher's role in planning and implementing the curriculum at three levels: classroom, school, and district. In his opinion, the teacher should be involved "in every phase" of curriculum making, including the planning of "specific goals . . . materials, content, and methods." Teachers should have a curriculum "coordinating body" to unify their work and develop relationships with "supervisors [and] other teachers" involved in the curriculum.[91]

Peter Oliva adopts a broader and ideal view of the teacher's role. For him, teachers are the "primary group in curriculum development." They constitute the "majority or the totality of the membership of curriculum committees and councils." Their role is to develop, implement, and evaluate curriculum. In his words, teachers work in committees and "initiate proposals . . . review proposals, gather data, conduct research, make contact with parents and other lay people, write and create curriculum materials . . . obtain feedback from learners and evaluation programs."[92]

The views of Doll and Oliva, along with those of McNeil, suggest a **bottom-up approach** to curriculum, in which the teacher has a major role to perform. This

---

[88]Boyd, "What School Administrators Do and Don't Do"; James T. Scarnati, "Beyond Technical Competence: Nine Rules for Administrators," *NASSP Bulletin,* 78 (1994): 76–83.

[89]Lewis Cohen, "It's Not About Management," *Phi Delta Kappan,* 87 (2006): 459–461; Thelbert L. Drake and William H. Roe, *The Principalship,* 6th ed. (Columbus, OH: Merrill, 2003); Michael Fullan, *Leadership and Sustainability* (Thousand Oaks, CA; Corwin Press, 2005).

[90]Joseph Murphy, "Principal Instructional Leadership," in P. W. Thurston and L. S. Lotto (eds.), *Advances in Educational Administration,* vol. 1B (Greenwich, CT: JAI Press, 1990), pp. 162–200; Murphy, "What's Ahead for Tomorrow's Principals," *Principal,* 78 (1998): 13–16. Also see Jerome Murphy, "Dancing Lessons for Elephants: Reforming Ed School Leadership Programs," *Phi Delta Kappan,* 87 (2006): 488–491.

[91]Doll, *Curriculum Improvement: Decision Making and Process,* p. 334.

[92]Peter Oliva, *Developing the Curriculum,* 7th ed. (Boston: Allyn and Bacon, 2008), p. 128.

view was popularized by Taba in her classic text on curriculum development, but actually first introduced and elaborated by Harold Rugg in 1930. Rugg argued that teachers needed to be released from all classroom duties "to prepare courses of study, and assemble materials, and develop outlines of the entire curriculum." Later Caswell and Campbell, in 1935, envisioned teachers participating in curriculum committees at the school, district, and state levels during the summers and sometimes as a special assignment during the school year.[93]

The Central (District) Office

On the other end of the continuum, Glatthorn makes little provision for teacher input, a view similar to Tyler's, which few people recognize of Tyler because of his overall popularity. Glatthorn discusses the role of the "coordinators" at the district level and the roles of the principal, assistant principal, and chair at the school level. Only in elementary schools is he willing to recognize the role of a "teacher specialist" as a member of a subject or grade-level team and mainly confined to "reading and mathematics."[94]

Other educators present an even more **top-down approach,** outlining a bureaucratic, big-city model in which the teacher is given the curriculum by the assistant principal or principal and is expected to teach that curriculum. Those teachers who are "master teachers" and capable of "mentoring other teachers" will climb a career ladder, become assistant principals or principals, and then serve as curriculum leaders in their school.[95]

According to Bolman and Deal, and other administrators,[96] the influence and contributions of the central office show up everywhere, although often they go unnoticed. In many school districts, the central office is crucial to curriculum development, instructional improvement, and assessment and evaluation. In fact, the central office administrators are expected to exhibit leadership and improve schools, although they are not always given credit. Not only does the central office provide support and foster leadership among teachers, supervisors, and principals, but also "central office leaders are effective, in part, because they are invisible, much as the skeleton in the body is invisible."[97]

Based on contemporary theories of social organization and open systems, and the latest we know about effective schools, we regard the teachers' role in curriculum making as central. They are part of a professional team, working with supervisors and administrators (and other colleagues) at all levels—school, district, and state. In small and medium-sized school districts, teachers also work with parents. Nevertheless, big-city and large school districts usually have centralized curriculum committees—a top-down model with minimal teacher input.

The Team Collaborative Approach

In our view, the teacher sees the curriculum as a whole and, at several points, serves as a resource and change agent: developing it in committees, implementing it in classrooms, and evaluating it as part of a technical team. To guarantee continuity and integration of the curriculum within and among subjects and grade levels, teachers must be actively involved in the curriculum, ideally as part of a curriculum team. An experienced teacher has a broad and deep understanding of teaching and learning; the needs and interests of students; and the content, methods, and materials that are realistic. Therefore, it is the teachers (not the supervisors or administrators) who have the best chance of taking curriculum making out of the realm of theory or judgment and translating it into practice and utility.

Accordingly, the school administration must see to it that every teacher is assigned to a *team* of teachers who share the same assignment (e.g., all fourth-grade elementary school teachers, all math teachers in high school). This team should meet on a regular basis to plan goals and objectives, prune and update content, review instructional materials and media and methods of assessment, and evaluate curriculum outcomes. Similarly, teachers need to engage in *peer observation* and receive feedback from peers (not only from supervisors).

---

[93] Harold Rugg, "The Foundations of Curriculum Making," in W. G. Whipple (ed.), *The Foundations of Curriculum Making,* Twenty-Sixth Yearbook of the NSSE, Part II (Bloomington, IL: Public School Publishers, 1930), pp. 439–440; Hollis L. Caswell and Doak S. Campbell, *Curriculum Development* (New York: American Book, 1935).

[94] Glatthorn, *Curriculum Leadership,* pp. 148–149.

[95] John C. Daresh, *Beginning the Assistant Principalship* (Thousand Oaks, CA: Corwin Press, 2004); Lester Golden, "The Secondary School Assistant Principal," *NASSP Bulletin, 79* (1995): 68–74; Barry Jentz, "First Time in a Position of Authority," *Phi Delta Kappan, 91* (2009): 56–60.

[96] Lee G. Bolman and Terrance Deal, "Leading with Soul and Spirit," *School Administrator,* 59 (2002): 21–26; Kathleen F. Grove, "The Invisible Role of the Central Office," *Educational Leadership,* 59 (2002): 45–47.

[97] Grove, "The Invisible Role of the Central Office," p. 46.

This would include new and experienced *study groups* on a regular basis, whereby they can share ideas, raise questions, discuss problems, and experiment. The administration needs to encourage teachers to become part of *action research*—committed to the improvement of curriculum and instruction.[98]

All teachers and supervisors should be expected to participate, on a regular basis throughout their professional careers, in curriculum committees, staff development/mentoring groups, *school improvement* (dealing with the school operation) and *school reform* (dealing with school change) task forces. The focus is on collaboration, collegiality, and teacher involvement—short and simple—in order to enhance school climate, professional growth, and student learning.

Throughout the literature there is the false assumption that educators know what collaboration means, how it is practiced, and what actually happens. **Collaboration** requires that professional teams and/or committee members interact with mutual respect and open communication; and jointly consider issues or problems, shared decision making, and joint ownership of purposes or programs. Collaboration among teachers, supervisors, and curriculum leaders involves sharing information or resources to meet a common goal—in our case, to implement change and innovation.[99] The collaborative exchange within a school should cut across grades, departments, and programs to involve a greater amount of communication and collegiality among staff members and to avoid departmentalization or turf problems.

Implementation as a Change Process

Whenever the curriculum leader attempts to implement the curriculum, the principles of change come into play. Much that is planned and developed often does not get implemented, much of what is new or innovative rarely gets off the ground, and what gets reported often gathers dust on shelves. Many charged with **curriculum implementation** neither have a good macro view of the change process nor realize that it occurs at different levels or in stages and must be monitored continually.

Although experienced leaders of curriculum realize that implementation is an essential aspect of curriculum development, only in recent years has implementation become a major concern—largely due to the nature of change and not curriculum. As two authors maintain in their review of change and innovation, "If there is one finding that stands out in our review, it is that effective implementation of . . . innovations required time, personal interaction and contacts, inservice training, and other forms of people-based support." Their research shows that the leadership style, personal relations, and personal contacts of implementers and planners are crucial to effect change and "implement most innovations."[100]

Incrementalism for Change

People want to change; yet they are also afraid of change, especially if it comes quickly or if they feel they have little control or influence over it. People become accustomed to the status quo and prefer to make modifications in behavior in small and gradual steps.

The professional world of the teacher does not allow for much receptivity to change. Many educators have described the teacher's daily routine as presenting little opportunity for interaction with colleagues. This isolation results partly from the school's organization into self-contained classrooms and partly from the teaching schedules. According to Seymour Sarason, the reality of the school has made teachers feel that professionally they are on their own: It is their responsibility, and theirs alone, to solve their own problems. This posture causes teachers to view change introduced into the program as an individual activity. Viewing their struggles as solitary, teachers often develop a psychological loneliness that results in hostility to administrators and outside change agents who seem insensitive to the teachers' plight.[101] Dan Lortie has noted that, in fact, many

[98]William A. Firestone and Carolyn Riehl, *A New Agenda for Research in Educational Leadership* (New York: Teachers College Press, Columbia University, 2005); John I. Goodlad, *In Praise of Education* (New York: Teachers College Press, Columbia University, 1998); Ann Lieberman and Lynn Miller, ed. *Teachers in Professional Communities,* rev. ed. (New York: Teachers College Press, Columbia University, 2008).

[99]Marilyn Friend and Lynne Cook, *Interactions: Collaboration Skills for School Professionals,* 2nd ed. (New York: Longman, 1996); James G. Henderson, et al., *Transformative Curriculum Leadership,* 3rd ed. (Columbus, OH: Merrill, 2007).

[100]Richard F. Elmore, *School Reform from the Inside Out* (Cambridge, MA: Harvard University Press, 2004); Michael Fullan, *The New Meaning of Educational Change,* 4th ed. (New York: Teachers College Press, Columbia University, 2007).

[101]Seymour B. Sarason, *The Case for a Change* (San Francisco: Jossey-Bass, 1994); Sarason, *Political Leadership and Educational Failure* (San Francisco: Jossey-Bass, 1998); Sarason, *Productive Learning* (Thousand Oaks, CA: Corwin Press, 2006).

factors detrimentally affect teachers' receptivity to change: "Teachers have a built-in resistance to change because they believe that their work environment has never permitted them to show what they can really do." Many proposals for change strike them as "frivolous and wasteful"—not addressing the real issues that deal with student disruptions or discipline, student reading problems, administrative support, and so on.[102]

Curriculum leaders must create an environment that encourages openness and trust and gives feedback so that teachers realize that their contributions are appreciated and their talents considered worthwhile. Teachers need time to "try" the new program to be implemented. They need time to reflect on new goals and objectives; to consider new content, learning experiences, and environments; and to try out new tasks. They need time to map out their tactics for meeting the challenges of the new program, and they need time to talk to their colleagues. Teachers can handle new programs if the changes demanded in their attitudes, behaviors, and knowledge are to be attained in manageable increments.

Curriculum implementation does not occur all at once with all teachers. Ideally, an implementation process allows sufficient time for certain groups of teachers to try out the new curriculum in "pieces." Researchers have found that teachers go through levels of use with a new curriculum. First, they orient themselves to the materials and engage in actions that will prepare them to deliver the curriculum. Their beginning use of the new curriculum is mechanical, and they follow the guide with little deviation. Their delivery of the curriculum becomes rather routine, and they take little initiative to make any changes in it. As they become more comfortable with the curriculum, they may begin to modify it, either to adjust it to their own educational philosophies or to better meet students' needs.[103]

Successful implementers appreciate that it takes time for teachers to "buy into" a new curriculum and to become skilled in delivering the new program. Curriculum leaders should anticipate teachers' questions and concerns and plan potential strategies for addressing them.

In planning **change** or **innovation**, those who will be affected by it experience various levels of concerns or anxieties: first, concern about self; second, concern about the mechanics or operation of the new program or curriculum; and third, concern about students (and others such as colleagues or the community).[104] These stages of concern are important for school leaders to recognize, especially those in charge of implementation of curriculum change. Effective administrators should be prepared first to deal with personal issues, then professional or technical issues, and finally client issues.

Resistance to Change

A curriculum leader who accepts that people are the key to successful curriculum activity and implementation is cognizant of the barriers that people place between themselves and change efforts. Perhaps the biggest barrier is inertia among the staff, the administration, or the community. Many people think that it is just easier to keep things as they are. If we think of ourselves as systems, we realize that we like to maintain steady states. We have traditions to which we adhere and institutions that we cherish—and we do not wish to change them. Many people are happy with the current school setup as a bureaucracy.

Wanting to keep things as they are is often mixed with believing that things do not need to be changed or that the change being suggested is unwise and will thus be unproductive in meeting school objectives. Educators themselves argue this point. Some say that the schools are fine and just need to be maintained, whereas others claim that the schools are not responsive to the times and require major modification. The status quo tends to be maintained if those suggesting change have not presented precise goals for the new program being suggested—that is, they have not planned adequately what the new program will look like or indicated ways in which the new program will be superior to the existing one.

Often, teachers have not been able or willing to keep up with scholarly development. They have not stayed abreast of the knowledge explosion that would allow them to feel committed to curriculum change and the implementation of new programs. Teachers frequently

---

[102]Dan Lortie, *Schoolteacher: A Sociological Study* (Chicago: University of Chicago Press, 1975), p. 235.

[103]Linda Darling-Hammond, *Professional Development Schools* (New York: Teachers College Press, Columbia University, 2005); Grant Wiggins and Jay McTighe, *Understanding by Design* (Columbus, OH: Merrill, 2006).

[104]Philip W. Jackson (ed.), *Contributing to Educational Change* (Berkeley, CA: McCutchan, 1988); Linda Lambert et al., *The Constructivist Leader,* 2nd ed. (New York: Teachers College Press, Columbia University, 2002); and Robert G. Owens and Thomas C. Valesky, *Organizational Behavior in Education: Adaptive Leadership and School Reform,* 10th ed. (Boston: Allyn and Bacon, 2011).

view change as just signaling more work—something else to add on to an already overloaded schedule for which little or no time is allotted. Usually, no extra money or reward is earmarked for the extra work either. Often they view new curricular programs as requiring them to learn new teaching skills, develop new competencies in curriculum development and the management of learning resources, or acquire new skills in interpersonal relations. In some instances, even staff development programs fail to develop those competencies necessary for teachers to become active participants in innovation.

Another reason administrators have difficulty getting teachers to accept innovation is, according to Edgar Friedenberg, people who go into teaching tend to be conformist in nature, not innovative. These people have succeeded in the school system as it has existed. They have learned to play it safe and to keep a low profile in a bureaucratic system run by administrators who do not like "waves" created.[105] They have found success and fulfillment first as students and now as teachers in this system, and for this reason many see no reason to change it. To many beginning teachers, the bureaucracy in place is a welcome and familiar support system, and they are often slow to change it.

Can educators cope with the demand for more change or for assuming change agent roles? Uncertainty fosters insecurity. Often educators who feel comfortable with the present are reluctant to change for a future they cannot comprehend or see clearly. People often prefer to stay with certain known deficiencies rather than venture forth to uncertain futures, even if the changes most likely would be improvements. Bringing new students or parents into the curriculum realm or organizing the program in new ways makes many teachers uneasy.

Another factor that causes people to resist change is the rapidity of change. Many people feel that if something is implemented this year, it will most likely be abandoned when another innovation appears and will thus make most of their efforts useless. There have, in fact, been enough bandwagons in education to make educators innovation-shy.

Sometimes people resist innovation and its implementation because they are ignorant. They either do not know about the innovation or have little information about it. Curriculum leaders must furnish all affected parties—teachers, pupils, parents, community members—with information about the nature of the program and its rationale. Ideally, all affected parties should be informed either directly or indirectly by school representatives of the reasons for the new program.

People often resist change, too, if no financial support or additional time is given for the effort. A project for which no monies are budgeted is rarely destined to be implemented. School districts often budget monies for materials but fail to allocate funds for the creation of the curriculum plan, its delivery within the classroom, or necessary in-service training. Also, we raise the question of whether a person who earns $50,000 (or slightly more) is supposed to be a **change agent.** Teachers are not paid enough to innovate; that is the role of a leader, not of a teacher. Teachers are required to implement change, but the school leader (principal) or school district leader (superintendent) should be the one to initiate change and provide the ingredients and processes for constructive change.

Conversely, teachers are an untapped source of energy and insight, capable of profoundly changing the schools if they act as a group. Many teachers desire to do something different or innovative, but have few ideas of what it is they wish to do or how to implement it. Most teachers have a deep sense of caring and desire to help children. They prefer to teach; they are motivated in helping young people, embedded in the ideas of "feminist" pedagogy, rather than serving as bureaucrats or technocrats.[106]

It may seem that administrators face insurmountable problems. But resistance to change is good because it requires change agents to think carefully about the innovations and to consider the human dynamics involved in implementing programs. Having to fight for change protects the organization from becoming proponents of just random change and educational bandwagonism.

Improving Receptivity to Change

Curriculum activity involves people thinking and acting. Leaders of curriculum development, and especially implementation, realize that the human equation is of

[105]Edgar A. Friedenberg, *Coming of Age in America* (New York: Random House, 1965).

[106]Margaret Smith Crocco, Petra Munro, and Kathleen Weiler, *Pedagogies of Resistance: Women Educator Activists* (New York: Teachers College Press, Columbia University, 1999); Madeleine Grumet, *Bitter Milk: Women and Teaching* (Amherst, MA: University of Massachusetts Press, 1988); Noddings, *Educating Moral People: A Caring Alternative to Character Education.*

paramount importance and that they must therefore understand how people react to change. Often people say they are willing to change but act as though they are unwilling to adjust. A successful change agent knows how people react to change and how to encourage them to be receptive to change.[107] A wise administrator understands that teachers often are reluctant to change their own behavior, because of habit, tradition, or laziness, but often feel that their colleagues need changing. People often say they want change, but not for themselves, and she must separate lip service from action. The change agent must listen carefully and move slowly in these situations in order to incorporate into the change process those who really prefer no change.

Curriculum innovation and implementation require face-to-face interaction—person-to-person contact. People charged with implementation must understand the interpersonal dimension of leadership. Curriculum innovation and implementation is a group process involving individuals working together. The group not only enables certain actions to occur but also serves to change its individual members.

Analysis of efforts over the past decade to improve schools has resulted in a much better understanding of the steps that must be taken to ensure that change and innovation efforts have a significant and lasting impact. Among the lessons learned from past change efforts are the following:

1. *Adaptive Problem Solving.* Change or innovation must be introduced in such a way that the staff can reasonably implement it.
2. *School-Level Focus.* The focus in bringing about change must be at the school level where the problems occur; teaching and learning take place at the school level, not the district level.
3. *Compatibility.* Successful reform depends on whether changes introduced are implementable, that is, if teachers perceive that they can use the reforms.
4. *Principal's Leadership.* Successful implementation requires change in institutional arrangements and structures; the building principal is the key person for making such decisions.
5. *Teacher Involvement.* To fully cooperate, teachers must have a voice in designing and implementing change. They must be given time, resources, and opportunity to collaborate and make decisions.
6. *Top-Down/Bottom-Up Approaches.* Both approaches have been underscored as important for change. The bottom-up approach encourages a sense of ownership among teachers. The top-down approach communicates to teachers: "We are trying a new approach, we are going to implement it, and we are going to help each other."
7. *Staff Development.* Staff development in terms of continuous participation, feedback, and support of the staff is essential for school improvement.
8. *School-Business Cooperation.* Some of the most promising reforms and innovations include partnerships between schools and business—sort of a revitalization or rediscovery of the old stewardship concept of the private sector.[108]

Curriculum leaders can also increase educators' willingness to change by linking the needs and expectations of the individuals with those of the organization. Each person has certain needs and interests that she expects to fulfill within the school organization. Every individual who comes into a system plays a multitude of roles; each professional brings to her role a personality as well. Rarely, however, are institutional expectations absolutely compatible with individual needs. Misalignment can cause conflict. Administrators need to recognize that they cannot always avoid this conflict; they must manage it. The way they manage it is reflected in their own personality and leadership behavior.

At the school level, the principal is the key person for matching individual needs and institutional expectations; he or she is crucial to creating school spirit and receptivity to change by promoting trust and teamwork. However, the principal can dampen spirit and change by promoting distrust and demoralization. What matters most to principals—values and attitudes—gets articulated (directly and indirectly) to the school staff. At the school district level, the same is true, only then the key person is the superintendent. What the superintendent values gets filtered down to the central administration, principals, and school staff. (See Administrative Advice 13–3.)

[107]Michael Fullan, "The Change Leader," *Educational Leadership,* 59 (2002): 16–21; Carl D. Glickman, "Educational Leadership: Failure to Use Our Imagination," *Phi Delta Kappan,* 87 (2006): 689–690.

[108]Daniel U. Levine and Allan C. Ornstein, "Effective Schools: What Research Says About Success," *High School Magazine,* 1 (1993): 32–34; Allan C. Ornstein, et al., *Foundations of Education,* 11th ed. (Boston, Houghton Mifflin, 2011).

ADMINISTRATIVE ADVICE 13–3

Information Checklist for Implementing Curriculum Change and Innovation

Administrators involved in curriculum implementation will have concerns about change and how teachers will react to it. People prefer the status quo when they are familiar and satisfied with it. This checklist consists of a number of questions that deal with the organization of information that school leaders might wish to include in a presentation to the staff. Their emphasis is mainly on teachers' personal and technical concerns.

1. What are the implications of the new program for staff development?
2. How much additional teacher preparation time will the new program require?
3. Do teachers feel the innovation is coming from outside or within the organization (school, school district)?
4. How does the new program fit in to the state standards?
5. What kind of resources and/or materials will be provided?
6. Does the new program benefit students (in terms of learning) or teachers (e.g. by bringing greater recognition or reward)?
7. How does the new program change content which students are expected to learn?
8. Are the new materials or content appropriate for the students' reading levels?
9. Do the leaders responsible for the new program show support for the change?
10. Who, specifically, can teachers rely on for gaining feedback or support?
11. Are new instructional procedures required? What kind of feedback or support will teachers receive regarding the new procedures?
12. How will collaborative action among staff members be implemented?
13. Which groups, if any, are threatened by the new program? Why?
14. How is classroom management affected by the new program? Does the new program make things more (or less) manageable?
15. How do parents feel about the program?
16. What new equipment, if any, will be required? Are the teachers familiar with the operation of this new equipment?
17. Does the new program coincide with the philosophical beliefs and learning principles of the majority of teachers? To what extent must opposing beliefs and feelings be addressed?
18. How is the new program to be evaluated?

Summary

1. Curriculum can be defined in many ways: as a plan, in terms of experiences, as a field of study, and in terms of subject matter and grade levels. Most curriculum leaders in schools are comfortable with three out of four definitions, except the one about a field of study, with which theoreticians and professors tend to feel more comfortable.
2. There are four basic approaches to developing curriculum: behavioral, managerial, systems, and humanistic. Most school administrators adhere to the first two approaches. The systems approach is a little more theoretical, and the humanistic approach tends to coincide with progressive thought. The nontechnical model relies on personal, philosophical, and reflective ideas; most administrators would consider the model to be impractical.
3. The classic method of curriculum development is based on the Tyler model, which is behaviorist in nature.

PRO CON DEBATE

Teaching Values

The crux of the issue can be simply stated: Should schools teach a set of values as a framework for determining, or at least influencing, subject content and its organization, broad issues and tasks, or what belief systems and attitudes should guide students' actions?

Question: Should schools implement a values-centered curriculum?

Arguments PRO

1. There are certain basic core values (or American values) that we should be able to agree upon and incorporate into curriculum.
2. Schools and classrooms are appropriate places for students to discuss values and share a diversity of opinions.
3. Organizing our values according to a generalized framework or set of criteria results in personal commitment, self-confidence, and social responsibility.
4. Schools have a responsibility to teach valuing.
5. Valuing is part of citizenship and national pride. Given our growing diverse population, agreed-to values can be the cement that holds the nation together.
6. A set of core values helps children and youth express themselves, make wise choices, and be responsible for their behavior. It also helps in the self-actualization and potential development of students.

Arguments CON

1. Values are subjective, not neutral, and therefore we cannot agree upon them. It boils down to whose values? Who speaks for the community?
2. Discussion of values results in peer pressure and school pressure—whatever is the dominant or prevailing attitude of the group.
3. Organizing our values according to a generalized framework or set of criteria results in group thinking and group behavior.
4. Valuing is the responsibility of the home and/or church.
5. Valuing is not part of citizenship, but it can lead to an "ism"—some form of indoctrination—such as nationalism, ethnocentrism, fascism, communism, and so forth.
6. Learning to make wise choices and take responsibility for one's actions is based on learning essential knowledge, which has enabled humankind to advance civilization; learning how to think, not feel, is the basis for self-actualization.

4. There are a number of fundamental questions that help determine the planning and implementation of curriculum, the function of subject matter, and the role of curriculum leaders and specialists.
5. Regardless of definition or approach, curriculum can be organized into three major components: content, experiences, and environment. Content basically answers the *what* of curriculum, and experiences and environment answer the *how*.
6. Curriculum implementation is largely a function of leadership style and involves personal interaction, program development, and organizational structures.
7. Successful change involves collaboration, collegiality, and communication—what the authors call the three Cs.
8. In implementing curriculum, administrators need to consider the principles of change and how they can influence change among staff members.
9. Ideally, curriculum leaders must understand how professional people can plan, implement, and evaluate change.
10. People often resist change, as well as accept it. An effective administrator can work with and convince the staff to be more receptive than resistant to change. A number of leadership characteristics improve receptivity to change among staff participants.

Key Terms

machine theory
curriculum engineering
curriculum development
sources of information
screen
goals
curriculum design
nontechnical model
content and experiences
balanced curriculum
cultural literacy
great books
general manager
curriculum-instructional leader
textbooks
toxic cultures
positive cultures
bottom-up approach
top-down approach
collaboration
curriculum implementation
change or innovation
change agent

Discussion Questions

1. What definition of curriculum do you prefer? Why?
2. What approach to curriculum do you prefer? Why?
3. In developing curriculum, what criteria for selecting content do you feel are important? What criteria not mentioned in the chapter would you add? In developing curriculum, what criteria for selecting experiences do you feel are important? What criteria not mentioned in the chapter would you add?
4. How can curriculum implementation be improved in your school? As a curriculum leader, how do you involve teachers and students, if at all, in curriculum making?
5. How can the change process in schools be improved? As a curriculum leader, what specific steps would you take to improve the receptivity to change in your school?

Suggested Readings

Deal, Terrence, E. and Kent D. Peterson. *The Leadership Paradox* (San Francisco: Jossey-Bass, 2000). The authors explain how leadership and management serve as complements for school improvement and curriculum reform.

Drucker, Peter. *The Leader of the Future* (San Francisco: Jossey-Bass, 1998). The author offers unique perspectives on management and leadership and how organizations and their leaders must evolve.

Fullan, Michael, and Clif St. Germain, *Learning Places: A Field Guide for Improving Schools.* (Thousand Oaks, CA: Corwin Press, 2007). A practical guide to inspiring school change and reform.

Glickman, Carl D., et al. *Supervision and Instructional Leadership,* 8th ed. (Boston, MA: Allyn and Bacon, 2010). The book describes a "bottom-up" administrative approach to supervising and evaluating instruction.

Ornstein, Allan C., Edward F. Pajak, and Stacey B. Ornstein, *Contemporary Issues in Curriculum,* 5th ed. (Boston: Allyn and Bacon, 2011). A comprehensive book that focuses on contemporary and controversial issues in curriculum.

Sarason, Seymour B. *Educational Reform: A Self-Scrutinizing Memoir* (New York: Teachers College Press, Columbia University, 2002). The author shares his thoughts about the future of school reform.

Tyler, Ralph W. *Basic Principles of Curriculum and Instruction* (Chicago: University of Chicago Press, 1949). This classic curriculum book largely exemplifies a behavioral and rational approach.

14

Analyzing and Improving Teaching

FOCUSING QUESTIONS

1 What is the difference between teacher processes and teacher products?

2 How can the interaction between the teacher and students in the classroom be measured?

3 What are the characteristics of a good teacher?

4 How can we determine teacher effectiveness?

5 How would you define an expert teacher and a novice teacher? How do experts and novices differ in the role they assume in classroom instruction and classroom management?

6 What are some current methods for understanding how teachers teach and what they are thinking about when they are teaching?

7 Should public school teachers be committed to teaching moral values? Why? Why not?

8 Should teachers be primarily evaluated on improving student test outcomes?

9 For what reasons do students from industrialized countries outperform U.S. students on math and science tests?

In this chapter, we present an overview of the research on effective teaching and five basic ways of analyzing teaching: teacher styles, teacher interactions, teacher characteristics, teacher effects, and teacher contexts. In the early stages of research, up to the mid-1970s, theorists were concerned with **teacher processes**—that is, what the teacher was doing while teaching. They attempted to define and explain good teaching by focusing on teacher styles, teacher interactions, and teacher characteristics. From about 1975 to 1990, researchers shifted their concerns to **teacher products**—that is, student outcomes—and the assessment focused on teacher effects. More recently, theorists have attempted to analyze the culture, language, and thoughts of teachers, combine (rather than separate) teaching and learning processes, and use qualitative methods to assess what they call **teacher contexts.** We intend to move the discussion one step further, as we reconceptualize teaching, and examine the need for **humanistic teaching.**

The second part of the chapter deals with teaching and testing. Beginning teachers in particular should expect to encounter some problems and frustrations, but with proper supervisory and administrative assistance they should be able to improve their technical skills and student test scores. International test comparisons, as well as national and state test scores, are examined in context with the notion of human capital.

Review of the Research on Teaching

Over the years thousands of studies have been conducted to identify the behaviors of successful and unsuccessful teachers. However, teaching is a complex act; what works in some situations with some teachers may not work in different school settings with different subjects, students, and goals. There will always be teachers who break many of the rules of procedures and methods and yet are profoundly successful. There will always be teachers who follow the rules and are unsuccessful.

Some educational researchers maintain that we cannot distinguish between "good" and "poor" or "effective" and "ineffective" teachers, that no one knows for sure or agrees on what the competent teacher is, that few authorities can "define, prepare for, or measure teacher competence."[1] They point out that disagreement over terms, problems in measurement, and the complexity of the teaching act are major reasons for the negligible results in judging teacher behavior. The result is that much of the data have been confusing, contradictory, or confirmations of common sense (a cheerful teacher is a good teacher), and that so-called acceptable findings have often been repudiated.[2] The more complex or unpredictable one views teaching as being, the more one is compelled to conclude that it is difficult to agree upon generalizations about successful teaching.[3]

Other researchers assert that appropriate teaching behaviors can be defined (and learned by teachers), that good or effective teachers can be distinguished from poor or ineffective teachers, and that the magnitude of the effect of these differences on students can be determined.[4] They conclude that the kinds of questions teachers ask, the ways they respond to students, their expectations of and attitudes toward students, their classroom management techniques, their teaching

---

[1]Bruce J. Biddle and William J. Ellena, "The Integration of Teacher Effectiveness," in B. J. Biddle and W. J. Ellena (eds.), *Contemporary Research on Teacher Effectiveness* (New York: Holt, Rinehart and Winston, 1964), p. 3.

[2]Allan C. Ornstein, "Successful Teachers: Who They Are," *American School Board Journal*, 180 (1993): 24–27; Ralph T. Putnam and Hilda Borko, "What Do New Views of Knowledge . . . Say About Research on Teaching?" *Educational Researcher*, 29 (2000), pp. 4–16.

[3]Homer Coker, Donald M. Medley, and Robert S. Soar, "How Valid Are Expert Opinions about Effective Teachers?" *Phi Delta Kappan*, 62 (1980): 131–134, 149; Lee S. Schulman, "A Union of Insufficiencies: Strategies for Teacher Assessment," *Educational Leadership*, 46 (1988): 35–41; Arthur E. Wise and Jane A. Leibbrand, "Standards and Teacher Quality," *Phi Delta Kappan*, 81 (2000): 612–621.

[4]Jere E. Brophy, "Classroom Management Techniques," *Education and Urban Society*, 18 (1986): 182–194; N. L. Gage and Margaret C. Needels, "Process-Product Research on Teaching," *Elementary School Journal*, 89 (1989): 253–300; Catherine E. Snow, "Knowing What We Know: Children, Teachers, Researchers," *Educational Researcher*, 30 (2001): 3–4.

methods, and their general teaching behaviors (sometimes referred to as "classroom climate") all make a difference. However, in some cases the positive effects of teachers upon student performance may be masked or washed out by the relative negative effects of other teachers in the same school.[5] The teachers may not be the only variable, or even the major one, in the teaching-learning equation, but they can make a difference, either positive or negative. Here it should be noted that negative teacher influences have greater impact than positive ones, in that students can be turned into nonlearners and experience loss of self-concept in a matter of weeks as a result of a hostile or intimidating teacher.

If teachers do not make a difference, then the profession has problems. If teachers do not make a difference, the notions of teacher evaluation, teacher accountability, and teacher performance are nonworkable; sound educational policy cannot be formulated, and there is little hope for many students and little value in trying to learn how to teach. However, even if we are convinced that teachers have an effect, it is still true that we are unable to assess with confidence the influence a teacher has on student performance because the learning variables are numerous and the teaching interactions are complex.

Teacher Styles

Teacher style is viewed as a broad dimension or personality type that encompasses teacher stance, pattern of behavior, mode of performance, and attitude toward self and others. Penelope Peterson defines teacher style in terms of how teachers utilize space in the classroom, their choice of instructional activities and materials, and their method of student grouping.[6] Still others describe teacher style as an *expressive* aspect of teaching (characterizing the emotional relationship between students and teachers, such as warm or businesslike) and as an *instrumental* aspect (how teachers carry out the task of instruction, organize learning, and set classroom standards).[7]

Regardless of which definition of teacher style you prefer, the notion of stability or pattern is central. Certain behaviors and methods are stable over time, even with different students and different classroom situations. There is a purpose of rationale—a predictable teacher pattern even in different classroom contexts. Aspects of teaching style dictated by personality can be modified by early experiences and perceptions and by appropriate training as a beginning teacher. As years pass, a teacher's style becomes more ingrained and it takes a more powerful set of stimuli and more intense feedback to make changes. If you watch teachers at work, including teachers in your school, you can sense that each one has a personal style for teaching, for structuring the classroom, and for delivering the lesson.

Research on Teacher Styles

Lippitt and White laid the groundwork for a more formal classification of what a teacher does in the classroom. Initially, they developed an instrument for describing the "social atmosphere" of children's clubs and for quantifying the effects of group and individual behavior. The results have been generalized in numerous research studies and textbooks on teaching. The classic study used classifications of authoritarian, democratic, and laissez-faire styles.[8]

The *authoritarian* teacher directs all the activities of the program. This style shares some characteristics with what is now called the *direct teacher.* The *democratic* teacher encourages group participation and is willing to let students share in the decision-making process. This behavior is typical of what is now called the *indirect*

[5]Thomas L. Good, Bruce J. Biddle, and Jere E. Brophy, *Teachers Make a Difference* (New York: Holt, Rinehart and Winston, 1975); Allan C. Ornstein, "A Look at Teacher Effectiveness Research: Theory and Practice," *NASSP Bulletin*, 74 (1990): 78–88; Pamela Tucker, "Helping Struggling Teachers," *Educational Leadership*, 58 (2001): 52–56.

[6]Penelope L. Peterson, "Direct Instruction Reconsidered," in P. L. Peterson and H. J. Walberg (eds.), *Research on Teaching: Concepts, Findings, and Implications* (Berkeley, CA: McCutchan, 1979), pp. 57–69. Also see Richard F. Elmore, Penelope L. Peterson, and Sarah J. McCarthy, *Restructuring in the Classroom* (San Francisco: Jossey-Bass, 1996).

[7]Donald R. Cruickshank and Donald Haefele, "Good Teachers, Plural," *Educational Leadership*, 58 (2001): 26–30; Susan L. Lytle and Marilyn Cochran-Smith, "Teacher Research as a Way of Knowing," *Harvard Educational Review*, 62 (1992): 447–474; Karen Zumwalt, "Alternate Routes to Teaching," *Journal of Teacher Education*, 43 (1992): 83–92.

[8]Ronald Lippitt and Ralph K.White, "The Social Climate of Children's Groups," in R. G. Barker, J. S. Kounin, and H. F. Wright (eds.), *Child Behavior and Development* (New York: McGraw-Hill, 1943), pp. 485–508. Also see Kurt Lewin, Ronald Lippitt, and Ralph K. White, "Patterns of Aggressive Behavior in Experimentally Created Social Climates," *Journal of Social Psychology*, 20 (1939): 271–299.

Table 14-1 Flanders's Classroom Interaction Analysis Scale

I. Teacher Talk

A. Indirect Influence

1. *Accepts Feelings.* Accepts and clarifies the tone of feeling of the students in an unthreatening manner. Feelings may be positive or negative. Predicting or recalling feelings is included.
2. *Praises or Encourages.* Praises or encourages student action or behavior. Jokes that release tension, but not at the expense of another individual, nodding head or saying "Um hm?" or "Go on" are included.
3. *Accepts or Uses Ideas of Student.* Clarifying, building, or developing ideas suggested by a student. As teacher brings more of his own ideas into play, shift to category 5.
4. *Asks Questions.* Asking a question about content or procedure with the intent that a student answer.

B. Direct Influence

5. *Lecturing.* Giving facts or opinions about content or procedure; expressing her own ideas, asking rhetorical questions.
6. *Giving Directions.* Directions, commands, or orders which students are expected to comply with.
7. *Criticizing or Justifying Authority.* Statements intended to change student behavior from unacceptable to acceptable pattern; bawling someone out; stating why the teacher is doing what he is doing; extreme self-reference.

II. Student Talk

8. *Student Talk: Response.* Talk by students in response to teacher. Teacher initiates the contact or solicits student statement.
9. *Student Talk: Initiation.* Talk initiated by students. If "calling on" student is only to indicate who may talk next, observer must decide whether student wanted to talk.

III. Silence

10. *Silence or Confusion.* Pauses, short periods of silence, and periods of confusion in which communication cannot be understood by the observer.

Source: Ned A. Flanders, *Teacher Influence, Pupil Attitudes, and Achievement* (Washington, DC: U.S. Government Printing Office, 1965), p. 20.

teacher. The *laissez-faire* teacher (now often considered to be an unorganized or ineffective teacher) provides no (or few) goals and directions for group or individual behavior.

One of the most ambitious research studies on teacher styles was conducted by Ned Flanders and his associates between 1954 and 1970. Flanders focused on developing an instrument for quantifying verbal communication in the classroom.[9] Every three seconds observers sorted teacher talk into one of four categories of *indirect* behavior or one of three categories of *direct* behavior. Student talk was categorized as response or initiation, and there was a final category representing silence or when the observer could not determine who was talking. The ten categories are shown in Table 14–1.

Flanders's indirect teacher tended to overlap with Lippitt and White's democratic teaching style, and the direct teacher tended to exhibit behaviors similar to their authoritarian teacher. Flanders found that students in the indirect classrooms learned more and exhibited more constructive and independent attitudes than students in the direct classrooms. All types of students in all types of subject classes learned more working with the indirect (more flexible) teachers. In an interesting side note, Flanders found that as much as 80 percent of the classroom time is generally consumed in teacher talk. We will return to this point later.

The following questions, developed by Amidon and Flanders, represent a possible direction for organizing and analyzing observations.

1. What is the relationship of teacher talk to student talk? This can be answered by comparing the total number of observations in categories 1 to 7 with categories 8 and 9.
2. Is the teacher more direct or indirect? This can be answered by comparing categories 1 to 4 (indirect) with categories 5 to 7 (direct).
3. How much class time does the teacher spend lecturing? This can be answered by comparing category 5

[9]Ned A. Flanders, *Teacher Influence, Pupil Attitudes, and Achievement* (Washington, DC: U.S. Government Printing Office, 1965); Flanders, *Analyzing Teaching Behavior* (Reading, MA: Addison-Wesley, 1970).

with the total number of observations in categories 1 to 4 and 6 to 7.

4. Does the teacher ask divergent or convergent questions? This can be answered by comparing category 4 to categories 8 and 9.[10]

The data obtained from this system do not show when, why, or in what context teacher-student interaction occurs, only how often particular types of interaction occur. Nonetheless, the system is useful for making teachers aware of their interaction behaviors in the classroom.

The Flanders system can be used to examine teacher-student verbal behaviors in any classroom, regardless of grade level or subject. Someone can observe the verbal behavior of a prospective, beginning, or even experienced teacher and show how direct or indirect the teacher is. (Most prospective and beginning teachers tend to exhibit direct behavior, since they talk too much. Professors also usually lecture and thus exhibit many direct behaviors while teaching.) In fact, education students and student teachers often associate good teaching with some form of lecturing, since most of their recent teaching models are professors who often do a lot of talking—the wrong method for younger students who lack the maturity, attentiveness, and focus to cope with a passive learning situation for any length of time. Beginning teachers, therefore, must often unlearn what they have learned from their experiences with their own professors. (See Administrative Advice 14–1.)

Teacher Interaction

An approach to the study of teacher behavior is based on systematic observation of **teacher-student interaction** in the classroom as, for example, in the work of Flanders, which we have already described. The analysis of interaction often deals with a specific teacher behavior and a series of these behaviors constituting a larger behavior, described and recorded by an abstract unit of measurement that may vary in size and time (for example, every 3 seconds a recording is made).

[10]Edmund J. Amidon and Ned A. Flanders, *The Role of the Teacher in the Classroom* (St. Paul, MN: Amidon & Associates, 1971). Also see Robert F. McNergney and Carol A. Carrier, *Teacher Development*, 2nd ed. (New York: Macmillan, 1991).

Verbal Communication

In a classic study of teacher-student interaction, Arno Bellack and colleagues analyzed the linguistic behavior of teachers and students in the classroom.[11] Classroom activities are carried out in large part by verbal interaction between students and teachers; few classroom activities can be carried out without the use of language. The research, therefore, focused on language as the main instrument of communication in teaching. Four basic verbal behaviors or "moves" were labeled.

1. *Structuring moves* serve the function of focusing attention on subject matter or classroom procedures and beginning interaction between students and teachers. They set the context for subsequent behavior. For example, beginning a class by announcing the topic to be discussed is a structuring move.
2. *Soliciting moves* are designed to elicit a verbal or physical response. For example, the teacher asks a question about the topic with the hope of encouraging a response from the students.
3. *Responding moves* occur in relation to and after the soliciting behaviors. Their ideal function is to fulfill the expectations of the soliciting behaviors.
4. *Reacting moves* are sometimes occasioned by one or more of the above behaviors, but are not directly elicited by them. Reacting behaviors serve to modify, clarify, or judge the structuring, soliciting, or responding behavior.[12]

According to Bellack, these pedagogical moves occur in combinations he called **teaching cycles**. A cycle usually begins with a structuring or soliciting move by the teacher, both of which are initiative behaviors; continues with a responding move from a student; and ends with some kind of reacting move by the teacher. In most cases the cycle begins and ends with the teacher. The investigators' analysis of the classroom also produced several insights.

1. Teachers dominate verbal activities. The teacher-student ratio in words spoken is 3:1. (This evidence corresponds with Flanders's finding that teachers' talk is 80 percent of classroom activity.)
2. Teacher and student moves are clearly defined. The teacher engages in structuring, soliciting, and

[11]Arno A. Bellack et al., *The Language of the Classroom* (New York: Teachers College Press, Columbia University, 1966).

[12]Ibid.

ADMINISTRATIVE ADVICE 14–1

Observing Other Teachers to Improve Teaching Patterns

The statement "Teachers are born, not made" fails to take into account the wealth knowledge we have about good teaching and how children learn. Teachers can supplement their pedagogical knowledge and practices by observing other good teachers. Supervisors or administrators are in a position to ensure that their school has a policy for inexperienced teachers or for those who need assistance, and to see how other teachers organize their classrooms and instruct their students. Here are some of the things teachers can observe.

Student-Teacher Interaction

- What evidence was there that the teacher truly understood the needs of the students?
- What techniques were used to encourage students' respect for each other's turn to talk?
- What student behaviors in class were acceptable and unacceptable?
- How did the teacher motivate students?
- How did the teacher encourage student discussion?
- In what way did the teacher see things from the students' point of view?
- What evidence was there that the teacher responded to students' individual differences?
- What evidence was there that the teacher responded to students' affective development?

Teaching-Learning Processes

- Which instructional methods interested the students?
- How did the teacher provide for transitions between instructional activities?
- What practical life experiences (or activities) were used by the teacher to integrate concepts being learned?
- How did the teacher minimize student frustration or confusion concerning the skills or concepts being taught?
- In what way did the teacher encourage creative, imaginative work from students?
- What instructional methods were used to make students think about ideas, opinions, or answers?
- How did the teacher arrange the groups? What social factors were evident within the groups?
- How did the teacher encourage independent (or individualized) student learning?
- How did the teacher integrate the subject matter with other subjects?

Classroom Environment

- How did the teacher utilize classroom space/equipment effectively?
- What did you like and dislike about the physical environment of the classroom?

reacting behaviors, while the student is usually limited to responding. (This also corresponds with Flanders's finding that most teachers dominate classrooms in such a way as to make students dependent.)

3. Teachers initiate about 85 percent of the cycles. The basic unit of verbal interaction is the soliciting-responding pattern. Verbal interchanges occur at a rate of slightly less than two cycles per minute.
4. In approximately two-thirds of the behaviors and three-fourths of the verbal interplay, talk is content oriented.
5. About 60 percent of the total discourse is fact oriented.

In summary, the data suggest that the classroom is teacher dominated, subject centered, and fact oriented. The student's primary responsibility seems to be to respond to the teacher's soliciting behaviors. As an instructional leader, you need to help teachers break this cycle of teaching.

Nonverbal Communication

According to Miles Patterson, nonverbal behavior in the classroom serves five teacher functions: (1) *providing information*, or elaborating upon a verbal statement; (2) *regulating interactions*, such as pointing to someone; (3) *expressing intimacy* or liking, such as smiling or touching a student on the shoulder; (4) *exercising social control*, reinforcing a classroom rule, say, by proximity or distance, and (5) *facilitating goals*, as when demonstrating a skill that requires motor activity or gesturing.[13] These categories are not mutually exclusive; there is some overlap, and nonverbal cues may serve more than one function depending on how they are used.

Although the teaching-learning process is ordinarily associated with verbal interaction, **nonverbal communication** operates as a silent language that influences the process. What makes the study of nonverbal communication so important and fascinating is that some researchers contend that it comprises about 65 percent of the social meaning of the classroom communication system.[14] As the old saying goes, "Actions speak louder than words."

In another study of 225 teachers (and school principals) in forty-five schools, Stephens and Valentine observed ten specific nonverbal behaviors: (1) smiles or frowns, (2) eye contact, (3) head nods, (4) gestures, (5) dress, (6) interaction distance, (7) touch, (8) body movement, (9) posture, and (10) seating arrangements.[15] In general, the first four behaviors are easily interpreted by the observer; some smiles, eye contact, head nods, and gestures are expected, but too many make students suspicious or uneasy. Dress is a matter of professional code and expectation. Distance, touch, body movement, posture, and seating are open to more interpretation, are likely to have personal meaning between communicators, and are based on personalities and social and cultural relationships.[16] Different types of these five behaviors, especially distance, touch, and body movement, can be taken as indications of the degree of formality in the relationship between the communicators, from intimate and personal to social and public. Teachers should maintain a social or public relationship—that is, a formal relationship—with their students. Behaviors that are inappropriate or could be interpreted as indicating intimate and personal relations must be avoided. It is difficult to define the point in a student-teacher relationship where friendliness can be misconstrued. To some extent that point differs for different students and teachers. It is fine to be warm, friendly, and caring—but too much warmth or friendliness in your interaction (distance, touch, body movement, posture) can get you in trouble as a teacher. Teachers need to be aware of the messages they are sending to students, especially if the students are teenagers and teachers are in their twenties.

When the teacher's verbal and nonverbal cues contradict one another, according to Charles Galloway, the students tend to read the nonverbal cues as a true reflection of the teacher's feelings. Galloway developed global guidelines for observing nonverbal communication of teachers, which he referred to as the "silent behavior of space, time, and body."[17]

1. *Space.* A teacher's use of space conveys meaning to students. For example, teachers who spend most of their time by the chalkboard or at their desk may convey insecurity, a reluctance to venture into student territory.
2. *Time.* How teachers utilize classroom time is an indication of how they value certain instructional activities. The elementary teacher who devotes a great deal of time to reading but little to mathematics is conveying a message to the students.
3. *Body Maneuvers.* Nonverbal cues are used by teachers to control students. The raised eyebrow, the pointed finger, the silent stare all communicate meaning.

Galloway suggests that various nonverbal behaviors of the teacher can be viewed as encouraging or restricting. By their facial expressions, gestures, and body movements, teachers affect student participation and performance in the classroom. These nonverbal behaviors—ranging from highly focused to minimal eye contact, a pat on the back to a frown, a supporting to an angry look—all add up

---

[13]Miles L. Patterson, *Nonverbal Behavior: A Functional Perspective* (New York: Springer, 1983).

[14]Sonia Nieto, *Language, Culture, and Teaching* (Mahwah, NJ: Erlbaum, 2002); Albert Oosterhof, *Developing and Using Classroom Assessments,* 2nd ed. (Columbus, OH: Merrill, 1999).

[15]Pat Stephens and Jerry Valentine, "Assessing Principal Nonverbal Communication," *Educational Research Quarterly,* 11 (1986): 60–68.

[16]D. Jean Claudinin and F. Michael Connelly, *Narrative Inquiry* (San Francisco: Jossey-Bass, 1999); Jane Roland Martin, *Cultural Miseducation* (New York: Teachers College Press, Columbia University, 2002).

[17]Charles M. Galloway, "Nonverbal Communication," *Theory into Practice* (December 1968): 172–175; Galloway, "Nonverbal Behavior and Teacher Student Relationships: An Intercultural Perspective," in A. Wolfgang (ed.), *Nonverbal Behavior: Perspectives, Applications, Intercultural Insights* (Toronto: Hogrefe, 1984), pp. 411–430.

to suggest approval and support or irritability and discouragement. In sum, these nonverbal behaviors influence teacher-student interactions. What teachers should do, both in their personal and professional pursuits, is to become aware of how their mannerisms influence their communication and relations with others.

Jacqueline Hausen makes a similar point, that when teachers' verbal and nonverbal behavior are incongruent, students will believe what they see and not what they hear. Teachers therefore can never be sure whether students receive the intended verbal message. She also points out that people communicate with others even when they do not talk; in fact, "up to 90% of what people say and feel is communicated through their actions, not their words." Students also have different zones of acceptable proximity, based on culture, age and personality. For example, Hispanics and Middle Eastern peers stand close together and accept teacher proximity more that white and Asian students. Preschoolers and primary children communicate at close range and touch others. As they mature, proximity correlates with culture, personality, and relationships.[18]

Teacher Expectations

Teachers communicate their expectations of students through verbal and nonverbal cues. It is well established that these expectations affect the interaction between teachers and students and, eventually, the performance of students. In many cases teacher expectations become **self-fulfilling prophecies;** that is, if the teacher expects students to be slow or exhibit deviant behavior, the teacher treats them accordingly, and in response they adopt such behaviors.

The research on teacher expectations is rooted in the legal briefs and arguments of Kenneth Clark, prepared during his fight for desegregated schools in the 1950s and in his subsequent description of the problem in New York City's Harlem schools.[19] He pointed out that prophesying low achievement for black students not only provides teachers with an excuse for their students' failure but also communicates a sense of inevitable failure to the students.

Clark's thesis was given empirical support a few years later by Rosenthal and Jacobsen's *Pygmalion in the Classroom,* a study of students in the San Francisco schools.[20] After controlling for the ability of students, experimenters told teachers there was reason to expect that certain students would perform better—and that expectancy was fulfilled. However, confidence in *Pygmalion* diminished when Robert Thorndike, one of the most respected measurement experts, pointed out that there were several flaws in the methodology and that the tests were unreliable.[21]

Interest in teacher expectations and the self-fulfilling prophecy reappeared in the 1970s and 1980s. Cooper, and then Good and Brophy, outlined how teachers communicate expectations to students and in turn influence student behavior.

1. The teacher expects specific achievement and behavior from particular students.
2. Because of these different expectations, the teacher behaves differently toward various students.
3. This interaction suggests to students what achievement and behavior the teacher expects from them, which affects their self-concepts, motivation, and performance.
4. If the teacher's interaction is consistent over time, it will shape the students' achievement and behavior. High expectations for students will influence achievement at high levels, and low expectations will produce lower achievement.
5. With time, student achievement and behavior will conform more and more to the original expectations of the teacher.[22]

The most effective teacher is realistic about the differences between high and low achievers. The teacher

[18]Jacqueline Hansen, "Teaching Without Talking," *Phi Delta Kappan* (September 2010): 35–40.

[19]Kenneth B. Clark, *Dark Ghetto* (NewYork: Harper & Row, 1965).

[20]Robert Rosenthal and Lenore Jacobson, *Pygmalion in the Classroom* (New York: Holt, Rinehart and Winston, 1968).

[21]Robert Thorndike, "Review of Pygmalion in the Classroom," *American Educational Research Journal, 5* (1968): 708–711.

[22]Jere E. Brophy and Thomas L. Good, *Teacher-Student Relationships* (New York: Holt, Rinehart and Winston, 1974); Harris M. Cooper, "Pygmalion Grows Up: A Model for Teacher Expectation Communication and Performance Influence," *Review of Educational Research,* 49 (1979): 389–410; Cooper and Good, *Pygmalion Grows* Up (New York: Longman, 1983); Thomas L. Good and Rhona G. Weinstein, "Teacher Expectations: A Framework for Exploring Classrooms," in K. Zumwalt (ed.), *Improving Teaching* (Alexandria, VA: Association for Supervision and Curriculum Development, 1986), pp. 63–85. Also see Iris C. Rotberg, "A Self-Fulfilling Prophecy," *Phi Delta Kappan,* 83 (2001): 170–171.

who develops a rigid or stereotyped perception of students is likely to have a harmful effect on them. The teacher who understands that differences exist and adapts realistic methods and content accordingly will have the most positive effect on students.

Teacher Characteristics

Of the reams of research published on teacher behavior, the greatest amount concerns **teacher characteristics**. The problem is that researchers disagree on which teacher characteristics constitute successful teaching, on how to categorize characteristics, and on how to define them. In addition, researchers use a variety of terms to name what they are trying to describe, such as *teacher traits, teacher personality, teacher performance,* or *teacher methods*. Descriptors or characteristics have different meanings to different people. "Warm" behavior for one investigator often means something different for another, just as the effects of such behavior may be seen differently. For example, it can be assumed that a warm teacher would have a different effect on students according to age, sex, achievement level, socioeconomic class, ethnic group, subject, and classroom context.[23]

Such differences tend to operate for every teacher characteristic and to affect every study on teacher behavior. Although a list of teacher characteristics may be suitable for a particular study, the characteristics (as well as the results) cannot always be compared with another study.

Yet as Lee Shulman points out, teacher behavior researchers often disregard factors such as the time of day, school year, and content, and combine data from an early observation with data from a later occasion. Data from the early part of the term may be combined with data from the later part of the term; data from one unit of content (which may require different teacher behaviors or techniques) are combined with those from other units of content.[24] All these aggregations assume that instances of teaching over time can be summed to have equal weights, which is rarely the case. The accuracy issue is further clouded when such studies are compared, integrated, and built upon each other to form a theory or viewpoint about which teacher characteristics are most effective.

Despite such cautions, many researchers feel that certain teacher characteristics can be defined, validated, and generalized from one study to another. In turn, recommendations can be made from such generalizations for use in a practical way in the classroom and elsewhere.

Research on Teacher Characteristics

Although researchers have named literally thousands of teacher characteristics over the years, A. S. Barr organized recommended behaviors into a manageable list.[25] Reviewing some fifty years of research, he listed and defined twelve successful characteristics, including resourcefulness, intelligence, emotional stability, buoyancy (or enthusiasm), and considerateness (or friendliness). Other authorities have made other summaries of teacher characteristics, but Barr's work is considered most comprehensive.

While Barr presented an overview of hundreds of studies of teacher characteristics, the single most comprehensive study was conducted by David Ryans.[26] More than 6000 teachers in 1700 schools were involved in the study over a six-year period. The objective was to identify through observations and self-ratings the most desirable teacher characteristics. Ryans developed a bipolar list of eighteen teacher characteristics (for example, original vs. conventional, patient vs. impatient, hostile vs. warm). Respondents were asked to identify the approximate position of teachers for each pair of characteristics on a seven-point scale. (A seven-point scale makes it easier for raters to avoid midpoint responses and neutral positions.)

The eighteen teacher characteristics were defined in detail and further grouped into three "patterns" of successful versus unsuccessful teachers:

1. *Pattern X:* understanding, friendly, responsive, versus aloof, egocentric.

[23]N. L. Gage, "Confronting Counsels of Despair for the Behavioral Sciences," *Educational Researcher,* 25 (1996): 5–16; Allan C. Ornstein, "A Look at Teacher Effectiveness Research," *NASSP Bulletin,* 73 (1990), 78–88; W. James Popham, "Why Standardized Tests Don't Measure Educational Quality," *Educational Leadership,* 56 (1999): 8–16.

[24]Lee S. Shulman, "Paradigms and Research Programs in the Study of Teaching," in M. C. Wittrock (ed.), *Handbook of Research on Teaching,* 3rd ed. (New York: Macmillan, 1986), pp. 3–36; Shulman, "Ways of Seeing, Ways of Knowing: Ways of Teaching, Ways of Learning About Teaching," *Journal of Curriculum Studies,* 23 (1991): 393–396.

[25]A. S. Barr, "Characteristics of Successful Teachers," *Phi Delta Kappan,* 39 (1958): 282–284.

[26]David G. Ryans, *Characteristics of Teachers* (Washington, DC: American Council of Education, 1960).

2. *Pattern Y:* responsible, businesslike, systematic, versus evading, unplanned, slipshod.
3. *Pattern Z:* stimulating, imaginative, original, versus dull, routine.

These three primary teacher patterns were the major qualities singled out for further attention. Elementary teachers scored higher than secondary teachers on the scales of understanding and friendly classroom behavior (Pattern X). Differences between women and men teachers were insignificant in the elementary schools, but in the secondary schools women consistently scored higher in Pattern X and in stimulating and imaginative classroom behavior (Pattern Z), and men tended to exhibit businesslike and systematic behaviors (Pattern Y). Younger teachers (under 45 years) scored higher than older teachers in patterns X and Z; older teachers scored higher in Pattern Y.

A similar but more recent list of teacher characteristics was compiled by Bruce Tuckman, who has developed a feedback system for stimulating change in teacher behavior.[27] His instrument originally contained twenty-eight bipolar items and was expanded to thirty items (for example, creative vs. routinized; cautious vs. outspoken; assertive vs. passive; quiet vs. bubbly) on which teachers were also rated on a seven-point scale.

Teacher Effects

Teacher behavior research has shown that teacher behaviors, as well as specific teaching principles and methods, make a difference with regard to student achievement. Rosenshine and Furst analyzed some forty-two correlational studies in their often-quoted review of process-product research. They concluded that there were eleven teacher processes (behaviors or variables) strongly and consistently related to products (outcomes or student achievement). The first five teacher processes showed the strongest correlation to positive outcomes:

1. *Clarity* of teacher's presentation and ability to organize classroom activities.
2. *Variability* of media, materials, and activities used by the teacher.
3. *Enthusiasm,* defined in terms of the teacher's movement, voice inflection, and the like.
4. *Task orientation* or businesslike teacher behaviors, structured routines, and an academic focus.
5. *Student opportunity to learn,* that is, the teacher's coverage of the material or content in class on which students are later tested.[28]

The six remaining processes were classified as promising: use of student ideas, justified criticism, use of structuring comments, appropriate questions in terms of lower and higher cognitive level, probing or encouraging student elaboration, and challenging instructional materials.

Rosenshine himself later reviewed his conclusions; his subsequent analysis showed that only two behaviors or processes consistently correlated with student achievement: (1) task orientation (later referred to as *direct instruction*), and (2) opportunity to learn (later referred to as *academic time, academic engaged time,* and *content covered*). On a third behavior, clarity, he wavered, pointing out that it seemed to be a correlate of student achievement for students above the fifth grade. The other eight processes appeared to be less important and varied in importance not only according to grade level but also according to subject matter, instructional groups and activities, and students' social class and abilities.[29] Nevertheless, the original review remains a valuable study on how teacher processes relate to student products.

The Gage Model

Nate Gage analyzed forty-nine process-product studies. He identified four clusters of behaviors that show a strong relationship to student outcomes: (1) *teacher indirectness,* the willingness to accept student ideas and feelings, and the ability to provide a healthy emotional climate; (2) *teacher praise,* support and encouragement,

---

[27]Bruce W. Tuckman, "Feedback and the Change Process," *Phi Delta Kappan,* 67 (1986): 341–344; Tuckman, "The Interpersonal Teacher Model," *Educational Forum,* 59 (1995): 177–185.

[28]Barak V. Rosenshine and Norma F. Furst, "Research in Teacher Performance Criteria," in B. O. Smith (ed.), *Research on Teacher Education* (Englewood Cliffs, NJ: Prentice Hall, 1971), pp. 37–42; Rosenshine and Furst, "The Use of Direct Observation to Study Teaching," in R. M. Travers (ed.), *Second Handbook of Research on Teaching* (Chicago: Rand McNally, 1973), pp. 122–183.

[29]Barak V. Rosenshine, "Content, Time and Direct Instruction," in Peterson and Walberg (eds.), *Research on Teaching: Concepts, Findings, and Implications,* pp. 28–56.

use of humor to release tensions (but not at the expense of others), and attention to students' needs; (3) *teacher acceptance,* clarifying, building, and developing students' ideas; and (4) *teacher criticism,* reprimanding students and justifying authority. The relationship between the last cluster and outcomes was negative—where criticism occurred, student achievement was low.[30] In effect, the four clusters suggest the traditional notion of a democratic or warm teacher (a model emphasized for several decades).

From the evidence on teacher effects upon student achievement in reading and mathematics in the elementary grades, Gage presented successful teaching principles and methods that seem relevant for other grades as well. These strategies are summarized below. Bear in mind that they are commonsense strategies. They apply to many grade levels, and most experienced teachers are familiar with them. Nonetheless, they provide guidelines for education students or beginning teachers who say, "Just tell me how to teach."

1. Teachers should have a system of rules that allow students to attend to their personal and procedural needs without having to check with the teacher.
2. A teacher should move around the room, monitoring students' work and communicating an awareness of their behavior while also attending to their academic needs.
3. To ensure productive independent work by students, teachers should be sure that the assignments are interesting and worthwhile, yet still easy enough to be completed by each student without teacher direction.
4. Teachers should keep to a minimum such activities as giving directions and organizing the class for instruction. Teachers can do this by writing the daily schedule on the board and establishing general procedures so students know where to go and what to do.
5. In selecting students to respond to questions, teachers should call on volunteers and nonvolunteers by name before asking questions to give all students a chance to answer and to alert the student to be called upon.
6. Teachers should always aim at getting less academically oriented students to give some kind of response to a question. Rephrasing, giving cues, or asking leading questions can be useful techniques for bringing forth some answer from a silent student, one who says "I don't know," or one who answers incorrectly.
7. During reading group instruction, teachers should give a maximum amount of brief feedback and provide fast-paced activities of the drill type.[31]

[30] N. L. Gage, *The Scientific Basis of the Art of Teaching* (New York: Teachers College Press, Columbia University, 1978).

The Good and Brophy Model

Over the last twenty years, Good and Brophy have identified several factors related to effective teaching and student learning. They focus on basic principles of teaching, but not teacher behaviors or characteristics, since both researchers contend that teachers today are looking more for principles of teaching than for prescriptions.

1. *Clarity* about instructional goals (objectives).
2. Knowledge about *content* and ways for teaching it.
3. *Variety* in the use of teaching methods and media.
4. *"With-it-ness,"* awareness of what is going on, alertness in monitoring classroom activities.
5. *"Overlapping,"* sustaining an activity while doing something else at the same time.
6. *"Smoothness,"* sustaining proper lesson pacing and group momentum, not dwelling on minor points or wasting time dealing with individuals, and focusing on all the students.
7. *Seatwork* instructions and management that initiate and focus on productive task engagement.
8. Holding students *accountable* for learning; accepting responsibility for student learning.
9. *Realistic expectations* in line with student abilities and behaviors.
10. *Realistic praise,* not praise for its own sake.
11. *Flexibility* in planning and adapting classroom activities.
12. *Task orientation* and businesslike behavior in the teacher.

[31] Ibid. The authors disagree with item 5. Most good teachers first ask the question, then call on a student so everyone in the class is required to listen; hence, no one knows who the teacher will call on.

13. *Monitoring* of students' understanding; providing appropriate feedback, giving praise, asking questions.
14. Providing student *opportunity to learn* what is to be tested.
15. Making comments that help *structure learning* of knowledge and concepts for students; helping students learn how to learn.[32]

The fact that many of these behaviors are classroom management techniques and structured learning strategies suggests that good discipline is a prerequisite for good teaching.

The Evertson-Emmer Model

The Evertson and Emmer model is similar to that of Good and Brophy (in fact, Evertson has written several texts and articles with Brophy). The models are similar in three ways: (1) Teacher effectiveness is associated with specific teaching principles and methods, (2) organization and management of instructional activities is stressed, and (3) findings and conclusions are based primarily on process-product studies.

Nine basic teaching principles represent the core of Evertson's work with Emmer (and, to a lesser extent, with Brophy). Effectiveness is identified in terms of raising student achievement scores.

1. *Rules and Procedures.* Rules and procedures are established and enforced and students are monitored for compliance.
2. *Consistency.* Similar expectations are maintained for activities and behavior at all times for all students. Inconsistency causes confusion in students about what is acceptable.
3. *Prompt Management of Inappropriate Behavior.* Inappropriate behavior is attended to quickly to stop it and prevent its spread.
4. *Checking Student Work.* All student work, including seatwork, homework, and papers, is corrected, errors are discussed, and feedback is provided promptly.
5. *Interactive Teaching.* This takes several forms and includes presenting and explaining new materials, question sessions, discussions, checking for student understanding, actively moving among students to correct work, providing feedback, and, if necessary, reteaching materials.
6. *Academic Instruction,* sometimes referred to as "academic learning time" or "academic engaged time." Attention is focused on the management of student work.
7. *Pacing.* Information is presented at a rate appropriate to the students' ability to comprehend it, not too rapidly or too slowly.
8. *Transitions.* Transitions from one activity to another are made smoothly, with minimal confusion about what to do next.
9. *Clarity.* Lessons are presented logically and sequentially. Clarity is enhanced by the use of instructional objectives and adequate illustrations and by keeping in touch with students.[33]

The Master Teacher

The national interest in education reform and excellence in teaching has focused considerable attention on teachers and the notion of the **master teacher.** The direct behaviors suggested by Rosenshine, and the Good, Brophy, and Evertson models, correspond with Walter Doyle's task-oriented and businesslike description of a master teacher. Such teachers "focus on academic goals, are careful and explicit in structuring activities . . . , promote high levels of student academic involvement and content coverage, furnish opportunities for controlled practice with feedback, hold students accountable for work, . . . have expectations that they will be successful in helping students learn, [and are] active in

[32]Thomas L. Good and Jere E. Brophy, "Teacher Behavior and Student Achievement," in M. C. Wittrock (ed.), *Handbook of Research on Teaching*, 3rd ed. (New York: Macmillan, 1986), pp. 328–375; Good and Brophy, *Looking into Classrooms*, 10th ed. (Boston: Allyn and Bacon, 2008).

[33]Edmund T. Emmer, Carolyn M. Evertson, and Jere E. Brophy, "Stability of Teacher Effects in Junior High Classrooms," *American Educational Research Journal*, 6 (1979): 71–75; Emmer et al., *Classroom Management for Middle and High School Teachers*, 8th ed. (Boston: Allyn and Bacon, 2010); Evertson, "Do Teachers Make a Difference?" *Education and Urban Society*, 18 (1986): 195–210; and Evertson et al., *Classroom Management for Elementary Teachers*, 8th ed. (Boston: Allyn and Bacon, 2009).

explaining concepts and procedures, promoting meaning and purpose for academic work, and monitoring comprehension."[34]

When 641 elementary and secondary teachers were asked to "rate criteria for recognition of a master teacher," they listed in rank order: (1) knowledge of subject matter, (2) encourages student achievement through positive reinforcement, (3) uses a variety of strategies and materials to meet the needs of all students, (4) maintains an organized and disciplined classroom, (5) stimulates students' active participation in classroom activities, (6) maximizes student instruction time, (7) has high expectations of student performance, and (8) frequently monitors student progress and provides feedback regarding performance.[35]

Although the sample of teachers was predominantly female (71 percent), so that it can be argued that the recommended behaviors reflect female norms, it must be noted that the teaching profession is predominantly female (67 percent, according to NEA survey data). Most important, the teachers surveyed were experienced (77 percent had been teaching for at least eleven years) and their rank order list of criteria corresponds closely to the principals' rank order list and to Doyle's notion of a master teacher.

In *Classroom Instruction that Works,* Robert Marzano identified nine instructional strategies that have positive effects on student achievement across the country: (1) identifying similarities and differences in content, (2) summarizing and note taking, (3) reinforcing effort and providing recognition, (4) homework and practice, (5) nonlinguistic recommendations, (6) cooperative learning, (7) providing feedback, (8) testing hypotheses, and (9) cues, questions and advance organizers.[36] These instructional strategies were considered as having "high probability of enhancing student achievement," and coincided with many of the direct and business-like behaviors from the Ryans and Rosenshine era to the Good, Brophy, and Doyle era. Although these instructional strategies worked in most schools, Marzano warned that we can expect in 20 to 40 percent of the studies these strategies will have no effect or even a negative effect.[37] In other words, we are dealing with people and different variables and human interaction—and not nuts and bolts.

Based on a study of several hundred teachers who teach in multiracial and multilinguistic schools, Martin Haberman's portrait of what he termed "star" urban teachers revealed a host of behaviors and attitudes that dismiss what many educators say makes master or effective teachers.[38] Star teachers develop an ideology—that is, a pervasive way of believing and acting. These teachers do not use theory to guide their practice; they do not refer to the axioms or principles of Piaget, Skinner, or the like. Star teachers do not consider the research on teacher effectiveness or school effectiveness. They are generally oblivious to and unconcerned with how researchers or experts in various subjects organize the content in their disciplines. Rather, they have internalized their own view of teaching, their own organization of subject matter, and their own practices through experience and self-discovery. Their behaviors and methods are not forms of knowledge learned in university courses. "Almost everything star teachers do that they regard as important," according to Haberman, "is something they believe they learned on the job after they started teaching."[39] Star teachers reflect on what they are doing in the classroom, why they are doing it, and the best way to do it. These teachers are also guided by the expectations that inner-city and poor children can learn, think, and reflect.

For the casual observer it may seem that teachers generally perform the same way. Going beyond the data, the inference is that star teachers or master teachers are different from the average; they have a well thought-out ideology that gives their performance a different meaning. They appear to be mavericks (or at least atypical) and confident in the way they organize and operate their own classrooms. They are sensitive

[34]Walter Doyle, "Effective Teaching and the Concept of Master Teacher," *Elementary School Journal*, 86 (1985): 30; Doyle, "Curriculum and Pedagogy," in P. W. Jackson (ed.), *Handbook of Research on Curriculum* (New York: Macmillan, 1992), pp. 486–516.

[35]Jann E. Azumi and James L. Lerman, "Selecting and Rewarding Master Teachers," *Elementary School Journal*, 88 (1987): 197.

[36]Robert J. Marzano, et al. *Classroom Instruction that Works* (Alexandria, Va: Association of Supervision and Curriculum Development, 2001).

[37]Robert J. Marzano, "Setting the Record Straight on 'High Yield' Strategies," *Phi Delta Kappan:* 91 (2009): 30–37.

[38]Martin Haberman, "The Pedagogy of Poverty versus Good Teaching," *Phi Delta Kappan,* 72 (1991): 290–294; Haberman, "The Ideology of Star Teachers of Children of Poverty," *Educational Horizons*, 70 (1992): 125–129; and Haberman, "The Dimensions of Excellence," *Peabody Journal of Education,* 70 (1995): 24–43.

[39]Martin Haberman and Linda Post, "Teachers for Multicultural Schools: The Power of Selection," *Theory into Practice*, 37 (1998): 99.

ADMINISTRATIVE ADVICE 14–2

Improving Support for Beginning Teachers

Whatever the existing policies regarding the induction period for entry teachers, there is a need to improve provisions for their continued professional development, to make the job easier, to make them feel more confident in the classroom and school, to reduce the isolation of their work settings, and to enhance interaction with colleagues. Here are some recommendations that administrators can implement for achieving these goals.

- Schedule beginning teacher orientation in addition to regular teacher orientation. Beginning teachers need to attend both sessions.
- Appoint someone to help beginning teachers set up their rooms.
- Provide beginning teachers with a proper mix of courses, students, and facilities (not all leftovers). If possible, lighten their load for the first year.
- Assign extra class duties of moderate difficulty and requiring moderate amounts of time, duties that will not become too demanding for the beginning teacher.
- Pair beginning teachers with master teachers to meet regularly to identify general problems before they become serious.
- Provide coaching groups, tutor groups, or collaborative problem-solving groups for all beginning teachers to attend. Encourage beginning teachers to teach each other.
- Provide for joint planning, team teaching, committee assignments, and other cooperative arrangements between new and experienced teachers.
- Issue newsletters that report on accomplishments of all teachers, especially beginning teachers.
- Schedule reinforcing events, involving beginning and experienced teachers, such as tutor-tutoree luncheons, parties, and awards.
- Provide regular (say, monthly) meetings between the beginning teacher and supervisor to identify problems as soon as possible and to make recommendations for improvement.
- Plan special and continuing in-service activities with topics directly related to the needs and interests of beginning teachers. Eventually, integrate beginning staff development activities with regular staff development activities.
- Carry on regular evaluation of beginning teachers; evaluate strengths and weaknesses, present new information, demonstrate new skills, and provide opportunities for practice and feedback with master teacher and/or supervisors.

to their students and teach in ways that make sense to their students, not necessarily according to what researchers or administrators and colleagues have to say about teaching. These teachers seem to be driven by their own convictions of what is right and not by how others interpret the teacher's role or teacher's pedagogy. See Administrative Advice 14–2. Most star teachers would reject the current notion that tries to correlate student test scores with teacher evaluations.

Cautions and Criticisms

Although the notions of teacher competencies or teacher effectiveness are often identified as something new in research efforts to identify good teaching, they are nothing more than a combination of teaching principles and methods that good teachers have been using for many years prior to this recent wave of research. What these product-oriented researchers have accomplished is to summarize what we have known for a long time, but often passed on in the form of "tips for teachers" or practical suggestions that were once criticized by researchers as being recipe oriented. These researchers confirm the basic principles and methods of experienced teachers. They give credibility to teaching practices by correlating teacher behaviors (processes) with student achievement (products). Product-oriented researchers also dispel the notion that teachers have little or no measurable effect on student achievement.

However, there is some danger in this product-oriented research. The conclusions overwhelmingly portray the effective teacher as task oriented, organized, and structured (nothing more than Ryans's Pattern Y teacher). But the teacher competency and teacher effectiveness models tend to overlook the friendly, warm, and democratic teacher; the creative teacher who is stimulating and imaginative; the dramatic teacher who bubbles with energy and enthusiasm; the philosophical teacher who encourages students to play with ideas and concepts; and the problem-solving teacher who requires that students think out the answers. In the product-oriented researchers' desire to identify and prescribe behaviors that are measurable and quantifiable, they overlook the emotional, qualitative, and interpretive descriptions of classrooms, and the joys of teaching; they tend to be driven by high-stake tests and the need for teachers to show evidence of student learning and progress on achievement tests.[40] Most of their research has been conducted at the elementary grade levels, where one would expect more social, psychological, and humanistic factors to be observed, recorded, and recommended as effective. A good portion of their work also deals with low achievers and at-risk students—perhaps the reason many of their generalizations or principles coincide with classroom management and structured and controlling techniques.[41]

Teacher Contexts: New Research, New Paradigms

For the last fifty years or more, research on teacher behavior has been linear and category-based, focused on specific teacher styles, interactions, characteristics, or effects. It focused on either the *process* of teaching (how the teacher was behaving in the classroom) or the *products* of teaching (student outcomes). As the 1990s unfolded, the research on teaching examined the multifaceted nature and context of teaching; it examined the relationship of teaching and learning, the subject-matter knowledge of the teacher, how knowledge was taught, and how it related to pedagogy.

The new emphasis on teaching goes beyond what the teacher is doing and explores teacher thinking from the perspective of teachers themselves. The teacher is depicted as one who copes with a complex environment and simplifies it, mainly through experience, by attending to a small number of important tasks, and synthesizing various kinds of information that continually evolve. The impact of professional knowledge (that is, both subject matter and pedagogical knowledge—knowing *what* you know, and how well you know it) is now considered important for defining how teachers and students construct meaning for their respective academic roles and perform tasks related to those roles.

An alternative for understanding the nature of teaching has evolved—one that combines teaching and learning processes, incorporates holistic practices, and goes beyond what teachers and students appear to be doing to inquire about what they are thinking. This model relies on language and dialogue, and not mathematical or statistical symbols, to provide the conceptual categories and organize the data. It uses the approaches that reformers, reconceptualists, and postliberal theoreticians have advocated: metaphors, stories, biographies and autobiographies, conversations (with experts), and voices (or narratives). Such research, which has surfaced within the last two decades, looks at teaching "from the inside." It focuses on the personal and practical knowledge of teachers, the culture of teaching, and the language and thoughts of teachers.

Metaphors

Teachers' knowledge, including the way they speak about teaching, not only exists in propositional form but also includes figurative language or **metaphors.** The thinking of teachers consists of personal experiences, images, and jargon, and therefore figurative language is central to the expression and understanding of the teachers' knowledge of pedagogy.[42]

---

[40]See Gerald W. Bracey, "How to Avoid Statistical Traps," *Educational Leadership*, 63 (2006): 78–82; Elliot W. Eisner, "Opening a Shuttered Window: A Special Section on the Arts and Intellect," *Phi Delta Kappan*, 87 (2005): 8–10; and W. James Popham, "Branded by a Test," *Educational Leadership,* 63 (2006): 86–87.

[41]Allan C. Ornstein, "Teacher Effectiveness Research: Theoretical Considerations," in H. C. Waxman and H. J. Walberg (eds.), *Effective Teaching* (Berkeley, CA: McCutchan, 1991), pp. 63–80; Allan C. Ornstein and Richard C. Sinatra, *K–8 Instructional Methods*: *A Literacy Perspective* (Boston: Allyn and Bacon, 2005).

[42]Christopher Clark, "Real Lessons from Imaginary Teachers," *Journal of Curriculum Studies,* 23 (1991): 429–434; Joy S. Richie and David E. Wilson, *Teacher Narrative as Critical Inquiry* (New York: Teachers College Press, Columbia University, 2000); Jennifer Tupper and Michael Cappello, "Teaching Treaties as (Un)Usual Narratives," *Curriculum Inquiry:* 38 (2008): 559–578.

Metaphors of space and time figure in the teachers' descriptions of their work ("pacing a lesson," "covering the content," "moving on to the next part of the lesson").[43] The studies on teacher style, examined in the earlier part of the chapter, represent concepts and beliefs about teachers that can be considered as metaphors: the teacher as a "boss," "coach," "comedian," or "maverick." The notions of a "master" teacher, "lead" teacher, "star" teacher, or "expert" teacher are also metaphors, or descriptors, used by current researchers to describe outstanding or effective teachers.

Metaphors are used to explain or interpret reality. In traditional literature, this process of understanding evolves through experience and study—without the influence of researchers' personal or cultural biases. But the use of metaphors can also be conceptualized in the literature of sociology to include ideas, values, and behaviors that derive in part from a person's position within the political and economic order. Similarly, critical pedagogists and liberal theorists argue that personal and cultural factors such as gender, class, and caste influence the formation of knowledge, especially metaphors as well as behavior.[44]

Stories

Increasingly, researchers are telling stories about teachers—their work and how they teach—and teachers are telling stories about their own teaching experiences. Most **stories** are narrative and descriptive in nature; they are rich and voluminous in language, and those about teachers make a point about teaching that would otherwise be difficult to convey with traditional research methods. The stories told reflect the belief that there is much to learn from "authentic" teachers who tell their stories about experiences they might otherwise keep to themselves or fail to convey to others.[45]

Stories have an important social or psychological meaning. Stories of teachers allow us to see connections between the practice of teaching and the human side of teaching. The stories of individual teachers allow us to see their knowledge and skills enacted in the real world of classrooms, and lead us to appreciate their emotional and moral encounters with the lives of the people they teach.

Stories by teachers such as Bel Kaufman, Herbert Kohl, Jonathan Kozol, and Sylvia Ashton-Warner have become best-sellers because of their rich descriptions, personal narratives, and the way they describe the very "stuff" of teaching. These stories are aesthetic and emotional landscapes of teaching and learning that would be missed by clinically based process-product research studies of teacher effectiveness. Still others criticize such personal teacher stories for lacking scholarly reliability and accuracy—flaws they see as grounded in egoism or exaggeration.

Stories of teachers by researchers are less descriptive, less emotional, and less well known. Nevertheless, they are still personal and rich encounters with teachers, and they provide us with teachers' knowledge and experiences not quite on their own terms, but in a deep way that helps us understand what teaching is all about. These stories provide unusual opportunities to get to know and respect teachers as people, on an emotional as well as intellectual level. Most important, these stories represent a shift in the way researchers are willing to convey teachers' pedagogy and understanding of teaching. However, some researchers point out that observers and authors construct different realities, so that different storytellers could write very different versions of the same teacher. But the author is only one variable. Subject matter, students, and school settings could lead to a striking contrast in portrayal and interpretation of the same teacher.[46]

Biographies and Autobiographies

Stories written by researchers about teachers tend to be biographical and stories written by teachers about themselves tend to be autobiographical. Both **biography** and **autobiography** encompass a "whole story"

[43]Tom Barone, "Science, Art, and the Predispositions of Educational Researchers," *Educational Researcher,* 30 (2001): 24–28; Kathy L. Carter, "The Place of Story in the Study of Teaching," *Educational Researcher,* 22 (1993): 5–12.

[44]Michael W. Apple, *Cultural Politics and Education* (New York: Teachers College Press, Columbia University, 1996); James A. Banks, *Cultural Diversity and Education,* 5th ed. (Needham Heights, MA: Allyn and Bacon, 2006).

[45]Sandra Golden et al., "A Teacher's Words Are Tremendously Powerful: Stories from the GED Scholars Initiative," *Phi Delta Kappan,* 87 (2005): 311–315; Allan C. Ornstein, "Beyond Effective Teaching," *Peabody Journal of Education,* 70 (1995): 2–23; John K. Smith, "The Stories Educational Researchers Tell About Themselves," *Educational Researcher,* 26 (1997): 4–1.

[46]Antoinette Errante, "But Sometimes You're Not Part of the Story," *Educational Researcher,* 24 (2000): 16–27; Shulman, "Ways of Seeing, Ways of Knowing"; Jeremy D. Stoddard, "The Ideological Implications of Using Educational Film to Teach Controversial Events," *Curriculum Inquiry,* 39 (2009): 407–433.

EXEMPLARY EDUCATIONAL ADMINISTRATORS IN ACTION

ART RAINWATER Superintendent, Madison Metropolitan School District, Wisconsin.

Words of Advice: The complexity and expectations of modern public education make it impossible to be an effective "lone wolf" administrator. A team of talented and committed people focused and working with a common vision can accomplish things that no one of us could accomplish alone. Several key points are essential in creating a successful collaborative team approach to administration:

- The children always come first.
- The leader must have a thorough understanding of his or her own personal nonnegotiable core beliefs and values about children and the learning process. These nonnegotiables must be communicated clearly to the team both initially and as the vision grows and changes.
- Common vision must be developed through ongoing discussion and negotiation between the leader and the team around all of the values and beliefs that make up the culture and working relationship of the team.
- Trust between the leader and the rest of the team is critical. There can never be an effective collaborative team in which members feel they have to look over their shoulder at the leader or at each other.
- The leader must establish trust, and it must be apparent that he or she: believes the team members will make quality, competent decisions; accepts the decisions team members make; never publicly rebukes a member, and is constantly guiding and developing team members' skills.
- To operate effectively, all team members must have the authority to act within their own area. Although authority can be delegated, responsibility always remains with the leader.
- Leadership is creating positive change. It only takes a manager to maintain the status quo. Every organization has a culture that is developed over many years. To lead change you must stay within the culture and ethos of the organization.

and represent the full depth and breadth of a person's experiences, as opposed to commentary or fragments. Unity and wholeness emerge as a person brings past experience to make present action meaningful—to make experiences understandable in terms of what a person has undergone.[47]

The essence of an autobiography is that it provides an opportunity for people to convey what they know and have been doing for years, and what is inside their heads, unshaped by others. Whereas the biography is ultimately filtered and interpreted by a second party, the autobiography permits the author (in this case the teacher) to present the information in a personal way on his or her own terms.

As human beings, we all have stories to tell. Each person has a distinctive biography or autobiography in which is shaped a host of experiences, practices, and a particular standpoint or way of looking at the world. For teachers, this suggests a particular set of teaching experiences and practices, as well as a particular style of teaching and pedagogy.

A biography or an autobiography of a teacher may be described as the life story of one teacher who is the central character based in a particular classroom or school, and of the classroom dynamics and school drama that unfolds around the individual. These types of stories are concerned with longitudinal aspects of personal and professional experiences that can bring much detailed and insightful information to the reader. They help us reconstruct teachers' and students' experiences that would not be available to use by reading typical professional literature on teaching.[48]

The accounts in biographies and autobiographies suggest that the author is in a position of "authority"

[47]William Ayers, *To Teach: The Journey of a Teacher* (New York: Teachers College Press, Columbia University, 2001); Donna Kagan, "Research on Teacher Cognition," in A. C. Ornstein (ed.), *Teaching: Theory and Practice* (Needham Heights, MA: Allyn and Bacon, 1995), pp. 226–238; and Selma Wassermann, *This Teaching Life: How I Taught Myself to Teach* (New York: Teachers College Press, Columbia University, 2004).

[48]Robert V. Bullough and Stefinee Pinnegar, "Guidelines for Quality in Autobiographical Forms of Self-Study," *Educational Researcher,* 30 (2001): 13–22; Robert Donmoyer, "Research as Advocacy and Storytelling," *Educational Researcher,* 26 (1997): 2–3; Brenda Trofanenko, "More than a Single Best Narrative," *Curriculum Inquiry*, 38 (2008): 579–603.

with respect to the particular segment of the life being described—hence the thoughts and experiences of the author take on a sense of reality and objectivity not always assumed in other stories.[49] However, when teachers write an autobiography (as opposed to someone else writing the story in biography form), they run the risk of being considered partial or writing self-serving descriptions of their teaching prowess.

Thus Madeleine Grumet suggests that researchers publish multiple accounts of teachers' knowledge and pedagogy, instead of a single narrative. The problem is that this approach suggests taking stories out of the hands of teachers.[50] Joint publications between teachers and researchers may be appropriate in some situations and a method for resolving this problem.[51]

The Expert Teacher

The **expert teacher** concept involves new research procedures—such as simulations, videotapes, and case studies—and a new language to describe the work, prestige, and authority of teachers.[52] The research usually consists of small samples and in-depth studies (the notion of complete lessons and analysis of what transpired), in which expert (sometimes experienced) teachers are distinguished from novice (sometimes beginning) teachers. Experts usually are identified through administrator nominations, student achievement scores, or teacher awards (e.g., Teacher of the Year). **Novice teachers** commonly are selected from groups of student teachers or first-year teachers.

Dreyfus and Dreyfus delineate five stages from novice to expert across fields of study. In stage 1, the novice is inflexible and follows principles and procedures the way they were learned; the advanced beginner, stage 2, begins to combine theory with on-the-job experiences. By stage 3, the competent performer becomes more flexible and modifies principles and procedures to fit reality. At stage 4, the proficient performer recognizes patterns and relationships and has a holistic understanding of the processes involved. Experts, stage 5, have the same big picture in mind but respond effortlessly and fluidly in various situations.[53] Cushing and others point out that "expert teachers make classroom management and instruction look easy," although we know that teaching is a complex act, requiring the teacher "to do many many things at the same time."[54]

Data derived from recent studies suggest that expert and novice teachers teach, as well as perceive and analyze information about teaching, in different ways. Whereas experts are able to explain and interpret classroom events, novices provide detailed descriptions of what they did or saw and refrain from making interpretations. Experts recall or see multiple interactions and explain interactions in terms of prior information and events, whereas novices recall specific facts about students or what happened in the classroom.

The data derived from experts are rich in conversational and qualitative information, but limited in statistical analysis and quantifiable information. What experts (or experienced teachers) say or do about teaching is now considered important for building a science of teaching. Studies of expert and novice teachers show they differ in many specific areas of teaching and instruction.

1. Experts are likely to refrain from making quick judgments about their students and tend to rely on their own experiences and gut feelings, whereas novices tend to lack confidence in their own

---

[49]Sara Day Hatton, *Teaching by Heart: The Foxfire Interviews* (New York: Teachers College Press, Columbia University, 2005); Myles Horton, Judith Kohl, and Herbert Kohl, *The Long Overhaul: An Autobiography* (New York: Teachers College Press, Columbia University, 1998); Betsy Rymes, *Conversational Borderlands* (New York: Teachers College Press, Columbia University, 2001).

[50]Madeleine R. Grumet, "The Politics of Personal Knowledge," *Curriculum Inquiry,* 17 (1987): 319–329.

[51]Donna Kagan and Deborah J. Tippins, "The Genesis of a School-University Partnership," *Educational Forum,* 60 (1995): 48–62; Allan C. Ornstein, "Critical Issues in Teaching" in A. C. Ornstein, E. Pajak, and S. B. Ornstein (eds.), *Contemporary Issues in Education,* 4th ed. (Boston: Allyn and Bacon, 2007), pp. 82–98.

[52]Robert J. Garmston, "Expert Teachers Carry a Satchel of Skills," *Journal of Staff Development,* 19 (1998): 54–56; Randi Nevins Stanulis and Robert E. Floden, "Intensive Mentoring as a Way to Help Beginning Teachers," *Journal of Teacher Education,* 60 (2009): 112–122; Scott Willis, "Creating a Knowledge Base for Teaching," *Educational Leadership,* 59 (2002): 6–11.

[53]Hubert L. Dreyfus and Stuart E. Dreyfus, *Mind over Machine* (New York: Free Press, 1986).

[54]Katherine S. Cushing, Donna S. Sabers, and David C. Berliner, "Investigations of Expertise in Teaching," *Educational Horizons,* 70 (1992): 109; Daniel M. Levin, et al. "Novice Teachers' Attention to Student Teaching," *Journal of Teacher Education* 60 (2009): 142–154.

judgments and are not sure where to start when they begin teaching.

2. Experts tend to analyze student cues in terms of instruction, whereas novices analyze them in terms of classroom management.
3. Experts make the classroom their own, often changing the instructional focus and methods of the previous teacher.
4. Experts engage in a good deal of intuitive and improvisational teaching.
5. Experts seem to have a clear understanding of the types of students they are teaching and how to teach them.[55]
6. Expert teachers are less egocentric and more confident about their teaching.

In short, expert teachers see the big picture, understand human behavior and relationships, perform in an easy and fluid manner, have their own style or way of doing things, and set up routines or take precautionary steps to avoid trouble or potential problems in their classrooms.

Voice

The notion of **voice** sums up the new linguistic tools for describing what teachers do, how they do it, and what they think when they are teaching. Voice corresponds with such terms as the *teacher's perspective, teacher's frame of reference,* or *getting into the teacher's head.* The concern with voice permeates the teacher empowerment movement and the work of researchers who collaborate with teachers in teacher effectiveness projects. The idea of voice should be considered against the backdrop of previous teacher silence and impotence in deciding on issues and practices that affect their lives as teachers. The fact that researchers are now willing to give credibility to teachers' knowledge, teachers' practices, and teachers' experiences helps redress an imbalance that in the past gave little recognition to teachers. Now teachers have a right and a role in speaking for themselves and about teaching.[56]

Although there are some serious attempts to include teachers' voices, the key issue is to what extent these new methods permit the "authentic" expression of teachers to influence the field of teacher effectiveness research and teacher preparation programs. In the past, it has been difficult for teachers to establish a voice, especially one that commanded respect and authority, in the professional literature. The reason is simple: the researchers and theoreticians have dominated the field of inquiry and decided on what should be published. Now big government and big business are imposing complieated and flawed testing procedures to rate teachers.

With the exception of autobiographies and stories written by teachers, teachers' voices generally are filtered through and categorized by researchers' writings and publications. For decades, firsthand expressions of teacher experiences and wisdom (sometimes conveyed in the form of advice or recommendations) were considered nothing more than "recipes" or lists of "dos and don'ts"—irrelevant to the world of research on teaching. Recently, however, under umbrella terms such as *teacher thinking, teacher processes, teacher cognition, teacher practices,* and *practical knowledge,* it has become acceptable and even fashionable to take what teachers have to say, adapt it, and turn it into *professional knowledge, pedagogical knowledge,* or *teacher knowledge.* Yet, although researchers are now collaborating with practitioners, taking teacher views seriously, and accepting teachers on equal terms as part of teacher-training programs, teachers still do not always receive credit where it is due. Whereas in scholarly publications researchers and practitioners are named as coauthors, practitioners may be acknowledged only by pseudonyms such as "Nancy" or "Thomas." The culture of schools and universities, and of teachers and professors, should be compatible enough to bridge this gap in the near future.

Reconceptualizing Teaching

To argue that good teaching boils down to a set of prescriptive behaviors, methods, or proficiency levels, that teachers must follow a "new" research-based

[55]David C. Berliner et al., "The Vision Thing," *Educational Researcher,* 26 (1997): 12–20; Kathy Carter, Walter Doyle, and Mark Riney, "Expert-Novice Differences in Teaching," in A. C. Ornstein (ed.), *Teaching: Theory and Practice* (Needham Heights, MA: Allyn and Bacon, 1995), pp. 259–272; Scott Mandel, "What New Teachers Really Need," *Educational Leadership,* 63 (2006): 66–69.

[56]Barnett Berry, "Recruiting and Retaining Board-Certified Teachers for Hard-to-Staff Schools," *Phi Delta Kappan,* 87 (2005): 290–297; Andy Hargreaves, "Revisiting Voice," *Educational Researcher,* 25 (1996): 12–19. Also see Robin Fogarty and Brian Pete, "Professional Learning 101," *Phi Delta Kappan,* 91 (2009): 32–34.

teaching plan or evaluation system, or that decisions about teacher accountability can be assessed in terms of students passing some standardized or multiple-choice test is to miss the human aspect of teaching—the "essence" of what teaching is all about.

The stress on standards (or outcomes), assessments, and evaluation systems today illustrates that behaviorism has won at the expense of humanistic psychology. The ideas of Thorndike and Skinner have prevailed over the ideas of Dewey and Kilpatrick. It also suggests that school administrators, policymakers, and researchers focus on the *science* of teaching—behaviors and outcomes that can be observed, counted, or measured—rather than on the *art* of teaching with its humanistic and hard-to-measure variables.

Researchers contend that assessment of teachers and students can be easily mandated, implemented, and reported, and thus has wide appeal under the guise of "reform." Although these assessment systems are supposed to improve education, they don't necessarily do so.[57] New assessment systems tied to standardized test scores have significant margins of error and often rank the "best" teachers (where parents are begging principals to have their children put in their classes) with the lowest ratings.

Real reform is complex and costly (for example, reducing class size, raising teacher salaries, introducing special reading and tutoring programs, extending the school day and year), and it takes time before the results are evident. People, such as politicians and business leaders, who seem to be leading this latest wave of reform want a quick, easy, and cheap fix. Thus, they will always opt for assessment since it is simple and inexpensive to implement. It creates heightened media visibility, the feeling that something is being done, and the "Hawthorne effect" (novelty tends to elevate short-term gains). This assessment focus (which is a form of behaviorism) also provides a rationale for teacher education programs, because it suggests that we can separate the effects of teachers from other variables and identify good teaching. Yet it is questionable, given our current knowledge of teaching and teacher education and the human factor that goes with teaching and learning, whether new teachers can be properly prepared in terms of both pedagogical rigor and practical reality.

[57]W. James Popham, "The Age of Compliance," *Educational Leadership,* 63 (2005): 84–86; Popham, "Those [Fill-in-Blank] Tests," *Educational Leadership,* 63 (2006): 85–88; and Richard J. Stiggins, "From Formative Assessment to Assessment for Learning: A Path to Success in Standards-Based Schools," *Phi Delta Kappan,* 87 (2005): 324–328.

For those in the business of preparing teachers, there is need to provide a research base and rationale showing that teachers who enroll and complete a teacher education program are more likely to be effective teachers than those who lack such training. The fact is there are several alternative certification programs for teachers in more than forty states, in which nearly 5 percent (as high as 16 percent in Texas and 22 percent in New Jersey) of the nationwide teaching force entered teaching.[58] This makes teachers of teachers (professors of education) take notice and try to demonstrate that their teacher preparation programs work and that they can prepare effective teachers. Indeed, there is need to identify teacher behaviors and methods that work under certain conditions—leading many educators to favor behaviorism (or prescriptive ideas and specific tasks) and assessment systems (close-ended, tiny, measurable variables) that correlate teaching behaviors (or methods) and learning outcomes.

The reason is, there is a growing body of literature informing us that traditional certification programs and education courses make little difference in teacher effectiveness; therefore, they should be curtailed to allow alternative certification programs to expand. For the time being, Linda Darling-Hammond assures us that the bulk of the research suggests that teachers who are versed in both pedagogical knowledge and subject knowledge are more successful in the classroom than teachers who are versed only in subject matter. It is also true that teachers who hold standard certificates are more successful than teachers who hold emergency licenses, or who attend "crash" programs in the summer and are then temporarily licensed.[59]

Being able to describe detailed methods of teaching and how and why teachers do what they do should improve the performance of teachers. But all the new research hardly tells the whole story of teaching—what leads to teacher effectiveness and student learning: Being able to describe teachers' thinking or decision making, analyzing their stories and reflective practices, suggests that we understand and can improve teaching. The new research on teaching—with its stories, biographies,

[58]Abby Goodnough, "Regents Create a New Path to Teaching," *New York Times,* July 15, 2000, pp. B4, B7.

[59]Linda Darling-Hammond, "The Challenge of Staffing Our Schools," *Educational Leadership,* 58 (2001): 12–17; Darling-Hammond, "Keeping Good Teachers," in A. C. Ornstein et al. *Contemporary Issues in Curriculum,* 4th ed. (Boston: Allyn and Bacon, 2007), pp. 139–146; Darling-Hammond, "America's Commitment to Equity will Determine Our Future," *Phi Delta Kappan,* 91 (2010): 8–14.

reflective practices, and qualitative methods—provides a platform and publication outlet for researchers. It promotes their expertise (which in turn continues to separate them from practitioners) and permits them to continue to subordinate teaching to research. It also provides a new paradigm for analyzing teaching since the older models (teacher styles, teacher personality, teacher characteristics, teacher effectiveness, etc.) have become exhausted and repetitive. The issues and questions related to the new paradigm create new educational wars and controversy between traditional and nontraditional researchers, between quantitative and qualitative advocates. It is questionable whether this new knowledge base about teaching really improves teaching and learning or leads to substantial and sustained improvement.

The Need for Humanistic Teaching

The focus of teacher research should be on the learner, not the teacher; on the feelings and attitudes of the students, not on knowledge and information (since feelings and attitudes will eventually determine what knowledge and information are sought and acquired); and on long-term development and growth of the students, not on short-term objectives or specific teacher tasks. But if teachers spend more time with the learners' feelings and attitudes, as well as on social and personal growth, teachers may be penalized when cognitive student outcomes (little pieces of information) are correlated with their behaviors and methods in class.

Students need to be encouraged and nurtured by their teachers, especially when they are young. They are too dependent on approval from significant adults—first their parents, then their teachers. Parents and teachers need to help young children and adolescents establish a source for self-esteem by focusing on their strengths, supporting them, discouraging negative self-talk, and helping them take control of their lives in context with their own culture and values.

People (including children) with high self-esteem achieve at high levels, and the more one achieves, the better one feels about oneself. The opposite is also true: Students who fail to master the subject matter get down on themselves and eventually give up. Students with low self-esteem give up quickly. In short, student self-esteem and achievement are directly related. If we can nurture students' self-esteem, almost everything else will fall into place, including achievement scores and academic outcomes. Regardless of how smart or talented a child is, if he or she has personal problems, then cognition will be detrimentally effected.

This builds a strong argument for creating success experiences for students to help them feel good about themselves. The long-term benefits are obvious: The more students learn to like themselves, the more they will achieve; and the more they achieve, the more they will like themselves. But that takes time, involves a lot of nurturing, and does not show up on a standardized test within a semester or school year; moreover, it doesn't help the teacher who is being evaluated by a content- or test-driven school administrator who is looking for results now. It certainly does not benefit the teacher who is being evaluated by a behaviorist instrument that measures how many times he or she attended departmental meetings, whether the shades in the classroom were even, whether his or her instructional objectives were clearly stated, whether homework was assigned or the computer was used on a regular basis.

It is obvious that certain behaviors contribute to good teaching. The trouble is that there is little agreement on exactly what behaviors or methods are most important. There are some teachers who gain theoretical knowledge of "what works" but are unable to put the ideas into practice. Some teachers act effortlessly in the classroom, while others with similar preparation consider teaching a chore. All this suggests that teaching cannot be described in terms of a checklist or a precise model. It also suggests that teaching is a humanistic activity that deals with people (not tiny behaviors or competencies) and how people (teachers and students) behave in a variety of classroom and school settings.

While the research on teacher effectiveness provides a vocabulary and a system for improving our insight into good teaching, there is a danger that it may lead some of us to become too rigid in our view of teaching. Following only one teacher model or evaluation system can lead to too much emphasis on specific behaviors that can be easily measured or prescribed in advance—at the expense of ignoring humanistic behaviors that cannot be easily measured or prescribed in advance such as aesthetic appreciation, emotions, values, and moral responsibility.

Although some educators recognize that humanistic factors influence teaching, we continue to define most teacher performance in terms of behaviorist and cognitive factors. Most teacher evaluation instruments tend to de-emphasize the human side of teaching because it is difficult to observe or measure. In an attempt to be scientific, to predict and control behavior, we sometimes lose sight of the attitudes and feelings of teachers and their relations with students. As Maxine Greene asserts, good teaching and learning involve feelings, insights, imagination, creative inquires—an existential and philosophical encounter—which cannot be readily quantified. By overlooking hard-to-measure aspects of teaching, we miss a substantial part of teaching, what Greene calls the "stuff" of teaching, what Eisner calls the "artful elements" of teaching, and what others refer to as drama, tones, and flavor.[60]

Teacher behaviors that correlate with measurable outcomes often lead to rote learning, "learning bits" and not the whole picture, to memorization and automatic responses, not high-order thinking. These evaluation models seem to miss moral and ethical outcomes, as well as social, personal, and self-actualizing factors related to learning and life—in effect, the affective domain of learning and the psychology of being human. In their attempt to observe and measure what teachers do, and detail whether students improve their performance on reading or math tests, current models ignore the learner's imagination, fantasy, and intuitive thinking, their dreams, hopes, and aspirations, and how teachers have an impact on these hard-to-define-and-measure but very important aspects of students' lives.

In providing feedback and evaluation for teachers, many factors must be considered so the advice or information does not fall on deaf ears. Teachers must be permitted to incorporate specific behaviors and methods according to their own unique personality and philosophy, to pick and choose from a wide range of research and theory, and to discard other teacher behaviors that conflict with their own style without the fear of being considered ineffective. Many school districts, even state departments of education, have developed evaluation instruments and salary plans based exclusively on prescriptive and product-oriented behaviors. Even worse, teachers who do not exhibit these behaviors are often penalized or labeled as "marginal" or "incompetent."[61]

There is an increased danger that many more school districts and states will continue to jump on this bandwagon and make decisions based on prescriptive behaviors (or student outcomes) without recognizing or giving credence to other teacher behaviors or methods that might deal with feelings, emotions, and personal connections with people—what some educators label as fuzzy or vague criteria.

Examples of Humanistic Teaching

In traditional terms, humanism is rooted in the fourteenth- and fifteenth-century Renaissance period of Europe, where there was a revival of classical humanism expressed by the ancient Greek and Latin culture. The philosophers and educators of the Renaissance, like the medieval Scholastics before them (who were governed and protected by the church), found wisdom in the past and stressed classical manuscripts. Unlike the Scholastics, they were often independent of the church, and were concerned with the experiences of *humans* and not God-like or religious issues.[62]

In the early twentieth century, humanistic principles of teaching and learning were envisioned in the theories of progressive education: in the *child-centered* lab school directed by John Dewey at the University of Chicago from 1896 to 1904; the *play-centered* methods and materials introduced by Maria Montessori that were designed to develop the practical, sensory, and formal skills of prekindergarten and kindergarten children in the slums of Italy starting in 1908; and the *activity-centered* practices of William Kilpatrick who in the 1920s and 1930s urged the elementary teachers to organize classrooms around social activities, group enterprises, and group projects, and allow children to say what they think.

All of these progressive theories were highly humanistic and stressed the child's interests, individuality, and creativity—in short, the child's freedom to develop naturally, freedom from teacher domination, and freedom from the weight of rote learning. But progressivism failed because, in the view of Lawrence Cremin, there weren't enough good teachers to implement progressive thought in classrooms and schools.[63] To be sure,

---

[60]Maxine Greene, *The Dialectic of Teaching* (New York: Teachers College Press, Columbia University, 1998); Greene, *Variations on a Blue Guitar* (New York: Teachers College Press, Columbia University, 2001); Elliot W. Eisner, *The Educational Imagination,* 3rd ed. (Columbus, OH: Merrill, 2002).

[61]Gary D. Borich, *Effective Teaching Methods,* 6th ed. (Columbus, OH: Merrill, 2007); Allan C. Ornstein, *Teaching and Schooling in America: Pre- and Post-September 11* (Boston: Allyn and Bacon, 2003); and Allan C. Ornstein and Thomas J. Lasley, *Strategies for Effective Teaching,* 4th ed. (Boston: McGraw-Hill, 2004).

[62]The religious scholar of the medieval period, versed in scriptures and theological logic, was no longer the preferred model; rather, it was the Courtier—man of style, wit, and elegance, liberally educated, a diplomat, politician, or successful merchant. See Baldesar Catiglione, *The Book of the Courtier,* rev. ed. (Garden City, NY: Doubleday, 1959). Niccolò Machiavelli's *The Prince* is a perfect example of the preferred philosophy, advice, and behavior for this Renaissance period.

[63]Lawrence A. Cremin, *The Transformation of the School* (New York: Random House, 1961).

it is much easier to stress knowledge, rote learning, and right answers than it is to teach about ideas, to consider the interests and needs of students, and to give them freedom to explore and interact with each other without teacher constraints.

By the end of the twentieth century, the humanistic teacher was depicted by William Glasser's "positive" and "supportive" teacher who could manage students without coercion and teach without failure.[64] It was also illustrated by Robert Fried's "passionate" teachers and Vito Perrone's "teacher with a heart"—teachers who live to teach young children and refuse to submit to apathy or criticism that may infect the school in which they work.[65] These teachers are dedicated and caring; they actively engage students in their classrooms, and they affirm their identities. The students do not have to ask whether their teacher is interested in them, thinks of them, or knows their interests or concerns. The answer is definitely "yes."

Good teaching, according to Alfie Kohn, requires that we accept students for who they are rather than what they do or how much they achieve. All children and youth need to know that their parents will accept them unconditionally, but Kohn goes one step further and maintains that unconditional teaching is also important.[66] For their own self-esteem and ego identity, all children and youth need to feel loved, understood, and valued; this idea is based on Carl Rogers' classic notion of effective teaching and learning, William Glasser's concept of a successful school, and Abraham Maslow's notion of personal healthy growth and development.[67] These are basic sociopsychological principles that date back more than a half century—and they are still relevant today. Now all students need support and encouragement from teachers, but lower-achieving students and disadvantaged learners are more in need of support and positive reinforcement from their teachers.

[64]William Glasser, *Schools Without Failure* (New York: Harper & Row, 1969); Glasser, *The Quality School* (New York: HarperCollins, 1990).

[65]Fried, *The Passionate Teacher;* Vito Perrone, *Teacher with a Heart* (New York: Teachers College Press, Columbia University 1998).

[66]Alfie Kohn, *Unconditional Parenting: Moving from Rewards and Punishments to Love and Reason* (New York: Atria Books, 2005).

[67]Glasser, *Schools Without Failure;* Abraham Maslow, *Motivation and Personality* (New York: Harper & Row, 1954); and Carl Rogers, *On Becoming a Person* (Boston: Houghton Mifflin, 1961).

"Unconditional teachers are not afraid to be themselves with students—to act like real human beings rather than controlling authority figures." These are the kind of teachers who act informally—"write notes to students, have lunch with them [and] . . . listen carefully to what kids say and remember details about their lives."[68]

The humanistic teacher is also portrayed by Ted Sizer's mythical teacher called "Horace," who is dedicated and enjoys teaching, treats learning as a humane enterprise, inspires his students to learn, and encourages them to develop their powers of thought, taste, and character.[69] Yet, the system forces Horace to make a number of compromises in planning, teaching, and grading that he knows he would not make if we lived in an ideal world (with more than twenty-four hours in a day). Horace is a trouper; he hides his frustration. Critics of teachers don't really want to hear him or face facts; they don't even know what it is like to teach. Sizer simply states: "Most jobs in the real world have a gap between what would be nice and what is possible. One adjusts."[70] Hence, most caring, dedicated teachers are forced to make some compromises and accommodations and take some shortcuts. So long as no one gets upset and no one complains, the system permits a chasm between rhetoric (the rosy picture) and reality (slow burnout).

There is also a humanistic element in Nel Noddings's ideal teacher who focuses on the nurturing of "competent, caring, loving, and lovable persons." To that end, she describes teaching as a caring profession in which teachers should convey to students the caring way in thinking about one's self, siblings, and strangers, and about animals, plants, and the physical environment. She stresses the affective aspect of teaching: the need to focus on the child's strengths and interests, the need for an individualized curriculum built around the child's abilities and needs, and the need to develop sound character.[71]

Caring, according to Noddings, cannot be achieved by a formula or checklist. It calls for different behaviors for different situations—from tenderness to tough

[68]Alfie Kohn, "Unconditional Teaching," *Educational Leadership,* 63 (2005): 20–24.

[69]Theodore R. Sizer, *Horace's Compromise* (Boston: Houghton Mifflin, 1985).

[70]Ibid, p. 20.

[71]Nel Noddings, *The Challenge to Care in Schools,* 2nd ed. (New York: Teachers College Press, Columbia University, 2005).

love. Good teaching, like good parenting, requires continuous effort, trusting relationships, and continuity of purpose—the purpose of caring, appreciating human connections, and respecting people and ideas from a historical, multicultural, and diverse perspective. The teacher is not only concerned about educating students to be proficient in reading and mathematics but also about making classrooms happy places and helping students become happy with life.[72]

Actually, the humanistic teacher is someone who highlights the personal and social dimension in teaching and learning, as opposed to the behavioral, scientific, or technological aspects. We might argue that everything the teacher does is "human" and the expression "humanistic teaching" is a cliché. However, the authors also use the term in a loose sense to describe the teacher who emphasizes the arts as opposed to the sciences, and people instead of numbers. Although the teacher understands the value of many subjects, including the sciences and social sciences, he or she feels there is the need for students to understand certain *ideas* and *values,* some rooted in 3000 years of philosophy, literature, art, music, theater, etc. Without certain agreed-on content, what Arthur Bestor and Allan Bloom would call the "liberal arts," what E. D. Hirsch and Diane Ravitch would call "essential knowledge," and what Robert Hutchins and Mortimer Adler would call "the Great Books," our heritage would crumble and we would be at the mercy of chance and ignorance; moreover, our education enterprise would be subject to the whim and fancy of local fringe groups.

Humanistic education, according to Jacques Barzun, the elegant and eloquent writer of history and humanism, leads to a form of knowledge that helps us deal with the nature of life, but it does not guarantee us a more gracious or noble life. "The humanities will not sort out the world's evils and were never meant to cure [our] troubles. . . . They will not heal diseased minds or broken hearts any more than they will foster political democracy or settle international disputes." The so-called humanities (and if we may add, the humanistic teacher) "have meaning," according to Barzun, "because of the inhumanity of life; what they depict is strife and disaster";[73] and, if we may add, by example, they help us deal with the human condition and provide guidelines for moral behavior, good taste, and the improvement of civilization.

On a schoolwide level, the authors would argue that humanism (what Fried calls "passion," Perrone calls "heart," Sizer calls "dedication," Noddings calls "caring," and Barzun calls "the well-rounded person") means that we eliminate the notion that everyone should go to college since it creates frustration, anger, and unrealistic expectations among large numbers of children and youth. According to Paul Goodman, it requires that society find viable occupational options for non–college graduates, and jobs that have decent salaries, respect, and social status.[74] It suggests, according to John Gardner, that we recognize various forms of excellence—the excellent teacher, the excellent artist, the excellent plumber, the excellent bus driver—otherwise, we create a myopic view of talent and subsequent tension that will threaten a democratic society.[75] It also means that we appreciate and nurture different student abilities, aptitudes, and skills, what Howard Gardner calls "multiple intelligences."[76]

We need to provide more options and opportunities for children and youth, not only preparation for jobs related to verbal and math skills or aptitudes (the ones usually emphasized in schools and tested on tests) but also skills and aptitudes that produce poets, painters, musicians, actors, athletes, mechanics, and public speakers or politicians. Both Gardners believe in performance and merit, although John calls it "talent" and Howard calls it "intelligence" (we call it "skills and aptitude"). John Gardner is more concerned about the social consequences if we only emphasize academic performance as a criterion for success and status. Similarly, Howard Gardner feels that emphasis on verbal-logical-mathematical learning is rooted in classic Piagetian theory, which ignores a pluralistic approach to cognition and a wider range of domains conducive to different cultures.

Moral and Civic Virtues

Teaching should be committed to a higher purpose, not just teaching knowledge for passing a standardized test; rather, a humanistic-moral purpose designed

[72]Nel Noddings, *Educating Moral People* (New York: Teachers College Press, Columbia University, 2001); Noddings, *The Challenge to Care in Schools;* and Noddings, *Happiness and Education* (Cambridge, MA: Cambridge University Press, 2003).

[73]Jacques Barzun, *Teachers in America,* rev ed. (Lanham, MD: University Press of America, 1972).

[74]Paul Goodman, *Compulsory Mis-Education* (New York: Horizon Press, 1964).

[75]John Gardner, *Excellence: Can We Be Equal Too?* (New York: Harper & Row, 1962).

[76]Howard Gardner, *Frames of Mind: The Theory of Multiple Intelligences* (New York: Basic Books, 1983).

for academic excellence as well as personal and social responsibility. It should be built around people and community, around respecting, caring for, and having compassion towards others. This means that teachers in the classroom would deal with social and moral issues—with the human condition and good and evil. Such teaching encourages students to ask "why?" as opposed to merely giving the "right" answer. The question should start with family conversation and then be nurtured in school during the formative years of learning so that students develop a sense of social and moral consciousness. But our teachers and schools register a disturbing deficit on this score, originally because morality was thought to tread on the spiritual domain and now because there is little time to inquire about and discuss important ideas and issues. Today's curriculum is test driven by items of knowledge and short-answer outcomes.

"Why?" is the existential question that every individual must be permitted to ask, and must receive an appropriate and meaningful answer, from those in power or who mete out of justice. Denial of the question means the individual has no basic rights. This ultimately creates a totalitarianism in which the individual is trivialized, as in the Roman empire, where the ruling classes' main amusement was watching humans being eaten by animals or fighting each other to the death; as in the cattle cars to the concentration camps of Auschwitz and Majdanek, where the individual was reduced to a serial number and human remains were often retrofitted into soap products, lamp shades, and gold rings; as in the Serbian ethnic cleansing and rape of Bosnia and Kosovo, and the cleansing and rape of Rwanda and Darfur, as well as many other tragic slaughters through history.

How many of us can locate Rwanda or Darfur on the map? asks one of the authors. Does anyone among us know where Auschwitz and Majdanek were located? How many among us, except for a few elderly statesmen, scholars, and descendants of the victims, care? Given the "luxury of late birth" and "geographical distance," recent and current generations are expected to do little more than cite a few numbers or statements to put the horrors of humanity into some context or understanding. Few students learn to care about the sufferings of all the folk groups, tribes, and nations since humanity emerged from the caves. Do any students any more know the names of one or two people who died in Nanking, at Pearl Harbor, in the Holocaust, at Juno or Utah Beach, in the killing fields of Cambodia, or in Croatia or Kosovo? Can they cite one name that appears on the Arc de Triomphe or the Vietnam Memorial? Can you?

How many of today's students know the name of the pilot (Paul Tibbets) who dropped the atomic bomb on Hiroshima—what his thoughts were as he approached the target or after the carnage and cloud of dust? Who among us cares to know or can explain what happened or why it happened that more than 100 million soldiers and civilians died in war (or related civilian activities) in the last century, in what one of the authors has called the most ruthless century—consisting of the most vile deeds and crimes against people? Can today's children weigh the value of Western technology and industry against the millions who died beside railroad tracks and in battle trenches using the most advanced killing machines?[77]

Note here that Louis Raths some thirty years ago talked about valuing as part of the teaching and learning—choosing, prizing, cherishing, affirming, and acting upon choices. Similarly, Carl Rogers sought ways for teachers to understand what goes on inside students' minds—their needs, wants, desires, feelings, and their ways of perceiving, appreciating, and valuing. Today, Nel Noddings talks about multiple aims—social, emotional, and spiritual—not just promoting reading and math skills. Similarly, Ted Sizer is worried about our democratic future and insists that we take time out from cognitive processes and educate for sound character and personal responsibility; to teach students to grapple with ideas, as well as enable them to understand the big picture and become active citizens in a democratic society.[78]

Moral practices start with the family and continue with the church and community, but teachers must also play an active role if our society is to become more compassionate, caring, and just. Teachers need to encourage open debate concerning the thorniest issues of the present and past, to welcome discussions without ad hominem attacks or stereotypes, and to build a sense of community (what the French call *civisme*) and character. For the educational system itself to be

---

[77]Allan C. Ornstein, *Teaching and Schooling in America: Pre- and Post-September 11* (Boston: Allyn and Bacon, 2003).

[78]Nel Noddings, "What Does It Mean to Educate the Whole Child?" *Educational Leadership,* 63 (2005): 8–13; Louis E. Raths, Merrill Harmin, and Sidney B. Simon, *Values and Teaching,* 2nd ed. (Columbus: Merrill, 1978); Carl Rogers, *Freedom to Learn,* 2nd ed. (Columbus OH: Merrill, 1983); Ted Sizer and Nancy Sizer, "Grappling," *Phi Delta Kappan,* 81 (1999): 184–190.

moral, teachers must be allowed to go beyond facts, raise thoughtful questions that stem from meaningful readings, and transcend the cognitive domain into the moral universe—at all grade levels.

As educational leaders, we have twenty-five or thirty years to make an imprint on the next generation, to remember the millions who are not in the encyclopedias and who no longer exist, to pass on their thoughts and deeds to the next generation. Our work requires that we understand what is at stake: improving and enriching society by making our children, and their children, care about what is morally right. We are obliged to motivate students to accomplish great things that exhibit the good side of humanity.

Active teaching and learning means that students be encouraged and rewarded for moral and community action, for helping others and volunteering their time and service. Therefore, character development and civic service should receive the same attention and recognition that we give to A students and star quarterbacks. Active teaching and learning call for special assemblies, special scholarships, and special staff development programs that promote character development, the desire to help others, and the expectation of social and civic involvement. It means giving character development—helping and caring for others, contributing back to the school and community—as much attention as we give academics and sports in school.

This does not require a special course or program to meet some "service-learning" mandate, but rather a school ethos or a common philosophy that teachers and administrators support. The idea must permeate the entire school and be expected of all students. One or two teachers attempting to teach moral responsibilities or civic participation cannot effect long-term change; it takes a team effort and schoolwide policy, demanding nothing less than a reconceptualization of the roles, expectations, and activities of students and teachers involved in the life of schools and communities. The idea flows back to the early philosophy and cardinal principles of progressive education of the 1910s and 1920s and the core curriculum of the 1930s and 1940s, which promoted the study of moral and social issues, social responsibility, and civic education and youth service for the community and nation.

In an era of high-stake testing and cognitive outcomes, school reform has become fixated on raising reading and math test scores. Such an approach has narrowed the curriculum and teaching emphasis. Elliot Eisner asks that we return to John Dewey's philosophy of teaching the "whole child." He warns that "children respond to educational situations not only intellectually, but emotionally and socially as well."[79] The contemporary stress on cognition is based on an Essentialist philosophy that reached its height of influence during the Cold War and has been propelled by a technical and competitive orientation to teaching, influenced by globalization and big business and big government.

In answer to the question, "What are schools for?" John Goodlad says they are established to develop individual potential and serve the needs of society. Both purposes call for a holistic process of teaching, embracing both the arts and sciences, and full development (not just cognitive) of children and youth.[80] Aristotle examined this idea in a clear, concise way more than 2000 years ago: "The habits we form from childhood make no small difference, but rather they make all the difference."

A humanistic, civic, and holistic view of education also means that we consider the basic school, conceived by Ernest Boyer and the Carnegie Foundation. Boyer focuses on the child (or adolescent) and community, where schools are kept small so that people work together and feel connected and empowered; and the school provides emotional and social support for children, beyond academics and test scores, to concentrate on the whole child and teach the importance of values, ethics, and moral responsibility.[81] Boyer's view coincides with a more recent view by Kenneth Strike concerning the advantages of small schools and prescriptions for reforming schools;[82] his view also suggests that a moral and civil society is a requirement for democracy to work, as so keenly described over 150 years ago in Alexis de Tocqueville's classic treatise *Democracy in America* and reaffirmed by John Dewey nearly 100 years ago in his book *Democracy and Education.*

Humanism emphasizes teaching the importance of connecting with nature and the ecology of our planet, to preserve our resources and ensure our future. This

---

[79]Elliot W. Eisner, "Back to the Whole," *Educational Leadership,* 63 (2005): 16.

[80]John I. Goodlad, *What Schools Are For,* 2nd ed. (Bloomington, IN: Phi Delta Kappan Educational Foundation, 1994); John I. Goodlad and Timothy J. McMannon (eds.), *The Public Purpose of Education and Schooling* (San Francisco: Jossey-Bass, 1997).

[81]Ernest L. Boyer, High School (New York: The Carnegie Foundation for the Advancement of Teaching, 1983).

[82]Kenneth A. Strike, *Small Schools and Strong Communities* (New York: Teachers College Press, Columbia University 2010).

philosophy requires that we bring competitiveness and social cohesion, excellence and equality, as well as material wealth and poverty, into harmony—not an easy task compared to squaring a circle. Ideally, we need to focus on the whole child, keenly expressed in the 1918 Cardinal Principles of Secondary Education, and not just cognitive outcomes. Educating the whole child includes health, leisure and recreation, civic participation, work, family life, ethics, and the fundamentals, as well.

Teaching, Testing, and the Achievement Gap

Today the focus on testing dominates the teaching process—a return to the era of World War I, when large-scale testing was first introduced and used to sort individuals by those qualified and less qualified for schools and colleges, employment, and the armed forces. The same testing and teaching ethos resurfaced during the post–Sputnik/Cold War era, a reaction to the Soviet military threat, which led to the proliferation of standardized testing; advanced placement high school courses; and, as well, as a focus on talented and gifted students, reforming or upgrading the curriculum (more academic courses, more homework, etc.) and emphasis on science and math.

The current threat perceived by Americans centers around economics, particularly with globalization, and the impact of tens of millions of skilled workers and technicians in Asia and Europe competing with American workers. One source claims that 40 to 50 million jobs can potentially be eliminated (as has happened with the auto industry) or outsourced to other countries (as with IBM, Cisco, and Hewlett-Packard) for 25 to 33 percent of the American wage. The need is to provide American students with scientific and technical skills so they can compete in the twenty-first century. In 2007, according to Marge Schever, the editor-in-chief of the Association for Supervision and Curriculum Development, U.S. students will take nearly 70 million standardized tests to meet the requirements of the No Child Left Behind Act alone, and possibly another 70 million involving international tests, **National Assessment of Educational Progress (NAEP)**, and the SATs and ACTs.[83]

Even when testing measures achievement, using assessment for feedback and learning has become secondary. The schools are more interested in measuring student results and rankings, improving proficiency levels, holding teachers and administrators accountable, and ensuring that everyone has complied with state and federal guidelines.[84] In this high-stake testing era, the scoreboard officially indicates whether a school has been successful or unsuccessful in showing test score improvement that state and federal assessment requires.

Teaching has become geared toward improving student test outcomes and getting measurable results, not whether students are really learning. Tests are driving curriculum in the form of content standards, and teachers are expected to teach toward those standards. There is little concern about whether students can critically think or solve problems, or whether their social, personal, and emotional needs are being met. Given the concern for compliance with state and federal testing programs, teachers and administrators have been depersonalized and deprofessionalized, reduced to technicians who are now told from the top down what strategies are needed to raise proficiency scores and what content should be scheduled. Increasingly, school administrators are planning workshops on "Teaching Toward Tests," "Raising Student Test Scores," and "Getting Results," while traditional staff development themes such as classroom management, lesson planning, and team teaching—the "nuts and bolts" of teaching—get forced to the wayside.

In *The Teaching Gap,* Stigler and Hiebert document that teaching (and learning to teach) is a cultural activity. Among industrialized countries they studied, teachers employ different classroom techniques.[85] There is no evidence of change in techniques among experienced teachers who are given in-service workshops or education courses. For example, Japanese math teachers stress concepts and relationships. In Hong Kong, teachers require students to practice procedures. In the U.S., math teachers review homework, recall information, and also practice procedures. The authors conclude that it matters little what we tell teachers to do or that we provide them with "best practices" or "what works." Teachers view their own methods and techniques "through

[83]Marge Schever, "Reclaiming Testing," *Educational Leadership,* 63 (2005): 9.

[84]Thomas R. Guskey, "Mapping the Road to Proficiency," *Educational Leadership,* 63 (2005): 32–38; W. James Popham, "The Age of Compliance," *Educational Leadership,* 63 (2005): 84–85; and Mike Rose, "Standards, Teaching and Learning," *Phi Delta Kappan*: 91 (2009): 21–27.

[85]James W. Stigler and James Hiebert, *The Teaching Gap: Best Ideas from the World's Teachers for Improving Education in the Classroom* (New York: Free Press 2009).

their own cultural lens and unintentionally distort key features" to fit their personality and training.[86] This view of culture is actually an extension or offshoot of the classic book, *Sociology of Teaching,* published in 1932—***sort of old wine bottled under a new label*** called *The Teaching Gap.*

Most important, however, what students learn or don't learn in class depends less on what teachers do and more on student input, that is their abilities and values. Teacher and school input combined, according to research, accounts for no more than 17 to 20 percent of the variance related to academic achievement.[87] This tends to be shoved underneath the rug because of its negative implications and because it is politically incorrect to hold students accountable; the "in" idea is to hold teachers accountable as if we were trying to fix an old TV: give it a kick—and see what happens.

Teaching and Learning

Throughout the 1980s and 1990s, a debate focused on whether schooling improved cognitive test scores and whether these outcomes affected economic earnings. Schooling explained only a modest amount of the variations related to academic achievement, highlighted by Jerome Coleman; and academic achievement explained a modest amount of the variation related to wages, highlighted by Christopher Jencks. Although employers value what students learn in school and are willing to pay for it, they also value other skills.

Most of the variation in economic outcomes can be attributed to noncognitive factors such as physical characteristics, personality, motivation, reliability, honesty, and creativity. Since social scientists have spent little effort analyzing these characteristics, the cognitive factors remain masked (by noncognitive factors) and for the time being appear to be less than what educators would like to hear.

The negligible impact of schooling was bolstered in the 1980s and 1990s by Erik Hanushek's review of the research, which confirmed—like the Coleman and Jencks reports—that schools have no measurable effect on students' test scores or future earnings, and there is no strong relationship between school spending and student performance.[88] Where research did show that school characteristics or school spending had positive effects, the relationship was small or shown to be contaminated by (1) methodological assumptions, (2) weighting procedures of school characteristics, and (3) unlike comparisons across schools, school districts, or states.[89] Despite these flaws in the research, student expenditures, smaller classrooms, and teacher experience (not salaries or education) demonstrated the most consistent effects. Nonetheless, other studies showed contradictory or inconsistent results among these factors.[90]

The 1990s also revived the argument of heredity, with Herrnstein and Murray's 1994 publication of *The Bell Curve,* which claimed that cognitive tests that predict life chances and economic earnings were measuring a collection of stable abilities. Psychologists, since Charles Spearman's research in 1904 often called this ability set *g,* for general intelligence.[91] The most important characteristic of *g* is the general ability to learn new skills and knowledge quickly and easily—exactly the type of "**human capital**" that employers seek and reward. It just so happens that "smart" people with a

[86]James W. Stigler and James Hiebert, "Closing the Teaching Gap," *Phi Delta Kappan* 91 (2009): 32–37.

[87]Christopher Jencks, *Inequality: A Reassessment of the Effect of Family and Schooling* (New York: Basic Books, 1972); Christopher Jencks and Meredith Phillips, eds., *The Black-White Test Score Gap* (Washington, DC: Brookings Institute 1998); Allan C. Ornstein, *Teaching and Schooling in America* (Boston: Allyn and Bacon, 2003).

[88]Eric A. Hanushek, "The Economics of Schooling." *Journal of Economic Literature,* 2 (1986): 1141–1176; Hanushek, "The Impact of Differential Expenditures on School Performance," *Educational Researcher* (May 1989): 45–51; and Hanushek, *Making Schools Work* (Washington, DC: Brookings Institute, 1994).

[89]Ronald F. Ferguson, "Teachers' Perceptions and Expectations and the Black-White Score Gap," in C. Jencks and M. Phillips (eds.), *The Black White Score Gap* (Washington, DC: Brookings Institute, 1998); Helen F. Ladd (ed.), *Holding Schools Accountable* (Washington, DC: Brookings Institute, 1996); and Robert Rothman, "Improving Student Learning Requires District Learning," *Phi Delta Kappan,* 91 (2009): 44–50.

[90]Gary Burtless (ed.), *Does Money Matter? The Effect of School Resources on Student Achievement and Advent Success* (Washington, DC: Brookings Institute, 1996); Stacey M. Childress, "Six Lessons for Pursuing Excellence and Equity at Scale," *Phi Delta Kappan,* 91 (2009): 13–18; Charles M. Payne, *So Much Reform, So Little Change* (Cambridge, MA: Harvard Education Press, 2008); and Helen F. Ladd (ed.), *Holding Schools Accountable: Performance-Based Reform in Education* (Washington, DC: Brookings Institution, 1996).

[91]Richard J. Herrnstein and Charles Murray, *The Bell Curve: Intelligence and Class Structures in American Life* (New York: Free Press, 1994). Also see Charles E. Spearman, "General Intelligence Objectivity Determined and Measured," *American Journal of Psychology* (April 1904): 201–293.

high *g* factor tend to go to school longer and get higher grades; it is not the amount of schooling or high test scores that are primarily associated with future earnings, but the *g* factor which leads to more schooling and better test scores, and greater job competency (because people with general intelligence become skilled in many social and work-related areas). Also, the authors argued that *g* was biological or genetic, not environmentally or socially based.

Aptitude, Achievement and Human Capital

The best analyses of education and earnings since *The Bell Curve* are by Susan Mayer (formerly the Jencks team) and Paul Peterson (a Harvard professor); those by David Grissmer and his colleagues at the Rand Corporation; and the publications of the Brookings Institution, Rand, and the Urban Institute. In general, theses reports do not repudiate Coleman and Jencks (see Chapter 10), or the unaccounted variances related to economic outcomes (what Jencks calls luck). We are told that schools help promote intergenerational mobility, although they do not themselves provide sufficient opportunity to break the general class structure. Given our information age, in which knowledge is crucial, formal education should increase social mobility in the future; however, we cannot dismiss growing economic inequality when students are completing more school years. Students at the bottom of the social order tend to be "frozen" in their parents' status, but for the small percentage who can rise above that status, the schools are the chief route to success.

Mayer and Peterson argue that both aptitude and achievement result in adult success but aptitude is more important because people who learn more quickly are more useful to their employers than people who learn slowly or with difficulty. Their model also assumes that "the entire school curriculum is a prolonged aptitude test, and that the specific skills and knowledge taught in school have no economic value" because people who easily learn Latin also easily learn algebra, computer skills, or financial banking skills.[92]

Most educators and policymakers prefer the achievement model, arguing that academic outcomes and schooling count, and what you know counts more than how hard you need to study to learn it. For this group, outcomes count more than the learning process. Math or verbal scores count because employers seek someone with math or verbal skills, not because the scores indicate the worker's ability to learn other skills. Mayer and Peterson ask us to imagine two groups of adults with similar math (or verbal) scores: one with less math training but high aptitude and the other with better math training but low aptitude. According to the achievement model, the two groups have an equal earning potential. The aptitude model assumes that the high aptitude group with less math training can learn more math in the long run and also can function better in other content areas and thus earn substantially more than the low aptitude group with better math training. Most people have no problem with this analysis until they realize that aptitude is a form of *g* and suggests heredity.

Mayer and Peterson further maintain that schools can exert considerable influence on the child's experiences, and these experiences affect achievement. In general, each additional year of schooling beyond high school increases wages 2 to 4 percent, not considering the effect of aptitude or intelligence. "But most of the variation in occupational status and salaries has little to do with education and is not measured by conventional tests. Employers seek reliable, creative, honest, and socially skilled persons." Pedigree, nepotism, parental social contacts, and how someone talks and dresses also affects economic outcomes. "But social scientists have devoted little time and effort to measuring the effects of these characteristics."[93] That said, before we alter the classroom and students' instructional experiences, we need to know how much achievement would vary if we treated all children alike and how assigning children with different aptitudes to different environments would alter the variance of achievement. In this way we could determine (in theory) which changes have the most influence and how our resources can be earmarked to improve achievement.

Grissmer takes us to the final step in the debate about family and school characteristics, and their effect on achievement. He speaks in terms of family capital and social capital. *Family capital* refers to characteristics within the family passed from parent to child, the family's quality and quantity of resources, and the allocation of these resources toward the child's educations and socialization. *Social capital* refers to long-term

[92]Susan E. Mayer and Paul E. Peterson *Earning and Learning: How Schools Matter* (Washington, D.C.: Brookings Institution, 1999).

[93]Allan C. Ornstein, *Class Counts: Education, Inequality and the Shrinking Middle Class* (Lanbaum, MD: Rowman & Littlefield, 2007) pp. 105–106.

capacities within the community and school district that affect achievement—for example, peer group, parents' trust in the community, the community's safety and support structure, and the community's ability to support and pay for schools and social institutions (community centers, theaters, athletic clubs, etc.)[94]

Grissmer infers that family capital is more important than social capital, and the authors agree because the family doesn't change while the school and community can change (simply by the family's moving) and the child's earliest experiences are rooted in the family. However, he points out that family and social capital are not independent, or randomly distributed, but are grouped together because of economics. "More social capital arises in communities and states having higher income and more educated families. Thus achievement scores across schools, communities and states differ partly because their families differ in their internal capacity to produce achievement and partially because families with similar characteristics are grouped in communities and states creating different levels of social capital."[95] In other words, high-income families tend to cluster in high-income communities that spend more on schooling and have smaller classes and better paid, and more experienced teachers.

Do School characteristics by themselves shape academic outcomes? No. Family and social capital differences lead to academic differences. For instance a review of the National Assessment of Educational Progress (NAEP) results, which now test students in 44 states and are considered the best indicators of national achievement, shows that achievement levels are directly related to family and social characteristics across states and only a tiny portion of test results is related to what schools do. Moreover, it is difficult to discern which school policies succeed because so many of the measures concerning school spending, classroom size, teacher education levels, and so on are related to family and social capital. There is some indication that changes in school spending and classroom size count, but these results are "inconsistent and unstable . . . to guide policy" and sometimes even based on "noncredible estimates."[96]

What do the recent scores in Texas tell us? On the surface, they tell us that teachers and schools can improve student performance and reduce differences in average scores among minority groups in only four years—results that bolsters the achievement model. Often referred to as the "Texas Miracle" because of the larger-scale increase in post-test scores, closer examination reveals intense test preparation in low-performing schools, large-scale cheating, and many students held back to show more improvement on the post-test than comparable students who move to the next grade. Most importantly, each school selected the students and classrooms that would be tested, thus screening out low-performing students on the post-tests.[97] Those factors are not unique. Other teachers, schools, and school districts involved in high-stakes testing, and showing large-scale or sudden gains, usually reveal similar findings that distort inferences from test-score gains. In a nutshell, it is difficult to put stock in the results of any standardized test when the stakes are high, claims are made in order to promote a policy or program, jobs are at stake, or black-Hispanic-white scores are being compared.

NAEP/State Standards and Test Scores

Thousands of publications exist showing relationships between social class and achievement and race/ethnicity and achievement. Since 1990, the NAEP, known as the **nation's "Report Card,"** has reported fourth-, eighth-, and twelfth-grade performance scores in reading and math, as well as other subject areas. It is considered perhaps the most comprehensive and reliable set of data, although some critics have questioned the instructional validity of the test items. Consistently, over the last fifteen years, lower-class students (eligible for free or reduced-priced lunch) and minority students (blacks and Hispanics) perform three to four grade levels below their middle-class and white counterparts by grade eight and this continues in grade twelve despite all the remediation, tutoring, and compensatory programs that have been introduced.[98]

In 2003, the average *reading* NAEP score at grade four was 218. For black students it was 198, for Hispanic students 200, and for white students 229. By grade eight the reading gap had increased. The average

[94]David Grissmer et al. *Improving Student Achievement* (Santa Monica, Ca: Rand Corporation, 2000).

[95]Ibid, p. 18.

[96]Ibid, pp. 29, 31.

[97]Stephen P. Klein, "What Do Test Scores in Texas Tell Us?," Issue Paper (Santa Monica, Ca: Rand Corporation, 2000); Ornstein, *Teaching and Schooling in American.*

[98]There was minimal reduction in the achievement gap between 1996 and 2000, which then leveled off between 2001 and 2004. See Eric A. Hanushek and Alfred A. Lindseth, *Schoolhouses, Courthouses, and Statehouses: Solving the Funding-Achievement Puzzle in America's Public Schools* (Princeton, NJ: Princeton University Press, 2009).

Table 14-2 Percent of Eighth Grade Reading and Math Scores of States at or Above Proficient, 2003

	NAEP		State Test		Difference Total
	Reading	Math	Reading	Math	Reading + Math
Tennessee	26	21	80	79	54 + 58 = 112
Texas	26	25	88	72	62 + 47 = 109
N. Carolina	29	32	86	82	57 + 50 = 107
W. Virginia	25	20	80	69	55 + 49 = 104
Oklahoma	30	20	79	73	49 + 53 = 102
Georgia	26	22	81	67	55 + 45 = 100
Ohio	34	30	87	71	53 + 41 = 94
Wisconsin	37	35	84	76	47 + 41 = 88
Colorado	36	34	86	68	50 + 34 = 84
Connecticut	37	35	77	77	40 + 42 = 82

Source: Adapted from "Quality Counts 2005: No Small Change," *Education Week*, January 6, 2005: 1–5.

reading score was 263. For black students it was 244, Hispanic students 245, and white students 272. Using class as an indicator: in grade four, in schools where 76 to 100 percent of the students were eligible for free or reduced-price lunch, the average score was 194, compared to schools where 0 to 10 percent of the students participated in the lunch program, where the average score was 238. By grade eight the scores were 239 for the low-income students and 280 for the middle- and upper-middle-class students.[99]

In *math*, the average NAEP gap in scores were similar by race and class. For example, at grade four, white students scored 27 points higher than blacks and 21 points higher than Hispanics. By grade eight, the white-black math gap was 36 points and white-Hispanic math gap was 29 points. In terms of class, in grade four the math gap between lower-class students and middle-class students was 34 points, and by grade eight it was 49 points.[100] In short, the NAEP achievement gap between minority and white students and between lower- and middle-class students increased by grade level, as originally pointed out in the Coleman Report in 1966.

Under the No Child Left Behind (NCLB) Act, fourth-grade and eighth-grade students in every state were required to participate in NAEP reading and math tests every other year, in part to verify state assessments. Such comparisons on state and national tests have never been possible or required before. The test content and benchmarks for passing varied dramatically by state, resulting in a variable definition of "proficiency." For example, in 2003, the highest proficiency rates were reported in Colorado and Mississippi: 87 percent of fourth graders passed their exams. But the Colorado proficiency rate fell a dramatic 50 points to 37 percent on the NAEP, and Mississippi fell 69 points to 18 percent, placing last among all the states. The comparisons were similar among fourth graders in math. Colorado showed a proficiency level of 86 percent, whereas the NAEP revealed it to be 34 percent—a 52-point difference. In Mississippi, 74 percent scored at or above proficient, but on the NAEP the score was 17 percent—a difference of 57 points. The same pattern existed at the eighth-grade level. Table 14–2 reports ten states with the greatest NAEP difference in scores of proficiency in reading and math at the eighth grade. All these states, in short, are misrepresenting their results and thus evading the real issues of student achievement and education reform.

According to NCLB, all students are required to reach proficiency on state reading and math tests by 2014. States are judged on yearly progress and penalized, including the loss of federal funds, if proficiency levels decline. Yet states continue to use their own definition of proficiency. Those "states that have the bar lower will have an easier time meeting the mark and avoiding federal sanctions,"[101] but it can be expected

[99]*The Condition of Education 2004* (Washington, DC: U.S. Government Printing Office, 2004), table 9–2, p. 120.

[100]Ibid, table 11–2, p. 128.

[101]Susan Saulny, "State to State, Varied Ideas of 'Proficient,'" *New York Times*, 19 January 2005, p. B8.

that eventually state officials and education policymakers will address these different standards.

Diane Ravitch, an education historian, is a vocal critic of state exams. She refers to them "as persistent dumbing down" by state education departments "and lying to the public." Administrators who are concerned about parental opinion claim that so long as Federal policies (such as NCLB) rely on state tests to measure school performance the tests are reliable and valid predictors of performance. But Michael Mulgrew, the president of the United Federation of Teachers, argues that the federal test (NAEP) results show that the state tests are unreliable and invalid, and that the states need to be more truthful.[102]

In 2003 no state performed better on the NAEP in fourth-grade reading than on the state's own exam, and only two did better at the eighth-grade level (Vermont, 3 percent difference; Missouri, 2 percent). Two states scored better on the NAEP fourth-grade math test than on their own state exams (Vermont, 2 percent; Massachusetts, 1 percent) and three states did better on the NAEP eighth-grade math test (Massachusetts by 1 percent, South Carolina by 7, and Missouri by 14).

More than three-fourths of the states require state proficiency tests to determine whether students will pass to the next grade or graduate from high school.[103] Minority students and low-income students fail these tests at rates of 50 to 90 percent, depending on the state and year. In Louisiana, for example, nearly 50 percent of poor and minority students failed the state tests, even after taking them a second time. In Georgia, two-thirds of low-income students failed the math and reading sections of the state competency tests. Almost half the students of Ohio from families with incomes below $20,000 failed the state exams, while 80 percent of students from families earning more than $30,000 passed.[104]

In Minnesota, the assessment program consisted of 47,300 students and the size of the sample suggested minimal statistical error. The overall mean difference between lunch and non-lunch program students was 6.9 raw points in the third grade, equivalent to more than one grade level. By the fifth grade the achievement gap by income was nearly two grade levels apart.[105] After matching pre- and posttest scores, it was rare to find any member of the disadvantaged group who made equal progress from grade three to five, never mind more progress; so the trend repeated itself for more than 95 percent of the students. The only low-income group to keep up with their more-advantaged group peers were the Asian disadvantaged, as their limited English proficiency declined.

As many as 26 states require passage of exams for high school graduation: fifteen states, including New Jersey, New York and Texas, use subject-based tests. This approach links course content to exit tests and most teachers believe the tests help clarify the curriculum they teach; eleven states use comprehensive verbal and mathematical exams (which can used under the NCLB law).[106]

All the states have softened standards, provided multiple chances to retake the tests, and/ or added alternative paths to a diploma in order to prop up graduation numbers. Standards have been lowered, then lowered again and again, because a disproportionate percent of minorities fail the tests, afterwards accompanied by law suits claiming that the tests are unfair. The outcome is that the high school diploma has diminished in value—in an information and global economy that requires literate and skilled workers to compete with other industrialized and emerging nations.

The data implies that once the achievement gap begins, it worsens over time. Students do not make up lost ground. Moreover, longitudinal data from the NAEP show similar gaps increasing in reading, math, and other subject areas from grade four, the earliest grade for which the tests are given. "Once [NAEP] achievement gaps between students group emerge, they tend to persist over time."[107] The groups most effected by declining achievement test scores are racial, ethnic, and

[102]"U.S. Math Tests Show Scant Progress," *New York Times*, October 15, 2009, pp. A1, A32.

[103]Martin Carnoy and Susanna Loeb, "Does External Accountability Affect Student Outcomes?" *Educational Evaluation and Policy Analysis* 24 (2002): 305–332.

[104]Jay Heubert, "First, Do No Harm," *Educational Leadership* 60 (2003): 26–30; David Sadker and Karen Zittleman, "Test Anxiety: Are Students Failing Tests—Or Are Tests Failing Students?" *Phi Delta Kappan* 85 (2004): 740–744, 751.

[105]Mark L. Davidson et al., "When Do Children Fall Behind?" *Phi Delta Kappan* 85 (2004): 752–761.

[106]Ian Urbina, "States Lower Test Standards For Diploma," *New York Times*, January 12, 2010, pp. 1A, 12A.

[107]Sharon Nichols and David C. Berliner, "Why High-Stakes Testing So Easily Slipped into American Contemporary Life," *Phi Delta Kappan* 89 (2008): 672–676; Mano Singham, "The Achievement Gap: Myths and Reality," *Phi Delta Kappan* 84 (2003): 586.

low socio-economic groups.[108] Whether the problem results from poverty, or inadequacies of students and their families, or teachers, or underlying racism, the solution is to prevent the gaps from emerging in the first place by focusing on infant and preschool education, and family conditions. But as critics point out, early childhood programs are diffuse, uncoordinated, and underfunded,[109] and family differences and issues lead to controversial and heated debates and politically complicated solutions.

In general, student achievement has remained flat based on the results of the NAEP tests in reading, math, and science for minority (black and Hispanic) students. Of the fifty states, the majority received a D, that is, minimal or limited progress, on the 2005 annual report card for closing achievement gaps between black and Hispanic students and their white and Asian counterparts.[110] The results, published by Fordham Foundation, a conservative education think tank, advised that progress has been negligible since the 1983 release of *A Nation at Risk,* which warned of the "rising tide of mediocrity" in American schools and the inability of the United States to economically compete on a global basis because of its workforce. The same trend has held true since 2002, when NCLB went into effect, despite government insistence that by 2014 the performance of white and minority students must be indistinguishable. In 2002, for example, 13 percent of the nation's black eighth-grade students were proficient in reading. By 2005 (the latest available data) the figure had dropped to 12 percent. In other words, the performance of black students had slightly declined.

The report contradicts the rhetoric of reform among education leaders. State educators and school superintendents reject the report as unusually "harsh" and not reflecting the problems encountered by the schools in educating low-income and minority students. Family background remains a reliable predictor of student performance. According to recent research, a public school that enrolls middle-class white children has a 25 percent (or 1 in 4) chance of earning high test scores on the NAEP two years in a row, whereas a school with mostly poor minority children has a 0.33 percent (or 1 in 300) chance.[111]

Race and Class

Explanations for the achievement gap run the gamut from differences in family and health conditions, to teacher expectations and experience, to school spending and changing student exclusion rates, to television viewing and "hip-hop" culture. Research by Paul Barton of the Educational Testing Service summarizes fourteen factors related to home and school conditions and student achievement for low-income and minority students for which they are disadvantaged. Home conditions include (1) low birth weights, (2) exposure to lead poisoning found in old houses, (3) hunger and malnutrition, (4) parents or adults who rarely read to young children, (5) watching lots of television, (6) significant percentages of one-family households (2.5 times higher among black children compared to white children), (7) high student mobility rates, (8) and minimal parent participation in school matters. School conditions include (9) easier courses, (10) teachers with fewer years of experience and larger absentee rates, (11) teachers with less preparation, and more of them out of license, (12) fewer computers available in school and less internet use at home, (13) larger class sizes, and (14) more unsafe schools.[112]

There was no mention in the report about school spending as a factor. The data about it are consistent, however. In wealthy states, average school spending between big-city school districts and nearby affluent suburbs runs 2 to 3 times as high, say, $10,000 versus $20,000 per student. Over a twelve-year period, the impact of $120,000 per student is substantial. Furthermore, the student poverty index in the majority of big-city school systems runs 25 percent or more, and in ten big cities it runs 40 to 50 percent, with Atlanta (51 percent) and Detroit (48 percent) having the highest poverty rates.[113] Clearly, poor and minority students have more social, psychological, and educational

---

[108]Davidson, "When Do Children Fall Behind?"; Ruth S. Johnson, *Using Data to Close the Achievement Gap* (Thousand Oaks, CA: Corwin Press, 2002).

[109]Gerald Bracey and Arthur Stellar, "Long-Term Studies of Preschool: Lasting Benefits Far Outweigh Costs," *Phi Delta Kappan* 84 (2003): 780–783, 797.

[110]*Quality Counts* (Washington, DC: Thomas B. Fordham, 2006). Also see Linda Jacobson, "States Get Poor Grades on Closing Achievement Gaps," *Education Week,* November 8, 2006, pp. 18–19; Joseph Murphy, "Closing the Achievement Gap," *Phi Delta Kappan,* 91 (2009): 8–12.

[111]Paul Tough, "Can Teaching Poor Children to Act More Like Middle-Class Children Help Close the Education Gap?" *New York Times Magazine,* November 26, 2006, pp. 44–51, ff.

[112]Paul E. Barton, *Passing the Achievement Gap* (Princeton, NJ: Educational Testing Service, 2003).

[113]*Digest of Education Statistics 2003* (Washington, DC: U.S. Government Printing Office, 2004), table 91, pp. 124–125.

problems than do affluent students, and therefore need more money (not less) to attempt to diminish achievement disparities. A conservative interpretation is that money and whatever the school attempts are not the main contributing factors—a reaffirmation of Coleman and Jencks. Once students begin to fall behind most will never catch up, which is the reason why the achievement gap has persisted so long.[114] This fact is unacceptable to liberal and minority reformers, and is considered a form of class and race bias.

For the nation as a whole, the disparity in school performance tied to race and class has become a major issue because of the social and economic implications of the continuous failure of schools to prepare tens of millions of children for the technological and information age, and to compete in the global economy. The inability of schools to close the achievement gap has led business and parent groups to lose faith in public schools, to insist on higher standards and more testing as an overall "solution" to the problem, and to insist on a variety of school alternatives. The concern is further heightened upon recognition that black and Hispanic students accounted for about one-third of the 54 million children in the nation's public schools in 2000 and are expected to increase to two-thirds by 2015.[115]

Another Option

There are no agreed-upon solutions to the education crisis afflicting U.S. society. After fifty years of compensatory funding and nearly $100 billion invested, the results are at best mixed; the programs and money spent have not had much impact on the achievement gap between low-income students and middle-income students and minority and white students. In order to neutralize the skepticism of the education establishment, reformers have developed a literature on *more effective schools* which purports that inner-city schools can successfully educate poor and minority students.

Advocates of this approach pay attention to schools as institutions (focusing on preschool and elementary schools), the environment in which they operate, and usually define success in terms of student achievement. This emphasis corresponds with environmental research data indicating that intervention is most critical in the early stages of human development, which is the most rapid period of cognitive growth (50 percent by age four, another 25 percent by age nine, according to Ben Bloom).[116]

Given the public concern for young children, and the fact that Americans have sufficient wealth as a nation to meet the education and special needs of all young children, it is surprising that we lack a national and sustainable program that supports a public investment in infant and toddler education. The research is consistent about the value of early childhood education for children who are "at risk" and coincides with the developmental theories of Jean Piaget and Ben Bloom. In several European countries, there has been a trend toward nationalization of education services for all children from as early as eighteen months in Sweden, two years in Belgium, and three years in Italy.[117] To date, most federal and state initiatives in the United States focus on Head Start education for children four to five years old. However, only 36 percent of eligible children receive Head Start services,[118] which borders on a national embarrassment.

The industrialized countries of Europe, Australia, and New Zealand spend on average 0.5 percent of their GNP on education for early childhood.[119] Given the education benefits (exemplified by a longitudal preschool study through age 27 by David Weikart of the University of Michigan, the early childhood education studies in Europe, and the benefits to working mothers and ultimate savings to society),[120] it would seem to our advantage to expand prekindergarten education in the United States downward to age three; to upgrade training in personnel and provide for certification; to ensure a consensus on philosophy and pedagogy; to monitor the participation of parents and staff; and

[114]Davidson, "When Do Children Fall Behind?" Julian Weissglass, "Racism and the Achievement Gap," *Education Week*, August 8, 2001, p. 8.

[115]Robert C. Johnston and Debra Viadero, "Unmet Promises: Raising Minority Achievement," *Education Week*, March 5, p. 19; *The Condition of Education* (2004), table 4–1, p. 112.

[116]Benjamin S. Bloom, *Stability and Change in Human Characters* (New York: Wiley, 1964).

[117]Michelle J. Neuman and John Bennett, "Starting Strong: Policy Implications for Early Childhood Education and Care in the U.S.," *Phi Delta Kappan* 83 (2001): 246–254.

[118]Pauline B. Gough, "The Best Place to Start," *Phi Delta Kappan* (November 2001): 182.

[119]*A Caring World: The New Social Policy Agenda* (Paris: OECD, 1999); *Starting Strong: Early Childhood Education and Care* (Paris: OCED, 2001).

[120]Ibid. Also see David Weikart, *Significant Benefits: The High/Scope Perry Preschool Study Through Age 27* (Ypsilanti, MI: High/Scope Press, 1993).

PRO CON DEBATE

Teacher Accountability

Parents and communities want what is best for children, and for many, high scholastic performance is the goal. In some communities, when the goal is not reached, school board members and/or administrators are replaced. But teachers have tenure and are exempt from such actions.

Question: Should teachers be accountable for high student performance?

Arguments PRO

1. It is important to relate dollars spent to student accomplishment, since 65 to 70 percent of the school budget is related to teacher/administrative salaries. Holding educational professionals accountable is wise policy, especially if we wish to focus on results. Failure to hold teachers accountable lets them off the hook.
2. The heart of the educational system is the classroom. It is here that teaching occurs and learning results. If anyone should be accountable for scholastic achievement, it should be the teacher.
3. Stringent teacher accountability would ensure that marginal teachers do not remain in the classroom. Why do we pay high salaries to teachers who can't get the job done?
4. All professionals are accountable for performing their work well. If teaching is a profession, then once standards have been identified, it is the responsibility of teachers to meet them.

Arguments CON

1. Many variables impact on student accomplishment. Student achievement is a joint responsibility among students, parents, teachers, administrators, board members, and taxpayers (or the community). The idea of holding teachers and administrators accountable, without considering family and student responsibility, is highly political and unwise.
2. The teacher works with many children, each of whom has different talents, different potential, and a different home life. It would be unfair to expect teachers to meet high standards when the raw material is so variable and complex.
3. If teachers are likely to be fired when students do not perform well, then teachers will concentrate on teaching to the tests that measure student performance. Our tests are not reliable enough to make or break careers.
4. As a rule, professionals see the immediate results of their work. Doctors know if an operation is successful. Lawyers know if the case is won. Engineers see bridges built. The results of teaching are not evident in the short term: The truly educated person takes years to evolve.

to pay sufficient wages to attract qualified personnel and reduce turnover. This combination could counteract the negative influence of a deprived environment and family discord.

As of 2000, about 2.6 million U.S. infants and toddlers were in some form of child care full time, or thirty-five hours a week, distributed among child-care centers (39 percent), relatives (27 percent), neighbors (27 percent), and nannies or babysitters (7 percent).[121] The Dependent Care Assistance Program allows families to deduct up to $5,000 per year for child-care expenses for children age fourteen and under. But again, who benefits? Certainly not the poor, who rely on relatives and neighbors to provide care.

Because a child's early years are so formative, it would be wise for the United States to commit to the care and education of its young and to make those compulsory, especially for "at risk" and poor children, in order to prepare or catch them up to grade level by the time they enter school. A few states, such as Massachusetts, Vermont, and West Virginia, do provide comprehensive programs for infants and toddlers, and the federal government in 2000 provided $3.5 billion in block grants to states for providing child-care services to assist working women with children (73 percent of women between ages twenty-five and thirty-four are

[121] "Nearly 5 million Infants and Toddlers in Child Care," *New Federalism* (June 2001): 2.

in the workforce).[122] The outcomes of this, however, are piecemeal and inadequate. More like $12 billion is needed—twice the appropriations for Head Start—to ensure that all our nation's poor or at-risk children receive appropriate services and education.

School nutrition programs; extended day, weekend, and required preschool programs; required summer school for primary students (grades one through three) to neutralize cognitive deficits as opposed to allowing them to increase; reading and tutoring programs; parenting education; and reducing class and school size—all are crucial.[123] The instruction recommended is prescriptive and diagnostic, emphasizing basic skill acquisition, review and guided practice, monitoring of student programs, prompt feedback and reinforcement to students, and mastery-learning opportunities. These actions point to a behaviorist, direct, convergent, systematic, and low cognitive level of instruction, as opposed to a problem-solving, abstract, divergent, inquiry-based, and high level of instruction. (Some critics would argue that this type of instruction is second rate and reflects our low expectations of low-achieving students. Perhaps. But the critics have had their opportunities and failed to close the achievement gap.) Plato may have been right: The state needs to intervene, if not to nationalize education then to provide the resources needed to educate children starting at a very young age.

Summary

1. Research on teacher behavior has looked at teacher styles, teacher-student interactions, teacher characteristics, teacher effects, and teacher contexts.
2. Although much remains to be learned about successful teaching, research has identified some teacher behaviors that seem to be effective and influence student performance.
3. Recent research on effective teaching has shifted from the process of teaching to the products of teaching and, most recently the context of teaching.
4. The classic, important research on teaching prior to the 1970s was the work of A. S. Barr, Arno Bellack, Ned Flanders, and David Ryans. These researchers focused on teacher styles, teacher-student interactions, and teacher characteristics—that is, the process, what was happening in the classroom or the behavior of the teacher.
5. In the 1970s and 1980s, the research on teaching was based on the work of Jere Brophy, Walter Doyle, Carolyn Evertson, N. L. Gage, Thomas Good, and Barak Rosenshine. Their research focused on teacher effectiveness and on the products or results of teaching.
6. Since the 1990s, two trends influenced research on teaching. One was the nature of expertise in teaching, and how expert and novice teachers differ in approach and in seeing and analyzing classroom events. The other promoted different forms of investigating teaching, based on language and dialogue: metaphors, stories, biographies, autobiographies, expert opinions, and voice. All these methods dismiss traditional qualitative methods of examining teacher behavior.
7. The need for humanistic teachers is highlighted in context with the history of effective teaching for the new century.
8. Evaluation of teachers is becoming increasingly linked to student test outcomes, at the expense of humanistic, inquiry-based, and creative instruction.
9. Data analysis shows that U.S. students are consistently outperformed by their foreign counterparts on international tests of science and mathematics, and older U.S. students fall further behind foreign students. Several reasons for this achievement gap are discussed.
10. Data analysis also shows that U.S. students consistently score higher on state reading and mathematic tests than on national tests, indicating that the states are dumbing down their tests in order to appease the public by making it appear that the local schools are doing an adequate job.

---

[122]Sharon L. Kagan and Lynda G. Hallmark, "Early Care and Education Policies in Sweden: Implications for the United States," *Phi Delta Kappan* 83 (2001): 237–245, 254; Sally Lubeck, "Early Childhood Education and Care in Cross National Perspective," *Phi Delta Kappan* 83 (2001): 213–215; and *Starting Strong: Early Childhood Education and Care.*

[123]Lorin Anderson and Leonard O. Pellicer, "Synthesis of Research on Compensatory and Remedial Education," *Educational Leadership* 48 (1990): 10–16; Allan C. Ornstein and Daniel U. Levine, "School Effectiveness and Reform: Guidelines for Action," *Clearing House* 64 (1990): 115–118: Michael Salmonowicz, "Meeting the Challenge of School Turnaround," *Phi Delta Kappan*, 91 (2009): 19–24. Georgina was the first state to require pre-K programs for all four-year-olds in the state. We recommend starting toddler programs at age three.

Key Terms

teacher processes
teacher products
teacher contexts
humanistic teaching
teacher style
teacher-student interaction
teaching cycles
nonverbal communication
self-fulfilling prophecies
teacher characteristics
master teacher
metaphors
stories
biography
autobiography
expert teacher
novice teachers
voice
humanistic education
human capital
National Assessment of Educational Progress (NAEP)
Nation's "Report Card"

Discussion Questions

1. How would you use the Flanders interaction analysis scale to provide feedback for a beginning teacher?
2. What teacher characteristics and competencies described in this chapter seem important for effective teaching in your school district? Why?
3. What behaviors listed by Gage, Good and Brophy, and Evertson coincide with the ideal teacher behavior in your school district?
4. To what extent does your school district provide peer coaching and technical coaching for teachers? Which do you prefer? Why?
5. How do you personally expect to use videos, computers, and the internet with your teaching practice? Explain.

Suggested Readings

Darling-Hammond, Linda, *The Flat World and Education* (New York: Teachers College Press, Columbia University, 2010). The path to U.S. and global well-being is related to educational opportunity and professional accountability.

Glatthorn, Allan A. and Jerry M. Jailall, *The Principal as Curriculum Leader,* 3rd ed. (Thousand Oaks, CA: Corwin Press, 2009). The author explains how the principal should work with teachers and provide leadership for schools.

Good, Thomas L., and Jere E. Brophy. *Looking into Classrooms,* 10th ed. (Boston: Allyn and Bacon, 2008). This important book helped move the field from the study of teacher processes to teacher products and presents a convincing argument that teachers do make a difference.

Goodlad, John I. *Teachers for Our Nation's Schools* (San Francisco: Jossey-Bass, 1994). As many as twenty-nine teacher training institutions are examined and nineteen postulates are set forth for reforming teacher education.

Ornstein, Allan C. *Teaching: Theory into Practice* (Needham Heights, MA: Allyn and Bacon, 1995). The author discusses the thoughts and behaviors of teachers, as well as the social and political contexts of teaching.

Popham, W. James. *America's Failing Schools* (New York: Routledge-Falmer, 2004). The book examines the implications of teaching toward standardized tests, particularly *No Child Left Behind.*

Strike, Kenneth A. and Johns F. Soltis. *The Ethics of Teaching,* 5th ed. (New York: Teachers College Press, Columbia University, 2009). A discussion of moral and ethical factors involved in teaching.

15

Human Resources Administration

FOCUSING QUESTIONS

1 What are the steps in the human resource management process?

2 Why is it important for school districts to plan their human resource needs?

3 How do school districts go about recruiting personnel?

4 What is the process used in selecting personnel?

5 Why are professional development programs needed? What are the most commonly used professional development methods?

6 How can employee performance be measured and improved? What are some common methods used?

7 What are the forms of intrinsic and extrinsic compensation, and how are they used to reward and motivate personnel?

8 How is a collective bargaining agreement negotiated and administered?

In this chapter, we attempt to answer these questions concerning human resources administration in schools. We begin our discussion with an overview of the human resource management process. Then we look at recruiting, selecting, and developing personnel. Performance appraisal and compensation are discussed next. Finally, we explore union-management relations, including the negotiation and administration of the collective bargaining agreement, incorporating new thinking concerning union-management relations.

The chapter deals with all aspects of human resources administration in schools. It is intended to help practicing and prospective school administrators (principals, central office staff, and superintendents) gain a better understanding of the entire human resource function, including both traditional and novel perspectives.

The Human Resource Management Process

The human resource management process comprises the following programs: human resource planning, recruitment, selection, professional development, performance appraisal, and compensation.[1] Figure 15–1 outlines the personnel management steps, which are affected by legislative constraints and union demands.

Human Resource Planning. Good **human resource planning** involves meeting current and future personnel needs. The school administrator ensures that personnel needs are met through ongoing analysis of performance objectives, job requirements, and available personnel, coupled with a knowledge of employment laws.

[1]L. Dean Webb and M. Scott Norton, *Human Resources Administration: Personnel Issues and Needs in Education,* 5th ed. (Upper Saddle River, NJ: Pearson Education, 2009).

Recruitment. Once personnel needs have been identified, **recruitment** involves locating qualified applicants to satisfy the organization's personnel plans.

Selection. After carefully evaluating applicants in the recruiting pool, the organization makes a **selection** of candidates who meet the job requirements.

Professional Development. **Professional development** involves improving employees' present skills and preparing them for additional responsibilities or advancement in the organization.

Performance Appraisal. **Performance appraisal** involves rating personnel performance in relationship to the organization's standards and goals. This step involves rewarding personnel, providing feedback, and maintaining communications between administrators and subordinates.

Compensation. **Compensation** involves decisions concerning salary, fringe benefits, and merit.

Human Resource Planning

School organizations typically plan their future needs for supplies, equipment, building capacity, and financing. School organizations must also plan to ensure that their human resource needs are satisfied. Human resource planning involves identifying staffing needs, forecasting available personnel, and determining what additions or replacements are required to maintain a staff of the desired quantity and quality to achieve the organization's mission.

The human resource planning function involves at least three different elements: job analysis, forecasting demand and supply, and legal constraints.

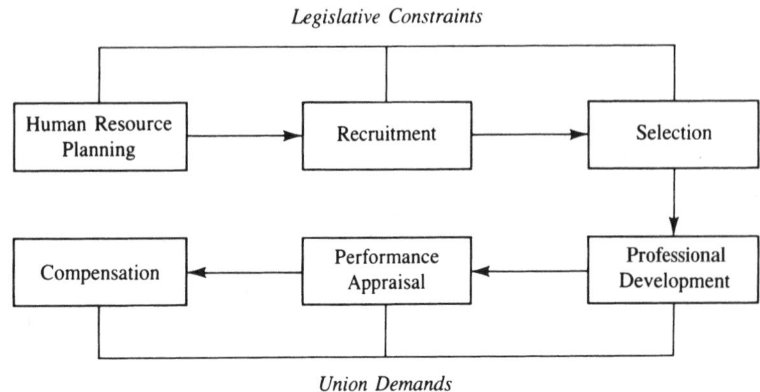

FIGURE 15–1

The Human Resource Management Process

Table 15–1 Job Description

Job Title:	School Principal
Job Goal:	To administer and supervise all activities and personnel within an assigned school, toward the fullest possible development of the skills and motivations of each pupil for fulfillment as a responsible and significant human being.
Reports to:	District Superintendent
Supervises:	All professional and nonprofessional staff assigned.

Job Responsibilities:

1. Supervises the school's instructional and extracurricular programs and all activities within the school.
2. Works toward the improvement of the instructional program within the school through faculty study groups and other evaluation processes.
3. Implements all school board policies and administrative rules and regulations.
4. Develops and encourages programs of orientation and self-improvement of teachers and others within the school.
5. Determines the work assignment of all professional personnel.
6. Plans and conducts faculty meetings.
7. Observes and reviews the performance of all personnel to provide a basis for effective counseling and for encouraging optimum performance.
8. Assists in the selection of teaching personnel and recommends to the assistant superintendent personnel candidates for positions.
9. Provides for the health, safety, and welfare of students and staff within the school.
10. Maintains standards of student discipline designed to command the respect of students and parents and to minimize school and classroom disruptions.
11. Coordinates the use of student transportation services provided for the school.
12. Develops working relationships among school staff and school system resource personnel available to the school.
13. Makes regular and thorough inspections of the school plant and school properties.
14. Supervises the preparation of all school reports, student records, and the school's internal accounts, and maintains a record-keeping system.
15. Approves or initiates requisitions for supplies, equipment, and materials necessary for the operation of the school.
16. Interprets activities and policies of the school to the community and encourages community participation in school life.
17. Makes recommendations to the district superintendent and the superintendent concerning policy, practice, or personnel for the purposes of improving the quality of the school system.
18. Other duties assigned.

Job Analysis

Superintendent, assistant superintendent, director of personnel, curriculum coordinator, legal counsel, labor relations specialist, principal, assistant principal, college president, dean, and professor are all jobs. To recruit and select the appropriate personnel for specific jobs, it is necessary to know what the jobs entail. **Job analysis** is the process of obtaining information about jobs through a systematic examination of job content.[2] A job analysis usually consists of two parts: a job description and a job specification. The **job description** is a written statement that outlines the duties and responsibilities expected of a job incumbent. It usually includes a job title, the title of the incumbent's immediate supervisor, a brief statement of the job goal, and a list of duties and responsibilities (see Table 15–1).[3] The **job specification** is a written document that outlines the qualifications that a person needs in order to accomplish the duties and responsibilities set forth in the job description.

Job analysis provides valuable information for forecasting future staffing needs and other personnel management functions. For example, the data produced by the job analysis can be used to develop appropriate

[2]U.S. Department of Labor, *Handbook for Job Analysis* (Washington, DC: U.S. Government Printing Office, 2011).

[3]The sample job description was provided by the New Orleans Public Schools.

recruitment and selection methods, to determine dimensions on which personnel should be evaluated, to determine the worth of jobs for compensation purposes, and to develop training programs for personnel.

Job Analysis Techniques A variety of techniques are available for conducting a job analysis. The technique most appropriate for a given situation depends on a number of factors, such as the type of job being analyzed, the resources available for doing a job analysis, the scope of the job, and the size of the organization. Some of the most commonly used techniques for conducting a job analysis include observation, work sampling, critical incidents, interviews, and questionnaires.[4]

Observation The most straightforward method of job analysis is **observation** of people performing the job. Observation can be a good way of examining jobs that consist mainly of observable physical activity. Jobs such as school custodian, groundskeeper, and machine operator are examples. Analyzing a job through observation is not appropriate where the job requires much abstract thinking, planning, or decision making (e.g., superintendent, labor relations specialist, college dean).

Work Sampling A variation of the observation technique is the **work sampling** approach. The job analyst periodically samples employees' activities and behavior on jobs that have long cycles, that have irregular patterns of activity, or that require a variety of different tasks. For example, research on the administrative demands of school principals consistently shows that they are fragmented and rapid fire.[5]

A personnel administrator could examine the job activities of twenty-five or thirty high school principals on a given day or randomly select twenty-five or thirty days of the school year and observe the job activities of one or two principals during those days. This approach is similar to the one used by Henry Mintzberg in his analysis of a school superintendent and that of Harry Wolcott in his study of school principals.[6] Both researchers, however, went well beyond the work sampling approach in their analysis of school principals and superintendents. They used a combination of ethnographic techniques including observation, interviews, document analysis, and structured questionnaires to obtain their data.[7]

Critical Incidents Another variation of the observation technique, known as **critical incidents**, examines only those job activities leading to successful or unsuccessful performance. This approach is similar to the trait approach used to identify effective and ineffective leaders. An outside consultant, an immediate supervisor, or a job incumbent can conduct this technique. Direct observation and the two variations thereof are frequently used in conjunction with interviewing.

Interviews Probably the most widely used technique for determining what a job entails is the **interview** technique, and its wide use attests to its advantages. Observation of a school district's labor relations specialist, for example, would only reveal that the district's chief negotiator conducts research, prepares proposals and counterproposals, confers with management's bargaining team, and negotiates at the bargaining table. This method fails to identify other important aspects of the job, such as analytic thinking and problem solving. Interviewing the labor relations specialist allows that person to describe important activities of the job that might not be revealed through direct observation.

Questionnaires Many organizations use job analysis **questionnaires** to elicit information concerning what a job entails. Such questionnaires have at least two advantages. First, they can pool the responses of numerous job incumbents and compare job activities across many jobs, using a standard set of common dimensions. Second, questionnaires can generate much information quickly and inexpensively. For example, a job analyst could administer a questionnaire to 100 job incumbents in less time than it would take to observe a single job or interview one job occupant.

Forecasting Demand and Supply

The second phase of human resource planning, **forecasting** demand and supply, involves using any number

[4] U.S. Department of Labor, *Handbook for Job Analysis.*

[5] Fred C. Lunenburg and Beverly J. Irby, *The Principalship: Vision to Action* (Belmont, CA: Wadsworth/Cengage Learning, 2006).

[6] Henry Mintzberg, *Mintzberg on Management: Inside Our Strange World of Organizations* (New York: Simon & Schuster, 2008). Harry F. Wolcott, *The Man in the Principal's Office* (New York: Altamira Press, 2003).

[7] Robert C. Bogdan and Sari Knopp Biklen, *Qualitative Research for Education: An Introduction to Theories and Methods*, 5th ed. (Boston: Allyn and Bacon, 2007).

of sophisticated statistical procedures based on analysis and projections. Such forecasting techniques are beyond the scope of this discussion.

At a more practical level, forecasting demand involves determining the numbers and kinds of personnel that the school district will need at some point in the future. Most school administrators consider several factors when forecasting future personnel needs. The demand for the organization's product or service is paramount. Thus, in a school district, student enrollments are projected first. Then the personnel needed to serve the projected enrollment is estimated. Other factors typically considered when forecasting the demand for personnel include budget constraints; turnover due to resignations, terminations, transfers, and retirement; new technology in the field; decisions to upgrade the quality of services provided; and minority hiring goals.[8]

Forecasting supply involves determining what personnel will be available. The two sources are internal and external: people already employed by the school district and those outside the school district. Factors school administrators typically consider when forecasting the supply of personnel include promoting employees from within the organization; identifying employees willing and able to be trained; availability of required talent in local, regional, and national labor markets; competition for talent within the field; population trends (such as movement of families in the United States from the Northeast to the Southwest); and college and university enrollment trends in the needed field.[9]

Internal sources of employees to fill projected vacancies must be monitored. This is facilitated by the use of the human resource audit, or the systematic inventory of the qualifications of existing personnel. A **human resource audit** is simply an organizational chart of a unit or entire organization with all positions (usually administrative) indicated and keyed as to the promotability of each role incumbent.

Figure 15–2 depicts a human resource audit, or inventory chart, for a hypothetical school district. As Figure 15–2 shows, the superintendent can see where she stands with respect to future staff actions. The superintendent's successor is probably the assistant superintendent for instruction. This person has a successor, the director of elementary education, ready for promotion. Subordinates to the director of elementary education are two principals who are promotable now, three who will be ready for promotion in one or two years, two who are not promotable, and one who should be dismissed.

The other subordinate to the assistant superintendent of instruction, the director of secondary education, is satisfactory but not promotable. That person has two principals who are promotable now, one who will be promotable with further training, and one who is satisfactory but not promotable.

The assistant superintendent of business requires further training before being ready for promotion. Here is a person who knows the job of business management extremely well but lacks training in other aspects of the superintendency, such as curriculum development, personnel administration, public relations, and the like. Some of the accountants reporting to the assistant superintendent of business are promotable now, while others either are nonpromotable or require additional training before being ready for promotion.

The assistant superintendent of personnel, while occupying a very specialized function, is promotable now. Subordinates to that person occupy such specialized jobs that, although performing these roles satisfactorily, they require additional training before being ready for promotion to assistant superintendent of personnel.

The assistant superintendent of research and development was a newly created position in this hypothetical school district. Because of the specialized nature of the position, that person requires considerable training before being ready for promotion. Subordinates to that position are designated similarly.

The analysis provided in Figure 15–2 is very valuable to the school administrator. Future needs and the potential of the existing administrative staff have been identified, and weaknesses have been uncovered. These data can help administrators plan immediate promotions for personnel from within the school district who are promotable, plan for appropriate training and development of others, or dismiss those who are unsatisfactory. If there are an insufficient number of candidates inside the school district to fill vacancies, staffing specialists typically analyze labor markets.

Legal Constraints

Legislation designed to regulate hiring practices affects nearly every aspect of employment—from human resource planning to compensation. Our intent is not

[8]John T. Seyforth, *Human Resource Leadership for Effective Schools* (Boston: Allyn and Bacon, 2008).

[9]Ronald W. Rebore, *Human Resources Administration: A Management Approach* (Upper Saddle River, NJ: Prentice Hall, 2011).

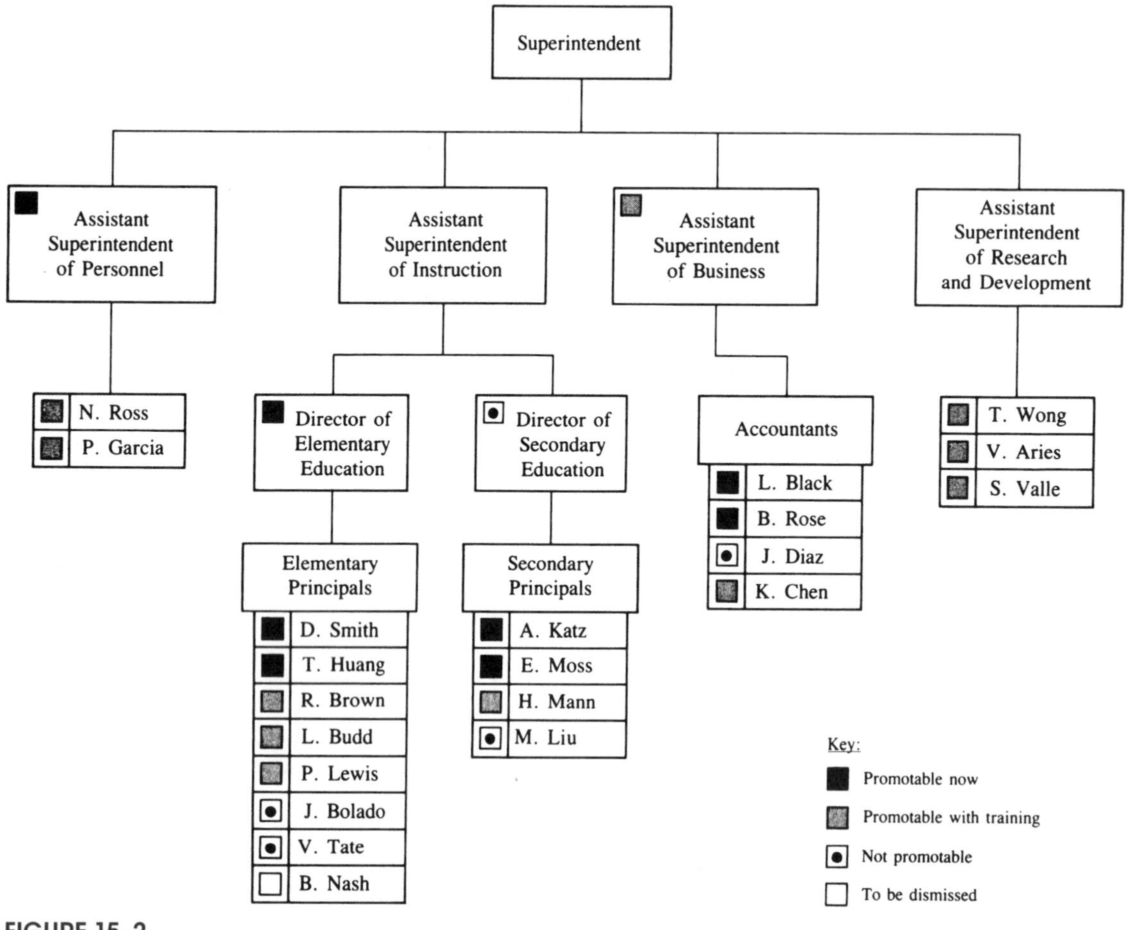

FIGURE 15-2

Human Resource Audit for Administrative Personnel

to make school administrators into attorneys but to examine the basic laws that relate to employment decisions. School administrators must avoid possible charges of discrimination on the basis of race, color, gender, national origin, age, or disability.[10] Table 15–2 summarizes some of the major laws pertaining to the personnel process.

Women and Minorities The landmark legislation designed to ensure equal employment opportunity is the Civil Rights Act of 1964. In 1965, President Lyndon B. Johnson issued Executive Order 11246 (amended by Executive Order 11375 in 1967). These executive orders obligated employers to go beyond the provisions of nondiscrimination of the Civil Rights Act and to actively seek out women and minorities and hire, train, develop, and promote them. In 1972, Congress established the **Equal Employment Opportunity Commission** (EEOC) and passed the Equal Employment Opportunity Act. This amendment to the Civil Rights Act of 1964 extended the jurisdiction of the EEOC and gave it the power to initiate court action against noncomplying organizations.

Older Workers Congress passed the Age Discrimination in Employment Act in 1967. The act originally prohibited discrimination in employment of those people forty to sixty-five years of age; the act was amended in 1978 to move the top age from sixty-five to seventy years; and in 1986, the upper age limit was removed. In essence, the law prohibits discrimination in hiring,

[10]John J. Moran, Employment Law (Upper Saddle River, NJ: Prentice Hall, 2011). See also Barry Cushway, *The Employer's Handbook: An Essential Guide to Employment Law: Personnel Policies and Procedures* (Milford, CT: Kogan Page, 2011).

Table 15–2 Major Laws Affecting Hiring Practices

Law	Basic Requirements
Title VII of the Civil Rights Act of 1964 (as amended)	Prohibits discrimination in employment on the basis of race, color, religion, gender, or national origin.
Age Discrimination in Employment Act of 1968 (as amended)	Prohibits discrimination in employment against any person forty years of age or over.
Equal Pay Act of 1963	Prohibits wage discrimination on the basis of gender; requires equal pay for equal work regardless of gender.
Rehabilitation Act of 1973	Requires employers to take affirmative action to employ and promote qualified handicapped persons.
Pregnancy Discrimination Act of 1978	Requires employers to treat pregnant women and new mothers the same as other employees for all employment-related purposes.
Vietnam Era Veterans' Readjustment Act of 1974	Requires employers to take affirmative action to employ disabled Vietnam War veterans.
Occupational Safety and Health Act (OSHA) of 1970	Establishes mandatory safety and health standards in organizations.

firing, compensating, or any other conditions of work of any person forty years of age or over. Exceptions to the legislation include tenured faculty and some high-salaried executives or for documented health- or performance-related reasons.

The Handicapped The Vocational Rehabilitation Act was passed in 1973 and amended in 1978. The act requires employers who have a contract with the federal government worth $2500 or more to take affirmative action to hire and promote qualified handicapped persons. A handicapped person is defined as any individual with a physical or mental disability that limits normal activities such as walking, seeing, speaking, or learning. The law stipulates that the handicapped individual must be capable of performing the particular job for which she is being considered.

Veterans The Vietnam Era Veterans' Readjustment Act of 1974 requires employers with federal contracts to take affirmative action to employ disabled veterans. The act also provides job assistance for Vietnam-era veterans in the form of job counseling, training, and placement.

Equal Employment Opportunity **Equal employment opportunity** (EEO) is the right of all persons to work and to advance on the basis of merit, ability, and potential without regard to race, color, religion, gender, or national origin. Table 15–2 summarizes the primary legal base for EEO and supporting legal activities. The provisions of these acts generally apply to all public and private organizations employing fifteen or more people. The EEOC administers and federally enforces the various equal employment opportunity acts. The EEOC provides assistance to employers in developing affirmative action programs and in resolving discrimination complaints brought against employers.

Affirmative Action Programs

Whereas EEO legislation prohibits discrimination in recruitment, hiring, promotion, compensation, and discharge, **affirmative action programs** are designed to increase employment opportunities for women and other minorities including veterans, the aged, and the handicapped. Based on two executive orders, originally issued by President Johnson, affirmative action requirements apply to public and private employers and educational institutions that either have contracts with or receive monies from the federal government. The intent of the program is to ensure that women and other minorities are represented in the organization in percentages similar to their percentage in the labor market from which the school district draws personnel. For example, if the labor pool in a community is 15 percent black and 5 percent Hispanic, then 15 percent and 5 percent of the labor force of an organization operating in that community should be black and Hispanic, respectively.

In general, affirmative action programs should include the following:[11] (1) making concerted efforts to recruit and promote women, minorities, the handicapped, and veterans, including recruiting through state employment services and at minority and women's colleges; (2) limiting the questions that can be asked in employment applications and interviews; (3) determining available percentages of women, minorities, and the handicapped in the labor market; (4) setting up goals and timetables for recruiting women, minorities, the handicapped, and veterans; and (5) avoiding testing unless it meets established guidelines.

Recruitment

All school districts, at one time or another, engage in recruiting to replace or expand their supply of personnel. Some organizations recruit better personnel than others, which is later reflected in the quality of their instructional programs. Recruitment refers to the process of generating a pool of competent applicants needed to fill the available positions in an organization. Emphasis on the word *competent* is important. No matter how personnel are later selected, developed, and compensated, it is important to begin with a group of high-caliber job applicants. Overall, sources of personnel available to fill vacant positions can be categorized as sources inside the organization and sources outside the organization.

Internal Sources

The existing pool of employees within the school system is one source of recruiting personnel. Individuals already employed by the district might possess excellent qualifications for a vacant position. There are some advantages to using **internal recruitment**. First, it allows administrators to observe an employee over a period of time and to evaluate that person's potential and job behavior. These factors cannot be easily observed off the job. Second, when employees see that competence is rewarded with promotion, their morale and performance will likely be enhanced. Third, employees are likely to identify their long-term interests with an organization that provides them with a chance for promotion and hence are less likely to leave. Fourth, employees can be better qualified than outside candidates: Even positions that do not appear unique require familiarity with the people, policies, procedures, and special characteristics of the school district. Finally, when carefully planned, promoting from within can act as a training device for developing middle- and top-level administrators such as principals, central office administrators, and superintendents.[12]

Internal recruiting sources include inventory charts, informal search, talent search, and job posting.[13]

Inventory Chart In filling administrative vacancies, a human resource audit of the type discussed earlier is helpful (see Figure 15–2). Many large school districts have computerized information on their administrators' qualifications and promotability. When a vacancy occurs at the administrative level, the computer can search the list of administrators having the qualifications that match the requirements of the position.

Informal Search In large school districts with a personnel department, the administrator of the division or school having a vacancy consults the personnel director, and together they consider one or more possible candidates for the position. The administrator or the director may interview one or more employees who appear to have the necessary qualifications for the position. After the interview, the position may be offered to one of the candidates.

While the informal search was commonly used in the past, it represents a **closed recruitment system;** that is, it tends to exclude most employees who might be interested in the position from applying. Legislation to ensure equal employment opportunity and affirmative action (see Table 15–2) has resulted in a more **open recruitment system,** which increases the in-house advertisement of all job vacancies.

Talent Search A closely related procedure that represents an open recruitment system is the *talent search*. The school district uses this method when it anticipates vacancies at the administrative level and wishes to promote from within the system. Contrary to the informal search, a talent search is widely advertised throughout the school district. Training programs are offered that will qualify personnel for promotion. Employees are asked

[11]Rachel Kranz, *Affirmative Action*, rev. ed. (New York: Facts on File, Inc., 2012).

[12]Bernard Barker, *Human Resource Management in Education: Contexts, Themes, and Impact* (New York: Routledge, 2011).

[13]Ibid.

to notify the personnel department or their building or division administrator if they are interested in participating in the training program. Some training programs are administered independently by the school district or collaboratively with a local university or consulting firm. Those who indicate an interest are administered a battery of cognitive or psychological tests and assessed in other ways. Employees who are selected are given appropriate training and then placed in a talent pool. They continue in their current jobs until an appropriate position for which they are qualified becomes vacant.

Job Posting Another procedure to facilitate implementation of a promotion-from-within policy is job posting. A job posting system gives every employee an opportunity to apply for a vacant position within the school district. The posting notification may be communicated on bulletin boards throughout the district, in the weekly or monthly school district newsletter, or in a special posting sheet from the personnel department, outlining all positions currently available. The job posting usually contains information regarding job title, a brief job description, salary range, and school or division location. Collective bargaining agreements may contain a provision for job posting. In such instances, job posting can be formal. Unions generally prefer that promotions be based on seniority, whereas administration prefers that decisions be based on merit.

Internal sources of recruitment, involving talent searches and job posting, have received attention recently because of equal employment opportunity and affirmative action programs. Government agencies monitoring employment practices frequently require school districts that previously did not practice open recruitment and solicit inside candidates to do so. The ultimate goal of such procedures is to prevent women and minorities from being kept in lower-paying, entry-level jobs.

External Sources

Internal sources do not always produce enough qualified applicants to fill vacant positions in the school district. Several **external recruitment** sources are available and include educational institutions, employment agencies, executive search firms, temporary help agencies, advertising, and unsolicited applicants.[14]

Educational Institutions Universities, colleges, vocational schools, technical schools, and high schools are all important sources of recruits for most school districts. High schools or vocational schools can provide service applicants such as plant-maintenance workers; business or secretarial schools can provide office staff such as bookkeepers and clerical personnel; colleges and universities can provide professional staff such as teachers, counselors, social workers, and school psychologists; and graduate schools can often provide administrative personnel such as superintendents and principals.

Most universities and colleges operate placement services. Potential employers can review credentials submitted by applicants. For professional positions in great demand, school districts may send recruiters to campuses for the purpose of interviewing job applicants. On-campus recruiting can be an expensive and time-consuming process. However, because there is a great deal of competition for the top graduating students in professional-type jobs, the recruiting visit may be worth the time and expense if a high-quality applicant is hired. Like the top business firms and athletic programs, school organizations need to do more active recruiting of top students graduating from universities and colleges.

Employment Agencies Every state in the United States operates a state employment agency under the umbrella of the U.S. Training and Employment Service (USTES) of the U.S. Department of Labor. There are 2400 such offices, which are staffed by state employees and funded by the federal government.[15] The service is free to all job applicants. These agencies have a poor image, which is no reflection on their competence or service. State employment agencies are perceived by job applicants as having few high-skilled jobs, and employers tend to view such agencies as having few high-quality applicants.

There are thousands of private employment agencies in the United States. Private agencies provide more services to an employer and are perceived to offer employers higher-quality applicants than public agencies do. For example, some private employment agencies advertise the position sought, screen applicants, and sometimes even provide a guarantee of satisfactory service to the hiring organization. For these services, a fee is charged, which is absorbed by the organization or the employee, or shared between the two. Such fees are usually set by state law. Private agencies can be sources of service, clerical, professional, and administrative personnel.

[14]Ibid.

[15]U.S. Department of Labor, *Employment and Training Report of the President* (Washington, DC: U.S. Government Printing Office, 2012).

Executive Search Firms Many major corporations, hospitals, universities, and large school districts now use executive search firms (or "headhunters," as they are commonly called) to recruit middle-level and top-level executives. In searching for a superintendent of schools, for example, whose compensation package may be in excess of $250,000 a year, the school district is often willing to pay a very high fee to locate precisely the right person to fill the vacant position. A fee of 25 to 35 percent of the superintendent's first year's salary, plus $500 a day for expenses is not uncommon. These firms have contacts throughout the United States and are especially well trained in contacting highly qualified candidates who are already employed. In fact, executive search firms will not accept unsolicited applications from persons seeking employment. This procedure, often referred to as "pirating," is a common practice today among the larger, more successful organizations.

Temporary Help Agencies Organizations such as Kelly Services and Manpower can provide school organizations with temporary help. Traditionally developed to supply secretarial, clerical, and semiskilled labor, the temporary help agencies have expanded to include skilled and technical areas. One such agency is Account Temps, which provides temporary help in the accounting and computer fields. School districts can rent on a day-rate basis people with a broad range of skills, such as engineers, computer technicians, or accountants. Employing temporary help may be more efficient than employing permanent staff during peak periods. Temporary employees do not receive the fringe benefit package required for permanent employees; and costly layoffs (paying unemployment compensation) during less active periods can be avoided.

Advertising Advertising in newspapers, trade magazines, and professional journals is a widely used method of external recruiting. A local newspaper can be a good source of service workers, clerical staff, and lower-level administrative personnel. Trade and professional journals enable school organizations to aim at more specialized employees. For example, the *Chronicle of Higher Education* is commonly used to recruit personnel in higher education. Administrative positions in the public schools can be advertised in the *School Administrator, Executive Educator, NASSP Bulletin, Principal, Educational Leadership, Educational Researcher,* or *Phi Delta Kappan.*

In contrast to print advertising in publications such as newspapers and trade and professional journals, other forms of recruitment advertising are used less frequently. These include television, radio, billboards, and the internet. Advertising usually generates a large pool of applicants who then must be screened carefully to determine those who are qualified.

Unsolicited Applicants Another source of prospective job applicants is the file, maintained at the school district office, of unsolicited candidates. Unsolicited applicants communicate with the school district by letter, by telephone, or in person. The qualifications of unsolicited applicants depend on several factors: the condition of the labor market, the school district's reputation, and the types of jobs available. Regardless of these factors, there will always be some unsolicited applicants in most school districts—people entering the labor force for the first time, women returning to work after a period of child rearing, or individuals improving their employment situation. Generally, the use of unsolicited applicants is prevalent in staffing clerical and plant-maintenance jobs. A school district with a good reputation can also rely on this source to fill professional positions including teachers and other support personnel.

Internal versus External Recruitment

Both internal recruitment and external recruitment have advantages and disadvantages to the school district (see Figure 15–3).

Promoting from within can work to the school district's advantage. Applicants are already familiar with the organization, have a known performance record within the district that can be examined, and may be less expensive to recruit than external candidates. As indicated previously, internal recruitment also improves morale and loyalty among employees because they believe that competence is rewarded with promotion. However, there are at least two disadvantages of internal recruitment: organizational inbreeding—a "but we've always done it that way" mentality—and increased political behavior if it is perceived that such behavior may result in a promotion.

External recruiting, on the other hand, infuses the organization with "new blood," which may broaden present ideas and knowledge and question traditional ways of doing things. The abundance of external sources almost guarantees that the school district will find an adequate number of candidates from which to choose. Promoting from outside the organization also provides an opportunity to recruit women and minorities at all levels in the school district. Exclusive reliance on promotions from within may further inhibit the entry of these

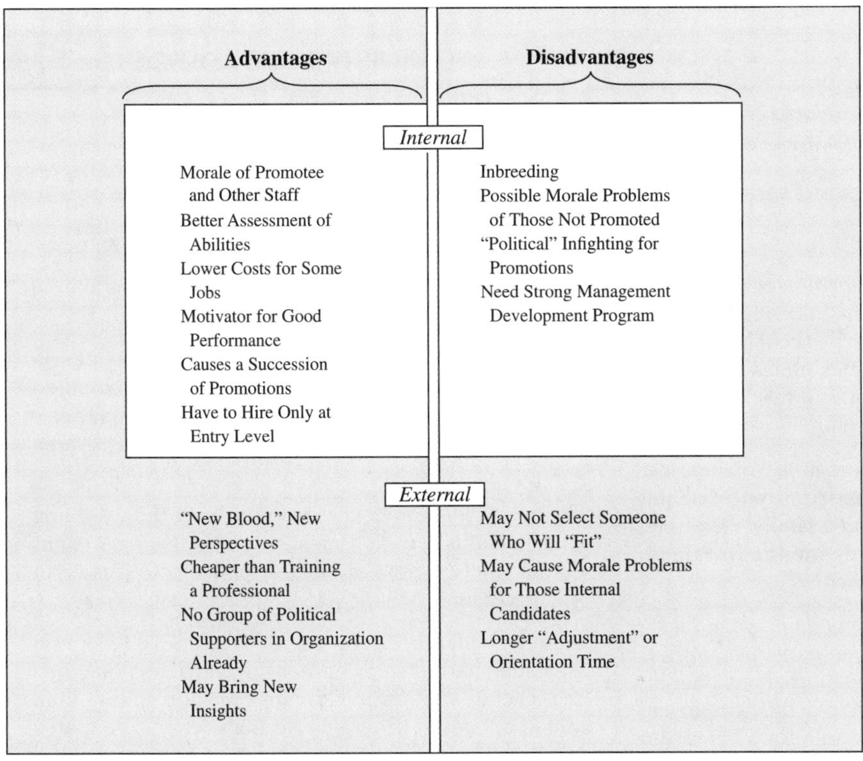

FIGURE 15–3

Internal and External Recruitment
Source: Adapted from Robert L. Mathis and John H. Jackson, *Personnel: Human Resource Management,* 5th ed., p. 229.

groups into higher-level positions in the school district, assuming that past underrepresentation of these groups exists. On the negative side, using external sources can be quite costly, particularly the hiring of middle-level and top executives. In general, most school districts use a mixture of internal and external sources of recruitment.

One of the most important instructional decisions a principal or superintendent makes is hiring his teaching personnel. School administrators share one of the same concerns faced by top-level managers everywhere: how to find great employees and keep them productive and satisfied while they're at work. (See Administrative Advice 15–1.)

Selection

Once applicants have been recruited, the school district must select the most qualified people to fill existing vacancies. A comprehensive discussion of selection techniques can be found in personnel administration texts. The most common procedure involves a series of steps including biographical information, reference checks, written tests, performance simulations, interviews, and physical exam results.[16] (See Figure 15–4.)

Biographical Information

The first step in the selection process is searching for evidence of past performance in a candidate's record. This information can be secured from an application blank, a résumé, a letter of application, writing samples, school records or college transcripts, and similar biographical data. Research shows that **biographical information** can predict future job performance because

[16]Webb and Norton, *Human Resources Administration: Personnel Issues and Needs in Education.*

ADMINISTRATIVE ADVICE 15–1

Recruiting the Next Generation of Teachers

Here are some tips for improving teacher recruitment for the next generation of teachers in your school or school district.

Retrain the best teachers to fill critical needs. Offer retraining and recredentialing opportunities to teachers with proven track records. This can be accomplished by having teachers enroll in university courses at the district's expense plus a $2000 incentive if teachers agree to remain for two years after retraining.

Institute a job-sharing or flex-time program. Job sharing offers dedicated teachers an opportunity to remain professionally active while raising a family. Flex time allows two or more teachers to divide the workload during time intervals suitable to each.

Recruit and train professionals from other career fields. Two sources provide access to personnel from other career fields: alternative certification programs offered in some states, and businesses that pay their employee salaries and tuition while they retrain for a career in teaching.

Tap the reservoir of retired people. Many retired people look for ways to get involved in meaningful work activities. Schools can use senior citizens in paraprofessional and support roles.

Grow your own. Teacher cadet programs and future teacher clubs, Future Teachers of America (FTA), can inject enthusiasm for the teaching profession among young people.

Capitalize on the talents of college students. College students will respond to requests to work with troubled youth. Examples include VISTA, "Teach for America," and Madison House, voluntary tutoring programs staffed by collegians.

Try part-time approaches. Teaching part time, serving as a consultant, or as a mentor to new teachers might entice teachers who are near retirement to remain in the profession.

Initiate cooperative programs with business. Business-education partnerships have the potential to strengthen the teacher workforce. Examples include college loan and scholarship programs for high school graduates interested in teaching; and summer internships, teacher enrichment programs, research grants, company-sponsored management training made available to faculty might aid in recruiting quality teachers.

Source: Adapted from Sara Snyder Crumpacker, "Recruiting the Next Generation of Teachers," School Administrator, 11 (1992): 38–39. Used by permission.

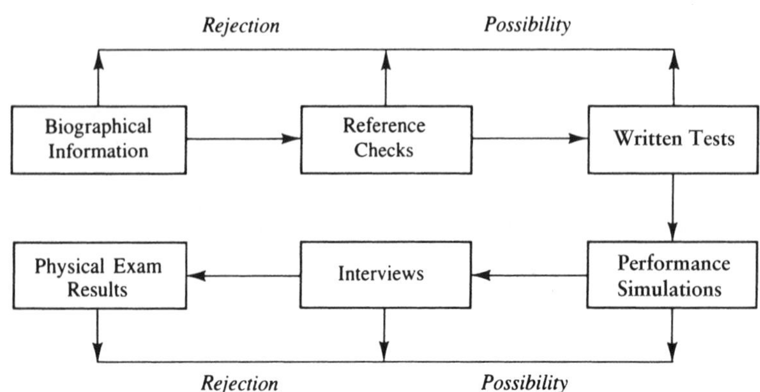

FIGURE 15–4

Steps in the Selection Process

a person's behavior is consistent over time.[17] The use of such information in making selection decisions is based on the idea that an effective predictor of future performance is past performance.

An approach that can be used to analyze biographical data is the *weighted method*. Statistically weighted biographical data can further enhance the predictability of job performance. The weighting procedure consists of identifying background factors on which high-performing employees tend to differ from low-performing employees. Differential weights are then assigned to these background factors. The weightings are based on a statistical analysis that has shown, over time, that there is a high correlation between some background factors or categories of information and high or low performance.[18] Each candidate for a job receives a final score based on this analysis. The administrator then hires personnel who obtain a high score when their biographical information is weighted using this method. Thus, school employers increase the likelihood of employing high-performing personnel.

In practice, most school districts use different background factors, depending on the job level. For professional and administrative personnel, for example, biographical data may include an application blank, a letter of application, a résumé, a writing sample, and undergraduate and graduate transcripts. For building maintenance, clerical, and other noncertificated staff, background factors might consist of a different application blank, school records, military records, and other biographical sources.

Reference Checks

Reference checks fall into two categories: letters of recommendation and subsequent telephone follow-up inquiries of the final candidates for a position. Letters of recommendation can be considered part of the biographical information or screening process and usually precede the interview. Telephone follow-up inquiries typically are made after all other steps in the selection process are completed and just prior to making the hiring decision. For example, the administrator may wish to contact by telephone the present employer or student-teaching supervisor of each of the three leading candidates for a teaching position. Some school organizations mistakenly omit this vital step.

Letters of recommendation are generally of little value in the selection process, for at least four reasons. First, job applicants usually ask for references from persons who are likely to write complimentary letters. As a result, letters of recommendation are biased in the applicant's favor. Second, the recommender may possess only limited knowledge of the applicant. Third, under the Privacy Act of 1974, people have the right to examine letters of reference concerning them unless they waive that right. Because of this privacy legislation, recommenders are reluctant to provide negative information about an applicant in writing for fear of being sued. Fourth, occasionally, recommenders will write a favorable letter of recommendation for an incompetent applicant in order to facilitate their leaving their current employment.

In one actual situation, the board of education of a suburban school district dismissed a teacher on the recommendation of the superintendent of schools. Later, the teacher sued the board and superintendent for damages. To avoid the legal costs of a trial, the superintendent was instructed by his board of education, at the urging of the dismissed teacher's attorney, to write a favorable letter of recommendation for the alleged incompetent teacher. The superintendent did so, and the lawsuit was dropped.

Despite their questionable value, school organizations typically require letters of recommendation as part of the selection process. There are ways to improve the validity of reference checks. First, telephone the references and ask for an oral recommendation. Most people are more likely to provide complete and frank statements orally than they would in writing. Second, contact people other than those referred by the job applicant. This increases the pool of information available about the candidate. Third, allow more credence to references provided by previous employers than those provided by other nonemployment sources such as colleagues, friends, ministers, and the like. Fourth, give more weight to references of those candidates who have waived their right to view their letters of recommendation. Fifth, contact the applicant's two previous employers. This provides wider coverage of previous employment. These techniques will strengthen the validity of reference checks. The rationale underlying reference checks, like biographical information, is that past performance will to a great extent predict future performance.

[17]Ralph D. Thomas, *Pre Employment Investigation* (Austin, TX: Thomas Publications, 1992).

[18]Henry C. Link, Employment Psychology: The Application of Scientific Methods to the Selection, Training, and Grading of Employees (Charleston, SC: Biblio Bazaar, 2011).

Written Tests

Written tests have a long history of use as a selection device. During the 1970s and 1980s, the use of written tests as a selection device declined. Many organizations had not validated them as job-related and some tests were considered discriminatory. However, during the past 20 years, we have witnessed a resurgence in the use of tests. A comprehensive survey of 2500 U.S. organizations revealed that more than 60 percent use testing as a device in hiring and promotion decisions.[19]

Many human resource experts believe that testing is the single best selection device. Tests yield more information about an applicant than do biographical information and letters of recommendation, and they are less subject to bias than interviews. The primary advantages of testing include finding the right person for the job, obtaining a high degree of job satisfaction for the applicant because of a good fit between the school district and the person, and reducing absenteeism and turnover.[20]

Although there are many kinds of tests available for school district use, they can be classified into three major groups: (1) intelligence or cognitive ability tests, (2) personality tests, and (3) interest inventories.[21]

Intelligence Tests **Intelligence tests** have proven to be particularly good predictors for jobs that require incumbents to perform mental activities, such as thinking, reasoning, and problem solving.[22] Intelligence quotient (IQ) tests, for example, are designed to measure an individual's general intellectual abilities. Popular college admission tests, such as the SAT and ACT and graduate admission tests in medicine (MCAT), law (LSAT), business (GMAT), and education (GRE) measure such general intellectual abilities. Testing firms do not make the claim that their tests assess intelligence, but experts in the field know that they do.[23]

It may interest you to know that many job applicants in business are discovering that employing organizations are requesting their SAT scores as a criterion in the selection process. A case in point is Donna Chan, a recent graduate of Wagner College in New York. Donna Chan discovered that one of the minimum requirements for many of the entry-level financial service jobs she was seeking was a combined SAT score of 1300. How competitive is a score of 1300? The maximum score on the old version of the SAT is 1600. [The new version has added a writing section, in addition to the traditional verbal and quantitative sections.] According to the College Board and Educational Testing Service, the firm that administers the exam, the average combined verbal and quantitative score of the freshman class of 2005 (the last class to take the old version of the SAT) was 1028. Donna Chan's score was in the "1200s." Although above average, Donna Chan's SAT score was not good enough to obtain any of the positions she was seeking despite her 3.9 grade-point average at Wagner College.[24]

Jobs differ in the demands required of organization members to use their intellectual abilities. The more complex a job is in terms of thinking, reasoning, and problem-solving skills, the more general intelligence will be needed to perform the job well.[25] For highly routine jobs with few information-processing demands, a high IQ is not as important to performing the job successfully.

Personality Tests The use of personality tests has increased in the past decade. Japanese car manufacturers, when staffing plants in the Unites States, have relied heavily on personality tests to identify candidates who will be high performers. Toyota puts candidates for entry-level, shop-floor jobs through fourteen hours of testing.[26] **Personality tests** attempt to measure personality

[19]Robert M. Guion, *Assessment, Measurement, and Prediction for Personnel Decisions* (Mahwah, NJ: Lawrence Erlbaum, 2010).

[20]Steven T. Hunt, *The Art and Science of Staffing, Assessment, and Employee Selection* (New York: Wiley, 2008). See also Mary Kennedy, *Teacher Assessment and the Quest for Teacher Quality* (New York: Wiley, 2011).

[21]Robert Edenborough, *Assessment Methods in Recruitment, Selection, and Performance: A Manager's Guide to Psychometric Testing, Interviews, and Assessment Centers* (Milford, CT: Kogan Page, 2008).

[22]Robert J. Gregory, *Psychological Testing: History, Principles, and Applications* (Boston: Allyn & Bacon, 2007).

[23]Gary Groth-Marnat, *Handbook of Psychological Assessment* (New York: Wiley, 2010). See also Mike Bryon, *Ultimate Psychometric Tests: Over 1,000 Verbal, Numerical, Diagrammatic, and IQ Practice Tests* (Milford, CT: Kogan Page, 2009).

[24]S. Foss, "Background Check—Background Search, *American Chronicle*, July 12, 2007; Kemba J. Dunham, "Career Journal: More Employers Ask Job Seekers for SAT Scores," *Wall Street Journal*, October 28, 2003, p. B1. Reported in Stephn B. Robbins and Timothy A. Judge, *Organizational Behavior*, 13th ed. (Upper Saddle River, NJ: Prentice Hall, 2009), p. 611.

[25]Groth-Marnat, *Handbook of Psychological Assessment.*

[26]Robbins and Judge, *Organizational Behavior.*

characteristics that might be important on the job, such as emotional stability, introversion and extroversion, self-confidence, aggressiveness or submissiveness, neurotic tendencies, and many other characteristics and traits.[27] In particular, many organizations use dimensions of the "Big Five" personality traits (see Chapter 5) in selection decisions. The traits that best predict job performance are conscientiousness and emotional stability.[28] This makes sense, since conscientious people tend to be motivated and dependable, and people who are emotionally stable are calm, steady, cool, self-confident and persistent: the personality traits you want school administrators and other education professionals to possess.

Interest Inventories **Interest inventories** attempt to measure an applicant's interest in performing various kinds of activities. The notion underlying the administration of interest tests to job applicants is that certain people perform jobs well because the job activities are interesting. The purpose of this type of test is to create a better "fit" between the applicant and the specific job.[29] Two popular interest tests are the Kuder Preference Record and the Strong-Campbell Interest Inventory.

In sum, many experts contend that intelligence tests are the *single best* selection device across jobs. Personality tests and interest inventories provide additional information concerning factors such as dependability, self-confidence, persistence, and "fit" with the job. The evidence is impressive that these tests are powerful in predicting job performance and employee behavior on the job, such as discipline problems, excessive absenteeism, and turnover.[30]

Performance Simulations

The idea behind **performance simulations** is to have applicants perform simulations of part or all of the job to determine whether applicants can do the job successfully. Examples include typing and dictaphone tests for secretaries, speed and accuracy tests for computer operators, and driving tests for driver education teachers. Candidates for the space program have to perform a variety of tasks on a specially constructed simulated test station at NASA's training facility in Houston, Texas.

Elaborate performance-simulation tests, specifically designed to evaluate a school administrator's potential, are administered in **assessment centers.** The National Association of Secondary School Principals (NASSP) Assessment Center is an approach to the selection of school principals that is rapidly gaining in popularity.[31] It is particularly good for selecting present school district employees for promotion to principal or assistant principal positions. A typical NASSP Assessment Center lasts two days, with groups of six to twelve assessees participating in a variety of administrative exercises. Most assessment centers include two in-basket tests, two leaderless-group exercises, a fact-finding exercise, and a personal interview. A panel of NAASP-trained assessors evaluate candidates individually on a number of dimensions, using a standardized scale. Later, by consensus, a profile of each candidate is devised.

Assessment centers are valid predictors of administrative success, and some business firms now use them for hiring technical workers. Assessment centers are also used to help design training and development programs for the purpose of improving the leadership skills of pre-service principals and in-service principals.[32]

Some universities use the assessment center to pinpoint areas of strengths and weaknesses on which graduate students can then focus during their doctoral studies in educational administration. For example, The University of Texas Executive Leadership Program puts each of its doctoral candidates in educational administration through a variation of a standardized NASSP Assessment Center during their first semester of study. Faculty and students then work together to develop the latter's skills based on the results of their assessment profile.

Interviews

The interview continues to be the most common selection device used by all organizations, including school districts.[33] Furthermore, the interview tends to have

[27]Raymond Cattell, *The Scientific Analysis of Personality* (Piscataway, NJ: Aldine Transaction, 2010).

[28]M.R. Barrick and M. K. Mount, "Select on Conscientiousness and Emotional Stability," in E. A. Lock (ed.), *Handbook of Principles of Organizational Behavior* (Malden, MA: Blackwell, 2004), pp. 15–28.

[29]Thomas P. Hogan, *Psychological Testing: A Practical Introduction* (New York: Wiley, 2007).

[30]Guion, *Assessment, Measurement, and Prediction for Personnel Decisions.*

[31]National Association of Secondary School Principals, *Leaders for the Future: Assessment and Development Programs* (Reston, VA: NASSP, n.d.).

[32]National Association of Secondary School Principals, *Professional Development and Assessment Programs* (Reston, VA: NASSP, n.d.).

[33]Rob Yeung, *Successful Interviewing and Recruitment* (Milford, CT: Kogan Page, 2011).

a disproportionate amount of influence on the hiring decision. The applicant who performs poorly in the job interview is likely to be eliminated from the applicant pool regardless of experience, test scores, or letters of recommendation. Very often the individual who is most skilled in interviewing techniques is the person hired, even though she may not be the best candidate for the position.[34] In addition, despite its widespread use, the interview is a poor predictor of job performance.[35] We will now discuss interviewing problems, followed by ways to improve the interview process.

Interviewing Problems The following interviewing problems should be avoided:[36]

Unfamiliarity with the Job. Interviewers frequently are unfamiliar with the job. When interviewers do not know what the job entails, they do not ask the right questions, interpret the obtained information differently, have faulty impressions of the information supplied, and spend time discussing matters irrelevant to the job.

Premature Decisions. Interviewers tend to make a decision about an applicant in the first few minutes of the interview before all relevant information has been gathered. Then they spend the rest of the interview seeking information that confirms their initial impression.

Emphasis on Negative Information. Interviewers tend to weight negative information supplied by the applicant more heavily than positive information. On occasion, the interviewer may change his or her mind, but the change tends to be from positive to negative rather than vice versa. In fact, in most cases, interviews tend to be a search for negative information.

Personal Biases. Some interviewers tend to have preconceptions and prejudices about people. Some examples follow: "fat people are lazy"; "people from the East are unfriendly and arrogant"; "people from the South are slow"; "people with low foreheads are stupid." Other biases may reflect negatively against some minority groups or in favor of those candidates who have backgrounds similar to the interviewer(s). As ridiculous as these prejudices may seem, many of these personal biases still exist. Furthermore, some interviewers are overly impressed with surface signs of composure, manner of speech, and physical appearance.

Applicant Order. Interviewers' ratings of an applicant are influenced by the order in which candidates are interviewed. For example, when an average applicant is interviewed immediately following one or more below-average applicants, the average applicant tends to be evaluated well above average. A similar process works in reverse. If an average applicant follows an outstanding applicant, the former is rated below average.

Hiring Quotas. Interviewers who have been given hiring quotas tend to rate applicants higher than interviewers who have not been given quotas. Thus, pressure to hire influences the interviewer's judgments of the applicant and thereby diminishes the usefulness of the interview as a selection technique.

Improving the Interview Process School organizations will continue to use interviews regardless of the problems. Thus, researchers have identified several techniques for improving the interview process:[37]

Use a Structured Interview Format. Interviews should be more structured. In a structured interview, questions are written in advance, scaled on a standardized rating scale, and asked of all job applicants. The

[34]See, for example recent books devoted to applicant interviewing techniques Brian Davis, *Top Notch Interviews: Tips, Tricks, and Techniques from the First Call to Getting the Job You Want* (Pompton Plains, NJ: Career Press, 2011); Matthew DeLuca, *Best Answers to the 201 Most Frequently Asked Questions*, 2nd ed. (New York: McGraw-Hill, 2011); Rebecca Corfield, *Knockout Interview Presentations: How to Present with Confidence, Beat the Competition, and Impress Your Way into a Top Job* (Milford, CT: Kogan Page, 2011); Denise Taylor, *Now You've Been Shortlisted: Step by Step, Your Guide to Being Successful at Interviews and Assessment Centers* (London: Harriman House, 2011); Rebecca Anthony, *Getting Hired: A Student Teacher's Guide to Professionalism, Resume Development, and Interviewing* (Dubuque, IA: Kendall/Hunt, 2011).

[35]David S. Cohen, *The Talent Search: A Behavioral Approach to Hiring, Developing, and Keeping Top Performers* (New York: Wiley, 2011).

[36]Ronald W. Fry, Ask the Right Questions: Hire the Best People (Pompton Plains, NJ: Career Press, 2011).

[37]Robert Yeung, *Successful Interviewing and Recruiting*; Donald L. Caruth, *Staffing the Contemporary Organization: A Guide to Planning, Recruiting, and Selecting for Human Resource Professionals* (Westport, CT: Greenwood, 2009); Bradford D. Smart, *The Smart Interviewer* (New York: Wiley, 2010).

structured interview has three major advantages. It brings consistency to the interview process; it provides an opportunity to develop questions that are relevant to the job; and it allows screening and refinement of questions that may be discriminatory. In addition, the structured interview is more defensible in court. A less-structured method can be used when interviewing administrative personnel. That is, the interview is still carefully planned in terms of content areas covered, but it allows more flexibility by the interviewer.

Train Interviewers. One way to improve the validity and reliability of the interview is to train interviewers. Effective interviewing requires specific skills including asking questions, probing, listening, observing, recording unbiased information, rating, and the like. Specifically designed workshops can teach these skills. A cadre of trained interviewers can then interview job applicants.

Keep a Written Record of Each Interview. Keeping a written record of each interview facilitates a comparison of the applicants interviewed. To make accurate comparisons among the candidates, maintain and preserve the details of their responses and impressions. Without such information, later deliberations and decision making will be less accurate and valid.

Use Multiple Interviewers. Using multiple interviewers facilitates a comparison of evaluations and perceptions. Specifically, it allows the school district to place greater confidence in areas where consensus of opinion exists. And it opens up discussion in specific areas where disagreement occurs, with the purpose of arriving at an equitable hiring decision. Personnel who have specific knowledge of the job and the candidate's immediate supervisor-to-be would provide a well-balanced interview team. Or the district may wish to use a cadre of trained interviewers in every interview situation.

Get the Applicant to Talk. The main purpose of an interview is to learn as much as possible about a job applicant. This can be accomplished by getting the applicant to talk. Establish a friendly, open rapport with the applicant early in the interview, with some brief comments about the organization and the job. Then shift to a preplanned question format. Listen carefully to content. Probe for answers to all questions and check for inconsistencies. Relate responses given to questions during the interview to written biographical information supplied earlier. Pay attention to nonverbal cues such as tone of voice, general personality, and emotional characteristics of the applicant. For example, failure of a candidate to maintain eye contact may be a danger sign. Thus, observation during an interview is as important as listening.

Use the Interview as One Aspect of the Selection Process. Avoid using the interview as the sole criterion for selecting applicants. By the same token, the interviewer(s) should not be the sole decision maker for who is or is not hired. Supplement the interview with data from other sources, including biographical information, results of tests, written references, and telephone inquiries. Interviewers may not be privy to the telephone reference checks, which may rest exclusively in the hands of the top-executive officer. When the aforementioned suggestions are implemented, the interview can be a useful source of information in the selection process.

An effective interview requires adequate preparation, a comfortable setting, and clear communication between interviewer and interviewee. (See Administrative Advice 15–2.)

Hiring Decision

The final step in the selection process is the hiring decision. The person who has successfully passed through the steps in the process is offered employment. The offer may be subject to the successful completion of a physical examination.

Professional Development

After recruiting and selecting new personnel, the next step is professional development. **Professional development** refers to teaching administrators and professionals the skills needed for both present and future positions.[38] School administrators need to help all personnel fulfill their potential by learning new skills and developing their abilities to the fullest. The three basic steps or phases in any professional development program are assessment, training, and evaluation.

[38]Bruce Joyce and Emily Calhoun, *Models of Professional Development* (Thousand Oaks, CA: Corwin Press, 2010).

ADMINISTRATIVE ADVICE 15–2

Tips for Interviewing

Here are some tips for conducting a successful interview, including interviewing steps, the role of the interviewer, interviewing techniques, and questioning.

Interviewing Steps

Step 1: Establish an atmosphere of interest in the interviewee. Establishing an atmosphere of interest can be accomplished in three ways: by showing friendliness, by maintaining eye contact, and by using a firm handshake.

Step 2: Become an active listener. It is the interviewer's responsibility to listen carefully to the spoken words of the interviewe, to direct the communication toward the final goal, and to remember key words that may add discussion or clarification.

Step 3: Make the purpose known. Typically, the school administrator's purpose is to approve or recommend an interviewee for a professional or paraprofessional position. Once the purpose of the interview is known, the interviewer directs the questions and focuses the interview toward that purpose.

Role of the Interviewer

Maximize the forces that lead to communication. These include a relaxed atmosphere, focus on the interview purpose, and indication of listening by both parties.

Measure the data collected. To measure the adequateness of a response, the interviewer must decide if the question was truly answered. If not, ask additional questions. If yes, reward the interviewee with a nod or murmur of understanding.

How to Interview

The interviewer should have a strong background in all aspects of the job.

The interview begins with observation. The interviewer must note what the interviewee says and what the interviewee does not say.

Question with a purpose. The purpose of every interview is to determine if the interviewee has the qualifications to do the job and fit in with the faculty and staff.

Pace your questions to the answers of the interviewee. Proceeding too rapidly can cause confusion or a missed response and may give the interviewee the appearance of being uninterested.

Questions

What if? Hypothetical situation questions allow the interviewer to determine values, and to determine if the interviewee has orderly thought processes.

Describe your philosophy of education. This helps the interviewer hear what the interviewee hopes his students will learn and how she has integrated the philosophy into teaching.

How would you set up a program (such as reading)? Look for one-to-one student-teacher communication, a set of checks and balances for assessing mastery, a plan to monitor the plan, where to seek resources, how to accommodate individual differences in students.

What are your weaknesses? Look for an admission that anyone can learn and an indication that the interviewee does not think she knows everything.

Define the principal's role. Look for those applicants who perceive the principal as fulfilling multiple roles: a resource for research, a facilitator and supporter, a mentor, an instructional leader.

Describe yourself. Look for enthusiasm, warmth, caring, emotional maturity, leadership skills, and a willingness to learn.

Source: Adapted from Cynthia Martin, "Hiring the Right Person: Techniques for Principals," *NASSP Bulletin*, *77*, no. 550 (1993): 79–83.

Assessment of Professional Development Needs

A *needs assessment* should precede the planning and execution of a professional development program. In a needs analysis, the school administrator or personnel department determines exactly what the staff professional development needs are before designing a program to meet them. A needs analysis typically has a threefold focus: *organizational analysis* (analyzing the needs of the entire school district now and in the future), *operational analysis* (analyzing the needs of a specific group of

EXEMPLARY EDUCATIONAL ADMINISTRATORS IN ACTION

RON SAUNDERS, Ed.D., Superintendent, Barrow County Schools, Winder, Georgia.

Words of Advice: Education will not get easier. The more diverse we become, the more that schools will be asked to do. Administrators must view this as an "opportunity to succeed" and not a "challenge to fail." When I was a principal of a high school. I had a student who was a member of a gang and did some very foolish things that led him to be expelled from the school system three times. After every expulsion he would return to my office at the end of his expulsion and ask for a second chance. After long discussions, I would let him back into the school and watch him closely. He had a teacher who also looked after him. As long as he came back asking for another chance, I was willing to go the distance with him. He finally did graduate from high school and is a successful citizen today. He contributes much of his success to me and his teacher for not giving up on him. I contribute it mostly to his "no quit" attitude and the chance that two adults did not lose hope. Try to see the good in each student no matter how hard it is. Find a teacher to work along with you in your mission to guide the troubled student. Good luck.

jobs or positions), and *individual analysis* (analyzing the needs of the specific individual).[39] A needs analysis helps specify professional development objectives, the criteria for professional development activities, and the criteria against which the programs will be evaluated.

There are several methods of determining which needs to focus on in the professional development programs. The first method is to evaluate the school district's output variables (see Figure 1–2 in Chapter 1). Such variables include performance levels and growth levels of students and employees, student dropout rates, employee turnover, student and employee absenteeism, school-community relations, employee-management relations, student attitudes toward school, employee job satisfaction, and the like. Another method for determining professional development needs is direct feedback from school district employees regarding what they feel are the organization's development needs. A final method of determining professional development needs involves projecting. If new programs, procedures, or equipment are predicted, some type of corresponding professional development will be needed.

Professional Development Techniques

Numerous techniques used for professional development are available. Table 15–3 presents the most common methods. The key is to match the technique with the objectives of the professional development program. For example, if the objective is for employees to learn school district policies and procedures, then assigned readings, lecture, and programmed learning might be an effective approach. If the objective is developing better human relations, group decision making, or communications, then case discussion, conference, role playing, and sensitivity training might work well. If the objective is to teach a skill, then behavior modeling, on-the-job training, and vestibule training might be the most appropriate techniques. Other considerations in selecting a staff development technique include cost, time constraints, number of employees, type of employee (maintenance, clerical, professional, or administrative), and who will do the training.

Evaluating the Professional Development Program

Evaluating the effectiveness of a professional development program is the final phase of a professional development effort. Evaluation generally occurs during four stages: before professional development begins, during professional development, immediately after the professional development experience, and after a length of time on the job. Several validated instruments are available to evaluate professional development programs.[40]

Ideally, the best method to use in evaluating the effectiveness of professional development is the controlled experiment. In a controlled experiment, one or more groups that receive training (experimental groups) and a group that does not receive training (control group)

[39]Ibid.

[40]Thomas R. Guskey, *Evaluating Professional Development* (Thousand Oaks, CA: Corwin Press, 2000).

Table 15-3 Common Professional Development Techniques

Methods	Comments
Assigned readings	Readings may or may not be specially prepared for training purposes.
Behavior modeling	Use of a videotaped model displaying the correct behavior, then trainee role playing and discussion of the correct behavior. Used extensively for supervisor training in human relations.
Simulation	Both paper simulations (such as in-basket exercises) and computer-based games teach management skills.
Case discussion	Small-group discussion of real or fictitious cases or incidents.
Conference	Small-group discussion of selected topics, usually with the trainer as leader.
Lecture	Oral presentation by the trainer, with limited audience participation.
On the job	Ranges from no instruction, to casual coaching by more experienced employees, to carefully structured explanation, demonstration, and supervised practice by a qualified trainer.
Programmed instruction	Self-paced method using text followed by questions and answers; expensive to develop.
Role playing	Trainees act out roles with other trainees, such as "boss giving performance appraisal" and "subordinate reacting to appraisal" to gain experience in human relations.
Sensitivity training	Called T-group and laboratory training, this is an intensive experience in a small group; individuals try new behaviors and give feedback; promotes trust, open communication, and understanding of group dynamics.
Vestibule training	Supervised practice on manual tasks in a separate work area with emphasis on safety, learning, and feedback.

Source: Adapted from Ricky W. Griffin, *Management,* 3rd ed., p. 363. Copyright © 1990 by Houghton Mifflin Company. Used by permission.

are used. Relevant data (e.g., some output variable[s]) are secured before and after the training for both the experimental group(s) and the control group. Then a comparison of the performance of the groups is made to determine to what extent any change in the relevant variable(s) occurred as a result of training. One study, which used a quasi-experimental design, found no change in principals' leadership effectiveness before and immediately following situational leadership training but did discover a change in effectiveness three years after training.[41]

Performance Appraisal

Once employees are trained and in place in their jobs, school administrators usually begin to appraise their performance.There are many reasons to appraise how well employees are performing. First, the school district needs a check on the effectiveness of its personnel-selection procedures, by comparing scores on various selection devices used with later performance on the job. Second, administrators use the evaluations to make decisions about compensation, promotions, transfers, and sometimes demotions or terminations. Third, performance appraisals show the school district where professional development programs are needed and later gauge whether these have been effective. Finally, if employees are to perform their jobs better in the future, they need to know how well they have performed them in the past. School administrators also use feedback about employees' performance to recognize them for a job well done and to motivate them.[42]

Performance Appraisal Methods

Organizations currently use several methods to appraise performance. For the sake of simplicity, we can group them into three categories: the judgmental approach, the absolute standards approach, and the results-oriented approach.

[41]Salvatore V. Pascarella and Fred C. Lunenburg, "A Field Test of Hersey and Blanchard's Situational Leadership Theory in a School Setting," *College Student Journal*, 21 (1988): 33–37.

[42] Ronald W. Rebore, *Human Resources Administration: A Management Approach* (Upper Saddle River, NJ: Prentice Hall, 2011).

Table 15-4 Abbreviated Graphic Rating Scale for School Administrators

Work Dimension	Rating				
	Unacceptable	Needs Improvement	Acceptable	Commendable	Outstanding
Leadership	1	2	③	4	5
Management	1	2	3	4	⑤
Personnel administration	1	2	③	4	5
Administrative teaming	1	②	3	4	5
Budgeting	1	2	③	4	5
Total: 16					

Source: Fred C. Lunenburg, "One Method of Determining Administrative Salaries," *New York State School Board Association Journal* (January 1986), p. 20. Used by permission.

Judgmental Approach Under this approach, a school administrator or performance appraiser is asked to compare an employee with other employees and rate the person on a number of traits or behavioral dimensions. These appraisal systems are based on the exercise of judgment by the superior. Four widely used judgmental approaches are graphic rating scales, ranking, paired comparison, and forced distribution.[43]

Graphic Rating Scales A popular, simple technique for evaluating employees is to use a **graphic rating scale.** Table 15–4 shows a typical rating scale for a school administrator. Note that the scale lists a number of important work dimensions (such as leadership and management) and a performance range for each one. For each work dimension, the evaluator circles the numerical value that best describes the employee's performance. A five-point evaluation scheme is typically used to assess the important work dimensions: (1) unacceptable, (2) needs improvement, (3) acceptable, (4) commendable, and (5) outstanding. The assigned values for each dimension are then added up and totaled.[44]

Ranking An alternative method to graphic rating scales involves administrators ranking their subordinates in order of their performance effectiveness from best to worst. The usual procedure requires the rater to write the name of the best subordinate on the top of a list, then the name of the worst at the bottom and continue this sequential procedure until all subordinates are listed. **Ranking** is most frequently used for making personnel decisions such as promotions or the merit salary increase each employee will receive.

Paired Comparison A modification of the ranking procedure is the **paired comparison** technique. The method overcomes the problem associated with differentiating between subordinates in the middle range of the distribution. Under paired comparisons, raters compare only two subordinates at a time until all two-way comparisons have been made among all employees. After rating all pairs, the administrator can put the subordinates into a rank order by counting up the number of times each employee has been judged superior.

Forced Distribution "Grading on a curve" is a good example of the forced distribution method of performance appraisal. With this technique, the rater places a predetermined percentage of ratees into four or five performance categories. For example, if a five-point scale is used, the school administrator might decide to distribute employees as follows: 5 percent in the "unacceptable" category, 25 percent in the "needs improvement" category, 40 percent in the "acceptable" category, 25 percent in the "commendable" category, and 5 percent in the "outstanding" category. The usual procedure for accomplishing such a distribution is to record each employee's name on a separate index card.

---

[43]John Ivancevich, *Human Resource Management* 8th ed. (New York: McGraw-Hill, 2010).

[44]The graphic rating scale shown in Table 15–4 was developed and used by the lead author to determine administrative salaries, while he served as superintendent of schools of a medium-sized school district.

Table 15-5 A Guide to Appraising School Administrators' Performance

Performance Factor	Outstanding	High Satisfactory	Satisfactory	Low Satisfactory	Unsatisfactory
Quality	Leaps tall buildings with a single bound	Needs running start to jump tall buildings	Can only leap small buildings	Crashes into buildings	Cannot recognize buildings
Timeliness	Is faster than a speeding bullet	Only as fast as a speeding bullet	Somewhat slower than a bullet	Can only shoot bullets	Wounds self with bullets
Initiative	Is stronger than a locomotive	Is stronger than a bull elephant	Is stronger than a bull	Shoots the bull	Smells like a bull
Adaptability	Walks on water consistently	Walks on water in emergencies	Washes with water	Drinks water	Passes water in emergencies
Communication	Talks with God	Talks with angels	Talks to himself	Argues with himself	Loses those arguments
Relationship	Belongs in general management	Belongs in executive ranks	Belongs in rank and file	Belongs behind a broom	Belongs with competitor
Planning	Too bright to worry	Worries about future	Worries about present	Worries about past	Too dumb to worry

Source: Anonymous.

Then, for each dimension being appraised (leadership, management, etc.), the employee's index card is placed in one of the five categories.

Absolute Standards Approach Most appraisal measures that employ an absolute standards approach are based on job analysis. As discussed earlier, this type of analysis can provide a more detailed description of the actual behavior necessary for effective performance. School administrators compare the performance of each employee to a certain standard instead of to the performance of other employees; thus, they rate the degree to which performance meets the standard. The most common performance appraisal processes in this group are checklists, essays, critical incidents, and behaviorally anchored rating scales.[45]

Checklists The most common technique in the absolute standards group is some sort of **checklist**. Checklists tend to be more behaviorally based than either graphic rating scales or other employee-comparison methods. Table 15–5 presents a humorous example of a checklist that might be used to appraise school administrators' performance. More elaborate procedures, such as weighted and forced choice checklists, are also available. Specific weights are assigned to a list of work behaviors in the *weighted checklist*. A *forced choice checklist* consists of job-behavior statements with two to five response items in each set that correlate with high- and low-performing employees. The end result is a single numerical rating that is useful for personnel decisions such as salary and promotion.

Essays The **essay** method requires the rater to describe in writing each employee's strengths and weaknesses, along with suggestions for ways to improve performance. Some school districts require every rater to respond to specific open-ended questions, whereas others allow more flexibility. Compared to employee comparison methods, the essay method is time-consuming and difficult to quantify. Variations in writing skills of raters is another limitation. Some school districts have combined the graphic and essay methods by providing space for comments on the graphic rating scale.

Critical Incidents The **critical incidents** technique begins by identifying job requirements for successful performance. Job requirements are those behaviors that determine whether the job is being done effectively or ineffectively. The school administrator keeps a log, for each subordinate, of both effective and ineffective "incidents" of on-the-job behaviors. The incidents are then analyzed and refined into a composite picture of the required essentials in a particular job. From this a checklist is developed, which constitutes

[45]Ibid.

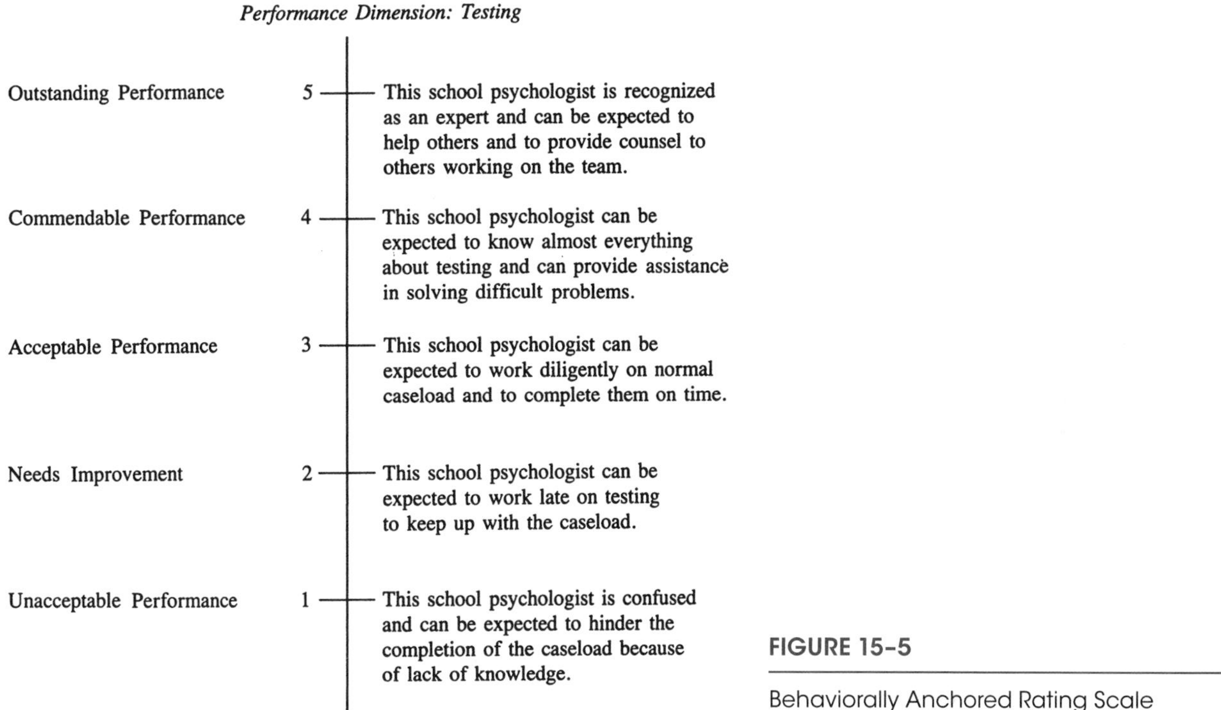

FIGURE 15–5

Behaviorally Anchored Rating Scale

the framework against which the subordinate is evaluated. During the evaluation conference, the administrator can refer to the critical incidents to correct work deficiencies, identify training needs, or praise successful performance.

Behaviorally Anchored Rating Scales A newer and somewhat related approach to the critical incidents technique is the **behaviorally anchored rating scale** (BARS). It was developed to cope with the problem of identifying scale anchor points. Specifically, the scale points such as unacceptable, needs improvement, acceptable, commendable, and outstanding (as shown in Table 15–4) may be difficult to define and may lead to unreliable or invalid appraisal results. Hence, the BARS defines scale points with specific behavior statements that describe varying degrees of performance. The form for a BARS generally covers six to eight specifically defined performance dimensions. A BARS should be developed for each dimension.

Figure 15–5 shows an example of a BARS for the testing competence-performance dimension for school psychologists. The scale anchors define the particular response categories for the evaluator. The response made by the evaluator is specific enough to be used as feedback in an appraisal interview with the school psychologists and is meaningful to the subordinate. For example, if the school psychologist were given a 3 on this dimension, the subordinate would be given the specific performance indicators that led to the evaluator's rating.

Results-Oriented Approaches In recent years, results-oriented approaches to performance appraisal have been suggested as an alternative to the judgmental and absolute standards approaches. As the name implies, the emphasis of results-oriented approaches is on the evaluation of results—both quantitative and qualitative. Put another way, the focus is on what the subordinate is supposed to accomplish on the job rather than a consideration of the subordinate's traits or on-the-job behaviors.[46]

---

[46]Clive Fletcher, *Appraisal, Feedback, and Development: Making Performance Review Work* (New York: Routledge, 2009). See also Ron Nash, *The Active Mentor: Practical Strategies for Supporting New Teachers* (Thousand Oaks, CA: Corwin Press, 2010).

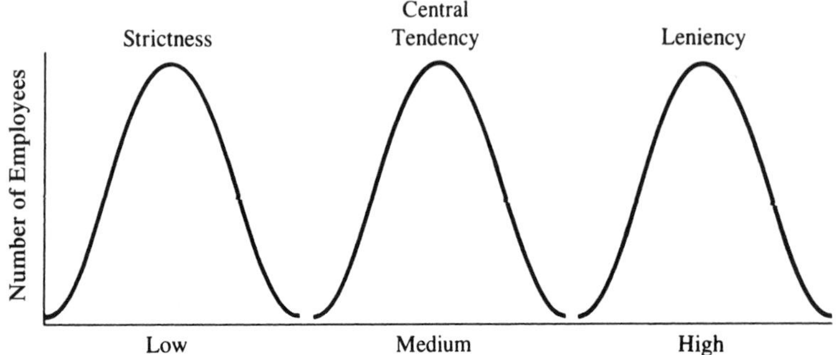

FIGURE 15-6

Strictness, Central Tendency, and Leniency Performance Ratings

Goal Setting One popular results-oriented approach is **goal setting**. We discussed goal-setting theory[47] in Chapter 4 and, more specifically, as a motivational technique. Goal setting can also serve as the foundation for a school district's performance appraisal system. It is particularly well suited to high-level administrative positions for which methods such as BARS may be inappropriate.

This program typically includes two major elements. First, the supervisor and the subordinate meet to discuss goals, which are established by the supervisor alone or jointly by the supervisor and the subordinate. Second, the supervisor and the subordinate meet to appraise the subordinate's performance in relation to the previously established goals. For example, suppose a high school principal sets a goal of increasing average daily attendance (ADA) in the building next year by 15 percent. At the end of the school year, this goal provides a framework for performance appraisal. If attendance has increased by 15 percent or more, a positive performance appraisal is likely. However, if ADA has increased by only 5 percent and if the principal is directly responsible for the results, a more negative evaluation may be in order. Then suggestions for improvement can be specified.

Other Results-Oriented Measures Besides goal setting, school administrators can use a variety of other results-oriented measures to assess subordinate performance. Some suggestions include measures of quantity of output, such as number of articles published, words typed, or items produced; measures of quality, such as reputation of the journal, typographical errors, or items rejected; measures of lost time, such as absenteeism or tardiness; or measures involving education, training, or experience, such as time in the field or time in a particular position. Although these measures tend to be nonjudgmental, they measure only one dimension of job performance. Such measures can also be tied to a goal-setting program.

Rating Errors

In conducting performance appraisals, school administrators must be careful to avoid making rating errors. Four of the more common rating errors are strictness or leniency, central tendency, halo effect, and recency of events.[48]

Strictness or Leniency Some supervisors tend to rate all their subordinates consistently low or high. These are referred to as **strictness and leniency errors**. The strict rater gives ratings lower than the subordinate deserves. This strictness error penalizes superior subordinates. The lenient rater tends to give higher ratings than the subordinate deserves. Just as the strictness error punishes exceptional subordinates, so does the leniency error. Strictness-leniency bias presents less of a problem when absolute standards and results-oriented approaches to performance appraisal are used.

Central Tendency Some raters are reluctant to rate subordinates as very high or very low. They dislike being too strict with anyone by giving them an extremely low rating, and they may believe that no one ever deserves to get the highest possible rating. The result of this type of attitude is that everyone is rated around average. Figure 15–6 depicts examples

[47]Edwin A. Locke and Gary P. Latham, *A Theory of Goal Setting and Task Performance*, 2nd ed. (Englewood Cliffs, NJ: Prentice Hall, 1994).

[48]Michael Deblieux, *Performance Appraisal Source Book: A Collection of Practical Samples* (Alpharetta, GA: Society for Human Resource Management, 2003).

of strictness, leniency, and central tendency biases. The distribution of ratings on the left of the figure indicates a strictness error; those in the middle indicate a central tendency error; and the cluster on the right indicates a leniency error.

Halo Effect When a single positive or negative dimension of a subordinate's performance is allowed to influence the supervisor's rating of that subordinate on other dimensions, a **halo effect** is operating. For example, the supervisor likes Tom because he is so cooperative. The halo effect leads Tom's supervisor to automatically rate him high on all appraisal dimensions, including leadership, management, personnel administration, administrative teaming, and even budgeting. The result is that subordinates are rated consistently high, medium, or low on all performance appraisal dimensions.

Recency of Events Ideally, performance appraisals should be based on data collected about a subordinate's performance over an entire evaluation period (usually six months to a year). However, as is often the case, the supervisor is likely to consider recent performance more strongly than performance behaviors that occurred earlier. This is called the **recency of events error**. Failure to include all performance behaviors in the performance appraisal of a subordinate can bias the ratings.

Strictness or leniency, central tendency, halo effect, and recency of events all result in inaccurate performance appraisals of employees. The absolute standards and results-oriented approaches to performance appraisal, particularly BARS and goal setting, attempt to minimize such rating errors.

Compensation

The compensation of employees is another important component of the personnel evaluation process.[49] A sound compensation program can help organizations attract qualified applicants, retain desirable employees, and motivate and reward high employee performance. The formal compensation system takes the form of wages and salaries and fringe benefits.

Wages and Salaries

Because wages and salaries affect every member of the organization, they are one of the most important parts of a compensation program. A successful compensation program involves three major decisions: wage level decisions, wage structure decisions, and individual wage decisions.

Wage Level Decisions To develop an equitable compensation program, human resource administrators determine wage and salary levels that are comparable for the industry and geographic area. *Wage leaders* are those organizations that pay employees more than the average paid for similar jobs in the industry and geographic area. One example of a wage leader is the Rochester (New York) Public Schools, known as the Rochester Experiment, which paid its teachers among the highest salaries in the nation—some at $70,000 a year more than twenty years ago.[50]

Wage followers pay less than the average for the industry and area. Most organizations make an effort to pay what the competition is paying. A **wage survey** can be used to determine what other organizations pay employees. Then personnel administrators can adjust wage levels to meet or exceed the comparable rates.

The salaries that a school district pays its certified employees vary by geographic area. There is published information on nonsupervisory jobs from which school organizations can draw. The Bureau of Labor Statistics has conducted a number of surveys covering various blue-collar and white-collar jobs in different regions of the country. Many professional associations also conduct surveys focused on specific jobs. For example, the National Association of Elementary School Principals (NAESP), National Association of Secondary School Principals (NASSP), American Association of School Administrators (AASA), and Association for School Business Officials (ASBO) survey wage levels, respectively, for elementary, middle, and high school principals, school superintendents, and school business officials. The American Association of University Professors (AAUP) annually surveys wage levels for college and university professors.

---

[49]WorldatWork, *The WorldatWork Handbook of Compensation, Benefits and Total Rewards* (New York: John Wiley, 2007); Bruce R. Ellig, *The Complete Guide to Executive Compensation* (New York: McGraw-Hill, 2007).

[50]Jerry Buckley, "The Rochester Experiment: A Blueprint for Better Schools," *U.S. News and World Report,* 104, no. 2 (1988): 60–65; Buckley, "The Rochester Experiment: School Reform, School Reality," *U.S. News and World Report*, 104, no. 24 (1988): 58–63.

Wage Structure Decisions Whereas wage level involves the comparison of wages and salaries paid in comparable organizations, wage structure describes the relative worth of particular jobs within the organization. To determine what jobs are worth, many organizations use a technique called **job evaluation**. The basic information necessary for a job evaluation is obtained during job analyses, discussed earlier. The results of job analyses describing such items as responsibilities, education, skill requirements, and physical requirements of the job are used to evaluate the job. The higher the evaluation, the higher the wages or salaries associated with the job.

The four principal systems of job evaluation are job ranking, the classification system, the point system, and the factor comparison method.[51]

Job Ranking **Job ranking** is the simplest form of job evaluation. Responsibilities and other characteristics associated with each job are examined, and the jobs are ranked from most demanding to least demanding. To facilitate this ranking, benchmark jobs are selected, and others are inserted between them. For example, the most highly skilled nonsupervisory job in a school district is computer programmer, and the lowest is that of maintenance worker. In between are numerous gradations of jobs. When a few of these nonsupervisory jobs are analyzed and placed on the scale, the remaining jobs can be ranked by comparing them with those already on the scale.

Classification System A **classification system** places jobs and salaries in levels. The U.S. Civil Service has eighteen classification levels (L1 through L18) that are used to determine salary ranges for its employees. These classification levels are assigned to jobs from most to least difficult and important. For example, school organizations typically have classification levels for clerical employees: Receptionists may be classified as level 1 (L1), secretaries L2, private secretaries L3, office managers L4, and the like. If such a job evaluation is districtwide, it ensures that there is some internal equity in the ranking of jobs based on hierarchical positions.

Point System One of the most widely used methods of job evaluation today is the **point system**. Under the point system, various factors are designated—for example, mental requirements, skill requirements, physical requirements, responsibilities, and supervision—and the maximum number of points allowable for each is determined. A computer programmer will then receive the maximum number of points for mental requirements, and other jobs proportionately less according to the number of mental requirements they require. Wage rates are then linked to the number of points assigned to the job.

Factor Comparison Method Like the point system, the **factor comparison method** also makes use of job factors. However, the factor comparison method creates a key scale for measuring jobs. This is the basic difference between it and the point system. Typically, twenty or thirty jobs in the organization are analyzed to form the key comparison scale. Each job is ranked by each factor in turn, and the portion of the total salary paid for this factor is determined. This in turn determines the weight to be given to each factor in arriving at a final ranking. Table 15–6 presents the factors used in a hypothetical school district's job-evaluation system and the percentage of total wages that determines each one.

The major advantage of the factor comparison method over the point system is that higher-level jobs can be added to an original system. The point system, for example, requires developing separate systems to handle maintenance, professional, and administrative tasks, whereas the factor comparison method can take care of each of these levels within a single system.

Individual Wage Decisions Once wage ranges are developed for jobs, how does an administrator determine what to pay an employee? The easiest decision is to pay a single rate for each wage classification. More typically, decisions about individual wages generally are based on a combination of factors. Employees are paid according to qualification level, that is, their prior work experience and their skill level. For example, a secretary (L2)

Table 15-6 Key Comparison Scale

Factor	Percentage
Mental requirements	20
Skill requirements	30
Physical requirements	5
Responsibilities	20
Supervision requirements	25
TOTAL	100

[51]Michael Armstrong et al., *Job Evaluation: A Guide to Achieving Equal Pay* (London: Kogan Page, 2006).

with five years of experience is likely to earn more than a beginner, because of superior skill development. Employees are also paid based on seniority, that is, the length of time they have worked for an organization or in their current job. For instance, most school districts use a lockstep salary schedule for determining pay increases for teachers based solely on job seniority. Finally, employees may be paid for their performance on the job, that is, their **merit**.

Benefits

Wages and salaries make up the major part of an organization's compensation package. Equally important are the benefits paid to employees. A recent survey reveals that benefits constitute nearly 40 percent of the cash compensation paid to employees, and in some industries, employee benefits represent two-thirds of payroll costs.[52] Some of these benefits are legally required. For example, the Social Security Act requires retirement pay, disability pay, and survivor's benefits. Unemployment compensation, also required by the act, provides subsistence payments to employees who have been laid off. All states have workers' compensation laws, which provide for those who suffer job-related illnesses and injuries. Voluntary benefits include health and dental insurance, life insurance, retirement benefits, paid vacations and holidays, sick-leave pay, credit unions, recreational programs, and payment for graduate courses completed.

Union-Management Relations

A **union** is an organization of employees formed for the purpose of influencing an employer's decisions concerning conditions of employment. **Union-management relations** is the ongoing relationship between a group of employees represented by a union and management in the employing organization. The basis for any union-management relationship is **collective bargaining**, the process of negotiating and administering a collective bargaining agreement or negotiated contract between a union and the employing organization. Collective bargaining agreements specify the rights and duties of employees and management with respect to wages, hours, working conditions, and other terms of employment. They constitute a major influence on the day-to-day operation of a school as well as the long-term administrative activities of the school district.[53]

Union Membership

The labor union movement in the United States began in response to undesirable management practices in industry. It has spread to include employees in the public sector, such as teachers and government workers. Teachers represent the largest group of employees in an educational institution. Today, all but nine states have enacted statutes specifically establishing some rights of employees in public schools to bargain collectively with boards of education. Over 80 percent of the nation's teachers belong to either the National Education Association (NEA), which has over 1.5 million members, or the American Federation of Teachers (AFT), which has about half a million members.[54]

Collective Bargaining

Collective bargaining is the process of negotiating between management and employees on the terms and conditions of employment. It is collective in the sense that the employees, as a unit, select representatives from their membership to meet with management to discuss issues that need to be resolved. The union bargains on items that represent the concerns of its membership. Management tries to advance the interests of the organization.

Bargaining Issues Collective bargaining agreements are complex and often lengthy, written contracts that are legally binding on both management and the union(s) representing its employees. A recent agreement between the Chicago Board of Education and the Chicago Teachers' Association is over 250 pages long.[55] It is more streamlined than most. Although the

[52]U.S. Chamber of Commerce, *Employee Benefits 2011* (Washington, DC: U.S. Chamber of Commerce, 2012).

[53]Todd DeMitchell, *Labor Relations in Education: Policies, Politics, Practices* (Lanham, MD: Rowman & Littlefield, 2011).

[54]U.S. Department of Labor, Bureau of Labor Statistics, *Employment and Earnings* (Washington, DC: U.S. Government Printing Office, 2008).

[55]Chicago Board of Education, *Chicago Board of Education-Chicago Teachers' Association* (*CBA-CTA Agreement 1997–2000* (Chicago Board of Education, Chicago, 2000).

specific provisions of collective bargaining agreements vary from one school district to another, the collective bargaining process and negotiated agreement generally address the following issues.[56] (Because teachers make up the largest group of employees in schools, we will limit our discussion to teachers' collective bargaining agreements. It should be noted, however, that school administrators collectively bargain with other employee unions as well.)

Management Rights During collective bargaining, unions strive to increase wages, protect job security, and improve the work conditions of employees. On the other hand, management tries to protect and clarify its rights as employer. Any rights not given to the union in the collective bargaining agreement are assumed to belong to management. These are called **management rights**. A strong management rights clause in the contract reinforces statutory rights of the board of education and aids in limiting the authority of an arbitrator in the grievance process. A common management rights clause is a lengthy list of specific management prerogatives, such as the right to supervise all operations; control all property and equipment; determine the size of the workforce; assign work to be done; introduce new methods, programs, or procedures; hire and fire employees; promote, demote, and transfer employees; and in general maintain an orderly, effective, and efficient operation.

Narrow Grievance Definition A grievance procedure is a formal system by which contract disputes are expressed, processed, and judged. The definition of a grievance in a written collective bargaining agreement determines which employee complaints are subject to binding grievance arbitration. A **narrow grievance definition** that limits employee complaints to the specific written agreement is recommended. Such an approach does not preclude other complaint procedures. It does limit what a grievance arbitrator can decide during the written terms of the negotiated agreement in force.

No-Strike Provision Federal law prohibits strikes by teachers. Most states have passed similar laws. Because teacher strikes occur despite the laws against them, additional protection can be gained through a **no-strike provision** in the collective bargaining agreement. Such a provision puts the union on record against strikes and involves the union in the enforcement of the laws prohibiting them. In addition, a no-strike provision usually permits management to impose monetary damages on teachers who engage in an illegal strike.

Zipper Clause A **zipper clause**, or waiver provision, stipulates that the written agreement is the complete and full contract between the parties and that neither party is required to bargain on other items during the term of the agreement. The purpose of such a provision is to avoid continuing negotiations after the contract has been ratified; when coupled with a strong management rights clause, it limits the role of past practice used by grievance arbitrators.

Such a provision, however, does not preclude the parties from negotiating further if both agree. New bargaining strategies, including collaborative or win-win bargaining, would be an exception to the use of a zipper clause. The idea of collaborative bargaining is that union and management negotiate continually during the year as problems arise.

Maintenance of Standards Management should avoid a **maintenance of standards** provision. Such a provision is routinely included in most union proposals and incorporates the school district's current practices on a wide range of items, many of which are not mandatory subjects of bargaining. Furthermore, a maintenance of standards provision leaves the district vulnerable to the role of past practice used by grievance arbitrators in settling contract disputes. It is the antithesis of a management rights provision and a zipper clause.

An example of a maintenance of standards provision is the following:

> All conditions of employment, including teaching hours, extra compensation for work outside regular teaching hours, relief periods, leaves and general working conditions shall be maintained at not less than the highest minimum standards, provided that such conditions shall be improved for the benefit of teachers, as required by the express provisions of this agreement. The agreement shall not be interpreted or applied to deprive teachers of professional advantages heretofore enjoyed, unless expressly stated herein.[57]

Management should avoid such a provision.

[56]Michael R. Carrell et al., *Labor Relations and Collective Bargaining*. (Upper Saddle River, NJ: Prentice Hall, 2010).

[57]Peggy Odell Gander, *Collective Bargaining* (Arlington, VA: American Association of School Administrators, 1981), p. 22.

Just Cause The term **just cause** is found in numerous collective bargaining agreements in public education and is routinely included in most union proposals. There is a danger in using such a term, from management's standpoint, because *just cause* has no clear definition. If a collective bargaining agreement has binding arbitration as the last step in the grievance procedure, then an arbitrator will decide what the term means. The arbitrator's interpretation of the term may be different from what management had intended. For example, suppose a collective bargaining agreement contained the following provision: "No teacher will be disciplined without *just cause*." What does *just cause* mean in this case? It will likely mean something different to management than to employees. The point is that the meaning of *just cause* must be spelled out clearly somewhere in the contract or eliminated entirely.

Reduction in Force Most all collective bargaining agreements have some form of **reduction in force** (RIF) provision. Seniority, or length of continuous service within a certificated field, is the key factor used in employee layoff and recall. Some agreements allow for **bumping**, which means that teachers laid off in one certificated field may replace another teacher in another certificated area who has less seniority in the field than the bumping teacher. A few RIF provisions stress other factors such as affirmative action and teacher merit. Such provisions are more favorable to management but are opposed by most teachers' unions.

Wages and Benefits Much time at the bargaining table is devoted to wage increases and fringe-benefit improvements. Wage and salary increases are often stated as across-the-board salary increases for steps on a lockstep salary schedule and **cost-of-living adjustments** (COLA) based on the Consumer Price Index in a designated geographic area. Besides salary increases, unions often demand improvements in various fringe benefits such as insurance programs (life, health, and dental); pension plans; merit pay; and sick leave, personal days, and paid religious holidays. Compensation costs in today's school districts often range from 75 to 85 percent of the total budget.

Other Issues Among other important bargaining issues are grievance arbitration, teacher evaluation, class size, school calendar, and the like. Binding grievance arbitration is not a problem providing the rest of the agreement protects management prerogatives. Likewise, teacher evaluation, class size, and school calendar should not be overly restrictive on the school district.

The Bargaining Process To bargain for these issues, management and the union each select a negotiating team. Opinions vary widely on who should conduct management negotiations. In small school districts, the superintendent or a board member often conducts negotiations with the teachers' union. Experts advise against this practice, however.[58] In large districts, a full-time administrator (director of employee relations, assistant superintendent, or director of personnel) usually serves as chief negotiator. Still other districts employ an outside negotiator—an attorney or labor relations specialist.

One of a superintendent's basic personnel decisions concerning collective **bargaining** is whether to have a labor relations specialist at the bargaining table to advise the school district or perhaps even represent the district during negotiations. When hiring a labor relations specialist, the superintendent must decide how much authority to give him or her.

One or more building administrators often are included on management's negotiating team. These people live with the contract day to day; they know its weak and strong points; they will administer the new agreement; and they will likely give the contract greater support if they can participate in the changes made in it. The union team generally consists of the local union president and other members of the local membership. Its team may also include an attorney or a labor relations specialist from a regional unit who negotiates for other teachers' unions in the region.

Once each side has selected its negotiating teams, the bargaining process begins. The bargaining takes place in face-to-face meetings between management and union representatives during which numerous proposals and counterproposals are exchanged. Several rounds of negotiations may be needed to reach agreement on all issues. When the two parties agree on the issues, a new negotiated contract is presented to the union membership and the board for a ratification vote. If both parties approve the agreement, it goes into effect. If they reject the agreement, each goes back to the bargaining table for another round of negotiations.

An **impasse** is said to exist when both parties are unable to reach agreement on a contract. State procedures

[58]DeMitchell, *Labor Relations in Education*.

vary when the union and the school board are deadlocked in negotiations. Most states have some provision for resolving impasses. Some states, like Wisconsin, have developed a procedure for resolving impasses. The procedure involves the following steps:

Mediation. The two contending parties meet with a neutral third person who attempts to persuade them to settle the remaining issues through discussion and by proposing compromise provisions to the contract. The mediator acts as a facilitator, however, and has no legal authority to force the parties to accept the suggestions offered.

Fact Finding. The state appoints a group or committee to investigate and report the facts that are presented by each party. The fact-finding committee's recommendations are generally made public, which places additional pressure on the parties to come to agreement.

Arbitration. If the parties are still at an impasse, state law may require the union and the school board to submit to arbitration or binding arbitration. Guidelines for teachers' contracts in Wisconsin, for example, stipulate that arbitrators must choose the proposal of either the school board or the teachers' union, but not a compromise solution. This forces the two contending parties to bring their contract proposals closer together. The result has been a decrease in teacher strikes in Wisconsin.[59]

Bargaining Tactics Negotiators use a number of tactics to improve their bargaining. Four tactics that are typically used are counterproposals, trade-offs, the caucus, and costing proposals.[60]

Counterproposals Collective bargaining consists of the exchange of proposals and counterproposals in an effort to reach settlement between the negotiating parties. A proposal is an offer presented by one party in negotiations for consideration by the other party. A **counterproposal**, which is designed to bring the parties closer together on an issue, is an offer suggested as an alternative to the previous proposal by the other party. Because it is the union that is seeking improved conditions of employment, it introduces the majority of proposals. Generally, management responds to the union's demands through counterproposals. Actually, there are at least two advantages to this approach for management: (1) The party that moves first on an issue is usually at a disadvantage, for it invariably reveals some information helpful to the other negotiator; and (2) the union, as the initiating party, is forced to work for every concession it gets.

Tradeoffs Another bargaining tactic is the **tradeoff**, which is giving one issue in return for another. For example, a teachers' union will make a number of proposals, such as (1) fair share, (2) salary increase, (3) increased sick leave, (4) increased personal days, (5) extra holiday(s), (6) hospitalization, (7) life insurance, (8) dental insurance, (9) maternity leave, (10) binding arbitration of grievances, (11) past practice provision, (12) reduction in force procedures, (13) teacher evaluations, (14) class size, (15) school calendar, and the like. Management then responds by stating that it will grant a 5 percent salary increase if the union withdraws its proposals for increased sick leave and personal days, hospitalization, life insurance, and dental insurance. Further, management will grant the past practice clause if the union drops its request for binding arbitration of grievances. All proposals are "packaged" in this manner until the teacher's union and the school board reach a settlement. While neither party wants to give up its item, each may perceive the exchange as a reasonable compromise.

Caucus A basic principle of negotiating is that only one person speaks at the bargaining table—the chief negotiator. The other members of the bargaining team must remain quiet. Remaining quiet at the bargaining table can be a frustrating demand for the other members of the bargaining team. A **caucus** is a private meeting of a bargaining team to decide what action to take on a particular phase of negotiations. It provides an opportunity to get needed input from other team members and to release built-up tensions that arise during stressful negotiations.

Costing Proposals All proposals in collective bargaining have direct, hidden, and administrative costs. Management must know the cost of all union proposals. Therefore, **costing proposals** is another important bargaining tactic.

[59]American Arbitration Association, *Arbitration and the Law* (Huntington, NY: Juris Publishing, 2010).

[60]Richard G. Neal, *Bargaining Tactics* (Manassas, VA: Richard Neal Associates, 1982); Fred C. Lunenburg, "Collective Bargaining in the Public Schools," *Journal of Collective Negotiations*, 29 (2000): 259–272; Michael Carrell, Negotiating Skills: Theory, Skills, and Practices (Upper Saddle River, NJ: Prentice Hall, 2007).

Preparation for this phase of bargaining should be a continual process throughout the school year. Such an approach will avoid errors made in costing proposals hastily during the heat of negotiations. The logical department in a school district to maintain a data bank and generate data for costing proposals is the business office. This office can then provide a database to the board's negotiating team at the beginning of the bargaining process.

The following guidelines for costing proposals are recommended:[61]

Cost Proposals Accurately. Typically, the union will request copies of all cost data that management prepares. Management can expect distribution of part or all of the data supplied. Therefore, prepare cost data carefully. All calculations must withstand the scrutiny of the public, a mediator, a fact-finding committee, or an arbitrator.

Cost Proposals Separately. Cost each union proposal separately. For example, the estimated cost of increasing the number of personal leave days must be costed independently of a proposal for increasing the number of sick days. Each must be based on historical data and cost projections.

Cost Proposals from Management's Viewpoint. Prepare costings from management's point of view. For example, proposals to reduce services must consider either the cost of replacing those services or the economic loss resulting from not having those services performed. In one school district in a midwestern state, a teachers' collective bargaining agreement stipulated that high school English teachers were required to teach only four classes a day (not exceeding twenty-five students in a class) in order to alleviate the heavy load of correcting daily written assignments. All other high school teachers in the district taught five classes a day. Because there were twenty-four high school English teachers in the district at an average salary of $50,000 a year, this provision in the contract cost the school district $240,000 a year ($10,000 × 24).

Cost Proposals as of a Common Date. Base all costings on data gathered as of a common date. The usual cycle used in school districts is the fiscal year beginning July 1.

Analyze Comparable Data from Neighboring Organizations. The board's chief negotiator must be able to analyze comparable data from neighboring school districts. For instance, cost data from neighboring school districts must not be considered in isolation. Public school financing is tricky business and comprises numerous factors. The personnel practices and curriculum of each situation are different. While the salary schedule in one district may be better than that in another, the work load in the latter district may be less demanding (e.g., see number 3). Or the salaries in the neighboring district may be distributed differently—higher at the top of the scale but lower at the bottom, for example. Therefore, the board's chief negotiator must be thoroughly familiar with the collective bargaining agreements in neighboring districts. It is a natural tendency for the teachers' union to seek the best of both worlds.

Supply Specifically Requested Information Only. Cost data should be pertinent to each proposal. Only management's chief negotiator should be provided with the raw data that was used to prepare summaries. Related data may suggest counterproposals. Never distribute raw data to the union and supply only specifically requested information.

Provide Management's Negotiating Team with a Budget Projection. The superintendent must provide management's negotiating team with a budget projection at the start of bargaining. The document can be used to set the tentative limits on the chief negotiator. The budget projections must provide a minimum and several alternatives, including factors that might influence the final budget.

The following are some important factors that influence a school district's final budget.[62] This information should be part of a school district's data bank. Such cost data can assist management's bargaining team in costing proposals.

- *Salary*
  - Salary schedules and placement of teachers (see Table 15–7)
  - Average salary of newly hired teachers
  - Average base salary of teachers, by school, level, department
  - Contract salaries distribution

[61] Ibid.

[62] Ibid.

Table 15-7 Salary Schedule for a Hypothetical School District

Step	B.A.	No. of Staff	Cost	Step	M.A.	No. of Staff	Cost	Step	Ph.D.	No. of Staff	Cost
1	$43,000	2	$86,000	1	$45,000	1	$45,000	1	$47,000		
2	45,000			2	48,000	2	96,000	2	51,000		
3	47,000			3	51,000	2	102,000	3	55,000		
4	49,000	2	98,000	4	54,000	4	216,000	4	59,000		
5	51,000			5	57,000	2	114,000	5	63,000		
6	53,000			6	60,000	3	180,000	6	67,000	1	67,000
7	55,000	2	110,000	7	63,000			7	71,000		
8	57,000	3	171,000	8	66,000	2	132,000	8	75,000		
9	59,000	1	59,000	9	69,000	1	69,000	9	79,000		
10	61,000	2	122,000	10	72,000			10	83,000		
11	63,000	2	126,000	11	75,000	3	225,000	11	87,000		
12	65,000	8	520,000	12	78,000	17	1,326,000	12	91,000	1	91,000
Totals		22	$1,292,000			37	$2,505,000			2	$158,000

Total number of teachers: 61
Total of teachers' salaries: $3,955,000
Average teacher salary: $64,836

Past record of salary schedule improvements (dollar amount and percentage)
Total cost of past schedule improvements
Past record of change in the salary schedule (steps and lanes)
Projected cost: normal increment, $100 on base schedule, 1 percent schedule increase

- *Fringe Benefits*

Fringe benefits as percentage of salaries paid
Cost of fringe benefits per new position
Leave history: policy and record
Separation pay: number of individuals, per diem rate, annual rate, average pay
Sabbatical leave: granted, denials, costs, subsequent separations
Retirements: mandatory versus actual, reason for retirement

- *Staffing*

Number of employees
Staffing ratios by school, level, department
Recruitment history: applicants, offers, acceptances
Separation history: number, reason, scale placement, turnover experience
General statistics: age, gender, race, marital status of employees
Scale placement: academic advancement record, payment for graduate credits, merit pay

- *Administration*

Cost of recruitment
Cost of selection
Cost of training
Cost of basic supplies and equipment for new employees
Cost of negotiations
Budget history/forecasting
Expenditure history
Enrollment history and projections
Per-pupil cost history
Reserve trends/forecasting
Building factors affecting conditions of employment

New Bargaining Strategies Currently, forty-one of the fifty states permit teachers to bargain collectively with school boards. Where such bargaining is allowed, almost all school districts employ traditional or adversarial bargaining. In recent years, a new unionism, one that connects teacher participation in educational

ADMINISTRATIVE ADVICE 15–3

Contrasts Between Industrial and Professional Unionism

Here industrial-style teacher unionism is contrasted with professional-style teacher unionism in three areas: responsibilities, relationships, and protection.

Industrial-Style Teacher Unionism

Emphasizes the separateness of labor and management:

- Separation of managerial and teaching work
- Separation between job design and its execution
- Strong hierarchical divisions

Motto: *"Boards make policy, managers manage, teachers teach."*

Emphasizes adversarial relationships:

- Organized around teacher discontent
- Mutual deprecation—lazy teachers, incompetent managers
- Win/lose distributive bargaining
- Limited scope contract

Motto: *"It's us versus them."*

- **Emphasizes protection of teachers:**
- Self-interest
- External quality control

Motto: *"Any grievant is right."*

The Emerging Union of Professionals

Emphasizes the collective aspect of work in schools:

- Blurring the line between teaching and managerial work through joint committees and lead teacher positions
- Designing and carrying out school programs in teams
- Flattened hierarchies, decentralization

Motto: *"All of us are smarter than any of us."*

Emphasizes the interdependency of workers and managers:

- Organized around the need for educational improvement
- Mutual legitimation of skill and capacity of management and union
- Interest-based bargaining
- Broad scope contract and other agreements

Motto: *"Be hard on the problem, not on each other."*

Emphasizes protection of teachers:

- Combination of self-interest and public interest
- Internal quality control

Motto: *"The purpose of the union is not to defend its least competent members."*

Source: Adapted from Charles T. Kerchner, "Building the Airplane as It Rolls Down the Runway," *School Administrator*, 10 (1993): 10. Used by permission.

decisions to taking responsibility for outcomes, has become apparent. Studies of a number of collaborative efforts in union-management relations describe reform initiatives in Rochester, Pittsburgh, Cincinnati, Glenview, IL, Greece, NY, Jefferson County, KY, and other cities.[63] This research describes professional unionism and how it contrasts sharply with the beliefs and practices of traditional industrial unionism. (See Administrative Advice 15–3.)

One consequence of professional unionism is the emergence of a new mode of principal leadership. While they vary in personal style, gender, and ethnicity, professional unions share similar management styles. They empower the people with whom they work. They use a hands-on approach. They are entrepreneurs; they gather and redistribute resources and encourage others to do so. They abide by a common realization that one leads best by developing the talent of others and gaining commitment rather than compliance with organizational rules.

[63]Charles T. Kerchner, Julia Koppich, and Joseph G. Weeres, *Taking Charge of Quality, How Teachers and Unions Can Revitalize Schools: An Introduction and Companion to United Mind Workers* (San Francisco: Jossey-Bass, 1998); Jane Hannaway et al., *Collective Bargaining in Education: Negotiating Change in Today's Schools* (Cambridge, MA: Harvard Education Publishing Group, 2006).

PRO CON DEBATE

Superintendent Searches

One of the most important decisions a school board can make is the appointment of a superintendent of schools. Some boards conduct a search on their own. Some work with their local intermediate unit or district superintendent. Minimal expense is incurred with either of these options. Other boards employ executive search firms or superintendent search consultants (generally, educational administration professors who specialize in this service). Search firms and search consultants charge large fees.

Question: Does the involvement of an executive search firm or a superintendent search consultant justify the expense?

Arguments PRO

1. Boards rarely have the expertise to conduct a legal search. Candidates' civil rights are protected by law and regulation. Without the guidance of experts, boards have been known to make serious errors in these areas.
2. Consultants and search firms can get inside information about candidates because they know the network and have the credibility to tap into the network. They are more likely to learn sensitive information about candidates from references and other sources.
3. Consultants and search firms are constantly on the alert for good candidates. They follow the careers of promising administrators and share perceptions with each other. They have an expert's knowledge of the candidates.
4. Aspiring superintendents know who the search consultants are and can strive to attract their attention.
5. The intermediate unit heads or district superintendents are expert at conducting searches. However, because the superintendent works in a dependent relationship to them, the intermediate unit or district superintendent has a vested interest in the identification of candidates who fit their profile, not the school district board's profile.
6. The use of professional researchers depoliticizes the process of identifying a superintendent. The consultant is an outside person without ties in the district who can be disinterested about the identification of candidates.

Arguments CON

1. Boards can learn how to conduct an appropriate search by consulting the state school board association and reviewing the literature.
2. Board members can learn what they need to know about candidates from a careful reading of résumés, telephone contact with references, thoughtful interviews, and site visits to candidates' workplaces.
3. Consultants and search firms are notorious for nurturing and recommending white males whom they perceive to be the best candidates in their network. Their network is the "old-boy" network.
4. The search experts become king makers. They gain power because aspiring administrators must stay in their good graces. Candidates call search consultants' interviews at national conferences "meat markets."
5. Intermediate unit heads or district superintendents are as expert at search consulting as the firms that charge for the service. In addition, they know the school district well and therefore can help the board find a candidate who will meet its unique needs.
6. The school board makes the final selection of the superintendent whether or not a search consultant is involved.

Consistent with professional unionism is collaborative bargaining (also known as win-win bargaining). Typically, collaborative bargaining focuses on ongoing problem solving rather than dealing with a buildup of issues presented at the bargaining table. Both management and union keep a "tickler file" of problems encountered in administering the current contract. Joint committees deal with the problems encountered. Then when contract language is finally discussed the parties present specific notes to support their positions. both parties establish agreed-on ground rules and specific time limits for negotiations, and write trust agreements and memoranda of understanding, and carefully select respected, credible members of negotiating teams. These procedures can help establish trust and a sense of collaboration to solve mutual problems throughout the school year and at the bargaining table.

Summary

1. The personnel process consists of the following steps: human resource planning, recruitment, selection, professional development, performance appraisal, and compensation. Of particular concern for today's administrators is the growing body of laws regulating the personnel process.
2. Human resource planning begins with a forecast of the number and types of employees needed to achieve the organization's objectives. Planning also includes preparation of job descriptions and specifications.
3. Recruitment involves the initial screening of prospective employees. Sources of prospective employees can be located inside or outside the organization.
4. Selection involves choosing an individual to hire from among the pool of applicants who have been recruited. Biographical information, testing, interviews, reference checks, and assessment centers are often used as aids in the selection process.
5. Professional development helps employees perform their jobs better and prepares them for future jobs. The professional development process involves determining development needs, designing and implementing the development program, and evaluating the development program.
6. Performance appraisal is the systematic observation and evaluation of employee behavior. Some of the most commonly used methods of appraisal include the judgmental approach, the absolute standards approach, and the results-oriented approach.
7. Compensation includes wages and salaries and fringe benefits. Wage and salary levels are usually tied to what other organizations in the field pay. Legally required benefits are Social Security, workers' compensation, and unemployment insurance. Other benefits include pension plans, insurance programs, leaves, educational benefits, and the like.
8. Most states permit teachers to bargain collectively with boards of education. Labor relations refers to dealing with employees when they are organized into a union. Management must engage in collective bargaining with the union in an effort to reach agreement on a contract. The most recent approaches to collective bargaining are referred to as "win-win bargaining."

Key Terms

human resource planning
recruitment
selection
professional development
performance appraisal
compensation
job analysis
job description
job specification
observation
work sampling
critical incidents
interview
questionnaires
forecasting
human resource audit
Equal Employment Opportunity Commission
equal employment opportunity
affirmative action program
internal recruitment
closed recruitment system
open recruitment system
external recruitment
biographical information

reference checks
written tests
intelligence tests
personality tests
interest inventories
performance simulations
assessment centers
professional development
graphic rating scale
ranking
paired comparison
forced distribution
checklist
essay
critical incidents
behaviorally anchored rating scale
goal setting
strictness and leniency errors
central tendency bias
halo effect
recency of events error
wage survey
job evaluation
job ranking
classification system
point system
factor comparison method
seniority
merit
union
union-management relations
collective bargaining
management rights
narrow grievance definition
no-strike provision
zipper clause
maintenance of standards
just cause
reduction in force
bumping
cost-of-living adjustments
ratification vote
impasse
mediation
fact finding
arbitration
counterproposal
tradeoff
caucus
costing proposals

Discussion Questions

1. What steps does your school/school district use in selecting personnel?
2. Discuss the advantages and disadvantages of internal and external recruiting. What techniques can administrators use to improve their recruiting and selection practices?
3. What are some of the federal laws and agencies that affect recruitment and selection of personnel?
4. Describe the procedure used to develop a wage and salary structure for a school district. What system does your school/school district use to compensate personnel?
5. What are the major issues that are negotiated at the bargaining table between the board of education and the teachers' union? Discuss some bargaining tactics that management can use to improve its position in the collective bargaining process. Discuss some of the new bargaining approaches that have emerged over the last decade.

Suggested Readings

David A. DeCenzo et al. *Fundamentals of Human Resource Management* (New York: John Wiley, 2010). This text provides the most practical, most comprehensive treatment available of the personnel function as it applies to educational administration.

Nigro, Felix A., and Lloyd G. Nigro. *The New Public Personnel Administration* (Belmont, CA: Wadsworth, 2007). The authors provide an excellent introduction to all aspects of personnel administration, including human resource planning, recruitment, selection, appraisal, development, compensation, and bargaining.

Rebore, Ronald W. *Human Resources Administration: A Management Approach*, 7th ed. (Upper Saddle River, NJ: Prentice Hall, 2011). The author provides a practical, comprehensive treatment of the personnel function as it operates from a central office perspective. The text emphasizes the management approach, which is organized around the processes and procedures necessary for effective personnel administration.

Sanders, James R. *Evaluating School Programs* (Thousand Oaks, CA: Sage, 2007). Aimed at providing a guide for evaluating educational and training programs, projects, and materials in a variety of settings, these thirty standards were compiled by the Joint Committee on Standards for Educational Evaluation from knowledge gained from the professional literature as well as from years of experience by educators and evaluation specialists.

Seyfarth, John T. *Human Resource Leadership for Effective Schools* (Boston, MA: Allyn and Bacon, 2007). The book emphasizes the relationship of personnel management to student learning. It also emphasizes personnel practice in schools with site-based management and shows practical applications for research related to personnel practice.

Webb, L. Dean, and M. Scott Norton. *Human Resources Administration: Personnel Issues and Needs in Education*, 5th ed. (Upper Saddle River, NJ: Pearson, 2009). The authors address all traditional topics in personnel administration, with care taken throughout to provide a strong human resources perspective. They underscore the realization that the human element is central to an organization's progress, and that the human resources function encompasses utilization, development, and the teaching environment.

Young, I. Phillip. *The Human Resource Function in Educational Administration*, 9th ed. (Upper Saddle River, NJ: Pearson, 2008). Issues that have been and continue to be the mainstay of the human resource function are examined from both traditional and novel perspectives.

Name Index

Italic page numbers indicate material in figures, footnotes or sources.

Subject Index

Note: page numbers in italic indicate figures; page numbers followed by a t *indicate tables.*

Case Index

Italic page numbers indicate footnotes.